The First Hebrew Shakespeare Translations

The First Hebrew Shakespeare Translations

Isaac Edward Salkinson's *Ithiel the Cushite of Venice* and *Ram and Jael*

A Bilingual Edition and Commentary

Lily Kahn

UCLPRESS

First published in 2017 by
UCL Press
University College London
Gower Street
London WC1E 6BT

Available to download free: www.ucl.ac.uk/ucl-press

A CIP catalogue record for this book is available from The British Library.

ISBN: 978-1-911307-99-0 (Hbk.)
ISBN: 978-1-911307-98-3 (Pbk.)
ISBN: 978-1-911307-97-6 (PDF)
ISBN: 978-1-911576-00-6 (epub)
ISBN: 978-1-911576-01-3 (mobi)
DOI: https://doi.org/10.14324/111.9781911307976

This book is dedicated with love to Panda.

Acknowledgements

I wish to express my very deepest gratitude to the Arts and Humanities Research Council for generously funding the fellowship that led to the production of this volume.

I am extremely grateful to the staff at UCL Press, in particular Lara Speicher, Chris Penfold, and Jaimee Biggins, for their support of the volume from its inception through the writing, submission, and production process.

My warmest thanks go to Ada Rapoport-Albert for her continual encouragement, as well as for generously giving of her time to review the entire volume and make countless positive contributions to it. I am also very grateful to the anonymous reader for providing a number of extremely helpful comments. Special thanks are due to Sacha Stern for his support of the project, and to Shai Heijmans, Tsila Ratner, Aaron Rubin, Andrea Schatz, and Riitta-Liisa Valijärvi for their invaluable discussion sessions and help with individual portions of the research.

Finally, I am eternally grateful to James Holz for his ceaseless support and numerous insightful suggestions.

Contents

Introduction

1 The historical and literary background to the first Hebrew Shakespeare translations

The first Hebrew Shakespeare translations are a product of the Haskalah, or Jewish Enlightenment, a hugely influential social and intellectual movement that emerged in Berlin in the 1770s around the German Jewish philosopher Moses Mendelssohn and his circle. The Haskalah evolved under the influence of the general European Enlightenment but with a specific focus on Jewish issues. Maskilim, adherents of the Haskalah, sought to promote greater integration of Jews into their European host societies with a view towards eventual emancipation. To this end they advocated educational reform, including engagement with science, mathematics, European languages, and other subjects that had been absent from the traditional Ashkenazic (Northern, Central, and Eastern European Jewish) educational system, which was dedicated solely to study of the canonical Jewish texts with a focus on the Babylonian Talmud. A central element of the Maskilic project was the creation of a modern literary culture in Hebrew including genres that had not previously existed among Ashkenazic Jewry. Early Maskilic literary production consisted primarily of critical essays, poetry, and some drama (Pelli 1979). At the time Hebrew was not a spoken language, having died out in the early centuries CE and remaining more or less solely a literary medium until its revernacularization in late nineteenth- and early twentieth-century Palestine (Sáenz-Badillos 1993). The Maskilim selected Hebrew as the chief vehicle of their literary project due to its central and venerable status in Jewish society as the language of its main religious, legal, and philosophical writings (Pelli 1979: 73–108; Shavit 1993; Schatz 2009; Eldar 2016). They typically expressed a preference for Biblical Hebrew over postbiblical varieties of the language, regarding the biblical stratum as the purest form (Shavit 1993: 117–18) – although not all early Maskilim supported a strictly purist biblical style (Schatz 2009). They rejected Yiddish, the Central and Eastern European vernacular, and sought to replace it with German as the Jews' spoken language (Shavit 1993: 114–15; Eldar 2016: 29). Over the course of the following decades, the Haskalah spread into Galicia and then further east into czarist Russia, where it gave rise to a much more extensive body of Hebrew literature including novels, short stories, novellas, and plays (Patterson 1988) in addition to a thriving press and other forms of non-fiction. Maskilic fiction included both original compositions and translations of European literature, mainly German or, in the later decades of the Haskalah, Russian (Toury 2012: 133, 162–72). The popularity of translations during the Haskalah was a product of the desire to expand the Hebrew literary canon (Toury 2012: 165), as in other cultures with newly emerging literary models (Even-Zohar 1990: 47).

Considering Shakespeare's status as one of the most highly regarded authors in the European canon, it is unsurprising that the early Maskilim became interested in his work as part of their drive to develop a new Hebrew literature based on European models. Shakespeare's particular eminence in Germany is especially relevant in this context both because of the great admiration for his work expressed by Lessing, Schiller, and Goethe – whom the Maskilic authors held in extremely high esteem – and because most Maskilim accessed and translated European literature through German intermediaries, with few of them trained in other European languages (Almagor 1975: 721–6; Toury 2012: 162–72). The early decades of the Haskalah saw the first attempt to translate Shakespeare into Hebrew, a rendition of fifteen lines of a speech by King Henry IV from *Henry IV Part Two* (via German) that appeared in a book on biblical poetics (Levisohn 1816). The translated excerpt was intended to serve as an example of the concept of the apostrophe (Toury 2012: 171).

Following this initial effort, there was a gap of twenty-five years before any further Shakespeare extracts appeared in Hebrew. Between the 1840s and 1870s, a small number of Maskilic writers produced half a dozen fragmentary translations, mostly monologues and all via German versions. These fragments include three excerpts from *Hamlet*; the first, by Fabius Mieses, was composed in 1842 but remained unpublished until 1891; the second, by Naphtali Poper Krassensohn, appeared in the Maskilic periodical *Kokheve Yiṣḥaq* in 1856; and the third, by the prominent Hebrew literary figure Peretz Smolenskin, consists of four short extracts embedded in his novel *The Joy of the Godless*, which was published in the literary journal *HaShaḥar* in 1872. There were also two excerpts from *Macbeth*; the first appeared in an article by Joshua Steinberg published in 1868 in the Maskilic periodical *HaKarmel*; the second was translated by an S. Medliger and published in the periodical *Haʿet* in 1871. Finally, an extract based on Herder's version of a song from Cymbeline was translated by Simon Bacher and published in *Kokheve*

Yiṣḥaq in 1862.[1] As Toury (2012: 171–2) observes, these fragments did very little to familiarize Maskilic readers with Shakespeare's work or to establish a position for him within the nascent Hebrew literary library: with the exception of Peretz Smolenskin, the translators were all minor or unknown literary figures, the translations were typically published in relatively peripheral journals, and some of them (such as those of Smolenskin) were further obscured by appearing embedded within novels or articles.

This early period of marginal Hebrew Shakespeare translation ended with the publication of Isaac Edward Salkinson's Hebrew version of Othello, *Ithiel the Cushite of Venice* (Vienna, 1874). Salkinson's *Ithiel* marked the beginning of a new era in the story of Shakespeare in Hebrew because it was the first rendition of a complete play to appear in the language and the first to gain widespread critical attention in Maskilic literary circles. In addition, it was the first Hebrew Shakespeare version to be translated directly from the English original, constituting a departure from the earlier practice of indirect translation via German. Salkinson's translations were thus the first to bring the English and Hebrew texts into a direct dialogue with each other, in contrast to the previous versions, which were shaped by the interpretive filter of the German intermediary. This is significant not only in the immediate context of early Hebrew Shakespeare translation, but in that of translated nineteenth-century Hebrew literature in more general terms, as throughout this period English literature in Hebrew was typically mediated via German, and the distinction between direct and indirect translation was relatively unknown (Toury 2012: 165–73). Salkinson's pivotal role in the history of Hebrew Shakespeare translation is rooted in his singular biographical circumstances, which will be discussed in Section 2.

2 Isaac Edward (Eliezer) Salkinson's life and works

Biographical information on Salkinson, in particular his early years, is relatively scant. He is believed to have been born in 1820 as Isaac Eliezer Salkinson in a small village near Shklov, a town in present-day Belarus that was then part of the Russian Empire. His father is thought to have been a poor scholar who was unsuccessful in securing a rabbinical post but served for a time as a judge in a rabbinical court in Shklov (Zitron 1925: 37–8); while some sources (e.g., Lapide 1984: 92) identify him as the Hebrew poet Solomon Salkind (1806–68), there does not seem to be any clear basis for this. Salkinson's father was married twice. He had three children with his first wife, of whom Salkinson was the youngest. He and his first wife

1 See Almagor (1975: 769–71) and Toury (2012: 171) for bibliographic details of these early fragmentary Hebrew Shakespeare translations, and Almagor (1975: 737–9) for a short discussion of them.

Figure 1 Isaac Edward (Eliezer) Salkinson (1820–83)

were divorced sometime during Salkinson's childhood; he subsequently remarried and had another two children (Zitron 1925: 38). According to the only book-length biography of Salkinson (Cohen 1942: 12), his family life was unhappy and he was cruelly treated by his stepmother. The same account states that Salkinson's mother died when he was seven and his father may have died around ten years later; by contrast, according to the short biographical sketch appearing in Dunlop (1894: 373), his father died seven years before his mother. Salkinson received a traditional Jewish education, which included study of the classical sources (the Hebrew Bible, the Mishnah, and especially the Talmud), and gained a reputation as an *ilui*, an outstanding scholar (Zitron 1925: 38). Like other Eastern European Jews of the period, his native vernacular was Yiddish.

When Salkinson was sixteen or seventeen he is believed to have left home and settled in Mogilev, a larger city in present-day Belarus, where he continued his studies of the traditional Jewish sources until he was forced into hiding at the house of an innkeeper in a nearby village in order to avoid being conscripted into the czarist army (Zitron 1925: 39–41). While in the village, the innkeeper introduced him to a man who exposed him to the Maskilic principle of secular education in addition to Torah study and encouraged him to study medieval Hebrew literature as well as the Talmud (Zitron 1925: 42–3). The innkeeper wanted Salkinson to marry his granddaughter, and when Salkinson refused his host attempted to prevent him from leaving the village. Salkinson's Maskilic friend helped him to obtain a travel permit and escape the village (Zitron 1925: 43–9). He travelled to Minsk and from there to Vilna, where he was introduced to Chayim Zalman Eliashevitz, a Maskil who took him in and introduced him to key Maskilic ideologies and texts. Under Eliashevitz's guidance he studied Hebrew grammar, Moses Mendelssohn's influential Judeo-German Bible translation, and the German and Russian languages. While Salkinson did not take to the study of Russian and abandoned it after a short time (Zitron 1925: 49), he immersed himself in the study of German language and literature with the intention of travelling to Germany to pursue further education (Cohen 1942: 18). While in Vilna he fell in love with Eliashevitz's daughter, but she did not return his affections, preferring a rabbinical student who used to frequent Eliashevitz's house (Zitron 1925: 50). According to Zitron, the rabbinical student would write Hebrew poetry for her, which impressed both her and her father. Apparently jealousy of his competitor spurred Salkinson to make his first attempt at literary translation into Hebrew, a rendition of the first act of Schiller's drama *Kabale und Liebe* called נכלים ואהבה 'Deceit and Love' (Zitron 1925: 50), which does not seem to have survived. While Eliashevitz and his Maskilic associates were impressed with the translation, it did not have the desired effect of winning over Eliashevitz's daughter, and the rejection caused Salkinson to leave Vilna (Zitron 1925:50). Lacking a foreign travel permit, he crossed the Prussian border illegally and made his way to Königsberg (present-day Kaliningrad), from whence he planned to continue on to Berlin (Zitron 1925: 52–3). The subsequent turn of events is somewhat unclear. According to Zitron (1925: 53), while working at the Königsberg port in order to make money for his trip to Berlin he met a converted Jewish ship's captain who offered him free passage to London and persuaded him that it would be easier for him to continue his studies there. By contrast, Dunlop (1894: 373) states that he decided to go the United States in order to train under a 'celebrated rabbi' and stopped off in London on the way.

Regardless of the circumstances of his journey, it is clear that Salkinson arrived in London in the late 1840s. According to Zitron (1925: 53–4), the ship's captain arranged for him to be taken to the London Missionary Society, an organization that was engaged in, among its many international missionary projects, converting London Jews to Christianity. At some point following this initial encounter Salkinson converted to Christianity, allegedly under the influence of an elderly converted Jewish couple who took him in, showed him hospitality, and encouraged him in his educational ambitions (Zitron 1925: 60–5; Cohen 1942: 21–3). Salkinson is one of a number of Eastern European Jewish translators and scholars to convert to

Christianity under missionary auspices in this period.[2] Following his conversion, Salkinson completed a four-year course at the college of the British Society for the Propagation of the Gospel among the Jews, subsequently becoming a missionary of the British Society in Scotland while training as a Presbyterian minister in Edinburgh and Glasgow. He received his ordination in Glasgow in 1859 (Dunlop 1894: 373).

Around this time Salkinson began to engage in earnest with his interest in Hebrew translation. In an autobiographical sketch published in Dunlop (1894: 373), he recalls how upon first encountering the New Testament – in a Hebrew translation – he felt the need for 'a version in idiomatic Hebrew'. Having acquired Greek language skills as part of his seminary training, he translated the Epistle to the Romans into Hebrew (Salkinson 1855 – although Salkinson himself cites a publication date of 1853). This was followed by a Hebrew translation of *Philosophy of the Plan of Salvation: A Book for the Times* (Walker 1841), an American missionary tract; the translation was commissioned by Salkinson's fellow students at the United Presbyterian Seminary and was published in 1858. Dunlop (1894: 375–7) contains details of this book and Salkinson's Hebrew translation of it. At some point he married a younger Jewish woman who had converted to Christianity and the couple had two children (Kamianski as cited in Zitron 1925: 71), but there is little additional information in this respect other than that his wife was 'his invaluable helpmate in the Mission Field' (Dunlop 1894: 382).

At this time Salkinson returned to literary translation, following a suggestion by his converted Jewish colleague Christian David Ginsburg that he produce a Hebrew version of Milton's *Paradise Lost* (Dunlop 1894: 374). He began his translation in 1861 and completed it in 1870, when it was published with Ginsburg's assistance under the title of ויגרש את האדם *'So He Drove Out the Man'*.[3] Reverend Joseph Rawson Lumby, Norrisian Professor of Divinity at Cambridge, commented (in Dunlop 1894: 377) that Salkinson's Hebrew translation 'sets forth Christian teaching almost as definitely as does the Apostles' Creed'. This contrasts sharply with Salkinson's later Shakespeare translations, in which he typically omits or Judaizes Christian elements, as discussed in Section 3.2.1.

At some point after Salkinson completed his studies in Scotland, the British Society posted him to Pressburg (present-day Bratislava), where there was a large Jewish community, in order to pursue his missionary activities there among his former coreligionists (Cohen 1942: 23). In 1876 he was transferred to Vienna, which

2 See Dunlop (1894) for a compilation of biographical sketches of Jewish converts to Christianity in Victorian Britain; see Ruderman (2015) for a discussion of the nineteenth-century missionary activity of the London Society for Promoting Christianity amongst the Jews, focusing on the central figure of Alexander McCaul. See also Endelman (1987).

3 This title is a citation of the beginning of Gen. 3:24, in which God drives Adam and Eve out of the Garden of Eden after they eat from the tree of knowledge. See Dikman (in Salkinson 1874/2015: 234–5) for a brief discussion of Salkinson's translation of *Paradise Lost*.

at the time was a pivotal hub of Maskilic literary culture, serving as the home of various major Hebrew writers (mostly émigrés from czarist Russia) and journals including the influential *HaShaḥar*, the chief forum for late nineteenth-century Hebrew literature (Holtzman 2010). In Vienna Salkinson met and became friends with Peretz Smolenskin, the Russian-born editor of *HaShaḥar* and an extremely prominent author of Maskilic Hebrew prose fiction. During his time in Vienna Salkinson seems to have spent a great deal of time associating with members of the Maskilic Hebrew literary circles, befriending well-known authors such as Judah Leib Gordon and Abraham Baer Gottlober; indeed, Zitron (1925: 67), who met Salkinson during his years in Vienna, suggests that this activity was more important to him than his missionary work. Hebrew writers who were acquainted with him seem to have regarded him as honest and upstanding, with a true love for the Hebrew language, and to have respected him (while simultaneously holding him in suspicion) for his openness regarding his missionary activities (Cohen 1942: 38).

Smolenskin had a longstanding desire to see Shakespeare's plays in Hebrew, but lacked the English skills to conduct a translation from the original himself. Upon meeting Salkinson, who was a fluent English speaker and had experience with literary translation into Hebrew, he saw the rare opportunity for this dream to be fulfilled and commissioned him to translate an entire play, *Othello*. Salkinson's acceptance of this commission is likely to have been rooted in his longstanding passion for literary translation, as well as in his evident desire to maintain a foothold in the Maskilic Hebrew cultural world despite his conversion. His *Othello* translation, entitled *Ithiel the Cushite of Venice*, was published in Vienna in 1874 with a lengthy preface by Smolenskin. This preface is itself a remarkable piece of early Hebrew Shakespeare criticism, which makes for fascinating reading in its own right. In it, Smolenskin analyses Shakespeare's significance as a playwright and provides a psychological assessment of the characters appearing in the play, with a particular focus on Ithiel (Othello), Doeg (Iago), Phichol (Brabantio), and Asenath (Desdemona); in addition, he evaluates the ways in which the play's themes are particularly relevant and instructive for a Jewish audience, and argues for his vision of good literature as a vehicle for the depiction of human nature in all its moral complexity.

The motivation behind Salkinson's and Smolenskin's selection of *Othello* as opposed to other Shakespearean works is unclear. Scolnicov (2001) proposes that the subject matter of *Othello* was particularly appealing to Salkinson because he identified with the protagonist's liminal status as a foreigner and convert. This was followed by a translation of *Romeo and Juliet*, called *Ram and Jael*, published in 1878.[4] Again, there is no explicit reason given for the selection of this particular play. Gilulah (2013: 50) suggests that the choice of *Othello* followed by

4 See Section 3.1 for further details of the publication and reception of these two translations.

Romeo and Juliet hints at a particular interest in the themes of jealousy and love. (If so, perhaps this interest was inspired by Salkinson's memories of his love for Eliashevitz's daughter and his unsuccessful rivalry for her affections.) During this time, Salkinson also rendered Christoph August Tiedge's early nineteenth-century German poetic work *Urania* into Hebrew at the request of the Reverend Jellinek in Vienna (Dunlop 1894: 374); the translation was published in 1877. Apparently he also translated Byron's 1815 volume *Hebrew Melodies* into Hebrew, but this does not seem to have survived (Oz in Salkinson 1878/2016: 190).

Despite his obvious affinity for Maskilic cultural activity, Salkinson's autobiographical sketch and letters to John Dunlop – secretary of the British Society – predictably paint a very different picture of his time in Vienna, focusing on his attempts to convert the local Jews to Christianity while downplaying his work as a literary translator. Salkinson (in Dunlop 1894: 380–2) describes visits to the Temple Library in Vienna, where he attended lectures on Midrash and the Hebrew Bible in an attempt to raise the issue of the Messiah with the Jewish audience, his discussions with a Jewish doctor with whom he discussed the tenets of Christianity, and a friend from Breslau who converted under his influence. Nevertheless, regardless of such efforts Salkinson did admit that he felt translation to be his chief purpose in life, stating that 'Hebrew translation seemes [sic] to be the only talent given to me, and it I have consecrated to the LORD' (Dunlop 1894: 382). It is thus unsurprising that even within the context of his missionary work, Salkinson's most memorable achievement was in the realm of translation. The British Society, like Smolenskin, recognized his singular talent in this area and in 1877 commissioned him to produce a Hebrew version of the New Testament. In his autobiographical sketch (Dunlop 1894: 375) he notes: 'I undertook the work with delight, the more so since many learned Jews repeatedly expressed to me their astonishment that I had not undertaken it long ago.'

Salkinson seems to have intended to continue juggling his Hebrew literary translation with his missionary activities. In the preface to *Ram and Jael*, Smolenskin puts forth his vision for a complete series of Hebrew Shakespeare plays translated by Salkinson. However, this dream was to go unrealized. According to the Hebrew writer David Isaiah Silberbusch (1936), following publication of *Ram and Jael* a fellow converted Jew called Josephus, who had taken a dislike to Smolenskin and was offended at his comparison of Shakespeare's work to the Holy Scriptures (made in the preface to Salkinson's *Ithiel*), took his anger out on Salkinson by reporting him to the British Society for neglecting his missionary work and New Testament commission while instead spending his time translating Shakespeare into Hebrew. The British Society dismissed Salkinson from his post for a year and banned him from returning until he had completed his New Testament translation. While Salkinson, unsurprisingly, does not reference this incident directly in his autobiographical sketch, there is perhaps a veiled allusion to it when he says: 'Under peculiar circumstances, I was induced to translate, in my own hours of recreation, "Othello," and "Romeo and Juliet"' (Dunlop 1894: 374). The reference to 'peculiar circumstances' and 'own hours of recreation' may suggest a reluctance to admit to the British Society, in whose volume the sketch was published, of his close association with the Jewish literary circles in Vienna and his engagement with Hebrew translation unrelated to his missionary work. In his letters to John Dunlop from the early 1880s he mentions his progress with the New Testament translation, noting that he does not wish to sell the manuscript and copyright to the British Society but rather to give it away freely (Dunlop 1894: 383). Whether the suspension of duty made him reluctant to return to literary translation or not is uncertain, but he did not turn his hand to further Shakespeare renditions. He died on 5 June 1883 in Vienna. At the time his New Testament translation was not quite finished and the British Society asked Christian David Ginsburg to complete it (Dunlop 1894: 384). The finished translation was published in 1885 by the London-based Trinitarian Bible Society as 'The Salkinson-Ginsburg Hebrew New Testament'. It has since been reissued in numerous editions and remains available to the present day.

3 Salkinson's Shakespeare translations

3.1 Publication and reception

As discussed in the previous sections, Salkinson's translations were the product of a longstanding Maskilic interest in Shakespeare. Like the first fragmentary renditions produced earlier in the nineteenth century, Salkinson's *Ithiel* and *Ram and Jael* were intended as purely literary endeavours, designed for private reading by the largely Maskilic circles with an interest in Hebrew fiction. They were not envisioned for performance on stage, as they were composed several decades before the establishment of the first Hebrew theatres (following some intermittent Hebrew-language performances in Łódź and Riga towards the end of the nineteenth century, the first permanent Hebrew theatres were launched in St Petersburg and Białystock in 1909[5]). *Ithiel* was published with Smolenskin's support in a thousand copies (Almagor 1975: 753) by the Viennese printer Spitzer and Holzwarth Junior as a standalone volume (in contrast to many Maskilic Hebrew novels, which were serialized in literary journals such as Smolenskin's *HaShaḥar*). According to the publication announcement printed in the leading Maskilic Hebrew periodical *HaMaggid* (10 March 1874), it was sold for eighty kopecks or three francs and could be purchased from the publishers or one of the agents selling *HaShaḥar*. The title page (Figures 2 and 3), which appeared in Hebrew and English, listed Salkinson

5 See Zer-Zion (2010) for discussion of the early Hebrew theatre.

only as 'J.E.S., translator of Paradise Lost', while acknowledging Smolenskin prominently as editor. (Salkinson was likewise listed only as J.E.S. on the title page of his other literary translations.) Upon its publication, *Ithiel* was very well received in the Maskilic literary circles at which it was aimed. The publication announcement in *HaMaggid* (10 March 1874: 97) described it in glowing terms, stating that its like had never before been seen, and that it was a precious jewel for the Hebrew language. A similarly positive review appeared in a slightly later issue of the same newspaper (*HaMaggid*, 26 May 1874: 185), in which it was praised as 'one of the best and most faithful Hebrew translations that have been carried out in our days'; Smolenskin's preface to the work was also lauded. However, in the following issue (*HaMaggid*, 2 June 1874: 193) the positive review was tempered by a notice drawing the reader's attention to the fact that the unknown J.E.S. had been discovered to be none other than Isaac Salkinson, a convert and well-known missionary. A similar review appeared in another Hebrew periodical, *HaLevanon* (10 June 1874: 338), noting that the translation was magnificent and had rightly received praise, but that the anonymous translator was 'not one of ours'.[6]

Smolenskin did not allow the criticism of Salkinson's personal circumstances to deter him from pursuing his goal of seeing Shakespeare in Hebrew and he encouraged Salkinson to continue work on a further Shakespeare translation, supporting him in the production of *Ram and Jael*, which was published in 1878 in Vienna by the printer Georg Brög, again in a thousand copies (Almagor 1975: 753). However, the controversy surrounding Salkinson's status is reflected in the fact that on the title page of this second translation, Smolenskin's role in the project is played down, with his name appearing in miniscule letters under the publisher's name (Figures 4 and 5). In his preface to *Ram and Jael* (which is much shorter than his preface to *Ithiel*), Smolenskin takes pains to explain to Salkinson that this decision should in no way be interpreted as an attempt to distance himself from his friend, but rather is rooted in a desire to spare Salkinson from the damage that would be done to the volume's reputation were Smolenskin's name to appear more prominently, given the latter's many enemies in Maskilic literary circles. Perhaps surprisingly, despite the previously mentioned announcement in *HaMaggid* revealing the translator's identity and convert status, when *Ram and Jael* was published a short review appeared in the prominent Hebrew periodical *HaMeliṣ* (11 March 1879: 190) praising the work and referring to the translator only as 'the anonymous author J.E.S.'. Another positive review appeared in the periodical *HaṢefira* (3 June 1879: 158), again without acknowledging the translator's identity.

6 See Cohen (1942: 63–64) and Almagor (1975: 744) for further discussion of these critical reactions to Salkinson's unusual status within the Jewish community; see also Salkinson (1874/2015: 226–9) for the announcements in *HaMaggid* and *HaLevanon*.

Although Smolenskin's dream of a complete series of Salkinson's Hebrew Shakespeare translations was to remain unfulfilled, *Ithiel* and *Ram and Jael* quickly inspired others to follow suit, and the two decades following the publication of Salkinson's groundbreaking work saw the appearance of another four translations of complete Shakespeare plays undertaken by various Eastern European Jewish authors. The first of these was Isaac Barb's *Macbeth* (1883), followed by Judah Leib Elkind's version of *The Taming of the Shrew* (1892), Samuel Leib Gordon's translation of *King Lear* (1890), and Hayim Yehiel Bornstein's *Hamlet* (1900–1). With the exception of Barb's *Macbeth*, which was translated via Schiller's early nineteenth-century German adaptation, all of these plays were (at least allegedly) translated directly from the English, a trend initiated by Salkinson. Although information on these authors is relatively scarce, Salkinson's work was undoubtedly familiar to them and most likely served as a model; an example of this may be Elkind's decision to name the Hebrew version of the protagonist Petruchio 'Peretz', which mirrors Salkinson's choice of name for the character Petruchio appearing in *Romeo and Juliet*.[7]

With the end of the Maskilic era and the rise of political Zionism in the late nineteenth century, the centre of Hebrew literary activity began to shift from Eastern Europe to Palestine. After the publication of Bornstein's *Hamlet* there was a gap of more than twenty years before another complete Shakespeare play appeared in Hebrew (although a number of fragmentary renditions, a prose adaptation, and some sonnet translations were produced in the intervening years[8]). The next translation of an entire play was David Frischmann's *Coriolanus*, which was published in Warsaw in 1924. Frischmann had come of age during the late Haskalah and had published his early works in Maskilic newspapers and literary journals such as *HaShaḥar* and *HaMeliṣ* (Bar-Yosef 2010), and as such would most likely have been familiar with Salkinson's Shakespeare translation. However, by the 1920s, Jewish society and the status of Hebrew had changed radically, with the language now established both as a fully fledged vernacular in Palestine and as a much more widespread literary vehicle; as such, Frischmann's translation belongs to a new generation of Hebrew Shakespeare rooted in a very different linguistic, literary, and cultural context from Salkinson's. Frischmann's *Coriolanus* was followed by Shimon Halkin's version of *The Merchant of Venice* (Berlin, 1929) and Saul Tchernikovsky's translation of *Twelfth Night* (Tel Aviv, 1930); a number of other plays were translated by Hebrew writers based in the United States during the 1930s (Almagor 1975: 752–3).

---

7 See *Ram and Jael*, First Part, note 359. See Almagor (1975) for a summary discussion of these late nineteenth-century works and Kahn (forthcoming b) for an analysis of Bornstein's *Hamlet*.

8 See Almagor (1975: 776–81) for a complete list.

Salkinson's *Ithiel* and *Ram and Jael* remained the only Hebrew translations of *Othello* and *Romeo and Juliet* in this period, and his work continued to be read and referenced in the new Palestinian context. *Ithiel* was reissued in Tel Aviv in 1930, although significantly, Salkinson's biblicized names for the characters[9] were replaced by the English originals, reflecting a shift in translatorial norms that had taken place since the Maskilic era. Moreover, *Ithiel* was performed (under the updated title of *Othello*[10]) in Mandate Palestine, at the Haifa Hebrew Theatre, under the direction of Benno Fraenkel and featuring the actor Avraham Shklarsh in the title role. It opened on 12 March 1936 and was reviewed by the prominent Hebrew poet Lea Goldberg in the Hebrew newspaper *Davar* (Goldberg 1936). It was revived as a one-man performance with Avraham Shklarsh at the HaOhel Theatre in Tel Aviv, debuting on 21 November 1946, and was reviewed in several different Hebrew newspapers (Malkin 1946; Roeh 1946; Zussman 1946). *Ram and Jael* does not seem to have been performed.

In the 1940s the Hebrew poets Lea Goldberg, Avraham Shlonsky, and Natan Alterman produced a new generation of Hebrew Shakespeare translations (Golomb 1998: 263–70). This included the first replacement for one of Salkinson's works, Natan Alterman's *Othello*, which was published in 1950. The translation was undertaken for Habima Hebrew Theatre, where it was first performed on 6 March 1950 in Tel Aviv. Alterman (1950; also cited in Almagor 1975: 743–4) acknowledged his debt to Salkinson's *Ithiel*, expressing great admiration for – and indeed envy of – his predecessor's work; however, he did not mimic Salkinson's domesticating style,[11] which was no longer the norm in Hebrew translation.[12] In 1957 the Israeli poet and translator Raphael Eliaz published a new version of *Romeo and Juliet*. Like Alterman's, Eliaz's translation was performed on the Israeli stage; it was first shown at Tel Aviv's Cameri Theatre in 1957. In the latter half of the twentieth century and the early twenty-first century new Hebrew Shakespeare versions reflecting contemporary linguistic and translatorial practices were produced by well-known Israeli poets and scholars including Dan Almagor, Ted Carmi, Ehud Manor, Dan Miron, Avraham Oz, Shimon Sandbank, Meir Wieseltier, and, most recently, Dori Parnes. Salkinson's work fell into obscurity (although certain respected literary figures such as the poet Ted Carmi continued to recall him with praise; Dikman in Salkinson 1874/2015: 243). This fate was not unique to Salkinson, but rather was part of a more general tendency to regard Maskilic literature as an antiquated body of writing reflecting awkward linguistic and literary conventions such as excessive

9 See Section 3.2.1.1 for discussion of this issue.

10 See the performance announcement in the Hebrew newspaper *Do'ar HaYom*, 23 February 1936: 7.

11 See Section 3.2.1 for analysis of this.

12 See Dikman (in Salkinson 1874/2015: 240–3) for a comparison of some aspects of Salkinson's and Alterman's *Othello* renditions.

reliance on biblical citations and *meliṣa*, a writing technique valued by Maskilim but later considered florid and bombastic (Shahevitch 1970; Pelli 1993; Kahn 2013). In the mid-to-late twentieth-century Israeli context, Salkinson's translations were rarely read or studied, being viewed as 'outdated curiosities' (Golomb 1998: 261).

This situation changed in 2015 and 2016 when Salkinson's *Ithiel* was reissued by the Israeli publisher Raav as the first in a series intended to bring forgotten works of Hebrew literature back into the public eye. The volume features an afterword on Salkinson's life and work by Aminadav Dikman, a literary scholar and himself a Hebrew translator. The edition emphasizes Salkinson's contribution to Hebrew literature and Dikman describes his *Ithiel* as a shining example of Hebrew literary translation that has been unjustly neglected. Upon its release the new edition of *Ithiel* was featured in two articles in the Israeli newspaper *Ha'aretz* (Arbel 2015; Ashkenazi 2015). In 2016, Salkinson's *Ram and Jael* was published as part of the same series with an afterword by Avraham Oz, a theatre scholar and prominent Hebrew Shakespeare translator. Like *Ithiel*, *Ram and Jael* was the subject of an article in *Ha'aretz* (Almagor 2016). The two Raav editions and the press coverage that they have received mark the beginning of a new chapter in Salkinson's reception history wherein his pioneering contribution to Hebrew literature is once again being given its rightful recognition. It is hoped that the present bilingual edition will continue this trend by making Salkinson's remarkable work accessible to readers with or without knowledge of Hebrew and by highlighting the multifaceted significance of his work. *Ithiel* and *Ram and Jael* are obviously of major importance for Hebrew literary history because they were the first complete Shakespearean dramas to appear in the language and paved the way for all subsequent Hebrew translations of the plays. Moreover, they are of particular relevance for translation studies specialists in that they constitute some of the only examples globally of Shakespeare adaptations in a largely unspoken language. Finally, they have much to offer scholars and students of multicultural Shakespeare by providing a rare and invaluable insight into the reception of the plays in a nineteenth-century European minority society.

3.2 Translation style

Salkinson's *Ithiel* and *Ram and Jael* exhibit various noteworthy characteristics that distinguish them markedly from the Shakespearean source text. In some respects, they can be regarded as relatively close to the original in that they often preserve the line divisions, do not omit significant amounts of material (with a few exceptions in *Ram and Jael*, which are indicated in the text of this edition as they occur), and usually render the overall sense of each character's lines. These tendencies can be contrasted with certain well-known earlier European-language

Shakespeare translations such as Pierre-Antoine de La Place and Jean-François Ducis' French adaptations (Schwartz-Gastine 2003: 225) and Christoph Martin Wieland's German prose versions (Williams 1990: 51–8, 69), which depart much more radically from the source text. However, Salkinson's translations are not at all literal: while he does not generally leave out lines and maintains the overall sense of individual speeches, the lines themselves are often merely paraphrases of the source text. This is due to a number of considerations, namely his domesticating translation style,[13] the difficulty of finding equivalents for Shakespeare's wording while relying heavily on the technique of *shibbuṣ* (the incorporation of biblical citations into a new composition),[14] and, in some cases, the need to find Hebrew rhymes that echo those appearing in the source text (this is a particular issue in *Ram and Jael*, which is rich in rhyming couplets). The key features of Salkinson's translations are outlined in the remainder of Section 3.2 and are discussed in further depth in the running commentary in the bilingual edition.

3.2.1 Domestication

Perhaps the most striking hallmark of Salkinson's translation is its highly domesticating nature.[15] Salkinson's domesticating approach is rooted in the fact that his *skopos*, or translatorial aim (Pym 2010: 43–50), was a product of the Maskilic perspective on translation, which was not seen in neutral terms, but rather was an explicit strand in the ideological drive to rejuvenate the Jewish nation and was linked to the often fraught relationship between Jews and non-Jews in Europe. Smolenskin's preface to *Ithiel* offers a striking illustration of this heavily loaded ideological attitude to literary translation, with its infamous (if perhaps somewhat tongue-in-cheek) description of Salkinson's Hebrew play as an act of 'revenge':[16]

> Today we get revenge on the British; they have taken our Holy Scriptures and treated them as one treats one's own property: they have translated them, scattered them to all corners of the earth as if they were their own, and so today we repay them for their deed, for we are taking the books which are as precious to them as the Holy Scriptures, the plays of Shakespeare, and we are bringing them into the treasure-house of our holy tongue; is this revenge not sweet?!

Smolenskin's comments reflect an attitude prevalent among Eastern European Maskilim regarding the pivotal role of the translator as an agent of Jewish cultural

13 Discussed in detail in Section 3.2.1.

14 See Section 3.2.1.5.

15 See Schleiermacher (1813), Venuti (2008), and Pym (2010: 30–3) for discussion of domesticating translation theory.

16 See Almagor (1975: 742–3), Golomb (1998: 255–9), and Scolnicov (2001: 184) for further discussion of Smolenskin's statement. See the beginning of Smolenskin's preface to *Ithiel* in this edition for the full text from which this citation is taken.

renewal, and of the Haskalah as a transformative acculturating project (Pelli 1979; Feiner 2002; Schatz 2009; Eldar 2016). It is not surprising that this Maskilic attitude to translation often resulted in a domesticating approach whereby non-Jewish elements appearing in European-language source texts underwent a process of Judaization when rendered into Hebrew.[17] It should be noted that domesticating translation into Hebrew is not a Maskilic innovation, but rather is a much older Jewish tradition attested as early as the medieval period (Needler 1977; Singerman 1988); a prominent example of this type of Judaizing tendency is the thirteenth-century Hebrew version of the legend of King Arthur.[18] The same approach is also commonly found in medieval and early modern translations into Yiddish, such as the Bovo-bukh, a sixteenth-century Yiddish adaptation of the English romance Bevis of Hampton via its Italian version Buovo d'Antona,[19] as well as Sephardic Jewish versions of Spanish ballads.[20]

At first glance it may appear surprising that Salkinson adopted a Judaizing translation strategy given his extremely liminal position in Jewish society as a Christian convert and missionary. However, his domesticating approach is not actually as remarkable as it may seem, being the logical product of his own background as well as the conditions surrounding the commission of his translations. As discussed in Section 2, Salkinson had received an advanced traditional Jewish education and as such was intimately familiar with canonical Hebrew and Aramaic texts including the Bible, Mishnah, and Talmuds (Cohen 1942: 12–3). Moreover, as mentioned previously, despite his conversion and missionary status he remained closely affiliated with the Jewish community, particularly during his time in Vienna. Finally, in contrast to his other translations, which were all of books with overt Christian content and designed to raise awareness of Christian tenets among a Hebrew readership, his Shakespeare translations were primarily literary endeavours not explicitly intended to deliver a Christian message to readers. Indeed, because *Ithiel* and *Ram and Jael* were commissioned by and conducted in close association with Peretz Smolenskin, a pillar of the Maskilic literary community, and were designed for a readership with a hostile attitude towards Christianity of which Salkinson would have been only too aware, it is perhaps only to be expected that he opted for a Judaizing strategy in keeping with Maskilic literary sensibilities despite his conversion and missionary status.

Salkinson's domesticating translation style manifests itself in six key areas: his treatment of characters' names; Christian rituals, institutions, and oaths; Classical

17 See Kahn (forthcoming c) for discussion of this type of approach in a Maskilic translation of a historical text.
18 See Leviant (2003), Rovang (2009), and Valles (2013: 38–76) for details of this text.
19 See Rosenzweig (2016) for a scholarly edition of this work.
20 See Armistead and Silverman (1965) for details.

mythology; other non-Jewish cultural references; the technique of *shibbuṣ* (the insertion of biblical verses and phrases into the composition); and foreign-language elements in the source text. The following is a brief summary of these strategies; the commentary accompanying the bilingual edition focuses on the same six areas and discusses each individual instance of domestication.

3.2.1.1 Names

One of Salkinson's most immediately noticeable domesticating strategies is the replacement of almost all of Shakespeare's characters' names with Hebrew equivalents, typically biblical ones. This practice is a common feature of Maskilic Hebrew translations generally (Dikman in Salkinson 1874/2015: 239). Salkinson's Hebraization of characters' names conforms to three main patterns. First, in many cases he selects the biblical names wholly or primarily on the basis of a sound correspondence. Often the names belong to minor biblical characters lacking any kind of particular associations for readers. Examples include the replacement of Roderigo with Raddai (based on 1 Chron. 2:14[21]) and of Gregory with Gera (based on Gen. 46:21 and several other locations in the Hebrew Bible[22]).

In other instances Salkinson chooses his Hebrew names not only on the basis of sound correspondence but also in order to indicate a particular quality relevant to the character in question. For example, he replaces Romeo with Ram, the namesake of King David's ancestor mentioned in Ruth 4:19;[23] readers would have associated this name with the positive qualities of the Davidic line as well as with the romantic plot of the Book of Ruth, the classic biblical love story.

In a number of instances Salkinson selects his Hebrew name purely on the basis of meaning without attempting to find an equivalent with sound correspondence. Such a case is Romeo's father Montague, whom he renames Abiram, which literally means 'father of Ram' and therefore links neatly to the title character, but also is the namesake of one of the members of Korach's rebellion against Moses recounted in Numbers 16 and as such has connotations of arrogance and spite;[24] another example is the replacement of Shakespeare's Rosaline with Shoshannah, a postbiblical Hebrew female name meaning 'rose'.[25]

3.2.1.2 Christian references

Given the widespread distrust of Christianity on the part of Salkinson's Eastern European Jewish audience, it is perhaps unsurprising that one of the main foci of his Judaizing translation strategy concerns Christian holidays, institutions, rituals,

21 See *Ithiel*, First Part, note 3.
22 See *Ram and Jael*, First Part, note 4.
23 See *Ram and Jael*, First Part, note 44.
24 See *Ram and Jael*, First Part, note 11.
25 See *Ram and Jael*, First Part, note 151.

and oaths. Salkinson has several different domesticating approaches to the translation of such terms. In some instances he simply omits them; this is particularly common in the case of Christian oaths. In other cases, he dechristianizes the reference but does not replace it with an explicitly Jewish one, instead choosing a religiously and culturally neutral equivalent. For example, in *Ram and Jael* he translates 'evening mass' as בֵּין הָעַרְבָּיִם 'twilight',[26] which eradicates any religious connotations but preserves the temporal associations of the original. In still other instances, he replaces a Christian reference with an unambiguously Jewish dynamic equivalent (a translation that differs formally from that of the source text but serves an equivalent function in the target culture, thus making the translation more accessible to readers[27]). Like the choice of biblical names, the selection of Jewish equivalents for Christian concepts has the effect of transforming the cultural context of the play into an unquestionably Jewish one. For example, Shakespeare's 'Easter' becomes חַג הַמַּצּוֹת 'Passover'.[28]

3.2.1.3 Classical mythology

Another prominent area of domestication concerns Shakespeare's references to figures from Classical mythology. Salkinson almost invariably domesticates such references just as he adapts the Christian allusions discussed previously. However, although the technique is the same, the reluctance to preserve Classical mythological elements has slightly different motivations. While explicit references to Christianity would have been seen as inappropriate for a Jewish readership, Maskilim generally professed an admiration for Classical literature, recognizing it as a central foundation of the European tradition upon which their own literary project was modelled. For example, in his preface to Salkinson's *Ithiel*, Smolenskin praises the writings of Homer as the greatest literary works in history alongside Shakespeare and the Hebrew Bible. Throughout the nineteenth century, Maskilic authors produced fragmentary Hebrew translations of Classical texts (e.g., Micah Joseph Lebensohn's 1849 adaptation of a portion of the Aeneid via Schiller's German version). However, the Maskilic admiration for Classical sources was a new development among Central and Eastern European Jews, who typically regarded Classical culture as irrelevant, or indeed antithetical, to Jewish society and did not traditionally study Greek or Latin. As such, in-depth knowledge of Classical language and literature was relatively rare even among Maskilim, and many of the mythological figures mentioned in Shakespeare's plays would likely have meant little to Salkinson's audience. Moreover, Naphtali Hirz Wessely, a prominent early Maskil, instructed the editors of the first Maskilic Hebrew periodical,

26 See *Ram and Jael*, Fourth Part, note 11.

27 See Nida (1964) and Nida and Taber (1969) for further discussion of dynamic equivalency.

28 See *Ram and Jael*, Third Part, note 10.

HaMe'assef, not to mention the names of Greek and Roman gods in their Hebrew translations (*HaMe'assef*, 1 October 1873: 7–8). In this light, Salkinson's decision to domesticate the Classical references in Shakespeare's texts is unsurprising. His earlier translation of *Paradise Lost* exhibits the same strategy, most likely for similar reasons (Dikman in Salkinson 1874/2015: 234–5). As in the case of the aforementioned Christian references (particularly oaths), in some instances Salkinson simply omits Classical allusions, while in others he substitutes a reference to a Classical figure with one to the monotheistic God. In many cases, he goes further and finds a dynamic equivalent from within the Jewish tradition. A striking example of this is his replacement of Shakespeare's 'Venus' (*Romeo and Juliet* 2.1.11) with 'Ashtoreth', a Canaanite goddess associated with love and fertility.[29]

3.2.1.4 Other non-Jewish cultural elements

In addition to domesticating Christian and Classical references, Salkinson has a tendency to Judaize other elements of the source text that he deemed inappropriate or irrelevant for his Hebrew translation. This includes European cultural references such as Queen Mab[30] and the legend of King Cophetua,[31] as well as flora and fauna lacking biblical equivalents, occupations not common among Eastern European Jews, and ethnic or geographical labels. Salkinson typically replaces such elements with dynamic equivalents familiar to Jewish readers from the Hebrew Bible, or with references to postbiblical Jewish religious culture, Eastern European Jewish realia and social conditions, and folk traditions. An example of this tactic is his substitution of Shakespeare's 'colliers' (*Romeo and Juliet* 1.1.2) with חֹטְבֵי עֵצִים 'woodcutters':[32] woodcutting would have been widely recognized among Hebrew readers as a classic form of manual labour due to its appearance in a well-known phrase from Joshua 9:21, 'woodcutters and water carriers', as well as due to the fact that it was a common occupation among Eastern European Jews.

3.2.1.5 *Shibbuṣ*

Another prominent domesticating strategy is the phenomenon of *shibbuṣ*, a common Hebrew literary technique whereby intact or adapted biblical verses or verse fragments are inserted into a new composition. *Shibbuṣ* is attested in numerous types of postbiblical Hebrew literature, but is commonly associated with Maskilic authors due to the fact that it was a particularly favoured technique for them. One of the reasons for the Maskilic penchant for *shibbuṣ* is ideological: as the Maskilic authors held the biblical text and language in extremely high esteem, incorporating

29 See *Ram and Jael*, Second Part, note 9.
30 See *Ram and Jael*, First Part, note 259.
31 See *Ram and Jael*, Second Part, note 12.
32 See *Ram and Jael*, First Part, note 7.

elements of it into their own writing served to raise the latter's linguistic and literary prestige. Another reason is a more practical one: as Hebrew was not a vernacular in the Maskilic era, drawing on familiar biblical phrases was a convenient method of aiding their creative expression in the language.[33] An example of biblical *shibbuṣ* in Salkinson's translations is the replacement of Shakespeare's 'Your son-in-law is far more fair than black' (*Othello* 1.3.291) with וְעַל חֲתָנְךָ הִנְנִי אֹמֵר: קָרַן עוֹר פְּנֵי הַכּוּשִׁי 'and regarding your son-in-law I hereby say: the skin of the Cushite's face shone',[34] based on קָרַן עוֹר פְּנֵי מֹשֶׁה 'and Moses' face shone' (Exod. 34:35). While some of Salkinson's *shibbuṣ* choices have symbolic meaning (which will be discussed in the commentary to the edition where relevant), in many cases he selected a given verse simply because it corresponded roughly in meaning to the equivalent line in the source text, without any deeper interpretive motivation.

While Salkinson's *shibbuṣ* is drawn primarily from biblical sources, contrary to common belief (as in Almagor 1975: 743; Scolnicov 2001: 185; Dikman in Salkinson 1874/2015: 243), his *Ithiel* also contains citations from rabbinic literature (the Babylonian Talmud) and a range of medieval and early modern sources well known to Eastern European Jews of his era, most typically the biblical commentaries of Rashi (eleventh century), Abraham Ibn Ezra (twelfth century), Isaac Abarbanel (fifteenth–sixteenth centuries), and Moses Alshekh (sixteenth century). Cases of *shibbuṣ* from postbiblical sources are indicated in the commentary to the edition. An example of *shibbuṣ* from a Mishnaic text is עֲבֵרָה גֹּרֶרֶת עֲבֵרָה 'one transgression brings another transgression', from Mishnah *Avot* 4:2, as a translation of Shakespeare's 'One unperfectness shows me another' (*Othello* 2.3.292–3).[35] An example of *shibbuṣ* from a medieval text is הֵן אֲדַמְּךָ אֲכַנְּךָ וְלֹא יְדַעְתִּיךָ בְּשֵׁם 'indeed I can imagine you and describe you, though I do not know you by name',[36] from Judah the Pious' twelfth-century Hymn of Glory, as a translation of Shakespeare's 'If thou hast no name to be known by' (*Othello* 2.3.277–8).

3.2.1.6 Foreign-language material

The final domesticating strategy evident in Salkinson's work concerns the foreign-language elements in *Othello* and *Romeo and Juliet.* Where French, Italian, or Latin words or phrases appear in the English, Salkinson routinely translates them into Hebrew, thus eradicating the linguistic variegation present in Shakespeare's text. As in the case of the references to Classical mythological figures, this approach stems from the fact that, while in much of Europe these languages were commonly studied and enjoyed a prestigious status, they were generally unfamiliar to Eastern

33 See Shahevitch (1970), Pelli (1993), and Kahn (2013) for further discussion of the use of *shibbuṣ* in Maskilic Hebrew literature.

34 See *Ithiel*, First Part, note 259.

35 See *Ithiel*, Second Part, note 228.

36 See *Ithiel*, Second Part, note 223.

European Jews (including Maskilim) and would have lacked any meaningful associations for Salkinson's readers. Examples of Salkinson's treatment of such linguistic elements include his replacement of the Friar's Latin greeting '*Benedicite*' (*Romeo and Juliet* 2.3.27) with the Hebrew !בָּרוּךְ הַבָּא 'welcome',[37] and his replacement of Shakespeare's '*bonjour*' (*Romeo and Juliet* 2.4.43–5) with הֲשָׁלוֹם לְךָ 'greetings'.[38]

3.2.2 Poetry

One of the most immediately conspicuous features of Salkinson's translations is that he has eradicated all of Shakespeare's distinctions between verse and prose, rendering everything into verse. Salkinson's verse is utterly free: it does not seem to exhibit either syllabic metre or a particular stress pattern; indeed, the only feature distinguishing it from prose is the formal distribution of the lines, which generally correspond more or less to Shakespeare's, and the fact that the text is vocalized, which was the convention in Maskilic Hebrew poetry (as in that of present-day Hebrew). Salkinson's poetry thus differs markedly from Shakespeare's in its lack of iambic pentameter or other features of an accentual-syllabic metrical system. Moreover, it diverges from the typical Maskilic poetic convention, which was a purely syllabic system consisting of a fixed number of syllables, with stress on the penultimate syllable but otherwise free (Hrushovski-Harshav 2007: 613–14). The main ways in which Salkinson's poetry resembles that of his Maskilic contemporaries are his frequent use of conjoint phrases (two juxtaposed synonymous or nearly synonymous expressions), a practice that echoes the parallelism that is a hallmark of biblical poetry,[39] and of course his use of *shibbuṣ*. Salkinson's poetic style likewise differs from that of the Hebrew Bible, which is defined chiefly by parallelism and exhibits an accentual system with free variation of numbers of stresses in a verse unit (Hrushovski-Harshav 2007: 596, 598–9, 605).

While *Ithiel* and *Ram and Jael* do not resemble their English source texts in terms of metre, they do mirror them in terms of rhyme: where Shakespeare's text contains rhymes, Salkinson finds Hebrew equivalents for them, but he does not add rhymes where they do not appear in the original. In most cases Salkinson's rhyme schemes are the same as Shakespeare's (typically rhyming couplets, but also ABAB, ABA, and ABBA patterns) and appear in the same line. However, occasionally Salkinson's scheme differs from the original (most commonly ABAB instead of a rhyming couplet); such changes are generally due to difficulties finding a suitable rhyme fitting the original pattern. In cases where it is difficult to find a suitable rhyme while preserving the source text's meaning, Salkinson typically prioritizes

---

37 See *Ram and Jael*, Second Part, note 125.

38 See *Ram and Jael*, Second Part, note 203.

39 See Gilulah (2013: 51–2) for analysis of some examples from *Ithiel*; see also Oz (in Salkinson 1878/2016: 193). See Toury (2012: 133, 139) for discussion of this practice in Maskilic writing in general.

the rhyme, often completely changing the sense of the lines in question. He does not typically seem to have regarded same-word rhymes in Shakespeare's text (e.g., flower/flower, wife/wife) as such, given that he rarely reproduces them in his translation. Salkinson's rhymes could be either masculine (i.e., stressed on the ultima) or feminine (i.e., stressed on the penult). As in the case of metre, this diverges from the Maskilic standard, which generally allowed only for feminine rhymes (Hrushovski-Harshav 2007: 613–15; Toury 2012: 151). This convention was inherited from earlier Italian Hebrew poetry, which was in turn based on the model of the Italian language, wherein nouns with penultimate stress were the norm. In the Sephardic (Southern and Southeastern European and North African) Hebrew pronunciation, only a small percentage of Hebrew words are stressed on the penult, whereas in the Ashkenazic pronunciation a much larger percentage of words have penultimate stress. When the Maskilim adopted the Italian Hebrew poetic convention, they allowed only words with penultimate stress according to the Sephardic pronunciation, despite the fact that their own Ashkenazic pronunciation would have given them a much larger repertoire on which to draw. This rule meant that Maskilic poets had to restrict themselves to a very marginal group of nouns, verbs, and prepositions on which to base their rhymes, with a concomitant constraining effect on their verse (Hrushovski-Harshav 2007: 614). It is possible that Salkinson broke away from this convention by including rhymes based on his Ashkenazic pronunciation (with its much larger range of penultimately stressed vocabulary) because it would have been too difficult for him to reproduce Shakespeare's rhymes while restricting his options to the small pool of penultimately stressed Sephardic lexis.

3.2.3 Hebrew language

The language of Salkinson's translations is predominantly biblicizing, which is in keeping with Maskilic authors' expressed preference for Biblical Hebrew over the postbiblical strata in the composition of fiction, particularly poetry. This is evident in the grammar of *Ithiel* and *Ram and Jael*, which favours biblical forms and constructions (e.g., the *wayyiqṭol* for preterite sequences; the cohortative and jussive; and conjunctions such as כִּי 'because, that, if/when' and אֲשֶׁר 'which, that') over their postbiblical counterparts, and in its lexis, which is typically drawn from the biblical corpus. A relatively common feature of Salkinson's work is a readiness to utilize rare biblical vocabulary including *hapax legomena* (words that appear only once in the Bible); this was a widespread Maskilic technique often employed as a means of lexical enrichment (Kahn 2013). He also frequently employs pausal forms (e.g., לָחֶם 'bread' instead of לֶחֶם) before punctuation and at the end of lines; such forms are most commonly associated with the Hebrew Bible, in which they typically appear together with disjunctive accents (symbols marking breaks in the text, similar to punctuation) and at the end of verses (Fassberg 2013). The dominance of biblical structures and vocabulary goes hand-in-hand with Salkinson's predilection for *shibbuṣ*, as he frequently imported biblical expressions and verses wholesale into his work. Salkinson's use of *shibbuṣ* reflects an extensive engagement with the entire Hebrew Bible, with all twenty-four books represented in his text at least once. However, certain books feature much more prominently than others: the most frequently appearing biblical intertexts are Psalms, Isaiah, and Proverbs, with more than 150 citations each, followed by Job, with approximately 130. By contrast, a few books, all from the Minor Prophets, are cited only one to three times (Haggai, Jonah, Nahum, Obadiah). Most of the remaining books are cited between twenty and a hundred times.

Despite Salkinson's preference for the biblical stratum of Hebrew, a not insignificant number of postbiblical (rabbinic, medieval, and Maskilic) elements are attested in both *Ithiel* and *Ram and Jael* (belying the common belief, as expressed in Gilulah 2013: 50, and Dikman in Salkinson 1874/2015: 239, 243, that the language of *Ithiel* is purely biblical). Like the biblical elements, these postbiblical features are both grammatical and lexical. Certain grammatical features are traceable to the classical rabbinic period; for example, the possessive particle שֶׁל 'of' and sequences of *qaṭal* and *yiqṭol* verbal forms. Constructions combining biblical and postbiblical elements are also attested (this is a common Maskilic phenomenon[40]). On occasion Salkinson employs grammatical constructions typical of nineteenth-century Eastern European Hebrew that lack precedent in the canonical sources (e.g., the *qaṭal* verbal conjugation to indicate a past progressive action[41]). Likewise, Salkinson utilizes numerous rabbinic vocabulary items throughout the two plays (e.g., רַצְעָן 'shoemaker', דִּין וּדְבָרִים 'grievance', פְּרוּצָה 'strumpet, whore'), as well as a number of medieval terms (e.g., תְּכוּנָה 'nature', יְדִיד נֶפֶשׁ 'beloved', מִגְרָעוֹת 'flaws') and innovations of the Maskilic era (e.g., כַּדּוּר 'bullet', קְנֵה רֹבֶה 'gun', חֳלִי רַע 'cholera').

3.3 Salkinson's source text edition

Salkinson did not specify which Shakespeare edition he used, and given the large number of English versions that appeared in the decade preceding the publication of his translations it is extremely difficult to establish this with any certainty. However, both *Ithiel* and *Ram and Jael* seem to be based on Folio rather than Quarto versions. In the case of *Ithiel*, this is evidenced by the inclusion of certain elements such as the Willow Song in Act 5. In *Ram and Jael*, this is made clear, for example, by the absence of the Prologue, which does not appear in the Folio versions; more specifically, the assignment of certain lines to Rezin the Priest (Friar Laurence) instead

40 See Kahn (2009) for discussion of this phenomenon.
41 See Kahn (2009: 80–3; 2015: 149–50) for details.

of Ram (Romeo) suggests that Salkinson may have been working with an edition based on the Second, Third, or Fourth Folio.[42] In addition to the English source text, Salkinson may have consulted the Schlegel-Tieck German translation of the two plays, which was very prominent and widely circulated, or perhaps another German version, but this is uncertain as he did not make explicit reference to it (in contrast to Smolenskin, who does mention consulting an unspecified German version of *Othello*, possibly Philipp Kaufmann's[43]).

4 This edition of *Ithiel the Cushite of Venice* and *Ram and Jael*

4.1 The Hebrew text

This edition reproduces the Hebrew text of Salkinson's translations as they first appeared in print in the 1870s. The original spelling and vocalization have been preserved even where they differ from what would be expected. In such cases the standard equivalent is provided in a footnote on the Hebrew side of the edition indicated by an asterisk. (Note that Smolenskin included a small number of footnotes in his prefaces to the plays, as did Salkinson in his introductory letters and occasionally in the body of the translations; these are indicated by an asterisk followed by a round bracket, as in the original editions.) The only corrections made to the vocalization consist of a handful of changes that were listed as errata at the end of the original editions of *Ithiel* and *Ram and Jael*, which I have incorporated into the text without comment. The numerous citations of biblical and postbiblical sources appearing in the translations have been marked in bold font so as to make it easier for readers to identify them. Such citations, as well as any other issues requiring comment, are indicated by a numbered footnote and explained in the running commentary to the edition.[44] The original format of the stage directions has largely been preserved, but inconsistencies have been ironed out.

4.2 The English back-translation

Salkinson's Hebrew text is accompanied by a facing English back-translation. The primary purpose of the back-translation is to make Salkinson's work accessible to readers without knowledge of Hebrew, whether scholars and students of multicultural Shakespeare, translation studies, comparative literature, or anyone with an interest in Shakespeare, Eastern European Jewish history, and/or Hebrew

42 See *Ram and Jael*, Second Part, notes 94 and 99.

43 See *Ithiel*, Publisher's Note, note 2.

44 See Section 4.3.

literature. With this in mind, I have favoured a relatively literal translation style so as to give readers as much of a feel for the Hebrew text as possible. However, I have modified Hebrew phrases or expressions that would be unidiomatic or very difficult to understand if rendered literally into English; in such cases literal translations are provided in footnotes. The translation tends towards a somewhat formal and slightly archaizing tone, which is designed to give readers a sense of Salkinson's biblicizing language. The English translations of Smolenskin's prefaces to the two plays (which are written in a cumbersome literary Hebrew style – not uncommon during this period – likewise replete with *meliṣa* and biblical references) are somewhat less literal while remaining relatively formal so as to match his style as closely as possible.

Each citation or allusion to a biblical or postbiblical textual source is marked in bold and accompanied by a numbered footnote. The English translations of the numerous biblical citations appearing in Salkinson's work are my own. However, in formulating my translations I have consulted various English Bible versions, including traditional texts (the Geneva Bible and King James Bible) as well as more recent versions (the New English Bible, New Revised Standard Version, and New International Version) in addition to the Jewish Publication Society's 1917 and 1985 editions. In most cases my translation choices are based on the King James Bible and Geneva Bible, which were felt to be the most appropriate as they lend an archaizing tone to the text that evokes the feel of Salkinson's biblicizing Hebrew while simultaneously corresponding most closely to the sixteenth- and seventeenth-century context of Shakespeare's own writing. Moreover, in many instances the particular phrasing appearing in the traditional versions is more familiar to English-speaking readers than those of the contemporary translations. However, in cases where the King James and Geneva Bible renditions are at odds with Salkinson's meaning, or contain archaic and unfamiliar vocabulary that might be confusing to readers, I have opted for a translation more closely resembling one of the modern versions. I have not usually indicated which English Bible version my back-translation is based on except in cases where the differences between them are relevant to the issue under discussion (e.g., the translation of the term כּוּשִׁי 'Cushite'[45]). The translations of Salkinson's citations of rabbinic literature are likewise my own, but I have consulted English translations where these exist (most commonly Danby 1933 for the Mishnah).

I have generally maintained Salkinson's punctuation except when it clashes markedly with English norms. Comparison of the Hebrew text with the facing English back-translation will make such cases clear.

---

45 See *Ithiel*, First Part, note 26.

4.3 The commentary

The bilingual edition of Salkinson's plays is accompanied by a running commentary indicated by numbered footnotes. The commentary serves five main purposes. First, it provides readers with a key to the various Hebrew textual sources (primarily biblical, but sometimes rabbinic and medieval) embedded in the translations. Second, it points out and analyses Salkinson's domesticating translation choices, comparing them with the source text and discussing the motivations behind the decisions. Third, it elucidates issues with which many readers may be unfamiliar (chiefly biblical and postbiblical figures, biblical locations, and aspects of Jewish history, law, ritual, and culture). Fourth, where possible, given the constraints of the volume, it raises points of comparison between Salkinson's and Shakespeare's texts regarding issues other than domestication (e.g., the use of rhyme, omission of lines, conversion of prose to verse, resemblances to the Folio versus Quarto versions). Finally, it discusses issues of relevance to students and scholars of Hebrew language and literature, such as Salkinson's use of particular lexical items or grammatical constructions that differ from the biblical standard (although due to space limitations and because these are not the primary focus of the edition, such issues are discussed only sparingly).

The rich array of biblical citations in Salkinson's translations vary in length from two-word collocations to most or all of a verse. For the sake of comprehensiveness I have included references to almost all such sources, including the shorter ones, as even these may be useful to readers both because they help to highlight the extent to which Salkinson's work is underpinned by intertextual references, and because they provide an explanation for what might otherwise seem to be unexpected or awkward turns of phrase lacking precedent in Shakespeare's text. The only exceptions to this policy comprise collocations that appear so many times in the Hebrew Bible and/or are such basic and commonly used elements of all forms of Hebrew that Salkinson's use of them is very unlikely to be directly traceable to a particular biblical source. When biblical phrases additionally appear in postbiblical Hebrew literature, these later sources are not cited in the footnotes because their ultimate source is the Bible.

When Salkinson incorporates a Hebrew textual source into his work without altering it, only the verse number is provided in the commentary. However, he often modifies his citations when inserting them into his translation; some such changes are intentional (e.g., changing the person or number of a possessive suffix in order to fit the story), but others (e.g., omitting or switching a preposition with no change in meaning) are most likely unintentional and are simply attributable to the fact that he was citing the sources from memory. When Salkinson's version differs from the original source, the source is provided for comparison along with an English translation of it. (In such cases the English translation of both the source and Salkinson's modified version may be the same.)

When a citation appears on multiple occasions in the plays, I have referenced it in each case. This has been done for the reader's convenience as well as to highlight the frequency of Salkinson's employment of particular biblical citations and facilitate the identification of any possible patterns in his selections. Where more than one biblical verse may have informed the text in question, the most relevant is provided first but the others, which may be similar but not quite as close, are listed as well.

In many cases I have refrained from commenting on the possible motivations for Salkinson's selection of a given biblical or postbiblical source. This is both because such an extended commentary is beyond the scope of this volume, and because in many instances Salkinson's choices were most likely driven primarily or solely by the fact that the meaning of the sources in question fit his translatorial purposes rather than due to a desire to convey any particular symbolism or deeper meaning. However, in certain instances the citation in question has clear and striking associations that would almost certainly have resonated with the target audience and play a role in shaping the sense of the Hebrew text; in such cases I have provided an explanatory note to draw the reader's attention to the significance of these overtones.

Although Smolenskin's prefaces to the two plays are likewise replete with biblical and sometimes postbiblical citations, I have not referenced these unless they are of particular relevance to his discussion or would be difficult to understand without explanation. Likewise, I have not referenced or commented on the biblical names for characters (e.g., Ithiel for Othello, Ram for Romeo) mentioned in the prefaces; these are discussed when they first appear in the plays themselves.

I have used the standard scholarly Arden Third Series editions of *Othello* and *Romeo and Juliet* for the English line numbers and citations. Note that Salkinson's *Ram and Jael* is based on the First Folio edition whereas the Arden version is based on the Second Quarto. Where there are differences between the Quarto and Folio editions reflected in Salkinson's translation, these are indicated in the commentary.

אִיתִיאֵל הַכּוּשִׁי מִוִּינֶעצְיָא

Ithiel the Cushite of Venice

פתח דבר*)

Preface*)

נקמות נעשה היום בהבריטאנים, המה לקחו את כתבי קדשנו ויעשו בהם כאדם העושה בשלו, העתיקום, פזרום לכל קצות הארץ כמו להם המה, וגם אנחנו נשלם להם היום פעלתם אל חיקם, כי נקח את הספרים היקרים בעיניהם ככתבי הקדש, את חזיונות שעקספיר ונביאם לאוצר שפת קדשנו, ואם לא מתוקה הנקמה הזאת?!

Today we get revenge on the British; they have taken our Holy Scriptures and treated them as one treats one's own property: they have translated them, scattered them to all corners of the earth as if they were their own, and so today we repay them for their deed, for we are taking the books which are as precious to them as the Holy Scriptures, the plays of Shakespeare, and we are bringing them into the treasure-house of our holy tongue; is this revenge not sweet?!

חזיונות שעקספיר בשפת קדש! לוא הבינו כל ישראל את שפת אבותם וחובבוה, ולוא הבינו כל המבינים שפת עבר וחובביה את השלל הגדול אשר יביא המעתיק את החזיונות האלה לאוצר שפתנו, כי אז היה היום אשר בו הופיע החזיון הראשון לשעקספיר בשפת עבר כיום חג נצחון, כי אמנם נצחון גדול הוא לשפת קדשנו אם אבני חן כאלה תכללנה יפיה. אבני חן כאלה יתנו לה לוית חן ונעורים בעת הזאת, למרות חפץ מנדיה אשר לא יבינוה שיאמרו: בלה היא, מטה לשחת, קברוה, כסו פניה בטמון ובשמה לא תזכירו עוד.

The plays of Shakespeare in the holy tongue! If the entire Jewish people understood the language of their forefathers and loved it, and if all of those who understood the language and loved it understood the great spoil that the translator of these plays is bringing into the treasure-house of our language, then the day on which the first Shakespeare play appeared in the Hebrew language would be like a victory holiday, because it is indeed a great victory for our holy tongue if such gems perfect its beauty. Such gems adorn it with grace and youth at this time, despite the desire of those who reject it, who do not understand it, who say that it is worn out, bound for the grave; who bury it, cover its face in obscurity and do not mention its name again.

*) לאלה אשר לא קראו את המחזה עד הנה, איעץ כי יקראו דברי אלה אחרי אשר קראו את החזיון עד תמו, כי דברים רבים יהיו להם כדברי הספר החתום.

*) For those who have not yet read the play, I recommend that they read this preface after they have read the play to the end, because much of what I say will be like a sealed book to them.

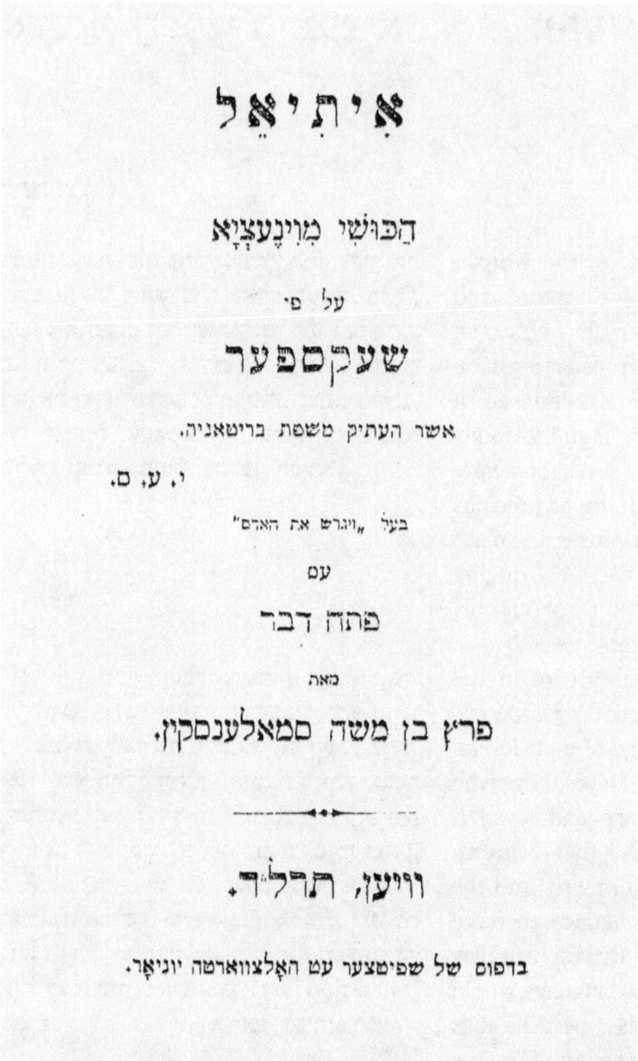

אִיתִיאֵל

הַכּוּשִׁי מִוִּינֶעצְיָא

על פי

שעקספער

אשר העתיק משפת בריטאניה.

י. ע. ס.

בעל „ויגרש את האדם"

עם

פתח דבר

מאת

פרץ בן משה סמאלענסקין.

ווין, תרל"ד.

בדפוס של שפיטצער עט האָלצוואַרטה יוניאָר.

Figure 2 (Hebrew title page of *Ithiel*)

The plays of Shakespeare, the greatest playwright without compare in all the languages and tongues, except for the Holy Scriptures and Homer, to whom have been revealed all the human heart's secret schemes, machinations, and wiles, who has displayed before

חזיונות שעקספיר, החוזה חזיונות הגדול מאין כמהו בכל השפות והלשונות, מלבד כתבי הקדש והאָמער, אשר לפניו נגלו כל צפוני חקרי לב אנוש ומזמותיו ותחבולותיו, אשר הציג לפנינו לב האדם ערום ונקרא בו כמעל ספר פתוח כל הרשום עליו בכתב החפץ והתאוה הנותנים יד לכל מחשבה, פעולה ומעשה לשבט או לחסד,

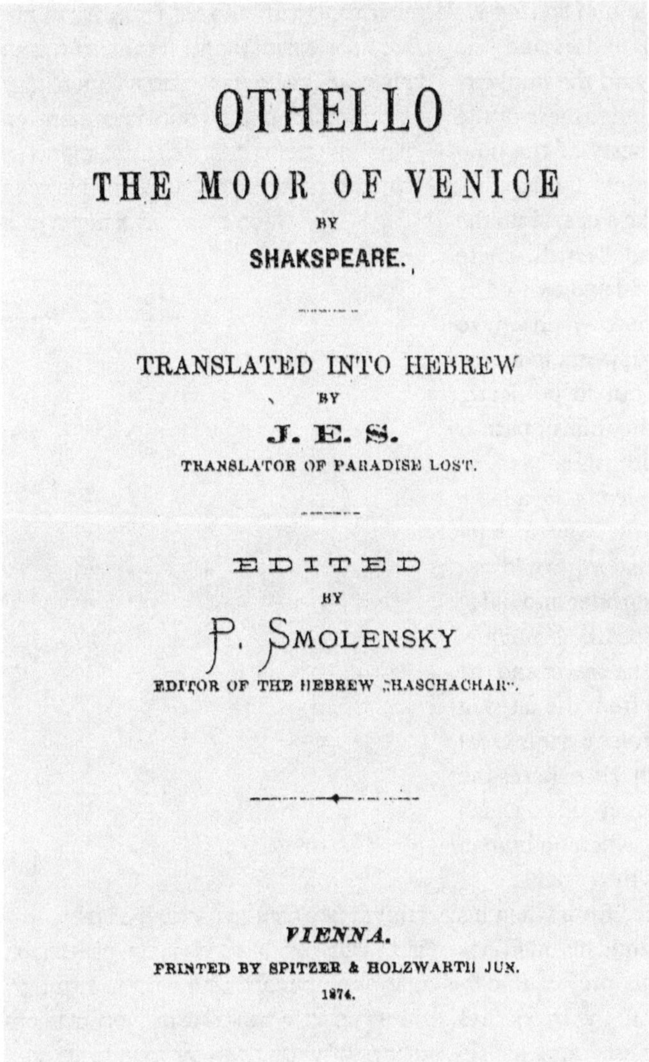

OTHELLO
THE MOOR OF VENICE
BY
SHAKSPEARE.

TRANSLATED INTO HEBREW
BY
J. E. S.
TRANSLATOR OF PARADISE LOST.

EDITED
BY
P. SMOLENSKY
EDITOR OF THE HEBREW „HASCHACHAR".

VIENNA.
PRINTED BY SPITZER & HOLZWARTH JUN.
1874.

Figure 3 (English title page of *Ithiel*)

us the naked human heart, so that we may read, as from an open book, everything that is inscribed upon it, the desire and the lust which, for good or for ill, have a share in every thought, deed, and action, and who can show us as well as he how man behaves and

ומי כמהו מורה אותנו דרכי האדם ויצרי מעלליו למען נדע ונבין מרמות ערומים ונכלי נוכלים, צדקת צדיקים וישר ישרי לב למען נדע ונשכיל ולא נלך כבהמה בבקעה[1] בתבל הבלולה הזאת. אשר בני האדם ישנו פניה ויעוו דרכיה עד כי לא נדע הדרך נלך בה. כי יש אשר נראה דרך צדקה והיא – מות, דרך רשע כסל והיא בצדקה תְּכּוֹנָן, והמורה הנאמן

the impulses that drive him so that we might recognize and understand the deceit of the cunning and the duplicity of scoundrels, the righteousness of the righteous and the honesty of the honest, so that we might know and be wise, rather than walking like a beast into the valley[1] on this confounded earth, where the apparent is so altered and twisted by men that we do not know which way to go. For at times what appears to be the righteous path turns out to be death, while the wicked or the foolish path is nevertheless paved with righteousness. But this faithful guide leads us, a lamp in his hand lighting the way to banish the darkness so that we would not stumble but see and consider and judge for ourselves. Shakespeare is unique; none but him has had the power and the courage to lift the veil from the faces of actors who play their roles on this great stage of ours, the earth. He exposes the deeds of nation and man alike, which take place in the dark, when no human eye would see them as they are.

הזה יוליכנו אחריו ונר מאיר הדרך בידו להגיה האפלה למען נראה ונתבונן ונשפוט ולא נכשל. אחד הוא שעקספיר ואין מלבדו, אשר בידו היה הכֹּח ובלבו האֹמץ להרים המסך מעל פני המשחקים בבמת משחק הגדולה הזאת, בתבל, ויצג לפנינו מעשי גוי ואדם יחד, אשר במחשך יֵעָשׂוּ ועין אדם לא תשורם כמו.

A long time passed from when his plays first appeared until his methods became known and his project understood; for a long time all the hypocrites and self-righteous priests and senseless authors were angry with him as those who rebel against light fight the sunlight; these bats banded together against him to extinguish the light of his plays and eradicate them from the face of the earth as they sought to darken all brightness and light, but a sapphire

ימים רבים עברו מעת אשר נראו חזיונותיו בטרם אשר הכירו דרכיו והבינו פעלו, ימים רבים נִחֲרוּ בו כל החנפים והכהנים המתקדשים והסופרים חסרי הדעה כאשר יריבו מורדי אור באור שמש; העטלפים האלה יחד עליו התמלאו לכבות אור חזיונותיו ולהשמידם מעל פני האדמה כאשר בקשו להקדיר כל נֹגה ואור, אך לא לעולם יתגולל ספיר בבוץ ולא לנצח יכסו עננים על פני השמש, הבוץ יוסר והספיר יראה בכל כבודו, העננים יכלו והשמש תשמח עין, וכן היה גם לשעקספיר כי גואליו קמו אחרי שתי מאות שנה ויראו לַכֹּל את ערך האבן היקרה אשר אמרו

1 The phrase 'like a beast into the valley' is a citation of Isa. 63:14, but Smolenskin seems to be using it to denote ignorance, whereas in Isaiah it refers to effortlessness.

להשביתה מטהרה בהשליכם עליה שקוצים, ואם אמנם גם עד היום הזה לא כל הקוראים יבינו את ערך החוזה חזיונות גדל דעה הזה, ועוד יקומו כפעם בפעם חסרי דעה וטעם לשים בו דפי, אך חכמי הלב נמנו וגמרו כלם כי המגדף את שעקספיר את נפשו הוא מגדף.

will not stay wallowing in mud for eternity, and clouds will not cover the face of the sun forever, the mud will be removed and the sapphire will appear in all its glory, the clouds will dissipate and the sun will make the eye rejoice, and so it was also for Shakespeare, for his redeemers arose after two hundred years and showed everyone the worth of the precious stone which they had tried to strip of its purity by besmirching it, and although admittedly until this day not all readers appreciate this brilliant playwright, and from time to time senseless and witless men still arise to malign him, nevertheless the wise men have made themselves counted and have all determined that one who reviles Shakespeare reviles himself.

ולא לפלא הוא אם רבים לא הבינו ולא יבינו עד היום לפעולות האדם הגדול הזה המורם מהסופרים, כי הרבים לא יבינו ולא ישכילו מה היא האמת, כי הסכינו מאז לקרוא לשקר אמת, ואם יראו את האמת אז לא יכירו פניה ויאמרו שקר היא! וכל אלה באשמת הסופרים המתעים את קוראיהם בכזבים נעימים למען קחת לבם. רוב הסופרים וחוזי חזיונות מבשרם יחזו כל איש ואת אשר יכשר בעיניהם אותו יתנו לפנינו כטוב וישר ועל כל אשר לזרא הוא לרוחם יָרְבוּ לשליך שקוצים. ברואי חזיונותיהם אשר כטובים וישרים יציגום לפנינו ידברו וישיחו רק מעלות רוח בוראיהם, וכל מדבר או עושה לא כחפץ לבם הוא רע ובליעל. סופרים כאלה ישימו מסוה על פעולות בני איש ומחשבותיהם ויתעו את קוראיהם לבלתי ראות את אשר יֵעָשֶׂה באמת, אחרי כי לא פעולות בני האדם וחפציהם יָרְאוּ לנו כי אם חפץ לבם המה, ואם ישגו בדרכי לביהם אז ירימו את השפל וישפילו את הגבה, יצדיקו את הרשע וירשיעו את התם. כזאת יעשו גם הסופרים הישרים בלבותם רק מאשר כי לא חננו ברוח נאמן לשפוט את הדבר כמו, כי אם מבשרם

But it is no wonder if many have not understood, and to this day do not understand, the works of this great man, the most exalted of writers, for the masses do not understand and do not realize what truth is, for they have long since grown accustomed to calling lies truth. And if they were to see the truth, they would not recognize it, and they would say that it was a lie! And all of this is the fault of the authors who mislead their readers with pleasant lies in order to capture their heart. Most authors and playwrights see everyone from their own perspective, and what is fitting to them they present to us as good and honest, while everything which they dislike, they besmirch. The characters they create in their plays, whom they present to us as good and upright, speak and converse only of the exalted spirit of their creators, and any of them who does not speak or do as their creators' heart desires is evil and a villain. Such authors mask men's actions and thoughts, misleading their readers so that they cannot see what is really being done, since they do not show us men's actions and desires but rather their own hearts' desires, and if they succeed in following their hearts, then they raise up that which is low and lower that which is high, acquit the wicked and condemn the innocent. Authors who are honest also do so, only since they cannot be trusted to judge the matter as it is, but rather see everything from their own perspective, they corrupt justice and lead their readers astray by showing them perversions, not maliciously but rather in error. But there are authors even more evil than these (and they are the majority), playwrights who do not prevail on earth for the sake of truth and knowledge, but rather only in order to make a name and money for themselves, and they maliciously destroy all sense of morality and love of truth, for they attempt to present to their community of readers only that which is pleasant to them; they sing in their ears songs that are pleasing to the ear and extol with their tongue indecency and desire, speaking lustfully of everyone who prevails on earth by means of their wanton schemes and the impulses that drive them; they present to us as heroes men who violate law and morality, who mock truth and hate innocence, and every innocent man is like a powerless creature in their eyes, and as such the plays are of little dignity, and the places in which they

יחזו הכל והמה יעותו משפט ויתעו את קוראיהם לחזות תהפוכות, לא בזדון כי אם בשגגה. אך ישנם סופרים עוד רעים מאלה (והמה הרבים), חוזי חזיונות אשר לא למען האמת והדעת יגברו בארץ, כי אם רק למען עשות להם שם וכסף, והמה ישחיתו כל רגש מוסר ואהבת האמת בזדון לב, כי המה יבקשו לתת לפני קהל קוראיהם אך את אשר ינעם להם, המה ישירו באזניהם שירים ערבים לאֹזן וירוממו תחת לשונם זמה ותאוה, ועגבים בפיהם לכל אשר יגברו בארץ במזמות תאותיו ויצרי מעלליו, כגבורים יציגו לפנינו אנשים אשר יפרעו חֹק ומוסר, אשר ילעגו לאמת וישנאו תֹּם, וכל תם דרך כגֹלם אין ידים לו בעיניהם, אשר על כן דל מאוד כבוד החזיונות ובתי המשחק, מקום אשר יציגו לעינינו גבורי המחזות האלה, אשר תכליתם היא להורות את העם דעת מוסר והשכל, היו כמערות פריצים, כבתי ספר להורות את בני הנעורים איך לרדוף אחרי זמה ותבל.

present to us the protagonists of these plays, the playhouses, whose purpose is to instruct the people in morality and wisdom, have become like thieves' dens, like schools for youth to instruct them in how to chase after indecency and disgrace.

Not so is the lot of Shakespeare (and like him, so too all honest authors who have eyes to see what is in front of them, even if their spirit is not as great as his); he sits at the seat of judgement like a god judging the exalted; before his seat of judgement stand both king and slave, both nation and individual, and he considers everything, investigates everything, does not show partiality to anyone and does not favour his protagonists; no one is loved by him and no one is hateful in his eyes; he weighs everyone's deeds on the scales and tells each man of the righteousness within him, even if he is a rogue and a villain, and he does not show partiality to the honest by ignoring their flaws, for no one is blameless in the land of the living. He does not refrain from pronouncing judgement for fear that hypocrites would rage at him, he does not pay heed to his audience for fear that the scene may displease them when they choose an opulently dressed lie over the naked truth. It is not in accordance with his own heart's desire or others' inclinations that he sets out a path for his characters and determines their end, but rather in accordance with the course, the rules, the accidents, and the circumstances of life, and therefore his plays contain a righteous man who perishes by his righteousness as he falls

לא כאלה חלק שעקספיר (וכמֹהו כן גם כל הסופרים הישרים אשר להם עינים לראות נכחה, אף אם כי לא כרוחו הכביר רוחם); הוא ישב לכסא משפט כאל שופט רמים, לפני כס משפטו יעמדו כמלך כעבד, כגוי כאדם, והוא יתבונן לכל, יחקור הכל, לא ישא פנים לאיש ולא יכיר פני גבוריו, אין אהוב לנפשו ואין שנוא לנגד עיניו, את מעשי כלם ישקול בפלס, ויגיד לאיש צקדתו אשר תמצא בו, אף אם הוא עַוָל ובליעל, ואת פני הישרים לא ישא ממום, כי אין נקי בארץ החיים. הוא לא יירא בדברו משפט פן יזעמוהו חנפים, לא ישים לבו לשומעי דבריו פן לא ינעם להם המחזה, כי יבחרו בשקר לבוש מכלול מאמת ערומה. לא לפי חפץ לבו או לרוח אחרים יַתְוֶה דרך לברואיו וישים קץ להם, כי אם על פי דרכי החיים ומשטריהם ומקריהם ומסבותיהם, אשר על כן יש בחזיונותיו צדיק אובד בצדקתו בנפלו בפח פועלי און ורשע מאריך ברעתו כי לו נתכנו עלילות, ויש אשר יד המקרה תנחת עליהם וצדיק ורשע יחד יסופו יתמו, כי כן המה דרכי החיים.

into the snare of evildoers, and a villain who lives long by his wickedness, because he is destined for great things, and there are those upon whom the hand of fate lands, when the righteous and the wicked together come to an end and meet their demise, for such are the paths of life.

On the paths of life we see each morning that the earth belongs to the mighty man, and the man who plots evil rules over everything, over the spirits of the innocent and their bodies, and in his cunning he makes even them into a weapon of destruction. On the paths of life we see that not only honesty triumphs over injustice, and the pure-hearted man does not always eat the fruits of his deeds. On the paths of life we observe that not all wrongdoers are brought to justice, as they know how to put a shield and buckler around themselves in their cunning, and justice is not powerful enough to punish many wicked men who have caused much suffering and ruin, even if their treachery is known in the community. Indeed, what is the punishment that should be borne by one who slanders his fellow with lies and deposes him from his position with the breath of his mouth, or brings him to the gates of death? The guileless man is led astray and falls, while the one who led him astray rises up and rejoices because he has accomplished his desire, or if a villain entices the innocent with a flattering tongue to do evil and spill blood, and the innocent man who commits the evil is judged and punished for his sin, whereas the villain who led him astray

בדרכי החיים נראה בבֹקר בבֹקר כי איש זרוע לו הארץ ובעל מזמות ישלוט בכל, ברוח תמימי לב ובגויתם ויעשן גם אותן לכלי משחית ביד ערמתו. בדרכי החיים נראה כי לא רק הישר על עול יתגבר, ולא כפרי מעלליו יאכל תמיד טהר לב. בדרכי החיים נתבונן כי לא כל עושי עול יובאו במשפט, בדעתם לשים עליהם צנה וסוחרה בערמתם, וידי המשפט תקצרנה מענוש רשעים רבים אשר הרבו עמל ושוד גם אם נודע מעלם בקהל. הן מה הוא העֹנש אשר ישא מלשין רעהו בשקר וממצבו יהדפנו ברוח פיו, או יביאהו עד שערי מות? הפתי נתעה ויפול והמתעה יקום וישמח כי חפצו הצליח בידו, או אם ידיח נבל את תמים, בחלקת לשון לעשות עול ולשפוך דם, התמים העושה העול ישא חטאתו במשפט והבליעל המתעהו בשוא, יעמוד ויראה בכרוע הנדח לטבח, ואם איש זרוע או אוצרות הוא המתעה אז ינחל גם כבוד חכמים ובסוד יועצים יחד כבודו, כי איש דעת הוא. מה יהיה משפט חנפים העובדים בכרם האמונה וממנה לחמם נמצא אם בשמה יעשקו עֹשק, או אם בסתר אהלם יעשו כל זמה ותועבה וילעגו לאמונתם ואלהיהם? אלה ישבו ספונים בטירותיהם ויד לא תגע בהם, ואם יקום איש דעת לחות משפט נגד האמונה אז עונו ישא. – במה יְוָסְרוּ גוזלי ארצות ועמים בלי ישר ומשפט וידכאו רב אדם תחת רגליהם? משפטם הוא כי יהיו לאדירי ארץ ומפניהם יֵחַתּוּ אלים ושמם ינשא על כל שפתים, ואם ישלח רעב את ידו בפת לחם רעהו, גנב ופושע הוא וכל העם יראו את המשפט אשר יעשו בו ויצדיקו עליו את הדין כמו המה טהורים ונקיים וכל עמלם אך בכשרון וצדק וישר בא להם. – מה הוא המוסר אשר ינחל אב אכזר

with a lie stands and watches as the one who was lured kneels for slaughter, and if the one who led astray is a mighty or wealthy man, then he will be greatly honoured by the sages and will be counted among the wise counsellors, as a knowledgeable man; what will be the judgement of godless ones who toil in the vineyard of faith and earn their living from it, even if they exploit others in its name, or if they commit every indecency and abomination in private and mock their faith and their God? These men sit sheltered in their castles, and no hand can touch them, and if a knowledgeable man arises to make a judgement against the faith then he will be punished for his iniquity. – What is the punishment of those who rob lands and nations dishonestly and unjustly, who trample many men under their feet? Their sentence is that they become mighty men of the land, feared by gods, and exalted upon all lips, but if a hungry man helps himself to his fellow's piece of bread, he is a thief and a criminal, and the whole nation sees the judgement which is brought against him and they consider it just, as if they were pure and blameless, and everything they do is achieved only through skill and justice and honesty. – How would the judges chastise a cruel father for ruling over his offspring like a cruel lord, reining in their spirit with a bit and bridle as if they were livestock bought with his money rather than his own flesh and blood, and for dealing with them in whichever way he fancies, forcing his son to take a wife not after his own

מאת השופטים על רדותו בפרי בטנו כאדון אכזר וישים מתג ורסן לרוחם כמו מקנת כספו ולא עצמו ובשרו המה, ויסחר בהם כהעולה על רוחו, יצוה במפגיע על בנו לקחת לו רעיה לא כלבבו כי אם כחפץ האב, אשר אל יחש משפחות או הון עתק יביט, יאסור ידי בתו אשר נפשה כלתה לאיש כלבבה ויתנה לאשר תבחל נפשה בו ויגזול אשרה וחייה, ויכביד עליה אכפו לסבב בכחש את אלוף נעוריה אשר ירכיב לראשה ואשר רק ידה לא לבה תתן לו ויביא רעות עליה ועל אהוב נפשה ושנוא נפשה אשר היה לבעל לה כאחד, כי הכבוד או הכסף עורו עיניו, ולא ישיב אל לבו כי נפשות הוא חומס, נפשות נקיות, נפש פרי בטנו יחבל, ואם יש משפט אשר ייסר כפעולתם אכזרים כאלה אשר לרגעים נראם? – או היש עין צופיה למעשי בעל אביר לב אשר יענה נפש אשתו באכזריות לב, יונה בדברים וימרר חייה בלי רגש חמלה אשר גם לעבדו לא יעשה כזאת מיראה פן יתפרץ מפניו, ולא לכלבו פן יעלה אפו וישכהו בשניו, בדעתו כי היא רפת ידים ותשא מכאוביה? הכֹּח הוא הישר, זאת יאמרו לנפשם כל בעלי הכֹּח, ואלה המה דרכיהם ולא חרב המשפט עליהם. הן אלה המה דרכי החיים, ואם לפלא הוא כי מספר הישרים מעט מעט מאוד והזדים יגברו ויעצמו בארץ, כי כל סר מרע משתולל הוא בעיני כל יודעיו ואיש אשר הצליח, לו כביר כֹּח לב יֵאָמֵר, ואם נשתומם עוד אם נראה צדיק אובד בצדקתו, אחרי כי עוזריו המה אך מעטים, ואוהבי העול, או היראים מפניו, המה כמעט כל בני האדם, ואם כן אם נחפוץ לתאר בעט אמת את דרכי בני האדם אז עלינו להציב יד למחזות מדאיבי לב כאלה, ואם אין, נעשה שקר בנפשנו כי רק חזון לבנו ולא מראה החיים נראה לקוראי דברינו. ואם אמנם נראה לא לעתים רחוקות כי גם רשעים בחבלי חטאתם יתמכו, כי ערומים ילכדו בערמתם ובפח טמנו תלכד רגלם המה, אך גם זאת נדע כי לא יד המשפט, ולא צקדת בני האדם אשר יבקשו אך צדק תעשינה זאת כי אם יד המקרה, אשר לא תכיר פני איש אם צדיק או רשע, ומה יועיל להתמימים אשר מרגשת פועלי און נכחדו אם לעת קץ תמלא גם

heart but rather in accordance with the wishes of the father, who is thinking of family pedigree or great wealth; who binds the hands of his daughter who yearns for a man after her heart, giving her to someone who repulses her, robbing her of her joy and her life, and leading her to deceive the husband he has forced on her, for she gives him only her hand and not her heart. He thus brings evil upon her, upon her beloved, and also upon the one whom she despises, who has become her husband, for glory or money blinded his eyes, and he does not notice that he is violating lives, blameless lives, the lives of his offspring, which he is ruining, yet is there a judgement which will appropriately rebuke such cruel men whom we see at every moment? – Or is there an eye watching over the deeds of a hard-hearted man who cruelly humiliates his wife, deceives her with words and embitters her life without any compassion, such things as he would not do even to his servant, out of fear that he might run away from him, nor to his dog lest he grow angry and bite him with his teeth, as he knows that she is weak and will endure her pains? Power is right, this is what all powerful men say, and this is how they behave, and the sword of justice does not hang over them. Indeed, these are the paths of life, and is it a wonder that the number of honest men is extremely small, while the wicked prevail and grow powerful on earth, for anyone who turns away from evil is regarded as a madman by those who know him, and it is said of a successful man that he has great

סאת הרשעים ויהיו עדי אובד, האם יחיו מתיהם ברדתם המה דומה? האם ירימו הנדכאים ראש עת אשר יְשְׁפְּלוּ משפיליהם? אך לא! נקל מאוד לעשות רעה, לבלע ולהשחית, להוריד רב אדם עד דכא אך ברוח פה, אבל לא לעשות טובה, לסמוך נופלים, להרים קרן אלה אשר השכינו לעפר כבודם. אם תוציא דבה על איש אז יאמין לך כל שומע כרגע מבלי בקש חשבונות רבים ואוזל לו יוסיף עליה כהנה וכהנה, ואם טוב תדבר על רעיך אז לא על נקלה תמצא אזנים קשובות ולב מאמין, אשר על כן תרבה הרעה מהטובה, כי לעשות רע לא דרוש כֹּח ועֹז וחכמה רק לב רע, ולעשות הטוב דרוש לא רק לב טוב, כי אם רוח נכון ואֹמץ ודעת ויגיע רבה.

strength of heart, so should we still be astonished if we see a righteous man perish in his righteousness, since his helpers are only few, and those who love evil, or who are in awe of it, comprise almost all men. Thus, if we desire to depict men's character with a true pen, then we must acknowledge such painful sights, as otherwise we deceive ourselves, for only the vision of our hearts and not that which is seen in life will be visible to our readers. Now admittedly we see not infrequently that wicked men are also caught in the bonds of their sin, for cunning men can be trapped in their cunning and their leg can be caught in the snare that they themselves set, but here too we know that it is not justice, nor the righteousness of men who seek only justice, that do this, but rather circumstance, which does not show partiality to anyone whether righteous or wicked, and how does it benefit the innocent who have been destroyed by the throng of evildoers if in the end the wicked get their just desserts, and they perish; will their dead live as they go down to the grave? Will the oppressed lift up their head when those who humiliate them are humiliated? Why, no! It is very easy to do evil, to annihilate and destroy, to reduce a multitude of men to dust with only a single breath, but not to do good, to support those who are falling, to exalt those who have surrendered their own honour. If you spread libel against a man, everyone who hears will immediately believe you without asking for much evidence, and will go on his way adding to it here and there. But if you speak well of your fellows, you will not easily find attentive ears and a believing heart, and therefore you will do more evil than good, for in order to do evil power and might and wisdom are not required, only an evil heart, whereas in order to do good not only is a good heart required, but a willing spirit and courage and knowledge and much toil.

On account of which, every man of sense will understand that those who describe for us how only pious and righteous men become great, whereas wrongdoers are scattered, are lying; they are flattering their readers and leading them astray with lies, and everything that they do is only wickedness or grievous harm, for it does not cause men to do good or consider their conduct or understand the paths of life.

אשר על כן יבין כל איש לבב כי אלה אשר יתארו לפנינו כי רק חסידים ותמימים ירימו ראש ובני עולה יתפרדו, כי אלה מכזבים המה, חנופה יעשו לקוראי דבריהם ויתעום בשקר וכל פעלם אך רעות רוח או רעה חולה, כי על ידו לא ייטיבו בני האדם מעלליהם ולא יתבוננו לדרכיהם ולא יבינו דרכי החיים.

Many may ask: what is the lesson of a play that presents us with wicked men who succeed in their deeds, and what is the moral that we should take from the sight of righteous men perishing in their righteousness? Indeed, if we see that the wicked prosper, then we shall envy all traitors and refrain from seeking to learn to do well. Not so if we are shown the chastisement and punishment of the wicked; in that case we shall learn to fear doing evil – so say many who preach morality without knowing what it is. Truth endures forever; it stands above all, higher than any feeling, even honesty and justice and morality, for without truth these are all meaningless. Such feelings change their appearance from generation to generation and from era to era, and

רבים ישאלו: מה הוא הלקח הטוב אשר יצא מאת חזיון המציג לפנינו רשעים מצליחים במעשיהם, ומה הוא המוסר אשר נקח ממראה צדיקים אובדים בצדקתם? הן אם נראה כי דרך רשעים צלחה אז נקנא בכל בוגדי בגד ולא נבקש להשכיל להיטיב, לא כן אם יראונו מוסר הזדונים וענשם אז נקח מוסר ונירא מעשות רע – כן יאמרו רבים אשר הסכינו לשאת מוסר על שפת לשונם מבלי דעת מה הוא. האמת לעולם תעמוד, היא נעלה ונשגבה מכל חפץ, מכל רגש גם מישר וצדק ומוסר, כי באין אמת כל אלה הבל. רגשות כאלה תמירנה פניהן מדור לדור ומעת עד עת, ויש אשר לפנים לו צדק, ישר ומוסר קראו ועתה הוא כמעשה תעתועים או רשע כסל, ויש אשר עתה נעריצהו ונכבדהו כמוסר נעלה ואם נשאל לימים ראשונים ונכונן לבנו לחקר דורות קדומים נראה כי לפנים בחלה נפש אוהבי מוסר בו, רק האמת לעולם תעמוד, היא לא תשנה פניה וגם יד בני האדם תשלוט אך לשים מסוה על פניה,

there are things that previously were called justice, honesty, and morality, but now are considered acts of delusion or foolish wickedness, and there are such things which we now admire and honour as high morality, but if we enquire as to the earliest days and resolve to investigate previous generations, we see that previously lovers of morality found them distasteful, but truth endures forever; it does not change its appearance and men are powerful enough only to put a veil over its face, to cast dust on it until it cannot be seen by the eye, or to besmirch it until it becomes repulsive, but they cannot strip it of its purity; the day will come when the curtain will be lifted from its face and its beauty will be visible to everyone. The point of all morality is to seek the truth, and those who speak untruths hate morality or do not know what it is. What is to be gained from us leading the readers astray with plays that are false, where catastrophe is brought upon the wicked and the moment of punishment upon all evildoers, while the truth stands and cries out: it is a lie! for this is not what is done to them? What would be the lesson of such plays that do not depict the paths of life, but rather visions drawn from a heart that devises falsehood? Why, such plays delude their viewers, so that they do not examine their conduct and do not investigate and turn away from it, for they say to themselves: surely punishment follows on the heels of iniquity, and if we have not been punished, it is a sign that we have not sinned. What is the benefit of the fear generated by such plays, which depict only the punishment of the wicked; after all, it is pointless,

לעפר בעפר לעומתה עד כי לא תֵרָאֶה לעין, או להשליך עליה שקוצים עד כי תהיה לגֹעל נפש, אך מטהרה לא ישביתוה, יבוא יום ויגל את המסך מעל פניה ותראה יפעתה לעין כל. תכלית כל מוסר היא לבקש אמת, ואלה אשר לא אמת שמיעונו המה שונאי מוסר המה או לא ידעו מה הוא. מה בצע כי נוליך את הקוראים שולל בחזיונות שוא, כי נביא על רשעים אידם, ועל כל עושי עול רגע פקודתם, אם האמת תעמוד ותצעק: שקר הוא! כי לא כן יעשה להם? מה הוא הלקח הטוב אשר יצא מחזיונות כאלה אשר לא דרכי החיים יַתְוּו לנו כי אם חזיונות מלב הוגה שקר? הלא בחזיונות כאלה יַשְׁלוּ את נפש רואיהם לבל יחפשו דרכיהם ולבל יחקרו וישובו מהם, כי ישיבו אל לבם: הן בעקב העון המוסר ילך ואם לא נוסרנו אות הוא כי לא עוינו. מה היא התועלת אשר תצא מהפחד אשר יביאו חזיונות כאלה אשר יתארו אך מוסר רשעים, הלא פחד שוא וכעבור רגע ואינו. הפחד הזה הוא כהפחד אשר יפילו על ילדים כי יקראו קריאת שמע[2] ואם אין יבוא שד או מת וישים מחנק לנפשם, והילד יאמין ויפחד, אך אחרי אשר נסה לישן מבלי קרוא שמע ושנתו ערבה לו, השדים לא עזבו מדורת שאול[3] והמתים לא התנערו מעפר אז יחדל מהאמין בכל, וכל אשר הורוהו לעשות ביראה ופחד ישליך אחרי גוו. וכן היא כל תורה אשר יקבלו רק אחרי אשר יכפו על המקבלים הר כגיגית, כל עוד שאת ההר תבעתם יחזיקו בה ועבר הפחד ישליכוה ככלי אין חפץ בו, וכן הוא המורא אשר יביאו חזיונות כאלה המתארים עֹנש רשעים, תמימי לב יאמינו בו עדי הפקח עיניהם ויראו כי האמינו בשוא נתעה כי לא כן חלק הרשע בארץ, כי לא כל פגע רק עליו יסל ארחות אידו, כי לא כל צרה רק אותו תקראהו לרגלו, ומה הוא המוסר אשר יקח ממראה עיניו? אז יאמר: „כל האדם כוזב, וגם חוזי החזיונות אשר אמרתי אלהים המה, גם המה כאדם יחמדו כזב ושקר ירבו“. לא כן פעולות החוזים גלויי העינים אשר יקראו כל מעשי אנוש ותחבולותיו ומזמות לבו ויצר מחשבותיו כמעל ספר פתוח ואותם יציגו לנגד

and it vanishes in an instant. This fear is like the fear put into children that they must recite the Shema[2] or else a demon or corpse will come and strangle them, and the child believes and fears, but after he has tried to sleep without reciting the Shema and has slept well enough – the demons did not leave the fire of Sheol[3] and the corpses did not shake themselves out of the dust – then he stops believing in anything, and he abandons everything that he has been instructed to do out of awe and fear. And so it is with any instruction that is accepted only after it has been forced like a burden upon those accepting it; as long as bearing the burden scares them, they will hold onto it, but when the fear has passed they will throw it away like an unwanted vessel; and it is such fear that is generated by this type of play, which depicts the punishment of the wicked; innocent men believe in it until their eyes are opened and they see that they believed in misguided falsehood, for this is not the lot of the wicked on earth, and not every injury lands directly upon him, not every woe affects only him, and so what is the moral which he should take from what he sees? Then he says: 'Every man lies, and even the playwrights whom I said were gods, even they, as men, covet falsehood and lie often.' Not so for the works of playwrights with open eyes, who read all of man's deeds and thoughts and impulses as from an open book, and present them before our eyes naked as the day they were born; they do not turn evil

עינינו ערומים כיום הולדם, לא יהפכו רע לטוב ומר למתוק, אז יצא לנו מדבריהם מוסר נעלה, כי נראה את האמת ונתבונן כי אנשים ישרים אך מעט מזער המה והמה הבחירים במין האדם, ואם נפשנו תתאוה להיות מן הבחירים אז לא עלינו לשית לב להבלי ההמון, כי רעיון רוחנו יאמצנו, והדעת כי נעשה טוב היא היא המשכֹרת היותר גדולה אשר בידי בן אנוש למצוא, עינינו תפקחנה לראות יצרי לבבנו אשר המה כראשית חטאת, ואם נטה אך מעט מהדרך הטוב, כי אז נלך מדחי אל דחי, כי ראשית כל חטאת היא כחוט השני[4] ואחריתה כעבותות העגלה,[5] זאת נראה ונבין ונדע להזהר אם נחפוץ, ואלה אשר לא יחפצו, להם לא יועיל כל מוסר וכל מטיף. והתועלת היוצאת מחזיונות נאמנים על פי דרכי החיים היא רבה ונכבדה מאוד, כי המה יעשונו לאנשי לב. לא ביד כל האדם לדעת ולהכיר ארחות אנשים לאלפים בחליפות תאותיהם ובהשנות מקרי הזמן, כי חיינו קצרים, ועיננו לא תחדור על הרוב עד משכיות לבב אנוש, כי על כן הסופרים הנאמנים המה לנו לעינים, המה יחזו בעיני הרוח ואת אשר יראו יגידו לנו ונדע, וספרים כאלה יהיו לנו למורים היותר טובים ונאמנים, כי ינהלונו בדרכי החיים בעינים פקוחות לבל נכשל. והמורה הגדול בכל המורים היה שעקספיר; הוא יראנו בחזיונותיו שלשלת הפעולות אשר תמשך לפעמים מאת מקרה קל, מאת תאוה קטנה מלב איש קטן והיא תרחב ותגדל מעת לעת בְּהִלָּוֹת עליה מקרים שונים עדי תהי לכלי משחית לחבל רב אדם. הוא יורנו ארחות התאוה איך תובילנה אל ירכתי בור את הנלכדים בשחיתותיה ואיך ימשכו אחריהם אלה הנלכדים גם תמימי דרך אל אבדון הפתוח לפניהם, איך כמֹהו אשר ידע לשקול בפלס כל מקרה קל, כל חפץ אשר בראשיתו היה כמהו כאין ובאחריתו היה לקטב ישוד צהרים. נביט נא אל החזיון הזה שלפנינו אשר הוא אחד מהיותר

2 A central Jewish prayer consisting of the biblical passages Deut. 6:4–9, 11:13–21, and Num. 15:37–41. The Shema is recited at the morning and evening daily prayers and at bedtime.

3 The biblical abode of the dead.

into good and bitter into sweet, so high morals emerge for us from their words, for we see the truth and observe that honest men are but very few, and they are the choicest of the human race, and if our soul longs to be one of the choicest, then we must not pay heed to the delusions of the masses, for our own ideas should strengthen us, and the knowledge that we are doing good is the greatest reward that a human can receive; our eyes will open to see the impulses of our heart, which are like a gateway to sin, and if we deviate even a little bit from the good path, then we will go from bad to worse, for the beginning of every sin is but a scarlet thread,[4] while its end is like the heavy cords of a cart;[5] we see this, and we understand and know to be careful if we want to, and as for those who do not want to, no instruction or preacher will benefit them. And the benefit that emerges from plays faithful to the paths of life is very great and weighty, for they transform us into men of sense. Not every man is able to recognize the ways of men in the thousands with their changing desires and with the shifting circumstances of time, for our lives are short, and for the most part our eye does not penetrate the imaginings of the human heart; therefore

טובים אשר הוליד ברוחו הכביר, וננסה נא לדבר משפט על כל ברואי דמיונו הבאים בו.

4 There are several biblical references to a scarlet thread, i.e., Gen. 38:28, 30, in which a scarlet thread is tied to the wrist of one of Tamar's twin sons as he is born to identify him as the older one; Josh. 2:18, 21, in which Rahab, a resident of Jericho who shelters Joshua's men from danger when they come to scout out the city, ties a scarlet thread to her window as an identifying sign so that they will know to avoid harming anyone in her house during their subsequent invasion; Song of Songs 4:3, in which it is used romantically as a simile for lips; and various locations in Exodus, in which it is one of the materials used to make the priestly garments. Smolenskin seems to be referring to the warning function of the scarlet thread as it appears in Josh. 2:18, 21, but is focusing on it being only a thin thread, as the mere possibility of sin first emerges.

5 This is a reference to Isa. 5:18, הֹ֛וֹי מֹשְׁכֵ֥י הֶעָוֺ֖ן בְּחַבְלֵ֣י הַשָּׁ֑וְא וְכַעֲבֹ֥ות הָעֲגָלָ֖ה חַטָּאָֽה 'woe to those that draw iniquity with cords of falsehood, and sin as with the ropes of a cart'.

reliable authors become our eyes; they see with the eyes of the spirit and what they see, they tell us so that we might know, and their books become the best and most reliable teachers for us, for they guide us on the paths of life with open eyes so that we do not stumble. And the greatest of all teachers was Shakespeare; in his plays he shows us the chain of actions that sometimes unfolds from a trifling event, from a small desire of a small man's heart, which expands and grows from day to day accompanied by various events until it becomes an instrument of destruction annihilating many men. He instructs us in the ways of desire, how it leads those trapped in its corrupt snares to the depths of the pit, and how the trapped ones also pull innocent men after them into the destruction that has opened up before them; there is none like him who knows how to weigh on a scale every trifling event, every object that at first was as nothing but in the end became a disaster that lays waste at midday. Let us look at this play before us, which is one of the best that he brought into existence with his great spirit, and let us try to make a judgement about each of the characters created by his imagination that appear in it.

'Shakespeare sought to depict jealousy for us in this play, just as he depicted for us in *Hamlet* a man at his wits' end, in *Romeo and Juliet* love, and in *The Merchant of Venice* revenge.' Many of those who speak about him and his books have expressed their opinion in this manner, but in truth Shakespeare's power is not one thing, he does not show us one desire, but rather his power is in

„שעקספיר בקש לתאר לפנינו את הקנאה בחזיון הזה כאשר תאר לנו בהאמלעט איש אובד עצות, בראמעאָ ויוליעט את האהבה ובהסוחר מוויניציא את הנקמה" כן השמיעו דעתם רבים מהמדברים אודותו ואודות ספריו, אבל באמת יד שעקספיר לא דבר אחד, לא תאוה אחת תראנו, כי ידו בכל, ובכל אשר יתאר נראה תאות האדם ורגשותיו בכל מראיהן ומסבותיהן. בחזיון הזה נראה לא רק יד קנאת איש לאשתו, אשר תכה בעורון ותוליד שולל גם ישרי דרך לעשות מעשה

everything, and in everything that he depicts we see the desire and feelings of man in all their manifestations and circumstances. In this play we see not only the power of a man's jealousy over his wife, which strikes one with blindness and leads even upright men astray, causing them to commit acts of delusion, but also a man's jealousy of his companion, which, like a maggot, eats the heart of its master and leads him astray on the paths of death; the love of false honour, which hardens the heart against even one's own offspring and turns a loving father into one as cruel as ostriches in the wilderness;[6] innocence, which at first gives rest to the one who possesses it, for it instils within him trust in his fellows, but can change its shape like clay under a seal, and when the one who possesses it falls into the trap of a flattering tongue, then it turns into a raging staff, destroying honest men; faithful love that does not depart even if it is not repaid in kind; we see all of these together in this play, and upon all of these is the hand of fate, which weaves things of trifling worth and makes them like the ropes of a cart, pulling into a trap everyone whose leg is caught in them. A thing of trifling worth that most readers may not notice becomes here the thread that ties together the whole play from beginning to end, and is the driving force for many deeds, uniting the events that follow it, and making them together into a tall and steep mountain. This trifling thing is the curses with which Asenath's

תעתועים כי אם גם קנאת איש מרעהו, אשר כרמה תאכל בקרב לב בעליה ותתעהו בדרכי מות; אהבת הכבוד הַמְדֻמֶּה, אשר תקשיח הלב גם מפרי בטן ותהפך מאב אוהב לאכזרי כיענים במדבר;[6] תם לב אשר תתן בתחלה מנוחה לבעליה, כי תתן בקרבו האמונה ברעים, אך תתהפך כחֹמר חותם, ובנפול בעליה בפח חלקת לשון אז תהיה גם היא כמטה זעם להכחיד ישרים; אהבה נאמנה אשר לא תמוש גם אם לא יְשֻׁלַּם לה כפעלה כל אלה יחד נראה בהחזיון הזה, ועל כל אלה יד המקרה אשר תארוג דברים קלי ערך ותעשה אותם כעבותות העגלה למשוך אחריה בחרמה כל אשר נלכדה רגלו בהמה. דבר קל ערך אשר רוב הקוראים אולי לא יתבוננו בו הנהו פה כחוט המשלב את כל החזיון מראשיתו עד אחריתו והוא המניע למעשים רבים, והוא יאחד את המקרים הבאים אחריו, לעשות אותם יחד להר גבה ותלול. הדבר הקל הזה הוא גדופי אבי אסנת (דעזדעמאנא) אשר חֵרְפָהּ ביום הפרדה מעליו ויאמר לאישה, שים עליה עינך כושי פן בגוד תבגוד גם בך כאשר בגדה באביה! הדבר הקל הזה היה לראשית חטאת לכל המקרה הנורא אשר בא אחריו. אך נשים נא בתחלה עין על הברואים ואחרי כן על המקרים אשר היו בעזרתם. נושא החזיון הוא איתיאל הכושי, אשר גם שמו נקרא עליו, ובזה הראנו הסופר כי האיש הזה הוא תכלית מעשהו, אף כי דואג (דיעגא[7]) הוא הפועל היותר גדול בכל החזיון והוא המניע לכל המעשים אשר יֵעָשׂוּ בו, כי ראשית חפצו היה להראות בחזיון הזה איך תם דרך יִכָּשֵׁל בהטותו אֹזן לחלקת לשון בוגד ואת יד הקנאה העורת, אשר תהפוך שה תמימה לנמר אכזרי לבלע ולהשחית גם אהובי נפשו ביום תוכחה. איתיאל הוא איש גבור חיל במלחמה, לו אֹמץ לב ורוח כביר מאין כמֹהו, אך רק למען התיצב נגד לוחמיו במלחמת תנופה אשר יראם בעיניו ויתבונן לכלי מלחמתם, לא כן נגד איש מזמות אשר בדרכו באֹפל יתהלך ולא יראהו. אנשים כמֹהו העומדים

6 This is a direct citation of Lam. 4:3. Ostriches were associated with cruelty in the Hebrew Bible as they were known for neglecting their eggs and young (Job 29:13–8; Berlin and Brettler 2004b: 1599).

(Desdemona's) father condemned her on the day she left him, when he said to her husband, 'Keep your eye on her, Cushite, lest she betray you too as she betrayed her father!' This trifling thing was the starting point for the whole terrible event that followed. But let us first turn our attention to the characters, and afterwards to the events they triggered. The subject of the play is Ithiel the Cushite, after whom it is also named, and in this the author has shown us that this man is the protagonist of his story, even though Doeg (Diego[7]) is the prime mover throughout the play, and he is the driving force for all the deeds that take place in it, for his primary desire was to show in this play how an innocent man can stumble by listening to the flattering tongue of a traitor, and the power of blind jealousy, which can turn an innocent lamb into a cruel leopard, annihilating and destroying even those who love it on the day of reckoning. Ithiel is a mighty man of valour in war, he has courage and a great spirit without equal, but only in order to position himself against his foes in an offensive war where he can see them with his eyes and observe their weapons; not so against a scheming man who goes about his business in the dark and whom he cannot see. Men like him who stand on the most elevated heights, and who have not tried to fight against everyday obstacles (which do not surround him

ברום המעלה, ואשר לא נסו ללחום את פגעי יום יום, אשר לא כלוחמים כי אם כזבובי מות יעטרונו לכאיב ולא להמית, אנשים כאלה אשר רק בשאון ותרועת מלחמה בלו ימיהם ומלחמת החיים לא ראו, בסוד רודפי תענוגי התבל לא באו ולא הכירו ארחותם, איך על מרמה תחש רגלם, אנשים כאלה אשר הסכינו כי האויב יקרא עליהם מלחמה, המה כילדים פותים ויאמינו לכל אשר תשמע אזניהם, המה יאמינו, יען כי הסכינו לראות רק עבדים לפניהם, עבדים אשר יכפו ראשם כאגמון בדברם אתם, עבדים אשר ייחלו לחסדם, עבדים אשר יפחדו וייראו מפניהם, ועל כן ידמו כי איש לא יערב לבו להוליכם בתֹהו, אותם, את הגבורים בעלי הזרוע אשר יתנו חתיתם בארץ חיים. ואחרי אשר בכל ימי חייהם הסכינו אך במלחמה גלויה לכן לא יבינו ערמת המורה חציו במו אֹפל, ואחרי אשר המה לא הונו איש מעודם, כי לא אכף עליהם הזמן, וגם לחרפה יחשבו זאת לנפשם לעשות כזאת בעוד אשר זרועם מושלה להם לכן לא יבינו למרמת ערומים, ואיש כזה היה גם איתיאל. ואולם גם בזה נראה מה כביר כח החוזה הזה הנעלה בחוזים, כי בחר לו*) איש חיל מקרב ממשלת ווינעציא, אשר בה היתה ממשלת העם ולא ממלכה. אם בחשבון או בלי חשבון עשה זאת לא נוכל לדעת, אך זאת נראה בעינים פקוחות כי רוחו הכביר הרימהו מעל כל שגיאה. הוא בחר בשר צבא מארץ אשר בה ממשלת העם ולא ממלכה, כי בארץ אשר בה מלך ישור, ומה גם בעת ההיא, היו הרוזנים ושרי הצבא הגדולים כעבדים נבזים לפני אדוניהם המלך, במרמה עלה איש מעלה מעלה, בשפת חנף לאהובי המלך, בחלקת לשון להשרות הרואות פני המלך, בלשון הרע, במלשינות ובמרמה פלס לו נתיב עד כי נתעלה, ושם התמים נשכח ואיש לא פנה אליו ואיש לא

7 Sic.

*) Although admittedly it has not escaped me that Shakespeare took this play from an Italian-language story in which almost all the characters in the play appear in identical form, nevertheless we can see in them the hand of Shakespeare who arranged them authoritatively and breathed new life into them with his greatness.

*) אם אמנם לא נכחד ממני כי את החזיון הזה לקח שעקספיר מספור בשפת אטאליא שבו באו כמעט כל הברואים בהמחזה כצלמם ותבניתם, בכל זאת נראה בהם למדי יד שעקספיר אשר ערך אותם במשטר ויפח בקרבם חיים חדשים ברוחו הכביר.

like warriors but instead like deadly flies seeking to wound rather than kill), such men, who have spent all their days in the din and thundering of war and have not seen the war of life, have not been admitted to the confidence of those who pursue perverse pleasures and are not familiar with their deceitful ways, such men who are used to the enemy calling them to battle, are like gullible children and believe everything they hear; they believe it because they are used to seeing before them only servants, servants who bow their heads like reeds when they speak to them, servants who wish for their mercy, servants who fear and are in awe of them. Therefore, they think that no man would take pleasure in leading them into the void, them, the mighty warriors who instil their terror in the land of the living. And because they have been accustomed to open war their entire lives, they do not understand the cunning of the man who shoots his arrows in the dark, and since they have never deceived anyone (because circumstance has not imposed this on them), and because they would consider it a disgrace to do so while in power, they do not understand the deceit of the cunning. Ithiel too was such a man. Indeed here too we see how great is the power of this

זכר את כשרונו וחכמתו, ועל כן לוא היה איתיאל שר צבא גדול בארץ אשר תעמוד למשפט מלך כי אז ידע כבר ארחות הרמיה ולא תמים לב היה, ולוא ידע ערמה ומזמה כי אז לא מהר להאמין בדברי איש מזמות כדואג, כי השיב כרגע אל לבו, אך משרה נכבדה יבקש ועל כן יחבל מזמות, אך שוחה הוא כורה על כשד (קאססיא) בקנאתו בו, כי כן יעשו כל אלה הרודפים אחרי משרה ופקודה, לא כן בארץ אשר על פי מחוקקים תשים משטרה ותקים שרים ותורידם לא על פי עצת חנפים כי אם במשפט וחשבון,*) יען כי לא אחד הוא היושב לכסא, אשר על נקלה ימשכוהו ברשת המזמה, רבים המה ועל כן כבד הדבר מאוד לשית בחלקות לכלם, אשר על כן יצליח יותר איש אשר לו כשרון, בארץ כזאת לא ראה דרכי המזמה העקלקלות, כי הוא הגיע למעלה מבלי חנופה רק בגבורתו וישרו ותמתו ובצדק נוכל לאמר עליו את אשר אמר דואג על נפשו: לוא הייתי איתיאל כי אז דואג לא הייתי כי אמנם כן הוא לאו היה דואג איש המעלה כאשר אותה נפשו כי אז לא תחש על מרמה רגלו, ולוא היה איתיאל דואג כי אז איתיאל לא היה כי אז היה איש מזמות ולא תם, אך הוא היה איתיאל איש תם ועל כן האמין בכל איש, ולא התבונן כי תאוה נמבזה תדיח את אחד מעבדיו לשים חחים באף לויתן כמהו ולשחק בו כצפור, הוא לא התבונן, יען כי איש כמהו לא יכול להתבונן לזאת, ומה גם אחרי אשר לאיש המדיחו נתכנו עלילות, דואג ידע היטיב כי נפש תמים לב כאיתיאל תשנא כל רמיה, ובשמעו שם בגד ורמיה תלהט נפשו גחלים ולא ירבה לבקש חשבונות רבים, ועל כן ידע להביא בלב איתיאל לאט לאט הספק בתמת

---

*) Although even in this republic deceit and roguery rule without end, and the hands of most of the ministers are defiled by violence, nevertheless it did have a benefit, for there was not *one man* ruling over the land, and the rulers had some slight knowledge of how to appreciate the worth of a warrior who could save the land with his strength, which did not happen – not even rarely – in governments ruled by a king, and we can see this here as well, for even Phichol, one of the counsellors of the realm, did not succeed in his desire to bring evil upon Ithiel unlawfully.

*) אף כי גם בממשלת העם הזאת שררה מרמה ונבלה לאין קץ, וידי רוב השרים נגאלו בשדד, בכל זאת יתרון היה לה, כי לא א ח ד משל בארץ, ודעת צרה ידעו המושלים ערוך ערך גבור אשר בידו להציל את הארץ בישע ימינו, אשר כזאת לא קרה אף לעתים רחוקות בהממשלות אשר מלך משל בהן, וזאת נראה גם פה, כי אף ידי פיכול אחד יועצי המלכה לא עשו חיל בחפצו להביא רעה על איתיאל לא במשפט.

most exalted of playwrights, for he chose for himself*) a military man from among the rulers of Venice, which had a republic rather than a monarchy. Whether he did this intentionally or unintentionally we cannot know, but we see clearly that his greatness elevated him above all error. He chose an army commander from a land which had a republic and not a monarchy, because in a land that is governed by a king, especially at that time, dukes and great army commanders were like lowly slaves before their lord the king; men advanced by means of deceit, speaking obsequiously to the king's friends, with a flattering tongue to the women of rank who have audiences with the king; they carved a path for themselves with gossip, informing on others, and paved their way with deceit until they became exalted, while the innocent were forgotten, with no one turning to them and no one remembering their talent or wisdom. Therefore, if Ithiel had been a great army commander in a land ruled by a king, he would already have been familiar with deceitful conduct and he would not have been innocent, and if he were familiar with cunning and schemes, he would not have been so quick to believe the words of a schemer like Doeg, for he would have stopped and said to himself, surely he wants an eminent position, and to this end he is devising schemes; why, he is digging a pit for Chesed (Cassio) because he envies him, for that is what those who pursue position and office do. Not so in a land which bases its government on lawmakers, appointing and dismissing ministers not according to the counsel of hypocrites, but rather by law and accounts,*) because there is not just one

אשתו, ואחרי כן הראהו באות נאמן כי היא בוגדה היא, כי היא סבבה גם את אביה בכחש, ובדבר הזה היה די להטות לב איש כאיתיאל להאמין כי אמנם בוגדה וסוררה היא מנֹער. הן גם את אביה רמתה בערמת ערומים באהבתה אותו, את איתיאל, ומי זה לידו יתקע אם לא תלכוד גם אותו בפח הרמיה באהבתה את איש זר? - פה הציצו הדברים הרעים אשר דבר אבי אסנת באכזריות לבו ויעשו שֹרש פרה ראש ולענה. אביה העיד בו ביום עזוב בתו אותו לאמר: שים עינך עליה כושי פן תבגוד גם בך כאשר בגדה באביה, ודואג הבליעל ידע לעשות את הדברים האלה לכלי משחית בידו בהזכירו את איתיאל כי אשתו בגדה באביה, ובכן היו דברי אביה לרשת פרושה ליד מעגל בתו ואישה, אשר בה נוקשו ונלכדו ויחד למות הָכְרָעוּ. איתיאל הוא צלם דמות כל פתי מאמין לכל דבר, אשר יהיה משחק לכל זד ובליעל, וכן המה כל אלה אשר לא ידעו ארחות התבל ומזמות אנשי מרמה כי יהיו לכלי משחית לחבל נפשם ונפש ישרים באולתם, אולת כזאת תסלף דרך תמימים כרשעה ותאוה, רק כי הרשע ברשעתו ירשיע והמה ברשע אחרים יאשמו.

man sitting on the throne who could easily be drawn into a web of schemes; there are many. Therefore it is very difficult to treat them all obsequiously, and as such a man who has talent will be more successful; in such a land he has not seen the crooked paths of schemes, for he has advanced without flattery, only with his greatness, his honesty, and his innocence, and we can justly say of him what Doeg said of himself: 'If I were Ithiel, I would not be Doeg.' For indeed it is so; if Doeg were the elevated man that he wanted to be, he would not have hastened to act deceitfully, and if Ithiel were Doeg, he would not be Ithiel, for he would be a schemer and not an innocent man; but he was Ithiel, an innocent man, and therefore he believed in everyone, and it did not occur to him that a loathsome desire might drive one of his servants to put hooks in the nose of a leviathan such as himself and toy with him like a bird. It did not occur to him because such a thing cannot occur to a man such as he; especially since the man who was deposing him was destined for great things. Doeg knew well that an innocent soul like Ithiel would hate all deception, and when he heard the words treachery and deception, he would blaze with fury and he would not really take stock, and therefore he knew how to put doubt gradually into Ithiel's soul regarding his wife's innocence, and afterwards he showed him reliably that she was unfaithful, for she had deceived her father as well. This was enough to lead a man like Ithiel to believe that she had indeed been unfaithful and wayward from her youth. Why, she had deceived even her father with great cunning by loving him, Ithiel, so who could guarantee him that she would not also trap him in the snare of deception by loving another man? – here the terrible things that Asenath's father had cruelly said sprouted and formed a root bearing poisonous fruit and wormwood. Her father had warned him on the day his daughter left him, 'Keep your eye on her, Cushite, lest she betray you as well, as she betrayed her father', and the villain Doeg knew how to make these words into an instrument of destruction in his hand by reminding Ithiel that his wife had betrayed her father. Her father's words thus became a net spread out on the path of his daughter and her husband, in which they were ensnared and trapped and together were doomed to die. Ithiel is the very image of every gullible person who believes everything, who becomes a game for every rogue and villain, and so are all of those who are not familiar with the ways of the earth and the schemes of the deceitful, for they become an instrument of destruction, annihilating themselves and honest men with their folly; such folly corrupts the path of the innocent like wickedness and lust, except that the wicked man condemns others in his wickedness, while they are found guilty by the wickedness of others.

The second character in the play, who is the first in every deed and the one who makes the whole play revolve, is Doeg. Through him, the very image of a man's envy of his companion and the symbol of treachery is displayed before our eyes. There are very many men among the living with hearts like Doeg's, half of them and perhaps even

השני בהחזיון אשר הוא הראשון בכל מעשה והמסבב את כל החזיון, הוא דואג. בו יציג לעינינו צלם דמות קנאת איש מרעהו וסמל הבגד. אנשים אשר לב להם כלב דואג רבים המה מאוד בין החיים, מחציתם ואולי עוד יותר, אנשים אשר יבקשו להיטיב מצבם בקנאתם ברעיהם ולא יסוגו אחור מפני כל מעשה רע, להלשין, להעיד שקר, לשלוח מדנים בין אחים ובין איש לאשתו, להרבות כזב על כזב אך למצוא

more; men who try to improve their situation out of envy of their companions, and who would not hold back from any wicked deed, informing, bearing false witness, sowing discord between brothers and between a man and his wife, acting with ever greater deceit, only in order to achieve their desire, or at least to bring down their companion who is too great for them to endure, for every man who is greater than them is hateful to them, and they regard him as an enemy, and therefore they wage war against him, but since he is greater than them, and hence more powerful, they hide like ambushers on his way to set snares at his foot. Such men are extremely numerous, most of the traders and merchants of the earth, most of the ministers and dukes of the land, nor is their number few among the sages and teachers of law and judgement, but not many are as clever as Doeg at making every trifling event into an instrument of destruction, and not many have the fortune to be given an instrument of destruction such as they desire, and therefore they do not gain a reputation. By contrast, those who have been trapped by circumstances gain the reputation of the most deceitful men on earth. Conversely, if circumstances are favourable to them from when they first set out on their corrupted path until they achieve their goal and attain all their desires, they do not acquire the reputation of evildoers, for if a man is successful and becomes wealthy and holds a position, then has he not gained his desire by his righteousness and honesty? So say all who

את אשר אותה נפשם, או למצער להוריד את רעם הגדול מהם משאתו, כי כל גדול מהם שנוא נפשם הוא וכאויב יחשבוהו ועל כן יערכו אתו קרב, אך אחרי כי הוא גדול ואם כן גם כחו רב, לכן יתחבאו כאורבים עלי דרכיו לשים מוקשים ברגלו, אנשים כאלה רבים המה מאוד, רֹב כנעני התבל וסוחריה, רֹב שרי הארץ ורוזניה, גם בחכמים ומורי דת ודין לא מעט מספרם רק לא רבים יחכמו כדואג לעשות כל מקרה קל לכלי משחית להם, ולא לרבים יאיר המקרה פניו לתת להם כלי משחית כאשר תאוה נפשם ועל כן לא יצא להם שם, לאלה אשר המקרה סך בעדם, כשם אנשי רמיה הגדולים אשר בארץ, או כי תהיה להפך כי המקרה יאיר אליהם פנים מראשית צאתם לדרכם הנשחתה עד תֹּם דרכיהם כי השיגו מטרתם וכל חפציהם בידם המה, גם אלה לא ינחלו שם בני עולה, כי אם יצליח איש ויעשיר וישא משרה על שכמו אז הלא בצדקתו ויֹשר לבבו מצא חפצו, כן יאמרו כל יודעיו, ומי יחפש אחרי הדרכים העקלקלות אשר בהן תחת שואה התגלגל[8] עד הגיעו למחוז חפצו אם ראשית הדרך ואחריתה נסתרות מעיני כל חי? ואחרי אשר השגה חיל הלא אז אין חפץ לו עוד במרמה כי אם ביד רמה יוכל לעשות חפצו בכֹּל, וכל יודעיו יודוהו ויאמרו כי הגדיל לעשות, וגם לוא הצליח בידי דואג ויהי לשר גם אז היה נכבד מאוד, ואיש לא העז פניו לקרוא לנדיב הזה נבל, לא כן העַוָל אשר המקרה הביא בידו להוציא עלילותיו לפעולות ואחרי כן בטרם יבוא לחפצו ישבור עליו חק ויסכל עצתו ויגלה לַכֹּל עונו, אותו יכירו וידעו כלם כי בוגד היה ובאחריתו יהיה נבל בפי כל יודעיו. הוא אשר אמרתי כי לב רבים כלב דואג, רק לא מרמת רבים תצא לפֹעל ידים ואם תצא לפֹעל לא תודע תמיד בקהל. רבים המה המקנאים באשר רעיהם וגדולתם, וראשית הקנאה הזאת היא העצלות; האיש אשר יאהב עבודה ועמל כפים בלב נאמן הוא יפלס לו נתיב בחיים על פי דרכו וישמח בעבודתו, עד כי לא יחפוץ להמירנה באחרת, ועל כן הוא שמח בחלקו, אף אם עמלו רב, כי אין נותן מנוחה לנפש ושלום בקרב ולב כהעבודה ביד חרוצים, ואלה לא יקנאו באשר

know him, and who would search for the crooked paths along which he rolled in the midst of the ruins[8] until he achieved his desire, if the beginning and end of the path are concealed from the eyes of every living being? And since he has acquired wealth, why, is it not the case that he no longer has any desire for deceit, for instead he can boldly do whatever he wants, and everyone who knows him praises him and says that he has done great things. Thus, if Doeg had achieved his desire and had become a minister, then he too would have been greatly respected, and no one would have dared to call this nobleman a scoundrel. It is not so for the fool whom circumstance allowed to realize his ambitions, but afterwards, before he had achieved his desire, brought him to justice and foiled his plans and revealed his iniquity to everyone; everyone recognizes that he was a traitor, and in the end he is called a scoundrel by all who know him. As I said, many have a heart like Doeg's, but not many manage to carry out their deceit, and if they do, it is not always made public. There are many who are envious of their fellows' happiness and greatness, and the starting point for this envy is sloth. The man who loves hard work makes his way through life in good faith, and rejoices in his work, so much so that he does not yearn to exchange it for another. Therefore he is

רעיהם ולא יחבלו מזמות להדיחם משאתם למען רשת מקומם, כי לבם מלא מחפץ עבודתם, אך אנשים כאלה לא רבים המה, ולעמתם העצלים אשר בלי כל עמל ועבודה יבקשו טוב הארץ רבים המה, ואחרי כי נרפים המה מעבודה ולבם ריק מחפץ המעשה וידיהם לא תעשינה תושיה לפלס להם בפֹעל כפיהם דרך טוב בחיים, לכן יתבוננו בקנאה רק לאשר רעיהם ויהגו מזמות כל היום עליהם כמו גוזלי טובם המה. אנשים כאלה ישנאו תכלית שנאה כל עשיר ונכבד, אנשים כאלה לא יכירו טובה להעושים טוב להם, כי את הטוב אשר יקבלו יחשבו רק כחלק קטן שִׁלּוּמים מכל אשר גזלו מהם, באנשים כאלה לא נוכל לבטוח כי יאהבו אותנו על אשר הרבינו לעזור אותם (צלם דמות אנשים כאלה לכל משפטיהם וחקותיהם ויצרי לבבם הרע, השכיל לתאר לנו ביד חרוצים מאין כמהו הסופר הנפלא דיקענס בספרו „האוהב לכלנו" בהציגו לפנינו את האיש המשחת סילאס וועגג), כי יבקשו וימצאו בכל עת תאֹנות לנו כי לא יצאנו ידי חובתנו בהטיבנו להם, אנשים כאלה נראה בדור הזה למאות, כי העצלים אשר בעצלותם הָשְׁפְּלוּ יאגדו אגודות ויקראו עצרות לבלע ולהשחית כל איש אשר בידו טובו, ומי ימנה מספר לאלה אשר רק בסתר אהלם ישנאו את כל מאֲשר מהם ויעוללו עלילות להביא עליו שואת פתאום. ועצלים כאלהּ אשר ידיהם תרפינה מעבודה לשונם לא תדע עצלות, היא תעבוד כל היום עבודתה, להפיח מדנים ולסכסך איש ברעהו ולהכות ישרים ברוח פיהם, כמעשה הנחש אשר אין לו ידים להלחם ולא קרנים לנגח כי ימחץ בלשונו לאין מרפא. ואחד מהאנשים או הנחשים כאלה הזוחלים על גחון למען מחץ פעמי העובר בטח, היה דואג; במלחמה לא רמה ידו ועל כן לא רמה קרנו, בעבודה ועמל כפים מאס ועל כן תחש על מרמה רגלו למצוא את אשר לא עלתה בידו למצוא בכשרון מעשהו. הוא חרש

8 This expression is a slightly modified citation of Job 30:14. The Hebrew in the biblical verse is somewhat enigmatic and has been translated in various ways, including 'in the desolation they rolled themselves' (King James Bible), 'amid the ruins they come rolling in' (New International Version), 'amid the crash they roll on' (New Revised Standard Version).

happy with his lot, even if he has a great deal of work, for nothing gives rest to the soul and peace to the heart like toil in the hands of the industrious. These men do not envy their fellows' happiness, and they do not plot to depose them from their high position and take their place, for their heart is full of love for their work. However, there are not many such men, and in contrast to them there are many slothful men who seek the good of the land without any toil or labour. Since they shy away from labour, have no desire to work, and are unsuccessful in forging a good path through life by means of their own toil, they look with envy upon their fellows' happiness, and all day they contemplate schemes regarding them, as if they were the ones robbing them of their prosperity. Such men have a passionate hatred for every rich and respected man; such men are not grateful to those who are good to them, because they consider the good things that they receive to be only a small fraction of the payment for everything of which they have been robbed. We cannot trust such men, for they love us because we have often helped them (the very image of such men in all their conduct, behaviour, and wicked inclinations has been described for us with incomparable diligence by the wonderful author Dickens in his book *Our Mutual Friend* when he presented us with the destructive Silas Wegg), for at every occasion they seek and find excuses to say that we have not fulfilled our obligation to be good to them. We see such men by the hundreds in this

רע על כשד אשר לא עשה לו רעה מעודו, וכל עונו היה כי הטבע חנן אותו בתאר הפנים ואֹמץ לב וכשרון כי על כן הצליח למשרה נכבדה על פי פעולתו. הוא שנא תכלית שנאה את איתיאל אף כי הרבה להיטיב עמדו, על כי לא הרימהו למעלה גבהה, ועל כן חרש מזמות להצמית שנואי נפשו אלה. אבל גם בזה נראה כביד כֹּח לב שעקספיר וטהר עיניו לחפוש חדרי בטן, כי לא הציג לפנינו את הבליעל הזה, אף כי בליעל היה, כעושה מעשים רעים בעינים פקוחות, לא! גם הרע והנשחת הזה בקש חשבונות להצדיק נפשו בעשותו העול הנורא, הוא אמר לנפשו כי יצדק במעשהו בכרותו שוחה לאיתיאל, כי לפי דברת רבים חלל איתיאל את יצועו ולכן לו הצדקה לעשות בו נקמות, ואף כי לא האמין בדבה הזאת, ומי יודע אם לא מלבו הרה והגה הדבה הזאת למען השלות נפשו, בכל זאת די היה לו להשקיט בה מוסר כליותיו, אשר יתעורר לפעמים גם בלב נשחת. וכמהו כן יעשו כל חורשי רע כי יכזבו בתחלה לנפשם ויתעו לבם במשאות שוא עד כי ישענו אחרי כן בכזב אשר הוליד רוחם למען התעות אחרים בדברי שקר. „היה נאמן לנפשך ותהיה נאמן לכל אדם" – יאמר פאלאניוס ללאערטוס בנו בחזיון האמלעט. ואמנם זאת היא תורת האדם; האיש אשר לא יעשה שקר בנפשו, אשר לא ישלה את נפשו בחזיונות שוא הוא לא ישקר גם לרעיו, אך זאת היא ראשית חטאת לכל אלה המתעים אנשים באמרי פיהם כי בתחלה יכזבו לנפשם, האחד יתברך בלבו כי הוא באמת נעלה על כל רעיו ואחרי כן יחפוץ להטות אותם לחפצו; השני ישיב אל לבו כי לא כגמול ידיו ולא ככשרונו יְשֻׁלַּם לו, ועל כן יחשוב כי לו הצדקה לעשוק גם אחרים, והשלישי יבקש להאמין כי אמנם הוא הנבחר לשופט רמים לנהל רב אדם בשבט ממשלתו וידכא רב אדם תחת רגליו, ואם יתפרץ איש מפניו ויבקש לפרוק עלו מעל צוארו יחשבהו כמורד בשופט רמים אשר מידו לו המשרה והגדולה, וכאלה רבות הנה הדרכים העקלקלות אשר בהן ילכדו המכזבים לנפשם למען יתעו אחרים בשקריהם. וכה השקיט גם הבליעל הזה מוסר כליותיו בתחלה ואחרי כן

generation, for slothful men who have been humiliated in their sloth gather together and unite to engulf and destroy every prosperous man; who can count the number of men that secretly hate all those happier than them, and hatch plots to bring sudden disaster upon them. Yet such slothful men who shy away from work have tongues that know no sloth; they do their work all day, stirring up quarrels and provoking one man against his fellow and striking honest men with the breath of their mouth, like the case of the serpent who had no hands for fighting and no horns for goring, so instead he inflicted irreparable wounds with his tongue. And Doeg was one of this type of men or serpents who crawl on their belly to wound the feet of the trusting passer-by; he was not mighty in battle, and therefore he did not become exalted; he despised work and manual labour, and therefore he rushed to achieve through deceit that which he had not succeeded in achieving through talent. He plotted evil against Chesed, who had never done him ill; his only iniquity was that nature had graced him with a handsome face and a courageous heart and talent, inasmuch as he had succeeded in achieving a respected position based on his actions. He hated Ithiel passionately even though he treated him very well, because he had not promoted him, and therefore he concocted schemes to destroy these men that he hated. But even in this we see how great Shakespeare's power is and how pure his eyes are in searching out the innermost depths, for he has not presented

כאשר כבר הרבה מזמות חמס אז חדל עוד מבקש חשבונות נפשו ויחשב רק דרכי מזמותיו עד כי בצע את אשר החל וַיָּבֵא רע על כל אנשי עברתו, אך גם הוא בערמתו נלכד ובעת קץ נודע מעלו ועל כן היה לאות לכל בוגד ופושע. דואג הוא צלם דמות העצלות אשר תוליד קנאת איש מרעהו ומרמה ובגד.

this villain to us – although he was a villain – as one who commits evil deeds with open eyes, no! Even this evil and corrupted man took stock, justifying himself in doing the terrible wrong; he told himself that he was justified in his deeds as he dug a pit for Ithiel, for according to what many people said, Ithiel had desecrated his bed, and therefore he had the right to exact revenge upon him. Even though he did not believe this libel – and who knows if he did not conceive and plot it on his own in order to delude himself – nevertheless, it was sufficient to silence the warnings of his conscience, which sometimes stirs even in a corrupted heart. And all those who plot evil do as he did: first they deceive themselves and lead themselves astray with false visions, and afterwards they come to rely on the deceit which they themselves had invented, so that they might lead others astray with lies. 'Be faithful to yourself and be faithful to every man' – Polonius says to his son Laertes in the play *Hamlet*. And indeed this is man's teaching; he who does not deceive himself, and does not delude himself with false visions, will likewise not lie to his fellow; indeed, this is the gateway to sin for all those who delude men with their speech, for first they deceive themselves; one boasts to himself that he is truly more exalted than all his fellows, and afterwards he desires to mould them to his will; a second one says to himself that he is not being paid as he deserves and in accordance with his talent, and therefore he thinks that he has the right to exploit others as well; and a third one wants to believe that he has been selected as a judge of elevated men to lead the multitudes with his authority and trample many men under his feet, and if a man breaks away from him and attempts to remove his yoke from his neck, he regards him as a rebel against the judge of elevated men who has dominion and majesty because of his power, and so numerous are the crooked paths upon which those who deceive themselves in order to lead others astray with their lies are caught. That is how this villain initially silenced the warnings of his conscience, and afterwards, when he had already concocted many violent schemes, he ceased taking stock of himself and he thought only about the practicalities of his schemes, until he finished what he had started and brought evil upon all the objects of his wrath. However, he too was trapped in his cunning and in the end his betrayal was revealed, and therefore he became a symbol for every traitor and criminal. Doeg is the very image of sloth, which begets envy of one man against his fellow, as well as deceit and betrayal.

The third character in the play is Phichol (Brabantio), Asenath's father, who was the starting point for all the evil that befell his daughter and her husband. Through him we are given a description of the love of false honour, which hardens the heart and blinds the one who possesses it until he cannot distinguish between good and evil or between truth and lies, and he does much evil, even if he has an honest heart, like all evildoers.

השלישי בהחזיון הוא פיכל (בראַבאַנטיא) אבי אסנת אשר היה ראשית חטאת לכל הרע אשר בא על בתו ואישה. בו תאר לפנינו אהבת הכבוד הַמְדֻמֶה, אשר תקשיח הלב ותכה בעורון את בעליה עד כי לא יבחין בין טוב לרע בין אמת לשקר וירבה הַרֵעַ, אף אם לב ישר לו, ככל המרעים.

Phichol, Asenath's father, was a great and wealthy minister, respected in his city and his country, and a counsellor in the government; as such, it goes without saying that since he had a daughter he intended to give her to a man as exalted as himself, and for such men, an exalted man is not one who has made a name for himself by his wisdom, courage, or talent; they honour and respect such men when they find them pleasing, but what nobleman would give his daughter to such a man? For the daughters of noblemen, a man from among the noblemen is required, whoever he may be: an unsuccessful man, a villain, someone who chases intoxication and lewdness, or is empty-headed; it does not matter, if only he has hereditary pedigree, for those with pedigree do not consider all these sins to be iniquities. Indeed, a man is called a drunkard only if he gets drunk on beer, but not if he gets drunk on champagne; in that case he is only called a lover of life, and there are many sins like these for which only men lacking a title are condemned, but not members of the elite, for ancestral pedigree purifies every impurity, cleanses all grime and makes the wise man who was clever enough to be born to noblemen privileged from the womb. So how great is the pain of Phichol, the minister and the counsellor, when he finds out that his daughter has given her heart to a man who acquired all his honour only by means of his toil and courage; consuming rage burned within him, and he forgot that he was his daughter's father, pushing her away with both hands and

פיכל אבי אסנת היה שר גדול ועשיר, נכבד בעירו וארצו ויועץ בממלכה, ואם כן מובן הדבר מעצמו כי אחרי אשר בת היתה לו חשב מחשבות לתת אותה לאיש המעלה כערכו, ואדם המעלה בעיני אנשים כאלה הוא לא איש אשר בחכמת לבו או אֹמץ רוחו או כשרון ידיו עשה לו יד ושם, את אנשים כאלה יוקירו ויכבדו בעת אשר ימצאו חפץ במו, אך מי מהאצילים יתן את בתו לאיש כזה? לבנות האצילים דרוש איש בן אצילים, יהיה מי שיהיה: גבר לא יצלח, או בליעל, רודף שכר וזמה או נבוב הלב, אחת היא, אם רק יחש משפחות לו, כי לבני היחש לא יחשבו כל החטאות האלה לעון. הן רק אם ביין-דגן ישכר איש אז לו שכור יאמר, אך לא אם יסבא יין שאמפניה לשכרה, לו רק אוהב החיים יאמר, וכהנה רבות הנה האשמות אשר רק על בני בלי שם תשלכנה שקוצים, אך לא על בני המעלה, כי יחש האבות תטהר כל טומאה, תנקה כל חלאה ותעשה את החכם, אשר השכיל להולד על ברכי אצילים, לנבחר מבטן. ומה רבו מכאובי פיכל השר והיועץ בהודע לו כי בתו נתנה את לבה לאיש אשר כל כבודו קנה לו רק בידיו ובאֹמץ לבו, חמתו בערה בו עד להשחית וישכח כי אב הוא לבתו וידחפנה בשתי ידיו ויאמר לה לעין כל: לא בתי את. הנה זאת היא אהבת רב האבות לבניהם, רק כל עוד אשר יעשו חפצם כעבדים נאמנים, רק כל עוד אשר ישלטו בגויתם גם ברוחם אז ינטלום וינשאום ויעמלו להם ויתפארו באהבתם, אך אם יעלה רגע רעיון על לב הבנים כי גם המה אנשים המה וגם להם לב ורגש ויחפצו לחיות על פי חפצם, אז לא יכירום האבות הרחמנים האלה ולא אבותיהם המה. כן יעשו רֹב האבות וכליותם לא ייסרום על העול הזה, כי זאת נחלו מאבותיהם ואבות אבותיהם. הן לוא השיב פיכל אל לבו מה צדקה יש לי על בתי למכרה כשפחה חרופה לאיש אשר נפשה תגעל בו? מי נתן לי המשפט לגזול את מחמד נפשה מאתה ולמרר חייה עד עולם? הן נפשה ולבה לה המה ותוכל לתתם לאשר ישר בעיניה, לוא בקש חשבונות כאלה כי אז השיב אל

saying to her in front of everyone, 'You are not my daughter.' Indeed, such is most fathers' love for their children; only as long as they do their bidding like faithful servants, only as long as they rule over their bodies as well as their souls, do they exalt them, elevate them, toil for them, and glory in their love, but if for a moment the idea enters the children's mind that they too are people and that they too have a heart and feelings and want to live in accordance with their desires, then these merciful fathers do not recognize them and are not their fathers. Most fathers act in this manner, and their conscience does not rebuke them for this iniquity, because they inherited it from their fathers and their fathers' fathers. Indeed, if Phichol had said to himself, 'What right do I have over my daughter to sell her like a contemptible maidservant to a man whom she reviles? Who gave me the authority to rob her of her heart's desire and to embitter her life forever? After all, her soul and her heart are hers, and she can give them to whomever she pleases'; if he had taken stock in this way he would have said to himself that indeed a daughter only spends a quarter of her life in her parents' house, but must spend three-quarters of her life in her husband's house, and if she is given to a man who is alien to her, why then all her days will be pain and anger, and she will prefer death to such a bitter life; if he had said such a thing to himself, perhaps he would have repented, regretted his thoughts, and had mercy on his daughter, and would not have pushed her away in anger. But like most

לבו: הן אך החלק הרביעי משני חייה תבלה הבת בבית הוריה ושלשת חלקי החיים עליה לבלות בבית אישה, ואם תנתן לאיש זר לרוחה, הלא אז יהיו כל ימיה מכאובים וכעס וייקר בעיניה המות מחיים מרים כאלה, לוא השיב כזאת אל לבו, אולי שב ונחם ממחשבתו ורחם את בתו ולא הדפה בזעם אפו, אך לא חשב כזאת כאשר לא יחשבו זאת רֹב האבות, ואהבת נפשו הדיחתו להקשיח לבו מבתו כמו זרה היתה לו, ואת כל רחמיו ואהבתו אליה לא זכר ביום העברה ההוא: אין לי עוד בת – קרא בעברתו – ולא שב מדברו. אמנם לוא רק זאת עשה, לוא רק התנכר לה, כי אז לא רבה רעתו, אך לא! הוא העמיק שַׁחֵת עוד הרבה יתר מבלי חשוב מה הוא עושה. הן לוא היתה אסנת זרה לו, האם העיז מצח לאמר לה קבל עם כי תהיה בימים הבאים לזונה, פרוצה? האם הרהיב עֹז בנפשו לאמר לאיש אשה נכריה לו: שים עינך עליה כי בגוד תבגוד בך! – כזאת לא עשה, ולוא עשה כזאת כי אז נשא עונו, או חרפתו שבה כפלים לחיקו, אך האב הרחמן הזה אשר לפני רגע אמר: אין לי עוד בת! ואם כן חשב את אסנת לזרה לו, ובכל זאת לא כלא זעמו ויוסף להתגרות בה ולחרפה לעין כֹּל, יען מה? יען כי אביה ה י ה ויחשוב כי עוד לו צדקה ומשפט עליה אחרי כי אביה היה שנים אחדות. ובמשפט הזה הביא עליה הרע אשר הצעידה לבור צלמות, כי הדברים אשר דבר באפו עשו פרי לענה על תלמי לבב איתיאל, אשר גם הוא ככל האדם לא הרבה מחשבות רבות, ולא השיב אל לבו, כי שקר בפי פיכל באמרו כי בתו בגדה בו, כי היא לא בגדה בו, ולהפך הוא בגד בה ויתנכר לה. אם לבבה בחר לה איש, בזה לא בגדה כי אם עשתה כחק הטבע, ואם בה העון אשר ביום הבראה נתן לה במקרה לב אשר בו היה חדר פתוח למשכן האהבה? היא לא בגדה באביה כי היא לא אמרה לו: לא אבי אתה, כי אם הוא בגד בה ויאמר: לא בתי את! ובכל זאת לא התעורר עליו איתיאל בשמעו מפיו גדופי אשתו, יען מה? יען כי גם הוא נתעה בשוא ככל האדם לחשוב כי אמנם יש ויש להאב המשפט והצדקה לעשות בבתו כחפצו, ואחרי כי נתעה לחשוב כזאת, לכן

חשב אותה כבוגדה באביה, ואחרי כי כבוגדה היתה בעיניו, לכן הטה אזנו לקול המלשין אשר הכה אותה בלשון לאמר: בגדה אסנת באישה כאשר בגדה באביה. זאת היא פעולת המשפטים המעקלים אשר מצאו קן בלב בני האדם וימאנו להרחיקם ממנו. המשפט המעקל הזה כי הצדקה להאבות לעשות את הבנים כחפצם השחיתה לב אביה לבל ירחם וידיח הרעה על בתו האהובה, ועל נפשו כי גם הוא מת מעֹצר רעה ויגון על בתו אשר חֲשָׁבָהּ לבוגדה, ואת לב אישה לבל יחוס עליה ביום זעמו, ולבל ישיב אל לבו כי לא בגדה באביה, ולוא גם בגדה בו, אין עוד אות נאמן כי בגדה בי, כי לא כהאב האיש, את האב לא בחרה לה כחפצה, ואת האיש בחר לבה ולא תבגוד בו, אך אחרי כי המשפט המעקל הכה גם אותו בסנורים לכן שמע בקול מלשין בסתר ויורד דומה את הנקיה החפה מכל עון. פיכל הוא צלם דמות אהבת הכבוד המדמה אשר על משפטים מעקלים תחיה ותמית את בעליה.

fathers, he did not consider such things, and his selfishness made him harden his heart against his daughter as if she were a stranger to him, and he did not remember all his mercy and love for her on that day of wrath; 'I no longer have a daughter' – he called out in his wrath – and did not repent. Indeed, if he had only done this, if he had only acted like a stranger to her, then his evil would not have been so great, but no! He wrought much more profound destruction without considering what he was doing. Indeed, if Asenath had been a stranger to him, would he have dared to tell her in public that she would become a whore, a strumpet in the future? Would he have had the nerve to tell a man that he had an adulterous wife? – 'Keep your eye on her, for she will surely betray you!' – he would not have done such a thing, and if he had done such a thing he would have been punished, and his disgrace would have returned to him twofold; but this merciful father who a moment previously had said, 'I no longer have a daughter!' and as such regarded Asenath as a stranger to him, nevertheless did not contain his fury, continuing to scold her and curse her in front of everyone, because of what? Because he *was* her father and he felt that he still had right and authority over her, since he had been her father for some years. With this judgement he brought the evil upon her that drove her to the grave, for the words that he spoke in his anger spawned a poisonous fruit in the furrows of Ithiel's heart, who, like any man, did not think much either, and did not tell himself that

Phichol might have been lying when he said that his daughter had betrayed him, for she had not betrayed him; on the contrary, he had betrayed her and alienated himself from her. Choosing a husband for herself did not constitute a betrayal; rather, she was acting in accordance with the law of nature. Was it her fault that on the day she was created fate gave her a heart which had an open chamber for love to settle in? She did not betray her father, in that she did not say to him: 'You are not my father'; rather he betrayed her, saying: 'You are not my daughter!' but nevertheless, Ithiel did not oppose him when he heard him insulting his wife, because of what? Because he too had been misled like every man to think that indeed the father has the authority and the right to do as he pleases with his daughter, and since he had been misled to think thus, he saw her as a traitor to her father, and since he saw her as a traitor, he paid heed to the informer who destroyed her with his speech, saying that Asenath had betrayed her husband as she had betrayed her father. This is the outcome of the perverted ruling that has become rooted in men's hearts, from which they have refused to distance themselves. This perverted ruling – that fathers have the right to do as they please with their children – corrupted her father so that he did not have mercy upon her and brought evil upon his beloved daughter, as well as upon himself (for he too died from affliction, evil, and sorrow over his daughter, whom he had considered a traitor), and her husband, so that he did not have mercy upon her on the day of his fury, and did not tell himself: 'Indeed she did not betray her father, and even if she had betrayed him, there is no other reliable indication that she has betrayed me, for a husband is not like a father; she did not choose her father of her own free will, whereas she chose her husband, and she would not betray him.' Instead, since he too had been blinded by the perverted ruling, he listened to someone who slandered in secret and brought about the death of this blameless girl, innocent of any iniquity. Phichol is the very image of the love of false honour, which lives on perverted rulings and kills those who possess it.

The rest of the men who appear in the story are not honourable in their actions; Chesed is a naive man who fell into the net of cunning unwittingly; Raddai is an empty-headed man chasing after desire who is trapped by his desire and goes to the grave because of his desire and folly.

יתר האנשים הבאים בהספור לא נכבדים המה במעשיהם; כשד הוא איש תם אשר נפל ברשת הערמה מבלי דעת; רדי הוא איש נבוב לב רודף תאוה אשר בתאותו נלכד וירד שחת בתאותו וסכלותו.

But Asenath is the very image of pure and faithful love, which knows no limits and sees no obstacles on its path; her love leads her to follow a man who has won over her conscience and heart; her love also sustains her to endure pain inflicted by her beloved, and her love does not abandon her even in death, and she blesses the name of her lover who destroyed her in his anger.

אבל אסנת היא צלם דמות האהבה הטהורה והנאמנה, אשר לא תדע כל מעצר ולא תראה כל שטן בדרכה, אהבתה תוליכנה ללכת אחרי איש אשר קנה כליותיה ולבה, אהבתה תסמכנה גם לשאת ולסבול מכאובים מידי אהוב נפשה, ואהבתה לא תעזבנה גם במות ותברך את שם אוהבה אשר טרף נפשה באפו.

This is the power of Shakespeare, for all the women who appear in his plays do not speak much and do not perform great deeds, but in few words we see them as if they were living before our eyes. Ophelia (in *Hamlet*),

זה הוא הכֹּח לשעקספיר כי כל הנשים הבאות בחזיונותיו לא תרבינה דַבֵּר ולא תגדלנה לעשות פעולות גדולות, כי אם במעט מלים נראה אותן כמו חיות לעינינו. דברי אפעליאַ (בהאמלעט), יוליאַ בראָמעאָ ויוליא[9], ואסנת (דעזדעמאנא) באיתיאל תדברנה אך מעט, ובכל

Julia in *Romeo and Julia,*[9] and Asenath (Desdemona) in *Ithiel* speak only little, but nevertheless we see the power of their limitless love. Even in death she did not abandon her love, and before her soul departed, she even tried to clear her beloved of any blame, saying, 'My hands did this', and these few words were potent enough to depict the power of love for us much better than entire books intensely praising its greatness and worth.

זאת נראה עזוז אהבתן עד בלי די. גם במות לא עזבה אהבתה, וטרם נפחה נפשה עוד בקשה להסיר כל אשמה מעל ראש אהובה ותאמר: ידי עשו אלה, ודי כֹּח בהמלים האחדות האלה לתאר לנו כֹּח האהבה הרבה יתר מספרים שלמים המרבים להלל גדלה וערכה.

Many have regarded Asenath's love as exaggerated, and now too many regard it as impossible, that this wretched girl who was murdered by the bridegroom of blood[10] not long after her wedding, that this wretched girl should still continue to love him and should take such great blame upon herself as her soul departed, saying, 'My hands did this to me!' But they do not understand women's hearts. Almost all women and children – as well as many men – who are not used to waging war with the vicissitudes of circumstance, feel desire only as long as it is far from their reach, whereas if it is given to them without toil they do not rejoice in it. So too with their love: if they obtain it without obstacles or misfortunes, then they do not value it. Only with a multitude of obstacles in their way does their love grow, does its intensity increase without them searching out schemes to achieve their desire. Instead, they sit and quarrel with their circumstances, feeling angry

רבים נמצאו אשר חשבו את אהבת אסנת כנפרזה, ורבים ימצאו גם עתה אשר יחשבו זאת לנמנע, כי העלובה הזאת אשר נרצחה מידי חתן הדמים[10] זמן לא כביר אחרי חפתה, כי העלובה הזאת עוד תוסיף אהבתו ותאשם אשמה גדולה כזאת כרגע אשר נפחה נפשה לאמר: ידי עשו זאת לי! אבל המה לא יבינו לב הנשים. כמעט כל הנשים כהילדים ורבים מהאנשים, אשר לא הסכינו לערוך מלחמה את הפגעים אשר ישלח בהם המקרה, המה ישגו בחפץ רק כל עוד אשר הוא רחוק מהם, ואם ינתן בידם מבלי עמל לא ישישו בו, וכן גם באהבתם, אם ימצאו אתה בלי שטן ופגע רע אז לא תיקר בעיניהם, ורק ברבות המכשולים על דרכם כן תרב אהבתם, היא תגדיל כֹּחה בלבם מבלי אשר יבקשו תחבולות להשיג חפצם, כי אם ישבו ויריבו בהמקרים ויאנפו בהפגעים ונפשם עליהם תאבל, ואחרי אשר לא הסכינו ל ע ש ו ת לכן יגבר הרעיון כֹּחו ויקח כל הלב לעבד לו, עד כי לא ימצאו און להסיר מחשבת אהבתם מלבם אף רגע, לא כן אלה אשר נסו לערוך מלחמה את מקרי החיים, אותם יעוררו הפגעים ל פ ע ו ל ה, להרים כל מכשול, להסיר כל שטן מעל פניהם, ואם יצלחו בדרכם ישישו בו,

9 Sic.

10 This is a reference to Exod. 4:25. See Fifth Act, note 73.

with their misfortunes and mourning over them, and since they are not accustomed to *act*, the idea grows more and more powerful, becoming master over their whole heart, until they cannot find the strength to stop thinking about their love even for a moment; not so are those who have experience waging war against the vicissitudes of life; misfortunes spur them to *action*, to do away with every stumbling block and remove every obstacle from their way. And if they are successful they rejoice, but if they see that they have been ineffectual, and all their toil has been in vain, they say to themselves: there's nothing for it, and toiling to no end is utter futility, and in this way they find some comfort and relief. But women, who for the most part are not accustomed to physical battle, are always intoxicated in their love. And each stumbling block and misfortune stirs them not to obtain their desire by practical means, but rather to desire more intensely. Because of this, if a man shows his beloved frequent signs of love, he does not cause her love to intensify; conversely, if he treats her like a stranger and appears not to seek her love, then the love is ignited in her heart like an infernal blaze, and a woman will bear everything calmly, even condemnations and abuse, even blows from her lover's hand, especially if she sees that he did it out of jealousy, for jealousy in her lover's heart – even if it treats her very badly and embitters her life and forces her to sit at home like a bird in a cage and not to speak a word to anyone – even brings joy to her heart, as she thinks: indeed he is only

ואם יראו כי אזלת יד, וכל עמלם שיעמלו עוד יהיה לריק אז ישיבו אל לבם: הדבר הזה אין להשיב עוד ולעמול לשוא אך הבל ורעות רוח הוא ובזאת ינחמו וימצאו מנוחה בפעל כפים, הנה תשגינה באהבתן תמיד, וכל מכשול ופגע לא יעוררו אותן למעשה למצוא חפצן כי אם להגדיל את החפץ בלבן ביתר שאת, אשר על כן אם ירבה איש להראות אותות אהבה לאהובתו אז לא יגדיל האהבה בלבה, לא כן אם יתנכר לה ויתראה כמו לא יבקש אהבתה, אז תצת האהבה בלבה כמדורת שאול, ואת כֹל תשא אשה במנוחה גם חרפות ונאצות גם מכות מידי אוהבה, ומה גם אם תראה כי מקנאה עשה זאת, כי הקנאה בלב אוהבה, אף אם תָּרֵעַ לה עד מאוד ותמרר חייה ותכביד עליה אכפה לשבת בית כצפור בכלוב ולבלי דבר דבר את איש, בכל זאת תתן הקנאה הזאת גם שמחה בלבה בחשבה: הן רק מאהבתו יקנא, והרעיון הזה די לה להשקיט רוחה, וגם אהבת אסנת לא רפתה בהדיח אותה אישה, ולהפך כי גברה עוד בלבה ביתר שאת, ומה גם בְּהִוָּכְחָה כי מקנאה עשה זאת, אז סלחה לו על כל אשמתו ותהי נכונה גם לנשק את הידים אשר עשו קץ לחייה, ולא לפלא הוא כי בקשה להסיר כל אשמה מראש אישה אהובה בחשבה כי רק למען אהבתה עשה זאת, והשקר אשר דברה היה כאמת וצדק בעיניה, כי בו חפצה להציל את אישה מחרפה או עֹנש.

jealous because of his love, and this idea is enough for her to silence herself, and so too Asenath's love did not weaken when her husband struck her down; on the contrary, it grew even more intense, especially as she was convinced that he had acted out of jealousy, so she forgave him for all of his wrongs, and she was even prepared to kiss the hands that had brought an end to her life. It is no wonder that she tried to clear her husband of all blame, her beloved, as she thought that he had acted only out of his love for her, and the lie that she told seemed to her like truth and justice, because through it she sought to save her husband from disgrace or punishment.

But she did not tell a lie, for indeed her hands had done this to her: she had failed because of her great love and innocence; she trusted in her love too much, and because of that she pressured Ithiel to restore Chesed to his position, and it never even occurred to her that what she was saying might be a burden to him, that she might be asking something of him which should not be done even for love – namely, issuing a corrupt ruling and desecrating his honour. Only senseless youths follow love with closed eyes wherever it leads them and do everything that it commands them, performing strange deeds and uttering perversities. Not so for men who have made their mark on the world by their might and uprightness, and whose honour, which they have obtained with great toil, is more precious to them than all of life's pleasures, even more than love, even more than life. A sense of honour is extremely precious to those who understand its value, and they will forcibly remove everything from their

אולם היא לא שקר דברה, כי אמנם ידיה עשו זאת לה, כי היא ברב אהבתה ותֻמת לבה נכשלה; היא בטחה באהבתה יתר מדי, ועל כן הציקה לאיתיאל בדברים להשיב את כשד על כנו, וגם שמץ מחשבה לא עלה על לבה, פן יהיו דבריה עליו למשא, פן תבקש ממנו דבר אשר גם למען האהבה לא יֵעָשֶׂה, והוא לעות משפט ולחלל כבודו. רק נערים חסרי דעה ילכו אחרי האהבה אל אשר תוליכם בעינים עצומות ויכשו* ככל אשר תפקוד עליהם, יעשו מעשים זרים וידברו תהפוכות, לא כן אנשים אשר בכח ידם וישר לבם הציבו להם יד בתבל, ואשר בעיניהם כבודם, אשר ברב עמל השיגוהו, יקר מכל חפצי החיים גם מהאהבה וגם מהחיים. רגש הכבוד יקר מאוד בעיני אלה אשר יבינו לערוך חין ערכו, וכל דבר אשר בידו לחלל כבודם אף במעט יסירו מעל פניהם בחזקת היד אף אם לבם ידוה מאוד על המעשה אשר יעשו. שופט נאמן אשר יצא לו שם בצדקתו לא יהפך למכיר פנים לחלל שם כבודו אף אם האהבה תצוהו לעשות כן, גבור מלחמה אשר בעזוז רוחו קנה לו שם גבורים לא ישבית מלחמה בעוד אויבו לנגדו גם אם האהבה תבקש זאת ממנו, איש הולך ברעיון לבו אשר התעורר לדבר אמת בשער להוכיח לנתעים אולתם ולחוטאים חטאתם על פניהם לא ישוב

* יעשו

path that has the power to tarnish their honour even slightly – even if the deed that they must do sickens them greatly. A faithful judge who has gained a reputation for his righteousness will not become biased, desecrating his honourable name, even if love commands him to do so; a warrior who has gained the reputation of a hero through his strength of spirit will not stop a war while his enemy is before him, even if love asks it of him; a man who has followed his conscience and stood up to speak the truth in public, rebuking misguided men for their folly and sinners for their sins, will not act deceitfully again, not even for love. Thus, no man who is sustained by a sense of honour and who found his path in life before he knew love will abandon his path for it, for the sense that had inspired him for a long time and had been like a light illuminating his path does not dim quickly; even if its voice is hidden for a day or two by the roar of love's voice, it will grow stronger in the end and will make itself heard with greater force. Only those who lack any noble yearnings in life wander after love like a beast into the valley,[11] going so far as to commit strange and perverse acts, for they would commit strange and perverse acts even without love, since they have not chosen a sound path for themselves. Many women fail to understand this and place too much trust in the power of love, asking of their lovers things that it is inappropriate for them to do; in this way they do themselves ill, for if once or twice the lover disregards and overrides his honour, the power of love is indeed thereby weakened, and woe to love if its

לעשות חֹנף גם למען האהבה, וכן כל איש אשר רגש הכבוד יחיהו ויפלס לו נתיב בחיים בטרם אשר הכיר דרכי האהבה לא יעזוב דרכו בעבורה, כי הרגש אשר מצא בלבו מסלות ימים רבים ויהי לו כאור מאיר בדרכיו לא יועם עד מהרה, וגם אם יום או יומים יֵחָבֵא קולו משאון קול האהבה, יגבר לאחרונה חילים וישמיע קולו ביתר עז, רק אלה אשר לבם ריק מכל חפץ נעלה בחיים המה יתעו כבהמה בבקעה[11] אחרי האהבה לעשות גם זרות ותהפוכות כי המה יעשו זרות ותהפוכות גם בלעדי האהבה, אחרי כי לא ברו להם דרך סלולה, וזאת לא תבינינה נשים רבות ותבטחנה בכח האהבה יתר מדי ותשאלנה מאת אוהביהן דברים אשר לא נאוה להם לעשות, ובזאת תרענה לנפשן, כי אם פעם אחת ושתים ימחול האוהב על כבודו ויעבור על מדתו, אך בזאת ירפה כֹּח האהבה, ואוי לה להאהבה אם כחה רפה אך מעט, כי אז תלך הלוך וחסור עד כי תסוף מלב ולא לעתים רחוקות תהפך לאיבה בהיותה למשא, אך נשים רבות לא תדענה זאת ותכרינה בידיהן קבר לאהבתן, קבר עולמים. וזאת היתה גם לאסנת, היא לא השכילה עשות בהציקה לאישה בדברים לעשות את אשר מֵאֵן לעשות, ולוא גם לא בא בעצמותיו רקב הקנאה, אשר זאת לא ידעה, גם אז לא בחכמה בקשה זאת ממנו, ולה היה לדעת כי לא לאשה להתערב במשטרי המדינה ומשפטי צבא המלחמה, לה היה לדעת זאת לוא ידעה ארחות התבל ולב הגברים, אך היא בתֹם לבה לא הבינה זאת, ועל כן היו לה תמתה ואהבתה לפח ולמוקש, ודואג הבליעל עשה גם אותן לכלי משחית לחבל נפשות זעומי נפשו ביעצו את כשד להרבות תחנה לפניה, ובדברו על לבה, כי תרב אמריה לאישה, ובהראותו לאיתיאל כי אך מאהבתה לכשד תעשה זאת, ועל נקלה מצאו דבריו הרעים מסלות בלבב איתיאל, אחרי כי דבריה היו לו למורת רוח גם בלעדי הקנאה, ולוא גם שמע לדבריה בפעם הזאת, כי אז בלי ספק קצף עליה לוא נסתה שנית לעשות כזאת. ובדברי אסנת המעטים השכיל שעקספיר מאין כמהו להורות דרך להנשים כי תדענה איך ללכת

11 See note 1.

power is weakened even slightly, for then it continues to diminish until it disappears and not infrequently turns into enmity, being a burden. However, many women are ignorant of this and dig a grave – an eternal grave – for their love with their own hands. This was the case for Asenath too; she did not act wisely in pressuring her husband to do what he had refused to do. Even if the rot of jealously had not set into his bones (which she did not know), it still would not have been wise of her to ask this of him; she should have known that a wife must not interfere with state governance and military judgements. She would have known this if she had been familiar with the ways of the world and men's hearts, but in her innocence she did not understand this. Thus her innocence and love became a trap and a snare, and the villain Doeg made even them into an instrument of destruction to obliterate those with whom he was angry by advising Chesed to plead repeatedly to her, convincing her to speak repeatedly to her husband, and showing Ithiel that she was only doing this because she loved Chesed. His evil words easily made inroads into Ithiel's heart, since what she was saying would have caused him grief even without the jealousy, and even if he had listened to her the first time, he would have undoubtedly grown angry at her if she had tried to do such a thing a second time. And through Asenath's few words, Shakespeare managed like none other to show women how to follow love without stumbling, without trusting too much in the power of love and without digging a grave for it with their own hands, over which they would cry all the days of their lives without a future or hope.

בעקבות האהבה לבל תכשלנה, לבל תרבינה לבטוח בכח האהבה יתר על המדה ולבל תכרינה בידיהן לה קבר, אשר עליו תבכינה כל ימי חייהן מבלי אחרית ותקוה.

In Milcah he has presented us with a woman on a lower level than Asenath, a woman who says decisively that she would not shy away from sin if she were to receive a great payment, and that it would not be her own fault, but rather the fault of her husband, the villain who had mistreated her (as indeed, according to her, all men do). The number of such women on earth, who are corrupted by their husbands and forget the honest way, is not small; indeed, it is much bigger than the number of women like Asenath.

במלכה הציג לפנינו אשה במעלה שפלה מאסנת, אשה אשר תאמר בפה מלא, כי לא תסוג אחור מחטא אם שכר הרבה תקח, ולא באשמתה, כי אם באשמת אישה הבליעל אשר התעמר בה, כאשר נשמע דבריה אודות האנשים, ומספר נשים כאלה אשר באשמת בעליהן תשחתנה ותשכחנה אורח ישר לא מעט הוא בתבל, והוא יגדל הרבה יתר ממספר נשים כאסנת.

Anah is a woman on the lowest level among women, equivalent to Raddai's level among men, about whom there is not much to say, and in these three we have been given a reliable portrait of almost all women, with the diversity of their characters and inclinations.

ענה היא אשה במדרגה היותר שפלה בין הנשים כמדרגת רדי בין האנשים, אשר אין לדבר אודותה הרבה, ובשלש אלה נתן לפנינו ציור נאמן כמעט מכל הנשים לפלגות דרכיהן ויצרי לבהן.

From all these, we see that this exalted play becomes like an illuminating light, like a faithful guide for the multitudes, instructing them in the ways of the world and the desires, schemes, and inclinations of men's hearts. For this playwright is not a playwright for one people or one land, he is a playwright for all peoples and all lands, for he does not show us the conduct of a member of a single people or individual men, but rather the conduct of men in general. Therefore he is like a teacher for all men, and should not be considered a stranger even to us in our language, for if we observe just a little, we see that among us too there are men like Ithiel and Phichol and Doeg and their ilk.

מכל אלה נראה כי החזיון הנעלה הזה יהיה כאור מאיר, כמורה דרך נאמן לרב אדם, להורותם דרכי התבל וארחות לבב בני האדם, תאותיהם, מזמותיהם ויצרי לבם. כי החוזה הזה לא חוזה לעם אחד או לארץ אחת הנהו, הוא חוזה לכל העמים ולכל הארצות, כי לא דרכי בן עם אחד או אנשים פרטיים יֵרָאֶה לנו כי אם דרכי האדם בכלל, ועל כן יהיה כמורה לכל בני האדם, וגם לנו בשפתנו לא כזר יחשב, כי אם נתבונן אך מעט אז נראה כי גם בנו יש ויש אנשים באיתיאל ופיכול ודואג ודומיהם.

Although admittedly we do not have great army commanders like Ithiel, who display their prowess and courage on the battlefield, instead we have in our midst members of the elite who are innocent in

אם אמנם שרי צבא גדולים כאיתיאל אשר יראו עזוז רוחם ואֹמץ ידם על שדי קטל אין לנו, אך תחת זאת יש ויש בקרבנו בני המעלה תמימי דרך, רבנים, מורים, ראשי העדה וגבירים בעם תמימי לב, אשר יטו אזן קשבת לדברי מלשינים

their conduct, innocent rabbis, teachers, community leaders, and rich men who turn an attentive ear to the words of those who slander in secret, to crooked-hearted men who would guide their leaders into oblivion in order to acquire money or a position, corrupting justice, pursuing blameless men who have done no wrong, and spreading quarrels and strife in each and every community. And the Jewish people are not at all lacking in men like Doeg; in almost each and every town, in each and every community, there are men like him by the dozens, who with their lying and deception set cities aflame, sow discord, and cause destruction. One calls on the name of faith and puts a God-fearing veil over his face in order to destroy many followers of the Haskalah by making judgements against those who have forgotten God, while another carries the banner of the Haskalah on his shoulders in order to oppress those whom he considers to be fools and simpletons, as they draw water from the well of faith in order to sustain themselves; and together they all surround the great ones with their deceit and the lesser ones with their fear or their intellect, and they cause a great deal of failure wherever they go. Indeed, all such men are Doeg's friends, and they camp under his banner.

בסתר, לנעוי לב אשר למען מצוא כסף או משרה יטו בתֹהו ראשיהם לעות משפט ולרדוף נקיים על לא חמס עשו ולהרבות ריב ומדון בעדה ועדה, ומאנשים כדואג לא אלמן ישראל מכל וכל; כמעט בכל עיר ועיר ובבל עדה ועדה נמצא אנשים כמֹהו לעשרות, אשר בשקרותם ותרמיתם יפיחו קריה, ישלחו מדנים וישימו שמות, זה יקרא בשם האמונה וישים מסוה יראת אלהים על פניו למען ירבה חללי ההשכלה בשומו שפטים בשוכחי אלהים, וזה ישא דגל ההשכלה על שכמו למען דכא האוילים והפתאים בעיניו, אשר מבאר האמונה ישאבו מים להם להחיות נפשם, וכלם יחד יסבבו את הגדולים בתרמיתם והקטנים ביראתם או בדעתם וירבו כושל על כל דרכיהם. הנה כל אלה חברי דואג המה ועל דגלו יחנו.

But men like Phichol, who are blinded by the desire for power, are perhaps even more numerous among the Jewish people than among all other peoples. There is almost no people on earth which regards its sons and daughters as livestock bought with its money, doing what it pleases with them, like the Jewish people do. Among all peoples we see that only their great men and leaders are

אבל אנשים כפיכל אשר תאות הכבוד תעור עיניהם רבים בבית ישראל אולי גם יתר מאשר בכל העמים. כמעט אין עם בארץ אשר יחשוב את בניו ובנותיו כמקנת כספו ויעשה בהם כחפצו כעם ישראל; בכל העמים נראה רק כי אדיריהם ומושליהם לא יפנו אל רגשות לב פרי בטניהם ויתנום לאשר ישר בעיניהם למען ינחלו כבוד ולהרבות כבוד משפחתם, ובישראל כמעט כלם מקטניהם עד גדוליהם, ממשכיליהם עד אויליהם כלם יחד בני מלכים הם וכבוד

indifferent to their offspring's feelings, marrying them off to whomever they deem suitable in order to gain honour and increase their family's honour, whereas among the Jewish people almost everyone, from the most insignificant to the greatest among them, from the wisest to the most foolish among them, are all the sons of kings, and family honour and pedigree are the things that make matches for them. But they falsely boast that no one is as merciful towards their children as they are, and that they toil their whole lives only in order to grant their children success, but in truth it is not for their children but rather for themselves, in order to increase their honour that they do so. If they were really thinking of their children's success, they would take care to make a path for them in life, to teach them a trade if they are not suited for study, and they would not constantly think about how this would ruin their pedigree. If they really wanted to grant their daughters success, they would not choose husbands for them by means of messengers and matchmakers, they would not consider familial honour, or a foolish rabbi who bestows his glory upon the whole family, or a rich man who has robbed strangers of their wealth and has become successful and bestowed the radiance of his gold upon all the members of his family.

המשפחות ויחש הם המה המזוגים זוגים להם. אך שקר יתפארו כי מרחמים על בניהם אין כמהם, וכי כל ימי חייהם יעמלו רק למען יצליחו את בניהם, כי באמת לא לבניהם כי אם למען נפשם, למען הרבות כבודם יעשו זאת. לוא הביטו אל הצלחת בניהם באמת, כי אז שמו לבם לפלס להם דרך סלולה בחיים, ללמדם עבודה ומלאכה אם לא יצלחו לדעת, ולא זכרו לרגעים את יחשם אשר יחלל על ידי הדבר הזה, לו חפצו באמת להצליח את בנותיהם, כי אז לא ביד מלאכים ושדכנים בחרו להן אנשים, כי אז לא הביטו אל כבוד משפחות, אל רב אוילי אשר יאציל מהודו על כל המשפחה כלה, אל גביר אשר גזל חיל זרים ויעשה חיל ויאציל מברק זהבו על כל בני משפחתו.

Indeed, what is the pedigree of most Jewish families? One has become rich through deception, and has managed to buy the sixth Torah portion and *maftir*[12]

הן מה הוא יחש רוב משפחות בני ישראל? האחד עשה עֹשר ברמיה וידו מצאה לקנות ששי ומַפטיר[12] שנים רבות ולעמוד בראש בבית התפלה ולקנות ספרי תורה[13] וכהנה ויהיה לפנת

12 This refers to the practice of dividing the Sabbath Torah reading in synagogues into seven portions and giving different members of the community the honour of being called up to recite the blessings over each portion. The sixth portion is particularly esteemed and is often assigned to learned members of the community. The *maftir* portion follows the seventh portion; it consists of the last few lines of the seventh portion followed by the *haftarah*, a selection from the Prophets with links to the Torah reading.

for many years, to occupy a leading position in the synagogue, and to buy Torah scrolls[13] and so forth, and he becomes a precious cornerstone for his entire family and all of his descendants derive their honour from him and mention his name with great pride. Another has borrowed money without repaying it on multiple occasions, yet nevertheless he is considered generous, for he is a friend of the burial societies and gives of his stolen money to charity; a third one acted corruptly and committed every indecency in his trading with partners from other lands in the days of his youth, and yet in his old age he sits in a prayer-shawl and phylacteries for two hours a day in the study-house and is called a righteous man, and all his sons and daughters boast of his honour; a fourth one made his wealth through deceit overnight on the stock market and became respected by all, and this man has a rabbi or *dayyan*[14] or ritual slaughterer in his family, whose honour is as naught in his eyes, and when he speaks to them he lords it over them because he is rich and they are poor, but on the day when it comes to discussing a marriage match for his son or daughter, he puffs himself up like a frog and mentions the name of the exalted man, because he too is illuminated by the light of his honour. And they all (except a small number of people, and they are very few, who with their hearts as well as their mouths seek only their children's happiness) see their sons and daughters only as a way of increasing the family honour, and even if the girl cries out bitterly: 'I have no desire

יקרת לכל משפחתו ותלו עליו כל הצאצאים ובשמו יזכירו וילבשו גאות כמדם. השני לוה ולא שלם פעמים ושלש ובכל זאת לו נדיב יֵאָמֵר כי חבר הוא לחברות קדושות ויעניק מכסף הגזל לצדקה, השלישי שחת דרכו ועשה כל זמה בסחרו אל ארצות לרגלי מסחרו בימי עלומיו ולעת זקנותו ישב בטלית ותפלין שתי שעות ביום בבית המדרש ולו צדיק יאמר ובכבודו יתימרו כל בניו ובנותיו, ורביעי עשה עֹשר ברמיה בין לילה על הבאֶרזע ויהי לנכבד לכל, ולזה רב או דין[14] או שוחט במשפחתו, אשר כבודם כאין בעיניו ובדברו אתם יגדיל עליהם עקב כי הוא עשיר והמה עניים, אך ביום שֶׁיְּדֻבַּר בבנו או בבתו אז יתנפח כצפרדע ויזכיר בשם הגבר הוקם על אשר יפיץ מאור כבודו גם עליו. וכלם כאחד (מלבד מתי מספר והמה מעטים מאוד, אשר בלבם כמו בפיהם יבקשו רק אֹשר בניהם) ישאו עיניהם אך להגדיל כבוד המשפחה על ידי בניהם ובנותיהם, ואם גם נפש הנערה מר תשוע: אין חפצי אל שנוא נפשי, יקר בעיני המות מתת חיי בידי איש אשר רוחו זרה לי, ואם גם יתחנן הבן: נפשי קצה בבת הגביר או המיחש הלז אשר תארה משחת ולבה ריק ואיכה אשליך חיי מנגד לבלות ימי באנחה? תצעקנה ותהמינה הנפשות הנענות האלה כהעולה על רוחן ושומע אין להן מאת אבותיהן מ ר ח מ י ה ן, אשר רק למענן יחיו ולמענן ירבו עמל ועבודה, ולמענן יעשו עֹשר ברמיה ונלוז. פה איש חסיד נבער מדעת יְלַמֵּד בתו שפה ולשון ולפרוט על פי הנבל ולצאת במחול משחקים והיא תלמד ותעשה חיל ותקנה לב ובאחריתה תהיה לאשה לנבל חסר דעת, חסיד ממשפחה מיחסת ונפשה תשוע: למה עכרתני אבי בתתך אותי ללמוד דעת ולפקוח עינים למען אראה שברי? לוא כאחת חסרות הדעת הייתי כי אז הייתי מאשרת, כי אז לא ידעתי תפארת אנשים כי אז לא הכרתי ערך האדם המעלה מן בזוי אדם ואתה הבאת שבר ברוחי בהביאך דעת בלבי ועתה תוסיף לגזול אשרי וחיי בקשרך אותי אל בול עץ! – תצעק תהמה כחפצה ואזני אביה הרחמן אטומות, כי

13 Sponsoring a scribe to produce a Torah scroll for the community is an extremely costly endeavour that is considered a great honour in Jewish society.

14 Judge in a rabbinical court.

למען אשרה יעשה זאת. שם יתרועע איש את משכילים וכחובב השכלה יֵרָאֶה למען ינחל כבוד ובתו למדה מנער לכבד משכילים והשכלה ולא תבקש עֹשר ומרכבות מרקדות והיכלי עֹנג כי אם איש אשר קנה כליותיה ולבבה, וביום שידבר בה יבחר אביה באיש אוצרות אף אם לא דעת ולא תבונה ולא תֹאר אדם לו, ולרגלי החמור הזה ישליך את בתו כי ידרוך עליה ברגל גאוה, כי איש עשיר תאוה נפשו וצרת נפש בתו לא תרך לבו כי לאשרה והצלחתה יתן כ ס ף לה. לו קבצו הדמעות הנובעות מעיני נפשות נענות כאלה למקום אחד כי אז היו לנחל שוטף, לוא התאחדו כל האנחות היוצאות מלבות נשברים כאלה כי אז היו לרוח סערה נוראה מאוד, אך איש לא יספרן ולא יקבצן ולא ישים לב להן, וימכרו את בניהם ובנותיהם כעבדים למען מלא תאות נפשם לכבוד, ובכן ירבו האמללים, ושלום אמת בבית איש ישראל (ומה גם בעת הזאת אשר נפלגו לבות בני ישראל למפלגות היראים והמשכילים) הוא דבר יקר מאוד; בארצות אשר עוד לא החזיקו בכל דרכי העמים נשמע מצה ומריבה בין איש לאשתו, נראה יום יום באים לבתי הדינים לתת ספר כריתות לאשתם אשר נתנו אבותיהם להם, גרושות אמללות, עגונות שוממות נראה על כל צעד, ובארצות אשר שם בוש יבושו לשלח את אשתם, כי חרפה היא, יפנו איש לדרכו, אחרי עיניו ולבו, ונשותיהם גם הנה תלמדנה ארחותיהם, וזאת היא ההצלחה אשר על במותיה ירכיבו האבות הרחמנים אשר יעמלו רק למען פרי בטנם, את בניהם ובנותיהם. יראו תלמידים פיכל אלה מבני ישראל הבוחרים בדרכיו, את דרכיהם ועלילותיהם בהמחזה הזה כבראי מלטש, ואולי יבינו לאחריתם, יראו תמימי לב כאיתיאל את דרכי הנוכלים הבוגדים וידעו להזהר מהם, יראה כל העם את דרכי הבוגדים כדואג ולא יזנו אחריהם. אחת היא על כן אמרתי, כי החזיון הזה גם לנו הוא כמו לכל העמים, ועל כן עלינו להכיר טובה להמעתיק הזה בהביאו אל אוצר שפתנו כלי חמדה כזה, כלי חמדה אשר לתפארת ולחפץ יהיה לשפתנו. ומה מאוד ישמח לבי בזכרי כי אני העירותי את רוח המעתיק לעשות המלאכה

for a man whom I despise; I would prefer to die rather than to give my life to a man who is alien to me,' and even if the son begs, 'I am repulsed by the daughter of this rich or pedigreed man who has a corrupted character and a hollow heart, so how can I endanger my life and spend my days groaning?' These afflicted souls cry out and howl how they feel, but there is no one to listen to them among their *merciful* fathers, who live only for them and toil intensively for them, and gain wealth for them through deceit and dishonesty. In one case a pious and ignorant man teaches his daughter languages, and how to strum on a harp, and how to go out to merrymakers' dances, and she studies and is successful and acquires knowledge, yet in the end she is to become the wife of an ignorant fool, a pious man from a pedigreed family, and she cries out: 'Why did you bring trouble upon me, father, by letting me acquire knowledge and open my eyes, so that I might see my destruction? If I were like one of the ignorant girls, then I would be happy, for I would not know the glory of men, I would not know the worth of an exalted man compared to a despicable man; but you have brought destruction upon me by giving me knowledge, and now you continue to rob me of my happiness and my life by tying me to a block of wood!' – She cries out and howls how she feels, but her merciful father's ears are closed, because he is doing this for her happiness. In another case a man befriends Maskilim and appears to be an enthusiast of the Haskalah in order to gain honour, and his daughter has learned since her youth to honour Maskilim and the Haskalah, seeking not wealth, dancing chariots, or palaces of pleasure, but rather a man who has won her mind and heart. But on the day when her match is arranged, her father chooses a wealthy man, even though he is devoid of knowledge, intellect, and manly qualities, and he throws his daughter at the foot of this ass in order for him to trample on her with a prideful foot, for he desires a rich man, and his daughter's distress does not soften his heart, for he is giving her *money* for her happiness and success. If the tears welling up from the eyes of these afflicted souls were gathered into one place, they would become a flowing stream; if all the groans emanating from such broken hearts were united, they would become a very fearsome storm wind, but no one counts them, no one gathers them, no one pays attention to them; they sell their sons and their daughters like slaves in order to satisfy their own desire for honour, and therefore wretched people proliferate, and true peace in a Jew's home (especially at this time, when the hearts of the Jewish people have been divided into the camps of the God-fearing and the Maskilim) is a very precious thing. In countries where the Jews have not yet adopted Gentile ways, we hear of strife and quarrels between a man and his wife; on a daily basis we see men going to the courthouses to grant bills of divorce to their wives whom their fathers had given them; we see miserable divorcées and desolate abandoned wives at every step. Meanwhile, in the countries where men are ashamed to get rid of their wives, because it is a disgrace, each man does as he pleases, following his eyes and heart, and their wives also learn their ways, and this is the success upon whose altars

הזאת, ועל משפטי נשען להוציא פעולתו לאור, כי ימים רבים כלתה נפשי לראות פעל ידי ראש החוזים לובשים אדרת שפתנו, ימים רבים בראותי כי סופרינו, כאלה אשר להם יאות שם סופרים כן אלה אשר יקחו להם השם הזה בלי כל צדקה, יפנו איש איש לספרים זרים להלבישם בלבוש שפתנו, ספרים זרים לעמנו, לרוחנו ולשפתנו, ספרים אשר לא יביא כל תֹּעלת ודעת, ספרים גם אשר אין שוה להדפיסם בשפה אשר נכתבו ואף כי להעתיקם לשפה אחרת, בספרים כאלה יבחרו סופרינו להעשיר בהם אוצר ספרתנו, בראותי כזאת אמרתי תמיד: האם בשגעון הֻכּוּ כלם לבחור רק רע ומשחת ואין מתעורר לתת לנו דברים טובים ומועילים. מי יתן וימצא איש מעתיק חזיונות שעקספיר לשפתנו ועליו תבוא ברכת כל אוהבי שפתנו אשר יבינו פעלו – כן אמרתי תמיד לאוהבי, והנה זה נמצא היום גואל לשפתנו אשר החל לנסות כחו במלאכה הזאת, נסה וגם הצליח במאוד מאוד, כאשר תחזינה עיני הקוראים, ומי יתן והיה את לבבו להוסיף במלאכתו זאת להאדיר קרן שפתנו, ולקרב לב רבים מקוראיה, אשר עוד לא יבינו משפט מה טוב ומה רע, לשים עיניהם ולבם אך לספרים טובים ונעלים כמו אלה, ופעלו הטוב יהי משכרתו, כי למשכרת אחרת לא ייחל ולא יקוה, כי אם להגדיל כבוד שפתנו ולהאדירה, וידעתי נאמנה כי לא יבוש משברו, כי כל הקוראים יודוהו על פי פעלו כאשר אודהו ואברכהו אני על הטוב אשר עשה.

וויען תשיעי לירח שבט שנת תרל"ד.[15]
פרץ בן משה סמאלענסקין.

the merciful fathers who toil only for the benefit of their offspring place their sons and daughters. These Jewish students of Phichol who choose to follow in his footsteps will see their conduct and their actions in this play as if in a polished mirror, and perhaps they will understand what lies in store for them; innocent men like Ithiel will see how traitorous scoundrels behave and will know to be wary of them; the entire people will see the behaviour of traitors like Doeg and will not go chasing after it. It is all the same; therefore I say that this play is also for us just as it is for all peoples, and therefore we must be grateful to this translator for bringing such a precious object into the treasure-house of our language, a precious object that will be a beauty and a delight for our language. And it gladdens my heart very much when I recall that I spurred the translator on to perform this labour, and that he relied upon my judgement to bring his work to light, because for a long time I had yearned to see the work of the greatest of playwrights dressed in the mantle of our language; for a long time, when I saw that our authors – those deserving of the title of author as well as those who take this title for themselves without any justification – were all turning to foreign books and dressing them in the garment of our language, books foreign to our people, our spirit, and our language, books that bring no benefit or knowledge, books not even worth printing in the language in which they were written, let alone translating into another language, our authors were choosing such books with which to enrich the treasure-house of our literature; when I saw such things, I always said: 'Have they all been stricken with madness, choosing only what is evil and corrupt, with no one stirring to give us good and beneficial words? If only a man could be found to translate the plays of Shakespeare into our language, he would receive the blessing of all lovers of our language who understood his work' – I always said this to my friends, and look, today someone to redeem our language has been found, someone who has begun to try his hand at this work; he has tried it and has succeeded most greatly, as readers will see. If only he should desire to continue with this labour of his, to glorify the prestige of our language, and to draw in many of its readers, who do not yet know how to judge what is good and what is bad, paying attention only to good and exalted books like these! May his good deed be his wages, for he does not wish or hope for any other wages, other than to increase and magnify the honour of our language, and I know with certainty that he will not be put to shame in his hope, because all readers will praise him for his work just as I praise him and bless him for the good that he has done.

Vienna, the ninth of the month of
Shevat, 5634.[15]
Peretz ben Moses Smolenskin.

---

15 This date on the Hebrew calendar corresponds to 27 January 1874.

Letter from the translator to the publisher

I have fulfilled your desire, my friend, and translated *Othello* from English into Hebrew. I have also obeyed you and called it *Ithiel* in Hebrew, which resembles *Othello* only in pronunciation, and not *Athlai*[16] as I had called it in the beginning, and which is its correct translation. But after I finished the work, I was disheartened, for while reading the original, each and every utterance chimed in my ears with a voice full of power and glory, like the voice of a living man emerging from Shakespeare's throat, but my translation was not like this, for its voice issued like a ghost from the ground, and my words spoke from the dust. And even though I knew well that I had translated the author's ideas faithfully and had not strayed from his thoughts to the right or the left, nevertheless the road is long between the living language emerging from the mouth of the greatest man among the Anakim[17] and the Hebrew language twittered by a man such as myself. It is in no way lost on me that the man contemplating the work of his own hands resembles a woman looking at her face in a polished mirror; she cannot know whether she is beautiful or not if she has not heard so from someone else's mouth; and thus is man; he should not be judge of the work of his hands or testify about it either for good or for ill, because the judgement is for others. Therefore

מכתב המעתיק אל המוציא לאור

מלאתי רצונך ידידי, והעתקתי את אָטעלא מאנגלית לעברית וגם שמעתי בקולך וקראתי שמו בישראל איתיאל, הדומה רק במבטא אל אטעלא ולא עַתְלַי,[16] כאשר קראתי לו בתחלה, ואשר הוא תרגומו הנכון. אך אחרי אשר כליתי את המלאכה, נפלו פני, כי מדי קראי במקור הספר, כל מאמר ומאמר מצלצל באזני בקול עז והדר, כקול איש חי היוצא מתוך גרונו של שעקספער, לא כן העתקתי, כי כאוב מארץ תתן קולה ומעפר תשח אמרתי. ואף כי ידעתי מאד, כי רעיון המחבר העתקתי באמונה ולא נטיתי ממחשבתו ימין ושמאל, בכל זאת רב הדרך, בין לשון חיה היוצאת מפי האדם הגדול בענקים[17] ובין לשון עברית אשר יצפצף איש כמוני. אפס לא נעלם ממני, כי האיש המתבונן במעשה ידיו, דומה הוא לאשה, אשר תראה את פניה בראי מלוטש, היא לא תוכל לדעת, אם יפה היא או לו*, אם לא שמעה כן מפי זולתה, וכן הוא האיש, אין לו להיות דיין ועד על מעשה ידיו, לא לטוב ולא לרע, כי המשפט לאחרים הוא. ואשר על כן הנני שולח לך בזה את ההעתקה, ואתה תחרוץ כטוב בעיניך: אם תאמר, כי בריאת בשר היא וגלגול הנפש מענגליש לעברית נעשה כהוגן, אז בידך היא להוציאה לאור ולהביאה בקהל ישראל, ואם תמצא כי טעם שעקספער לא עמד בקנקני, וריח שפת קדשנו נמר בהעתקתי, הגד לי כן בפה מלא, ואני הנני נכון לאבד מעשה ידי ונתתי את עמלי למאכולת אש, כי למה אני מכניס צפרדעים למצרים והעתקה רעה למחנה העברים? המעט להם העתקות רעות ונשחתות אשר שרצו סופרי ישראל כיאור מדור דור? או האין לי מלאכה אחרת בעולמי, בלתי להתעלל באשת יפת תאר ולתעב את יפיה, עד אשר תגעל בה נפש הרואה ונמצא שם שעקספער מתחלל

16 This minor biblical character, mentioned in Ezra 10:28, was a Judean who had intermarried but was influenced by the scribe Ezra to send away his foreign wife. See First Part, note 94. Apart from this brief statement and one editorial comment at the end of the play (see Publisher's Note, note 1), there does not seem to be any documented indication as to the extent of Smolenskin's changes to Salkinson's translation, nor as to how Salkinson might have regarded such alterations to his work.

17 'The greatest man among the Anakim' is a citation of Josh. 14:15; the Anakim or Anakites were a race of primordial giants mentioned on various occasions in the Hebrew Bible.

*) לא

I am hereby sending you the translation, and you must decide as you see fit: if you say that it is healthy and that the reincarnation from English to Hebrew has been conducted appropriately, then it is in your power to publish it and introduce it to the Jewish community, but if you find that Shakespeare's flavour has not remained in my jar, and the scent of our holy tongue has been altered in my translation, tell me so decisively, and I shall be prepared to destroy the work of my hand and to hand over my toil as fuel for the fire, for why should I bring frogs into Egypt and a bad translation into the camp of the Hebrews? Do they have too few bad and corrupted translations, with which Jewish authors have been swarming like the Nile for generation after generation? Or do I have no other work to keep me occupied, other than mistreating a beautiful woman and defiling her beauty, to the point where the viewer would be repulsed by her and Shakespeare's name would be desecrated at my hand? Indeed, it is true that I translated *Paradise Lost* and printed it and took it upon myself to ensure that it would see the light of day, without taking advice from knowledgeable people, but there were two reasons for that; the first reason is that this great and important book is constructed from beginning to end on the foundation of the Holy Scriptures, and because of my great love for the books of the LORD I determined to present this voluntary offering upon the altar of our language for the good of the Jewish people; and if they scorn my offering, I shall not take it to heart because the LORD, who sees into the heart, knows that I did this for His honour.*) And the

על ידי? הן אמת הדבר כי ספר Paradise Lost העתקתיו והדפסתיו על אחריותי שלי כי יצא לאור עולם, בלי קחת עצה מפי יודעי דת ודין, אך שני טעמים היו בדבר; הטעם הראשון, כי הספר הגדול והנכבד הזה, בנוי מתחלתו ועד סופו על יסוד ספרי הקדש, ומרוב אהבתי לספרי ה', אמרתי להגיש מנחת נדבה זו על מזבח שפתנו לטובת עם ישראל; ואם הם יבעטון במנחתי לא אשים לב כי השם הרואה ללבב, הוא יודע כי לכבודו עשיתי זאת*). והטעם השני כי הספר Paradise Lost איננו נודע כל כך בשערי ישראל, ויש רבים מראשי חכמיו וסופריו אשר שמעו את שמעו, כי מעשה ידי אמן גדול הוא, ובכל זאת לא קראו דבריו, לא ראו הודו ולא ידעו מה הוא, ועל כן נדרשתי ללא שאלוני, והעתקתי את הספר לבני עבר, למען ידעו ויכירו מה ערך האיש מילטאן הגדול בחסידי אומות העולם ומה פעל בספרו, אשר קראתיו בשם ויגרש את האדם,[18] כי נפלאות יחזו בו, אשר לא נבראו בכל הגוים עד היום הזה. לא כן שעקספער, ספריו נקראים בארבע כנפות הארץ בשבעים לשון, ואת חזיונותיו יראו הרואים על הבמה בכל עיר גדולה, על כן אין לי חפץ להביא ספריו בקהל ישראל בטרם אשמע מפי איש רב ושליט כמוך כי העתקתי נכונה ומותרת היא לבוא בקהל. ואם אחרי כן יבואו המבקרים וימצאו בה ערות דבר אתה ידידי לבדך תשא, ואני את נפשי הצלתי.

ידידך מוקירך ומכבדך
J.E.S.

*) If readers scorn the offering that he has brought them with his book *So He Drove Out the Man*, it is not because he was unsuccessful in his work, for all understanding readers have praised his work and have marvelled very greatly at his talent

*) אם הקוראים יבעטו בהמנחה אשר הביא להם בספרו "ויגרש את האדם" הוא לא יען כי לא הצליח במעשהו, כי כל הקוראים המבינים הוקירו פעלו ויתפלאו על כשרונו בהעתקה במאוד מאוד, אך ענין הספר לא ירצה לבן ישראל, ועל כן אם לא יתן לפעל המעתיק

second reason is that *Paradise Lost* is not so well known among the Jewish people; while there are many among its foremost sages and authors who have heard of it, and that it is the work of a great artist, nevertheless they have not read it, have not seen its glory and do not know what it is, and therefore I responded though no one had asked me, and translated the book for the Hebrews, in order that they might know and recognize the worth of Milton, the greatest of the righteous among the nations, and what he achieved with his book, which I have called by the title *So He Drove Out the Man*,[18] because wondrous things can be seen in it which have not been devised in any nation until this day. It is not so with Shakespeare; his books are read in the four corners of the world in seventy languages, and viewers can see his plays on the stage in every big city; therefore I have no desire to bring his books into the Jewish community before I hear from the mouth of a great and powerful man like yourself that my translation is correct and that it is permitted to enter the community. And if afterwards the critics come and find any indecency in it, you, my friend, will bear it on your own, and I shall have rescued myself.

Your friend who respects and
honours you
J.E.S.

---

in translating, but the subject of the book is not pleasing to a Jew, and therefore, if he does not highly value the translator's work, we cannot place the blame on the translator. However, with this translation that is not the case, because its subject matter is desirable and acceptable to all readers, and moreover the translator has succeeded greatly in his work. He can trust that this translation will be a desirable offering for all those who love the language of their forefathers – The Publisher.

תעצומות ועז לא נוכל לשים אשם נפשו, לא כן בהעתקה הזאת, אשר הענין יהיה רצוי ומקבל לכל הקוראים, וגם במלאכתו השכיל מאוד, בההעתקה הזאת יוכל לבטוח, כי תהיה למנחת רצון לכל אוהבי שפת אבותם - המו״ל.

18 The title of Salkinson's translation of *Paradise Lost* is a citation of the beginning of Gen. 3:24, in which God drives Adam and Eve out of the Garden of Eden after they eat from the tree of knowledge.

The names of the speakers

Duke. . . . . .The Prince of the Land *in Venice*[19]

Brabantio. . . . . Phichol *counsellor at the gate of the state*[20]

Senators . . . . .Two other counsellors

Gratiano . . . . .Gether *Phichol's brother*

Lodovico . . . . .Lud *Phichol's friend*

Othello the Moor . . . . .Ithiel *the Cushite*

Cassio . . . . .Chesed *his officer*

Jago[21] . . . . .Doeg *his standard-bearer*

Roderig[22] Raddai *one of the noblemen of Venice*

Montano . . . . .Kenaz *the governor on the island of Caphtor before Ithiel's arrival*

Chlown[23]. . . . . .Clown *attendant to Ithiel*

Herald. . . . . .Herold[24]

Desdemona . . . . Asenath *Phichol's daughter; Ithiel's wife*

Emilie[25]. . . . . .Milcah *Doeg's wife*

Bianco[26]. . . . . .Anah *Chesed's concubine*

Officers, noblemen, couriers, musicians, sailors, attendants, and others.

The scene in the first part is in Venice, and the rest of the scenes are on the seashore on the island of Caphtor [Cyprus].

19 Salkinson provided this English cast list alongside the Hebrew one.
20 In biblical times a city's gate served as the gathering place for its judges and other authority figures.
21 Sic; this appears in Salkinson's English cast list instead of the expected 'Iago'.
22 Sic; this appears in Salkinson's English cast list instead of the expected 'Roderigo'.
23 Sic; this appears in Salkinson's English cast list instead of the expected 'Clown'.
24 Sic; this appears in Salkinson's English cast list instead of the expected 'Herald'.
25 Sic; this appears in Salkinson's English cast list instead of the expected 'Emilia'.
26 Sic; this appears in Salkinson's English cast list instead of the expected 'Bianca'.

שמות המדברים

נשיא הארץ בוינעציא	Duke[19]
פִּיכל יועץ בשער[20] המדינה	Brabantio
שני יועצים אחרים.	Senators
גֶּתֶר אחי פיכל	Gratiano
לוד מודע לפיכל	Lodovico
אִיתִיאֵל הכושי	Othello the Moor
כֶּשֶׂד פקידו	Cassio
דוֹאֵג נושא דגלו	Jago[21]
רַדַּי אחד מאצילי וינעציא	Roderig[22]
קְנַז הנציב באי כפתור לפני בוא איתיאל	Montano
לֵץ משרת לאיתיאל	Chlown[23]
מכריז	Herold[24]
אָסְנַת בת פיכל אשת איתיאל.	Desdemona
מִלְכָּה אשת דואג	Emilie[25]
עֲנָה פלגש כשד	Bianco[26]

פקידים, אצילים, רצים, מנגנים, מלחים, משרתים ויתר העם.

המחזה בחלק ראשון בוינעציא. ויתר המחזות על חוף הים באי כפתור Cyprus

First Part[1]

חלק[1] ראשון

SCENE I	*Venice[2] – street(Raddai[3] and Doeg[4])*	וינעציא[2] – רחוב (רדי[3] ודואג[4])	מחזה א'
RADDAI	Be silent! Do not speak to me further	הַס! אַל תּוֹסֶף דַּבֵּר אֵלַי עוֹד	רדי
	Behold, my purse is perpetually open before you	הֵן כִּיס כַּסְפִּי פָּתוּחַ לְפָנֶיךָ תָּמִיד	
	And you know this – **I am deeply angry**.[5]	וְאַתָּה כָּזֹאת יָדַעְתָּ – הֵיטֵב חָרָה לִי.[5]	
DOEG	But why, devil![6] You are not listening to my words	אֲבָל מַדּוּעַ, שָׂטָן![6] לֹא תִשְׁמַע דְּבָרָי	דואג
	If I have turned my attention to this matter	אִם שַׂמְתִּי לִבִּי אֶל הַדָּבָר הַזֶּה	
	If I have ever pondered such a thing, you may indeed abhor me.	אִם הָגִיתִי כֵן מֵעוֹדִי תַּעֵב תְּתַעֵב אֹתִי.	
RADDAI	Why, you told me that you hate him.	הֲלֹא הִגַּדְתָּ לִי כִּי שָׂנֵאתָ אֹתוֹ.	רדי
DOEG	May I be a laughingstock if the matter is not so.	תְּהִי נַפְשִׁי לָבוּז אִם לֹא כֵן הַדָּבָר.	דואג
	Three of **the great men of the city**[7] urged him **from day to day**[8]	שְׁלֹשָׁה גְדוֹלֵי הָעִיר[7] הִפְצִירוּ בוֹ מִיּוֹם לְיוֹם[8]	

1 Salkinson uses the Hebrew word חלק 'part' rather than a more specific term for 'act', most likely because there was no widely established Hebrew theatre terminology at the time.

2 Salkinson retains the Italian place names appearing in Shakespeare's text. While this seems to deviate from his overall Judaizing strategy, it may be rooted in his recognition of the longstanding and prominent Jewish presence in Italy and could point to a concomitant decision to interpret his characters as Italian Jews (Kahn 2017).

3 1 Chron. 2:14. Raddai was the fifth son of Jesse and older brother of King David. Salkinson most likely selected the name primarily or solely on the basis of its sound correspondence with Shakespeare's 'Roderigo'.

4 1 Sam. 22:18, 22; Ps. 52:2. Doeg was an Edomite and chief herdsman to King Saul who carried out the execution of a large number of priests. Edom was an enemy nation for biblical Israel; in rabbinic literature, it became a symbol of the Jews' Roman conquerors and of Christianity in general. In light of these points, Scolnicov (2001: 186) proposes that Salkinson selected Doeg as the equivalent of Iago in order to highlight the character's murderous proclivities and to mark him as a Christian enemy in contrast to the Jewish Ithiel (see note 94). The partial sound correspondence with Shakepeare's 'Iago' most likely also played a role.

5 Jon. 4:9.

6 Cf. Shakespeare's 'Sblood' (1.1.3). Salkinson has neutralized the Christian connotations of this oath, a contraction of 'God's blood'. While 'Sblood' was expurgated from the text of the First Folio (Honigmann 1997: 115), it seems to have been present in the edition that Salkinson was using (which generally corresponds to the Folio in other respects). The Hebrew term typically means 'adversary' in the Bible, but takes on the sense of 'devil' or 'Satan' in postbiblical texts. Salkinson is using it in the latter meaning.

7 2 Kings 10:6.

8 Esther 3:7.

To raise me up and let me be an officer[9] for him	כִּי יְנַשְּׂאֵנִי וְיִתְּנֵנִי לִהְיוֹת לוֹ לְפָקִיד[9]
And I hereby swear by my faith that **my strength is sufficient for me**[10]	וְהִנְנִי נִשְׁבַּע בֶּאֱמוּנָתִי כִּי יָדַי רַב לִי[10]
And I am not unworthy to bear the obligation of such an office	וְלֹא קָטֹנְתִּי מִשְּׂאֵת מִשְׁמֶרֶת פְּקוּדָּה כַּזֹּאת
But he in his arrogance **has a different spirit with him**[11]	אַךְ הוּא בְּגַאֲוָתוֹ רוּחַ אַחֶרֶת אִתּוֹ[11]
And he replied to them with **false and misleading oracles**[12]	וַיָּשֶׁב אֶת פְּנֵיהֶם בְּמַשְׂאוֹת שָׁוְא וּמַדּוּחִים[12]
And he behaved deceitfully towards them, saying that it was a time of war	וַיִּתְנַכֵּל לָהֶם לֵאמֹר עֵת מִלְחָמָה הִיא
And that he would not be able to fulfil that which they had urged on my behalf	וְלֹא יוּכַל לְמַלֵּא אֵת אֲשֶׁר הִפְגִּיעוּ בַּעֲדִי
For he had already chosen an officer, **a man after his own heart.**[13]	כִּי כְבָר בָּחַר בְּאִישׁ פָּקִיד כִּלְבָבוֹ.[13]
And who is this officer? Who is the man after his own heart?	וּמִי הוּא הַפָּקִיד הַזֶּה? מִי הוּא הָאִישׁ כִּלְבָבוֹ?
A man by the name of **Chesed**,[14] a native of the city of Florence	אִישׁ כֶּשֶׂד[14] שְׁמוֹ, יְלִיד עִיר פְלָארֶענְץ
Who has understanding of the times[15] and is the servant of a beautiful concubine	יֹדֵעַ בִּינָה לָעִתִּים[15] וְעֶבֶד לְפִלֶגֶשׁ יָפָה
But to lead a troop in the field, to command an army of war	אַךְ לְהוֹלִיךְ גְּדוּד בַּשָּׂדֶה, לְפַקֵּד צְבָא מִלְחָמָה
He has no more knowledge than **one who grasps the spindle**[16]	אֵין לוֹ יִתְרוֹן דַּעַת עַל תֹּמֵךְ פָּלֶךְ.[16]

9 Cf. Shakespeare's 'lieutenant' (1.1.8). The Hebrew word פָּקִיד is much more general than the English 'lieutenant'; as Dikman (in Salkinson 1874/2015: 239) has observed, Salkinson uses it to translate distinct English terms ('lieutenant' and 'officer'), thus obscuring the differences between them.

10 Deut. 33:7 יָדָיו רָב לוֹ 'strengthen his hands', i.e., 'give him the strength'.

11 Num. 14:24 הָיְתָה רוּחַ אַחֶרֶת עִמּוֹ 'he had a different spirit with him'.

12 Lam. 2:14.

13 1 Sam. 13:14.

14 One of the sons of Abraham's brother Nahor mentioned in Genesis 22:22 (spelled Kesed in some English Bible translations). Salkinson most likely selected this name on the basis of its sound correspondence with Shakespeare's 'Cassio'.

15 1 Chron. 12:33 וּמִבְּנֵי יִשָּׂשכָר יוֹדְעֵי בִינָה לַעִתִּים 'And of the sons of Issachar, who had understanding of the times'.

16 Prov. 31:19 וְכַפֶּיהָ תָּמְכוּ פָלֶךְ 'and her hands grasp the spindle'. Salkinson appears to have taken Shakespeare's 'spinster' (1.1.23) to mean 'one who spins'.

For he has not experienced these, and he has learned war	כִּי לֹא נִסָּה בָאֵלֶּה וַיִּלְמוֹד מִלְחָמָה
Only from the book; he has no **counsel or might**[17]	רַק מֵעַל הַסֵּפֶר; לֹא עֵצָה וּגְבוּרָה[17] לוֹ
And no action on **a day of battle**[18] in the manner of a valiant man	וְלֹא עֲלִילָה בְּיוֹם קְרָב[18] כַּמִּשְׁפָּט לְבֶן חָיִל
Except for tongue and lips, and this is his whole lot.	בִּלְתִּי לָשׁוֹן וּשְׂפָתַיִם וְזֶה כָּל חֶלְקוֹ.
But he has chosen him, and placed the office on his shoulders	אָמְנָם הוּא בָּחַר בּוֹ וַיִּתֵּן הַמִּשְׂרָה עַל שִׁכְמוֹ
Whereas I am poor and wretched; though with his eyes he has seen	וַאֲנִי דַל וְאֻמְלָל; אַף כִּי בְעֵינָיו רָאָה
My ability and my might on the island of **Caphtor**[19] and Rhodes[20]	אֶת יָדִי וּגְבוּרָתִי בְּאִי כַפְתּוֹר[19] וְרוֹדוֹס[20]
In the Christians' **portion of land**[21] and among the people of a foreign god.	בְּחֶלְקַת שְׂדֵה[21] נוֹצְרִים וּבְקֶרֶב בְּנֵי אֵל נֵכָר.
I must place **a muzzle on my mouth**[22] and **bind my face in the hidden place**[23]	עָלַי לָשׂוּם מַחְסוֹם לְפִי[22] וְלַחֲבשׁ פָּנַי בַּטָּמוּן[23]
Lest the lender and the creditor oppress me because it is too heavy for me.	פֶּן יִלְחָצֵנִי הַמַּלְוֶה וְהַנֹּשֶׁא כִּי כָבֵד מִמֶּנִּי.
Look down from heaven and see[24] that **I have waited for your salvation**![25]	הַבֵּט מִשָּׁמַיִם וּרְאֵה[24] כִּי לִישׁוּעָתְךָ קִוִּיתִי![25]
Chesed has become an officer, whereas I am the Cushite's[26] standard-bearer!	כֶּשֶׁד הָיָה לְפָקִיד וַאֲנִי נוֹשֵׂא דֶגֶל הַכּוּשִׁי![26]

17 2 Kings 18:20 עֵצָה וּגְבוּרָה לַמִּלְחָמָה 'counsel and might for the war'.
18 Ps. 78:9; Zech. 14:3.
19 A place-name mentioned in various places in the Bible, the precise location of which is unclear. It is referred to as an island in Jeremiah 47:4 and is typically thought to correspond to Crete, although some argue that it denotes the southern coast of Turkey.
20 Somewhat unusually, Salkinson has not replaced this place-name with a biblical equivalent.
21 Gen. 33:19; 2 Sam. 23:11; Ruth 2:3, 4:3; 1 Chron. 11:13.
22 Ps. 39:2 אֶשְׁמְרָה לְפִי מַחְסוֹם 'I shall guard my mouth with a muzzle'.
23 Job 40:13 פְּנֵיהֶם חֲבֹשׁ בַּטָּמוּן 'bind their faces in the hidden place'.
24 Isa. 63:15; Ps. 80:15 (80:14 in English Bibles).
25 Gen. 49:18.
26 The Hebrew word כּוּשִׁי is a gentilic adjective appearing on numerous occasions in the Hebrew Bible (e.g., 2 Sam. 18:21; Jer. 13:23; Zeph. 2:12; Num. 12:1 [in the feminine form, referring to Moses' wife]; Amos 9:7 [in the plural]). It is based on the toponym כּוּשׁ, which is first mentioned in Gen. 2:13 and appears in various other places in the Hebrew Bible (e.g., 2 Kings 19:9; Isa. 11:11; Ps. 68:32 [68:31 in English

RADDAI	To bear him in order to hang him is better than bearing his standard.	לָשֵׂאת אֹתוֹ לִתְלוֹתוֹ טוֹב מִשֵּׂאת אֶת דִּגְלוֹ.	רדי
DOEG	There is no remedy for this illness; this is the curse of those who serve	אֵין מָזוֹר לְמַחֲלָה זוֹ, זֹאת הַמְּאֵרָה לָעוֹבְדִים	דואג
	That a man is not allowed to rise up the ladder of government,	כִּי לֹא יֻתַּן לָאִישׁ לַעֲלוֹת בְּסֻלַּם הַמֶּמְשָׁלָה,	
	Step after step, **a man on the heels of his brother**,[27]	מַדְרֵגָה אַחֲרֵי מַדְרֵגָה אִישׁ בַּעֲקֵב אָחִיו,[27]	
	But rather, by **partiality**[28] and according to **the mood of the ruler**[29]	כִּי אִם בְּהַכֵּר פָּנִים[28] וּלְפִי רוּחַ הַמּשֵׁל[29]	
	One rises up while another stays on the lowest step	זֶה יַעֲלֶה מַעְלָה וְזֶה יַעֲמֹד בְּשֵׁפֶל הַמַּדְרֵגָה	
	And now tell me sir, am I obliged	וְעַתָּה הַגִּידָה אֲדֹנִי הַאִם עָלַי הַחוֹבָה	
	To love the Cushite?	לְאַהֲבָה אֶת הַכּוּשִׁי?	
RADDAI	Leave him and do not continue to serve him.	עֲזֹב אֹתוֹ וְאַל תּוֹסֵף לְעָבְדוֹ.	רדי
DOEG	Do not fear, sir; I serve him for myself	אַל תִּירָא אֲדֹנִי, הִנְנִי עֹבֵד אֹתוֹ לְמַעֲנִי	דואג
	In order that I might also happen **to repay him his recompense**[30]	לְמַעַן יְאֻנֶּה לְיָדִי לְהָשִׁיב לוֹ גְּמוּלוֹ[30] גַּם אָנִי.	
	We cannot all be masters, but not every servant	לֹא נוּכַל לִהְיוֹת אֲדֹנִים כֻּלָּנוּ וְלֹא כָל עֶבֶד	
	Serves his master. There are senseless faithful men	עֹבֵד אֶת אֲדֹנָיו. יֵשׁ חַסְרֵי לֵב נֶאֱמָנִים	
	That bend a knee and bear a burden all the days,	שֶׁיִּכְרְעוּן בֶּרֶךְ וְיִשְׂאוּ עֹל כָּל הַיָּמִים,	

Bibles]). The location to which the toponym refers is uncertain, but is generally believed to denote a region in northeastern Africa (Koehler and Baumgartner 2001, 1: 466–7), possibly Ethiopia (Schulman 2007). This uncertainty is reflected in the English translations of both the toponym and its associated adjectives. Some translations (e.g., the New English Bible, New International Version, and English Standard Version) generally prefer the terms 'Cush' and 'Cushite', while others (e.g., the King James Bible, Jewish Publication Society Tanakh, and New Revised Standard Version) favour 'Ethiopia' and 'Ethiopian'. (Note, however, that there is internal inconsistency within individual translations; for example, the King James Bible uses 'Ethiopia' in Gen. 2:13 but 'Cush' in Isa. 11:11.) In the modern period, the adjective came to refer more generally to anyone of African descent. I have chosen the translation 'Cushite' here as it more closely resembles the Hebrew and is geographically less specific, which is in keeping with the uncertainty surrounding the meaning of Shakespeare's 'Moor'.

27 Gen. 25:26 וְיָדוֹ אֹחֶזֶת בַּעֲקֵב עֵשָׂו 'and his hand was grasping Esau's heel'.

28 Prov. 24:23, 28:21.

29 Eccles. 10:4.

30 Psalms 28:4 הָשֵׁב גְּמוּלָם לָהֶם 'repay them their recompense'.

They serve their masters, like asses for **straw and fodder**,[31]	יְשָׁרְתוּן אֲדֹנֵיהֶם, כַּחֲמוֹרִים בְּעַד תֶּבֶן **וּמִסְפּוֹא**,[31]
Who send them away in their old age like **a wife forsaken**[32]	אֲשֶׁר יְשַׁלְּחוּם לְזִקְנָתָם כְּאִשָּׁה כִּי תִמָּאֵס[32]
And of them it is said: **'a rod for the back of fools'**.[33]	וַעֲלֵיהֶם יֵאָמֵר: שֵׁבֶט לְגֵו כְּסִילִים.[33]
Whereas others appear outwardly to be as faithful servants	וּכְמוֹ עֲבָדִים נֶאֱמָנִים אֲחֵרִים יִתְרָאוּ לָעֵינַיִם
But they are faithful to themselves, for by their apparent service	וְהֵם נֶאֱמָנִים לְנַפְשָׁם, כִּי בַּעֲבֹדָתָם לְמַרְאֵה עָיִן
They prosper before their masters, they accumulate a fortune, fill their bags	יִצְלְחוּ לִפְנֵי אֲדֹנֵיהֶם, יִצְבְּרוּ הוֹן יְמַלְאוּ שַׂקֵּיהֶם
And in their latter days they become masters. These are men of sense	וּבְאַחֲרִיתָם יִהְיוּ אֲדֹנִים. אֵלֶּה בַּעֲלֵי לֵב הֵם
And I am as one of them. On your name Raddai I swear	וַאֲנִי כְּאַחַד מֵהֶם. בְּשִׁמְךָ רַדַּי נִשְׁבַּעְתִּי
If I were the Cushite, I would no longer be Doeg,	לוּ הָיִיתִי אֲנִי הַכּוּשִׁי לֹא עוֹד דּוֹאֵג הָיִיתִי,
And I go after him in order to arrive **at my desired haven**[34]	וַאֲנִי הוֹלֵךְ אַחֲרָיו לְמַעַן אַגִּיעַ לִמְחוֹז **חֶפְצִי**[34]
Not out of love or innocence of heart – **as God is my witness!**[35]	לֹא מֵאַהֲבָה וּמִתָּם־לֵב – **שָׂהֲדִי בַּמְּרוֹמִים!**[35]
But rather **with a flattering mouth**[36] until I arrive at the target	כִּי אִם **בְּפֶה חָנֵף**[36] עַד בּוֹאִי אֶל הַמַּטָּרָה
For God forbid that I should reveal by the work of my hand and my service	כִּי חָלִלָה לִי מֵהַרְאוֹת בְּמַעֲשֵׂה יָדַי וַעֲבֹדָתִי
What my desires and my hidden thoughts are,	מַה־מַּאֲוַיֵּי נַפְשִׁי וּמַצְפּוּנֵי לְבָבִי פְּנִימָה,
Lest I reveal my heart in the assembly **in broad daylight**[37]	פֶּן אֲגַלֶּה אֶת לִבִּי בַּקָּהָל נֶגֶד הַשָּׁמֶשׁ[37]

31 Gen. 24:32.
32 Isa. 54:6 וְאֵשֶׁת נְעוּרִים כִּי תִמָּאֵס 'and the wife of one's youth when forsaken'.
33 Alshekh to Prov. 10.
34 Ps. 107:30 אֶל־מְחוֹז חֶפְצָם 'to their desired haven'.
35 Job 16:19.
36 Prov. 11:9.
37 Num. 25:4; 2 Sam. 12:12.

	So that **ravens of the valley might pick it out**,[38] not thus am I with myself	וְיִקְּרוּהוּ עֹרְבֵי נָחַל,[38] לֹא כֵן אָנֹכִי עִמָּדִי	
	I am not the man **in the heart, as you see me in the eyes**.[39]	אֵינֶנִּי הָאִישׁ לַלֵּבָב כַּאֲשֶׁר אַתָּה רֹאֵנִי לָעֵינַיִם.[39]	
RADDAI	What great **wealth and riches**[40] this big-lipped one will have	מָה רַב הוֹן וָעֹשֶׁר[40] לְבַעַל שְׂפָתַיִם הַלָּזֶה	רדי
	If he can carry out his plan!	אִם יְבַצַּע זְמָמוֹ!	
DOEG	Call her father, wake him up from his sleep	קְרָא אֶת אָבִיהָ, עוֹרְרָה אֹתוֹ מִשְּׁנָתוֹ	דואג
	Do not let go[41] of him; put hemlock in his pleasures	אַל תֶּרֶף[41] מִמֶּנּוּ, שִׂים רוֹשׁ בְּתַעֲנוּגָיו	
	Proclaim his name outside and rouse all the members of her family.	הַשְׁמַע שְׁמוֹ בַּחוּץ וְהָסֵת כָּל בְּנֵי מִשְׁפַּחְתָּהּ.	
	Release flies upon him so that they bite him **in a peaceful abode**[42]	שַׁלַּח בּוֹ זְבוּבִים וְנָשְׁכוּ אֹתוֹ בִּנְוֵה שָׁלוֹם[42]	
	And if his face glows from joy, **may his eye grow dim from grief**.[43]	וְאִם פָּנָיו צָהֲלוּ מִשָּׂשׂוֹן, תֵּכַהּ מִכַּעַשׂ עֵינוֹ.[43]	
RADDAI	This is **her father's house**;[44] behold, I shall call out loud.	זֶה הוּא בֵּית אָבִיהָ,[44] הִנֵּה אֶקְרָא בְּקוֹל.	רדי
DOEG	Call out in **a sound of terror**,[45] in a **sound of loud rumbling**[46]	קְרָא בְּקוֹל פְּחָדִים,[45] בְּקוֹל רַעַשׁ גָּדוֹל[46]	דואג
	Like one who calls out while fire devours a peaceful city at night.	כַּקּוֹרֵא בַּאֲכוֹל אֵשׁ בְּקִרְיָה שַׁאֲנַנָּה בַּלָּיְלָה.	
RADDAI	Ho, ho, **Phichol**![47] My lord Phichol, arise!	הוֹי הוֹי פִּיכֹל![47] פִּיכֹל אֲדֹנִי, קוּם!	רדי
DOEG	Arise, Phichol, wake up! Thieves, **robbers in the night**![48]	קוּמָה פִּיכֹל, הָקִיצָה! גַּנָּבִים, שׁוֹדְדֵי לָיְלָה![48]	דואג

38 Prov. 30:17.

39 1 Sam. 16:7 הָאָדָם יִרְאֶה לַעֵינַיִם וַיהוָה יִרְאֶה לַלֵּבָב 'man sees the outward appearance, but the Lord sees the heart'.

40 Ps. 112:3.

41 Josh. 10:6; Prov. 4:13; Ps. 138:8.

42 Isa. 32:18.

43 Ps. 6:8 (6:7 in English Bibles) עָשְׁשָׁה מִכַּעַס עֵינִי 'my eye grows dim from grief'; also Ps. 31:10 (31:9 in English Bibles).

44 Gen. 38:11; Lev. 22:13; Num. 30:17; Deut. 22:20; Josh. 6:25; Judg. 19:2, 3.

45 Job 15:21.

46 Ezek. 3:12, 3:13.

47 Commander of Abimelech's army, mentioned in Gen. 21:22, 32, 26:26. Abimelech was a Philistine king contemporaneous with the patriarch Abraham. Salkinson may have selected the name in order to evoke associations of leadership and prowess, as there is no clear sound correspondence between Phichol and Shakespeare's Brabantio.

48 Obad. 1:5.

	Thieves! Thieves!	גַּנָּבִים! גַּנָּבִים!	
	Look to your house, look to your daughter and your bags of money,	רְאֵה בֵיתְךָ, רְאֵה בִתְּךָ וּצְרוֹרוֹת כַּסְפֶּךָ,	
	Thieves, thieves!	גַּנָּבִים! גַּנָּבִים!	
	(Phichol looks out through the window)[49]	(פיכל נשקף בעד החלון[49])	
PHICHOL	What is **the sound of shouting**[50] there? What is this I hear?	מַה־קּוֹל הַצְּעָקָה[50] שָׁם? מַזֶּה אָנֹכִי שֹׁמֵעַ?	פיכל
RADDAI	Are all the members of your household, my lord, inside the house?	הַאִם בְּנֵי בֵיתְךָ אֲדֹנִי, כֻּלָּם בְּתוֹךְ הַבָּיִת?	רדי
DOEG	Are the doors closed?	הַאִם הַדְּלָתוֹת סְגוּרוֹת?	דואג
PHICHOL	Why do you ask such a thing? Why do you ask such a thing?	לָמָּה תִשְׁאֲלוּ כָזֹאת? לָמָּה כָזֹאת תִּשְׁאָלוּ?	פיכל
DOEG	Why,[51] you have been robbed, my lord!	הֲלֹא[51] שֻׁדַּדְתָּ אֲדֹנִי!	דואג
	(But put on your robe, for you are naked)	(אַךְ לְבַשׁ כֻּתָּנְתְּךָ כִּי עֵירֹם אָתָּה)	
	Your heart has been torn to pieces, **and your flesh has been half consumed**[52]	לִבְּךָ נִקְרַע לִקְרָעִים וַיֵּאָכֵל חֲצִי בְשָׂרֶךָ[52]	
	Behold, now at this very moment, an old black ram	הִנֵּה עַתָּה בְּרֶגַע זֶה, תַּיִשׁ שָׁחֹר זָקֵן	
	Is pounding your ewe purer than milk. **Arise, go**[53]	יָדוּשׁ רְחֵלְךָ הַזַּכָּה מֵחָלָב. קוּם לֵךְ[53]	
	With **the sound of the ram's horn and shouting,**[54] and assemble the citizens	בְּקוֹל שׁוֹפָר וּתְרוּעָה[54] וְהַקְהֵל אֶת בְּנֵי הָעִיר	
	Who are sprawled on their beds.[55] If you wait a bit longer	הַסְּרוּחִים עַל עַרְשׂוֹתָם.[55] אִם תּוֹחִיל עוֹד מְעָט	
	Soon you will be embracing your grandchild, that son of Azazel.[56]	מַהֵר תְּחַבֵּק אֶת נֶכְדְּךָ, אֶת בֶּן עֲזָאזֵל[56] הַהוּא.	

49 Judg. 5:28 בְּעַד הַחַלּוֹן נִשְׁקְפָה 'she peered out through the window' (Sisera's mother).
50 1 Sam. 4:14.
51 Cf. Shakespeare's 'Zounds' (1.1.85); Salkinson has removed the Christian oath.
52 Num. 12:12 וַיֵּאָכֵל חֲצִי בְשָׂרוֹ 'and its flesh has been half consumed'.
53 Gen. 28:2; Num. 22:20; Deut. 10:11; 1 Kings 17:9; Jer. 13:6; Jon. 1:2, 3:2.
54 2 Sam. 6:15 בִּתְרוּעָה וּבְקוֹל שׁוֹפָר 'with shouting and the sound of the ram's horn'.
55 Amos 6:4.
56 The term Azazel appears in Lev. 16:8–10, in the description of the Yom Kippur ritual whereby the sins of the community were symbolically placed upon a goat that was sent out into the wilderness, 'to Azazel'.

	Arise, I proclaim to you!	קוּם הֲלֹא הִשְׁמַעְתִּיךָ!	
PHICHOL	Are you mad?	הַאִם מְשֻׁגָּעִים אַתֶּם?	פיכל
RADDAI	My chief and lord, do you recognize my voice?	אַלּוּפִי וַאֲדֹנִי, הֲתַכִּיר אֶת קוֹלִי?	רדי
PHICHOL	I do not recognize you; who are you?	לֹא אַכִּירֶךָ; מִי אָתָּה?	פיכל
RADDAI	My name is Raddai.	רַדַּי שְׁמִי.	רדי
PHICHOL	As such my anger and fury at your coming here is doubled,	לָכֵן בּוֹאֲךָ הֵנָּה עַל אַפִּי וַחֲמָתִי כִּפְלָיִם,	פיכל
	Why, I have warned you not to lie in wait at the door of my house	הֵן הִזְהַרְתִּיךָ לְבַל תֶּאֱרֹב אֶל פֶּתַח בֵּיתִי	
	And I have said clearly to your ears that my daughter will not be for you	וָאַגֵּד בְּאָזְנֶיךָ מְפֹרָשׁ כִּי לֹא לְךָ תִהְיֶה בִתִּי	
	Yet now you have come from your carousing, behaving like a madman from the evening's wine	וְעַתָּה בָאתָ מִסָּבְאֲךָ מִשְׁתַּגֵּעַ מִיֵּין הָעֶרֶב	
	With **a spirit of confusion mixed within you,**[57] in order to disturb my rest.	**וְרוּחַ עִוְעִים מָסוּךְ בְּקִרְבְּךָ**[57] לְהַפְרִיעַ מְנוּחָתִי.	
RADDAI	My lord, my lord…	אֲדֹנִי, אֲדֹנִי...	רדי
PHICHOL	Indeed know that **my strength is sufficient**[58]	אָכֵן דַּע לְךָ **כִּי יָדִי רַב לִי**[58]	פיכל
	And your end will be bitter.	וּמָרָה תִּהְיֶה אַחֲרִיתֶךָ.	
RADDAI	Please, my lord, please, wait a little while.	בִּי אֲדֹנִי אָנָּא, הוֹחִילָה מְעַט רֶגַע.	רדי
PHICHOL	What did you tell me about **quarrel and strife?**[59]	מָה הִגַּדְתָּ לִי עַל דְּבַר **שׁוֹד וְחָמָס**?[59]	פיכל

The meaning of this term is uncertain: some English Bible versions (e.g., the King James Bible and the New International Version) translate it as 'scapegoat', while others (e.g., the English Standard Version, the Jewish Publication Society Tanakh, and the New Revised Standard Version) translate it as 'Azazel'. In rabbinic literature, Azazel is interpreted variously as an area of mountainous cliffs from which the goat was pushed to its death; as the name of the goat (possibly based on a fusion of the names of two fallen angels, Uzza and Azael, whose sins it was intended to atone for); or as the name of a demon (Ahituv 2007). The thirteenth-century Jewish commentator Nahmanides supports the latter interpretation, and the association of Azazel with a demon has remained dominant in Jewish tradition. Salkinson's translation is based on this interpretation.

57 Isa. 19:14 יְהוָה מָסַךְ בְּקִרְבָּהּ רוּחַ עִוְעִים 'the Lord has mixed a spirit of confusion within her'.

58 Deut. 33:7 יָדָיו רָב לוֹ 'strengthen his hands' (more literally: 'let his hands be sufficient for him'); i.e., 'give him the power'.

59 Hab. 1:3.

	This is, after all, the city of Venice, and my house is a wall house –	הֲלֹא זֹאת הָעִיר וִינֶעצְיָא וּבֵיתִי בֵּית חוֹמָה –	
RADDAI	Honourable sir, with an innocent and pure heart I have come to you –	אָדוֹן נִכְבָּד, בְּלֵב תָּמִים וְטָהוֹר בָּאתִי אֵלֶיךָ –	רדי
DOEG[60]	You,[61] my lord, are like one of the men	הֲלֹא[61] אַתָּה אֲדֹנִי, כְּאַחַד מִן הָאֲנָשִׁים	דואג[60]
	Who afflict the mouth of the devil when he commands them	הַמַּמְרִים פִּי הַשָּׂטָן לְעֵת יִפְקֹד עֲלֵיהֶם	
	To serve God. Behold, we come for your own good	לַעֲבֹד אֶת הָאֱלֹהִים. הֵן נַחְנוּ בָּאִים לְטוֹבָתְךָ	
	Yet you would make us out to be villains.	וְאַתָּה תִּתֵּן אֹתָנוּ לִפְנֵי בְּנֵי בְלִיָּעַל.	
	Is it good in your eyes that an ass[62] **should cleave to your daughter**	הֲטוֹב בְּעֵינֶיךָ כִּי יִדְבַּק חֲמוֹר[62] בְּבִתֶּךָ	
	And they become one flesh[63] and it be said of the offspring of the ass	וְהָיוּ לְבָשָׂר אֶחָד[63] וְעַל זֶרַע הַחֲמוֹר יֵאָמֵר	
	That he is your offspring?	כִּי זַרְעֲךָ הוּא?	
PHICHOL	Who are you? **A mouth speaking folly?**[64]	מִי אַתָּה? פֶּה דֹבֵר נְבָלָה?[64]	פיכל
DOEG[65]	I am the man who has come to tell you:	אֲנִי הוּא הָאִישׁ אֲשֶׁר בָּאתִי לְהַגֶּד לְךָ:	דואג[65]
	Behold, right now your daughter stands before the Cushite	הִנֵּה זֶה עַתָּה בִּתְּךָ עֹמֶדֶת לִפְנֵי הַכּוּשִׁי	
	As if she were **standing before a steer, a bull to lie with her.**[66]	כְּעוֹמֶדֶת לִפְנֵי שׁוֹר פַּר לְרִבְעָהּ.[66]	
PHICHOL	**Your mouth testifies against you**[67] that you are a villain.	פִּיךָ יַעֲנֶה בְּךָ[67] כִּי נָבָל אַתָּה.	פיכל

60 This speech is prose in the original (1.1.107–12).
61 Cf. Shakespeare's 'Zounds' (1.1.107); as previously, Salkinson has omitted the Christian oath.
62 Cf. Shakespeare's 'Barbary horse' (1.1.110), i.e., a North African horse (Honigmann 1997: 123, note 110). Salkinson has removed this geographic reference and replaced the horse with an ass. Scolnicov (2001: 187) suggests that this replacement serves to preserve Shakespeare's bestial imagery via a veiled allusion to Ezek. 23:20, וַתַּעְגְּבָה עַל פְּלַגְשֵׁיהֶם אֲשֶׁר בְּשַׂר־חֲמוֹרִים בְּשָׂרָם וְזִרְמַת סוּסִים זִרְמָתָם 'for she doted upon their paramours, whose flesh is as the flesh of asses, and whose issue is as the issue of horses'.
63 Gen. 2:24 עַל־כֵּן יַעֲזָב־אִישׁ אֶת־אָבִיו וְאֶת־אִמּוֹ וְדָבַק בְּאִשְׁתּוֹ וְהָיוּ לְבָשָׂר אֶחָד 'therefore a man leaves his father and his mother and cleaves to his wife and they become one flesh'.
64 Isa. 9:16 (9:17 in English Bibles).
65 This speech is prose in the original (1.1.114–15).
66 Lev. 18:23 וְאִשָּׁה לֹא־תַעֲמֹד לִפְנֵי בְהֵמָה לְרִבְעָהּ 'and a woman must not stand before a beast to lie with it'.
67 2 Sam. 1:16 כִּי פִיךָ עָנָה בְךָ 'for your mouth has testified against you'.

DOEG	**Your mouth testifies against you**[68] that you are a counsellor.	**פִּיךָ יַעֲנֶה בְךָ**[68] כִּי יוֹעֵץ אָתָּה.	דואג
PHICHOL	You will bear all of these yourself, for I know you, Raddai.	לְבַדְּךָ תִּשָּׂא כָּל אֵלֶּה כִּי יְדַעְתִּיךָ, רַדַּי.	פיכל
RADDAI	All of these I shall bear, just please listen to me:	כָּל אֵלֶּה אֶשָּׂא, רַק אָנָּא שְׁמָעֵנִי:	רדי
	If this matter had been from my lord	אִם מֵאֵת אֲדֹנִי נִהְיָה הַדָּבָר הַזֶּה	
	And it were the desire of your heart that your delicate daughter	וְחֵפֶץ לִבְּךָ הוּא כִּי בִתְּךָ הָעֲדִינָה	
	Should be brought **in the middle of the night and the darkness**[69] by one of the sailors	תּוּבַל **בְּאִישׁוֹן לַיְלָה וַאֲפֵלָה**[69] עַל יַד אַחַד הַמַּלָּחִים	
	To set her in the bosom of the Cushite, a man of lust and desires	לְהוֹשִׁיבָהּ בְּחֵיק הַכּוּשִׁי, אִישׁ תַּאֲוָה וַעֲגָבִים	
	In order that **he abuse her**;[70] if it is your heart's desire	**לְמַעַן יִתְעַלֶּל בָּהּ**;[70] אִם חֵפֶץ לִבְּךָ הוּא	
	Then we have erred very gravely, and **our sin is too great to bear**.[71]	הִנֵּה שָׁגִינוּ הַרְבֵּה מְאֹד **וְגָדוֹל עֲוֹנֵנוּ מִנְּשׂוֹא**.[71]	
	But if you were not aware of the matter, it is my opinion and my belief that	אַךְ אִם נֶעְלַם הַדָּבָר מִמֶּךָּ, עַל דַּעְתִּי וֶאֱמוּנָתִי	
	Your rebuking us is not fair and not just.	כִּי גַּעֲרָתְךָ בָּנוּ לֹא בְיֹשֶׁר וְלֹא בְצֶדֶק.	
	Please don't, my lord! I am not insane	אַל נָא אֲדֹנִי! לֹא חֲסַר דֵּעָה אָנִי	
	That I should come to mock you. And I hereby say further	כִּי אָבוֹא לְצַחֶק בָּךְ. וְהִנְנִי מוֹסִיף לֵאמֹר	
	If the girl has acted on her own volition **and has not sought your counsel**[72]	אִם מִלִּבָּהּ עָשְׂתָה הַנַּעֲרָה **וְאֶת פִּיךָ לֹא שָׁאָלָה**[72]	
	She is profaning her father. – How can a daughter of good sense	אָבִיהָ הִיא מְחַלֶּלֶת. – אֵיךְ בַּת טוֹבַת טָעַם	

68 2 Sam. 1:16 כִּי פִיךָ עָנָה בְךָ 'for your mouth has testified against you'.

69 Prov. 7:9.

70 Judg. 19:25 וַיִּתְעַלְּלוּ־בָהּ כָּל־הַלַּיְלָה 'and they abused her all night' (as part of a gruesome incident whereby a Levite man allows the men of Gibeah to rape and kill his concubine, this reference would have had strong associations for Salkinson's readers).

71 Gen. 4:13 גָּדוֹל עֲוֹנִי מִנְּשֹׂא 'my iniquity is too great to bear' (Cain speaking to God after killing his brother Abel).

72 Josh. 9:14 וְאֶת־פִּי יְהוָה לֹא שָׁאָלוּ 'but they did not ask the Lord's counsel'.

	A beautiful, educated daughter, let herself be sold to a **foreign man**![73]	בַּת יָפָה מַשְׂכֶּלֶת, תִּתְמַכֵּר **לְאִישׁ נָכְרִי**![73]	
	A noble daughter[74] like her, to a **fugitive and a wanderer**[75] like a **fool**![76]	**בַּת נָדִיב**[74] כָּמוֹהָ, **לָנָע וָנָד**[75] **כְּאַחַד הָרֵקִים**![76]	
	And now see, if you can find her in the house or in the chamber	וְעַתָּה רְאֵה אִם תִּמְצָאֶנָּה בַּבַּיִת אוֹ בֶחָדֶר	
	Pronounce me guilty at the gate of judgement for I have wearied you falsely	תַּרְשִׁיעֵנִי בְּשַׁעַר מִשְׁפָּט כִּי בְכָזָב הֶלְאֵתִיךָ	
PHICHOL	Hurry, bring out fire! – Bring light at once!	מַהֲרוּ הוֹצִיאוּ אֵשׁ! – הָבוּ נֵר כְּרָגַע! –	פיכל
	Call all of my men to me – behold, this matter	קִרְאוּ לִי כָּל אֲנָשַׁי – הִנֵּה מִקְרֶה זֶה	
	Disturbs me like a bad dream; I fear lest the matter is true	כַּחֲלוֹם רָע יְפַעֲמֵנִי; יָרֵאתִי פֶּן אֱמֶת הַדָּבָר	
	Dreams do not speak in vain – light! Light!	חֲלוֹמוֹת לֹא שָׁוְא יְדַבֵּרוּ – נֵר! נֵר!	
	(Exits from the window)	(הולך מעל החלון)	
DOEG	Behold, I am going to my place, and as for you, farewell to you, Raddai	הִנְנִי הוֹלֵךְ לִמְקוֹמִי וְאַתָּה שָׁלוֹם לְךָ רַדַּי	דואג
	I shall not stand with you any longer lest the matter be discovered	לֹא אֶעֱמֹד עִמְּךָ עוֹד פֶּן יִוָּדַע הַדָּבָר	
	That I am one of those who rebel against the Cushite, and **I destroy my inheritance**.[77]	כִּי מִמִּתְקוֹמְמֵי הַכּוּשִׁי אֲנִי **וְשִׁחַתִּי אֶת נַחֲלָתִי**.[77]	
	I know that the prince of the land **writes bitter things against him**[78]	אֶת נְשִׂיא הָאָרֶץ יָדַעְתִּי כִּי **יִכְתֹּב עָלָיו מְרֹרוֹת**[78]	
	But he **will not depose him from his station**[79] at this time of war.	אַךְ לֹא **יֶהְדְּפֶנּוּ מִמַּצָּבוֹ**[79] בְּעֵת מִלְחָמָה הַזֹּאת.	

73 Deut. 17:15; Eccles. 6:2.
74 Song of Songs 7:2 (7:1 in English Bibles).
75 Gen. 4:12 (referring to Cain's fate after killing Abel).
76 2 Sam. 6:20.
77 Ruth 4:6 פֶּן־אַשְׁחִית אֶת־נַחֲלָתִי 'lest I destroy my inheritance'.
78 Job 13:26 כִּי־תִכְתֹּב עָלַי מְרֹרוֹת 'for you write bitter things against me'.
79 Isa. 22:19 וַהֲדַפְתִּיךָ מִמַּצָּבֶךָ 'and I shall depose you from your station'.

	And he has already arranged to go down with the ships **to perform service**[80] in Caphtor	וּכְבָר נוֹעַד לָרֶדֶת בַּצִּים **לִצְבֹּא צָבָא**[80] בְּכַפְתּוֹר	
	For he is a valiant man; **there is none like him in the land.**[81]	כִּי בֶן חַיִל הוּא **אֵין כָּמוֹהוּ בָּאָרֶץ.**[81]	
	And even though I despise him like the **pains of Sheol**[82]	וְאַף כִּי אָנֹכִי **כְּחֶבְלֵי שְׁאוֹל**[82] שְׂנֵאתִיהוּ	
	Nevertheless I sense that the matter is necessary	בְּכָל זֹאת אָחִישׁ לִי כִּי הַדָּבָר נָחוּץ	
	To raise the banner as a sign that **his banner over me is love.**[83]	לְהָרִים הַדֶּגֶל לְאוֹת כִּי **דִגְלוֹ עָלַי אַהֲבָה.**[83]	
	And you will surely find him if you instruct the guards	וְאַתָּה תִּמְצָאֵנּוּ לְנָכוֹן כִּי תַנְחֶה אֶת הַשֹּׁמְרִים	
	And search for him in a certain inn[84]	וּתְבַקְשֶׁנּוּ בְּבֵית מָלוֹן פְּלוֹנִי אַלְמֹנִי[84]	
	For there you will find him and me together. *(Exits)*	כִּי שָׁם תִּמְצָא אֹתוֹ וְאֹתִי גַּם יָחַד. (הולך)	
	(Phichol and servants with torches)	(פיכל ומשרתים עם לפידים)	
PHICHOL	**This evil has surely befallen me,**[85] **the girl is gone**[86]	**רָעָה הַזֹּאת בָּאַתְנִי**[85] לְנָכוֹן, **הַיַּלְדָּה אֵינֶנָּה**[86]	פיכל
	What will be the end of my days except for **poison and wormwood?**[87]	מָה אַחֲרִית יְמֵי חֶלְדִּי בִּלְתִּי **רוֹשׁ וְלַעֲנָה.**[87]	
	Tell me Raddai! Where did you see her?	הַגִּידָה לִי רַדַּי! אֵיפֹה רָאִיתָ אֹתָהּ?	
	Where has the wretched girl been cast? With the Cushite, you told me?	אָנָה נִדְחֲתָה הָאֻמְלָלָה*? עִם הַכּוּשִׁי הִגַּדְתָּ לִּי?	
	Who should want to be a father? Who would raise up maidens?	מִי יַחְפֹּץ לִהְיוֹת אָב? מִי יְרוֹמֵם בְּתוּלוֹת?	
	How did you recognize her, that it was her you saw there?	אֵיךְ הִכַּרְתָּ אֹתָהּ, כִּי אֹתָהּ רָאִיתָ שָׁם?	

80 Num. 4:23, 8:24.

81 Job 1:8, 2:3.

82 2 Sam. 22:6; Ps. 18:6. Sheol is the biblical abode of the dead. Salkinson has found a particularly close Hebrew equivalent to Shakespeare's 'hell-pains' (1.1.52).

83 Song of Songs 2:4.

84 Salkinson has generalized Shakespeare's reference to a specific inn, the Sagittary, an inn with the sign of Sagittarius (the Centaur, mythological half-man half-horse – see Honigmann 1997: 126, note 156), which would have had little meaning to nineteenth-century Hebrew readers.

85 Rashi to Job 21:28 הרעה אשר באתני 'the evil which has befallen me'.

86 Gen. 37:30 הַיֶּלֶד אֵינֶנּוּ 'the boy is gone'.

87 Deut. 29:17 (29:18 in English Bibles).

* הָאֻמְלָלָה

	Now I know well that you have deceived me	עַתָּה יָדַעְתִּי מְאֹד כִּי כִחַשְׁתְּ לִי	
	And you have spoken lies to me[88] – what did she say to you?	**וַתְּדַבֵּר אֵלַי כְּזָבִים**[88] – מַה־דִּבְּרָה אֵלֶיךָ?	
	Bring lamps and torches – call all my relatives! –	הָבִיאוּ נֵרוֹת וְלַפִּידִים – קִרְאוּ לְכָל קְרוֹבַי! –	
	Do you think, Raddai, that she is also married?[89]	הֲתַחְשֹׁב רַדַּי כִּי גַּם בְּעוּלָה[89] הִיא?	
RADDAI	I think so now, that she is married.	כֵּן חָשַׁבְתִּי עַתָּה כִּי בְּעוּלָה הִיא.	רדי
PHICHOL	How did **the daughter of a perverse and rebellious woman**[90] get out?	אֵיכָכָה יָצְאָה הַחוּצָה **בַּת נַעֲוַת הַמַּרְדּוּת!**[90]	פיכל
	Fathers, do not trust your daughters any more –	אַל לָכֶם אָבוֹת לִבְטֹחַ עוֹד בִּבְנוֹתֵיכֶם –	
	Is the matter true, that a maiden **in the days of her youth**[91]	הַאִם אֱמֶת הַדָּבָר כִּי בְתוּלָה **בִּימֵי נְעוּרֶיהָ**[91]	
	Might heed the voice of charmers[92] to hand over her honour?	**תִּשְׁמַע לְקוֹל מְלַחֲשִׁים**[92] לְהַסְגִּיר אֶת כְּבוֹדָהּ?	
	Have you read, Raddai, things such as this in books?	הַאִם קָרָאתָ רַדַּי, כַּדְּבָרִים הָאֵלֶּה עַל הַסֵּפֶר?	
RADDAI	Yes, my lord, I have read such things in books.	כֵּן אֲדֹנִי, כֵּן קָרָאתִי בַּסֵּפֶר.	רדי
PHICHOL	Call my brother for me – if only *you* had married her –	קִרְאוּ לִי לְאָחִי – לוּ נָשָׂאתָ אֹתָהּ אָתָּה –	פיכל
	Go some this way, some that way –	לְכוּ אֵלֶּה לְכֹה וְאֵלֶּה לְכֹה –	
	Do you know where we may catch her and the Cushite?	הֲיָדַעְתָּ אֵיפוֹ נוּכַל לִלְכֹּד אֹתָהּ וְאֶת הַכּוּשִׁי?	
RADDAI	I shall surely find him if you give me guards	אָנֹכִי אֶמְצָאֶנּוּ לְנָכוֹן אִם תִּתֵּן שֹׁמְרִים בְּיָדִי	רדי
	And you also go with us.	וְגַם פָּנֶיךָ יֵלְכוּ אִתָּנוּ.	
PHICHOL	Come, lead us.	לֵךְ נְחֵה אֹתָנוּ.	פיכל

88 Judg. 16:10.
89 In postbiblical forms of Hebrew this can also mean 'one who has lost her virginity' (Even-Shoshan 2003, 1: 191); Scolnicov (2001: 186) argues that Salkinson intended the latter meaning.
90 1 Sam. 20:30 בֶּן־נַעֲוַת הַמַּרְדּוּת 'son of a perverse and rebellious woman'.
91 Ezek. 16:60 בִּימֵי נְעוּרָיִךְ 'in the days of your youth'.
92 Ps. 58:6 (58:5 in English Bibles) אֲשֶׁר לֹא־יִשְׁמַע לְקוֹל מְלַחֲשִׁים 'that does not heed the voice of charmers'.

	Behold, I shall enter every house, even if **with a strong hand**![93]	הִנְנִי אָבוֹא לְכָל בַּיִת וְאַף אִם **בְּיָד חֲזָקָה**![93]	
	Bring weapons and guards who surround the city at night –	הָבִיאוּ כְלֵי נֶשֶׁק וְשֹׁמְרִים הַסֹּבְבִים בָּעִיר לָיְלָה –	
	Lead, Raddai, my friend, there is payment for your labour. *(Exeunt)*	נְחֵה רַדַּי יְדִידִי, יֵשׁ שָׂכָר לַעֲמָלֶךָ. (הולכים)	
SCENE 2	*A city street in a different place (Ithiel,[94] Doeg, and attendants)*	רחוב העיר במקום אחר (איתיאל[94] דואג ומשרתים)	מחזה ב'
DOEG	Even though I have killed men in the battles of war	אַף כִּי אֲנָשִׁים הָרַגְתִּי בְּמַעַרְכוֹת הַמִּלְחָמָה	דואג
	My heart does not permit me to kill a soul with malicious forethought	לִבִּי לֹא יִתְּנֵנִי לְהָמִית נֶפֶשׁ בִּצְדִיָּה	
	For I am not wicked enough to do evil even for my own good.	כִּי יַד רִשְׁעָתִי קְצָרָה מֵהָרַע אַף לְטוֹבָתִי.	
	How many times have I raised my hand **to strike him in the belly**.[95]	כַּמֶּה פְעָמִים הֵנַפְתִּי יָדִי **לְהַכּוֹת אֶל הַחֹמֶשׁ**.[95]	
ITHIEL	It is good that you did not strike him.	טוֹב כִּי לֹא הִכִּיתָ אֹתוֹ.	איתיאל
DOEG	But who can hear ridicule and disgrace from his mouth	אַךְ מִי יוּכַל לִשְׁמֹעַ לַעַג וּנְאָצָה מִפִּיו	דואג
	As he scorned your name and **spoke rebellion against you**,[96]	כִּי נִאֵץ שִׁמְךָ **וַיְדַבֵּר עָלֶיךָ סָרָה**,[96]	

93 Exod. 3:19, 6:1, 13:9; Deut. 5:15, 6:21, 7:8, 9:26, 26:8; Ezek. 20:33–4; Ps. 136:12; Dan. 9:15.

94 This is the name of two minor biblical characters, a) one of two addressees of Agur's oracle, mentioned in Prov. 30:1, and b) a Benjaminite returning from Babylonian exile to Jerusalem, mentioned in Neh. 11:7. The name seems to have been selected primarily on the basis of the sound correspondence with Shakespeare's 'Othello'. Note that, as mentioned in his letter to Smolenskin directly preceding the beginning of the play, Salkinson originally planned to name his protagonist Athlai, after the minor biblical character the mentioned in Ezra 10:28, a Judean who had intermarried but was influenced by the scribe Ezra to send away his foreign wife. This likewise corresponds in sound to 'Othello', although perhaps not as closely as Ithiel. Scolnicov (2001: 186) argues that the selection of Ithiel, an Israelite name for Othello (as opposed to most of the other characters, who bear the names of non-Israelites), serves to highlight the fact that Salkinson regarded his protagonist as a Jew and used the name to underscore his foreignness in the Venetian context. If this was indeed the intention, Salkinson's initial choice would have made the point more vividly, since the biblical Athlai is known precisely for his status as a Judean with a foreign wife.

95 2 Sam. 4:6, 20:10.

96 Jer. 29:32 כִּי־סָרָה דִבֶּר עַל־יְהוָה 'for he has spoken rebellion against the Lord'.

	I would have **grown weary of enduring**[97] his words had the fear of heaven not prevented me	נִלְאֵתִי לְהָכִיל[97] דְּבָרָיו לוּלֵי יִרְאַת שָׁמַיִם עֲצָרַתְנִי	
	But **I shall ask you one thing;**[98] inform me whether the wedding was **according to the law?**[99]	**אַךְ אַחַת אֶשְׁאָלְךָ**[98] וְהוֹדִיעֵנִי אִם הָיְתָה הַחֲתֻנָּה **כַּדָּת?**[99]	
	You know that the counsellor is **dear and honourable**[100]	יָדַעְתָּ אֶת הַיּוֹעֵץ כִּי יָקָר וְנִכְבָּד[100] הוּא	
	And he is as powerful at the gate as our lord the prince of the land	וְיָדָיו רַב לוֹ בַּשַּׁעַר כִּנְשִׂיא הָאָרֶץ אֲדֹנֵנוּ	
	And he will force you to give a **bill of divorce**[101] to your wife	וְהוּא יְאַלֵּץ אֹתְךָ לָתֵת סֵפֶר **כְּרִיתוּת**[101] לְאִשְׁתֶּךָ	
	Or punishment will be meted out against you according to the laws of the land	אוֹ עֹנֶשׁ יוּשַׁת עָלֶיךָ לְפִי חֻקֵּי הַמְּדִינָה	
	Which he has the power to impose however he desires.	אֲשֶׁר בְּיָדוֹ לְהַטּוֹתָם אֶל כָּל אֲשֶׁר יַחְפֹּץ.	
ITHIEL	Let him do whatever is in his power.	יַעֲשֶׂה כְּכֹל אֲשֶׁר לְאֵל יָדוֹ.	איתיאל
	My service for the government will mollify all of his complaints.	עֲבֹדָתִי לִפְנֵי הַמֶּמְשָׁלָה תַּשְׁבִּיחַ כָּל תְּלוּנוֹתָיו.	
	In my heart there would also be the courage to boast **in the midst of the assembly and congregation**[102]	גַּם בִּלְבָבִי אֹמֶץ לְהִתְהַלֵּל **בְּתוֹךְ קָהָל וְעֵדָה**[102]	
	If I knew that a boaster would be honoured by his own mouth.	לוּ יָדַעְתִּי כִּי כָבוֹד יִנְחַל מִתְהַלֵּל בְּמוֹ פִיו.	
	I am also from a family of rulers; I **came out of the loins**[103] of kings	גַּם אֲנִי מִמִּשְׁפַּחַת שָׂרִים מִיֶּרֶךְ מְלָכִים **יָצָאתִי**[103]	
	And the honour which I have taken for myself **with my sword and my bow**[104]	וְהַכָּבוֹד אֲשֶׁר לָקַחְתִּי לִי **בְּחַרְבִּי וּבְקַשְׁתִּי**[104]	

97 Jer. 6:11 וְאֵת חֲמַת יְהוָה ׀ מָלֵאתִי נִלְאֵיתִי הָכִיל 'and I am filled with the wrath of the LORD; I am weary of enduring it'.
98 Ps. 27:4 אַחַת ׀ שָׁאַלְתִּי מֵאֵת־יְהוָה 'one thing I have asked of the LORD'.
99 Esther 1:8, 4:16.
100 Alshekh to Ps. 36:8.
101 Deut. 24:1.
102 Prov. 5:14.
103 Exod. 1:5 כָּל־נֶפֶשׁ יֹצְאֵי יֶרֶךְ־יַעֲקֹב 'all the souls who came out of the loins of Jacob'.
104 Ps. 44:7 כִּי לֹא בְקַשְׁתִּי אֶבְטָח וְחַרְבִּי לֹא תוֹשִׁיעֵנִי 'for I shall not trust in my bow, neither will my sword save me'. Salkinson has inverted the meaning of this citation, but the resemblance suggests that he may have had it in mind.

	Is greater than the honour of the counsellors who boast with their head-covering.	רַב מִכְּבוֹד הַיּוֹעֲצִים אֲשֶׁר בְּמִגְבַּעְתָּם יִתְאַמָּרוּ.	
	And who would scorn me saying that I am **a fugitive and a wanderer**?[105]	וּמִי יִבְזֵנִי לֵאמֹר כִּי נָע וָנָד[105] אָנֹכִי?	
	Indeed **I love to wander**[106] and to be free in the land	הֵן אָהַבְתִּי לָנוּעַ[106] וְלִהְיוֹת חָפְשִׁי בָּאָרֶץ	
	And had not the love of **Asenath**[107] kept me dwelling at home	וְלוּלֵא אַהֲבַת אָסְנַת[107] תַּעַצְרֵנִי לָשֶׁבֶת בָּיִת	
	A far-flung journey[108] would be better for me than all the abundance of the sea,	טוֹבָה לִי טַלְטֵלָה גָּבֶר[108] מִכֹּל שִׁפְעַת הַיָּם,	
	But look, what are these torches coming up from there?	אַךְ רְאֵה מַה־לַּפִּידִים אֵלֶּה עֹלִים מִשָּׁם?	
	(Chesed and attendants with torches in their hands enter from afar)	(כשד ומשרתים ולפידים בידיהם באים מרחוק)	
DOEG	Her father and her relatives are coming here **in anger and great wrath**.[109]	אָבִיהָ וּקְרוֹבֶיהָ בָּאִים הֵנָּה בְּחֵמָה וְקֶצֶף גָּדוֹל.[109]	דואג
	Please get into the house.	בּוֹאָה נָא הַבָּיְתָה.	
ITHIEL	No, rather I shall stand here	לֹא, כִּי פֹּה אֶעֱמֹד	איתיאל
	Should such a man as I flee?[110] **I shall not turn away from anyone**[111]	הַאִישׁ כָּמוֹנִי יִבְרָח?[110] לֹא אָשׁוּב מִפְּנֵי כל[111]	
	But are these the men?	אַךְ הַאִם הֵם אֵלֶּה?	

105 Gen. 4:12 (referring to Cain's fate after killing Abel).

106 Jer. 14:10 כֵּן אָהֲבוּ לָנוּעַ 'thus they love to wander'.

107 Asenath is Joseph's wife. In Gen. 41:45, 50, 46:20 she is identified as the daughter of the Egyptian priest Potiphera. In some places in rabbinic literature (e.g., *Genesis Rabbah*) she is said to be the daughter of Potiphar's wife, while in others (e.g., *Pirqe deRabbi Eliezer*) she is said to be the daughter of Joseph's sister Dinah. See Standhartinger (2009) for discussion of Asenath in Jewish literary tradition. Scolnicov (2001: 186) suggests that Salkinson selected this name for his version of Desdemona because Asenath was a non-Hebrew married to a prominent Hebrew; she argues that this was designed to underscore Salkinson's interpretation of Ithiel as a lone Jew among Christians, an ethnic outsider like Othello. Unlike many of the other Hebrew names in the play, there is no obvious sound correspondence between Asenath and Desdemona.

108 Isa. 22:17.

109 Deut. 29:27 (29:28 in English Bibles) וּבְחֵמָה וּבְקֶצֶף גָּדוֹל 'and in anger and in great wrath'; also Jer. 21:5.

110 Neh. 6:11.

111 Responsa of Spanish Talmudic authority Isaac ben Sheshet Perfet (1326–1408, known as Ribash), section 394. First published in Constantinople in 1546, these responsa were widely studied and would have been familiar to Salkinson.

DOEG	As my lord lives,[112] these are not the men.	חֵי אֲדֹנִי[112] כִּי לֹא אֵלֶּה הֵם.	דואג
ITHIEL	Why, they are the servants of the prince with my officer Chesed.	הֲלֹא הֵם עַבְדֵי הַנָּשִׂיא עִם כֶּשֶׂד פְּקִידִי.	איתיאל
	Greetings, my brothers! What news is in your mouth?	שָׁלוֹם בּוֹאֲכֶם אַחַי! מֶה חֲדָשׁוֹת בְּפִיכֶם?	
CHESED	The prince enquires after your health, **army commander**[113]	הַנָּשִׂיא פֹּקֵד לִשְׁלוֹמְךָ **שַׂר הַצָּבָא**[113]	כשד
	And asks to see you at once.	וּמְבַקֵּשׁ לִרְאוֹת אֶת פָּנֶיךָ כְּרֶגַע.	
ITHIEL	Do you know what he desires?	הֲיָדַעְתָּ מַה חֶפְצוֹ?	איתיאל
CHESED	In my opinion it is on the matter of Caphtor	לְפִי דַעְתִּי בִּדְבַר כַּפְתּוֹר הוּא	כשד
	For regarding that the matter was urgent.	כִּי עַל כֵּן הָיָה הַדָּבָר נָחוּץ.	
	Messenger after messenger and courier after courier in the night	צִיר אַחֲרֵי צִיר וְרָץ אַחֲרֵי רָץ בַּלַּיְלָה	
	Went out hastened and rushed[114] by the men of the ships	יָצְאוּ מְבֹהָלִים וּדְחוּפִים[114] מֵאֵת אַנְשֵׁי הַצִּיִּים	
	And the counsellors were called and gathered before the prince in his palace	וְהַיּוֹעֲצִים נִקְרְאוּ וְנֶאֶסְפוּ לִפְנֵי הַנָּשִׂיא בְּהֵיכָלוֹ	
	And he also sent for you but you could not be found at home	וְגַם אֵלֶיךָ שָׁלַח וְלֹא נִמְצֵאתָ בַּבָּיִת	
	Therefore they again sent other messengers from the council house	לָכֵן שָׁלְחוּ עוֹד מַלְאָכִים אֲחֵרִים מִבֵּית הַמּוֹעֵצָה	
	Who appointed three leaders to look for you throughout the whole city.	אֲשֶׁר שָׂמוּ שְׁלֹשָׁה רָאשִׁים לְבַקֶּשְׁךָ בְּכָל הָעִיר.	
ITHIEL	It is good that you found me.	טוֹב כִּי אַתָּה מְצָאתַנִי.	איתיאל
	Wait a little while so that I may give some orders to the household	הוֹחִילָה מְעַט רֶגַע וַאֲצַוֶּה מַה־בַּבָּיִת	
	And afterwards let us go together. *(Exits into the house)*	וְאַחֲרֵי כֵן נֵלְכָה יַחְדָּו. (הולך אל הבית)	

112 Salkinson has replaced Shakespeare's 'by Janus' (1.2.33) with this expression, which lacks any associations with Classical mythology but resembles the common biblical oath חֵי יהוה 'as the LORD lives'.

113 Cf. Shakespeare's 'general' (1.2.36); this phrase appears numerous times in the Bible; for example, 1 Sam. 17:55; 1 Kings 1:19; Jer. 52:25.

114 Esther 3:15 הָרָצִים יָצְאוּ דְחוּפִים בִּדְבַר הַמֶּלֶךְ 'the couriers went out, hastened by the king's command'.

CHESED	Tell me, **standard-bearer**,[115] what is he doing here?	הַגֵּד **בַּעַל הַנֵּס**,[115] מָה הוּא עֹשֶׂה הֲלֹם?	כשד
DOEG	He captured **a mighty ship**[116] tonight	הוּא לָכַד **צִי אַדִּיר**[116] בַּלַּיְלָה הַזֶּה	דואג
	And if his action is **according to the law**[117] let him be **a successful man**.[118]	וְאִם מַעֲשֵׂהוּ **כַּדָּת**[117] וְכַדִּין **אִישׁ מַצְלִיחַ**[118] יֶהִי.	
CHESED	Your words are **too wondrous for me**;[119] I do not understand your language.	**נִפְלְאוּ מִמֶּנִּי**[119] דְּבָרֶיךָ לֹא אָבִין שְׂפָתֶךָ.	כשד
DOEG	He was married tonight.	אִשָּׁה נָשָׂא הַלַּיְלָה.	דואג
CHESED	And whose daughter is she? *(Ithiel re-enters from the house)*	וּבַת מִי הִיא? (איתיאל שב מן הבית)	כשד
DOEG	Will you go, army commander? Will you go right now?	הֲתֵלֵךְ שַׂר הַצָּבָא? הֲתֵלֵךְ זֶה עָתָּה?	דואג
ITHIEL	Behold, I am going, and who would stop me.	הִנְנִי הוֹלֵךְ וּמִי זֶה יַעַצְרֵנִי.	איתיאל
CHESED	Behold, another troop is coming here to look for you.	הִנֵּה גְּדוּד אַחֵר בָּא הֲלוֹם לְבַקֶּשְׁךָ.	כשד
	(Phichol, Raddai and the guards who surround the city with torches and weapons)	(פיכל, רדי ושומרים הסבבים בעיר עם לפידים וכלי נשק)	
DOEG	Behold, Phichol is coming; guard yourself from him, army commander	הִנֵּה פִּיכֹל בָּא, הִשָּׁמֵר מִפָּנָיו שַׂר הַצָּבָא	דואג
	For he **plots evil**.[120]	כִּי הוּא **חֹרֵשׁ רָעָה**.[120]	
ITHIEL	Desist, stand!	הֶרֶף, עֲמֹד!	איתיאל
RADDAI	My lord Phichol, here is the Cushite.	פִּיכֹל אֲדֹנִי, הִנֵּה זֶה הַכּוּשִׁי.	רדי
PHICHOL	Behold, this is the robber! Destroy, destroy!	הִנֵּה זֶה הַשּׁוֹדֵד! הַשְׁמֵד, הַשְׁמֵד!	פיכל
	(They draw their swords on either side)	(שולפים חרבותם אלה מזה ואלה מזה)	

115 This collocation appears in the Babylonian Talmud *Nidda* 31a, with a different meaning, namely 'someone who has experienced a miracle' (the Hebrew word נֵס can mean 'miracle' or 'banner, standard').

116 Isa. 33:21.

117 Esther 1:8, 4:16.

118 Gen. 39:2.

119 Prov. 30:18.

120 Prov. 6:14.

DOEG	Prepare yourself Raddai, come, **let us face each other.**[121]	הִכּוֹן נָא רַדַּי, בּוֹא וְנִתְרָאֶה פָּנִים.[121]	דואג
ITHIEL	Let each man return his sword to its sheath	הָשִׁיבוּ אִישׁ חַרְבּוֹ אֶל נְדָנָהּ	איתיאל
	Lest rot appear on the blade from the droplets of dew.	לְבַל יָבוֹא רָקָב בַּלַּהַב, מֵרְסִיסֵי טָל.	
	And you Phichol, **I said a multitude of days should speak**[122]	וְאַתָּה פִיכוֹל, אָמַרְתִּי רֹב יָמִים יְדַבֵּרוּ[122]	
	For the mouth of an elder like you is better than **the edge**[123] **of your sword.**[124]	כִּי פִּי זָקֵן כָּמוֹךָ, טוֹב מִפִּי[123] חַרְבֶּךָ.[124]	
PHICHOL	**Kidnapper,**[125] foul barbarian! Where have you hidden my daughter?	גֹּנֵב נֶפֶשׁ,[125] פָּרִיץ נִמְאָס! אֵיפֹה הִסְתַּרְתָּ בִתִּי?	פיכל
	With cords of magic you have pulled her after you, **man whom I have determined to destroy?**[126]	בְּחַבְלֵי קֶסֶם מָשַׁכְתָּ אֹתָהּ אַחֲרֶיךָ אִישׁ חֶרְמִי[126]	
	For if her hands are not bound with chains of enchantment	כִּי אִם יָדֶיהָ לֹא אֲסֻרוֹת בַּעֲבוֹתוֹת כְּשָׁפִים	
	Who **with sense**[127] would believe that a **tender and delicate**[128] maiden	מִי נְבוֹן דָּבָר[127] יַאֲמִין, כִּי עַלְמָה רַכָּה וַעֲנֻגָּה[128]	
	Who has never desired to marry any man	אֲשֶׁר מֵעוֹדָהּ לֹא שָׁתָה לֵב לְהִנָּשֵׂא לְאִישׁ	
	And who has hidden her face from the **desirable young men,**[129] the honourable ones of our nation;	וַאֲשֶׁר הִסְתִּירָה פָּנֶיהָ מִבַּחוּרֵי חֶמֶד[129] נִכְבַּדֵּי עַמֵּנוּ;	
	That such a pleasant maiden would deceive her father	עַלְמָה נֶחֱמָדָה כָּזֹאת, תִּגְנֹב אֶת לֵב אָבִיהָ	
	And flee to **everlasting disgrace,**[130] to lie in your bosom, despicable Cushite	וְתִבְרַח לִכְלִמַּת עוֹלָם,[130] לִשְׁכַּב בְּחֵיקְךָ כּוּשִׁי נִבְזֶה	

121 2 Kings 14:8; 2 Chron. 27:17 (both in the context of battle).

122 Job 32:7 אָמַרְתִּי יָמִים יְדַבֵּרוּ וְרֹב שָׁנִים יֹדִיעוּ חָכְמָה 'I said, days should speak and multitude of years should teach wisdom'.

123 Lit. 'mouth' (play on words with 'mouth' in the beginning of the line).

124 Gen. 34:26 לְפִי־חָרֶב 'with the edge of the sword' (referring to Jacob's sons killing Shechem for raping their sister).

125 Deut. 24:7.

126 1 Kings 20:42.

127 1 Sam. 16:18 (referring to King David).

128 Deut. 28:56 הָרַכָּה בְךָ וְהָעֲנֻגָּה 'the most tender and delicate woman among you'.

129 Ezek. 23:6, 12, 23.

130 Jer. 20:11.

	Whose face is like a furnace,[131] to cast dread upon children	אֲשֶׁר פָּנֶיךָ כְּכִבְשָׁן,[131] לְהַטִּיל אֵימָה עַל יְלָדִים	
	And damsels do not love you? – Understand, **judges of the earth**[132]	וַעֲלָמוֹת לֹא יֶאֱהָבוּךָ? – הַשְׂכִּילוּ **שׁוֹפְטֵי אֶרֶץ**[132]	
	Whether I have spoken truly, that he came to her with charms	אִם לֹא כֵן דִּבַּרְתִּי, כִּי בִלְחָשִׁים בָּא אֵלֶיהָ	
	And gave her a cup of intoxicants to drink, or a mixture from **a cup of poison**[133]	וַיַּשְׁקֶהָ כּוֹס סַמִּים, אוֹ מֶסֶךְ **מִסַּף רַעַל**[133]	
	Which takes a maiden's heart and incites the flame of desire in her.	אֲשֶׁר יִקַּח לֵב נַעֲרָה וְיַצִּית בָּהּ אֵשׁ הַחֵשֶׁק.	
	With this I have proven sufficiently, that **the matter has substance**[134]	בָּזֶה הוֹכַחְתִּי לְמַדַּי, כִּי **יֵשׁ רַגְלַיִם לַדָּבָר**[134]	
	And also a reliable sign that he has committed this abomination	וְגַם אוֹת נֶאֱמָן, כִּי עָשָׂה הַנְּבָלָה הַזֹּאת	
	And therefore I have come to imprison him, as one who violates the laws of the state	וְלָכֵן בָּאתִי לְאָסְרוֹ, כְּפֹרֵץ חֻקֵּי הַמְּדִינָה	
	And as one who engages in the craft of sorcery, which must not be done	וּכְעֹשֶׂה בִּמְלֶאכֶת הַכְּשָׁפִים אֲשֶׁר לֹא תֵעָשֶׂה	
	Catch him quickly, and if **he stands against you**[135]	תִּפְשׂוּ אֹתוֹ מְהֵרָה וְאִם **יִתְיַצֵּב בִּפְנֵיכֶם**[135]	
	Lay a hand on him,[136] for **his blood is on his head.**[137]	שִׁלְחוּ בוֹ יָד,[136] כִּי **דָּמוֹ בְרֹאשׁוֹ.**[137]	
ITHIEL	Be silent, calm down all of you, let no man raise his hand	הַחֲרִישׁוּ, הֵרָגְעוּ כֻּלְּכֶם, אִישׁ אַל יָרִים יָדוֹ	איתיאל
	Both on this side and that side. If I desired to fight	גַּם מֵעֵבֶר מִזֶּה וּמִזֶּה. לוּ חָפַצְתִּי לְהִלָּחֵם	
	My arm would save me and I would not call for help	תּוֹשִׁיעַ לִי זְרוֹעִי וְלֹא אֶקְרָא לְעֶזְרָה	

131 An indirect reference to Shakespeare's 'sooty bosom' (1.2.70).
132 Isa. 40:23.
133 Zech. 12:2.
134 This is a postbiblical expression first appearing in the Mishnah (e.g., *Oholot* 16:3 רגלים לדבר 'the matter has substance').
135 Deut. 7:24 לֹא־יִתְיַצֵּב אִישׁ בְּפָנֶיךָ 'no man will be able to stand against you'; see also Deut. 11:25.
136 i.e., with intent to kill; this is a common biblical idiom.
137 Josh. 2:19; Ezek. 33:4.

	But you choose yourselves, where must I go	אַךְ בַּחֲרוּ לָכֶם אַתֶּם, אָנָה עָלַי לָלֶכֶת	
	To give a response to the judges, for **my transgression and my sin?**[138]	לָתֵת מַעֲנֶה לַשֹּׁפְטִים, עֲלֵי פִשְׁעִי וְחַטָּאתִי?[138]	
PHICHOL	To the prison house you will go, until the appointed day comes	לְבֵית הַכֶּלֶא תֵּלֵךְ, עַד בֹּא יוֹם נָכוֹן	פיכל
	When you stand before the judges, to prove your innocence for your life.	וְעָמַדְתָּ לִפְנֵי הַשֹּׁפְטִים, לְהִצְטַדֵּק עַל נַפְשֶׁךָ.	
ITHIEL	If I go in compliance with your command, what will our lord the prince[139] say	אִם אֵלֵךְ כִּדְבָרְךָ, מַה־יַּעֲנֶה הַנָּשִׂיא[139] אֲדֹנֵנוּ	איתיאל
	He who sent messengers to me, who stand here next to me	אֲשֶׁר שָׁלַח אֵלַי מַלְאָכִים, הָעֹמְדִים פֹּה אֶצְלִי	
	To bring me before him, so that he might say something to me	לַהֲבִיאֵנִי לְפָנָיו, לְמַעַן יְדַבֵּר אִתִּי דָּבָר	
	Regarding the affairs of state?	עַל אֹדוֹת דִּבְרֵי הַמְּדִינָה?	
THE OFFICER	The matter is thus, honourable lord	כֵּן הַדָּבָר אָדוֹן נִכְבָּד	הפקיד
	The prince sits here, in the company of his counselling ministers	הַנָּשִׂיא יוֹשֵׁב בָּזֶה, בְּסוֹד שָׂרֵי עֲצָתוֹ	
	And you, too, have been called to come amongst those summoned.	וְגַם אַתָּה נִקְרֵאתָ לָבוֹא בְּתוֹךְ הַקְּרוּאִים.	
PHICHOL	The prince sits in the company of his council on this night	הַנָּשִׂיא בְּסוֹד עֲצָתוֹ יוֹשֵׁב בַּלַּיְלָה הַזֶּה	פיכל
	Bring him before him. My quarrel is not a small quarrel	הָבִיאוּ אֹתוֹ לְפָנָיו. רִיבִי אֵינֶנּוּ רִיב קָטָן	
	Both the prince himself and my brothers the counsellors of the nation	גַּם הַנָּשִׂיא בְּנַפְשׁוֹ גַּם אַחַי יוֹעֲצֵי הַמְּדִינָה	
	Will consider this violence against me as **violence and robbery**[140] against themselves.	יַחְשְׁבוּ חֲמָסִי זֶה כְּחָמָס וָשֹׁד[140] לְנַפְשָׁם.	

138 Exod. 34:7 עָוֹן וָפֶשַׁע וְחַטָּאָה 'iniquity and transgression and sin'; see also Lev. 16:16, 21; Ps. 32:5; Dan. 9:24 for similar collocations.

139 Cf. Shakespeare's 'duke' (1.2.14).

140 Jer. 6:7, 20:8; Ezek. 45:9; Amos 3:10.

	If such deeds can be done and no one **stands at the breach**[141]	אִם מַעֲשִׂים כָּאֵלֶּה יֵעָשׂוּ וְאֵין **עֹמֵד בַּפָּרֶץ**[141]	
	Servants and foreigners will before long rule the land. *(All exit)*	עֲבָדִים וְנָכְרִים יִמְשְׁלוּ עַד מְהֵרָה בָּאָרֶץ. (הולכים כלם)	
SCENE 3	*The council house (The prince and the counsellors sit at the table and attendants stand over them)*	בית המועצה (הנשיא והיועצים יושבים אל השלחן ומשרתים עומדים עליהם)	מחזה ג'
THE PRINCE	The reports that are arriving do not correspond to each other	הַשְּׁמֻעוֹת הַבָּאוֹת אֵינָן מַקְבִּילוֹת אַחַת אֶל אֶחָת	הנשיא
	And one can hardly believe them.	וְכִמְעַט אֵין לְהַאֲמִין בָּהֶן.	
COUNSELLOR 1	**One says this way and another says that way**[142]	**זֹאת אֹמֶרֶת בְּכֹה וְזֹאת בְּכֹה**[142]	יועץ א'
	In my letters it is written a hundred and seven ships.	בְּאִגְּרוֹתַי כָּתוּב מֵאָה וְשִׁבְעָה צִיִּים.	
THE PRINCE	And in my letters, a hundred and forty.	וּבְאִגְּרוֹתַי, מֵאָה וְאַרְבָּעִים.	הנשיא
COUNSELLOR 2	And in *my* letters, two hundred;	וּבְאִגְּרוֹתַי שֶׁלִּי, מָאתָיִם;	יועץ ב'
	Although the number is not the same, as is the way of rumours	אֶפֶס אִם הַמִּסְפָּר אֵינֶנּוּ שָׁוֶה כְּדֶרֶךְ הַשְּׁמֻעוֹת	
	Regardless, they are **unanimous**[143] that the **Turks**[144]	בְּכָל זֹאת **פֶּה אֶחָד**[143] לָהֶן כִּי **הַתּוֹגַרְמִים**[144]	
	Are descending on ships to Caphtor.	יוֹרְדִים בָּאֳנִיּוֹת לְכַפְתּוֹר.	
THE PRINCE	**One who understands matters precisely**[145] will admit that it is thus	**הַמֵּבִין דָּבָר לַאֲשֻׁרוֹ**,[145] יוֹדֶה כִּי כֵן הוּא	הנשיא

141 Ezek. 22:30; see also a similar collocation in Ps. 106:23.

142 1 Kings 3:23 זֹאת אֹמֶרֶת זֶה־בְּנִי הַחַי וּבְנֵךְ הַמֵּת וְזֹאת אֹמֶרֶת לֹא 'one says, my son is the living one and your son is the dead one, and the other one says no'.

143 Josh. 9:2; 1 Kings 22:13; 2 Chron. 18:12.

144 The Hebrew epithet תּוֹגַרְמָה 'Togarmah' appears in Gen. 10:3, where it denotes one of Japheth's grandsons. It also appears in Ezek. 27:14 and 38:6, where it is referred to as a nation from the far north, possibly in a region corresponding to today's Armenia (Koehler and Baumgartner 2001, 2: 1688). In the medieval and Maskilic periods it became identified with Turkey (Even-Shoshan 2003, 6: 1984); this is the sense in which Salkinson is using it.

145 Prov. 14:15 פֶּתִי יַאֲמִין לְכָל־דָּבָר וְעָרוּם יָבִין לַאֲשֻׁרוֹ 'the simple man believes everything, but the prudent man considers his steps'.

	And who would rely on numerical errors to **live in safety**[146]	וּמִי יִסְמֹךְ עַל שִׁגְגוֹת הַמִּסְפָּר לָשֶׁבֶת **בֶּטַח**[146]	
	It is enough for us with this report, to hurry and take heed.	דַּי לָנוּ בַּשְּׁמֻעָה זֹאת, לְהָחִישׁ וְלָשִׁית לֵב.	
	(A sailor knocks outside) Open the door for me.	(מלח דופק מבחוץ) פִּתְחוּ לִי הַדֶּלֶת.	
	(An attendant brings the sailor)	(משרת אחד מביא את המלח)	
THE ATTENDANT	This is a messenger sent by the men of the ships.	הִנֵּה זֶה צִיר שָׁלוּחַ מֵאֵת אַנְשֵׁי הַצִּיִּים.	המשרת
THE PRINCE	What does he have to say?	מַה־בְּפִיו?	הנשיא
THE SAILOR	The Turks' army is headed for Rhodes	חֵיל הַתּוֹגַרְמִים פְּנֵיהֶם מוּעָדוֹת לְרוֹדוֹס	המלח
	Thus the **military commander**[147] ordered me to tell the prince.	כֵּן צִוַּנִי **שַׂר הָאֶלֶף**[147] לְהַגִּיד לִפְנֵי הַנָּשִׂיא.	
THE PRINCE	What do you think about this new matter?	מַה־תְּחַשְּׁבוּן אֶל דָּבָר חָדָשׁ הַזֶּה?	הנשיא
COUNSELLOR I	The matter is not so; it is only deceit for the eyes	אֵין הַדָּבָר כֵּן רַק מִרְמָה הוּא לָעֵינַיִם	יועץ א'
	To pull us by a misleading bridle in a different direction.	לְמָשְׁכֵנוּ בְּרֶסֶן מַתְעֶה אֶל עֵבֶר אַחֵר.	
	Let us first consider with **good judgement and knowledge**[148]	נִתְבּוֹנֵן נָא תְּחִלָּה בְּטוּב **טַעַם וָדַעַת**[148]	
	What the island of Caphtor is worth to the Turks	מַה־נֶּחְשָׁב אִי כַפְתּוֹר לִפְנֵי הַתּוֹגַרְמִים	
	And how much higher its value is than Rhodes in their eyes	וּמַה־מְּאֹד נַעֲלָה עֶרְכּוֹ מִן רוֹדוֹס בְּעֵינֵיהֶם	
	For it is easy for them to besiege it and conquer it	כִּי נָקֵל לָהֶם לָצוּר עָלָיו וּלְכָבְשׁוֹ	

146 Deut. 12:10 וִישַׁבְתֶּם־בֶּטַח 'and you will live in safety'; 1 Sam. 12:11 וַתֵּשְׁבוּ בֶּטַח 'and you lived in safety'.
147 1 Sam. 18:13.
148 Ps. 119:66.

	Since a **peaceful and secure people**[149] inhabits the island	אַחֲרֵי אֲשֶׁר יוֹשֵׁב הָאִי עַם שֹׁקֵט וּבֹטֵחַ[149]	
	And there is no army or weaponry to stand against the enemy.	וְאֵין שָׁם חַיִל וָנֶשֶׁק לְהִתְיַצֵּב בִּפְנֵי הַצָּר	
	Not so is Rhodes, a place of citadel and weapons of war	לֹא כֵן רוֹדוֹס מְקוֹם מִבְצָר וּכְלֵי מִלְחָמָה	
	And therefore if the **wisdom** of the Turks has not **decayed**[150]	וְלָכֵן אִם לֹא נִסְרְחָה חָכְמַת[150] הַתּוֹגַרְמִים	
	They will not abandon the island which is easy for them to possess	לֹא יַעַזְבוּ אֶת הָאִי אֲשֶׁר נָקֵל לָהֶם לְרִשְׁתּוֹ	
	In order to go and try to take possession of Rhodes	לָלֶכֶת לְנַסּוֹת דָּבָר לְהַבְקִיעַ אֶל רוֹדוֹס	
	Because their work will be made difficult and they will not find reward there.	אֲשֶׁר תִּכְבַּד עֲבֹדָתָם וְשָׂכָר לֹא יִמְצְאוּ שָׁם.	
THE PRINCE	My **heart is resolved**[151] that they are not **advancing**[152] on Rhodes.	סָמוּךְ לִבִּי[151] כִּי לֹא לְרוֹדוֹס מְגַמַּת פְּנֵיהֶם.[152]	הנשיא
THE ATTENDANT	Behold, another messenger.	הִנֵּה שָׁלִיחַ אַחֵר.	המשרת
THE MESSENGER	Please, honourable lords! The Turks' ships	בִּי אֲדֹנִים נִכְבָּדִים! אֳנִיּוֹת הַתּוֹגַרְמִים	השליח
	Which have gone towards the island of Rhodes	אֲשֶׁר הָלְכוּ לְנֹכַח פְּנֵי הָאִי רוֹדוֹס	
	Have joined there with other ships.	הִתְחַבְּרוּ שָׁמָּה עִם אֳנִיּוֹת אֲחֵרוֹת.	
COUNSELLOR I	I knew that this would happen –	יָדַעְתִּי כִּי כָאֵלֶּה תִּקְרֶאנָה –	יועץ א'
	What is the number of additional ships?	מַה־מִּסְפַּר הָאֳנִיּוֹת הַנּוֹסָפוֹת?	
THE MESSENGER	About thirty. But behold, now they have gone back and turned around	כִּשְׁלֹשִׁים. וְהִנֵּה עַתָּה שָׁבוּ וְהָפְכוּ פְּנֵיהֶן	השליח

149 Judg. 18:27.
150 Jer. 49:7 נִסְרְחָה חָכְמָתָם 'their wisdom has decayed'.
151 Ps. 112:8 סָמוּךְ לִבּוֹ לֹא יִירָא 'his heart is resolved; he does not fear'.
152 Hab. 1:9.

	Going back towards Caphtor.	הָלוֹךְ וָשׁוֹב לְכַפְתּוֹר.	
	And **Kenaz,**[153] **the bravest of the warriors**[154] and a faithful servant of the government	וּקְנַז[153] אַמִּיץ בַּגִּבּוֹרִים[154] וְעֶבֶד נֶאֱמָן לְהַמֶּמְשָׁלָה	
	Has enquired after your wellbeing, saying that you may trust his words.	פָּקַד לִשְׁלוֹמְכֶם לֵאמֹר כִּי תִסְמְכוּ עַל דְּבָרָיו.	
THE PRINCE	It is clear to us that they are advancing towards Caphtor –	בָּרוּר הַדָּבָר לְפָנֵינוּ כִּי לְכַפְתּוֹר מְגַמָּתָם –	הנשיא
	Is Marcos[155] in the city?	הַאִם מַרְקוֹס[155] בָּעִיר?	
COUNSELLOR I	He has gone to Florence.	הוּא הָלַךְ לִפְלָארֶענְץ.	יועץ א'
THE PRINCE	Write to him in my name to hurry and return on horseback.	כְּתֹב אֵלָיו בִּשְׁמִי לְהָחִישׁ וְלָשׁוּב עַל כַּנְפֵי הָרָכֶשׁ.	הנשיא
COUNSELLOR I	Behold, here comes Phichol with the valiant warrior the Cushite.	הִנֵּה פִיכֹל בָּא עִם הַכּוּשִׁי גִּבּוֹר הֶחָיִל.	יועץ א'
	(Phichol, Ithiel, Doeg, Raddai, and attendants)	(פיכל איתיאל דואג רדי ומשרתים)	
THE PRINCE	Ithiel, valiant warrior! Look, I hereby command you	אִיתִיאֵל גִּבּוֹר הַחַיִל! רְאֵה הִנֵּה הִפְקַדְתִּיךָ	הנשיא
	To go out towards the army of the Turks, our enemies.	לָצֵאת לִקְרַאת חֵיל הַתּוֹגַרְמִים בַּעֲלֵי מִלְחַמְתֵּנוּ.	
	(To Phichol) Greetings, dear Phichol!	(אל פיכל) שָׁלוֹם בּוֹאֲךָ פִּיכֹל הַיָּקָר!	
	I am not seeing you here to seek **counsel and sound wisdom**[156] from your mouth.	לֹא רְאִיתִיךָ בָזֶה לְבַקֵּשׁ עֵצָה וְתוּשִׁיָּה[156] מִפִּיךָ.	

153 This is the name of three minor biblical characters, namely a son of Esau's son Eliphaz (Gen. 36:11, 15, 42; 1 Chron. 1:36, 53); Caleb's brother and the judge Othniel's father (Josh. 15:17; Judg. 1:13, 3:9, 11; 1 Chron. 4:13); and the son of Caleb's son Elah (1 Chron. 4:15). The motivation for Salkinson's selection of this name as an equivalent of Shakespeare's Montano is unclear, as there is no sound correspondence between the two and no obvious parallel in meaning.

154 Amos 2:16 וְאַמִּיץ לִבּוֹ בַּגִּבּוֹרִים 'and the bravest of the warriors'.

155 Cf. Shakespeare's Marcus Luccicos (1.3.45). This is the only name in the play that Salkinson does not Hebraize (cf. Balthasar and Peter in *Ram and Jael*; see *Ram and Jael*, First Part, note 18 and Second Part, note 210 respectively). There does not seem to be a clear motivation for his decision. Salkinson has changed 'Marcus' to 'Marcos', possibly in order to echo the second name Luccicos, which he has omitted.

156 Prov. 8:14.

PHICHOL	And I too am not seeing you to ask for such things from your mouth	גַּם אֲנִי לֹא רְאִיתִיךָ לְבַקֵּשׁ כָּאֵלֶּה מִפִּיךָ	פיכל
	Please pardon me, prince of our nation! It is not the burden of my obligation	שָׂא נָא נְשִׂיא עַמֵּנוּ! לֹא מַשָּׂא מִשְׁמַרְתִּי	
	Nor the report of war that has brought me here from my bed	וְלֹא שְׁמוּעַת מִלְחָמָה הֱבִיאַתְנִי פֹּה מִמִּשְׁכָּבִי	
	And neither can I devote attention to the concerns of the state	וְגַם לְדַאֲגַת הַמְּדִינָה לֹא אוּכַל לָשִׁית לֵב	
	For **the distress of my soul**[157] has engulfed me **like a storm against the wall**[158]	כִּי צָרַת נַפְשִׁי[157] שְׁטָפַתְנִי כְּזֶרֶם קִיר[158]	
	And all the distresses of others have sunk in **the sea of my distress**[159]	וְכָל צָרוֹת אֲחֵרִים צָלְלוּ בְּיַם צָרָתִי[159]	
	And I do not know anything except for pain before me.	וַאֲנִי לֹא אֵדַע מָה, בִּלְתִּי מַכְאֹב לְנֶגְדִּי.	
THE PRINCE	What is wrong with you? What has happened?	מַה־לְּךָ? מַה־נִּהְיָתָה?	הנשיא
PHICHOL	My daughter, my daughter! Oh, **the fruit of my loins**![160]	בִּתִּי, בִּתִּי! אֲהָהּ פְּרִי בִטְנִי![160]	פיכל
COUNSELLOR	Is she dead?	הַאִם מֵתָה הִיא?	יועץ
PHICHOL	To me she is dead	עָלַי הִיא מֵתָה	פיכל
	For she is defiled and deflowered, **stolen by night**[161]	כִּי הִיא טְמֵאָה וַחֲלָלָה גְּנֻבְתִי לָיְלָה[161]	
	By magic and poison wine of **spellcasters**[162]	עַל יְדֵי קְסָמִים וְיֵין רַעַל חֹבְרֵי חָבֶר[162]	
	For an innocent, educated, and sensible soul such as her	כִּי נֶפֶשׁ תְּמִימָה מַשְׂכֶּלֶת וְטוֹבַת טַעַם כָּמוֹהָ	
	Would not be capable of erring by committing such follies	לֹא תוּכַל לִשְׁגּוֹת לַעֲשׂוֹת תַּעְתּוּעִים כָּאֵלֶּה	

157 Gen. 42:21 צָרַת נַפְשׁוֹ 'the distress of his soul'.
158 Isa. 25:4.
159 Zech. 10:11.
160 Mic. 6:7.
161 Gen. 31:39 (Jacob speaking to Laban).
162 Deut. 18:11 וְחֹבֵר חָבֶר 'and a spellcaster'; also Ps. 58:6 (58:5 in English Bibles).

	Except by sorcery.	בִּלְתִּי עַל יְדֵי כְשָׁפִים.	
THE PRINCE	As I live! Indeed that man	חַי אָנִי! כִּי הָאִישׁ הַהוּא	הנשיא
	Who tricked your daughter and enticed her away from you	אֲשֶׁר הִשִּׁיא בִתְּךָ וְהִדִּיחַ אֹתָהּ מֵאַחֲרֶיךָ	
	Shall bear his guilt[163] in judgement according to the book of statute and law	יִשָּׂא עֲוֹנוֹ[163] בִּפְלִילִים כְּסֵפֶר הַחֹק וְהַמִּשְׁפָּט	
	Which you shall read to him **well and plainly**[164] in his ears,	אֲשֶׁר תִּקְרָאֶנּוּ אַתָּה בָּאֵר הֵיטֵב[164] בְּאָזְנָיו,	
	Even if he is one of my own **he shall not go unpunished.**[165]	וְאִם יֶשְׁנוֹ בְּבָנַי לֹא יִנָּקֶה.[165]	
PHICHOL	Let me find favour in your eyes, my lord, for you have comforted me.	אֶמְצָא חֵן בְּעֵינֶיךָ אֲדֹנִי כִּי נִחַמְתָּנִי.	פיכל
	The man is this Cushite who stands before you	הָאִישׁ, הוּא הַכּוּשִׁי הַזֶּה הָעֹמֵד לְפָנֶיךָ	
	For you have called him regarding affairs of state.	כִּי קָרָאתָ לוֹ עַל אֹדת דִּבְרֵי הַמְּדִינָה.	
THE PRINCE AND THE COUNSELLORS	We are very sorry.	צַר לָנוּ מְאֹד.	הנשיא והיועצים
THE PRINCE	*(To Ithiel)* What do you have to say to prove yourself innocent?	(אל איתיאל) מַה־יֵּשׁ בְּפִיךָ לְהַצְדִּיק* נַפְשֶׁךָ?	הנשיא
PHICHOL	There is nothing save to confess his sin.	אֵין דָּבָר בִּלְתִּי לְהִתְוַדּוֹת אֶת עֲוֹנוֹ.	פיכל
ITHIEL	Honourable rulers, **judges of righteousness and truth,**[166]	שָׂרִים נִכְבָּדִים, שׁוֹפְטֵי צֶדֶק וָאֱמֶת,[166]	איתיאל
	Ones who know law and judgement! Indeed the matter is true	יוֹדְעֵי דָת וָדִין! הֵן אֱמֶת הַדָּבָר	
	The daughter of this elder, I took her for myself as a wife	בַּת הַזָּקֵן הַזֶּה לְקַחְתִּיהָ לִי לְאִשָּׁה	
	And this is the whole of my crime and my sin from root to branch	וְזֶה כָל פִּשְׁעִי וְחַטָּאתִי מִשֹּׁרֶשׁ וְעַד עָנָף	

163 Exod. 28:38.
164 Deut. 27:8.
165 Prov. 6:29; also 11:21, 16:5, 17:5, 19:5, 19:9, 28:20.
166 *Pirqe DeRabbi Eliezer* 14; Abarbanel to Exod. 22 and 2 Sam. 24 שופט צדק ואמת 'judge of righteousness and truth'.

*) לְהַצְדִּיק

And there is no other iniquity. **I am not a man of words**[167]	וְעָוֹן אַחֵר אָיִן. **לֹא אִישׁ דְּבָרִים אָנֹכִי**[167]
And I do not know how **to speak clearly**[168] like the inhabitants of **quiet resting places**[169]	**וּלְדַבֵּר צַחוֹת**[168] כִּבְנֵי **מְנוּחוֹת שַׁאֲנַנּוֹת**[169] לֹא יָדַעְתִּי
For from the days of my youth when I was seven years old	כִּי מִימֵי שַׁחֲרוּתִי בִּהְיוֹתִי בֶּן שֶׁבַע שָׁנִים
Until nine months ago, in which time I have rested,	עַד לִפְנֵי תִשְׁעָה חֳדָשִׁים אֲשֶׁר נַחְתִּי בָּהֶם
I wandered from tent to tent to teach my hands battle	הִתְהַלַּכְתִּי מֵאֹהֶל לְאֹהֶל לְלַמֵּד יָדַי לַקְּרָב
Upon the open field, and I know nothing on the earth	עַל פְּנֵי הַשָּׂדֶה וְלֹא יָדַעְתִּי דָבָר בָּאָרֶץ
Except the din of weapons and the noise of war	כִּי אִם שְׁאוֹן כְּלֵי נֶשֶׁק וְרַעַשׁ מִלְחָמָה
And therefore I have not come with **grace of lips**[170] to prove my innocence here.	וְלָכֵן לֹא **בְּחֵן שְׂפָתַיִם**[170] בָּאתִי לְהִצְטַדֵּק פֹּה.
But if you let me **open my mouth**[171] in your kindness	אַךְ אִם תִּתְּנוּ לִי **פִּתְחוֹן פֶּה**[171] בְּחַסְדְּכֶם
I shall tell the ways of love in an honest and sincere language	אֲסַפֵּר אָרְחוֹת אֲהָבָה בְּשָׂפָה יְשָׁרָה וּתְמִימָה
In order that you may know the magic and the charms and the sorceries	לְמַעַן תֵּדְעוּ אֶת הַקְּסָמִים וְאֶת הַלְּחָשִׁים וְהַנְּחָשִׁים
The secrecies of sorcerous wonders which have been calculated as guilt against me	סִתְרֵי פְּלִיאוֹת הַכְּשָׁפִים אֲשֶׁר נֶחְשְׁבוּ לִי לְאַשְׁמָה
And according to which I enticed the heart of the lass to myself.	וַאֲשֶׁר עַל פִּיהֶן פִּתֵּיתִי לִי לֵב הַנַּעֲרָה.
PHICHOL A lass who has never known brazenness	פיכל נַעֲרָה אֲשֶׁר עַזּוּת לֹא יָדְעָה מֵעוֹדָהּ
For she walks modestly in a spirit of humility and quietness	כִּי תַצְנֵעַ לֶכֶת בְּרוּחַ עֲנָוָה וְהַשְׁקֵט

167 Exod. 4:10.
168 Isa. 32:4.
169 Isa. 32:18.
170 Prov. 22:11 חֵן שְׂפָתָיו 'the grace of his lips'.
171 Ezek. 16:63, 29:21.

So that even at **the sound of marching**[172] her face reddens from shame;	עַד גַּם לְקוֹל צְעָדָה[172] יַאֲדִימוּ פָּנֶיהָ מְבוּשָׁה;
Would she risk her soul – a soft and delicate soul	הֲהִיא תַשְׁלִיךְ אֶת נַפְשָׁהּ – נֶפֶשׁ רַכָּה וַעֲדִינָה
Forgetting **her father's house**[173] and her native land	לִשְׁכֹּחַ אֶת בֵּית אָבִיהָ[173] וְאֶת אֶרֶץ מוֹלַדְתָּהּ
And all of her precious things, to cleave to the love of a man	וְאֶת כָּל מַחֲמַדֶּיהָ, לְדָבְקָה בְּאַהֲבַת אִישׁ
At whose face she feared to look? Such a thing has not been seen	אֲשֶׁר יָרְאָה לְהַבִּיט בְּפָנָיו? לֹא נִרְאֲתָה כָּזֹאת
Such a thing has not been, and indeed will not be;	לֹא נִהְיְתָה כָּזֹאת וְהָיֹה לֹא תִהְיֶה;
And only a senseless, witless, and mindless one	וְרַק סָר טַעַם חֲסַר דֵּעָה וְהַשְׂכֵּל
Would believe such strange things, for **there is perversity in his heart**[174]	יַאֲמִין זָרוֹת כָּאֵלֶּה כִּי תַהְפֻּכוֹת בְּלִבּוֹ[174]
And by means of false tricks, deceit of demons	וְעַל יְדֵי תַחְבּוּלוֹת שָׁוְא, נִכְלֵי בְּנֵי שַׁחַת
He means to prove **in the sight of the sun**[175] that the matter is thus.	יֹאמַר לְהוֹכִיחַ לְעֵינֵי הַשֶּׁמֶשׁ[175] כִּי כֵן הַדָּבָר.
And therefore I say one thing: this is the attestation of my mouth	וְלָכֵן אַחַת אָמַרְתִּי: זֹאת תְּעוּדַת פִּי
That with a mixture which ignites a fire in the blood	כִּי בְמֶזֶג אֲשֶׁר יַבְעִיר אֵשׁ בַּדָּם
Or with **water that brings a curse**[176] he enticed her away from me.	אוֹ בְמַיִם מְאָרְרִים[176] הִדִּיחַ אֹתָהּ מֵאַחֲרָי.
THE PRINCE Such an attestation of the mouth is not like **trustworthy testimony**;[177]	הנשיא תְּעוּדַת פֶּה כָּזֹאת אֵינֶנָּה כְּעֵדוּת נֶאֱמָנָה;[177]

172 2 Sam. 5:24.
173 Gen. 38:11; Lev. 22:13; Num. 30:17; Deut. 22:20; Josh. 6:25; Judg. 19:2, 3.
174 Prov. 6:14.
175 2 Sam. 12:11.
176 Num. 5:22.
177 Ps. 19:8 (19:7 in English Bibles) עֵדוּת יְהוָה נֶאֱמָנָה 'the testimony of the LORD is trustworthy'.

	But perhaps you have stronger and more trustworthy signs	אַךְ אוּלַי יֵשׁ לְךָ מוֹפְתִים נֶאֱמָנִים וַחֲזָקִים	
	Than this thin and insubstantial testimony **which has no basis.**[178]	מִתְעוּדָה קַלָּה וְרָזָה זאת אֲשֶׁר אֵין לָהּ שָׁחַר.[178]	
COUNSELLOR I	Pray tell, Ithiel	הַגֶּד נָא אִיתִיאֵל	יועץ א'
	Whether you captured the soul of the lass by **crooked paths**[179]	הַאִם שָׁבִיתָ נֶפֶשׁ הַנַּעֲרָה בְּאָרְחוֹת עֲקַלְקַלּוֹת[179]	
	And forced her **with a strong hand**[180] to give you her love	וַתִּלְחַץ אֹתָהּ בְּיָד חֲזָקָה[180] לָתֵת לְךָ דֹּדֶיהָ	
	Or drew her in with pleasing words and supplications	אוֹ מָשַׁכְתָּ אֹתָהּ בְּדִבְרֵי רָצוֹן וְתַחֲנוּנִים	
	As is the custom of one person to another and **the way of a man with a maiden?**[181]	כְּחָק־נֶפֶשׁ לַנֶּפֶשׁ וּכְדֶרֶךְ גֶּבֶר בְּעַלְמָה?[181]	
ITHIEL	Please call to the woman of a certain house[182]	קִרְאוּ נָא לָאִשָּׁה מִבֵּית פְּלֹנִי אַלְמֹנִי[182]	איתיאל
	And ask her before her father and **in broad daylight**[183]	וְשַׁאֲלוּ אֶת פִּיהָ נֶגֶד אָבִיהָ וְנֶגֶד הַשָּׁמֶשׁ[183]	
	If according to her words you may find iniquity in me	אִם לְפִי דְבָרֶיהָ תִּמְצְאוּ בִי עָוֹן	
	Not only may you punish me by taking me down from my station,	לֹא לְבַד מִמַּצָּבִי תִּשְׁפְּטוּ לְהוֹרִיד אֹתִי,	
	But also by **taking my soul down to Sheol.**[184]	כִּי אִם גַּם לְהוֹרִיד אֶת נַפְשִׁי שְׁאוֹלָה.[184]	
THE PRINCE	Bring Asenath here.	הָבִיאוּ אֶת אָסְנַת הֵנָּה.	הנשיא
ITHIEL	Go with them Doeg, for you know her location.	לֵךְ דוֹאֵג עִמָּהֶם כִּי יָדַעְתָּ אֶת מְקוֹמָהּ.	איתיאל
	(Doeg and attendants exit)	(דואג ומשרתים הולכים)	

---

178 Isa. 8:20 אֲשֶׁר אֵין־לוֹ שָׁחַר 'which has no basis'.
179 Judg. 5:6.
180 Exod. 3:19, 6:1, 13:9; Deut. 5:15, 6:21, 7:8, 9:26, 26:8; Ezek. 20:33–34; Ps. 136:12; Dan. 9:15.
181 Prov. 30:19.
182 See note 84.
183 Num. 25:4; 2 Sam. 12:12.
184 Gen. 42:38 וְהוֹרַדְתֶּם אֶת־שֵׂיבָתִי בְּיָגוֹן שְׁאוֹלָה 'and you will take my grey head in sorrow down to Sheol'.

	But before she comes I shall tell some **words of truth**[185] in your ears	אַךְ בְּטֶרֶם תָּבוֹא אַגִּיד דִּבְרֵי אֱמֶת[185] בְּאָזְנֵיכֶם	
	I shall conceal nothing, as from God in heaven	לֹא אֲכַחֵד דָּבָר כְּמִפְּנֵי אֵל בַּשָּׁמָיִם	
	In order that you might know how I won the heart of the **gracious woman**[186]	לְמַעַן תֵּדְעוּ בַּמֶּה קָנִיתִי, אֶת לֵב אֵשֶׁת חֵן[186]	
	And how she won *my* heart.	וּבַמֶּה קָנְתָה הִיא, אֶת לִבִּי גַּם הִיא.	
THE PRINCE	Speak.	דַּבֵּר.	הנשיא
ITHIEL	Her father loved me and called me to come to his house	אָבִיהָ אָהַב אֹתִי וַיִּקְרָאֵנִי לָבוֹא לְבֵיתוֹ	איתיאל
	Not once and not twice,[187] for he desired to hear from my mouth	לֹא אַחַת וְלֹא שְׁתַּיִם,[187] כִּי חָפֵץ לִשְׁמֹעַ מִפִּי	
	All the chronicles of **the days of the years of my life**[188]	כָּל דִּבְרֵי הַיָּמִים מִתּוֹלְדוֹת יְמֵי שְׁנֵי חַיָּי[188]	
	All the wars and the sieges and the hardships that had befallen me	כָּל הַמִּלְחָמוֹת וְהַמְּצוּרוֹת וְהַתְּלָאוֹת הַמֹּצְאוֹת אֹתִי	
	And so I fulfilled his desire and I told him of all the times	וְכֵן מִלֵּאתִי רְצוֹנוֹ וַאֲסַפֵּר לוֹ כָּל הָעִתִּים	
	That I had been through from the days of my childhood onwards, **from beginning to end**;[189]	אֲשֶׁר עָבְרוּ עָלַי מִימֵי יַלְדוּתִי* הָחֵל וְכַלֵּה;[189]	
	Every disaster and misfortune and all the great terrors	כָּל אָסוֹן וָפֶגַע וְכָל הַמּוֹרָאִים הַגְּדוֹלִים	
	Whether by sea or on land; how I escaped from the fangs of death	בֵּין בַּיָּם בֵּין בַּיַּבָּשָׁה; אֵיךְ נִמְלַטְתִּי מִשִּׁנֵּי הַמָּוֶת	
	When I **stood in the breach**;[190] how I **fell into the hand of the enemy**[191]	לְעֵת עָמַדְתִּי בַּפֶּרֶץ;[190] אֵיךְ נָפַלְתִּי בְּיַד צָר[191]	

185 Eccles. 12:10.
186 Prov. 11:16.
187 2 Kings 6:10.
188 Gen. 25:7, 47:9; 2 Sam. 19:35.
189 1 Sam. 3:12.
190 Ezek. 22:30 וְעֹמֵד בַּפֶּרֶץ 'and stand in the breach'; Ps. 106:23 לוּלֵי מֹשֶׁה בְחִירוֹ עָמַד בַּפֶּרֶץ 'had not Moses his chosen one stood in the breach'.
191 Lam. 1:7 בִּנְפֹל עַמָּהּ בְּיַד־צָר 'when her people fell into the hand of the enemy'.

* יַלְדוּתִי

And was sold as a captive of the sword and how I was redeemed **from the house of bondage.**[192]	וְנִמְכַּרְתִּי כִּשְׁבוּי חֶרֶב וְאֵיךְ נִפְדֵּיתִי מִבֵּית עֲבָדִים.[192]
In addition to what my eyes saw on **each and every journey**[193]	מִלְּבַד אֲשֶׁר רָאוּ עֵינַי בְּכָל מַסַּע וָמַסַּע[193]
Huge fearsome caves and **barren howling wilderness**[194]	מְעָרוֹת גְּדוֹלוֹת נוֹרָאוֹת וְתֹהוּ יְלֵל יְשִׁימוֹן[194]
Rock quarries, mountain ranges, rocks, and **everlasting hills**[195]	מַקֶּבֶת צוּרִים רְכָסִים כֵּפִים וְהַרְרֵי עַד[195]
Whose peaks touch the clouds. And thus **I made known that which surely was,**[196]	אֲשֶׁר שִׂיאָם לָעָב יַגִּיעַ. וְכֵן הוֹדַעְתִּי נֶאֱמָנָה[196]
For I responded to what they asked me about, about **wild men in the wilderness**[197]	כִּי נִדְרַשְׁתִּי לַאֲשֶׁר שְׁאָלוּנִי עַל פְּרָאִים בַּמִּדְבָּר[197]
Who eat men and each man lives on the flesh of his fellow	אֹכְלֵי נֶפֶשׁ אָדָם וְאִישׁ עַל בְּשַׂר רֵעֵהוּ יִחְיוּן
And strange men whose faces are like those of a hunchback	וַאֲנָשִׁים זָרִים אֲשֶׁר פְּנֵיהֶם כִּפְנֵי גִבֵּן
And their heads are under their shoulders. These strange things	וְרֹאשָׁם מִתַּחַת לְשִׁכְמָם. דְּבָרִים זָרִים הָאֵלֶּה
Drew in the ear of Asenath to hear them from my mouth with eagerness	מָשְׁכוּ אֹזֶן אָסְנַת לְשָׁמְעָם מִפִּי בְּחֵפֶץ לִבָּהּ
And when they summoned her to attend to **the affairs of her household**[198]	וְכַאֲשֶׁר קָרְאוּ לָהּ לָשׂוּם עַיִן לַהֲלִיכוֹת בֵּיתָהּ[198]
Thus she hastily performed all of her actions and her work	כֵּן עָשְׂתָה בְחִפָּזוֹן כָּל מַעֲשֶׂיהָ וּמְלַאכְתָּהּ
And quickly she returned like a thirsty woman to hear my words.	וְעַד מְהֵרָה שָׁבָה כַּצְּמֵאָה לִשְׁמֹעַ דְּבָרָי.

192 Exod. 13:3 and many other locations in the Hebrew Bible.

193 Leviticus Rabbah 36.

194 Deut. 32:10.

195 Hab. 3:6.

196 Hosea 5:9.

197 Job 24:5. In the biblical verse פְּרָאִים means 'wild donkeys'; since Shakespeare does not mention donkeys but rather cannibals and men whose heads grow beneath their shoulders (1.3.143–6), it is more likely that Salkinson is using the word in the sense of 'wild men', which it acquired only in the medieval period (Even-Shoshan 2003, 5: 1524).

198 Prov. 31:7.

My eye saw this and I also did not delay	זאת רָאֲתָה עֵינִי* וְלֹא אֵחַרְתִּי גַם אָנִי
To find **an acceptable moment**[199] of rest and give her the opportunity	לִמְצוֹא **עֵת רָצוֹן**[199] וּמְנוּחָה וְלָתֵת לָהּ יָדַיִם
Until she stood and implored me ardently	עַד אֲשֶׁר עָמְדָה וַתִּפְצַר בִּי בְּחוֹם לְבָבָהּ
To tell her again the whole account of my life and my experiences	לְסַפֵּר לָהּ שֵׁנִית כָּל תּוֹלְדוֹת חַיַּי וְקוֹרוֹתַי
As she had not heard **a word spoken properly**[200]	אֲשֶׁר לֹא שָׁמְעָה **דָּבָר דָּבֻר עַל אָפְנָיו**[200]
But rather separate parts, fragments.	כִּי אִם חֲלָקִים נִפְרָדִים קְרָעִים קְרָעִים.
And I acquiesced to her and several times I succeeded	וְאָנֹכִי נֶעְתַּרְתִּי לָהּ וְכַמֶּה פְּעָמִים הִשְׂכַּלְתִּי
In bringing forth, with that which dropped from my lips, drops of water from her eyes	לְהוֹצִיא בְּנִטְפֵי שְׂפָתַי נִטְפֵי מַיִם מֵעֵינֶיהָ
For she was filled with pity upon hearing **my affliction and my misery**[201] from my youth	כִּי מָלְאָה חֶמְלָה בְּשָׁמְעָהּ **עָנְיִי וּמְרוּדִי**[201] מִנְּעוּרָי
When my words were finished she gave me sufficient recompense	כַּאֲשֶׁר תַּמּוּ דְבָרַי נָתְנָה לִי דֵּי שְׂכָרִי
For she sighed from **the chambers of her heart**[202] and spread her palms saying:	כִּי נֶאֶנְחָה **מִקִּירוֹת לִבָּהּ**[202] וַתִּפְרֹשׂ כַּפֶּיהָ לֵאמֹר:
'On my life, these are strange things – wondrously strange –	חֵי נַפְשִׁי זָרוֹת הֵנָּה – זָרוֹת הֵנָּה עַד לְהַפְלִיא –
My **heart is faint**[203] hearing such things – my heart is very faint –	**לִבִּי דָוֶה**[203] לִשְׁמֹעַ כָּזֹאת – דָּוֶה לִבִּי עַד מְאֹד –
If only I had not heard such things – if only I had found such a man!'	לוּ לֹא שָׁמַעְתִּי כָזֹאת – לוּ מָצָאתִי אִישׁ כָּזֶה!
Afterwards she gave her hand to thank me for my kindness	אַחַר נָתְנָה יָדָהּ לְהוֹדוֹת לִי עַל חַסְדִּי

199 Ps. 69:14 (69:13 in English Bibles).
200 Prov. 25:11.
201 Lam. 3:19.
202 Jer. 4:19.
203 Lam. 5:17 עַל־זֶה הָיָה דָוֶה לִבֵּנוּ 'for this our heart is faint'.

* עֵינִי

	And she said further to me that if I had a friend and companion	וַתֹּסֶף לֵאמֹר לִי: אִם יֵשׁ לִי רֵעַ וּמוֹדָע	
	Who desired her, it would be well for me to instruct him	אֲשֶׁר נַפְשׁוֹ חָשְׁקָה בָהּ, טוֹב לִי לְהוֹרוֹתוֹ	
	To tell the account of my life in her ears and she would be his.	לְסַפֵּר תּוֹלְדוֹת חַיַּי בְּאָזְנֶיהָ וְאָז תִּפֹּל בְּגוֹרָלוֹ.	
	And I hastened to contemplate what her words were hinting at	וַאֲנִי מִהַרְתִּי לְהִתְבּוֹנֵן מַה־יִּרְזְמוּן מִלֶּיהָ	
	And I lifted my eyes to her **and my soul clove to her soul**;[204]	וָאֶשָּׂא עֵינַי אֵלֶיהָ וַתִּדְבַּק נַפְשִׁי בְנַפְשָׁהּ;[204]	
	She loved me for **passing as a man through a sea of trouble**[205]	הִיא אֲהֵבַתְנִי, עַל עָבְרִי כַּגֶּבֶר בְּיָם צָרָה[205]	
	And I loved her because **her compassion was stirred**[206] for me.	וַאֲנִי אֲהַבְתִּיהָ, עַל אֲשֶׁר נִכְמְרוּ רַחֲמֶיהָ[206] עָלָי.	
	This is the charm and the sorcery that I worked	זֶה הוּא הַלַּחַשׁ וְזֶה הַקֶּסֶם אֲשֶׁר קָסַמְתִּי	
	Now behold, the woman comes before us; let her arise and testify against me.	וְהִנֵּה הָאִשָּׁה בָּאָה לְפָנֵינוּ תָּקוּם וְתַעֲנֶה בִּי.	
	(Asenath, Doeg, and attendants)	(אסנת דואג ומשרתים)	
THE PRINCE	Such a clever and **smooth speech**[207] would be powerful enough	חֶלְקַת לָשׁוֹן[207] מְלִיצָה כָּזֹאת רַב כֹּחָהּ	הנשיא
	To entice my daughter too.	לְפַתּוֹת גַּם אֶת בִּתִּי.	
	Phichol my friend, I counsel you, your vessel has broken in two.	פִּיכֹל יְדִידִי אִיעָצְךָ, כֶּלְיְךָ נִשְׁבַּר לִשְׁנָיִם	
	Take the good half out of the two parts	קַח לְךָ הַחֲצִי הַטּוֹב מִתּוֹךְ שְׁנֵי הַשְּׁבָרִים	
	A broken weapon is better than empty hands in war.	טוֹב כְּלִי נֶשֶׁק נִשְׁבָּר מִיָּדַיִם רֵקוֹת בַּמִּלְחָמָה.	
PHICHOL	Please consent to hear **the testimony of her mouth.**[208]	אָנָּא הוֹאֶל נָא לִשְׁמֹעַ עֵדוּת פִּיהָ[208]	פיכל

204 Gen. 34:3 וַתִּדְבַּק נַפְשׁוֹ בְּדִינָה 'and his soul clove to Dinah'; Alshekh to Gen. 34 דבקה נפשו בנפשה 'his soul clove to her soul'.

205 Zech. 10:11 וְעָבַר בַּיָּם צָרָה 'and they will pass through the sea of trouble'.

206 1 Kings 3.26.

207 Prov. 6:24.

208 Ps. 119:88 עֵדוּת פִּיךָ 'the testimony of Your mouth'.

	If she admits before you that her hand is also among the conspirators	אִם תּוֹדֶה לְפָנֶיךָ כִּי גַם יָדָהּ בַּקֹּשְׁרִים	
	I shall die if I place iniquity on his head.	תָּמוּת נַפְשִׁי אִם אָשִׁית עָוֺן עַל רֹאשׁוֹ.	
	Listen, **my daughter, my only one**![209] Look at the faces of those gathered here	שִׁמְעִי בִתִּי יְחִידָתִי![209] רְאִי פְּנֵי הַנֶּאֱסָפִים פֹּה	
	Which of ours will you obey more than his fellow?	לְמִי מִשֶּׁלָּנוּ תִּשְׁמְעִי בְקוֹלוֹ מִקּוֹל זוּלָתוֹ?	
ASENATH	There are **two opinions before me, and I must hobble between them both**[210]	שְׁתֵּי סְעִיפִּים לְפָנַי וְעָלַי לִפְסֹחַ עַל שְׁתֵּיהֶן[210]	אסנת
	I am yours, as is everything that belongs to me, for you gave me life	לְךָ אֲנִי וְכָל אֲשֶׁר לִי, כִּי נָתַתָּ לִי חַיִּים	
	And also raised me, and therefore I **indeed honour you**[211]	וְגַם גִּדַּלְתָּ אֹתִי וְלָכֵן כַּבֵּד אֲכַבֶּדְךָ[211]	
	According to **the law and the commandment**;[212] you are lord at my head	כְּפִי הַתּוֹרָה וְהַמִּצְוָה;[212] אַתָּה אָדוֹן לְרֹאשִׁי	
	And I am your daughter, your maidservant. However, there is my husband in front of me	וַאֲנִי בִּתְּךָ אֲמָתֶךָ. אָכֵן שָׁם בַּעְלִי כְּנֶגְדִּי	
	And therefore all the honour which my mother gave to you	וְלָכֵן כָּל הַכָּבוֹד אֲשֶׁר עָשְׂתָה לְךָ אִמִּי	
	As she forgot **her father's house**[213] and went after her lord	כִּי שָׁכְחָה בֵּית אָבִיהָ[213] וַתֵּלֶךְ אַחֲרֵי אֲדֹנֶיהָ	
	Such honour I too give to my lord the Cushite.	כַּכָּבוֹד הַזֶּה גַּם אֲנִי אֶעֱשֶׂה לְכוּשִׁי אֲדֹנִי.	
PHICHOL	Go after him in peace – **there are no more words on my tongue**[214] –	לְכִי אַחֲרָיו בְּשָׁלוֹם – אֵין מִלָּה עוֹד בִּלְשׁוֹנִי[214] –	פיכל

209 Gen. 22:2 קַח־נָא אֶת־בִּנְךָ אֶת־יְחִידְךָ 'take your son, your only one'.
210 1 Kings 18:21 עַד־מָתַי אַתֶּם פֹּסְחִים עַל־שְׁתֵּי הַסְּעִפִּים 'how long will you hobble between two opinions'.
211 Num. 22:17, 24:11 ('honour' in these contexts refers to a monetary reward).
212 2 Chron. 14:3 (14:4 in English Bibles). This collocation also appears in various rabbinic and medieval Hebrew texts; in these postbiblical sources the first word, תּוֹרָה, refers to the Torah (which in its narrow definition denotes the Pentateuch and in its broader definition the whole of Jewish law and tradition), while the second word, מִצְוָה, refers to the biblical commandments as interpreted through the framework of rabbinic Judaism.
213 Gen. 38:11; Lev. 22:13; Num. 30:17; Deut. 22:20; Josh. 6:25; Judg. 19:2, 3.
214 Ps. 139:4 כִּי אֵין מִלָּה בִּלְשׁוֹנִי 'for there is no word on my tongue'.

	Bring the prince! Turn to the affairs of state.	הָבָה נָּא הַנָּשִׂיא! פְּנֵה לְדִבְרֵי הַמְּדִינָה.	
	It would be better for me to collect a son from a market than to beget offspring of my loins.	טוֹב לִי לֶאֱסֹף בֵּן מִשּׁוּק מֵהוֹלִיד זֶרַע מִבָּטֶן.	
	Approach me, O Cushite! I hereby give you my daughter	גְּשָׁה לִי הַכּוּשִׁי! הִנְנִי נֹתֵן לְךָ בִּתִּי	
	Since you married her in secret,	אַחֲרֵי אֲשֶׁר קָנִיתָ אֹתָהּ לְאִשָּׁה בַּסֵּתֶר,	
	For if you had not already married her, I would not give her to you now.	שֶׁלּוּלֵא קִדַּמְתָּ לִקְנוֹתָהּ, לֹא נְתַתִּיהָ לְךָ עַתָּה.	
	And you, **delightful daughter**,[215] **have put joy in my heart**[216]	וְאַתְּ בַּת שַׁעֲשׁוּעִים[215] נָתַתְּ שִׂמְחָה בְּלִבִּי[216]	
	That you are my only child and I have no other daughter	עַל כִּי יְחִידָה אַתְּ וְאֵין לִי בַּת אַחֶרֶת	
	For your flight from my house would have made me merciless to your sister	כִּי מְנוּסָתֵךְ מִבֵּיתִי שָׂמַתְנִי לְאַכְזָר לַאֲחוֹתֵךְ	
	Enclosing her with planks of cedar.[217] – My words are finished.	לָצוּר עָלֶיהָ לוּחַ אָרֶז.[217] – כָּלוּ דְבָרָי.	
THE PRINCE	Desist so that I may propose some words to be **a little help**[218]	הֶרֶף וְאַעֲרִיךְ מִלִּים לִהְיוֹת לְעֵזֶר מְעָט[218]	הנשיא
	As the entrance to the dwelling of peace, to **turn the heart of the father to the children**:[219]	כְּמָבוֹא לִמְעוֹן הַשָּׁלוֹם לְהָשִׁיב לֵב אָב לְבָנִים:[219]	
	In the absence of healing for the break, let worry and terror retreat[220]	בְּאֶפֶס אֲרֻכָה לַשֶּׁבֶר תָּסוּר דְּאָגָה וּמְחִתָּה[220]	
	For a man girds himself to bear the distress in its time;	כִּי יִתְאַזֵּר הַגֶּבֶר לָשֵׂאת הַצָּרָה בְּעִתָּהּ;	

215 Jer. 31:20 יֶלֶד שַׁעֲשֻׁעִים 'delightful child'.
216 Ps. 4:8 (4:7 in English Bibles) נָתַתָּה שִׂמְחָה בְלִבִּי 'you (masc.) have put joy in my heart'.
217 Song of Songs 8:9 נָצוּר עָלֶיהָ לוּחַ אָרֶז 'we shall enclose her with planks of cedar'.
218 Dan. 11:34.
219 Mal. 3:24 (4:6 in English Bibles) וְהֵשִׁיב לֵב־אָבוֹת עַל־בָּנִים 'he will turn the heart of the fathers to the children'.
220 This and the next line form a rhyming couplet, mirroring Shakespeare's 'ended/depended' (1.3.203–4).

	Do not cry out **with a bitter soul**[221] over that which has passed and is no more.[222]	לַאֲשֶׁר עָבַר וְאֵינֶנּוּ אַל תִּזְעַק בְּנֶפֶשׁ מָרָה[222,221]	
	For this is the way to create distress twice;	כִּי זֶה הַדֶּרֶךְ לְהָקִים פַּעֲמַיִם צָרָה;	
	If the ewe has gone and the stray cannot be returned[223]	אִם אָזְלָה הַכִּבְשָׂה וְאֵין לְהָשִׁיב הַנִּדָּחָה[223]	
	With long forbearance[224] the damage will turn into gain;	בְּאֹרֶךְ אַפַּיִם[224] יִתְהַפֵּךְ הַנֶּזֶק לִרְוָחָה;	
	When a robbed man laughs, he steals a portion from the plunderer[225]	שָׁדוּד כִּי יִשְׂחַק חֹמֵס חֵלֶק מֵהַשּׁוֹלֵל[225]	
	But he steals from himself if he cries out like a madman.	וְהוּא חֹמֵס נַפְשׁוֹ אִם יִצְעַק כְּמִשְׁתּוֹלֵל.	
PHICHOL	Thus if the Turks dare to go up to Caphtor[226]	כֵּן אִם הַתּוֹגַרְמִים לַעֲלוֹת לְכַפְתּוֹר יָהִינוּ[226]	פיכל
	It will not be torn away from us but rather **our mouths will be filled with laughter**;[227]	לֹא תִקָּרַע מִמֶּנּוּ כִּי **יִמָּלֵא שְׂחֹק פִּינוּ**;[227]	
	Happy is he who rejoices in his judgement and delights even in the inferno[228, 229]	אַשְׁרֵי הַשָּׂמֵחַ בְּדִינוֹ וּמִתְעַנֵּג גַּם בַּתֹּפֶת[228, 229]	
	From poison he extracts sweetness for himself, from wormwood he sucks pure honey;	מֵרוֹשׁ יוֹצִיא לוֹ מָתוֹק מִלַּעֲנָה יָמֹץ נֹפֶת;	
	But woe to him who has **a worried heart**[230] and no patience in his spirit[231]	וְאוֹי לַאֲשֶׁר לוֹ **לֵב רַגָּז**[230] וּלְרוּחוֹ אֵין אֹרֶךְ[231]	

221 Job 21:25.
222 This and the next line form a rhyming couplet, mirroring Shakespeare's 'gone/on' (1.3.205–6).
223 This and the next line form a rhyming couplet, mirroring Shakespeare's 'takes/makes' (1.3.207–8).
224 Prov. 25:15.
225 This and the next line form a rhyming couplet, mirroring Shakespeare's 'thief/grief' (1.3.209–10).
226 This and the next line form a rhyming couplet, mirroring Shakespeare's 'beguile/smile' (1.3.211–12).
227 Ps. 126:2.
228 This word appears on a number of occasions in the Hebrew Bible (2 Kings 23:10; Jer. 7:31, 32, 19:6, 11–14) but as a place-name, Topheth, a location in Jerusalem where idol-worshippers would sacrifice their children; in the medieval period it became a label for hell (Even-Shoshan 2003, 6: 2030), and this is the sense in which Salkinson is employing it.
229 This and the next line form a rhyming couplet, mirroring Shakespeare's 'bears/hears' (1.3.213–14).
230 Deut. 28:65.
231 This and the next line form a rhyming couplet, mirroring Shakespeare's 'sorrow/borrow' (1.3.215–16).

	For when he is judged he is tormented by pain and despondency;	כִּי יִתְעַנֶּה בְּהִשָּׁפְטוֹ מִפְּנֵי מַכְאֹב וָמֹרֶךְ;	
	And parables, why they are as sharp as an ox-goad or a nail[232]	וּמְשָׁלִים הֲלֹא הֵמָּה חַדִּים כְּדָרְבָן וּמַסְמֵרָה[232]	
	To one like sugar cane; to another, more bitter than gall;	לְאֶחָד כְּקָנֶה דְבַשׁ לַשֵּׁנִי מַר מִמְּרֵרָה;	
	But what do **mere words**[233] have that they might **be good medicine**?[234, 235]	**אַךְ מַה־לִּדְבַר שְׂפָתַיִם**[233] **כִּי יֵיטִיב גֵּהָה**[234, 235]	
	Can healing for **a broken spirit**[236] go in through the ears? –	הֲיַעֲלֶה דֶרֶךְ אָזְנַיִם אֲרֻכָה לְ**רוּחַ נְכֵאָה**?[236] –	
	Now please resolve to turn your attention to the affairs of state.	עַתָּה אָנָּא הוֹאֵל לָשִׁית לֵב לְדִבְרֵי הַמְּדִינָה.	
THE PRINCE[237]	The Turks **with a great army**[238] are descending towards Caphtor	הַתּוֹגַרְמִים **בְּחַיִל כָּבֵד**[238] יֹרְדִים לִקְרַאת כַּפְתּוֹר	הנשיא[237]
	And you, Ithiel, know well the citadel of that place	וְאַתָּה אִיתִיאֵל יָדַעְתָּ הֵיטֵב מִבְצַר הַמָּקוֹם הַהוּא	
	And as for the governor whom we have, though he is a valiant man	וְהַנָּצִיב אֲשֶׁר לָנוּ, אַף כִּי בֶּן חַיִל הוּא	
	Everyone says **unanimously**[239] that you **excel in dignity and power**[240]	יֹאמְרוּ כֻלָּם **פֶּה אֶחָד**[239] כִּי לְךָ **יֶתֶר שְׂאֵת וָעָז**[240]	
	And therefore for several days you must cease taking pleasure in your light	וְלָכֵן יָמִים אֲחָדִים תֶּחְדַּל מֵהִתְעַנֵּג בְּאוֹרְךָ	
	Which is shining for you like a new star, in order to set your feet	הַזֹּרֵחַ לְךָ כְּכוֹכָב חָדָשׁ, לְמַעַן תָּשִׂים פְּעָמֶיךָ	

232 This and the next line form a rhyming couplet, mirroring Shakespeare's 'gall/equivocal' (1.3.217–18).
233 2 Kings 18:20; Isa. 36:5.
234 Prov. 17:22 לֵב שָׂמֵחַ יֵיטִב גֵּהָה 'a joyful heart is good medicine'.
235 This and the next line form a rhyming couplet, mirroring Shakespeare's 'hear/ear' (1.3.219–20).
236 Prov. 15:13, 17:22, 18:14.
237 This speech is prose in the original (1.3.222–9).
238 2 Kings 18:17; Isa. 36:2.
239 Josh. 9:2; 1 Kings 22:13; 2 Chron. 18:12.
240 Gen. 49:3 יֶתֶר שְׂאֵת וְיֶתֶר עָז 'excelling in dignity and excelling in power'.

	On a road of snares and uneven ground and a field of din and shouting	לְדֶרֶךְ מוֹקְשִׁים וּרְכָסִים וְלִשְׂדֵה שָׁאוֹן וּתְרוּעָה	
	For you shall go at the head of the company to command the army of war.	כִּי תֵלֵךְ בְּרֹאשׁ הַחַיִל לְפַקֵּד צְבָא הַמִּלְחָמָה.	
ITHIEL	The hand of cruel time has taught me like a nurse from youth	יַד הַזְּמָן הָאַכְזָר לִמְּדַתְנִי כָּאֹמֶנֶת מִנֹּעַר	איתיאל
	To lie in a field of war on a bed of **iron and lead**[241]	לִשְׁכַּב בִּשְׂדֵה מִלְחָמָה עַל עֶרֶשׂ **בַּרְזֶל וָעֹפֶרֶת**[241]	
	As on a pillow of fur and down, and a spirit of power and might	כְּעַל כַּר שֵׂעָר וָנוֹצָה, וְרוּחַ עֹז וּגְבוּרָה	
	Spurs me to perform any service, even to fight against the Turks.	יְפַעֲמֵנִי לַעֲבֹד כָּל עֲבֹדָה, אַף כִּי לְהִלָּחֵם בַּתּוֹגַרְמִים.	
	And therefore **I hereby present my plea before the honour of the rulership**[242]	וְלָכֵן **הִנְנִי מַפִּיל תְּחִנָּתִי לִפְנֵי** כְּבוֹד הַמֶּמְשָׁלָה[242]	
	To be a shield and protector for my wife who stands here	לִהְיוֹת לְמָגֵן וּלְמַחֲסֶה לְאִשְׁתִּי הַנִּצֶּבֶת פֹּה	
	To support her in an established house as befits the house of her birth.	לְכַלְכֵּל אֹתָהּ בְּבַיִת נָכוֹן כְּנָכוֹן לְבֵית מוֹלַדְתָּהּ.	
THE PRINCE	If you are willing, she may stay in **her father's house.**[243]	אִם יֵשׁ אֶת נַפְשְׁךָ תֵּשֵׁב **בְּבֵית אָבִיהָ.**[243]	הנשיא
PHICHOL	Her father refuses to allow her to return to his house.	מֵאֵן אָבִיהָ לְתִתָּהּ לָשׁוּב לְבֵיתוֹ.	פיכל
ITHIEL	As do I.	כֵּן גַּם אָנִי.	איתיאל
ASENATH	As do I; for I have no desire	וְכֵן גַּם אָנִי; כִּי אֵין לִי חֵפֶץ	אסנת
	To disturb my father's peace whenever he sees me in his house.	לְהַפְרִיעַ שְׁלוֹם אָבִי מִדֵּי יִרְאֵנִי בְּבֵיתוֹ.	
	And to you, O prince, I raise my eyes that you might be an advocate for me	וְאֵלֶיךָ הַנָּשִׂיא נָשָׂאתִי עֵינַי כִּי תִהְיֶה לִי לְמֵלִיץ	
	To take hold of that which I ask with an innocent heart.	לְהַחֲזִיק אֶת שְׁאֵלָתִי אֲשֶׁר אֶשְׁאַל בְּתָם־לֵב.	

241 Job 19:24.
242 Jer. 38:26 מַפִּיל־אֲנִי תְחִנָּתִי לִפְנֵי הַמֶּלֶךְ 'I have presented my plea before the king'.
243 Gen. 38:11; Lev. 22:13; Num. 30:17; Deut. 22:20; Josh. 6:25; Judg. 19:2, 3.

THE PRINCE	**What is your request,**[244] Asenath?	מַה־בַּקָּשָׁתֵךְ[244] אָסְנַת?	הנשיא
ASENATH	That I love the Cushite in order that I might live with him	כִּי אָהַבְתִּי אֶת הַכּוּשִׁי לְמַעַן אֶחְיֶה עִמּוֹ	אסנת
	Is known in all the land, since I left my father	מוּדַעַת בְּכָל הָאָרֶץ, אַחֲרֵי אֲשֶׁר אָבִי עֲזַבְתִּי	
	And went out from his house in a storm, **for I saw the heart of my husband**[245]	וּבִסְעָרָה יָצָאתִי מִבֵּיתוֹ, כִּי לִלְבַב בַּעְלִי רָאִיתִי[245]	
	And my soul clove to his soul,[246] until I forgot my kindred	וַתִּדְבַּק נַפְשִׁי בְּנַפְשׁוֹ,[246] עַד אֲשֶׁר נָשִׁיתִי מוֹלַדְתִּי	
	And all of my precious things from previously, in order that I be called by his name	וְכָל מַחֲמַדֵּי מִקֶּדֶם, לְמַעַן יִקָּרֵא שְׁמוֹ עָלַי	
	To revel in the glory of his power, and with his honour my honour might be joined.	לְהִתְפָּאֵר בְּתִפְאֶרֶת עֻזּוֹ וּבִכְבוֹדוֹ יֵחַד כְּבוֹדִי.	
	And now, honourable ministers! If he goes to the war	וְעַתָּה שָׂרִים נִכְבָּדִים! אִם הוּא הוֹלֵךְ לַמִּלְחָמָה	
	And I stay here like **a lonely bird on a rooftop**[247]	וְאָנֹכִי אֶשָּׁאֵר פֹּה כְּצִפּוֹר בּוֹדֵד עַל גָּג[247]	
	What will remain with me, of all my desire and my love?	מַה־נִּשְׁאַר עִמָּדִי מִכָּל חֶפְצִי וְאַהֲבָתִי?	
	How can I sit many days, without a father, without a husband	אֵיכָה אֵשֵׁב יָמִים רַבִּים, בְּאֵין אָב, בְּאֵין בַּעַל	
	Alone, abandoned like an orphan and like a widow, **a widow whose husband is alive?**[248]	גַּלְמוּדָה עֲזוּבָה כִּיתוֹמָה וּכְאַלְמָנָה אַלְמְנוּת חַיּוּת?[248]	
	Let me go with him.	תְּנוּ לִי לָלֶכֶת עִמּוֹ.	
ITHIEL	Please consent, ministers! To give her her desire;	אָנָּא הוֹאִילוּ שָׂרִים! לָתֵת לָהּ חֶפְצָהּ;	איתיאל
	My witness is in heaven! That I do not yearn for this before you	עֵדִי בַשָּׁמַיִם! כִּי לֹא אוֹחִילָה לִפְנֵיכֶם	

244 Esther 5:3, 6, 7:2, 9:12.

245 1 Sam. 16:7 הָאָדָם יִרְאֶה לַעֵינַיִם וַיהוָה יִרְאֶה לַלֵּבָב 'man sees the outward appearance, but the LORD sees the heart'.

246 Gen. 34:3 וַתִּדְבַּק נַפְשׁוֹ בְּדִינָה 'and his soul clove to Dinah'; Alshekh to Ruth 1 דבקה נפשי בנפשך 'my soul clove to your soul'.

247 Ps. 102:8 (102:7 in English Bibles).

248 2 Sam. 20:3.

Because I desire to satisfy the hunger of my soul

בַּעֲבוּר כִּי חָשַׁקְתִּי לְמַלֵּא רַעֲבוֹן נַפְשִׁי

And to drink new wine from my own vineyard for I am thirsty

וְלִשְׁתּוֹת מִכַּרְמִי שֶׁלִּי יַיִן חָדָשׁ כִּי צָמֵאתִי,

It is for nothing other than to fulfil her wishes that I have asked.

אֵין זֹאת, כִּי אִם לְמַלֵּא מִשְׁאֲלוֹתֶיהָ שָׁאָלְתִּי.

And God forbid you should say that when she goes with me

וְחָלִלָה לָכֶם לֵאמֹר כַּאֲשֶׁר תֵּלֵךְ עִמָּדִי

I shall abandon the labour which you have entrusted into my hand.

פֶּן אֶעֱזֹב אֶת הַמְּלָאכָה אֲשֶׁר נְתַתֶּם בְּיָדִי.

If I have given myself up to **the delights of men, many concubines**,[249]

אִם הִתְמַכַּרְתִּי לְתַעֲנֻגוֹת **בְּנֵי אָדָם שִׁדָּה וְשִׁדּוֹת**[249]

And have become like the target for **arrows of love**[250] from the hand of **an archer**[251]

וָאֶהְיֶה כַּמַּטָּרָה לְחִצֵּי **אַהֲבָה**[250] מִיַּד **רֹבֶה קַשָּׁת**[251]

Which seizes the heart of its master and casts sluggishness upon his delights

אֲשֶׁר יִקַּח לֵב בְּעָלָיו וְיַפִּיל עַצְלָה בְּשַׁעֲשֻׁעָיו

So as not to engage in the labour which keeps its master alive,

לְבִלְתִּי עֲשׂוֹת בַּמְּלָאכָה, אֲשֶׁר תְּחַיֶּה אֶת בְּעָלֶיהָ,

May my wife grind grain for another man;[252] may my honour turn into shame;

תִּטְחַן לְאַחֵר אִשְׁתִּי;[252] כְּבוֹדִי יֵהָפֵךְ לְקָלוֹן;

And may **the bronze helmet on my head**[253] become the cooking women's pot!

וְכוֹבַע נְחֹשֶׁת עַל רֹאשִׁי,[253] יְהִי לְסִיר הַמְבַשְּׁלוֹת!

THE PRINCE Look, you have the power to choose as is best in your eyes

הנשיא רְאֵה הִנֵּה בְיָדְךָ לִבְחֹר כַּטּוֹב בְּעֵינֶיךָ

But choose for yourself quickly, whether you will go or whether you will leave off

אַךְ מַהֵר בְּחַר לְךָ, אִם תֵּלֵךְ וְאִם תֶּחְדָּל

---

249 Eccles. 2:8 וְתַעֲנוּגֹת בְּנֵי הָאָדָם שִׁדָּה וְשִׁדּוֹת 'and the delights of men, many concubines'.
250 Salkinson has deleted the reference to Classical mythology in this translation of Shakespeare's 'light-winged toys/Of feathered Cupid' (1.3.269–70).
251 Gen. 21:20.
252 Job 31:10.
253 1 Sam. 17:5 וְכוֹבַע נְחֹשֶׁת עַל־רֹאשׁוֹ 'and there was a bronze helmet on his head'.

	For the matter is extremely urgent, and you are due to leave tonight.	כִּי הַדָּבָר נָחוּץ מְאֹד וּבַלַּיְלָה אַתָּה הוֹלֵךְ.	
ASENATH	Tonight?	בַּלַּיְלָה?	אסנת
THE PRINCE	This very night.	בַּלַּיְלָה הַזֶּה.	הנשיא
ITHIEL	Behold, I shall go with all my heart.	הִנְנִי הוֹלֵךְ בְּכָל לְבָבִי.	איתיאל
THE PRINCE	Tomorrow **at the morning watch**[254] we shall gather here again	לְמָחָר בְּאַשְׁמֹרֶת הַבֹּקֶר[254] נִתְאַסֵּף פֹּה עוֹד	הנשיא
	Ithiel, please appoint one of your men to stay behind you	הַצִּיגָה נָא אִיתִיאֵל, אֶחָד מֵאֲנָשֶׁיךָ אַחֲרֶיךָ	
	And he will bring to your hand our document of attestation	וְהוּא יָבִיא לְיָדְךָ כְּתַב הַתְּעוּדָה שֶׁלָּנוּ	
	With the rest of the supplies required for you on the way.	עִם יֶתֶר הַחֲפָצִים הַדְּרוּשִׁים לְךָ עַל הַדָּרֶךְ.	
ITHIEL	I shall appoint my standard-bearer, an honest and faithful man	הִנְנִי לְהַצִּיג נוֹשֵׂא דִּגְלִי, אִישׁ יָשָׁר וְנֶאֱמָן	איתיאל
	Whom I shall assign[255] to bring me my wife	אֲשֶׁר אֶמְסֹר[255] עַל יָדוֹ, לְהָבִיא לִי אֶת אִשְׁתִּי	
	With the rest of the things that you will send **as is fitting in your eyes.**[256]	עִם יֶתֶר הַדְּבָרִים אֲשֶׁר תִּשְׁלְחוּ **כַּטּוֹב בְּעֵינֵיכֶם.**[256]	
THE PRINCE	Let it be so – go in peace, **each man to his house.**[257]	יְהִי כֵן – לְכוּ לְשָׁלוֹם **אִישׁ לְבֵיתוֹ.**[257]	הנשיא
	And you, noble Phichol! Listen to the wise pronouncement of the ruler	וְאַתָּה פִיכֹל הַנָּדִיב! שְׁמַע מְשַׁל הַמֹּשֵׁל	
	Indeed I shall honour a man of valour, as long as I still have my sense[258]	אִישׁ חַיִל כַּבֵּד אֲכַבְּדֶנּוּ, כָּל עוֹד בִּי חוּשִׁי[258]	

254 Exod. 14:24; 1 Sam. 11:11 (sometimes translated as 'last watch of the night').

255 This verb appears only once in the Hebrew Bible (Num. 31:16), with unclear meaning; it becomes commonly used only in postbiblical texts starting with the Mishnah (Even-Shoshan 2003, 3: 1026).

256 Gen. 19:18; Esther 8:8.

257 Judg. 20:8; 1 Sam. 10:25; 2 Sam. 6:19; 1 Kings 12:24, 22:17; Hag. 1:9; 1 Chron. 16:43; 2 Chron. 11:4, 18:16.

258 This and the next line form a rhyming couplet, mirroring Shakespeare's 'lack/black' (1.3.290–1).

	And regarding your son-in-law I hereby say: **the skin of the Cushite's face shone.**[259]	וְעַל חֲתָנְךָ הִנְנִי אֹמֵר: קָרַן עוֹר פְּנֵי הַכּוּשִׁי.[259]	
COUNSELLOR I	Go in peace, Ithiel; do well by your wife Asenath.	לֵךְ לְשָׁלוֹם אִיתִיאֵל, הֵיטִיבָה לְאָסְנַת אִשְׁתֶּךָ.	יועץ א'
PHICHOL	Keep your eye on her, Cushite, for **there is deceit in her mouth**[260, 261]	שִׂים עֵינְךָ עָלֶיהָ כּוּשִׁי, כִּי מִרְמָה בְּפִיהָ[260, 261]	פיכל
	Lest she **cheat**[262] you as she cheated her father.	פֶּן תַּעֲקֹב[262] בַּעְלָהּ כַּאֲשֶׁר עָקְבָה אָבִיהָ.	
	(The prince, the counsellors, and the attendants exit)	(הנשיא והיועצים והמשרתים הולכים)	
ITHIEL	**I shall vouch for**[263] my wife with my life – my dear Doeg!	אֶת אִשְׁתִּי בְּנַפְשִׁי אֶעֶרְבֶנָּה[263] – דוֹאֵג יַקִּירִי!	איתיאל
	Know that I hereby give her over to your charge	דַּע כִּי עַל יָדְךָ הִנֵּה אֲנִי נֹתֵן אֹתָהּ	
	Command your wife to stand at attendance and serve before her	צַו אֶת אִשְׁתְּךָ לַעֲמֹד וּלְשָׁרֵת לְפָנֶיהָ	
	And as for you, bring both of them to me according to your best ability.	וְאַתָּה תָּבִיא אֶת שְׁתֵּיהֶן כְּיָדְךָ הַטּוֹבָה אֵלָי.	
	Come to me Asenath, only a few moments	בּוֹאִי אֵלַי אָסְנַת, רַק רְגָעִים אֲחָדִים	
	Have been given to us as **a time of love,**[264] for the appointed time cannot be moved.	נְתֻנִים לָנוּ לְעֵת דֹּדִים,[264] כִּי אֵין לְהַעֲבִיר הַמּוֹעֵד.	
	(Ithiel and Asenath exit)	(איתיאל ואסנת הולכים)	
RADDAI	Doeg!	דוֹאֵג!	רדי

259 Exod. 34:35 קָרַן עוֹר פְּנֵי מֹשֶׁה 'the skin of Moses' face shone' (after speaking with God). This phrase also appears in the thirteenth-century Hebrew book of fables *Meshal haQadmoni* by the poet and scholar Isaac ben Solomon abi Sahula, where it refers to a husband whose wife has been unfaithful to him by playing on the homonymy of the word קֶרֶן, which can mean 'ray of light' or 'horn'. Sahula draws on the medieval European notion of the wronged husband wearing horns. It is possible that Salkinson was aware of the text and its interpretation, and had it in mind when selecting this particular phrase. Thanks to Marc Sapirstein for this observation.
260 Isa. 53:9 וְלֹא מִרְמָה בְּפִיו 'and there was no deceit in his mouth'.
261 This and the next line form a rhyming couplet, mirroring Shakespeare's 'see/thee' (1.3.293–4).
262 Gen. 27:36 וַיַּעְקְבֵנִי זֶה פַעֲמַיִם 'for he has tricked me twice now'.
263 Gen. 43:9 אָנֹכִי אֶעֶרְבֶנּוּ 'I shall be surety for him'.
264 Ezek. 16:8.

DOEG	What do you say, **willing-hearted one?**[265]	מָה אַתָּה מְדַבֵּר נְדִיב לֵב?[265]	דואג
RADDAI	Tell me, what should I do now?	הַגֵּד לִי, מָה אֶעֱשֶׂה עַתָּה?	רדי
DOEG	Go to your house and lie on your bed.	לֵךְ לְבֵיתְךָ וּשְׁכַב עַל מִשְׁכָּבֶךָ.	דואג
RADDAI	I am going to drown in the river momentarily.	הִנְנִי הוֹלֵךְ לִטְבֹּעַ בַּנָּהָר כְּרָגַע.	רדי
DOEG[266]	If you do so, I shall not continue	אִם כֵּן תַּעֲשֶׂה, לֹא אוֹסִיף עוֹד	דואג[266]
	To love you. But why, my dear fool?	לְאַהֲבָה אֶת נַפְשֶׁךָ. אַךְ מַדּוּעַ פֶּתִי יַקִּירִי?	
RADDAI	Because it is folly to keep myself alive	יַעַן כִּי פְתַיּוּת הִיא, לְהַחֲיוֹת אֶת נַפְשִׁי	רדי
	Since life is cholera[267] and death is the doctor.	בַּאֲשֶׁר הַחַיִּים חֳלִי רַע[267] וְהַמָּוֶת הוּא הָרֹפֵא.	
DOEG	**You are speaking like a shameless one.**[268]	כְּאַחַד הַנְּבָלִים תְּדַבֵּר.[268]	דואג
	Approximately four times seven years have passed on my head	כְּאַרְבַּע פְּעָמִים שֶׁבַע שָׁנִים עָבְרוּ עַל רֹאשִׁי	
	And from the day that I started to distinguish **between good and evil**[269]	וּמִיּוֹם הַחִלּוֹתִי לְהַבְדִּיל בֵּין טוֹב וּבֵין רָע[269]	
	I have not found a single man who knew how to honour himself.	לֹא מָצָאתִי אִישׁ אֶחָד הַיּוֹדֵעַ לְהוֹקִיר נַפְשׁוֹ.	
	As for myself, instead of going to drown because of a beautiful hen	וַאֲנִי תַּחַת לֶכְתִּי לִטְבֹּעַ בִּגְלַל תַּרְנְגוֹלֶת יָפָה	
	I would go to exchange my life for the life of a monkey.	הָיִיתִי הוֹלֵךְ לְהָמִיר חַיַּי בְּחַיֵּי אַחַד הַקֹּפִים.	
RADDAI	But I do not know what I should do –	אֲבָל לֹא אֵדַע מָה אֶעֱשֶׂה –	רדי
	Shamefacedly I admit that my love has grown greater than **the strength of bearing the burden**[270]	בְּבֹשֶׁת פָּנִים אוֹדֶה כִּי אַהֲבָתִי גָּבְרָה מִכֹּחַ הַסַּבָּל[270]	

265 Exod. 35:22; 2 Chron. 29:31.

266 This and the following speeches until Raddai's line 'Where shall we see each other tomorrow' are prose in the original (1.3.307–73).

267 Cf. Shakespeare's 'to live is torment; and then have we a prescription to die' (1.3.309–10). Cholera was the most common infectious disease affecting Eastern European Jews in the second half of the nineteenth century (see Markel 1997: esp. 87–8). Cf. *Ram and Jael*, Fifth Part, note 28.

268 Job 2:10 כְּדַבֵּר אַחַת הַנְּבָלוֹת תְּדַבֵּרִי 'you are speaking like a shameless woman'.

269 Lev. 27:12, 14 (with a slightly different meaning: 'whether good or evil').

270 Neh. 4:4 (4:10 in English Bibles).

And **I have no more spirit**[271] to extinguish the flame.

וְאֵין בִּי עוֹד רוּחַ[271] לְכַבּוֹת אֶת הַתַּבְעֵרָה.

DOEG Your spirit is futility;

דואג רוּחֲךָ הֶבֶל הוּא;

For the strength is in our hands to be thus or thus.

כִּי הַכֹּחַ בְּיָדֵינוּ הוּא, לִהְיוֹת כֵּן אוֹ כֵן.

Man's body is a garden, and the master of the garden is the will;

גּוּף הָאָדָם הוּא גַּן וּבַעַל הַגָּן הוּא הָרָצוֹן;

I have the power to plant weeds in it and to sow greens in it,

בְּיָדִי לִנְטֹעַ בּוֹ חֲרֻלִים וְלִזְרֹעַ בּוֹ יָרָק,

When I will it hyssop rises up, and when I will it that which my hand has planted is torn up,

בִּרְצוֹתִי יַעֲלֶה אֵזוֹב וּבִרְצוֹתִי יֵעָקֵר מַטַּע יָדִי,

When I will it I sow one species, or **species of different kinds**,[272]

בִּרְצוֹתִי אֶזְרַע מִין אֶחָד, אוֹ מִינִים מִמִּינִים שׁוֹנִים,[272]

It is in my power to make it like **the field of a slothful man**,[273] **neither pruned nor weeded**[274]

בְּיָדִי לַעֲשׂוֹתוֹ כִּשְׂדֵה אִישׁ עָצֵל,[273] **לֹא יִזָּמֵר, לֹא יֵעָדֵר**[274]

Or like the garden of an industrious man full of blessed fruit,

אוֹ כְּגַן אִישׁ חָרוּץ מָלֵא פְּרִי בְרָכָה,

All these come into being in accordance with my desire, which is ruler over everything.

כָּל אֵלֶּה תִּהְיֶינָה לְפִי רְצוֹנִי הַשַּׁלִּיט בַּכֹּל.

If you ponder the way of life[275] and there is no sense on the scale

אֹרַח חַיִּים אִם תְּפַלֵּס[275] וְאֵין שֵׂכֶל בְּכַף הַמֹּאזְנַיִם

To outweigh the scale[276] full of desire and lusts

לְהַכְרִיעַ אֶת הַכָּף[276] הַמְּלֵאָה תַאֲוָה וַעֲגָבִים

Who could stand up against **the inclination of the heart, which is evil from one's youth**![277]

מִי יַעֲמֹד לִפְנֵי יֵצֶר הַלֵּב הָרַע מִנְּעוּרָיו![277]

But indeed, our sense is with us, and the strength is in our hands

אָכֵן שִׂכְלֵנוּ אִתָּנוּ וְהַכֹּחַ בְּיָדֵינוּ הוּא

271 Josh. 5:1 וְלֹא־הָיָה בָם עוֹד רוּחַ 'and they had no more spirit'; 1 Kings 10:5 וְלֹא־הָיָה בָהּ עוֹד רוּחַ 'and she had no more spirit'.

272 Abarbanel to 1 Kings 11.

273 Prov. 24:30.

274 Isa. 5:6 לֹא יִזָּמֵר וְלֹא יֵעָדֵר 'neither pruned nor weeded'.

275 Prov. 5:6 אֹרַח חַיִּים פֶּן־תְּפַלֵּס 'lest you (or: she) ponder the way of life'.

276 Mishnah *Avot* 2:9 אם יהיו כל חכמי ישראל בכף מאזנים ורבי אליעזר בן הרקנוס בכף שניה מכריע את כולם 'if all the sages of Israel were in one pan of a scale and Eliezer ben Hyrcanus were in the other, he would outweigh them all'.

277 Gen. 8:21 יֵצֶר לֵב הָאָדָם רַע מִנְּעֻרָיו 'the inclination of man's heart is evil from his youth'.

	To put out the fire of lust and the desire of **the life of the flesh**.[278]	לְכַבּוֹת אֵשׁ הַתְּשׁוּקָה וְתַאֲוַת חַיֵּי בְּשָׂרִים.[278]	
	And therefore the desire in your heart, which you have called by the name of love	וְלָכֵן חֵשֶׁק לִבֵּךְ, אֲשֶׁר בְּשֵׁם אַהֲבָה קָרָאתָ	
	Is an alien branch in your garden **and a foreign vine**.[279]	סְעִיף נֵכָר הוּא בְּגַנְּךָ וּזְמֹרַת זָר.[279]	
RADDAI	God forbid, do not say such a thing.	חָלִלָה, אַל תֹּאמַר כֵּן.	רדי
DOEG	The soul of desire is in the blood, and the will can rule over it;	נֶפֶשׁ הַתַּאֲוָה בַּדָּם הִיא וְהָרָצוֹן יִמְשָׁל בָּהּ,	דואג
	Arise, be a man, and do not chatter like a fool	קוּמָה הֱיֵה לְאִישׁ וְאַל תְּבַטֵּא כַּסָּכָל	
	About destroying yourself with your hands; throw **vermin and mice**[280] in the water	לְאַבֵּד נַפְשְׁךָ בְּיָדַיִם; הַשְׁלֵךְ שֶׁקֶץ וְעַכְבָּר[280] בַּמָּיִם	
	Or puppies, puppies without eyes.	אוֹ יַלְדֵי כְלָבִים, יְלָדִים בְּלִי עֵינָיִם.	
	As for me, my soul is tied to you by unbreakable bonds	וַאֲנִי נַפְשִׁי קְשׁוּרָה בְךָ בַּעֲבוֹתוֹת לֹא יִנָּתֵקוּ	
	And now the time has come to help you with my love.	וְעַתָּה בָּא הַמּוֹעֵד לְהוֹעִיל לְךָ בְּאַהֲבָתִי.	
	Put money in your purse and go after the army of war,	שִׂים כֶּסֶף בְּכִיסְךָ וְלֵךְ אַחֲרֵי צְבָא הַמִּלְחָמָה,	
	Disguise yourself with a long beard and do not forget your bag of money;	הִתְחַפֵּשׂ בְּזָקָן אָרוּךְ וְאַל תִּשְׁכַּח צְרוֹר כַּסְפְּךָ,	
	Indeed, Asenath will not love the Cushite for long,	הֵן לֹא לְאֹרֶךְ יָמִים, תֶּאֱהַב אָסְנַת אֶת הַכּוּשִׁי	
	Therefore put money in your purse – and he will not love her forever	לָכֵן שִׂים כֶּסֶף בְּכִיסֶךָ – וְהוּא לֹא יֶאֱהָבֶנָּה לָעַד	
	A love that is hasty at its beginning soon reaches its end.	אַהֲבָה מְבֹהֶלֶת בְּרֵאשִׁיתָהּ קְרוֹבָה לָבוֹא אַחֲרִיתָהּ.	
	And therefore, just put the **money in the mouth of your sack**[281]	וְלָכֵן אַךְ אֶת הַכֶּסֶף תָּשִׂים בְּפִי אַמְתַּחְתֶּךָ[281]	

278 Prov. 14:30.

279 Isa. 17:10.

280 Isa. 66:17 וְהַשֶּׁקֶץ וְהָעַכְבָּר 'and the vermin and the mice'.

281 Gen. 42:27 וַיַּרְא אֶת־כַּסְפּוֹ וְהִנֵּה־הוּא בְּפִי אַמְתַּחְתּוֹ 'and he saw that his money was at the mouth of his sack'; see also Gen. 43:21 for a similar phrasing.

Indeed the Cushites change the desire of their hearts like clothing	הֲלֹא בְנֵי הַכּוּשִׁיִּים כַּלְּבוּשׁ יַחֲלִיפוּ חֵשֶׁק לִבָּם
So therefore, fill your sack with money.	וַאֲשֶׁר לְזֹאת אֵיפוֹ, מַלֵּא אַמְתַּחְתְּךָ כָּסֶף.
The food which is as sweet to him today as **pure honey**[282]	הָאֹכֶל אֲשֶׁר יִמְתַּק לוֹ הַיּוֹם כְּנֹפֶת **צוּפִים**[282]
Will be as bitter to him tomorrow as the **venom of asps**.[283]	יֵמַר לוֹ לְמָחֳרָתוֹ כְּמוֹ **רֹאשׁ פְּתָנִים**.[283]
And moreover, she is tender in years; she will desire a change and replacements	וְגַם הִיא רַכָּה בְשָׁנִים, תִּתְאַו לִתְמוּרָה וַחֲלִיפוֹת
When she has had her fill of his flesh, she will recognize her mistake	כַּאֲשֶׁר תִּשְׂבַּע מִבְּשָׂרוֹ כֵּן תַּכִּיר שִׁגְגָתָהּ
And she will set her sights on a change, and her change will surely come;	וְלִתְמוּרָה תָּשִׂים עֵינֶיהָ וּתְמוּרָתָהּ בּוֹא תָבוֹא,
Therefore I say to you, prepare your bag of money.	לָכֵן אָמַרְתִּי אֵלֶיךָ הָכֵן לְךָ צְרוֹר כַּסְפֶּךָ.
But if you want to send your soul down to the land of the dead	וְאִם חָפֵץ אַתָּה לְהוֹרִיד נַפְשְׁךָ לַאֲבַדּוֹן
Choose for yourself **the death of the righteous**,[284] and do not descend into the depths	בְּחַר לְךָ מוֹת יְשָׁרִים[284] וּבַמְּצוּלָה אַל תֵּרֵד
Arise, collect all the money that you have to hand.	קוּם לְקֹט כָּל הַכֶּסֶף הַנִּמְצָא תַּחַת יָדֶךָ.
Behold, my hand is stretched out and the whole **assembly of the dead**[285] is with me	הֵן יָדִי נְטוּיָה וְכָל קְהַל הָרְפָאִים[285] עִמִּי
To nullify the link between this foreign **sojourner**[286]	לְהָפֵר אֶת הַקֶּשֶׁר בֵּין הַגֵּר[286] הַלּוֹעֵז הַזֶּה

282 Ps. 19:11 (19:10 in English Bibles). It is unclear whether Salkinson chose this translation in order to avoid the non-kosher connotations of the original 'locusts' (1.3.349), or because he was aware of the interpretation according to which the English term refers to the sweet juice of the carob (see Honigmann 1997: 157, note 349; Crystal and Crystal 2002: 266).

283 Deut. 32:33; Job 20:16; פְּתָנִים is sometimes translated as 'cobras' or 'vipers'.

284 Num. 23:10.

285 Prov. 21:16.

286 Cf. Shakespeare's 'Barbarian' (1.3.356). In the Hebrew Bible this term denotes a resident foreigner in Israelite territory (Lieber 2007). Conversely, in rabbinic and later Jewish literature, as well as in Yiddish, it refers to a convert to Judaism (Rabinowitz and Eichhorn 2007). As Salkinson's readers would have been familiar with both meanings of the word, the translation can be understood on two levels: Ithiel is at once a foreigner residing in Venice, and a convert to a different religion, which echoes Othello's implied conversion to Christianity in the original text. See *Ram and Jael*, First Part, note 340 for a similar use of this word.

	And that **deceitful soul,**[287] the beautiful daughter of Venice	וּבֵין נֶפֶשׁ רְמִיָּה[287] זֹאת בַּת וִינֶעצְיָא הַיָּפָה	
	And if my **power is not gone,**[288] **you will go in to her and be her husband**[289]	וְאִם לֹא אָזְלַת יָדִי,[288] תָּבוֹא אֵלֶיהָ וּבְעַלְתָּהּ[289]	
	Therefore, prepare your money – and let your plan to drown in the river	לָכֵן הָכֵן לְךָ כַּסְפְּךָ – וַעֲצָתְךָ לִטְבֹּעַ בַּנָּהָר	
	Become **a bane and a curse,**[290] for this is not a good plan.	תְּהִי לִמְאֵרָה וְלִקְלָלָה,[290] כִּי זוּ עֵצָה לֹא טוֹבָה.	
	It is better for you to be hanged in peace and honour on a tree	טוֹב לְךָ לְהִתָּלוֹת בְּשָׁלוֹם וּבְכָבוֹד עַל הָעֵץ	
	After you have drunk your fill of **stolen water**[291]	אַחֲרֵי אֲשֶׁר שָׁתִיתָ מִמַּיִם גְּנוּבִים[291] לִרְוָיָה	
	Than to go die in the depths before you have tasted a thing.	מִלֶּכֶת לִגְוֹעַ בִּמְצוּלָה טֶרֶם טָעַמְתָּ דָּבָר.	
RADDAI	If I do as you say	אִם אֶעֱשֶׂה כִדְבָרְךָ	רדי
	Will you stand at my right-hand side to grant me my desires **when there is a chance?**[292]	הֲתַעֲמֹד לִימִינִי לְהָפִיק מַאֲוַיַּי לְעֵת מְצוֹא?[292]	
DOEG	**Let your heart be firm because you trust in me.**[293]	יְהִי נָכוֹן לִבְּךָ כִּי בִי בָטוּחַ.[293]	דואג
	Go and gather up all the money that you have to hand; why, I have already told you	לֵךְ וְצַרְתָּ הַכֶּסֶף בְּיָדְךָ; הֵן כְּבָר הִגַּדְתִּי	
	And I shall tell you a second time and a third time that **with absolute hatred**	וְעוֹד אֶשְׁנֶה אֲשַׁלֵּשׁ לְהַגִּידְךָ, כִּי תַכְלִית שִׂנְאָה	
	I **hate the Cushite,**[294] and I do not hate him **for nothing**[295]	שָׂנֵאתִי אֶת הַכּוּשִׁי[294] וְלֹא עַל חִנָּם[295] שְׂנֵאתִיו	

287 Prov. 19:15; in the biblical verse the word רְמִיָּה is translated as 'idle', but in Salkinson's text it has the meaning of 'deceitful', which corresponds to Shakespeare's 'super-subtle' (1.3.357, used in the sense of 'crafty'; see Honigmann 1997: 158, note 357). This latter meaning of רְמִיָּה is attested in a different collocation in Mic. 6:12 (Koehler and Baumgartner 2001, 2: 1243–4) and is also standard in later forms of Hebrew.

288 Deut. 32:36 אָזְלַת יָד '[their] strength is gone'.

289 Deut. 21:13.

290 Abarbanel to Numbers 5 מארה וקללה 'a bane and a curse'.

291 Prov. 9:17.

292 Ps. 32:6.

293 Ps. 112:7 נָכוֹן לִבּוֹ בָּטֻחַ בַּיהוָה 'his heart is steadfast, trusting in the Lord'.

294 Ps. 139: 22 תַּכְלִית שִׂנְאָה שְׂנֵאתִים 'I hate them with absolute hatred'.

295 This collocation is first attested in rabbinic literature; for example, Babylonian Talmud *Sanhedrin* 22b.

Just like your hatred, **the root of the matter is found for it**[296] as well

כַּאֲשֶׁר גַּם שִׂנְאָתְךָ שֹׁרֶשׁ דָּבָר נִמְצָא בָהּ.[296]

Come, let us take counsel together in order to exact revenge upon him;

לְכָה וְנִוָּעֲצָה יַחְדָּו לַעֲשׂוֹת נְקָמָה בוֹ,

If you **desecrate his bed**,[297] you will be pleased and I shall laugh.

כִּי תְחַלֵּל יְצוּעוֹ,[297] יִנְעַם לְךָ וַאֲנִי אֶשְׂחָק

And who else then **knows what the day will bring**.[298]

וּמִי אֵיפוֹ יוֹדֵעַ עוֹד, מַה־יֵּלֶד יוֹם.[298]

For much counsel runs this way and that

כִּי תַחְבּוּלוֹת רַבּוֹת כָּהֵנָּה וְכָהֵנָּה מִתְרֹצְצוֹת

Until it emerges from the womb when the days of conception are complete.

עַד תֵּצֶאנָה מֵרֶחֶם בִּמְלֹאת יְמֵי הַהֵרָיוֹן.

Go and prepare your money, and tomorrow we shall speak further.

לְכָה וְהָכֵן כַּסְפְּךָ וּלְמָחָר נוֹסִיף לְדַבֵּר עוֹד.

RADDAI Where shall we see each other tomorrow?

רדי אָנָה נִרְאֶה אִישׁ אֶת רֵעֵהוּ לְמָחָר?

DOEG At my house.

דואג בְּבֵיתִי.

RADDAI Early in the morning I shall come to see you.

רדי בַּבֹּקֶר הַשְׁכֵּם אָבוֹא לִרְאוֹתֶךָ.

DOEG Go in peace – do you hear me, Raddai?

דואג לֵךְ לְשָׁלוֹם – הַאִם שְׁמַעְתַּנִי רַדָּי?

RADDAI What do you ask of me?

רדי מַה־תְּבַקֵּשׁ מִיָּדִי?

DOEG Do not talk further of drowning in the river – do you hear?

דואג אַל תֹּאמַר עוֹד לִטְבֹּעַ בַּנָּהָר – הֲשׁוֹמֵעַ אָתָּה?

RADDAI **My heart is turned within me**;[299] I shall sell **the field of my possession**.[300]

רדי נֶהְפַּךְ לִבִּי בְּקִרְבִּי[299] הִנְנִי לִמְכֹּר שְׂדֵה אֲחֻזָּתִי.[300]

DOEG Go in peace! Put enough money in your purse. *(Raddai exits)*

דואג לֵךְ לְשָׁלוֹם! שִׂים דֵּי כֶסֶף בְּכִיסֶךָ. (רדי הולך)

---

296 Job 19:28 וְשֹׁרֶשׁ דָּבָר נִמְצָא־בִי 'and the root of the matter is found in me'.
297 1 Chron. 5:1 וּבְחַלְּלוֹ יְצוּעֵי אָבִיו 'and when he defiled his father's bed' (referring to Jacob's son Reuben, who slept with his father's concubine).
298 Prov. 27:1 כִּי לֹא־תֵדַע מַה־יֵּלֶד יוֹם 'for you do not know what the day will bring'.
299 Lam. 1:20.
300 Lev. 27:16, 22, 28 מִשְּׂדֵה אֲחֻזָּתוֹ 'of the field of his possession'.

Thus I shall find for myself a bag of money, by means of this **senseless man**[301]

כֵּן אֶמְצָא לִי צְרוֹר כֶּסֶף, בְּכַנְפֵי אִישׁ בַּעַר[301] זֶה

For it would be a disgrace for a shrewd man like me to waste pleasant words

כִּי חֶרְפָּה לְעָרוּם כָּמוֹנִי לְהַשְׁחִית דְּבָרִים נֶחֱמָדִים

In the ears of a fool like him, if not for profit and amusement.

בְּאָזְנֵי כְסִיל כָּמוֹהוּ, אִם לֹא לְיִתְרוֹן וְשַׁעֲשֻׁעִים.

And I hate the Cushite, and many even say

וַאֲנִי שׂוֹנֵא אֶת הַכּוּשִׁי וּמַה־גַּם כִּי רַבִּים אֹמְרִים

That he has gone up on my bed; and even though I do not know

כִּי עַל יְצוּעִי עָלָה; וְאַף כִּי לֹא אֵדָע

Whether the matter is indeed true, nevertheless I shall recompense him

אִם אֱמֶת נָכוֹן הַדָּבָר, בְּכָל זֹאת אֶגְמֹל עָלָיו

Solely **for what my ears have heard**,[302] as if I had seen it with my eyes.

לְמִשְׁמַע אָזְנַי[302] לְבַד, כְּמוֹ אִם רָאִיתִי בְּעֵינָי.

And because of his great trust in my faithfulness, as quick as lightning he will fall into my hunting-net

וּמֵרֹב בִּטְחוֹנוֹ בֶּאֱמוּנָתִי, חִישׁ קַל יִפֹּל בִּמְצוּדָתִי

And Chesed is the man who will be like a desired tool in my hand;

וְכֶשֶׂד הוּא הָאִישׁ אֲשֶׁר יִהְיֶה כִּכְלִי חֵפֶץ בְּיָדִי;

But how **will he be of profit to me**[303] if not to dispossess him

אַךְ בַּמֶּה יִסְכָּן־לִי[303] אִם לֹא לְהוֹרִישׁוֹ

In order to take his office and satiate my eye with vengeance

לְמַעַן קַחַת פְּקוּדָתוֹ וּלְהַשְׂבִּיעַ עֵינִי נְקָמָה

Because with a desired tool like him I shall carry out a double act of deceit.

כִּי בִכְלִי חֵפֶץ כָּמוֹהוּ אֲבַצַּע מִרְמָה אַחַת כִּפְלָיִם.

But how will the deceit succeed? Desist – I shall ponder the matter

אַךְ אֵיךְ תִּצְלַח הַמִּרְמָה? הֶרֶף – אֶתְבּוֹנֵן בַּדָּבָר

In several days, I shall report him to the Cushite's ears, saying

כַּעֲבֹר יָמִים אֲחָדִים, אַלְשִׁינוֹ בְּאָזְנֵי הַכּוּשִׁי לֵאמֹר

That **I saw him sporting with the lady Asenath**[304]

כִּי רְאִיתִיו מְצַחֵק אֶת אָסְנַת הַגְּבִירָה[304]

---

301 Ps. 92:7 (92:6 in English Bibles).

302 Isa. 11:3 וְלֹא־לְמִשְׁמַע אָזְנָיו 'and not by what his ears hear'.

303 Job 35:3 מַה־יִּסְכָּן־לָךְ 'what profit is it to you'.

304 Gen. 26:8 וַיַּרְא וְהִנֵּה יִצְחָק מְצַחֵק אֵת רִבְקָה אִשְׁתּוֹ 'and he saw Isaac sporting with his wife Rebecca'.

And the spirit of jealousy will come upon him,[305] thinking that his wife has strayed

וַעֲבָרוֹ רוּחַ קִנְאָה[305] לַחֲשֹׁב כִּי שָׂטְתָה אִשְׁתּוֹ

For **her soul desired the officer,**[306] a man with **a flattering tongue**[307] and lips

כִּי חָשְׁקָה נַפְשָׁהּ בַּפָּקִיד,[306] אִישׁ מַחֲלִיק לָשׁוֹן[307] וּשְׂפָתָיִם

As he is also **handsome in form and appearance.**[308]

בַּאֲשֶׁר גַּם יְפֵה תֹאַר וִיפֵה מַרְאֶה[308] הוּא.

And the Cushite in his innocence will not recognize my cunning

וְהַכּוּשִׁי בְּתָם־לִבּוֹ, אֶת עָרְמָתִי לֹא יַכִּיר

For he considers me to be faithful, as I appear in his eyes

כִּי לְנֶאֱמָן יַחְשְׁבֵנִי, כַּאֲשֶׁר נִרְאָה אֲנִי לְעֵינָיו

And he will go where I lead him, like an ass pulled by the bridle.

וְאֶל אֲשֶׁר אוֹלִיכֶנּוּ יֵלֵךְ, כַּחֲמוֹר הַנִּמְשָׁךְ בְּמֶתֶג.

Aha! Just now, I have conceived a sin in the world,[309]

הֶאָח! זֶה עַתָּה, הָרִיתִי אָוֶן בְּחָלֶד[309]

And Sheol and the darkness answer: behold, evil is born.

וּשְׁאוֹל וְצַלְמָוֶת יַעֲנוּ: הִנֵּה עָמָל יוּלָּד.

(Exits)

(הולך)

End of First Part.

תם חלק ראשון.

305 Num. 5:14 וְעָבַר עָלָיו רוּחַ־קִנְאָה 'and the spirit of jealousy comes upon him'; see also Num. 5:30.
306 Gen. 34:8 חָשְׁקָה נַפְשׁוֹ בְּבִתְּכֶם 'his soul desires your daughter'.
307 Prov. 28:23.
308 Gen. 39:6 וַיְהִי יוֹסֵף יְפֵה־תֹאַר וִיפֵה מַרְאֶה 'and Joseph was handsome in form and appearance'.
309 This and the following line form a rhyming couplet, mirroring Shakespeare's 'night/light' (1.3.402–3).

Second Part

חלק שני

SCENE I	*A town by the seashore on Caphtor Stage overlooking the courtyard (Kenaz and two men)*	עיר על חוף הים בכפתור במה על פני החצר (קנז ושני אנשים)	מחזה א'
KENAZ	What do you see there on the face of the sea?	מָה אַתֶּם רֹאִים שָׁם עַל פְּנֵי הַיָּם?	קנז
MAN I	I see nothing except the **breakers of the stormy sea**[1]	אֵינֶנִּי רֹאֶה מְאוּמָה בִּלְתִּי מִשְׁבְּרֵי יָם סֹעֵר[1]	איש א'
	And there is no mast or ship between the heavens and the depths.	וְאֵין תֹּרֶן וּסְפִינָה בֵּין שָׁמַיִם לִתְהוֹם.	
KENAZ	The storm is growing stronger over the dry land	הַסַּעַר הוֹלֵךְ הָלוֹךְ וְחָזֵק עַל פְּנֵי הַיַּבָּשָׁה	קנז
	Because of it towers are trembling, **rampart and wall**[2] are quaking	מִפָּנָיו יָחִילוּ מִגְדָּלִים חֵל וָחוֹמָה[2] יִתְגָּעֲשׁוּ	
	And if it whirls over the sea every mast will break	וְאִם יִתְחוֹלֵל עַל הַיָּם יִשָּׁבֵר כָּל תֹּרֶן	
	The strength of oak will not withstand it and the ships will split apart	חֹסֶן אַלּוֹנִים לֹא יַעֲמֹד וְהַסְּפִינוֹת תִּתְבַּקַּעְנָה	
	From **the mass of great water**[3] that rises and falls like mountains	מֵחֹמֶר מַיִם אַדִּירִים[3] הָעֹלִים וְנֹפְלִים כֶּהָרִים	
	But what report is heard of the Turks' ships?	וּמַה־שְּׁמוּעָה נִשְׁמַע מִן אֳנִיּוֹת הַתּוֹגַרְמִים?	
MAN 2	That they have been broken in the heart of the sea and the Turks are no more.	כִּי נִשְׁבְּרוּ בְּלֵב הַיָּם וְהַתּוֹגַרְמִים עוֹד אֵינָם.	איש ב'
	Stand here on the shore whose face is white with foam	עֲמֹד פֹּה עַל הַחוֹף אֲשֶׁר פָּנָיו יַלְבִּינוּ מִקֶּצֶף	
	And look at the depths which are throwing their waters up to the clouds	וּרְאֵה אֶת הַתְּהוֹם הַזֹּרֵק מֵימָיו עַד הֶעָבִים	
	And its waves are rising to the heavens to extinguish **the Pleiades and Orion**[4]	וְגַלָּיו יַעֲלוּ שָׁמַיִם לְכַבּוֹת כִּימָה וּכְסִיל[4]	

---

1 Ps. 93:4.
2 Lam. 2:8.
3 Hab. 3:15 חֹמֶר מַיִם רַבִּים 'a mass of great waters'.
4 Amos 5:8.

	And **the Bear with its cubs**[5] and all of the constellations of the heavens	וְעַיִשׁ עַל בָּנֶיהָ[5] עִם כָּל מַזָּרוֹת שְׁחָקִים	
	Such a raging sea as this my eye has never seen.	יָם זֹעֵף כָּזֶה מֵעוֹדִי לֹא רָאֲתָה עֵינִי.	
KENAZ	The Turks' ships have sunk if they have not reached the shore	אֳנִיּוֹת הַתּוֹגַרְמִים טָבְעוּ אִם לֹא הִגִּיעוּ לַחוֹף	קנז
	For who could withstand such **a storm and tempest**.[6]	כִּי מִי יַעֲמֹד לִפְנֵי סוּפָה וּסְעָרָה[6] כָּזֹאת.	
	(A third man enters)	(איש שלישי בא)	
MAN 3	There are good tidings in my mouth; we are no longer at war	בְּשׂרָה טוֹבָה בְּפִי, מִלְחָמָה אֵין לָנוּ עוֹד	איש ג'
	The storm struck the Turks and foiled their plan	הַסַּעַר נָגַע בַּתּוֹגַרְמִים וַיְסַכֵּל אֶת עֲצָתָם	
	The men on the ship from Venice saw their calamity from afar	אַנְשֵׁי הַסְפִינָה מִוִּינֶעצְיָא רָאוּ אֵידָם מֵרָחוֹק	
	For they were smashed to pieces in the storm and most of their ships were broken.	כִּי הִתְפַּצְּצוּ בַּסְּעָרָה וְרֹב אֳנִיּוֹתָם נִשְׁבָּרוּ.	
KENAZ	What are you telling us?	מָה הִגַּדְתָּ לָנוּ?	קנז
MAN 3	The ship stands at the shore and Chesed has come up from within it,	הַסְּפִינָה עֹמֶדֶת בַּחוֹף וְכֶשֶׂד עָלָה מִתּוֹכָהּ,	איש ג'
	He is the officer of Ithiel the Cushite, **a mighty man of valour**[7]	הוּא הַפָּקִיד לְאִיתִיאֵל הַכּוּשִׁי, **אִישׁ גִּבּוֹר חָיִל**[7]	
	And he is also crossing over the sea, to come to us, to Caphtor	וְגַם הוּא עֹבֵר בַּיָּם, לָבוֹא אֵלֵינוּ לְכַפְתּוֹר	
	For the Prince has sent him, to become leader here.	כִּי שְׁלָחוֹ הַנָּשִׂיא, לִהְיוֹת פֹּה לְרֹאשׁ.	
KENAZ	You have brought me a good report, for the man is very honourable.	שְׁמוּעָה טוֹבָה הִשְׁמַעְתַּנִי, כִּי נִכְבָּד הָאִישׁ מְאֹד.	קנז
MAN 3	But that Chesed, who told us of the destruction of the Turks	אֲבָל כֶּשֶׂד הַהוּא, הַמַּגִּיד לָנוּ שֶׁבֶר הַתּוֹגַרְמִים	איש ג'
	Is distressed about the Cushite lest a disaster befall him	נֶעֱצָב אֶל הַכּוּשִׁי פֶּן יִקְרֶנּוּ אָסוֹן	
	Since he was separated from him in a great storm.	אַחֲרֵי אֲשֶׁר נִפְרַד מִמֶּנּוּ בִּסְעָרָה גְּדוֹלָה.	

5 Job 38:32.
6 Isa. 29:6.
7 Ruth 2:1.

KENAZ	If only the LORD would protect him from every woe.	אַחֲלַי לִפְנֵי הַשֵּׁם כִּי יִשְׁמְרֵהוּ מִכָּל צָרָה.	קנז
	I served in the army under the standard of this warrior,	אָנֹכִי עָבַדְתִּי בַּצָּבָא עַל דֶּגֶל הַגִּבּוֹר הַזֶּה,	
	He is very great in strength and commands like a man of war.	כַּבִּיר כֹּחַ הוּא מְאֹד וּמְפַקֵּד כְּאִישׁ מִלְחָמָה.	
	But let us all go see the men of the ship	אַךְ נֵלְכָה נָּא כֻּלָּנוּ לִרְאוֹת אֶת אַנְשֵׁי הַסְּפִינָה	
	On the seashore, and let our eyes look out for the Cushite's ship	עַל שְׂפַת הַיָּם וְעֵינֵינוּ תְּצַפֶּינָה לְצִי הַכּוּשִׁי	
	For we shall not leave there until we can no longer distinguish	כִּי לֹא נָמוּשׁ מִשָּׁם עַד לֹא נַכִּיר עוֹד	
	Between the blue hue of the sky and the hue of the sea's surface.	בֵּין עֵין תְּכֵלֶת הָרָקִיעַ וּבֵין עֵין פְּנֵי הַיָּם.	
MAN 3	Come, let us go	לְכוּ וְנֵלְכָה	איש ג'
	For new faces are soon to arrive.	כִּי פָנִים חֲדָשִׁים לִרְגָעִים יָבוֹאוּ.	
CHESED	Please take my blessing, men of valour who inhabit the island!	קְחוּ נָא בִרְכָתִי, אַנְשֵׁי הַחַיִל יוֹשְׁבֵי הָאִי!	כשד
	For you have spoken well regarding Ithiel the Cushite	כִּי דִבַּרְתֶּם טוֹב עַל אִיתִיאֵל הַכּוּשִׁי	
	And I raise my eyes to God Most High, that He might protect him from upheavals and accidents	וַאֲנִי עֵינַי לְאֵל עֶלְיוֹן כִּי יִשְׁמְרֵהוּ מֵרַעַשׁ וָפֶגַע	
	For I was separated from him in the heart of a most raging sea.	כִּי נִפְרַדְתִּי מִמֶּנּוּ בְּלֵב יָם זוֹעֵף מְאֹד.	
KENAZ	Is his ship good and strong?	הַאִם אֳנִיָּתוֹ טוֹבָה וַחֲזָקָה?	קנז
CHESED	Its planks are cedar and oak, and the oarsmen and captain	לוּחוֹתֶיהָ בְּרוֹשִׁים וְאַלּוֹנִים, וְהַשָּׁטִים וְרַב הַחֹבֵל	כשד
	Are all wise and experienced in dealing with great waters.	כֻּלָּם נְבוֹנִים מְלֻמְּדֵי מְלָאכָה בְּמַיִם רַבִּים	
	Therefore I have not lost hope that he will indeed arrive safely.	לָכֵן לֹא אָבְדָה תִקְוָתִי כִּי בוֹא יָבוֹא בְּשָׁלוֹם.	
	(A voice from outside, Ship coming, ship!*)*	(קול מחוץ, אֳנִיָּה בָּאָה, אֳנִיָּה!)	
	(A fourth man enters)	(איש רביעי בא)	
CHESED	What is this voice?	מָה הַקּוֹל הַזֶּה?	כשד

MAN 4	**The town is abandoned**[8] and empty, and a crowd of many people	הָעִיר עֲזוּבָה[8] וְרֵיקָה וְהָמוֹן אֲנָשִׁים רַבִּים	איש ד'
	Is standing on the seashore and shouting, 'ship, ship'.	עֹמְדִים עַל שְׂפַת הַיָּם וּמְרִיעִים אֳנִיָּה אֳנִיָּה.	
CHESED	Perhaps the army commander is arriving, for I have waited for him.	אוּלַי בָּא שַׂר הַצָּבָא כִּי קִוִּיתִי לוֹ.	כשד
	(Sound of cannons)	(קול כלי המורים)	
MAN 2	Behold, the sound of the cannons to welcome him with honour	הִנֵּה קוֹל כְּלֵי הַמּוֹרִים לְקַדֵּם פָּנָיו בְּכָבוֹד	איש ב'
	And if he is not there, it is our allies who are coming.	וְאִם הוּא אֵינֶנּוּ שָׁם, בַּעֲלֵי בְרִיתֵנוּ הֵם הַבָּאִים.	
CHESED	Go see and tell us who the ones coming are.	לֵךְ רְאֵה וְהַגֵּד לָנוּ מִי הֵמָּה הַבָּאִים?	כשד
MAN 2	I am your servant. *(Exits)*	הִנְנִי עַבְדֶּךָ. (הולך)	איש ב'
KENAZ	Tell me officer, is your master married?	הַגֵּד לִי הַפָּקִיד, אִם אֲדֹנְךָ בַּעַל אִשָּׁה הוּא?	קנז
CHESED	He found a good woman whose **graceful proportion**[9] is beyond description	הוּא מָצָא אִשָּׁה טוֹבָה חִין עֶרְכָּהּ[9] אֵין לְמַלֵּל	כשד
	And **the pen of a scribe**[10] is not enough to praise **her splendour and majesty,**[11]	וּלְהַלֵּל הוֹדָהּ וַהֲדָרָהּ[10] עֵט סֹפֵר[11] אֵין דָּי,	
	She is unique among women, there is none like her **among the daughters of the land**[12]	אַחַת הִיא בַּנָּשִׁים בִּבְנוֹת הָאָרֶץ[12] אֵין כָּמוֹהָ.	
	(To man 2 as he reenters) Who is coming there in the ship?	(אל איש ב' בשובו) מִי בָא שָׁם בָּאֳנִיָּה?	
MAN 2	A man called Doeg, the army commander's standard-bearer.	אִישׁ דּוֹאֵג שְׁמוֹ, נוֹשֵׂא הַדֶּגֶל לְשַׂר הַצָּבָא.	איש ב'
CHESED	He set out on his way beforehand and has succeeded in arriving safely.	הוּא הִקְדִּים* לַעֲשׂוֹת דַּרְכּוֹ וַיַּצְלִיחַ לָבוֹא בְשָׁלוֹם.	כשד

8 Jer. 4:29 כָּל־הָעִיר עֲזוּבָה 'each town is abandoned'.
9 Job 41:4 (41:12 in English Bibles) וְחִין עֶרְכּוֹ 'and his graceful proportion' (referring to the mythological sea creature Leviathan).
10 Ps. 45:2 (45:1 in English Bibles).
11 Ps. 45:4 הוֹדְךָ וַהֲדָרֶךָ 'Your splendour and majesty'; Ps. 21:6 הוֹד וְהָדָר 'splendour and majesty', also Ps. 96:6, 104:1, 111:3; Job 40:10; 1 Chron. 16:27.
12 Gen. 34: 1.

* הִקְדִּים

	A storm wind,[13] a raging sea, and a great upheaval	גַּם רוּחַ סְעָרָה[13] יָם זֹעֵף וְרַעַשׁ גָּדוֹל	
	Teeth of rock, cliffs, and heaps of sand and mud	שִׁנֵּי סְלָעִים מְצוּקִים וַעֲרֵמוֹת חוֹל וָרֶפֶשׁ	
	That lie in wait to hunt ships, have all forgotten to lay waste this time	הָאוֹרְבִים לָצוּד אֳנִיּוֹת, שָׁכְחוּ לְהַשְׁחִית הַפַּעַם	
	Because they had mercy on a beautiful woman of good judgement	כִּי נָשְׂאוּ פָנִים לְאִשָּׁה יָפָה טוֹבַת טָעַם	
	And they let the happy Asenath pass safely.	וַיָּנִיחוּ לַעֲבֹר בְּשָׁלוֹם אֶת אָסְנַת הַמְאֻשָּׁרָה.	
KENAZ	Who is this Asenath?	מִי אָסְנַת הַזֹּאת?	קנז
CHESED	She is the woman whom I mentioned, **a crown for the Cushite's head**[14]	הִיא הָאִשָּׁה אֲשֶׁר אָמַרְתִּי, עֲטֶרֶת לְרֹאשׁ הַכּוּשִׁי[14]	כשד
	And who was given to Doeg for him to bring her here	וַאֲשֶׁר נִתְּנָה עַל יַד דּוֹאֵג לַהֲבִיאָהּ הֲלֹם	
	And he came quickly, a week before I imagined.	וְהוּא מִהֵר לָבוֹא שָׁבוּעַ בְּטֶרֶם אֲשֶׁר דִּמִּיתִי.	
	God of the sea and the dry land![15] Grant **the shield of Your salvation**[16] to Ithiel	אֱלֹהֵי הַיָּם וְהַיַּבָּשָׁה![15] תְּנָה מָגֵן יִשְׁעֲךָ[16] לְאִיתִיאֵל	
	And with the spirit of Your noble breath guide his ship safely	וּבְנִשְׁמַת רוּחֲךָ הַנְּדִיבָה נְחֵה אֶת אֳנִיָּתוֹ בְּשָׁלוֹם	
	So that he arrives at the port, **at this desired haven of his**[17]	לְמַעַן יַגִּיעַ לְחוֹף אֳנִיּוֹת,לִמְחוֹז חֶפְצוֹ[17] הַזֶּה	
	To embrace the bosom of his beloved, to enjoy himself with his wife Asenath	לְחַבֵּק חֵיק אֲהוּבָתוֹ, לְהִתְעַלֵּס בְּאָסְנַת אִשְׁתּוֹ	
	And to restore the breath of life to all of us, **for our soul has sunk down into the dust**[18]	וּלְהָשִׁיב רוּחַ חַיִּים לְכֻלָּנוּ, כִּי שָׁחָה לֶעָפָר נַפְשֵׁנוּ[18]	
	And to be a sign of blessing to all inhabitants of this island.	וְלִהְיוֹת לְאוֹת בְּרָכָה, לְכָל יוֹשְׁבֵי הָאִי הַזֶּה.	

13 Ezek. 1:4; Ps. 107:25, 148:8.
14 Prov. 12:4 אֵשֶׁת־חַיִל עֲטֶרֶת בַּעְלָהּ 'a woman of valour is her husband's crown'.
15 Cf. Shakespeare's 'great Jove' (2.1.77); Salkinson has replaced the reference to a Classical deity with one to the monotheistic God.
16 2 Sam. 22:36; Ps. 18:36 (18:35 in English Bibles).
17 Ps. 107:30 אֶל־מְחוֹז חֶפְצָם 'to their desired haven'.
18 Ps. 44:26 (44:25 in English Bibles).

	(Asenath, Milcah,[19] *Doeg, Raddai, and attendants enter)*	אסנת מלכה[19] דואג רדי ומשרתים (באים)	
	Behold **the treasure-house of a precious vessel**[20] from the ship on the dry land	רְאוּ **אוֹצַר כְּלִי חֶמְדָּה**[20] מִן הָאֳנִיָּה בַּיַּבָּשָׁה	
	Bend your knee before her, all inhabitants of the island	כִּרְעוּ בֶרֶךְ לְפָנֶיהָ כָּל יוֹשְׁבֵי הָאִי	
	Welcome, lady! Welcome to Caphtor!	בָּרוּךְ בּוֹאֵךְ הַגְּבִירָה! בָּרוּךְ בּוֹאֵךְ לְכַפְתּוֹר!	
	May the God of the heavens be gracious to you and crown you with **mercy and compassion.**[21]	יָחְנֵךְ אֱלֹהֵי הַשָּׁמַיִם וִיעַטְּרֵכִי **חֶסֶד וְרַחֲמִים.**[21]	
ASENATH	**Thank you,**[22] dear and honourable Chesed!	**תְּשֻׁאוֹת חֵן חֵן**[22] לָךְ, כֶּשֶׂד הַיָּקָר וְהַנִּכְבָּד!	אסנת
	Can you tell me about the health of my husband and lord?	הֲיָדַעְתָּ לְהַגִּיד לִי, מִשְּׁלוֹם אִישִׁי אֲדֹנִי?	
CHESED	I know nothing, except that he is well	לֹא יָדַעְתִּי דָבָר, בִּלְתִּי כִּי שָׁלוֹם לוֹ	כשד
	And **he is indeed coming and will not delay.**[23]	**וּבוֹא יָבוֹא לֹא יְאַחֵר.**[23]	
ASENATH	My heart trembles within me – how were you separated from him?	לִבִּי חָרֵד בְּקִרְבִּי – אֵיךְ נִפְרַדְתָּ מִמֶּנּוּ?	אסנת
CHESED	Storms of the heavens on the sea separated me from him.	סַעֲרוֹת שְׁחָקִים בַּיָּם, הִפְרִידוּ בֵּינִי וּבֵינוֹ.	כשד
	But listen to the voice of the crowd –	אַךְ שִׁמְעִי קוֹל הֶהָמוֹן –	
	(Voice from outside: Ship, ship! *Afterwards the sound of the cannons)*	(קול מחוץ: אֳנִיָּה אֳנִיָּה! אחרי כן קול המורים)	
MAN 2	The sound of the cannons from a ship before the citadel	קוֹל כְּלֵי הַמּוֹרִים מֵאֳנִיָּה, לְנֹכַח פְּנֵי הַמְּצוּדָה	איש ב'

19 This is the name of two biblical characters, a) Abraham's brother Nahor's wife, mentioned in Gen. 11:29, 22:20, 23, 24, 24:15, 24, 47 and b) one of Zelophehad's daughters, mentioned in Num. 26:33, 27:1, 36:11; Josh. 17:3. Salkinson is likely to have selected the name based on its partial sound correspondence with Shakespeare's Emilia, as well as perhaps because of the qualities of strength and independence associated with Zelophehad's daughters: in the biblical narrative they made a successful public protest against the unjustness of the law barring daughters from inheriting land, and are recognized for their bravery in subsequent Jewish tradition (e.g., the Babylonian Talmud, *Bava Batra* 119b).

20 Hosea 13:15 הוּא יִשְׁסֶה אוֹצַר כָּל־כְּלִי חֶמְדָּה 'he will plunder the treasure-house of every precious vessel'.

21 Zech. 7:9; Ps. 103:4.

22 Zech. 4:7; lit. 'shouts of grace, grace'. This expression was used in the sense of 'thank you' in the medieval and early modern periods, as well as in early revernacularized Modern Hebrew (Even-Shoshan 2003, 2: 580).

23 Hab. 2:3.

	As a sign that they are **our trusted friends.**[24]	לְאוֹת כִּי אַנְשֵׁי שְׁלוֹמֵנוּ[24] הֵם.	
CHESED	Go see who the ones coming are? *(Man 2 exits)*	לֵךְ רְאֵה מִי הֵם הַבָּאִים? (איש ב' הולך)	כשד
	Greetings, standard-bearer!	הֲשָׁלוֹם נוֹשֵׂא הַדָּגֶל!	
	(To Milcah) Greetings, **woman of valour!**[25] **Let it not be displeasing in your eyes,**[26] Doeg,	(אל מלכה) שָׁלוֹם בּוֹאֵךְ אֵשֶׁת חָיִל[25]! אַל יֵרַע בְּעֵינֶיךָ[26] דּוֹאֵג	
	That I honour your wife, for I have been educated to do so from my youth *(Kisses her)*	כִּי אֲכַבֵּד פְּנֵי אִשְׁתְּךָ כִּי כֵן לָמַדְתִּי מִנְּעוּרָי (נושק אותה)	
DOEG	If she responds to you with her lips as she is accustomed to respond to me with her tongue	לוּ תָשִׁיב לְךָ בִּשְׂפָתֶיהָ, כְּדַרְכָּהּ לְהָשִׁיב לִי בִלְשׁוֹנָהּ	דואג
	You will have more than enough.	יִהְיֶה לְךָ דַּי וְהוֹתֵר.	
ASENATH	Why, **there is not a word on her tongue.**[27]	הֲלֹא אֵין מִלָּה בִלְשׁוֹנָהּ.[27]	אסנת
DOEG	She has an endless number of words;	מִלֶּיהָ רַבּוֹת לְאֵין קֵץ;	דואג
	For I have found her thus, when I want to **give sleep to my eyes**[28]	כִּי מְצָאתִיהָ כֵן, בְּחֶפְצִי לָתֵת שְׁנָת לְעֵינָי[28]	
	But before you, my lady, **her tongue cleaves to the roof of her mouth**[29]	אַךְ לְפָנַיִךְ גְּבִרְתִּי, תִּדְבַּק לְשׁוֹנָהּ לְחִכָּהּ[29]	
	And only in her heart does she rebel, **but her voice is not heard.**[30]	וְרַק בִּלְבָבָהּ תִּתְקוֹטֵט וְקוֹלָהּ לֹא יִשָּׁמֵעַ.[30]	
MILCAH	You attack me baselessly, for **you have found no fault in me.**[31]	חִנָּם תִּתְגֹּלֵל עָלַי, כִּי לֹא מָצָאתָ בִי מְאוּמָה.[31]	מלכה
DOEG	A woman **in the streets and squares**[32] resembles a picture on a scroll;	אִשָּׁה בַּשְּׁוָקִים וּבָרְחֹבוֹת,[32] דָּמְתָה לִתְמוּנָה עֲלֵי גִלָּיוֹן	דואג

24 Jer. 38:22 אַנְשֵׁי שְׁלֹמֶךָ ‘your trusted friends’; also Obad. 1:7.
25 Prov. 12:4, 31:10; Ruth 3:11.
26 Gen. 21:12; 2 Sam. 11:25.
27 Ps. 139:4 כִּי אֵין מִלָּה בִּלְשׁוֹנִי ‘for there is no word on my tongue’.
28 Prov. 6:4 אַל־תִּתֵּן שֵׁנָה לְעֵינֶיךָ ‘do not give sleep to your eyes’.
29 Ps. 137:6 תִּדְבַּק־לְשׁוֹנִי ׀ לְחִכִּי ‘may my tongue cleave to the roof of my mouth’.
30 1 Sam. 1:13.
31 1 Sam. 29:3 וְלֹא־מָצָאתִי בוֹ מְאוּמָה ‘and I have found no fault in him’.
32 Song of Songs 3:2.

	At home, **clanging cymbals**;[33] and in the cooks' house **an evil beast**;[34]	בַּבַּיִת לְצִלְצְלֵי תְרוּעָה[33] וּבְבֵית הַמְּבַשְּׁלוֹת לְחַיָּה רָעָה,[34]	
	She is too modest to rebuke others but a villain when she herself is rebuked.	צְנוּעָה הִיא לְיַסֵּר אֲחֵרִים וּבַת בְּלִיַּעַל בְּהִוָּסֵר נַפְשָׁהּ.	
	She plays during her work, and she is **a woman of valour**[35] in bed.	מְשַׂחֶקֶת בְּעֵת מְלַאכְתָּהּ וְאֵשֶׁת חַיִל[35] הִיא בַּמִּטָּה.	
ASENATH	How do you know no shame, **talebearer**![36]	אֵיךְ לֹא תֵדַע כְּלִמָּה, הוֹלֵךְ רָכִיל![36]	אסנת
DOEG	May I be called a Turk if the matter is not so.	יִקָּרֵא שְׁמִי תּוֹגַרְמִי אִם לֹא כֵן הַדָּבָר.	דואג
	You arise from your sleep to play and go to bed for work.	מִשְּׁנַתְכֶן תָּקוּמְנָה לְצַחֵק וְעַל הַיְצוּעַ תַּעֲלֶינָה לִמְלָאכָה	
MILCAH	I shall not ask my praise to be written in the book by *your* hand.	לֹא מִיָּדְךָ אֲבַקֵּשׁ לִכְתֹּב תְּהִלָּתִי בַּסֵּפֶר.	מלכה
DOEG	Do not ask me, for I shall not do it.	אַל תְּבַקְשִׁי מִמֶּנִּי, כִּי לֹא אֶעֱשֶׂה זֹאת.	דואג
ASENATH	What would you write about me, if you wanted to praise me?	מַה־תִּכְתֹּב עָלַי, לוּ חָפַצְתָּ לְהַלֵּל אֹתִי?	אסנת
DOEG	**Do not urge me**,[37] my lady, to come with **the tool of a scribe**[38]	אַל תִּפְגְּעִי בִי[37] גְּבִרְתִּי, לָבוֹא בְּשֵׁבֶט סֹפֵר[38]	דואג
	For I have no power save with the staff of punishment.	כִּי אֵין כֹּחִי, כִּי אִם בְּשֵׁבֶט בִּקֹּרֶת.	
ASENATH	Please try with all that is in your power –	נַס נָא בְּכָל אֲשֶׁר בְּכֹחֶךָ –	אסנת
	Has anyone gone to the shore?	הַאִם הָלַךְ אִישׁ אֶל הַחוֹף?	
DOEG	Yes, my dear lady, one man has gone from here.	הֵן, גְּבִרְתִּי הַיְקָרָה, אִישׁ אֶחָד הָלַךְ מִזֶּה.	דואג
ASENATH	My heart is not at peace, but I disguise myself with a laughing face	לִבִּי לֹא יִשְׁקֹט, אַךְ אֶתְחַפֵּשׂ בְּפָנִים שׂחֲקִים	אסנת
	Lest it be discovered that I am sad of spirit –	לְבַל יִוָּדַע כִּי עֲצוּבַת רוּחַ אָנִי –	

33 Ps. 150:5.
34 Gen. 37:20, 33; Lev. 26:6; Ezek. 14:15, 34:25.
35 Prov. 12:4, 31:10; Ruth 3:11.
36 Prov. 11:13, 20:19.
37 Ruth 1:16.
38 Judg. 5:14; שֵׁבֶט typically means 'staff' or 'rod'.

	Say what kind of commendation and praise you would give me with your mouth?	דַּבֵּר מַה־תִּתֵּן לִי שֶׁבַח וּתְהִלָּה בְּפִיךָ?	
DOEG	Right now your servant is indeed pondering from the depths of the heart	עַתָּה זֶה הֹגֶה עַבְדֶּךָ, הָגוֹ מִלֵּב עָמֹק	דואג
	And conceiving as a woman conceives and goes into labour, and now **I have come to the moment of birth**[39]	וְהָרוֹ כְאִשָּׁה הָרָה מְצֵרָה וְהִנֵּה **בָּאתִי עַד מַשְׁבֵּר**[39]	
	And this is what I have given birth to:	וְזֶה הוּא אֲשֶׁר יָלָדְתִּי:	
	If the woman is beautiful and wise – wisdom and beauty are friends[40]	אִם הָאִשָּׁה יָפָה וּמַשְׂכֶּלֶת – הַשְׂכֵּל וְיֹפִי חֲבֵרִים[40]	
	Wisdom is pleasing to the soul, and beauty to the soul of others.	הַשְׂכֵּל לַנֶּפֶשׁ יִנְעָם וְיֹפִי לְנֶפֶשׁ אֲחֵרִים.	
ASENATH	**Your praise is fitting,**[41] but what if she is black and wise?	**נָאוָה תְהִלָּתְךָ**,[41] אַךְ אִם הִיא שְׁחוֹרָה וּמַשְׂכָּלֶת?	אסנת
DOEG	If she is as black as a Cushite woman and she has a portion of wisdom[42]	אִם הִיא כְּכוּשִׁית שְׁחוֹרָה וְחֵלֶק לָהּ בַּבִּינָה[42]	דואג
	A man with white **on his wing will cover her like a shield**.[43]	אִישׁ לָבָן **בְּאֶבְרָתוֹ, יָסֶךְ לָהּ כַּצִּנָּה**.[43]	
ASENATH	Stop, lest you go from evil to evil.	הֶרֶף, פֶּן תֵּצֵא מֵרַע אֶל רָע.	אסנת
MILCAH	And what would you say about a beautiful and senseless woman?	וּמַה־תֹּאמַר עַל אִשָּׁה יָפָה וְסָרַת טָעַם?	מלכה
DOEG	There is no beautiful woman without the sense to do good and evil[44]	אֵין אִשָּׁה יָפָה, בִּבְלִי דַעַת לְהֵיטִיב וּלְהָרַע[44]	דואג
	For even in her folly, she is wise enough to produce offspring.	כִּי גַם בְּאִוַּלְתָּהּ, תַּשְׂכִּיל לְהַזְרִיעַ זָרַע.	
ASENATH[45]	These are old sayings, to serve as amusement for fools	מְשָׁלִים יְשָׁנִים הֵם, לִהְיוֹת לִצְחֹק לָאֱוִילִים	אסנת[45]

39 2 Kings 19:3; Isa. 37:3 בָּ֣אוּ בָנִ֔ים עַד־מַשְׁבֵּ֔ר 'children have come to the moment of birth'.
40 This and the next line form a rhyming couplet, mirroring Shakespeare's 'wit/it' (2.1.129–30).
41 Ps. 33:1 לַ֝יְשָׁרִ֗ים נָאוָ֥ה תְהִלָּֽה 'praise is fitting for the upright'; also Ps. 147:1.
42 This and the next line form a rhyming couplet, mirroring Shakespeare's 'wit/fit' (2.1.132–3).
43 Ps. 91:4 בְּאֶבְרָת֨וֹ ׀ יָ֣סֶךְ לָ֭ךְ וְתַֽחַת־כְּנָפָ֣יו תֶּחְסֶ֑ה צִנָּ֖ה וְֽסֹחֵרָ֣ה אֲמִתּֽוֹ 'with his wing he will cover you and under his wings you will find shelter; his faithfulness will be your shield and buckler'.
44 This and the next line form a rhyming couplet, mirroring Shakespeare's 'fair/heir' (2.1.136–7).
45 This speech is prose in the original (2.1.138–40).

	And melodies to drinkers of alcohol; but what **wicked slander**[46]	וּנְגִינוֹת לְשֹׁתֵי שֵׁכָר; אֲבָל מַה־דִּבָּה רָעָה[46]	
	Would you bring forth **with the lash of your tongue**,[47] concerning a despised and foolish woman?	תּוֹצִיא בְשׁוֹט לְשׁוֹנְךָ,[47] עַל שְׂנוּאָה וּפְתַיָּה?	
DOEG	There is no despised and foolish woman innocent of sin and folly[48]	אֵין שְׂנוּאָה וּפְתַיָּה, נְקִיָּה מֵאָוֶן וְאִוֶּלֶת[48]	דואג
	For **she twists and turns on her ways**[49] like a beautiful wise woman.	כִּי מְשָׂרֶכֶת דְּרָכֶיהָ[49] כִּיפַת תֹּאַר מַשְׂכָּלֶת.	
ASENATH[50]	This way of yours is **wickedness of folly**,[51] for you favour the wicked woman	זֶה דַרְכְּךָ רֶשַׁע כֶּסֶל,[51] כִּי תֶהְדַּר פְּנֵי הָרָעָה	אסנת[50]
	Over her better. But **tell me, do not conceal**[52]	מִן הַטּוֹבָה מִמֶּנָּה, אוּלָם הַגֵּד אַל תְּכַזֵּב[52]	
	What is fitting praise for a happy, honourable woman	מַה־תְּהִלָּה נָאוָה לְאִשָּׁה כְּבוּדָה מְאֻשָּׁרָה	
	For whom even **injustice shuts its mouth**[53] before the righteousness of her soul?	אֲשֶׁר לִפְנֵי יִשְׁרַת נַפְשָׁהּ, גַּם עַוְלָתָה תִּקְפָּץ פִּיהָ?[53]	
DOEG	A woman **of perfect beauty**[54] but **a stranger and alien**[55] to pride[56]	אִשָּׁה כְּלִילַת יֹפִי[54] וּלְגַאֲוָה מוּזָרָה וְנָכְרִיָּה[55,56]	דואג
	Her tongue is **a learned tongue**[57] and she is not wayward or riotous	לְשׁוֹנָהּ לְשׁוֹן לִמּוּדִים[57] וְאֵינֶנָּה סֹרֵרָה וְהֹמִיָּה	
	Wealth and riches are in her house,[58] yet she does not have many jewels or sashes[59]	הוֹן וָעֹשֶׁר בְּבֵיתָהּ[58] וְלֹא תַרְבֶּה עֲדִי וְקִשּׁוּרִים[59]	

46 Ecclesiastes Rabbah 9.
47 Job 5:21 בְּשׁוֹט לָשׁוֹן 'from the lash of the tongue'.
48 This and the next line form a rhyming couplet, mirroring Shakespeare's 'thereunto/do' (2.1.141–2).
49 Jer. 2:23.
50 This speech is prose in the original (2.1.143–7).
51 Eccles. 7:25.
52 Josh. 7:19 וְהַגֶּד־נָא לִי מֶה עָשִׂיתָ אַל־תְּכַחֵד מִמֶּנִּי 'and tell me what you have done; do not conceal it from me'.
53 Job 5:16 וְעֹלָתָה קָפְצָה פִּיהָ 'and injustice shuts its mouth'.
54 Ezek. 27:3; Lam. 2:15.
55 Ps. 69:9 (69:8 in English Bibles) מוּזָר הָיִיתִי לְאֶחָי וְנָכְרִי לִבְנֵי אִמִּי 'I have become a stranger to my brothers, an alien to my mother's sons'.
56 This and the next line form a rhyming couplet, mirroring Shakespeare's 'proud/loud' (2.1.148–9).
57 Isa. 50:4.
58 Ps. 112:3 הוֹן־וָעֹשֶׁר בְּבֵיתוֹ 'wealth and riches are in his house'.
59 This and the next line form a rhyming couplet, mirroring Shakespeare's 'gay/may' (2.1.150–1).

	She scorns the grapes of lust **even when it is the time of the first ripe fruits**[60]	תָּבוּז עִנְּבֵי תַאֲוָה וְהַיָּמִים יְמֵי בִכּוּרִים[60]	
	And even in anger and jealousy and **destructive revenge that has already been decreed**[61, 62]	וְגַם בְּקֶצֶף וְקִנְאָה וּנְקָמָה **נֶחֱרָצָה וְכָלָה**[61,62]	
	She says to her anger, 'desist', and to her jealousy 'be gone'	תֹּאמַר לְקִצְפָּהּ הֶרֶף וּלְקִנְאָתָהּ גְּשִׁי הָלְאָה	
	And her mind examines in order to know what is elevated and low[63]	וְלִבָּהּ יִבְחַן לָדַעַת מָה רָמִים וּשְׁפָלִים[63]	
	For **the tail of lions is better than the head of foxes**[64]	כִּי **זָנָב לָאֲרָיוֹת טוֹב מֵרֹאשׁ לַשּׁוּעָלִים**[64]	
	And **she has counsel and sound wisdom**[65] yet does not disclose her words[66]	וְלָהּ עֵצָה וְתוּשִׁיָּה[65] וְלֹא תְגַלֶּה דְבָרֶיהָ[66]	
	And she does not look back if there are bachelors behind her –	וְלֹא תַבִּיט אֲחֹרַנִּית אִם בַּחוּרִים אַחֲרֶיהָ –	
	Such a woman is one in a thousand – and **it is her due**[67] –	אִשָּׁה כָּזֹאת אַחַת מֵאֶלֶף – **וְלָהּ יָאָתָה**[67] –	
ASENATH	And what is her due?	וּמַה יָּאֲתָה לָהּ?	אסנת
DOEG	To uncover a breast to suckle fools and to serve drinkers of alcohol.	לַחֲלֹץ שַׁד לְהָנִיק אֱוִילִים וּלְשָׁרֵת אֶת שׁוֹתֵי שֵׁכָר.	דואג
ASENATH[68]	Who has heard such perverse words?	מִי שָׁמַע דִּבְרֵי סֶלֶף כָּאֵלֶּה	אסנת[68]
	Milcah, do not learn his ways, even though he is your husband.	מִלְכָּה אַל תִּלְמְדִי אָרְחוֹתָיו, אַף כִּי בַּעֲלֵךְ הוּא.	
	What do you say Chesed, to this bad counsellor and villain?	מַה־תֹּאמַר כֶּשֶׂד, לְיוֹעֵץ רָע וּבְלִיַּעַל הַזֶּה?	
CHESED[69]	**There is one who speaks like the piercings of a sword**;[70] but it is as a soldier	**יֵשׁ בּוֹטֶה כְּמַדְקְרוֹת חָרֶב**;[70] אֲבָל הוּא כְּאִישׁ חַיִל	כשד[69]

60 Num. 13:20 וְהַיָּמִים יְמֵי בִּכּוּרֵי עֲנָבִים 'now it was the time of the first ripe fruits of the grape'.
61 Isa. 10:23, 28:22; Dan. 9:27.
62 This and the next line form a rhyming couplet, mirroring Shakespeare's 'nigh/fly' (2.1.152–3).
63 This and the next line form a rhyming couplet, mirroring Shakespeare's 'frail/tail' (2.1.154–5).
64 Mishnah *Avot* 4:20 והוי זנב לאריות, ואל תהי ראש לשועלים 'and be the tail of lions, rather than the head of foxes'. This is comparable in meaning to the English 'be a small fish in a big pond rather than a big fish in a small pond'.
65 Prov. 8:14 לִי־עֵצָה וְתוּשִׁיָּה 'I have counsel and sound wisdom'.
66 This and the next line form a rhyming couplet, mirroring Shakespeare's 'mind/behind' (2.1.156–7).
67 Jer. 10:7 לְךָ יָאָתָה 'it is your due'.
68 This speech is prose in the original (2.1.161–4).
69 This speech is prose in the original (2.1.165–6).
70 Prov. 12:18.

	That he will please you, my lady, and not as a scholar.	יָפִיק רָצוֹן מִמֵּךְ גְּבִרְתִּי, וְלֹא כְּיוֹדֵעַ סֵפֶר.	
DOEG[71]	*(Speaking to himself)* He holds her hand and whispers in her ears	(מדבר אל עצמו) הוּא אֹחֵז בְּיָדָהּ וְלוֹחֵשׁ בְּאָזְנֶיהָ	דואג[71]
	With these spider-webs, I shall hunt a fly as big as Chesed.	בְּקוּרֵי עַכָּבִישׁ אֵלֶּה, אָצוּד זְבוּב גָּדוֹל כְּכֶשֶׂד.	
	Make your face shine at her[72] and babble pleasantries into her ears	הַצְהֵל לָהּ פָּנִים[72] וְהַטֵּף נְעִימוֹת בְּאָזְנֶיהָ	
	And prepare for yourself the trap in which your soul will be caught.	וְהָכֵן לְךָ אֶת הַפַּח, בּוֹ תִּלָּכֵד נַפְשֶׁךָ.	
	If you knew your end, that another will take your office	לוּ יָדַעְתָּ אַחֲרִיתְךָ כִּי פְקוּדָתְךָ יִקַּח אַחֵר	
	You would not touch her hand and you would not kiss your fingers in front of her	לֹא נָגַעְתָּ בְּיָדָהּ וְלֹא נָשַׁקְתָּ אֶצְבְּעוֹתֶיךָ נִכְחָהּ	
	But you err, fool, by kissing your fingers again	וְאַתָּה סָכָל תִּשְׁגֶּה, לְנַשֵּׁק אֶצְבְּעוֹתֶיךָ שֵׁנִית	
	It would be better for you, if **your thumbs were cut off**.[73]	טוֹב הָיָה לְךָ, לוּ בְּהֹנוֹת יָדֶיךָ קֻצָּצוּ[73].	
	(Sound of a blast)	(קול תרועה)	
	Behold, this is the Cushite, for I know the blast of that horn.	הִנֵּה זֶה הַכּוּשִׁי כִּי יָדַעְתִּי תְּרוּעַת הַקֶּרֶן.	
CHESED	I also know the sound of that blast.	גַּם אֲנִי יוֹדֵעַ קוֹל הַתְּרוּעָה.	כשד
ASENATH	Come, let us go receive him.	לְכוּ וְנֵלְכָה לְקַדֵּם פָּנָיו.	אסנת
CHESED	Behold, he is coming towards us.	הִנֵּה הוּא הוֹלֵךְ לִקְרָאתֵנוּ.	כשד
	(Ithiel and his men)	(איתיאל ואנשיו)	
ITHIEL	Greetings, **my love**,[74] daughter of valour **on the day of battle**![75]	הֲשָׁלוֹם רַעְיָתִי,[74] בַּת חַיִל בְּיוֹם נָשֶׁק![75]	איתיאל
ASENATH	Greetings, Ithiel, my beloved!	שָׁלוֹם אִיתִיאֵל יְדִיד נַפְשִׁי!	אסנת
ITHIEL	To the wonderment of my heart and to my joy, you have arrived here first.	לְתִמְהוֹן לְבָבִי וּלְשִׂמְחָתִי, קִדַּמְתָּ לָבוֹא הֵנָּה.	איתיאל

71 This speech is prose in the original (2.1.167–78).
72 Ps. 104:15 לְהַצְהִיל פָּנִים מִשָּׁמֶן 'to make one's face shine from oil'.
73 Judg. 1:7 בְּהֹנוֹת יְדֵיהֶם וְרַגְלֵיהֶם מְקֻצָּצִים 'with their thumbs and big toes cut off'.
74 Song of Songs 1:9, 15, 2:2, 10, 13, 4:1, 7, 5:2, 6:4.
75 Ps. 140:8 (140:7 in English Bibles).

	See, my soul's delight, if after every storm	רְאִי חֶמְדַּת נַפְשִׁי, אִם אַחֲרֵי כָל סְעָרָה	
	Such a pleasant calm as this should arise, I would laugh at **storm and tempest**[76]	תָּקוּם דְּמָמָה נְעִימָה כָזֹאת, אֶשְׂחַק **לְסֹעָה וָסַעַר**[76]	
	I would not fear if the earth gave way,[77] and Sheol would not terrify me	לֹא אֶפְחַד **בְּהָמִיר אָרֶץ**[77] וּשְׁאוֹל לֹא יְבַעֲתֵנִי	
	For I would be at peace in my ship, even if it rose up towards the heavens	כִּי אֶשְׁקֹט בָּאֳנִיָּתִי, אַף כִּי תַעֲלֶה שָׁמַיִם	
	Went down to the depths, or **was like to break apart**[78] **in the heart of the sea**.[79]	תֵּרֵד תְּהוֹמוֹת וּתְחַשֵּׁב **לְהִשָּׁבֵר**[78] **בְּלֵב־יָם**.[79]	
	If my end were to come today, I would die in peace now	לוּ בָא קִצִּי הַיּוֹם, בְּשָׁלוֹם אָמוּתָה הַפָּעַם	
	For I fear very much that such a great delight	כִּי יָרֵאתִי מְאֹד פֶּן עֹנֶג רַב כָּזֶה	
	I shall not see again in all the days to come.	לֹא אֶרְאֶה עוֹד בְּכָל הַיָּמִים הַבָּאִים.	
ASENATH	May the One Who Dwells on High forbid it!	חָלִלָה לְשֹׁכֵן שְׁחָקִים!	אסנת
	I trust in Him, that just as He multiplies our days	בּוֹ בָּטְחָה נַפְשִׁי, כִּי כַּאֲשֶׁר יַרְבֶּה יָמֵינוּ	
	So He will continue to multiply our **love with delights**.[80]	כֵּן יוֹסֵף לָנוּ, רֹב **אַהֲבָה בַּתַּעֲנוּגִים**.[80]	
ITHIEL	Amen! – May God say so –	אָמֵן! – כֵּן יֹאמַר אֱלֹהִים –	איתיאל
	How inadequate my heart is to contain this great delight	אֵיךְ קָצַר לִבִּי מֵהָכִיל הָעֹנֶג הַגָּדוֹל הַזֶּה	
	And how weak my tongue is to tell the excitement of my joy	וְאֵיךְ רָפָה לְשׁוֹנִי מֵהַגֵּד רִגְשַׁת שִׂמְחָתִי	
	I cannot speak further, for **my soul yearns**[81] *(Kisses her)*	לֹא אוּכַל דַּבֵּר עוֹד, כִּי **כָלְתָה נַפְשִׁי**[81] (נושק אותה)	

76 Ps. 55:9 (55:8 in English Bibles) מֵרוּחַ סֹעָה מִסָּעַר 'from the stormy wind and tempest'.
77 Ps. 46:3 (46:2 in English Bibles) לֹא־נִירָא בְּהָמִיר אָרֶץ 'we will not fear, though the earth give way'.
78 Jon. 1:4 וְהָאֳנִיָּה חִשְּׁבָה לְהִשָּׁבֵר 'and the ship was like to break apart'.
79 Exod. 15:8; Prov. 23:34, 30:19.
80 Song of Songs 7:7 (7:6 in English Bibles).
81 Ps. 84:3 (84:2 in English Bibles).

	If only our hearts might be undivided for eternity	מִי יִתֵּן וְלֹא יֵחָלֵק לִבֵּנוּ עַד עוֹלָם	
	Let only the **sound of rejoicing**[82] and jubilation be heard in our land	רַק יִשָּׁמַע בִּגְבוּלֵנוּ קוֹל **שָׂשׂוֹן**[82] וְרִנָּה	
	The sound of lovers' kisses, like this and like this…	קוֹל נְשִׁיקוֹת דּוֹדִים, כָּזֹאת וְכָזֹאת...	
DOEG	*(Speaking to himself)* Your heart is set on rejoicing, but I swear on my faith	(מדבר אל עצמו) לִבְּכֶם נָכוֹן לְרַנֵּן וַאֲנִי נִשְׁבַּעְתִּי בֶּאֱמוּנָתִי	דואג
	That I shall set the strings for a song of mourning rather than of joy.	כִּי אֲכוֹנֵן הַמֵּיתָרִים לְקִינָה וְלֹא לְרִנָּה.	
ITHIEL	Let us go to the palace; haven't you heard, my brothers	נֵלְכָה נָּא אֶל הָאַרְמוֹן, הֲלֹא שְׁמַעְתֶּם אַחַי	איתיאל
	We are no longer at war, the Turks **have been drowned in the sea.**[83] –	מִלְחָמָה אֵין לָנוּ עוֹד, הַתּוֹגַרְמִים **טֻבְּעוּ בַיָּם.**[83]–	
	How fare my companions of old, all my acquaintances on this island? –	הֲשָׁלוֹם לְרֵעַי מִקֶּדֶם, לְכָל מְיֻדָּעַי בְּאִי הַזֶּה? –	
	I know that they will greet you **with love and favour,**[84] **my love**[85]	יָדַעְתִּי כִּי **בְּאַהֲבָה וְרָצוֹן**[84], יְקַדְּמוּ פָּנַיִךְ **רַעְיָתִי**[85]	
	For since I sojourned with them they have loved me greatly.	כִּי מֵאָז גַּרְתִּי עִמָּהֶם גָּדְלָה אַהֲבָתָם אֵלָי.	
	See, the one **whom my soul loves,**[86] from my much musing and joy in you	רְאִי **שֶׁאָהֲבָה נַפְשִׁי,**[86] מֵרֹב הֲגִיגִי וְשִׂמְחָתִי בָךְ	
	My speech is disordered and my lips are like **the lips of those who sleep.**[87]	שִׂיחִי בְּלֹא סְדָרִים וּשְׂפָתַי **כְּשִׂפְתֵי יְשֵׁנִים.**[87]	
	Go Doeg, bring the baggage from the ship	לְכָה דוֹאֵג הָבִיאָה אֶת הַכֵּלִים מִן הַסְּפִינָה	
	The captain will also come with you to the palace	גַּם רַב הַחֹבֵל יָבוֹא אִתְּךָ אֶל הָאַרְמוֹן	
	In order that I might do him kindness and honour him according to his great worth.	לְמַעַן אֶעֱשֶׂה עִמּוֹ חֶסֶד וְכִבַּדְתִּיו כְּעֶרְכּוֹ הָרָב.	

82 Jer. 7:34, 16:9, 25:10, 33:11.
83 Exod. 15:4 וּמִבְחַר שָׁלִשָׁיו טֻבְּעוּ בְיַם־סוּף 'and his choicest officers were drowned in the Sea of Reeds'.
84 Alshekh to Lev. 20.
85 Song of Songs 1:9, 15, 2:2, 10, 13, 4:1, 7, 5:2, 6:4.
86 Song of Songs 1:7, 3:1, 2, 3.
87 Song of Songs 7:10 (7:9 in English Bibles).

	And now I call again, welcome, Asenath!	וְהִנְנִי קֹרֵא עוֹד הַפַּעַם, בָּרוּךְ בּוֹאֵךְ אָסְנַת!	
	Welcome to Caphtor!	בָּרוּךְ בּוֹאֵךְ לְכַפְתּוֹר!	
	(Ithiel, Asenath, and their attendants exit)	(איתיאל אסנת ומשרתיהם הולכים)	
DOEG[88]	*(To Raddai)* Go forth to the shore and let us meet together there.	(אל רדי) צֵא אֶל הַחוֹף וְשָׁם נִפָּגְשָׁה יַחְדָּו.	דואג[88]
	If you are brave of heart (as they say,	אִם אַמִּיץ לֵב אַתָּה (כַּאֲשֶׁר יֹאמְרוּ הָאֹמְרִים	
	Love increases bravery even in a wicked and corrupt heart)	אַהֲבָה תוֹסִיף אֹמֶץ גַּם בְּלֵב רָע וְנִשְׁחָת)	
	Then you will understand my words. You see, the officer Chesed	אָז תָּבִין דְּבָרָי. הִנֵּה כֶּשֶׂד הַפָּקִיד	
	Will be standing before the citadel on his guard duty tonight –	יַעֲמֹד לִפְנֵי הַמְּצוּדָה עַל מִשְׁמַרְתּוֹ בַּלַּיְלָה –	
	But you must first know that Asenath loves him.	רַק עָלֶיךָ לָדַעַת בַּתְּחִלָּה, כִּי אָסְנַת אֹהֶבֶת אֹתוֹ.	
RADDAI	She loves *him*? **This cannot be so.**[89]	אֹתוֹ הִיא אֹהֶבֶת – **זֹאת לֹא זֹאת.**[89]	רדי
DOEG	**Put your hand on your mouth**[90] and **take heed of my wisdom**:[91]	**שִׂים יָדְךָ עַל פִּיךָ**[90] **וְלִבְּךָ תָּשִׁית לְדַעְתִּי**:[91]	דואג
	She loves the Cushite with a powerful and strong love	בְּאַהֲבָה עַזָּה וַחֲזָקָה אֹהֶבֶת אֶת הַכּוּשִׁי	
	Only on account of **the moving of his lips**[92] and worthless words of wonder	רַק בַּעֲבוּר **נִיד שְׂפָתָיו**[92] וְדִבְרֵי נִפְלָאוֹת שָׁוְא	
	So now, then, do you think that her love will continue?	וְעַתָּה הֲתַחְשֹׁב אֵיפוֹא, כִּי אַהֲבָתָהּ תִּמָּשֵׁךְ?	
	Do not think thus, if you have understood a little.	אַל יֶהְגֶּה לִבְּךָ כֵּן, אִם נָבֹנוֹת מְעָט.	
	Why, this woman seeks to satisfy her eyes	הֵן הָאִשָּׁה הַזֹּאת מְבַקֶּשֶׁת לְהַשְׂבִּיעַ עֵינֶיהָ	

88 This and the following speeches until Raddai's exit are prose in the original (2.1.212–83).
89 Ezek. 21:31 (21:26 in English Bibles).
90 Judg. 18:19.
91 Alshekh to Prov. 22 and Song of Songs 7.
92 Job 16:5 וְנִיד שְׂפָתַי 'and the moving of my lips' (sometimes translated as 'the solace of my lips').

So what could she see in the Cushite, what could she see in the face of Azazel?[93]	וּמַה־תֶּחֱזֶה בַּכּוּשִׁי, מַה־תֶּחֱזֶה בִּפְנֵי הָעֲזָאזֵל?[93]
When the fire of her love goes out and her blood is cold within her	בִּכְלוֹת אֵשׁ אַהֲבָתָהּ וְדָמָהּ קַר בְּקִרְבָּהּ
She will seek a new face to refresh the hunger of her soul	תְּבַקֵּשׁ פָּנִים חֲדָשִׁים לְחַדֵּשׁ רַעֲבוֹן נַפְשָׁהּ
And only a man **young in years,**[94] **handsome in form and appearance**[95]	וְרַק אִישׁ נַעַר בְּשָׁנִים[94] יְפֵה תֹאַר וּמַרְאֶה[95]
And resplendent with grace and glory, he is the man that she will choose	וְהָדוּר בְּחֵן וְתִפְאֶרֶת, הוּא הָאִישׁ אֲשֶׁר תִּבְחַר
And not this Cushite who lacks all of these;	וְלֹא הַכּוּשִׁי הַזֶּה אֲשֶׁר יֶחְסַר כָּל אֵלֶּה;
For a woman of good sense like her will grow sick of a man	כִּי טוֹבַת טַעַם כָּמוֹהָ תָּקוּץ מִפְּנֵי גֶבֶר
Who has flaws and not a single advantage	אֲשֶׁר מִגְרָעוֹת בּוֹ וְאֵין לוֹ יִתְרוֹן מְאוּמָה,
And quick as lightning she will regret and sigh **with the anguish of her spirit**[96]	וְחִישׁ קַל תִּנָּחֵם וְתֵאָנַח בְּמַר נַפְשָׁהּ[96]
And instead of the scorned Cushite she will seek for herself **a man after her own heart**.[97]	וְתַחַת הַכּוּשִׁי הַנִּמְאָס תְּבַקֵּשׁ לָהּ אִישׁ כִּלְבָבָהּ.[97]
And now who is the one closest to her, whose lot it will be to seize her	וְעַתָּה מִי הַקָּרוֹב לָהּ אֲשֶׁר יִלְכְּדֶנָּה בְּגוֹרָלוֹ
If not this Chesed, **an industrious man**[98] and a villain,	אִם לֹא כֶּשֶׂד הַזֶּה, אִישׁ חָרוּץ[98] וּבְלִיַּעַל,
A man who appears to pursue innocence and honesty	אִישׁ אֲשֶׁר לְעֵינַיִם, רֹדֵף תֹּם וָיֹשֶׁר
But inwardly he sets his ambush,[99] to perform every abomination of his heart?	וּבְקִרְבּוֹ יָשִׂים אָרְבּוֹ,[99] לַעֲשׂוֹת כָּל תּוֹעֲבַת לִבּוֹ?

93 See note 56.
94 Abarbanel to 1 Kings 14 and the introductions to Jeremiah and Ezekiel.
95 Gen. 39:6 וַיְהִי יוֹסֵף יְפֵה־תֹאַר וִיפֵה מַרְאֶה 'and Joseph was handsome in form and appearance'.
96 Job 7:11, 10:1 בְּמַר נַפְשִׁי 'with the anguish of my spirit'.
97 1 Sam. 13:14 אִישׁ כִּלְבָבוֹ 'a man after his own heart'.
98 Ibn Ezra to Prov. 12; Alshekh to Prov. 22.
99 Jer. 9:7 (9:8 in English Bibles).

	Who could seize her other than him? There is no man, there is no man!	מִי יִלְכְּדֶנָּה בִּלְתּוֹ? אֵין אִישׁ, אֵין אִישׁ!	
	For there is none as quick in **cunning and schemes**[100] as he	כִּי אֵין כָּמוֹהוּ מְהִיר עָרְמָה וְתַחְבּוּלָה[100]	
	Who knows how to keep his appointed time and utter **a word in due season**[101]	הַיּוֹדֵעַ לִשְׁמֹר מוֹעֲדוֹ וּלְהוֹצִיא דָבָר בְּעִתּוֹ[101]	
	And even from **absolutely nothing**[102] can find advantage and **great reward**.[103]	וְגַם מֵאֶפֶס וָאַיִן[102] יִמְצָא לוֹ יִתְרוֹן וְעֵקֶב רָב.[103]	
	And only he is the adversary[104] for us, because he is still young in days	וְרַק הוּא הַשָּׂטָן[104] לָנוּ כִּי עוֹדֶנּוּ צָעִיר לְיָמִים	
	With beautiful eyes, a comely appearance[105] and **he is perfect in his splendour**[106]	יְפֵה עֵינַיִם טוֹב רֹאִי[105] וְכָלִיל הוּא בַּהֲדָרוֹ[106]	
	Whom foolish young damsels seek to love	אֲשֶׁר עֲלָמוֹת רַכּוֹת פּוֹתוֹת תְּבַקֵּשְׁנָה לְאַהֲבָה	
	And the woman has already raised her eyes to this villain.	וְהָאִשָּׁה כְּבַר נָשְׂאָה עֵינֶיהָ אֶל בֶּן־בְּלִיַּעַל הַזֶּה.	
RADDAI	I cannot believe this **wicked slander**[107] about her	לֹא אוּכַל לְהַאֲמִין דִּבָּה רָעָה[107] זוּ עָלֶיהָ	רדי
	For she is honourable, and full of **blessings of heaven**.[108]	כִּי כְבוּדָּה הִיא וּמְלֵאָה בִּרְכוֹת שָׁמַיִם.[108]	
DOEG	Full of false blessings –	מְלֵאָה בִּרְכוֹת שָׁוְא –	דואג
	The wine that she drinks, even it is grape juice.[109]	הַיַּיִן אֲשֶׁר תִּשְׁתֶּה, גַּם הוּא מִיץ עֲנָבִים.[109]	

100 Abarbanel to Gen. 32, Exod. 30, 2 Sam. 24.
101 Prov. 15:23.
102 Alshekh to Job 40.
103 Ps. 19:12 (19:11 in English Bibles).
104 Alternatively, 'devil' (based on the postbiblical meaning of the word).
105 1 Sam. 16:12 יְפֵה עֵינַיִם וְטוֹב רֹאִי 'with beautiful eyes and a comely appearance' (referring to King David in his youth).
106 *She'ilat Yaveṣ* part 2, 143 (a well-known work of responsa by the prominent German rabbi Jacob Emden [1697–1776]).
107 Ecclesiastes Rabbah 9.
108 Gen. 49:25.
109 Cf. Shakespeare's 'the wine she drinks is made of grapes' (2.1.249–50), which may be a mocking reference to sacramental wine (Schwarz 2004: 101) but is somewhat vague and subject to interpretation (Honigmann 1997: 179, notes 249–50); Salkinson has transformed this into an unambiguous and religiously neutral example of falseness.

	If she were full of **blessings of heaven,**[110] she would not cling to the Cushite;	לוּ מָלְאָה **בִּרְכוֹת שָׁמַיִם,**[110] לֹא דָבְקָה בַּכּוּשִׁי;	
	And what are her blessings? Didn't you see	וּמָה הֵנָּה בִּרְכוֹתֶיהָ? הַאִם לֹא רָאִיתָ	
	How she placed her fingers smoothly on his palm?	אֵיךְ שָׁתָה אֶצְבְּעוֹתֶיהָ עַל כַּפּוֹ לְמִשְׁעִי?	
	Didn't you see this? –	הֲזֹאת לֹא רָאִיתָ? –	
RADDAI	She did this as a sign that he pleased her.	זֹאת עָשְׂתָה לְאוֹת, כִּי מָצָא חֵן בְּעֵינֶיהָ.	רדי
DOEG	As a sign of lewdness and lusts, and this is the opening for **indecent behaviour**.[111]	לְאוֹת זִמָּה וַעֲגָבִים וְזֶה – פֶּתַח **דְּבַר עֶרְוָה**.[111]	דואג
	When they spoke mouth to mouth, they brought their lips close	כַּאֲשֶׁר דִּבְּרוּ פֶּה אֶל פֶּה, הִקְרִיבוּ שִׂפְתוֹתֵיהֶם	
	As if for lovers' kisses, and that is enough to understand, Raddai,	כְּמוֹ לִנְשִׁיקוֹת דּוֹדִים וְדַי בָּזֶה לְהָבִין רַדַּי,	
	That they are plotting evil, and after **secret love**[112]	כִּי הֵם חֹרְשִׁים רָעָה וְאַחֲרֵי **אַהֲבָה מְסֻתֶּרֶת**[112]	
	They will of course carry out their plot **and become one flesh.**[113]	הֲלֹא יְבַצְּעוּ זְמָמָם **וְהָיוּ לְבָשָׂר אֶחָד.**[113]	
	And now listen to me, for this is why I brought you from Venice.	וְעַתָּה שְׁמַע בְּקוֹלִי, כִּי לְזֹאת הֲבֵאתִיךָ מִוִּינֶעצְיָא	
	Stand watch tonight as I shall show you	עֲמֹד עַל הַמִּשְׁמָר בַּלַּיְלָה הַזֶּה כַּאֲשֶׁר אַרְאֶךָּ	
	For I shall keep guard opposite and shall not go far from you.	כִּי אֲנִי אֶשְׁמֹר מִנֶּגֶד וְלֹא אֶרְחַק מִמֶּךָּ.	
	And when you see the officer, who will consider you a stranger,	וְהָיָה בִּרְאוֹתְךָ אֶת הַפָּקִיד, אֲשֶׁר לְזָר יַחְשְׁבֶךָּ	
	Look for a pretext to provoke him and anger him	תְּבַקֵּשׁ לְךָ תֹּאֲנָה, לְהַמְרוֹת עֵינָיו וּלְהַכְעִיסוֹ	
	With harsh and bitter words, or with mockery and lies	בִּדְבָרִים קָשִׁים וּמָרִים, אוֹ בִשְׂחֹק וּמַהֲתַלּוֹת	
	Whatever you find occasion for.[114]	**כַּאֲשֶׁר תִּמְצָא יָדֶךָ.**[114]	

110 Gen. 49:25.
111 Mishnah *Giṭṭin* 9:10.
112 Prov. 27:5.
113 Gen. 2:24 (referring to Adam and Eve).
114 Judg. 9:33.

RADDAI	And afterwards –	וְאַחֲרֵי כֵן –	רדי
DOEG	He is quick to anger and his rage rises up within a moment	הוּא מְהִיר חֵמָה וְקִצְפּוֹ יַעֲלֶה כְּרֶגַע בְּאַפּוֹ	דואג
	And when he lifts his hand against you, provoke him with words	וְכַאֲשֶׁר יָרִים יָדוֹ עָלֶיךָ, הִתְגָּרֶה בּוֹ בִּדְבָרִים	
	So that he strikes you with his staff. As for my part, this blow will be enough for me	לְמַעַן יַכְּךָ בְּמַטֵּהוּ. וַאֲנִי דַּי לִי בְּמַכָּה זוֹ	
	To rouse the inhabitants of Caphtor to conspire to rebel	לְעוֹרֵר יוֹשְׁבֵי כַפְתּוֹר לְהִתְקַשֵּׁר לִמְרֹד מֶרֶד	
	And **they will not be at peace and will not rest**[115] until Chesed is banished from here.	**וְלֹא יִשְׁקְטוּ וְלֹא יָנוּחוּ**[115] עַד הִגָּרֵשׁ כֶּשֶׂד מִזֶּה.	
	And thereby your hope will come, for I am going to help you	וּבְזֹאת תָּבוֹא תִקְוָתְךָ, כִּי הִנְנִי לַעֲזֹר לָךְ	
	For after the obstacle is gone and there is no more **adversary or misfortune**[116]	כִּי אַחֲרֵי סוּר הַמּוֹקֵשׁ **וְאֵין שָׂטָן וּפֶגַע**[116] עוֹד	
	Who will stop me from fulfilling your soul's every desire?	מִי יַעֲצֹר אֹתִי, לְמַלֵּא כָל תַּאֲוַת נַפְשֶׁךָ.	
RADDAI	I shall do as you say if I can find the opportunity.	כֵּן אֶעֱשֶׂה כִּדְבָרְךָ אִם אֶמְצָא לִי יָדַיִם.	רדי
DOEG	Take my palm, for you will succeed on your way.	הֵא לְךָ כַּפִּי כִּי תַצְלִיחַ בְּדַרְכֶּךָ.	דואג
	Go to the citadel and there we shall speak further	לֵךְ אֶל הַמְּצוּדָה וְשָׁם נְדַבֵּר עוֹד	
	And as for me, I am going to bring his baggage from the ship.	וַאֲנִי הִנְנִי הוֹלֵךְ לְהָבִיא כֵלָיו מִן הַסְּפִינָה.	
RADDAI	Go in peace. *(Raddai exits)*	לֵךְ לְשָׁלוֹם. (רדי הולך)	רדי
DOEG	How easy to believe that Chesed desires to take her to his bed	מַה־נָּקֵל לְהַאֲמִין, כִּי כֶּשֶׂד מִתְאַוֶּה לְדַעְתָּהּ	דואג
	And who would vouch for her that she might not desire as well	וּמִי יֶעֶרְבֶנָּה כִּי לֹא תוּכַל לְהִתְאַוּוֹת גַּם הִיא	
	But the Cushite, who is hateful in my eyes, is a dear and innocent man	וְהַכּוּשִׁי הַנִּמְאָס בְּעֵינַי הוּא אִישׁ יָקָר וְתָמִים	

115 Job 3:26 וְלֹא שָׁקַטְתִּי וְלֹא־נָחְתִּי 'and I have no peace and no rest'.
116 1 Kings 5:18 (5:4 in English Bibles) אֵין שָׂטָן וְאֵין פֶּגַע רָע 'there is no adversary and there is no misfortune'.

And **the expression of his face testifies to**[117] his love and faithfulness for his wife.

וְהַכָּרַת פָּנָיו תַּעֲנֶה בוֹ[117] אַהֲבָתוֹ וֶאֱמוּנָתוֹ לְאִשְׁתּוֹ.

And I am determined to love her as well;

וַאֲנִי הִנְנִי נָכוֹן לְאַהֲבָה אֹתָהּ גַּם אָנִי;

Not out of passion and lust, like **the sins of my youth**[118]

לֹא מֵחֶמְדָּה וְתַאֲוָה, כְּפִי חַטְּאוֹת נְעוּרָי[118]

But rather out of the spirit of jealousy, after hearing **the slander of many**[119]

כִּי אִם מֵרוּחַ קִנְאָה, אַחֲרֵי שָׁמְעִי דִבַּת רַבִּים[119]

Saying that the Cushite desecrated my bed in secret.

לֵאמֹר חִלֵּל הַכּוּשִׁי אֶת מִשְׁכָּבִי בַּסָּתֶר.

And this spirit of jealousy has stirred like **rot in my bones**[120]

וְרוּחַ קִנְאָה הַזֹּאת נוֹסְסָה כְּרָקָב בַּעֲצָמָי[120]

And I cannot calm it until I am avenged of it

וְלֹא אוּכַל לְהַרְגִּיעַ עַד אֲשֶׁר אֶנָּקֵם מִמֶּנּוּ

With the seah[121] that he has measured for me – **a wife for a wife.**[122]

בַּסְּאָה[121] אֲשֶׁר מָדַד לִי – **אִשָּׁה תַּחַת אִשָּׁה.**[122]

And if I do not succeed in this desire

וְאִם חֵפֶץ זֶה לֹא יִצְלַח בְּיָדִי

I shall ignite the fire of jealousy in the heart of **this man whom I have appointed for destruction**[123]

אַצִּית אֵשׁ הַקִּנְאָה בִּלְבַב אִישׁ חֶרְמִי[123]

Until the waters of his wisdom are unable to extinguish the blaze.

עַד אֲשֶׁר מֵי תְבוּנָתוֹ לֹא יוּכְלוּ לְכַבּוֹת הַתַּבְעֵרָה.

And the fool of Venice, instead of **chasing the east wind**[124]

וְהַכְּסִיל מִוֵּינֶעצְיָא, תַּחַת רָדְפוֹ קָדִים[124]

Is prepared for **the rod of punishment**,[125] and he will be the instrument of my scheme,

נָכוֹן לְשֵׁבֶט מוּסָר[125] וְהוּא יִהְיֶה הַכְּלִי לִמְזִמָּתִי,

---

117 Isa. 3:9 הַכָּרַת פְּנֵיהֶם עָנְתָה בָּם 'the expression of their faces testifies against them'.

118 Ps. 25:7.

119 Jer. 20:10; Ps. 31:14 (31:13 in English Bibles).

120 Hab. 3:16.

121 A measurement used in the Hebrew Bible and rabbinic literature, equivalent to approximately 13.3 litres.

122 Exod. 21:24 עַיִן תַּחַת עַיִן שֵׁן תַּחַת שֵׁן יָד תַּחַת יָד רֶגֶל תַּחַת רָגֶל 'an eye for an eye, a tooth for a tooth, a hand for a hand, a foot for a foot'; Lev. 24:20 שֶׁבֶר תַּחַת שֶׁבֶר עַיִן תַּחַת עַיִן שֵׁן תַּחַת שֵׁן 'a breach for a breach, an eye for an eye, a tooth for a tooth'.

123 1 Kings 20:42.

124 Hosea 12:2 (12:1 in English Bibles) אֶפְרַיִם רֹעֶה רוּחַ וְרֹדֵף קָדִים 'Ephraim feeds on the wind and chases the east wind' (denotes pointlessness).

125 Prov. 22:15.

For if he stands on his watch as I instructed him

כִּי אִם יַעֲמֹד עַל מִשְׁמַרְתּוֹ כַּאֲשֶׁר הוֹרֵיתִיהוּ

Chesed will fall into my hunting-net, **he who stands as an adversary against me on the way**[126]

יִפֹּל כֶּשֶׂד בִּמְצוּדָתִי, הַנִּצָּב לְשָׂטָן לִי בַּדָּרֶךְ[126]

For I shall strike him down with my tongue and incite the Cushite to destroy him

כִּי אַכֵּהוּ בַלָּשׁוֹן וְאָסִית אֶת הַכּוּשִׁי לְבַלְּעוֹ

And he will love me more and will give me my sufficient reward

וְהוּא יֶאֱהָבֵנִי עוֹד וְנָתַן לִי דֵּי שְׂכָרִי

In exchange for managing to lead him **like a beast into the valley**[127]

תַּחַת אֲשֶׁר הִשְׂכַּלְתִּי לְהַנְחוֹתוֹ כַּבְּהֵמָה בַּבִּקְעָה[127]

And disturbing his peace and his rest until he goes mad.

וּלְהַפְרִיעַ שְׁלוֹמוֹ וּמְנוּחָתוֹ עַד לְהִשְׁתַּגֵּעַ.

Here my scheme is yet, confused in **desolation by night**[128]

פֹּה עוֹד מְזִמָּתִי, נְבוֹכָה בְּשׁוֹאָה וָאֶמֶשׁ[128]

Like every deceit and abomination, before it emerges into the light of the sun.[129] *(Exits)*

כְּכָל מִרְמָה וּנְבָלָה, טֶרֶם תֵּצֵא לְאוֹר הַשָּׁמֶשׁ.[129] (הולך)

SCENE 2 *(Herald on the town street with many people before him)*

מחזה ב' (מכריז ברחוב העיר ועם רב לפניו)

HERALD[130] In the name of the army commander, our lord the leader Ithiel,

מכריז[130] בְּשֵׁם שַׂר הַצָּבָא, אִיתִיאֵל אֲדֹנֵנוּ הָרֹאשׁ

Be informed that the Turks' ships have been destroyed in the sea

הִתְבַּשְּׂרוּ כִּי אֳנִיּוֹת הַתּוֹגַרְמִים אָבְדוּ בַּיָּם

And therefore today is for you **a day of feasting and joy**[131]

וְלָכֵן הַיּוֹם הַזֶּה לָכֶם, יוֹם מִשְׁתֶּה וְשִׂמְחָה[131]

A day of celebrations and delights, bonfires and dances

יוֹם הִלּוּלִים וְתַעֲנֻגִים, מְדוּרוֹת אֵשׁ וּמְחוֹלוֹת

For each man **as his soul desires**.[132] And this joy for you is doubled

לְאִישׁ אִישׁ כְּאַוַּת נַפְשׁוֹ.[132] וְשִׂמְחָה זוּ לָכֶם לְמִשְׁנֶה

---

126 Num 22:22 וַיִּתְיַצֵּב מַלְאַךְ יְהוָה בַּדֶּרֶךְ לְשָׂטָן לוֹ 'and the angel of the LORD stood on the way as an adversary against him'.

127 Isa. 63:14. Like Smolenskin (*Ithiel*, Preface, note 1), Salkinson seems to be using this citation to denote ignorance, whereas in Isaiah it refers to effortlessness.

128 Job 30:3 אֶמֶשׁ שׁוֹאָה וּמְשֹׁאָה 'by night in desolation and waste'.

129 This and the next line form a rhyming couplet, mirroring Shakespeare's 'confused/used' (2.1.309–10).

130 This speech is prose in the original (2.2.1–12).

131 Esther 9:17, 18.

132 Alshekh to Prov. 21.

	For on this day you will celebrate the army commander's wedding	כִּי בַיּוֹם הַזֶּה תָּחֹגּוּ חַג חֲתֻנַּת שַׂר הַצָּבָא	
	And you will rejoice with him at the head of his joy, in all the chambers of the palace	וְתַעַלְזוּ עִמּוֹ בְּרֹאשׁ שִׂמְחָתוֹ, בְּכָל חַדְרֵי הָאַרְמוֹן	
	For they will be open for all those who come	כִּי פְּתוּחִים יִהְיוּ, לִקְרַאת כָּל הַבָּאִים	
	To eat, to drink, and to laugh there, until the middle of the night.	לֶאֱכֹל לִשְׁתּוֹת וּלְצַחֵק שָׁם, עַד חֲצוֹת הַלָּיְלָה.	
	Long live the inhabitants of Caphtor! Long live Ithiel the army commander! *(Exeunt)*	יִחְיוּ יוֹשְׁבֵי כַפְתּוֹר! יְחִי אִיתִיאֵל שַׂר הַצָּבָא! (הולכים)	
SCENE 3	*The innermost chamber*[133] *of the palace (Ithiel, Asenath, Chesed, and attendants)*	דביר[133] בארמון (איתיאל אסנת כשד ומשרתים)	מחזה ג'
ITHIEL	Pay attention, Chesed, on the watch tonight	שִׂים עֵינְךָ כֶּשֶׂד, עַל הַמִּשְׁמָר בַּלַּיְלָה	איתיאל
	We would do well to be careful, to fulfil all service and duty	טוֹב לָנוּ לְהִזָּהֵר, לְמַלֵּא כָּל עֲבֹדָה וּמִשְׁמֶרֶת	
	Even in times of pleasure, lest we forget what our task is.	וְגַם בְּתַעֲנֻגִים בַּל נִשְׁכַּח מַה־פְּקוּדָתֵנוּ.	
CHESED	I have appointed Doeg to do the things that must be done	אֶת דּוֹאֵג הִפְקַדְתִּי לַעֲשׂוֹת אֶת אֲשֶׁר תֵּעָשֶׂינָה	כשד
	And I am also with him, and **my eyes are upon all his ways.**[134]	וְגַם אֲנִי עִמּוֹ וְעֵינַי עַל כָּל דְּרָכָיו.[134]	
ITHIEL	He is a loyal man in his service. Go in peace, Chesed	הוּא אִישׁ נֶאֱמָן בַּעֲבֹדָתוֹ. לֵךְ לְשָׁלוֹם כֶּשֶׂד	איתיאל
	Tomorrow early in the morning **come appear before me.**[135]	לְמָחָר בַּבֹּקֶר הַשְׁכֵּם תָּבוֹא לֵרָאוֹת אֶת פָּנָי.[135]	
	(To Asenath) And you **whom my soul loves!**[136]	(אל אסנת) וְאַתְּ שֶׁאָהֲבָה נַפְשִׁי![136]	

133 This word is attested in the Hebrew Bible, but assumes the sense of 'innermost chamber in a palace' only from the medieval period onwards (Even-Shoshan 2003, 1: 291).
134 Jer. 16:17 עֵינַי עַל־כָּל־דַּרְכֵיהֶם 'my eyes are upon all their ways'.
135 Exod. 34:24 לֵרָאוֹת אֶת־פְּנֵי יְהוָה 'to appear before the Lord'; also Deut. 31:11.
136 Song of Songs 1:7, 3:1, 2, 3.

	Come, let us satiate ourselves from the tree which we planted **with the sweat of our brow**[137, 138]	בּוֹאִי וְנִשְׂבְּעָה מֵעֵץ נָטַעְנוּ בְּזֵעַת אַפָּיִם[137, 138]	
	The tree is desirable to look upon and the fruit is a delight for the eyes.[139]	הָעֵץ נֶחְמָד לְמַרְאֶה וְהַפְּרִי תַּאֲוָה לָעֵינָיִם.[139]	
	(Ithiel, Asenath, and their men exit and Doeg enters)	(איתיאל אסנת ואנשיהם הולכים ודואג בא)	
CHESED	Greetings Doeg; let us make our way to the watch duty.	שָׁלוֹם בּוֹאֲךָ דוֹאֵג, נָשִׂימָה אֶל הַמִּשְׁמָר פְּעָמֵינוּ.	כשד
DOEG[140]	Not on this watch; the commander ordered us to go	לֹא בְּאַשְׁמוּרָה זוּ; הַשָּׂר צִוָּנוּ לָלֶכֶת	דואג[140]
	Before the appointed time, for the love of Asenath was pressing upon him.	טֶרֶם בָּא הַמּוֹעֵד, כִּי אַהֲבַת אָסְנַת הֱצִיקַתְהוּ	
	But we shall not condemn him in this **night of his pleasure**[141]	וַאֲנַחְנוּ לֹא נַרְשִׁיעֶנּוּ בְּנֶשֶׁף חִשְׁקוֹ[141] הַזֶּה	
	The first-night marital pleasures for **a loving and graceful doe**[142]	עוֹנַת לַיְלָה הָרִאשׁוֹנָה לְיַעֲלַת חֵן וַאֲהָבִים[142]	
	Whose **graceful proportion**[143] is so great as **to cheer God and men.**[144]	אֲשֶׁר חִין עֶרְכָּהּ[143] רַב לְשַׂמַּח אֱלֹהִים וַאֲנָשִׁים.[144]	
CHESED	She is a woman **very much praised for her beauty.**[145]	הִיא אִשָּׁה יָפָה לְהַלֵּל עַד מְאֹד.[145]	כשד
DOEG	And she has a heart for laughter and delights.	וְלָהּ לֵב לִצְחֹק וְשַׁעֲשׁוּעִים.	דואג
CHESED	She is **tender and delicate,**[146] like a budding rose.	רַכָּה הִיא וַעֲנֻגָּה,[146] כְּשׁוֹשַׁנָּה בְּאִבָּהּ.	כשד

137 Gen. 3:19 בְּזֵעַת אַפֶּיךָ תֹּאכַל לֶחֶם 'by the sweat of your brow you shall eat bread' (referring to Adam after eating from the tree of knowledge).

138 This and the next line form a rhyming couplet, mirroring Shakespeare's 'ensue/you' (2.3.9–10).

139 Gen. 3:6 טוֹב הָעֵץ לְמַאֲכָל וְכִי תַאֲוָה־הוּא לָעֵינַיִם וְנֶחְמָד הָעֵץ 'the tree was good for food and it was a delight to the eyes and the tree was desirable'.

140 This and the following speeches until Chesed's exit are prose in the original (2.3.13–44).

141 Isa. 21:4 אֵת נֶשֶׁף חִשְׁקִי שָׂם לִי לַחֲרָדָה 'my night of pleasure he has turned to terror'.

142 Prov. 5:19 אַיֶּלֶת אֲהָבִים וְיַעֲלַת־חֵן 'a loving hind and graceful doe'.

143 Job 41:4 (41:12 in English Bibles) וְחִין עֶרְכּוֹ 'and his graceful proportion' (referring to the mythological sea creature Leviathan).

144 Judg. 9:13 הֶחֳדַלְתִּי אֶת־תִּירוֹשִׁי הַמְשַׂמֵּחַ אֱלֹהִים וַאֲנָשִׁים 'should I leave my wine, which cheers God and men?' This is Salkinson's translation of Shakespeare's 'she is sport for Jove' (2.3.17), with the Classical reference removed.

145 2 Sam. 14:25 וּכְאַבְשָׁלוֹם לֹא־הָיָה אִישׁ־יָפֶה בְּכָל־יִשְׂרָאֵל לְהַלֵּל מְאֹד 'but in all Israel there was none to be so much praised as Absalom for his beauty'.

146 Isa. 47:1 כִּי לֹא תוֹסִיפִי יִקְרְאוּ־לָךְ רַכָּה וַעֲנֻגָּה 'for you shall no longer be called tender and delicate'.

DOEG	How beautiful her eyes are, like arrows she shoots in the heart of those who see her.	מַה־נָּאווּ עֵינֶיהָ, כְּחִצִּים תּוֹרָה בְּלֵב רֹאֶיהָ.	דואג
CHESED	Her eyes radiate grace and humility together.	עֵינֶיהָ מְפִיקוֹת חֵן וַעֲנָוָה יַחְדָּו.	כשד
DOEG	And how pleasant her speech is, like **a herald**[147] of love.	וּמַה־נָּעִים מִדְבָּרָהּ, כְּקוֹל **קֹרֵא**[147] לְאַהֲבָה.	דואג
CHESED	She is wholly beautiful, and **she is without blemish**.[148]	כֻּלָּהּ יָפָה **וּמוּם אֵין בָּהּ**.[148]	כשד
DOEG	Let them take their pleasure on their bed in peace.	יִתְעַנְּגוּ עַל מִשְׁכְּבוֹתָם בְּשָׁלוֹם.	דואג
	And now, officer, listen to me; I have a little wine here	וְעַתָּה הַפָּקִיד שְׁמָעֵנִי, הִנֵּה מְעַט יַיִן אִתִּי	
	And **the desirable young men**[149] of the town are standing there outside	**וּבַחוּרֵי חֶמֶד**[149] מִבְּנֵי הָעִיר עֹמְדִים שָׁם בַּחוּץ	
	And want to drink a cup to the life of the lord and the lady.	וּמְבַקְשִׁים לִשְׁתּוֹת כּוֹס לְחַיֵּי הָאָדוֹן וְהַגְּבִירָה.	
CHESED	Not this night, my dear; I cannot drink wine	לֹא בַלַּיְלָה הַזֶּה יַקִּירִי; לֹא אוּכַל לִשְׁתּוֹת יַיִן	כשד
	It is too strong for me. If only a different pleasure	חָזָק הוּא מִמֶּנִּי. מִי יִתֵּן וְעֹנֶג אַחֵר	
	Could be found instead of drinking **wine to make life merry**.[150]	יִמָּצֵא תַּחַת **יַיִן לְשַׂמַּח חַיִּים**.[150]	
DOEG	**Do not refuse me**;[151] behold, there are beloved companions outside	**אַל תָּשֵׁב פָּנַי**;[151] הִנֵּה רֵעִים אֲהוּבִים בַּחוּץ	דואג
	Won't you drink one cup, and I shall drink the rest instead of you.	הֲלֹא תִשְׁתֶּה כּוֹס אַחַת וְהַנּוֹתָר אֶשְׁתֶּה אֲנִי תַּחְתֶּיךָ.	
CHESED	Indeed I have already drunk one cup tonight **mixed with water**[152]	הֵן שָׁתִיתִי הַלַּיְלָה כּוֹס אַחַת **מָהוּל בַּמָּיִם**[152]	כשד
	And my insides are turning over like fire for the wine inflames me	וּבְקִרְבִּי יִתְהַפֵּךְ כְּמוֹ אֵשׁ כִּי הַיַּיִן יַדְלִיקֵנִי	

147 This expression derives from Isa. 40:3 קוֹל קוֹרֵא בַּמִּדְבָּר 'a voice crying out in the wilderness', but the meaning of 'herald' is thought to have originated in the modern period (Even-Shoshan 2003, 5: 1638). It could alternatively be translated 'a voice crying out for love', following the biblical meaning.

148 Num. 19:2 (a description of the red heifer, a cow brought to the priests for sacrifice and whose ashes were used for ritual purification).

149 Ezek. 23:6, 12, 23.

150 Eccles. 10:19 וְיַיִן יְשַׂמַּח חַיִּים 'and wine makes life merry'.

151 Ps. 132:10; 2 Chron. 6:42.

152 Isa. 1:22.

One cup is too much for me; I am no champion in drinking.

כּוֹס אַחַת רַב מִמֶּנִּי; גִּבּוֹר לִשְׁתּוֹת אֵינֶנִּי.

This is a weakness of my soul, and I cannot violate my rule.

זֶה רִפְיוֹן נַפְשִׁי וְלַעֲבֹר חֻקִּי לֹא אוּכַל.

DOEG Why are you babbling pointlessly? Indeed, tonight is a night of celebrations

דואג לָמָּה תְבַטֵּא חִנָּם הֵן הַלַּיְלָה לֵיל הִלּוּלִים

And you cannot abstain from the wishes of the **desirable young men.**[153]

וּמֵחֵפֶץ בַּחוּרֵי חֶמֶד[153] לֹא תִמְנַע אָתָּה.

CHESED So where are they?

כשד וְאָנָה אֵיפֹה הֵם?

DOEG They are standing at the door; go bring them into the house.

דואג הֵם עֹמְדִים לַפֶּתַח לְכָה נָא הֲבִיאֵם הַבָּיְתָה.

CHESED I shall do so **without desire.**[154] *(Chesed exits)*

כשד בְּלֹא חֶמְדָּה[154] אֶעֱשֶׂה כֵּן. (כשד הולך)

DOEG If I manage to give him one cup to drink

דואג אִם יַעֲלֶה בְיָדִי לְהַשְׁקוֹתוֹ כּוֹס אַחַת

In addition to the first cup that he drank this evening

נוֹסַף עַל הַכּוֹס הָרִאשׁוֹנָה אֲשֶׁר שָׁתָה בָּעֶרֶב

He will hasten to quarrel and fight like the small dog in my mistress' lap

יָחִישׁ לָרִיב וּלְהִתְקוֹטֵט כַּכֶּלֶב הַקָּטָן בְּחֵיק גְּבִרְתִּי

And Raddai, who in the sickness of his love **sees strange things and perversities**[155]

וְרַדַּי אֲשֶׁר בָּחֳלִי אַהֲבָתוֹ יִרְאֶה זָרוֹת וְתַהְפֻּכוֹת[155]

Has emptied bottles of wine to Asenath's life not once or twice

הֵרִיק אֲשִׁישֵׁי יַיִן לְחַיֵּי אָסְנַת לֹא אֶחָד וּשְׁנָיִם

And he stands on the watch with the three lads

וְהוּא יַעֲמֹד עַל הַמִּשְׁמָר עִם שְׁלֹשֶׁת הַבַּחוּרִים

The noblest of the sons of Caphtor, **proudly exulting**[156] and **easily angered**[157]

אֲצִילֵי בְנֵי כַפְתּוֹר עַלִּיזֵי גַאֲוָה[156] וּבַעֲלֵי אָף[157]

Whom I have already given drink until their heart was warm.

אֲשֶׁר כְּבַר הִשְׁקִיתִים עַד כִּי חַם לִבָּם.

---

153 Ezek. 23:6, 12, 23.

154 2 Chron. 21:20.

155 Prov. 23:33 עֵינֶיךָ יִרְאוּ זָרוֹת וְלִבְּךָ יְדַבֵּר תַּהְפֻּכוֹת 'your eyes see strange things, and your heart utters perversities'.

156 Isa. 13:3 עַלִּיזֵי גַּאֲוָתִי 'my proudly exulting ones'; Zeph. 3:11 עַלִּיזֵי גַּאֲוָתֵךְ 'your proud exulting ones'.

157 Prov. 22:24 אַל־תִּתְרַע אֶת־בַּעַל אָף 'do not associate with one easily angered'.

	And among this gang of drunkards I shall stir up Chesed	וּבֵין עֲדַת שִׁכּוֹרִים אֵלֶּה אָעִיר אֶת כֶּשֶׂד	
	To do something to anger all the inhabitants of the island.	לַעֲשׂוֹת דָּבָר לְמוֹרַת רוּחַ כָּל בְּנֵי הָאִי.	
	And behold, here they all come; **they stagger from strong drink**[158] –	וְהִנֵּה הִנָּם בָּאִים כֻּלָּם **תָּעוּ בַּשֵּׁכָר**[158] –	
	If my dream is true and its meaning emerges into the light[159]	אִם חֲלוֹמִי אֱמֶת וּפִתְרוֹנוֹ יֵצֵא לָאוֹר[159]	
	It will come quickly like a boat in the wind and the flow of the stream	יָחִישׁ לָבוֹא כִּכְלִי שַׁיִט בָּרוּחַ וְשֶׁטֶף הַיְאוֹר	
	(Chesed returns with Kenaz and the lads of the town)	(כשד שב עם קנז ובחורי העיר)	
CHESED	As I live! They have already given me too much to drink.	חַי אָנִי! כְּבַר הִשְׁקוּנִי יֶתֶר עַל הַמִּדָּה.	כשד
KENAZ[160]	On my word and my faith! One small measure	עַל דְּבָרִי וֶאֱמוּנָתִי! מִדָּה אַחַת קְטַנָּה	קנז[160]
	Not more than a log.[161]	לֹא יֶתֶר מִלֹּג.[161]	
DOEG	Bring wine. *(Holds a cup in his hand and sings)*	הָבוּ יַיִן. – (אוחז כוס בידו ומזמר)	דואג
	Drink my spiced mixed drink sweeter than song[162]	שְׁתוּ מִסְכִּי מָתוֹק מִזֶּמֶר[162]	
	Do not be bitterness for **the chief cupbearer**[163]	**לְשַׂר הַמַּשְׁקִים**[163] אַל תִּהְיוּ לְמֶמֶר;	
	A man of valour, a man of palate and throat	אִישׁ חַיִל, אִישׁ חֵיךְ וְגַרְגֶּרֶת	
	And the measure of the days of a man's life is a little finger	וּמִדַּת יְמֵי חַיֵּי אִישׁ, זֶרֶת	
	And therefore a man of valour must drink wine. –	וְלָכֵן אִישׁ חַיִל יִשְׁתֶּה חָמֶר. –	
	Bring wine! *(Wine is brought)*	הָבוּ יַיִן! (יין מובא)	

158 Isa. 31:11 וּבַשֵּׁכָר תָּעוּ 'and they stagger from strong drink'.

159 This and the next line form a rhyming couplet, mirroring Shakespeare's 'dream/stream' (2.3.59–60).

160 This and the following speeches (except the two songs) until Chesed's exit are prose in the original (2.3.62–115).

161 A small liquid measure equivalent to a sixth of a litre.

162 This song is composed of two pairs of rhyming lines. It differs substantially from the original, which reads 'And let me the cannikin clink, clink/And let me the cannikin clink./A solider's a man,/O, man's life's but a span,/Why then let a soldier drink!' (2.3.65–9).

163 Gen. 40:2, 9, 20; 41:9.

CHESED	How dear and pleasant is the song.	מַה־יָּקָר וְנָעִים הַזֶּמֶר.	כשד
DOEG	I learned this song in England	זֶמֶר זֶה לָמַדְתִּי בְּעֶנְגְלַאנְד	דואג
	For the men of England are **heroes in drinking wine.**[164]	כִּי אַנְשֵׁי עֶנְגְלַאנְד גִּבּוֹרִים לִשְׁתּוֹת יָיִן.[164]	
	Next to them the men of Germany, Denmark, or Holland	לְנֶגְדָּם אַנְשֵׁי אַשְׁכְּנַז דֶּענְמַארְק אוֹ הָאלְלַאנְד	
	Are all **as naught and nothing.**[165]	כֻּלָּם כְּאֶפֶס וּכְאָיִן.[165]	
CHESED	Do the men of England have great power in drinking?	הַאִם אַנְשֵׁי עֶנְגְלַאנְד רַב כֹּחָם בַּשְׁתִיָּה?	כשד
DOEG	Who can withstand a native of England?	מִי יַעֲמֹד לִפְנֵי יְלִיד עֶנְגְלַאנְד?	דואג
	Why, a man of Denmark would spin around, sway, and fall down like a dead man	הֵן אִישׁ דֶּענְמַארְק יָחֹג יָנוּעַ וְיִפֹּל כַּמֵּת	
	A man of the land of Germany would wallow under the table	אִישׁ אֶרֶץ אַשְׁכְּנַז יִתְגַּלֵּל תַּחַת הַשֻּׁלְחָן	
	And a man of Holland would surely spew **vomit and filth with no place untouched**[166]	וְאִישׁ הָאלְלַאנְד יָקִיא קִיא צוֹאָה בְּלִי מָקוֹם[166]	
	Before the Englishman had opened the second bottle.	טֶרֶם יִפְתַּח בֶּן עֶנְגְלַאנְד בַּקְבּוּק הַשֵּׁנִי	
CHESED	I hereby raise my glass to the life of the army commander.	הִנֵּה אֶשָּׂא כוֹסִי לְחַיֵּי שַׂר הַצָּבָא.	כשד
KENAZ	As do I; my mouth is like your mouth; I shall not deceive.	וְכֵן גַּם אָנִי; פִּי כְּפִיךָ לֹא אֲכַזֵּב.	קנז
DOEG	Dear England! *(Sings)*	עֶנְגְלַאנְד אֶרֶץ יְקָרָה הִיא! (מזמר)	דואג
	A man of many deeds was King Split[167]	אִישׁ רַב פְּעָלִים הָיָה הַמֶּלֶךְ פֶּקַע[167]	
	And he wore cloth trousers, two for a silver shekel[168]	וּמִכְנְסֵי בַד לָבַשׁ בְּשֶׁקֶל כֶּסֶף[168] שְׁנַיִם	

164 Isa. 5:22.

165 Isa. 41:12 כְּאַיִן וּכְאֶפֶס ‘as nothing and naught’.

166 Isa. 28:8 כִּי כָּל־שֻׁלְחָנוֹת מָלְאוּ קִיא צֹאָה בְּלִי מָקוֹם ‘for all the tables are filled with vomit and filth with no place untouched’.

167 In the Hebrew this song forms an ABAB rhyme. The king’s name, which is a nonsensical replacement for Shakespeare’s ‘Stephen’ (2.3.85), appears to have been chosen because it rhymes with the last word of the third line.

168 A shekel is a biblical weight (commonly used with reference to silver and gold) corresponding to approximately ten grams.

	And he complained because half a shekel had been added to his price	וַיִּתְאוֹנֵן כִּי הוֹסִיף עַל מְחִירוֹ בֶּקַע	
	And he called the trousers' tailor a dirty dog.	וְכֶלֶב טָמֵא קָרָא לְתֹפֵר הַמִּכְנָסַיִם.	
	He was mighty and elevated in **the highest places of the city**[169]	הוּא הָיָה אַדִּיר וְנִשָּׂא **בִּמְרֹמֵי קָרֶת**[169]	
	Whereas you **sit in a low place**;[170] you were born for labour and toil,	וְאַתָּה **יֹשֵׁב בַּשֶּׁפֶל**[170] נוֹלַדְתָּ לְעָמָל וּתְלָאָה,	
	Land after land is ruined because of pride	אֶרֶץ אֶרֶץ מִפְּנֵי גַאֲוָה נֶעְכָּרֶת	
	Arise, don your coat, a worn and patched coat.	קוּם לְבַשׁ אַדַּרְתְּךָ אַדֶּרֶת בָּלָה וּמְטֻלָּאָה.	
	Bring wine. –	הָבוּ יַיִן. –	
CHESED	This song is even more pleasant than the first.	הַמִּזְמוֹר הַזֶּה נָעִים גַּם מִן הָרִאשׁוֹן.	כשד
DOEG	Do you want to hear it again?	הֲתַחְפֹּץ לְשָׁמְעוֹ שֵׁנִית?	דואג
CHESED	I do not wish it –	לֹא חָפַצְתִּי בוֹ –	כשד
	A man who does this will not be prepared to stay at his post –	אִישׁ הָעֹשֶׂה זֹאת לֹא יִכּוֹן לְהִשָּׁאֵר עַל מַעֲמָדוֹ –	
	The heavens are above us – many will inherit eternal life	הַשָּׁמַיִם מִמַּעַל לָנוּ – רַבִּים יִירְשׁוּ חַיֵּי עוֹלָם	
	But many will not inherit it.	וְרַבִּים לֹא יִירָשׁוּ.	
DOEG	**You have spoken well**,[171] dear and pleasant officer.	**כֵּן דִּבַּרְתָּ**[171] פָּקִיד יַקִּיר וְנָעִים.	דואג
CHESED	And I expect to be one of the inheritors	וַאֲנִי מְצַפֶּה לִהְיוֹת אֶחָד מִן הַיּוֹרְשִׁים	כשד
	Not to the **bitterness of spirit**[172] of either the army commander or one of the ministers.	לֹא **לְמֹרַת רוּחַ**[172] שַׂר הַצָּבָא וְלֹא לְאַחַד הַשָּׂרִים.	
DOEG	And so do I.	וְכֵן גַּם אָנִי.	דואג
CHESED	You will not come into your inheritance before *I* have inherited	לֹא תָבוֹא לִירֻשָּׁתְךָ טֶרֶם יָרַשְׁתִּי אָנִי	כשד

169 Prov. 9:3.
170 Eccles. 10:6 וַעֲשִׁירִים בַּשֵּׁפֶל יֵשֵׁבוּ 'while the rich sit in a low place'.
171 Exod. 10:29.
172 Gen. 26:35.

	For the officer comes before the standard-bearer.	כִּי הַפָּקִיד רִאשׁוֹן לְנוֹשֵׂא הַדֶּגֶל.	
	But that's enough for us – let us go on our way	אַךְ רַב לָנוּ – נֵלְכָה נָּא לְדַרְכֵּנוּ	
	Forgive all iniquity! Each man to his work –	כָּל עָוֹן תִּשָּׂא! אִישׁ אִישׁ לִמְלַאכְתּוֹ –	
	Do not think, my brothers, that I am drunk,	אַל תַּחְשְׁבוּ אַחַי, כִּי מִשְׁתַּכֵּר אָנִי,	
	This is my standard-bearer – this is my right hand –	זֶה נוֹשֵׂא דִגְלִי – זֹאת הִיא יְמִינִי –	
	And this is my left hand – I am not an intoxicated drunk now	וְזֹאת הִיא שְׂמֹאלִי – שֹׁתֶה שִׁכּוֹר אֵינֶנִּי עַתָּה	
	Why, I am standing and not swaying, and my lips speak clearly.	הֵן אֶעֱמֹד וְלֹא אָנוּעַ וּשְׂפָתַי בָּרוּר תְּמַלֵּלְנָה.	
ALL	**Your speech is comely**[173] and pleasant.	מִדְבָּרֵךְ נָאוֶה[173] אַף נָעִים.	כלם
CHESED	If so, then do not consider me drunk. *(Exits)*	אִם כֵּן אֵיפוֹ לְמִשְׁתַּכֵּר אַל תַּחְשְׁבוּנִי. (הולך)	כשד
KENAZ	Arise, let us go to the camp and set the watch.	קוּמוּ וְנֵלְכָה הַמַּעֲרָכָה וְעָרַכְנוּ אֶת הַמִּשְׁמָר.	קנז
DOEG	Did you see the man who went out from here?	הֲרָאִיתָ אֶת הָאִישׁ אֲשֶׁר יָצָא יָצָא מִזֶּה?	דואג
	He is a man of valour; **he could stand before kings**[174]	הוּא אִישׁ חַיִל לִפְנֵי מְלָכִים יִתְיַצָּב[174]	
	But his carousing destroys him, for his soul contains good and evil	אַךְ סָבְאוֹ יַשְׁחִיתֶנּוּ, כִּי נַפְשׁוֹ תָּכִיל טוֹב וָרָע	
	Like **light and darkness**[175] in turn, this against that –	כְּאוֹר וְחֹשֶׁךְ[175] חֲלִיפוֹת, זֶה לְעֻמַּת זֶה –	
	My compassion is stirred for him,[176] and I also worry about the army commander	נִכְמְרוּ נִחוּמַי[176] עָלָיו וְגַם לְשַׂר הַצָּבָא דָאַגְתִּי	
	Lest **he be put to shame because of his hope,**[177] as he has placed much trust in him	פֶּן יֵבוֹשׁ מִמַּבָּטוֹ[177] אֲשֶׁר בָּטַח בּוֹ עַד מְאֹד	

173 Song of Songs 4:3.

174 Prov. 22:29. Cf. Shakespeare's 'He is a soldier fit to stand by Caesar' (2.3.118). Salkinson has replaced the culturally specific 'Caesar' with a more generic biblical reference to royalty.

175 Job 38:19.

176 Hosea 11:8.

177 Isa. 20:5 וְחַתּוּ וָבֹשׁוּ מִכּוּשׁ מַבָּטָם 'and they will be afraid and put to shame because of Cush their hope'.

	For with misfortune he will bring about confusion in the land.	כִּי בְמִקְרֶה לֹא טוֹב יַעֲשֶׂה לָאָרֶץ תּוֹעָה.	
KENAZ	Is this his usual way?	הַאִם כֵּן דַּרְכּוֹ כְּפַעַם בְּפָעַם?	קנז
DOEG	This is always his way; before he lay down on his bed	זֶה־דַּרְכּוֹ תָּמִיד; טֶרֶם יִשְׁכַּב עַל מִשְׁכָּבוֹ	דואג
	He would be able to keep a second watch	יֶשׁ לְאֵל יָדוֹ לִשְׁמֹר מִשְׁמֶרֶת מִשְׁנֶה	
	If only the drinking did not cast **sleep over his eyelids.**[178]	לוּלֵא תַפִּיל הַשְּׁתִיָּה תְּנוּמָה עַל עַפְעַפָּיו.[178]	
KENAZ	In my opinion the obligation is upon us to inform the army commander of the matter.	לְדַעְתִּי הַמִּצְוָה עָלֵינוּ לְהוֹדִיעַ הַדָּבָר לְשַׂר הַצָּבָא	קנז
	Maybe he is unaware of this, or he closes his eyes	אוּלַי נֶעְלָם זֶה מִמֶּנּוּ, אוֹ עֹצֵם עֵינָיו	
	Against seeing the shame of his officer, instead of the good that is in him;	מֵרְאוֹת בִּקְלוֹן פְּקִידוֹ, תַּחַת הַטּוֹב הַנִּמְצָא בוֹ,	
	What do you think?	מַה־יֶּהְגֶּה לִבֶּךָ?	
	(Raddai enters)	(רדי בא)	
DOEG	*(In a whisper)* What is wrong with you, Raddai? Go hurry after the officer.	(בלחש) מַה־לְּךָ רַדַּי? לֵךְ מַהֵר אַחֲרֵי הַפָּקִיד.	דואג
	(Raddai exits)	(רדי הולך)	
KENAZ	I am very sorry to see that the noble Cushite	צַר לִי מְאֹד לִרְאוֹת כִּי הַכּוּשִׁי הַנָּדִיב	קנז
	Has chosen as his second-in-command a man who has **a grievous evil**[179] within him	בָּחַר לְמִשְׁנֶה לוֹ אִישׁ אֲשֶׁר רָעָה חוֹלָה[179] בוֹ	
	Surely, it is **good and upright**[180] to reveal the matter to his ears.	הֲלֹא טוֹב וְיָשָׁר[180] לְגַלּוֹת הַדָּבָר לְאָזְנָיו.	
DOEG	Even if you gave me the island as my payment, I would not do this	אִם תִּתֵּן לִי הָאִי בִּשְׂכָרִי לֹא אֶעֱשֶׂה זֹאת	דואג
	For I am a friend to Chesed and seek a cure for his illness.	כִּי אֲנִי אֹהֵב לְכֶשֶׂד וּמְבַקֵּשׁ מָזוֹר לְמַחֲלָתוֹ.	
	But what is this voice? –	אַךְ מָה הַקּוֹל הַזֶּה? –	

178 Prov. 6:4 אַל־תִּתֵּן שֵׁנָה לְעֵינֶיךָ וּתְנוּמָה לְעַפְעַפֶּיךָ 'do not give sleep to your eyes, nor slumber to your eyelids'.
179 Eccles. 5:12 (5:13 in English Bibles).
180 Ps. 25:8.

	(A voice from outside, Save us, save us! Chesed is chasing Raddai!*)*	קול מחוץ הושיעה, הושיעה! כשד רודף (אחרי רדי)	
CHESED	Scoundrel! Villain![181] –	נָבָל! בְּלִיַּעַל![181] –	כשד
KENAZ	What is wrong with you, officer? What is this?	מַה־לְּךָ הַפָּקִיד? מַזֶּה?	קנז
CHESED	I shall strike and wound this scoundrel.	אֶת הַנָּבָל הַזֶּה אַכֶּה הַכֵּה וּפָצוֹעַ.	כשד
RADDAI	Strike me, please strike me.	הַכֵּנִי נָא הַכֵּנִי.	רדי
CHESED	Do you still open your mouth wide, scoundrel? *(Strikes Raddai with a powerful blow)*	הַעוֹד תַּרְחִיב פִּיךָ נָבָל? (מכה את רדי מכה עזה)	כשד
KENAZ	Please don't, officer! Stay your hand! *(Grasps his hands)*	אַל נָא הַפָּקִיד! הָשֵׁב אֶת יָדְךָ! (מאחז בידיו)	קנז
CHESED	Let go; why should I strike a blow to the cheek to you as well?	הַרְפֵּה, לָמָּה אַכֶּכָּה מַכַּת לֶחִי גַּם אוֹתְךָ?	כשד
KENAZ	Go out, go out, why, you are drunk –	צֵא צֵא, הֲלֹא שִׁכּוֹר אָתָּה –	קנז
CHESED	I am drunk? *(They fight each other with their swords)*	שִׁכּוֹר אָנִי? (נלחמים יחדו בחרבותם)	כשד
DOEG	*(In a whisper to Raddai)* Go quickly outside and call mutiny, mutiny!	(בלחש אל רדי) צֵא מַהֵר הַחוּצָה וּקְרָא קֶשֶׁר קֶשֶׁר!	דואג
	(Raddai exits)	(רדי הולך)	
	Please don't, officer, my friend! Please don't, sirs! –	אַל נָא הַפָּקִיד יְדִידִי! אַל נָא אֲדֹנִים! –	
	Help, help us! Desist, Chesed! Kenaz, my lord! –	עִזְרוּ עִזְרוּ לָנוּ! הֶרֶף כֶּשֶׁד! קְנַז אֲדֹנִי! –	
	Desist, my lord! – Help, rescue – why are you silent?	הֶרֶף אֲדֹנִי! – עִזְרוּ הוֹשִׁיעוּ – לָמָּה תַּחְרִישׁוּ?	
	Is this the watch? – *(Sound of the tower bell clamouring)*	הֲזֶה הוּא הַמִּשְׁמָר? – (קול פעמון המגדל הומה)	
	Who is making **a rumbling sound**?[182] – Why, **the whole town is astir**[183]	מִי מַשְׁמִיעַ קוֹל רַעַשׁ?[182] – הֲלֹא תֵהוֹם כָּל הָעִיר[183]	
	Desist Chesed, let go! Lest you become a disgrace	הֶרֶף כֶּשֶׁד הַנִּיחָה! פֶּן תִּהְיֶה לְבֹשֶׁת	

181 Cf. Shakespeare's 'Zounds, you rogue! you rascal!' (2.3.141); Salkinson has omitted the Christian oath.

182 Ezek. 3:12.

183 Ruth 1:19 וַתֵּהֹם כָּל־הָעִיר 'and the whole town was astir'.

	And your shame can never be erased.[184]	**וְחֶרְפָּתְךָ לֹא תִמָּחֶה**.[184]	
	(Ithiel and his men enter)	(איתיאל ואנשיו באים)	
ITHIEL	What is this?	מַה־זֹּאת?	איתיאל
KENAZ	My blood is spilling onto the earth,[185] he stabbed me with deathly cuts	דָּמַי מֻגָּרִים אָרְצָה,[185] הוּא דְקָרַנִי מַדְקְרוֹת מָוֶת	קנז
	Indeed he will also die –	מוֹת יָמוּת גַּם הוּא –	
ITHIEL	Stay your hands, for your lives depend on it.	הָשִׁיבוּ יְדֵיכֶם, כִּי בְנַפְשְׁכֶם הוּא.	איתיאל
DOEG	Stay your hand, officer! My lord Kenaz! –	הָשֵׁב יָדֶיךָ הַפָּקִיד! קְנַז אֲדֹנִי! –	דואג
	Look, sirs! –	רְאוּ אֲדֹנִים! –	
	Do you not have the sense to know what you and your deeds are?	הַאֵין לָכֶם לֵב לָדַעַת, מָה אַתֶּם וּמַעֲשֵׂיכֶם?	
	And do you not have an eye to see **before whom you stand?**[186]	וְאֵין לָכֶם עַיִן לִרְאוֹת, **לִפְנֵי מִי אַתֶּם עֹמְדִים?**[186]	
	You have gone too far, men – the army commander is speaking here –	רַב לָכֶם אֲנָשִׁים – שַׂר הַצָּבָא מְדַבֵּר פֹּה –	
	How do you know no shame –	אֵיךְ לֹא תֵדְעוּ כְלִמָּה –	
ITHIEL	Ah, what is this? From whence has this woe come upon us?	אֲהָהּ מַה־זֹּאת? מֵאַיִן בָּאַתְנוּ הַצָּרָה הַזֹּאת?	איתיאל
	Have we risen up instead of the Turks to swallow each other	הֲתַחַת הַתּוֹגַרְמִים קַמְנוּ לִבְלוֹעַ אִישׁ אָחִיו	
	Since they have been powerless to do us ill?	אַחֲרֵי אֲשֶׁר הֵם אָזְלַת יָדָם מֵהָרַע לָנוּ?	
	Feel shame, feel humiliation because of your waywardness, **cease to do evil**[187]	בּוֹשׁוּ הִכָּלְמוּ מִמְּשׁוּבֹתֵיכֶם, **חִדְלוּ הָרֵעַ**[187]	
	The man who causes further disturbances will be **condemned to death**[188]	הָאִישׁ הַפֹּרֵעַ פְּרָעוֹת עוֹד, **בֶּן מָוֶת**[188] הוּא	

184 Prov. 6:33 וְחֶרְפָּתוֹ לֹא תִמָּחֶה 'and his shame will never be erased'.
185 Cf. Shakespeare's 'Zounds, I bleed still' (2.3.160); Salkinson has removed the Christian oath.
186 Babylonian Talmud *Berakhot* 28b.
187 Isa 1:16.
188 1 Sam. 20:31; 2 Sam. 12:5.

	If he lifts his hand and his foot, he will surely be put to death within a moment.	אִם יָרִים יָדוֹ וְרַגְלוֹ, מוֹת יָמוּת כְּרָגַע.	
	Bring down the man who is ringing the tower bell,	הוֹרִידוּ אֶת הָאִישׁ הַמְצַלְצֵל בְּפַעֲמוֹן הַמִּגְדָּל,	
	This tumult of this bell is frightening all the inhabitants of the town.	הוֹלֵם פַּעֲמוֹן הַזֶּה יַחֲרִיד כָּל יוֹשְׁבֵי הָעִיר.	
	And you, dear Doeg, I see that your face	וְאַתָּה דוֹאֵג הַיָּקָר, רֹאֶה אֲנִי אֶת פָּנֶיךָ	
	Has fallen from sadness and grief, say who had a hand in this disloyalty?	כִּי נָפְלוּ מֵעֶצֶב וְיָגוֹן, דַּבֵּר מִי בַּמַּעַל הַזֶּה	
	Do not conceal anything from me;[189] indeed I command you.	אַל תְּכַחֵד מִמֶּנִּי דָּבָר[189] הֲלֹא אָנֹכִי צִוִּיתִיךָ.	
DOEG	I know nothing; in the beginning they were sitting together	לֹא יָדַעְתִּי מְאוּמָה, בַּתְּחִלָּה יָשְׁבוּ יַחְדָּו	דואג
	Friends like a groom and bride before they go to their bed,	חֲבֵרִים כְּחָתָן וְכַלָּה טֶרֶם יֵלְכוּ לְמִשְׁכָּבָם,	
	But within a moment the wheel turned, and led them astray	וּכְרֶגַע נֶהְפַּךְ הַגַּלְגַּל וַיּוֹלֶךְ אֹתָם שׁוֹלָל	
	For they **drew their flashing swords**[190] and they struck each other	כִּי הֵרִיקוּ בְּרַק חַרְבָּם[190] וַיַּכּוּ אִישׁ בְּרֵעֵהוּ	
	Until blood spilled upon them **and their swords devoured flesh**[191]	עַד שְׁפָךְ דָּם עֲלֵיהֶם וְחַרְבָּם אָכְלָה בָשָׂר[191]	
	And I still do not know what the grievance between them was.	וְעוֹדֶנִּי לֹא אֵדַע, מַה־דִּין וּדְבָרִים בֵּינֵיהֶם.	
	If only I could have died on the battlefield with honour	מִי יִתֵּן מוּתִי בִּשְׂדֵה הַמִּלְחָמָה בְּכָבוֹד	
	Before I came to see such indecency in our camp.	טֶרֶם בָּאתִי לִרְאוֹת עֶרְוַת דָּבָר כָּזֶה בְּמַחֲנֵנוּ.	
ITHIEL	What was wrong with you, Chesed, that you did this?	מֶה הָיָה לְךָ כֶּשֶׂד, כִּי עָשִׂיתָ זֹאת?	איתיאל
CHESED	Please forgive me, my lord! I cannot speak.	שָׂא נָא אֲדֹנִי! דַּבֵּר לֹא אוּכָל.	כשד

189 Jer. 38:14.

190 Deut. 32:41 אִם־שַׁנּוֹתִי בְּרַק חַרְבִּי 'when I sharpened my flashing sword'.

191 Deut. 32:42 וְחַרְבִּי תֹּאכַל בָּשָׂר 'and my sword devours flesh'.

ITHIEL	Kenaz! Indeed you have long been dear and honourable	קְנַז! הֲלֹא יָקָר וְנִכְבָּד הָיִיתָ מֵאָז	איתיאל
	Blameless and good-hearted in the land, and wise men have mentioned your name	תָּמִים וּבַר־לֵבָב בָּאָרֶץ וְשִׁמְךָ נָשְׂאוּ חֲכָמִים	
	What came over you that **you sullied your reputation**[192] within a moment	מֶה הָיָה לְךָ כִּי הִבְאַשְׁתָּ רֵיחֲךָ[192] כְּרָגַע	
	You cast down your name which was like **precious ointment**,[193] and you made another name for yourself	שִׁמְךָ כַּשֶּׁמֶן הַטּוֹב[193] מִגַּרְתָּ וַתַּעַשׂ לְךָ שֵׁם אַחֵר	
	As **a man of contention**[194] and blows? Will you not answer, Kenaz!	כְּאִישׁ מָדוֹן[194] וּמַהֲלֻמּוֹת? הֲלֹא תַעֲנֶה קְנַז!	
KENAZ	Look, honourable Ithiel, I have been struck a mortal blow	רְאֵה אִיתִיאֵל הַנִּכְבָּד, מַכַּת מָוֶת הֻכֵּיתִי	קנז
	Your servant Doeg saw, and will surely tell you everything	דּוֹאֵג עַבְדְּךָ רָאָה וְהַגֵּד יַגִּיד לְךָ כֹּל	
	Whereas I shall **refrain from speaking**,[195] for speech is difficult for me;	וַאֲנִי אֶעֱצֹר בְּמִלִּין[195] כִּי הַדִּבֵּר קָשֶׁה לִי;	
	Only this I shall say, that I have not done wrong tonight	רַק זֹאת אַגִּידָה, כִּי לֹא הֶעֱוֵיתִי הַלָּיְלָה	
	And I have not sinned with a word of the mouth nor with a deed of the hand	וְלֹא חָטָאתִי בִּדְבַר פֶּה וְלֹא בְמַעֲשֵׂה יָד	
	If it is not considered a sin for a man to save himself	אִם לֹא חֵטְא יֵחָשֵׁב, לְאִישׁ הַמַּצִּיל אֶת נַפְשׁוֹ	
	And an iniquity for one to guard his life from violence and murder.	וְעָוֹן לִשְׁמֹר אֶת חַיָּיו, מִפְּנֵי חָמָס וָרֶצַח.	
ITHIEL	**My heart grows hot within me;**[196] **I have no more rule over my spirit**[197]	חַם לִבִּי בְּקִרְבִּי[196] אֵין מַעְצֹר לְרוּחִי[197] עוֹד	איתיאל

192 Exod. 5:21 הִבְאַשְׁתֶּם אֶת־רֵיחֵנוּ 'you have sullied our reputation'.
193 Eccles. 7:1 טוֹב שֵׁם מִשֶּׁמֶן טוֹב 'a good name is better than precious ointment'.
194 Jer. 15:10.
195 Job 4:2 וַעְצֹר בְּמִלִּין מִי יוּכָל 'but who can refrain from speaking'.
196 Ps. 39:4 (39:3 in English Bibles).
197 Prov. 25:28 אִישׁ אֲשֶׁר אֵין מַעְצָר לְרוּחוֹ 'a man who has no rule over his spirit'.

	And instead of justice my soul's unrest rises up there;	וּבִמְקוֹם הַמִּשְׁפָּט שָׁם תַּעֲלֶה רִגְשַׁת נַפְשִׁי;	
	If I now arise[198] and raise my outstretched arm	אִם עַתָּה אָקוּם[198] וְאֶשָּׂא זְרוֹעִי הַנְּטוּיָה	
	Even the best of you will perish; from my rebuke he will become as nothing.	גַּם הַטּוֹב בָּכֶם יֹאבַד, מִגַּעֲרָתִי יְהִי לָאָיִן.	
	Speak, how did the quarrel break out? **Whose hand has been first in the trespass?**[199]	דַּבְּרוּ אֵיךְ פָּרַץ הָרִיב? יַד מִי בַּמַּעַל רִאשׁוֹנָה?[199]	
	And the man whose iniquity is in him, even if he is my brother,	וְהָאִישׁ אֲשֶׁר עֲוֹנוֹ בוֹ, אַף אִם אָחִי הוּא	
	I shall **by no means clear him**,[200] for I shall not favour a brother or friend.	נַקֵּה לֹא אֲנַקֵּהוּ,[200] כִּי אָח וְאֹהֵב לֹא אַכִּיר.	
	Is it really possible in a time of war, in a town full of terror and fear	הֲיִתָּכֵן בְּעֵת מִלְחָמָה, בְּעִיר מְלֵאָה מָגוֹר וָפַחַד	
	To stir up a quarrel at night, before the guards in the citadel?	לְעוֹרֵר רִיב בַּלַּיְלָה, לִפְנֵי הַשֹּׁמְרִים בַּמְּצוּדָה?	
	It is an outrage and a disgrace; Doeg, who started the outburst?	נְבָלָה הִיא וְשַׁעֲרוּרָה, דּוֹאֵג, מִי הֵחֵל בַּפָּרֶץ?	
KENAZ	If out of **love and brotherhood**,[201] you add to a word of truth	אִם מֵאַהֲבָה וְאַחְוָה,[201] תּוֹסִיף עַל דְּבַר אֱמֶת	קנז
	Or take away from it, you are not a man of valour.	אוֹ תִגְרַע מִמֶּנּוּ, לֹא אִישׁ חַיִל אָתָּה.	
DOEG	That's enough from you. –	רַב לָךְ. –	דואג
	May my tongue cleave to the roof of my mouth[202] if I speak a word	תִּדְבַּק לְשׁוֹנִי לְחִכִּי,[202] אִם אֲדַבֵּר דָּבָר	
	To cause pain to Chesed's heart; God forbid that I should do him ill	לְהַכְאִיב לֵב כֶּשֶׂד, חָלִלָה לִּי מֵהָרַע לוֹ	
	But nevertheless **my heart is resolved**[203] that I shall not deceive.	וּבְכָל זֹאת סָמוּךְ לִבִּי,[203] כִּי לֹא אֲכַזֵּב.	

198 Cf. Shakespeare's 'Zounds, if I once stir' (2.3.203); Salkinson has omitted the oath.
199 Ezra 9:2 וְיַ֤ד הַשָּׂרִים֙ וְהַסְּגָנִ֔ים הָיְתָ֛ה בַּמַּ֥עַל הַזֶּ֖ה רִאשׁוֹנָֽה 'and the hand of the princes and rulers has been first in this trespass'.
200 Exod. 34:7 וְנַקֵּה֙ לֹ֣א יְנַקֶּ֔ה 'and He will by no means clear [the guilty]'.
201 Babylonian Talmud *Berakhot* 16b and elsewhere in rabbinic and medieval Hebrew literature.
202 Ps. 137:6.
203 Ps. 112:8 סָמ֣וּךְ לִ֭בּוֹ לֹ֣א יִירָ֑א 'his heart is resolved; he does not fear'.

So now, listen, commander! The matter was thus:

וְעַתָּה שְׁמַע הַשָּׂר! כֵּן הָיָה הַדָּבָר:

I was sitting and talking with Kenaz

אֲנִי הָיִיתִי יוֹשֵׁב וּמְדַבֵּר עִם קְנַז

When all of a sudden a man came, crying out to save him

וְהִנֵּה אִישׁ בָּא פִּתְאֹם, מְצָעֵק לְהוֹשִׁיעַ לוֹ

While Chesed, with drawn sword, was chasing after him in order to strike him

וְכֶשֶׂד בְּחֶרֶב שְׁלוּפָה רֹדֵף אַחֲרָיו לְהַכּוֹתוֹ

Then Kenaz approached and urged him to put his sword back in its sheath

וַיִּגַּשׁ קְנַז וַיִּפְצַר בּוֹ לְהָשִׁיב חַרְבּוֹ אֶל תַּעְרָהּ

And meanwhile the man had fled outside

וּבֵין כֹּה וָכֹה וְהָאִישׁ בָּרַח הַחוּצָה

Crying out in a loud voice as he fled, and I ran after him

בָּרוֹחַ וּמְצָעֵק בְּקוֹל גָּדוֹל וְאָנֹכִי רַצְתִּי אַחֲרָיו

In order that he not make his voice heard, lest he frighten the inhabitants of the town,

לְבַל יַשְׁמִיעַ קוֹלוֹ פֶּן יַחֲרִיד יוֹשְׁבֵי הָעִיר,

But he, light on his feet, fled from me and was gone,

אַךְ הוּא קַל בְּרַגְלָיו נָס מִפָּנַי וְאֵינֶנּוּ,

And I was in a rush to come back into the house

וַאֲנִי נֶחְפָּז הָיִיתִי לָשׁוּב וְלָבוֹא הַבָּיְתָה

Since I heard the sound of quarrelling and the sound of weapons

אַחֲרֵי אֲשֶׁר שָׁמַעְתִּי קוֹל רִיב וְקוֹל נֶשֶׁק

And curses and condemnations from Chesed; I had never heard such things.

וּנְאָצוֹת וְגִדּוּפִים מִפִּי כֶשֶׂד, לֹא שָׁמַעְתִּי כֵן מֵעוֹדִי.

And when I arrived I found the two of them with **their swords against each other**[204]

וּבְבוֹאִי מָצָאתִי אֶת שְׁנֵיהֶם חֶרֶב אִישׁ בְּרֵעֵהוּ[204]

As you saw with your own eyes when you arrived as well.

כַּאֲשֶׁר רָאִיתָ בְּעֵינֶיךָ בְּבוֹאֲךָ גַּם אָתָּה.

With this I have told you everything that I know

בְּזֹאת הִגַּדְתִּי לְפָנֶיךָ כֹּל אֲשֶׁר יָדַעְתִּי

For I know nothing more than this.

כִּי יֶתֶר מִזֹּאת אֵינֶנִּי יוֹדֵעַ מְאוּמָה.

Indeed, this is the way of men, and even the most upright among them

אָמְנָם זֶה דֶרֶךְ אֲנָשִׁים וְגַם הַיָּשָׁר בָּהֶם

204 Judg. 7:22; 1 Sam. 14:20.

	Stumbles **when there is a chance.**[205] Indeed, it is true that Chesed	יִכָּשֵׁל **לְעֵת מְצֹא.**[205] הֵן אֱמֶת כִּי כֶּשֶׂד	
	Strayed from the righteous path and rushed to raise his hand against Kenaz	נָטָה מִדֶּרֶךְ הַיָּשָׁר וְנִמְהַר לְהָרִים יָדוֹ בִּקְנַז	
	As a man does to his fellow, in his anger and rage	כַּאֲשֶׁר יַעֲשֶׂה גֶּבֶר לְרֵעֵהוּ, בְּזַעְמוֹ וַחֲרוֹן אַפּוֹ	
	Despite this, in my opinion the iniquity is on the head of the man that fled	בְּכָל זֹאת לְדַעְתִּי, הֶעָוֹן בְּרֹאשׁ הָאִישׁ הַנָּס	
	Who aroused his rage and his fury **until there was no remedy.**[206]	אֲשֶׁר הֶעֱלָה אַפּוֹ וַחֲמָתוֹ **עַד לְאֵין מַרְפֵּא.**[206]	
ITHIEL	I know Doeg, that in your love and your faithfulness to Chesed	יָדַעְתִּי דוֹאֵג, כִּי בְּאַהֲבָתְךָ וֶאֱמוּנָתְךָ לְכֶשֶׂד	איתיאל
	You are trying to make light of his iniquity. –	תִּתְאַמֵּץ לְהָקֵל עֲוֹנוֹ. –	
	Listen to me, Chesed! I love you with all my heart	שְׁמָעֵנִי נָא כֶּשֶׂד! בְּכָל לִבִּי אֲהַבְתִּיךָ	
	But you will no longer be my officer **from this time forth and forevermore.**[207]	אַךְ פְּקִידִי לֹא תִהְיֶה עוֹד **מֵעַתָּה וְעַד עוֹלָם.**[207]	
	Because I am making you an example for many.	כִּי מוֹפֵת שַׂמְתִּיךָ לָרַבִּים.	
	(Asenath and attendants)	(אסנת ומשרתיה)	
ASENATH	What has happened here, my dear one?	מַה־נִּהְיְתָה פֹּה יַקִּירִי?	אסנת
ITHIEL	Rest **has been restored;**[208] let us return to our rest.	הַמְּנוּחָה **שָׁבָה לְאֵיתָנָהּ,**[208] נָשׁוּבָה נָּא לִמְנוּחָתֵנוּ.	איתיאל
	And as for your wounds, Kenaz, I shall heal them	וְאֶת פְּצָעֶיךָ קְנַז, אֲנִי אֶרְפָּא אֹתָם	
	Lead the man off from here. – *(They lead Kenaz off)*	הוֹלִיכוּ אֶת הָאִישׁ מִזֶּה. – (מוליכים את קנז)	
	Doeg, guard the town, quieten **quarrel and strife.**[209]	שְׁמֹר דוֹאֵג עַל הָעִיר, הַשְׁקֵט **רִיב וּמָדוֹן.**[209]	

205 Ps. 32:6.
206 2 Chron. 36:16.
207 Isa. 9:6, 59:21; Mic. 4:7; Ps. 113:2, 115:18, 121:8, 125:2, 131:3.
208 Exod. 14:27 וַיָּשָׁב הַיָּם לִפְנוֹת בֹּקֶר לְאֵיתָנוֹ 'and in the morning the sea returned to its normal course'.
209 Hab. 1:3.

	Come back, Asenath **my love**,[210] let us return to our bed. –	שׁוּבִי אָסְנַת רַעְיָתִי,[210] נָשׁוּבָה אֶל עַרְשֵׂנוּ. –	
	This is the lot of man, the lot of one who bears his weapon[211]	זֶה חֵלֶק לָאִישׁ, חֵלֶק לְנוֹשֵׂא נִשְׁקוֹ[211]	
	That **the sound of tumult**[212] and shouting should wake him up in **his night of pleasure.**[213]	קוֹל שָׁאוֹן[212] וּתְרוּעָה, יְעִירֻנוּ בְּנֶשֶׁף חִשְׁקוֹ.[213]	
	(All exit, but Doeg and Chesed remain)	(כלם הולכים ודואג וכשד נשארים)	
DOEG	What is wrong with you, officer? Is there a wound in your flesh?	מַה־לְּךָ הַפָּקִיד? הֲיֵשׁ פֶּצַע בִּבְשָׂרֶךָ?	דואג
CHESED	There is indeed, but there is no remedy for my wound.	יֵשׁ וָיֵשׁ וְאֵין מָזוֹר לְפִצְעִי	כשד
DOEG	God forbid.	חָלִלָה לְּךָ מֵאלֹהִים.	דואג
CHESED[214]	My honourable name, my honourable name, woe, for I have lost it!	שֵׁם כְּבוֹדִי, שֵׁם כְּבוֹדִי, אוֹי כִּי גָלָה מִמֶּנִּי!	כשד[214]
	My only glory in life has gone and is no more	תְּהִלָּתִי יְחִידָתִי בַּחַיִּים, אָזְלָה לָהּ וְאֵינֶנָּה	
	And what remains in my flesh is unclean like the flesh of a beast	וְהַנּוֹתָר בִּבְשָׂרִי, פִּגּוּל הוּא כִּבְשַׂר בְּהֵמָה	
	My honourable name, Doeg, oh, my honourable name!	שֵׁם כְּבוֹדִי, דּוֹאֵג, הָהּ שֵׁם כְּבוֹדִי!	
DOEG	By my faithful life! Indeed I thought that you had been struck	חֵי נַפְשִׁי הַנֶּאֱמָנָה! אָמוֹר אָמַרְתִּי כִּי הֻכֵּיתָ	דואג
	Or had borne a severe wound which causes more pain than any blow to the soul.	אוֹ נָשָׂאתָ פֶּצַע רָע, הַמַּכְאִיב מִכָּל נֶגַע בַּנָּפֶשׁ.	
	Of what account[215] is an honourable name? Why, it is **pointlessness and futility**![216]	בַּמֶּה נֶחְשָׁב[215] שֵׁם כָּבוֹד הֲלֹא שָׁוְא וְהֶבֶל[216] הוּא!	
	Many acquire one without a price, and are stripped of it for no reason	רַבִּים יִקְנוּהוּ בְּלֹא מְחִיר וְיִתְנַצְּלוּ אֹתוֹ חִנָּם	

210 Song of Songs 1:9, 15, 2:2, 10, 13, 4:1, 7, 5:2, 6:4.
211 This and the next line form a rhyming couplet, mirroring Shakespeare's 'life/strife' (2.3.253–4).
212 Isa. 13:4, 66:6.
213 Isa. 21:4 אֵת נֶשֶׁף חִשְׁקִי שָׂם לִי לַחֲרָדָה 'my night of pleasure he has turned to terror'.
214 This and the following speeches until Chesed's exit are prose in the original (2.3.258–330).
215 Isa. 2:22 כִּי־בַמֶּה נֶחְשָׁב הוּא 'for of what account is he?'
216 Alshekh to Job 7.

And your honourable name has not departed unless you announce so yourself.

וְשֵׁם כְּבוֹדְךָ לֹא סָר לוּלֵא תַשְׁמִיעַ כֵּן אָתָּה.

Get up, be a man, many ways are open for us

קוּמָה הֱיֵה לְאִישׁ, רַבִּים דְּרָכִים פְּתוּחִים לָנוּ

To make amends with the army commander; he removed you from your position

לְכַפֵּר פְּנֵי שַׂר הַצָּבָא; הוּא הֲדָפְךָ מִמַּצָּבֶךָ

Not out of **enmity and hate**,[217] but for a different reason

לֹא מֵאֵיבָה וְשִׂנְאָה,[217] רַק מִסִּבָּה אַחֶרֶת

Like a man who strikes his dog that has not sinned against him

כְּאִישׁ הַמַּכֶּה אֶת כַּלְבּוֹ אֲשֶׁר לֹא חָטָא לוֹ

Just in order to scare the lion. And now entreat him

רַק לְהַפְחִיד אֶת הָאֲרִי. וְעַתָּה חַל אֶת פָּנָיו

And he will favour you and be well disposed towards you.

וְהוּא יְחָנְּךָ וְיִרְצֶךָּ.

CHESED It would be better for me become a disgrace to than to be an officer to Ithiel

כשד תְּהִי נַפְשִׁי לְבֹשֶׁת, מִהְיוֹת פָּקִיד לְאִיתִיאֵל

Desecrating his honour with a servant as drunk, worthless, and despicable as me.

לְחַלֵּל כְּבוֹדוֹ בְּעֶבֶד שִׁכּוֹר, קַל וְנִבְזֶה כָּמוֹנִי.

For what am I now? A drunken, **reviling, and blaspheming**[218] man

כִּי מָה אֲנִי עַתָּה? אִישׁ שִׁכּוֹר מְחָרֵף וּמְגַדֵּף[218]

A man of strife[219] and blows, **stammering in a tongue that cannot be understood**[220]

אִישׁ רִיב[219] וּמַהֲלֻמּוֹת, נִלְעַג לָשׁוֹן אֵין בִּינָה[220]

Like a crane or a swallow chattering with its mouth[221] or like a madman playing with his shadow.

כְּסוּס עָגוּר מְצַפְצֵף בְּפִיו[221] וּכְסָר טַעַם מְשַׂחֵק בְּצִלּוֹ.

Oh, evil and destructive spirit that hides within wine!

הוֹי רוּחַ רָע וּמַשְׁחִית הַמִּסְתַּתֵּר בְּקֶרֶב הַיַּיִן!

217 Abarbanel to Gen. 32 and numerous other locations therein.

218 Ps. 44:17 (44:16 in English Bibles).

219 Isa. 15:10.

220 Isa. 33:19.

221 Isa. 38:14 כְּסוּס עָגוּר כֵּן אֲצַפְצֵף 'Like a crane or a swallow I chatter'.

	Indeed **I can imagine you and describe you, though I do not know you**[222] by name	הֵן אֲדַמְּךָ אֲכַנְּךָ וְלֹא יְדַעְתִּיךָ[222] בְּשֵׁם	
	If your name is not Satan. –	אִם לֹא הַשָּׂטָן שְׁמֶךָ. –	
DOEG	Who was the man whom you were chasing with your sword?	מִי הָיָה הָאִישׁ אֲשֶׁר רָדַפְתָּ אַחֲרָיו בְּחַרְבֶּךָ?	דואג
	What evil did he do to you?	מֶה עָשָׂה לְךָ רָעָה?	
CHESED	I do not know.	אֵינֶנִּי יוֹדֵעַ.	כשד
DOEG	The matter is very strange.	זָר הַדָּבָר מְאֹד.	דואג
CHESED	Like a dream **from too much activity**,[223] and nothing is clear to me	כַּחֲלוֹם בְּרֹב עִנְיָן[223] וְאֵין דָּבָר בָּרוּר לִי	כשד
	I remember words of a quarrel, but I do not know what about.	הִנְנִי זֹכֵר דִּבְרֵי רִיב וְלֹא יָדַעְתִּי עַל מָה.	
	How can a man bring **a foe and enemy**[224] inside himself	אֵיךְ יָבִיא אָדָם צַר וְאוֹיֵב[224] אֶל קִרְבּוֹ	
	Which captures his heart? How can we rejoice at the wine banquet	אֲשֶׁר יִקַּח אֶת לִבּוֹ? אֵיךְ נָשִׂישׂ בְּמִשְׁתֵּה הַיַּיִן	
	And **leap and dance**[225] so that we resemble a beast?	וּנְפַזֵּז וּנְכַרְכֵּר[225] עַל אֲשֶׁר נִדְמִינוּ לִבְהֵמָה?	
DOEG	Why are you still complaining, when the wine has left you?	לָמָּה תִּתְאוֹנֵן עוֹד וְהַיַּיִן יָצָא מִמֶּךָ	דואג
	See how quick as lightning **your soul has become upright within you.**[226]	רְאֵה אֵיךְ חִישׁ קַל, יָשְׁרָה נַפְשְׁךָ בָּךְ.[226]	
CHESED	The wine, one evil spirit, has indeed left me	הַיַּיִן, רוּחַ רַע אֶחָד, יָצֹא יָצָא מִמֶּנִּי	כשד
	But another spirit has come instead of it; it is anger and rage	וְרוּחַ אַחֵר בָּא תַּחְתָּיו, הוּא רֹגֶז וָכַעַס	
	One transgression brings another transgression,[227] and therefore I despise myself.	עֲבֵרָה גּוֹרֶרֶת עֲבֵרָה[227] וְלָכֵן מָאַסְתִּי נַפְשִׁי.	

222 Hymn of Glory, a twelfth-century acrostic hymn appearing at the end of the Shabbat morning liturgy. The hymn is attributed to Judah the Pious or to his father Samuel the Pious. Judah the Pious was an extremely prominent medieval scholar based in Speyer and Regensburg.

223 Eccles. 5:2 (5:3 in English Bibles) כִּי בָּא הַחֲלוֹם בְּרֹב עִנְיָן 'for a dream comes from too much activity'.

224 Lam. 4:12; Esther 7:6.

225 2 Sam. 6:16 וַתֵּרֶא אֶת־הַמֶּלֶךְ דָּוִד מְפַזֵּז וּמְכַרְכֵּר לִפְנֵי יְהוָה 'and she saw King David leaping and dancing before the LORD' (referring to David's wife Michal, watching him receive the Ark in Jerusalem).

226 Hab. 2:4 לֹא־יָשְׁרָה נַפְשׁוֹ בּוֹ 'his soul is not upright within him'.

227 Mishnah *Avot* 4:2.

DOEG	Desist, that's enough from you, do not chastise yourself too much	הֶרֶף, רַב לָךְ, אַל תְּיַסֵּר נַפְשְׁךָ יֶתֶר מִדָּי	דואג
	If only that which happened to us had not happened	מִי יִתֵּן וְלֹא קָרָה אֵת אֲשֶׁר קָרָה לָנוּ	
	But be insightful and wise, and turn the incident into good.	אַךְ הַשְׂכִּילָה וַחֲכָם וַהֲפֹךְ הַמִּקְרֶה לְטוֹבָה.	
CHESED	When I entreat him to return me to my position	כִּי אֲחַלֶּה אֶת פָּנָיו, לְהוֹשִׁיבֵנִי עַל כַּנִּי	כשד
	And he says to me: 'Why, you're a drunkard':	וְהוּא יֹאמַר אֵלָי: הֲלֹא שִׁכּוֹר אָתָּה:	
	What shall I answer him with my mouth? Even if I had a thousand mouths[228]	מָה אָשִׁיב לוֹ בְּפִי? וְאִם אֶלֶף פִּיּוֹת לִי[228]	
	Why, every mouth would be blocked, for I cannot find a response.	הֲלֹא יִסָּכֵר כָּל פֶּה, כִּי לֹא אֶמְצָא מַעֲנֶה.	
	Who would have said to a man of sense that he should turn into a brute!	מִי מִלֵּל לְבַעַל דַּעַת, כִּי יִתְהַפֵּךְ לְבַעַר!	
	Cursed be the cup **which is not according to the law**![229] Its wine is the wine of sea- serpents![230]	אֲרוּרָה הַכּוֹס אֲשֶׁר לֹא כַדָּת![229] יֵינָהּ יֵין תַּנִּינִים![230]	
DOEG	Please don't, Chesed, do not curse the wine	אַל נָא כֶּשֶׂד אַל תָּאֹר אֶת הַיַּיִן	דואג
	For it is very good if **it goes down smoothly**.[231]	כִּי טוֹב הוּא מְאֹד אִם יִתְהַלֵּךְ בְּמֵישָׁרִים.[231]	
	And of course you know that I love you with a pure heart.	וְאַתָּה הֲלֹא יָדַעְתָּ כִּי אֲהַבְתִּיךָ בְּלֵב תָּמִים.	
CHESED	And as a sign, I satisfied your desire and drank the cup from your hand.	וּלְאוֹת מִלֵּאתִי רְצוֹנְךָ וָאֵשְׁתְּ הַכּוֹס מִיָּדֶךָ.	כשד
DOEG	This way or that, a man may get drunk two or three times	כָּזֹאת וְכָזֹאת יִשְׁתַּכֵּר אָדָם פַּעֲמַיִם שָׁלֹשׁ	דואג
	Nonetheless he is not a drunkard. And now come, I shall advise you	בְּכָל זֹאת סֹבֵא אֵינֶנּוּ. וְעַתָּה לֵךְ אִיעָצְךָ	

228 Cf. Shakespeare's 'had I as many mouths as Hydra' (2.3.299); Salkinson has neutralized the Classical mythological reference.

229 Esther 4:16.

230 The translation 'sea-serpents' (which appears in the Creation story in Gen. 1:21 and in various other locations in the Hebrew Bible) seems to be intended as an equivalent to Shakespeare's 'devil' (2.3.303).

231 Prov. 23:31.

	Behold, the lady Asenath rules over the army commander	הִנֵּה אָסְנַת הַגְּבִירָה מֹשֶׁלֶת בְּשַׂר הַצָּבָא	
	For her beauty captures his heart and her splendour is like a spell over him	כִּי יָפְיָהּ יִקַּח לִבּוֹ וַהֲדָרָהּ כְּקֶסֶם לְנֶגְדּוֹ	
	Pour out your heart in her bosom, and you will be saved by her.	שְׁפֹךְ לִבְּךָ בְּחֵיקָהּ וְעַל יָדָהּ תִּוָּשֵׁעַ.	
	For she is most merciful, and she has **a willing spirit**[232]	כִּי רַבַּת חֶסֶד הִיא וְרוּחָהּ **רוּחַ נְדִיבָה**[232]	
	And if you urge her, to sew up the bond of love	וְאִם תִּפְצַר בָּהּ, לִתְפֹּר קֶשֶׁר הָאַהֲבָה	
	Whose threads have been severed, between you and her husband	אֲשֶׁר נִתְּקוּ חוּטָיו, בֵּינְךָ וּבֵין בַּעְלָהּ	
	I warrant you that the bond will be twice as strong	אָנֹכִי עָרַבְתִּי לְךָ, כִּי יִתְחַזֵּק הַקֶּשֶׁר	
	As it was before.	כִּפְלַיִם מֵאֲשֶׁר הָיָה לְפָנִים.	
CHESED	Your advice is good.	עֲצָתְךָ טוֹבָה.	כשד
DOEG	My advice stems from my honesty, from a source of faithful love.	עֲצָתִי נֹבַעַת מִתֻּמָּתִי, מִמְּקוֹר אַהֲבָה נֶאֱמָנָה.	דואג
CHESED	So my heart tells me; tomorrow early in the morning	כֵּן לְבָבִי יַגִּיד לִי; לְמָחָר בַּבֹּקֶר הַשְׁכֵּם.	כשד
	I shall come to beseech her to help me in my wretchedness	אָבוֹא לְהִתְחַנֵּן אֵלֶיהָ, לַעֲזֹר לִי בְּעָנְיִי	
	And if my request does not come to pass, I shall know that I am lost.	וְאִם לֹא תָבוֹא שְׁאֵלָתִי, אֵדַע כִּי אָבַדְתִּי.	
DOEG	Thus your path is straight ahead. Go to your bed in peace.	כֵּן דַּרְכְּךָ לְנֹכַח; לֵךְ אֶל מִשְׁכָּבְךָ בְּשָׁלוֹם.	דואג
	Meanwhile, I'll go to my watch.	וַאֲנִי הִנְנִי הוֹלֵךְ אֶל מִשְׁמַרְתִּי.	
CHESED	Go in peace, faithful Doeg. *(Chesed exits)*	לֵךְ לְשָׁלוֹם דּוֹאֵג הַנֶּאֱמָן. (כשד הולך)	כשד
DOEG	Who would say of me, that I am a villain? –	מִי יֹאמַר עָלַי, כִּי בֶן בְּלִיַּעַל אָנִי? –	דואג
	Why, I have given him **good and sound advice**[233]	הֲלֹא **עֵצָה טוֹבָה וּנְכוֹנָה**[233] נָתַתִּי לוֹ	

232 Ps. 51:14 (51:12 in English Bibles).

233 Ibn Ezra to Exod. 18; *Sefer Ḥasidim* section 134 (a twelfth- or thirteenth-century work by Judah the Pious on the daily life of medieval German Jews; it was well known among later Ashkenazic Jewish readers and would have been familiar to Salkinson).

Of **how he might regain favour with**[234] the Cushite, for how easy it would be	בַּמֶּה יִתְרַצֶּה אֶל[234] הַכּוּשִׁי, כִּי מַה־נָּקֵל
To persuade Asenath to intercede on his behalf	לְפַתּוֹת אֶת לֵב אָסְנַת אֲשֶׁר תַּפְגִּיעַ בַּעֲדוֹ
And if she intercedes, the Cushite will not turn her away	וְאִם הִיא תַפְגִּיעַ לֹא יָשִׁיב הַכּוּשִׁי אֶת פָּנֶיהָ
For he is ensnared in her love and **after she speaks he will not change anything.**[235]	כִּי נִלְכָּד הוּא בְּאַהֲבָתָהּ וְאַחֲרֵי דְבָרֶיהָ לֹא יְשַׁנֶּה.[235]
And if she told him to separate himself from the congregation of the Lord[236]	וְכִי תֹאמַר אֵלָיו, לְהִבָּדֵל מִקְּהַל אֲדֹנָי[236]
Or to **risk his life,**[237] he would not refuse her	אוֹ לְהַשְׁלִיךְ נַפְשׁוֹ מִנֶּגֶד,[237] לֹא יִמְנַע מִמֶּנָּה
For he is weak **and she rules over him.**[238]	כִּי רְפֵה כֹחַ הוּא וְהִיא תִמְשָׁל בּוֹ.[238]
And since I have given Chesed sound advice to help him,	וְאַחֲרֵי אֲשֶׁר יָעַצְתִּי לְכֶשֶׂד, עֵצָה נְכוֹנָה לְעֶזְרָתוֹ
Who would consider me a bad counsellor and villain? –	מִי זֶה יַחְשְׁבֵנִי, לְיוֹעֵץ רָע וּבְלִיַּעַל? –
Except that my paths are **the way to Sheol, going down to the chambers of death**[239]	אֶפֶס דַּרְכֵי שְׁאוֹל נְתִיבָתַי, יוֹרְדוֹת חַדְרֵי מָוֶת[239]
For both the devil and I **put on righteousness as a cloak**[240]	כִּי כַשָּׂטָן כָּמוֹנִי, נִלְבַּשׁ כַּמְּעִיל צְדָקָה[240]
So that we might do evil. For when this simpleton in his innocence	לְמַעַן נוּכַל לְהָרֵעַ. כִּי פֶּתִי הַזֶּה בְּתֻמָּתוֹ
Beseeches Asenath to restore him to his position	כַּאֲשֶׁר יִתְחַנֵּן אֶל אָסְנַת, לַהֲשִׁיבוֹ עַל כַּנּוֹ

---

234 1 Sam. 29:4 וּבַמֶּה יִתְרַצֶּה זֶה אֶל־אֲדֹנָיו 'and how might he regain favour with his master'.

235 Job 29:22 אַחֲרֵי דְבָרִי לֹא יִשְׁנוּ 'after I spoke they did not speak again'; Ps. 89:35 וּמוֹצָא שְׂפָתַי לֹא אֲשַׁנֶּה 'and I shall not alter what has gone forth from my lips'.

236 Salkinson has removed the explicitly Christian content of Shakespeare's 'to renounce his baptism' (2.3.338).

237 Judg. 9:17 וַיַּשְׁלֵךְ אֶת־נַפְשׁוֹ מִנֶּגֶד 'and he risked his life'.

238 Gen. 3:16 וְהוּא יִמְשָׁל־בָּךְ 'and he will rule over you' (God speaking to Eve about her husband Adam).

239 Prov. 7:27 דַּרְכֵי שְׁאוֹל בֵּיתָהּ יֹרְדוֹת אֶל־חַדְרֵי־מָוֶת 'her house is the way to Sheol, going down to the chambers of death'.

240 Isa. 59:17 וַיִּלְבַּשׁ צְדָקָה כַּשִּׁרְיָן [...] וַיַּעַט כַּמְּעִיל קִנְאָה 'he put on righteousness as a breastplate [...] and wrapped himself in zeal as a cloak'.

And she intercedes on his behalf to her husband the Cushite,

וְהִיא תַפְגִּיעַ בַּעֲדוֹ, אֶל בַּעֲלָהּ הַכּוּשִׁי

Then I shall whisper in his ears that it is only because she desires him

אֲלַחֵשׁ אָז בְּאָזְנָיו, כִּי רַק מֵאֲשֶׁר חָשְׁקָה בּוֹ

That she intercedes on his behalf like this, and the more determined she is

תַּפְגִּיעַ בַּעֲדוֹ כָּזֹאת, וְכָל עוֹד אֲשֶׁר תִּתְאַמֵּץ

To do kindness to Chesed, the more she will fall in her husband's eyes

לִגְמֹל חֶסֶד לְכֶשֶׂד, כֵּן תִּפֹּל בְּעֵינֵי בַעֲלָהּ

And the kindness which she planned to do, will be a snare for her

וְהַחֶסֶד אֲשֶׁר חָשְׁבָה לַעֲשׂוֹת, יִהְיֶה לָהּ לְמוֹקֵשׁ

And her goodness will become brimstone and all her kindness will become pitch

וְנֶהְפַּךְ טוּבָהּ לְגָפְרִית וְכָל חַסְדָּהּ לְזֶפֶת

And from there fire will come out and devour them all. –

וּמִשָּׁם תֵּצֵא אֵשׁ וְתֹאכַל אֶת כֻּלָּם. –

(To Raddai as he enters) Are you well, Raddai?

(אל רדי בבואו) הֲשָׁלוֹם לְךָ רַדַּי?

RADDAI[241] I am running here and there, not like a dog hunting prey

רדי[241] הִנְנִי רָץ כֹּה וָכֹה, לֹא כְּכֶלֶב לָצוּד צַיִד

But rather barking at the hunters.

כִּי אִם בִּלְתִּי לִנְבֹּחַ מֵאַחֲרֵי הַצַּיָּדִים.

Indeed I have been struck this night, **blows to the innermost parts of the belly**[242]

הֵן הֻכֵּיתִי בַּלַּיְלָה הַזֶּה, מַכּוֹת חַדְרֵי בָטֶן[242]

And my money has gone from my purse, so **why should I wait any longer**?[243]

וְכַסְפִּי אָזַל מִכִּיסִי **וּמָה אוֹחִיל עוֹד**?[243]

Is this the fruit of my labour, that I should return to Venice

הֲזֶה הוּא פְּרִי עֲמָלִי, כִּי אָשׁוּב לְוִינֶעצְיָא

With the benefit of little knowledge, with **a cruel chastisement**,[244] and with no money.

בְּיִתְרוֹן דַּעַת מְעָט, בְּמוּסָר **אַכְזָרִי**[244] וְאֵין כָּסֶף.

241 These lines are prose in the original (2.3.358–64).

242 Prov. 20:30.

243 2 Kings 6:33 מָה־אוֹחִיל לַיהוָה עוֹד 'why should I wait for the LORD any longer?'

244 Jer. 30:14.

DOEG	How wretched is man, if he has no patience?	מֶה אֻמְלָל הָאִישׁ, אִם אֵין לוֹ אֹרֶךְ רוּחַ?	דואג
	Who can cure the sick man, if not gradually?	מִי יְרַפֵּא אֶת הַחֹלֶה, אִם לֹא עַל יַד עַל יָד?	
	And after all, you know that we are bringing our work to light	וְאַתָּה הֲלֹא יָדַעְתָּ, כִּי נוֹצִיא פְּעֻלָּתֵנוּ לָאוֹר	
	By counsel, wisdom, and cunning, and not by witchcraft	בְּעֵצָה חָכְמָה וְתַחְבּוּלָה וְלֹא עַל יְדֵי כְשָׁפִים	
	And therefore our work must take its time, and must not be rushed	וְלָכֵן תִּמָּשֵׁךְ פְּעֻלָּתֵנוּ וְלֹא מְבֹהֶלֶת תִּהְיֶה	
	Lest its end not be blessed. Has your way not been successful?	פֶּן לֹא תְבֹרַךְ אַחֲרִיתָהּ. הַאִם דַּרְכְּךָ לֹא צָלֵחָה?	
	Chesed struck you a small blow and you deposed him from his position	כשֶׁד* הִכְּךָ מַכָּה קְטַנָּה וְאַתָּה הוֹרַדְתָּהוּ מִמַּצָּבוֹ	
	And what is wrong with you, that you cried out?[245] Plants grow in the sun	**וּמַה־לְּךָ כִּי נִזְעָקְתָּ?**[245] נְטִיעִים לִפְנֵי שֶׁמֶשׁ יִצְמָחוּ	
	But their fruit does not ripen before they bud and bloom.	אַךְ לֹא יַבְשִׁילוּ פִּרְיָם, טֶרֶם יָצִיצוּ וְיַפְרִיחוּ.	
	Wait a moment and you will eat **the fruit of your deeds.**[246]	הוֹחִילָה מְעַט רֶגַע **וּפְרִי מַעֲלָלֶיךָ תֹּאכַל.**[246]	
	But look, **the morning has dawned,**[247] with much work and joy	אַךְ רְאֵה **הַבֹּקֶר אוֹר,**[247] בְּרֹב עֲבֹדָה וְשִׂמְחָה	
	The night is over and gone,[248] quick, return to the place of your watch	**הַלַּיְלָה חָלַף הָלַךְ לוֹ,**[248] מַהֵר שׁוּב לִמְקוֹם מִשְׁמַרְתֶּךָ	
	And I shall tell you the rest of **the pleasing words**[249] at the appointed time.	וְיֶתֶר **דִּבְרֵי חֵפֶץ,**[249] אַשְׁמִיעֲךָ לְעֵת מוֹעֵד.	
	Why do you still hesitate? Hurry, do not stay standing.	לָמָּה תִּתְמַהְמַהּ עוֹד? חוּשָׁה אַל תַּעֲמֹד.	

245 Judg. 18:23. Although the meaning of the root ז.ע.ק. means 'gather' or 'assemble' in the *nif'al* stem, Salkinson seems to have had in mind the meaning of the *qal*, 'cry out'; the likelihood of this is reinforced by the fact that he uses the same expression in other contexts where it clearly has the sense of 'cry out' (see Fifth Part, note 19 and *Ram and Jael*, First Part, note 315).

246 Isa. 3:10 פְּרִי מַעַלְלֵיהֶם יֹאכֵלוּ 'they will eat the fruit of their deeds'.

247 Gen. 44:3.

248 Song of Songs 2:11 הַגֶּשֶׁם חָלַף הָלַךְ לוֹ 'the rain is over and gone'.

249 Eccles. 12:10.

(Raddai exits)

(רדי הולך)

With two things my plan will be complete, I shall send my wife

בִּשְׁתַּיִם תִּכּוֹן עֲצָתִי, אֶת אִשְׁתִּי אֶשְׁלְחָה

To convince her lady to go out to save Chesed

לְדַבֵּר עַל לֵב גְּבִרְתָּהּ, לָצֵאת לְהוֹשִׁיעַ לְכֶשֶׂד

And as for the Cushite, I shall lead him astray, **by speaking to him privately**[250]

וְאֶת הַכּוּשִׁי אַטֵּהוּ, לְדַבֵּר אִתּוֹ בַּשֶּׁלִי[250]

And bring him without knowledge to a place where he will find Chesed

וְלַהֲבִיאוֹ בִּבְלִי דַעַת, בַּאֲשֶׁר יִמְצָא אֶת כֶּשֶׂד

Pleading before his wife. –

בְּהִתְחַנְּנוֹ לִפְנֵי אִשְׁתּוֹ. –

This is the way and the gate,[251] to execute a scheme and a deception[252]

זֶה הַדֶּרֶךְ וְהַשַּׁעַר,[251] לְבַצַּע מְזִמָּה וּרְמִיָּה[252]

And indeed the appointed time is close, **and my hands will achieve success.**[253]

וְהֵן הַמּוֹעֵד קָרוֹב וְיָדַי תַּעֲשֶׂינָה תוּשִׁיָּה.[253]

(Exits)

(הולך)

End of Second Part.

תם חלק שני.

250 2 Sam. 3:27.
251 Isa. 30:21 זֶה הַדֶּרֶךְ 'this is the way'; Ps. 118:20 זֶה־הַשַּׁעַר לַיהוָה 'this is the gate of the Lord'.
252 This and the next line form a rhyming couplet, mirroring Shakespeare's 'way/delay' (2.3.382–3).
253 Job 5:12 וְלֹא־תַעֲשֶׂינָה יְדֵיהֶם תּוּשִׁיָּה 'and their hands do not achieve success'.

Third Part

חלק שלישי

SCENE I	*In front of the citadel (Chesed and musicians)*	לפני המצודה (כשד ומנגנים)	מחזה א'
CHESED	Musicians, I shall pay your wages and you will play well	מְנַגְּנִים אֲנִי אֶתֵּן שְׂכַרְכֶם וְאַתֶּם הֵיטִיבוּ נַגֵּן	כשד
	Receiving the army commander with a song of blessing for the dawn.	לְקַדֵּם פְּנֵי שַׂר הַצָּבָא בְּשִׁיר בִּרְכַּת הַשַּׁחַר.	
	(The musicians cheer and the clown emerges from the house)	(המנגנים מריעים והלץ יוצא מן הבית)	
THE CLOWN[1]	What are these instruments in your hand, are they from Naples	מָה הַכֵּלִים הָאֵלֶּה בְּיֶדְכֶם, הֲמִן נֵיאַפּוֹל הֵם	הלץ[1]
	That they issue their sound like a sound coming out of the nostrils?	כִּי יִתְּנוּ קוֹלָם כְּקוֹל הַיּוֹצֵא מִן הַנְּחִירַיִם?	
THE MUSIC DIRECTOR	What is wrong with you, my friend, that you ask such a thing?	מַה־לְּךָ רֵעִי, כִּי תִשְׁאַל כָּזֹאת?	המנצח
THE CLOWN	Tell me, are these called wind instruments?	הַגִּידָה לִי הַאֵלֶּה כְּלֵי תְרוּעָה נִקְרָאִים?	הלץ
THE MUSIC DIRECTOR	Yes, my friend, that is what they are called.	כֵּן רֵעִי, כֵּן הֵם נִקְרָאִים.	המנצח
THE CLOWN	I know that their wind is futility and has no benefit.	יָדַעְתִּי כָּל אֲשֶׁר בְּרוּחָם, הֶבֶל הוּא וְאֵין מוֹעִיל.	הלץ
THE MUSIC DIRECTOR	**Our spirit[2] is willing within us,[3]** and we are not planning evil.	רוּחֵנוּ[2] נְכוֹנָה בְּקִרְבֵּנוּ[3] וְאֵין אָנוּ חֹרְשִׁים רָעָה.	המנצח
THE CLOWN	The wind instruments release all their wind, and hot air[4] comes out of their mouths.	כְּלֵי הַתְּרוּעָה כָּל רוּחָם יוֹצִיאוּ וְהֶבֶל[4] יֵצֵא מִפִּיהֶם,	הלץ
	But here is money for you, sufficient for your wages	אַךְ הֵא לָכֶם כֶּסֶף דֵּי שְׂכַרְכֶם	

1 This and the following speeches until Doeg's entrance are prose in the original (3.1.3–4).
2 This is a play on words referring back to 'wind' in the previous line, as the word רוּחַ means both 'wind' and 'spirit'.
3 Ps. 51:12 וְרוּחַ נָכוֹן חַדֵּשׁ בְּקִרְבִּי 'and renew a willing spirit within me'.
4 Can also mean 'futility'.

	Now the army commander said that the sound of your playing is very pleasant	וְשַׂר הַצָּבָא אָמַר, כִּי קוֹל זְמִרַתְכֶם עָרֵב מְאֹד	
	Therefore save it for another day, and do not play it today.	לָכֵן חִשְׂכוּ אוֹתוֹ לְיוֹם אַחֵר וְהַיּוֹם אַל תַּשְׁמִיעוּהוּ.	
THE MUSIC DIRECTOR	If it does not please him, we shall not continue further.	אִם לֹא יִנְעַם לוֹ לֹא נוֹסִיף עוֹד.	המנצח
THE CLOWN	If you know how to play without making a sound,	אִם מִבְּלִי הַשְׁמֵעַ קוֹל לְנַגֵּן תַּשְׂכִּילוּ	הלץ
	Do as is best in your eyes, but if **the sound of song**[5] is heard	עֲשׂוּ כַּטּוֹב בְּעֵינֵיכֶם, אַךְ קוֹל זִמְרָה[5] כִּי יִשָּׁמַע	
	It will not please the ears of the army commander, so those who know him say.	לֹא יֶעֱרַב לְאָזְנֵי שַׂר הַצָּבָא, יוֹדְעָיו יֹאמֵרוּ.	
THE MUSIC DIRECTOR	We do not know how to play as you wish.	לְנַגֵּן כְּחֶפְצְךָ לֹא יָדָעְנוּ.	המנצח
THE CLOWN	If so, then put your instruments in your sacks	אִם כֵּן אֵיפוֹא שִׂימוּ כְלֵיכֶם בְּאַמְתְּחוֹתֵיכֶם	הלץ
	For I shall go from here, and as for you, watch and do as I do.	כִּי אֵלְכָה מִזֶּה וְאַתֶּם רְאוּ וַעֲשׂוּ כָמֹנִי.	
	(The musicians exit)	(המנגנים הולכים)	
CHESED	Please listen to the word of my mouth, my honest friend.[6]	שִׁמְעָה נָּא דְּבַר פִּי רֵעִי הַיָּשָׁר.[6]	כשד
THE CLOWN	I shall listen to the word of your mouth and not the mouth of your honest friend.[7]	דְּבַר פִּיךָ אֲנִי שֹׁמֵעַ וְלֹא פִּי רֵעֲךָ הַיָּשָׁר.[7]	הלץ
CHESED	Do away with laughter and deceit, and take this shekel[8] from my hand;	הָסֵר צְחֹק וּמַהֲתַלּוֹת וְקַח שֶׁקֶל[8] זֶה מִיָּדִי;	כשד
	And if the woman who attends the lady rises from her bed	וְאִם הָאִשָּׁה הַמְשָׁרֶתֶת אֶת הַגְּבִירָה קָמָה מִמִּשְׁכָּבָהּ	
	Say to her that Chesed is asking to see her.	אֱמֹר אֵלֶיהָ כִּי כֶשֶׁד מְבַקֵּשׁ לִרְאוֹת אֶת פָּנֶיהָ.	

5 Isa. 51:3; Ps. 98:5.

6 This is a double-entendre; it could also mean 'the word of the mouth of your honest friend'.

7 This response is based on the double-entendre from the previous line; it is a close parallel of Shakespeare's 'Dost thou hear, mine honest friend?/No, I hear not your honest friend, I hear you' (3.1.21–2).

8 Cf. Shakespeare's 'a poor piece of gold' (3.1.23–4). A shekel is a biblical weight (commonly used with reference to silver and gold) corresponding to approximately ten grams.

	Will you do this for me?	הֲתַעֲשֶׂה לִי זֹאת?	
THE CLOWN	She is rising from her bed, and when she arises to come here	הִיא קָמָה מִמִּשְׁכָּבָהּ וְכִי תָקוּם לָבוֹא הֵנָּה	הלץ
	I shall indeed tell the matter to her.	הַגֵּד אַגִּיד לָהּ הַדָּבָר.	
CHESED	Go and do as you say, my friend.	לֵךְ עֲשֵׂה כִּדְבָרְךָ יְדִידִי.	כשד
	(The clown exits and Doeg enters)	(הלץ הולך ודואג בא)	
	You have come at **a favourable time**,[9] Doeg.	בְּעֵת רָצוֹן[9] בָּאתָ הֵנָּה דוֹאֵג.	
DOEG	Have you not lain down on your bed all night?	הַאִם לֹא שָׁכַבְתָּ עַל מִשְׁכָּבְךָ כָּל הַלָּיְלָה?	דואג
CHESED	No, for **the morning had dawned**[10] before we parted.	לֹא, כִּי **הַבֹּקֶר אוֹר**[10] טֶרֶם נִפְרַדְנוּ.	כשד
	Just now I sent for your wife to be called to me	הִנֵּה זֶה שָׁלַחְתִּי, לִקְרֹא לִי אֶת אִשְׁתְּךָ	
	So that I might ask her whether she can take me	לְמַעַן אֶשְׁאַל אֶת פִּיהָ, אוּלַי תוּכַל לַהֲבִיאֵנִי	
	To see the lady Asenath.	לִרְאוֹת אֶת פְּנֵי אָסְנַת הַגְּבִירָה.	
DOEG	I shall send her to you immediately	הִנְנִי אֶשְׁלָחֶנָּה אֵלֶיךָ כְּרָגַע	דואג
	And I shall seek a pretext to lead the Cushite somewhere else	וְתֹאֲנָה אֲבַקֵּשׁ לְהוֹלִיךְ אֶת הַכּוּשִׁי לְעֵבֶר אַחֵר	
	In order that you might **speak with the lady, according to everything which is in your heart**,[11]	לְמַעַן **תְּדַבֵּר עִם הַגְּבִירָה, כְּכֹל אֲשֶׁר בִּלְבָבְךָ**,[11]	
	And there will be no stranger with you. *(Exits)*	וְאֵין זָר אִתְּכֶם. (הולך)	
CHESED	With all my heart I thank you for this great kindness of yours	בְּכָל לִבִּי אוֹדֶה לְךָ חַסְדְּךָ הַגָּדוֹל הַזֶּה	כשד
	For such a man of great kindness and such a faithful friend in sorrow as you	כִּי אִישׁ רַב חֶסֶד וִידִיד נֶאֱמָן בַּצָּרָה כָּמוֹךָ	
	I have not found even in Florence, my native city.	גַּם בְּפְלָארֶנְץ עִיר מוֹלַדְתִּי, לֹא מָצָאתִי.	

9 Isa. 49:8.
10 Gen. 44:3.
11 1 Kings 10:2 וַתְּדַבֵּר אֵלָיו אֵת כָּל־אֲשֶׁר הָיָה עִם־לְבָבָהּ 'and she spoke to him about everything that was in her heart'.

MILCAH	Welcome, dear officer!	בָּרוּךְ בּוֹאֲךָ, פָּקִיד יָקָר!	מלכה
	Your sorrow is my sorrow and I am distressed at your distress	יְגוֹנְךָ יְגוֹנִי הוּא וּבְצָרָתְךָ לִי צָר	
	But quickly, **go out into a spacious place**[12] **and sorrow and sighing will flee.**[13]	אַךְ מַהֵר **תֵּצֵא לַמֶּרְחָב**[12] **וְנָסוּ יָגוֹן וַאֲנָחָה.**[13]	
	The army commander and his wife are speaking about you	שַׂר הַצָּבָא וְאִשְׁתּוֹ מְדַבְּרִים עַל אֹדוֹתֶךָ	
	She is striving with all her might to have you acquitted	הִיא מִתְאַמֶּצֶת בְּכָל מְאֹדָהּ לְהַצְדִּיק אֶת נַפְשֶׁךָ	
	And he is responding that the man whom you gave many wounds	וְהוּא מֵשִׁיב כִּי הָאִישׁ אֲשֶׁר הִרְבֵּיתָ פְּצָעָיו	
	Is honourable among his people and his family is exalted in the land	נִכְבָּד הוּא בְּעַמּוֹ וּמִשְׁפַּחְתּוֹ רָמָה בָּאָרֶץ	
	Therefore he has pronounced his sentence, to remove you **until the anger passes.**[14]	לָכֵן חָרַץ מִשְׁפָּטוֹ לְהַרְחִיקְךָ **עַד יַעֲבָר זָעַם.**[14]	
	However, he is saying that you are dear in his eyes	אָכֵן הוּא מַגִּיד כִּי נַפְשְׁךָ יְקָרָה בְעֵינָיו	
	And his love for you will supplicate on your behalf even without any entreating	וְאַהֲבָתוֹ אֵלֶיךָ תַּעְתִּיר בַּעַדְךָ גַּם מִבְּלִי מַפְגִּיעַ	
	And indeed he will wait for an appropriate time to restore you to your position.	וְחַכֵּה יְחַכֶּה לְיוֹם מוֹעֵד לַהֲשִׁיבְךָ אֶל כַּנֶּךָ.	
CHESED	Indeed, if only you would listen to me, do me a kindness	אַךְ אִם אַתְּ לוּ שְׁמָעִינִי, עֲשִׂי עִמִּי חָסֶד	כשד
	And ask that I be given the opportunity to see the lady	וּבַקְּשִׁי לָתֵת לִי יָדַיִם לִרְאוֹת אֶת הַגְּבִירָה	
	In order that I might speak a few words with her alone.	לְמַעַן אוּכַל דַּבֵּר דְּבָרִים אֲחָדִים עִמָּהּ לְבַדָּהּ.	
MILCAH	Come into the house; I shall give you the opportunity	בֹּא נָא הַבַּיְתָה הִנְנִי אֶתֵּן לְךָ יָדַיִם	מלכה
	So that you might **pour out your lament**[15] which is in your heart.	לְמַעַן **תִּשְׁפֹּךְ שִׂיחֲךָ**[15] כַּאֲשֶׁר עִם לְבָבֶךָ.	

12 2 Sam. 22:20 וַיֹּצֵא לַמֶּרְחָב אֹתִי 'and He brought me out into a spacious place'.
13 Isa. 35:10.
14 Isa. 26:20.
15 Ps. 102:1 וְלִפְנֵי יְהוָה יִשְׁפֹּךְ שִׂיחוֹ 'and he pours out his lament before the Lord'.

CHESED	I shall never forget this kind deed of yours. *(Exeunt)*	גְּמוּלֵךְ זֶה לֹא אֶשְׁכַּח כָּל הַיָּמִים. (הולכים)	כשד
SCENE 2	*A chamber in the citadel (Ithiel, Doeg, and a few noblemen)*	חדר במצודה (איתיאל דואג ואצילים אחדים)	מחזה ב'
ITHIEL	Give these letters, Doeg, to the ship's captain	הַמִּכְתָּבִים הָאֵלֶּה דוֹאֵג, תֵּן לְרַב הַחֹבֵל	איתיאל
	So that he might give them to our lord the prince of the nation	לְמַעַן יִמְסֹר אֹתָם, לִנְשִׂיא הָאָרֶץ אֲדֹנֵנוּ	
	As for me, I am going to inspect **the ramparts and walls**[16] in the citadel	וַאֲנִי הִנְנִי הוֹלֵךְ לְבַקֵּר חֵל וְחוֹמָה[16] בַּמִּבְצָר	
	And there you will find me.	וְשָׁם תִּמְצָאֵנִי.	
DOEG	Yes, my lord.	הִנְנִי אֲדֹנִי.	דואג
ITHIEL	Will you go with me, ministers, to see the citadel?	הֲתֵלְכוּ עִמִּי שָׂרִים לִרְאוֹת אֶת הַמִּבְצָר?	איתיאל
THE NOBLEMEN	We shall follow our lord. *(Exeunt)*	הִנְנוּ הוֹלְכִים אַחֲרֵי אֲדֹנֵנוּ. (הולכים)	האצילים
SCENE 3	*In front of the citadel (Asenath, Chesed, and Milcah)*	לפני המצודה (אסנת כשד ומלכה)	מחזה ג'
ASENATH	Do not fear, dear Chesed, may your heart be confident	אַל תִּירָא כֶּשֶׂד הַיָּקָר יְהִי לִבְּךָ בָּטוּחַ	אסנת
	That I shall do everything which is in my power to save you.	כִּי כְּכָל אֲשֶׁר בְּכֹחִי אֶעֱשֶׂה לְהוֹשִׁיעַ לָךְ.	
MILCAH	Do so, my lady, for my husband is greatly distressed	עֲשִׂי כֵן גְּבִרְתִּי כִּי צַר לְבַעֲלִי מְאֹד	מלכה
	And it grieves his heart[17] just like the anguish of his own soul.	וְהוּא מִתְעַצֵּב אֶל לִבּוֹ[17] כְּעַל צָרַת נַפְשׁוֹ.	
ASENATH	It is a testimony to your husband that he is faithful of spirit.	עֵדוּת לְבַעֲלֵךְ כִּי נֶאֱמָן רוּחַ הוּא.	אסנת

16 Lam. 2:8.

17 Gen. 6:6 וַיִּתְעַצֵּב אֶל־לִבּוֹ 'and it grieved His heart' (referring to God's regret at having made humans after seeing how wicked they had become).

	As for you, Chesed, do not fear, for I shall make peace	וְאַתָּה כֶּשֶׁד אַל תִּירָא, כִּי שָׁלוֹם אֶעֱשֶׂה	
	Between you and my husband, and you will be friends as before.	בֵּינְךָ וּבֵין בַּעֲלִי וְאֹהֲבִים תִּהְיוּ כְּקֶדֶם.	
CHESED	My generous lady! **Your generosity has made me great;**[18]	גְּבִרְתִּי הַנְּדִיבָה! נְדָבָתֵךְ תַּרְבֵּנִי,[18]	כשד
	Consider me your faithful servant, **and let come on me what may.**[19]	לְעֶבֶד נֶאֱמָן לָךְ תְּשִׂימֵנִי וְיַעֲבֹר עָלַי מָה.[19]	
ASENATH	I give you my thanks, for you are a friend to my husband	תּוֹדָתִי לְךָ נְתוּנָה, כִּי אֹהֵב אַתָּה לְבַעֲלִי	אסנת
	And you have been a man of his confidence and faithful to his house for many days	וְאִישׁ סוֹדוֹ וְנֶאֱמַן בֵּיתוֹ הָיִיתָ מִיָּמִים רַבִּים	
	And although he may be acting as a stranger to you, his heart is not distant from you	וְאִם יִתְנַכֵּר לְךָ, לֹא רָחַק לִבּוֹ מִמֶּךָּ	
	Other than by **outward appearance.**[20]	כִּי אִם בִּלְתִּי לְמַרְאֵה עֵינָיִם.[20]	
CHESED	So it is, my lady;	כֵּן הוּא גְּבִרְתִּי;	כשד
	Except that the outward appearance may continue for many days	אֶפֶס מַרְאֵה עֵינַיִם, יוּכַל לְהִמָּשֵׁךְ לְיָמִים רַבִּים	
	For it grazes on **wind and fills its stomach with the east wind**[21]	כִּי יִרְעֶה רוּחַ וִימַלֵּא קָדִים בִּטְנוֹ[21]	
	Or he might find a new pretext **not to bring back his banished one**[22]	אוֹ יִמְצָא תֹּאֲנָה חֲדָשָׁה, לְבִלְתִּי הָשֵׁב אֶת נִדְחוֹ[22]	
	And since I have been abandoned and another is taking my office	וְאַחֲרֵי אֲשֶׁר נֶעֱזַבְתִּי וּפְקוּדָתִי יִקַּח אַחֵר	
	The army commander will forget my love and will no longer remember my service.	יִשְׁכַּח שַׂר הַצָּבָא אֶת אַהֲבָתִי וַעֲבֹדָתִי לֹא יִזָּכֵר־עוֹד	
ASENATH	God forbid, do not say such a thing; behold, I stand as surety	חָלִלָה אַל תֹּאמַר כֵּן, הִנֵּה עָרְבָה נַפְשִׁי	אסנת

---

18 2 Sam. 22:36 וַעֲנֹתְךָ תַּרְבֵּנִי 'and Your gentleness has made me great'; also Ps. 18:36 (18:35 in English Bibles).

19 Job 13:13.

20 This phrase derives from Eccles. 6:9, where it appears with the meaning 'what the eye can see', but seems to be used here with the meaning of a similar collocation מראית עין 'outward appearance', which appears numerous times in rabbinic and later Hebrew literature and denotes a principle of Jewish law whereby one should refrain from engaging in behaviour that, although permissible, might mistakenly appear to an onlooker to constitute a prohibited activity.

21 Job 15:2 הֶחָכָם יַעֲנֶה דַעַת־רוּחַ וִימַלֵּא קָדִים בִּטְנוֹ 'would a wise man answer with windy knowledge, and fill his stomach with the east wind?'

22 2 Sam. 14:13 לְבִלְתִּי הָשִׁיב הַמֶּלֶךְ אֶת־נִדְּחוֹ 'in that the king does not bring back his banished one'.

	In the sight of this Milcah that you shall return to your position	לְעֵינֵי מִלְכָּה הַזֹּאת, כִּי תָשׁוּב אֶל כַּנֶּךָ	
	And let your heart be resolute; if a word has gone out of my mouth	וְלִבְּךָ יְהִי סָמוּךְ אִם יָצָא דָבָר מִפִּי	
	That I shall ensure to fulfil it, **and I shall not alter what has gone out of my lips**[23]	כִּי אֶשְׁמֹר לְמַלְּאוֹתוֹ וּמוֹצָא שְׂפָתַי לֹא אֲשַׁנֶּה[23]	
	For I shall urge my husband and I shall not give him rest	כִּי אֶפְצַר בְּבַעֲלִי וְלֹא אֶתֵּן מַרְגּוֹעַ לוֹ	
	But rather I shall pressure him with words and I shall make his bed like a school	כִּי אֲצִיקֵהוּ בִּדְבָרִים וְאֶעֱשֶׂה מִטָּתוֹ כְּבֵית סֵפֶר	
	And his table like **a set table**[24] filled with chastisement and rebuke	וְשֻׁלְחָנוֹ כְּשֻׁלְחָן עָרוּךְ[24] מָלֵא מוּסָר וְתוֹכֵחָה	
	And everywhere that he turns he shall hear Chesed's case from my mouth,	וּבְכָל אֲשֶׁר יִפְנֶה יִשְׁמַע רִיב כֶּשֶׁד מִפִּי,	
	Therefore make your heart merry for your salvation is near	לָכֵן הֵיטִיבָה לִבְּךָ כִּי תְשׁוּעָתְךָ קְרוֹבָה	
	For I shall give myself over to death rather than abandon arguing your case.	כִּי אֶתֵּן לַמָּוֶת נַפְשִׁי, מֵעֲזֹב לָרִיב רִיבֶךָ.	
	(Ithiel and Doeg enter from afar)	(איתיאל ודואג באים מרחוק)	
MILCAH	My lady, my lord is coming towards us over there.	גְּבִרְתִּי הִנֵּה אֲדֹנִי בָּא שָׁמָּה לִקְרָאתֵנוּ.	מלכה
CHESED	My lady, I shall go from here.	גְּבִרְתִּי הִנְנִי הוֹלֵךְ מִזֶּה.	כשד
ASENATH	But why are you going? Stay, so that I might speak about you.	וְלָמָּה אַתָּה הוֹלֵךְ? הִתְיַצֵּב וַאֲדַבֵּר עָלֶיךָ.	אסנת
CHESED	I can stay no longer, for my soul is terrified	לֹא אוּכַל לַעֲמֹד עוֹד, כִּי נַפְשִׁי נִבְהָלָה	כשד
	And my spirit is not prepared within me to please my lord.	וְרוּחִי לֹא נְכוֹנָה בְּקִרְבִּי לְהָפֵק רָצוֹן מֵאֲדֹנִי.	
ASENATH	If so, turn around and go in accordance with your heart's desire. *(Chesed exits)*	אִם כֵּן סֹב וְלֶךְ־לְךָ לְפִי חֵפֶץ לִבֶּךָ. (כשד הולך)	אסנת

23 Ps. 89:35 (89:34 in English Bibles).

24 Ezek. 23:41; this phrase is also the title of Joseph Caro's authoritative code of Jewish law (first published in Venice, 1564–5).

DOEG	This matter is not good in my eyes.	לֹא טוֹב הַדָּבָר הַזֶּה בְּעֵינָי.	דואג
ITHIEL	What is this that you said?	מַה־זֶּה אָמַרְתָּ?	איתיאל
DOEG	Nothing, commander, or I do not know what I said.	אֵין מְאוּמָה הַשָּׂר, אוֹ לֹא יָדַעְתִּי מָה אָמַרְתִּי.	דואג
ITHIEL	Is that not Chesed, who parted from my wife there?	הַאֵין זֶה כֶּשֶׂד, אֲשֶׁר נִפְרַד שָׁם מֵאִשְׁתִּי?	איתיאל
DOEG	Chesed? No, my lord! My heart does not allow me to consider	כֶּשֶׂד? לֹא אֲדֹנִי! לִבִּי לֹא יִתְּנֵנִי לַחֲשׁוֹב	דואג
	That upon seeing your face, he would steal away to leave here	כִּי בִּרְאוֹתוֹ אֶת פָּנֶיךָ, יִתְגַּנֵּב לָצֵאת מִזֶּה	
	Like a criminal and guilty man.	כְּפֹשֵׁעַ וְאָשֵׁם.	
ITHIEL	Yet my heart tells me that he was there.	וּלְבָבִי יַגִּיד לִי, כִּי הוּא הָיָה שָׁם.	איתיאל
ASENATH	Listen to me, my husband, my lord! Behold, I have just spoken here	שְׁמָעֵנִי אִישִׁי אֲדֹנִי! הִנֵּה דִבַּרְתִּי בָּזֶה	אסנת
	With a sad and wretched man who **yearns for you**[25]	עִם אִישׁ נֶעְצָב וְאֻמְלָל, הַנֹּשֵׂא נַפְשׁוֹ אֵלֶיךָ[25]	
	For he despairs from your rebuke and is dying in your anger.	כִּי נָמֵס הוּא מִגַּעֲרָתְךָ וְגֹוֵעַ בַּחֲרוֹן אַפֶּךָ.	
ITHIEL	And who is this about whom you are speaking?	וּמִי הוּא זֶה, אֲשֶׁר תְּדַבְּרִי עָלָיו?	איתיאל
ASENATH	Why, it is your officer Chesed. If I have found favour in your eyes	הֲלֹא הוּא כֶּשֶׂד פְּקִידֶךָ. אִם מָצָאתִי חֵן בְּעֵינֶיךָ	אסנת
	And if I have power to guide you, won't you grant his request	וְאִם כֹּחַ בִּי לְהַטּוֹתְךָ, הֲלֹא תִשָּׂא פָנָיו	
	For he went astray in error, and not with wilful intent[26] or deceit	כִּי הֶעֱוָה בִשְׁגָגָה וְלֹא בְזָדוֹן[26] וּבְמִרְמָה	
	For if you have not found his heart to be faithful before you	כִּי אִם אֶת לְבָבוֹ לֹא מָצָאתָ נֶאֱמָן לְפָנֶיךָ	
	Who is he, and where is he,[27] who is faithful in the land?	מִי הוּא זֶה וְאֵי זֶה הוּא[27] נֶאֱמָן בָּאָרֶץ?	
	So now, please, my dear one, please call upon him to return.	וְעַתָּה אָנָּא יַקִּירִי, קְרָא נָא לוֹ לָשׁוּב.	

25 Ps. 86:4 כִּי אֵלֶיךָ אֲדֹנָי נַפְשִׁי אֶשָּׂא 'because I yearn for You, O Lord'.

26 The terms בשגגה 'in error' and בזדון 'with wilful intent' are concepts in Jewish law discussed in various sources including the Babylonian Talmud, in Moses Maimonides' twelfth-century legal guide *Mishneh Torah* (*Hilkhot Teshuva* 1:1), and in the Yom Kippur liturgy.

27 Esther 7:5.

ITHIEL	Has he gone from here?	הַאִם הוּא הָלַךְ מִזֶּה?	איתיאל
ASENATH	With **a broken heart**[28] he went from me and left his grief in my bosom.	בְּלֵב נִשְׁבָּר[28] הָלַךְ מִמֶּנִּי וַיַּעֲזֹב יְגוֹנוֹ בְּחֵיקִי	אסנת
	And I am very distressed at his distress. Please, **the one whom my soul loves**[29]	וּבְצָרָתוֹ צַר לִי מְאֹד. נָא **שֶׁאָהֲבָה נַפְשִׁי**[29]	
	Summon him to return.	קְרָא לוֹ לָשׁוּב.	
ITHIEL	Not now, pleasant Asenath, but at another time.	לֹא עַתָּה אָסְנַת הַנְּעִימָה, כִּי אִם לְעֵת אַחֶרֶת.	איתיאל
ASENATH	But when? Will he come soon?	אַךְ לְמָתַי? אִם בְּקָרוֹב יָבוֹא?	אסנת
ITHIEL	He will come quickly, for your sake.	בִּמְהֵרָה יָבוֹא לְמַעֲנֵךְ.	איתיאל
ASENATH	This evening at mealtime?	בָּעֶרֶב הַזֶּה לְעֵת הָאֹכֶל?	אסנת
ITHIEL	Not this evening.	לֹא בָעֶרֶב הַזֶּה.	איתיאל
ASENATH	Tomorrow for the noontime meal?	לְמָחָר אֶל לֶחֶם הַצָּהֳרָיִם?	אסנת
ITHIEL	At noon I shall not sit at home	בַּצָּהֳרַיִם לֹא אֵשֵׁב בַּבָּיִת	איתיאל
	For I shall dine with **the military men**[30] in the citadel.	כִּי אֶסְעַד עִם **חֲלוּצֵי הַצָּבָא**[30] בַּמְּצוּדָה.	
ASENATH	If so, then tomorrow in the evening	אִם כֵּן אֵיפוֹא, לְמָחָר בָּעֶרֶב	אסנת
	Or on Tuesday in the morning, at noon, or in the evening	אוֹ בַּיּוֹם הַשְּׁלִישִׁי בַּבֹּקֶר, בַּצָּהֳרַיִם אוֹ בָּעֶרֶב	
	Or on Wednesday morning. Please set the appointed time	אוֹ בַּבֹּקֶר הָרְבִיעִי. נָא הַגְבֵּל אֶת הַמּוֹעֵד	
	But do not postpone it more than three days.	אַךְ אַל תַּרְחִיקֶנּוּ יוֹתֵר מִשְּׁלֹשֶׁת יָמִים.	
	On my life! Indeed he **confesses and repents**[31] with all his heart	חֵי נַפְשִׁי! כִּי **מוֹדֶה וְעֹזֵב**[31] הוּא בְּכָל לִבּוֹ	
	Even though his iniquity is trivial in men's eyes.	אַף כִּי עֲוֹנוֹ קַל הוּא בְּעֵינֵי בְנֵי הָאָדָם.	
	Indeed the matter is true that punishing one who is dear and honourable	הֵן אֱמֶת הַדָּבָר, כִּי עֲנֹשׁ לְיָקָר וְנִכְבָּד	
	Is good and proper at a time of war, to make him an example for many	טוֹב וְנָכוֹן בְּעֵת מִלְחָמָה, לְתִתּוֹ מוֹפֵת לָרַבִּים	

28 Ps. 51:19 (51:17 in English Bibles).
29 Song of Songs 1:7, 3:1, 2, 3.
30 Josh. 4:13.
31 Prov. 28:13.

	But the rebuke is enough for him, on account of his small mistake.	אַךְ דַּי לוֹ הַגְּעָרָה, עֵקֶב שִׁגְגָתוֹ הַקְּטַנָּה.	
	Speak, Ithiel, when may he come? As for me, I wonder[32] very much	דַּבֵּר אִיתִיאֵל, מָתַי יָבוֹא? וַאֲנִי אֶתְפַּלָּא[32] מְאֹד	
	If you were to ask something of me, whether I would be able to refuse you	לוּ שָׁאַלְתָּ דָּבָר מִמֶּנִּי, אִם יָכֹלְתִּי הָשֵׁב פָּנֶיךָ	
	And turn here and there like you. Is it not Chesed	וְלִפְנוֹת כֹּה וָכֹה כָּמוֹךָ. הֲאִם לֹא כֶּשֶׁד הוּא	
	Who came with you to bring me into the covenant of your love	אֲשֶׁר בָּא עִמְּךָ לַהֲבִיאֵנִי בִּבְרִית אַהֲבָתֶךָ	
	And whenever I refused, he guided my heart towards you	וּבְכָל עֵת אֲשֶׁר מֵאַנְתִּי, הִטָּה אֶת לִבִּי אֵלֶיךָ	
	So how is the matter to be atoned for now so weighty?	וְאֵיךְ כָּבֵד הַדָּבָר לְכַפֵּר עָלָיו עָתָּה?	
	If it were me instead of you, believe me –	לוּ הָיִיתִי אֲנִי תַחְתֶּיךָ הַאֲמֵן לִי –	
ITHIEL	Please, that's enough from you! Indeed he can come at any time;	אָנָּא רַב לָךְ! הֵן יוּכַל לָבוֹא בְּכָל עֵת;	איתיאל
	For I cannot refuse you.	כִּי לֹא אָשִׁיב אֶת פָּנָיִךְ.	
ASENATH	It is not kindness from you; just as if I had implored you	לֹא חֶסֶד הוּא מִיָּדְךָ; כְּמוֹ לוּ הִפְצַרְתִּי בָךְ	אסנת
	To eat food, to put on a garment, and to protect yourself from cold	לֶאֱכָל־לֶחֶם, לִלְבֹּשׁ בֶּגֶד וְלִשְׁמֹר נַפְשְׁךָ מִקֹּר	
	Or to do something for your own good	אוֹ לַעֲשׂוֹת דָּבָר לְמַעַן טוֹב לָךְ	
	Who would consider it kindness, that you did this?	מִי יַחְשׁוֹב לְךָ לְחֶסֶד, כִּי עָשִׂיתָ זֹאת?	
	But if I should come to seek kindness and compassion from you	אֲבָל אִם חֶסֶד וַחֲנִינָה, אָבוֹא לִדְרֹשׁ מִיָּדֶךָ	
	To test the power of your love, I would not come with a small matter	לְנַסּוֹת כֹּחַ אַהֲבָתֶךָ, לֹא בְּדָבָר קָטֹן אָבוֹאָה	
	But rather I would seek to ask difficult and weighty things	כִּי אִם אֲקַשֶּׁה לִשְׁאוֹל קָשׁוֹת וְנִכְבָּדוֹת	

32 This meaning of the verbal root .פ.ל.א in the *hitpa'el* stem is first attested in the medieval period (Even-Shoshan 2003, 5: 1483). While the form occurs in the Hebrew Bible, it has a different meaning, 'to display marvellous power' (Job 10:16).

	Until **terror seized your soul**[33] to fulfil my request.	עַד אֲשֶׁר לְמַלֵּא שְׁאֵלָתִי, **תֹּאחַז נַפְשְׁךָ פַּלָּצוּת**.[33]	
ITHIEL	I shall deny you nothing –	לֹא אֶמְנַע דָּבָר מִמֵּךְ –	איתיאל
	Just one thing I ask of you; grant me this request of mine	רַק אַחַת שָׁאַלְתִּי מֵאִתֵּךְ, תְּנִי לִי שְׁאֵלָתִי זֹאת	
	Wait for me a little bit so that I may speak with myself alone.	חַכִּי לִי מְעַט רֶגַע וְאָשִׂיחָה עִם נַפְשִׁי לְבַדִּי.	
ASENATH	Shall I deny you anything? I am going.	הַאֲנִי אֶמְנַע דָּבָר מִמֶּךָּ? הִנְנִי הוֹלֶכֶת.	אסנת
ITHIEL	Go in peace. I shall come to see you quick as lightning.	לְכִי לְשָׁלוֹם. חִישׁ מַהֵר אָבוֹא לִרְאוֹת פָּנָיִךְ.	איתיאל
ASENATH	Do as you desire, my husband	עֲשֵׂה בַּעֲלִי כִּרְצוֹנֶךָ	אסנת
	For everything which you say, I **shall do and obey**.[34]	כִּי כָל אֲשֶׁר תֹּאמַר נַפְשְׁךָ, כֵּן **אֶעֱשֶׂה וְאֶשְׁמָעָה**.[34]	
	(Exits with Milcah)	(הולכת עם מלכה)	
ITHIEL	Beautiful and wretched one! May death destroy me if I do not love you;	יָפָה וְאֻמְלָלָה! מָוֶת יִקְטְבֵנִי אִם לֹא אֶאֱהָבֵךְ,	איתיאל
	Your love is stored in my heart, and if I should not love you any longer	אַהֲבָתֵךְ בְּלִבִּי צְפוּנָה, וְאִם לֹא אֶאֱהָבֵךְ עוֹד	
	Then everything would revert to void.	אָז יָשׁוּב הַכֹּל לְתֹהוּ.	
DOEG	**Noble-spirited**[35] lord –	**אָדוֹן יְקַר רוּחַ**[35] –	דואג
ITHIEL	What do you say, Doeg?	מָה אַתָּה מְדַבֵּר, דּוֹאֵג?	איתיאל
DOEG	Did Chesed know before you married the lady	הַאִם כֶּשֶׂד יָדַע, בְּטֶרֶם נָשָׂאתָ אֶת הַגְּבִירָה	דואג
	That you desired her?	כִּי חָשַׁקְתָּ בָהּ?	
ITHIEL	He was my man of confidence from the beginning to the end.	הוּא הָיָה אִישׁ סוֹדִי מֵהָחֵל וְעַד כַּלֵּה.	איתיאל
	But why do you ask such a thing?	אַךְ לָמָּה תִּשְׁאַל כָּזֹאת?	
DOEG	I wanted to know this in order to calm the thoughts of my heart	חָפַצְתִּי לָדַעַת זֹאת, לְהַשְׁקִיט מַחְשְׁבוֹת לִבִּי	דואג

33 Job 21:6 וְאָחַז בְּשָׂרִי פַּלָּצוּת 'and terror seizes my flesh'.

34 Exod. 24:7 וַיֹּאמְרוּ כֹּל אֲשֶׁר־דִּבֶּר יְהוָה נַעֲשֶׂה וְנִשְׁמָע 'and they said, "Everything which the Lord has spoken to us we shall do and obey"'; in rabbinic Judaism this phrase serves as a model for the way in which Jews should follow Jewish law, by observing the laws even when their significance is unclear.

35 Prov. 17:27.

	And there is nothing to disturb your spirit.	וְאֵין דָּבָר לְהַפְרִיעַ אֶת רוּחֶךָ.	
ITHIEL	And what are the thoughts of your heart?	וּמָה הֵנָּה מַחְשְׁבוֹת לִבֶּךָ?	איתיאל
DOEG	I did not imagine that Chesed had known her since then.	לֹא דִמִּיתִי, כִּי כֶשֶׂד יָדַע אֹתָהּ מֵאָז.	דואג
ITHIEL	It is so, and he was also the messenger between us	כֵּן הוּא, וְגַם הוּא הָיָה הַצִּיר בֵּינֵינוּ	איתיאל
	Whom we sent from time to time.	אֲשֶׁר שְׁלַחְנוּהוּ כְּפַעַם בְּפָעַם.	
DOEG	He was the messenger? –	הוּא הָיָה הַצִּיר? –	דואג
ITHIEL	He was the messenger! He and not another –	הוּא הָיָה הַצִּיר! הוּא וְלֹא אַחֵר –	איתיאל
	What strange things do you see here? Is he not faithful?	מַה־זָּרוֹת תִּרְאֶה פֹּה? הַאִם לֹא נֶאֱמָן הוּא?	
DOEG	Faithful?	נֶאֱמָן? –	דואג
ITHIEL	Faithful, I said.	נֶאֱמָן אָמַרְתִּי.	איתיאל
DOEG	According to what I think, my lord –	לְפִי אֲשֶׁר אָנֹכִי חֹשֵׁב, אֲדֹנִי –	דואג
ITHIEL	What do you think?	מָה אַתָּה חֹשֵׁב?	איתיאל
DOEG	What do I think, my lord?	מָה אֲנִי חֹשֵׁב, אֲדֹנִי?	דואג
ITHIEL	'Think, my lord'	„חֹשֵׁב, אֲדֹנִ"	איתיאל
	As I live, it is like a heavenly echo,[36] he is repeating my words	חַי אָנִי כִּי כְּבַת קוֹל,[36] הוּא שׁוֹנֶה אֶת דְּבָרַי	
	As if his heart were full of strange and terrible thoughts.	כְּמוֹ אִם לִבּוֹ מָלֵא מַחֲשָׁבוֹת זָרוֹת וְנוֹרָאוֹת.	
	If thoughts have arisen in your heart, tell them **in the sight of the sun**.[37]	אִם מַחֲשָׁבוֹת עָלוּ עַל לִבְּךָ, הַגֵּד לְעֵינֵי הַשָּׁמֶשׁ.[37]	
	When Chesed went away from my wife, I heard you say	כַּאֲשֶׁר הָלַךְ כֶּשֶׂד מֵאִשְׁתִּי, כֵּן שְׁמַעְתִּיךָ אֹמֵר	
	That 'the matter is not good'; what is not good in your eyes?	כִּי „לֹא טוֹב הַדָּבָר" מַה לֹּא טוֹב בְּעֵינֶיךָ?	
	And when you heard that he was my man of confidence in my love	וְכַאֲשֶׁר שָׁמַעְתָּ, כִּי הוּא הָיָה אִישׁ סוֹדִי בְּאַהֲבָתִי	

36 The heavenly echo (Hebrew בת קול *bat qol*, lit. 'daughter of a voice'), is a concept in the Mishnah, Talmud, and other rabbinic literature, denoting a divine voice that reveals God's will to humans (see Rothkoff 2007).

37 2 Sam. 12:11.

	And he was the messenger between us, you called out **in bewilderment of heart**,[38]	וְהוּא הָיָה הַצִּיר בֵּינֵינוּ, קָרָאתָ בְּתִמְהוֹן לֵבָב[38]	
	'He was the messenger?' And your face pursed up suddenly[39]	הוּא הָיָה הַצִּיר? וּפָנֶיךָ קָמְטוּ פִּתְאֹם[39]	
	As if a terrible idea had arisen in your heart and led your thoughts astray.	כְּמוֹ רַעְיוֹן נוֹרָא עָלָה עַל לִבְּךָ וַיַּתְעֶה עֶשְׁתֹּנוֹתֶיךָ.	
	If you love me **truly and sincerely**,[40] tell me your thoughts.	אִם אֲהַבְתַּנִי בֶּאֱמֶת וּבְתָמִים,[40] הַגֵּד לִי מַחְשְׁבוֹתֶיךָ.	
DOEG	You know, my lord, that I love you.	אַתָּה אֲדֹנִי יָדַעְתָּ, כִּי אֲהַבְתִּיךָ.	דואג
ITHIEL	I know that it is so;	יָדַעְתִּי כִּי כֵן הוּא;	איתיאל
	And because I trust that your love is pure	וְיַעַן כִּי בָטוּחַ אֲנִי, כִּי אַהֲבָתְךָ זַכָּה	
	And because you weigh your words on a scale before they pass your lips	וְכִי תִשְׁקֹל דְּבָרֶיךָ בְּפֶלֶס, טֶרֶם יַעַבְרוּן שְׂפָתֶיךָ	
	Therefore the signs of your face and your few words frighten me.	לָכֵן אוֹתוֹת פָּנֶיךָ וּדְבָרֶיךָ הַמְּעַטִּים יַפְחִידוּנִי.	
	If a cunning man and a scoundrel does such a thing it is deception	עָרוּם וְנָבָל אִם יַעֲשֶׂה כָּזֹאת מִרְמָה הִיא	
	As these are his ways, continually to deceive and lead astray his fellow;	וְאֵלֶּה דְרָכָיו תָּמִיד לְהוֹנוֹת וּלְהַתְעוֹת רֵעֵהוּ;	
	But in a **pure-hearted**[41] man like you, they are a faithful testimony	אָכֵן בְּבַר לֵבָב[41] כָּמוֹךָ, יָעִידוּ עֵדוּת נֶאֱמָנָה	
	That there is a war within you which you cannot sustain.	כִּי מִלְחָמָה בְקִרְבְּךָ שֶׁכַּלְכֵּל אוֹתָהּ לֹא תוּכָל.	
DOEG	I can trust in Chesed and can also say on oath	בְּחֶסֶד אוּכַל לִבְטֹחַ וְגַם לְהַגִּיד בִּשְׁבוּעָה	דואג
	That he is faithful.	כִּי נֶאֱמָן הוּא.	
ITHIEL	I also think him to be so.	כֵּן חֲשַׁבְתִּיהוּ גַּם אָנִי.	איתיאל
DOEG	A man should always be in secret as in the open	לְעוֹלָם יִהְיֶה אָדָם בַּסֵּתֶר כְּמוֹ בַּגָּלוּי	דואג

38 Deut. 28:28.
39 This verb originates in the rabbinic period (Even-Shoshan 2003, 5: 1675); although the root in this stem is attested in the Hebrew Bible (in Job 22:16), it has a different meaning, 'to be snatched'.
40 Judg. 9:16, 19.
41 Ps. 24:4.

	And not one man in the open and another man in secret.	וְלֹא אֶחָד בַּגָּלוּי וְאִישׁ אַחֵר, בַּסָּתֶר.	
ITHIEL	To be one man in mouth and heart, **this is the instruction for mankind**.[42]	לִהְיוֹת אֶחָד בְּפֶה וּבְלֵב, זֹאת תּוֹרַת הָאָדָם.[42]	איתיאל
DOEG	Therefore my heart thinks that Chesed is faithful.	לָכֵן יַחְשׁוֹב לִבִּי, כִּי כֶשֶׁד נֶאֱמָן הוּא.	דואג
ITHIEL	But apart from that, there are other things in your heart	אֲבָל זוּלַת זֹאת, יֵשׁ בִּלְבָבְךָ נוֹסָפוֹת עוֹד	איתיאל
	Please tell me everything that your heart whispers	הַגֶּד נָא לִי, כֹּל אֲשֶׁר יִרְחַשׁ לִבֶּךָ	
	Let your lips utter clearly even an evil and bitter matter	וְגַם דָּבָר רָע וָמָר, בָּרוּר תַּבַּעְנָה שְׂפָתֶיךָ	
	For evil tidings should only be made known with bitter words.	כִּי בְשׂוֹרָה רָעָה רַק בִּדְבָרִים מָרִים תִּוָּדֵעַ.	
DOEG	Please forgive me, my noble lord:	שָׂא נָא אֲדֹנִי הַנָּדִיב:	דואג
	Indeed I am prepared to keep all your commandments[43]	אָמְנָם נָכוֹן אָנֹכִי לִשְׁמֹר אֶת כָּל מִצְוֹתֶיךָ[43]	
	But not to do something which even a despicable slave would not do.	וְלֹא לַעֲשׂוֹת דָּבָר אֲשֶׁר גַּם עֶבֶד נִבְזֶה לֹא יַעֲשֶׂנּוּ.	
	Shall I reveal the hidden treasures of my heart, if my heart is pondering calamities?	הֲגַם אֲגַלֶּה מַצְפּוּנֵי לִבִּי, אִם לִבִּי יַחְשֹׁב הַוּוֹת?	
	And shall I not restrain **the fruit of my lips**,[44] if I have conceived destruction and disaster?	וְלֹא אֶכְלָא נִיב שְׂפָתַי,[44] אִם הָרִיתִי שָׁוְא וָאָוֶן?	
	Where is the palace through which an unclean thing has not passed?	אַיֵּה הוּא הַהֵיכָל, לֹא עָבַר בּוֹ דָּבָר טָמֵא	
	Or a pure heart which has never turned aside to accuse	אוֹ לֵב טָהוֹר, לֹא נָטָה לְהַרְשִׁיעַ מֵעוֹדוֹ	
	And has not made **a perverted judgement**[45] like a truthful and righteous judge?	וּמִשְׁפָּט מְעֻקָּל[45] לֹא הוֹצִיא כְּדַיָּן אֱמֶת וָצֶדֶק?	

42 2 Sam. 7:19.

43 Cf. Shakespeare's 'every act of duty' (3.3.137); Salkinson has replaced this with an explicitly Jewish formulation of duty, mitzvoth, or commandments.

44 Isa. 57:19 נִיב שְׂפָתָיִם 'the fruit of the lips'.

45 Hab. 1:4.

ITHIEL If you are thinking in your heart that a man has done me an injustice

איתיאל אִם תֶּהְגֶּה בִלְבָבְךָ כִּי אִישׁ עָשָׂה לִי עָוֶל

And you do not reveal it to me, you too, Doeg, are among the conspirators.

וְאֵינְךָ גֹּלֶה אֶת אָזְנִי, גַּם אַתָּה דוֹאֵג בַּקְּשָׁרִים.

DOEG I admit before you, commander, regarding my affliction and my pain

דואג אוֹדֶה לְפָנֶיךָ הַשָּׂר, עֲלֵי נִגְעִי וּמַכְאֹבִי

That this is my way at times, to spy out with an evil eye

כִּי זֶה דַרְכִּי לְעִתִּים, לָתוּר בְּעַיִן רָעָה

And to find iniquity in men who are innocent of any iniquity

וְלִמְצוֹא עָוֹן בַּאֲנָשִׁים, הַנְּקִיִּים מִכָּל עָוֹן

For out of my great zeal for my lord, or also out of **sorrow of heart**[46]

כִּי מֵרֹב קִנְאָתִי לַאֲדֹנִי, אוֹ גַּם מֵרֹעַ לֵב[46]

I see the shadow of mountains as mountains;[47] therefore I beg of you

אֶחֱזֶה צֵל הָרִים כֶּהָרִים;[47] לָכֵן אוֹחִילָה לְפָנֶיךָ

Do not take heed of my words and do not make trouble for yourself

אַל תָּשִׂים לִבְּךָ לִדְבָרַי וְלֹא תָבִיא עָמָל לְנַפְשֶׁךָ

For my knowledge is very trivial and the visions of my heart lead me astray

כִּי דַעְתִּי קַלָּה מְאֹד וְחֶזְיוֹן לִבִּי יַתְעֵנִי

And you will not find rest in my words, nor benefit to you

וְלֹא תִמְצָא דְבָרַי לִמְנוּחָה וְגַם לֹא לְהוֹעִיל לָךְ

Nor is it an advantage or wisdom for me to inform you of what is in my ponderings.

וְלֹא לְיִתְרוֹן וּלְחָכְמָה לִי, לְהוֹדִיעֲךָ אֶת אֲשֶׁר בַּהֲגִיגִי.

ITHIEL **What do your words hint at?**[48]

איתיאל מַה־יִּרְזְמוּן מִלֶּיךָ?[48]

DOEG A reputation is better for a man and a woman than any glory or jewel.

דואג טוֹב שֵׁם לְאִישׁ וּלְאִשָּׁה, מִכָּל פְּאֵר וַעֲדִי לְנַפְשָׁם.

The one who steals my bag of money steals dirt and dust

הַגֹּנֵב צְרוֹר כַּסְפִּי, הוּא גֹנֵב עָפָר וָאָבָק

For it is as naught and nothing, the money was in my hand

כִּי כְּאֶפֶס וּבְלִימָה הוּא, הַכֶּסֶף הָיָה בְיָדִי

And now it is in his hand, as it was in the hands of others before me.

וְעַתָּה בְיָדוֹ הוּא, כַּאֲשֶׁר הָיָה בִּידֵי אֲחֵרִים לְפָנָי.

---

46 Neh. 2:2.

47 This expression denoting paranoid exaggeration is thought to have originated in the modern era (Even-Shoshan 2003, 2: 422), but is based loosely on Judg. 9:36 אֵת צֵל הֶהָרִים אַתָּה רֹאֶה כָּאֲנָשִׁים 'you see the shadow of the mountains as if they were men' (which is uncertain in meaning; see Amit 2004: 532).

48 Job 15:12 וּמַה־יִּרְזְמוּן עֵינֶיךָ 'and what do your eyes wink at?' Cf. Shakespeare's 'Zounds! What dost thou mean?' (3.3.157).

	But the one who **sullies my reputation**[49] wrongs my soul,	אַךְ הַמַּבְאִישׁ אֶת רֵיחִי,[49] הוּא חֹמֵס נַפְשִׁי,	
	For the wrong does not enrich him and **he has made me like an empty vessel**.[50]	כִּי הֶחָמָס לֹא יַעְשְׁרֶנּוּ וְאֹתִי הִצִּיגַנִי כִּכְלִי רִיק.[50]	
ITHIEL	As I live, I shall not turn aside until I know your thoughts.	חַי אָנִי אִם אָסוּרָה, עַד אֵדַע עֶשְׁתֹּנוֹתֶיךָ.	איתיאל
DOEG	You will not be able to know them, not even if my heart were in your hand	לֹא תוּכַל לְדַעְתָּן, לוּ גַם הָיָה לִבִּי בְּיָדְךָ	דואג
	As long as I am still master over it.	וְאַף כִּי בְעוֹדֶנִּי אֲנִי אָדוֹן לוֹ.	
ITHIEL	Indeed?	הַאֻמְנָם?	איתיאל
DOEG	Guard yourself from the spirit of jealousy, for it comes like rot	הִשָּׁמֵר לְךָ מֵרוּחַ קִנְאָה, כִּי כְּרָקָב תָּבוֹא	דואג
	And like a maggot it scorns the food upon which it lives.	וּכְרִמָּה תְּשַׁקֵּץ אֶת הַלֶּחֶם, אֲשֶׁר תִּחְיֶה עָלָיו.	
	Happy is the one who turns a blind eye to his wife, if she is adulterous,	אַשְׁרֵי הַמַּעֲלִים עֵינָיו מֵאִשְׁתּוֹ, אִם הִיא נֹאָפֶת,	
	He does not warm himself in her love, yet the fire of jealousy does not devour him	בְּאַהֲבָתָהּ לֹא יִתְחַמָּם וְאֵשׁ קִנְאָה לֹא תֹאכְלֶנּוּ	
	But woe to the husband who loves and is jealous over his wife	וְאוֹי לוֹ לַבַּעַל הָאֹהֵב וְהַמְקַנֵּא אֶת אִשְׁתּוֹ	
	Both his love and his jealousy become, like death and Sheol, an abode for him.	גַּם אַהֲבָתוֹ וְקִנְאָתוֹ, כַּמָּוֶת וְכִשְׁאוֹל לִזְבוּל לוֹ.	
ITHIEL	Woe is me, wretched man!	אוֹי לִי אֻמְלָל!	איתיאל
DOEG	Poor and happy in his lot, he is the man of great wealth	דַּל וְשָׂמֵחַ בְּחֶלְקוֹ, הוּא הֶעָשִׁיר הַגָּדוֹל	דואג
	But the man of great wealth who constantly fears lest he become poor	אַךְ הֶעָשִׁיר הַגָּדוֹל, הַמְפַחֵד תָּמִיד פֶּן יִדַּל	
	There is none so poor as he. – O **God of the spirits**![51]	אֵין דַּל כָּמוֹהוּ. – **אֵל אֱלֹהֵי הָרוּחוֹת**![51]	
	Please save my tribe[52] from the spirit of jealousy.	הַצִּילָה נָּא אֶת בְּנֵי בְרִיתִי[52] מֵרוּחַ קִנְאָה.	

49 Exod. 5:21 הִבְאַשְׁתֶּם אֶת־רֵיחֵנוּ 'you have sullied our reputation'.
50 Jer. 51:34 הִצִּיגַנִי כְּלִי רִיק 'he has made me an empty vessel'.
51 Num. 16:22 אֵל אֱלֹהֵי הָרוּחֹת לְכָל־בָּשָׂר 'God of the spirits of all flesh', also Num. 27:16.
52 Salkinson has chosen to translate Shakespeare's 'my tribe' (3.3.177) with an expression that is used in rabbinic and later literature to refer specifically to Jews (Even-Shoshan 2003, 1: 211); see, for example, Mishnah *Bava Qamma* 1:2.

ITHIEL	Why are you speaking your words? Does jealousy graze on my soul?	לָמָּה תְּדַבֵּר דְּבָרֶיךָ? הֲקִנְאָה תִּרְעֶה נַפְשִׁי?	איתיאל
	Or do I change my face in the mornings, like the changes of the face of the moon	אוֹ אֲשַׁנֶּה פָּנַי לַבְּקָרִים, כַּחֲלִיפוֹת פְּנֵי הַיָּרֵחַ	
	To search here and there, in case I might find **some indecent thing?**[53]	לְבַקֵּשׁ כֹּה וָכֹה, אוּלַי אֶמְצָא **עֶרְוַת דָּבָר?**[53]	
	It is not so, Doeg; if my wife has caused me	לֹא כֵן דּוֹאֵג, אִם אִשְׁתִּי הֵסַבָּה לִי	
	To fear whether she has been unfaithful to me, then I have already made my judgement.	לְפַחֵד אוּלַי מָעֲלָה בִי, כְּבָר מִשְׁפָּטִי חָרַצְתִּי.	
	It is better for me to be like a goat in the forest	טוֹב לִי לִהְיוֹת, כְּאַחַד הַשְּׂעִירִים בַּיַּעַר	
	Than to watch after a woman lest **she go whoring away from me.**[54]	מֵהַבֵּט אַחֲרֵי אִשָּׁה, פֶּן **זָנֹה תִזְנֶה מֵאַחֲרָי.**[54]	
	If it is said in my ears that my wife is beautiful	אִם יֵאָמֵר בְּאָזְנַי, כִּי אִשְׁתִּי יָפָה הִיא	
	Loves banquets and companions, her mouth is open **to speak clearly**[55]	אֹהֶבֶת מִשְׁתֶּה וְרֵעִים, פִּיהָ פָּתוּחַ **לְדַבֵּר צָחוֹת**[55]	
	And she knows how to play well, to sing and to dance	וְיוֹדַעַת לְנַגֵּן הֵיטֵב, לָשִׁיר וְלָחוּל בַּמְּחוֹלוֹת	
	All this will not arouse the spirit of jealousy within me	כָּל זֹאת לֹא תְעוֹרֵר רוּחַ קִנְאָה בְּקִרְבִּי	
	For these additions add charm to an honest woman.	כִּי נוֹסָפוֹת אֵלֶּה, לְאִשָּׁה יְשָׁרָה יוֹסִיפוּ חֵן.	
	Nor is it because I am unworthy that I fear lest she betray me	גַּם לֹא מֵאֲשֶׁר קָטֹנְתִּי אָגוּרָה פֶּן תִּבְגֹּד בִּי	
	Going after strangers who are greater than me in my worth	לָלֶכֶת אַחֲרֵי זָרִים הַגְּדוֹלִים מִמֶּנִּי בְּעֶרְכִּי	
	For she saw me with her eyes and she chose me with her soul's desire,	כִּי הִיא רָאַתְנִי בְּעֵינֶיהָ וַתִּבְחַר בִּי בְּאַוַּת נַפְשָׁהּ,	
	Therefore I say one thing: I shall not judge her	לָכֵן אַחַת אָמַרְתִּי: לֹא יָדוֹן רוּחִי בָהּ	

53 Deut. 23:15 (23:14 in English Bibles), 24:1.
54 Hosea 1:2 כִּי־זָנֹה תִזְנֶה הָאָרֶץ מֵאַחֲרֵי יְהוָה 'for the land goes whoring away from the LORD'.
55 Isa. 32:4.

Until I see **what disgrace is found in her**[56]	עַד אֲשֶׁר אֶרְאֶה, מַה־שֶּׁמֶץ דָּבָר נִמְצָא בָּהּ[56]
And when I find some flaw in her, then I shall investigate and enquire	וְכַאֲשֶׁר אֶמְצָא בָהּ מְאוּם, כֵּן אֶחְקֹר וְאֶדְרֹשׁ
And if there is iniquity in her, there will be no more discussion	וְאִם יֵשׁ בָּהּ עָוֹן, אֵין דִּין וּדְבָרִים עוֹד
For **destruction will be decreed**,[57] and love and jealousy will be no more.	כִּי כָלָה וְנֶחֱרָצָה[57] וְאֶפֶס אַהֲבָה וְקִנְאָה.
DOEG I am happy to hear this from your mouth, for now I am prepared	דואג שָׂמַחְתִּי לִשְׁמֹעַ זֹאת מִפִּיךָ, כִּי עַתָּה הִנְנִי נָכוֹן
To show you my love and my service, without obstacles or hindrances.	לְהַרְאוֹתְךָ אַהֲבָתִי וַעֲבֹדָתִי, בְּלִי מִכְשׁוֹל וּמַעְצוֹר.
So now, listen to my word and I shall tell everything which is in my heart	וְעַתָּה שִׁמְעָה דְּבָרִי וְכֹל אֲשֶׁר בִּלְבָבִי אַגִּידָה
But I shall not **present my case**;[58] what evidence is in my hand?	וְלֹא אָשִׂים דִּבְרָתִי[58] מָה עֵדוּת יֵשׁ בְּיָדִי
But I shall say at the start, keep your eye on your wife	כִּי אִם אֹמַר בַּתְּחִלָּה, שִׂים עֵינְךָ עַל אִשְׁתֶּךָ
And observe her when she is sitting together with Chesed	וְהִתְבּוֹנֵן בָּהּ בְּשִׁבְתָּהּ עִם כֶּשֶׁד יַחְדָּו
Not with a jealous eye, nor with too much trust	לֹא בְעֵין קִנְאָה וְלֹא בְּבִטָּחוֹן יֶתֶר מִדַּי
For I fear that a sinful thing might be done	כִּי חָרֵד אָנֹכִי, לְבַל יֵעָשֶׂה דְּבַר נְבָלָה
To a noble-hearted man such as you, and therefore I say guard yourself.	לִנְדִיב לֵב כָּמוֹךָ וְלָכֵן אָמַרְתִּי הִשָּׁמֶר לָךְ.
For the women of Venice do things in secret	וּבְנוֹת וִינֶעצְיָא, תַּעֲשֶׂינָה מַעֲשִׂים בַּסֵּתֶר
Which they would not do before their husbands' eyes	אֲשֶׁר לֹא תַעֲשֶׂינָה לִפְנֵי עֵינֵי בַעֲלֵיהֶן
And every **meditation of their hearts**[59] is only to hide their deeds	וְכָל הָגוּת לִבָּן,[59] רַק לְהַסְתִּיר מַעֲשֵׂיהֶן

56 Job 26:14 וּמַה־שֵּׁמֶץ דָּבָר נִשְׁמַע־בּוֹ 'and how faint (or: whispering) a word is heard of Him'; Salkinson seems to have been using the word שֶׁמֶץ in its medieval sense of 'condemnation' or 'disgrace' (Even-Shoshan 2003, 6: 1921).

57 Isa. 10:23, 28:22; Dan. 9:27.

58 Job 5:8.

59 Ps. 49:4 (49:3 in English Bibles) וְהָגוּת לִבִּי 'and the mediation of my heart'.

	And not to keep iniquity far away.	וְלֹא לְהַרְחִיק אָוֶן.	
ITHIEL	Is this the testimony of your mouth?	הֲכֵן עֵדוּת פִּיךָ?	איתיאל
DOEG	Why, she deceived her father when she married you	הֲלֹא אֶת לֵב אָבִיהָ גָּנְבָה, בְּהִנָּשְׂאָהּ לָךְ	דואג
	And while she was acting as a stranger, as if she were afraid	וּלְעֵת אֲשֶׁר הִתְנַכְּרָה, כְּמוֹ אִם יָרְאָה	
	To look you in the eye, she already desired you.	לְהַבִּיט אֵלֶיךָ עַיִן בְּעַיִן, כְּבָר חָשְׁקָה נַפְשָׁהּ בָּךְ.	
ITHIEL	The matter is true.	אֱמֶת הַדָּבָר.	איתיאל
DOEG	If one as tender in years as she is possesses such cunning	אִם רַכָּה בְשָׁנִים כָּמוֹהָ, עָמְדָה לָהּ עָרְמָתָהּ	דואג
	To cover her father's eyes with a blanket lest he see anything	לְכַסּוֹת עֵינֵי אָבִיהָ בַּשְּׂמִיכָה, לְבַל יִרְאֶה דָבָר	
	Until he believed that it was witchcraft –	עַד אֲשֶׁר הֶאֱמִין, כִּי מַעֲשֵׂה כְשָׁפִים הוּא –	
	Indeed I fear greatly, lest I have sinned with my lips,	אָמְנָם אָגוּרָה מְאֹד, פֶּן חָטָאתִי בִשְׂפָתַי,	
	Forgive me my lord, for your great love has pressured me.	סְלַח לִי אֲדֹנִי, כִּי רֹב אַהֲבָתְךָ הֱצִיקַתְנִי.	
ITHIEL	I shall never forget your great love and kindness for all days.	רֹב אַהֲבָתְךָ וְחַסְדְּךָ, לֹא אֶשְׁכַּח כָּל הַיָּמִים.	איתיאל
DOEG	I see that your heart has sunk.	רֹאֶה אֲנִי, כִּי נָפַל לִבְּךָ עָלֶיךָ.	דואג
ITHIEL	No, no, it is nothing.	לֹא לֹא, אֵין דָּבָר.	איתיאל
DOEG	But I see that you are saddened,	וַאֲנִי הִנְנִי רֹאֶה, כִּי נֶעֱצַבְתָּ,	דואג
	Indeed I hope that you will have the wisdom to see	אָמְנָם תְּקַוֶּה נַפְשִׁי, כִּי תַשְׂכִּיל לִרְאוֹת	
	That my words spring from a source of love and friendship,	כִּי דְבָרַי נֹבְעִים מִמְּקוֹר אַהֲבָה וִידִידוּת,	
	But I am distressed to see you **grieved in your heart**[60]	אַךְ צַר לִי לִרְאוֹתְךָ, מִתְעַצֵּב אֶל לִבֶּךָ[60]	
	And therefore please, my lord, do not think deeply in order to find in my words	וְלָכֵן אָנָּא אֲדֹנִי, אַל תַּעֲמֵק לִמְצוֹא בִּדְבָרַי	
	A different notion and interpretation; I have only come to warn you.	רַעְיוֹן וּפִתְרוֹן אַחֵר; בִּלְתִּי לְהַזְהִיר נַפְשְׁךָ בָּאתִי.	

60 Gen. 6:6 וַיִּתְעַצֵּב אֶל־לִבּוֹ 'and it grieved His heart' (referring to God's regret at having made humans upon seeing how wicked they had become).

ITHIEL	I do not seek a different interpretation.	לֹא אֲבַקֵּשׁ פִּתְרוֹן אַחֵר.	איתיאל
DOEG	For a different interpretation would lead you into **the wasteland where there is no path**[61]	כִּי פִּתְרוֹן אַחֵר יוֹלִיכְךָ **בְּתֹהוּ לֹא דָרֶךְ**[61]	דואג
	Which my words do not contain and which has not occurred to me	אֲשֶׁר דְּבָרַי לֹא יָכִילוּ וְלֹא עָלְתָה עַל לִבִּי	
	As Chesed is my faithful friend – but I see	וְכֶשֶׁד הוּא אֹהֲבִי הַנֶּאֱמָן – אַךְ הִנְנִי רֹאֶה	
	That my lord's face has fallen, and your **spirit is troubled**[62] within you.	כִּי נָפְלוּ פְּנֵי אֲדֹנִי וְרוּחֲךָ **תִּפָּעֵם**[62] בְּקִרְבֶּךָ.	
ITHIEL	Only very little –	אַךְ מְעַט מִזְעָר –	איתיאל
	For in my opinion, Asenath's spirit is faithful to me.	כִּי לְפִי דַעְתִּי, רוּחַ אָסְנַת נֶאֱמָנָה אִתִּי.	
DOEG	If only it were so, and so may it be in your eyes	מִי יִתֵּן וְהָיְתָה כֵן וְכֵן תִּהְיֶה בְעֵינֶיךָ	דואג
	For all time.	לְאֹרֶךְ יָמִים.	
ITHIEL	But **the heart is devious**[63] and easily **turns away from the path.**[64]	אַךְ **הַלֵּב עָקֹב**[63] וְעַל נְקַלָּה **יָסוּר מִנִּי אֹרַח.**[64]	איתיאל
DOEG	This is the **stumbling block;**[65] and therefore I also say	זֹאת הִיא **אֶבֶן הַנֶּגֶף;**[65] וְלָכֵן גַּם אֲנִי אָשִׂיחָה	דואג
	That the woman is baffling in my eyes, and she has a strange way about her.	כִּי פְּלִיאָה הָאִשָּׁה בְּעֵינַי וְאֹרַח זָר לָהּ.	
	Indeed many **desirable young men**[66] possessing good looks and splendour	הֵן **בַּחוּרֵי חֶמֶד**[66] רַבִּים, בַּעֲלֵי תֹאַר וְהָדָר	
	From among the most honourable men of her native land, urged her to marry them	מִנִּכְבַּדֵּי אֶרֶץ מוֹלַדְתָּהּ, הִפְצִירוּ בָהּ לְקַחְתָּהּ	
	But she turned her back and refused to look at them	וְהִיא פָּנְתָה עֹרֶף וַתְּמָאֵן לְהַבִּיט בָּם	
	Not in the manner of damsels and not **according to the manner of all the earth**[67]	לֹא כְּאֹרַח עֲלָמוֹת וְלֹא **כְּדֶרֶךְ כָּל הָאָרֶץ**[67]	

61 Ps. 107:40.
62 Gen. 41:8 וַתִּפָּעֶם רוּחוֹ 'and his spirit was troubled'; also Dan. 2:3.
63 Jer. 17:9.
64 Isa. 30:11 סוּרוּ מִנֵּי־דֶרֶךְ הַטּוּ מִנֵּי־אֹרַח 'turn away from the road; go off the path'.
65 Isa. 8:14.
66 Ezek. 23:6, 12, 23.
67 Gen. 19:31.

	So who would not say that there is a **spirit of confusion within her**?[68]	וּמִי לֹא יֹאמַר, כִּי רוּחַ עִוְעִים בְּקִרְבָּהּ.[68]	
	But please forgive me my lord, I am not a slanderer	אַךְ שָׂא נָא אֲדֹנִי, לֹא מוֹצִיא דִבָּה אָנִי	
	And I would not disparage her, if I were not very worried	וְדֹפִי לֹא אֶתֵּן בָּהּ, לוּלֵא דָאַגְתִּי מְאֹד	
	Lest she open her eyes to weigh on the balance of her mind	פֶּן תִּפְקַח אֶת עֵינֶיהָ, לִשְׁקֹל בְּמֹאזְנֵי שִׂכְלָהּ	
	The men of her land against your worth, and deduct from your worth.	אֶת אַנְשֵׁי אַרְצָהּ בְּעֶרְכְּךָ וְגָרְעָה מֵעֶרְכֶּךָ.	
ITHIEL	Go in peace –	לֶךְ־לְךָ לְשָׁלוֹם –	איתיאל
	If you find anything else, please tell me	אִם תִּמְצָא עוֹד דָּבָר, הַגֵּד תַּגִּיד לִי	
	Order your wife to keep her watch with open eyes.	צַו אֶת אִשְׁתְּךָ לִשְׁמֹר מִשְׁמַרְתָּהּ בְּעֵינַיִם פְּקֻחוֹת.	
	And now go and leave me alone.	וְעַתָּה לֵךְ וְהַנִּיחֵנִי לְבַדִּי.	
DOEG	I am going, my lord. *(He makes to exit)*	הִנְנִי הוֹלֵךְ אֲדֹנִי. (חפץ ללכת)	דואג
ITHIEL	Why did I take a wife for myself?	לָמָּה זֶה לָקַחְתִּי לִי אִשָּׁה?	איתיאל
	This blameless man **uncovers a handbreadth and covers two handbreadths**[69]	וְאִישׁ תָּמִים הַזֶּה, מְגַלֶּה טֶפַח וּמְכַסֶּה טְפָחַיִם[69]	
	And out of what he has seen or knows, **he has not told me the half**.[70]	וּמֵאֲשֶׁר רָאָה אוֹ יָדַע, לֹא הִגִּיד לִי הַחֵצִי.[70]	
DOEG	Please let me entreat you; please do not question **either in the depths**	אָנָּה אֲחַלֶּה פָּנֶיךָ, אַל נָא תַּעֲמֵק שְׁאָלָה	דואג
	Or in the heights above;[71] every unknown thing will be made known	וְאַל תַּגְבֵּהַּ לְמָעְלָה;[71] כָּל נֶעְלָם יִוָּדַע	
	And will be revealed in time. And if you have determined	וְיִגָּלֶה בְּקֶרֶב הַיָּמִים. וְאִם חָרַצְתָּ אֹמֶר	
	To restore Chesed, for he is a man of valour,	לְהָשִׁיב אֶת כֶּשֶׂד, כִּי אִישׁ חַיִל הוּא	
	And keeps his watch in faith, it would be better after a few days	וְשׁוֹמֵר מִשְׁמַרְתּוֹ בֶּאֱמוּנָה, טוֹב לְאַחַר יָמִים אֲחָדִים	

68 Isa. 19:14 יְהוָה מָסַךְ בְּקִרְבָּהּ רוּחַ עִוְעִים ‘the Lord has mixed a spirit of confusion within her’.
69 Babylonian Talmud *Nedarim* 20b מגלה טפח ומכסה טפח ‘he uncovers a handbreadth and covers a handbreadth’. Cf. Shakespeare’s ‘sees and knows more – much more – than he unfolds’ (3.3.247).
70 1 Kings 10:7 לֹא־הֻגַּד־לִי הַחֵצִי ‘not even the half had been told to me’.
71 Isa. 7:11 הַעְמֵק שְׁאָלָה אוֹ הַגְבֵּהַּ לְמָעְלָה ‘ask either in the depth or in the heights above’.

	So that you might familiarize yourself with him in his ways, because **he will make himself known by his actions**[72]	לְמַעַן תַּכִּירֶנּוּ בִּדְרָכָיו, כִּי בְּמַעֲלָלָיו יִתְנַכֵּר[72]	
	And examine your wife as well when she intercedes on his behalf	וְגַם אֶת אִשְׁתְּךָ תִּבְחָן לְעֵת תַּפְגִּיעַ בַּעֲדוֹ	
	And observe her, how she pressures you intensely to restore him	וְתִתְבּוֹנֵן בָּהּ אֵיךְ תְּצִיקְךָ בְּחָזְקָה לַהֲשִׁיבוֹ	
	For with this touchstone[73] her heart can be well examined.	כִּי בְּאֶבֶן בֹּחַן[73] הַזֹּאת יִבָּחֵן לִבָּהּ הֵיטֵב.	
	But you will do well if you consider me hasty	אַךְ טוֹב תַּעֲשֶׂה, אִם לְנִמְהָר תַּחְשְׁבֵנִי	
	And mock my fear, because I am afraid for nothing,	וְתִלְעַג עַל חֶרְדָּתִי, כִּי חָרַדְתִּי חִנָּם,	
	For she is pure and there is no iniquity in her	כִּי נְקִיָּה הִיא וְעָוֹן לֹא נִמְצָא בָהּ	
	And regarding this I beseech you to listen to the voice of your servant.	וְעַל זֹאת אֶתְחַנָּן, כִּי תִשְׁמַע בְּקוֹל עַבְדֶּךָ.	
ITHIEL	I know how to control my spirit; do not worry about me.	יָדַעְתִּי לִמְשׁוֹל בְּרוּחִי, אַל תִּדְאַג לִי.	איתיאל
DOEG	Now I am going, in accordance with your words. *(Exits)*	עַתָּה הִנְנִי הוֹלֵךְ כִּדְבָרֶךָ. (הולך)	דואג
ITHIEL	This man is honest and faithful, and he has **a proud soul**[74]	הָאִישׁ הַזֶּה יָשָׁר וְנֶאֱמָן וְלוֹ נֶפֶשׁ רְחָבָה[74]	איתיאל
	Understanding the ways of men and their deeds, both small and large.	לְהַשְׂכִּיל דַּרְכֵי בְּנֵי אָדָם וַעֲלִילוֹתָם כַּקָּטֹן כַּגָּדוֹל.	
	If I find that my wife has strayed from me	אִם אֶמְצָא כִּי שָׂטְתָה אִשְׁתִּי תַחְתָּי	
	Even though I have kept her close to me, **like a seal on my heart**[75]	אַף כִּי הִדְבַּקְתִּי אֹתָהּ, כַּחוֹתָם עַל לִבִּי[75]	
	And I have tied her with bonds of love, like frontlets on my arm[76]	וָאֶקְשְׁרֶהָ בְּחַבְלֵי אַהֲבָה, כַּטֹּטָפוֹת עַל זְרוֹעִי[76]	

72 Prov. 20:11.

73 This expression derives originally from Isa. 28:16, but the meaning of 'touchstone' or 'acid test' is thought to be a modern innovation (Even-Shoshan 2003, 1: 8).

74 Mishnah *Avot* 5:19.

75 Song of Songs 8:6 שִׂימֵנִי כַחוֹתָם עַל־לִבֶּךָ 'place me like a seal on your heart'.

76 Cf. Shakespeare's 'jesses' (3.3.265), straps attached between a hawk's leg and the falconer's wrist (Honigmann 1997: 225, note 265; Crystal and Crystal 2002: 247). Salkinson has domesticated this image by replacing the falconry term with an allusion to the Jewish commandment of tying *tefillin*, or phylacteries, on the arm for weekday morning prayers.

I shall sever the ties from my arms like thread[77]	אֲנַתֵּק אֶת הַקְּשָׁרִים מֵעַל זְרוֹעוֹתַי כַּחוּט[77]
And send her away like a swallow to fly where the wind is.	וְשִׁלַּחְתִּיהָ כַּדְּרוֹר לָעוּף אֶל אֲשֶׁר יִהְיֶה שָׁם הָרוּחַ.
Maybe all of this has come upon me because I am black and a Cushite	אוּלַי כָּל זֹאת בָּאַתְנִי, כִּי שָׁחֹר וְכוּשִׁי אָנִי
And there is no honey under my tongue[78] to speak flattery and smoothness;	**וְאֵין דְּבַשׁ תַּחַת לְשׁוֹנִי**[78] לְדַבֵּר חֹנֶף וַחֲלָקוֹת;
Or because I am old, past half my days and more,	אוֹ מֵאֲשֶׁר בָּאתִי בַּיָּמִים, מֵחֲצִי יָמַי וָמָעְלָה,
But despite this it is not right that she should have been unfaithful to me.	אַךְ בְּכָל זֹאת לֹא תִצְדַּק כִּי מָעֲלָה בִּי.
Woe is me, woe is me! The unfaithful girl is not mine –	אוֹי לִי, אוֹי לִי! הַשּׁוֹבֵבָה לֹא לִי הִיא –
And all **my comfort in my wretchedness**[79] is that I might loathe her.	וְכָל **נֶחָמָתִי בְעָנְיִי**,[79] כִּי תִגְעַל נַפְשִׁי בָהּ.
I took her for myself as a curse, and her beauty is a heartache to me	לִקְלָלָה לְקַחְתִּיהָ לִי וְיָפְיָהּ לִי לִכְאֵב לֵב
I am ashamed that I trusted, for she is not mine. –	בּוֹשְׁתִּי כִּי בָטַחְתִּי, כִּי לֹא לִי הִיא. –
It would be better for me to be a locust, **to hop over the earth**[80]	טוֹב לִי לִהְיוֹת חָגָב, **לְנַתֵּר עַל הָאָרֶץ**[80]
Or to live on mist and steam in a prison	וְלִחְיוֹת עַל אֵד וְקִיטוֹר, בְּאַחַד בָּתֵּי כְלָאִים
Than to dwell with my soul's beloved one when strangers have a share of her	מִשֶּׁבֶת עִם אֲהוּבַת נַפְשִׁי וְיֵשׁ לְזָרִים חֵלֶק בָּהּ
This is the lot of commanders and the inheritance of the earth's great men,	זֶה גּוֹרַל הַשָּׂרִים וְנַחֲלָה לִגְדוֹלֵי אָרֶץ,
Because it is not for us to **live in safety**,[81] like the poor masses	כִּי לֹא לָנוּ **לָשֶׁבֶת בֶּטַח**,[81] כַּהֲמוֹן דַּלַּת הָעָם

77 Cf. Shakespeare's 'I'd whistle her off' (3.3.266); as previously (see preceding note), Salkinson has exchanged Shakespeare's falconry reference for an image of Jewish prayer with *tefillin*.

78 Song of Songs 4:11 דְּבַשׁ וְחָלָב תַּחַת לְשׁוֹנֵךְ 'there is honey and milk under your tongue'.

79 Ps. 119:50.

80 Lev. 11:21 אַךְ אֶת־זֶה תֹּאכְלוּ מִכֹּל שֶׁרֶץ הָעוֹף הַהֹלֵךְ עַל־אַרְבַּע אֲשֶׁר־לוֹ כְרָעַיִם מִמַּעַל לְרַגְלָיו לְנַתֵּר בָּהֵן עַל־הָאָרֶץ 'but these you may eat of every flying creeping thing that goes on all four, which has legs above its feet with which to hop upon the earth'.

81 Deut. 12:10 וִישַׁבְתֶּם־בֶּטַח 'and you will live in safety'; 1 Sam 12:11 וַתֵּשְׁבוּ בֶּטַח 'and you lived in safety'.

	And as soon as we have left the womb, evil pursues us	וְכִמְעַט יָצָאנוּ מֵרֶחֶם, תִּרַדֵּף רָעָה נַפְשֵׁנוּ	
	And lies in wait like death at the door – but Asenath is at the door.	וְתֶאֱרֹב כַּמָּוֶת לַפֶּתַח – אַךְ אָסְנַת בַּפֶּתַח.	
	(Asenath enters with Milcah)	(אסנת באה עם מלכה)	
	If she is unfaithful, **even the heavens are not pure in my eyes**[82]	אִם הִיא בָּגוֹדָה, גַּם **שָׁמַיִם לֹא זַכּוּ בְעֵינָי**[82]	
	But I shall not yet plan evil for her without cause.	אַךְ עוֹד לֹא אַחֲרֹשׁ עָלֶיהָ רָעָה חִנָּם.	
ITHIEL	Ithiel, my beloved, what is wrong with you?	אִיתִיאֵל יְדִיד נַפְשִׁי מַה־לָּךְ?	אסנת
	The noontime meal is prepared, and the honourable men of the town who have been invited	לֶחֶם הַצָּהֳרַיִם עָרוּךְ וְנִכְבַּדֵּי הָעִיר הַקְּרוּאִים	
	Are waiting for your arrival.	שׁוֹמְרִים אֶת בּוֹאֶךָ.	
ITHIEL	It was not right of me to be late.	לֹא צָדַקְתִּי כִּי אֵחַרְתִּי.	איתיאל
ASENATH	What is wrong with you, my husband, that you speak **so seriously**?[83]	מַה־לְּךָ בַּעֲלִי, כִּי תְדַבֵּר **בְּכֹבֶד רֹאשׁ**?[83]	אסנת
	Do you not feel well?	הַאֵין שָׁלוֹם בַּעֲצָמֶיךָ?	
ITHIEL	**My head, my head**[84] –	**רֹאשִׁי רֹאשִׁי**[84] –	איתיאל
ASENATH	Because you are often wakeful and do not sleep enough;	יַעַן כִּי תִשְׁקֹד הַרְבֵּה וְלֹא תִישַׁן דַּיֶּךָ,	אסנת
	Let me bind your head with my handkerchief,[85] and your pain will pass in a moment.	אֶחְבְּשָׁה רֹאשְׁךָ בְּמִטְפַּחְתִּי[85] וּכְאֵבְךָ יַעֲבֹר כְּרָגַע.	
ITHIEL	Your handkerchief is too small to bind my head	מִטְפַּחְתֵּךְ קְטַנָּה מֵחֲבשׁ אֶת רֹאשִׁי	איתיאל
	Come into the chamber; I shall come after you.	בּוֹאִי נָא הַחַדְרָה, הִנְנִי אָבוֹא אַחֲרַיִךְ.	
	(Removes the handkerchief from his head and drops it on the ground)	(מסיר המטפחת מעל ראשו ומפילה ארצה)	

82 Job 15:15 וְשָׁמַיִם לֹא־זַכּוּ בְעֵינָיו 'even the heavens are not pure in His eyes'.
83 Mishnah *Berakhot* 5:1 (also appears in the Tosefta and in later rabbinic literature).
84 2 Kings 4:19.
85 This word appears twice in the Hebrew Bible (Isa. 3:22 and Ruth 3:15), where it means 'shawl' or 'cloak'. From the rabbinic period onwards it more commonly means 'handkerchief'; Salkinson is using it in the latter sense.

ASENATH	I am sorry for your pain. *(Ithiel and Asenath exit)*	צַר לִי בְּמַכְאוֹבֵךְ. (איתיאל ואסנת הולכים)	אסנת
MILCAH	To my heart's joy I have found this handkerchief here	לְשִׂמְחַת לְבָבִי מָצָאתִי פֹּה הַמִּטְפַּחַת הַזֹּאת	מלכה
	It is the first present that he gave her **as a sign of their covenant**.[86]	הִיא הַמַּתָּנָה* הָרִאשׁוֹנָה נִתְּנָה לָהּ לְאוֹת בְּרִית.[86]	
	My fickle and strange husband has urged me a hundred times	בַּעֲלִי הֲפַכְפַּךְ וָזָר הִפְצִיר בִּי מֵאָה פְעָמִים	
	To steal it and give it to him; but it is precious in her eyes	לְגָנְבָהּ וּלְתִתָּהּ לוֹ; אַךְ יְקָרָה הִיא בְעֵינֶיהָ	
	In keeping with the Cushite's oath for her to keep it as an eternal memento[87]	כִּשְׁבוּעַת הַכּוּשִׁי עָלֶיהָ, לְשָׁמְרָהּ לְמַזְכֶּרֶת[87] עוֹלָם	
	And she carries it by her bosom continually and keeps it like a precious amulet	וְהִיא תִשָּׂאֶנָּהּ בְּחֵיקָהּ תָּמִיד וְתִשְׁמְרֶנָּהּ כִּסְגֻלָּה יְקָרָה	
	And she also utters words to it and kisses it in her love	וְגַם תּוֹצִיא לָהּ מִלִּין וּתְנַשֵּׁק אֹתָהּ בְּאַהֲבָתָהּ	
	But now that I have found it, I shall give it to my husband Doeg.	וְעַתָּה כִּי מְצָאתִיהָ אֶתְּנֶהָ לְדוֹאֵג בַּעֲלִי.	
	I cannot understand what he will do with the stolen item –	לֹא אוּכַל לְהָבִין, מַה־יַּעֲשֶׂה אֶת הַגְּנֵבָה	
	God alone knows, and I do not know what	הָאֱלֹהִים לְבַדּוֹ יוֹדֵעַ וַאֲנִי אֵינֶנִּי יוֹדַעַת מָה	
	But I shall do this, in order to calm his spirit.	אַךְ אֶעֱשֶׂה זֹאת, לְהַשְׁקִיט אֶת רוּחוֹ.	
DOEG	What are you doing here by yourself?	מַה־תַּעֲשִׂי פֹה לְבַדֵּךְ?	דואג
MILCAH	Do not argue with me, when in my hand there is something to give you.	אַל תִּתְקוֹטְטִי בִּי וּבְיָדִי דָבָר לְתִתּוֹ לָךְ.	מלכה
DOEG	Something for me? **Something wherein there is no pleasure**[88] –	דָּבָר לְמַעֲנִי? דָּבָר אֵין חֵפֶץ בּוֹ[88] –	דואג
MILCAH	In what do you have no pleasure?	בַּמָּה אֵין חֶפְצֵךְ?	מלכה

86 Gen. 9:13, 17:11.

87 This noun is attested in Num. 5:15, but the sense of 'memento' in which Salkinson is using it is thought to be a medieval innovation (Even-Shoshan 2003, 3: 924).

88 Jer. 22:28, 48:38; Hosea 8:8.

* הַמַּתָּנָה

DOEG	In **a foolish wife.**[89]	**בְּאֵשֶׁת כְּסִילוּת.**[89]	דואג
MILCAH	And therefore you find pleasure in **the tongue of the sly**[90] and **destructive words**[91]	וְלָכֵן תִּמְצָא חֵפֶץ, בִּלְשׁוֹן עֲרוּמִים[90] וְדִבְרֵי בָלַע[91]	מלכה
	But what would you say if I gave you the handkerchief?	אַךְ מַה־תֹּאמַר, אִם אֶתֵּן לְךָ הַמִּטְפַּחַת?	
DOEG	Which handkerchief?	אֵיזוֹ מִטְפַּחַת?	דואג
MILCAH	The handkerchief that the Cushite gave to Asenath as a memento	הַמִּטְפַּחַת אֲשֶׁר נָתַן הַכּוּשִׁי לְאָסְנַת לְזִכָּרוֹן	מלכה
	And which you have urged me several times to steal.	וַאֲשֶׁר הִפְצַרְתָּ בִּי, כַּמֶּה פְּעָמִים לְגָנְבָהּ.	
DOEG	And you have stolen it.	וְאַתְּ גָּנַבְתְּ אֹתָהּ.	דואג
MILCAH	God forbid that I steal it, it only happened to fall	חָלִלָה לִּי מִגְּנֹב, רַק בְּמִקְרֶה נָפָלָה	מלכה
	And I was summoned here and found the lost item	וְאָנֹכִי נִקְרֵאתִי פֹּה וָאֶמְצָא אֶת הָאֲבֵדָה	
	Look; here it is in my hand.	רְאֵה הִנֶּהָ בְּיָדִי.	
DOEG	I knew that you were **a woman of valour**[92] – give it to me.	יָדַעְתִּי כִּי **אֵשֶׁת חַיִל**[92] אָתְּ – תְּנִיהָ לִּי.	דואג
MILCAH	But tell me, what does the handkerchief have to do with you?	אַךְ הַגֵּד לִי, מַה לְּךָ וְלַמִּטְפַּחַת?	מלכה
	What do you want to do with it, that you persuaded me to obtain it?	מָה חֶפְצְךָ לַעֲשׂוֹת בָּה*, כִּי פִּתִּיתַנִי לְהַשִּׂיגָהּ?	
DOEG	What's it to you to know that? *(Snatches the handkerchief from her hand)*	מַה־לָּךְ לָדַעַת זֹאת? (יחטף המטפחת מידה)	דואג
MILCAH	What gain is there for you in this handkerchief? Give it back to me	מַה־בֶּצַע לְךָ בְּמִטְפַּחַת זוּ? הֲשִׁיבֶהָ לִּי	מלכה
	Lest my lady lose her wits when she sees that it is gone.	פֶּן תִּשְׁתּוֹלֵל גְּבִרְתִּי, בִּרְאוֹתָהּ כִּי אֵינֶנָּה.	
DOEG	See that no one finds out, lest you become a disgrace	רְאִי לְבַל יִוָּדַע לְאִישׁ, פֶּן תִּהְיִי לְבֹשֶׁת	דואג
	But I want it; get up and go. *(She exits)*	וַאֲנִי יֶשׁ־לִי חֵפֶץ בָּהּ; קוּמִי וּלְכִי לָךְ. (הולכת)	

89 Prov. 9:13.
90 Job 15:5.
91 Ps. 52:6 (52:4 in English Bibles).
92 Prov. 12:4, 31:10; Ruth 3:11.

* בָּהּ

	I shall throw this handkerchief into Chesed's chamber when no one is looking	הַמִּטְפַּחַת הַזֹּאת אַשְׁלִיךְ בַּחֲדַר כֶּשֶׂד בְּאֵין רֹאֶה	
	And he will find it there. A jealous man believes	וְהוּא יִמְצָאֶנָּהּ שָׁם. בַּעַל קִנְאָה יַאֲמִין	
	In signs more trifling than vapour as in wonders more reliable than the heavens.	בְּאוֹתוֹת קַלִּים מֵהֶבֶל, כְּמוֹפְתִים נֶאֱמָנִים מִשָּׁמָיִם.	
	And this will thus provide a small benefit and will not come back empty-handed,	וְזֹאת אֵיפוֹא תּוֹעִיל מְעָט וְלֹא תָשׁוּב רֵיקָם,	
	As **the cup of reeling**[93] which I have poured for the Cushite has already started to take its effect	וְכוֹס הַתַּרְעֵלָה[93] מָסַכְתִּי לַכּוּשִׁי כְּבָר הֵחֵלָּה פְּעֻלָּתָהּ	
	For deceitful words, like poisoned water, are pleasing to the palate	כִּי דִבְרֵי רְמִיָּה, כְּמֵי רַעַל עֲרֵבִים לְחֵיךְ	
	Until they mix with the blood and turn into **a stream of brimstone**.[94]	עַד אֲשֶׁר יִתְעָרְבוּ בַּדָּם וְנֶהֶפְכוּ **לְנַחַל גָּפְרִית**.[94]	
	(Ithiel enters)	(איתיאל בא)	
	Behold, he comes towards me – no intoxicating water or mixed wine	הִנֵּה הוּא בָא לִקְרָאתִי – כָּל מֵי רוֹשׁ וּמִמְסָךְ	
	And no **balm or remedy**[95] will bring **the sleep to your eyes**	**וְכָל צֳרִי וּמַרְפֵּא**,[95] **לֹא יִתְּנוּ שֵׁנַת לְעֵינֶיךָ**	
	Nor the slumber to your eyelids[96] which was so sweet for you last night.	**וְלֹא תְנוּמָה לְעַפְעַפֶּיךָ**,[96] אֲשֶׁר מָתְקָה לְךָ אֶמֶשׁ.	
ITHIEL	Has she indeed betrayed me? Has she betrayed *me*? –	הֲבָגוֹד בָּגְדָה בִי? בִּי הִיא בָגְדָה? –	איתיאל
DOEG	That's enough from you, army commander, of speaking about this matter.	רַב לְךָ שַׂר הַצָּבָא, לְדַבֵּר בַּדָּבָר הַזֶּה.	דואג
ITHIEL	**Stand back**![97] After all, you are the one who has brought the distress upon me;	**גֶּשׁ הָלְאָה**![97] הֲלֹא אַתָּה הֲבֵאתַנִי בַּמְּצָרִים,	איתיאל

93 Isa. 51:17.
94 Isa. 30:33.
95 Alshekh to Exod. 13, Deut. 4, Prov. 6, 18, 19.
96 Prov. 6:4 אַל־תִּתֵּן שֵׁנָה לְעֵינֶיךָ וּתְנוּמָה לְעַפְעַפֶּיךָ 'do not give sleep to your eyes, nor slumber to your eyelids'.
97 Gen. 19:9.

	I swear, I would prefer the woman's infidelity to be in secret	בִּי נִשְׁבַּעְתִּי, טוֹב לִי מַעַל הָאִשָּׁה בַּסֵּתֶר	
	Than to hear about the infidelity, **its edge but not all of it**.[98]	מִשְּׁמוֹעַ דְּבַר הַמַּעַל **אֶפֶס קָצֵהוּ וְלֹא כֻלּוֹ**.[98]	
DOEG	What is my lord talking about?	מָה אֲדֹנִי דֹבֵר?	דואג
ITHIEL	I knew nothing of **her harlotry**[99] in secret	מִן **נַאֲפוּפֶיהָ**[99] בַּמִּסְתָּרִים לֹא יָדַעְתִּי מְאוּמָה	איתיאל
	I did not notice or take heed, and I lacked for nothing,	לֹא שַׂמְתִּי עֵינִי וְלִבִּי וְלֹא חָסַרְתִּי דָּבָר,	
	I was calm previously **and my sleep was pleasant**[100]	שָׁלֵו הָיִיתִי מִתְּמוֹל **וּשְׁנָתִי עָרְבָה לִּי**[100]	
	And I did not find the kisses of Chesed's mouth upon her lips.	וּנְשִׁיקוֹת פִּי כֶשֶׂד, לֹא מָצָאתִי עַל שְׂפָתֶיהָ.	
	A robbed man who does not recognize what has been stolen from him	שָׁדוּד אֲשֶׁר לֹא יַכִּיר מַה־שֻּׁדַּד מִיָּדוֹ	
	Is not a robbed man, unless an informant has told him.	אֵין זֶה שָׁדוּד, בִּלְתִּי אִם הִגִּיד לוֹ הַמַּגִּיד.	
DOEG	I am sorry to hear your words.	צַר לִי לִשְׁמֹעַ דְּבָרֶיךָ.	דואג
ITHIEL	If only the men of the army, each insignificant and honourable man in the camp,	לוּ אַנְשֵׁי הַצָּבָא, כָּל נִקְלֶה וְנִכְבָּד בַּמַּחֲנֶה	איתיאל
	Tasted **bread in secrecy from my bread and stolen water**[101] from my well	טָעֲמוּ **לֶחֶם סְתָרִים** מִלַּחְמִי **וּמַיִם גְּנוּבִים**[101] מִבְּאֵרִי	
	And I did not know anything, I would be calm and quiet in my happiness	וְנַפְשִׁי לֹא יָדְעָה מָה שָׁלַוְתִּי וְשָׁקַטְתִּי בְּאָשְׁרִי	
	But now **my heart fails me**;[102] I cannot continue to rejoice in my lot. –	אַךְ עַתָּה **עֲזָבַנִי לִבִּי**,[201] לֹא אוֹסִיף לִשְׂמֹחַ בְּחֶלְקִי. –	
	What do I have to do with you any more, all **armed men carrying bows**![103]	מַה לִּי וְלָכֶם עוֹד, כָּל **נוֹשְׁקֵי רוֹמֵי קָשֶׁת**![103]	

98 Num. 23:13 אֶפֶס קָצֵהוּ תִרְאֶה וְכֻלּוֹ לֹא תִרְאֶה 'you will see its edge, but you will not see all of it'.
99 Hosea 2:4.
100 Jer. 31:26.
101 Prov. 9:17 מַיִם־גְּנוּבִים יִמְתָּקוּ וְלֶחֶם סְתָרִים יִנְעָם 'stolen water is sweet, and bread eaten in secret is pleasing'.
102 Ps. 40:13 (40:12 in English Bibles).
103 Ps. 78:9.

	What do I have to do with you any more, all of my glorious troops	מַה־לִּי וְלָכֶם עוֹד, כָּל גְּדוּדֵי תִפְאַרְתִּי	
	Which take pleasure in battles and boast **with sword and spear**![104]	אֲשֶׁר קְרָבוֹת תֶּחְפָּצוּן **וּבְחֶרֶב וַחֲנִית**[104] תִּתְיַמָּרוּ!	
	Remove, take away from me the sound of the horses' neighing	הַרְחִיקוּ הָסִירוּ מִמֶּנִּי, קוֹל מִצְהֲלוֹת הַסּוּסִים	
	The sound of timbrel and cymbals and all the thundering of weapons of war.	קוֹל תֹּף וּמְצִלְתַּיִם וְכָל תְּרוּעַת כְּלֵי מִלְחָמָה.	
	Remove from me **standard and banner**[105] and all **the shields of gold**[106]	הָסִירוּ מִמֶּנִּי, **נֵס וָדֶגֶל**[105] וְכָל **שִׁלְטֵי הַזָּהָב**[106]	
	Remove my **splendid chariots**[107] and all my **glorious beauty**,[108]	הָסִירוּ **מַרְכְּבוֹת כְּבוֹדִי**[107] וְכָל **צְבִי תִפְאַרְתִּי**,[108]	
	And you, instruments of the angels of death, **from whose mouth arrogance comes out**[109]	וְאַתֶּם כְּלֵי מַלְאֲכֵי מָוֶת אֲשֶׁר **עָתָק יֵצֵא מִפִּיכֶם**[109]	
	Like the lightning of the God of the heavens[110] and like the roar of His mighty thunder	כִּבְרַק אֱלֹהֵי שָׁמַיִם[110] וְכִשְׁאוֹן רַעַם גְּבוּרָתוֹ	
	Turn away, leave me alone! For the might of Ithiel is finished.	סוּרוּ חִדְלוּ מִמֶּנִּי! כִּי כָלוּ גְבוּרוֹת אִיתִיאֵל.	
DOEG	Who would believe it, hearing such a thing?	מִי הֶאֱמִין לִשְׁמֹעַ כָּזֹאת?	דואג
ITHIEL	Look, villain! You must establish	רְאֵה בֶּן בְּלִיַּעַל! עָלֶיךָ לְהָקִים הַדָּבָר	איתיאל
	That my beloved is committing adultery. *(Seizes him by his neck)*	כִּי אֲהוּבַת נַפְשִׁי מְנָאָפֶת. (יאחז אותו בערפו)	
	For if it is not so, **I swear by the One who lives forever**[111]	כִּי אִם לֹא זֹאת, **בְּחֵי הָעוֹלָם נִשְׁבַּעְתִּי**[111]	
	That your end will be bitter. It would be much better for you	כִּי מָרָה תִהְיֶה אַחֲרִיתֶךָ. טוֹב טוֹב הָיָה לָךְ	

104 1 Sam. 17:45, 47.
105 Alshekh to Isa. 59.
106 1 Sam. 8:7; 1 Chron. 18:7.
107 Isa. 22:18 מַרְכְּבוֹת כְּבוֹדֶךָ 'your glorious chariots'.
108 Isa. 28:1 צְבִי תִפְאַרְתּוֹ 'its glorious beauty', also Isa. 28:4.
109 1 Sam. 2:3 יֵצֵא עָתָק מִפִּיכֶם 'let [not] arrogance come out of your mouth'.
110 Cf. Shakespeare's 'Jove's dread clamours' (3.3.359); Salkinson has replaced this with a reference to the monotheistic God.
111 Dan. 12:7 וַיִּשָּׁבַע בְּחֵי הָעוֹלָם 'and he swore by the One who lives forever'.

	To have been a dog from the womb, than to stand before my wrath.	לִהְיוֹת כֶּלֶב מִבֶּטֶן, מֵעֲמֹד לִפְנֵי זַעְמִי.	
DOEG	Have we come to this?	הֲזֹאת הָיְתָה לָּנוּ?	דואג
ITHIEL	Show me **the vile thing**;[112] give me a reliable sign	הַרְאֵנִי דְּבַר הַנְּבָלָה;[112] תֶּן־לִי אוֹת נֶאֱמָן	איתיאל
	Which cannot be criticized; and if there is no such thing	אֲשֶׁר אֵין לְבַקֵּר אַחֲרָיו; וְאִם אֵין זֹאת	
	Woe to you, woe to you!	אוֹי לְךָ אוֹי לָךְ! –	
DOEG	My noble lord! –	אֲדֹנִי הַנָּדִיב! –	דואג
ITHIEL	If you have slandered her in order to torture me	אִם הֵבֵאתָ דִּבָּתָהּ רָעָה, בַּעֲבוּר לְעַנּוֹת אֹתִי	איתיאל
	Do not implore favour any more. **Go frowardly in the way of your heart!**[113]	אַל תִּתְחַנֵּן עוֹד. **לֵךְ שׁוֹבָב בְּדֶרֶךְ לִבְּךָ!**[113]	
	Add horror to horror **with a high hand**;[114]	הוֹסֵף **בְּיָד רָמָה**[114] שַׁעֲרוּרָה עַל שַׁעֲרוּרָה;	
	Shake the heavens,[115] **make the earth tremble**[116] with your iniquity	**הַרְעֵשׁ שָׁמַיִם**[115] **הַרְגֵּז אֶרֶץ**[116] בַּעֲוֹנֶךָ	
	And all these things will not add guilt to your guilt.	וְכָל אֵלֶּה לֹא יוֹסִיפוּ אַשְׁמָה עַל אַשְׁמָתֶךָ.	
DOEG	Hurry, angels of mercy come to protect me!	מַלְאֲכֵי רַחֲמִים חוּשׁוּ, בּוֹאוּ לְהָגֵן בַּעֲדִי!	דואג
	Are you a man? Do you have a soul and a spirit?	הַאִם אִישׁ אָתָּה? הֲיֵשׁ לְךָ נֶפֶשׁ וָרוּחַ?	
	Take my office from me – and may God help you.	קַח אֶת פְּקוּדָתִי מִמֶּנִּי – וֵאלֹהִים יִהְיֶה בְּעֶזְרֶךָ.	
	Whereas I am a fool and a wretch, for I have lived[117]	וַאֲנִי סָכָל וְאֻמְלָל, כִּי חָיִיתִי עַד הַיּוֹם[117]	
	To see my honesty considered as a sin.	לִרְאוֹת אֶת אֱמוּנָתִי, נֶחְשְׁבָה לִי לַחֲטָאָה.	
ITHIEL	But wait a bit more, perhaps you are honest and faithful.	אֲבָל חַכֵּה עוֹד מְעַט, אוּלַי יָשָׁר וְנֶאֱמָן אָתָּה.	איתיאל

---

112 Judg. 19:24.
113 Isa. 57:17 וַיֵּלֶךְ שׁוֹבָב בְּדֶרֶךְ לִבּוֹ 'but he went frowardly in the way of his heart'.
114 Exod. 14:8; Num. 15:30, 33:3.
115 Hag. 2:21 אֲנִי מַרְעִישׁ אֶת־הַשָּׁמַיִם 'I am going to shake the heavens'.
116 Isa. 14:16 הָאִישׁ מַרְגִּיז הָאָרֶץ 'the man who made the earth tremble'.
117 The source text has a rhyming couplet here 'hence/offence' (3.3.382–3) which Salkinson has not reproduced.

DOEG	But I am not wise, because the honest man is a fool	אֲבָל לֹא נָבוֹן אָנֹכִי, יַעַן הַיָּשָׁר סָכָל הוּא	דואג
	And does not obtain that which he seeks.	וְלֹא יַשִּׂיג אֵת אֲשֶׁר יְבַקֵּשׁ.	
ITHIEL	Sometimes I believe that my wife is faithful	פַּעַם אֲנִי מַאֲמִין בְּאִשְׁתִּי, כִּי נֶאֱמָנָה הִיא	איתיאל
	And sometimes not; sometimes I believe	וּפַעַם לֹא כֵן; פַּעַם אֲנִי מַאֲמִין בְּךָ	
	That you are honest, and sometimes not.	כִּי יָשָׁר אַתָּה וּפַעַם לֹא כֵן.	
	Therefore I say one thing; you must prove the matter to my eyes.	לָכֵן אַחַת אָמַרְתִּי, אָלֶיךָ לְהוֹכִיחַ הַדָּבָר לְעֵינָי.	
	Indeed there are sufficient fetters with me, a knife and a deathly wrath	הֵן דֵּי כְּבָלִים אִתִּי, מַאֲכֶלֶת וַחֲמַת מָוֶת	
	And also enough fire and water to exact revenge upon those who despise me[118]	וְגַם בְּדֵי אֵשׁ וּמַיִם, לִנְקֹם נָקָם מִמְּנַאֲצַי[118]	
	For I have grown tired of bearing it; I cannot endure it any longer	כִּי נִלְאֵיתִי נְשֹׂא, לְהָכִיל לֹא אוּכַל עוֹד	
	I seek only a true investigation at the start.	רַק בִּקֹּרֶת אֱמֶת, תְּבַקֵּשׁ נַפְשִׁי בַּתְּחִלָּה.	
DOEG	Look, your heart burns like an oven, and fire consumes your bones	רְאֵה לִבְּךָ בֹּעֵר כַּתַּנּוּר* וְאֵשׁ אֹכֶלֶת עַצְמוֹתֶיךָ	דואג
	I regret that I ignited this fire for you	נִחַמְתִּי כִּי אֲנִי הִבְעַרְתִּי לְךָ אֶת הַבְּעֵרָה	
	But after all, you seek a true investigation.	אַךְ בִּקֹּרֶת אֱמֶת, הֲלֹא תְבַקֵּשׁ נַפְשְׁךָ.	
ITHIEL	I seek it, and I shall not desist until I find it.	אֹתָהּ אֲנִי מְבַקֵּשׁ וְלֹא אֶרֶף עַד אֶמְצָאֶנָּה.	איתיאל
DOEG	Indeed you may find it as you seek, but what might suffice for you?	הֵן תִּמְצָא כַּאֲשֶׁר תְּבַקֵּשׁ, אַךְ מַה־יִּשְׂפֹּק לָךְ?	דואג
	Would you stand watching with your eyes, while Chesed bends over her?	הֲתַעֲמֹד לִרְאוֹת בְּעֵינֶיךָ, לְעֵת כֶּשֶׂד יִכְרַע עָלֶיהָ?	

118 Salkinson has omitted Shakespeare's 'Her name, that was as fresh/As Dian's visage, is now begrimed and black/As mine own face' (3.3.389–91), which appears directly before this sentence in the Folio editions. (This entire speech is missing from the Quarto, but the fact that Salkinson has retained most of it indicates that he was working from a source text that included it.)

* תַּנּוּר

ITHIEL	O, **death and destruction**![119]	אִי מָוֶת וַאֲבַדּוֹן![119]	איתיאל
DOEG	It is not easy to see shameful acts before one's eyes	לֹא עַל נְקַלָּה יֵרָאֶה מַעֲשֵׂה זִמָּה לְעֵינַיִם	דואג
	If you find them drawing near and approaching like an arrow in the quiver	אִם תִּמְצָא אֹתָם קְרֵבִים וּבָאִים כַּחֵץ בָּאַשְׁפָּה	
	Why, **you will stab both of them in their bellies.**[120]	הֲלֹא תִדְקֹר אֶת שְׁנֵיהֶם אֶל קֳבָתָם.[120]	
	What, then, shall I say now? What shall we do?	מָה אֵיפוֹא אֲדַבֵּר עַתָּה? מַה־נַּעֲשֶׂה לָּנוּ?	
	After all, you will not be able to see their nakedness	הֵן לֹא תוּכַל לִרְאוֹת אֶת עֶרְוָתָם	
	Even if they have given themselves over to desire and their lust is the lust of goats,	אַף אִם הִתְמַכְּרוּ לְתַאֲוָה וְעֹנָתָם עֹנַת שְׂעִירִים,	
	If their heat is the heat of monkeys and their flesh is the flesh of wolves	חֹם קֹפִים חֻמָּם וּבְשַׂר זְאֵבִים בְּשָׂרָם	
	And they have been inflamed beyond sense, as if drunk on the wine of lust	וְגַם נִבְעֲרוּ מִדַּעַת, כִּשְׁכּוֹרִים מִיֵּין עֲגָבִים	
	Your eye will not be able to see them joined together.	לֹא תַשִּׂיג* עֵינְךָ לִרְאוֹתָם מְצֻמָּדִים יַחְדָּו.	
	But if **signs and wonders**,[121] which give evidence like witnesses,	אַךְ אִם **אוֹתוֹת וּמוֹפְתִים**,[121] הַמַּגִּידִים כְּמוֹ עֵדִים	
	Are sufficient to make a judgement, you will find them if you seek them.	יַסְפִּיקוּ לְהוֹצִיא מִשְׁפָּט, תִּמְצָאֵם כִּי תְבַקְשֵׁם.	
ITHIEL	I require a **pure and refined**[122] test from you	בְּחִינָה **צְרוּפָה וּמְזֻקָּקָה**[122] אֲנִי דֹרֵשׁ מִיָּדְךָ	איתיאל
	So that I may know surely that she has been unfaithful to me.	לְמַעַן אֵדַע אֶל נָכוֹן כִּי מָעֲלָה בִי.	
DOEG	This matter is not pleasing in my eyes	לֹא לְרָצוֹן הַדָּבָר הַזֶּה בְּעֵינַי	דואג

119 Job 28:22 אֲבַדּוֹן וָמָוֶת 'destruction and death'.

120 Num. 25:8 וַיִּדְקֹר אֶת־שְׁנֵיהֶם אֵת אִישׁ יִשְׂרָאֵל וְאֶת־הָאִשָּׁה אֶל־קֳבָתָהּ 'and he pierced both of them through, the Israelite and the woman through her belly' (referring to Phineas, Aaron's grandson, driving a spear through an Israelite man and Moabite woman out of disapproval at intermarriage between the two groups).

121 Neh. 9:10; similar collocations with these two nouns appear in numerous other locations in the Hebrew Bible (referring to God's signs and wonders), e.g., Exod. 7:3; Deut. 4:34.

122 Ps. 12:7 (12:6 in English Bibles) כֶּסֶף צָרוּף בַּעֲלִיל לָאָרֶץ מְזֻקָּק שִׁבְעָתָיִם 'pure silver in an earthen furnace, refined seven times'.

* תַשִּׂיג

	Indeed after I started to uncover **disgrace**[123]	אָכֵן אַחֲרֵי הַחִלִּי, לְגַלּוֹת שֶׁמֶץ דָּבָר[123]	
	Because my great love and faith pressured me	כִּי הֱצִיקַתְנִי אַהֲבָתִי וֶאֱמוּנָתִי כִּי רַבָּה	
	I shall finish that which I started. One time at night	אֲכַלֶּה אֵת אֲשֶׁר הַחִלּוֹתִי. פַּעַם אַחַת בַּלַּיְלָה	
	I was sleeping with Chesed in the bed, and because of a powerful toothache	יָשַׁנְתִּי עִם כֶּשֶׂד בַּמִּטָּה וּמִכְּאֵב שִׁנַּי כִּי חָזַק	
	I could not sleep. You know that there are people	לֹא יָכֹלְתִּי לִישׁוֹן. וְהִנֵּה יֵשׁ בְּנֵי אָדָם	
	Who talk in their sleep, the secrets of their heart's inclination	אֲשֶׁר יָשִׂיחוּ בִּשְׁנָתָם, סִתְרֵי יֵצֶר לִבָּם	
	And Chesed is one of them. And so he called out in his sleep in my ears	וְכֶשֶׂד כְּאַחַד מֵהֶם. וְכֵן קָרָא בִשְׁנָתוֹ לְאָזְנָי	
	'Asenath, **whom my soul loves**![124] **Let us take sweet counsel together**[125]	אָסְנַת שֶׁאָהֲבָה נַפְשִׁי![124] נַמְתִּיק סוֹד יַחְדָּו[125]„	
	And let our love be kept secret'. After that he seized my hand	וְאַהֲבָתֵנוּ מְסֻתֶּרֶת תְּהִי" אַחֲרֵי כֵן אָחַז בְּיָדִי	
	And called: '**My darling, my beautiful one**!'[126] **And he kissed me with the kisses of his mouth**[127]	וַיִּקְרָא: רַעְיָתִי יָפָתִי![126] וַיִּשָּׁקֵנִי מִנְּשִׁיקוֹת פִּיהוּ[127]	
	As one kisses kissing lips, and he rested his leg on my thigh	כְּנשֵׁק שְׂפָתַיִם נשְׁקוֹת וַיַּנַּח שׁוֹקוֹ עַל יְרֵכִי	
	And he sighed and embraced and kissed and called out in a bitter voice	וַיֵּאָנַח וַיְחַבֵּק וַיְנַשֵּׁק וַיִּקְרָא בְּקוֹל מַר	
	'An evil and cruel fate gave you to the Cushite'.	מִקְרֶה רַע וְאַכְזָרִי נְתָנֵךְ אֶל הַכּוּשִׁי.	
ITHIEL	**I grow faint from hearing.**[128]	נַעֲוֵיתִי מִשְּׁמֹעַ.[128]	איתיאל

123 Job 26:14 וּמַה־שֵּׁמֶץ דָּבָר נִשְׁמַע־בּוֹ 'and how faint (or: whispering) a word is heard of Him'. See note 56 for discussion of Salkinson's use of this expression.

124 Song of Songs 1:7, 3:1, 2, 3.

125 Ps. 55:15 (55:14 in English Bibles) יַחְדָּו נַמְתִּיק סוֹד 'we took sweet counsel together'.

126 Song of Songs 2:10.

127 Song of Songs 1:2 יִשָּׁקֵנִי מִנְּשִׁיקוֹת פִּיהוּ 'let him kiss me with the kisses of his mouth'.

128 Isa. 21:3.

DOEG	Indeed he did not say this, except in a dream.	אָכֵן לֹא דִבֵּר זֶה, כִּי אִם בַּחֲלוֹם.	דואג
ITHIEL	But there is no dream without some business beforehand	אֲבָל אֵין חֲלוֹם, בְּלֹא עִנְיָן תְּחִלָּה	איתיאל
	And such evil dreams do not speak falsely.	וַחֲלוֹמוֹת רָעִים כָּאֵלֶּה, לֹא שָׁוְא יְדַבֵּרוּ.	
DOEG	And this may also be of benefit in reinforcing other tests	וְגַם זֶה יְהִי לְהוֹעִיל לְחַזֵּק בְּחִינוֹת אֲחֵרוֹת	דואג
	In order that we may rely on them, even though they be small.	לְמַעַן נִסָּמֵךְ עֲלֵיהֶן אַף כִּי קְטַנּוֹת הֵנָּה.	
ITHIEL	**I am going to tear her apart as one tears apart a kid**[129] –	**הִנְנִי לְשַׁסַּע אֹתָהּ כְּשַׁסַּע הַגְּדִי**[129] –	איתיאל
DOEG	Do not be hasty in your spirit, lest she is faithful	אַל תְּהִי נִמְהָר בְּרוּחֲךָ, פֶּן נֶאֱמָנָה הִיא	דואג
	And has not transgressed **a holy covenant**;[130] but tell me this	וְלֹא עָבְרָה **בְּרִית קֹדֶשׁ**;[130] אַךְ זֹאת הַגֵּד לִי	
	Have you seen a handkerchief in her hand with woven[131] pomegranates[132] on it?	הֲרָאִיתָ מִטְפַּחַת בְּיָדָהּ וּמִקְלְעוֹת[131] רִמּוֹנִים[132] עָלֶיהָ?	
ITHIEL	I gave her such a one, and it was the first gift from my hand.	כָּזֹאת נָתַתִּי לָהּ וְהִיא מַתַּת יָדִי הָרִאשׁוֹנָה.	איתיאל
DOEG	That was not known to me. Indeed today I noticed	זֶה לֹא נוֹדַע לִי, אֲבָל הַיּוֹם הִתְבּוֹנַנְתִּי	דואג
	That it was with a silk handkerchief which I had seen in your wife's hand	כִּי בְמִטְפַּחַת מֶשִׁי אֲשֶׁר רָאִיתִי בְּיַד אִשְׁתְּךָ	
	That Chesed was wiping the sweat from his face.	מָחָה חֶשֶׁד זֵעָה מֵעַל אַפָּיו.	

129 Judg. 14:6 וַיְשַׁסְּעֵהוּ כְּשַׁסַּע הַגְּדִי 'and he tore it apart as one tears apart a kid' (Samson tearing apart a lion with his bare hands).

130 Dan. 11:28, 30.

131 This word is attested in the Hebrew Bible (1 Kings 6:29, 32, 7:31), but has the meaning of 'carvings' or 'engravings'; the sense of 'weaving' in which Salkinson is using it originates in the modern period (Even-Shoshan 2003, 3: 1082).

132 Cf. Shakespeare's 'strawberries' (3.3.438). Salkinson's translation of 'pomegranates' has distinct connotations in Jewish culture. It is one of the seven fruits of the Land of Israel mentioned in Deut. 8:8, and is also frequently mentioned in the Song of Songs as well as in rabbinic literature. For example, a well-known reference (Song of Songs Rabbah 6:11) compares rows of students studying Torah to the rows of seeds in the pomegranate. Moreover, pomegranates are traditionally eaten on Rosh HaShanah, the Jewish New Year. Pomegranates also feature prominently in Jewish art, for example, the silver decorations covering the rollers on Torah scrolls are called *rimmonim* 'pomegranates'. See Feliks (2007) for discussion of pomegranates in Jewish tradition.

ITHIEL	Was it precisely that one? –	אם* רַק זאת הִיא? –	איתיאל
DOEG	If it was that one, or another one which she has	אִם זאת הִנֵּה, אוֹ אַחֶרֶת אֲשֶׁר לָהּ	דואג
	I cannot say; it is as naught whether this one or another	לֹא אוּכַל לְהַגִּיד; אֶפֶס בֵּין זאת וּבֵין אַחֶרֶת	
	After all, it will testify against her that she is guilty.	הֲלֹא הִיא תַעֲנֶה בְּפָנֶיהָ, כִּי אַשְׁמָתָהּ בָּהּ.	
ITHIEL	If only that despicable slave	מִי יִתֵּן וְהָיָה עֶבֶד נִבְזֶה הַזֶּה	איתיאל
	Had many lives instead of one life	בַּעַל נְפָשׁוֹת רַבּוֹת תַּחַת נֶפֶשׁ אַחַת	
	For one is not enough to sink my wrath into.	כִּי בְאַחַת אֵין דַּי, לְהָנִיחַ חֲמָתִי בוֹ.	
	Now I know, Doeg, that the matter is true	עַתָּה יָדַעְתִּי דוֹאֵג, כִּי אֱמֶת הַדָּבָר	
	And therefore I shall scatter my love **to the four winds of the heavens**[133]	וְלָכֵן אֱזֶרֶה אַהֲבָתִי לְאַרְבַּע רוּחוֹת הַשָּׁמָיִם[133]	
	I shall blow upon it and it will be gone –	אָפִיחַ בָּהּ וְאֵינֶנָּה –	
	Come, jealous wrath! Rise up from **the depths of Sheol**[134]	בּוֹאִי חֲמַת קִנְאָה! עֲלִי מִשְּׁאוֹל תַּחְתָּיו[134]	
	And fill all the chambers of my heart with hatred instead of love	וּמַלְאִי כָל חַדְרֵי לְבָבִי, שִׂנְאָה תַּחַת ידידת**	
	And enmity instead of affection, for I have been bitten	וְאֵיבָה תַּחַת אַהֲבָה, כִּי נָשׁוּךְ אָנֹכִי	
	And moreover my **belly is swollen**[135] from **the cruel venom of asps**[136]	וְגַם בִּטְנִי צָבְתָה[135] מֵרֹאשׁ פְּתָנִים אַכְזָר.[136]	
DOEG	Hold your spirit in check.	תְּנָה מַעְצֹר לְרוּחֶךָ.	דואג
ITHIEL	I am thirsty, Doeg, I am thirsty for blood.	צָמֵא אֲנִי דוֹאֵג, צָמֵא אֲנִי לְדָם.	איתיאל
DOEG	Calm the roar of your anger, lest you regret it in the end.	הַשְׁבֵּחַ שְׁאוֹן קִצְפְּךָ, פֶּן תִּנָּחֵם בָּאַחֲרוֹנָה.	דואג
ITHIEL	I shall never regret it; for like the Pontic sea[137]	לֹא אֶנָּחֵם לָנֶצַח; כִּי כְמוֹ יַם פָּאנְטוֹס[137]	איתיאל

133 Dan. 8:8, 11:4 see also Zech. 2:10 for a similar phrase.
134 Deut. 32:22.
135 Num. 5:27 וְצָבְתָה בִטְנָהּ 'and her belly will swell' (describing the punishment for adulterous women).
136 Deut. 32:33.
137 Somewhat unusually, Salkinson has not replaced this name with a biblical equivalent.

* אִם
** יְדִידֹת

	Flowing ahead in a stream of **mighty waters**[138]	הוֹלֵךְ וְשׁוֹטֵף לְפָנָיו בְּזֶרֶם מַיִם אַדִּירִים[138]	
	It will not rest and will not repose and will not turn back	לֹא יִשְׁקֹט לֹא יָנוּחַ וְלֹא יָשׁוּב אֲחֹרַנִּית	
	Until it pours out in the harbour[139] of Pont	עַד אֲשֶׁר יִשְׁתַּפֵּךְ* בְּמוֹ אֵילַת[139] פָּאנְט*)	
	So the flood of my spirit passes by **in a burst of anger**[140]	כֵּן שֶׁטֶף רוּחִי יַעֲבֹר **בְּשֶׁצֶף קֶצֶף**[140]	
	It will not look back and will not remember youthful love	לֹא יַבִּיט לְאָחוֹר וְלֹא יִזְכֹּר אַהֲבַת נְעוּרִים	
	Until it is swallowed up in the rage of the great sea	עַד אֲשֶׁר יִתְבַּלַּע בְּזַעַף יָם הַגָּדוֹל	
	That is the sea of revenge. And now, before the heavens above!	הוּא יַם הַנְּקָמָה. וְעַתָּה לְעֵינֵי הַשָּׁמַיִם מִמַּעַל!	
	(He kneels on his knees)	(כורע על ברכיו)	
	I raise my hand **in a curse and an oath**[141] that I shall not violate my word.	הֲרִימוֹתִי יָדִי **בְּאָלָה וּשְׁבוּעָה**[141] כִּי לֹא אָפִיר דְּבָרִי.	
DOEG	Wait for me a bit – *(He kneels as well)*	חַכֵּה לִי מְעַט – (כורע גם הוא)	דואג
	You are witnesses today, **bright lights of heaven**![142]	עֵדִים אַתֶּם הַיּוֹם, **מְאוֹרֵי אוֹר בַּשָּׁמַיִם**![142]	
	And the earth below is a witness! That Doeg has dedicated his life	וְעֵדָה הָאָרֶץ מִתָּחַת! כִּי דֹּאֵג הִקְדִּישׁ נַפְשׁוֹ	
	And has given himself up with all his might to serve Ithiel zealously	וַיִּתְמַכֵּר בְּכָל מְאֹדוֹ לְקַנֵּא קִנְאַת אִיתִיאֵל	
	And to roll away the shame from him, in everything that he commands him	וְלָגֹל חֶרְפָּה מֵעָלָיו, לְכָל אֲשֶׁר יְצַוֶּנּוּ	
	And he will not pull back his hand even from spilling blood.	וְגַם מִשְּׁפֹּךְ דָּם, לֹא יָשִׁיב יָדוֹ.	
ITHIEL	And I also thank you, not with empty words	וְגַם אֲנִי אוֹדְךָ, לֹא בִּדְבָרִים רֵקִים	איתיאל

138 Exod. 15:10.

139 The word used here is Elath, a proper noun denoting a port city on the Red Sea (modern-day Eilat at Israel's southern tip), mentioned in Deut. 2:8; 2 Kings 14:22, 16:6.

140 Isa. 54:8.

141 Neh. 10:30 (10:29 in English Bibles) בְּאָלָה וּבִשְׁבוּעָה 'in a curse and an oath'.

142 Ezek. 32:8.

* יִשְׁתַּפֵּךְ

Hellespont (*

	Your love is precious in my eyes and **your work shall be rewarded**[143]	אַהֲבָתְךָ תֵּיקַר בְּעֵינַי וְ**שָׂכָר לִפְעֻלָּתְךָ יֵשׁ**[143]	
	And now do not delay your work! **Within three days**[144]	וְעַתָּה עֲבוֹדָתְךָ אַל תְּאַחֵר! **בְּעוֹד שְׁלֹשֶׁת יָמִים**[144]	
	Announce to me that Chesed **has been cut off from the land of the living.**[145]	הַשְׁמִיעֵנִי כִּי כֶשֶׁד **נִגְזַר מֵאֶרֶץ חַיִּים.**[145]	
DOEG	**In accordance with your word, so be it**[146] – my friend Chesed is dead,	**כִּדְבָרְךָ כֶּן־הוּא**[146] – כֶּשֶׁד אֹהֲבִי מֵת,	דואג
	But have mercy on your wife, please have mercy and indeed let her live.	אֲבָל חוּסָה עַל אִשְׁתֶּךָ, חוּסָה נָא וְחָיֹה תִחְיֶה.	
ITHIEL	Destroy the cursed whore! Destroy her without mercy!	הַשְׁמֵד זוֹנָה אֲרוּרָה! הַשְׁמֵד מֵאֵין חֶמְלָה!	איתיאל
	Go with me to another place so that I may obtain a weapon of destruction	לְכָה אִתִּי לְמָקוֹם אַחֵר וְאֶקְחָה לִּי כְּלִי מַשְׁחִית.	
	In order **to take the beautiful daughter of Sheol down to Sheol in blood.**[147]	**לְהוֹרִיד בְּדָם שְׁאוֹלָה בַּת שְׁאוֹל יְפֵה פִיָּה.**[147]	
	And I make you today my officer instead of Chesed.	וַאֲנִי נְתַתִּיךָ הַיּוֹם לְפָקִיד תַּחַת כֶּשֶׁד.	
DOEG	I shall be your servant forever. *(Exeunt)*	הִנְנִי עַבְדְּךָ לָנֶצַח. (הולכים)	דואג
SCENE 4	*(Asenath, Milcah, and the clown)*	(אסנת מלכה והלץ)	מחזה ד'
ASENATH[148]	Hurry, call Chesed for me, do you know his abode?[149]	חוּשָׁה קְרָא לִי לְכֶשֶׁד, הֲיָדַעְתָּ אֶת מְגוּרוֹ?[149]	אסנת[148]
THE CLOWN	I fear for my life to say that he has an abode.[150]	פָּחַדְתִּי לְנַפְשִׁי לֵאמֹר, כִּי יֶשׁ־לוֹ מָגוֹר.[150]	הלץ
ASENATH	And why is it that you fear?	וְלָמָּה זֶה תִּפְחָד?	אסנת

143 Jer. 31:16 כִּי יֵשׁ שָׂכָר לִפְעֻלָּתֵךְ 'for your work shall be rewarded'.
144 Gen. 40:13, 19; Josh. 1:11.
145 Isa. 53:8.
146 Gen. 44:10 כְדִבְרֵיכֶם כֶּן־הוּא 'in accordance with your words, so be it'; also Josh. 2:21.
147 1 Kings 2:9 וְהוֹרַדְתָּ אֶת־שֵׂיבָתוֹ בְּדָם שְׁאוֹל 'and you will bring his grey head in blood down to Sheol'.
148 All of the lines between this and the clown's exit are prose in the original (3.4.1–22).
149 This word is a homonym with the additional meaning of 'fright'.
150 See preceding note.

THE CLOWN	Because he is a soldier, and if I were to say of a soldier	יַעַן הוּא בֶּן חַיִל וְכִי אֹמַר עַל בֶּן חַיִל	הלץ
	That he has fright,[151] **I would endanger my head**[152]	כִּי יֶשׁ־לוֹ מָגוֹר[151] **וְחִיַּבְתִּי אֶת רֹאשִׁי.**[152]	
ASENATH	Please don't; indeed, where does he reside?	אַל נָא, אֲבָל אַיֵּה הוּא שׁוֹכֵן?	אסנת
THE CLOWN	If I were to tell you, my lady, where he resides, **I would be dealing falsely against my own life.**[153]	כִּי אַגִּיד לָךְ גְּבִרְתִּי, אַיֵּה הוּא שׁוֹכֵן **אֶעֱשֶׂה שֶׁקֶר בְּנַפְשִׁי.**[153]	הלץ
ASENATH	Is there reason and sense in this man's words?	הֲיֵשׁ טַעַם וָשֵׂכֶל בְּדִבְרֵי הָאִישׁ הַזֶּה?	אסנת
THE CLOWN	I do not know his residence, and if I were to say that he resides there	לֹא יָדַעְתִּי מִשְׁכָּנוֹ וְכִי אֹמַר הוּא שׁוֹכֵן שָׁם	הלץ
	Or resides here, I would be speaking **lies.**[154]	אוֹ שׁוֹכֵן פֹּה, הֲלֹא אוֹצִיא **דְּבַר שֶׁקֶר.**[154]	
ASENATH	Go forth and look for his residence; ask others so that they may tell you.	צֵא וּדְרוֹשׁ לְשִׁכְנוֹ; שְׁאַל אֲחֵרִים וְיֹאמְרוּ לָךְ.	אסנת
THE CLOWN	I shall look in all the land, and I shall bring many questions and answers.[155]	אֶדְרשׁ בְּכָל הָאָרֶץ וְאֶעֱשֶׂה שְׁאֵלוֹת וּתְשׁוּבוֹת[155] לָרֹב.	הלץ
ASENATH	Go and seek him and bring him here when you find him.	לֵךְ בַּקֵּשׁ אֹתוֹ וַהֲבִיאוֹ הֵנָּה כִּי תִמְצָאֶנּוּ	אסנת
	Tell him that I have entreated my husband on his behalf	אֱמוֹר לוֹ כִּי חִלִּיתִי בַעֲדוֹ אֶת פְּנֵי בַעֲלִי	
	And I shall make peace between the two of them.	וְשָׁלוֹם אֶעֱשֶׂה בֵּין שְׁנֵיהֶם.	
THE CLOWN	This matter is not elevated beyond the limit of human wit	הַדָּבָר הַזֶּה לֹא נִשְׂגָּב מֵחֹק שֵׂכֶל אֱנוֹשׁ	הלץ
	And therefore I shall rush to do it. *(Exits)*	וְלָכֵן אָחִישׁ לַעֲשׂוֹתוֹ. (הולך)	

151 See note 149.
152 Dan. 1:10 וְחִיַּבְתֶּם אֶת־רֹאשִׁי לַמֶּלֶךְ 'you would endanger my head with the king'.
153 2 Sam. 18:13 בְנַפְשִׁי שֶׁקֶר אוֹ־עָשִׂיתִי 'otherwise I would have dealt falsely against my own life'.
154 Prov. 13:5, 29:12.
155 This collocation is commonly used in Hebrew to denote rabbinic responsa, i.e., the written rulings on questions regarding various aspects of Jewish law given by legal authorities. See Ta-Shma, Tal, and Slae (2007) for discussion of responsa literature.

ASENATH	Where did I leave my handkerchief, Milcah?	אָן עָזַבְתִּי אֶת מִטְפַּחְתִּי, מִלְכָּה?	אסנת
MILCAH	I do not know, my lady.	לֹא יָדַעְתִּי גְּבִרְתִּי.	מלכה
ASENATH	The loss of my handkerchief is more severe in my eyes than a bag of gold shekels[156]	אֲבֵדַת מִטְפַּחְתִּי קָשָׁה בְּעֵינַי מִצְּרוֹר שִׁקְלֵי זָהָב[156]	אסנת
	For how easy it would be for my husband to think strange thoughts	כִּי מַה־נָּקֵל לְבַעֲלִי, לַחְשׁוֹב מַחְשָׁבוֹת זָרוֹת	
	Were he not **pure-hearted**[157] and **the spirit of jealousy had not come upon him.**[158]	**לוּלֵא בַר לֵבָב**[157] **הוּא וְרוּחַ קִנְאָה לֹא עֲבָרוֹ.**[158]	
MILCAH	**Has the spirit of jealousy never come upon him?**[159]	**הַאִם לֹא עָבַר עָלָיו רוּחַ קִנְאָה**[159] **מֵעוֹדוֹ?**	מלכה
ASENATH	God forbid, the sun in his native land	חָלִלָה לוֹ מִזֹּאת, הַשֶּׁמֶשׁ בְּאֶרֶץ מוֹלַדְתּוֹ	אסנת
	Dried out all the damp of jealousy from his bones.	הוֹבִישׁ כָּל לֵחַ קִנְאָה מֵעַצְמוֹתָיו.	
MILCAH	Look, who's this coming over there?	הַבִּיטִי מִי זֶה בָּא שָׁמָּה?	מלכה
ASENATH	I shall not relent from him until he presently restores	לֹא אֶרֶף מִמֶּנּוּ עַד אֲשֶׁר יָשִׁיב עַתָּה	אסנת
	Chesed to his position.	אֶת כֶּשֶׂד עַל כַּנּוֹ.	
	(To Ithiel upon his entrance) Greetings my husband, my lord!	(לאיתיאל בבואו) הֲשָׁלוֹם אִישִׁי אֲדֹנִי!	
ITHIEL	Are you well, **my love**?[160] *(To himself)* It is difficult to speak **with a double heart**[161]	הֲשָׁלוֹם לָךְ **רַעְיָתִי**?[160] (אל עצמו) קָשֶׁה לְדַבֵּר **בְּלֵב וָלֵב**[161]	איתיאל
	Do you lack anything, Asenath?	הַאֵין מַחְסֹר לָךְ אָסְנַת?	
ASENATH	I lack nothing, my lord.	אֵין מַחְסוֹר כָּל דָּבָר אֲדֹנִי.	אסנת
ITHIEL	Give me your hand; your hand is very soft.	תְּנִי לִי יָדֵךְ, יָדֵךְ רַכָּה מְאֹד.	איתיאל
ASENATH	It has not yet lived through many years	עוֹד לֹא עָבְרוּ עָלֶיהָ שָׁנִים רַבּוֹת	אסנת

156 Cf. Shakespeare's 'crusadoes' (3.4.26), Portuguese coins marked with a cross (Crystal and Crystal 2002: 109). A shekel is a biblical weight (commonly used with reference to silver and gold) corresponding to approximately ten grams.

157 Ps. 24:4.

158 Num. 5:14 וְעָבַר עָלָיו רוּחַ־קִנְאָה 'and the spirit of jealousy comes upon him'; see also Num. 5:30.

159 Num. 5:14 וְעָבַר עָלָיו רוּחַ־קִנְאָה 'and the spirit of jealousy comes upon him'; see also Num. 5:30.

160 Song of Songs 1:9, 15, 2:2, 10, 13, 4:1, 7, 5:2, 6:4.

161 Psalms 12:3 (12:2 in English Bibles).

	Nor many sorrows.	וְלֹא צָרוֹת רַבּוֹת.	
ITHIEL	Therefore you are fruitful, and your spirit is **a willing spirit**[162]	לָכֵן פֹּרִיָּה אַתְּ וְרוּחֵךְ **רוּחַ נְדִיבָה**[162]	איתיאל
	And your hand is hot and soft; indeed it would be better for you to be closed in	וְיָדֵךְ חַמָּה וְרַכָּה; הֲלֹא טוֹב לָךְ לְהִסָּגֵר	
	So that you might sit alone to fast, to afflict yourself, and to pray	לְמַעַן תֵּשְׁבִי בָדָד לָצוּם לְהִתְעַנּוֹת וּלְהִתְפַּלֵּל	
	For an unfaithful spirit has resided in you since your youth	כִּי רוּחַ בֹּגֵדָה שׁוֹכֵן בָּךְ מִנְּעוּרָיִךְ	
	Yet your hand is good and willing.	וְיָדֵךְ טוֹבָה וּנְדִיבָה.	
ASENATH	**You have spoken well**[163]	**כֵּן דִּבַּרְתָּ**[163]	אסנת
	As you acquired my hand, you acquired my heart.	בַּאֲשֶׁר קָנִיתָ אֶת יָדִי, קָנִיתָ אֶת לִבִּי.	
ITHIEL	As a sign that your hand is willing. In olden times the acquisition of the heart	לְאוֹת כִּי יָדֵךְ נְדִיבָה. קִנְיַן לֵב לְפָנִים	איתיאל
	Preceded the acquisition of the hand, but now a hand is a hand and not a heart.	הָיָה רִאשׁוֹן לְקִנְיַן יָד וְעַתָּה יָד יָד וְלֹא לֵב.	
ASENATH	I do not know of that; but please make good on the matter	זֹאת לֹא יָדַעְתִּי; אַךְ אָנָּא הָקֵם הַדָּבָר	אסנת
	That you promised me.	אֲשֶׁר הִבְטַחְתָּ לִי.	
ITHIEL	Which matter, my dove?	אֵיזֶה דָבָר, יוֹנָתִי?	איתיאל
ASENATH	Why, I sent for Chesed to be summoned to come and speak with you.	הֵן שָׁלַחְתִּי לִקְרֹא לְכֶשֶׂד, לָבוֹא וּלְדַבֵּר אִתָּךְ.	אסנת
ITHIEL	I have a pain in my nose, for a cold has seized me	כְּאֵב לִי בְּאַפִּי, כִּי הַקֹּר אֲחָזַנִי	איתיאל
	Lend me your handkerchief.	הַשְׁאִילִי לִי אֶת מִטְפַּחְתֵּךְ.	
ASENATH	Here it is, my lord.	הֵא לְךָ אֲדֹנִי.	אסנת
ITHIEL	The one that I gave you.	אֹתָהּ אֲשֶׁר נְתַתִּיהָ לָךְ.	איתיאל
ASENATH	It is not with me.	הִיא אֵינֶנָּה עִמָּדִי.	אסנת
ITHIEL	It is not?	הִיא אֵינֶנָּה?	איתיאל

162 Ps. 51:14 (51:12 in English Bibles).
163 Exod. 10:29.

ASENATH	It is not with me, my lord.	אֵינֶנָּה עִמָּדִי, אֲדֹנִי.	אסנת
ITHIEL	I consider this as a sin on your part. Indeed this handkerchief	זאת אָשִׁית לְחַטָּאת עָלַיִךְ, הֵן מִטְפַּחַת זוּ	איתיאל
	Was originally given to my mother by an Egyptian witch	נִתְּנָה לְאִמִּי בַּתְּחִלָּה, מִיַּד מְכַשֵּׁפָה מִצְרִית	
	Who knew how **to examine the kidneys and the heart**[164] with her witchcraft,	אֲשֶׁר יָדְעָה לִבְחֹן כְּלָיוֹת וָלֵב[164] בִּכְשָׁפֶיהָ,	
	And she said to my mother that as long as she kept it	וְהִיא אָמְרָה לְאִמִּי, כָּל עוֹד אֲשֶׁר תִּשְׁמְרֶנָּה	
	She would find favour in the eyes of those who saw her and my father **would be intoxicated in her love**,[165]	תִּמְצָא חֵן בְּעֵינֵי רֹאֶיהָ וְאָבִי יִשְׁגֶּה בְּאַהֲבָתָהּ,[165]	
	But if indeed she lost it, or gave it to a stranger	וְאִם אַבֵּד תְּאַבְּדֶנָּה, אוֹ תִתְּנֶנָּה לְאִישׁ זָר	
	My father would be disgusted by her and would turn his eyes to other women	תִּגְעַל בָּהּ נֶפֶשׁ אָבִי וְנָשָׂא עֵינָיו לְנָשִׁים אֲחֵרוֹת	
	And my mother before her death gave it to me and commanded me	וְאִמִּי לִפְנֵי מוֹתָהּ, נָתְנָה אוֹתָהּ אֵלַי וַתְּצַוֵּנִי	
	To give it to my wife before my wedding, and so I did.	לְתִתָּהּ לְאִשְׁתִּי לִפְנֵי חֲתֻנָּתִי וְכֵן עָשִׂיתִי אָנִי.	
	Therefore take heed of its great worth, guard it like **the apple of your eye**[166]	לָכֵן שִׁיתִי לִבֵּךְ לִיקָרָתָהּ, שִׁמְרִי אֹתָהּ כְּבָבַת עֵינֵךְ[166]	
	For if it indeed gets lost and falls into the hands of strangers, you will be guilty.	כִּי אִם אָבֹד תֹּאבַד וְתִפֹּל בִּידֵי זָרִים וְאָשָׁמְתְּ.	
ASENATH	Are you speaking **truly and sincerely**?[167]	הַאִם בֶּאֱמֶת וּבְתָמִים[167] תְּדַבֵּר?	אסנת
ITHIEL	The matter is true and sure; the weave is magic,	אֱמֶת וְנָכוֹן הַדָּבָר; הָאֶרֶג מַעֲשֵׂה קֶסֶם הוּא,	איתיאל
	A witch who had seen the sun two hundred times in its cycle	מְכַשֵּׁפָה אֲשֶׁר רָאֲתָה הַשֶּׁמֶשׁ מָאתַיִם בִּתְקוּפָתוֹ	

164 Jer. 11:20 בֹּחֵן כְּלָיוֹת וָלֵב ‘examines the kidneys and the heart’ (i.e., the thoughts and mind).
165 Prov. 5:19 בְּאַהֲבָתָהּ תִּשְׁגֶּה תָמִיד ‘may you always be intoxicated in her love’.
166 Zech. 2:12 (2:8 in English Bibles) כִּי הַנֹּגֵעַ בָּכֶם נֹגֵעַ בְּבָבַת עֵינוֹ ‘for whoever touches you touches the apple of his own eye’.
167 Judg. 9:16, 19.

	When the Spirit rested upon her[168] sewed it and did the embroidery	כְּנוֹחַ עָלֶיהָ הָרוּחַ,[168] תָּפְרָה וְעָשְׂתָה הָרִקְמָה	
	And the silk was spun by worms from a holy place	וְאֶת הַמֶּשִׁי טָווּ, תּוֹלָעִים מִמָּקוֹם קָדוֹשׁ	
	And it was **painted with vermillion**[169] which the Egyptian woman had prepared in her wisdom	וּמְשׁוּחָה הִיא בַּשָּׁשַׁר[169] אֲשֶׁר הֵכִינָה הַמִּצְרִית בְּחָכְמָתָהּ	
	From the hearts of virgins embalmed in the coffin.	מִלֵּב הַבְּתוּלוֹת הַחֲנוּטוֹת בָּאָרוֹן.	
ASENATH	Why, surely you are mocking me.	הֲלֹא אַךְ תְּהַתֵּל בִּי.	אסנת
ITHIEL	**My mouth speaks the truth**;[170] therefore take heed of its value.	אֱמֶת יֶהְגֶּה חִכִּי;[170] לָכֵן שִׁיתִי לִבֵּךְ לְעֶרְכָּהּ.	איתיאל
ASENATH	If only I had never seen your handkerchief.	מִי יִתֵּן אֵיפוֹא וְלֹא רָאִיתִי מִטְפַּחְתְּךָ מֵעוֹדִי.	אסנת
ITHIEL	Why then?	וּמַדּוּעַ?	איתיאל
ASENATH	Why do you speak in haste and look at me with a penetrating eye?	מַדּוּעַ תְּדַבֵּר בְּחִפָּזוֹן וְתֶחֱזֶה בִּי בְּעַיִן חֹדֶרֶת?	אסנת
ITHIEL	Speak; is it lost? Or is it not here in your hand?	דַּבְּרִי הַאִם אָבְדָה? אוֹ אֵינֶנָּה פֹּה בְּיָדֵךְ?	איתיאל
ASENATH	Save me, God in heaven, save us!	הוֹשִׁיעָה אֵל אֱלֹהִים, הוֹשִׁיעָה לָנוּ מִשָּׁמַיִם!	אסנת
ITHIEL	But speak –	אֲבָל דַּבֵּרִי –	איתיאל
ASENATH	I have not lost it; but what if I had?	לֹא אָבְדָה מִמֶּנִּי; וְלוּ אַף אִם אָבָדָה?	אסנת
ITHIEL	What did you say?	מָה הִגַּדְתְּ?	איתיאל
ASENATH	I have not lost it, I say.	לֹא אָבְדָה הִגַּדְתִּי.	אסנת
ITHIEL	Go and bring it, so that I might see it with my eyes.	לְכִי הָבִיאִי אֹתָהּ, לְמַעַן אֶרְאֶנָּה בְּעֵינָי.	איתיאל
ASENATH	I can do so, but I am not going to now	יֵשׁ בְּיָדִי לַעֲשׂוֹת כֵּן וְרַק לֹא אֶעֱשֶׂה עַתָּה	אסנת
	Because you are searching for a pretext to distance me from my desire.	כִּי תֹאֲנָה אַתָּה מְבַקֵּשׁ לְהַרְחִיקֵנִי מִדְּבַר חֶפְצִי.	
	Please restore your officer Chesed to his place.	אָנָּא הָשֵׁב נָא אֶת כֶּשֶׂד פְּקִידְךָ לִמְקוֹמוֹ.	

168 Num. 11:25 וַיְהִי כְּנוֹחַ עֲלֵיהֶם הָרוּחַ וַיִּתְנַבְּאוּ 'and when the Spirit rested upon them they prophesied'.
169 Jer. 22:14 וּמָשׁוֹחַ בַּשָּׁשַׁר 'and painted with vermillion'.
170 Prov. 9:7.

ITHIEL	Bring me the handkerchief; my heart tells me evil things.	הָבִיאִי לִי אֶת הַמִּטְפַּחַת; לְבָבִי יַגִּיד לִי רָעָה.	איתיאל
ASENATH	Stop it;	חֲדַל לָךְ;	אסנת
	A better officer than him you will not find in all the land.	פָּקִיד טוֹב מִמֶּנּוּ, לֹא תִמְצָא בְּכָל הָאָרֶץ.	
ITHIEL	The handkerchief –	הַמִּטְפַּחַת –	איתיאל
ASENATH	I want to speak about Chesed now.	עַל אֹדֹת כֶּשֶׂד, חָפַצְתִּי לְדַבֵּר עַתָּה.	אסנת
ITHIEL	The handkerchief –	הַמִּטְפַּחַת –	איתיאל
ASENATH	Why, he is the man who has honoured your life more than gold	הֲלֹא הוּא הָאִישׁ, אֲשֶׁר הוֹקִיר נַפְשֵׁךְ מִפָּז	אסנת
	Your love is wonderful to him, more than any item or amulet[171]	**אַהֲבָתֵךְ נִפְלְאַתָה לוֹ, מִכָּל חֵפֶץ וּסְגֻלָּה**[171]	
	And in every **distress and anguish**[172] **he has taken his life in his hands**[173] in order to rescue you.	וּבְכָל **צָרָה וְצוּקָה**,[172] **שָׂם נַפְשׁוֹ בְכַפּוֹ**[173] לְהַצִּילֵךְ.	
ITHIEL	The handkerchief –	הַמִּטְפַּחַת –	איתיאל
ASENATH	**You are not just, I tell you…**[174]	**לֹא צָדַקְתָּ, אֶעֱנֶךָּ…**[174]	אסנת
ITHIEL	Depart from me! *(Ithiel exits)*	סוּרִי מִמֶּנִּי! (איתיאל הולך)	איתיאל
MILCAH	**Has not the spirit of jealousy come upon**[175] this man?	אִם לֹא הָאִישׁ הַזֶּה, **רוּחַ קִנְאָה עֲבָרוֹ?**[175]	מלכה
ASENATH	I have never seen such a thing apart from today	לֹא רָאִיתִי כָזֹאת מֵעוֹדִי בִּלְתִּי הַיּוֹם	אסנת
	And there must be nothing other than witchcraft in the handkerchief	וְאֵין זֶה כִּי אִם מַעֲשֵׂה כְשָׁפִים בַּמִּטְפַּחַת	
	I am very sorry that I lost it.	צַר לִי מְאֹד כִּי אָבְדָה מִיָּדִי.	
MILCAH	We cannot know the nature of a man in one or two years	לֹא בְשָׁנָה וּשְׁנָתַיִם נַכִּיר תְּכוּנַת גֶּבֶר	מלכה
	Men are like a stomach, and we are all like a meal to them	הַגְּבָרִים הֵם כַּקֵּבָה וַנַּחְנוּ כֻלָּנוּ כְּמַאֲכָל לָמוֹ	

171 2 Sam. 1:26 נִפְלְאַתָה אַהֲבָתְךָ לִי מֵאַהֲבַת נָשִׁים 'your love was wonderful to me, more than the love of women'.
172 Isa. 30:6; Prov. 1:27.
173 1 Sam. 19:5.
174 Job 33:12.
175 Num. 5:14 וְעָבַר עָלָיו רוּחַ־קִנְאָה 'and the spirit of jealousy comes upon him'; also Num. 5:30.

	When they are hungry they swallow us, and after they are satiated they spew us out	לְרַעֲבוֹן נַפְשָׁם יִבְלָעוּנוּ וְאַחֲרֵי שָׂבְעָם יְקִיאוּנוּ	
	But look, Chesed and my husband are coming over there.	אַךְ רְאִי הִנֵּה כֶשֶׂד וּבַעֲלִי בָּאִים שָׁמָּה.	
	(Doeg and Chesed)	(דואג וכשד)	
DOEG	There is no other way, except for her to save you	אֵין דֶּרֶךְ אַחֶרֶת, בִּלְתִּי יָדָהּ תּוֹשִׁיעַ לָךְ	דואג
	And to our salvation we have found her here; approach and beseech her.	וְלִתְשׁוּעָתֵנוּ מְצָאנוּהָ פֹּה, קְרַב וְהִתְחַנֵּן לְפָנֶיהָ.	
ASENATH	Is there a word of news in your mouth, dear Chesed?	הֲיֵשׁ דָּבָר חָדָשׁ בְּפִיךָ כֶּשֶׂד הַיָּקָר?	אסנת
CHESED	I am going to renew my plea, intercede on my behalf, my lady	הִנְנִי לְחַדֵּשׁ תְּחִנָּתִי, הַפְגִּיעִי בַעֲדִי גְּבִרְתִּי	כשד
	Do not delay any longer, so that I might return to my lord	אַל תְּאַחֲרִי עוֹד, לְמַעַן אָשׁוּב לַאֲדֹנִי	
	Whom I love like my own life, and be as an ally in his house	אֲשֶׁר אֲהַבְתִּיו כְּנַפְשִׁי וְהָיִיתִי כְּבֶן בְּרִית בְּבֵיתוֹ	
	To stand before him and serve him, as I did previously,	לַעֲמֹד לְפָנָיו וּלְשָׁרְתוֹ, כַּאֲשֶׁר הָיִיתִי לְפָנִים,	
	But if **my iniquity is too great to bear**,[176] he will not remember my faith and service	וְאִם **עֲוֹנִי גָדוֹל מִנְּשֹׂא**,[176] אֱמוּנָתִי וַעֲבֹדָתִי לֹא יִזְכֹּר	
	And he will not consider **my affliction and my misery**,[177] because he has no desire for me	וְלֹא יַבִּיט **עָנְיִי וּמְרוּדִי**,[177] כִּי אֵין לוֹ חֵפֶץ בִּי	
	Then it would be better for me to know that there is no more hope	טוֹב לִי אָז לָדַעַת, כִּי אֵין תִּקְוָה עוֹד	
	For through this I would find new strength to sustain my spirit	כִּי בָזֹאת אַחֲלִיף כֹּחַ לְכַלְכֵּל אֶת רוּחִי	
	I would go out and don black and seek out one of the priesthoods	אֵצֵא וְאֶלְבַּשׁ שְׁחֹרִים וַאֲבַקֵּשׁ אַחַת הַכְּהֻנּוֹת	
	In whichever place I might find, to eat a crust of bread.	בַּמָּקוֹם אֲשֶׁר אֶמְצָא, לֶאֱכֹל פַּת לָחֶם.	

176 Gen. 4:13 גָּדוֹל עֲוֹנִי מִנְּשֹׂא 'my iniquity is too great to bear' (Cain speaking to God after killing his brother Abel).
177 Lam. 3:19.

ASENATH	Oh, dear-spirited Chesed! Today I would intercede in vain	אֲהָהּ כֶּשֶׁד יְקַר רוּחַ! לַשָּׁוְא אַפְגִּיעַ הַיּוֹם	אסנת
	My prayer would become a sin; my husband has become another man;	תְּפִלָּתִי תִּהְיֶה לַחֲטָאָה; בַּעְלִי הָיָה לְאִישׁ אַחֵר;	
	He is no longer my husband. If **the Cushite were to change his skin**[178]	אֵינֶנּוּ בַּעְלִי עוֹד. **אִם יַהֲפֹךְ הַכּוּשִׁי עוֹרוֹ**[178]	
	As he has changed his heart, I would no longer recognize him.	כַּאֲשֶׁר הָפַךְ אֶת לִבּוֹ, לֹא אַכִּירֶנּוּ עוֹד.	
	May all the angels of mercy intercede on my behalf	יַפְגִּיעוּ כֵן בַּעֲדִי, כָּל מַלְאֲכֵי רַחֲמִים	
	As I have supplicated in order to arouse his mercy for you	כַּאֲשֶׁר הֶעְתַּרְתִּי דְבָרִים לְעוֹרֵר רַחֲמָיו עָלֶיךָ	
	And I have not held back from speaking so harshly as to arouse his rage against me.	וְלֹא נִמְנַעְתִּי מִדַּבֵּר קָשׁוֹת עַד לְעוֹרֵר זַעְמוֹ עָלָי.	
	So now go wait further and I shall do everything that is in my power	וְעַתָּה לֵךְ הוֹחִילָה עוֹד וְכָל אֲשֶׁר בְּכֹחִי אֶעֱשֶׂה	
	For I care for you more than I care for myself.	כִּי אָחוּשׁ לְנַפְשְׁךָ יֶתֶר מֵאֲשֶׁר אָחוּשׁ לְנַפְשִׁי.	
DOEG	Is the commander angry?	הַאִם חָרָה אַף הַשָּׂר?	דואג
MILCAH	He left here full of anger and wrath.	הוּא הָלַךְ מִזֶּה מָלֵא כַעַס וָקָצֶף.	מלכה
DOEG	Is he angry and wrathful? Indeed I have seen the cannon	הַהוּא יִכְעַס וְיִקְצֹף? הֵן רָאִיתִי קְנֵה הַמּוֹרֶה	דואג
	Which felled a great multitude from the army of his ranks to the ground	אֲשֶׁר הִפִּיל מֵחֵיל שׁוּרוֹתָיו הָמוֹן רָב אָרְצָה	
	And also snatched away his brother **like a robber**[179] from his right hand	וְגַם אֶת אָחִיו, חָתַף **כְּחֶתֶף**[179] מִימִינוֹ	
	And he did not tremble and did not rage, yet now **his face is angry**?[180]	וְלֹא זָע וְלֹא זָעַם, וְעַתָּה **פָּנָיו זוֹעֲפִים**?[180]	

178 Jer. 13:23 הֲיַהֲפֹךְ כּוּשִׁי עוֹרוֹ 'can a Cushite change his skin?'

179 Prov. 23:28.

180 Dan. 1:10 לָמָּה יִרְאֶה אֶת־פְּנֵיכֶם זֹעֲפִים 'why should he see your faces looking haggard'. Salkinson seems to have had this particular collocation in mind, but is using the root ז.ע.ף in its alternative sense of 'to rage, to be angry'.

	It is indeed a matter – I shall go to him and see him,	הֲלֹא דָבָר הוּא – אֵלְכָה לִקְרָאתוֹ וְאֶרְאֶנּוּ,	
	For it is not without cause that **smoke is rising from his nostrils.**[181]	כִּי לֹא עַל חִנָּם, **יַעֲלֶה עָשָׁן בְּאַפּוֹ.**[181]	
ASENATH	Do so, my friend – *(Doeg exits)*	עֲשֵׂה כֵן יְדִידִי – (דואג הולך)	אסנת
	It is nothing other than reports from Venice that are alarming him	אֵין זֶה כִּי אִם שְׁמוּעוֹת יְבַהֲלוּהוּ מִוִּינֶעצְיָא	
	Or his spirit has suddenly been stirred up by a conspiracy of traitors on Caphtor	אוֹ נֶעְכַּר רוּחוֹ פִּתְאֹם מִקֶּשֶׁר בֹּגְדִים בְּכַפְתּוֹר	
	For so is the way of a man when others vex him	כִּי כֵן דֶּרֶךְ גֶּבֶר כַּאֲשֶׁר יַכְעִיסוּהוּ אֲחֵרִים	
	He pours out his wrath[182] and his anger on the members of his household.	**יִשְׁפֹּךְ חֲמָתוֹ**[182] וְכַעֲסוֹ עֲלֵי אַנְשֵׁי בֵיתוֹ.	
	In this way we know well that from a pain in the little finger	כֵּן יָדַעְנוּ מְאֹד, מִכְּאֵב אֶצְבַּע קְטַנָּה	
	Our whole body hurts, for a man is flesh and not a god	כָּל בְּשָׂרֵנוּ יִכְאַב, כִּי אָדָם בָּשָׂר וְלֹא אֵל	
	And we cannot expect **a time of love**[183] every day.	וְלֹא נוּכַל לְצַפּוֹת **לְעֵת דֹּדִים**[183] בְּכָל יוֹם.	
	Look, Milcah, I have almost become a **quarrelsome woman**[184]	רְאִי מִלְכָּה כִּמְעַט **לְאֵשֶׁת מְדָנִים**[184] הָיִיתִי	
	For I began **to cry out that I had been wronged**[185] because he had grieved me,	כִּי הוֹאַלְתִּי **לִצְעֹק חָמָס,**[185] עַל אֲשֶׁר הֶעֱצִיבַנִי,	
	But now I know that the testimony of my mouth is not reliable	אָכֵן עַתָּה יָדַעְתִּי, כִּי עֵדוּת פִּי לֹא נְכוֹנָה	
	And I have no right to fall upon him undeservedly.	וְאֵין לִי צְדָקָה, לְהִתְגֹּלֵל עָלָיו חִנָּם.	

181 2 Sam. 22:9 עָלָה עָשָׁן בְּאַפּוֹ 'smoke rose from his nostrils'; also Ps. 18:9 (18:8 in English Bibles).

182 Jer. 10:25 שְׁפֹךְ חֲמָתְךָ 'pour out Your wrath'; similar collocations appear in Ezek. 14:19, 20:8, 13, 21, 22:22, 30:15, 36:18; Ps. 79:6. The phrasing from Jer. 10:25 and Ps. 79:6 is also very well known from its appearance in the Passover Haggadah.

183 Ezek. 16:8.

184 Prov. 26:21 וְאִישׁ מִדְיָנִים 'and a quarrelsome man'.

185 Job 19:7 אֶצְעַק חָמָס 'I cry out that I have been wronged'.

MILCAH	If only it were as you say, that it is because of a matter of state	לוּ יְהִי כִדְבָרֵךְ, כִּי מֵעִנְיַן הַמְּדִינָה הוּא	מלכה
	And not because he has let himself be fooled into becoming jealous over you.	וְלֹא מֵאֲשֶׁר נִפְתָּה לְקַנֵּא אֶת נַפְשֵׁךְ.	
ASENATH	Oh! Indeed from me there has been no cause for his jealousy.	אֲהָהּ! הֵן מֵאִתִּי לֹא הָיְתָה נְסִבָּה לְקִנְאָתוֹ.	אסנת
MILCAH	A jealous man does not need a reason for his jealousy	אֵין בַּעַל קִנְאָה דֹּרֵשׁ סִבָּה לְקִנְאָתוֹ	מלכה
	But rather, he is jealous because he is a jealous man.	כִּי אִם יְקַנֵּא יַעַן בַּעַל קִנְאָה הוּא.	
	For jealousy is a worm that infests the flesh beneath it.	כִּי הַקִּנְאָה תּוֹלַעַת אֲשֶׁר יָרֻם הַבָּשָׂר מִתַּחְתָּיו.	
ASENATH	My God! Save Ithiel's soul from this worm.	אֵלִי! הַצִּילָה מִתּוֹלַעַת זוּ אֶת נֶפֶשׁ אִיתִיאֵל.	אסנת
MILCAH	**Amen and amen.**[186]	אָמֵן וְאָמֵן.[186]	מלכה
ASENATH	I'll go look for him, and you, Chesed, walk about here	אֵלְכָה לִּי לְבַקְּשׁוֹ וְאַתָּה כֶשֶׂד הִתְהַלֵּךְ פֹּה	אסנת
	And if I find him **at a favourable time**[187] I shall strive with all my might	וְאִם אֶמְצָאֶנּוּ בְּעֵת רָצוֹן[187] אֶתְאַמֵּץ בְּכָל מְאֹדִי	
	To entreat him to grant your heart's desires.	לְחַלּוֹת אֶת פָּנָיו לְמַלֵּא מִשְׁאֲלוֹת לִבֶּךָ.	
CHESED	I thank the lady's kindness with the humbleness of my heart.	חַסְדֵי הַגְּבִירָה אוֹדֶה בְּעַנְוַת לִבִּי.	כשד
	(Asenath and Milcah exit)	(אסנת ומלכה הולכות)	
ANAH[188]	Greetings Chesed, my beloved.	שָׁלוֹם כֶּשֶׂד יְדִיד נַפְשִׁי.	ענה[188]
CHESED	What has brought you here, beautiful and pleasant Anah?	מָה הֱבִיאֵךְ הֲלֹם, עֲנָה הַיָּפָה וְהַנְּעִימָה?	כשד
	Are you well? I was almost about to go to your lodgings.	הֲשָׁלוֹם בּוֹאֵךְ? כִּמְעַט הוֹאַלְתִּי לָלֶכֶת לִמְעוֹנֵךְ.	

186 Ps. 41:14 (41:13 in English Bibles), 72:19, 89:53 (89:52 in English Bibles).

187 Isa. 49:8.

188 The mother of one of Esau's wives, mentioned in Gen. 36:2, 14, 18. (Note that many interpretations of this verse, including that of the prominent medieval Jewish commentator Rashi, understand Anah to be a man.) Salkinson's motivation for selecting this name as an equivalent of Shakespeare's Bianca is unclear, as there is no obvious correspondence in meaning or sound. It is possible that he saw the shared 'an' sound in both names as a partial correspondence, and/or that he was inspired by the biblical Anah's associations with idolatry and immorality.

ANAH	Whereas I had set out to look for you in your residence.	וַאֲנִי שַׂמְתִּי פְּעָמַי, לְבַקֶּשְׁךָ בְּבֵית מְגוּרֶךָ.	ענה
	I haven't seen you for a week; seven days night and day;	זֶה שָׁבוּעַ לֹא רְאִיתִיךָ; שִׁבְעַת יָמִים לַיְלָה וָיוֹם;	
	A hundred and sixty-eight **degrees on the sundial**[189]	**מֵאָה שִׁשִּׁים וּשְׁמֹנֶה מַעֲלוֹת בְּצֵל הַמַּעֲלוֹת בַּשֶּׁמֶשׁ**[189]	
	And each degree for a woman in her love is longer than a whole day	וְכָל מַעֲלָה לְאִשָּׁה בְּאַהֲבָתָהּ, אֲרֻכָּה מִיּוֹם תָּמִים	
	My soul is too tired to calculate all these.	עָיְפָה נַפְשִׁי מֵחֲשֹׁב כָּל אֵלֶּה.	
CHESED	Forgive me Anah	סִלְחִי לִי עֲנָה	כשד
	Great sorrows have enveloped me for the past few days	צָרוֹת גְּדוֹלוֹת אֲפָפוּנִי, זֶה יָמִים אֲחָדִים	
	And when I see relief, **I shall turn back the sundial.**[190]	וְכִי אֶרְאֶה הָרְוָחָה, **אָשִׁיב צֵל הַמַּעֲלוֹת אֲחֹרַנִּית.**[190]	
	(Gives her Asenath's handkerchief)	(נותן לה מטפחת אסנת)	
	But take this from me and make me another one like it.	אַךְ קְחִי זֹאת מִיָּדִי וַעֲשִׂי לִי אַחֶרֶת כָּמוֹהָ.	
ANAH	Where did you get this, Chesed? Who gave you this,	זֹאת מֵאַיִן לְךָ כֶּשֶׂד? מִי נָתַן לְךָ זֹאת?	ענה
	If not a new companion? You have acquired it for yourself recently	אִם לֹא רַעְיָה חֲדָשָׁה, קָנִיתָ לְךָ מִקָּרֹב	
	And did she give you this handkerchief as a token of love?	וּמִטְפַּחַת זוּ נָתְנָה לְךָ הִיא לְמַזְכֶּרֶת אַהֲבָה?	
	Now I know the reason why you have not come to see me.	עַתָּה יָדַעְתִּי הַסִּבָּה מַדּוּעַ לֹא בָאתָ לִרְאוֹתֵנִי.	
CHESED	**Stand back,**[191] woman –	**גְּשִׁי הָלְאָה**[191] אִשָּׁה –	כשד
	The devil's hand is with you in this evil slander	יַד הַשָּׂטָן אִתֵּךְ בְּדִבָּה רָעָה הַזֹּאת	

189 Isa. 38:8 הִנְנִי מֵשִׁיב אֶת־צֵל הַמַּעֲלוֹת אֲשֶׁר יָרְדָה בְמַעֲלוֹת אָחָז בַּשֶּׁמֶשׁ אֲחֹרַנִּית עֶשֶׂר מַעֲלוֹת 'Behold, I shall turn back the degrees, which have gone down on the sundial of Ahaz, by ten degrees'. Cf. Shakespeare's 'hours' (3.4.174).

190 Isa. 38:8 הִנְנִי מֵשִׁיב אֶת־צֵל הַמַּעֲלוֹת אֲשֶׁר יָרְדָה בְמַעֲלוֹת אָחָז בַּשֶּׁמֶשׁ אֲחֹרַנִּית עֶשֶׂר מַעֲלוֹת 'Behold, I shall turn back the degrees, which have gone down on the sundial of Ahaz, by ten degrees'.

191 Gen. 19:9 גֶּשׁ־הָלְאָה 'stand back'.

	For he has incited you against me and has instilled the spirit of jealousy within you	כִּי הוּא הֱסִיתֵךְ בִּי וַיִּפַּח בָּךְ רוּחַ קִנְאָה	
	By saying that the token is in my hand that I have entered a new covenant,	לֵאמֹר הָאוֹת בְּיָדִי כִּי בָאתִי בִּבְרִית חֲדָשָׁה,	
	You have erred, Anah, you have erred greatly.	שָׁגִית עֲנָה שָׁגִית מְאֹד.	
ANAH	If so, then whose is the handkerchief?	אִם כֵּן אֵיפוֹא, לְמִי הַמִּטְפַּחַת?	ענה
CHESED	I do not know, my daughter, for I found it in my chamber	לֹא יָדַעְתִּי בִתִּי, כִּי מְצָאתִיהָ בַּחֲדָרַי	כשד
	And its craftsmanship is very beautiful; therefore I desire	וּמְלַאכְתָּהּ יָפָה עַד מְאֹד עַל כֵּן חָפַצְתִּי	
	For you to make me another one based on this pattern,	כִּי תַעֲשִׂי לִי אַחֶרֶת עַל פִּי הַתַּבְנִית הַזֹּאת,	
	Before the person who lost it comes to demand it from me.	טֶרֶם יָבוֹא בַּעַל הָאֲבֵדָה, לִדְרֹשׁ אֹתָהּ מִיָּדִי.	
	Go and do so for me, and leave me alone.	לְכִי וַעֲשִׂי לִי כֵן וְעִזְבִי אֹתִי לְבַדִּי.	
ANAH	But why must I leave you now?	וְלָמָּה אֶעֱזָבְךָ עָתָּה?	ענה
CHESED	Because I am waiting here to speak to the army commander	כִּי מְחַכֶּה אֲנִי פֹּה, לְדַבֵּר אֶת שַׂר הַצָּבָא	כשד
	And he will not regard it in my favour if he sees a woman at my right hand.	וְלֹא לְיִתְרוֹן יֵחָשֶׁב־לִי, בִּרְאוֹתוֹ אִשָּׁה לִימִינִי.	
ANAH	Why do you think such a thing?	לָמָּה חָשַׁבְתָּ כָּזֹאת?	ענה
CHESED	It is not because my love for you has departed that I think such a thing.	לֹא מֵאֲשֶׁר מָשָׁה אַהֲבָתֵךְ מִמֶּנִּי, חָשַׁבְתִּי כֵן.	כשד
ANAH	This is the matter, that your love for me has departed from your heart;	זֶה הוּא הַדָּבָר, כִּי אַהֲבָתִי מָשָׁה מִלִּבֶּךָ;	ענה
	But lead me on the way a little and say whether you will see me in the evening.	אַךְ נְחֵנִי בַדֶּרֶךְ מְעַט וֶאֱמֹר אִם תִּרְאֵנִי בָּעֶרֶב.	
CHESED	I shall lead you a little distance; I shall not go far from here	הִנְנִי לַנְחוֹתֵךְ כִּבְרַת אֶרֶץ, לֹא אֶרְחַק מִזֶּה	כשד

	And if nothing stops me, I shall come to dinner.	וְאִם דָּבָר לֹא יַעַצְרֵנִי, אָבוֹא לַאֲרוּחַת הָעֶרֶב.	
ANAH	The word of your mouth is good; it has calmed my heart[192]	אִמְרַת פִּיךָ טוֹבָה, אֶת לִבִּי הִשְׁקִיטָה[192]	ענה
	I know that a woman like me is only good in her time.	יָדַעְתִּי כִּי אִשָּׁה כָּמוֹנִי, טוֹבָה רַק בְּעִתָּהּ.	
	(Both exit)	(הולכים שניהם)	

End of Third Part. תם חלק שלישי.

192 In the Hebrew these two lines form a rhyming couplet, which lacks a parallel in Shakespeare's single-line statement 'Tis very good; I must be circumstanced' (3.4.202).

	## Fourth Part	## חלק רביעי	
SCENE I	*(Ithiel and Doeg)*	(איתיאל ודואג)	מחזה א'
DOEG	Do you believe this, commander?	הֲיַאֲמִין זאת לִבְּךָ הַשַּׂר?	דואג
ITHIEL	Do I believe this? Doeg?	הַאַאֲמִין זאת? דּוֹאֵג?	איתיאל
DOEG	Is it possible? To kiss in secret!	הֲיִתָּכֵן? לְנַשֵּׁק בַּסֵּתֶר!	דואג
ITHIEL	Secret kisses are stolen kisses.	נְשִׁיקוֹת סְתָרִים, נְשִׁיקוֹת גְּנוּבוֹת הֵן.	איתיאל
DOEG	Is it possible that a naked woman would lie with a stranger in bed	הֲיִתָּכֵן כִּי אִשָּׁה עֲרוּמָּה תִּשְׁכַּב עִם זָר בַּמִּטָּה	דואג
	And say that they did not have ill intent?	וְלֵאמֹר כִּי לֹא חָשְׁבוּ רָעָה?	
ITHIEL	Naked with a stranger in bed, and say that they did not have ill intent,	עֲרוּמָּה עִם זָר בַּמִּטָּה וְלֵאמֹר לֹא חָשְׁבוּ רָעָה,	איתיאל
	Even the devil would scold them, saying that it is ungodliness.	גַּם הַשָּׂטָן יִגְעַר בָּם לֵאמֹר כִּי חֲנֻפָּה הִיא.	
	And if blameless ones do this, the devil tests them	וְאִם נְקִיִּים עֹשִׂים זאת, הַשָּׂטָן מְנַסֶּה אֹתָם	
	And they test their Creator.	וְהֵם מְנַסִּים אֶת יוֹצְרָם.	
DOEG	If they have not committed lewdness and indecency, they will be forgiven;	אִם זִמָּה וּנְבָלָה לֹא עָשׂוּ וְנִסְלַח לָהֶם;	דואג
	However, if I had given a handkerchief to my wife –	אָכֵן לוּ נָתַתִּי מִטְפַּחַת לְאִשְׁתִּי –	
ITHIEL	And then?	וְאָז?	איתיאל
DOEG	The handkerchief would be hers, and she would have the right to give it to a stranger.	הַמִּטְפַּחַת לָהּ הִיא, וְלָהּ הַמִּשְׁפָּט לְתִתָּהּ לַזָּר.	דואג
ITHIEL	Her honour is also hers; should she give her honour to a stranger?	גַּם כְּבוֹדָהּ לָהּ הוּא, הֲתִתֵּן כְּבוֹדָהּ לַזָּר?	איתיאל
DOEG	Honour is not visible to the eye, and the hand cannot touch it	הַכָּבוֹד לֹא יֵרָאֶה לְעַיִן וְיָד לֹא תְמַשְּׁנּוּ	דואג
	There are many who inherit honour, but shame is their due,	יֵשׁ נוֹחֲלֵי כָבוֹד רַבִּים, וְלָהֶם קָלוֹן יָאָתָה,	
	But the handkerchief –	אֲבָל הַמִּטְפַּחַת –	
ITHIEL	If only I could forget it – you told me –	מִי יִתֵּן וּשְׁכַחְתִּיהָ מִלֵּב – אַתָּה הִגַּדְתָּ לִי –	איתיאל

	Like a raven that flies speedily to the stench of the houses of the sick	כָּעֹרֵב חָשׁ לָעוּף לְצַחֲנַת בָּתֵּי הַחוֹלִים	
	Which becomes an evil omen to the eyes of the afflicted ones in the house,	אֲשֶׁר יִהְיֶה לְאוֹת רָע לְעֵינֵי הַמְנֻגָּעִים בַּבָּיִת,	
	So is the memory of the handkerchief for me – because it is in his hand.	כֵּן זִכְרוֹן הַמִּטְפַּחַת לְנֶגְדִּי – כִּי בְיָדוֹ הִנֶּהָ.	
DOEG	Is its worth still great in your eyes?	הַעוֹד עֶרְכָּהּ רַב בְּעֵינֶיךָ?	דואג
ITHIEL	Its worth is as naught in my eyes.	עֶרְכָּהּ כְּאַיִן בְּעֵינָי.	איתיאל
DOEG	What if you heard me say that I had seen him desecrating your bed	לוּ שְׁמַעְתַּנִי אֹמֵר: כִּי רְאִיתִיו בְּחַלְּלוֹ יְצוּעֶךָ	דואג
	Or that I had heard **this vile thing**[1] from his lips	אוֹ שָׁמַעְתִּי מִשְּׂפָתָיו, **דְּבַר הַנְּבָלָה הַזֹּאת**[1]	
	In the manner of villains who tempt their companions' wives	כְּאֹרַח בְּנֵי בְלִיַּעַל, אֲשֶׁר יְפַתּוּן נְשֵׁי רֵעֵיהֶם	
	And **do not cover up the sin**,[2] but rather **speak rashly of it with their lips**[3] –	**וְהַפֶּשַׁע לֹא יְכַסּוּן**,[2] כִּי אִם **יְבַטְּאוּ בִשְׂפָתֵיהֶם**[3] –	
ITHIEL	Did he say anything with his mouth?	הַאִם הִגִּיד דְּבַר מַה בְּפִיו?	איתיאל
DOEG	He said the thing; but believe me, my lord	הוּא הִגִּיד הַדָּבָר; אַךְ הַאֲמֵן אֲדֹנִי	דואג
	That just as he said it, so he will deny it **with a curse and an oath**.[4]	כִּי כַּאֲשֶׁר הִגִּיד, כֵּן יְכַחֵשׁ **בְּאָלָה וּבִשְׁבוּעָה**.[4]	
ITHIEL	And what did he say?	וּמָה הִגִּיד?	איתיאל
DOEG	That he was with her – but I – I do not know more.	כִּי הָיָה אֶצְלָהּ – וַאֲנִי – אֲנִי לֹא אֵדַע יוֹתֶר.	דואג
ITHIEL	What did he say that he did?	מָה הִגִּיד כִּי עָשָׂה?	איתיאל
DOEG	He lay –	שָׁכַב –	דואג
ITHIEL	With her?	עִמָּהּ?	איתיאל
DOEG	With her, on her, reckon it as you see fit.	עִמָּהּ, עָלֶיהָ, חֲשׁוֹב כְּהָעוֹלֶה עַל רוּחֶךָ.	דואג
ITHIEL[5]	With her? – On her? – Indecency![6] –	עִמָּהּ? – עָלֶיהָ? – נְבָלָה![6] –	איתיאל[5]

1 Judg. 19:24.
2 Prov. 28:13 מְכַסֶּה פְשָׁעָיו לֹא יַצְלִיחַ 'he who covers up his sins will not prosper'.
3 Ps. 106:33 וַיְבַטֵּא בִּשְׂפָתָיו 'and he spoke rashly with his lips'.
4 Neh. 10:30 (10:29 in English Bibles) בְּאָלָה וּבִשְׁבוּעָה 'in a curse and an oath'.
5 This speech is prose in the original (4.1.35–43).
6 Cf. Shakespeare's 'zounds, that's fulsome!' (4.1.36).

	He must confess – handkerchief – he must confess – handkerchief –	יִתְוַדֶּה – מִטְפַּחַת – יִתְוַדֶּה – מִטְפַּחַת –	
	He must confess and be hung upon a tree – No! He must be hung upon a tree	יִתְוַדֶּה וְיִתָּלֶה עַל הָעֵץ – לֹא! יִתָּלֶה עַל הָעֵץ	
	And then he must confess. And as for me, **trembling has gripped me**[7]	וְאַחֲרֵי כֵן יִתְוַדֶּה. וַאֲנִי **פַּלָּצוּת בִּעֲתַתְנִי**[7]	
	It is **a grim vision**,[8] and it is not without cause that it has terrorized me.	**חָזוּת קָשָׁה**[8] הִיא וְלֹא עַל חִנָּם תְּבַעֲתַנִי.	
	It is not the sound of words, but rather a picture before my eyes	לֹא קוֹל דְּבָרִים, כִּי אִם תְּמוּנָה לְנֶגֶד עֵינָי	
	Noses – ears – lips – what is this that I see?	אַפַּיִם – אָזְנַיִם – שְׂפָתַיִם – מַזֶּה אֲנִי רֹאֶה?	
	Confess – handkerchief – oh, destruction! –	הִתְוַדֵּה – מִטְפַּחַת – הוֹי אֲבַדּוֹן! –	
	(Falls unconscious)	(נופל מתעלף)	
DOEG	Do your work, my medicine, give him an intoxicating cup to drink,	פְּעַל פְּעוּלָּתְךָ סַמִּי, הַשְׁקֵהוּ כּוֹס שִׁכָּרוֹן,	דואג
	Such fools are caught in the snare of deception	פְּתָאִים כָּאֵלֶּה וְכָאֵלֶּה יִלָּכְדוּ בְּפַח הָרְמִיָּה	
	And even the best of the righteous women become **a shame and disgrace**.[9] –	וְגַם הַטּוֹבוֹת בִּנְשֵׁי צֶדֶק תִּהְיֶינָה **לְבֹשֶׁת וּכְלִמָּה**.[9] –	
	Oh, army commander! What is wrong with you, army commander Ithiel?	הוֹי שַׂר הַצָּבָא! מַה־לְּךָ אִיתִיאֵל שַׂר הַצָּבָא!	
	(Chesed enters)	(כשד בא)	
	My lord Ithiel! – What do you have to say, Chesed?	אִיתִיאֵל אֲדוֹנִי! – מַה־בְּפִיךָ כֶּשֶׂד?	
CHESED	What has happened here?	מַה־קָּרָה פֹּה?	כשד
DOEG	**A convulsion has seized my lord**[10] and he has fainted twice now.	**אֲדֹנִי הַשָּׁבָץ אֲחָזָהוּ**[10] וַיִּתְעַלֵּף זֶה פַּעֲמָיִם.	דואג

7 Isa. 21:4.
8 Isa. 21:2.
9 Ps. 35:26.
10 2 Sam. 1:9 אֲחָזַנִי הַשָּׁבָץ 'agony has seized me'; the word שָׁבָץ appearing in this verse is a *hapax legomenon* with somewhat uncertain meaning (having been interpreted as 'death throes', 'agony', or 'convulsions'; Koehler and Baumgartner 2001, 2: 1402). Salkinson uses it as a translation of Shakespeare's 'epilepsy' (4.1.50). The same citation is used in a different sense in *Ram and Jael*; see *Ram and Jael*, Third Part, note 99.

CHESED	Anoint his temple.	מְשַׁח אֶת רַקָּתוֹ.	כשד
DOEG	Leave him be	הַנַּח־לוֹ	דואג
	It is no good to wake him up before the end of the deep sleep,	אֵין טוֹב לְהָעִיר אֹתוֹ עַד תֹּם הַתַּרְדֵּמָה,	
	Lest he bring forth drool from his mouth and behave madly like a lunatic.	פֶּן יוֹצִיא רִירוֹ מִפִּיו וְיִשְׁתַּגַּע כַּחֲסַר טָעַם.	
	See, behold, he is stirring, and soon he will arise	רְאֵה הִנֵּה הוּא מִתְעוֹרֵר וְעַד מְהֵרָה יָקוּם	
	And go to his home; therefore go out from here	וְיֵלֶךְ לוֹ לְבֵיתוֹ; לָכֵן צֵא מִזֶּה הַחוּצָה	
	And return to me **in a little while,**[11] because I have a matter for you.	וְשׁוּב אֵלַי כִּמְעַט קָט,[11] כִּי דָּבָר לִי אֵלֶיךָ.	
	(Chesed exits)	(כשד יוצא)	
	What happened, army commander? Is your head not injured?	מַה־קָּרְךָ שַׂר הַצָּבָא? הַאֵין רֹאשְׁךָ פָּצוּעַ?	
ITHIEL	Are you mocking me?	הַאַתָּה תְּשַׂחֵק עָלָי?	איתיאל
DOEG	Am I mocking? God forbid that I should mock	הֶאָנֹכִי אֶשְׂחָק? חָלִלָה לִּי מִשְּׂחֹק	דואג
	Rather, my whole aim is only that you should bear the changes of the time like a man	וְרַק כָּל מְגַמָּתִי כִּי תִשָּׂא כַּגֶּבֶר חֲלִיפוֹת הַזְּמָן	
	And face your fate like a man.[12]	וְתַעֲמֹד לְגוֹרָלְךָ כָּאִישׁ.[12]	
ITHIEL	The man whose wife has been unfaithful to him	הָאִישׁ אֲשֶׁר אִשְׁתּוֹ מָעֲלָה בוֹ מָעַל	איתיאל
	Resembles a goat, or one of the **wild asses in the wilderness.**[13]	לְשָׂעִיר נִדְמָה וּלְאַחַד הַפְּרָאִים בַּמִּדְבָּר.[13]	
DOEG	If so, you can find many goats and a multitude of wild asses	אִם כֵּן אֵיפוֹא, תִּמְצָא שְׂעִירִים רַבִּים וַהֲמוֹן פְּרָאִים	דואג
	In every big city.	בְּכָל קִרְיָה גְדוֹלָה.	
ITHIEL	Has he confessed with his own mouth?	הַאִם הוֹדָה בְּמוֹ פִיו?	איתיאל
DOEG	My lord, be a man,	אֲדֹנִי הֱיֵה לְאִישׁ,	דואג

11 Ezek. 16:47.

12 In Hebrew this and the previous line employ two different words for 'man'.

13 Job 24:5. Cf. Shakespeare's 'A horned man's a monster, and a beast' (4.1.62). Salkinson's replacement of 'monster' with 'goat' may be an attempt to preserve an element of the English expression 'horned man'.

	Many honourable men bear the burden of a woman on their neck	נִכְבָּדִים רַבִּים יִשְׂאוּ עֹל אִשָּׁה עַל צַוָּארָם	
	And let them bear the burden like you; thousands of thousands of men	וְיִמְשְׁכוּ בָעֹל כָּמוֹךָ; אַלְפֵי אֲלָפִים אֲנָשִׁים	
	Lie down in the night on their bed which is impure	יַעֲלוּ בַלַּיְלָה עַל מִשְׁכָּבָם אֲשֶׁר לֹא טָהוֹר	
	And boast in their heart, saying[14] that their bed is honourable,	וְהִתְבָּרְכוּ בִּלְבָבָם לֵאמֹר,[14] כִּי מִטָּתָם כְּבוּדָה,	
	But your fate is better than theirs; they embrace and kiss	וְאַתָּה גּוֹרָלְךָ טוֹב מֵהֶם, הֵם יְחַבְּקוּן יְנַשְּׁקוּן	
	A whoring and defiled wife[15] like an upright and modest wife	**אִשָּׁה זוֹנָה וַחֲלָלָה**,[15] כְּאִשָּׁה יְשָׁרָה וּצְנוּעָה	
	Filling the devil's mouth with laughter, and the sons of Sheol clap their hands,	לְמַלֵּא פִּי הַשָּׂטָן שְׂחֹק וּבְנֵי הַשְּׁאוֹל יִמְחֲאוּ־כָף,	
	But you, it is better for you to know who you are	וְאַתָּה טוֹב לְךָ לָדַעַת, מִי הוּא אַתָּה	
	And who **the wife of your covenant**[16] is.	וּמִי **אֵשֶׁת בְּרִיתֶךָ**.[16]	
ITHIEL	Indeed every mouth would admit that you are wise	כִּי נָבוֹן דָּבָר אַתָּה יוֹדֶה כָל פֶּה.	איתיאל
DOEG	Go and hide opposite and wait there a little while.	לֵךְ הִסָּתֵר מִנֶּגֶד וְהוֹחִילָה שָׁם מְעַט רֶגַע.	דואג
	Chesed was here while you were lying on **the bed of languishing**[17]	כֶּשֶׁד הָיָה פֹּה לְעֵת שָׁכַבְתָּ **עַל עֶרֶשׂ דְּוָי**[17]	
	For you had swooned due to great agitation and anger	כִּי עֻלְּפָה נַפְשְׁךָ מֵרֹב רֹגֶז וָכַעַס	
	Which is not fitting for a brave-hearted man such as yourself.	אֲשֶׁר לֹא יָאֲתָה כֵן לְאַמִּיץ לֵב כָּמוֹךָ.	
	I lied to him, saying that **a deep sleep had fallen upon you**,[18]	וַאֲנִי כִחַשְׁתִּי לוֹ לֵאמֹר, **תַּרְדֵּמָה נָפְלָה עָלֶיךָ**,[18]	
	And he will indeed return here, as I commanded him	וְהוּא שׁוֹב יָשׁוּב הֵנָּה, כַּאֲשֶׁר אָנֹכִי צִוִּיתִיו	

14 Deut. 28:18 (28:19 in English Bibles) וְהִתְבָּרֵךְ בִּלְבָבוֹ לֵאמֹר 'and he boasts in his heart, saying'.

15 Lev. 21:7.

16 Mal. 2:14.

17 Ps. 41:4 (41:3 in English Bibles).

18 Gen. 15:12 וְתַרְדֵּמָה נָפְלָה עַל־אַבְרָם 'a deep sleep fell upon Abram'.

	Therefore hide there so that you are not visible	לָכֵן הִתְחַבֵּא שָׁם לְבַל תֵּרָאֶה לָעַיִן	
	In order that you might hear with your own ears everything that he says to me	לְמַעַן תִּשְׁמַע בְּאָזְנֶיךָ, כָּל אֲשֶׁר יְדַבֵּר עִמִּי	
	And you will see the mockery and the derision from between his eyelids	וְרָאִיתָ אֶת הַלַּעַג וְאֶת הַקֶּלֶס מִבֵּין עַפְעַפָּיו	
	And **the shameful spewing from his lips, which he pours over your honour.**[19]	וְאֶת הַקִּיקָלוֹן מִשְּׂפָתָיו, אֲשֶׁר יִשְׁפֹּךְ עַל כְּבוֹדֶךָ.[19]	
	For I shall guide the topic until he tells me again	כִּי אֲסַבֵּב בִּדְבָרִים, עַד אֲשֶׁר יְסַפֵּר לִי שֵׁנִית	
	How he came to your wife on such-and-such a day and in such-and-such a place	אֵיךְ בָּא אֶל אִשְׁתְּךָ בְּיוֹם פְּלֹנִי וּבְמָקוֹם פְּלֹנִי	
	And how many times he has come and when he will come to her again.	וְכַמֶּה פְעָמִים בָּא וּלְמָתַי יָבוֹא אֵלֶיהָ עוֹד.	
	Indeed, observe his speech and examine the expression of his face	אַךְ הִתְבּוֹנֵן אֶל שִׂיחוֹ וְהַכָּרַת פָּנָיו תִּבְחָן	
	But restrain yourself greatly and sit quietly	רַק הִתְאַפֵּק מְאֹד וְדוּמָם תֵּשֵׁב תַּחְתֶּיךָ	
	Because if not, one who sees you will say	כִּי אִם לֹא כֵן, יֹאמַר עָלֶיךָ הָרֹאֶה	
	That your sense has departed and there is no human spirit within you.	הֵן רוּחֲךָ סָרָה וְנֶפֶשׁ אָדָם בְּאַפֶּיךָ אָיִן.	
ITHIEL	Listen to me, Doeg, I shall sit as quiet as a stone	שְׁמָעֵנִי דוֹאֵג, אֲנִי אֵשֵׁב דוּמָם כָּאָבֶן	איתיאל
	But afterwards (do you hear?!) I shall arise as **a man of blood.**[20]	וְאַחֲרֵי כֵן (הֲלֹא שָׁמַעְתָּ!) אָקוּם כְּאִישׁ דָּמִים.[20]	
DOEG	Thus you must do and not sin, but **do the thing in its time.**[21]	כֵּן תַּעֲשֶׂה וְלֹא תֶחֱטָא, אַךְ עֲשֵׂה דָבָר בְּעִתּוֹ.[21]	דואג
	And now go and hide *(Ithiel hides and Doeg continues speaking to himself)*	וְעַתָּה לֵךְ וְהִסָּתֵר, (איתיאל מסתתר ודואג מדבר עוד אל עצמו)	
	Meanwhile, I shall ask Chesed about the concubine Anah	וַאֲנִי אֶשְׁאַל אֶת כֶּשֶׂד, עַל עֲנָה הַפִּלֶגֶשׁ	

19 Hab. 2:16 וְקִיקָלוֹן עַל־כְּבוֹדֶךָ 'and shameful spewing upon your honour'.

20 2 Sam. 16:8; translated as 'a murderer' in some English Bible versions (e.g., Geneva Bible and New International Version).

21 Prov. 15:23 וְדָבָר בְּעִתּוֹ 'and a word (or: matter) in its time'.

	Who sells him her love for bread and a garment	הַמֹּכֶרֶת לוֹ דֹדֶיהָ, בְּעַד לֶחֶם וְשִׂמְלָה	
	And she loves him with all the desire of her heart	וְהִיא אֹהֶבֶת אֹתוֹ, בְּכָל חֵשֶׁק לְבָבָהּ	
	Because such is the way of the whore; she deceives many men	כִּי כֵן מִשְׁפַּט הַזּוֹנָה, הִיא תּוֹנֶה רַבִּים	
	And one man deceives her, and when he hears her name from my mouth	וְאֶחָד יוֹנֶה אוֹתָהּ, וְכַאֲשֶׁר יִשְׁמַע שְׁמָהּ מִפִּי	
	He will deride and scoff and will not be able to stop himself from laughing	כֵּן יִלְעַג וִיהַתֵּל וְלֹא יַעֲצֹר פִּיו מִשְּׂחֹק	
	And as he laughs, so Ithiel will grow madder	וְכַאֲשֶׁר הוּא יִשְׂחַק, כֵּן יוֹסֵף אִיתִיאֵל לְהִשְׁתַּגֵּעַ	
	For in his jealousy he will think that the wretched Chesed	כִּי הוּא בְקִנְאָתוֹ יַחְשֹׁב, כִּי כֶּשֶׂד הָאֻמְלָל	
	Is mocking his wife Asenath –	מְהַתֵּל בְּאָסְנַת אִשְׁתּוֹ –	
	(To Chesed upon his return) Are you well, officer Chesed?	(אל כשד בשובו) הֲשָׁלוֹם כֶּשֶׂד הַפָּקִיד?	
CHESED	**There is no wellness in my bones,**[22] and the title of my office from your mouth	**אֵין שָׁלוֹם בַּעֲצָמַי**[22] וְשֵׁם פְּקוּדָתִי מִפִּיךָ	כשד
	Increases my sorrow unto death.	יַרְבֶּה עִצְּבוֹנִי עַד מָוֶת.	
DOEG	Entreat Asenath, if you are not succeeding on your path.	חַל נָא פְּנֵי אָסְנַת, אִם לֹא תַצְלִיחַ בְּדַרְכֶּךָ.	דואג
	(In a whisper)	(בלחש)	
	If only it were Anah instead of her, she would already have **brought your soul out of trouble.**[23]	לוּ הָיְתָה עֲנָה תַּחְתֶּיהָ, כְּבָר **הוֹצִיאָה מִצָּרָה נַפְשֶׁךָ.**[23]	
CHESED	**Silly senseless heifer**[24] –	**עֶגְלָה פוֹתָה אֵין לֵב**[24] –	כשד
ITHIEL	*(To himself)* See how he opens his mouth wide in laughter.	(אל עצמו) רְאֵה אֵיךְ יִפְעַר פִּיו בִּשְׂחֹק.	איתיאל
DOEG	Her love for you is great; I have not seen her equal among women.	גְּדוֹלָה אַהֲבָתָהּ אֵלֶיךָ, לֹא רָאִיתִי כָמוֹהָ בַּנָּשִׁים.	דואג

22 Ps. 38:4.
23 Ps. 143:11 תּוֹצִיא מִצָּרָה נַפְשִׁי 'bring my soul out of trouble'.
24 Hosea 7:11 וַיְהִי אֶפְרַיִם כְּיוֹנָה פוֹתָה אֵין לֵב 'Ephraim is like a silly senseless dove'.

CHESED	Perhaps this poor wretch desires me **truly and sincerely**.[25]	עֲנִיָּה זוּ אוּלַי חָשְׁקָה בִי, בֶּאֱמֶת וּבְתָמִים.[25]	כשד
ITHIEL	*(To himself)* He denies the matter as if mocking, and his derision testifies against him.	(אל עצמו) מְכַחֵשׁ הַדָּבָר כִּמְהַתֵּל וְלַעֲגוֹ יַעֲנֶה בְּפָנָיו.	איתיאל
DOEG	Are you listening?	הֲשׁוֹמֵעַ* אָתָּה?	דואג
ITHIEL	*(To himself)* Now he urges him to discuss his love;	(אל עצמו) עַתָּה יִפְצַר בּוֹ לְסַפֵּר דִּבְרֵי אֲהָבָיו;	איתיאל
	He is a wise man in his ways.	אִישׁ מַשְׂכִּיל הוּא בִּדְרָכָיו.	
DOEG	She is saying in the town that you are going to take her to wife	הִיא אֹמֶרֶת בָּעִיר, כִּי אַתָּה תִקָּחֶנָּה לְאִשָּׁה	דואג
	Do you want to take her?	הֶחָפֵץ אַתָּה לְקַחְתָּהּ?	
ITHIEL[26]	*(To himself)* Do you laugh now? Do you laugh, son of Florence?[27]	(אל עצמו) הֲכִי תִשְׂחַק עַתָּה, הֲכִי תִשְׂחַק בֶּן פְלָארֶענְץ?[27]	איתיאל[26]
CHESED[28]	Am I insane, that I should take a whore to wife?	הַחֲסַר־דֵּעָה אָנִי, כִּי אֶשָּׂא זוֹנָה לְאִשָּׁה?	כשד[28]
	Please do not ascribe to me words that are not so	אָנָּא אַל תְּחַפֵּא עָלַי, דְּבָרִים אֲשֶׁר לֹא כֵן	
	And do not degrade my worth with such laughter and mockery.	וְאַל תַּשְׁפִּיל עֶרְכִּי, בִּצְחֹק וּמַהֲתַלּוֹת כָּאֵלֶּה.	
ITHIEL	*(To himself)* He commits adultery with a woman and **fills his mouth with laughter**.[29, 30]	(אל עצמו) נֹאֵף אִשָּׁה, יְמַלֵּא שְׂחֹק פִּיהוּ.[29, 30]	איתיאל
DOEG	The report has gone out in the town, that you are indeed going to marry her.	הַשְּׁמוּעָה יָצְאָה בָּעִיר, כִּי נָשׂא תִשָּׂאֶנָּה.	דואג
CHESED	Please speak the truth; do not lie.	דַּבֵּר נָא אֱמֶת אַל תְּשַׁקֵּר.	כשד
DOEG	You may consider me a villain if I have not spoken the truth.	לְבֶן־בְּלִיַּעַל תַּחְשְׁבֵנִי, אִם לֹא אֱמֶת דִּבַּרְתִּי.	דואג

25 Judg. 9:16, 19.
26 Salkinson has omitted Cassio's immediately preceding line 'Ha, ha, ha' (4.1.118).
27 Cf. Shakespeare's 'Do ye triumph, Roman, do you triumph?' (4.1.119), an ironic reference to the Roman entrance ceremony by a victorious general (Honigmann 1997: 262, note 119). Salkinson has simplified this into a straightforward reference to Chesed's native city.
28 This and the following speeches until the arrival of Lud, Asenath, and the servants are all prose in the original (4.1.120–212).
29 Ps. 126:2 אָז יִמָּלֵא שְׂחוֹק פִּינוּ 'then our mouths will fill with laughter'.
30 As previously, Salkinson has omitted Shakespeare's 'Ha, ha, ha!' appearing at the end of Cassio's speech in the previous line (4.1.122).

* הֲשׁוֹמֵעַ

ITHIEL	*(To himself)* To cover me with **everlasting disgrace**,[31] you say that the matter is good.	(אל עצמו) לְהַעֲטוֹת עָלַי כְּלִמַּת* עוֹלָם[31] תֹּאמַר טוֹב** הַדָּבָר.	איתיאל
CHESED	Only from the mouth of the she-ass has this report gone out	רַק מִפִּי הָאָתוֹן יָצְאָה הַשְּׁמוּעָה הַזֹּאת	כשד
	Because her love is so great, she boasts in vain	מֵאַהֲבָתָהּ כִּי גָדְלָה, תִּתְבָּרֵךְ בְּנַפְשָׁהּ לַשָּׁוְא	
	That I shall indeed marry her, although I have said nothing.	כִּי נָשֹׂא אֶשָּׂאֶנָּה וַאֲנִי לֹא דִּבַּרְתִּי דָּבָר.	
ITHIEL	*(To himself)* Doeg is waving a hand at me to listen, for now he is going to begin	(אל עצמו) דּוֹאֵג מֵנִיף לִי יָד לִשְׁמֹעַ, כִּי יָחֵל עַתָּה	איתיאל
	To tell of **the lewdness of his fornication**.[32]	לְסַפֵּר זִמַּת זְנוּתוֹ.[32]	
CHESED	And here too she met me a few moments ago	וְגַם פֹּה פָּגְשָׁה אֹתִי לִפְנֵי רְגָעִים אֲחָדִים	כשד
	For she is always running after me. Yesterday I stood	כִּי תָרוּץ אַחֲרַי תָּמִיד. בְּיוֹם אֶתְמוֹל עָמַדְתִּי	
	With guests from Venice on the seashore	עִם אֹרְחִים מִוִּינֶעצְיָא עַל שְׂפַת הַיָּם	
	And the fool came suddenly and fell upon my neck –	וְהַפְּתַיָּה בָּאָה פִּתְאֹם וַתִּפֹּל עַל צַוָּארִי –	
ITHIEL	*(To himself)* And she called out, Chesed, my love, my chosen one…	(אל עצמו) וַתִּקְרָא כֶּשֶׂד, אֲהֻבִי, בְּחִירִי...	איתיאל
CHESED	And she embraced and kissed me and wept upon my neck	וַתְּחַבֵּק וַתְּנַשֵּׁק אֹתִי וַתֵּבְךְּ עַל צַוָּארִי	כשד
	And drew me to go after her…	וַתִּמְשְׁכֵנִי לָלֶכֶת אַחֲרֶיהָ...	
ITHIEL	*(To himself)* Now he will tell of how she drew him in her love	(אל עצמו) עַתָּה יְסַפֵּר אֵיךְ מָשְׁכָה אֹתוֹ בְּאַהֲבָתָהּ	איתיאל
	And brought him to my bedchamber. I see now	וַתְּבִיאֵהוּ לַחֲדַר מִטָּתִי. הִנְנִי רֹאֶה עַתָּה	
	Your nose on your face, but not the dog	אֶת אַפְּךָ בְּפָנֶיךָ, אַךְ לֹא אֶת הַכֶּלֶב	
	Before which I shall throw it.	אֲשֶׁר אַשְׁלִיכֶנּוּ לְפָנָיו.	

31 Jer. 20:11.
32 Jer. 13:27 זִמַּת זְנוּתֵךְ 'the lewdness of your fornication'.

* כְּלִמַּת
** טוֹב

CHESED	And therefore I have determined to leave her and to sever the bond of our covenant.	וְלָכֵן חָרַצְתִּי לְעָזְבָהּ וּלְנַתֵּק קֶשֶׁר בְּרִיתֵנוּ.	כשד
DOEG	But look over there, who is coming towards us.	אַךְ רְאֵה נָא שָׁמָּה, מִי הַבָּאָה לִקְרָאתֵנוּ.	דואג
	(Anah enters)	(ענה באה)	
CHESED	Here comes this Lilith[33] **perfumed with myrrh and frankincense**[34] –	הִנֵּה לִילִית[33] הַזֹּאת בָּאָה מְקֻטֶּרֶת מֹר **וּלְבֹנָה**[34] –	כשד
	What is there between you and me, Anah, that you constantly pursue me?	מַה־לִּי וָלָךְ עֲנָה, כִּי תִרְדְּפִינִי תָּמִיד?	
ANAH	May Azazel and all of the evil angels[35] pursue you!	יִרְדָּפְךָ עֲזָאזֵל וְכָל מַלְאֲכֵי רָעִים;[35]	ענה
	Indeed, what is the story with you and the handkerchief that you gave me?	אַךְ מַה־לְּךָ וְלַמִּטְפַּחַת אֲשֶׁר נָתַתָּ בְּיָדִי?	
	How could I have been so stupid as to believe that you found	אֵיךְ נִסְכַּלְתִּי לְהַאֲמִין כִּי אֲבֵדָה יְקָרָה כָּזֹאת	
	Such a precious lost item in your lodgings, and that you do not know who its owner is?	מָצָאתָ בְּבֵית מְלוֹנְךָ וְלֹא יָדַעְתָּ מִי בְעָלֶיהָ?	
	Why, this is the gift of a woman as a token of love	הֲלֹא זֹאת מַתְּנַת יַד אִשָּׁה לְמַזְכֶּרֶת אַהֲבָה	
	So how could you give it to me to make another one like it?	וְאֵיךְ תִּתְּנֶהָ לִי לַעֲשׂוֹת אַחֶרֶת כָּמוֹהָ?	
	Take it and give it back to the woman whom you have chosen	קַח לְךָ וַהֲשִׁיבֶנָּה אֶל הָאִשָּׁה אֲשֶׁר בָּחַרְתָּ בָּהּ	
	For my hands will not be doing such work.	כִּי מְלָאכָה כָּזֹאת יָדַי לֹא תַעֲשֶׂינָּה.	

33 Cf. Shakespeare's 'fitchew' (4.1.145), a polecat, skunk, or prostitute (Crystal and Crystal 2002: 177). Although Lilith is almost totally absent from the Bible (there is a single somewhat opaque attestation of the name in Isaiah 34:14), she became prominent in postbiblical Jewish literature, featuring in the Babylonian Talmud, in rabbinic midrash (homiletical and narrative commentary on the Hebrew Bible), and in medieval mystical texts. She is a familiar feature of Eastern European Jewish folklore as Adam's first wife who became a she-demon given to kidnapping and murdering new-born boys (Petrovsky-Shtern 2010).

34 Song of Songs 3:6.

35 Cf. Shakespeare's 'the devil and his dam' (4.1.147). The name Azazel first appears in Lev. 16:8, 10 in the description of a Yom Kippur ritual whereby a goat was sent into the wilderness symbolically bearing the community's sins. The meaning of the name is unclear. In Talmudic times there were variant interpretations of the term, one of which was as a demonic figure (Ahituv 2007); this is the sense in which Salkinson is using it. The phrase 'evil angels' appears in Ps. 78:49. See First Part, note 56 for further discussion of the name Azazel.

CHESED	Please don't, Anah, please don't, pleasant Anah.	אַל נָא עֲנָה, אַל נָא עֲנָה הַנְּעִימָה	כשד
	Why do you rage without cause?	לָמָּה זֶה תִּקְצְפִי חִנָּם?	
ITHIEL	*(To himself)* On my life, that's my handkerchief.	(אל עצמו) חֵי נַפְשִׁי, מִטְפַּחְתִּי הִיא זֹאת.	איתיאל
ANAH	If so, then come to dinner today	אִם כֵּן אֵיפוֹא, בּוֹא לַאֲרֻחַת הָעֶרֶב הַיּוֹם	ענה
	And if you do not want to today, I shall wait until you do want to. *(Exits)*	וְאִם לֹא חָפַצְתָּ הַיּוֹם, אוֹחִילָה עַד שֶׁתֶּחְפָּץ. (הולכת)	
DOEG	Go forth and follow her.	צֵא וְלֵךְ אַחֲרֶיהָ.	דואג
CHESED	I'll go with her, so that she does not talk about me outside.	הִנְנִי הוֹלֵךְ עִמָּהּ, לְבַל תָּשִׂיחַ בִּי בַּחוּץ.	כשד
DOEG	Will you go to her house, to eat with her in the evening?	הֲתֵלֵךְ אֶל בֵּיתָהּ, לֶאֱכֹל עִמָּהּ בָּעֶרֶב?	דואג
CHESED	I shall do so.	כֵּן אֶעֱשֶׂה.	כשד
DOEG	Maybe I shall come to see you there, for I have news to tell you.	אוּלַי אָבוֹא לִרְאוֹתְךָ שָׁם, כִּי חֲדָשׁוֹת בְּפִי לְהַגִּידָךְ.	דואג
CHESED	Do so, my friend, as you have said.	כֵּן תַּעֲשֶׂה רֵעִי, כַּאֲשֶׁר דִּבַּרְתָּ.	כשד
DOEG	Go in peace, until we see each other.	לֵךְ־לְךָ לְשָׁלוֹם עַד נִרְאֶה אִישׁ אֶת רֵעֵהוּ.	דואג
	(Chesed exits)	(כשד הולך)	
ITHIEL	How shall I kill him, Doeg?	בַּמָּה אֶהֶרְגֵהוּ דּוֹאֵג?	איתיאל
DOEG	Did you see how he laughed about having committed the indecency?	הֲרָאִיתָ אֵיךְ שָׂחַק עַל כִּי עָשָׂה אֶת הַנְּבָלָה?	דואג
ITHIEL	I saw.	רָאִיתִי.	איתיאל
DOEG	And did you also see the handkerchief?	וְגַם אֶת הַמִּטְפַּחַת רָאִיתָ?	דואג
ITHIEL	But is this the one?	אַךְ אִם זוּ הִיא?	איתיאל
DOEG	It is your handkerchief, on your life! And now, see	מִטְפַּחְתְּךָ הִיא חֵי נַפְשֶׁךָ! וְעַתָּה רְאֵה נָא	דואג
	How esteemed your wife, this foolish woman, is in his eyes	בַּמֶּה נֶחְשְׁבָה אִשְׁתְּךָ הַפְּתַיּוּת הַזֹּאת בְּעֵינָיו	
	If he took the gift of her hand and gave it as **a whore's fee**.[36]	אִם מַתְּנַת יָדָהּ לָקַח וַיִּתְּנָה לְאֶתְנַן זוֹנָה.[36]	
ITHIEL	If I had the power to slay him, it would be a killing lasting nine years.	לוּ תַשִּׂיג יָדִי לַהֲמִיתוֹ, בַּהֲרֵגָה מִמֻשֶּׁכֶת תֵּשַׁע שָׁנִים.	איתיאל

36 Deut. 23:19 (23:18 in English Bibles).

	Is this the woman of whom they say that she is **of perfect beauty**[37]	הֲזֹאת הָאִשָּׁה שֶׁיֹּאמְרוּ, **כְּלִילַת יֹפִי**[37] הִיא	
	Unique among women and pure to the husband of her covenant!	אַחַת הִיא בַּנָּשִׁים וּבָרָה לְבַעַל בְּרִיתָהּ!	
DOEG	Remove all this from your heart, and remember her beauty no longer.	הַעֲבֵר כָּל זֹאת מִלִּבְּךָ וְיָפְיָהּ אַל תִּזְכָּר־עוֹד.	דואג
ITHIEL	May her bones rot in the grave and may destruction cover her guilt	יִרְקְבוּן עַצְמוֹתֶיהָ בַּשַּׁחַת וַאֲבַדּוֹן יְכַסֶּה אַשְׁמָתָהּ	איתיאל
	For she shall not live any longer, and she shall not see the light of dawn.	כִּי לֹא תִחְיֶה עוֹד וְלֹא תִרְאֶה אוֹר בֹּקֶר.	
	And as for me, my heart is harder than a stone and **I have set my face like flint**[38] –	וַאֲנִי לְבָבִי קָשֶׁה מִסֶּלַע וּפָנַי **שַׂמְתִּי כַּחַלָּמִישׁ**[38] –	
	Who has seen such a beautiful woman as she in all the land?	מִי רָאָה אִשָּׁה יָפָה כָּמוֹהָ בְּכָל הָאָרֶץ	
	Kings look at her **and put the royal crown on her head.**[39]	מְלָכִים יֶחֱזוּ בָהּ **וְיָשִׂימוּ כֶּתֶר מַלְכוּת בְּרֹאשָׁהּ.**[39]	
DOEG	But you, commander, do not look at her thus.	וְאַתָּה הַשָּׂר, לֹא כֵן תֶּחֱזֶה בָּהּ.	דואג
ITHIEL	May **the king of terrors**[40] take her! I can only speak of **her graceful proportion,**[41]	יִקָּחֶנָּה **מֶלֶךְ בַּלָּהוֹת!**[40] **רַק חִין עֶרְכָּהּ**[41] אֲמַלֵּל,	איתיאל
	She is praised for her handiwork and she plays magnificently	מַעֲשֵׂי יָדֶיהָ יְהַלְלוּהָ וּנְגִינוֹתֶיהָ תְּנַגֵּן לְהִתְפָּאֵר	
	Every heart softens at her voice and indeed every stone melts,	לְקוֹלָהּ יֵרַךְ כָּל לֵב וְאֶבֶן הַמֵּס יִמָּס,	
	In **skilful crafts**[42] she is **ten times better**[43]	גַּם **בִּמְלֶאכֶת מַחֲשֶׁבֶת**,[42] **לָהּ עֶשֶׂר יָדוֹת**[43]	
	And in wisdom, understanding, and wit she surpasses all of her companions.	וּבְחָכְמָה, בִּינָה וְהַשְׂכֵּל, עָלְתָה עַל כָּל רְעוּתֶיהָ.	
DOEG	Therefore her guilt is seven times greater.	לָכֵן גָּדְלָה אַשְׁמָתָהּ שִׁבְעָתַיִם.	דואג

---

37 Ezek. 27:3; Lam. 2:15.

38 Isa. 50:7 שַׂמְתִּי פָנַי כַּחַלָּמִישׁ 'I have set my face like flint'.

39 Esther 2:7 וַיָּשֶׂם כֶּתֶר־מַלְכוּת בְּרֹאשָׁהּ 'and he put the royal crown on her head'.

40 Job 18:14 (an epithet for Death; see Gruber 2004: 1528).

41 Job 41:4 (41:12 in English Bibles) וְחִין עֶרְכּוֹ 'and his graceful proportion' (referring to the mythological sea creature Leviathan).

42 Exod. 35:33 בְּכָל־מְלֶאכֶת מַחֲשָׁבֶת 'in every skilful craft'.

43 Dan. 1:20.

ITHIEL	It is seventy-seven times greater – although her spirit is willing.	גָּדְלָה שִׁבְעִים וְשִׁבְעָה – אָמְנָם רוּחָהּ נְדִיבָה.	איתיאל
DOEG	Too willing.	נְדִיבָה יֶתֶר מִדַּי.	דואג
ITHIEL	Too much, and therefore **my compassion is stirred;**[44]	יֶתֶר עַל הַמִּדָּה וְלָכֵן **נִכְמְרוּ נִחוּמָי;**[44]	איתיאל
	How can I not be compassionate, Doeg, how can I not have mercy on her!	אֵיךְ לֹא אָחוּס דּוֹאֵג, אֵיךְ לֹא אֶחְמֹל עָלֶיהָ!	
DOEG	If her lewdness is good in your eyes, allow her to sin	אִם זִמָּתָהּ טוֹבָה בְּעֵינֶיךָ, הַנַּח לָהּ לַחְטֹא	דואג
	And no one will take heed of her, and the sin will be yours alone	וְאִישׁ לֹא יָשִׁית אֵלֶיהָ לִבּוֹ וּלְךָ לְבַדְּךָ חַטָּאָה	
ITHIEL	**I shall cut her into pieces**[45] – would she take strangers instead of her husband?	**אֲנַתַּח אֹתָהּ לִנְתָחֶיהָ**[45] – הֲתַחַת אִישָׁהּ תִּקַּח זָרִים?	איתיאל
DOEG	How great is the vileness!	מָה רַבָּה הַנְּבָלָה! –	דואג
ITHIEL	To lie with my servant –	לִשְׁכַּב אֶת עַבְדִּי –	איתיאל
DOEG	It is double vileness.	נְבָלָה הִיא כִּפְלַיִם.	דואג
ITHIEL	Prepare for me, Doeg, a cup of poison tonight.	הָכֵן לִי דּוֹאֵג, כּוֹס רַעַל בַּלַּיְלָה הַזֶּה	איתיאל
	I shall not come to argue with her again	לֹא בְדִין וּדְבָרִים, אָבוֹא עִמָּהּ עוֹד	
	Lest her beauty blind my eyes and her splendour captivate my heart	פֶּן יָפְיָהּ יְעַוֵּר עֵינַי וַהֲדָרָהּ יִקַּח לִבִּי	
	Prepare the cup for me tonight.	הָכֵן לִי הַכּוֹס הַלַּיְלָה.	
DOEG	Do not give her a cup of poison to drink; choose to strangle her	אַל תַּשְׁקֶנָּה כּוֹס רַעַל, בְּחַר מַחֲנַק לְנַפְשָׁהּ	דואג
	On her bed, on the bed which she has desecrated.	בְּעֶרֶשׂ יְצוּעָה, בַּמִּטָּה אֲשֶׁר חִלְּלָה.	
ITHIEL	Your judgement is true and righteous, and so I shall do as you have determined.	מִשְׁפָּטְךָ אֱמֶת וָצֶדֶק וְכֵן אֶעֱשֶׂה כַּאֲשֶׁר חָרַצְתָּ.	איתיאל
DOEG	And to make a judgement against Chesed, leave him in my hands	וְלַעֲשׂוֹת מִשְׁפָּט בְּכֶשֶׂד, תְּנָה אֹתוֹ בְּיָדִי	דואג
	And at midnight you will hear how the matter has been resolved.	וְכַחֲצֹת הַלַּיְלָה תִּשְׁמַע אֵיךְ נָפַל הַדָּבָר.	

44 Hosea 11:8.

45 Lev. 1:6 וְנִתַּח אֹתָהּ לִנְתָחֶיהָ 'and he must cut it into pieces'.

	(The sound of a trumpet from outside)	(קול תרועה מחוץ)	
ITHIEL	Your word is very good – but what is the sound of the trumpet?	טוֹב דְּבָרְךָ מְאֹד – אַךְ מַה קוֹל הַתְּרוּעָה?	איתיאל
DOEG	Lud[46] has come here from Venice, as the prince has sent him.	לוּד[46] מִוִּינֶעצְיָא בָּא הֵנָּה, אֲשֶׁר שְׁלָחוֹ הַנָּשִׂיא	דואג
	And your wife is with him.	וְהִנֵּה אִשְׁתְּךָ עִמּוֹ.	
	(Lud, Asenath, and attendants)	(לוד אסנת ומשרתים)	
LUD	Long live the army commander!	יְחִי שַׂר הַצָּבָא!	לוד
ITHIEL	Welcome!	שָׁלוֹם בּוֹאֶךָ!	איתיאל
LUD	The prince and counsellors give you their greetings.	הַנָּשִׂיא וְשָׂרֵי הָעֵצָה, פֹּקְדִים לְשָׁלוֹם לָךְ.	לוד
	(Hands over a letter)	(נותן אגרת בידו)	
ITHIEL	God be with you, honourable messenger who brings me their greetings.	אֱלֹהִים עִמְּךָ צִיר נִכְבָּד, הַמֵּבִיא לִי פְּקוּדָתָם.	איתיאל
	(Opens and reads the letter)	(פותח וקורא באגרת)	
ASENATH	What news is in your mouth, Lud, my **flesh and blood**?[47]	מֶה חֲדָשׁוֹת בְּפִיךָ, לוּד עַצְמִי וּבְשָׂרִי?[47]	אסנת
DOEG	I am happy to see your face, my lord; welcome to Caphtor!	שָׂמַחְתִּי לִרְאוֹת פָּנֶיךָ אֲדֹנִי, שָׁלוֹם בּוֹאֲךָ לְכַפְתּוֹר!	דואג
LUD	Are you well, Doeg? Is officer Chesed well?	הֲשָׁלוֹם לְךָ, דּוֹאֵג? הֲשָׁלוֹם לְכֶשֶׂד הַפָּקִיד?	לוד
DOEG	He still lives.	הוּא עוֹדֶנּוּ חָי.	דואג
ASENATH	**Quarrel and strife**[48] have broken out between him and my lord husband	רִיב וּמָדוֹן[48] פָּרַץ בֵּינוֹ וּבֵין אִישִׁי אֲדֹנִי	אסנת
	But you, my kin, will make peace between them.	אַךְ אַתָּה קְרוֹבִי, תָּשִׂים שָׁלוֹם בֵּינֵיהֶם.	
ITHIEL	Do you know this definitely?	הֲיָדַעַתְּ זֹאת אֶל נָכוֹן?	איתיאל
ASENATH	Of what does my lord speak?	מָה אֲדֹנִי דֹּבֵר?	אסנת

46 This is the name of one of the sons of Noah's son Shem, mentioned in Gen. 10:22 and 1 Chron. 1:17; it also appears in Isa. 66:19 and Ezek. 27:10, 30:5 as the name of a foreign nation. Salkinson seems to have chosen the name as an equivalent of Shakespeare's Lodovico based on the sound correspondence between the two.

47 Gen. 29:14; 2 Sam. 19:13, 14 (19:12, 13 in English Bibles).

48 Hab. 1:3.

ITHIEL	*(Reads the letter)* 'Please act in accordance with your desire; **do not turn from it**'[49]	(קורא באגרת) „עֲשֵׂה נָא כְּחֶפְצְךָ אַל תָּסוּר מִמֶּנּוּ"[49]	איתיאל
LUD	He was not speaking to you, but rather is pondering the letter;	לֹא אֵלַיִךְ דִּבֵּר, כִּי הֹגֶה הוּא בָּאִגֶּרֶת,	לוד
	Have there been **matters of controversy**[50] between your husband and Chesed?	הֲיֵשׁ דִּבְרֵי רִיבוֹת[50] בֵּין בַּעֲלֵךְ וּבֵין כֶּשֶׂד?	
ASENATH	Unfortunately, there have been, to **the anguish of my spirit**;[51]	בְּמִקְרֶה לֹא טוֹב, יֵשׁ וְיֵשׁ לְמֹרַת רוּחִי;[51]	אסנת
	And I desire that they make amends, due to my great love for Chesed.	וְנַפְשִׁי חָשְׁקָה כִּי יַשְׁלִימוּ, מֵרֹב אַהֲבָתִי לְכֶשֶׂד.	
ITHIEL	Oh, **fire and brimstone**![52]	הוֹי אֵשׁ וְגָפְרִית![52]	איתיאל
ASENATH	My lord husband –	אִישִׁי אֲדֹנִי –	אסנת
ITHIEL	**Does your sense remain in you**?[53]	הַאִם עָמַד טַעֲמֵךְ בָּךְ?[53]	איתיאל
ASENATH	Is my lord angry?	הַאִם חָרָה לַאֲדֹנִי?	אסנת
LUD	Perhaps he is angry after reading the letter	אוּלַי חָרָה לוֹ, אַחֲרֵי אֲשֶׁר קָרָא בָּאִגֶּרֶת	לוד
	Because he must return to Venice, and Chesed is to replace him.	כִּי עָלָיו לָשׁוּב לְוִינֶעצְיָא וְכֶשֶׂד יְמַלֵּא מְקוֹמוֹ.	
ASENATH	As for me, I am happy to hear these good tidings.	וַאֲנִי שָׂמַחְתִּי לִשְׁמוֹעַ בְּשׂוֹרָה טוֹבָה זֹאת.	אסנת
ITHIEL	Are you happy?	הַאִם שָׂמַחַתְּ?	איתיאל
ASENATH	My lord husband –	אִישִׁי אֲדֹנִי –	אסנת
ITHIEL	I am happy to see you **without sense**.[54]	אֶשְׂמַח לִרְאוֹתֵךְ סָרַת טָעַם.[54]	איתיאל
ASENATH	Why do you speak thus, Ithiel my beloved?	מַדּוּעַ תְּדַבֵּר כֹּה, אִיתִיאֵל אֲהוּבִי?	אסנת
ITHIEL	Daughter of Sheol! *(Strikes her with his hand)*	בַּת שְׁאוֹל! (מכה אותה בידו)	איתיאל
ASENATH	Aah! What is my crime?	הָהּ! מֶה אַשְׁמָתִי?	אסנת

49 Josh. 1:7.
50 Deut. 17:8.
51 Gen. 26:35 מֹרַת רוּחַ 'bitterness of spirit'.
52 Ezek. 38:22; Ps. 11:6.
53 Jer. 48:11 עָמַד טַעְמוֹ בּוֹ 'its flavour (can also mean 'sense') remained in it'.
54 Prov. 11:22.

LUD	If I tell this in Venice, they will not believe the report;	אִם אֲסַפֵּר זאת בְּוִינֶעצְיָא, לֹא יַאֲמִינוּ לַשְּׁמוּעָה,	לוד
	You have done a strange deed which should not be done, commander	מַעֲשֶׂה זָר אֲשֶׁר לֹא יֵעָשֶׂה, עָשִׂיתָ הַשָּׂר	
	And now please go humble yourself, for she is crying.	וְעַתָּה לֵךְ נָא הִתְרַפֵּס, כִּי בֹכִיָּה הִיא.	
ITHIEL	Oh, daughter of **Sheol and destruction**![55] –	הוֹי בַּת **שְׁאוֹל וַאֲבַדּוֹן**![55] –	איתיאל
	If the earth could bring forth seeds from women's tears	אִם מִדִּמְעוֹת הָאִשָּׁה, תּוֹצִיא הָאָרֶץ זָרַע	
	From every tear that fell to the earth, **a twisting serpent**[56] would come forth –	מִכָּל דֶּמַע הַנֹּפֵל אָרְצָה, יֵצֵא **נָחָשׁ עֲקַלָּתוֹן**[56] –	
	Be gone from my sight.	צְאִי מִנֶּגֶד עֵינָי.	
ASENATH	I am leaving, so as not to vex you further. *(Exits)*	הִנְנִי אֵצֵאָה, לְבִלְתִּי הַכְעִיסְךָ עוֹד. (יוצאת)	אסנת
LUD	Indeed this is a woman who obeys her husband.	אַךְ זאת הִיא אִשָּׁה, הַשּׁוֹמַעַת בְּקוֹל בַּעֲלָהּ.	לוד
	Please, army commander, call her to come back.	אָנָּא שַׂר הַצָּבָא קְרָא לָהּ לָשׁוּב.	
ITHIEL	Come back, woman! –	שׁוּבִי אִשָּׁה! –	איתיאל
ASENATH	Here I am, my lord.	הִנְנִי אֲדֹנִי.	אסנת
ITHIEL	Noble Lud, do you have something to discuss with her?	הֲיֵשׁ לְךָ לוּד הַנָּדִיב, לְדַבֵּר אִתָּהּ?	איתיאל
LUD	I have nothing to discuss with her.	לִי אֵין דָּבָר לְדַבֵּר אִתָּהּ.	לוד
ITHIEL	Well, *you* wanted me to call her to come back	הֲלֹא אַתָּה חָפַצְתָּ, כִּי אֶקְרָא לָהּ לָשׁוּב	איתיאל
	And she can come back and go out and come back again	וְהִיא תוּכַל לָשׁוּב וְלָצֵאת וְלָשׁוּב עוֹד	
	And she can cry and obey me, as my lord says	וְתוּכַל לִבְכּוֹת וְלִשְׁמוֹעַ בְּקוֹלִי, כַּאֲשֶׁר אֲדֹנִי דִבֵּר	
	For she has an attentive ear, an overly attentive ear.	כִּי לָהּ אֹזֶן קַשֶּׁבֶת, אֹזֶן קַשֶּׁבֶת יֶתֶר מִדָּי.	
	Pour out your tears, woman, **give yourself no respite**[57]	שִׁפְכִי אִשָּׁה דִּמְעָתֵךְ, **אַל תִּתְּנִי פוּגַת לָךְ**[57]	

55 Prov. 15:11.
56 Isa. 27:1 (referring to the mythological sea creature Leviathan). Cf. Shakespeare's 'crocodile' (4.1.245).
57 Lam. 2:18.

	You know how to pretend; be gone from here until I send for you.	יוֹדַעַת אַתְּ לְהִתְחַפֵּשׂ; צְאִי מִזֶּה עַד אֶשְׁלַח אַחֲרָיִךְ.	
	And as for the letter, I am to return to Venice –	וְעַל אֹדוֹת הָאִגֶּרֶת, הִנְנִי לָשׁוּב לְוִינֶעצְיָא –	
	Be gone from here immediately. – *(Asenath exits)*	צְאִי מִזֶּה כְּרָגַע. – (אסנת יוצאת)	
	Chesed is to take my office – and I anticipate that your noble self	כֶּשֶׁד יִקַּח פְּקוּדָתִי – וּלְפָנֶיךָ הַנָּדִיב אוֹחִילָה	
	Will come eat with me in the evening.	כִּי תָבוֹא לֶאֱכָל־לֶחֶם אִתִּי בָּעֶרֶב.	
	Welcome to Caphtor! Welcome goats and monkeys!	שָׁלוֹם בּוֹאֲךָ לְכַפְתּוֹר! שָׁלוֹם שְׂעִירִים וְקֹפִים!	
	(Exits)	(הולך)	
LUD	Is this the mighty Cushite in whom	הֲזֶה הוּא הַכּוּשִׁי הָאַדִּיר, אֲשֶׁר בּוֹ בָטְחוּ	לוד
	All the counselling ministers have trusted as the pillar of the nation?	כָּל שָׂרֵי הָעֵצָה, כְּעַמּוּד הַתָּוֶךְ בַּמַּמְלָכָה?	
	Is this the powerful man, the hero who rules over his spirit	הֲזֶה הוּא הָעִזּוּז וְהַגִּבּוֹר הַמֹּשֵׁל בְּרוּחוֹ	
	And is this his strength of heart, he of whom they say	וְזֶה הוּא עֹז לִבּוֹ אֲשֶׁר יֹאמְרוּ עָלָיו	
	He regards the enemy's arrows as straw, and the rattling of the scimitar is a game to him?[58]	חִצֵּי אוֹיֵב יַחְשׁוֹב לְקַשׁ וְרַעַשׁ כִּידוֹן מִשְׂחָק לוֹ?[58]	
DOEG	**His heart is turned within him**[59] and he has become a different man.	לִבּוֹ נֶהְפַּךְ בְּקִרְבּוֹ[59] וַיְהִי לְאִישׁ אַחֵר.	דואג
LUD	Are his wits straight, and his sense has not departed?	הַאִם דַּעְתּוֹ יְשָׁרָה וְטַעֲמוֹ לֹא סָר?	לוד
DOEG	You see him as he is; I cannot give my opinion	הִנֵּה הוּא אֲשֶׁר הוּא; לְחַוּוֹת דֵּעִי לֹא אוּכָל	דואג
	If only he were now, as he was previously	מִי יִתֵּן וְהָיָה הוּא עַתָּה, כַּאֲשֶׁר הָיָה לְפָנִים	
	And not as he is today.	וְלֹא כַּאֲשֶׁר הוּא הַיּוֹם.	
LUD	But to strike his wife **for no fault**[60] –	אֲבָל לְהַכּוֹת אִשְׁתּוֹ בְּלִי עָוֺן[60] –	לוד
DOEG	On my life! This deed is not good	חֵי נַפְשִׁי! לֹא טוֹב הַמַּעֲשֶׂה הַזֶּה	דואג

58 Job 41:21 (41:29 in English Bibles) כְּקַשׁ נֶחְשְׁבוּ תוֹתָח וְיִשְׂחַק לְרַעַשׁ כִּידוֹן 'a club is regarded as a piece of straw, and he laughs at the rattling of the scimitar' (referring to the mythological sea creature Leviathan).

59 Lam. 1:20 נֶהְפַּךְ לִבִּי בְּקִרְבִּי 'my heart is turned within me'.

60 Ps. 59:5 (59:4 in English Bibles).

	But if only it were all his sin.	אַךְ מִי יִתֵּן וְהָיָה זֶה כָּל חַטָּאתוֹ.	
LUD	Is this his way, that he has grown accustomed to doing so,	הַאִם זֶה דַּרְכּוֹ, כִּי הִסְכִּין לַעֲשׂוֹת כֵּן	לוד
	Or perhaps the matter of the letter has made his blood boil today?	אוֹ אוּלַי דְּבַר הָאִגֶּרֶת, הִרְתִּיחַ דָּמוֹ הַיּוֹם?	
DOEG	My loyalty does not allow me to tell what I have seen and know	אֱמוּנָתִי לֹא תִתְּנֵנִי, לְהַגִּיד אֲשֶׁר רָאִיתִי וְיָדַעְתִּי	דואג
	But observe him and his ways will testify against him	אַךְ הִתְבּוֹנֵן בּוֹ וּדְרָכָיו יַעֲנוּ בְּפָנָיו	
	As for me, I shall put my hand to my mouth. Please go after him and see	וַאֲנִי אָשִׂים יָדִי לְפִי. לְכָה נָא אַחֲרָיו וּרְאֵה	
	What else he does.	מַה יּוֹסֵף לַעֲשׂוֹת.	
LUD	I am very sorry that my hope has been disappointed.	צַר לִי מְאֹד, כִּי בוֹשְׁתִּי מִתִּקְוָתִי.	לוד

SCENE I[61]	*A chamber in the citadel (Ithiel and Milcah)*	חדר במצודה (איתיאל ומלכה)	מחזה א'[61]
ITHIEL	And you did not see anything?	וְאַתְּ לֹא רָאִית דָּבָר?	איתיאל
MILCAH	Nor did I hear anything, and it did not occur to me.	וְגַם לֹא שָׁמַעְתִּי דָּבָר וְלֹא עָלָה עַל לִבִּי.	מלכה
ITHIEL	But nevertheless you saw her together with Chesed.	וּבְכָל זֹאת רָאִית אֹתָהּ עִם חֶסֶד יַחְדָּו.	איתיאל
MILCAH	But I saw no wrongdoing, although I heard	אֲבָל לֹא רָאִיתִי כָּל אָוֶן; אַף כִּי שָׁמַעְתִּי	מלכה
	Every single word that came out of their mouths.	כָּל מִלָּה וּמִלָּה*, אֲשֶׁר יָצְאָה מִפִּיהֶם.	
ITHIEL	Did they not whisper?	הַאִם לֹא הִתְלַחֲשׁוּ?	איתיאל
MILCAH	I never saw them whispering.	מֵעוֹדִי לֹא רְאִיתִים מִתְלַחֲשִׁים.	מלכה
ITHIEL	Did they not sometimes send you away from them?	הַאִם לֹא שִׁלְּחוּךְ** לְעִתִּים מֵעַל פְּנֵיהֶם?	איתיאל
MILCAH	They did not send me away from them, not even once.	לֹא שִׁלְּחוּנִי*** מֵעַל פְּנֵיהֶם, אַף לֹא פַּעַם אֶחָת.	מלכה
ITHIEL	To fetch something from outside, or from another chamber?	לְהָבִיא אֵיזֶה דָּבָר מִחוּץ, אוֹ מֵחֶדֶר אַחֵר?	איתיאל

61 Sic; should read 'SCENE 2'.

* מִלָּה וּמִלָּה
** שִׁלְּחוּךְ
*** שִׁלְּחוּנִי

MILCAH	They did not send me to fetch anything.	לֹא שְׁלָחוּנִי לְהָבִיא מְאוּמָה.	מלכה
ITHIEL	The matter is strange in my eyes.	זָר הַדָּבָר בְּעֵינָי.	איתיאל
MILCAH	I place my own life as surety that she is pure and blameless,	אֲנִי בְנַפְשִׁי אֶעֶרְבֶנָּה, כִּי טְהוֹרָה וּנְקִיָּה הִיא,	מלכה
	And now my lord, please remove wicked thoughts from within you	וְעַתָּה הָסֵר אֲדֹנִי, מַחְשָׁבָה רָעָה מִקִּרְבֶּךָ	
	For this is not fitting for a **pure-hearted**[62] man such as you.	כִּי כֵן לֹא יָאֲתָה לְבַר לֵבָב[62] כָּמוֹךָ.	
	And if some villain has incited you against her	וְאִם הֱסִיתְךָ בָּהּ, אֶחָד מִבְּנֵי בְלִיַּעַל	
	He is as cursed as the serpent under the LORD's heavens,	אָרוּר הוּא כַּנָּחָשׁ תַּחַת שְׁמֵי אֲדֹנָי,	
	For if your wife is not honest, pure, and innocent,	כִּי אִם אֵין אִשְׁתְּךָ יְשָׁרָה בָּרָה וּתְמִימָה	
	There is no good woman on the earth and there is no helpmeet for man	אֵין אִשָּׁה טוֹבָה בָּאָרֶץ וְעֵזֶר לָאָדָם אָיִן	
	And even the best one among them is as much of an abomination as a slanderer in secret.	וְגַם הַטּוֹבָה בְּכֻלָּן, תּוֹעֵבָה הִיא כִּמַלְשִׁין* בַּסָּתֶר.	
ITHIEL	Go and tell her to come here. *(She exits)*	לְכִי וְאִמְרִי לָהּ לָבוֹא הֵנָּה. (הולכת)	איתיאל
	Who would listen to the testimony of her mouth, for she says her words	מִי יִשְׁמַע לְעֵדוּת פִּיהָ, כִּי תַגִּיד דְּבָרֶיהָ	
	Like any whorehouse madam. But my wife is a cunning whore	כְּכָל בַּעֲלַת בֵּית זוֹנָה. וְאִשְׁתִּי זוֹנָה עֲרוּמָה	
	She commits her vile acts behind lock and key,	תַּעֲשֶׂה אֶת תּוֹעֲבוֹתֶיהָ מִבַּעַד לְמַנְעוּל וּבְרִיחַ,	
	And nevertheless my eyes have seen that she kneels to her God	וּבְכָל זֹאת רָאוּ עֵינַי, כִּי תִכְרַע לֵאלֹהֶיהָ	
	And does not reduce her prayers.	וּתְפִלָּתָהּ לֹא תִגְרָע.	
	(Milcah re-enters with Asenath)	(מלכה שבה עם אסנת)	
ASENATH	Here I am, my lord – what do you seek from me?	הִנְנִי אֲדֹנִי – מַה תְּבַקֵּשׁ מֶנִּי?	אסנת

62 Ps. 24:4.

* כְּמַלְשִׁין

ITHIEL	Come, my dove, come to me.	בּוֹאִי נָא יוֹנָתִי, בּוֹאִי נָא אֵלָי.	איתיאל
ASENATH	Here I am – what is your desire?	הִנֵּנִי – מָה חֶפְצֵךְ?	אסנת
ITHIEL	Show me your eyes, look me in the eye.	הַרְאִינִי אֶת עֵינַיִךְ, הַבִּיטִי בִי עַיִן בְּעָיִן.	איתיאל
ASENATH	What further **strange things and perversities**[63] do you seek from me?	מַה־זָּרוֹת וְתַהְפֻּכוֹת[63] תְּבַקֵּשׁ מֶנִּי עוֹד?	אסנת
ITHIEL	*(To Milcah)* Do your office with the whores;	(אל מלכה) עֲשִׂי פְקוּדָתֵךְ אִם הַזּוֹנוֹת,	איתיאל
	Leave the two lovers alone and close the door,	הַנִּיחִי לִשְׁנֵי הַנֶּאֱהָבִים לְבַדָּם וְסִגְרִי אֶת הַדֶּלֶת,	
	And if someone comes, sneeze and whistle to warn us;	וְהָיָה אִם יָבֹא אִישׁ, תְּזוֹרְרִי וְתִשְׁרְקִי לְהַזְהִירֵנוּ,	
	Quickly, leave here and stand at your post.	מַהֲרִי צְאִי מִזֶּה וְעִמְדִי עַל מִשְׁמַרְתֵּךְ.	
	(Milcah exits)	(מלכה הולכת)	
ASENATH	On my knees I beg before you, explain your words to me,	עַל בִּרְכַּי אֶתְחַנָּן לְפָנֶיךָ בָּאֵר לִי דְבָרֶיךָ,	אסנת
	Your fury terrifies me, and I do not understand the words of your mouth.	זַעַף אַפְּךָ יְבַעֲתַנִי וְאִמְרֵי פִיךָ לֹא אָבִין.	
ITHIEL	Tell me who you are?	הַגִּידִי לִי מִי אָתְּ?	איתיאל
ASENATH	I am **the wife of your bosom,**[64] my lord, the faithful **wife of your covenant**.[65]	**אֵשֶׁת חֵיקְךָ**[64] אֲדֹנִי, **אֵשֶׁת בְּרִיתְךָ**[65] הַנֶּאֱמָנָה.	אסנת
ITHIEL	Swear to me falsely, in order that your iniquity be completed	הִשָּׁבְעִי לִי לַשֶּׁקֶר לְמַעַן יִמָּלֵא עֲוֹנֵךְ	איתיאל
	And so that evil angels will no longer be able to say in their heart	וְלֹא יֹאמְרוּ עוֹד מַלְאָכִים רָעִים בִּלְבָבָם	
	That you fear God and be afraid to touch you,	יְרֵאַת אֱלֹהִים אַתְּ וּפָחֲדוּ מִנְּגֹעַ בָּךְ,	
	Therefore, swear on your soul that you have not desecrated your covenant	לָכֵן הִשָּׁבְעִי בְנַפְשֵׁךְ כִּי לֹא חִלַּלְתְּ בְּרִיתֵךְ	

63 Prov. 23:33 עֵינֶיךָ יִרְאוּ זָרוֹת וְלִבְּךָ יְדַבֵּר תַּהְפֻּכוֹת 'your eyes see strange things, and your heart utters perversities'.
64 Deut. 13:7 (13:6 in English Bibles).
65 Mal. 2:14.

	And your soul will be doubly guilty.	וְאָשְׁמָה נַפְשֵׁךְ כִּפְלָיִם.	
ASENATH	**By the faithful witness in heaven,**[66] I am pure.	**עֵד בַּשַּׁחַק נֶאֱמָן,**[66] כִּי טְהוֹרָה אָנִי.	אסנת
ITHIEL	**By the faithful witness in heaven,**[67] you are false.	**עֵד בַּשַּׁחַק נֶאֱמָן,**[67] כִּי כֹזֶבֶת אָתְּ.	איתיאל
ASENATH	To whom have I then been false? When have I spoken falsely?	לְמִי אֵיפוֹא כִּזַּבְתִּי? מָתַי דִּבַּרְתִּי כְּזָבִים?	אסנת
ITHIEL	It is bitter for me, Asenath, bitter; get out, get out of my sight.	מַר לִי מָר אָסְנַת, צְאִי צְאִי מֵעַל פָּנָי.	איתיאל
ASENATH	Oh, bitter day! Why do you weep, Ithiel?	אֲהָהּ לַיּוֹם הַמָּר! לָמָּה זֶּה תִבְכֶּה אִיתִיאֵל?	אסנת
	Have I caused your tears? Perhaps you are saying in your heart	הֶאָנֹכִי סִבֹּתִי בְדִמְעָתֶךָ? אוּלַי תֹּאמַר בִּלְבָבֶךָ	
	That on the advice of my father at the gate you have been summoned to return from here?	כִּי בַּעֲצַת אָבִי בַּשַּׁעַר, נִקְרֵאתָ לָשׁוּב מִזֶּה;	
	But what am I, that you place iniquity upon me?	אַךְ מָה אֲנִי, כִּי תָשֶׁת עָלַי עָוֹן?	
	If he has abandoned you and has refused to be a father to you	אִם הוּא עֲזָבְךָ וַיְמָאֵן לִהְיוֹת לְךָ לְאָב	
	Then I have also been abandoned, and am regarded as a stranger to him.	כֵּן נֶעֱזַבְתִּי גַם אֲנִי וְנָכְרִיָּה נֶחְשַׁבְתִּי לוֹ.	
ITHIEL	If only God would test me with great **distress and anguish**;[68]	לוּ יְנַסֵּנִי אֱלֹהִים, בְּרֹב **צָרָה וְצוּקָה**;[68]	איתיאל
	If only He would rain down on my head **fire and brimstone from the heavens**;[69]	לוּ יַמְטִיר עַל רֹאשִׁי, **אֵשׁ וְגָפְרִית מִן הַשָּׁמַיִם**;[69]	
	If He were to give my possessions over as plunder so that I lacked my food and my clothing;	יִתֵּן רְכוּשִׁי לְבִזָּה וְלַחְמִי וְשִׂמְלָתִי אֶחְסַר;	
	Or if He were to take me into captivity, with no **hope or future**,[70]	אוֹ יוֹלִיכֵנִי בַּשִּׁבְיָה, בְּאֶפֶס **תִּקְוָה וְאַחֲרִית**[70]	

66 Ps. 89:38 (89:37 in English Bibles).
67 Ps. 89:38 (89:37 in English Bibles).
68 Isa. 30:6; Prov. 1:27.
69 Midrash Tanḥuma to Gen. 18:1–22:24; Alshekh to Exod. 16 and 2 Sam. 22.
70 Jer. 29:11 אַחֲרִית וְתִקְוָה 'a future and a hope'.

	I would still find comfort as long as my soul was within me.	עוֹד אֶמְצָא נֹחַם, כָּל עוֹד נַפְשִׁי בִי.	
	But to set me up as the target for arrows of **scorn and derision**[71]	אַךְ לְהַצִּיבֵנִי כְּמַטָּרָה, לְחִצֵּי לַעַג וָקֶלֶס[71]	
	To become a spectacle all day and an amusement for every passer-by	לִהְיוֹת לְרַאֲוָה כָּל הַיּוֹם וּלְמִשְׂחָק לְכָל עֹבֵר	
	Aah, who could endure it?	אֲהָהּ מִי יוּכַל לַעֲמֹד!	
	But even in such an **iron furnace**[72] perhaps I shall prevail, and emerge refined	וְגַם בְּכוּר בַּרְזֶל[72] כָּזֶה, אוּלַי אֶתְגַּבֵּר וְאֵצֵא מְזֻקָּק	
	But it has destroyed the spring **from which comes the source of my life**[73]	אַךְ הוּא הִשְׁחִית הַמַּבּוּעַ מִמֶּנּוּ תּוֹצְאוֹת חַיָּתִי[73]	
	And my well on which I live, or I would cease to be,	וּבְאֵרִי, עָלֶיהָ אֲנִי חַי, אוֹ חָדֵל אָנִי,	
	Has become **a strange narrow well**,[74] full of **scum and refuse.**[75]	הָיְתָה לִבְאֵר צָרָה נָכְרִיָּה,[74] מְלֵאָה סְחִי וּמָאוֹס.[75]	
	In it **a snail melts as it goes along**,[76] and frogs dance there	בָּהּ שַׁבְּלוּל תֶּמֶס יַהֲלֹךְ[76] וּצְפַרְדְּעִים יְכַרְכְּרוּ שָׁם	
	And who could still have hope in this **valley of troubles**![77] –	וּמִי יְיַחֵל עוֹד בְּעֵמֶק עָכוֹר[77] הַזֶּה! –	
ASENATH	I hope, my lord, that you regard me as faithful.	קִוְּתָה נַפְשִׁי אֲדֹנִי, כִּי לְנֶאֱמָנָה תַּחְשְׁבֵנִי.	אסנת
ITHIEL	I regard you as the summer flies in the slaughterhouse	חֲשַׁבְתִּיךְ כִּזְבוּבֵי קַיִץ, בְּבֵית הַמִּטְבָּח	איתיאל
	Who leave their eggs in the meat, and **that which is crushed hatches into a maggot**[78]	הָעֹזְבִים בַּבָּשָׂר בֵּיצֵיהֶם וְהַזּוּרָה תִּבָּקַע רִמָּה[78]	

71 Ps. 44:14 (44:13 in English Bibles), 79:4.
72 Deut. 4:20; 1 Kings 8:51; Jer. 11:4.
73 Prov. 4:23 כִּי־מִמֶּנּוּ תּוֹצְאוֹת חַיִּים 'for from it come the sources of life'.
74 Prov. 23:27 כִּי־שׁוּחָה עֲמֻקָּה זוֹנָה וּבְאֵר צָרָה נָכְרִיָּה 'for a whore is a deep pit, and a strange woman is a narrow well'.
75 Lam. 3:45.
76 Ps. 58:9 (58:8 in English Bibles). The meaning of this biblical expression is unclear, although it seems to form part of a curse (Berlin and Brettler 2004a: 1345).
77 Joshua 7:24, 15:7; Isa. 65:10; Hosea 2:17 (originally a place name, the Valley of Achor, this term came to be used as an epithet for a place of suffering and trouble; see Even-Shoshan 2003, 4: 1373).
78 Isa. 59:5 וְהַזּוּרֶה תִּבָּקַע אֶפְעֶה 'and that which is crushed hatches into a viper'.

	Woe, **alien vine**![79] How beautiful your appearance is	הוֹי זְמֹרַת זָר![79] מַרְאֵךְ מַה־נָּאוֶה	
	And how pleasant is **the fragrance of your oils**[80] – if only you had not emerged into the light of the world.	וּמַה־נֶּחְמָד רֵיחַ שְׁמָנַיִךְ[80] – לוּ לֹא יָצָאת לְאוֹר עוֹלָם.	
ASENATH	What is my crime, and what is my sin? How have I erred, inform me?	מַה־פִּשְׁעִי וּמַה חַטָּאתִי? מַה־שָּׁגִיתִי הוֹדִיעֵנִי?	אסנת
ITHIEL	How can a splendid paper have the name of whore inscribed upon it?	אֵיךְ גִּלָּיוֹן הָדוּר, יִכָּתֵב עָלָיו שֵׁם זוֹנָה?	איתיאל
	A scroll more precious than gold, with the name of prostitute[81] on the title page? –	סֵפֶר יָקָר מִפָּז, שֵׁם קְדֵשָׁה[81] עַל הַשַּׁעַר? –	
	How have I erred, you ask, a whore **in an open place**![82]	מַה־שָּׁגִיתִי תִּשְׁאָלִי, זוֹנָה **בְּפֶתַח עֵינָיִם**![82]	
	When I tell your sin, my cheeks will redden like fire,	כִּי אַגִּיד חַטָּאתֵךְ, יַאְדִּימוּ לְחָיַי כָּאֵשׁ,	
	And my humility will disappear from my face like straw in **a heated oven**;[83]	וַעֲנָוָתִי תִּכְלֶה מֵעַל פָּנַי, כְּקַשׁ **בְּתַנּוּר בֹּעֵרָה**;[83]	
	If I made known in public what you did in secret	אִם אַשְׁמִיעַ בַּגָּלוּי, אֵת אֲשֶׁר עָשִׂית בַּסָּתֶר	
	The moon would be too abashed to listen, and the sun would be ashamed[84]	**וְחָפְרָה הַלְּבָנָה** מִשְּׁמֹעַ **וּבוֹשָׁה הַחַמָּה**[84]	
	And the earth would not endure your disgrace, **sly-hearted whore**![85]	וְהָאָרֶץ לֹא תָכִיל חֶרְפָּתֵךְ, **זוֹנָה נְצוּרַת לֵב**![85]	
ASENATH	**I raise my hand up on high**,[86] that you attack me without cause.	**הֲרִימֹתִי יָדִי** לַמָּרוֹם,[86] כִּי תִּתְגּוֹלֵל עָלַי חִנָּם.	אסנת

79 Isa. 17:10.

80 Song of Songs 1:3, 4:10.

81 In the Hebrew Bible this word is typically translated as ‘cult prostitute’, ‘temple prostitute’, or ‘shrine prostitute’ (see, e.g., Deut. 23:18 [23:17 in English Bibles]), and is generally understood as referring to sacred prostitution, which was a common feature of the ancient Near East and is particularly associated with the Canaanite goddess Astarte. However, Salkinson seems to be using it in the straightforward sense of ‘prostitute, whore’, which is thought to have evolved in the modern period (Even-Shoshan 2003, 5: 1632).

82 Gen. 38:18 (referring to Judah’s daughter-in-law Tamar, who dressed up as a temple prostitute in order to trick Judah into honouring his broken vow to her).

83 Hosea 7:4.

84 Isa. 24:23 וְחָפְרָה הַלְּבָנָה וּבוֹשָׁה הַחַמָּה ‘the moon will be abashed and the sun ashamed’.

85 Prov. 7:10 שִׁית זוֹנָה וּנְצֻרַת לֵב ‘dressed as a whore and sly-hearted’.

86 Gen. 14:22 הֲרִימֹתִי יָדִי אֶל־יְהוָה ‘I raise my hand up to the Lord’.

ITHIEL	Are you not an adulteress?	לֹא מְנָאֶפֶת אָתְּ?	איתיאל
ASENATH	On my faith, by the God of my salvation,[87] I am innocent of any crime;	בֶּאֱמוּנָתִי בֵּאלֹהֵי יִשְׁעִי,[87] חַפָּה אֲנִי מִפֶּשַׁע,	אסנת
	If I have guarded my vessels so that no stranger's hand might touch them	אִם שָׁמַרְתִּי אֶת כֵּלַי מִנְּגֹעַ בָּהֶם יַד זָר;	
	And have known only my husband, and have not given my honour to another,	וְאֶת אִישִׁי לְבַדּוֹ יָדַעְתִּי וּכְבוֹדִי לְאַחֵר לֹא נָתַתִּי,	
	If this is a righteous path and not a treacherous path,	אִם זֹאת דֶּרֶךְ יְשָׁרָה וְלֹא דֶּרֶךְ בּוֹגֵדָה,	
	Then I am not a treacherous woman.	אִשָּׁה בּוֹגֵדָה אֵינֶנִּי.	
ITHIEL	And are you not a prostitute?[88]	וְלֹא קְדֵשָׁה[88] אָתְּ?	איתיאל
ASENATH	No, no, may God help me.	לֹא, לֹא, יְהִי כֵן אֱלֹהִים בְּעֶזְרִי.	אסנת
ITHIEL	Is the matter so?	הַאִם כֵּן הַדָּבָר?	איתיאל
ASENATH	Please save me, my God, please save us!	אָנָּא הוֹשִׁיעָה אֵלִי, הוֹשִׁיעָה נָּא לָנוּ!	אסנת
ITHIEL	Forgive me this time;	סִלְחִי לִי הַפָּעַם;	איתיאל
	Here I in my haste thought you to be a cunning whore from Venice.	וַאֲנִי בְּחָפְזִי חֲשַׁבְתִּיךְ לְזוֹנָה עֲרוּמָה מִוִּינֶעצְיָא	
	And Ithiel became her husband – come back, Milcah.	וְאִיתִיאֵל הָיָה לָהּ לְבַעַל – שׁוּבִי מִלְכָּה.	
	(Milcah re-enters)	(מלכה שבה)	
	The key to the heavens is in the hand of Petros,[89] and the key to Sheol is in your hand;	מַפְתֵּחַ הַשָּׁמַיִם בְּיַד פֶּטְרוֹס[89] וּמַפְתֵּחַ הַשְּׁאוֹל בְּיָדֵךְ,	
	You are the woman – you are she, and no other –	אַתְּ הִיא הָאִשָּׁה – אַתְּ הִיא וְלֹא אַחֶרֶת –	

87 Mic. 7:7; Hab. 3:18; Ps. 25:5; Ps. 27:9. Cf. Shakespeare's 'as I am a Christian' (4.2.84). Salkinson's version is religiously neutral; however, Scolnicov (2001: 188) suggests that his selection of the word יִשְׁעִי 'my salvation' was intended as a veiled punning reference to יֵשׁוּעַ 'Jesus'.

88 See note 81.

89 Cf. Shakespeare's 'Saint Peter' (4.2.93). This is noteworthy as one of the only instances in either of Salkinson's Shakespeare translations in which he leaves a Christian reference intact. Note the Italianate suffix -os, comparable to 'Marcos' (First Part, note 155).

	Indeed we have completed the matter of our desire; here's money for your wages	הֵן כִּלִּינוּ דְבַר חֶפְצֵנוּ, הֵא לָךְ כֶּסֶף בִּשְׂכָרֵךְ	
	Open the door for me and let no man enter our confidence. *(Exits)*	פִּתְחִי לִי הַדֶּלֶת וְאַל יָבוֹא אִישׁ בְּסוֹדֵנוּ. (הולך)	
MILCAH	This man, I do not know what has happened to him –	הָאִישׁ הַזֶּה, לֹא יָדַעְתִּי מֶה הָיָה לוֹ –	מלכה
	What is wrong with you, my lady, what is wrong with you, my precious lady?	מַה־לָּךְ גְּבִרְתִּי, מַה־לָּךְ גְּבִרְתִּי הַיְקָרָה?	
ASENATH	I am like one dreaming.	כְּחוֹלֶמֶת אָנִי.	אסנת
MILCAH	Tell me, my lady, what has happened to my lord?	הַגִּידִי לִי גְּבִרְתִּי, מֶה הָיָה לַאֲדֹנִי?	מלכה
ASENATH	To which lord?	לְאֵי־זֶה אָדוֹן?	אסנת
MILCAH	To my lord, I say.	לַאֲדֹנִי אָמַרְתִּי.	מלכה
ASENATH	Who is your lord?	מִי הוּא אֲדֹנֵךְ?	אסנת
MILCAH	Your lord is my lord.	אֲדֹנֵךְ הוּא אֲדֹנִי.	מלכה
ASENATH	I have no lord; do not speak further to me Milcah	אֵין לִי אָדוֹן; אַל תּוֹסִיפִי דַּבֵּר אֵלַי מִלְכָּה	אסנת
	I have no strength to weep; my **fountain of tears**[90] has dried up	אֵין בִּי כֹחַ לִבְכּוֹת, מְקוֹר דִּמְעָתִי[90] יָבֵשׁ	
	And I cannot give a reply. Put my wedding garments	וְתֵת מַעֲנֶה לֹא אוּכָל. שִׁיתִי בִּגְדֵי חֲתֻנָּתִי	
	On my bed tonight; remember this, and do not forget	עַל מִטָּתִי הַלַּיְלָה; זִכְרִי זֹאת וְאַל תִּשְׁכָּחִי	
	And call your husband to me.	וְקִרְאִי לִי אֶת בַּעְלֵךְ.	
MILCAH	*(As she exits)* How her day has changed for her!	(בלכתה) אֵיךְ נֶהְפַּךְ עָלֶיהָ יוֹמָהּ!	מלכה
ASENATH	Is he treating me as I deserve today?	הַאִם כִּגְמוּל יָדַי הוּא עֹשֶׂה לִי הַיּוֹם?	אסנת
	What wrong, **what disgrace**[91] has he found in me	מֶה עָוֶל, מַה־שֶּׁמֶץ דָּבָר[91] מָצָא בִי	

90 Jer. 8:23 (9:1 in English Bibles) מִי־יִתֵּן רֹאשִׁי מַיִם וְעֵינִי מְקוֹר דִּמְעָה 'if only my head were waters and my eye a fountain of tears'.

91 Job 26:14 וּמַה־שֵּׁמֶץ דָּבָר נִשְׁמַע־בּוֹ 'and how faint (or: whispering) a word is heard of Him'. See Third Part, note 56 for discussion of Salkinson's use of this expression.

	That he accuses me without cause and places a great sin upon me?	כִּי יַרְשִׁיעֵנִי חִנָּם וַיָּשֶׁת עָלַי חֲטָאָה גְדֹלָה?	
	(Milcah re-enters with Doeg)	(מלכה שבה עם דואג)	
DOEG	How is the lady? What is her command, and it will be done.	הֲשָׁלוֹם לַגְּבִירָה? מַה־פְּקוּדָתָהּ וְתֵעָשׂ.	דואג
ASENATH	I cannot answer. One who disciplines a child	לֹא אוּכַל לַעֲנוֹת. הַמּוֹכִיחַ לַיֶּלֶד	אסנת
	Chastises him with a light rebuke and does not push him away with both hands	יְיַסְּרֶנּוּ בְּמוּסָר קַל וְלֹא יַדִּיחֶנּוּ בִּשְׁתֵּי יָדַיִם	
	So why did he not also chastise me in this manner	וְלָמָּה לֹא יְסְּרַנִי גַּם הוּא כַּמִּשְׁפָּט הַזֶּה	
	For with respect to enduring rebukes and reprimands, I am still a girl.	כִּי לָשֵׂאת גְּעָרָה וְתוֹכַחַת, עוֹדֶנִּי יַלְדָּה אָנִי.	
DOEG	What has happened here, my lady?	מַה־נִּהְיְתָה פֹּה גְּבִרְתִּי?	דואג
MILCAH	Oh, Doeg, my lord called her **a wife of whoredom**[92]	אֲהָהּ דוֹאֵג, אֲדֹנִי קָרָא לָהּ **אֵשֶׁת זְנוּנִים**[92]	מלכה
	And poured contempt and shame on **a precious soul**,[93] **too much to bear**.[94]	וַיִּשְׁפֹּךְ בּוּז וְקָלוֹן עַל **נֶפֶשׁ יְקָרָה**[93] **מִרְבָּה לְהָכִיל**.[94]	
ASENATH	Is this name fitting for me?	הֲנָכוֹן לִי הַשֵּׁם הַזֶּה?	אסנת
DOEG	Which name?	אֵיזֶה שֵׁם?	דואג
ASENATH	The name that your wife said, which my husband gave to me.	הַשֵּׁם נָקְבָה אִשְׁתְּךָ, אֲשֶׁר נָתַן לִי בַּעֲלִי.	אסנת
MILCAH	He called her a whore. Even a pauper through whom wine has flowed	זוֹנָה קָרָא לָהּ. גַּם אֶבְיוֹן אֲשֶׁר יַיִן עֲבָרוֹ	מלכה
	Would not give this name to his wife because she vexes him.	לֹא יִתֵּן הַשֵּׁם הַזֶּה לְאִשְׁתּוֹ כִּי תַכְעִיסֶנּוּ.	
DOEG	So why did he do this?	וּמַדּוּעַ עָשָׂה זֹאת?	דואג
ASENATH	This I do not know; I know only one thing	זֹאת לֹא יָדַעְתִּי, רַק אַחַת יָדַעְתִּי	אסנת

92 Hosea 1:2.
93 Prov. 6:26.
94 Ezek. 23:32.

	That he has never seen **an indecent thing**[95] in me.	**כִּי עֶרְוַת דָּבָר**,[95] לֹא רָאָה בִּי מֵעוֹדוֹ.	
DOEG	Restrain your voice, my lady, **restrain your voice from weeping**[96]	מִנְעִי קוֹלֵךְ גְּבִרְתִּי, **מִנְעִי קוֹלֵךְ מִבֶּכִי**[96]	דואג
	Woe to the day!	אֲהָהּ לַיּוֹם!	
MILCAH	Did she indeed refuse princes who wanted to take her	הֲכִי הֵשִׁיבָה פְּנֵי שָׂרִים אֲשֶׁר רָצוּ לְקַחְתָּהּ	מלכה
	And leave her land, her native land, and her father	וַתַּעֲזֹב אֶת אַרְצָהּ, אֶת מוֹלַדְתָּהּ וְאֶת אָבִיהָ	
	In order to be called by the name of whore? Now, who would not **fall down weeping**?[97]	לְהִקָּרֵא בְּשֵׁם זוֹנָה? וּמִי לֹא **יוֹרֵד בַּבֶּכִי**?[97]	
ASENATH	Such is my wicked fate.	כֵּן הוּא גוֹרָלִי הָרָע.	אסנת
DOEG	Raise your voice to him and rebuke him	הָרִימִי קוֹלֵךְ עָלָיו וְגַעֲרִי בוֹ	דואג
	Who has mixed this spirit of confusion within him?[98]	**מִי מָסַךְ בְּקִרְבּוֹ רוּחַ עִוְעִים** זֶה?[98]	
ASENATH	God only knows.	הָאֱלֹהִים לְבַדּוֹ יוֹדֵעַ.	אסנת
MILCAH	I'll give my soul to killers if it is not **one of the foolish fellows**[99]	נַפְשִׁי אֶתֵּן לַמְּמִיתִים, אִם לֹא **אַחַד הָרֵקִים**[99]	מלכה
	A rascal and a cunning hypocrite, **a despicable slave**[100] and a villain	נָבָל וְחָנֵף עָרוּם, **עֶבֶד נִבְזֶה**[100] וּבְלִיַּעַל	
	Has brought the libel against her in order to obtain one of the offices	הוֹצִיא הַדִּבָּה עָלֶיהָ, לְמַעַן הַשֵּׂג אַחַת הַכְּהֻנּוֹת	
	If his hand is not in this, I'll give my soul to killers.	אִם לֹא יָדוֹ בָזֹּאת, אֶתֵּן נַפְשִׁי לַמְּמִיתִים.	
DOEG	It is a vain oath; there is no such man on earth.	שְׁבוּעַת שָׁוְא הִיא; אֵין אִישׁ כָּזֶה בָּאָרֶץ.	דואג
ASENATH	But if there is such a one on earth, may God forgive him.	וְאִם יֶשְׁנוֹ בָּאָרֶץ, הָאֱלֹהִים יְכַפֵּר בַּעֲדוֹ.	אסנת
MILCAH	May only a noose pardon him	רַק הַחֶבֶל יְכַפֵּר בַּעֲדוֹ	מלכה

95 Deut. 23:15 (23:14 in English Bibles), 24:1.
96 Jer. 31:16.
97 Isa. 15:3.
98 Isa. 19:14 יְהוָה מָסַךְ בְּקִרְבָּהּ רוּחַ עִוְעִים 'the LORD has mixed a spirit of confusion within her'.
99 2 Sam. 6:20.
100 Alshekh to Eccles. 10.

	And may his bones be broken apart in hell. Why did he call her a whore?	וְעַצְמוֹתָיו יִתְפָּרְקוּ בְּגֵיהִנֹּם. לָמָּה קָרָא לָהּ זוֹנָה?	
	Who has come to her? To whom has she raised her eyes?	מִי בָּא אֵלֶיהָ? אֶל מִי נָשְׂאָה עֵינֶיהָ?	
	On which day, in which place? Does this lie have substance?[101]	בְּאֵיזֶה יוֹם, בְּאֵיזֶה מָקוֹם? הֲיֵשׁ רַגְלַיִם[101] לַשֶּׁקֶר הַזֶּה?	
	It is nothing other than that the Cushite, falsely seduced, led astray	אֵין זֶה כִּי אִם הַכּוּשִׁי, נִדַּח בַּשָּׁוְא נִתְעֶה	
	By cunning of **the son of a base man,**[102] **a disgraceful and shameful son**[103]	בְּעָרְמַת **בֶּן בְּלִי שֵׁם,**[102] **בֵּן מֵבִישׁ וּמַחְפִּיר**[103]	
	An **abominable and vile**[104] rascal. If only the heavens	**נָבָל נִתְעָב וְנֶאֱלָח.**[104] מִי יִתֵּן וְהַשָּׁמַיִם	
	Would reveal the iniquity of this man and the hand of every honest man	יְגַלּוּ עֲוֹן הָאִישׁ הַזֶּה וְיַד כָּל אָדָם יָשָׁר	
	Would seize **a rod for whipping**[105] and lead the worthless one naked	תֹּאחַז **בְּמַקֵּל חֹבְלִים**[105] וְהוֹלִיכוּ אֶת הַנִּקְלֶה עָרוֹם	
	Smiting him as they led him all over the land, from east to west.	הוֹלֵיךְ וְהַכּוֹת אֹתוֹ בְּכָל הָאָרֶץ, מִמִּזְרָח וְעַד מַעֲרָב.	
DOEG	Slowly, slowly, woman, do not make your voice heard outside.	לְאַט לְאַט אִשָּׁה, אַל תַּשְׁמִיעִי קוֹלֵךְ הַחוּצָה.	דואג
MILCAH	May mention of him be ignominy outside. Maybe this is the villain	יְהִי זִכְרוֹ לְקָלוֹן בַּחוּץ. אוּלַי הוּא זֶה הַבְּלִיָּעַל	מלכה
	Who led you astray as well, saying	אֲשֶׁר הוֹלִיכֵךְ שׁוֹלָל גַּם אַתְּ לֵאמֹר	
	That the Cushite **had spread his garment over me.**[106]	הַכּוּשִׁי **פָּרַשׂ כְּנָפוֹ עָלָי.**[106]	
DOEG	That's enough from you, foolish woman, arise and get out.	רַב לָךְ אֵשֶׁת אִוֶּלֶת, קוּמִי וּצְאִי לָךְ.	דואג
ASENATH	Tell me, dear Doeg, what then should I do	הַגִּידָה דוֹאֵג הַיָּקָר, מָה אֵיפוֹא אֶעֱשֶׂה	אסנת

101 This is a postbiblical expression first appearing in the Mishnah (e.g., *Oholot* 16:3 רגלים לדבר 'the matter has substance').

102 Job 30:8 בְּנֵי־נָבָל גַּם־בְּנֵי בְלִי־שֵׁם 'sons of fools, indeed sons of base men'.

103 Prov. 19:26.

104 Job 15:16.

105 This is a modern expression based on Zech. 11:7 וָאֶקַּח־לִי שְׁנֵי מַקְלוֹת לְאַחַד קָרָאתִי נֹעַם וּלְאַחַד קָרָאתִי חֹבְלִים 'and I took two rods; I called one Beauty and the other Bands' (see Even-Shoshan 2003, 3: 1081).

106 Ruth 3:9 וַתֹּאמֶר אָנֹכִי רוּת אֲמָתֶךָ וּפָרַשְׂתָּ כְנָפֶךָ עַל־אֲמָתְךָ 'and she said, "I am your maidservant Ruth; spread your garment over your maidservant"' (i.e., marry your maidservant).

	In order to win back the heart of my husband? You go and speak kindly to him.	לְהָשִׁיב לֵב בַּעֲלִי, לֵךְ אַתָּה וְדַבֵּר עַל לִבּוֹ.	
	I raise my hand up on high[107] that I do not know why he has turned away from me.	הֲרִימֹתִי יָדִי לַמָּרוֹם,[107] אִם יָדַעְתִּי לָמָּה חָמַק מִמֶּנִּי.	
	Before the One who **examines the kidneys and the heart**,[108] on my knees I say	לִפְנֵי הַבֹּחֵן כְּלָיוֹת וָלֵב,[108] עַל בִּרְכַּי הִנְנִי מַגֶּדֶת	
	If I have violated my holy covenant between me and my husband;	אִם הֵפַרְתִּי בְּרִית קָדְשִׁי, בֵּינִי וּבֵין בַּעֲלִי;	
	If I have ever sinned, in speech, in thought, or in deed	אִם חָטָאתִי מֵעוֹדִי, בְּאֹמֶר בְּמַחֲשָׁבָה וּבְמַעֲשֶׂה	
	And have desired a stranger's form, rather than his;	וָאֶחְשַׁק בְּתֹאַר זָר בִּלְתִּי תֹאַר פָּנָיו;	
	If my love for him is not as strong today as previously	אִם לֹא עַזָּה אַהֲבָתִי אֵלָיו הַיּוֹם כְּקֶדֶם	
	And if my love departs, even if he drives me out from his house,	וְאִם תָּמוּשׁ אַהֲבָתִי, אַף כִּי יְשַׁלְּחֵנִי מִבֵּיתוֹ	
	Do not save me, my God! –	אַל תּוֹשִׁיעֵנִי אֱלֹהָי! –	
	Harsh matters, matters too harsh for me, and his harsh hand may kill me,	דְּבָרִים קָשִׁים, קָשִׁים מִמֶּנִּי וְיָדוֹ הַקָּשָׁה תְּמִיתֵנִי	
	But until I die I shall not remove my love.	אַךְ עַד אֶגְוַע לֹא אָסִיר אַהֲבָתִי.	
	I cannot bring the name whore to my lips	לֹא אוּכַל לְהַעֲלוֹת שֵׁם זוֹנָה עַל שְׂפָתַי	
	And when I mention it on this day **all my bones tremble**[109]	וְכִי אַזְכִּירוֹ בַּיּוֹם הַזֶּה יִרְחֲפוּ כָּל עַצְמוֹתָי[109]	
	But to commit the sin and be called by the name of my deed	אַךְ לַעֲשׂוֹת הַחֲטָאָה וּלְהִקָּרֵא עַל שֵׁם פְּעוּלָּתִי	
	Even if the earth were given to me as my wages, I would not do this.	אִם תִּנָּתֵן לִי הָאָרֶץ בִּשְׂכָרִי, לֹא אֶעֱשֶׂה זֹאת.	
DOEG	Please be strong, my lady, distress will not arise twice;	הִתְחַזְּקִי נָא גְּבִרְתִּי, לֹא תָקוּם צָרָה פַּעֲמַיִם,	דואג
	Why, it is due to matters of the nation that **his spirit is broken**[110] at this time	הֲלֹא מִדִּבְרֵי הַמְּדִינָה רוּחוֹ נְכֵאָה[110] הַפַּעַם	

107 Gen. 14:22 הֲרִימֹתִי יָדִי אֶל־יְהוָה 'I raise my hand up to the Lord'.

108 Jer. 11:20.

109 Jer. 23:9 רָחֲפוּ כָּל־עַצְמוֹתַי 'all my bones tremble'.

110 Prov. 15:13 רוּחַ נְכֵאָה 'a broken spirit', also 17:22, 18:14.

	And therefore **he has exhausted his fury on you.**[111]	וְלָכֵן כִּלָּה חֲמָתוֹ בָּךְ.[111]	
ASENATH	If only it were nothing other than that.	לוּ אֵין דָּבָר בִּלְעֲדֵי זֹאת.	אסנת
DOEG	Other than that there is nothing.	בִּלְעֲדֵי זֹאת אֵין כָּל מְאוּמָה.	דואג
	(The sound of a bell)	(קול פעמון)	
	But listen, the sound of the bell calling for the evening meal	אַךְ הַקְשִׁיבִי קוֹל הַפַּעֲמוֹן הַקֹּרֵא לַאֲרֻחַת הָעֶרֶב	
	There the noblemen of the nation, the messengers of Venice are gathered	שָׁם נְדִיבֵי הָעָם, מַלְאֲכֵי וִינֶעצְיָא נֶאֱסָפוּ	
	Refrain your eyes from tears[112] and come eat bread with them	מִנְעִי עֵינַיִךְ מִדִּמְעָה[112] וּבוֹאִי לֶאֱכָל־לֶחֶם עִמָּהֶם	
	And wait for the conclusion of the matter, because it will work out well for you.	וְהוֹחִילִי לְאַחֲרִית דָּבָר, כִּי יִפֹּל לְטוֹב לָךְ.	
	(Asenath exits with Milcah and Raddai enters)	(אסנת הולכת עם מלכה ורדי בא)	
	What do you have to say, Raddai?	מַה־בְּפִיךָ רַדַּי?	
RADDAI[113]	Thus far I have not found that you are dealing with me in good faith.	עַד כֹּה לֹא מָצָאתִי, כִּי תִסְחַר עִמִּי בֶּאֱמוּנָה.	רדי[113]
DOEG	Not in good faith?	לֹא בֶּאֱמוּנָה?	דואג
RADDAI	Each and every day **you brush me off with some excuse**[114]	מִדֵּי יוֹם בְּיוֹמוֹ, דָּחֹה תַדִּיחֵנִי בְּקַשׁ[114]	רדי
	And you do not let me see **a doorway of good hope,**[115]	וְלֹא תִתְּנֵנִי לִרְאוֹת, פֶּתַח תִּקְוָה[115] טוֹבָה,	
	And even I cannot continue to endure it, for **the strength of the burden-bearer has given out**[116]	וְגַם אֲנִי לֹא אוֹסִיף לְהָכִיל, כִּי כָשַׁל כֹּחַ הַסַּבָּל[116]	
	Nor shall I be quiet or sit silently any longer	וְגַם לֹא אֶשְׁקֹט וְלֹא אֵשֵׁב כְּמַחֲרִישׁ עוֹד	

111 Ezek. 6:12 וְכִלֵּיתִי חֲמָתִי בָּם 'and I shall exhaust my fury on them'.
112 Jer. 31:16 מִנְעִי קוֹלֵךְ מִבֶּכִי וְעֵינַיִךְ מִדִּמְעָה 'refrain your voice from weeping, and your eyes from tears'.
113 The remainder of this scene is in prose in the original (4.2.175–246).
114 This is a postbiblical expression traceable to the Babylonian Talmud, *Ḥullin* 27b. Salkinson's use of the phrase includes an infinitive absolute, which is a more characteristically biblical form.
115 Hosea 2:17 (2:15 in English Bibles).
116 Neh. 4:4 (4:10 in English Bibles).

Regarding everything which I have borne like a senseless man until now.

עַל כָּל אֲשֶׁר נָשָׂאתִי, כַּחֲסַר לֵב עַד הֵנָּה.

DOEG Will you give me an attentive ear?

דואג הֲתִתֵּן לִי אֹזֶן קַשֶּׁבֶת?

RADDAI On my faith, I have listened to you too much

רדי עַל אֱמוּנָתִי, הִקְשַׁבְתִּי לְקוֹלְךָ יֶתֶר מִדַּי

For your words and your deeds do not fit together.

כִּי דְבָרֶיךָ וּמַעֲשֶׂיךָ לֹא יַתְאִימוּ יַחְדָּו.

DOEG You rebuke me without cause, and unfairly and unjustly.

דואג עַל חִנָּם תּוֹכִיחֵנִי וְלֹא בְּיֹשֶׁר וּבְצֶדֶק.

RADDAI Not without cause, but rather fairly and justly.

רדי לֹא עַל חִנָּם, כִּי אִם בְּיֹשֶׁר וּבְצֶדֶק

Indeed I have freely distributed my property and my possessions and precious stones and jewels

הֵן הוֹנִי וּרְכוּשִׁי פִּזַּרְתִּי וְאַבְנֵי חֵפֶץ וַעֲדָיִים

Half of which would be enough to tempt even the heart of a priest's daughter[117]

אֲשֶׁר דַּי בְּחֶצְיָם לְפַתּוֹת גַּם לֵב בַּת כֹּהֵן[117]

I handed them over to you to give them as a gift to Asenath

מָסַרְתִּי בְיָדְךָ לְתִתָּם תְּשׁוּרָה אֶל אָסְנַת

And you promised me that soon she would come

וְאַתָּה הִבְטַחְתָּ לִי, כִּי בִמְהֵרָה תָבוֹא

To delight herself with me in love[118] and to restore my spirit,[119]

לְהִתְעַלֵּס אִתִּי בָּאֳהָבִים[118] וְלִהְיוֹת לִי לְמְשִׁיבַת נָפֶשׁ[119]

But there is no sound and no response.[120]

וְאֵין קוֹל וְאֵין קָשֶׁב.[120]

DOEG Go forth, go forth, the matter is good.

דואג צֵא צֵא, טוֹב הַדָּבָר.

RADDAI 'Go forth, go forth, the matter is good'; I cannot go forth

רדי „צֵא צֵא, טוֹב הַדָּבָר" לֹא אוּכַל לָצֵאת

Nor is the matter good, but rather very bad

וְגַם לֹא טוֹב הַדָּבָר, כִּי אִם רַע מְאֹד

---

117 Cf. Shakespeare's 'votarist' (i.e., 'nun'; see Crystal and Crystal 2002: 484). The specifically Jewish connotations of Salkinson's expression would have been obvious to his readers: it is typically used to denote a *bat kohen* or daughter of a Cohen (member of the priestly class), a status that has certain implications in Jewish law. This changes the sense somewhat, as a Cohen's daughter (as indeed a priest's daughter) would not be bound by the rules of chastity governing the life of a nun.

118 Prov. 7:18 נִתְעַלְּסָה בָּאֳהָבִים 'let us delight ourselves in love'.

119 Ruth 4:15 וְהָיָה לְךָ לְמֵשִׁיב נֶפֶשׁ 'and he will restore your spirit'.

120 2 Kings 4:31.

	For now my eyes have been opened to see lies and deception.	כִּי עַתָּה נִפְקְחוּ עֵינַי לִרְאוֹת כַּחַשׁ וּרְמִיָּה.	
DOEG	The matter is very good.	טוֹב הַדָּבָר מְאֹד.	דואג
RADDAI	I testify to you today that the matter is not very good	הַעִידֹתִי בְךָ הַיּוֹם, כִּי לֹא טוֹב הַדָּבָר מְאֹד	רדי
	Look, I am going to go tell the matter to Asenath;	רְאֵה הִנְנִי הוֹלֵךְ לְהַגִּיד הַדָּבָר לְאָסְנַת	
	If she returns the jewels to me, I shall turn away and let her be	אִם תָּשִׁיב לִי הָעֲדָיִים, אָסוּר וְאֶרֶף מִמֶּנָּה	
	And **I shall smite my thigh**[121] because I desired **not according to the law**[122]	**וְסָפַקְתִּי עַל יָרֵךְ**,[121] עַל אֲשֶׁר חָמַדְתִּי **לֹא כַדָּת**[122]	
	But if she does not return them to me, I shall indeed demand them from you.	וְאִם לֹא תְשִׁיבֵם לִי, דָּרוֹשׁ אֶדְרֹשׁ מִיָּדֵךְ.	
DOEG	Just now you have told me everything that is in your heart.	זֶה עַתָּה הִגַּדְתָּ לִי כָּל אֲשֶׁר בִּלְבָבֶךָ.	דואג
RADDAI	Thus I have told you, and thus I shall do today	כֵּן אֵיפוֹא הִגַּדְתִּי וְכֵן אֶעֱשֶׂה הַיּוֹם	רדי
	And I have not said anything which I shall not do.	וְלֹא הִגַּדְתִּי דָבָר, אֵת אֲשֶׁר לֹא אֶעֱשֶׂה.	
DOEG	Behold, now I know that you are **mighty in strength and understanding**[123]	הִנֵּה עַתָּה יָדַעְתִּי, כִּי **כַבִּיר כֹּחַ לֵב**[123] **אָתָּה**	דואג
	And therefore I place my trust in you today, more than I did previously	וְלָכֵן שַׁתִּי בְךָ מִבְטַחִי הַיּוֹם, מִכֹּל אֲשֶׁר שַׁתִּי מֵאָז	
	For **your hands will achieve success.**[124] Give me your hand, Raddai,	**כִּי יָדֶיךָ תַעֲשֶׂינָה תוּשִׁיָּה.**[124] תְּנָה לִי יָדְךָ רַדַּי,	
	You are right to argue with me; nevertheless **I shall instruct you and teach you**[125]	צָדַקְתָּ כִּי רִיבוֹת אֵלַי, בְּכָל זֹאת **אַשְׂכִּילְךָ וְאוֹרְךָ**[125]	
	That all my deeds are good for you.	כִּי כָל מַעֲשַׂי טוֹבִים אֵלֶיךָ.	
RADDAI	I have not noticed such a thing until now.	לֹא הִשְׂכַּלְתִּי כָזֹאת עַד כֹּה.	רדי

121 Jer. 31:19 (a sign of abhorrence, regret, or grief); see also Ezek. 21:17.
122 Esther 4:16.
123 Job 36:5.
124 Job 5:12 וְלֹא־תַעֲשֶׂינָה יְדֵיהֶם תּוּשִׁיָּה 'and their hands do not achieve success'.
125 Ps. 32:8.

DOEG	I know that you have not noticed, and therefore your complaint against me is strong	יָדַעְתִּי כִּי לֹא הִשְׂכַּלְתָּ וְלָכֵן חֲזָקָה תְּלוּנָתְךָ עָלַי	דואג
	With **words that are right**[126] to the ear. But if you are a man of valour	**בִּדְבָרִים נְכֹחִים**[126] לְאֹזֶן. אַךְ אִם אִישׁ חַיִל אַתָּה	
	More so than I thought in days gone by	יֶתֶר עַל אֲשֶׁר חֲשַׁבְתִּיךָ בְּיָמִים עָבָרוּ	
	And moreover do not lack discretion and great bravery and strength,	וְגַם לֹא תֶחְסַר מְזִמָּה וְרֹב אֹמֶץ וָכֹחַ	
	Prepare yourself tonight to carry out **the end of the matter**.[127]	הִכּוֹן לְךָ הַלַּיְלָה הַזֶּה, לְבַצַּע **אַחֲרִית דָּבָר**.[127]	
	And if you do not rejoice over Asenath tomorrow	וְאִם לֹא תָשִׂישׂ עַל אָסְנַת בְּיוֹם מָחָר	
	You may prepare **instruments of violence**[128] for yourself and ambush me in order to take my life.	תָּכִין לְךָ **כְּלֵי חָמָס**[128] וְתֶאֱרֹב עַל נַפְשִׁי לְקַחְתָּהּ.	
RADDAI	And what do I have to do, in order to carry out **the end of the matter**?[129]	וּמָה עָלַי לַעֲשׂוֹת, לְבַצַּע **אַחֲרִית דָּבָר**?[129]	רדי
	Is this deed possible for me? Will it succeed for me?	הֲיִתָּכֵן לִי הַמַּעֲשֶׂה? הֲיִצְלַח בְּיָדַי?	
DOEG	The messengers of Venice have come in order to move Ithiel from here	מַלְאֲכֵי וִינֶעצְיָא בָּאוּ, לְהַעֲבִיר אֶת אִיתִיאֵל מִזֶּה	דואג
	And to install Chesed in his place.	וּלְהוֹשִׁיב אֶת כֶּשֶׂד תַּחְתָּיו.	
RADDAI	If so, why then Ithiel and Asenath will return to Venice.	אִם כֵּן הֲלֹא יְשׁוּבוּן אִיתִיאֵל וְאָסְנַת לְוִינֶעצְיָא.	רדי
DOEG	He is going to an eastern land,[130] and he will take Asenath with him	הוּא הוֹלֵךְ לְאֶרֶץ קֶדֶם[130] וְאֶת אָסְנַת יִקַּח עִמּוֹ	דואג
	Except if a snare is set for him which will stop him from leaving here	לוּלֵא מוֹקֵשׁ יִנָּתֵן לוֹ, אֲשֶׁר יַעַצְרֶנּוּ מֵעֲבֹר מִזֶּה	
	And there is no snare ready for him except if Chesed	וְאֵין מוֹקֵשׁ נָכוֹן לוֹ בִּלְתִּי אִם כֶּשֶׂד	
	Is removed from the earth.[131]	**יִכָּחֵד מִן הָאָרֶץ**.[131]	

126 Prov. 24:26.
127 Eccles. 7:8.
128 Gen. 49:5.
129 Eccles. 7:8.
130 Cf. Shakespeare's 'Mauretania' (4.2.226), the North African homeland of the Moors (Honigmann 1997: 287, note 226). Salkinson's substitution fits in with his reshaping of the play's protagonist as a Cushite – or, alternatively, as Scolnicov (2001) suggests, a Jew (despite the fact that he is not labelled as such).
131 Exod. 9:15 וַתִּכָּחֵד מִן־הָאָרֶץ 'and you will be removed from the earth'.

RADDAI	And how **will he be removed from the earth?**[132]	וְאֵיךְ יִכָּחֵד מִן הָאָרֶץ?[132]	רדי
DOEG	If you smash his skull, **he will be removed from the earth**[133]	אִם תָּרֹץ אֶת גֻּלְגָּלְתּוֹ יִכָּחֵד מִן הָאָרֶץ[133]	דואג
	And he will no longer sit on Ithiel's chair.	וְעַל כִּסֵּא אִיתִיאֵל לֹא יֵשֵׁב עוֹד.	
RADDAI	And you are telling me to do this work?	וְלִי תֹאמַר לַעֲשׂוֹת אֶת הַמְּלָאכָה הַזֹּאת?	רדי
DOEG	If there is strength in your right hand and you want to be of benefit to yourself	אִם יֵשׁ עֹז בִּימִינְךָ וְחָפֵץ אַתָּה לְהוֹעִיל לְנַפְשֶׁךָ	דואג
	The work is fitting for you. Behold, he is eating bread	הַמְּלָאכָה יָאֲתָה לָךְ. הִנֵּה הוּא אֹכֵל לֶחֶם	
	In the whore's house tonight, and there I shall join up with him	בְּבֵית זוֹנָה הַלַּיְלָה וְשָׁם אֶתְחַבֵּר עִמּוֹ	
	And he does not yet know that **his horn is exalted high.**[134]	וְהוּא אֵינֶנּוּ יוֹדֵעַ עוֹד, כִּי רָמָה קַרְנוֹ[134] לְמָעְלָה.	
	If you lie in wait for him when he returns after midnight	אִם תֶּאֱרֹב עָלָיו בְּשׁוּבוֹ אַחֲרֵי חֲצוֹת הַלַּיְלָה	
	You will find his life in your hand, and I shall keep watch opposite	תִּמְצָא אֶת נַפְשׁוֹ בְּיָדֶךָ וַאֲנִי אֶשְׁמֹר מִנֶּגֶד	
	To be of assistance to you, and he will be killed by the hand of us both.	לִהְיוֹת לְעֵזֶר לָךְ וּבְיַד שְׁנֵינוּ יוּמָת.	
	Do not look at me as if **pricked in the heart**[135] – rise up and go with me	אַל תַּבֵּט בִּי מִשְׁתּוֹנֵן[135] – קוּם וְלֵךְ עִמָּדִי	
	And I shall teach you that death is necessary and very good for him	וְהוֹרֵתִיךָ כִּי הַמָּוֶת נָחוּץ וְטוֹב לוֹ מְאֹד	
	And also that it is your right to kill him. But mealtime is approaching –	וְגַם לְךָ הַמִּשְׁפָּט לַהֲמִיתוֹ. אַךְ עֵת הָאֹכֶל בָּאָה	
	And midnight is near; arise and let us go on our way.	וַחֲצוֹת הַלַּיְלָה קְרוֹבָה, קוּמָה וְנֵלְכָה לְדַרְכֵּנוּ.	

132 See preceding note.

133 See note 131.

134 1 Sam. 2:1 רָמָה קַרְנִי בַּיהוָה 'my horn is exalted in the LORD', indicating joy or strength. Cf. Shakespeare's 'his honourable fortune' (4.3.236).

135 Ps. 73:21 וְכִלְיוֹתַי אֶשְׁתּוֹנָן 'and I was pricked in the heart'.

RADDAI	Teach me your way so that I may know.	הוֹרֵנִי דַּרְכְּךָ וְאֵדָעָה.	רדי
DOEG	And you will see, and your soul will rejoice.	וְאַתָּה תִּרְאֶה וְתָגֵל נַפְשְׁךָ.	דואג
	(Both exit)	(הולכים שניהם)	
SCENE 3	*The citadel (Ithiel, Lud, Asenath Milcah, and attendants)*	בית המצודה (איתיאל לוד אסנת מלכה ומשרתים)	מחזה ג'
LUD	Please do not trouble yourself, commander, to go with me in order to send me off.	אַל נָא תַּעֲמֹל הַשַּׂר, לָלֶכֶת אִתִּי לְשַׁלְּחֵנִי.	לוד
ITHIEL	But it will do me good to walk around a bit outside.	אַךְ יִיטַב לִי, לְהִתְהַלֵּךְ מְעַט בַּחוּץ.	איתיאל
LUD	Take my blessing, lady, according to the honour which you have done me.	שְׂאִי בִרְכָתִי הַגְּבִירָה, כַּכָּבוֹד אֲשֶׁר כִּבַּדְתִּנִי.	לוד
ASENATH	Go in peace, my lord; I am honoured by your honour.	לֵךְ לְשָׁלוֹם אֲדוֹנִי, בִּכְבוֹדְךָ נִכְבַּדְתִּי אָנִי.	אסנת
ITHIEL	Are you not going? –	הַאִם לֹא הוֹלֵךְ אָתָּה? –	איתיאל
	And you, Asenath –	וְאַתְּ אָסְנַת –	
ASENATH	Here I am, my husband, my lord!	הִנְנִי אִישִׁי אֲדֹנִי!	אסנת
ITHIEL	Hurry to your bed, and I shall come soon	מַהֲרִי אֶל מִשְׁכָּבֵךְ וַאֲנִי אָבוֹא עַד מְהֵרָה	איתיאל
	And send the woman who attends you out of the room	וְאֶת הָאִשָּׁה הַמְשָׁרֶתֶת אִתָּךְ, שַׁלְּחִי מִתּוֹךְ הֶחָדֶר	
	Remember this, and do not forget.	זִכְרִי זֹאת וְאַל תִּשְׁכָּחִי.	
ASENATH	I shall do so, my lord.	כֵּן אֶעֱשֶׂה אֲדֹנִי.	אסנת
	(Ithiel, Lud, and the attendants exit)	(איתיאל לוד והמשרתים הולכים)	
MILCAH	What do you say now? Why, his anger has left him.	מַה־תֹּאמְרִי עַתָּה? הֲלֹא סָר אַפּוֹ מִמֶּנּוּ.	מלכה
ASENATH	He told me that he will return quickly	הוּא הִגִּיד לִי, כִּי יָשׁוּב עַד מְהֵרָה	אסנת
	And he commanded me to lie upon my bed and to send you away.	וְאֹתִי צִוָּה לִשְׁכַּב עַל מִטָּתִי וּלְשַׁלְּחֵךְ.	
MILCAH	And to send me away?	וּלְשַׁלְּחֵנִי?	מלכה
ASENATH	So he commanded me; therefore give me, Milcah,	כֵּן צִוָּה אֹתִי; לָכֵן תְּנִי לִי מִלְכָּה	אסנת

	My garment for bed tonight and go in peace;	כְּסוּתִי לְמִשְׁכַּב הַלַּיְלָה וּלְכִי לָךְ לְשָׁלוֹם;	
	We had best be careful, so as not to vex him further.	טוֹב לָנוּ לְהִזָּהֵר, לְבִלְתִּי הַכְעִיסוֹ עוֹד.	
MILCAH	If only, my lady, you had never seen him.	מִי יִתֵּן גְּבִרְתִּי, וְלֹא רָאִית אֹתוֹ מֵעוֹלָם.	מלכה
ASENATH	Whereas **the desires of my heart**[136] are not so, for he is pleasant in his rebuking	**וּמִשְׁאֲלוֹת לִבִּי**[136] לֹא כֵן, כִּי נֶחְמָד הוּא בְּגַעֲרָתוֹ	אסנת
	And **my insides are moved for him**[137] despite his **anger so cruel**.[138]	**וּמֵעַי יֶהֱמוּ לוֹ**,[137] אַף **בְּעֶבְרָתוֹ כִּי קָשָׁתָה**.[138]	
	Yea, unfasten the hooks for me and remove my robe.	אַךְ פִּתְחִי לִי הַקְּרָסִים וְהַפְשִׁיטִי אֶת כֻּתָּנְתִּי.	
MILCAH	Behold, I have placed the garments on your bed as you commanded.	הִנֵּה שַׂמְתִּי הַשְּׂמָלוֹת עַל מִטָּתֵךְ כַּאֲשֶׁר צִוִּית.	מלכה
ASENATH	What is the difference between one garment and another? Why, one is like the other;	מַה־בֵּין שִׂמְלָה לְשִׂמְלָה? הֲלֹא זֹאת כְּמוֹ זֹאת,	אסנת
	How we resemble children, and **folly is bound up in our hearts**[139] –	אֵיךְ לְעוֹלְלִים נִדְמִינוּ **וְאִוֶּלֶת קְשׁוּרָה בְּלִבֵּנוּ**[139] –	
	If I die before you die, dress my corpse, Milcah,	אִם אָמוּת בְּטֶרֶם תָּמוּתִי, הַלְבִּישִׁי מִלְכָּה אֶת גְּוִיָּתִי	
	In this **linen robe**.[140]	אֶת **תַּכְרִיךְ בּוּץ**[140] הַזֶּה.	
MILCAH	Do not bring forth such words from your lips.	אַל תּוֹצִיאִי בִּשְׂפָתַיִךְ כַּדָּבָר הַזֶּה.	מלכה
ASENATH	My mother had **a maidservant who was promised to a man**,[141] and her name was Azubah[142]	לְאִמִּי הָיְתָה **שִׁפְחָה נֶחֱרֶפֶת לְאִישׁ**[141] וּשְׁמָהּ עֲזוּבָה[142]	אסנת

136 This is a postbiblical expression traceable to the Babylonian Talmud (*Berakhot* 16b) and appearing elsewhere in rabbinic, medieval, and early modern literature.

137 Jer. 31:20 הָמוּ מֵעַי לוֹ 'my insides are moved for him'; see also a similar phrase in Song of Songs 5:4.

138 Gen. 49:7 וְעֶבְרָתָם כִּי קָשָׁתָה 'and their fury so cruel'.

139 Prov. 22:15 אִוֶּלֶת קְשׁוּרָה בְלֶב־נָעַר 'folly is bound up in the heart of a child'.

140 Esther 8:15. In the biblical verse, the linen robe appears in a celebratory context; Salkinson seems to have borrowed the phrase without intending to evoke these positive connotations.

141 Lev. 19:20.

142 Cf. Shakespeare's 'Barbary' (4.3.24). Azubah is the name of two minor biblical characters, the wife of Caleb mentioned in 1 Chron. 2:18, and the mother of the king Jehoshaphat mentioned in 1 Kings 22:42 and 2 Chron. 20:31. Salkinson seems to have intended it as a play on words, as the name literally means 'abandoned (fem.)'; see also note 144.

	And her beloved lost his mind and abandoned her and went away.	וְאֹהֲבָהּ שִׁנָּה אֶת טַעֲמוֹ וַיַּעַזְבֶהָ וַיֵּלֶךְ לוֹ.	
	And in her mouth there was an ancient song by the name of '**Willows of the Brook**'[143]	וּבְפִיהָ הָיְתָה שׁוּמָה שִׁירַת קֶדֶם, בְּשֵׁם: עַרְבֵי נַחַל.[143]	
	Whose words were pleasant for **a sad-spirited woman like Azubah**[144]	אֲשֶׁר עָרְבוּ דְבָרֶיהָ, לַעֲצוּבַת רוּחַ כַּעֲזוּבָה[144]	
	And she sang this song as her soul departed.	וַתָּשַׁר אֶת הַשִּׁירָה הַזֹּאת, לְעֵת צֵאת נַפְשָׁהּ.	
	And **I have set this song before my eyes tonight**[145]	וַאֲנִי שִׁוִּיתִי הַלַּיְלָה הַשִּׁירָה הַזֹּאת לְנֶגֶד עֵינָי[145]	
	And I almost wanted to sing, as Azubah did –	וְכִמְעַט חָפַצְתִּי לָשִׁיר, כַּאֲשֶׁר עָשְׂתָה עֲזוּבָה –	
	But hurry, finish your work.	אַךְ מַהֲרִי כַּלִּי מְלַאכְתֵּךְ.	
MILCAH	Shall I go bring you the nightgown?	הַאֵלֵךְ לְהָבִיא לָךְ אֶת כְּסוּת הַלַּיְלָה?	מלכה
ASENATH	Loosen the ties for me first –	הַתִּירִי לִי הַלֻּלָאוֹת רִאשׁוֹנָה –	אסנת
	How good and precious is the man Lud, my relative.[146]	מַה־טּוֹב וְיָקָר, הָאִישׁ לוּד קְרוֹבִי.[146]	
MILCAH	He is an honourable man and very handsome.	אִישׁ הָדוּר הוּא וְנֶחְמָד מְאֹד.	מלכה
ASENATH	And how pleasant is his speech.	וּמִדְבָּרוֹ מַה־נָּאוֶה.	אסנת
MILCAH[147]	I know a woman in Venice who would not see it as a burden	יָדַעְתִּי אִשָּׁה בְּוִינֶעצְיָא, אֲשֶׁר לֹא לְטֹרַח יְהִי לָהּ	מלכה[147]
	To walk barefoot to the Holy Land[148] for a kiss of his lips.	לָלֶכֶת יָחֵף לָאָרֶץ* הַקְּדוֹשָׁה,[148] בְּעַד נְשִׁיקַת שְׂפָתָיו.	

143 Lev. 23:40; Job 40:22.

144 Isa. 54:6 כִּי־כְאִשָּׁה עֲזוּבָה וַעֲצוּבַת רוּחַ קְרָאָךְ יְהוָה 'for the Lord has called you like a wife abandoned and sad-spirited' (this is a play on words, as עֲזוּבָה is both the name 'Azubah' and the word 'abandoned [fem.]').

145 Ps. 16:8 שִׁוִּיתִי יְהוָה לְנֶגְדִּי תָמִיד 'I have set the Lord before me continually'.

146 Salkinson has added the word קְרוֹבִי 'my relative', which does not feature in the original (4.3.34-5).

147 These lines are prose in the original (4.3.37–8).

148 Cf. Shakespeare's 'Palestine' (4.3.38); Salkinson's translation is a very commonly used Hebrew term for the Land of Israel.

* לָאָרֶץ

(Asenath sings)	(אסנת תשיר)
Beneath an **oak of weeping**[149] an abandoned woman[150] weeps over **the bridegroom of her youth**[151]	**תַּחַת אַלּוֹן בָּכוּת**[149] עֲזוּבָה[150] מְבַכָּה עַל **בַּעַל נְעוּרֶיהָ**[151]
Willows[152] weep, sway to the destruction of the wretched one in love	עֲרָבִים[152] יִבְכּוּ יָנוּעוּ לְשֵׁבֶר הָאֻמְלָלָה בָּאֳהָבִים
Her hand on her head and her head between her knees	יָדָהּ עַל רֹאשָׁהּ וְרֹאשָׁהּ בֵּין בִּרְכֶּיהָ
Cry, wail, oh! Willows, willows, willows.	זַעֲקוּ הֵילִילוּ הָהּ! עֲרָבִים עֲרָבִים עֲרָבִים.
The brook opposite answers, wails to the sound of her wailing	הַנַּחַל יַעֲנֶה מִנֶּגֶד יְיֵלִיל לְקוֹל יִלְלָתָהּ
Willows weep, sway at the destruction of the wretched one in love	עֲרָבִים יִבְכּוּ יָנוּעוּ לְשֵׁבֶר הָאֻמְלָלָה בָּאֳהָבִים
Her eyes are red from weeping and the stones grow wet from her tears	אָדְמוּ עֵינֶיהָ מִבֶּכִי וַאֲבָנִים רָטְבוּ מִדִּמְעָתָהּ
(To Milcah) Put that down, Milcah –	(אל מלכה) הַנִּיחִי זֹאת מִיָּדֵךְ מִלְכָּה –
Cry, wail, oh! Willows, willows, willows!	זַעֲקוּ הֵילִילוּ הָהּ! עֲרָבִים עֲרָבִים עֲרָבִים!
(To Milcah) Hurry, finish your work, he will be coming any moment –	(אל מלכה) מַהֲרִי כַּלִּי מַעֲשַׂיִךְ, הוּא יָבוֹא כְּרֶגַע –
With the willows of the brook upon my death, make a garland for me	בְּעַרְבֵי הַנַּחַל בְּמוֹתִי, עַטְרוּ לִי עֲטָרָה

149 Gen. 35:8; in the biblical verse the oak tree is the location where the matriarch Rebecca's nurse Deborah was buried; in most English Bibles the phrase 'oak of weeping' is translated as a proper name, Allon(-)bacuth.

150 Or 'Azubah'; see notes 142 and 144.

151 Joel 1:8.

152 Scolnicov (2001: 189) argues that Salkinson's selection of the plural form here, in contrast to Shakespeare's singular 'willow' (4.3.40ff), is intended as a reference to Ps. 137:1–2, which contains a mention of willows (in the plural) as part of a lament about exile from Zion; as such, Salkinson is linking the sadness of spurned lovers to the Jews' mourning for loss of a national homeland. While it is possible that Salkinson had such associations in mind, it is perhaps more likely that the use of the plural is rooted primarily or solely in a desire to maintain consistency with the initial appearance of the word in Asenath's speech (as the song's title), which is in the plural because it is a citation of Lev. 23:40 and Job 40:22 (see note 143).

	They will weep at my destruction, they will sway to the wretched one in love	הֵם לְשִׁבְרִי יִבְכָּיוּן, יָנוּדוּ לָאֻמְלָלָה בָּאֳהָבִים	
	Even in his rage I love him, do not speak ill of him	גַּם בְּזַעְמוֹ אֲהַבְתִּיהוּ, אַל תְּדַבְּרוּ בוֹ סָרָה	
	Cry, wail, oh, willows, willows, willows	זַעֲקוּ הֵילִילוּ הָהּ עֲרָבִים עֲרָבִים עֲרָבִים	
	(To Milcah) Behold, he knocks –	(אל מלכה) הִנֵּה הוּא דוֹפֵק –	
MILCAH	It is not he, but only the wind blowing.	לֹא הוּא רַק הָרוּחַ נוֹשָׁבֶת.	מלכה
	(Asenath sings)	(אסנת תשיר)	
	I called him deceitful,[153] and he answered me with **the sweetness of his lips**[154] –	אַכְזָב[153] שְׁמוֹ קָרָאתִי וְהוּא בְּמֶתֶק שְׂפָתָיו[154] עָנָנִי –	
	Willows weep, sway to the destruction of the wretched one in love –	עֲרָבִים יִבְכּוּ יָנוּעוּ לְשֵׁבֶר הָאֻמְלָלָה בָּאֳהָבִים –	
	'Do not go after strange men, and I shall not approach a strange woman'	„אַל תֵּלְכִי אַחֲרֵי זָרִים וְאֶל זָרָה לֹא אֶקְרַב אָנִי"	
	Cry, wail, oh! Willows, willows, willows.	זַעֲקוּ הֵילִילוּ הָהּ! עֲרָבִים עֲרָבִים עֲרָבִים.	
	Now **my eyes grow dim**;[155] is that a sign of weeping?	עַתָּה עָשְׁשׁוּ עֵינַי;[155] הַאוֹת הוּא לְבֶכִי?	
MILCAH	**I do not know the interpretation of the matter.**[156]	לֹא יָדַעְתִּי פֵּשֶׁר דָּבָר.[156]	מלכה
ASENATH	Whereas I have heard such a thing – men are harsher than us –	וַאֲנִי כֵן שָׁמַעְתִּי – הָאֲנָשִׁים קָשִׁים מִמֶּנִּי –	אסנת
	Tell me, Milcah, is it possible for a woman	הַגִּידִי לִי מִלְכָּה, הֲיֵשׁ בְּיַד אִשָּׁה	
	To violate a covenant and oath and to be unfaithful to **the bridegroom of her youth**?[157]	לְהָפֵר בְּרִית וּשְׁבוּעָה וְלִמְעָל מַעַל בְּבַעַל נְעוּרֶיהָ?[157]	

---

153 Salkinson's choice of this word is particularly appropriate in the context of this song, as its single biblical appearance (in Jer. 15:18) is often translated as 'deceptive brook', referring to a seasonally dry brook or river.

154 Prov. 16:21 וּמֶתֶק שְׂפָתַיִם 'and sweetness of lips'.

155 Ps. 6:8 (6:7 in English Bibles) עָשְׁשָׁה מִכַּעַס עֵינִי 'my eye grows dim from grief'; also Ps. 31:10 (31:9 in English Bibles).

156 Eccles. 8:1 וּמִי יוֹדֵעַ פֵּשֶׁר דָּבָר 'and who knows the interpretation of a matter'.

157 Joel 1:8.

MILCAH	It is, it is.	יֵשׁ וָיֵשׁ.	מלכה
ASENATH	Would you commit this vile deed, for the whole earth?	הֲתַעֲשִׂי הַנְּבָלָה הַזֹּאת, בְּעַד כָּל הָאָרֶץ?	אסנת
MILCAH	And why would I not do so; wouldn't you?	וְלָמָּה לֹא אֶעֱשֶׂה כֵן, הַאִם לֹא תַעֲשִׂין אָתְּ?	מלכה
ASENATH	Before the sun! I swear I would not do this thing.	נֶגֶד פְּנֵי הַשֶּׁמֶשׁ! אִם אֶעֱשֶׂה הַדָּבָר הַזֶּה.	אסנת
MILCAH	Before the sun, I would not do it either	נֶגֶד פְּנֵי הַשֶּׁמֶשׁ, לֹא אֶעֱשֶׂה גַם אָנִי	מלכה
	But in the darkness of the night –	אֶפֶס בְּחֶשְׁכַּת הַלָּיְלָה –	
ASENATH	And if the earth were to be given to you, would you do this evil thing?	וְאִם הָאָרֶץ תִּנָּתֶן לָךְ, תַּעֲשִׂי הָרָעָה הַזֹּאת?	אסנת
MILCAH	The earth is a huge payment for this small iniquity.	הָאָרֶץ שָׂכָר רָב, בְּעַד עָוֹן קָטֹן זֶה.	מלכה
ASENATH	Whereas I think that you would not do this, God forbid.	וַאֲנִי חָשַׁבְתִּי, כִּי חָלִלָה לָּךְ מֵעֲשׂוֹת זֹאת.	אסנת
MILCAH[158]	I do not think so, but rather I would sin and then repent.	לֹא כֵן חָשַׁבְתִּי אָנִי, כִּי אִם אֶחְטָא וְאָשׁוּב,	מלכה[158]
	Indeed I would not do this for a gift of trifling value,	הֵן לֹא אֶעֱשֶׂה זֹאת, בְּעַד אֶתְנָן קַל הָעֵרֶךְ	
	For **a ring and a necklace**,[159] for two cubits[160] of linen and silk;	בְּעַד טַבַּעַת וְכוּמָז,[159] בְּעַד שְׁתֵּי אַמּוֹת[160] בַּד וָמֶשִׁי;	
	But for the whole earth, why, that is a matter.	אֲבָל בְּעַד כָּל הָאָרֶץ, הֲלֹא דָבָר הוּא.	
	Who would not be unfaithful to her husband, in order to make him	מִי לֹא תִמְעַל בְּאִישָׁהּ, לְבַעֲבוּר עֲשׂוֹת אֹתוֹ	
	King over the whole earth?[161] For such a great gift	לְמֶלֶךְ עַל כָּל הָאָרֶץ?[161] בְּעַד אֶתְנָן רַב כָּזֶה	
	Even the inferno[162] would be a laughing matter to me, and I would not fear the fire of hell.	גַּם הַתֹּפֶת[162] מִשְׂחָק לִי וּמֵאֵשׁ גֵּיהִנֹּם לֹא אֶפְחָד.	

158 These lines are prose in the original (4.3.70–6).
159 Exod. 35:22.
160 A measurement equivalent to approximately 45cm.
161 Zech. 14:9.
162 Cf. Shakespeare's 'purgatory' (4.3.76). Salkinson has replaced the Christian term with a close Jewish equivalent. The word appears on a number of occasions in the Hebrew Bible (2 Kings 23:10; Jer. 7:31, 32, 19:6, 11–4) but as a place-name, Topheth, a location in Jerusalem where idol-worshippers would sacrifice their children; in the medieval period it became a label for hell (Even-Shoshan 2003, 6: 2030), and this is the sense in which Salkinson is employing it.

ASENATH	As for me, on my life, I would not commit the sin	וַאֲנִי חֵי נַפְשִׁי! אִם אֶעֱשֶׂה הַחֲטָאָה	אסנת
	Even if the whole earth were given to me as my payment.	וְאַף אִם תִּנָּתֵן לִי, כָּל הָאָרֶץ בִּשְׂכָרִי.	
MILCAH	Why, this sin can only be done on earth	הֲלֹא הַחֲטָאָה הַזֹּאת, תֵּעָשֶׂה רַק בָּאָרֶץ	מלכה
	And since the earth would be yours, the sin would be yours alone	וְאַחֲרֵי אֲשֶׁר לָךְ הָאָרֶץ לָךְ לְבַדֵּךְ חַטָּאת	
	And afterwards you could repent, and who could tell you what you must do.	וְאַחֲרֵי כֵן תּוּכְלִי לָשׁוּב וּמִי יֹאמַר מַה־תַּעֲשִׂין.	
ASENATH	But my heart tells me that there is no such woman on earth.	וּלְבָבִי יַגִּיד לִי, אֵין אִשָּׁה כָּזֹאת בָּאָרֶץ.	אסנת
MILCAH	There is a great number on earth, in accordance with the number of pleasure seekers.	יֵשׁ מִסְפָּר רַב בָּאָרֶץ, לְמִסְפַּר רֹדְפֵי הַתַּעֲנוּגִים.	מלכה
	However, the snare of the women comes on account of the iniquity of their husbands	אָמְנָם מוֹקֵשׁ הַנָּשִׁים, יָבוֹא בַּעֲוֹן בַּעֲלֵיהֶן	
	Who do not fulfil that which is lacking for them, or scatter their might	אֲשֶׁר לֹא יְמַלְּאוּ מַחְסוֹרָן, אוֹ יְפַזְּרוּ חֵילָם	
	In the laps of strange and alien women, or are jealous regarding their wives without cause	בְּחֵיק זָרוֹת נָכְרִיּוֹת; אוֹ יְקַנְּאוּ אֹתָן חִנָּם	
	And lock them up for nothing; or raise their hand to strike them;	וְיַעַצְרוּן עַל לֹא דָבָר; אוֹ יָרִימוּ יָדָם לְהַכּוֹתָן;	
	Or hold back our money in order to hurt us	אוֹ יַעַצְרוּ כַּסְפֵּנוּ, לְהַכְאִיב אֶת נַפְשֵׁנוּ	
	And do not notice that we also have a heart	וְלֹא יָשִׂימוּ אֶל לִבָּם, כִּי גַם לָנוּ לֵב	
	And after our patience, we also take revenge.	וְאַחֲרֵי אֹרֶךְ אַפֵּנוּ נִנְקֹם נָקָם גַּם אָנוּ.	
	For why do they not notice that their wives also	כִּי לָמָּה לֹא יִתְבּוֹנְנוּ, כִּי גַם לִנְשֵׁיהֶם	
	Have an eye to see, a nose to smell, and a palate to taste sweet and bitter?	עַיִן לִרְאוֹת, אַף לְהָרִיחַ וְחֵיךְ לִטְעֹם מָתוֹק וָמָר?	
	Why, for pleasure they exchange us for other women	הֲלֹא הֵמָּה לְתַעֲנוּג, יַחְלִיפוּ אֹתָנוּ בַּאֲחֵרוֹת	

	And the love of pleasure comes from desire of the flesh	וְאַהֲבַת הַתַּעֲנוּג תָּבוֹא, בַּעֲקֵב תַּאֲוַת הַבָּשָׂר	
	And desire of the flesh comes from weakness of the soul	וְתַאֲוַת הַבָּשָׂר תָּבוֹא, בַּעֲקֵב רִפְיוֹן הַנֶּפֶשׁ	
	Therefore they should know that we also have a portion	לָכֵן עֲלֵיהֶם לָדַעַת, כִּי גַּם לָנוּ חֵלֶק	
	In weakness of the soul, in desire of the flesh, and in the love of pleasure.	בְּרִפְיוֹן הַנֶּפֶשׁ, בְּתַאֲוַת הַבָּשָׂר וּבְאַהֲבַת הַתַּעֲנוּג.	
	And now take instruction, men, and do well with the wives of your bosom.[163]	וְעַתָּה הִוָּסְרוּ בְּנֵי אָדָם, וְהֵיטִיבוּ לִנְשֵׁי חֵיקְכֶם.[163]	
	But if you do not do well, and iniquity is found in us,	וְאִם לֹא תֵיטִיבוּ וְעָוֹן יִמָּצֵא בָנוּ	
	Know that it was planted by your hand, for we have learned your deeds.	וִידַעְתֶּם כִּי מַטַּע יֶדְכֶם הוּא, כִּי לָמַדְנוּ מַעַלְלֵיכֶם.	
ASENATH	Go in peace – my rock![164] Instruct me in the way of salvation[165]	לְכִי לָךְ לְשָׁלוֹם – צוּרִי![164] הוֹרֵנִי דֶּרֶךְ יֶשַׁע[165]	אסנת
	To choose good over evil and not to learn **iniquity and transgression**.[166]	לִבְחֹר טוֹב מֵרָע וְלֹא לִלְמֹד **עָוֹן וָפֶשַׁע**.[166]	
	(Exeunt)	(הולכות)	

End of Fourth Part.

תם חלק רביעי.

163 This rhymes with the last word of the speech's last line, echoing Shakespeare's 'know/so' (4.3.101–2) except that the latter is a rhyming couplet. Salkinson most likely opted for a different pattern because he could not find a workable rhyme for the last two lines of the speech. He has employed the pausal form of the Hebrew word for 'bosom' (as opposed to the standard חֵיקְכֶם) for purposes of the rhyme.

164 A designation for God (see, e.g., 2 Sam. 22:3; Ps. 18:3 [18:2 in English Bibles]).

165 This and the next line form a rhyming couplet, mirroring Shakespeare's 'send/mend' (4.3.103–4).

166 Exod. 34:7; Num. 14:18.

Fifth Part

חלק חמישי

SCENE I	*A Street in the Town (Doeg and Raddai)*	רחוב העיר (דואג ורדי)	מחזה א'
DOEG	Stand here behind the wall; he is coming towards us	עֲמֹד פֹּה מֵאַחֲרֵי הַקִּיר, הוּא הוֹלֵךְ לִקְרָאתֵנוּ	דואג
	Draw your sword and strike him like **a skilled warrior**[1]	שְׁלֹף אֶת חַרְבְּךָ וּפְגַע בּוֹ כְּגִבּוֹר מַשְׂכִּיל[1]	
	Do not fear and do not lose heart,[2] for I shall save you;	אַל תִּירָא וְאַל תֵּחָת,[2] כִּי אָנֹכִי לְהוֹשִׁיעֶךָ,	
	Remember that this night is the end for us;	זְכֹר כִּי הַלַּיְלָה הַזֶּה, הוּא הַקֵּץ לָנוּ;	
	On it we shall act and succeed; or we shall fall and perish	בּוֹ נַעֲשֶׂה וְנַצְלִיחַ אוֹ נֵרֵד וְנֹאבֵד	
	Therefore **be strong and courageous.**[3]	לָכֵן חֲזַק וֶאֱמָץ.[3]	
RADDAI	Position yourself opposite me, lest I miss with my sword when I strike.	הִתְיַצֵּב מִנֶּגֶד לִי, פֶּן אַחֲטִיא בְּחַרְבִּי בְּהַכּוֹתִי.	רדי
DOEG	I shall position myself opposite; hold fast to your sword, **go up and succeed.**[4]	אֲנִי אֶתְיַצֵּב מִנֶּגֶד, הַחֲזֵק בְּחַרְבְּךָ עֲלֵה וּצְלַח.[4]	דואג
	(Doeg goes and positions himself opposite)	(דואג הולך ומתיצב מנגד)	
RADDAI	I have no desire to commit this act	חֶמְדָּה אֵין לִי, לְהִתְעוֹלֵל עֲלִילָה זֹאת	רדי
	But he tricked me and persuaded me with the wisdom of his words,	אַךְ הוּא הִשִּׁיאַנִי וַיְפַתֵּנִי בְּשֵׂכֶל מִלָּיו,	
	That only one soul will go to its eternal home[5] –	כִּי רַק נֶפֶשׁ אַחַת תֵּלֵךְ אֶל בֵּית עוֹלָמָהּ[5] –	
	Awaken, my sword, and strike this **man who must die**![6]	עוּרִי חַרְבִּי וּפִגְעִי בְּבֶן־מָוֶת[6] הַזֶּה!	
	(Goes and stands in his position)	(הולך ועומד במקומו)	

1 Jer. 50:9.
2 Deut. 1:21; Josh. 8:1; 1 Chron. 22:13, 28:20.
3 Deut. 31:7, 23; Josh. 1:6, 7, 9, 18; 1 Chron. 22:13.
4 1 Kings 22:15 עֲלֵה וְהַצְלַח 'go up and succeed'.
5 Eccles. 12:5 כִּי־הֹלֵךְ הָאָדָם אֶל־בֵּית עוֹלָמוֹ 'for man goes to his eternal home'.
6 1 Sam. 20:31; 2 Sam. 12:5.

	As for this rash man, I have touched **his wound and his bruise,**[7]	אִישׁ נִמְהָר הַזֶּה, נָגַעְתִּי בְּפִצְעוֹ וַחֲבֻרָתוֹ[7]	דואג
	And out of his pain **he has cried out against me,**[8] and now he will kill Chesed	וּמִכְּאֵבוֹ נָתַן עָלַי בְּקוֹלוֹ[8] וְעַתָּה יָמִית אֶת כֶּשֶׂד	
	Or Chesed will kill him, or they will kill each other;	אוֹ כֶּשֶׂד יָמִית אֹתוֹ, אוֹ יַהַרְגוּ אִישׁ אֶת רֵעֵהוּ	
	Any of these three will be of benefit to me.	כָּל אַחַת מִשְּׁלָשׁ־אֵלֶּה, תִּהְיֶה לְהוֹעִיל לִי.	
	If Raddai survives, he will surely demand from me	אִם יִשָּׁאֵר רַדַּי בַּחַיִּים, דָּרשׁ יִדְרשׁ מִיָּדִי	
	Gold and precious stones, which I took from him	זָהָב וַאֲבָנִים יְקָרוֹת, אֲשֶׁר לָקַחְתִּי מִמֶּנּוּ	
	To give to Asenath, and therefore I seek to take his life	לְתִתָּם אֶל אָסְנַת וְלָכֵן אֲבַקֵּשׁ נַפְשׁוֹ לְקַחְתָּהּ	
	Whereas if Chesed lives, I will not be able to withstand him	וְאִם כֶּשֶׂד יִחְיֶה, לֹא אוּכַל לַעֲמוֹד לְפָנָיו	
	For he **has more beautiful eyes and a more comely appearance**[9] than me,	כִּי יְפֵה עֵינַיִם וְטוֹב רֹאִי[9] הוּא מִמֶּנִּי,	
	And moreover, perhaps the Cushite will tell him of my plan for him	וְגַם אוּלַי הַכּוּשִׁי, יַגִּיד לוֹ מַחֲשַׁבְתִּי עָלָיו	
	And therefore **he must die**[10] – but here he comes.	וְלָכֵן בֶּן־מָוֶת[10] הוּא – אַךְ הִנֵּה הוּא בָא.	
	(Chesed passes by)	(כשד עובר)	
RADDAI	I hear the sound of his feet; **your blood is on your head,**[11] rascal!	קוֹל רַגְלָיו אֲנִי שׁוֹמֵעַ; דָּמְךָ בְּרֹאשְׁךָ[11] נָבָל!	רדי
	(Runs and strikes him with his sword)	(רץ ומכה בו בחרבו)	
CHESED	You tried to strike me down like a foe with a single blow	לְהַכּוֹת אֹתִי אָמַרְתָּ כַּצָּר בְּמַכָּה אַחַת	כשד
	But you did not know that my armour is tougher than the edge of your sword	וְלֹא יָדַעְתָּ כִּי שִׁרְיוֹנִי* קָשֶׁה מִפִּי חַרְבֶּךָ	
	And now I shall also try.	וְעַתָּה אֲנַסֶּה גַם אָנִי.	

7 Isa. 1:6 פֶּצַע וְחַבּוּרָה 'a wound and a bruise'.
8 Jer. 12:8 נָתְנָה עָלַי בְּקוֹלָהּ 'she has cried out against Me'.
9 1 Sam. 16:12 וְהוּא אַדְמוֹנִי עִם־יְפֵה עֵינַיִם וְטוֹב רֹאִי 'and he was ruddy with beautiful eyes and a comely appearance' (referring to King David in his youth).
10 1 Sam. 20:31; 2 Sam. 12:5.
11 Josh. 2:19 דָּמוֹ בְרֹאשׁוֹ 'his blood is on his head'.

* שִׁרְיוֹנִי

	(Draws sword and wounds Raddai)	(שולף ופוצע את רדי)	
RADDAI	Aah, I am dead! –	אֲהָהּ מֵת אָנִי! –	רדי
	(Doeg runs and strikes an injurious blow to Chesed's leg from behind him and flees to his position)	(דואג רץ ומכה מכת פצע על שוק כשד מאחריו ונס למקומו)	
CHESED	Aah, I am wounded – murderers! Murderers! *(Falls to the ground)*	אֲהָהּ פָּצוּעַ אָנִי – מְרַצְּחִים! מְרַצְּחִים! (נופל ארצה)	כשד
	(Ithiel enters from afar)	(איתיאל בא מרחוק)	
ITHIEL	**The voice is the voice of Chesed;**[12] Doeg has kept his promise.	הַקּוֹל קוֹל כֶּשֶׂד;[12] דּוֹאֵג הֵקִים אֶת דְּבָרוֹ.	איתיאל
RADDAI	Woe is me, for I have done wrong –	אוֹי לִי כִּי הֶעֱוֵיתִי –	רדי
ITHIEL	Let me listen to the voice again – it is his voice.	אֶשְׁמְעָה עוֹד אֶת הַקּוֹל – קוֹלוֹ הוּא זֶה.	איתיאל
CHESED	Come to my aid – bring light, and a surgeon for my wound.	בּוֹאוּ לְעֶזְרָתִי – הֵבִיאוּ* נֵר וְחֹבֵשׁ לְפִצְעִי.	כשד
ITHIEL	It is definitely his voice; Doeg is a man of valour	קוֹלוֹ הוּא אֶל נָכוֹן; דּוֹאֵג אִישׁ חַיִל הוּא	איתיאל
	An honest and faithful man, who fights his friend's fight as his own	אִישׁ יָשָׁר וְנֶאֱמָן, אֲשֶׁר רָב רִיב אֹהֲבוֹ כְּנַפְשׁוֹ	
	You have been a model to me, my friend –	לְמוֹפֵת הָיִיתָ לִי יְדִידִי –	
	As for you, **tender and delicate one,**[13] see, your lover **is slain by the sword**[14]	וְאַתְּ רַכָּה וַעֲנֻגָּה,[13] רְאִי עֹגְבֵךְ חֲלַל חָרֶב[14]	
	And the time of your punishment is also coming; I am on my way to you, adulteress	וְגַם עֵת פְּקוּדָתֵךְ בָּאָה; הִנְנִי אֵלַיִךְ נֹאָפֶת	
	Beautiful-eyed one, abomination, I despise your youthful love[15]	יְפַת עֵינַיִם תּוֹעֵבָה, מָאַסְתִּי אַהֲבַת נְעוּרָיִכִי[15]	
	And the bed which you have desecrated will be stained with your lifeblood.	וְהַמִּטָּה אֲשֶׁר חִלַּלְתְּ, תִּתְגָּאַל בְּדַם חַיָּיִכִי.	

12 Gen. 27:22 הַקֹּל קוֹל יַעֲקֹב וְהַיָּדַיִם יְדֵי עֵשָׂו 'the voice is the voice of Jacob, but the hands are the hands of Esau'.

13 Isa. 47:1, in reference to Babylon, which is prophesied destruction and will no longer be called tender or delicate. Cf. Shakespeare's 'minion' (5.1.33), which commonly means 'darling' but here is used in the sense of 'hussy' (Honigmann 1997: 298, note 33; Crystal and Crystal 2002: 282). The negative context of the biblical citation suggests that Salkinson was aware of the insulting sense of the English original and expected his readers to interpret the Hebrew endearment ironically.

14 Num. 19:16.

15 This and the next line form a rhyming couplet, mirroring Shakespeare's 'blotted/spotted' (5.1.35–6).

* הָבִיאוּ

	(Ithiel exits)	(איתיאל הולך)	
	(Lud and Gether[16] from afar)	(לוד וגתר[16] מרחוק)	
CHESED	Are there no night watchmen? Does no one pass by?	הַאֵין שׁוֹמְרֵי לָיְלָה? הַאֵין אִישׁ עֹבֵר?	כשד
	I have been murdered! I have been murdered!	נִרְצַחְתִּי! נִרְצָחְתִּי!	
GETHER	I hear an anguished voice, **a voice crying bitterly**.[17]	קוֹל שֶׁבֶר אֲנִי שׁוֹמֵעַ, קוֹל מַר צֹרֵחַ.[17]	גתר
CHESED	Arise to my aid…	קוּמוּ לְעֶזְרָתִי...	כשד
LUD	Listen to the voice.	שְׁמַע נָא אֶת הַקּוֹל.	לוד
RADDAI	Cursed be the villain!	אָרוּר בֶּן הַבְּלִיַּעַל!	רדי
LUD	Two or three shout, and there is **a heavy darkness**[18] tonight;	שְׁנַיִם אוֹ שְׁלֹשָׁה יִצְעֲקוּ וְהַלַּיְלָה **חֹשֶׁךְ אֲפֵלָה**,[18]	לוד
	Perhaps they shout deceitfully; we cannot come to their voice	אוּלַי בְּמִרְמָה הֵם צֹעֲקִים, לֹא נוּכַל לָבוֹא לְקוֹלָם	
	Unless there are other men with us.	בִּלְתִּי אִם אֲנָשִׁים אֲחֵרִים אִתָּנוּ.	
RADDAI	No one comes to my aid, and my blood is spilling onto the earth.	אֵין אִישׁ לְעֶזְרָתִי וְדָמַי נִגָּרִים אָרְצָה.	רדי
	(Doeg enters with a torch in his hand)	(דואג בא ולפיד בידו)	
LUD	Look, who goes there?	רְאֵה מִי בָא שָׁמָּה?	לוד
GETHER	Behold, a man in his robe, with a torch and weapons in his hand.	הִנֵּה אִישׁ בְּכֻתָּנְתּוֹ וְלַפִּיד וּכְלֵי נֶשֶׁק בְּיָדוֹ.	גתר
DOEG	Who is there? Who cried out there, 'I have been murdered'?	מִי הוּא שָׁם? מִי צָעַק שָׁם נִרְצָחְתִּי?	דואג
LUD	We do not know.	אֲנַחְנוּ לֹא יָדָעְנוּ.	לוד
DOEG	Did you not hear the voice crying out?	הַאִם לֹא שְׁמַעְתֶּם קוֹל הַצְּעָקָה?	דואג
CHESED	Hurry, come here, hurry to my aid –	חוּשׁוּ בֹּאוּ הֵנָּה, חוּשׁוּ לְעֶזְרָתִי –	כשד
DOEG	**What is wrong with you there, that you cried out?**[19]	**מַה־לְּךָ שָׁם, כִּי נִזְעָקְתָּ?**[19]	דואג

16 This is Shem's grandson and Aram's son, mentioned in Gen. 10:23 and 1 Chron. 1:17. Salkinson has selected the name based on its sound correspondence with Shakespeare's Gratiano.

17 Zeph. 1:14 קוֹל יוֹם יְהוָה מַר צֹרֵחַ שָׁם גִּבּוֹר 'the voice of the day of the LORD, wherein the mighty man cries bitterly'.

18 Exod. 10:22 (referring to the darkness that afflicted Egypt as one of the ten plagues).

19 Judg. 18:23. Although the meaning of the root ז.ע.ק. means 'gather' or 'assemble' in the *nif'al* stem, Salkinson seems to have had in mind the meaning of the *qal*, 'cry out'. (See also Second Part, note 245 and *Ram and Jael*, First Part, note 316.)

GETHER	This is Ithiel's standard-bearer.	זֶה הוּא נוֹשֵׂא הַדֶּגֶל לְאִיתִיאֵל.	גתר
LUD	I know him, for he is a man of valour.	יְדַעְתִּיו כִּי בֶּן־חַיִל הוּא.	לוד
DOEG	Who are you there, making the sound of your wailing heard?	מִי אַתֶּם שָׁם, כִּי תַשְׁמִיעוּ קוֹל יִלְלַתְכֶם?	דואג
CHESED	Come to me, Doeg, robbers **have struck me and wounded me**[20]	בּוֹאָה אֵלַי דּוֹאֵג, שׁוֹדְדִים **הִכּוּנִי פְּצָעוּנִי**[20]	כשד
	Hurry to my aid.[21]	**חוּשָׁה לְעֶזְרָתִי.**[21]	
DOEG	Chesed, my dear officer, who laid a hand on you?	כֶּשֶׂד פְּקִידִי יַקִּירִי, מִי שָׁלַח בְּךָ יָד?	דואג
CHESED	One of the robbers is lying close to me	אֶחָד מִן הַשּׁוֹדְדִים שׁוֹכֵב קָרוֹב לִי	כשד
	For he cannot move from his position.	כִּי לֹא יוּכַל לָמוּשׁ מִמְּקוֹמוֹ.	
DOEG	Where are they, where are they, **bloodthirsty and deceitful men**?[22]	אַיָּם אֵיפֹה הֵם, **אַנְשֵׁי דָמִים וּמִרְמָה**?[22]	דואג
RADDAI	Please save me.	נָא הוֹשִׁיעָה לִּי.	רדי
CHESED	That is one of them.	זֶה הוּא אֶחָד מֵהֶם.	כשד
DOEG	Are you **a bloodthirsty and deceitful man**?[23]	הַאַתָּה הוּא **אִישׁ דָּמִים וּמִרְמָה**?[23]	דואג
	(Doeg stabs Raddai)	(דואג דוקר את רדי)	
RADDAI	Oh, despicable dog! Ignominy of men! –	הוֹי כֶּלֶב נִבְזֶה! קְלוֹן בְּנֵי הָאָדָם! –	רדי
	Oh! Oh! Oh!…	הוֹ! הוֹ! הוֹ! ...	
DOEG	Would you murder a soul in the dark? Where are the rest of the robbers?	הֲתִרְצַח נֶפֶשׁ בַּחֹשֶׁךְ? אַיֵּה יֶתֶר הַשּׁוֹדְדִים?	דואג
	The whole town sits quietly, while murderers are on its streets.	כָּל הָעִיר יֹשֶׁבֶת וְשׁוֹקֶטֶת וּמְרַצְּחִים בְּחוּצוֹתֶיהָ.	
	And who are you there – are you good or evil?	וּמִי אַתֶּם שָׁמָּה – הֲטוֹבִים אַתֶּם אִם רָעִים?	
LUD	**As we consider ourselves, so shall you call us.**[24]	**כַּאֲשֶׁר נְשָׁעֵר בְּנַפְשֵׁנוּ, כֵּן תְּכַנֶּה אֹתָנוּ.**[24]	לוד
DOEG	Are you the noble Lud?	הַאַתָּה הוּא לוּד הַנָּדִיב?	דואג

20 Song of Songs 5:7.
21 Ps. 38:23 (38:22 in English Bibles).
22 Ps. 55:24 (55:23 in English Bibles).
23 Ps. 5:7 (5:6 in English Bibles).
24 Prov. 23:7 כִּי | כְמוֹ־שָׁעַר בְּנַפְשׁוֹ כֶּן־הוּא 'for as he considers himself, so he is'.

LUD	I am he.	אֲנִי הוּא.	לוד
DOEG	Please pardon me; behold, Chesed lies here	שָׂא נָא אֶת פָּנַי; הִנֵּה כֶשֶׂד שׁוֹכֵב פֹּה	דואג
	Beaten and wounded by the robbers.	מֻכֶּה וּפָצוּעַ מִן הַשּׁוֹדְדִים.	
GETHER	Chesed?	כֶּשֶׂד?	גתר
DOEG	Is there a wound in your flesh, my brother?	הֲיֵשׁ פֶּצַע בִּבְשָׂרְךָ אָחִי?	דואג
CHESED	My leg has been cut in half.	שׁוֹקִי נִגְזְרָה עַד חֶצְיָהּ.	כשד
DOEG	God forbid you should say so; show me in the light of the lamp	חָלִלָה אַל תֹּאמַר כֵּן; הָאִירוּ לִי בְּאוֹר הַנֵּר	דואג
	So that I may bind the wound with my robe.	וְאֶחְבֹּשׁ אֶת הַפֶּצַע בְּכֻתָּנְתִּי.	
ANAH	What is this? **Who cried out a great and bitter cry**?[25]	מַה־זֹּאת? מִי צָעַק צְעָקָה גְדוֹלָה וּמָרָה?[25]	ענה
DOEG	Are you asking who it is that cried out?	הַאַתְּ תִּשְׁאֲלִי, מִי הוּא אֲשֶׁר צָעַק?	דואג
ANAH	Woe is me, Chesed **my glory and my splendour**![26]	אוֹי לִי, כֶּשֶׂד הוֹדִי וַהֲדָרִי![26]	ענה
	Woe is me, Chesed, Chesed, Chesed!	אוֹי לִי כֶּשֶׂד כֶּשֶׂד כֶּשֶׂד!	
DOEG	Be quiet, whore, strumpet! What do you think, Chesed	הַחֲרִישִׁי זוֹנָה פְּרוּצָה. מַה־תַּחְשׁוֹב כֶּשֶׂד	דואג
	Who wounded your leg?	מִי מָחַץ שׁוֹקֶךָ?	
CHESED	I do not know.	לֹא יָדָעְתִּי.	כשד
GETHER	I am sorry that it is thus for you; I had gone to seek you.	צַר לִי שֶׁכָּכָה לָךְ וַאֲנִי הָלַכְתִּי לְבַקֶּשְׁךָ.	גתר
DOEG	Lend me a belt so that I may bind the wound	הַשְׁאִילוּ לִי חֲגוֹרָה וְאֶחְבֹּשׁ אֶת הַמַּכָּה	דואג
	And bring me a chair to bear him in comfort.	וְהָבִיאוּ לִי כִסֵּא, לָשֵׂאת אֹתוֹ בְּנַחַת.	
ANAH	Woe is me, he is fainting – Chesed, Chesed, Chesed!	אוֹי לִי הוּא מִתְעַלֵּף – כֶּשֶׂד כֶּשֶׂד כֶּשֶׂד!	ענה
DOEG	Listen to me, minsters, my heart tells me	שְׁמָעוּנִי שָׂרִים, אֲנִי לְבָבִי יַגִּיד לִי	דואג

25 Gen. 27:34 וַיִּצְעַק צְעָקָה גְּדֹלָה וּמָרָה 'and he cried out a great and bitter cry'.
26 Alshekh to Prov. 14 and Dan. 4.

	That this **sack of filth**[27] has also had a hand in the conspiracies	כִּי חֵמַת־צֹאָה[27] הַזֹּאת, גַּם יָדָהּ בַּקְּשָׁרִים	
	But it is not the time to investigate; **be strong and show yourself courageous**,[28] Chesed.	אַךְ אֵין עֵת לְבַקֵּר; חֲזַק וְהִתְחַזֵּק[28] כֶּשֶׁד.	
	Bring the lamp over; do you know this man's face?	הָבִיאוּ הַנֵּר מֵעֵבֶר מִזֶּה; הַיְדַעְתֶּם פְּנֵי הָאִישׁ הַזֶּה?	
	Why, he is my friend and companion, a son of my native city.	הֲלֹא הוּא אֹהֲבִי וְרֵעִי, בֶּן־עִיר מוֹלַדְתִּי.	
	Is this Raddai? No, no, but perhaps it is him	הַהוּא זֶה רַדָּי? לֹא לֹא, וְאוּלַי הוּא הִנֵּהוּ	
	Shudder, O heavens![29] It is Raddai and none other –	שֹׁמּוּ שָׁמַיִם![29] רַדַּי הוּא וְלֹא אַחֵר –	
GETHER	Raddai of Venice?	רַדַּי מִוִּינֶעצְיָא?	גתר
DOEG	Yes, my lord; do you know him?	כֵּן אֲדֹנִי, הֲיָדַעְתָּ אֹתוֹ?	דואג
GETHER	Indeed I do know him.	יְדַעְתִּיו גַּם יְדַעְתִּיו.	גתר
DOEG	These severe woes have not allowed me to welcome you	צָרוֹת קָשׁוֹת אֵלֶּה, לֹא נְתָנוּנִי לְקַדֵּם פָּנֶיךָ	דואג
	With the honour befitting you; indeed I beg your pardon.	בְּכָבוֹד הַנָּכוֹן לָךְ, אָכֵן אִתְּךָ הַסְּלִיחָה.	
GETHER	I am happy to see your face.	שָׂמַחְתִּי לִרְאוֹת פָּנֶיךָ.	גתר
DOEG	What can I do for you, Chesed? – Bring another chair –	מָה אֶעֱשֶׂה לְךָ כֶּשֶׂד? – הָבִיאוּ כִּסֵּא עוֹד –	דואג
	(A second chair is brought)	(כסא שני מובא)	
GETHER	Raddai?…	רַדָּי? ...	גתר
DOEG	It is he – who among us, kind men,	הוּא הוּא זֶה – מִי אִתָּנוּ אַנְשֵׁי חֶסֶד	דואג
	Will carry him in comfort away from here, while I call the doctor.	יִשָּׂאוּהוּ בְּנַחַת מִזֶּה וַאֲנִי אֶקְרָא אֶת הָרֹפֵא.	
	(To Anah) As for you, woman, do not labour in vain	(אל ענה) וְאַתְּ אִשָּׁה, אַל תַּעַמְלִי לַשָּׁוְא	
	Did you know that the stricken Chesed was my best friend –	הֲיָדַעַתְּ כִּי כֶשֶׂד הַמֻּכֶּה, הָיָה אֹהֲבִי בְּחִירִי –	
	What was the quarrel between you?	מֶה הָיָה הָרִיב בֵּינֵיכֶם?	

27 Babylonian Talmud *Shabbat* 152a אשה חמת מלא צואה 'a woman is a sack full of filth'.
28 2 Sam. 10:12 חֲזַק וְנִתְחַזַּק 'be strong and let us show ourselves courageous'.
29 Jer. 2:12.

CHESED	There was no quarrel between us, nor do I know the man.	רִיב לֹא הָיָה בֵּינֵינוּ וְגַם לֹא יָדַעְתִּי אֶת הָאִישׁ.	כשד
DOEG	*(To Anah)* Now why is it that your face grows pale? –	(אל ענה) וְלָמָּה זֶה יֶחְוְרוּ פָּנָיִךְ? –	דואג
	Take them both away from the street.	הוֹצִיאוּ אֶת שְׁנֵיהֶם אֶל מִחוּץ לָרְחוֹב.	
	(Chesed and Raddai are taken out in their chairs)	(כשד ורדי מוצאים בכסאותם)	
	Stand and look, ministers, why is it that her face grows pale	עִמְדוּ הַבִּיטוּ שָׂרִים, לָמָּה זֶה יֶחְוְרוּ פָּנֶיהָ	
	Look at her face to face; the look in her eyes testifies against her.	הַבִּיטוּ אֵלֶיהָ פָּנִים בְּפָנִים, אוֹתוֹת עֵינֶיהָ יַעֲנוּ בָהּ.	
	If you look thus at us, we shall draw out the hidden matters of your heart,	אִם כֹּה תֶחֱזִי בָנוּ, נִדְלֶה מַצְפּוּנֵי לִבֵּךְ,	
	The wickedness will issue its voice, even if her lips are dumb.	הָרִשְׁעָה תִּתֵּן קוֹלָהּ, אַף אִם שְׂפָתֶיהָ תֵּאָלַמְנָה.	
MILCAH	What has happened? What has happened, my husband?	מֶה הָיָה הַדָּבָר? מֶה הָיָה הַדָּבָר בַּעֲלִי?	מלכה
DOEG	Raddai and other men fell upon Chesed in the dark;	רַדַּי וַאֲנָשִׁים אֲחֵרִים, נָפְלוּ עַל כֶּשֶׂד בַּמַּחְשָׁךְ,	דואג
	The men fled for their lives; Chesed is still alive	הָאֲנָשִׁים נִמְלְטוּ לְנַפְשָׁם; כֶּשֶׂד עוֹד נִשְׁמָתוֹ בוֹ	
	But Raddai is dead.	וְרַדַּי מֵת.	
MILCAH	My soul weeps for the dead man, and my heart for dear-spirited Chesed.	נַפְשִׁי תִבְכֶּה לַמֵּת וְלִבִּי לְכֶשֶׂד יְקַר רוּחַ.	מלכה
DOEG	This is the fruit of whoredom; go, Milcah, and enquire	זֶה־פְּרִי הַזְּנוּת; לְכִי מִלְכָּה וְדִרְשִׁי	דואג
	Where Chesed ate his bread tonight.	אָנָה אָכַל כֶּשֶׂד אֶת לַחְמוֹ הַלָּיְלָה.	
	(To Anah) Now why is it that trembling has seized you?	(אל ענה) וְלָמָּה זֶה חֲרָדָה אֲחָזַתֵךְ?	
ANAH	He ate in my house; but trembling has not seized me.	הוּא אָכַל בְּבֵיתִי; אַךְ חֲרָדָה לֹא אֲחָזַתְנִי.	ענה
DOEG	If so, then go with me to be put to the test.	אִם כֵּן אֵיפוֹא, עִמִּי תֵלְכִי לְהִבָּחֵן.	דואג

MILCAH	May shame cover you, **wife of whoredom**.[30]	כְּלִמָּה תְכַסֵּךְ אֵשֶׁת זְנוּנִים.[30]	מלכה
ANAH	I am not **a wife of whoredom**,[31] but rather an honest woman	לֹא אֵשֶׁת זְנוּנִים[31] אָנִי, כִּי אִם אִשָּׁה יְשָׁרָה	ענה
	Like you, who insults me without cause.	כָּמוֹךְ אֲשֶׁר תְּגַדְּפִינִי חִנָּם.	
MILCAH	**Taunts and insults**[32] are fitting for a woman like you.	חֲרָפוֹת וְגִדּוּפִים,[32] נְכוֹנִים לְאִשָּׁה כָּמוֹךְ.	מלכה
DOEG	Go with me, ministers, so that we may give Chesed a remedy	לְכוּ אִתִּי שָׂרִים, וְנָשִׂים מָזוֹר לְחֶשֶׁד	דואג
	And as for you, woman, go with us and tell us everything.	וְאַתְּ אִשָּׁה תֵּלְכִי עִמָּנוּ וְתַגִּידִי לָנוּ כֹּל.	
	Hurry, Milcah, to the citadel, to the commander and the lady	מַהֲרִי מִלְכָּה אֶל הַמְּצוּדָה, אֶל הַשָּׂר וְהַגְּבִירָה	
	And tell them what has happened. *(To himself)* As for me, tonight I shall run[33]	וַאֲשֶׁר קָרָה הַגִּידִי. (אל עצמו) וַאֲנִי הַלַּיְלָה אָרוּץ[33]	
	In order to arrive **at my desired haven**,[34] or to **decreed destruction**.[35]	לָבוֹא לִמְחוֹז חֶפְצִי,[34] אוֹ לְכִלָּיוֹן חָרוּץ.[35]	
	(All exit)	(הולכים כלם)	
SCENE 2	*The bedchamber – Asenath sleeps and a light burns*	חדר המטה – אסנת ישנה ונר דולק	מחזה ב'
ITHIEL	Why, the matter is true, the matter is true, on my life!	הֲלֹא אֱמֶת הַדָּבָר, אֱמֶת הַדָּבָר חֵי נַפְשִׁי!	איתיאל
	But I shall not mention the abomination, before the pure stars;	אַךְ לֹא אַזְכִּיר הַתּוֹעֵבָה, נֶגֶד הַכּוֹכָבִים הַזַּכִּים;	
	And even if the matter is true, I shall not spill her blood,	וְאַף אִם אֱמֶת הַדָּבָר, לֹא אֶשְׁפֹּךְ דָּמָהּ,	
	I shall not tear the skin of her flesh; it is whiter than snow	לֹא אֶקְרַע עוֹר בְּשָׂרָהּ, לָבָן הוּא מִשֶּׁלֶג	

30 Hosea 1:2.
31 Hosea 1:2.
32 Ezek. 5:15 חֶרְפָּה וּגְדוּפָה 'a taunt and an insult'.
33 This and the next line form a rhyming couplet, mirroring Shakespeare's 'night/quite' (5.1.128–9).
34 Ps. 107:30 אֶל־מְחוֹז חֶפְצָם 'to their desired haven'.
35 Isa. 10:22.

And as smooth as a marble memorial stone. *(Removes his sword from his thigh)*	וְחָלָק כְּמַצֶּבֶת שָׁיִשׁ. (מסיר חרבו מעל ירכו)
Nevertheless she shall surely die, so that she cannot seduce another man.	בְּכָל זֹאת מוֹת תָּמוּת, לְבַל תּוֹסֵף לְהַדִּיחַ אִישׁ.
I shall put out the light here and put out the light there,	אֲכַבֶּה אֶת הַנֵּר פֹּה וַאֲכַבֶּה אֶת הַנֵּר שָׁם,
If I put out the light of the chamber, I can light it again should I have regrets	אִם כִּבֵּיתִי נֵר הַחֶדֶר, אוּכַל לְהַדְלִיקוֹ כִּי נִחָמְתִּי
But if I put out the light of the LORD, the ultimate **work of the hands of a skilled craftsman**[36]	וְכִי כִבֵּיתִי נֵר אֲדֹנָי, תַּכְלִית מַעֲשֵׂה יְדֵי אָמָּן[36]
That illuminates the innermost parts, who can light it again?	הַמֵּאִיר בְּחַדְרֵי בָטֶן, מִי יוּכַל לְהַדְלִיקוֹ עוֹד?
Even **an angel and a seraph**[37] cannot light the wick again.[38]	גַּם מַלְאָךְ וְשָׂרָף,[37] לֹא יַדְלִיק עוֹד הַפְּתִילָה.[38]
If I pluck a rose from its stalk, it cannot be planted again	אִם קָטַפְתִּי שׁוֹשַׁנָּה מִגִּזְעָהּ, אֵין לִנְטֹעַ אֹתָהּ שֵׁנִית
For it shall surely wilt; I can smell it now	כִּי נָבוֹל תִּבּוֹל; אָרִיחַ בָּהּ עַתָּה
While it is still on its stalk. *(Kisses Asenath)*	בְּעוֹדָהּ עַל גִּזְעָהּ. (נושק את אסנת)
Your scent is pleasant and comely; you still have enough power	רֵיחֵךְ עָרֵב וְנָעִים; עוֹד כֹּחֵךְ רַב לָךְ
To persuade the judge to let the sword of justice fall from his hand	לְפַתּוֹת אֶת הַשּׁוֹפֵט, לְהַפִּיל חֶרֶב הַמִּשְׁפָּט מִיָּדוֹ
I shall kiss you once more – once more again –	אֶשָּׁקֵךְ עוֹד הַפַּעַם – עוֹד זֹאת הַפַּעַם –
You were comely in life and you will be comely in your death as well –	נְעִימָה הָיִית בַּחַיִּים – וּנְעִימָה תִּהְיִי גַּם בְּמוֹתֵךְ
I shall kill you with my hand, and afterwards I shall love you again[39]	הִנְנִי אֲמִיתֵךְ בְּיָדִי וְאַחֲרֵי כֵן אֶרְחָמֵךְ עוֹד[39]

36 Song of Songs 7:2 (7:1 in English Bibles).

37 Midrash Tanḥuma to Exod. 30:11–34:35; Alshekh to Isa. 6 and Song of Songs 1.

38 Cf. Shakespeare's 'I know not where is that Promethean heat/That can thy light relume' (5.2.12–13); Salkinson has omitted the Classical reference.

39 Or: 'continue to love you'; either meaning of the Hebrew עוד 'still', 'again' is a possible translation for Shakespeare's 'I will kill thee and love thee after' (5.2.18–19).

	And this is my last kiss – the kiss of the angel of death –	וְזֹאת נְשִׁיקָתִי הָאַחֲרוֹנָה – נְשִׁיקַת מַלְאַךְ הַמָּוֶת –	
	My compassion is stirred for you,[40] yet I spill the tears of a cruel man	נִכְמְרוּ רַחֲמַי אֵלַיִךְ[40] וְאֶשְׁפֹּךְ דִּמְעוֹת אַכְזָר	
	Like **the fearsome king most high**[41] who gathers in those He loves.	כְּמֶלֶךְ עֶלְיוֹן נוֹרָא,[41] אֶת אֲשֶׁר יֶאֱהַב יַאַסְפֶנּוּ.	
	But she awakens –	אַךְ הִיא מְקִיצָה –	
ASENATH	Who is this? Ithiel?	מִי הוּא זֶה? אִיתִיאֵל?	אסנת
ITHIEL	It is I, Asenath.	אֲנִי הוּא, אָסְנַת.	איתיאל
ASENATH	Will you lie with me in the bed, my lord?	הֲתִשְׁכַּב עִמִּי בַּמִּטָּה אֲדֹנִי?	אסנת
ITHIEL	Have you prayed tonight?	הַאִם הִתְפַּלַּלְתְּ הַלַּיְלָה?	איתיאל
ASENATH	I have not forgotten my prayer.	לֹא נָשִׁיתִי תְפִלָּתִי.	אסנת
ITHIEL	If there is still iniquity in you and you have not entreated your God,	אִם עוֹד עָוֹן בָּךְ וְאֶת פְּנֵי אֱלֹהַיִךְ לֹא חִלִּית	איתיאל
	Hurry, entreat Him now.	מַהֲרִי חַלִּי אֶת פָּנָיו עַתָּה.	
ASENATH	Oh, my lord! **What do your words hint at?**[42]	אֲהָהּ אֲדֹנִי! מַה־יִּרְזְמוּן מִלֶּיךָ?[42]	אסנת
ITHIEL	Pray a short prayer, and I shall stand afar	הִתְפַּלְּלִי תְּפִלָּה קְצָרָה וַאֲנִי אֶעֱמֹד מִנֶּגֶד	איתיאל
	I cannot kill you before you reconcile yourself with the **God of the spirits**[43]	לֹא אוּכַל לַהֲמִיתֵךְ, טֶרֶם תִּתְרַצִּי אֶל אֱלֹהֵי הָרוּחוֹת[43]	
	God forbid that I should destroy the spirit with the body.	חָלִלָה לִּי מֵהַשְׁחִית, אֶת הָרוּחַ עִם הַגְּוִיָּה.	
ASENATH	Do you intend to kill me?	הֲתֹאמַר לַהֲמִיתֵנִי?	אסנת
ITHIEL	Yes.	הֵן.	איתיאל
ASENATH	My God, my God, have mercy on me!	אֵלִי אֵלִי חוּסָה עָלָי!	אסנת
ITHIEL	Amen and amen!	אָמֵן וְאָמֵן!	איתיאל

40 Gen. 43:30 וַיְמַהֵר יוֹסֵף כִּי־נִכְמְרוּ רַחֲמָיו אֶל־אָחִיו 'And Joseph hurried out, for his compassion was stirred for his brother'.
41 Ps. 47:3 (47:2 in English Bibles) כִּי־יְהוָה עֶלְיוֹן נוֹרָא מֶלֶךְ גָּדוֹל עַל־כָּל־הָאָרֶץ 'for the Lord on high is fearsome; a great king over the whole earth'.
42 Job 15:12 וּמַה־יִּרְזְמוּן עֵינֶיךָ 'and what do your eyes wink at?'
43 Num. 16:22 אֵל אֱלֹהֵי הָרוּחֹת לְכָל־בָּשָׂר 'God of the spirits of all flesh', also Num. 27:16.

ASENATH	If you say amen, I hope that you will not kill me.	אִם אָמֵן אָמַרְתָּ, הוֹחַלְתִּי כִּי לֹא תְמִיתֵנִי.	אסנת
ITHIEL	Whereas I do not hope so.	וַאֲנִי לֹא כֵן אוֹחִילָה.	איתיאל
ASENATH	I fear your roaming eyes, for you are fearsome	יָרֵאתִי מֵעֵינֶיךָ הַמְשׁוֹטְטוֹת, כִּי נוֹרָא אָתָּה	אסנת
	Although I do not know why I fear you	אַף כִּי לֹא יָדַעְתִּי, לָמָּה אִירָא מִפָּנֶיךָ	
	For I have not sinned against you and have not done you ill.	כִּי לֹא חָטָאתִי לְךָ וְלֹא גְמַלְתִּיךָ רָעָה.	
	Nevertheless, **deathly horror has overwhelmed me.**[44]	בְּכָל זֹאת **אֵימוֹת מָוֶת נָפְלוּ עָלָי.**[44]	
ITHIEL	Pay heed to your iniquities.	שִׁיתִי לִבֵּךְ אֶל עֲוֹנָיִךְ.	איתיאל
ASENATH	To my love which I have for you.	אֶל אַהֲבָתִי אֲשֶׁר אֲהַבְתִּיךָ.	אסנת
ITHIEL	And therefore you deserve to die.	וְלָכֵן מִשְׁפַּט מָוֶת לָךְ.	איתיאל
ASENATH	Death **is unjust;**[45] for who would kill someone	מָוֶת **לֹא בְמִשְׁפָּט;**[45] כִּי מִי הוֹרֵג נֶפֶשׁ	אסנת
	Because she loved him? Indeed, why do you **purse your lips**[46]	עֵקֶב אֲשֶׁר אֲהֵבַתְהוּ? אַךְ לָמָּה **תִקְרַץ בִּשְׂפָתֶיךָ**[46]	
	And tremble where you stand,[47] like one who plans **to engulf and destroy**[48] all?	**וְתַחְתֶּיךָ תִּרְגַּז,**[47] כְּחֹשֵׁב **לְבַלַּע וּלְהַשְׁחִית**[48] כֹּל?	
	They are terrible signs; nevertheless, I hope and await	אוֹתוֹת נוֹרָאִים הֵם; בְּכָל זֹאת קִוִּיתִי הוֹחַלְתִּי	
	That it is not upon me, Ithiel, not upon me that **you will pour out your wrath.**[49]	כִּי לֹא עָלַי אִיתִיאֵל, לֹא **עָלַי תִּשְׁפֹּךְ חֲמָתֶךָ.**[49]	
ITHIEL	Be silent; do not speak further.	הַחֲרִישִׁי, אַל תּוֹסִיפִי דַבֵּר.	איתיאל
ASENATH	I shall not speak further, but what else do you seek?	לֹא אוֹסֵף דַּבֵּר, וּמַה־תְּבַקֵּשׁ עוֹד?	אסנת
ITHIEL	The handkerchief which is precious to me, which I gave you as a gift	הַמִּטְפַּחַת הַיְקָרָה לִי, אֲשֶׁר נָתַתִּי לָךְ לְמַתָּת	איתיאל

44 Ps. 55:5.

45 Jer. 17:11.

46 Prov. 16:30 קֹרֵץ שְׂפָתָיו כִּלָּה רָעָה 'he purses his lips and brings about evil'.

47 Hab. 3:16 וְתַחְתַּי אֶרְגָּז 'and I tremble where I stand'.

48 Abarbanel to Ezek. 7; Alshekh to Gen. 27 and numerous other locations therein.

49 Jer. 10:25 שְׁפֹךְ חֲמָתְךָ 'pour out Your wrath'; similar collocations appear in Ezek. 14:19, 20:8, 13, 21, 22:22, 30:15, 36:18; Ps. 79:6. The phrasing from Jer. 10:25 and Ps. 79:6 is also very well known from its appearance in the Passover Haggadah.

	You gave it to Chesed –	נָתַתְּ אֹתָהּ אֶל כֶּשֶׂד –	
ASENATH	On my life and soul! Indeed I did not do this	חֵי נַפְשִׁי וְרוּחִי! כִּי לֹא עָשִׂיתִי זֹאת	אסנת
	Send for and summon the man, and ask him.	שְׁלַח וּקְרָא אֶת הָאִישׁ וּשְׁאַל אֶת פִּיהוּ.	
ITHIEL	Guard yourself, **precious soul,**[50] guard yourself from **a false oath**[51]	הִשָּׁמְרִי לָךְ **נֶפֶשׁ יְקָרָה**,[50] הִשָּׁמְרִי **מִשְּׁבוּעַת שָׁקֶר**[51]	איתיאל
	You are lying in the bed from which you will not get out.	אַתְּ שׁוֹכֶבֶת בַּמִּטָּה אֲשֶׁר לֹא תֵרְדִי מִמֶּנָּה.	
ASENATH	But not to die in it tonight.	אַךְ לֹא לָמוּת בָּהּ הַלָּיְלָה.	אסנת
ITHIEL	Indeed you shall die momentarily; therefore make confession	מוֹת תָּמוּתִי כְּרֶגַע; לָכֵן תְּנִי תוֹדָה	איתיאל
	For all of your iniquities; if you deceive **with a curse and an oath**[52]	עַל כָּל עֲוֹנַיִךְ; אִם תְּכַזְּבִי **בְּאָלָה וּבִשְׁבוּעָה**[52]	
	Saying, 'I have not sinned', it will not benefit you and will not save you	לֵאמֹר לֹא חָטָאתִי, לֹא יוֹעִילֵךְ וְלֹא יַצִּילֵךְ	
	The word has gone out of my mouth, to **the anguish of my spirit**,[53] and it cannot be put back;	דָּבָר יָצָא מִפִּי **לְמֹרַת רוּחִי**[53] וְאֵין לְהָשִׁיב,	
	Indeed you shall die, Asenath.	מוֹת תָּמוּתִי אָסְנַת.	
ASENATH	Have mercy upon me, God in heaven!	חוּסָה עָלַי אֵל בַּשָּׁמַיִם!	אסנת
ITHIEL	I too **shall lift up my hands**[54] and say amen.	גַּם **אֲנִי אֶשָּׂא כַפַּי**[54] וְאֹמַר אָמֵן.	איתיאל
ASENATH	If so, then have mercy upon me too	אִם כֵּן אֵיפוֹא, חוּסָה עָלַי גַּם אַתָּה	אסנת
	I have not transgressed your covenant, and I do not love Chesed	לֹא עָבַרְתִּי בְּרִיתְךָ וְאֵת כֶּשֶׂד לֹא אָהַבְתִּי	
	Except in that he is a person; I love him like any person	כִּי אִם בַּאֲשֶׁר הוּא אָדָם, אֲהַבְתִּיו כְּכָל אָדָם	

50 Prov. 6:26.
51 Zech. 8:17.
52 Neh. 10:30 (10:29 in English Bibles) בְּאָלָה וּבִשְׁבוּעָה 'in a curse and an oath'.
53 Gen. 26:35 מֹרַת רוּחַ 'anguish of spirit'.
54 Ps. 63:5 (63:4 in English Bibles), 119:48.

	According to the law and the commandment;[55] but I have not given him a token.	כַּתּוֹרָה וְכַמִּצְוָה;[55] אַךְ אוֹת לֹא נָתַתִּי לוֹ.	
ITHIEL	On my life! Indeed I saw my handkerchief in his hand	חֵי נַפְשִׁי! כִּי מִטְפַּחְתִּי רָאִיתִי בְיָדוֹ	איתיאל
	And you, in your lying, force me to harden my heart like a rock	וְאַתְּ בְּכַחְשֵׁךְ תְּאַלְּצִינִי לְהַקְשׁוֹת לִבִּי כַּסָּלַע	
	To complete my task as a murderer and not as one sacrificing a burnt offering or a sin offering	לְכַלּוֹת מְלַאכְתִּי כְּרֹצֵחַ וְלֹא כְּמַקְרִיב עוֹלָה וַחֲטָאָה	
	For indeed with my eyes I saw the handkerchief.	כִּי הֵן בְּעֵינַי רָאִיתִי אֶת הַמִּטְפַּחַת.	
ASENATH	If so, then he found it	אִם כֵּן אֵיפוֹא, הוּא מָצָא אֹתָהּ	אסנת
	For I never gave it to him	כִּי אָנֹכִי מֵעוֹדִי, לֹא נְתַתִּיהָ לוֹ	
	Summon him here so that he may tell you the truth.	קְרָא אֹתוֹ הֵנָּה, וְיַגִּיד לְךָ דְּבַר אֱמֶת.	
ITHIEL	He has already told the matter.	כְּבָר הִגִּיד הַדָּבָר.	איתיאל
ASENATH	And what did he tell you, my lord?	וּמָה הִגִּיד לְךָ אֲדֹנִי?	אסנת
ITHIEL	That he came to you.	כִּי בָא אֵלַיִךְ.	איתיאל
ASENATH	He came to me?	הוּא בָא אֵלַי?	אסנת
ITHIEL	Yes.	כֵּן.	איתיאל
ASENATH	Such a thing he cannot say.	דָּבָר כָּזֶה, לֹא יוּכַל לְהַגִּיד.	אסנת
ITHIEL	Because his mouth is blocked –	יַעַן כִּי סָתוּם פִּיהוּ –	איתיאל
	Doeg, the most faithful in all my house, fulfilled my instructions.	דּוֹאֵג הַנֶּאֱמָן בְּכָל בֵּיתִי, מִלֵּא אַחֲרֵי דְבָרִי.	
ASENATH	Have I understood your words, and he is dead as I fear?!	הַאִם בַּנְתִּי לִדְבָרֶיךָ וְהוּא מֵת כַּאֲשֶׁר יָגוֹרְתִּי!	אסנת
ITHIEL	If there were as many lives inside him as hairs on his flesh	לוּ הָיוּ בְקִרְבּוֹ נְפָשׁוֹת רַבּוֹת כְּשַׂעֲרוֹת בְּשָׂרוֹ	איתיאל
	The stomach of my revenge would not be too small to swallow him entirely.	לֹא קָצְרָה בֶטֶן נִקְמָתִי לִבְלֹעַ אֹתוֹ כָּלִיל.	
ASENATH	Oh! He has been caught in the snare, and I am done for, done for.	אֲהָהּ! הוּא נִלְכַּד בַּפָּח וַאֲנִי אָבַדְתִּי אָבָדְתִּי.	אסנת

55 2 Chron. 14:3 (14:4 in English Bibles) הַתּוֹרָה וְהַמִּצְוָה 'the law and the commandment'. See First Part, note 212 for discussion of this collocation.

ITHIEL	Does your heart dare, whore, to weep for him to my face?	הֲיָעֹז לִבֵּךְ זוֹנָה, לְבַכּוֹת אֹתוֹ עַל פָּנָי?	איתיאל
ASENATH	Send me to prison, my lord, **but please do not kill me.**[56]	שַׁלְּחֵנִי אֲדֹנִי לְבֵית כֶּלֶא וְהָמֵת אַל תְּמִיתֵנִי.[56]	אסנת
ITHIEL	Your end approaches, whore.	בָּא קִצֵּךְ זוֹנָה.	איתיאל
ASENATH	Please kill me in the morning, but let me live tonight.	הָרְגֵנִי נָא בַּבֹּקֶר וּתְנָה לִי נַפְשִׁי הַלָּיְלָה.	אסנת
ITHIEL	If you resist me –	אִם תִּתְיַצְּבִי בְּפָנַי –	איתיאל
ASENATH	Let go of me, just for a few moments.	הַרְפֵּה מִמֶּנִּי, אַךְ רְגָעִים אֲחָדִים.	אסנת
ITHIEL	Your time has come, and the appointed time cannot be delayed.	בָּאָה עִתֵּךְ וְאֵין לְאַחֵר הַמּוֹעֵד.	איתיאל
ASENATH	Let me pray a short prayer.	הַנִּיחֵנִי לְהִתְפַּלֵּל תְּפִלָּה קְצָרָה.	אסנת
ITHIEL	The appointed time has already passed. *(Strangles her)*	כְּבָר עָבַר הַמּוֹעֵד. (מחנק אותה)	איתיאל
MILCAH	*(From outside)* Open up for me, commander, please open the door for me	(מחוץ) פְּתַח לִי הַשָּׂר, אָנָּא פְּתַח לִי הַדֶּלֶת	מלכה
	Hurry, my lord – !	חוּשָׁה אֲדֹנִי! –	
ITHIEL	What is the sound of shouting there? – Your soul is still within you!	מֶה קוֹל הַצְּעָקָה שָׁם? – עוֹד נַפְשֵׁךְ בָּךְ!	איתיאל
	There still remains breath in you? Although I am cruel	עוֹד נוֹתְרָה בָךְ נְשָׁמָה? אַף כִּי אַכְזָר אָנִי	
	I cannot prolong your death pangs without cause	לֹא אוּכַל לְהַאֲרִיךְ חֶבְלֵי מוֹתֵךְ חִנָּם	
	I shall press my hand heavily upon you,[57] a little here, a little there[58]	אַכְבִּיד עָלַיִךְ אַכְפִּי,[57] זְעֵיר פֹּה זְעֵיר שָׁם[58]	
	And that is it for you.	וְדַי לָךְ.	
MILCAH	*(From outside)* Please, my lord, my lord!…	(מחוץ) אָנָּא אֲדֹנִי אֲדֹנִי! ...	מלכה

56 1 Kings 3:26 וְהָמֵת אַל־תְּמִיתֻהוּ 'and do not kill him'.
57 Job 33:7 וְאַכְפִּי עָלֶיךָ לֹא־יִכְבָּד 'and my hand will not be heavy upon you'.
58 Isa. 28:10 זְעֵיר שָׁם זְעֵיר שָׁם 'a little here, a little there'.

ITHIEL	Who knocks there?	מִי דוֹפֵק שָׁם?	איתיאל
MILCAH	*(From outside)* My dear lord, I have something to tell you.	(מחוץ) אֲדֹנִי הַיָּקָר, דָּבָר יֵשׁ בְּפִי לְהַגֶּד־ךָ.	מלכה
ITHIEL	It is Milcah – stand there for a brief moment –	מִלְכָּה הִיא – עִמְדִי שָׁם מְעַט רֶגַע –	איתיאל
	Behold, she is dead, and this one comes to bring me the tidings	הִנֵּה מֵתָה הִיא וְזֹאת בָּאָה לְבַשְּׂרֵנִי	
	That Chesed is dead, for she raises her voice like a herald.	לֵאמֹר כֶּשֶׂד מֵת, כִּי כִמְבַשֶּׂרֶת תִּתֵּן קוֹלָהּ.	
	Do you still move? No, no, she is already dead	הֲנוֹעַ תָּנוּעַ עוֹד? לֹא לֹא כְּבָר גָּוָעָה	
	And she lies as still as the grave – shall I open the door for Milcah –	וְדוּמָם תִּשְׁכַּב כַּקָּבֶר – הַאֶפְתַּח הַדֶּלֶת לְמִלְכָּה –	
	Perhaps there is still breath in her nostrils – no, there is no feeling[59] in her.	אוּלַי עוֹד נְשָׁמָה בְּאַפָּהּ – לֹא, רֶגֶשׁ[59] בָּהּ אָיִן.	
	And if I open the door, Milcah will indeed come	וְאִם אֶפְתַּח הַדֶּלֶת, בּוֹא תָבוֹא מִלְכָּה	
	To speak to my wife – oh, who is my wife now?	לְדַבֵּר אֶל אִשְׁתִּי – אֲהָהּ מִי אִשְׁתִּי עוֹד?	
	Oh, woe to this day! The sun above has grown dark upon me	אֲהָהּ לַיּוֹם הַזֶּה! חָשַׁךְ עָלַי הַשֶּׁמֶשׁ מִמַּעַל	
	The moon is clothed in darkness,[60] and the earth crumbles underneath.	הַיָּרֵחַ יִלְבַּשׁ קַדְרוּת[60] וְהָאָרֶץ תִּתְפּוֹרֵר מִתָּחַת.	
MILCAH	*(From outside)* Have mercy, open up for me, commander, so that I may speak a word to you.	(מחוץ) חָנֵּנִי פְּתַח לִי הַשָּׂר, וַאֲדַבֵּר דָּבָר אֵלֶיךָ.	מלכה
ITHIEL	I almost forgot you, Milcah, please come here –	שְׁכַחְתִּיךְ מִלְכָּה כִמְעַט, בּוֹאִי נָא הֵנָּה –	איתיאל
	Indeed I shall hurry to spread the curtain over the bed –	אַךְ אָחִישׁ לִפְרֹשׂ הַמָּסָךְ עַל פְּנֵי הַמִּטָּה –	
	Where are you, where are you? What is wrong with you, that you called out?	אַיֵּךְ אֵיפֹה אַתְּ? מַה־לָּךְ כִּי קָרָאתְ*?	

59 This word is attested in the Hebrew Bible, but it is a *hapax legomenon* (appearing in Ps. 55:15 [55:14 in English Bibles]) with the meaning of 'throng' or 'unrest'. Salkinson is instead using it in the sense of 'feeling' or 'sensation', which dates to the modern period (Even-Shoshan 2003, 5: 1748).

60 Isa. 50:3 אַלְבִּישׁ שָׁמַיִם קַדְרוּת 'I clothe the heavens in darkness'.

* קָרָאת

	(Opens the door)	(פותח את הדלת)	
MILCAH	Oh, my lord! There are murderous deeds in our midst.	הוֹי אֲדֹנִי! עֲלִילוֹת רֶצַח בְּקִרְבֵּנוּ.	מלכה
ITHIEL	When did it happen?	מָתַי נִהְיָה?	איתיאל
MILCAH	Just now.	זֶה עָתָּה.	מלכה
ITHIEL	This is the fault of the moon, for it has drawn near to the earth	זאת שִׁגְגַת הַיָּרֵחַ, כִּי הִקְרִיב אֶל הָאָרֶץ	איתיאל
	And struck its inhabitants with madness.	וַיַּךְ אֶת יֹשְׁבֶיהָ בְּשִׁגָּעוֹן.	
MILCAH	Chesed struck one of the lads, Raddai of Venice.	כֶּשֶׂד הִכָּה אַחַד הַבַּחוּרִים, רַדַּי מְוִינֶעצְיָא.	מלכה
ITHIEL	Raddai has been killed? And Chesed has been killed?	רַדַּי הוּמַת? וְכֶשֶׂד הוּמַת?	איתיאל
MILCAH	Chesed has not been killed.	כֶּשֶׂד לֹא הוּמָת.	מלכה
ITHIEL	If Chesed has not been killed, there is no advantage to the murder	אִם כֶּשֶׂד לֹא הוּמַת אֵין יִתְרוֹן לָרֶצַח	איתיאל
	And the revenge is not sweet.	וְהַנְּקָמָה אֵינֶנָּה מְתוּקָה.	
ASENATH	Without cause I have been murdered, for nothing.	חִנָּם נִרְצַחְתִּי, עַל לֹא דָבָר.	אסנת
MILCAH	What is this voice?	מָה הַקּוֹל הַזֶּה?	מלכה
ITHIEL	What voice?	אֵיזֶה קוֹל?	איתיאל
MILCAH	It is the voice of my lady, oh, come, hurry to save her –	קוֹל גְּבִרְתִּי הוּא, הוֹי בּוֹאוּ חוּשׁוּ לִישׁוּעָתָה* –	מלכה
	Speak again, my lady! Speak, dear Asenath, speak!	דַּבְּרִי עוֹד גְּבִרְתִּי! דַּבְּרִי אָסְנַת הַיְקָרָה דַּבֵּרִי!	
ASENATH	I die blameless.	נְקִיָּה אֲנִי מֵתָה.	אסנת
MILCAH	Who has laid a hand on you?	מִי שָׁלַח בָּךְ יָד?	מלכה
ASENATH	My hand did this, and there is no one besides me.	יָדִי עָשְׂתָה זאת וְאֵין אִישׁ זוּלָתִי.	אסנת
	Farewell! And commend me to my noble husband.	חֲיִי בְשָׁלוֹם! וְהִזְכַּרְתִּנִי אֶל בַּעֲלִי הַנָּדִיב.	
	Farewell, farewell! – *(Dies)*	חֲיִי חֲיִי בְשָׁלוֹם**! – (מתה)	
ITHIEL	How, then, has she been killed?	אֵיךְ אֵיפוֹא נֶהֶרְגָה?	איתיאל
MILCAH	Who indeed knows?	מִי אֵיפוֹא יוֹדֵעַ?	מלכה
ITHIEL	Well, you heard from her mouth that I did not kill her.	הֲלֹא שָׁמַעַתְּ מִפִּיהָ, כִּי לֹא אָנֹכִי הֲרַגְתִּיהָ.	איתיאל

* לִישׁוּעָתָהּ

** בְּשָׁלוֹם

MILCAH	I did hear this from her mouth, and as I heard, so shall I tell.	כֵּן שָׁמַעְתִּי מִפִּיהָ וְכַאֲשֶׁר שָׁמַעְתִּי אַגִּידָה.	מלכה
ITHIEL	There is lying under her tongue, and she will go down to Sheol as a liar	כָּזָב תַּחַת לְשׁוֹנָהּ וּכְכֹזֶבֶת תֵּרֵד שְׁאוֹלָה	איתיאל
	For I killed her with my hand.	כִּי אָנֹכִי בְּיָדִי הֲרַגְתִּיהָ.	
MILCAH	Therefore, then, she resembles one of the **angels on high**[61]	לָכֵן אֵיפוֹא דָּמְתָה הִיא, לְאֶחָד מִמַּלְאֲכֵי עֶלְיוֹן[61]	מלכה
	And you are one of the **evil angels**.[62]	וְאַתָּה אֶחָד הִנְּךָ, מִן מַלְאֲכֵי רָעִים.[62]	
ITHIEL	She went astray **like a shameless woman**,[63] for she was a whore.	הִיא שָׂטְתָה כְּאַחַת הַנְּבָלוֹת,[63] כִּי זוֹנָה הָיָתָה.	איתיאל
MILCAH	You are speaking like a demon, and **you are bearing false witness against her**.[64]	כְּאַחַד הַשֵּׁדִים תְּדַבֵּר וְתַעֲנֶה בָהּ עֵד שָׁקֶר.[64]	מלכה
ITHIEL	The falseness has borne witness against her; her recklessness resembled water.	הַשֶּׁקֶר עָנָה בְּפָנֶיהָ, פַּחְזוּתָהּ דָּמְתָה לַמָּיִם.	איתיאל
MILCAH	And you are as rash as fire, and your wicked libel is worthless and false;	וְאַתָּה נִמְהָר כָּאֵשׁ וְדִבָּתְךָ הָרָעָה שָׁוְא וָשָׁקֶר;	מלכה
	She was as pure **as the very heavens**.[65]	זַכָּה הָיְתָה כְּעֶצֶם הַשָּׁמַיִם.[65]	
ITHIEL	Chesed defiled her, ask your husband and he will tell you.	כֶּשֶׁד טִמֵּא אוֹתָהּ, שַׁאֲלִי אֶת בַּעֲלֵךְ וְיַגִּידֵךְ.	איתיאל
	I would go down to **the depths of Sheol**[66] if I did not know well	לִשְׁאוֹל תַּחְתִּית[66] אֵרֵדָה, לוּלֵי יָדַעְתִּי מְאֹד	
	That I killed her justly, and your husband knows and is witness.	כִּי הֲרַגְתִּיהָ בַּמִּשְׁפָּט וּבַעֲלֵךְ יוֹדֵעַ וָעֵד.	
MILCAH	My husband is witness?	בַּעֲלִי עֵד?	מלכה
ITHIEL	Your husband is witness.	בַּעֲלֵךְ עֵד.	איתיאל
MILCAH	That she defiled herself in a stranger's bed?	כִּי נִטְמְאָה בְּמִשְׁכַּב זָר?	מלכה
ITHIEL	Chesed lay with her;	כֶּשֶׁד שָׁכַב אִתָּהּ,	איתיאל

---

61 This expression is extremely well known from its appearance in the liturgical song שלום עליכם מלאכי השרת 'welcome, ministering angels' traditionally sung in Jewish homes immediately before the Friday night meal; it is also attested in numerous locations in the commentaries of Ibn Ezra, Abarbanel, and Alshekh.

62 Ps. 78:49.

63 Job 2:10 כְּדַבֵּר אַחַת הַנְּבָלוֹת תְּדַבֵּרִי 'you are speaking like a shameless woman'.

64 Exod. 20:16 לֹא־תַעֲנֶה בְרֵעֲךָ עֵד שָׁקֶר 'you shall not bear false witness against your neighbour'.

65 Exod. 24:10.

66 Deut. 32:22.

	If she had been true to me, **I raise my hand up on high**[67]	לוּ הָיְתָה בְּאָמְנָה אִתִּי, הֲרִימוֹתִי יָדִי לַמָּרוֹם[67]	
	That I would not have exchanged her for **all the earth and the fullness thereof**[68]	אִם לָקַחְתִּי תְּמוּרָתָהּ, כָּל הָאָרֶץ וּמְלֹאָהּ[68]	
	Even if its dust were gold and its stones were gems of Ophir.[69]	אַף כִּי עַפְרָהּ זָהָב וַאֲבָנֶיהָ אַבְנֵי אוֹפִיר.[69]	
MILCAH	My husband is witness?	בַּעֲלִי עֵד?	מלכה
ITHIEL	He was the first who opened my eyes,	הוּא הָיָה הָרִאשׁוֹן, אֲשֶׁר פָּקַח אֶת עֵינַי,	איתיאל
	For he is a faithful man and despises **the daubing of whitewash**[70]	כִּי אִישׁ נֶאֱמָן הוּא וּמְתָעֵב טִיחַ תָּפֵל[70]	
	Over **wicked men**.[71]	עַל פְּנֵי בְנֵי עַוְלָה.[71]	
MILCAH	My husband?	בַּעֲלִי?	מלכה
ITHIEL	Why have you asked twice? Why, I've said your husband.	לָמָּה זֶּה־תִּשְׁאֲלִי פַּעֲמַיִם? הֲלֹא בַּעֲלֵךְ אָמַרְתִּי.	איתיאל
MILCAH	Deceit has increased in the land, and **love has stumbled in the street**,[72]	גָּבְרָה הַמִּרְמָה בָּאָרֶץ וְאַהֲבָה בָּרְחוֹב כָּשָׁלָה,[72]	מלכה
	Did my husband really say that my lady is an adulteress?	הַאֻמְנָם בַּעֲלִי הִגִּיד כִּי גְבִרְתִּי מְנָאָפֶת?	
ITHIEL	Your husband, woman, your husband I said with **pure speech**[73]	בַּעֲלֵךְ, אִשָּׁה, בַּעֲלֵךְ אָמַרְתִּי בְּשָׂפָה בְרוּרָה[73]	איתיאל
	Do you not yet know who your husband is? He is Doeg, my faithful friend.	הֲטֶרֶם תֵּדְעִי מִי בַּעֲלֵךְ? הוּא דוֹאֵג אֹהֲבִי הַנֶּאֱמָן.	
MILCAH	If he said such a thing, may rot eat his flesh	אִם הוּא הִגִּיד כָּזֹאת, רָקָב יֹאכַל בְּשָׂרוֹ	מלכה
	One grain a day; for he has spoken deceit from his heart	גַּרְגַּר גַּרְגַּר לַיּוֹם; כִּי כָזָב דִּבֵּר מִלִּבּוֹ.	

67 Gen. 14:22 הֲרִימֹתִי יָדִי אֶל־יְהוָה 'I raise my hand up to the LORD'.
68 Deut. 33:16; Isa. 34:1; Jer. 8:16, 47:2; Ezek. 19:7, 30:12; Mic. 1:2.
69 A region renowned in the Hebrew Bible for its wealth; see, for example, 1 Kings 10:11, which describes the riches that King Solomon received from Ophir.
70 Based on Ezek. 22:28 וּנְבִיאֶיהָ טָחוּ לָהֶם תָּפֵל 'and her prophets have daubed them with whitewash'.
71 2 Sam. 3:34, 7:10; 1 Chron. 17:9.
72 Isa. 59:14 כִּי־כָשְׁלָה בָרְחוֹב אֱמֶת 'for truth has stumbled in the street'.
73 Zeph. 3:9.

	Her love was too great, for **a bridegroom of blood**[74]	גָּדְלָה אַהֲבָתָהּ יֶתֶר מִדַּי, אֶל **חֲתַן דָּמִים**[74]	
	To an **abominable and vile**[75] man –	אֶל אִישׁ **נִתְעָב וְנֶאֱלָח**[75] –	
ITHIEL	How dare you?	הֲיָעֹז פִּיךָ?	איתיאל
MILCAH	Do whatever is in your power; your deed is worthy of **God's law**[76]	עֲשֵׂה כָל אֲשֶׁר בְּכֹחֶךָ; שָׁוֶה מַעֲשֶׂךָ **לְתוֹרַת אֱלֹהִים**[76]	מלכה
	Just as you were worthy of a pure woman like her.	כַּאֲשֶׁר שׁוֶֹה* הָיִיתָ, בְּאִשָּׁה בָרָה כָּמוֹהָ.	
ITHIEL	I advise you to put a hand to your mouth.	אִיעָצְךָ לָשִׂים יָד לְפֶה.	איתיאל
MILCAH	I have more ability to suffer than any ill you could do to me.	כֹּחִי רַב לִי לִסְבֹּל, מִכָּל אֲשֶׁר תּוּכַל לְהָרַע לִי.	מלכה
	Strong-boned ass![77] **Wild donkey**![78] As brutish as a pig in muck!	**חֲמוֹר גָּרֶם**![77] **עַיִר פֶּרֶא**![78] נִבְעָר כַּחֲזִיר בָּרֶפֶשׁ!	
	You have done an evil deed – I do not fear **your flashing sword**[79]	אַתָּה הִשְׁחַתָּ עֲלִילָה – לֹא אִירָא **מִבְּרַק חַרְבֶּךָ**[79]	
	For twenty times **I would risk my life**[80]	כִּי עֶשְׂרִים פְּעָמִים, **אַשְׁלִיךְ נַפְשִׁי מִנֶּגֶד**[80]	
	To make your deeds known at the gates – oh, oh! Hurry, come!	וְאַשְׁמִיעַ בַּשְּׁעָרִים מַעֲשֶׂיךָ – הוֹי, הוֹי! חוּשׁוּ, בֹּאוּ!	
	The Cushite has killed my lady – murderer! Murderer!	הַכּוּשִׁי הָרַג אֶת גְּבִרְתִּי – מְרַצֵּחַ! מְרַצֵּחַ!	
	(Kenaz, Gether, and Doeg enter)	(קנז גתר ודואג באים)	
KENAZ	What has happened here? What is wrong with you, army commander?	מַה־קָּרָה פֹּה? מַה־לְּךָ שַׂר הַצָּבָא?	קנז
MILCAH	You have done well to come, Doeg, since the murderer	הֵטִיבוֹתָ לָבוֹא דוֹאֵג, אַחֲרֵי אֲשֶׁר הַמְרַצֵּחַ	מלכה

74 Exod. 4:25. This expression appears in a very different context in the biblical source; it is uttered by Moses' wife Zipporah in an enigmatic episode whereby she circumcizes her son and touches Moses' feet with the blood. See Ben-Shushan (2006) for a detailed study of the 'bridegroom of blood' motif in biblical and postbiblical Hebrew literature.

75 Job 15:16.

76 Josh. 24:26; this is also a very common phrase in all postbiblical forms of Hebrew meaning 'God's Torah'. Salkinson has chosen this phrase as a translation for Shakespeare's 'heaven' (5.2.156), in an undermotivated act of Judaization.

77 Gen. 49:14.

78 Job 11:12.

79 Deut. 32:41 אִם־שַׁנּוֹתִי בְּרַק חַרְבִּי 'when I sharpened my flashing sword'.

80 Judg. 9:17 וַיַּשְׁלֵךְ אֶת־נַפְשׁוֹ מִנֶּגֶד 'and he risked his life'.

* שָׁוֶה

	Has placed his iniquity upon your head.	שָׁת עֲוֹנוֹ עַל רֹאשֵׁךְ.	
GETHER	What has happened here?	מַה־נִּהְיְתָה פֹּה?	גתר
MILCAH	If you are a man, testify against the villain's lies	אִם אִישׁ הִנְּךָ, עֲנֵה כַחֲשׁוֹ בִּפְנֵי הַפָּרִיץ	מלכה
	He says you told him that his wife was unfaithful to him	הוּא אֹמֵר אַתָּה הִגַּדְתָּ, כִּי אִשְׁתּוֹ מָעֲלָה בוֹ	
	But I know well that you did not say so	וַאֲנִי יָדַעְתִּי מְאֹד כִּי כֵן לֹא הִגַּדְתָּ	
	For you are not a villain; speak, for **my heart is hot**.[81]	כִּי לֹא בְלִיַּעַל אַתָּה; דַּבֵּר כִּי חַם לִבִּי.[81]	
DOEG	I told him everything that I knew	אָנֹכִי הִגַּדְתִּי לוֹ, כְּכָל אֲשֶׁר יָדַעְתִּי	דואג
	And I did not add anything that he did not find	וְלֹא הוֹסַפְתִּי דָבָר, אֲשֶׁר לֹא מָצָא הוּא	
	To be so.	כִּי כֵן הוּא.	
MILCAH	But did you also say that his wife was whoring?	אֲבָל הֲגַם הִגַּדְתָּ, כִּי זָנְתָה אִשְׁתּוֹ?	מלכה
DOEG	Yes.	כֵּן.	דואג
MILCAH	You have spoken lies and falsehood; lies, falsehood, and slander	שֶׁקֶר וְכָזָב דִּבַּרְתָּ, שֶׁקֶר כָּזָב וָדֹפִי	מלכה
	As the Lord lives! Indeed you have deliberately spoken lies.	חַי אֲדֹנָי! כִּי שֶׁקֶר דִּבַּרְתָּ בְּזָדוֹן.	
	Did this blameless one lie with Chesed?	הֲכִי הַנְּקִיָּה הַזֹּאת, שָׁכְבָה עִם כֶּשֶׂד?	
	With Chesed, you said?	עִם כֶּשֶׂד הֲלֹא אָמַרְתָּ?	
DOEG	I told you, woman, Chesed is the man	הִגַּדְתִּי לָךְ אִשָּׁה, כֶּשֶׂד הוּא הָאִישׁ.	דואג
	But hurry, get out of here and hold your tongue.	אַךְ מַהֲרִי צְאִי מִזֶּה וּתְנִי מַעְצֹר לִלְשׁוֹנֵךְ.	
MILCAH	Behold, it is time to speak, and I shall not hold my tongue	הִנֵּה עֵת לְדַבֵּר וְלֹא אֶתֵּן מַעְצֹר לִלְשׁוֹנִי	מלכה
	My lady lies here, murdered on her bed.	גְּבִרְתִּי שׁוֹכֶבֶת פֹּה, נִרְצָחָה עַל מִשְׁכָּבָהּ.	
ALL	May God forbid.	חָלִלָה זֹאת מֵאֱלֹהִים.	כלם

81 Ps. 39:4 (39:3 in English Bibles).

MILCAH	And you, **with the lash of your tongue**,[82] caused the murder.	וְאַתָּה בְּשׁוֹט לְשׁוֹנְךָ,[82] סַבֹּתָ אֶת הָרֶצַח.	מלכה
ITHIEL	Do not stare, brothers; behold, the matter is true.	אַל תִּשְׁתָּאוּ אַחִים, הִנֵּה אֱמֶת הַדָּבָר.	איתיאל
GETHER	The matter is dreadful, **and who can endure it.**[83]	נוֹרָא הַדָּבָר וּמִי יְכִילֶנּוּ.[83]	גתר
KENAZ	A most **appalling and horrible thing**![84]	שַׁמָּה וְשַׁעֲרוּרָה[84] גְדוֹלָה! –	קנז
MILCAH	Deceit, deceit, and vileness! –	מִרְמָה מִרְמָה וּנְבָלָה! –	מלכה
	My spirit makes diligent search inside of me and I commune with my heart[85]	רוּחִי יְחַפֵּשׂ בְּקִרְבִּי וְעִם לְבָבִי אָשִׂיחָה[85]	
	While I muse a fire burns,[86] for thus I thought previously	בַּהֲגִיגִי תִבְעַר אֵשׁ,[86] כִּי כֵן חִשַּׁבְתִּי מִקֶּדֶם,	
	I shall kill myself, for my pain is too great to bear	אֶשְׁלַח יָד בְּנַפְשִׁי, כִּי גָדַל כְּאֵבִי מִנְּשׂא	
	Oh, deceit and vileness! –	הוֹי מִרְמָה וּנְבָלָה! –	
DOEG	Have you lost your senses? Get out and go to your house.	הַאִם סָר טַעֲמֵךְ! צְאִי וּלְכִי לָךְ לְבֵיתֵךְ.	דואג
MILCAH	Forgive me, ministers, so that I may speak; I must obey him	שָׂאוּנִי שָׂרִים וַאֲדַבֵּרָה; יֶשׁ־לִי לִשְׁמֹעַ בְּקוֹלוֹ	מלכה
	But not now; who yet knows, Doeg,	אֲבָל לֹא עָתָּה; מִי יוֹדֵעַ עוֹד דוֹאֵג	
	Perhaps I shall never again go to my house.	אוּלַי לֹא אֵלֵךְ עוֹד לְבֵיתִי עַד עוֹלָם.	
ITHIEL	*(Bending down over his wife)* Woe, woe, woe! –	(שוחח על אשתו) אוֹיָה, אוֹיָה, אוֹיָה! –	איתיאל
MILCAH	**Roll around in the dust**[87] and wail; you murdered a pure soul	הִתְפַּלֵּשׁ בֶּעָפָר[87] וְהֵילֵל; אַתָּה רָצַחְתָּ נֶפֶשׁ זַכָּה	מלכה
	A precious, blameless soul; there is none like her among women.	נֶפֶשׁ נְקִיָּה יְקָרָה, אֵין כָּמוֹהָ בַּנָּשִׁים.	
ITHIEL	*(Rising)* She was a deceitful soul –	(בקומו) נֶפֶשׁ רְמִיָּה הָיְתָה –	איתיאל
	I did not recognize you, my uncle; here lies your niece	לֹא הִכַּרְתִּיךָ דוֹדִי; פֹּה שׁוֹכֶבֶת בַּת אָחִיךָ	

82 Job 5:21 בְּשׁ֣וֹט לָ֭שׁוֹן תֵּחָבֵ֑א 'you will be hidden from the lash of the tongue'.
83 Joel 2:11.
84 Jer. 5:30.
85 Ps. 77:7 עִם־לְבָבִ֥י אָשִׂ֑יחָה וַיְחַפֵּ֥שׂ רוּחִֽי 'I commune with my heart, and my spirit makes diligent search'.
86 Ps. 39:4 (39:3 in English Bibles).
87 Mic. 1:10 עָפָ֖ר התפלשתי הִתְפַּלָּֽשִׁי 'roll around in the dust'.

	Who died here, for I strangled her with my hand.	אֲשֶׁר גָּוְעָה בָזֶה, כִּי חִנַּקְתִּיהָ בְיָדִי.	
	I know that the deed is evil, the deed of a cruel man's hands.	יָדַעְתִּי כִּי רַע הַמַּעֲשֶׂה, מַעֲשֵׂה יְדֵי אַכְזָר.	
GETHER	My daughter, my daughter Asenath! It is well for your father that he died in his misery	בִּתִּי בִּתִּי אָסְנַת! טוֹב לְאָבִיךְ כִּי מֵת בְּעָנְיוֹ	גתר
	For the thread of his life was severed by the bond of your covenant at that time	כִּי פְּתִיל חַיָּיו נִתַּק בְּקֶשֶׁר בְּרִיתֵךְ מֵאָז	
	If he were still alive, he would go mad now at the sight of his eyes	לוּ עוֹדֶנּוּ חַי, יִשְׁתּוֹלֵל עַתָּה לְמַרְאֵה עֵינָיו	
	And he would brazenly reproach his God and die as **a reviler and a blasphemer**.[88]	וְיָזִיד לְחָרֵף אֱלֹהָיו וְלָמוּת כִּמְחָרֵף וּמְגַדֵּף.[88]	
ITHIEL	**Evil and bitter is the deed**;[89] but Doeg knows	רַע וּמַר הַמַּעֲשֶׂה;[89] אֶפֶס דּוֹאֵג הוּא יֹדֵעַ	איתיאל
	That she committed vile deeds with Chesed a hundred times;	כִּי עָשְׂתָה נְבָלָה עִם כֶּשֶׂד מֵאָה פְּעָמִים;	
	Chesed confessed and did not deny it, and she, in her love for him,	כֶּשֶׂד הוֹדָה וְלֹא כִחֵד וְהִיא בְּאַהֲבָתָהּ אֹתוֹ	
	Gave him as a gift that very token	נָתְנָה לוֹ לְמַתָּת אֶת עֶצֶם הָאוֹת הַהוּא	
	Which I had given her, and which I saw in his hand	אֲשֶׁר אָנֹכִי נָתַתִּי לָהּ וַאֲשֶׁר רְאִיתִיו בְּיָדוֹ	
	Why, it is an embroidered silk handkerchief from antiquity	הֲלֹא הִיא מִטְפַּחַת מֶשִׁי מְרֻקָּמָה מִשָּׁנִים מִקֶּדֶם	
	Which my father originally gave my mother as a token of love.	אֲשֶׁר נָתַן אָבִי לְאִמִּי, לְמַזְכֶּרֶת אַהֲבָה בַּתְּחִלָּה.	
MILCAH	Oh God, oh **God of hosts**![90] –	אֵל אֱלֹהִים! אֵל **אֱלֹהֵי הַצְּבָאוֹת**![90] –	מלכה
DOEG	Be silent, restrain yourself.[91]	הַחֲרִישִׁי הִתְאַפְּקִי.[91]	דואג
MILCAH	**The spirit within me compels me**,[92] and **a fire is shut up in my bones**[93]	רוּחַ בִּטְנִי הֱצִיקַתְנִי[92] וְאֵשׁ עֲצוּרָה בְעַצְמוֹתַי[93]	מלכה

88 Ps. 44:17 (44:16 in English Bibles).
89 Abarbanel to 1 Sam. 16; Alshekh to Deut. 12 and Prov. 5, 20.
90 Hosea 12:6 (12:5 in English Bibles); Amos 3:13, 6:14.
91 Cf. Shakespeare's 'Zounds, hold your peace' (5.2.216).
92 Job 32:18 הֱצִיקַתְנִי רוּחַ בִּטְנִי 'the spirit within me compels me'.
93 Jer. 20:9 כְּאֵשׁ בֹּעֶרֶת עָצֻר בְּעַצְמֹתָי 'like a burning fire shut up in my bones'.

	I cannot control myself; shall I be silent this time?	הִתְאַפֵּק לֹא אוּכָל; הֶאָנֹכִי אַחֲרִישׁ הַפַּעַם?	
	Not so, my husband; **I must speak that I may find relief.**[94]	לֹא כֵן בַּעֲלִי, **אֲדַבְּרָה וְיִרְוַח לִי.**[94]	
	And even if heavens and earth and all men	וְאַף כִּי שָׁמַיִם וָאָרֶץ וְכָל בְּנֵי הָאָדָם	
	As well as all the **evil angels**[95] should surely scorn me	גַּם **מַלְאֲכֵי רָעִים**[95] כֻּלָּם בּוֹז יָבוּזוּ לִי	
	I shall not hold back from speaking and shall not control myself any longer.	לֹא אַחֲרִישׁ מִדַּבֵּר וְלֹא אֶתְאַפֵּק עוֹד.	
DOEG	Listen, be wise and go to your house.	שִׁמְעִי, הַשְׂכִּילִי וּלְכִי לְבֵיתֵךְ.	דואג
MILCAH	I shall not go.	לֹא אֵלֵךְ.	מלכה
	(Doeg raises his sword against his wife)	(דואג מניף חרבו על אשתו)	
GETHER	How can you raise a sword against a woman? It is a disgrace.	אֵיךְ תָּנִיף חֶרֶב עַל אִשָּׁה? חֶרְפָּה הִיא.	גתר
MILCAH	Listen, senseless Cushite, the handkerchief of which you speak	הַקְשֵׁב כּוּשִׁי חֲסַר דֵּעָה, הַמִּטְפַּחַת אֲשֶׁר אָמַרְתָּ	מלכה
	I happened to find it and gave it to my husband	אָנֹכִי בְּמִקְרֶה מְצָאתִיהָ וָאֶתְּנֶהָ אֶל בַּעֲלִי	
	For he had urged me several times to steal it.	כִּי כַּמֶּה פְּעָמִים הִפְצִיר בִּי לִגְנֹב אֹתָהּ.	
DOEG	**You are speaking like a shameless woman.**[96]	**כְּאַחַת הַנְּבָלוֹת תְּדַבֵּרִי.**[96]	דואג
MILCAH	Did she give the handkerchief to Chesed? God forbid; I found it	הַהִיא נָתְנָה הַמִּטְפַּחַת לְכֶשֶׂד? חָלִלָה, אֲנִי מְצָאתִיהָ	מלכה
	And gave it to my husband.	וָאֶתְּנֶהָ אֶל בַּעֲלִי.	
DOEG	**You speak lies,**[97] despicable woman.	**שֶׁקֶר דִּבַּרְתְּ,**[97] אִשָּׁה נִמְאָסָה.	דואג
MILCAH	I have not lied, as the LORD lives! I have not lied, ministers;	לֹא שִׁקַּרְתִּי, חַי אֲדֹנָי! לֹא שִׁקַּרְתִּי שָׂרִים;	מלכה
	Oh, foolish murderer! What could a **senseless man**[98] like you have to do	הוֹי מְרַצֵּחַ אֱוִילִי! מַה־לְּאִישׁ **בַּעַר**[98] כָּמוֹךָ	

94 Job 32:20.
95 Ps. 78:49.
96 Job 2:10 כְּדַבֵּר אַחַת הַנְּבָלוֹת תְּדַבֵּרִי 'you are speaking like a shameless woman'.
97 Zech. 13:3 שֶׁקֶר דִּבַּרְתָּ 'you speak lies'.
98 Ps. 92:7 (92:6 in English Bibles).

	With an honourable woman like her?	וּלְאִשָּׁה כְבוּדָה כָּמוֹהָ?	
	(Doeg stabs Milcah and flees)	(דואג דוקר את מלכה ונס)	
ITHIEL	Are there no **stones of fire**[99] in the heavens, with which to stone this villain!	הַאֵין **אַבְנֵי אֵשׁ**[99] בַּשָּׁמַיִם, לִרְגֹּם אֶת הַנָּבָל הַזֶּה!	איתיאל
GETHER	The woman is falling; he has killed his wife.	הָאִשָּׁה נֹפֶלֶת, הוּא הֵמִית אֶת אִשְׁתּוֹ.	גתר
MILCAH	Behold, I am dying; lay me next to my lady.	הֵן מֵתָה אָנִי, הַשְׁכִּיבוּנִי אֵצֶל גְּבִרְתִּי.	מלכה
GETHER	He has fled for his life, and his wife has been killed by his hand.	הוּא נִמְלַט לְנַפְשׁוֹ וְאִשְׁתּוֹ הוּמְתָה בְּיָדוֹ.	גתר
KENAZ	Does such a villain exist! – Take this sword	הֲנִמְצָא בְלִיַּעַל כָּזֶה! – קַח אֶת הַחֶרֶב הַזֹּאת	קנז
	Which I took from the Cushite's hand, and guard the door from outside	אֲשֶׁר לָקַחְתִּי מִיַּד הַכּוּשִׁי וּשְׁמֹר עַל הַפֶּתַח מִחוּץ	
	Lest he leave the doors of his house, and if he passes by, stab him.	לְבַל יֵצֵא מִדַּלְתֵי בֵיתוֹ וְאִם יַעֲבֹר דָּקְרֵהוּ.	
	Meanwhile, I shall run after this villain.	וַאֲנִי אָרוּצָה, אַחֲרֵי אִישׁ הַבְּלִיַּעַל הַזֶּה.	
	(Kenaz and Gether exit)	(קנז וגתר יוצאים)	
ITHIEL	I am no longer a man of valour;	בֶּן־חַיִל אֵינֶנִּי עוֹד;	איתיאל
	Even one of the youths may take my sword from my hand.	גַּם אֶחָד הַנְּעָרִים, יִקַּח אֶת חַרְבִּי מִיָּדִי.	
	But what is the benefit of might, when I have no justness	אַךְ מַה־בֶּצַע בִּגְבוּרָה וּצְדָקָה לִי אָיִן	
	Therefore, then, I lose everything in one day.	לָכֵן אֵיפוֹא אֶשְׁכַּל הַכֹּל בְּיוֹם אֶחָד.	
MILCAH	Asenath! What is the song that you sang before your death	אָסְנַת! מָה הַשִּׁירָה, שַׁרְתְּ לִפְנֵי מוֹתֵךְ	מלכה
	I too shall follow in your footsteps, and like you, I shall sing as I die	גַּם אֲנִי אֵצֵא בְעִקְבוֹתַיִךְ וְכָמוֹךְ בְּמוֹתִי אָשִׁירָה	
	Willows, willows, willows…	עֲרָבִים עֲרָבִים עֲרָבִים…	
	Listen to me, cruel Cushite! Your wife kept her covenant	שְׁמָעֵנִי כּוּשִׁי אַכְזָרִי! אִשְׁתְּךָ שָׁמְרָה בְרִיתָהּ	
	And loved you with an eternal love; if there is a lie in my mouth	וְאַהֲבַת עוֹלָם אֲהֵבַתְךָ; אִם שֶׁקֶר בְּפִי	

99 Ezek. 28:14, 16.

	Do not save me, my God! – And I shall utter with my tongue	אַל תּוֹשִׁיעֵנִי אֱלֹהָי! – וַאֲנִי אֶהְגֶּה בִלְשׁוֹנִי	
	What my heart utters, and **with the meditation of my tongue and my heart**[100]	כַּאֲשֶׁר יֶהְגֶּה לְבָבִי **וּבְהֶגְיוֹן לְשׁוֹנִי וּלְבָבִי**[100]	
	I shall vent my spirit[101] and die. *(Dies)*	**אוֹצִיא רוּחִי**[101] וְאֶגְוָעָה. (מתה)	
ITHIEL	I have another sword, in the depths of this chamber	עוֹד יֶשׁ־לִי חֶרֶב, בְּיַרְכְּתֵי הַחֶדֶר הַזֶּה	איתיאל
	It is sharpened and also polished,[102] from the weapons house in Spain	הוּחַדָּה הִיא וְגַם מְרוּטָה,[102] מִבֵּית הַנֶּשֶׁק בִּסְפָרַד.	
	Open the door for me, Gether my uncle, so that I may indeed go out.	פְּתַח לִי גֶּתֶר דּוֹדִי, וְיָצוֹא אֵצֵא הַחוּצָה.	
GETHER	Forbear, and do not go out, **for it will cost you your life**[103]	חֲדַל לְךָ וְאַל תֵּצֵא, **כִּי בְנַפְשְׁךָ הוּא**[103]	גתר
	There is no weapon in your hand, and **your blood will be on your head**.[104]	נֶשֶׁק אֵין בְּיָדְךָ **וְדָמְךָ יְהִי בְרֹאשֶׁךָ**.[104]	
ITHIEL	If so, then come into the house to speak with me[105]	אִם כֵּן אֵיפוֹא, בּוֹא הַבַּיְתָה לְדַבֵּר אִתִּי[105]	איתיאל
	Lest I break out and attack you with no sword or spear.	פֶּן אֶפְרֹץ וְנָפַלְתִּי עָלֶיךָ בְּאֵין חֶרֶב וַחֲנִית.	
	(Gether enters the house)	(גתר בא הביתה)	
GETHER	What do you want from me?	מַה־תְּבַקֵּשׁ מֶנִּי?	גתר
ITHIEL	Look, there is a sword in my hand	רְאֵה חֶרֶב בְּיָדִי	איתיאל
	You have not seen a better one than it **on a warrior's thigh**.[106]	טוֹבָה מִמֶּנָּה, לֹא רָאִיתָ **עַל יָרֵךְ גִּבּוֹר**.[106]	
	I remember the days when with this sword of mine in my hand	זָכַרְתִּי אֶת הַיָּמִים, אֲשֶׁר בְּחַרְבִּי זוּ בְּיָדִי	
	I split a way for myself between twenty obstacles like you	בָּקַעְתִּי לִי דֶרֶךְ, בֵּין עֶשְׂרִים פְּגָעִים כָּמוֹךָ	

100 Ps. 19:15 (19:14 in English Bibles) אִמְרֵי־פִי וְהֶגְיוֹן לִבִּי 'the words of my mouth and the meditation of my heart'.
101 Prov. 29:11 כָּל־רוּחוֹ יוֹצִיא כְסִיל 'a fool vents all of his spirit'.
102 Ezek. 21:14 (21:9 in English Bibles) חֶרֶב הוּחַדָּה וְגַם־מְרוּטָה 'a sword, sharpened and also polished'.
103 Prov. 7:23 וְלֹא־יָדַע כִּי־בְנַפְשׁוֹ הוּא 'and he does not know that it will cost him his life'.
104 1 Kings 2:37 דָּמְךָ יִהְיֶה בְרֹאשֶׁךָ 'your blood will be on your head'.
105 Salkinson has not reproduced Shakespeare's rhyming couplet 'me/thee' (5.2.255).
106 Ps. 45:4 (45:3 in English Bibles).

But in vain I boast now, for the wheel has turned	אַךְ לַשָּׁוְא אֶתְהַלֵּל עַתָּה, כִּי נֶהְפַּךְ הַגַּלְגַּל
And who might turn back its cycle? Do not fear me	וּמִי יָשִׁיב תְּקוּפָתוֹ? אַל תִּירָא מִפָּנַי
And let my sword not frighten you. Indeed, I have come to my end;	וְחַרְבִּי אַל תְּבַעֲתֶךָּ. הֵן בָּאתִי עַד קִצִּי;
Here is the limit of my lifespan. Here is the shore for my ship	פֹּה הוּא גְּבוּל חֶלְדִּי, פֹּה הַחוֹף לָאֳנִיָּתִי
So why should you fear me? Even from the waving of a soft reed	וְלָמָּה זֶה תֵּחַת מִפָּנַי? גַּם מִתְּנוּפַת קָנֶה רַךְ
Ithiel would retreat – but where should I go?	יִסּוֹג אִיתִיאֵל לְאָחוֹר – אַךְ אָנָה אֲנִי בָא?
How do I see your face, cursed, despoiled, wretched girl	אֵיךְ אֶרְאֶה פָּנַיִךְ, זְעוּמָה שְׁדוּדָה אֻמְלָלָה
Your face is white as snow and your flesh is cold as ice.	פָּנַיִךְ לְבָנִים כַּשֶּׁלֶג וּבְשָׂרֵךְ קַר כַּקָּרַח.
When we stand in judgement, why, at the sight of my eyes	כַּאֲשֶׁר נַעֲמֹד בַּמִּשְׁפָּט, הֲלֹא לְמַרְאֵה עֵינַי
I shall fall from the heavens to Sheol, among **evil angels**.[107]	אֶתְנַפֵּל מִשָּׁמַיִם שְׁאוֹלָה, בֵּין **מַלְאֲכֵי רָעִים**.[107]
You are cursed, wicked slave! Insolent destroyer of my soul! –	אָרוּר אַתָּה עֶבֶד נוֹכֵל! זֵד עֹכֵר נַפְשִׁי! –
Come, devils and demons, strike me, tear me to pieces	בּוֹאוּ שְׂעִירִים וְשֵׁדִים, הַכּוּנִי גְּזָרוּנִי לִגְזָרִים
So that I do not gaze there at my eyes' delight	לְבַל אַבִּיט שָׁמָּה אֶל מַחְמַד עֵינָי.
Put my flesh into **a stream of brimstone**,[108] sow my dust into the wind	תְּנוּ בְשָׂרִי **בְּגָפְרִית בֹּעֵרָה**,[108] זְרוּ עֲפָרִי לָרוּחַ
And take my soul down to **rivers and streams of fire**[109] –	וְהוֹרִידוּ אֶת נַפְשִׁי **לְנַהֲרֵי נַחֲלֵי אֵשׁ**[109] –
Asenath, **whom my soul loves**?[110] Asenath, Asenath, Asenath! –	אָסְנַת **שֶׁאָהֲבָה נַפְשִׁי**?[110] אָסְנַת, אָסְנַת, אָסְנַת! –
(Lud, Kenaz, Chesed laid out on a chair and attendants with Doeg bound in shackles)	(לוד, קנז, כשד מוטל בכסא ומשרתים עם דואג אסור בנחשתים)

107 Ps. 78:49.
108 Isa. 30:33.
109 Job 20:17 נַהֲרֵי נַחֲלֵי דְּבַשׁ וְחֶמְאָה 'rivers and streams of honey and butter'.
110 Song of Songs 1:7, 3:1, 2, 3.

LUD	Where is that rash, wretched man?	אַיֵּה הוּא הַגֶּבֶר הַנִּמְהָר הָאֻמְלָל הַהוּא?	לוד
ITHIEL	I am the man who was called Ithiel.	אֲנִי הוּא הַגֶּבֶר, אֲשֶׁר אִיתִיאֵל נִקְרֵאתִי.	איתיאל
LUD	And the wicked viper, where is he? Bring him before us.	וְהַפֶּתֶן הָרָע אַיֵּהוּ? הָבִיאוּ אֹתוֹ לְפָנֵינוּ.	לוד
ITHIEL	I want to look upon him, what the soles of his feet are	חָפַצְתִּי לְהִתְבּוֹנֵן בּוֹ, מַה־כַּפּוֹת רַגְלָיו	איתיאל
	But maybe it is a fable that the fable-tellers **devised from their own hearts**[111] –	אַךְ אוּלַי מָשָׁל הוּא, אֲשֶׁר **בָּדְאוּ** הַמּשְׁלִים **מִלִּבָּם**[111] –	
	If you are a demon, indeed I cannot kill you.	אִם אַחַד הַשֵּׁדִים הִנְּךָ, יָכֹל לֹא אוּכַל לְהָרְגֶךָ.	
	(Ithiel strikes Doeg an injurious blow)	(איתיאל מכה בדואג מכת פצע)	
LUD	Take his sword from his hand.	קְחוּ אֶת חַרְבּוֹ מִיָּדוֹ.	לוד
DOEG	My blood is spilling onto the earth, but I have not been struck a mortal blow.	דָּמִי נִגָּר אָרְצָה וּמַכַּת מָוֶת לֹא הֻכֵּיתִי.	דואג
ITHIEL	My eye is not distressed to see you, for you are still alive	לֹא צָרָה עֵינִי לִרְאוֹתְךָ, כִּי עוֹדְךָ חָי	איתיאל
	There is nothing better for you than death, and there is nothing more bitter for you than life.	אֵין טוֹב לְךָ מִמָּוֶת וְאֵין מַר לְךָ מֵחַיִּים.	
LUD	Ithiel! You were dear and noble in the days of old	אִיתִיאֵל! יָקָר וְנָדִיב הָיִיתָ בְּיָמִים מִקֶּדֶם	לוד
	But after you fell into the pit of this wicked slave	וְאַחֲרֵי אֲשֶׁר נָפַלְתָּ בִּשְׁחִיחוּת* עֶבֶד נוֹכֵל הַזֶּה	
	What can we say, how would we speak of you?	מַה־נֹּאמַר מַה־נְּדַבֵּר עָלֶיךָ?	
ITHIEL	Call me a murderer, if it is good in your eyes	קִרְאוּ לִי מְרַצֵּחַ, אִם טוֹב בְּעֵינֵיכֶם	איתיאל
	But please know and see that it was not out of insolence	אַךְ דְּעוּ נָא וּרְאוּ, כִּי לֹא בְזָדוֹן	
	But rather with innocence of heart that I did what I did.	כִּי אִם בְּתָם־לֵב, עָשִׂיתִי מַה שֶּׁעָשִׂיתִי.	
LUD	This villain has almost confessed to all his crimes;	הַנָּבָל הַזֶּה כִּמְעַט הוֹדָה עַל כָּל פְּשָׁעָיו;	לוד

111 1 Kings 12:33 בַּחֹדֶשׁ אֲשֶׁר־בָּדָא מלבד מִלִּבּוֹ 'in the month which he had devised from his own heart'.

* שְׁחִיתוּת

	Did you act together with him, to kill Chesed?	הַאִם הָיְתָה יָדְךָ עִמּוֹ, לַהֲרֹג אֶת כֶּשֶׁד?	
ITHIEL	Yes.	הֵן.	איתיאל
CHESED	My lord, army commander! How have I ever sinned against you?	אֲדֹנִי שַׂר הַצָּבָא! מֶה חָטָאתִי לְךָ מֵעוֹדִי?	כשד
ITHIEL	Now I know that you are in the right; please forgive me.	עַתָּה יָדַעְתִּי כִּי צָדַקְתָּ; אָנָּא סְלַח לִי.	איתיאל
	And now, please ask this evil destroyer	וְעַתָּה שַׁאֲלוּ נָא, אֶת הַמַּשְׁחִית הָרָע הַזֶּה	
	Why he gave himself over to corrupting my soul and my body together.	מַדּוּעַ הִתְמַכֵּר לְשַׁחֵת נַפְשִׁי וּגְוִיָּתִי כְּאֶחָת.	
DOEG	Do not ask me anything; you know what you know	אַל תִּשְׁאֲלוּנִי דָּבָר; יְדַעְתֶּם אֵת אֲשֶׁר יְדַעְתֶּם	דואג
	And from now on, I shall not open my mouth to speak a word.	וּמִזֶּה וָמַעְלָה, לֹא אֶפְתַּח פִּי לְדַבֵּר דָּבָר.	
LUD	But will you not open your mouth even for prayer?	וְלֹא תִפְתַּח פֶּה גַּם לִתְפִלָּה?	לוד
GETHER	Pains will open your lips.	מַכְאוֹבִים יִפְתְּחוּ אֶת שְׂפָתֶיךָ.	גתר
ITHIEL	Choose for yourself what is best in your eyes.	בְּחַר לְךָ אֶת הַטּוֹב בְּעֵינֶיךָ.	איתיאל
LUD	And you, my lord, must know that which you do not yet know	וְעָלֶיךָ אֲדֹנִי לָדַעַת, אֵת אֲשֶׁר לֹא יָדַעְתָּ עוֹד	לוד
	That we found letters in the pocket of the slain Raddai	כִּי מִכְתָּבִים מָצָאנוּ, בְּכִיס רַדַּי הַנֶּהֱרָג	
	And from one letter we know that there was an order between them	וּמִמִּכְתָּב אֶחָד נֵדַע, כִּי מַאֲמָר הָיָה בֵּינֵיהֶם	
	For Chesed to be killed by Raddai's hand.	לְהָמִית אֶת כֶּשֶׁד, עַל יְדֵי רַדָּי.	
ITHIEL	Is there any villain like him?	הֲיֵשׁ נָבָל כָּמוֹהוּ?	איתיאל
CHESED	Even among the followers of a foreign god none like him can be found.	גַּם בִּבְנֵי אֵל נֵכָר, לֹא נִמְצָא כָּמוֹהוּ.	כשד
LUD	And furthermore there is a letter of complaint which Raddai wrote to Doeg	וְעוֹד מִכְתַּב תְּלוּנָה, כָּתַב רַדַּי אֶל דּוֹאֵג	לוד
	But before he sent it, Doeg came and stabbed him.	אַךְ בְּטֶרֶם שְׁלָחוֹ, בָּא דוֹאֵג וַיִּדְקְרֵהוּ.	

ITHIEL	Evil and despicable dog –	כֶּלֶב רָע וְנִבְזֶה –	איתיאל
	But tell me, Chesed, how did	אַךְ הַגִּידָה לִי כֶּשֶׂד, אֵיכָה בָּאָה לְיָדְךָ	
	The handkerchief which belonged to my wife come into your hand?	הַמִּטְפַּחַת אֲשֶׁר לְאִשְׁתִּי?	
CHESED	I found it in my lodgings.	אֲנִי מְצָאתִיהָ בִּמְלוֹנִי.	כשד
	And he with his own mouth said here that he had thrown it there	וְהוּא בְּפִיו הִגִּיד בָּזֶה, כִּי הִשְׁלִיכָהּ שָׁם	
	In order to carry out the scheme of his heart.	לְמַעַן יוֹצִיא מְזִמַּת לְבָבוֹ.	
ITHIEL	How I have become a fool, a stupid fool **with no wisdom**![112]	אֵיךְ לֶאֱוִיל הָיִיתִי, אֱוִיל כְּסִיל וְאֵין תְּבוּנָה![112]	איתיאל
CHESED	And even Raddai in his letters **cries out that he has been wronged**[113] by Doeg	וְגַם רַדַּי בְּמִכְתָּבוֹ, יִצְעַק חָמָס[113] עַל דּוֹאֵג	כשד
	Because he incited him to become involved in a fight with me on the watch	עַל אֲשֶׁר הֱסִיתוֹ, לְהִתְגָּרוֹת בִּי עַל הַמִּשְׁמָר	
	For which I was removed from my position	אֲשֶׁר בַּעֲבוּר זֶה, נִדַּחְתִּי מֵעַל מַצָּבִי	
	And when he was dying, before he passed away he cried, 'Doeg struck me,	וּבְמוֹתוֹ טֶרֶם גָּוַע צָעַק „דּוֹאֵג הִכַּנִי	
	Doeg led me astray'.	דּוֹאֵג הֱדִיחָנִי".	
LUD	*(To Ithiel)* As for you, come out of the house, for you must go with us;	(אל איתיאל) וְאַתָּה צֵא מִן הַבַּיִת כִּי תֵלֵךְ עִמָּנוּ;	לוד
	Your post has been stripped from you and has been placed on Chesed's shoulders	הַמִּשְׂרָה נִקְרְעָה מֵעָלֶיךָ וּנְתוּנָה עַל שְׁכֶם כֶּשֶׂד	
	He is in charge on Caphtor. And with respect to this wicked man	הוּא הַמּשֵׁל בְּכַפְתּוֹר. וְעַל אֹדוֹת הַזֵּד הַזֶּה	
	If **the chastisement of a cruel man**,[114] painful, malicious, and prolonged, can be found	אִם יִמָּצֵא מוּסַר אַכְזָרִי,[114] מַכְאִיב מַמְאִיר וּמְמֻשָּׁךְ	
	Let him be disciplined and afflicted thereby. As for you, you will stay in prison	יִוָּסֵר וִיעֻנֶּה בוֹ. וְאַתָּה תֵּשֵׁב בְּבֵית כֶּלֶא	

112 Prov. 21:30.
113 Job 19:7 אֶצְעַק חָמָס 'I cry out that I have been wronged'.
114 Jer. 30:14.

	Until your judgement goes forth from the gate of Venice.	עַד אֲשֶׁר יֵצֵא מִשְׁפָּטְךָ מִשַּׁעַר וִינֶעצְיָא.	
	Go and bring him to the watch.	לְכוּ וְהוֹלִיכוּ אֹתוֹ אֶל הַמִּשְׁמָר.	
ITHIEL	Before you leave here, wait for me a little while	בְּטֶרֶם תֵּצְאוּ מִזֶּה, הוֹחִילוּ לִי מְעַט רֶגַע	איתיאל
	So that I may speak a few words. Indeed it is known in Venice	וַאֲדַבֵּר דְּבָרִים אֲחָדִים. הֵן מוּדַעַת בְּוִינֶעצְיָא	
	That I served her faithfully and you do not have to mention this	כִּי בֶּאֱמוּנָה עֲבַדְתִּיהָ וְלֹא לָכֶם לְהַזְכִּיר זֹאת	
	But when you write the chronicles in a book	אַךְ כַּאֲשֶׁר תִּכְתְּבוּ דִּבְרֵי הַיָּמִים עַל סֵפֶר	
	And the evil which has found us, mention my name in the prescribed manner	וְהָרָעָה אֲשֶׁר מְצָאַתְנוּ, הַזְכִּירוּ אֶת שְׁמִי כַּמִּשְׁפָּט	
	Do not show me partiality and do not condemn me without cause.	אַל תִּשְׂאוּ לִי פָנִים וְאַל תַּרְשִׁיעוּ אֹתִי חִנָּם.	
	And this is what you must say: that I loved **without wisdom**[115]	וְזֶה אֲשֶׁר תֹּאמְרוּ, כִּי אָהַבְתִּי **בְּאֵין תְּבוּנָה**[115]	
	But my love was complete; the spirit of jealousy is strange to me	אַךְ אַהֲבָתִי תְּמִימָה; רוּחַ קִנְאָה מוּזָר לִי	
	But when it passed over me, **it overflowed and reached the neck**[116]	אַךְ אַחֲרֵי אֲשֶׁר עֲבָרַנִי, **שָׁטַף וְעָבַר עַד צַוָּאר**[116]	
	Until I acted foolishly and was ensnared like that Judean[117]	עַד אֲשֶׁר נוֹאַלְתִּי וְנוֹקַשְׁתִּי כַּיְהוּדִי[117] הַהוּא	
	Who threw a sapphire[118] from his hand more precious than all the wealth of Israel.[119]	אֲשֶׁר הִשְׁלִיךְ סַפִּיר[118] מִיָּדוֹ, יָקָר מִכָּל הוֹן יִשְׂרָאֵל.[119]	

115 Prov. 21:30.

116 Isa. 8:8.

117 Alternatively, 'Jew'. Cf. Shakespeare's 'Indian' (Quarto and Second, Third, and Fourth Folios) or 'Judean' (First Folio) (5.2.345). The Hebrew word יְהוּדִי typically means 'Judean' (i.e., someone of the tribe of Judah) in the Hebrew Bible, but in later biblical texts (e.g., Esther) it begins to be used in the sense of 'Jew', which becomes standard in the postbiblical period. Salkinson's readers would have been aware of both meanings, and as such, the reference would have had unmistakeably Jewish associations. In addition, Scolnicov (2001: 189) points out that, as the name 'Judah' is the Hebrew equivalent of 'Judas', Salkinson's Ithiel is drawing an explicit comparison between his actions and the betrayal of Jesus.

118 Cf. Shakespeare's 'pearl' (5.2.345). The Hebrew word is sometimes translated as 'lapis lazuli'; see Exod. 24:10, 28:18; Ezek. 1:26, 10:1, 28:13; Job 28:6, 16; Lam. 4:7.

119 Salkinson has replaced Shakespeare's undefined 'his tribe' (5.3.346) with this very specific reference, which can be interpreted either as an allusion to biblical Israel (in keeping with 'Judean' in the preceding line) or as a label for the Jewish people, which 'Israel' commonly denotes in postbiblical usage.

	And my eyes, which from my youth had not learned to shed a tear	וְעֵינַי אֲשֶׁר מִנְּעוּרַי, לֹא לָמְדוּ לִשְׁפֹּךְ דִּמְעָה	
	Drip drops of water like **olive trees**[120] in Arabia.	תִּטֹּפְנָה נִטְפֵי מַיִם, כַּעֲצֵי שֶׁמֶן[120] בַּעֲרָב.	
	And you must also tell this: when I was in **Aram-zobah**[121]	וְגַם זֹאת תְּסַפְּרוּ, כַּאֲשֶׁר הָיִיתִי בַּאֲרַם צוֹבָה[121]	
	I saw an Ishmaelite,[122] **an arrogant, haughty man**[123] in his turban	רָאִיתִי אִישׁ יִשְׁמְעֵאלִי[122], זֵד יָהִיר[123] בְּמִצְנַפְתּוֹ	
	Strike one of our brothers to the disgrace of the nation of Venice	מַכֶּה אֶחָד מֵאַחֵינוּ, לְחֶרְפַּת עַם וִינֶעצְיָא	
	And I seized that circumcized dog and thrust my sword into his stomach	וְהֶחֱזַקְתִּי בַּכֶּלֶב הַנִּמּוֹל הַהוּא וָאֶתְקַע חַרְבִּי בְּבִטְנוֹ	
	Like this – *(Thrusts his sword into his stomach)*	כָּזֹאת – (תוקע חרבו בבטנו)	
LUD	Oh, **decreed destruction!**[124]	אֲהָהּ כִּלָּיוֹן חָרוּץ![124]	לוד
GETHER	Indeed **grace of lips**[125] is in vain; everything that is said is marred.	אַךְ לַשָּׁוְא חֵן שְׂפָתַיִם,[125] כָּל אֹמֶר נִשְׁחָת.	גתר
ITHIEL	*(Falls on Asenath)* I kissed you before I killed you	(נופל על אסנת) נְשַׁקְתִּיךְ טֶרֶם הֲרַגְתִּיךְ	איתיאל
	I made you cleave to me in my life; so shall I make you cleave to me in my death.	הִדְבַּקְתִּיךְ אֵלַי בְּחַיַּי, כֵּן בְּמוֹתִי אַדְבִּיקָה.	
	I lay hand on myself, and I die with a kiss.	שָׁלַחְתִּי יָד בְּנַפְשִׁי וְהִנְנִי מֵת בִּנְשִׁיקָה.	
	(Dies)	(מת)	
CHESED	This is what I feared, for I know his **breadth of heart**[126]	זֶה הוּא אֲשֶׁר יָגוֹרְתִּי, כִּי יָדַעְתִּי רֹחַב לִבּוֹ[126]	כשד
	But I thought one thing, that there was no weapon in his hand.	אַךְ אַחַת חָשַׁבְתִּי, כִּי אֵין נֶשֶׁק בְּיָדוֹ.	

120 1 Kings 6:23, 31, 32, 33.
121 Cf. Shakespeare's 'Aleppo' (5.3.350). Ps. 60:2 (60:1 in English Bibles); an Aramean state in southern Syria that arose in the late second millennium or early first millennium BCE, mentioned only here in the Hebrew Bible. The name is associated with the city of Aleppo in medieval and later Jewish tradition (see Ashtor 2007: 613), and is therefore an appropriate translation for 'Aleppo'.
122 The Ishmaelites, descendants of the biblical patriarch Abraham's elder son Ishmael, are equated with the Arabs in postbiblical Jewish tradition.
123 Prov. 21:24.
124 Isa. 10:22.
125 Prov. 22:11 חֵן שְׂפָתָיו 'the grace of his lips'.
126 1 Kings 5:9 (1 Kings 4:29 in English Bibles).

LUD	*(To Doeg)* Bold-spirited[127] dog!	לוד (אל דואג) כֶּלֶב עַז נֶפֶשׁ![127]
	More evil than any affliction, than hunger, plague, or a flood of water	רַע מִכָּל פֶּגַע, מֵרָעָב, דֶּבֶר וּמַבּוּל מָיִם
	Look at the slain ones who lie here in the bed	הַבֵּט אֶל הַנֶּהֱרָגִים, הַשּׁוֹכְבִים פֹּה בַּמִּטָּה
	They were killed by your hand; the outcome of the deeds of your hands.	חַלְלֵי יָדְךָ הֵם, תַּכְלִית מַעֲשֵׂי יָדֶיךָ.
	Who could see this sight and still have breath left in him –	מִי יִרְאֶה הַמַּרְאֶה הַזֶּה וְקָמָה עוֹד רוּחַ בּוֹ –
	Hide all of these; hide them from the eye of observers.	הַסְתִּירוּ כָּל אֵלֶּה, הַסְתִּירוּ מֵעֵין הָרֹאֶה.
	Arise, Gether, take possession of the house and all the property of the Cushite	קוּם גֶּתֶר, רֵשׁ אֶת הַבַּיִת וְכָל נַחֲלַת הַכּוּשִׁי
	For you shall succeed him. As for you, Chesed, governor of the land,	כִּי אַתָּה תִנְחָלֶנּוּ. וְאַתָּה כֶּשֶׁד נְצִיב הָאָרֶץ,
	Make a terrible judgement against this destroyer	עֲשֵׂה מִשְׁפָּט נוֹרָא, בָּאִישׁ הַמַּשְׁחִית הַזֶּה
	Recompense him according to his deeds;[128] do not look compassionately upon him.	**כְּמַעֲלָלָיו תָּשִׁיב לוֹ**,[128] אַל תָּחוֹס עֵינֶיךָ.
	As for me, **in the bitterness of my soul**[129] I shall go to sea by ship	**וַאֲנִי בְּמַר נַפְשִׁי**,[129] אֵרֵד הַיָּם בַּסְּפִינָה
	To tell at the gates of Venice all the words of lament.	לְהַגִּיד בְּשַׁעֲרֵי וִינֶעצְיָא, כָּל דִּבְרֵי הַקִּינָה.
	(All exit)	(הולכים כלם)

The end of the book. — תם הספר.

127 Cf. Shakespeare's 'Spartan' (5.3.359).
128 Hosea 12:3 (12:2 in English Bibles) כְּמַעֲלָלָיו יָשִׁיב לוֹ 'He will recompense him according to his deeds'.
129 Job 7:11.

Publisher's note

On page 197[130] the translator translated: 'more precious than all the tribes of Israel', but I changed the translation and wrote: 'more precious than all the wealth of Israel'.

And it seems to me that I am correct in this change, for in the English language it says 'richer' and this word has two senses; the first is wealth and the second is honour, and I chose the first sense, and so did the German translator[131] as well, for he did not translate *Besser als sein Stamm, sondern: reicher als sein Stamm*, and the difference between these two translations is very great, as every perceptive reader will understand on his own.

הערה מאת המו"ל

בדף 197[130] העתיק המעתיק: יָקָר מִכָּל שִׁבְטֵי יִשְׂרָאֵל, ואני שניתי ההעתקה וכתבתי: יָקָר מִכָּל הוֹן יִשְׂרָאֵל.

ואני אדמה כי צדקתי בהשנוי הזה, כי בשפת אנגלית יאמר richer ולמלה הזאת שתי הוראות; האחת לעשר והשנית לכבוד, ואני בחרתי בהוראה הראשונה, וכן עשה גם המעתיק האשכנזי[131] כי לא העתיק Besser als sein Stamm, sondern: reicher als sein Stamm, והשנוי אשר בין שתי העתקות האלה גדול מאוד כאשר כל קורא מבין יבין מדעתו.

130 In the original edition of *Ithiel*. As in the case of Smolenskin's request that Salkinson change the name of the play (see Letter from the Translator to the Publisher, note 1), there is no attested indication of Salkinson's opinion regarding this alteration.

131 Smolenskin does not name the German translator to whom he refers, but the phrase 'reicher als sein Stamm' appears in Philipp Kaufmann's *Othello* translation of 1832 (Kaufmann 1832: 184); interestingly, it does not appear in the influential Schlegel-Tieck German translation that was the standard throughout much of the nineteenth century.

Ram and Jael

Letter to the translator

Vienna, fifteenth of Ab 5638.[1]

My honourable friend!

You asked me for my opinion regarding the translation of the wonderful play *Romeo and Julia*,[2] the love song *par excellence*, like our Song of Songs, as wise men have called it, and whose name you have changed – with good sense – to *Ram and Jael*, so that it could also bear a Hebrew name, since in the Hebrew clothing wherein you have dressed it no one would recognize that the hands of a Hebrew had not created it, the hands of a Hebrew who speaks the language of his own playwrights and performs as wondrously as they do in his tongue. You ask for my opinion, but surely you should have known it even before you asked me, for it is no secret to you that I admire the exalted playwright who created *Ithiel* and *Ram and Jael* and the rest of his plays (which I pray will also have the good fortune to be written in Hebrew) and I envy the British, for he belongs to them, and since there is none amongst us who can write as wonderfully as he does, I hereby exalt the work of an honest man who sacrifices his time and his toil to do only kindness to our wretched language, made wretched at

1 This Hebrew date corresponds to 14 August 1878.

2 Sic.

רָם וְיָעֵל

מכתב אל המעתיק

וויען חמשה עשר באב תרל"ח.[1]

ידידי הנכבד!

את דעתי שאלתני על אודות העתקת המחזה הנפלא ראָמע ויוליא, שיר השירים להאהבה כאשר כנוהו יודעי טעם, ואשר אתה בטוב טעם שנית שמו ל ר ם ו י ע ל, למען גם שם עברי יקרא עליו, אחרי אשר בלבוש עבר אשר הלבשתו לא יכירהו איש כי לא ידי עברי כוננוהו, ידי עברי המדבר בשפת חוזיו ומפליא לעשות כמהם בניבו, את דעתי תשאלני ואותה הלא לך לדעת גם בטרם שאלתני, כי לא נכחד ממך כי אעריץ את שם החוזה הנעלה יוצר איתיאל ורם ויעל ויתר חזיונותיו (אשר אני תפלה כי יזכו גם המה לְהִכָּתֵב עברית) ואקנא בהבריטאנים, כי להם הוא, ואם אין אתנו מפליא לעשות כמהו, הנה אשגיב פֹּעל אדם ישר, אשר יקריב עתו ועמלו לעשות אך חסד את שפתנו העלובה, עלובה על ידי מחרפיה ועוד יותר עלובה על ידי רֹב אוהביה, אשר ישליכו עליה שקוצים באהבתם אותה הרבה יתר מאלה שיבזו צלמה, כי אלה ישטו ויעברו וסר צלם מעליה והיא תוסיף להפיץ נגוהות ואלה עליה יסבו ורקדו במחולות סביבה ובאבק רגליהם יכסו פניה עד כי תהי לזעוה, ואיך לא אכיר מעבדי האיש אשר עֹז בידו להראות יפיה וחנה לעיני כל, אשר קסמים בידו לשים בפי שעקספיר החוזה דברים כדברי ישעיהו הנביא, ורעיונות החוזה לא בכבדות יעברו על דל הנביא ודברי הנביא כלבוש ילבשו עשתונות החוזה וכפי כתנתם יאזרום.[2] וכל אלה הלא כבר ידעת, כבר הגדתי והשמעתיך, כי אך אתה הוא האיש אשר בידך להביא את הַיְקָר הזה אל בית אוצר שפתנו

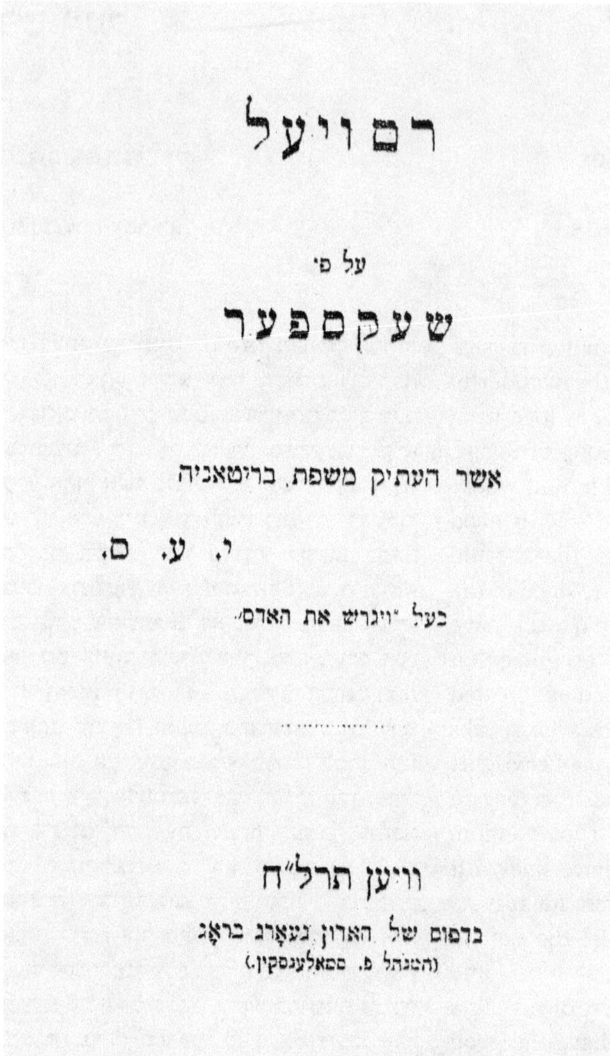

רם ויעל

על פי

שעקספער

אשר העתיק משפת בריטאניה

י. ע. ס.

בעל "ויגרש את האדם"

וויען תרל"ח

בדפוס של הארון געאָרג בראָג

(המנהל פ. סמאלענסקין.)

Figure 4 (Hebrew title page of *Ram and Jael*)

the hands of those who mock it and even more wretched at the hands of most of those who love it, who in their love for it besmirch it much more than those who scorn its image, for those who scorn its image turn their backs on it and pass it by, never darkening

וכבר בקשתיך והתחננתי לפניך כי כה תעשה, כי אם לא אתה תעשה זאת אין אתנו יודע לעשות זאת כמך, ואת ברכתי ותודתי אתן לך מקרב לבי בעד הברכה החדשה הזאת כאשר ברכתיך אז בהביאך מנחת איתיאל, כי פעלך זה לא נופל מפעל ההוא ואולי עוד נעלה עליו.

Shakspeares

ROMEO & JULIET

Translated into Hebrew

by

J. E. S.

WIEN 1878.

Buchdruckerei von Georg Brög in Wien, IX., Maria Theresienstrasse 19.

Unter der Leitung von P. Smolensky.

Image 5 (English title page of *Ram and Jael*)

it with their shadow and leaving it to spread its radiance, whereas those who love it close in on it and dance around it and cover its face with the dust of their feet until it becomes repulsive. So how could I not recognize the labours of the man who has the power to show its beauty and charm to everyone, who has the magical ability to put in the mouth of the playwright Shakespeare words like those of the prophet Isaiah? For the playwright's ideas would cross the prophet's lips without any difficulty and, equally, the prophet's words don the playwright's thoughts like a well-fitting garment. But after all, you already know all these things; I have already told you and let you know that indeed you are the man who has the power to bring this precious object into the treasure-house of our language, and I have already asked and begged you to do so, for if you do not do this, there is no one among us who knows how to do this like you, and I give you my blessing and my thanks from the bottom of my heart for this new blessing just as I blessed you when you brought me the offering of *Ithiel*, for this work of yours is not inferior to that work, and is perhaps even more exalted than it.

But indeed, if despite all these things I am not taking upon myself the work of publishing this book and putting my name on the translation do not wonder; indeed, you have heard the words of the grumblers who instead of blessing you for your labour and me for spurring you to do this precious work, have banded together against us and have made you and me an example, as if together we had dug a deep pit for our people into which they will fall and will not be able to get out, the fathers and sons alike, and even those who have lost the faith and it has been severed from their hearts, even they have seized on the spade of faith with which to dig dirt in order to fling it at

ואולם אם בכל אלה לא אקח עלי העבודה להוציא את הספר הזה לאור ולקרוא שמי על ההעתקה אל תתמה; הן שמעת דברי הנרגנים, אשר תחת לברך אותך על פעל כפך ואותי על כי עוררתיך לפעל היקר הזה, התמלאו יחד עלינו וישימוך אותך ואותי למשל, כמו לוא שוחה עמוקה כרינו יחד לעמנו ובה יפלו ולא יקומו האבות והבנים יחד, ואף אלה אשר אבדה האמונה ונכרתה מלבם אף המה אחזו בקרדום האמונה לחפור בו עפר לְעַפֵּר לעומתו[3] ונהי יחד כחוטאים, ומה איפו אוסיף להביא עצים להגדיל המדורה?

him,[3] and together we have become like sinners, so why therefore should I bring more wood to make the bonfire bigger?

But do not imagine that, out of my fear for myself lest shameless men damage my honour again, I cower and fear to add my name to your book; it is not so! I am already used to hear the whistling of the arrows that such archers shoot at me, and they pass by me and do not touch me, and I do not even notice them, but I know with certainty that it is not as they said deceitfully when they placed your sin on me, it is not so in truth but rather the opposite; you are being punished for *my* iniquity; if you had joined the authors' ranks in the first instance and had not made an alliance with me, they would have treated you like a prince, all those who now are shouting loudly against you and me; they would have lionized you and given you glorious praise in their hope that the day would come when you would recompense them according to their deeds, and indeed that you would exalt them and praise them as they had praised you. Indeed, by setting your foot over the threshold of the Hebrew language you would undoubtedly choose the way of its priests, praising and extolling anyone who praises and extols. However, by allying yourself with me, a man of quarrel and strife with Rabbi Akiva[4] and his friends

אבל אל תדמה בנפשך כי מיראתי לנפשי פן יפגעו שנית עזי נפש בכבודי לכן זחלתי ואירא מקרוא גם שמי על ספרך, לא זאת! אני כבר הסכנתי לשמוע שריקות החצים אשר יורו בי בעלי חצים כאלה והמה יעברו ממני והלאה ובי לא יגעו גם לא אשים לב אליהם, אך ידעתי נאמנה כי לא כאשר דברו במרמה וישימו בי חטאתך כן הוא באמת כי אם להפך, אתה ע ו נ י תשא, לוא יצאת בפעם הראשונה במערכת הסופרים ולי לא נתת יד כי אז קרבוך כמו נגיד, כל אלה אשר עתה יריעו תרועה גדולה עליך ועלי, כי אז גם בקשו קרבתך וישימו כבוד תהלתך בתקותם כי יבא יום וגם אתה תשלם להם כפעלם ואף אתה תרים להם קרן ותודה אותם כאשר הודו אותך המה. הן בהציגך כף רגלך על מפתן שפה עבריה בלי ספק תבחר דרך כהניה, להודות ולהלל לכל מי שיודה ויהלל. אולם בהתחברך אלי, איש ריב ומדון ברבי עקיבא[4] וחבריו ובבן מנחם[5] וסעיתו*, אשר לא ישא פנים להמהללים ולא יֵחַת מפני המחללים לכן גם אתה עוני תשא וגם אותך יציבו למטרה לחציהם, וכאשר קצרה ידם למצוא מגרעות בפעלך לכן יבקשו מומים בך – ומה לך לעורר עוד חמת נקם? וזאת היא שנתנה בלבי למשוך ידי מספרך זה, בן יקיר לי במאד מאד, ואם טובה תהיה לך אהבתי המסתרת לפעלך זה, הנני אומר לך, כי שש הייתי מאד מאד בקראי את ההעתקה הנפלאה הזאת ומקרב לבי ברכתיך וכן אברך אותך גם בימים הבאים, וכן יברך שמך כל אוהב שערי ציון ויכיר מעבדך, כי אחד מראשי הבונים הנה הנך בשערים האלה וישאר לזכרון לעד לדור.

אוהבך הנאמן
פ. סמאלענסקין.

3 Sic; 'us' would be expected.

4 Akiva (c. 50–135 CE) was one of the most influential rabbis and greatest scholars of the early rabbinic period. He features prominently in the Mishnah, was a key figure in the development of Jewish law, and was teacher to a large number of influential disciples.

* וסיעתו

and Ben Menachem[5] and his companions, who does not show partiality to those who praise and does not fear those who profane, you too are punished for my iniquity and they set you up too as a target for their arrows, and as they are unable to find weaknesses in your work, they seek flaws in you – so why should you stir up the vengeful anger still further? This is what made me decide to withdraw my hand from this book of yours, my most very dear son, and if my concealed love for this work of yours is good enough for you, then I hereby say to you that I rejoiced very greatly upon reading this wonderful translation, and from the bottom of my heart I blessed you, and I shall likewise bless you in the coming days as well, and likewise everyone who loves the gates of Zion will bless your name and recognize your work, for indeed you are one of the chief builders at these gates, and it will remain as an eternal memorial for future generations.

Your faithful friend
P. Smolenskin

5 Moses Mendelssohn, central figure of the early Haskalah.

Message from the translator

I found three snares before me in the translation of this book; the first snare is that the book's original (like all the rest of Shakespeare's books) is replete from beginning to end with paranomasia or parody, that is to say *meliṣa*,[6] as Jewish authors call it, wordplay. And even though it is one of the most precious treasures of the Hebrew language, nevertheless it is very difficult to translate such *meliṣa* and render it properly from language to language. The second snare is Jael's nurse, who was an obstacle to me at every turn. This woman, as Shakespeare presents her to us, has no graceful lips and no learned tongue, and does not even know how to distinguish one letter of the alphabet from another, but she is boisterous with excessive speech and a clumsy tongue, and all of her conversation is mixed up and full of errors so as to arouse laughter and amusement in the eyes of those watching her on the stage. But nevertheless, she has a great part in everything that happens in this drama, for only through her could Jael do everything that she planned to do. I realized that I would not manage to render all her lines into Hebrew as they appeared with stammering speech in English; therefore I rendered some of her lines in a manner that was true to the Hebrew rather than following the rules of a faithful translation. If the critic catches me in this iniquity, perhaps he might reconsider and have a little mercy on me as one who has confessed his sins. But the third snare is the chief among the three, for it closed

דברי המעתיק

שלשה מוקשים מצאתי לפני בהעתקת הספר הזה, המוקש הראשון הוא מקור הספר (ככל יתר ספרי שעקספער) מלא מפה לפה פַּאַרָאנָאמַסְיָא או פַּאַרָאדִי, היא המליצה[6] אשר יקראו לה סופרי היהודים, לשון נופל על לשון. ואף כי היא אחת מסגולות היקרות בשפת עבר, בכל זאת קשה הדבר מאד, להעתיק מליצה כזאת ולעשות אותה כמתכֻּנתה מלשון אל לשון. המוקש השני היא אומנת יעל אשר עמדה לשטן לי בדרך. האשה הזאת כאשר יציגנה שעקספער לעינינו, אין לה שפתי חן ולא לשון למודים ואף באלפא ביתא לא ידעה להבדיל בין אות לאות, אבל הומיה היא בשפת יתר ובלשון עלגים וכל שיחתה בלולה ומלאה שגיאות לעורר שחוק ומהתלות לעיני הרואים בה על פני הבמה. ובכל זאת לה חלק רב בכל אשר נעשה בדראמא הזאת, כי רק על ידה יכלה יעל לעשות ככל אשר יזמה לעשות. ואנכי נוכחתי כי לא תצלח בידי לשים כל דבריה בעברית כאשר הם בלעגי שפה בלשון ענגליש, על כן שמתי מקצת הדברים בפיה כמשפט הלשון ולא כמשפט העתקה נאמנה. ואם יתפשני המבקר בעון זה, אולי ישוב ירחמני מעט, כמודה על פשעיו. אך המוקש השלישי הוא ראש בשלשה, כי סגר עלי כגדר ולא נתנני לעבר בשנים שלשה מקומות, עד אשר אמרתי בלבי, בכל מקום אשר לא יתנני לעבר בו, כי אין לפרץ הגדר, אז אתנשא אדלג ואעבר עליו. ובכן דלגתי על המקומות אשר לא מצאתי בם דרך פתוחה לפני. והפגע הרע הזה אשר גדר בעדי, הוא מריות, מערקוטיא נער חרוץ מגדולי הארץ, אשר לו יד בחכמה בדעת ובלשונות זרות, רק אוהב לצון הוא ולעגו ישפך על כל הקרב אליו, כי באהבתו את הצחוק בין אוהב לאויב לא יכיר, ואין די לו להתלוצץ בשפה אחת, כי אם גם ישא מלה צרפתית על לשונו או איטאלקית ובכן יבטא בשפתיו אמרי הבל וריק כזורה מֹץ ברוח, גם אמרים נמרצים כיורה זיקים וחצים שנונים. ואני

6 This term denotes a writing style strongly associated with Maskilic Hebrew and characterized by flowery language replete with biblical citations. See Shahevitch (1970), Pelli (1993), and Kahn (2013) for discussion of *meliṣa*.

me in like a fence and did not allow me to pass in two or three places, until I said to myself, everywhere that it does not allow me to pass because the fence cannot be broken through, I shall rise above it, skip over it, and pass by it. And so I skipped over the places where I did not find a way open before me. And this terrible obstacle which fenced me in is Meraioth, Mercutio, a diligent lad, one of the earth's greatest men, who had much wisdom, knowledge, and skill in foreign languages, but was a lover of clowning and poured his scorn on everyone near him, for in his love of joking he did not distinguish friend from foe, and it was not enough for him to clown in one language, but rather there was also a French word on his tongue, or an Italian one, and as such he uttered with his lips empty and meaningless words like one who scatters chaff in the wind, as well as powerful words like one who shoots sparks and sharpened arrows. I trust that every understanding reader will admit that a Hebrew author does not have the power to translate all the words of Mercutio as they are. Authors of Shakespeare's biography have already told us that one of his acquaintances asked him why he did not let Mercutio live until the end of the whole story, and he answered as follows: 'If I had not arisen early to kill him, he would have killed me.' And thus I say as well, if I had not shortened his words, he would have shortened my life, for he would have killed me with the breath of his lips. –

סמוך לבי כי כל קורא מבין יודה כי אין ביד סופר עברי להעתיק כל דברי מערקוטיא כאשר הם. וכבר ספרו לנו סופרי תולדות חיי שעקספער, כי איש אחד ממכיריו שאל אותו, על מה זה לא האריך ימי חיי מערקוטיא עד תם כל המעשה, והוא ענה לאמר: לולא השכמתי להרגו, היה הוא הורג אותי. וכן גם אני אומר, לולא הקצרתי דבריו, היה הוא מקצר חיי, כי המיתני ברוח שפתיו. –

And now I shall justify myself to those who love the Hebrew language. I know that they are the people of the Lord and they do not deem it appropriate to encounter vileness or foul language in their holy tongue, and

ועתה הנני להצטדק לפני אוהבי שפת עבר. ידעתי כי עם ה' הם ואין טוב בעיניהם למצוא ערות דבר או נבול פה בשפת קדשם, ועל כן יבואו במשפט עמדי, על אשר תרגמתי במקומות אחדים בספר הזה דברים ככתבם, אשר לקולם תצלנה אזני נקיי הדעת במחנה העברים, וטוב

טוב היה לי לקחת את השמלה, להסב פני אחרנית ולכסות ערות אבי המשוררים.[7] ועל זאת אני משיב, הנה שעקספער סופר נאמן הוא לפני אלהים ואנשים, ובלהקת אנשים שונים המצחקים על פני הבמה (על פני הארץ) יציג לפנינו איש איש ואת שיחו כאשר הוא, ואם יש שם פוחזים ורקים המדברים דברי נבלה ומטמאים את פיהם, הם עתידים לתת את הדין, כמאמר התלמודי, כל המנבל את פיו מעמיקין לו גיהנם, אבל הסופר הנאמן, או המעתיק העושה מלאכתו באמונה נקי. כי אם לא כן קורא יקר, למה לא תריב גם באיש החכם מכל אדם,[8] על אשר הציג לעינינו אשה זרה, אשר החליקה אמריה[9] באזני נער חסר לב, ובמצח אשה זונה השמיעה דברים, אשר אין לבר לבב לשמוע. וכי תאמר כי רק להזהיר בא, ולהורות לנו מוסר טוב עשה כל זאת, גם אני אשאלך למה זה לא תדין לכף זכות גם את שעקספער. פתח נא את הספר הזה צד 32[10] והקשב לדברי מריות, אשר פער פיו לבלי חק והעתיק מפיו מלים לא בלשון נקיה, עד אשר נלאה רם לשמוע ויגער בו ויאמר: רב לך מריות לבטא הבל וריק! ומה ענה אותו מריות? על דברי חלומות הן אני מדבר, כי בנים רקים הם ילדי מחשבות שוא ותפל.....רצונו בזה להוכיח, כי חלומות והרהורים רעים באים מן הלב, כי יצר לב האדם רק רע כל היום, על כן החי יתן אל לבו. וידעת היום ובחנת אחי, כי איש רדף טוב יקח מוסר ולקח טוב גם מדברי זדים ופי אנשי בליעל, כמו מפי צדיקים וחסידים, ולכן עולה לא תמצא עוד בשפתי שעקספער ולא ערות דבר בדבריו, כי דבריו נכחים למבין וכל דרכיו ישרים, צדיקים ילכו בם ופשעים יכשלו בם. –

therefore they will make a judgement against me, because in some places in this book I translated utterances as they were written, at whose sound the ears of the pure-minded ones in the camp of the Hebrews will tingle, and they will say that it would have been much better for me to take the garment, turn my face backwards, and cover the nakedness of the father of poets.[7] And to this I respond that indeed Shakespeare is a trustworthy author before God and men, and out of all the various men who act upon the stage (upon the earth), he displays before us each man and his speech as it is, and if there are rash and worthless men among them who speak foully and sully their mouths, they will be judged, as the Talmud says; there will be a deeper hell for everyone with a foul mouth, but the trustworthy author or the translator who does his work faithfully is blameless. For if it is not so, dear reader, why do you not also quarrel with the wisest man of all[8] because he presented us with an adulterous woman who spoke flattering words[9] in the ears of a senseless youth, and with the brazenness of a whore uttered words that pure-hearted men should not hear. And if you say that he intended only to warn us, and that he did all of this to instruct us in good morals, then I shall also ask you why you do not judge Shakespeare favourably as well. Open this book to page 32[10] and listen to the words of Meraioth, who opened

7 This is a reference to Gen. 9:23, in which Noah's sons Shem and Japheth take a garment to cover their father's nakedness with their faces turned away while he lies in a drunken sleep.

8 King Solomon, traditionally considered the author of the biblical books Proverbs and Ecclesiastes.

9 This is a reference to Prov. 2:16 and 7:5, which advise caution against flattering adulteresses.

10 In the original edition; see *Ram and Jael*, First Part, note 273 in this edition.

his mouth without restraint and issued forth such unclean language that Ram grew weary of hearing it and scolded him, saying: 'That's enough from you, Meraioth, rashly speaking in vain and to no purpose!' And what did Meraioth answer him? 'Indeed I am speaking about matters of dreams, for they are frivolous sons, the children of pointless and insipid thoughts…' In saying this, he sought to prove that bad dreams and thoughts come from the heart, for the inclination of man's heart is only evil continually; therefore the living should take this to heart. Know today and consider, my brother, that a man who pursues good takes instruction and sound teaching even from the speech of wicked men and the mouth of villains just as from the mouth of righteous and pious men. Hence, you must no longer find sin on Shakespeare's lips or vileness in what he says, for what he says is plain to one who understands, and all his ways are honest; righteous men walk upon them, whereas sinners stumble upon them. –

Regarding the book's value I have nothing to say, for I am its relative and friend; if it contains anything desirable, let a stranger praise it, rather than me. But I would like to anticipate the reader when he asks me the following: is it good for Jewish youth to study such a book, which begins with madness and lust, and ends in murder, killing, and destruction? To this I respond that in my opinion the book is very good for Jewish youth, and will benefit them as they go through their life, for in it they can see not only the fruit of hatred and strife, which have felled many victims, but

על דבר יקרת ערך הספר, אין לי לדבר דבר, כי קרוב ומודע אני לו, ואם נמצא בו דבר חפץ, יהללנו זר ולא פי. אך לקדם פני הקורא חפצתי כי ישאלני לאמר: הטוב לנערי בני ישראל להגות בספר כזה, אשר ראשיתו הוללות ועגבים ואחריתו רצח הרג ואבדן? ועל זאת הנני משיב לדעתי טוב הספר מאד לנערי בני ישראל להועיל למו בדרכי חייהם, כי בו יראו, לא לבד מה פרי שנאה ומדנים אשר רבים חללים הפילו, כי אם גם מה רבו חללי האהבה ומה עצמו הרוגיה. הציגה נא קורא יקר לעיניך את בן אבירם, הוא בחור נחמד ונעים, אשר לו עשר גבורה ותפארת, אך תוכו רצוף אהבה בבלי מצרים. בתחלה נשא עיניו על נערה אחת ותדבק נפשו בה, אך באשר היא לא שתה אליו לבה, הלך כל היום קודר

also how many victims of love there are and how numerous those slain by it are. Consider, dear reader, the son of Abiram, a desirable and pleasant boy, who has a wealth of might and glory, but is consumed by unbounded love. In the beginning he had set his sights on a certain girl and clung to her, but since she paid him no heed, he went around all day gloomy under the weight of his heart, and at night he could not sleep. After days of sorrow and mourning, dark days when he loathed his life, he met another girl, better than the first one, and the fire of his love burned within him again like the flame of the Lord, and she too joined him in the bond of the covenant, but her parents, his enemies, were willing for both him and their daughter to be stabbed to death, rather than letting them enter this covenant. In dangerous circumstances he managed to see her once in secret in the dead of night, and he kissed her as he parted from her in bitterness; with this kiss he forfeited his entire future, for this was the reward for all his toil, and from that time onwards he found no rest until he killed himself and the girl of his youthful covenant did likewise, and the fire of love devoured both of them. And this is what I meant when I said that this book will present lessons and manners and good education to the youth who studies it, for he will recognize how to take care to keep his eyes open wherever he goes, and if it comes time for him to fall in love, he will enter only into a covenant of love by which he may live, rather than becoming attached to a graceful maiden on account of whom he will die.

בלחץ לבו ובלילה שנה בעיניו לא ראה. אחרי ימי יגון ואנחה, ימי חשך אשר קץ בחייו, פגש בנערה אחרת טובה מן הראשנה ותבער בו עוד אש אהבתו כשלהבת יה, וגם היא באה עמו במסרת הברית, אך אבותיה שנואי נפשו נכונו לדקור גם אותו גם את בתם, מתת ידם להקים את הברית הזאת. ובמסבות מתהפכות הצליח לראותה פעם אחת במסתר באישון לילה, וינשק לה בהפרדו ממנה במר נפש, בנשיקה הזאת מכר את כל עולמו, כי זה היה חלקו מכל עמלו, ומעת הזאת ומעלה, לא מצא מנוח לכף רגלו, עד אשר שלח יד בנפשו וגם בת ברית נעוריו עשתה כמוהו, ותאכל אש האהבה גם את שניהם. וזה הוא הדבר אשר אמרתי, כי תורה ודרך ארץ ומוסר טוב ישים הספר הזה לפני הנער ההוגה בו, כי ידע להזהר לשים עין פקוחה על כל דרכיו, ואם באה עתו עת דודים, יבוא רק בברית האהבה אשר יחיה בה ולא יתמכר לבת חן אשר ימות בה.

The names of the speakers

English	Hebrew
Escalus[12]	Eshcol[11] *the prince in Verona*
Paris	Paris *a young nobleman and friend of the prince*
Montague	Abiram
Capulet	Abiel
two heads of ancestral houses between whom there is a quarrel and war	
Uncle to Capulet	Elder
Romeo	Ram *Abiram's son*
Mercutio	Meraioth *acquaintance of the prince and Ram's friend*
Benvolio	Benaiah *Abiram's nephew and Ram's friend*
Tybalt	Tubal *nephew of Abiel's wife*
Friar Laurence	Rezin
Iohn	Hanan
two Christian priests	
Balthasar	Balthasar *Ram's servant*
Sampson	Shimshai
Gregory	Gera
Abiel's servants	
Peter	Peter *servant of Jael's nurse*
Abram	Bera *Abiram's servant*
An Apothecary	Apothecary *of medicines*
Musicians	Musicians
Chorns[13]	Chorus of singers
Two Pages	Two youths *attendants to Paris*
Lady Montague	Abiram's wife
Lady Capulet	Abiel's wife
Juliet	Jael *Abiel's daughter*
Nurse to Juliet	Nurse *to Juliet*

Natives of the city of Verona; men and women related to the two ancestral houses; people wearing masks over their eyes; guards; night watchmen and attendants.

Four of the scenes[14] are in Verona, and the fifth scene is in Mantua.

11 This is the name of an Amorite allied with Abraham (Gen. 14:13, 24).

12 Salkinson provided this English cast list alongside the Hebrew one.

13 Sic; this appears in Salkinson's English cast list instead of the expected 'Chorus'.

14 Salkinson is clearly referring to acts rather than scenes, but uses a word that he elsewhere employs in the sense of 'scene'.

שמות המדברים

אֶשְׁכֹּל[11] הנסיך בְּוֵירוֹנָה (Verona)		Escalus[12]
פָּרִיז בן נדיב נער ומודע לנסיך		Paris
אֲבִירָם	שני ראשי בתי אבות אשר ריב ומלחמה ביניהם	Montague
אֲבִיעֶל		Capulet
זקן דוד אביעל		Uncle to Capulet
רָם בן אבירם		Romeo
מְרָיוֹת מודע לנסיך ואוהב לרם		Mercutio
בְּנָיָה בן אחי אבירם ואוהב לרם		Benvolio
תּוּבַל בן אחי אשת אביעל		Tybalt
רְצִין	שני כהנים נוצרים	Friar Laurence
חָנָן		„ „ Iohn
בֵּלְטַאזָר עבד לרם		Balthasar
שִׁמְשִׁי	עבדים לאביעל	Sampson
גֵּרָא		Gregory
פֶּטֶר עבד לאומנת יעל		Peter
בֶּרַע עבד לאבירם		Abram
רוֹקֵחַ בסמי הרפואה		An Apothecary
מנגנים		Musicians
מקהלת משוררים		Chorns[13]
שני נערים משרתים לפריז		Two Pages
אשת אבירם		Lady Montague
אשת אביעל		Lady Capulet
יָעֵל בת אביעל		Juliet
אוֹמֶנֶת ליעל		Nurse to Juliet

בני העיר וֵירוֹנָה; אנשים ונשים קרובים לשני בתי האבות; נושרי אֲפֵר על עיניהם; אנשי משמר; שומרי לילה ומשרתים.

ארבעה המחזות[14] בְּוֵירוֹנָה והמחזה החמישי בְּמַנְטוּבָה. (Mantua)

First Part

חלק ראשון

SCENE I[1]	*A street in Verona[2] (Shimshai[3] and Gera[4] carrying shields and bearing swords)*	רחוב בוירונה[2] (שמשי[3] וגרא[4] נושאי מגן וחגורי חרב)	מחזה א'[1]
SHIMSHAI[5]	I say one thing, Gera; we shall no longer cut wood.	אַחַת דִּבַּרְתִּי גֵּרָא, לֹא נַחְטֹב עוֹד עֵצִים.	שמשי[5]
GERA	**You have spoken well,**[6] for why should we be woodcutters?[7]	כֵּן דִּבַּרְתָּ,[6] כִּי לָמָּה נִהְיֶה חֹטְבֵי עֵצִים.[7]	גרא
SHIMSHAI	Why, what I am saying is this: when smoke rises from my nose,[8] **I draw my sword.**[9]	הֲלֹא זֶה דְּבָרִי, בַּעֲלוֹת עָשָׁן בְּאַפִּי[8] אָרִיק חַרְבִּי.[9]	שמשי
GERA	As long as there is breath in your nose, draw your neck from your neck-chain.[10]	כָּל עוֹד נְשָׁמָה בְאַפֶּךָ, הָרֵק צַוָּארְךָ מֵעֲנָקֶיךָ.[10]	גרא
SHIMSHAI	I strike quick as lightning when my heart is angered.	הִנְנִי מַכֶּה חִישׁ קַל, כִּי יֵחַם לִבִּי.	שמשי
GERA	But your heart is not angered to strike quick as lightning.	אַךְ לֹא יֵחַם לִבְּךָ לְהַכּוֹת חִישׁ קַל.	גרא

1 Salkinson's translation seems to be based on the Folio version of *Romeo and Juliet*, as it omits the prologue ('Two households, both alike in dignity…') appearing in the Quarto versions.

2 As in *Ithiel*, Salkinson preserves the Italian place names appearing in Shakespeare's text. See Kahn (2017) for discussion of the possibility that this strategy is rooted in an acknowledgement of the longstanding and prominent Jewish presence in Italy.

3 A scribe mentioned in Ezra 4:8, 9, 17, and 23. Salkinson seems to have chosen this name based purely on its sound correspondence with Shakespeare's Sampson; he most likely chose this minor character over the more similar-sounding שִׁמְשׁוֹן 'Samson' because he wanted to avoid the strong associations of the latter, a prominent figure well known from Judges 13–16. In addition, Salkinson may have been motivated by the fact that the Hebrew root on which the name Shimshai is based means 'to serve', making it a particularly appropriate choice for a servant of the Abiel household.

4 A name referring to various minor biblical characters, namely one of Benjamin's sons (Gen. 46:21); the judge Ehud's father (Judg. 3:15); and the father of Shimei the Benjaminite, who cursed David (2 Sam. 16:5). Gera is also listed as Benjamin's grandson in 1 Chron. 8:3. The name may denote a particular Benjaminate family, and so the aforementioned instances may not all refer to different individuals. Salkinson most likely selected the name on the basis of its sound correspondence with Shakespeare's Gregory.

5 This and the following speeches until Benaiah's next line are prose in the original (1.1.1–61).

6 Exod. 10:29.

7 Salkinson's 'cut wood' and 'woodcutters' replace Shakespeare's 'carry coals' (1.1.1) and 'colliers' (1.1.2). These substitutions are explicitly Judaizing dynamic equivalents to the original English terms: woodcutting was a common occupation among Eastern European Jews well into the twentieth century (Salsitz 2002: 84–7); moreover, it would have been widely recognized among Hebrew readers as a classic form of manual labour due to its appearance in a well-known phrase from Joshua 9:21, חֹטְבֵי עֵצִים וְשֹׁאֲבֵי־מַיִם 'woodcutters and water carriers'.

8 i.e., 'when I grow angry' – the nose growing hot is a biblical idiom denoting anger.

9 Exod. 15:9.

10 Salkinson seems to have chosen to use the word 'nose' with two different senses, and the verb 'to draw' in this and the preceding line, to echo Shakespeare's pun on choler/collar 'an we be in choler' (1.1.3) and 'draw your neck out of collar' (1.1.4).

SHIMSHAI	Even a dog from the house of Abiram[11] would arouse all my anger.	גַּם כֶּלֶב מִבֵּית אֲבִירָם[11], יָעִיר כָּל חֲמָתִי.	שמשי
GERA	One who is aroused in his anger moves, whereas a warrior stands	הַנֵּעוֹר בַּחֲמָתוֹ יָנוּעַ, וְגִבּוֹר חַיִל יָקוּם	גרא
	And therefore, when you are aroused you flee for your life.	וְלָכֵן כַּאֲשֶׁר נֵעוֹר אַתָּה תָּנוּס לְנַפְשֶׁךָ.	
SHIMSHAI	A dog from this family would arouse my anger to take a stand before him	כֶּלֶב מִמִּשְׁפָּחָה הַזֹּאת, יָעִיר חֲמָתִי לְהִתְיַצֵּב בְּפָנָיו	שמשי
	And I would chase away every man and woman of the whole house of Abiram	וְכָל אִישׁ וְאִשָּׁה לְכָל בֵּית אֲבִירָם	
	As **one who pisses against the wall,**[12] and the wall would be mine.	אַבְרִיחַ כְּמַשְׁתִּין בְּקִיר[12] וְהָיָה לִי הַקִּיר.	
GERA	And this is a sign for me that you are **faint-hearted**[13]	וְזֶה לִּי לְאוֹת כִּי רַךְ לֵבָב[13] אָתָּה	גרא
	For every weakling leans against the wall.	כִּי כָל חַלָּשׁ יִסָּמֵךְ אֶל הַקִּיר.	
SHIMSHAI	Indeed the matter is true, for they push the women	הֵן אֱמֶת הַדָּבָר, כִּי יִדְחֲקוּן אֶת הַנָּשִׁים	שמשי
	For they are soft, to lean against the wall	כִּי רַכּוֹת הֵנָּה, לְהִסָּמֵךְ אֶל הַקִּיר	
	And therefore I shall do this to the house of Abiram when I push	וְלָכֵן זֹאת אֶעֱשֶׂה לְבֵית אֲבִירָם כִּי אֶהְדֹּף	
	The males away from the wall and press the females to the wall.	הַזְּכָרִים מִן הַקִּיר וְהַנְּקֵבוֹת אֶלְחַץ אֶל הַקִּיר.	

11 Salkinson's choice of אֲבִירָם 'Abiram' as an equivalent for Shakespeare's 'Montague' does not take sound correspondence into account, but rather is based solely on the name's significance. This choice functions on two distinct levels in Hebrew. First, it literally means 'Ram's father'. As Salkinson's has dubbed his equivalent of Romeo 'Ram' (see note 44), this name would have served explicitly to establish the familial link between the father and son in Hebrew readers' minds. Second, the biblical figure of Abiram would have been familiar to Salkinson's audience from his appearance in Numbers 16, as one of the members of Korach's rebellion against Moses' leadership of the Israelites during their forty-year sojourn in the desert following their liberation from Egypt. Abiram would thus have been synonymous with spite, arrogance, and disloyalty, not to mention the horrifying punishment of being swallowed by the earth.

12 This phrase appears in several locations in the Hebrew Bible (1 Sam. 25:22, 25:34; 1 Kings 14:10, 16:11, 21:21; 2 Kings 9:8), as an idiom meaning 'male'; here, Salkinson takes advantage of the fact that it contains the word קיר 'wall', thereby serving as a play on the same word in the following clause.

13 2 Chron. 13:7.

GERA	The quarrel is between our master and their master, and between us, the men.	הָרִיב בֵּין אֲדֹנֵינוּ וּבֵין אֲדֹנֵיהֶם וּבֵינֵינוּ הַגְּבָרִים.	גרא
SHIMSHAI	I do not distinguish between man and woman like a cruel tyrant;	לֹא אַבְדִּיל בֵּין אִישׁ לְאִשָּׁה כְּעָרִיץ אַכְזָרִי;	שמשי
	When I have fought against the lads, I shall fight with **furious cruelty**[14]	כַּאֲשֶׁר נִלְחַמְתִּי בַּנְּעָרִים אֶלְחַם בְּאַכְזְרִיּוּת חֵמָה[14]	
	Against the virgin lasses, and smash their head.	אֵת הַנְּעָרוֹת הַבְּתוּלוּת* וּמָחַצְתִּי אֶת רֹאשָׁן.	
GERA	Will you smash the head of the virgins?	הֲתִמְחַץ רֹאשׁ הַבְּתוּלוֹת?	גרא
SHIMSHAI	I shall smash the head of the virgins, or the head of their virginity[15]	אֲנִי אֶמְחַץ רֹאשׁ הַבְּתוּלוֹת, אוֹ רֹאשׁ בְּתוּלֵיהֶן[15]	שמשי
	And you must understand my words in accordance with your good sense.	וְעָלֶיךָ לְהָבִין דְּבָרַי לְפִי טוּב טַעֲמֶךָ.	
GERA	Only those who have their feeling within them to perceive sense will understand your words.	רַק אֵלֶּה יָבִינוּ דְבָרֶיךָ, אֲשֶׁר חוּשָׁם בָּם לִטְעֹם טָעַם.	גרא
SHIMSHAI	But they[16] will know my sense and my bow, for it sits firmly	וְהֵנָּה[16] תֵּדַעְנָה טַעֲמִי וְקַשְׁתִּי כִּי בְּאֵיתָן תֵּשֵׁב	שמשי
	And it is not concealed from anyone's eyes that I am great of flesh.	וְלֹא נֶעֱלָם מֵעֵינֵי כֹל, כִּי רַב בָּשָׂר אָנִי.	
GERA	You are great of flesh, and not a thin fish	רַב בָּשָׂר אַתָּה וְלֹא דָג רָזֶה	גרא
	But lift up your weapons; behold, there are two Abirams opposite.	אַךְ שָׂא אֶת כֵּלֶיךָ, הִנֵּה שְׁנֵי אֲבִירָמִים מִנֶּגֶד.	
	(Bera[17] and Balthasar[18] enter)	(ברע[17] ובלטאזר[18] באים)	

14 Prov. 27:4.

15 This is a relatively literal translation of Shakespeare's 'the heads of the maids, or their maidenheads' (1.1.24); in contrast to the English 'maidenheads', the Hebrew phrase 'head of their virginity' is not an established phrase and does not constitute a true play on words.

16 The Hebrew pronoun is feminine, referring specifically to the maidens.

17 Salkinson has chosen to alter the one biblical name that actually appears in Shakespeare's text, changing Abra(ha)m into בֶּרַע 'Bera'. This likely reflects a reluctance for Montague's retainer to bear the name of the first biblical patriarch and symbolic father of the Jewish people (Almagor 1975: 748). The choice of 'Bera', the king of Sodom mentioned in Genesis 14:2, indicates that Salkinson regarded a minor biblical character with negative associations (and dating to the same period as the great patriarch) to be a more appropriate equivalent.

18 This is one of the only names in the play that Salkinson has not Hebraized. Instead, he has transliterated the English name into Hebrew. As in the case of Marcos in *Ithiel* (First Part, note 155), there is no clear

* הַבְּתוּלוֹת

SHIMSHAI	Why, my sword is drawn; provoke them, and I shall be behind you.	הֵן חַרְבִּי נְטוּיָה, הִתְגָּר בָּם וַאֲנִי אַחֲרֶיךָ.	שמשי
GERA	And you will turn away from me and turn your back to flee?	וְאַתָּה תָּשׁוּב מֵאַחֲרַי וְתִפְנֶה עֹרֶף לִבְרֹחַ?	גרא
SHIMSHAI	**Do not let it cross your mind**[19] that I am afraid.	**אַל יַעֲלֶה עַל רוּחֲךָ**[19] כִּי יָרֵא אָנֹכִי.	שמשי
GERA	Indeed it would not cross my mind; would a man such as you flee?	כֵּן לֹא יַעֲלֶה עַל רוּחִי, הָאִישׁ כָּמוֹךָ יִבְרָח?	גרא
SHIMSHAI	Let them begin the quarrel so that the law will be with us.	יִפְתְּחוּ הֵם אֶת הָרִיב לְמַעַן לָנוּ יִהְיֶה הַמִּשְׁפָּט.	שמשי
GERA	I shall wink an eye at them, and let them answer as is good in their eyes.	אֲנִי אֶקְרֹץ עַיִן לִקְרָאתָם וְהֵם יַעֲנוּ כַּטּוֹב בְּעֵינֵיהֶם.	גרא
SHIMSHAI	Not as is good in their eyes, but rather as they are able;	לֹא כַטּוֹב בְּעֵינֵיהֶם, כִּי אִם כַּאֲשֶׁר לְאֵל יָדָם;	שמשי
	While I shall put my thumb in my mouth to mock them	וַאֲנִי אָשִׂים בֹּהֶן יָדִי בְּמוֹ פִי לְהַתֵּל בָּמוֹ	
	And it will be a disgrace for them if they do not respond.	וּתְהִי לָהֶם לְחֶרְפָּה אִם לֹא יָשִׁיבוּ דָבָר.	
BERA	Did you put your thumb in your mouth to mock us?	הֲשַׂמְתָּ בֹּהֶן יָדְךָ בְּפִיךָ לְהַתֵּל בָּנוּ?	ברע
SHIMSHAI	I put my thumb in my mouth –	בֹּהֶן יָדִי שַׂמְתִּי בְּפִי –	שמשי
BERA	Was it to mock us that you put your thumb in your mouth?	הַאִם לְהַתֵּל בָּנוּ שַׂמְתָּ בֹּהֶן יָדְךָ בְּפִיךָ?	ברע
SHIMSHAI	*(In a whisper to Gera)* If I say yes, with whom will the law be?	(בלחש אל גרע) אִם אֹמַר הֵן, לְמִי יִהְיֶה הַמִּשְׁפָּט?	שמשי
GERA	*(In a whisper to Shimshai)* Then the law will not be with us.	(בלחש אל שמשי) אָז לֹא לָנוּ הַמִּשְׁפָּט.	גרא
SHIMSHAI	It was not to mock you that I put my thumb in my mouth	לֹא לְהַתֵּל בָּכֶם שַׂמְתִּי בֹּהֶן יָדִי בְּפִי	שמשי
	I just put my thumb in my mouth –	לְבַד בֹּהֶן יָדִי שַׂמְתִּי בְּפִי –	
GERA	Do you quarrel with us?	הֲתָרִיב עִמָּנוּ?	גרא

motivation for this. The decision not to domesticate this name is particularly surprising given the existence of the similar-sounding Hebrew בֵּלְטְשַׁאצַּר 'Belteshazzar', another name for the biblical Daniel. It is possible that Salkinson chose to avoid this solution out of a reluctance to name Ram's servant after the venerated biblical figure, but it is unclear why he did not select another Hebrew name as he did in most other cases.

19 Alshekh to Gen. 6 and many other locations therein.

BERA	Would I quarrel? **The matter is not so.**[20]	הֶאָנֹכִי אָרִיב? לֹא כֵן הַדָּבָר.[20]	ברע
SHIMSHAI	If you would quarrel with us, I am ready for you	אִם תָּרִיב בָּנוּ הִנְנִי לִקְרָאתֶךָ	שמשי
	The master whom I serve is not inferior to your master.	הָאָדוֹן אֲשֶׁר אֲנִי עֹבֵד אֵינֶנּוּ נֹפֵל מֵאֲדֹנֶךָ.	
BERA	Nor better than him.	וְגַם לֹא טוֹב מִמֶּנּוּ.	ברע
SHIMSHAI	And what else will you answer?	וּמַה תַּעֲנֶה עוֹד?	שמשי
	(Benaiah[21] enters from opposite)	(בניה[21] בא מנגד)	
GERA	*(To Shimshai)* Say better than him; behold, an acquaintance of our master is coming.	(אל שמשי) אֱמֹר טוֹב מִמֶּנּוּ; הִנֵּה מוֹדַע לַאֲדֹנֵנוּ בָּא.	גרא
SHIMSHAI	He is better, better than him.	טוֹב הוּא, טוֹב הוּא מִמֶּנּוּ.	שמשי
BERA	You lie.	שֶׁקֶר בְּפִיךָ.	ברע
SHIMSHAI	Draw your swords if you are men – remember, Gera,	שִׁלְפוּ חַרְבְּכֶם אִם אֲנָשִׁים אַתֶּם – זְכֹר גֵּרָא	שמשי
	All the prideful words which you uttered. *(They fight each other)*	כָּל דִּבְרֵי רַהַב אֲשֶׁר הוֹצֵאתָ בְּפִיךָ. (נלחמים יחדו)	
BENAIAH	Desist, senseless men! Return your swords to their sheaths	חִדְלוּ חַסְרֵי לֵב! הָשִׁיבוּ חַרְבְּכֶם אֶל נְדָנָהּ	בניה
	Why, you do not know what you are doing. *(Strikes with his sword and knocks their swords from their hands)*	הֲלֹא אֵינְכֶם יֹדְעִים מָה אַתֶּם עֹשִׂים. (מכה בחרבו ומפיל חרבותם מידם)	
TUBAL[22]	Are you, with a drawn sword, involving yourself with these lowly servants?	הַאַתָּה בְּחֶרֶב שְׁלוּפָה, תִּתְעָרֵב בַּעֲבָדִים שְׁפָלִים אֵלֶּה?	תובל[22]
	Desist, Benaiah; there is but a footstep between you and death.	חֲדַל לְךָ בְּנָיָה, כְּפֶשַׂע בֵּינְךָ וּבֵין הַמָּוֶת.	
BENAIAH	I only came to silence the quarrel; put back your sword in peace	רַק לְהַשְׁקִיט הָרִיב בָּאתִי; הָשֵׁב חַרְבְּךָ בְּשָׁלוֹם	בניה

20 2 Sam. 20:21.

21 This is the name of various minor characters mentioned in a number of locations in the Hebrew Bible, the most prominent of which is a warrior loyal to King David (e.g., 2 Sam. 23:20–3). Salkinson most likely chose the name because of its sound correspondence with Shakespeare's 'Benvolio'.

22 One of Noah's grandsons, mentioned in Gen. 10:2; Salkinson most likely selected this name on the basis of its close sound correspondence with Shakespeare's 'Tybalt'.

	Or brandish it to help me separate the brawlers.	אוֹ הָנֵף אֹתָהּ לְעָזְרֵנִי לְהַפְרִיד אֶת הַנִּלְחָמִים.	
TUBAL	What does peace have to do with a drawn sword? I hate your peace	מַה־לְּשָׁלוֹם וּלְחֶרֶב נְטוּיָה? מְתָעֵב אֲנִי שְׁלוֹמֶךָ	תובל
	Like Sheol,[23] like the house of Abiram and like your despised self!	כִּשְׁאוֹל,[23] כְּבֵית אֲבִירָם וּכְנַפְשְׁךָ הַנִּמְאָסָה!	
	Come towards me, **weak-handed one**![24] *(They fight each other)*	צֵא לִקְרָאתִי רְפֵה יָדָיִם![24] (נלחמים יחדו)	
	(Several men from among the allies of the two families approach the fight, and afterwards the townspeople come with axes and hammers)	(מספר אנשים מבעלי ברית שתי המשפחות נגשים לקרב ואחרי כן באים בני העיר בכשיל וכילפות)	
ONE OF THE TOWNSPEOPLE	Hurry townspeople, strike **with axes and hammers**[25]	מַהֲרוּ בְּנֵי הָעִיר, הַכּוּ **בְּכַשִּׁיל וְכֵילַפּוֹת**[25]	אחד מבני העיר
	Destroy the Abiels![26] Destroy the Abirams!	הַשְׁמִידוּ אֶת הָאֲבִיעֵלִים![26] הַשְׁמִידוּ אֶת הָאֲבִירָמִים!	
	(Abiel wrapped in a coat, and his wife)	(אביעל עוטה מעיל ואשתו)	
ABIEL	What is the sound of confusion? Give me my large sword.	מַה־קּוֹל הַמְּהוּמָה? תְּנוּ לִי חַרְבִּי הַגְּדוֹלָה.	אביעל
ABIEL'S WIFE	A staff for **one who leans on a staff**;[27] what use have you for the sword?	פֶּלֶךְ לְמַחֲזִיק בַּפֶּלֶךְ,[27] מַה־לְּךָ וְלַחֶרֶב?	אשת אביעל
ABIEL	I said to give me my sword; there old Abiram	חַרְבִּי אָמַרְתִּי לָתֶת לִי, שָׁם אֲבִירָם הַזָּקֵן	אביעל

23 The biblical abode of the dead.

24 2 Sam. 17:2.

25 Ps. 74:6.

26 The name אֲבִיעֵל 'Abiel', Salkinson's translation of Shakespeare's 'Capulet', literally means 'Jael's father', referring to the fact that Salkinson has named his version of Juliet 'Jael' (see note 174). In selecting the name 'Abiel', Salkinson has created an exact parallel to 'Abiram', his translation for 'Montague' (which literally means 'Ram's father'; see note 11). The name אֲבִיעֵל does not actually appear in the Hebrew Bible, but is pronounced identically to the name אֲבִיאֵל 'Abiel', which denotes two different biblical characters, the grandfather of King Saul mentioned in 1 Sam. 9:1 and 14:51, and one of King David's warriors mentioned in 1 Chron. 11:32.

27 2 Sam. 3:29. Cf. Shakespeare's 'A crutch, a crutch!' (1.1.74).

	Is waving the blade of his sword in order to vex me.	מְעוֹפֵף לַהֶבֶת חַרְבּוֹ לְהַכְעִיסֵנִי.	
	(Abiram and his wife)	(אבירם ואשתו)	
ABIRAM	Come, you villain Abiel! – let go of me, so that I may go forth to him.	הָבָה אֲבִיעֵל בְּלִיַּעַל! – הַרְפִּי מִמֶּנִּי וְאֵצֵא לִקְרָאתוֹ.	אבירם
ABIRAM'S WIFE	You shall not step from here even one step to seek an enemy for yourself.	לֹא תִצְעַד מִזֶּה אַף צְעָדָה לְבַקֶּשׁ לְךָ אוֹיֵב.	אשת אבירם
	(The prince enters with his guards)	(הנסיך בא עם שומרי ראשו)	
THE PRINCE	Oh, **assembly of traitors**![28] Peace-hating people!	הוֹי עֲצֶרֶת בֹּגְדִים![28] עַם שֹׂנְאֵי שָׁלוֹם!	הנסיך
	Ones who desecrate **an iron weapon**[29] with their brothers' flesh	הַמְחַלְלִים נֶשֶׁק בַּרְזֶל[29] בִּבְשַׂר אֲחֵיהֶם	
	Are you not listening? – You are wild asses, not men	הַאִם לֹא תַקְשִׁיבוּ? – פְּרָאִים לֹא אֲנָשִׁים אַתֶּם	
	Who put out the fire of your rage in a fountain of blood flowing from your veins.	הַמְכַבִּים אֵשׁ זַעַמְכֶם בִּמְקוֹר דָּמִים נוֹזְלִים מֵעֹרְקֵיכֶם.	
	Throw the **instruments of violence**[30] from your hands, which are full of blood.	הַשְׁלִיכוּ כְּלֵי חָמָס[30] מִיְדֵיכֶם* אֲשֶׁר דָּמִים מָלֵאוּ.	
	Lest you bear your iniquity **in a furnace of affliction**[31] with **a burden on your loins**[32]	פֶּן תִּשְׂאוּ עֲוֺנְכֶם בְּכוּר עֹנִי[31] וּמוּעָקָה בְּמָתְנֵיכֶם[32]	
	And listen to the words of your masters, whom you have vexed today.	וְשִׁמְעוּ דִבְרֵי אֲדֹנֵיכֶם אֲשֶׁר הִכְעַסְתֶּם הַיּוֹם.	
	Three times now there has been the sound of **distress and cries of lament in our squares**[33]	זֶה שָׁלֹשׁ פְּעָמִים קוֹל פֶּרֶץ וּצְוָחָה בִּרְחֹבֹתֵינוּ[33]	

28 Jer. 9:1 (9:2 in English Bibles).
29 Job 20:24.
30 Gen. 49:5.
31 Isa. 48:10.
32 Ps. 66:11.
33 Ps. 144:14 אֵין־פֶּרֶץ וְאֵין יוֹצֵאת וְאֵין צְוָחָה בִּרְחֹבֹתֵינוּ 'may there be no breaches or going out [into captivity], and no cries of lament in our squares'.

* מִידֵיכֶם

As **stirring up anger by words more trifling than breath**

כִּי מִיץ אַפַּיִם בִּדְבָרִים קַלִּים מֵהֶבֶל

Between Abiel and Abiram has brought forth quarrel and strife[34]

בֵּין אֲבִיעֵל וַאֲבִירָם הוֹצִיא רִיב וּמָדוֹן[34]

Until it has led Verona astray, and its citizens and elders

עַד עֲשׂוֹת לְוֵירוֹנָה תוֹעָה וְאֶזְרָחֶיהָ וּזְקֵנֶיהָ

Have stripped off their ornaments[35] and their honour and have seized worn swords

הִתְנַצְּלוּ עֶדְיָם[35] וּכְבוֹדָם וַיַּחֲזִיקוּ בִּבְלוֹאֵי חֲרָבוֹת

And rotten iron tools with which to destroy the rot of their hatred.

וּכְלֵי בַרְזֶל רָקָב לְכַלּוֹת רְקַב שִׂנְאָתָם בָּם.

If you break out again and disturb the peace in the city

אִם עוֹד תִּפְרְצוּ פֶּרֶץ וְתַפְרִיעוּ שְׁלוֹם הָעִיר

I shall have but one law: to put to death,[36] and **your blood will be on your heads.**[37]

אַחַת דָּתִי לְהָמִית[36] וְדִמְכֶם יְהִי בְּרָאשֵׁיכֶם.[37]

And now all those gathered here, go, each man to his house

וְעַתָּה כָּל הַנֶּאֱסָפִים פֹּה, לְכוּ לָכֶם אִישׁ לְבֵיתוֹ

Only you, Abiel, shall indeed go with me

רַק אַתָּה אֲבִיעֵל, הָלֹךְ תֵּלֵךְ עִמָּדִי

And moreover you, Abiram, shall come to me **when midday is past**[38]

וְאַף אַתָּה אֲבִירָם, אֵלַי תָּבוֹא כַּעֲבֹר הַצָּהֳרַיִם[38]

And I shall announce my words **at the gate of judgement**[39] in the town of Horon[40]

וְאַשְׁמִיעֲךָ דְּבָרַי בְּשַׁעַר הַמִּשְׁפָּט[39] בְּקִרְיַת חֹרוֹן[40]

---

34 Prov. 30:33 וּמִיץ אַפַּיִם יוֹצִיא רִיב 'and stirring up anger brings forth quarrels'.

35 Exod. 33:6 וַיִּתְנַצְּלוּ בְנֵי־יִשְׂרָאֵל אֶת־עֶדְיָם מֵהַר חוֹרֵב 'and the children of Israel stripped off their ornaments by Mount Horeb'.

36 Esther 4:11 אַחַת דָּתוֹ לְהָמִית 'he has but one law: to put to death'.

37 Ezek. 33:4 דָּמוֹ בְרֹאשׁוֹ יִהְיֶה 'his blood will be on his head'.

38 1 Kings 18:29.

39 Alshekh to Gen. 19.

40 This is Salkinson's translation of Shakespeare's 'Freetown' (1.1.100). Horon is part of the place name Beth-Horon, which denotes two neighbouring towns mentioned on various occasions in the Hebrew Bible. These towns do not have any particular associations with law or judgements, either in the biblical period or later (although several Talmudic scholars came from Beth-Horon). Rather, the selection of this name in the present context is likely be rooted in the phonetic similarity between חֹרוֹן 'Horon' and the rabbinic word חורין 'free' (which most commonly appears in the phrase בן חורין 'free man'), thereby evoking echoes of the English 'Freetown'.

	And as for all of those gathered here, I order you again	וּלְכָל הַנִּצָּבִים פֹּה, אֲנִי מְצַוֶּה עוֹד הַפַּעַם	
	Go back, each man on his way, for **it will cost you your lives.**[41]	שׁוּבוּ אִישׁ אִישׁ לְדַרְכּוֹ, **כִּי בְּנַפְשְׁכֶם הוּא.**[41]	
	(The prince exits, and after him his attendants, Abiel and his wife, Tubal, and all the inhabitants of the city)	(הנסיך הולך ואחריו משרתיו, אביעל ואשתו ותובל וכל בני העיר)	
ABIRAM	Whose hand renewed the old quarrel today?	יַד מִי הָיְתָה הַיּוֹם, לְחַדֵּשׁ הַתִּגְרָה הַנּוֹשָׁנָה?	אבירם
	Tell me, my nephew, did you see how it began?	הַגֶּד־לִי בֶּן אָחִי, הֲרָאִיתָ אֵיךְ הֵחֵלָּה?	
BENAIAH	Your enemy's servants were fighting with your servants	עַבְדֵי אִישׁ אֹיִבְךָ, הָיוּ נִלְחָמִים בַּעֲבָדֶיךָ	בניה
	Before I reached them, for I sought to separate them,	טֶרֶם בָּאתִי אֲלֵיהֶם, כִּי הוֹאַלְתִּי לְהַפְרִידָם	
	Suddenly the rash Tubal came with drawn sword	וְהִנֵּה פִּתְאֹם בָּא תּוּבַל הַנִּמְהָר בְּחֶרֶב שְׁלוּפָה	
	And provoked me to fight against him; and he was raising and lowering his sword	וַיִּתְגָּר בִּי לַעֲרֹךְ נֶגְדּוֹ; וְהוּא מַעֲלֶה וּמוֹרִיד חַרְבּוֹ	
	Brandishing it in every direction, as if striking the wind around him	מֵנִיף לְכָל עֵבֶר, כְּמַכֶּה אֶת הָרוּחַ סְבִיבוֹ	
	But the wind was not struck by its striker, and whistled as if mocking him	וְהָרוּחַ לֹא הֻכָּה מִיַּד מַכֵּהוּ וַיִּשְׁרֹק כְּלֹעֵג לוֹ	
	And while we rushed to fight with blows and beatings in turn	וּבְעוֹד חַשְׁנוּ לְהִתְעַשֵּׁק בְּמַדְחֵפוֹת וּמַהֲלֻמוֹת חֲלִיפוֹת	
	A great crowd came and each man struck straight ahead **with a high hand**[42, 43]	בָּא הָמוֹן רָב וַיַּכּוּ אִישׁ נֶגְדּוֹ **בְּיָד רָמָה**[42, 43]	
	Until the prince came and scattered all the fighting men.	עַד אֲשֶׁר בָּא הַנָּסִיךְ וַיָּפֶץ כָּל אַנְשֵׁי הַמִּלְחָמָה.	

41 Prov. 7:23 וְֽלֹא־יָדַע כִּֽי־בְנַפְשׁוֹ הֽוּא 'and he does not know that it will cost him his life'.

42 Exod. 14:8; Num. 15:30, 33:3.

43 This and the next line form a rhyming couplet, mirroring Shakespeare's 'part/part' (1.1.112–13). This is unusual, as Salkinson does not usually recognize same-word rhymes in his translation.

ABIRAM'S WIFE	Where is my son Ram?[44] Have you seen him today, Benaiah?[45]	אֵי רָם[44] בְּנִי? הֲרָאִיתָ אֹתוֹ הַיּוֹם בְּנָיָה?[45]	אשת אבירם
	It is enough for me that he was not in this quarrel.	רב* לִי כִּי בַּמְּרִיבָה הַזֹּאת לֹא הָיָה.	
BENAIAH	Before the dawn had broken, ere from the windows of the firmament	עַד לֹא עָלָה הַשַּׁחַר, טֶרֶם יָצִיץ מֵחַלּוֹנֵי רָקִיעַ	בניה
	The glory of the sun peeked from the east, I arose **to stroll in the field.**[46]	הוֹד שֶׁמֶשׁ מִקָּדִים, קַמְתִּי לָשׂוּחַ בַּשָּׂדֶה.[46]	
	For **my spirit constrained me,**[47] and at that time I saw your son	כִּי הֱצִיקַתְנִי רוּחִי[47] וָאֶרְאֶה אָז אֶת בִּנְךָ	
	Walking back and forth between the boulevards of sycamores	מִתְהַלֵּךְ הֵנָּה וָהֵנָּה בֵּין שְׂדֵרוֹת הַשִּׁקְמִים	
	Which are to the west of the city, and when I turned towards him	אֲשֶׁר מִמַּעֲרַב לָעִיר וְכַאֲשֶׁר פָּנִיתִי לִקְרָאתוֹ	
	His eye saw me and he stole away **under the shady trees**[48] in the woods[49]	רָאַתְנִי עֵינוֹ וַיִּתְגַּנַּב תַּחַת צֶאֱלִים[48] בַּחֹרְשָׁה[49]	
	And I, from how **my face was set**, recognized how **his face was set**[50]	וַאֲנִי מִמְּגַמַּת פָּנַי הִכַּרְתִּי מַה מְּגַמַּת פָּנָיו[50]	

44 Salkinson selected 'Ram' as the Hebrew equivalent of 'Romeo' on the basis of both sound correspondence and meaning. Ram is a biblical character mentioned in Ruth 4:19 as the ancestor of King David. Because King David and his genealogical line are exalted in Jewish tradition, and readers of Salkinson's text would have been familiar with the biblical Ram from the annual synagogue recitation of the Book of Ruth during the festival of Shavuot, they would have associated Shakespeare's protagonist with the positive qualities of the Davidic line. Likewise, the fact that the name derives from the Book of Ruth is itself significant: as Ruth is the archetypal biblical love story, the name would have had romantic associations in readers' minds.

45 This and the next line form a rhyming couplet, mirroring Shakespeare's 'today/fray' (1.1.114–15).

46 Gen. 24:63.

47 Job 32:18 הֱצִיקַתְנִי רוּחַ בִּטְנִי 'the spirit within me constrains me'.

48 Job 40:21. The word צֶאֱלִים appears only twice in the Hebrew Bible (here and in the following verse, Job 40:22), and its meaning is somewhat unclear. The translation 'shady trees' is based on the King James Bible, and has been selected because it most closely parallels Shakespeare's 'the covert of the wood' (1.1.123), but other possibilities include 'bramble bush' and 'bough' (Koehler and Baumgartner 2001, 2: 992), as well as 'lotus plants' (e.g., New Revised Standard Version, English Standard Version).

49 This form appears in the Hebrew Bible but seems to be a place name; the meaning of 'woods' is believed to have originated in the modern period (Even-Shoshan 2003, 2: 615).

50 Hab. 1:9 מְגַמַּת פְּנֵיהֶם קָדִימָה 'their faces are set as the east wind'.

* רַב

	For I, like he, sought to converse with myself alone	כִּי אֲנִי כָמוֹהוּ בִּקַּשְׁתִּי לָשִׂיחַ עִם נַפְשִׁי לְבַדִּי	
	Lest someone be **a hindrance to me, for I was a burden to myself**[51]	**לְבַל יְהִי לִי אָדָם לְמִפְגָּע, כִּי אֲנִי עָלַי לְמַשָּׂא**[51]	
	And therefore I went on my way and I turned away from him as my soul desired	וְלָכֵן הָלַכְתִּי לְדַרְכִּי וָאֵט מֵעָלָיו בְּאַוַּת נַפְשִׁי	
	Just as he, as his soul desired, fled and turned away from me.	כַּאֲשֶׁר הוּא בְּאַוַּת נַפְשׁוֹ נָס וַיֵּט מִפָּנָי.	
ABIRAM	Thus he has been seen two or three times, walking back and forth there in the woods	כֵּן נִרְאָה פַּעֲמַיִם שָׁלֹשׁ, מִתְהַלֵּךְ שָׁם בַּחֹרְשָׁה	אבירם
	His eyes drip water to supplement the dewdrops	עֵינָיו תִּטֹּפְנָה מַיִם לָשִׁית נוֹסָפוֹת עַל אֶגְלֵי טָל	
	And with the groaning of his spirit he clouds his surroundings, multiplying the morning clouds	וּבְאֶנְקַת רוּחוֹ יָעִיב סְבִיבוֹ לְהַכְבִּיר עַנְנֵי בֹקֶר	
	And when the dawn stirs and rolls back the curtain	וְכַאֲשֶׁר יֵעוֹר הַשַּׁחַר וְגָלַל אֶת הַמָּסָךְ	
	From the chambers of the east and the sun emerges from its canopy[52]	מֵעַל חַדְרֵי מִזְרָח וְהַשֶּׁמֶשׁ יֵצֵא מֵחֻפָּתוֹ[52]	
	To make the soul of every living being rejoice, thus my son returns home	לְשַׂמֵּחַ נֶפֶשׁ כָּל חַי, כֵּן יָשׁוּב בְּנִי הַבַּיְתָה	
	Gloomy with the oppression of his heart; he closes and blocks the windows of his chamber	קֹדֵר בְּלַחַץ לִבּוֹ, יִסְגֹּר יַאְטֵם חַלּוֹנֵי חַדְרוֹ	
	Lest light come from its dwelling-place and make morning of his darkness.	לְבַל יָבוֹא אוֹר בְּמוֹשָׁבוֹ וְשָׂם לוֹ בֹּקֶר לְצַלְמָוֶת.	
	This **broken spirit**[53] has been a mortal illness from the beginning[54]	**רוּחַ נְכֵאָה**[53] זוּ, מַחֲלָה אֲנוּשָׁה הִיא לְמִבָּרִאשֹׁנָה[54]	

51 Job 7:20 לָמָּה שַׂמְתַּנִי לְמִפְגָּע לָךְ וָאֶהְיֶה עָלַי לְמַשָּׂא 'why have You set me as your target, so that I am a burden to myself?'; Salkinson seems to be using the word מִפְגָּע, which means 'target' in the biblical text, in the sense of 'hindrance' or 'obstacle', which is first attested in the modern period (Even-Shoshan 2003, 3: 1050).

52 Cf. Shakespeare's 'the shady curtains from Aurora's bed' (1.1.134); Salkinson has removed the reference to Aurora, the Roman goddess of the dawn, which would have had little meaning or relevance in the Eastern European Jewish context.

53 Prov. 15:13, 17:22, 18:14.

54 This and the next line form a rhyming couplet, mirroring Shakespeare's 'prove/remove' (1.1.139–40).

	And if we do not find a remedy, **it will be bitterness in the end**.[55]	וְאִם לֹא נִמְצָא אֲרוּכָה, מָרָה תִּהְיֶה בָּאַחֲרֹנָה.[55]	
BENAIAH	My noble uncle, do you know what **his anguish of spirit**[56] is?	דּוֹדִי הַנָּדִיב, הֲיָדַעְתָּ מַה־מֹּרַת נַפְשׁוֹ?[56]	בניה
ABIRAM	Several times have I enquired, and many others too	כַּמֶּה פְּעָמִים דָּרַשְׁתִּי אֲנִי וְגַם רַבִּים אֲחֵרִים	אבירם
	But he is concealing the matter, and will not reveal his secret	אַךְ הוּא מַסְתִּיר דָּבָר וְאֶת סוֹדוֹ לֹא יְגַלֶּה	
	And everyone who enquires and seeks of him is like one who enquires of **a flower of the field**[57]	וְכָל דֹּרֵשׁ וּמְבַקֵּשׁ מִמֶּנּוּ כְּדֹרֵשׁ אֶל צִיץ הַשָּׂדֶה[57]	
	Whose insides have been eaten by a maggot and **it withers and dries**[58]	אֲשֶׁר רִמָּה אָכְלָה תוֹכוֹ וְהוּא יְמוֹלֵל וְיָבֵשׁ[58]	
	Before it has spread out its foliage to be seen and **its glorious beauty**[59] to the sun	בְּטֶרֶם פִּתַּח עָלֵהוּ לְמַרְאֶה וּצְבִי תִפְאַרְתּוֹ[59] לַשָּׁמֶשׁ.	
	If **we could find the root of the matter**[60] on account of which his soul is wretched[61]	לוּ מָצָאנוּ שֹׁרֶשׁ דָּבָר,[60] עַל מָה נַפְשׁוֹ אֻמְלָלָה[61]	
	It would not be impossible to find **a remedy**.[62]	לֹא יִבָּצֵר מִמֶּנּוּ לִמְצֹא לוֹ רְפֻאוֹת תְּעָלָה.[62]	
	(Ram can be seen from afar)	(רם נראה מרחוק)	
BENAIAH	Please turn aside, my lord; here he comes towards me[63]	סוּרָה נָּא אֲדֹנִי הַצִּדָּה, הִנֵּה הוּא בָא לִקְרָאתִי[63]	בניה
	And I shall question him and enter his confidence, for I shall urge him with my love.	וַאֲנִי אֶחְקְרֵהוּ אָבוֹא בְּסוֹדוֹ, כִּי אֶפְצַר בּוֹ בְּאַהֲבָתִי.	
ABIRAM	If only profound worry could be drawn out from a pit of water[64]	מִי יִתֵּן וְדָלֹה תִדְלֶה דְּאָגָה עֲמֻקָּה מִבּוֹר מָיִם[64]	אבירם

55 2 Sam. 2:26.
56 Gen. 26:35 מֹרַת רוּחַ 'anguish of spirit'.
57 Isa. 40:6; Ps. 103:15.
58 Ps. 90:6.
59 Isa. 28:1, 4.
60 Job 19:28 וְשֹׁרֶשׁ דָּבָר נִמְצָא־בִי 'and the root of the matter is found in me'.
61 This and the next line form a rhyming couplet, mirroring Shakespeare's 'grow/know' (1.1.152–3).
62 Jer. 30:13, 46:11.
63 This and the next line form a rhyming couplet, mirroring Shakespeare's 'aside/denied' (1.1.154–5).
64 This and the next line form a rhyming couplet, mirroring Shakespeare's 'stay/away' (1.1.156–7). Salkinson's insertion of the phrase לְמַעַן תֵּת לָהֶם יָדַיִם 'in order to give them space', which has no basis in the original, seems to have been rooted solely in a desire to make these two lines rhyme.

	Arise, my wife, and let us go from here to give them space.	קוּמִי אִשְׁתִּי וְנֵלְכָה מִזֶּה לְמַעַן תֵּת לָהֶם יָדָיִם.	
	(Abiram and his wife exit)	(אבירם ואשתו הולכים)	
BENAIAH	I am happy to have met you this morning; are you well, my brother?[65]	לְשִׂמְחָתִי פְּגַשְׁתִּיךָ בַּבֹּקֶר זֶה, הֲשָׁלוֹם לְךָ אָחִי?[65]	בניה
RAM	And I thought that **the morning watch**[66] had passed	וַאֲנִי דִמִּיתִי, כִּי **אַשְׁמֹרֶת הַבֹּקֶר**[66] עָבָרָה	רם
	Time is long for **the man whose path is hidden.**[67]	אֲרֻכָּה הָעֵת **לַגֶּבֶר אֲשֶׁר דַּרְכּוֹ נִסְתָּרָה.**[67]	
	But who hurried to go away from here? Was it my father?	אַךְ מִי נֶחְפָּז לָלֶכֶת מִזֶּה? הַאִם אָבִי הוּא?	
BENAIAH	Yes. But who is making your days lengthy and evil?[68]	הֵן. אַךְ מִי מֵשִׂים יָמֶיךָ מְמֻשָּׁכִים וְרָעִים?[68]	בניה
RAM	Indeed my lot is not such that the days pass by like moments.	כִּי אֶחְסַר הַחֵלֶק בּוֹ יַעַבְרוּ יָמִים כִּרְגָעִים.	רם
BENAIAH	Are you lovesick?	הַחֹלֵה אַהֲבָה אָתָּה?	בניה
RAM	I am loveless.	חֲסַר אַהֲבָה אָנִי.	רם
BENAIAH	Is your soul lacking love?	הַאִם אַהֲבָה תֶּחְסַר לְנַפְשֶׁךָ?	בניה
RAM	I am lacking **the one whom my soul loves,**[69] for she has abandoned me.	אֹתָהּ **שֶׁאָהֲבָה נַפְשִׁי**[69] אֶחְסָר, כִּי הִיא עֲזָבַתְנִי.	רם
BENAIAH	What is more pleasant than delicate love, **at a time when favour**[70] is upon its lips?[71]	מַה־נָּעִים מֵאַהֲבָה עֲדִינָה, **בְּעֵת רָצוֹן**[70] עַל שְׂפָתֶיהָ?[71]	בניה
	And who is as cruel as it is, without mercy at a time when it hides its face?[72]	וּמִי כָמוֹהָ אַכְזָר בְּלִי חֲנִינָה, לְעֵת תַּסְתִּיר פָּנֶיהָ?[72]	

65 This is the Hebrew dynamic equivalent of Shakespeare's nonspecific kinship term 'cousin' (1.1.158) (see Weis 2012: 135, note 158, and Crystal and Crystal 2002: 105 for discussion of Shakespeare's use of 'cousin' in this sense).

66 Exod. 14:24; 1 Sam. 11:11.

67 Job 3:23.

68 This and the next line form a rhyming couplet, mirroring Shakespeare's 'young/long' (1.1.158–9).

69 Song of Songs 1:7, 3:1, 2, 3.

70 Isa. 49:8.

71 This and the next line form a rhyming couplet. There is no precedent for this in the original, though perhaps Salkinson interpreted Shakespeare's 'view/proof' (1.1.167–8) as a rhyme.

72 The expression 'hide one's face' appears on many occasions in the Hebrew Bible (e.g., Deut. 31:18; Isa. 8:17; Ezek. 39:23; Ps. 27:9) and refers to God turning away from the Israelites in punishment for their sins. This concept of *hester panim*, or divine concealment (lit. 'hiding one's face'), is a theme in Jewish philosophy. See Wolpe (1997) for a discussion of *hester panim* in modern Jewish thought.

RAM	And how does this love with its eyes covered **twist and turn on its ways**[73, 74]	וְאֵיךְ אַהֲבָה זוּ בִּכְסוּת עֵינַיִם דְּרָכֶיהָ מְשָׂרֶכֶת[73, 74]	רם
	And in blindness pave a path to the place where it desires to go? –	וּבְעִוָּרוֹן תָּסֹל מְסִלָּה אֶל אֲשֶׁר תַּחְפֹּץ לָלֶכֶת? –	
	Where shall we dine at noon? – Woe, for there is **strife and violence in the city**[75]	אָנָה נֹאכַל בַּצָּהֳרָיִם? – אוֹי. כִּי רִיב וְחָמָס בָּעִיר[75]	
	But cease telling me, for I have heard everything.	אַךְ חֲדַל לְךָ מְסַפֵּר לִי, כִּי שָׁמַעְתִּי אֶת כֹּל.	
	We have had enough of quarrelling with enmity and doubly with love.	יֶשׁ לָנוּ רַב לְהִתְגָּרוֹת בְּאֵיבָה וְכִפְלַיִם בְּאַהֲבָה.	
	Oh woe, love full of brawling! Hatred mixed with affection![76]	הוֹי אַהֲבָה מְלֵאָה תִגְרָה! מַשְׂטֵמָה בְּלוּלָה בִּידִידוּת![76]	
	You are something created out of nothing, a matter trifling yet too heavy to bear	הִנְּךָ יֵשׁ נִבְרָא מֵאַיִן, דָּבָר קַל וְכָבֵד מִנְּשׂא	
	Pointlessness full of weighty matters, an image that is despised yet pleasing to the sight.	הֶבֶל מָלֵא נִכְבָּדוֹת, פֶּסֶל נִמְאָס וְנֶחְמָד לְמַרְאֶה	
	A wing of lead, bright smoke, and a cold flame	כְּנַף עֹפֶרֶת, עָשָׁן בָּהִיר וְשַׁלְהֶבֶת קָרָה	
	Healthy of flesh[77] yet sick of soul, **a spirit of deep sleep**[78] yet an alert heart;	בְּרִיאַת בָּשָׂר[77] וְחוֹלַת נֶפֶשׁ, רוּחַ תַּרְדֵּמָה[78] וְלֵב עֵר;	
	This is my love, strange and shifting before the eye[79]	זֹאת אַהֲבָתִי מוּזָרָה וּמִתְהַפֶּכֶת לְמַרְאֵה עָיִן[79]	
	And this is the lot of my soul, **drunk, but not with wine**.[80] –	וְזֶה חֵלֶק לְנַפְשִׁי שְׁכֻרַת וְלֹא מִיָּיִן.[80] –	
	Do you not laugh?	וְאַתָּה לֹא תִצְחָק?	

73 Jer. 2:23 מְשָׂרֶכֶת דְּרָכֶיהָ 'she twists and turns on her ways'.
74 This and the next line form a rhyming couplet, mirroring Shakespeare's 'still/will' (1.1.169–70).
75 Ps. 55:10 (55:9 in English Bibles) חָמָס וְרִיב בָּעִיר 'violence and strife in the city'.
76 The last word in this line does not rhyme with the last word in the following line, in contrast to Shakespeare's 'hate/create' (1.1.174–5). However, the final vowel of the last word of both lines is *ḥolem* (*o*), which may suggest that Salkinson was unable to find a fully rhyming translation and selected these two words because of their partial sound correspondence.
77 Gen. 41:2 וּבְרִיאֹת בָּשָׂר 'and fat (lit. healthy) of flesh'.
78 Isa. 29:10.
79 This and the next line form a rhyming couplet, mirroring Shakespeare's 'is/this' (1.1.179–80).
80 Isa. 51:21.

BENAIAH	Not so, my brother; I want to weep.	לֹא כֵן אָחִי, מְבַקֵּשׁ אֲנִי לִבְכּוֹת.	בניה
RAM	But for what, my beloved friend?	וְעַל מָה יְדִיד לִבֵּי?	רם
BENAIAH	For the distress of your soul, because I know its pain.	עַל צָרַת נַפְשְׁךָ, כִּי יָדַעְתִּי מַכְאֹבָהּ.	בניה
RAM	Why, this is the law of love, a bad law	הֲלֹא זֹאת חֻקַּת הָאַהֲבָה חֻקָּה לֹא טוֹבָה.	רם
	The oppression of my heart is severe, and my spirit crushes me like **a millstone**[81, 82]	לַחַץ לְבָבִי קָשֶׁה וְרוּחִי כְּפֶלַח **רֶכֶב**[81] תִּלְחָצֵנִי[82]	
	And you, because you are distressed on account of my distress, harass me further	וְאַתָּה כִּי צַר לְךָ בְּצָרָתִי, תָּשִׁית נוֹסָפוֹת לְהַצִּיקֵנִי	
	And your faithful love for me, which has been demonstrated to me,[83]	וְאַהֲבָתְךָ הַנֶּאֱמָנָה לִי, אֲשֶׁר לָדַעַת הָרְאֵיתִי[83]	
	Adds anguish to my anguish, which I have grown weary of bearing.	תּוֹסִיף מְצוּקָה עַל מְצוּקָתִי, אֲשֶׁר מִנְּשֹׂא נִלְאֵיתִי.	
	Love is the smoke of hearts rising from an excess of sighs[84]	הָאַהֲבָה הִיא עֲשַׁן הַלְּבָבוֹת, מֵאֲנָחוֹת כִּי יַכְבִּירוּ[84]	
	And when the smoke is cleansed it burns, and the lovers' eyes shine	וְכִי יְזֻקַּק הֶעָשָׁן יִבְעַר וְעֵינֵי הַנֶּאֱהָבִים יַזְהִירוּ	
	But it transforms itself with the sound of rebuke and becomes **a river of tears**.[85, 86]	וּמִקּוֹל גְּעָרָה יִתְהַפֵּךְ וְהָיָה **לְנַחַל דִּמְעָה**[85, 86]	
	And what else is love? Madness with much scheming	וּמָה הָאַהֲבָה עוֹד? שִׁגָּעוֹן בְּרֹב מְזִמָּה	
	More bitter than **the poison of asps**[87] and sweeter than all delights.	מַר **מֵרוֹשׁ פְּתָנִים**[87] וּמָתוֹק מִכָּל עֲדָנִים.	
	And now, farewell – *(Makes to exit)*	וְעַתָּה שָׁלוֹם – (הוא רוצה ללכת)	
BENAIAH	Wait and we'll go together; I desire your company[88]	הוֹחִילָה וְנֵלְכָה יַחְדָּו, בְּחֶבְרָתְךָ חָפֵץ הִנֵּנִי[88]	בניה

81 Judg. 9:53; 2 Sam. 11:21.
82 This and the next line form a rhyming couplet, mirroring Shakespeare's 'breast/pressed' (1.1.184–5).
83 This and the next line form a rhyming couplet, mirroring Shakespeare's 'shown/own' (1.1.186–7).
84 This and the next line form a rhyming couplet, mirroring Shakespeare's 'sighs/eyes' (1.1.188–9).
85 Lam. 2:18.
86 This and the next line form a rhyming couplet, mirroring Shakespeare's 'discreet/ sweet' (1.1.191–2).
87 Deut. 32:33; Job 20:16.
88 This and the next line form a rhyming couplet, mirroring Shakespeare's 'along/wrong' (1.1.193–4).

	Please listen to me, do not abandon me.	שְׁמַע נָא בְּקוֹלִי אַל נָא תַּעַזְבֵנִי.	
RAM	I have also been abandoned, and so I do not understand[89]	גַּם אֲנִי נֶעֱזַבְתִּי וְאֵיפוֹ אֲנִי לֹא אָבִינָה[89]	רם
	Ram is not here; he is wandering lost **at every corner**.[90]	רָם אֵינֶנּוּ פֹּה תֹּעֶה הוּא אֵצֶל כָּל פִּנָּה.[90]	
BENAIAH	Tell me, who is she whom you desire?	הַגִּידָה לִּי מִי הִיא אֲשֶׁר חָשַׁקְתָּ בָּהּ?	בניה
RAM	Should I groan bitterly, telling you who she is?	הֲכִי אֶאֱנַח בִּמְרִירוּת לְהַגִּיד לְךָ מִי הִיא?	רם
BENAIAH	Do not groan bitterly; pour out your heart and say who she is.	אַל תֵּאָנַח בִּמְרִירוּת, שְׁפוֹךְ לִבְּךָ וֶאֱמֹר מִי הִיא.	בניה
RAM	When you tell **a suffering man**,[91] hurry to make a will for your household[92]	כִּי תֹאמַר לְאִישׁ מַכְאֹבוֹת:[91] צַו לְבֵיתְךָ חוּשָׁה:[92]	רם
	At this **his heart melts**,[93] for he regards his blow to be mortal	לַדָּבָר הַזֶּה יִמַּס לִבּוֹ,[93] כִּי יַחְשֹׁב מַכָּתוֹ אֲנוּשָׁה	
	Only this shall I say in sadness, that I love a woman.	רַק זֹאת אַגִּידָה בְּעֶצֶב, כִּי אִשָּׁה אֲנִי אֹהֵב.	
BENAIAH	Before you told me, I thought so as well.	בְּטֶרֶם הִגַּדְתָּ לִי, חָשַׁבְתִּי כֵּן גַּם אָנִי.	בניה
RAM	You are a wise thinker, and my beloved is good-looking.	חֹשֵׁב נָבוֹן אַתָּה וַאֲהוּבָתִי טוֹבַת מַרְאֶה הִיא.	רם
BENAIAH	It is easy to shoot at a good-looking target, and you have struck well.	לְמַטָּרָה טוֹבַת מַרְאֶה נָקֵל לִירוֹת וְהֵיטֵב קִלַּעְתָּ.	בניה
RAM	You have shot your words for nothing, and you have not hit the target	חִנָּם יָרִיתָ דְּבָרְךָ וּבְמַטָּרָה לֹא נָגַעְתָּ	רם
	She laughs at the arrow-shooters,[94] and stands like **a fortified city**[95]	הִיא תִשְׂחַק לְבַעֲלֵי חִצִּים[94] וְתַעֲמֹד כְּעִיר בְּצוּרָה[95]	

89 This and the next line form a rhyming couplet, mirroring Shakespeare's 'here/otherwhere' (1.1.195–6).
90 Prov. 7:12.
91 Isa. 53:3.
92 This and the next line form a rhyming couplet, mirroring Shakespeare's 'will/ill' (1.1.200–1).
93 i.e., in fear; Josh. 2:11 וַיִּמַּס לְבָבֵנוּ 'and our heart melted'; see also Josh. 5:1, 7:5.
94 Cf. Shakespeare's 'Cupid's arrow' (1.1.207); Salkinson has replaced the Classical mythological reference with an expression devoid of any particular cultural overtones.
95 Isa. 47:10.

	Her mind is like God's mind;[96] there is no **counsel or strength**[97] before her	לִבָּהּ כְּלֵב אֱלֹהִים,[96] לְנֶגְדָּהּ אֵין עֵצָה וּגְבוּרָה[97]	
	The shield of her perfection is strong, and the whole fortress of her strength is stone[98]	מָגֵן תֻּמָּתָהּ חָזָק וְכָל מִבְצַר עֻזָּהּ אֶבֶן[98]	
	She does not fear **a drawn bow**;[99] she regards arrows of love as straw	לֹא תִירָא מִקֶּשֶׁת דְּרוּכָה,[99] חִצֵּי אַהֲבָה תַּחְשֹׁב לְתֶבֶן	
	Pleading does not help; she does not look favourably upon words of love[100]	לֹא יוֹעִילוּ תַּחֲנוּנִים, לֹא תִשְׁעֶה לְדִבְרֵי אֲהָבִים[100]	
	She is not moved by tears, and she turns her gaze away from arrogant eyes	דְּמָעוֹת לֹא תַבִּיט וְתָסֵב עֵינֶיהָ מֵעֵינֵי רְהָבִים	
	She has no desire for gold, she scorns wealth[101]	זָהָב לֹא תַחְפֹּץ בּוֹ, בְּעֹשֶׁר תִּתֵּן דֹּפִי[101]	
	Her great wealth is the charm of her face, and poverty would follow her	עָשְׁרָהּ רַב בְּחֵן פָּנֶיהָ וְעֹנִי יָבוֹא אַחֲרֶיהָ	
	For on the day of her death, beauty will die with her.	כִּי בְיוֹם מוֹתָהּ עִמָּהּ יָמוּת יֹפִי.	
BENAIAH	Has she sworn a vow to abstain from men, to sit barren all her days?[102]	הַאִם נָדְרָה לְהִנָּזֵר מֵאִישׁ, לָשֶׁבֶת כָּל יָמֶיהָ עֲקָרֶת?[102]	בניה
RAM	By abstaining she withholds her love, but indeed she is missing out	בְּנִזְרָהּ מֹנַעַת דֹּדֶיהָ וְהִיא אַךְ מְחַסֶּרֶת	רם

96 Cf. Shakespeare's 'She hath Dian's wit' (1.1.207). Salkinson has replaced Diana, the Roman goddess of hunting, with the monotheistic God. This differs from the many cases in which he simply removes references to Classical mythological figures. It is possible that he chose to retain the divine associations of the original phrase in order to preserve the point that Rosaline/Shoshana has a superhuman mind (in contrast to other cases, such as the directly preceding reference to Cupid, where the sense of the English can be conveyed without recourse to the divine).

97 2 Kings 18:20; Isa. 11:2, 36:5.

98 This and the next line form a rhyming couplet, mirroring Shakespeare's 'hit/wit' (1.1.206–7).

99 Isa. 21:15.

100 This and the next line form a rhyming couplet, mirroring Shakespeare's 'armed/uncharmed' (1.1.208–9).

101 This and the following two lines form an ABA rhyme, mirroring the original except that the latter has instead a rhyming couplet in the last two lines of the speech, 'poor/store' (1.1.213–14). This difference may suggest that Salkinson was unable to find a suitable rhyme in the two adjacent lines and decided on this solution as a partial correspondence to the English version.

102 This last word in Benaiah's line rhymes with the last word of the following line (spoken by Ram), echoing the English original (again, split between Benvolio and Romeo) 'chaste/waste' (1.1.215–16).

	For the beautiful maiden in her virginity, who refuses to build a house,[103]	כִּי הַיָּפָה בִּבְתוּלֶיהָ אֲשֶׁר תְּמָאֵן לִבְנוֹת בָּיִת[103]	
	Will not bequeath to eternity the fruit of her womb like olive shoots.	לֹא תַנְחִיל לַדּוֹר פְּרִי בִטְנָהּ כִּשְׁתִילֵי זָיִת.	
	She denies her great beauty, and she calls the life of the flesh the shadow of death[104]	לְיָפְיָהּ כִּי רַב תִּתְעַקֵּשׁ וְתִקְרָא לְחַיֵּי בְשָׂרִים צַלְמָוֶת[104]	
	In her hope to inherit eternal life, she has brought me to **the gates of death**[105]	בְּתִקְוָתָהּ לִנְחֹל חַיֵּי עַד, הֱבִיאַתְנִי עַד שַׁעֲרֵי מָוֶת[105]	
	She has issued a ban on touching **the tree of knowledge,**[106] **to my anger and my wrath**[107, 108]	מִנְּגֹעַ בְּעֵץ הַדַּעַת[106] אָסְרָה אִסָּר עַל אַפִּי וַחֲמָתִי[107, 108]	
	And from this ban I am dying, and live only to tell you of my love.	וּבְאִסָּר זֶה גֹּוֵעַ אֲנִי וְרַק חַי לְהַגִּיד לְךָ אַהֲבָתִי.	
BENAIAH	Listen, and forget it from your heart, and do not ponder the core of the obsession.[109]	הַקְשֵׁב וּשְׁכַח מִלֵּב וְאַל תֶּהְגֶּה בְּבַת שִׁגָּיוֹן.[109]	בניה
RAM	Teach me how to forget, lest I ponder all thoughts.	הוֹרֵנִי אֵיךְ לִשְׁכֹּחַ, לְבַל אֶהְגֶּה כָּל הִגָּיוֹן.	רם
BENAIAH	Look around you and see if the daughters of your land[110]	שָׂא אֶת עֵינֶיךָ מִסָּבִיב וּרְאֵה בִּבְנוֹת אַרְצֶךָ[110]	בניה
	Are not as good as anyone whom your soul desires.	אִם לֹא טֹבֹת הֵנָּה כְּכֹל אֲשֶׁר תְּאַוֶּה נַפְשֶׁךָ.	
RAM	Indeed this is the way	אַךְ זֹה הַדֶּרֶךְ	רם
	To teach me that my beautiful one is unique among women.	לְהוֹרוֹת לִי כִּי יָפָתִי, אַחַת הִיא בַּנָּשִׁים.	
	What could I say of a black veil over the face of a charming girl?	מָה אֹמַר לְמַסְוֶה שָׁחֹר עַל פְּנֵי בַת חֵן?	

103 This and the next line form a rhyming couplet, mirroring Shakespeare's 'severity/posterity' (1.1.217–18).
104 This and the next line form a rhyming couplet, mirroring Shakespeare's 'fair/despair' (1.1.219–20).
105 Ps. 9:14, 107:18; Job 38:17.
106 Gen. 2:9, 17.
107 Jer. 32:31 עַל־אַפִּי וְעַל־חֲמָתִי 'to my anger and my wrath'.
108 This and the next line form a rhyming couplet, mirroring Shakespeare's 'vow/now' (1.1.221–2).
109 This last word in Benaiah's line rhymes with the last word of the following line (spoken by Ram). There is no precedent for this in Shakespeare's 'her/think' (1.1.223–4).
110 This and the following line form a rhyming couplet. This lacks precedent in the source text; Salkinson may have understood Shakespeare's 'eyes/beauties' (1.1.225–6) as a rhyme, although it is not generally recognized as one (Weis 2012: 419).

	Except to distinguish between the veil and that which is behind the veil	בִּלְתִּי לְהַבְדִּיל בֵּין הַמַּסְוֶה וּבֵין אֲשֶׁר מִבַּעַד לַמַּסְוֶה	
	Can a blind man forget how sweet was the light of the sun	הֲיִשְׁכַּח עִוֵּר עֵינַיִם מַה־מָּתוֹק אוֹר הַשֶּׁמֶשׁ	
	Which he had seen previously, before he was struck with blindness?	אֲשֶׁר רָאָה לְפָנִים טֶרֶם הֻכָּה בָעִוָּרוֹן?	
	If I find a beautiful maiden, she will only be a reminder to me	אִם אֶמְצָא נַעֲרָה יָפָה, תִּהְיֶה לִּי רַק לְאוֹת	
	Which multiplies by the power of ten and yet does not reach its full measure	הַמַּעֲלֶה אֶת הַמִּסְפָּר לַעֲשָׂרוֹת וְעַד הַמִּסְפָּר לֹא בָא	
	So how can you advise me to forget the one who is superior to all of them![111]	וְאֵיךְ תִּיעָצֵנִי לִשְׁכֹּחַ אֹתָהּ, אֲשֶׁר עַל כֻּלָּנָה עָלָה![111]	
BENAIAH	If my advice is not good, I **shall go down to Sheol mourning.**[112, 113]	אִם לֹא טוֹבָה עֲצָתִי, אֵרֵד אָבֵל שְׁאוֹלָה.[112,113]	בניה
	(Exeunt)	(הולכים)	
SCENE 2[114]	*Street (Abiel, Paris,[115] and attendants)*	רחוב (אביעל פריז[115] ומשרתים)	מחזה שני[114]
ABIEL	Abiram was also warned like me that a punishment would be imposed upon him	גַּם אֲבִירָם נִזְהַר כָּמוֹנִי, פֶּן עֹנֶשׁ יוּשַׁת עָלָיו	אביעל
	And he has measured a judgement for both of us with a single line; but for elders like us	וּמִשְׁפָּט מָדַד לִשְׁנֵינוּ בְּקַו אֶחָד; אַךְ לִזְקֵנִים כָּמוֹנוּ	
	I do not regard it as a burden to seek ways of peace.	לֹא לְמַשָּׂא חָשַׁבְתִּי לְבַקֵּשׁ דַּרְכֵי שָׁלוֹם.	
PARIS	Why, you are both considered to be among the greatest and most respected men in the city	הֲלֹא שְׁנֵיכֶם נֶחְשַׁבְתֶּם מִגְּדוֹלֵי הָעִיר וְנִכְבַּדֶּיהָ	פריז

111 This last word in Ram's line rhymes with the last word of the following line (spoken by Benaiah), echoing the English original (again, split between Romeo and Benvolio) 'forget/debt' (1.1.235–6).

112 Gen. 37:35 כִּי־אֵרֵד אֶל־בְּנִי אָבֵל שְׁאֹלָה 'indeed I shall go down to my son to Sheol mourning'.

113 Cf. Shakespeare's 'I'll pay that doctrine, or else die in debt' (1.2.236); Salkinson has neutralized the Christian connotations of the source text's 'doctrine'.

114 Salkinson typically uses numerals to designate scenes, but in a few cases, such as this one, he uses ordinals spelled out as words. This English translation mirrors the Hebrew in all cases.

115 Cf. Shakespeare's 'Paris'. Salkinson has chosen to use the Hebrew name of the city.

	Therefore we are greatly distressed that you have not made peace long ago.	לָכֵן צַר לָנוּ מְאֹד, כִּי לֹא הִשְׁלַמְתֶּם מֵאָז.	
	But what do you say to me, who desires your daughter?	אַךְ מַה־תֹּאמַר לְנַפְשִׁי אֲשֶׁר חָשְׁקָה בְּבִתֶּךָ?	
ABIEL	Behold, I say today that which I said long ago	הִנְנִי אֹמֵר הַיּוֹם אֶת אֲשֶׁר אָמַרְתִּי מֵאָז	אביעל
	My daughter has not yet seen many days in her lifetime	בִּתִּי עוֹד לֹא רָאֲתָה יָמִים רַבִּים בְּחֶלְדָּהּ	
	She has not yet seen the passing of fourteen years	אַרְבַּע־עֶשְׂרֵה שָׁנָה עוֹד לֹא עָבְרוּ עָלֶיהָ	
	Therefore we shall let her see another two years **in her greenness**[116, 117]	לָכֵן נִתֵּן לָהּ לִרְאוֹת עוֹד שְׁנָתַיִם בְּאִבָּהּ[116, 117]	
	Then her time will come to be wed to a man whom she loves.	אָז יִמָּלְאוּן יָמֶיהָ לְהִנָּשֵׂא לְאִישׁ בְּאַהֲבַת לִבָּהּ.	
PARIS	I have seen a girl younger than her, **a joyous mother of children.**[118]	צְעִירָה מִמֶּנָּה רָאִיתִי, **אֵם־הַבָּנִים שְׂמֵחָה.**[118]	פריז
ABIEL	When a young girl takes a husband, she ages before her time.	צְעִירָה כִּי תִבָּעֵל תִּזְקַן בְּלֹא עֵת־זִקְנָתָהּ.	אביעל
	All my treasures from the days of yore have been swallowed up and been obliterated	כָּל מַחֲמַדֵּי מִקֶּדֶם נִבְלְעוּ הָלְכוּ לַאֲבַדּוֹן	
	And only my daughter is the **reviver of my soul**[119] and will inherit my estate.	וְרַק בִּתִּי לְבַדָּהּ **מְשִׁיבַת נַפְשִׁי**[119] וְיוֹרֶשֶׁת נַחֲלָתִי.	
	As for you, dear Paris, go befriend her	וְאַתָּה פָּרִיז הַיָּקָר, לֵךְ הִתְרֹעַע אִתָּהּ	
	And turn her heart towards you with good and faithful words[120]	וְהַטֵּה אֶת לִבָּהּ אֵלֶיךָ בִּדְבָרִים טוֹבִים וְנֶאֱמָנִים[120]	
	And if she desires you and is willing after two years	וְאִם הִיא תַחְפֹּץ בְּךָ וְתֹאבֶה אַחֲרֵי שְׁתֵּי שָׁנִים	

116 Job 8:12 עֹדֶנּוּ בְאִבּוֹ לֹא יִקָּטֵף 'while it is still in its greenness and not cut down'. The relatively literal translation 'in her/its greenness' follows the King James Bible; other translations include 'green', 'in flower', or 'growing'.

117 This and the next line form a rhyming couplet, mirroring Shakespeare's 'pride/bride' (1.2.10–11).

118 Ps. 113:9.

119 Ps. 19:8 (19:7 in English Bibles) מְשִׁיבַת נָפֶשׁ 'a reviver of the soul'; see also Ruth 4:15 and Lam. 1:16 for similar constructions.

120 This and the next line form a rhyming couplet, mirroring Shakespeare's 'heart/part' (1.2.15–16). Note that here, and in the following rhyming couplets, the Hebrew pairs of lines do not correspond exactly to their English counterparts.

To be a wife for you, I shall not refuse to give her.[121]	לִהְיוֹת לְךָ לְאִשָּׁה, אֲנִי לֹא אֶמְנַע לְתִתָּהּ.[121]
This evening I am holding a banquet, as I have done every year	בָּעֶרֶב הַזֶּה מִשְׁתֶּה לִי, כַּאֲשֶׁר עָשִׂיתִי מִיָּמִים יָמִימָה
And many are the guests, whose company is pleasant to me	וְרַבִּים הֵם הַקְּרוּאִים אֲשֶׁר חֶבְרָתָם לִי נְעִימָה
And you are also counted as one of the guests[122]	וְגַם אַתָּה כְּאֶחָד נִמְנֶה בֵּין הַקְּרוּאִים[122]
To increase their number and add to our delights	לְהַגְדִּיל אֶת מִסְפָּרָם וּלְהוֹסִיף לָנוּ שַׁעֲשׁוּעִים
Please come tonight to my house when the wealthiest gather[123]	בּוֹאָה נָּא הַלַּיְלָה לְבֵיתִי בְּהִתְאַסֵּף רָאשֵׁי הֶחָיִל[123]
And there you will see the lights of the land illuminating the darkness of night.	וְשָׁם תִּרְאֶה מְאֹרֹת הָאָרֶץ הַמְּאִירִים חֶשְׁכַּת הַלָּיִל.
Like youths who love rejoicing and are happy about everything,[124]	כִּנְעָרִים אֹהֲבֵי גִיל הַשְּׂמֵחִים עַל כָּל דָּבָר,[124]
They revel at **the time of singing of birds**[125] after **the winter is past**[126]	יָשִׂישׂוּ לְעֵת הַזָּמִיר[125] אַחֲרֵי אֲשֶׁר הַסְּתָיו עָבָר[126]
Thus will you revel on this night in the delights and glory all around[127]	כֵּן תָּשִׂישׂ בַּלַּיְלָה הַזֶּה עַל חֶמְדָּה וּפְאֵר מִסָּבִיב[127]
Indeed they are the delicate women who are as delightful as the blossoms in spring.	הֵן הֵנָּה הַנָּשִׁים הָרַכּוֹת, הָעֲנֻגּוֹת כַּנִּצָּנִים בָּאָבִיב.
Set your eyes on beauty and hear that which is pleasing to the ears.[128]	תֵּן עֵינֶיךָ בְּיֹפִי וּשְׁמַע אֵת אֲשֶׁר עָרֵב לְאָזְנַיִם.[128]
And afterwards weigh on the scales which girl is better than all of them	וְאַחֲרֵי כֵן תִּשְׁקֹל מִי הַטּוֹבָה בְּכֻלָּן בְּמֹאזְנַיִם

121 This and the next line form a rhyming couplet, mirroring Shakespeare's 'choice/voice' (1.2.17–18). The single Hebrew rhyme extends over three lines.

122 This and the next line form a rhyming couplet, mirroring Shakespeare's 'feast/guest' (1.2.19–20). 'Feast' and 'guest' rhymed in early modern English (Crystal 2011: 304).

123 This and the next line form a rhyming couplet, mirroring Shakespeare's 'store/more' (1.2.21–2).

124 This and the next line form a rhyming couplet, mirroring Shakespeare's 'night/light' (1.2.23–4).

125 Song of Songs 2:12. This is Salkinson's translation of Shakespeare's 'well-apparelled April' (1.2.26), reflecting a desire to avoid reference to the Gregorian calendar.

126 Song of Songs 2:11.

127 This and the next line form a rhyming couplet, mirroring Shakespeare's 'feel/heel' (1.2.25–6).

128 This and the next line form a rhyming couplet, mirroring Shakespeare's 'delight/night' (1.2.27–8).

	And when you raise your eyes up again, **like a shepherd seeking out his flock**[129, 130]	וְכַאֲשֶׁר תִּשָּׂא עֵינֶיךָ שֵׁנִית, כְּבַקָּרַת רֹעֶה עֶדְר[129, 130]	
	Knowing who is thin and flawed, and who is honourable and splendid	לָדַעַת לְמִי רָזוֹן וּמִגְרֶעֶת וּלְמִי יְקָר וְאֵדֶר	
	Regard my daughter as a ewe of the weak sort and not the strong sort[131, 132]	חֲשֹׁב בִּתִּי כְּכִבְשָׂה מֵהָעֲטֻפִים וְלֹא מֵהַקְּשֻׁרִים[131, 132]	
	And choose the first of the flock for yourself, **for this is what young men do.**[133]	וּבְחַר לְךָ רֵאשִׁית הַצֹּאן, כִּי כֵן יַעֲשׂוּ הַבַּחוּרִים.[133]	
	(Gives a missive to his servant) Go around the city and invite the people mentioned[134]	(נותן כתב אל עבדו) לֵךְ סֹב בָּעִיר וּקְרָא לָאֲנָשִׁים הַנְּקוּבִים[134]	
	As their names are written on this scroll,	כַּאֲשֶׁר בְּגִלָּיוֹן זֶה הֵם בִּשְׁמוֹתָם בַּכְּתוּבִים	
	Say that my table is set and my house is wide open[135]	אֱמֹר כִּי שֻׁלְחָנִי עָרוּךְ וּבֵיתִי פָּתוּחַ לִרְוָחָה[135]	
	And I am waiting for their arrival at the **family sacrifice.**[136]	וַאֲנִי מְחַכֶּה לְבוֹאָם אֶל זֶבַח הַמִּשְׁפָּחָה.[136]	
	(Abiel and Paris exit)	(אביעל ופריז הולכים)	
THE SERVANT[137]	I must find the men who are on the list	עָלַי לִמְצוֹא אֶת הָאֲנָשִׁים אֲשֶׁר הֵם בַּכְּתוּבִים	העבד[137]
	I know what is written: there is no craftsman without tools:	יָדַעְתִּי אֶת הַכָּתוּב: אֵין אָמָן בְּלֹא כֵלִים;	
	There is no tailor without an awl, no shoemaker	אֵין תֹּפֵר בְּגָדִים בִּבְלִי מַרְצֵעַ; אֵין עֹשֵׂה	

129 Ezek. 34:12.
130 This and the next line form a rhyming couplet, mirroring Shakespeare's 'see/be' (1.2.29-30).
131 This is a reference to Gen. 30:42 וּבְהַעֲטִיף הַצֹּאן לֹא יָשִׂים וְהָיָה הָעֲטֻפִים לְלָבָן וְהַקְּשֻׁרִים לְיַעֲקֹב 'but when the sheep and goats were weaker, he did not put them in, so the weaker ones went to Laban and the stronger ones went to Jacob', in which Jacob tricked his uncle Laban by separating the flocks that he was herding for Laban to his own advantage.
132 This and the next line form a rhyming couplet, mirroring Shakespeare's 'one/none' (1.2.31–2).
133 Judg. 14:10.
134 This and the next line form a rhyming couplet, mirroring Shakespeare's 'about/out' (1.2.33–4).
135 This and the next line form a rhyming couplet, mirroring Shakespeare's 'say/stay' (1.2.35–6).
136 1 Sam. 20:29 זֶבַח מִשְׁפָּחָה 'a family sacrifice'.
137 This speech is prose in the original (1.2.37–43).

	Without a needle, no fisherman without a pen,	נְעָלִים בִּבְלִי מַחַט; אֵין דַּיָּג בִּבְלִי חֶרֶט	
	And no painter without a net, but how can I find the people	וְאֵין צַיָּר בִּבְלִי מְצוּדָה, וְאֵיךְ אֶמְצָא אֶת הָאֲנָשִׁים	
	Who are on the list, when I do not know what the writer wrote	אֲשֶׁר הֵם בַּכְּתוּבִים וַאֲנִי לֹא יָדַעְתִּי מַה־כָּתַב	
	In this missive? – Indeed I shall go seek advice	הַכֹּתֵב בִּכְתָב זֶה? – אַךְ אֵלְכָה לִּי לְהִוָּעֵץ	
	From those who know how to read; perhaps I shall succeed in my desire.	אֶת יוֹדְעֵי סֵפֶר, אוּלַי יִצְלַח חֶפְצִי בְּיָדִי.	
	(Benaiah and Ram)	(בניה ורם)	
BENAIAH	Why, a burn can be healed with a burn, by adding **burning fire**[138, 139]	הֲלֹא כְוִיָּה תֵּרָפֵא בִכְוִיָּה, בְּהוֹסֵף **אֵשׁ בֹּעֶרֶת**[138, 139]	בניה
	And the pain of your soul will depart with the pain of another soul;	וּמַכְאֹב נַפְשְׁךָ יָסוּר בְּמַכְאֹב נֶפֶשׁ אַחֶרֶת;	
	If **your heart flutters**,[140] spin and move to calm yourself	אִם לִבְּךָ סְחַרְחַר,[140] תָּחוֹג וְתָנוּעַ לְהַרְגִּיעֶךָ	
	And let your companion's bruises and wounds cleanse your bruises and wounds;[141]	וּלְחַבֻּרוֹת פִּצְעֲךָ תַּמְרוּק חַבֻּרוֹת פֶּצַע רֵעֶךָ;[141]	
	If **evil has come upon you which you do not understand**[142, 143]	אִם רָעָה בָּאַתְךָ אֲשֶׁר לֹא תֵדַע שַׁחְרָהּ[142, 143]	
	Seek **to bring down disaster upon yourself**[144] and you will be able to pacify the evil.	בַּקֵּשׁ לְהַפִּיל הֹוָה עָלֶיךָ[144] וְאֶת הָרָעָה תּוּכַל כַּפְּרָהּ.	
RAM	Your leaf[145] is a good medicine and a remedy for this break.	עָלְךָ[145] מָזוֹר טוֹב וּמַרְפֵּא לַשֶּׁבֶר הַזֶּה.	רם
BENAIAH	For which break?	לְאֵיזֶה שֶׁבֶר?	בניה

138 Jer. 20:9.
139 This and the next three lines form two rhyming couplets, mirroring the source text except that the latter has an ABAB rhyming pattern: 'burning/anguish/turning/languish' (1.2.44–7).
140 Ps. 38:11 (38:10 in English Bibles) לִבִּי סְחַרְחַר 'my heart flutters'.
141 Prov. 20:30 חַבֻּרוֹת פֶּצַע תמריק תַּמְרוּק בְּרָע 'bruises and wounds cleanse evil'.
142 Isa. 47:11 וּבָא עָלַיִךְ רָעָה לֹא תֵדְעִי שַׁחְרָהּ 'and evil will come upon you which you do not understand'.
143 This and the next line form a rhyming couplet, mirroring Shakespeare's 'eye/die' (1.2.49).
144 Isa. 47:11 וְתִפֹּל עָלַיִךְ הֹוָה 'and disaster will fall upon you'.
145 Salkinson has simplified Shakespeare's 'plantain leaf' (1.2.50).

RAM	For your broken leg.	לְרַגְלְךָ הַנִּשְׁבָּרָה.	רם
BENAIAH	Are you mad?	הַמְשֻׁגָּע אָתָּה?	בניה
RAM	I am not mad, but I am bound like a madman	מְשֻׁגָּע אֵינֶנִּי, רַק אָסוּר אֲנִי כְּאַחַד הַמְּשֻׁגָּעִים	רם
	And trapped in prison without food or sustenance	וְעָצוּר בְּבֵית כֶּלֶא בִּבְלִי מָזוֹן וּמִחְיָה	
	My body is given over to abusers and my soul to oppressors and also –	גֵּוִי נָתוּן לְמַכִּים וְנַפְשִׁי לְלֹחֲצִים וְגַם –	
	(To the servant) What do you seek, my fellow? Are you well?	(אל העבד) מַה־תְּבַקֵּשׁ רֵעִי? הֲשָׁלוֹם?	
THE SERVANT	May the peace of the LORD be with you, my lord; tell me, can you read?	שְׁלוֹם אֲדֹנָי עִמְּךָ אֲדֹנִי, הַגִּידָה הֲתוּכַל קְרֹא?	העבד
RAM	Because of all that has befallen me, I can read my future.	מִכָּל הַמֹּצְאוֹת אֹתִי, אוּכַל קְרֹא עֲתִידֹתָי.	רם
THE SERVANT	You learned that without a book, but tell me	זֹאת לָמַדְתָּ בִּבְלִי סֵפֶר, אַךְ הַגֶּד־לִי	העבד
	Do you understand how to read every piece of writing that you see?	הֲמֵבִין אַתָּה לִקְרֹא כָּל כְּתָב אֲשֶׁר תִּרְאֶה?	
RAM	If I know the letters of the writing and the words of the language.	אִם יָדַע אֲנִי אוֹתוֹת הַכְּתָב וּמִלּוֹת הַלָּשׁוֹן.	רם
THE SERVANT	You have spoken honestly here – and now farewell to you.	כֵּן דִּבַּרְתְּ* בָּזֶה – וְעַתָּה שָׁלוֹם לָךְ.	העבד
RAM	Do not leave, man, I know how to read.	אַל תֵּלֵךְ מִזֶּה בֶּן אָדָם, יָדַע אֲנִי לִקְרֹא.	רם
	(Takes the missive and reads it)	(לוקח את הכתב וקורא בו)	
	Commander Marsena[146] with his wife and daughters	הָאַלּוּף מַרְסְנָה[146] עִם אִשְׁתּוֹ וּבְנוֹתָיו	
	Minister Shalmon[147] and his pleasant sisters	הַשַּׂר שַׁלְמוֹן**[147] וְאַחְיוֹתָיו הַנְּעִימוֹת	

146 One of the seven princes of Persia mentioned in Esther 1:14; Salkinson most likely selected this name on the basis of its sound correspondence with Shakespeare's 'Martino' (1.2.63).

147 This is likely to be a typographical error for Salmon, who is listed in Ruth 4:20–1 as one of the ancestors of King David. Salkinson probably suggested this name on the basis of its sound correspondence with Shakespeare's 'Anselm' (1.2.64).

* דִּבַּרְתָּ
** שַׂלְמוֹן

The lady widow of Ahitub[148]	הָאִשָּׁה הַגְּבִירָה אַלְמְנַת אֲחִיטוּב[148]
Commander Pelatiah[149] and his brother's pleasant daughters	הָאַלּוּף פְּלַטְיָה[149] וּבְנוֹת אָחִיו הַנֶּחֱמָדוֹת
Meraioth[150] and his brother Gibbethon[151]	מְרָיוֹת[150] וְגִבְּתוֹן[151] אָחִיו
My uncle Abiel with his wife and daughters	אֲבִיעֵל דוֹדִי עִם אִשְׁתּוֹ וּבְנוֹתָיו
My brother's daughter Shoshannah,[152] the most beautiful among girls, with Livia[153]	שׁוֹשַׁנָּה[152] בַּת אָחִי הַיָּפָה בַּבָּנוֹת עִם לִוְיָה[153]
Count Irad[154] with **his close relative**[155] Tubal	הָרֹזֶן עִירָד[154] עִם תּוּבָל **שְׁאֵרוֹ הַקָּרוֹב לוֹ**[155]
Luz[156] with the gracious Hilne.[157]	לוּץ[156] עִם הִילְנֵי[157] בַּת חָיִל.

148 This name appears in various locations in the Hebrew Bible. It can refer to the grandson of Eli the priest mentioned in 1 Sam. 14:3 and the father of Zadok, a priest in the time of King David mentioned in 2 Samuel 8:17, as well as possibly one or two other minor figures mentioned in Nehemiah and 1 Chronicles. Salkinson may have selected it on the basis of its partial sound correspondence with Shakespeare's 'Vitruvio' (1.2.65).

149 This name can refer to four different minor biblical characters, namely the son of Benaiah mentioned in Ezekiel 11:1, one of the signatories of the covenant mentioned in Neh. 10:23 (Neh. 10:22 in English Bibles), the son of Hananiah and grandson of Zerubbabel mentioned in 1 Chron. 3:21, and a captain of a band of marauders in the reign of King Hezekiah mentioned in 1 Chron. 4:42. Salkinson most likely chose the name on the basis of its sound correspondence with Shakespeare's 'Placentio' (1.2.66).

150 This name appears in several locations in the Hebrew Bible and refers to various minor characters; for example, the head of a priestly house mentioned in Neh. 12:15 and a descendant of Aaron's son Eleazar mentioned in 1 Chron. 5:32 (6:6 in English Bibles). Salkinson most likely selected the name because of its sound correspondence with Shakespeare's 'Mercutio' (1.2.67).

151 This is the name of a town allotted to the tribe of Dan in Josh. 19:44. It is unclear why Salkinson selected this name as a translation of Shakespeare's 'Valentine' (1.2.67), since it denotes a location rather than a person. The location does not have any particular associations with the English name, and does not clearly correspond in sound.

152 Shoshannah is a common postbiblical Hebrew female name meaning 'rose'. Salkinson most likely selected this name as the translation of 'Rosaline' (1.2.69) because, in contrast to most other names appearing in the play, it has a transparent meaning with an easily identifiable Hebrew equivalent.

153 This is not a Hebrew name but rather a word meaning 'decorative wreath' (Even-Shoshan 2003, 3: 829); Salkinson most likely selected it because of its exact sound correspondence with Shakespeare's 'Livia' (1.2.69).

154 Enoch's son, mentioned in Gen. 4:18.

155 Lev. 21:2 שְׁאֵרוֹ הַקָּרֹב אֵלָיו 'his close relative'; this collocation also appears in Num. 27:11. Cf. Shakespeare's 'cousin' (1.2.70).

156 This is not a Hebrew name or word. Salkinson most likely chose it simply as a Hebraized transliteration of Shakespeare's Lucio (1.2.71). However, it resembles the Hebrew verbal root ל.י.ץ. 'mock', which may have played some role in his decision. Note that I have transliterated it according to the traditional convention in English Bibles whereby the Hebrew letter צ *tsadi* is rendered as *z*.

157 This is not a Hebrew name or word; as in the case of Luz (see preceding note) it seems simply to be a Hebraized transliteration of Shakespeare's Helena (1.2.71).

	(Returning the missive) A select gathering, but where will they gather?	(בהשיבו את הכתב) אֲסֵפָה נִבְחָרָה, וְאָנָה יִתְאַסָּפוּ?	
THE SERVANT	In an upper room.	בַּעֲלִיָּה.	העבד
RAM	In which house?	בְּאֵיזֶה בָּיִת?	רם
THE SERVANT	In our house for the evening banquet.	בְּבֵיתֵנוּ אֶל מִשְׁתֵּה הָעֶרֶב.	העבד
RAM	In whose house?	בְּבֵית מִי?	רם
THE SERVANT	In my master's house.	בְּבֵית אֲדֹנִי.	העבד
RAM	If only I had asked this in the beginning.	לוּ שָׁאַלְתִּי זֹאת בַּתְּחִלָּה.	רם
THE SERVANT[158]	I shall answer before you ask: my master is	אֲנִי אֶעֱנֶה טֶרֶם תִּשְׁאַל: אֲדֹנִי הוּא אֲבִיעֵל	העבד[158]
	The great and honourable Abiel; and if you are not from the house of Abiram	הַגָּדוֹל וְהַנִּכְבָּד; וְאִם אַתָּה אֵינְךָ מִבֵּית אֲבִירָם	
	Come as well to empty a cup of wine – and farewell to you. *(Exits)*	בֹּא גַּם אַתָּה לְהָרִיק כּוֹס יַיִן – וְשָׁלוֹם לָךְ. (הולך)	
BENAIAH	Abiel holds this banquet **from year to year**[159]	הַמִּשְׁתֶּה הַזֶּה אֲבִיעֵל עֹשֶׂה מִדֵּי שָׁנָה בְּשָׁנָה[159]	בניה
	And Shoshannah, whom you love, will also be there	וְשָׁם תִּהְיֶה גַּם שׁוֹשַׁנָּה אֲשֶׁר נַפְשְׁךָ אָהֶבֶת	
	Among **the precious daughters of Verona, comparable to fine gold**[160]	בֵּין בְּנוֹת וֵירוֹנָה הַיְקָרוֹת הַמְסֻלָּאוֹת בַּפָּז[160]	
	Come and with a clear eye compare her face	בֹּא וְהִתְבּוֹנֵן בְּעַיִן זַכָּה, מַה־בֵּין פָּנֶיהָ	
	To the faces of other girls that the hand of the one who lies in wait will show you[161]	וּבֵין פְּנֵי אֲחֵרוֹת אֲשֶׁר תַּרְאֶךָּ יַד הָאוֹרֵב[161]	

158 These lines are prose in the original (1.2.78–82).
159 1 Sam. 7:16; Zech. 14:16; 2 Chron. 24:5.
160 Lam. 4:2 בְּנֵי צִיּוֹן הַיְקָרִים הַמְסֻלָּאִים בַּפָּז 'the precious sons of Zion, comparable to fine gold'.
161 This and the next line form a rhyming couplet, mirroring Shakespeare's 'show/crow' (1.2.87–8). Salkinson's seemingly puzzling selection of the phrase יַד הָאוֹרֵב 'the hand of the one who lies in wait' instead of Shakespeare's 'I' (1.2.87) is motivated simply by the necessity of finding a rhyme for the word עֹרֵב 'crow' at the end of the following line.

	And then your beautiful dove will appear as a crow in your eyes.	וְאָז יוֹנָתְךָ יָפָתְךָ תִּהְיֶה בְּעֵינֶיךָ כְּעֹרֵב.	
RAM	If my eyes see as your senseless heart sees[162]	אִם עֵינַי תֶּחֱזֶינָה כַּחֲזוֹת לִבְּךָ סָר טָעַם[162]	רם
	The fountain of my tears[163] will become **a blazing scorching fire**[164]	יֵהָפֵךְ מְקוֹר דִּמְעָתִי[163] **לִיקוֹד אֵשׁ צָרֶבֶת**[164]	
	And my eyes, which have drowned in tears and disappeared from time to time,	וְעֵינַי אֲשֶׁר טָבְעוּ בִּדְמָעוֹת וְנִמְלְטוּ כְּפַעַם בְּפָעַם	
	Will burn **like heretics and apostates**[165] in a blaze.	שָׂרֹף תִּשָּׂרַפְנָה כְּמִינִים וְאַפִּיקְרְסִים[165] בְּשַׁלְהֶבֶת.	
	Even the sun above, which sees everything before the eyes,[166]	גַּם שֶׁמֶשׁ מִמַּעַל, הָרֹאֶה אֶת כֹּל לָעֵינָיִם[166]	
	Has not seen anyone more beautiful than my beautiful one since the day when the earth and heavens were created.	לֹא רָאָה יָפָה מִיָּפָתִי, מִיּוֹם בְּרֹא אֶרֶץ וְשָׁמָיִם.	
BENAIAH	You found her beautiful by the balance, by the scales which you made[167]	יָפָה מְצָאתָ אֹתָהּ בַּפֶּלֶס, בַּמֹּאזְנַיִם אֲשֶׁר עָשִׂיתָ[167]	בניה
	The trays of your balance were your eyes, and you saw her with one.	כַּפּוֹת מֹאזְנֶיךָ הָיוּ הָעֵינַיִם וְאֹתָהּ בְּאַחַת רָאִיתָ.	
	Without a weight on the other one to tell you that you had erred	בִּבְלִי אֶבֶן מִשְׁקַל בַּשְּׁנִיָּה, לְהוֹרוֹתְךָ כִּי שָׁגִיתָ.	
	If your beautiful one were weighed against another maiden[168]	לוּ תִשָּׁקֵל יָפָתְךָ לְעֻמַּת נַעֲרָה אַחֶרֶת[168]	
	Whom I shall show you at the banquet **as clear as the very heavens**,[169]	אֲשֶׁר אַרְאֶךָ בַּמִּשְׁתֶּה כְּעֶצֶם הַשָּׁמַיִם לָטֹהַר[169]	

162 This and the subsequent three lines form an ABAB rhyming sequence, mirroring Shakespeare's 'eye/fires/die/liars' (1.2.89–92).

163 Jer. 8:23 (9:1 in English Bibles) מִי־יִתֵּן רֹאשִׁי מַיִם וְעֵינִי מְקוֹר דִּמְעָה 'if only my head were waters and my eye a fountain of tears'.

164 Isa. כִּיקוֹד אֵשׁ 'like a blazing fire'; Prov. 16:27 כְּאֵשׁ צָרָבֶת 'like a scorching fire'.

165 Abarbanel to Ezek. 5.

166 This and the next line form a rhyming couplet, mirroring Shakespeare's 'sun/begun' (1.2.93–4).

167 This and the next line form a rhyming couplet, mirroring Shakespeare's 'by/eye' (1.2.95–6). The Hebrew rhyme extends over three lines rather than two.

168 This and the subsequent three lines form an ABAB rhyming sequence, mirroring the original except that the latter is made up of two rhyming couplets: 'weighed/maid', 'feast/best' (1.2.97–100).

169 Exod. 24:10.

	You would say of the one who is now better in your eyes than all the charming and glorious maidens	וְהַטֹּבָה בְּעֵינֶיךָ עַתָּה מִכָּל בְּנוֹת חֵן וְתִפְאֶרֶת	
	That she has neither splendour nor radiance.	תֹּאמַר כִּי לָהּ אֵין הָדָר אַף לֹא זֹהַר.	
RAM	I shall go with you, not to see another light[170]	אֲנִי אֵלֵךְ אִתְּךָ, לֹא לִרְאוֹת אוֹר אַחֵר[170]	רם
	But rather to take delight in my light, like **the morning star, son of the dawn.**[171]	כִּי אִם לְהִתְעַנֵּג בְּאוֹרִי, כְּהֵילֵל בֶּן־שָׁחַר.[171]	
	(Exeunt)	(הולכים)	
THIRD SCENE	*A chamber in Abiel's house (Abiel's wife and the nurse)*	חדר בבית אביעל (אשת אביעל והאומנת)	מחזה שלישי
ABIEL'S WIFE	Nurse! Where is my daughter? Call her to come to me.	אֹמֶנֶת! אַיֵּה בִתִּי? קִרְאִי לָהּ לָבוֹא אֵלָי.	אשת אביעל
THE NURSE	On my life! Indeed when she was twelve years old	חֵי נַפְשִׁי! כִּי בַת שְׁתֵּים עֶשְׂרֵה שָׁנָה –	האומנת
	I called her then – but what is wrong with you, **graceful doe!**[172]	קְרָאתִי לָהּ אָז – אַךְ מַה־לָּךְ יַעֲלַת חֵן![172]	
	What is wrong with you, **sparrow?**[173] God forbid! –	מַה־לָּךְ צִפּוֹר דְּרוֹר![173] – חָלִילָה לָּךְ מֵאלֹהִים! –	
	Where is the girl, then? – Are you coming, Jael?[174]	אַיֵּה אֵיפֹא הַיַּלְדָּה? – הַאִם בָּאת יָעֵל?[174]	

170 This word and the last word of the following line do not rhyme visually or in Modern Hebrew pronunciation, but would have done so in Salkinson's Ashkenazic pronunciation. As such, the two lines echo Shakespeare's rhyming couplet 'shown/own' (1.2.101–2).

171 Isa. 14:12. This expression is associated with the planet Venus in postbiblical Hebrew literature (see Even-Shoshan 2003, 2: 381). This phrase lacks an equivalent in the original, which reads 'But to rejoice in splendour of mine own' (1.2.102). Salkinson most likely inserted it primarily or solely out of the desire to find a rhyme for the previous line.

172 Prov. 5:19. This is also a play on words referring to the heroine יָעֵל Jael (Juliet): the name literally means 'mountain goat' (sometimes translated as 'ibex' or 'deer'), and the noun יְעֵלָה or יַעֲלָה translated above as 'doe' denotes the female of the same species (Even-Shoshan 2003, 2: 704). See note 174 for further discussion of the name Jael.

173 This collocation is traceable to Rabbinic Hebrew, appearing in, for example, Mishnah *Nega'im* 8:4 and Babylonian Talmud *Beṣa* 24a.

174 Salkinson's selection of יָעֵל 'Jael' as a translation of 'Juliet' is rooted partially in sound correspondence, but has symbolic connotations as well. Jael would have been well known among Jewish audiences as the protagonist of the biblical story recounted in Judges 4 and 5, in which she saved the Israelites from crushing defeat and conquest by the Canaanites when she courageously lured the enemy general Sisera into her tent and killed him. Moreover, Jael has a prominent place in postbiblical Jewish tradition, with the Babylonian Talmud (*Nazir* 23b) considering her to be more meritorious than even the four biblical matriarchs Sarah, Rebecca, Rachel, and Leah. As such, by bestowing the name Jael upon Shakespeare's

JAEL	Who called me?	מִי קָרָא לִי?	יעל
THE NURSE	Your mother called you.	אִמֵּךְ קָרְאָה לָךְ.	האומנת
JAEL	Here I am, my lady mother, what is your desire with me?	הִנְנִי אִמִּי הַגְּבִירָה, מָה חֶפְצֵךְ עִמָּדִי?	יעל
ABIEL'S WIFE	This is the matter of my desire – go away from here, Nurse.	זֶה דְּבַר חֶפְצִי – לְכִי לָךְ אֹמֶנֶת מִזֶּה	אשת אביעל
	We have a secret matter – come back, Nurse, and **let us take sweet counsel together**[175]	דְּבַר סֵתֶר לָנוּ – שׁוּבִי אֹמֶנֶת וְיַחְדָּו נַמְתִּיק סוֹד[175]	
	You know, after all, that my daughter is soon to become a young woman.	הֲלֹא יָדַעַתְּ כִּי בִתִּי, בָּאָה עֵת נְעוּרֶיהָ.	
THE NURSE	I know the days of her life **from day to day**.[176]	הִנְנִי יֹדַעַת מִסְפַּר יְמֵי חַיֶּיהָ מִיּוֹם אֶל יוֹם.[176]	האומנת
ABIEL'S WIFE	Why, she is fourteen years old today.	הֲלֹא בַּת אַרְבַּע עֶשְׂרֵה שָׁנָה הִיא הַיּוֹם.	אשת אביעל
THE NURSE	I shall give my fourteen teeth if she is fourteen today	אַרְבַּע עֶשְׂרֵה שִׁנַּי אֶתֵּן, אִם הִיא אַרְבַּע עֶשְׂרֵה הַיּוֹם	האומנת
	Even though there are no more than four in my mouth;	אַף כִּי אֵין בְּפִי כִּי אִם אַרְבַּע;	
	She is not fourteen, for such-and-such a holiday	הִיא אֵינֶנָּה אַרְבַּע עֶשְׂרֵה, כִּי חַג פְּלֹנִי אַלְמֹנִי	
	On the first night of the fifth month has not yet come[177]	בַּלַּיְלָה הָרִאשׁוֹן לַחֹדֶשׁ הַחֲמִישִׁי עוֹדֶנּוּ לֹא בָא[177]	
	When will that holiday come?	מָתַי יָבוֹא הֶחָג הַהוּא?	
ABIEL'S WIFE	In two weeks and two or three days.	אַחֲרֵי שְׁבֻעַיִם וְיָמִים שְׁנַיִם אוֹ שְׁלֹשָׁה.	אשת אביעל

heroine, Salkinson has chosen to cast her unambiguously in the model of a strong, independent biblical figure who is unafraid to risk death in defence of her beliefs.

175 Ps. 55:15 (55:14 in English Bibles) יַחְדָּו נַמְתִּיק סוֹד 'we took sweet counsel together'.

176 Num. 30:15 (30:14); 1 Chron. 16:23.

177 The English original (1.3.16) refers to Lammastide, the Anglo-Saxon holiday marking the wheat harvest that takes place on the first of August. Salkinson replaces this with 'such-and-such a holiday' that takes place on the first day of the fifth month. The reference to the 'first night of the fifth month' is a veiled allusion to Lammastide: the first month in the Hebrew Bible corresponds approximately to April on the Gregorian calendar, and as such the fifth month would equate to August. Thus, Salkinson's translation serves to neutralize the Christian connotations of the original name (which has no established Hebrew equivalent and would not have been familiar to Jewish readers in any case) by substituting it with a nondescript label and placing it within the context of the biblical calendar. It is likely that Salkinson chose this strategy in the present instance because there is no Jewish holiday that falls at a similar time to and could easily be equated with Lammastide. (Note that in order to introduce this description of the holiday, Salkinson has substantially rephrased and expanded on the original.)

THE NURSE	The day of that holiday is the day of her birth	יוֹם הֶחָג הַהוּא הוּא יוֹם הֻלֶּדֶת אֹתָהּ	האומנת
	It is **a night of vigil**[178] for me **each and every year**[179]	לֵיל שִׁמֻּרִים[178] הוּא לִי בְּכָל שָׁנָה וְשָׁנָה[179]	
	And at that time she will turn fourteen.	וְאָז יִמָּלְאוּן לָהּ אַרְבַּע עֶשְׂרֵה שָׁנָה.	
	And Shoshannah[180] was the same age as her; she was born with her in the same year.[181]	וְשׁוֹשַׁנָּה[180] בַּת גִּילָהּ נוֹלְדָה עִמָּהּ בְּשָׁנָה אֶחָת.[181]	
	But she is not with us, for **she walks with God**.[182]	וְהִיא אֵינֶנָּה אִתָּנוּ, כִּי תִתְהַלֵּךְ אֶת־הָאֱלֹהִים.[182]	
	And I already said on the first of the fifth she will be fourteen	וּכְבַר אָמַרְתִּי בָּרִאשׁוֹן לַחֲמִישִׁי תִּהְיֶה בַּת אַרְבַּע עֶשְׂרֵה	
	For I remember well; it is eleven years since the earthquake	כִּי זֹכֶרֶת אֲנִי הֵיטֵב: זֶה עַשְׁתֵּי עֶשְׂרֵה אַחֲרֵי הָרַעַשׁ	
	On the day when she was weaned, and I shall never forget that day	בְּיוֹם הִגָּמֵל אֹתָהּ וְאֶת הַיּוֹם הַהוּא לֹא אֶשְׁכַּח לְעוֹלָם	
	For it is unique in the year; there is none like it among all the days.	כִּי אֶחָד הוּא בַּשָּׁנָה, אֵין כָּמוֹהוּ בְּכָל הַיָּמִים.	
	For in order to wean her from the milk of my breasts, I put wormwood on my bosom	כִּי לְגָמְלָהּ מֵחֲלֵב שָׁדַי, שַׂמְתִּי לַעֲנָה עַל דַּדַּי	

178 Exod. 12:42.

179 Esther 9:21, 27.

180 The name Susan derives from the Hebrew word and female name שׁוֹשַׁנָּה, meaning 'lily' or 'rose', and as such Shoshannah is an appropriate equivalent. As a result, the two characters Rosaline and Susan share a name in Salkinson's version.

181 Salkinson has omitted the Christian expression appearing in the original, 'Susan and she, God rest all Christian souls,/Were of an age' (1.3.19–20). This is a typical strategy that he adopts with respect to oath formulas and other phatic expressions containing allusions to Christian figures and concepts.

182 Gen. 5:24 וַיִּתְהַלֵּךְ חֲנוֹךְ אֶת־הָאֱלֹהִים 'and Enoch walked with God'. Cf. Shakespeare's 'Susan is with God' (1.3.20). Enoch is one of the figures appearing in a genealogical table chronicling the first generations of humankind. His account is enigmatic because, in contrast to the other figures in the list, it is not stated explicity that he died, but rather simply that he walked with God and was no more, for God took him. This ambiguity has led to various proposals relating to his fate, including the proposal appearing in rabbinic literature (e.g., certain midrashim and Targumim) that he was a righteous man who ascended to the heavens without suffering the throes of death (Sarna 2007). While it is uncertain whether Salkinson had these associations in mind when settling on this translation, the fact that he has omitted Shakespeare's 'She was too good for me' (1.3.21), which directly follows 'Susan is with God', may support the possibility that he chose the verse intentionally in order to suggest to readers that Shoshannah, like Enoch, was taken to heaven due to her righteousness, and that he felt the following line to be unnecessary.

While I was sitting under the dovecote in the courtyard	בְּעוֹד אֲנִי יֹשֶׁבֶת תַּחַת שׁוֹבֵךְ הַיּוֹנִים בֶּחָצֵר
And you, my lady, were at that time with my lord in Mantua[183]	וְאַתְּ גְּבִרְתִּי, הָיִית עִם אֲדֹנִי אָז בְּמַנְטוּבָה[183]
And I remember well, as I have already told the matter	וַאֲנִי זֹכֶרֶת הֵיטֵב, כַּאֲשֶׁר כְּבַר הִגַּדְתִּי הַדָּבָר
That as soon as she touched with her mouth and sucked the nipple	כִּי כִמְעַט נָגְעָה בְּפִיהָ וַתָּמָץ רֹאשׁ הַדַּד
The pleasant fool went mad when she tasted the wormwood	הִשְׁתּוֹלְלָה הַפְּתַיָּה הַנְּעִימָה בְּטָעֳמָהּ אֶת הַלַּעֲנָה
And became enraged at my breasts because it was very bitter to her	וַתִּתְרַגֵּז אֶל שָׁדַי כִּי מָרָה לָהּ מְאֹד
And suddenly the dovecote shook to and fro because the earthquake had begun	וּפִתְאֹם הִתְפּוֹרֵר שׁוֹבֵךְ הַיּוֹנִים כִּי הֵחֵל הָרַעַשׁ
And I saw that there was no way out except to flee **from the midst of the destruction**[184]	וָאֵרֶא כִּי אֵין פְּלֵטָה, כִּי אִם לָנוּס מִתּוֹךְ הַהֲפֵכָה[184]
And it is eleven years since the day of that event	וְזֶה עַשְׁתֵּי עֶשְׂרֵה שָׁנָה לְיוֹם הַמַּעֲשֶׂה הַהוּא
And at that time she could walk and run to every corner[185]	וְהִיא יָכְלָה אָז לָלֶכֶת וְלָרוּץ לְכָל פִּנָּה[185]
Because before that day, she fell to the ground on her forehead	כִּי לִפְנֵי הַיּוֹם הַהוּא, נָפְלָה עַל מִצְחָהּ אָרְצָה
And my husband, peace be upon him[186] (he was a good man, with **a merry heart**[187])	וּבַעֲלִי עָלָיו הַשָּׁלוֹם[186] (אִישׁ טוֹב הָיָה וְלֵב שָׂמֵחַ[187])
Set the girl upright **and spoke tenderly to her,**[188] saying	הֵקִים אֶת הַיַּלְדָּה וַיְדַבֵּר עַל לִבָּהּ[188] לֵאמֹר

183 Note that Salkinson has retained this Italian place name, like the others appearing in his two Shakespeare translations. This may be rooted in a recognition and acknowledgement of the prominent and longstanding Jewish presence in Italy and concomitant decision to interpret his characters as Italian Jews (Kahn 2017).

184 Gen. 19:29.

185 Salkinson has omitted Shakespeare's overtly Christian phatic expression 'by th' rood' (1.3.37), i.e., 'by Christ's cross' (Weis 2012: 151, note 37).

186 The Hebrew expression used here is the one traditionally uttered after mentioning a departed relative or loved one. This lends a specifically Jewish nuance to the nurse's speech.

187 Prov. 15:13, 17:22.

188 Gen. 34:3 וַיְדַבֵּר עַל־לֵב הַנַּעֲרָ 'and he spoke tenderly to the maiden'; similar constructions occur in Gen. 50:21 and 2 Chron. 32:6.

	'Today you have fallen on your face, but when you grow wise, you will fall backwards;	„הַיּוֹם נָפַלְתְּ עַל אַפַּיִךְ וְכַאֲשֶׁר תַּשְׂכִּילִי תִּפְּלִי אֲחֹרַנִּית	
	Is it not so, Jael?' And I swear	הַאִם לֹא כֵן יָעֵל?" וַאֲנִי בִּי נִשְׁבַּעְתִּי	
	That that foolish girl heard and fell silent and said, 'Yes'	כִּי הַפּוֹתָה הַזֹּאת שָׁמְעָה וַתִּדֹּם וַתֹּאמֶר „הֵן"	
	And now do you not understand the jest that she made of us,	וְעַתָּה הֲלֹא תָבִינִי אֶת הַצְּחֹק אֲשֶׁר עָשְׂתָה לָנוּ,	
	If I were to live a thousand years, on my life I would never forget this	אִם אֶלֶף שָׁנִים אֶחְיֶה, חֵי נַפְשִׁי אִם אֶשְׁכַּח זֹאת	
	For when he said this thing, 'Is it not so, Jael?'	כִּי בְּאָמְרוֹ כַּדָּבָר הַזֶּה „הַאִם לֹא כֵן יָעֵל?"	
	She stopped crying in her folly and fell silent and said, 'Yes'.	חָדְלָה בְסִכְלוּתָהּ לִבְכּוֹת וַתִּדֹּם וַתֹּאמֶר „הֵן".	
ABIEL'S WIFE	That's enough from you now, do not speak further of this matter.	רב* לָךְ עַתָּה, אַל תּוֹסִיפִי דַּבֵּר בַּדָּבָר הַזֶּה.	אשת אביעל
THE NURSE	But how, my lady, can I contain myself and not laugh	אַךְ אֵיךְ גְּבִרְתִּי אֶתְאַפַּק וְלֹא אֶשְׂחַק	האומנת
	When I remember that she stopped crying and with her mouth said 'Yes'	בְּזָכְרִי כִּי חָדְלָה לִבְכּוֹת וּבְפִיהָ אָמְרָה „הֵן"	
	And despite that, on my faith, she had a wound as big as an egg	וּבְכָל זֹאת עַל אֱמוּנָתִי, כִּי חַבֻּרָה גְדוֹלָה כְּבֵיצָה	
	On her forehead, and **she issued a lamentation and bitter weeping**[189]	הָיְתָה לָהּ עַל מִצְחָהּ וּנְהִי בְכִי תַמְרֻרִים הִשְׁמִיעָה[189]	
	But when my husband said 'Indeed you have fallen on your face	אַךְ כַּאֲשֶׁר אָמַר בַּעֲלִי „הֵן נָפַלְתְּ עַל אַפַּיִךְ	
	Wait until you become advanced in years, and then you will fall backwards	חַכִּי עַד בּוֹאֵךְ בַּיָּמִים וְאָז תִּפְּלִי אֲחֹרַנִּית	
	Is it not so, Jael?' She ceased and said 'Yes'.	הַאִם לֹא כֵן יָעֵל?" חָדְלָה הִיא וַתֹּאמֶר „הֵן".	

189 Jer. 31:15 קוֹל בְּרָמָה נִשְׁמָע נְהִי בְּכִי תַמְרוּרִים 'a voice was heard in Ramah, lamentation and bitter weeping'.

* רַב

JAEL	Listen to me, Nurse, and cease you too.	שִׁמְעִי נָא לִי אֹמֶנֶת וְחִדְלִי גַּם אָתְּ.	יעל
THE NURSE	Indeed I have listened and ceased, and may God help you!	הֵן שָׁמַעְתִּי וָאֶחְדָּל וְהָאֱלֹהִים יִהְיֶה בְּעֶזְרֵךְ!	האומנת
	How much more beautiful, how much more pleasant you are than all the infants that I nursed!	מַה־יָּפִית מַה־נָּעַמְתְּ מִכָּל הָעוֹלְלִים אֲשֶׁר הֵינַקְתִּי!	
	And only this is my entire desire, to see you **married to a husband.**[190]	וְרַק זֶה כָּל חֶפְצִי לִרְאוֹתֵךְ בְּעֻלַת **בָּעַל***.[190]	
ABIEL'S WIFE	I too wish to speak about the matter of husbands	עַל דְּבַר הַבְּעָלִים חָפַצְתִּי לְדַבֵּר גַּם אָנִי	אשת אביעל
	What do you say, my daughter Jael, to discussion of you being married?	מַה־תֹּאמְרִי יָעֵל בִּתִּי, כִּי יְדֻבַּר בָּךְ לְהִבָּעֵל.	
JAEL	Such an honour has not occurred to me, while waking or in a dream.	כָּבוֹד כָּזֶה לֹא עָלָה עַל לִבִּי לֹא בְּהָקִיץ וְלֹא בַחֲלוֹם.	יעל
THE NURSE	Who will merit this honour? – If I were not your nurse,	מִי יִנְחַל הַכָּבוֹד הַזֶּה? – לוּלֵא הָיִיתִי מֵינִקְתֵּךְ	האומנת
	I would say that you had suckled from breasts of wisdom from the time that you came out of the womb.	אָמַרְתִּי מִשְּׁדֵי בִינָה יָנַקְתְּ מֵעֵת צֵאתֵךְ מִבָּטֶן.	
ABIEL'S WIFE	Turn your attention to the matter of the wedding now; girls younger than you in Verona	שִׁיתִי לִבֵּךְ לִדְבַר הַחֲתֻנָּה, צְעִירוֹת מִמֵּךְ בְּוֵירוֹנָה	אשת אביעל
	From among the daughters of the city's noblemen are embracing their babies.	מִבְּנוֹת נְדִיבֵי הָעִיר, חֹבְקוֹת הֵנָּה אֶת עוֹלֵיהֶן.	
	And I was your mother by the time I had reached your age,	וַאֲנִי אִמֵּךְ הָיִיתִי כִּמְלֹאת לִי מִסְפַּר הַשָּׁנִים	
	And you are still a virgin; so to tell you everything I say:	אֲשֶׁר עוֹדֵךְ אַתְּ בִּבְתוּלַיִךְ; וּלְהַגִּיד לָךְ כֹּל אֹמַר:	

190 Gen. 20:3; Deut. 22:22.

* בָּעַל

	Behold, Paris, a man of valour, desires you for his wife.	הִנֵּה פָּרִיז אִישׁ חַיִל, חָשְׁקָה נַפְשׁוֹ בָּךְ לְקַחְתֵּךְ.	
THE NURSE	Oh, **noble daughter!**[191] He is a man of valour without equal	הָאָח בַּת נָדִיב![191] אִישׁ חַיִל הוּא אֵין כָּמוֹהוּ	האומנת
	He is splendid and complete in his beauty like **a statue cast by a craftsman.**[192]	הָדוּר וְכָלִיל הוּא בְּיָפְיוֹ כְּפֶסֶל נָסַךְ חָרָשׁ.[192]	
ABIEL'S WIFE	Even in Verona in the summer there is no flower as pleasant as he.[193]	גַּם בְּוֵירוֹנָה בַּקַּיִץ, אֵין צִיץ נֶחְמָד כָּמוֹהוּ.[193]	אשת אביעל
THE NURSE	He is a pleasant and agreeable flower! **A cluster of henna blossoms in the vineyards of Verona!**[194]	צִיץ נֶחְמָד וְנָעִים הוּא! אֶשְׁכֹּל הַכֹּפֶר בְּכַרְמֵי וֵירוֹנָה![194]	האומנת
ABIEL'S WIFE	Tell me, my daughter, would you want to be wed to a man like him?[195]	הַגִּידִי לִי בִּתִּי, הֲתִרְצִי לִהְיוֹת לְאִישׁ כָּמוֹהוּ?[195]	אשת אביעל
	Tonight you will see him at the banquet, for he is one of a thousand[196]	הַלַּיְלָה תִּרְאִי אוֹתוֹ בַּמִּשְׁתֶּה, כִּי אֶחָד הוּא מֵאֶלֶף[196]	
	Study him like a book, for there is a good treasure in him	הִתְבּוֹנְנִי בוֹ כְּמוֹ בְסֵפֶר, כִּי אוֹצָר טוֹב בּוֹ הוּא	
	Deep wisdom and **goodly words**;[197] there is no deceit in him	חָכְמָה עֲמֻקָּה וְאִמְרֵי שֶׁפֶר,[197] אֵין בּוֹ סֶלֶף	
	So you will find the Parisian when you see the expressions of his face **as one**[198]	כֵּן תִּמְצְאִי אֶת הַפְּרִיזִי בִּרְאוֹתֵךְ אוֹתוֹת פָּנָיו לַאֲחָדִים[198]	

191 Song of Songs 7:2 (7:1 in English Bibles).

192 Isa. 40:19.

193 Salkinson has not reproduced the same-word rhyming couplet 'flower/flower' (1.3.78–9) in the source text.

194 Song of Songs 1:14 אֶשְׁכֹּל הַכֹּפֶר | דּוֹדִי לִי בְּכַרְמֵי עֵין גֶּדִי 'my beloved is to me a cluster of henna blossoms in the vineyards of En-gedi'. This has no basis in the source text, in which the speech consists of a single sentence.

195 This and the subsequent three lines form an ABAB rhyming sequence. This differs from the English, which has an ABBA scheme: 'gentleman/feast/face/pen' (1.3.80–4).

196 The phrase 'for he is one of a thousand' lacks precedent in the original. As in several other cases discussed elsewhere in this volume, Salkinson most likely included it solely in order to find a rhyme for the last word in the previous line. Such cases illustrate the difficulties in finding Hebrew equivalents for the English wordplays that Salkinson alluded to in his introduction to the translation.

197 Gen. 49:21.

198 This and the following line form a rhyming couplet, mirroring Shakespeare's 'lineament/content' (1.3.84–5).

One by one[199] they are comely, and together they are pleasant	אֶחָד לְאֶחָד[199] נָאוֶה וְכֻלָּם כְּאֶחָד נֶחְמָדִים
And if you find in this book something obscure or insipid[200]	וְאִם תִּמְצְאִי בַּסֵּפֶר הַזֶּה דָּבָר סָתוּם אוֹ תָפֵל[200]
Look in the scroll of his eyes **and the spark of his fire will make the darkness shine**[201]	הַבִּיטִי בְגִלְיוֹן עֵינָיו וּשְׁבִיב אִשׁוֹ יַגִּיהַּ אֹפֶל[201]
And this precious book has made a glorious name for itself[202]	וְהַסֵּפֶר הַיָּקָר הַזֶּה, עָשָׂה לוֹ שֵׁם לְתִפְאֶרֶת[202]
And he lacks nothing save **good glue**[203] in the binding.	וְאֵין לוֹ מַחְסוֹר, כִּי אִם דֶּבֶק טוֹב[203] בְּמַחְבֶּרֶת.
Indeed he walks in the open space, like a fish that swims in the depths[204]	הֵן הוּא הוֹלֵךְ בַּמֶּרְחָב, כַּדָּג יָשׁוּט בַּמְּצוּלָה[204]
And who is suitable to hunt him, if not my virgin daughter!	וּלְמִי יָאֲתָה לָצוּד אֹתוֹ, אִם לֹא לְבִתִּי הַבְּתוּלָה!
Many regard him as **a jewel of fine gold;**[205] **he is a delight to the eyes**[206, 207]	רַבִּים יַחְשְׁבֻהוּ כִּכְלִי־פָז,[205] תַּאֲוָה הוּא לָעֵינָיִם[206, 207]
And **his interior is inlaid with love,**[208] whose value cannot be matched by **the gold of Parvaim**[209]	וְתוֹכוֹ רָצוּף אַהֲבָה[208] לֹא תְסֻלֶּה בִּזְהַב פַּרְוָיִם[209]
And therefore you will have all, if you have him as your husband[210]	וְלָכֵן לָךְ הַכֹּל, אִם יִהְיֶה לָךְ לְבַעַל[210]

---

199 Ezek. 37:17 וְקָרַ֨ב אֹתָ֜ם אֶחָ֧ד אֶל־אֶחָ֛ד לְךָ֖ לְעֵ֣ץ אֶחָ֑ד וְהָי֥וּ לַאֲחָדִ֖ים בְּיָדֶֽךָ ‘and join them one to another into one stick, and they will be as one in your hand’.

200 This and the following line form a rhyming couplet, mirroring Shakespeare’s ‘lies/eyes’ (1.3.86–7).

201 Job 18:5 וְֽלֹא־יִ֝גַּ֗הּ שְׁבִ֣יב אִשּֽׁוֹ ‘and the spark of his fire shall not shine’.

202 This and the following line form a rhyming couplet, mirroring Shakespeare’s ‘lover/cover’ (1.3.88–9).

203 Isa. 41:7 אֹמֵ֤ר לַדֶּ֙בֶק֙ ט֣וֹב ה֔וּא ‘he says of the welding, “it is good”’. This citation is used idiomatically to indicate acceptance of a marriage match (Even-Shoshan 2003, 1: 292); Salkinson has capitalized on it to make a bookbinding pun based on the fact that the word דֶּבֶק ‘welding’ also means ‘glue’.

204 This and the following line form a rhyming couplet, mirroring Shakespeare’s ‘pride/hide’ (1.3.90–1).

205 Job 28:17.

206 Gen. 3:6.

207 This and the following line form a rhyming couplet, mirroring Shakespeare’s ‘glory/story’ (1.3.92–3).

208 Song of Songs 3:10.

209 2 Chron. 3:6. Parvaim is a geographical name of uncertain reference, possibly a region of Arabia (Koehler and Baumgartner 2001, 2: 964). Beginning in the modern period the expression ‘the gold of Parvaim’ came to be used in Hebrew to denote something extremely pure and precious (Even-Shoshan 2003, 5: 1529).

210 This and the following line form a rhyming couplet, mirroring Shakespeare’s ‘possess/less’ (1.3.94–5).

	And of that which is yours he will not take even a thread or a shoelace.[211]	וּמֵאֲשֶׁר לָךְ לֹא יִקַּח, מִחוּט וְעַד שְׂרוֹךְ־נַעַל.[211]	
THE NURSE	A woman takes the wealth of her husband, but what does he take from her hands?[212]	אִשָּׁה תִקַּח חֵיל בְּעָלֶיהָ; וּמַה־יִּקַּח מִיָּדֶיהָ?[212]	האומנת
ABIEL'S WIFE	Speak, my daughter, is Paris good in your eyes or not?	דַּבְּרִי בִתִּי, הֲטוֹב פָּרִיז בְּעֵינַיִךְ אִם אָיִן?	אשת אביעל
JAEL	Behold, I shall raise my eye to him if he attracts me with his appearance	הִנֵּה אֶשָּׂא עֵינִי אֵלָיו אִם יִמְשְׁכֵנִי לְמַרְאֵה עָיִן.	יעל
	But I shall control my spirit and **shall not go following after my eyes**[213, 214]	אֶפֶס כִּי אֶמְשֹׁל בְּרוּחִי וְלֹא* אָתוּרָה אַחֲרֵי עֵינַי[213, 214]	
	More than would be pleasing to you and more than your counsel guides me.	יֶתֶר מֵאֲשֶׁר יִהְיֶה לִרְצוֹנֵךְ וּמֵאֲשֶׁר עֲצָתֵךְ תַּנְחֵנִי.	
THE SERVANT[215]	My lady, the guests have arrived; the table is already set	גְּבִרְתִּי, הֵן הַקְּרוּאִים בָּאוּ; הַשֻּׁלְחָן כְּבַר עָרוּךְ	העבד[215]
	The people gathered are waiting for your arrival and are enquiring where the lady's daughter is	הַנֶּאֱסָפִים מְחַכִּים לְבוֹאֵךְ וְדֹרְשִׁים אַיֵּה בַּת הַגְּבִירָה	
	In the house of the cooking women they are cursing the nurse and they are all in great confusion	בְּבֵית הַמְבַשְּׁלוֹת יָאֹרוּ אֶת הָאֹמֶנֶת וְכֻלָּם בִּמְבוּכָה גְדוֹלָה	
	And I am in a hurry to return to my post; please come quickly after me.	וַאֲנִי אָץ לָשׁוּב אֶל מִשְׁמַרְתִּי; אָנָּא מַהֵרְנָה לָבוֹא אַחֲרָי.	

211 Gen. 14:23 אִם־מִחוּט וְעַד שְׂרוֹךְ־נַעַל וְאִם־אֶקַּח מִכָּל־אֲשֶׁר־לָךְ 'I would not take even a thread or a shoelace of anything that is yours'.

212 Salkinson's translation does not retain Shakespeare's play on words 'No less? Nay, bigger – women grow by men' (1.3.96).

213 While this does not rhyme with the last word in the following line visually or in Modern Hebrew pronunciation, it would have been a near rhyme in Salkinson's Ashkenazic pronunciation, and as such it is likely that he intended the two lines to correspond to Shakespeare's rhyming couplet 'eye/fly' (1.3.99–100).

214 Num. 15:39 וְלֹא־תָתֻרוּ אַחֲרֵי לְבַבְכֶם וְאַחֲרֵי עֵינֵיכֶם 'and not to follow after your hearts and your eyes'. This extract makes up part of the Shema, a central prayer in the Jewish liturgy.

215 This speech is prose in the original (1.3.101–4).

* לא

ABIEL'S WIFE	We are coming after you – Jael, the lord wants to see you.[216]	אֲנַחְנוּ בָאוֹת אַחֲרַיִךְ – יָעֵל, הַשַּׂר יִרְאֶה פָּנָיִךְ.[216]	אשת אביעל
THE NURSE	Go and find for yourself delightful nights for your delightful days.	לְכִי וְתִמְצְאִי לָךְ לֵילוֹת תַּעֲנֻגִים לִימֵי תַעֲנֻגָיִךְ.	האומנת
	(Exeunt)	(הולכות)	
FOURTH SCENE	*Street (Ram, Meraioth, Benaiah with men dressed in masks and carrying torches, and other men)*	רחוב (רם, מריות, בניה עם אנשים מתחפשים בַּאֲפֵר ונושאי לפידים ואנשים אחרים)	מחזה רביעי
RAM	Must we say anything about why we have come?	הֲיֵשׁ לָנוּ לְדַבֵּר דָּבָר, עַל מֶה אֲנַחְנוּ בָאִים?	רם
	Or shall we come to the house without **an excuse**?[217]	אוֹ נָבוֹא אֶל הַבַּיִת בִּבְלִי פִתְחוֹן פֶּה?[217]	
BENAIAH	The old custom of coming with **an excuse**[218] has already ceased	כְּבַר חָדַל הַמִּנְהָג הַיָּשָׁן לָבוֹא בְּפִתְחוֹן פֶּה[218]	בניה
	And none of us is coming like an idol[219] with covered eyes	וְלֹא אֶחָד מֵאִתָּנוּ יָבוֹא כֶּאֱלִיל[219] בִּכְסוּת עֵינַיִם	
	Whose bow is **painted with vermillion**[220] like a bow of **the children of Kedar**[221]	אֲשֶׁר קַשְׁתּוֹ מְשׁוּחָה בְּשָׁשַׁר[220] כְּקֶשֶׁת בְּנֵי קֵדָר[221]	
	The quiver rattles against it,[222] casting terror over the women	וְעָלָיו תִּרְנֶה אַשְׁפָּה[222] לְהַטִּיל אֵימָה עַל הַנָּשִׁים	
	Like the figure of an archer in the presence of **every winged bird**[223]	כִּדְמוּת רֹבֶה קַשָּׁת לְעֵינֵי עוֹף כָּל כָּנָף[223]	

216 This and the following line form a rhyming couplet, mirroring Shakespeare's 'stays/days' (1.3.105–6).

217 This expression appears in Ezek. 16:63, 29:21 in the sense of 'the ability to speak'; in the rabbinic period it began to mean 'excuse', 'pretext' (Even-Shoshan 2003, 5: 1560); it is used here in the postbiblical sense.

218 See preceding note.

219 As elsewhere in his work, Salkinson has chosen not to translate Shakespeare's 'Cupid' (1.4.4), and has replaced it with a generic reference to an 'idol' (which itself reflects the traditional Jewish perception of Classical mythological figures).

220 Jer. 22:14 וּמָשׁוֹחַ בַּשָּׁשַׁר 'and painted with vermillion'.

221 Kedar is a nomadic tent-dwelling biblical nation descended from Ishmael's second son (mentioned in Gen. 25:13) from a region that most likely corresponds to somewhere in northwestern Arabia. Salkinson selected the children of Kedar as the equivalent of Shakespeare's 'Tartar' (i.e., Mongol). His choice is likely to be rooted in the fact that they are mentioned in Isa. 21:17 in conjunction with archery (וּשְׁאָר מִסְפַּר־קֶשֶׁת גִּבּוֹרֵי בְנֵי־קֵדָר יִמְעָטוּ 'and the remainder of the number of archers, the warriors of the childen of Kedar, will be few'), which corresponds to Shakespeare's 'Bearing a Tartar's painted bow of lath' (1.4.5).

222 Job 39:23.

223 Gen. 7:14; Ezek. 17:23, 39:4, 17.

	And we shall not meet the people gathered even with **a learned tongue**[224]	וְגַם לֹא בִּלְשׁוֹן לִמּוּדִים[224] נְקַדֵּם אֶת פְּנֵי הַנֶּאֱסָפִים	
	For what do their thoughts which they will think about us have to do with us?	כִּי מַה־לָּנוּ וּלְמַחְשְׁבוֹתֵיהֶם אֲשֶׁר יַחְשְׁבוּ עָלֵינוּ	
	After all, they understand that it is time to dance and not time to speak	הֲלֹא יָבִינוּ כִּי עֵת רְקוֹד וְלֹא עֵת לְדַבֵּר	
	And we came **to go forth in the dances of the merrymakers**[225] until we leave.	וְלָצֵאת בִּמְחוֹל מְשַׂחֲקִים[225] בָּאנוּ עַד אֲשֶׁר נֵצֵא.	
RAM	And I shall carry a torch, for **I do not have the heart**[226] for this galloping;	וַאֲנִי לַפִּיד אֶשָּׂא, כִּי אֵין נַפְשִׁי[226] לְדַהֲרוֹת אֵלֶּה;	רם
	The light grows dark in my tent,[227] and I shall carry a torch to give me light.	אוֹר חָשַׁךְ בְּאָהֳלִי[227] וְלַפִּיד אֶשָּׂא לְהָאֵר לִי.	
MERAIOTH	Not so, Ram my friend; you will leap with us.	לֹא כֵן רָם יְדִידִי, אַתָּה תְּפַזֵּז עִמָּנוּ.	מריות
RAM	The matter is too weighty for me; your feet in the shoes are light	כָּבֵד הַדָּבָר מִמֶּנִּי; פְּעָמֶיךָ בַּנְּעָלִים קַלִּים	רם
	And you are light on your feet; not so am I with myself	וְאַתָּה קַל בְּרַגְלֶיךָ, לֹא כֵן אָנֹכִי עִמָּדִי	
	My soul inside of me is lead, and my feet cannot move under me.	נַפְשִׁי בְקִרְבִּי עֹפֶרֶת וּפְעָמַי לֹא יָמוּשׁוּ מִתַּחְתָּי.	
MERAIOTH	Indeed you are known to love; go borrow wings for yourself from it[228]	יָדוּעַ אַהֲבָה הִנְּךָ, קוּם שְׁאַל לְךָ מִמֶּנָּה כְּנָפַיִם[228]	מריות
	And fly up above and **let your soul not bow down to the dust.**[229, 230]	וְהַגְבֵּהַּ לָעוּף לְמַעְלָה וְאַל תָּשַׁח לֶעָפָר נַפְשֶׁךָ.[229, 230]	

224 Isa. 50:4.
225 Jer. 31:4 וְיָצָאת בִּמְחוֹל מְשַׂחֲקִים 'and you will go forth in the dances of the merrymakers'.
226 Jer. 15:1.
227 Job 18:6 אוֹר חָשַׁךְ בְּאָהֳלוֹ 'the light grows dark in his tent'.
228 Salkinson has replaced Shakespeare's 'borrow Cupid's wings' (1.4.17) with this neutral mention of 'love' (thereby rendering the reference to wings somewhat opaque).
229 Ps. 44:26 (44:25 in English Bibles) כִּי שָׁחָה לֶעָפָר נַפְשֵׁנוּ 'for our soul is bowed down to the dust'.
230 Salkinson has not replicated Shakespeare's cross-line internal rhyme here 'ground/bound' (1.4.16–18) (see Weis 2012: 157, note 18).

RAM	**Love's arrows have struck me,**[231] and **my neck has been placed in an iron collar**[232]	חִצֵּי אַהֲבָה נִחֲתוּ בִי[231] וּבַרְזֶל בָּאָה נַפְשִׁי[232]	רם
	And how can a prisoner like me fly on wing and feather?	וְאֵיךְ יָעוּף אָסוּר כָּמוֹנִי עַל אֶבְרָה וָנוֹצָה?	
	Love is a burden to me, and **I lie beneath my burden.**[233]	הָאַהֲבָה עָלַי לְמַשָּׂא וְרֹבֵץ אֲנִי תַּחַת מַשָּׂאִי[233]	
MERAIOTH	If you lie, be a burden to your love	אִם רֹבֵץ אַתָּה, הֱיֵה לְמַשָּׂא עַל אַהֲבָתְךָ	מריות
	Which is too tender to bear a burden as heavy as you.	אֲשֶׁר רַכָּה הִיא מִנְּשֹׂא מַשָּׂא כָּבֵד כָּמוֹךָ.	
RAM	Is love tender? It is heavier than **the burden of sand**[234]	הַאִם הָאַהֲבָה רַכָּה הִיא? כְּבֵדָה הִיא מִנֵּטֶל הַחוֹל[234]	רם
	Harder than **a rod of iron,**[235] and as piercing as **a painful thorn.**[236]	קָשָׁה מִמְּטִיל בַּרְזֶל[235] וְדֹקֶרֶת כְּקוֹץ מַכְאִיב.[236]	
MERAIOTH	If love is heavy upon you, **make your hand heavy upon it**[237]	אִם הָאַהֲבָה כְּבֵדָה עָלֶיךָ, הַכְבֵּד אַכְפְּךָ עָלֶיהָ[237]	מריות
	And indeed stab it, thrust upon thrust. –	וְדָקֹר תִּדְקַר אֹתָהּ, מַדְקֵרָה תַּחַת מַדְקֵרָה. –	
	Give me a mask to cover my face *(Places mask on his face)*	תְּנוּ לִי אֲפֵר לְכַסּוֹת אֶת פָּנַי (משים אפר על פניו)	
	One disguised man against another! Now, why should I worry further?	מִתְחַפֵּשׂ לְנֶגֶד מִתְחַפֵּשׂ! וּמָה אֶדְאַג עוֹד?	
	If a penetrating eye finds **disgrace**[238] in my face	אִם עַיִן חוֹדְרָה תִּמְצָא שֶׁמֶץ דָּבָר[238] בְּפָנַי	
	Why, the form of my face over my face will blush on my account.	הֲלֹא תַּבְנִית פָּנַי עַל פָּנַי, יַאֲדִימוּ פָנֶיהָ בַּעֲדִי.	
BENAIAH	Come on, knock on the door and let us go into the house	קוּמוּ דִּפְקוּ עַל הַדֶּלֶת וְנָבוֹאָה הַבַּיְתָה	בניה
	And there each man who has legs will spin and move.	וְשָׁם יָחוֹג יָנוּעַ אִישׁ אִישׁ אֲשֶׁר לוֹ שׁוֹקַיִם.	

231 Ps. 38:3 (38:2 in English Bibles) כִּי־חִצֶּיךָ נִחֲתוּ בִי 'for Your arrows have struck me'.
232 Ps. 105:18 בַּרְזֶל בָּאָה נַפְשׁוֹ 'his neck has been placed in an iron collar'.
233 Exod. 23:5 חֲמוֹר שֹׂנַאֲךָ רֹבֵץ תַּחַת מַשָּׂאוֹ 'the ass of one who hates you lying under his burden'.
234 Prov. 27:3 כֹּבֶד־אֶבֶן וְנֵטֶל הַחוֹל 'a stone is heavy, and sand is a burden'.
235 Job 40:18.
236 Ezek. 28:24.
237 Job 33:7 וְאַכְפִּי עָלֶיךָ לֹא־יִכְבָּד 'nor should my hand be heavy upon you'.
238 Job 26:14 וּמַה־שֵּׁמֶץ דָּבָר נִשְׁמַע־בּוֹ 'and how faint [or: whispering] a word is heard of Him'. See *Ithiel*, Third Part, note 56 for discussion of Salkinson's use of this expression.

RAM	But give me a torch; lads who love rejoicing are dancing	אַךְ תְּנוּ לַפִּיד בְּיָדִי; נְעָרִים אֹהֲבֵי גִיל יְרַקֵּדוּן	רם
	And trampling the place where **reeds and rushes**[239] are spread out over the floor	וּמִשְׁטַח קָנֶה וָסוּף[239] עַל פְּנֵי הַקַּרְקַע יִרְמָסוּן	
	And I shall repeat with my own mouth a proverb[240] **greatly timeworn**[241]	וַאֲנִי אֲשַׁנֶּה בְּמוֹפִי פִּתְגָּם[240] יָשָׁן נוֹשָׁן[241]	
	'The one who holds a candle for others sees **but does not share in their joy**'[242, 243]	„הָאֹחֵז נֵר לַאֲחֵרִים, יִרְאֶה וְלֹא יִתְעָרֵב בְּשִׂמְחָתָם"[242, 243]	
	For **as for joy, what does it accomplish**,[244] when I have finished my dances.	כִּי לְשִׂמְחָה מַה־זֹּה עֹשָׂה[244] וַאֲנִי אֶת מְחוֹלַי גָּמַרְתִּי.	
MERAIOTH	You have finished the first dance, but the second dance is starting;	מָחוֹל רִאשׁוֹן גָּמַרְתָּ וּמָחוֹל שֵׁנִי תָּחֵל;	מריות
	And if like the ball of a children's game[245] you have been pushed into a place of mire[246]	וְאִם כְּכַדּוּר מִשְׂחַק הַיְלָדִים,[245] נִדַּחְתָּ לִמְקוֹם רֶפֶשׁ[246]	
	We shall pull you out to remove the discharge of love and the filth of the soul –	נִמְשָׁכְךָ לְהַדִּיחַ מִקִּרְבְּךָ זוֹב הָאַהֲבָה וְחֶלְאַת הַנֶּפֶשׁ –	
	Indeed come with us, lest the torches burn at dawn.[247]	אַךְ לְכָה אִתָּנוּ, לְבַל יִבְעֲרוּ הַלַּפִּידִים בַּשַּׁחַר.[247]	
RAM	Why **do you speak rashly with your lips**[248] of **a matter which has no basis**?[249]	לָמָּה תְּבַטֵּא בִשְׂפָתֶיךָ[248] כַּדָּבָר אֲשֶׁר אֵין לוֹ שָׁחַר?[249]	רם

239 Isa. 19:6.

240 This word appears in the Hebrew Bible, where it means 'decree' (see Eccles. 8:11 and Esther 1:20); Salkinson is using it in the sense of 'proverb', which originates in the modern period (Even-Shoshan 2003, 5: 1557).

241 Num. 5:17.

242 Prov. 14:10 וּבְשִׂמְחָתוֹ לֹא־יִתְעָרַב זָר 'and a stranger does not share in its joy'.

243 Salkinson has not reproduced the rhyming couplet 'on/dun' (1.4.38–9) in the source text.

244 Eccles. 2:2.

245 This translation differs markedly from the original 'If thou art dun' (1.4.41). Salkinson's translation may be based on a commentary noting that 'Dun is in the mire' seems to be a reference to an old Christmas game (see Weis 2012: 160, note 41).

246 This and the next line form a rhyming couplet. There is no basis for this in Shakespeare's 'mire/stickest' (1.4.41–2).

247 This last word in Meraioth's line rhymes with the last word of the following line (spoken by Ram), echoing the English original (again, split between Mercutio and Romeo) 'ho/so' (1.4.43–4).

248 Ps. 106:33 וַיְבַטֵּא בִּשְׂפָתָיו 'and he spoke rashly with his lips'.

249 Isa. 8:20 אִם־לֹא יֹאמְרוּ כַּדָּבָר הַזֶּה אֲשֶׁר אֵין־לוֹ שָׁחַר 'if they do not speak according to this word, it is because they have no basis'.

MERAIOTH	This is my word: if we delay on account of **empty words**[250, 251]	זֶה דְּבָרִי: אִם נִתְמַהְמַהּ בַּעֲבוּר דְּבַר **שְׂפָתַיִם**[250, 251]	מריות
	The torches burn pointlessly like **a candle at noon**[252]	הַלַּפִּידִים דֹּלְקִים לְלֹא הוֹעִיל **כַּנֵּר בַּצָּהֳרָיִם**[252]	
	But treat my thinking favourably, for **the meditation of our heart**[253, 254]	אַךְ רְצֵה אֶת הֶגְיוֹנִי, כִּי חָמֵשׁ פְּעָמִים בַּמִּדָּה[253]	
	Has five times the truth of any parable or riddle.	**הָגוּת לִבֵּנוּ**[254] נְכֹחָה מִכָּל מְלִיצָה חִידָה.	
RAM	Even as we go to the dances, **the meditation of our heart**[255] is true[256]	גַּם בְּלֶכְתֵּנוּ אֶל הַמְּחוֹלוֹת **הָגוּת לִבֵּנוּ**[255] נְכֹחָה[256]	רם
	But one who understands riddles would not desire to go.	אַךְ הַמֵּבִין חִידוֹת לֹא יִרְצֶה לָלֶכֶת.	
MERAIOTH	But why?	וּמַדּוּעַ?	מריות
RAM	Because I dreamt a dream tonight.[257]	כִּי חֲלוֹם חָלַמְתִּי הַלָּיְלָה.[257]	רם
MERAIOTH	So did I in my dream.	גַּם אֲנִי בַּחֲלוֹמִי.	מריות
RAM	And what did you see?	וּמֶה רָאִיתָ?	רם
MERAIOTH	I saw that those who dream see **false and misleading oracles.**[258, 259]	רָאִיתִי כִּי הַחֹלְמִים יֶחֱזוּ **מַשְׂאוֹת שָׁוְא וּמַדּוּחִים.**[258, 259]	מריות
RAM	And there are those who see truths while they are sprawled on their beds.	וְיֵשׁ אֲשֶׁר יִרְאוּ נְכֹחוֹת בְּעוֹדָם עַל עַרְשׂתָם סְרֻחִים.	רם
MERAIOTH	Perhaps the spirit which governs night visions[260] has come to you	אוּלַי בָּאָה אֵלֶיךָ הָרוּחַ, הַמּוֹשֶׁלֶת בְּחֶזְיוֹנוֹת לָיְלָה[260]	מריות

250 2 Kings 18:20; Isa. 36:5; Prov. 14:23.
251 This and the following line form a rhyming couplet, mirroring Shakespeare's 'delay/day' (1.4.44–5).
252 Rashi to the Babylonian Talmud *Ḥullin* 3 and *Shabbat* 6.
253 Ps. 49:4 (49:3 in English Bibles) וְהָגוּת לִבִּי תְבוּנוֹת 'and the meditation of my heart will be understanding'.
254 This and the following line form a rhyming couplet, mirroring Shakespeare's 'sits/wits' (1.4.46–7).
255 Ps. 49:4 (49:3 in English Bibles) וְהָגוּת לִבִּי תְבוּנוֹת 'and the meditation of my heart will be understanding'.
256 In Salkinson's Ashkenazic pronunciation this word forms a near rhyme with Meraioth's next line, mirroring the original (also split between Romeo and Mercutio) 'masque/ask' (1.4.48–9).
257 This word rhymes with the last word in Ram's next line. In this respect it corresponds to the original, except that in the latter the rhyme starts one utterance later and as such is split between Mercutio's lines 'I/lie' (1.4.50–1).
258 Lam. 2:14.
259 This last word in Meraioth's line rhymes with the last word of the following line (spoken by Ram), echoing the source text (although in the latter the rhyme is one line later, and as such is split between Romeo and Mercutio rather than the other way around) 'true/you' (1.4.52–3).
260 Cf. Shakespeare's 'Queen Mab' (1.4.53). It is likely that Salkinson chose to avoid a direct translation of the fairy's name because it would have had no meaning for his readers; his paraphrased description of Queen

After all, she is the midwife of the beautiful daughters of demons[261]	הֲלֹא הִיא הַמְיַלֶּדֶת לִבְנוֹת הַשֵּׁדִים[261] יְפוֹת תֹּאַר
And she is as small as an opal[262] in a ring which the town elder	וּקְטַנָּה הִיא כְּלֶשֶׁם[262] בְּטַבַּעַת אֲשֶׁר זְקַן הָעִיר
Wears on his finger; her team of horses is **like fine dust**[263]	יִשָּׂא עַל אֶצְבָּעוֹ; צֶמֶד סוּסֶיהָ כְּאָבָק דָּק[263]
And she comes to sleeping men through their nostrils.	וְהִיא תָּבוֹא אֶל הָאֲנָשִׁים הַיְשֵׁנִים דֶּרֶךְ נְחִירֵיהֶם.
The poles of her chariot are a lizard's feet and its canopy is a locust's wings	בַּדֵּי מִרְכַּבְתָּהּ רַגְלֵי שְׂמָמִית וּרְפִידָתָהּ כַּנְפֵי יֶלֶק
Her seat is **a spider's web**[264] and the horses' ornaments and sashes	מֶרְכָּבָהּ קוּרֵי עַכָּבִישׁ[264] וַעֲדִי הַסּוּסִים וְקִשּׁוּרֵיהֶם
Are like rays of moonlight, moister than **the droplets of the night.**[265]	כְּקַוֵּי אוֹר הַלְּבָנָה לַחִים מֵרְסִיסֵי לָיְלָה.[265]
The whip is a thin hair grasped in a cricket's leg	הַשּׁוֹט הוּא שֵׂעָר דַּק אָחוּז בְּשׁוֹק הַצְּלָצַל
The charioteer is a small ant, like **a moth that eats wool**[266]	הָרַכָּב נְמָלָה קְטַנָּה כְּסָס הָאֹכֵל צֶמֶר[266]
And the chariot is the seed of a small nut whose insides have been eaten by worms	וְהַמֶּרְכָּבָה זַג אֱגוֹז קָטֹן אֲשֶׁר תּוֹכוֹ אָכְלוּ תוֹלָעִים
For they are the builders of the chariot belonging to the beautiful daughters of demons.	כִּי הֵם בּוֹנֵי הַמֶּרְכָּבָה לִבְנוֹת הַשֵּׁדִים יְפוֹת תֹּאַר.

Mab is not based directly on the original but sums up her role as overseer of dreams that is detailed by Meraioth/Mercutio later in this speech.

261 Cf. Shakespeare's 'faeries'. 'Demons' is a dynamic Hebrew equivalent reflecting the fact that faeries do not occupy a meaningful position in Jewish culture, whereas demons feature relatively prominently; they are first mentioned in the Hebrew Bible (e.g., Deut. 32:17), and appear throughout rabbinic, medieval, and early modern Jewish literature (Trachtenberg 2004; Petrovsky-Shtern 2010).

262 Cf. Shakespeare's 'agate stone' (1.4.55). The term לֶשֶׁם appears in Exod. 28:19 and 39:12 as one of the gemstones on the High Priest's breastplate. Its precise meaning is uncertain; in addition to 'opal' (which is its meaning in Modern Hebrew), it has been translated in various English Bible versions as 'jacinth', 'ligure', and 'topaz'. Oddly, the word לֶשֶׁם is directly followed in these two biblical verses by the name of another gemstone, שְׁבוֹ, which is typically translated as 'agate', and therefore would have been a much closer equivalent to Shakespeare's term.

263 Isa. 29:5.

264 Isa. 59:5.

265 Song of Songs 5:2.

266 Isa. 51:8 וְכַצֶּמֶר יֹאכְלֵם סָס 'and the moth will eat them like wool'.

In this **bounding chariot**,[267] the midwife travels every night	בְּמֶרְכָּבָה מְרַקֵּדָה[267] זאת, תִּסַּע הַמְיַלֶּדֶת בְּכָל לַיְלָה
And visits the houses of thought belonging to those who know love	וּתְבַקֵּר בְּבָתֵּי הַמַּחֲשָׁבָה אֲשֶׁר לְיוֹדְעֵי אַהֲבָה
And afterwards each man dreams in accordance with his **soul's desire**.[268]	וְאַחֲרֵי כֵן יַחְלְמוּ אִישׁ אִישׁ **כְּאַוַּת נַפְשׁוֹ**.[268]
Those who serve at the royal court dream of how to bend their knee;	הַבָּאִים בַּחֲצַר מַלְכוּת, יַחְלְמוּ אֵיךְ לִכְרֹעַ בִּרְכָּם;
The advocates in the courthouses calculate on their fingers what their wages are	הַמְּלִיצִים בְּבָתֵּי מִשְׁפָּט, יַחְשְׁבוּ בְּאֶצְבָּעָם מַה־שְּׂכָרָם
And when she touches women's lips, they dream of kisses	וְכַאֲשֶׁר תִּגַּע בְּשִׂפְתֵי הַנָּשִׁים, הֵן רֹאוֹת נְשִׁיקוֹת בַּחֲלוֹם
And when she grows angry at them because the breath of their mouth is spoiled	וְכַאֲשֶׁר תִּקְצֹף עֲלֵיהֶן כִּי הֲבֵל פִּיהֶן נִשְׁחָת
From sweets which they have eaten to excess, she punishes their iniquity with a pox.	מִמַּמְתַּקִּים אֲשֶׁר אָכְלוּ לָרֹב, תַּעֲנֹשׁ בַּאֲבַעְבֻּעוֹת עֲוֹנָן.
And when she passes by and touches the nose of those who serve the king	וְכִי תַעֲבֹר וְתִגַּע בְּאַף הָרֹאִים פְּנֵי מֶלֶךְ
Quick as lightning they scent that their time to be elevated has come	חִישׁ מַהֵר יְרִיחוּן כִּי בָאָה עִתָּם לְהִתְנַשֵּׂא
And if she touches the nose of the priests of the congregation[269] with a hair or a feather[270]	וְאִם בְּאַף כֹּהֲנֵי הָעֵדָה,[269] תִּגַּע בְּשֵׂעָר אוֹ בְנוֹצָה[270]
They dream that one of the priestly appointments[271] has been added to their lot.	יִרְאוּ בַחֲלוֹם כִּי אַחַת הַכְּהֻנּוֹת[271] נוֹסְפָה עַל חֶלְקָם.

267 Nah. 3:2.

268 Deut. 18:6; Jer. 2:24.

269 Cf. Shakespeare's 'parson's nose' (1.4.79). The Hebrew term כֹּהֵן can refer to a Christian priest, but also has strong associations with the priests of the biblical Temple in Jerusalem, as well as with the descendants of the priestly class in later Jewish society (who have a particular standing in Jewish law). See Haran, Stern, and Blidstein (2007) for further information about the priestly class in the biblical and postbiblical periods.

270 Cf. Shakespeare's 'tithe-pig's tail', a pig paid to settle the tithe on produce pledged to the Church (Weis 2012: 163, note 79). Salkinson's translation is religiously neutral.

271 Cf. Shakespeare's 'benefice' (1.4.81), meaning a permanent church appointment; Salkinson's translation lacks these Christian associations.

And if she passes in her chariot over the necks of soldiers	וְכִי תַעֲבֹר בְּמֶרְכַּבְתָּהּ עַל צַוְּארֵי אַנְשֵׁי הַצָּבָא
They dream that they have cut off their enemies' heads	יַחְלְמוּ חֲלוֹם כִּי כָרְתוּ רָאשֵׁי בַעֲלֵי מִלְחַמְתָּם
And that they have breached, ambushed, and plundered a fortune and weapons	וְכִי פָרְצוּ אָרְבוּ וְשָׁלְלוּ הוֹן וּכְלֵי נָשֶׁק
And they are drinking wine from a faithful spring which does not deceive;	וְהֵם שׁוֹתִים יַיִן מִמָּקוֹר נֶאֱמָן אֲשֶׁר לֹא יְכַזֵּב;
But suddenly they stir, they awaken to the sound of a drum in their ears	אַךְ פִּתְאֹם יִתְעוֹרְרוּ יָקִיצוּ לְקוֹל הַתֹּף בְּאָזְנֵיהֶם
Then they tremble, **they utter a grievous curse**[272] and fall asleep again.	אָז יִרְגְּזוּ **יְקַלְלוּ קְלָלָה נִמְרֶצֶת**[272] וַיִּישְׁנוּ שֵׁנִית.
This is the witch that stretches out a hand against the hairs of the horses' necks at night	זֹאת הַמְכַשֵּׁפָה הַשֹּׁלַחַת יָד בְּשַׂעֲרוֹת צַוְּארֵי הַסּוּסִים לָיְלָה
Or **the locks of men's heads**[273] until they interlace	אוֹ **בְּמַחְלְפוֹת רָאשֵׁי אֲנָשִׁים**[273] עַד אֲשֶׁר יִשְׂתָּרְגוּ
And they become thick, fastened ropes stuck with the filth of their head	וְהָיוּ לַעֲבוֹתִים עָבִים מְצֻמָּדִים מְדֻבָּקִים בְּחֶלְאַת רֹאשָׁם
And if they are separated or shaved, their owners will consider it a bad sign for themselves.	וְאִם יִפָּרְדוּ אוֹ יְגֻלְּחוּ, יַחְשְׁבוּ בַעֲלֵיהֶם לְאוֹת רָע לָמוֹ.
And she is the one who presses the virgins lying on their backs in bed[274]	וְהִיא הַלֹּחֶצֶת הַבְּתוּלוֹת הַשֹּׁכְבוֹת עַל גַּבָּן בַּמִּטָּה

272 1 Kings 2:8 וְהוּא קִלְלַנִי קְלָלָה נִמְרֶצֶת 'and he uttered a grievous curse against me'. In selecting this verse, Salkinson has replaced Shakespeare's 'prayer' (1.4.87) with קְלָלָה 'curse'. His choice may reflect an understanding of Shakespeare's 'swears' in a negative sense, but it may equally lack deeper significance. There is no clear motivation for the translation in the Schlegel-Tieck German translation, which has *Gebete* 'prayers'.

273 Judg. 16:13 אִם־תַּאַרְגִי אֶת־שֶׁבַע מַחְלְפוֹת רֹאשִׁי 'if you weave the seven locks of my head'. This line is spoken by Samson to Delilah, who has enquired about the source of his physical strength. The same collocation also appears in Judg. 16:19. Salkinson has chosen this as an equivalent of Shakespeare's 'elf-locks' (1.4.90), a term denoting knotted locks of hair (Weis 2012: 164, note 90); the reference to Samson is apt as the description of his hair may have referred to dreadlocks.

274 This and the following line are the ones to which Smolenskin refers in his preface to *Ram and Jael*.

	So that they learn to bear the burden of men upon them	לְבַעֲבוּר תִּלְמַדְנָה לָשֵׂאת מַשָּׂא הָאֲנָשִׁים עֲלֵיהֶן[274]	
	And moreover she…	וְגַם הִיא.....	
RAM	That's enough from you, Meraioth, rashly speaking **in vain and to no purpose.**[275]	רַב לְךָ מְרָיוֹת, לְבַטֵּא הֶבֶל וָרִיק.[275]	רם
MERAIOTH	Indeed I am speaking about matters of dreams	עַל דִּבְרֵי חֲלוֹמוֹת הֵן אֲנִי מְדַבֵּר	מריות
	For they are frivolous sons, the children of pointless and insipid thoughts	כִּי בָנִים רֵקִים הֵם, יַלְדֵי מַחְשְׁבוֹת שָׁוְא וָתָפֵל	
	Their foundation is as thin as shadow and lighter than a blowing wind	יְסוֹדָם דַּק כַּצֵּל וְקַל מֵרוּחַ נֹשָׁבֶת	
	It is the wind which sometimes embraces the bosom of ice	הוּא הָרוּחַ אֲשֶׁר פַּעַם יְחַבֵּק חֵיק הַקֶּרַח	
	Lying naked before it in **the uttermost parts of the north,**[276] and sometimes changes direction	הַשֹּׁכֵב עָרוֹם נֶגְדּוֹ בְּיַרְכְּתֵי **צָפוֹן**[276] וּפַעַם יְשַׁנֶּה פָנָיו	
	And rolls onto **the layer of dew**[277] in **the chambers of the south.**[278]	וְיִתְגּוֹלֵל עַל **שִׁכְבַת הַטַּל**[277] **בְּחַדְרֵי תֵימָן.**[278]	
BENAIAH	And it is the wind which pushes and distances our hearts	וְהוּא הָרוּחַ אֲשֶׁר יֶהְדֹּף וְיַרְחִיק אֶת לִבֵּנוּ	בניה
	Outside the border of our souls. But mealtime has passed	מִחוּץ לִגְבוּל נַפְשֵׁנוּ. אַךְ עֵת הָאֹכֶל עָבָרָה	
	And we are going to arrive after the appointed time.	וַנַחְנוּ נָבוֹא כַּעֲבֹר הַמּוֹעֵד.	
RAM	I fear that we are rushing **before the appointed time**[279]	הִנְנִי יָרֵא כִּי אָצִים אָנוּ **לִפְנֵי הַמּוֹעֵד**[279]	רם
	My heart tells me that evil has looked down from the stars	לְבָבִי יַגֶּד לִי, כִּי רָעָה נִשְׁקָפָה מֵאֵת הַכּוֹכָבִים	

275 Isa. 30:7.
276 Isa. 14:13; Ezek. 38:6, 15, 39:2; Ps. 48:3 (48:2 in English Bibles).
277 Exod. 16:13, 14.
278 Job 9:9.
279 Mishnah *Mo'ed Qaṭṭan* 1:3.

	And on this night of rejoicing begins to run the path of its course	וּבְלֵיל שְׂמָחוֹת זֶה תָּחֵל לָרוּץ אֹרַח תְּקוּפָתָהּ	
	And it will put an end to my soul, which has grown weary of its life	וְתָשֵׂם קֵץ לְנַפְשִׁי אֲשֶׁר קָצָה בְחַיִּים חַיָּתָהּ	
	And which has become a snare bringing death **before its time**;[280]	וַאֲשֶׁר הָיְתָה לְמוֹקֵשׁ לְהָבִיא מָוֶת **בְּלֹא יוֹמוֹ**;[280]	
	But my ship is in the hand of the sailor; he will guide it where he wishes	אַךְ סְפִינָתִי בְּיַד הַמַּלָּח אֶל אֲשֶׁר יִרְצֶה יַטֶּנָּה.	
	Let us go, merry friends! Let us go to the dances.	לְכוּ חֲבֵרִים עַלִּיזִים! נָבוֹאָה אֶל הַמְּחוֹלוֹת.	
BENAIAH	Come, strike the drum. *(All exit)*	הָבוּ הַכּוּ בַּתֹּף. (הולכים כלם)	בניה
FIFTH SCENE	*The palace of the Abiel household (Musicians stand and attendants enter)*	ארמון בית אביעל (מנגנים עומדים ומשרתים באים)	מחזה חמישי
ATTENDANT 1[281]	Where is Ben Mahbi?[282] Help us to clear up the house;	אַיֵּכָּה בֶּן מַחְבִּי?[282] עֲזָר לָנוּ לְפַנּוֹת אֶת הַבָּיִת;	משרת א'[281]
	Is it time to lick the plates and eat that which remains with your hands?	הַעֵת לְלַקֵּק הַקְּעָרוֹת, וְלֶאֱכֹל הַנּוֹתָר בְּיָדַיִם?	
ATTENDANT 2[283]	These are the good traits that I was given	אִלּוּ הַמִּדּוֹת הַטּוֹבוֹת לִי הָיוּ נְתוּנוֹת	משרת ב'[283]
	To keep them in these hands of mine that are stained with the filth of choice fruits	לְשָׁמְרָן בְּיָדַי אֵלֶּה הַמְּגֹאָלוֹת בְּחֶלְאַת הַמְּגָדִים	
	What will become of the glory of the traits? –	מַה־יִּהְיֶה מִתִּפְאֶרֶת הַמִּדּוֹת? –	

280 Job 15:32.

281 The servants' dialogue (from here until the next stage direction) is in prose in the original (1.5.1–15). Salkinson's 'Servant 1' corresponds to Shakespeare's 'Head Servingman'.

282 This name, which corresponds to Shakespeare's 'Potpan' (1.5.1), is comprised of the word בֵּן 'son' (used in the formation of Jewish patronymics), followed by a diminutive of מַחֲבַת, meaning 'griddle' or 'pan'. The name evokes associations with certain rabbinic sages; for example, Ben Azzai and Ben Zoma.

283 Salkinson has conflated two characters from the original (1 and 2 Servingman) into one (Servant 2). This Servant 2 seems to speak as Ben Mahbi (in contrast to Shakespeare's Potpan, who does not have any lines).

ATTENDANT 1	Take the household vessels away from here and put back the silver vessels in the chest	שְׂאוּ מִזֶּה כְּלֵי הַבַּיִת וְהָשִׁיבוּ כְּלֵי הַכֶּסֶף בָּאַרְגָּז	משרת א'
	And you will do well to find me **a couple of cakes**[284, 285]	וְאַתָּה טוֹב תַּעֲשֶׂה כִּי תִמְצָא לִי שְׁתֵּי **לְבִבוֹת**[284, 285]	
	And tell the gatekeeper to open up for Shoshannah[286] and Sebabah,[287] the daughters of Rechab.[288, 289]	וְאָמַרְתָּ אֶל הַשּׁוֹעֵר לִפְתֹּחַ לְשׁוֹשַׁנָּה[286] וּשְׂבָבָה[287] בְּנוֹת רֵכָב.[288, 289]	
	Where are you, Puti[290] Ben Mahbi? –	אַיֶּכָּה פּוּטִי[290] בֶּן מַחְבִּי? –	
ATTENDANT 2	I did as you commanded me.	עָשִׂיתִי כַּאֲשֶׁר צִוִּיתָנִי.	משרת ב'
ATTENDANT 1	Hurry into the chamber, for they have asked about you	מַהֲרָה אֶל הַחֶדֶר פְּנִימָה, כִּי שָׁאֲלוּ עָלֶיךָ	משרת א'
	And their eye is expecting to see your face.	וְעֵינָם צוֹפִיָּה לִרְאוֹת אֶת פָּנֶיךָ.	
ATTENDANT 2	We cannot be in two places at once.	לֹא נוּכַל לִהְיוֹת בִּשְׁנֵי מְקוֹמוֹת כְּאֶחָד.	משרת ב'
	Be happy, rejoice, lads! Do not be sad today	שִׂישׂוּ גִּילוּ בַּחוּרִים! אַל תֵּעָצְבוּ הַיּוֹם	
	Give in to your masters with graceful meekness, for **the meek shall inherit the earth.**[291]	הִכָּנְעוּ בְּעַנְוַת חֵן לַאֲדֹנֵיכֶם, כִּי עֲנָוִים יִירְשׁוּ אָרֶץ.[291]	

284 2 Sam. 13:6.

285 2 Sam. 13:6, 8, 10. Salkinson has replaced Shakespeare's term 'marchpane' (1.5.8), i.e., marzipan, with this less specific label.

286 As in the case of the nurse's daughter, Salkinson's Shoshannah replaces the English Susan (see note 180).

287 Salkinson's motivation for selecting Sebabah here is unclear, as it is not a Hebrew name or word. It resembles the root ש.י.ב., meaning 'to be grey-haired, old', and Salkinson may have created the form Sebabah in order to evoke a female name denoting something like 'grey-haired woman'. Presumably Salkinson's Sebabah is intended as a translation of Shakespeare's 'Nell' (1.5.9; see note 289), but there is no obvious correspondence in either sound or meaning between these two names. Note that I have transliterated it according to the traditional convention in English Bibles whereby the Hebrew letter ב *vet* is rendered as *b*.

288 This is the name of three different biblical characters: a captain in the service of Saul's son Ish-bosheth (mentioned in 2 Sam. 4:2); the ancestor of the Rechabite tribe (mentioned in 1 Chron. 2:55); and the father of Malchiah, ruler of the Beth-haccherem district in Jerusalem after the return from Babylonian exile (Neh. 3:14).

289 This list of names corresponds to Shakespeare's 'Susan Grindstone, Nell, and Anthony' (1.5.9). Salkinson has designated the first two characters as the daughters of the third, which lacks precedent in the original.

290 Salkinson's choice of this name may be rooted in the sound correspondence between it and Shakespeare's 'Potpan'. His decision to give the character a first name has no basis in the original (which refers only to 'Potpan'). Puti is itself not a Hebrew name, but Salkinson might have had it in mind as a shortened version of the biblical Putiel (the name of a man whose daughter married Aaron's son Eleazar, mentioned in Exod. 6:25).

291 Ps. 37:11.

	(The attendants retreat)	(המשרתים שבים לאחור)	
	(Abiel, Abiel's wife, Tubal, and the members of the household with the guests wearing masks on their faces.)	(אביעל, אשת אביעל, יעל, תובל ובני הבית עם הקרואים נושאי אֵפֶר על פניהם.)	
ABIEL	Welcome, friends! The women whose toes	בּוֹאוּ לְשָׁלוֹם יְדִידִים! הַנָּשִׁים אֲשֶׁר בְּהֹנוֹת רַגְלֵיהֶן	אביעל
	Are not afflicted with a painful root expect **to go forth in the dances of the merrymakers**[292]	**לֹא יֻגְּעוּ בְשֹׁרֶשׁ מַכְאִיב, צוֹפוֹת לָצֵאת בִּמְחוֹל מְשַׂחֲקִים**[292]	
	Come, daughters of valour! The one among you who refuses to dance	בֹּאנָה בְּנוֹת חַיִל! מִי מִכֶּן תְּמָאֵן לִרְקוֹד	
	Is the woman who has an affliction on the toes of her feet.	הִיא הָאִשָּׁה אֲשֶׁר נֶגַע לָהּ בִּבְהֹנוֹת רַגְלֶיהָ.	
	And you too, new faces! Friends, welcome	וְגַם אַתֶּם פָּנִים חֲדָשִׁים! יְדִידִים בּוֹאֲכֶם לְשָׁלוֹם	
	I remember the day when I wore a mask over my eyes	זָכַרְתִּי אֶת הַיּוֹם אֲשֶׁר נָשָׂאתִי אֵפֶר עַל עֵינָי	
	And put pleasant words in the ears of a beautiful girl	וָאָשִׂים דְּבָרִים נְעִימִים בְּאָזְנֵי יְפַת תֹּאַר	
	But the day has passed, the day has passed and will not return.	אַךְ הַיּוֹם עָבַר, עָבַר הַיּוֹם וְלֹא יָשׁוּב.	
	Welcome, friends! Musicians, play well	בֹּאוּ לְשָׁלוֹם יְדִידִים! מְנַגְּנִים הֵיטִיבוּ נַגֵּן	
	Make room! Make room! Go forth, **damsels playing timbrels**![293]	פַּנּוּ מָקוֹם! פַּנּוּ מָקוֹם! צֶאֶינָה **עֲלָמוֹת תּוֹפֵפוֹת!**[293]	
	(The musicians play and people go forth dancing two by two)	(המנגנים מנגנים ושנים שנים יוצאים במחול)	
	(To the attendants) Bring more candles and bear the tables away from here	(אל המשרתים) הָבִיאוּ נֵרוֹת עוֹד וּשְׂאוּ הַשֻּׁלְחָנוֹת* מִזֶּה	
	And put out the fire in the oven, for it is very hot in the house.	וְכַבּוּ אֶת הָאֵשׁ בַּתַּנּוּר, כִּי חָזָק הַחֹם בַּבָּיִת.	
	How my heart rejoices to see the guests dancing	מַה־יִּשְׂמַח לִבִּי לִרְאוֹת בִּרְקוֹד הָאֹרְחִים	

292 Jer. 31:4 וְיָצָאת בִּמְחוֹל מְשַׂחֲקִים 'and you will go forth in the dances of the merrymakers'.
293 Ps. 68:26 (68:25 in English Bibles).

* הַשֻּׁלְחָנוֹת

	Whom I have not invited[294] – sit with me, my brother[295] Abiel	אֲשֶׁר לֹא קְרָאתִים[294] – שְׁבָה אִתִּי אֲבִיעֵל אָחִי[295]	
	For our dancing days are done. What is the number of years	כִּי חָלְפוּ יְמֵי מְחוֹלֵנוּ. מַה־מִּסְפַּר הַשָּׁנִים	
	From the day when we danced together with a mask on our face?	מִיּוֹם אֲשֶׁר רָקַדְנוּ יַחְדָּו וְהַמַּסְוֶה עַל פָּנֵינוּ?	
SECOND ABIEL[296]	About thirty years.	כִּשְׁלֹשִׁים שָׁנָה.	אביעל השני[296]
ABIEL	What are you talking about? Why, you have added to the number	מָה אַתָּה דֹבֵר? הֲלֹא הוֹסַפְתָּ עַל הַמִּסְפָּר	אביעל
	For on the next festival of Shavuot[297] it will be twenty-five years	כִּי בְּחַג הַשָּׁבֻעוֹת[297] הַבָּא יִהְיֶה עֶשְׂרִים וְחָמֵשׁ שָׁנִים	
	To the day of Luz's[298] wedding, and that is the day when we last danced.	לְיוֹם חֲתֻנַּת לוּץ[298] וְהוּא הַיּוֹם אֲשֶׁר רָקַדְנוּ בָּאַחֲרֹנָה.	
SECOND ABIEL	More than twenty-five, for his son is older than that,	לְמַעְלָה מֵעֶשְׂרִים וְחָמֵשׁ, כִּי בְנוֹ לְמַעְלָה מִזֶּה,	אביעל השני
	His son is around thirty.	בְּנוֹ הוּא כְּבֶן שְׁלֹשִׁים.	
ABIEL	Do not speak like this, for it is two years	אַל תְּדַבֵּר כַּדָּבָר הַזֶּה כִּי זֶה שְׁנָתַיִם	אביעל
	Since I have seen his son, **and he was still a youth.**[299]	מִיּוֹם רָאִיתִי אֶת בְּנוֹ וְהוּא עוֹדֶנּוּ נָעַר.[299]	

294 Cf. Shakespeare's 'Ah, sirrah, this unlooked-for sport comes well' (1.5.29). Shakespeare's 'unlooked-for', meaning 'unexpected', refers to the dancing, whereas Salkinson has changed it into a reference to the uninvited guests (Ram, Benaiah, and Meraioth). There is no basis for Salkinson's change in the Schlegel-Tieck German translation of the play, which he may have consulted.

295 Cf. Shakespeare's 'cousin' (1.2.30); see note 65.

296 Cf. Shakespeare's 'Cousin Capulet'.

297 Cf. Shakespeare's 'Pentecost' (1.5.36). The Jewish festival of Shavuot, which commemorates the giving of the Torah at Mount Sinai, is the dynamic equivalent of the Christian Pentecost as the former is the historical antecedent of the latter and both fall at a similar time of the year, in late spring or early summer. Moreover, Salkinson would have struggled to find another way of translating the term given the lack of a recognized Hebrew label for Pentecost. The substitution also serves to neutralize the Christian connotations of the original and replace them with explicitly Jewish ones, given that Salkinson's audience would have automatically understood the reference as being to the Jewish holiday rather than to the Christian one.

298 Salkinson has conflated his translation of Shakespeare's 'Lucentio' (1.5.35) with that of 'Lucio' (1.2.71); see note 156.

299 2 Chron. 34:3.

RAM *(To one of the attendants)*	Who is the damsel	מִי זֹאת הָעַלְמָה	רם (אל אחד המשרתים)
	Leaning there on the captain's arm at the dance?	הַמִּתְרַפֶּקֶת שָׁמָּה עַל יַד הַשָּׁלִישׁ בַּמָּחוֹל?	
THE ATTENDANT	I do not know who she is, my lord.	אֵינֶנִּי יוֹדֵעַ אֲדֹנִי, מִי הִיא.	המשרת
RAM	She teaches the candles to illuminate and to spread light[300]	הִיא תוֹרָה לַנֵּרוֹת, לְהָאִיר וּלְהָפִיץ אוֹרָה[300]	רם
	The sparkle of her splendour can be seen on the face of the night	בְּרַק יִפְעָתָהּ יֵרָאֶה עַל פְּנֵי הַלָּיִל	
	Like an emerald stone[301] in the ear of a black Cushite[302] woman	כְּמוֹ אֶבֶן בָּרֶקֶת[301] בְּאֹזֶן כּוּשִׁית[302] שְׁחוֹרָה	
	She is elevated above **those who dwell in houses of clay;**[303] she is without compare in wealth or riches.	מִשֹּׁכְנֵי בָתֵּי חֹמֶר[303] נִשְׂגָּבָה, לֹא תְסֻלֶּא בְּהוֹן וָחָיִל.	
	Like a dove purer than snow soaring among crows[304]	כְּיוֹנָה זַכָּה מִשֶּׁלֶג בְּקֶרֶב עוֹרְבִים מְרַחֶפֶת[304]	
	So this **noble daughter**[305] looks down from among her companions.	כֵּן בַּת נָדִיב[305] זוּ מִבֵּין רֵעוֹתֶיהָ נִשְׁקֶפֶת.	
	After this dance I'll observe where she rests from her toil[306]	אַחַר הַמָּחוֹל הַזֶּה אֶשְׁמֹר אֵיפֹה תָּנוּחַ מֵעֲמָלָהּ[306]	
	And if only I might touch her hand, **my soul will live because of her.**[307]	וְאִם אַךְ אֶגַּע בְּיָדָהּ וְחָיְתָה נַפְשִׁי בִּגְלָלָהּ.[307]	
	As I live! I shall never love another from this day forth[308]	חַי אָנִי! אִם אֹהַב אַחֶרֶת מִיּוֹם זֶה וָמָעְלָה[308]	

300 This and the subsequent three lines form an ABAB rhyming sequence; this can be contrasted with the original, which is comprised of two rhyming couplets 'bright/night', 'ear/dear' (1.5.43–6).
301 Exod. 28:17, 39:10. This is translated as 'beryl' in some English Bible versions.
302 Cf. Shakespeare's 'Ethiop' (1.5.45). The Hebrew term translated here as 'Cushite' is often associated with Ethiopia, and is translated as 'Ethiopian' in a number of English Bible versions. See *Ithiel*, First Part, note 26.
303 Job 4:19 (denoting ordinary mortals). Cf. Shakespeare's 'for earth too dear' (1.5.46).
304 This and the following line form a rhyming couplet, mirroring Shakespeare's 'crows/shows' (1.5.47–8).
305 Song of Songs 7:2 (7:1 in English Bibles).
306 This and the following line form a rhyming couplet, mirroring Shakespeare's 'stand/hand' (1.5.49–50).
307 Gen. 12:13 וְחָיְתָה נַפְשִׁי בִּגְלָלֵךְ 'and my soul will live because of you'.
308 This and the following line form a rhyming couplet, mirroring Shakespeare's 'sight/night' (1.5.51–2).

	For never have I seen **perfect beauty**[309] other than tonight.	כִּי מֵעוֹדִי לֹא רָאִיתִי **כְּלִילַת יֹפִי**[309] בִּלְתִּי הַלָּיְלָה.
TUBAL	His voice testifies against him that he is from the house of Abiram –	תובל קוֹלוֹ יַעֲנֶה בּוֹ, כִּי הוּא מִבֵּית אֲבִירָם –
	Who is on my side, who?[310] Bring me my sword – this villain	מִי אִתִּי מִי?[310] הָבֵא לִי חַרְבִּי – הַבְּלִיַּעַל הַזֶּה
	What is he doing here, that **he has disguised himself in a strange mask**[311]	מַה־לּוֹ פֹּה כִּי **הִתְחַפֵּשׂ בַּאֲפֵר**[311] זָר
	And has come to see our nakedness[312] and mock us at our festival.	**וַיָּבוֹא לִרְאוֹת עֶרְוָתֵנוּ**[312] וּלְהָתֵל בָּנוּ בְּחַגֵּנוּ.
	By the name of my father's house I swear, and by the honour of my great family[313]	בְּשֵׁם בֵּית אָבִי נִשְׁבַּעְתִּי וּבִכְבוֹד מִשְׁפַּחְתִּי הַגְּדוֹלָה[313]
	That it would not be considered an iniquity for me **to bring him in blood down to Sheol.**[314]	אִם לְעָוֹן יֵחָשֶׁב לִי, **לְהוֹרִידוֹ בְּדָם שְׁאוֹלָה.**[314]
ABIEL	What is wrong with you, **my flesh and blood?**[315] **What is wrong with you, that you cried out?**[316]	אביעל **מַה־לְּךָ שְׁאֵרִי וּבְשָׂרִי?**[315] **מַה־לְּךָ כִּי נִזְעָקְתָּ?**[316]
TUBAL	Look, my uncle, one of the Abirams, **hated of our souls**,[317, 318]	תובל רְאֵה דוֹדִי, אֶחָד מֵהָאֲבִירָמִים **שְׂנוּאֵי נַפְשֵׁנוּ**[317, 318]
	Has come here to cause **anguish of spirit**,[319] to mock us on the night of our festival.	בָּא הֵנָּה **לְמֹרַת רוּחַ**,[319] לְצַחֵק בָּנוּ בְּלֵיל חַגֵּנוּ.
ABIEL	Is he Ram, son of Abiram?	אביעל הַאִם רָם בֶּן אֲבִירָם הוּא?
TUBAL	He is the villain Ram.	תובל הוּא רָם הַבְּלִיַּעַל.

309 Ezek. 27:3; Lam. 2:15.

310 2 Kings 9:32.

311 1 Kings 20:38 וַיִּתְחַפֵּשׂ בָּאֲפֵר 'and he disguised himself with a mask (or: bandage)'.

312 Gen. 42:9 מְרַגְּלִים אַתֶּם לִרְאוֹת אֶת־עֶרְוַת הָאָרֶץ בָּאתֶם 'you are spies; you have come to see the nakedness of the land'.

313 This and the following line form a rhyming couplet, mirroring Shakespeare's 'kin/sin' (1.5.57–8).

314 1 Kings 2:9 וְהוֹרַדְתָּ אֶת־שֵׂיבָתוֹ בְּדָם שְׁאוֹל 'and you must bring his grey head down in blood to Sheol'.

315 Prov. 5:11 בְּשָׂרְךָ וּשְׁאֵרֶךָ 'your flesh and body' (used literally in this verse, but idiomatically in Salkinson's text).

316 Judg. 18:23. Although the meaning of the root ז.ע.ק. means 'gather' or 'assemble' in the *nif'al* stem, Salkinson seems to have had in mind the meaning of the *qal*, 'cry out'. See also *Ithiel*, Second Part, note 245 and Fifth Part, note 19.

317 2 Sam. 5:8 שְׂנֻאֵי נֶפֶשׁ דָּוִד 'hated of David's soul'.

318 This and the next line form a rhyming couplet, echoing but differing from the original, in which the rhyme begins a line earlier, in Capulet's speech, and is split between Capulet and Tybalt 'so?/foe' (1.5.59–60).

319 Gen. 26:35.

ABIEL	Please let him go, my son, let him go, let him be	נָא הֶרֶף מִמֶּנּוּ בְּנִי הֶרֶף הַנַּח־לוֹ	אביעל
	For **his speech is comely**[320] and his gait is like the steps of a nobleman	כִּי מִדְבָּרוֹ נָאוֶה[320] וַהֲלִיכוֹתָיו כְּפַעֲמֵי נָדִיב	
	And moreover all the sons of the city tell of his glory at the gate.	וְגַם כָּל בְּנֵי הָעִיר יְסַפְּרוּ תְהִלָּתוֹ בַּשָּׁעַר.	
	For he is a valiant man, **a wise son**[321] who **has control over his spirit**[322]	כִּי בֶן חַיִל הוּא, בֵּן מַשְׂכִּיל[321] מֹשֵׁל בְּרוּחוֹ[322]	
	Even if you were to give me the treasures of this entire city	אִם תִּתֶּן לִי אוֹצְרוֹת כָּל הָעִיר הַזֹּאת	
	I would not let a single one of his hairs fall to the ground[323] after **he came under the shelter of my roof**[324]	לֹא אַפִּיל מִשַּׂעֲרָתוֹ אַרְצָה[323] אַחֲרֵי בוֹאוֹ בְּצֵל קֹרָתִי.[324]	
	Therefore restrain your spirit, and do not pay heed to him	לָכֵן תְּנָה מַעְצֹר לְרוּחֲךָ וְאַל תָּשִׂים אֵלָיו לִבֶּךָ	
	And if you seek my wellbeing, please **let your heart be merry**[325]	וְאִם שְׁלוֹמִי אַתָּה דֹרֵשׁ הוֹאֶל־נָא וְיִיטַב לִבֶּךָ[325]	
	Remove the **angry countenance**[326] and do not **make the joy of our festival cease.**[327, 328]	הַעֲבֵר פָּנִים נִזְעָמִים[326] וְאַל תַּשְׁבֵּת מְשׂוֹשׂ חַגֵּנוּ.[327, 328]	
TUBAL	An **angry countenance**[329] is fitting for me, if a villain such as he	נְכוֹנִים לִי פָּנִים נִזְעָמִים,[329] אִם אִישׁ נָבָל כָּמוֹהוּ	תובל
	Interferes with the joy of our festival; I shall not endure him.	יִתְעָרֵב בְּשִׂמְחַת חַגֵּנוּ; אָנֹכִי לֹא אֶשָּׂא פָנָיו.	
ABIEL	Whereas I shall endure him.	וַאֲנִי פָּנָיו אֶשָּׂא.	אביעל
	And what can you say, young man? Indeed, I have said	וּמַה־תֹּאמַר אִישׁ נַעַר? הֵן אָנֹכִי אָמַרְתִּי	

320 Song of Songs 4:3 וּמִדְבָּרֵיךְ נָאוֶה 'and your words are comely'.

321 Prov. 10:5.

322 Prov. 16:32.

323 2 Sam. 14:11 חַי־יְהוָה אִם־יִפֹּל מִשַּׂעֲרַת בְּנֵךְ אָרְצָה 'as the LORD lives, not a single one of your son's hairs shall fall to the ground'; similar constructions appear in 1 Sam. 14:45 and 1 Kings 1:52.

324 Gen. 19:8 כִּי־עַל־כֵּן בָּאוּ בְּצֵל קֹרָתִי 'because therefore they have come under the shelter of my roof'.

325 Judg. 19:9 וְיִיטַב לְבָבֶךָ 'and let your heart be merry'.

326 Prov. 25:23.

327 Lam. 5:15 שָׁבַת מְשׂוֹשׂ לִבֵּנוּ 'the joy of our hearts has ceased'; a similar construction appears in Isa. 24:8.

328 Salkinson has not replicated the rhyming couplet 'feast/guest' (1.5.73–4) between this and the next line in the source text (possibly because he did not recognize the rhyme as such).

329 Prov. 25:23.

	That I shall endure him. Are you the master of the house	כִּי פָנָיו אֶשָּׂא. הַאַתָּה הוּא בַּעַל הַבַּיִת	
	Or am I the master of the house? Go out and boast that you will not endure him	אוֹ בַּעַל הַבַּיִת אָנִי? צֵא הִתְפָּאֵר כִּי לֹא תִשָּׂא פָנָיו	
	I know that you want to bring confusion among the guests	יָדַעְתִּי כִּי חָפַצְתָּ לְהָבִיא מְבוּכָה בֵּין הַקְּרוּאִים	
	And stand at the head of them all, like a mighty rooster[330] among the birds.	וְלַעֲמֹד בְּרֹאשׁ כֻּלָּם, כְּתַרְנְגֹל[330] עַז בָּעוֹף.	
TUBAL	It is a disgrace, my uncle, a disgrace to us.	חֶרְפָּה הִיא דוֹדִי, חֶרְפָּה הִיא לָנוּ.	תובל
ABIEL	That's enough from you, stubborn lad; this is your way, to vex me continually	רַב לְךָ נַעַר עִקֵּשׁ, זֶה דַרְכְּךָ לְהַכְעִיסֵנִי תָּמִיד	אביעל
	Guard yourself from **the force of your hand,**[331] **lest you be swallowed up**[332] –	הִשָּׁמֶר לְךָ מִתִּגְרַת יָדְךָ,[331] פֶּן יְבֻלַּע לָךְ[332] –	
	Make your hearts merry, friends; celebrate well at the dance! –	הֵיטִיבוּ לִבְּכֶם יְדִידִים, הֵיטִיבוּ לָחוֹג בַּמָּחוֹל! –	
	I said to you be silent, senseless one, **rooster with no understanding**![333] –	דּוֹם אָמַרְתִּי לְךָ חֲסַר לֵב, שֶׂכְוִי אֵין בִּינָה![333] –	
	Bring more candles, attendants – and as for you, **sit silently**[334] –	הָבִיאוּ נֵרוֹת עוֹד מְשָׁרְתִים – וְדוּמָם תֵּשֵׁב[334] אָתָּה –	
	Make your hearts merry, friends!	הֵיטִיבוּ לִבְּכֶם יְדִידִים!	
TUBAL	**Control over the spirit**[335] **with a strong hand**[336] and a blocked fire of wrath[337]	מַעְצָר לָרוּחַ[335] בְּחֶזְקַת הַיָּד[336] וְאֵשׁ חֵמָה עֲצוּרָה[337]	תובל

330 This seems to be based on Shakespeare's 'cock-a-hoop' (1.5.80), which is actually an idiom for starting a riot, with 'cock' meaning the tap or stopcock of a barrel of ale (the idiom derives from the idea that setting the stopcock on top of the hoop, or barrel, would lead to free-flowing ale, resulting in intoxication and lack of restraint; see Weis 2012: 172, note 80). Salkinson seems to have understood the word to mean 'rooster'.

331 Ps. 39:11 (39:10 in English Bibles).

332 2 Sam. 17:16 פֶּן יְבֻלַּע לַמֶּלֶךְ וּלְכָל־הָעָם אֲשֶׁר אִתּוֹ 'lest the king and all the people who are with him be swallowed up'.

333 Job 38:36 מִי־נָתַן לַשֶּׂכְוִי בִינָה 'who gave the rooster understanding?'

334 Isa. 47:5 שְׁבִי דוּמָם 'sit silently'.

335 Prov. 25:28 אִישׁ אֲשֶׁר אֵין מַעְצָר לְרוּחוֹ 'a man who has no control over his spirit'.

336 Isa. 8:11 כְּחֶזְקַת הַיָּד 'with a strong hand'.

337 This and the following line form a rhyming couplet, mirroring Shakespeare's 'meeting/greeting' (1.5.88–9).

	Have met together in my bones, like a bellows in a bonfire	נִפְגְּשׁוּ יַחְדָּו בְּעַצְמוֹתַי, כְּמַפֻּחַ בְּמוֹ מְדוּרָה	
	But I shall restrain myself and go forth, although the interloper among us is not acceptable to me[338]	אַךְ אֶתְאַפַּק וְאֵצֵא וְהַמִּתְעָרֵב בָּנוּ לֹא לִרְצוֹנִי[338]	
	The dance will please him for a moment; **afterwards he will bite like an adder.**[339]	רֶגַע יֶעֱרַב לוֹ הַמָּחוֹל, **אַחַר יִשֹּׁךְ כְּצִפְעוֹנִי.**[339]	
	(Exits)	(יוצא)	
RAM *(To Jael)*	When my hand touches holiness, the hem of one who is pure and awesome[340]	כִּי תִגַּע יָדִי בַּקֹּדֶשׁ, בִּכְנַף בָּרָה אֲיֻמָּה[340]	רם (אל יעל)
	I shall give this ransom, and distance the profane from the holy	כֹּפֶר זֶה אֶתֵּן וְחוֹל מִקֹּדֶשׁ אַרְחִיקָה	
	Indeed I am a sojourner[341] with you and with a lip red from shame	הֵן גֵּר[341] אֲנִי עִמָּךְ וּבְשָׂפָה מִבֹּשֶׁת אֲדֻמָּה[342]	
	I shall wipe clean the touch of my hand and atone for my iniquity with a kiss.	אֶמְחֶה מַגַּע יָדִי וַאֲכַפֵּר עַל עֲוֹנִי בִּנְשִׁיקָה.	
JAEL	Do not detract from the worth of your hand, dear and pleasant guest[342]	אַל תִּגְרַע מֵעֶרֶךְ יָדְךָ אֹרֵחַ יַקִּיר וְנָעִים[343]	יעל
	You have not violated good manners and your hand is not a burden upon me	לֹא פָרַעְתָּ מוּסָר וְלֹא יָדְךָ עָלַי לָטֹרַח	

338 This and the following line form a rhyming couplet, mirroring Shakespeare's 'shall/gall' (1.5.91).

339 Prov. 23:32 אַחֲרִיתוֹ כְּנָחָשׁ יִשָּׁךְ וּכְצִפְעֹנִי יַפְרִשׁ 'in the end it bites like a serpent and stings like an adder'.

340 This and the subsequent three lines form an ABAB rhyming sequence, echoing Shakespeare's 'hand/this/stand/kiss' (1.5.92–5).

341 Cf. Shakespeare's 'pilgrims' (1.5.94). In the Hebrew Bible, the word גֵּר denotes a resident foreigner in Israelite territory constituting a distinct class in the biblical legal system (Lieber 2007). By contrast, in rabbinic and later Jewish literature, as well as in Salkinson's Yiddish vernacular, the term refers to a convert to Judaism (Rabinowitz and Eichhorn 2007). Both the biblical and postbiblical meanings of the word would have been familiar to Salkinson's readers. As such, the translation can be understood on two levels, each of which retains the notion of religious migration while situating the utterance within an unambiguously Jewish frame of reference. See *Ithiel*, First Part, note 286 for a similar use of this word.

342 This and the subsequent three lines form an ABAB rhyming sequence, mirroring Shakespeare's 'much/this/touch/kiss' (1.5.96–9).

	Sojourners[343] touch the hands of holy men,[344] and the holy men the hands of new arrivals	גֵּרִים[344] יִגְּעוּ בִידֵי קְדוֹשִׁים וְהַקְּדוֹשִׁים בִּידֵי הַבָּאִים	
	For this is the way of peace for all wayfarers.	כִּי זֶה דֶּרֶךְ שָׁלוֹם לְכָל עֹבְרֵי אֹרַח.	
RAM	Why, holy men as well as guests have lips like your lips.[345]	הֲלֹא לִקְדוֹשִׁים וְאֹרְחִים גַּם שְׂפָתַיִם יֵשׁ כִּשְׂפָתַיִךְ.[345]	רם
JAEL	They have lips like my lips, which I open for my prayer.	יֵשׁ לָהֶם שְׂפָתַיִם כִּשְׂפָתַי אֲשֶׁר אֶפְתַּח לִתְפִלָּתִי.	יעל
RAM	Therefore I spread my palms and with my lip I entreat you!	לָכֵן אֵיפוֹא אֶפְרֹשׂ כַּפַּי וּבִשְׂפָתִי אֲחַלֶּה־פָּנַיִךְ!	רם
	And you, as a **holy angel,**[346] must listen, lest I despair of my faith.	וְאַתְּ כְּעִיר וְקַדִּישׁ[346] תִּשְׁמָעִי, פֶּן אֵבוֹשׁ מֵאֱמוּנָתִי.	
JAEL	Holy men do not move though they might hear a supplication.[347]	הַקְּדוֹשִׁים לֹא יָנוּעוּ אַף כִּי יִשְׁמְעוּ תְחִנָּה.[347]	יעל
RAM	Therefore stand at the ready and I shall test you with a touchstone[348]	לָכֵן עִמְדִי הָכֵן וְאֶבְחָנֵךְ בְּאֶבֶן הַבְּחִנָּה[348]	רם
	Behold, my lips touch yours **and my iniquity is removed.**[349, 350]	הִנֵּה נָגְעוּ שְׂפָתַי בִּשְׂפָתַיִךְ וְסָר עֲוֹנִי.[349, 350]	
	(Kisses her)	(נושק אותה)	
JAEL	And now I have sinned with my lips on your mouth, my lord.	וְעַתָּה אֲנִי חָטָאתִי בִּשְׂפָתַי עַל פִּיךָ אֲדֹנִי.	יעל
RAM	I hereby wipe the sin clean, for **I repent in dust and ashes.**[351]	הִנְנִי מֹחֶה הַחֵטְא, כִּי נִחַמְתִּי עַל עָפָר וָאֵפֶר.[351]	רם
	(Kisses her again)	(נושק אותה שנית)	

343 See note 341.
344 This is Salkinson's religiously more neutral translation of Shakespeare's 'saints' (1.5.98).
345 This and the subsequent three lines form an ABAB rhyming sequence, mirroring Shakespeare's 'too/prayer/do/despair' (1.5.100–4).
346 This is a medieval expression (Even-Shoshan 2003, 4: 1371) based on Dan. 4:10, 20.
347 This forms a rhyming couplet with the following line, echoing the English 'Saints do not move, though grant for prayers' sake./Then move not while my prayer's effect I take' (1.5.104–5).
348 This is not a recognized collocation in Hebrew, but is clearly based on the similar expression אֶבֶן בֹּחַן 'touchstone', a modern idiom derived from the appearance of the phrase (with a different meaning) in Isa. 28:16 (Even-Shoshan 2003, 1: 8). Salkinson has altered the final word of the phrase in order to fit in with his rhyme scheme.
349 Isa. 6:7 וְסָר עֲוֹנֶךָ 'and your iniquity is removed'.
350 This and the following three lines form two rhyming couplets, mirroring the original except that the latter has an ABAB pattern: 'purged/took/urged/book' (1.5.106–9).
351 Job 42:6.

JAEL	You know how to kiss according to what is written in the book.	אַתָּה יוֹדֵעַ לְנַשֵּׁק לְפִי הַכָּתוּב בַּסֵּפֶר.	יעל
THE NURSE	**Noble daughter,**[352] your mother desires to speak a word to you.	**בַּת נָדִיב,**[352] אִמֵּךְ חֲפֵצָה לְדַבֵּר דָּבָר אֵלָיִךְ.	האומנת
RAM	Who is her mother?	מִי הִיא אִמָּהּ?	רם
THE NURSE	Her mother is the mistress of the house, a wise **woman of valour**[353]	אִמָּהּ הִיא בַּעֲלַת הַבַּיִת, **אֵשֶׁת חַיִל**[353] מַשְׂכֶּלֶת	האומנת
	And I am nurse to her daughter, who stands with you here;	וַאֲנִי מֵינֶקֶת לְבִתָּהּ הַנִּצֶּבֶת עִמְּךָ בָּזֶה;	
	And you, young man, I'll have you know, **a word has left my mouth**[354]	וְאַתָּה בָּחוּר דַּע לְךָ, **דָּבָר יָצָא מִפִּי**[354]	
	That the one who finds her finds life.[355]	**כִּי מוֹצְאָהּ מָצָא חַיִּים.**[355]	
RAM	Is she the daughter of Abiel?	הֲבַת אָבִיעֵל הִיא?	רם
	I grow faint from hearing[356] that I have been caught in the enemy's hand.	**נַעֲוֵיתִי מִשְּׁמֹעַ**[356] כִּי נִסְגַּרְתִּי בְּיַד אוֹיֵב.	
BENAIAH	Come, let us go while they are still dancing to the sound of **timbrel and harp**[357, 358]	לְכָה וְנֵלְכָה בְּעוֹדָם רוֹקְדִים לְקוֹל **תֹּף וָנֵבֶל.**[357, 358]	בניה
RAM	I fear that this dance is becoming an occasion of mourning for me.	יָרֵאתִי כִּי הַמָּחוֹל הַזֶּה יֵהָפֵךְ לִי לְאֵבֶל.	רם
ABIEL	No, friends, do not rush to depart from here	אַל לָכֶם יְדִידִים, אַל תָּאִיצוּ לָלֶכֶת מִזֶּה	אביעל
	Various choice delicacies to restore the soul have yet been prepared.	עוֹד מְגָדִים שׁוֹנִים לְהָשִׁיב נֶפֶשׁ נְכוֹנִים.	

352 Song of Songs 7:2 (7:1 in English Bibles).
353 Prov. 12:4, 31:10; Ruth 3:11.
354 Esther 7:8 הַדָּבָר יָצָא מִפִּי הַמֶּלֶךְ 'as soon as the word left the king's mouth'.
355 Prov. 8:35 כִּי מֹצְאִי מצאי מָצָא חַיִּים 'for the one who finds Me finds life'.
356 Isa. 21:3.
357 1 Sam. 10:5 נֵבֶל וְתֹף 'harp and timbrel'.
358 This and the next line form a rhyming couplet, mirroring the original except that in the latter there are two rhyming couplets instead of one in the corresponding lines: 'Capulet/debt', 'best/unrest' (1.5.117–19).

	But if the appointed time for your departure has come, take my blessing	וְאִם מוֹעֵד צֵאתְכֶם בָּא, שְׂאוּ אֶת בִּרְכָתִי	
	And go in peace, friends! – Bring torches here	וּצְאוּ לְשָׁלוֹם יְדִידִים! – הָבִיאוּ לַפִּידִים הֵנָּה	
	Go to your houses in peace! *(To the second Abiel)* Go in peace, my brother	בּוֹאוּ לְבָתֵּיכֶם לְשָׁלוֹם! (לאביעל השני) צֵא לְשָׁלוֹם אָחִי	
	Indeed, the night will soon be over and I seek rest.	הֵן הַלַּיְלָה קָרוֹב לַעֲבוֹר וּמְנוּחָה אֲנִי מְבַקֵּשׁ.	
	(All exit except for Jael and the nurse)	(כלם הולכים לבד יעל והאומנת)	
JAEL	Look there, my nurse, who is that man?	רְאִי שָׁמָּה אֹמַנְתִּי, מִי הוּא הָאִישׁ הַהוּא?	יעל
THE NURSE	He is the son and heir of Tabrimon.[359]	הוּא בֶּן טַבְרִימוֹן[359] הַיּוֹרֵשׁ.	האומנת
JAEL	And whose son is the youth going out at the door?	וּבֶן מִי זֶה הָעֶלֶם, הַיּוֹצֵא בַּפֶּתַח?	יעל
THE NURSE	That is the son of Peretz[360] the Pirathonite.[361]	זֶה הוּא בֶּן פֶּרֶץ[360] הַפִּרְעָתוֹנִי.[361]	האומנת
JAEL	And who is this one going out after him, who refused to dance?	וּמִי זֶה הַיּוֹצֵא אַחֲרָיו, אֲשֶׁר מֵאֵן לִרְקֹד?	יעל
THE NURSE	I do not know.	אֵינֶנִּי יוֹדַעַת.	האומנת
JAEL	Ask what his name is; if the man is **a woman's husband**[362, 363]	שַׁאֲלִי מַה־שְּׁמוֹ; אִם בַּעַל אִשָּׁה[362] הוּא הַגֶּבֶר[363]	יעל

359 The father of Ben-hadad, king of Aram, mentioned in 1 Kings 15:18. Salkinson seems to have chosen this name based on its sound correspondence with Shakespeare's 'Tiberio' (1.5.128).

360 This name denotes two different biblical characters, a) the son of Judah and Tamar whose story is told in Genesis 38, and b) an ancestor of Boaz, protagonist of the Book of Ruth mentioned in Ruth 4:18. Salkinson most likely chose this name on the basis of its sound correspondence with Shakespeare's 'Petruchio' (1.5.130). Note that Judah Leib Elkind, who translated *The Taming of the Shrew* into Hebrew in 1892, chose Peretz for his version of Petruchio, possibly inspired by Salkinson (see Kahn [forthcoming a] for discussion of the symbolism of this choice in Elkind [1892]). It is unclear why Salkinson has made this character the son of Peretz, while in Shakespeare's version the reference is to Petruchio, not his son.

361 This is a gentilic adjective denoting a native of the town of Pirathon; it appears in Judg. 12:13, 15; 2 Sam. 23:30; and 1 Chron. 11:31, 27:14. As in the case of the personal name Peretz (see preceding note), Salkinson undoubtedly selected this name based on its sound correspondence with the original 'Petruchio' (1.5.130). However, it is uncertain why he chose to add the gentilic adjective, which has no basis in the source text.

362 Exod. 21:3.

363 This and the next line form a rhyming couplet, mirroring Shakespeare's 'married/bed' (1.5.133–4).

	I know that the palanquin to my wedding will be my grave.	יָדַעְתִּי כִּי אַפִּרְיוֹן לַחֲתֻנָּתִי, יִהְיֶה לִּי הַקֶּבֶר.	
THE NURSE	That is Ram, only son of Abiram, your greatest enemy.	זֶה רָם בֶּן יָחִיד לַאֲבִירָם רֹאשׁ שֹׂנְאֵיכֶם.	האומנת
JAEL	**From the quarry of an ancient hate a great love has been dug for me**[364, 365]	מִמַּקֶּבֶת שִׂנְאָה נוֹשָׁנָה, אַהֲבָה רַבָּה לִי נֻקָּרָה[364, 365]	יעל
	I saw his face early, and came to know his name late	קִדַּמְתִּי לִרְאוֹת פָּנָיו וְלָדַעַת שְׁמוֹ אֵחַרְתִּי	
	This is a **froward generation**[366] and this is a strange love	זֶה דוֹר תַּהְפֻּכֹת[366] וְזוּ אַהֲבָה זָרָה	
	To a man whom I hate like death, I say 'you are my life'.	לְאִישׁ שְׂנֵאתִי כַּמָּוֶת „חַיַּתִי אַתָּה" אָמַרְתִּי.	
THE NURSE	What is this matter? What is your tongue speaking of?	מָה הַדָּבָר הַזֶּה? מַה־תֶּהְגֶּה לְשׁוֹנֵךְ?	האומנת
JAEL	Two rhyming lines which I learned here	טוּרִים חֲרוּזִים שְׁנַיִם, אֲשֶׁר לָמַדְתִּי בָּזֶה	יעל
	From the mouth of a boy my age at the dance.	מִפִּי בֶן גִּילִי בַּמָּחוֹל.	
	(A voice calls from inside)	(קול קורא מבפנים)	
	Jael!	יָעֵל!	
THE NURSE	Indeed we shall come in the blink of an eye[367] –	הֵן בָּאוֹת אֲנַחְנוּ כְּהֶרֶף עַיִן[367] –	האומנת
	Come, let us depart from this place, for there is no one here. *(Exeunt)*	לְכִי וְנֵלְכָה מִזֶּה כִּי אִישׁ פֹּה אַיִן. (הולכות)	

364 Isa. 51:1 הַבִּיטוּ אֶל־צוּר חֻצַּבְתֶּם וְאֶל־מַקֶּבֶת בּוֹר נֻקַּרְתֶּם 'look to the rock from which you were hewn, and the quarry from which you were dug'.

365 This and the following three lines form an ABAB rhyme, mirroring the original except that the latter is composed of two rhyming couplets: 'hate/late', 'me/enemy' (1.5.137–40).

366 Deut. 32:20.

367 This and the next line form a rhyming couplet, mirroring Shakespeare's 'anon/gone' (1.5.143).

CHORUS OF SINGERS[368]	The first desire has fallen, and is soon to die on its bed[369]	חֵשֶׁק הָרִאשׁוֹן נָפַל וְקָרוֹב לָמוּת עַל מִטָּתוֹ[369]	מקהלת משוררים[368]
	And its eye is watching for desire's son to succeed it.	וְחֵשֶׁק בֶּן חֵשֶׁק לְהוֹרִישׁוֹ עֵינוֹ צוֹפִיָּה.	
	Who said to Ram, who was ill and sickly in his love	מִי מִלֵּל לְרָם, אֲשֶׁר חָלָה וַיֵּאָנֵשׁ בְּאַהֲבָתוֹ	
	That he should arise and shake himself free, **to embrace the bosom of a strange woman.**[370]	כִּי יָקוּם וְיִתְנַעֵר, לְחַבֵּק חֵיק נָכְרִיָּה.[370]	
	Indeed the love of Ram and Jael sprang up overnight[371]	אָמְנָם בִּן־לַיְלָה עָלְתָה אַהֲבַת רָם וְיָעֵל[371]	
	For they were pulled by ropes of magic, **in tumult**[372] **and without rest**[373]	כִּי נִמְשְׁכוּ בְּחַבְלֵי קֶסֶם, **בְּרֶגֶשׁ**[372] **וְאֵין נָחַת**[373]	
	He trembles and complains, how an enemy might be made his wife	הוּא יִרְגַּז וְיִתְאוֹנֵן, אֵיךְ שְׂנוּאָה תִּבָּעֵל	
	And she gathers morsels of love from **the sides of the mouth of the chasm**[374, 375]	וְהִיא תְלַקֵּט פְּתוֹתֵי אֲהָבִים מֵעֶבְרֵי **פִּי־פָחַת.**[374, 375]	
	He cannot approach the house of his enemy Abiel out of fear	אֶל בֵּית אֲבִיעֵל שׂנְאוֹ, לֹא יוּכַל קְרֹב מִפַּחַד	
	So how then can he swear to his daughter that his love is pure and powerful?	וְאֵיפוֹ יִשָּׁבַע לְבִתּוֹ כִּי אַהֲבָתוֹ זַכָּה וַעֲצוּמָה?	

368 In Salkinson's version this speech appears at the end of the First Part, while in the original it typically marks the beginning of Act 2. It is possible that Salkinson was working from an English version that placed it at the end of Act 1, although this is difficult to establish with certainty.

369 This and the following three lines form an ABAB rhyming sequence, mirroring Shakespeare's 'lie/heir/die/fair' (2.0.1–4).

370 Prov. 5:20 וּתְחַבֵּק חֵק נָכְרִיָּה 'and embrace the bosom of a strange woman'.

371 This and the following three lines form an ABAB rhyming sequence, mirroring Shakespeare's 'again/looks/complain/hooks' (2.0.5–8).

372 Ps. 55:15 (55:14 in English Bibles). This phrase is often translated as 'among the crowd', 'in the throng', or 'in company', but Salkinson is using it in the sense of 'tumult' or 'agitation', which is the chief meaning of the root.

373 Prov. 29:9.

374 Jer. 48:28.

375 This and the following three lines form an ABAB rhyming sequence, mirroring Shakespeare's 'access/swear/less/anywhere' (2.0.9–12).

And as for her, her soul like his soul is filled with love and terror alike	וְהִיא נַפְשָׁהּ כְּנַפְשׁוֹ, מְלֵאָה אַהֲבָה וּמָגוֹר יַחַד
And it is beyond the maiden to do anything.	וַיִּפָּלֵא בְּעֵינֵי הַבְּתוּלָה לַעֲשׂוֹת מְאוּמָה.
But love has wings, and the lovers fly upon them.[376]	אַךְ כְּנָפַיִם לָאַהֲבָה וְהַנֶּאֱהָבִים יָעוּפוּ עֲלֵיהֶן.[376]
And **two ends**[377] will meet, if they both have one wind.[378]	וּשְׁתֵּי **קְצָוֹת**[377] תִּפָּגַשְׁנָה, אִם רוּחַ[378] אַחַת לִשְׁתֵּיהֶן.
(Exeunt)	(הולכים)

End of First Part.

תם חלק ראשון.

376 This and the next line form a rhyming couplet, mirroring Shakespeare's 'meet/sweet' (2.0.13–14).
377 Exod. 28:25, 39:18.
378 This has a double sense, as רוּחַ also means 'spirit'.

Second Part | חלק שני

SCENE I	*Open street before Abiel's vineyard, surrounded by a wall*	רחוב פתוח לפני כרם אביעל המוקף חומה	מחזה א'
RAM	How can I return to my way when my soul, my only one, is there?	אֵיךְ אָשׁוּב לְדַרְכִּי וְנַפְשִׁי יְחִידָתִי שָׁמָּה?	רם
	I am a house of clay without a soul or spirit	בֵּית חֹמֶר אָנֹכִי בְּלֹא נֶפֶשׁ וָרוּחַ	
	I seek my soul – *(Ascends the wall and leaps into the vineyard)*	אֲבַקֵּשׁ אֶת נַפְשִׁי – (עולה על החומה ודולג אל הכרם פנימה)	
	(Benaiah and Meraioth)	(בניה ומריות)	
BENAIAH	Where are you, Ram? Where are you, Ram, my brother?[1]	אַיֶּכָּה רָם? אַיֶּכָּה רָם אָחִי?[1]	בניה
MERAIOTH	He is a wise man, for he has gone in secret to his house	אִישׁ נָבוֹן הוּא, כִּי הָלַךְ חֶרֶשׁ לְבֵיתוֹ	מריות
	And lain down upon his bed.	וַיִּשְׁכַּב עַל מִטָּתוֹ.	
BENAIAH	He has ascended the wall and jumped into the vineyard.[2]	הוּא עָלָה עַל הַחוֹמָה וַיְדַלֵּג אֶל הַכֶּרֶם[2] פְּנִימָה	בניה
	Please call to him.	קְרָא נָא לוֹ.	
MERAIOTH	I shall also make him swear that **he is listening to the voice of charmers**[3] –	הִנְנִי גַם לְהַשְׁבִּיעֵהוּ כִּי יִשְׁמַע בְּקוֹל מְלַחֲשִׁים[3] –	מריות
	Ram! Hasty to love! Fool! **The man of the spirit is mad!**[4]	רָם! מְהִיר אַהֲבָה! אֱוִילִי! מְשֻׁגָּע אִישׁ הָרוּחַ![4]	
	Make the sound of your sighing heard to me; or one or two words	הַשְׁמִיעֵנִי קוֹל אֶנְקָתְךָ; אוֹ מִלָּה אַחַת וּשְׁתַּיִם	
	From **the noise of your songs**[5] with which **your insides moan**[6] and it will be enough for me;	מֵהֲמוֹן שִׁירֶיךָ[5] אֲשֶׁר יֶהֱמוּ מֵעֶיךָ[6] וְדַי לִי;	
	Call as was your way previously, 'Oh, **my dove, my undefiled one**!'[7,8]	קְרָא כְּדַרְכְּךָ* מֵאָז „אֲהָהּ יוֹנָתִי תַּמָּתִי"[7,8]	

---

1 Cf. Shakespeare's 'cousin' (2.1.3); see First Part, note 65.
2 Cf. Shakespeare's 'orchard' (2.1.5). Salkinson's substitution is most likely rooted in the fact that vineyards feature more prominently in the Hebrew Bible than orchards.
3 Ps. 58:6 (58:5 in English Bibles) אֲשֶׁר לֹא־יִשְׁמַע לְקוֹל מְלַחֲשִׁים 'so that it does not listen to the voice of charmers'.
4 Hosea 9:7.
5 Ezek. 26:13.
6 Isa. 16:11 עַל־כֵּן מֵעַי לְמוֹאָב כַּכִּנּוֹר יֶהֱמוּ 'therefore my insides moan for Moab like a harp'.
7 Song of Songs 5:2, 6:9.
8 These last two words rhyme in Hebrew, mirroring the English 'love' and 'dove' (2.1.10).

* כְּדַרְכְּךָ

Or call on the name of Ashtoreth,[9] **weary from adultery**[10]	אוֹ קְרָא בְּשֵׁם עַשְׁתֹּרֶת[9] בָּלָה נְאֻפִים[10]
And on the name of the heir to her house, a blind child and an archer	וּבְשֵׁם יוֹרֵשׁ בֵּיתָהּ יֶלֶד עִוֵּר וְרֹבֶה קַשָּׁת
Who shot his flaming arrows[11] into the heart of King So-and-So[12]	אֲשֶׁר יָרָה זִיקָיו[11] בְּלֵב מֶלֶךְ פְּלֹנִי אַלְמֹנִי[12]
Until he fell ill in his love of a poor and needy girl. –	עַד אֲשֶׁר חָלָה בְּאַהֲבָתוֹ אֶת בַּת עָנִי וְאֶבְיוֹן. –
But what has happened to him, that he does not listen to me?	אַךְ מֶה הָיָה לוֹ, כִּי אֵינֶנּוּ שֹׁמֵעַ לִי?
I have called **but no one answers; I have cried out but there is no voice and no one pays attention**[13]	קָרָאתִי וְאֵין עֹנֶה, צָעַקְתִּי וְאֵין קוֹל וְאֵין קָשֶׁב[13]
The young hart[14] is dead; but I shall raise him up with sorcery	עֹפֶר הָאַיָּלִים[14] מֵת הוּא; וַאֲנִי אַעֲלֶנּוּ בִּלְחָשִׁים.
I adjure you by the name of Shoshannah whom you love	הִנְנִי מַשְׁבִּיעֲךָ בְּשֵׁם שׁוֹשַׁנָּה אֲשֶׁר נַפְשְׁךָ אֹהֶבֶת
By the flash of the light of her eyes, by the splendour of her brow and **the grace of her lips**[15, 16]	בִּבְרַק אוֹר עֵינֶיהָ בַּהֲדַר מִצְחָהּ וּבְחֵן שְׂפָתֶיהָ[15, 16]
By the glory of her legs and her thighs, and by the treasure of all her chambers	בְּתִפְאֶרֶת שׁוֹקֶיהָ וִירֵכָהּ וּבְאוֹצַר כָּל חֲדָרֶיהָ

9 Cf. Shakespeare's 'Venus' (2.1.11). Ashtoreth was one of the chief goddesses of the Canaanite pantheon and is associated with love and fertility (Frymer 2007: 581); moreover, she has been linked to Aphrodite in Ancient Near Eastern sources from the first millennium BCE (Ackerman 2009). In the Hebrew Bible the Israelites are condemned on multiple occasions for worshipping Ashtoreth (e.g., Judg. 2:13–14, 10:6–7, 1 Sam. 7:3–4, 12:10). Salkinson was clearly aware of the links between Ashtoreth and the Greek and Roman goddess of love, and thus selected her as a suitable domesticating equivalent.

10 Ezekiel 23:43.

11 Salkinson has omitted Shakespeare's mention of 'Abraham Cupid' (2.1.13). The omission of 'Cupid' is a typical example of his avoidance of Classical mythological figures, and the omission of the biblical Abraham is likely due to the fact that including this reference on its own might have lacked relevance in the context and caused confusion to readers.

12 Cf. Shakespeare's 'King Cophetua' (2.1.14), referring to the legend of a king who falls in love with a beggar. Salkinson most likely made this replacement because his Eastern European Jewish audience would not have been familiar with Cophetua.

13 1 Kings 18:29 וְאֵין־קוֹל וְאֵין־עֹנֶה וְאֵין קָשֶׁב 'but there was no voice, and no one answered, and no one paid attention'.

14 Song of Songs 2:9, 17; 8:14. Salkinson has chosen this as a translation of Shakespeare's 'The ape is dead' (2.1.16), possibly because the word קוֹף 'ape, monkey' is a rare feature of the Hebrew Bible, appearing only twice (1 Kings 10:22 and 2 Chron. 9:21), whereas deer are mentioned more frequently. This substitution changes the sense of the line, as the original 'ape' was meant in the sense of 'fool' (Weis 2012: 182, note 16), whereas Salkinson's version lacks such a nuance.

15 Prov. 22:11 חֵן שְׂפָתָיו 'the grace of his lips'.

16 This and the next line form a rhyming couplet, mirroring Shakespeare's 'thigh/lie' (2.1.19–20).

	By all of these I adjure you to reveal yourself to us at once.	בְּכָל אֵלֶּה אֲנִי מַשְׁבִּיעֲךָ לְהִגָּלוֹת אֵלֵינוּ כְּרֶגַע.	
BENAIAH	With such words you will vex him and arouse his wrath.	בִּדְבָרִים כָּאֵלֶּה תַּרְגִּיזֶנּוּ וְתַעֲלֶה אֶת חֲמָתוֹ.	בניה
MERAIOTH	I shall not arouse his wrath with this. If I had adjured a ghost	לֹא אַעֲלֶה חֲמָתוֹ בָּזֹאת. לוּ הִשְׁבַּעְתִּי אַחַד הָרְפָאִים	מריות
	To enter his beloved's sphere and not move from there	לָבוֹא עַד מַעְגַּל אֲהֻבָתוֹ וּמִשָּׁם לֹא יָמוּשׁ	
	Until with her magic she made it bow before her feet on the ground	עַד אֲשֶׁר בִּקְסָמֶיהָ תַּכְרִיעֵהוּ לְרַגְלֶיהָ אַרְצָה	
	Then would his wrath rise up; but he will be pleased with the whisper of my lips	אָז תַּעֲלֶה חֲמָתוֹ בְּאַפּוֹ; אַךְ לַחַשׁ שְׂפָתַי יִרְצֶה	
	For I have adjured him by the name of his beloved **truly and sincerely**[17]	כִּי אֹתוֹ הִשְׁבַּעְתִּי בְּשֵׁם אֲהֻבָתוֹ בֶּאֱמֶת וּבְתָמִים[17]	
	To rise from the dead.	לַעֲלוֹת מִן הַמֵּתִים.	
BENAIAH	Come, let us go, for he has hidden in the trees of the garden	לְכָה וְנֵלְכָה, כִּי הוּא הִתְחַבֵּא בַּעֲצֵי הַגָּן	בניה
	And **his eye waits for twilight**,[18] keeping company with gloom	וְעֵינוֹ שָׁמְרָה נֶשֶׁף[18] לְהִתְרֹעֵעַ אֶת צַלְמָוֶת	
	His love has no eyes, and therefore over light he chooses darkness.	אַהֲבָתוֹ אֵין לָהּ עֵינַיִם וְלָכֵן מֵאוֹר יִבְחַר חֹשֶׁךְ.	
MERAIOTH	If love has no eyes, how can it send its arrows to the target?[19]	אִם אֵין עֵינַיִם לָאַהֲבָה, אֵיךְ תְּשַׁלַּח חִצֶּיהָ לְמַטָּרָה?[19]	מריות
	And he is sitting under the tree, and his only desire now	וְהוּא יוֹשֵׁב תַּחַת הָעֵץ וְכָל חֶפְצוֹ עַתָּה	
	Is that his beautiful one should become a pomegranate,[20] and he a palm branch[21]	כִּי יָפָתוֹ תִּהְיֶה לְרִמּוֹן[20] וְהוּא לְכַף תָּמָר[21]	

17 Judg. 9:16, 19.

18 Job 24:15 וְעֵין נֹאֵף | שָׁמְרָה נֶשֶׁף 'and the eye of the adulterer waits for twilight'.

19 This and the following line form a rhyming couplet, mirroring the original except that the latter starts one line earlier and is split between Benvolio and Mercutio: 'dark/mark' (2.1.32–3).

20 Cf. Shakespeare's 'medlar' (2.1.34–5), a fruit similar to an apple. The pomegranate is mentioned on numerous occasions in the Hebrew Bible, including in a romantic context in Song of Songs 4:3 and 6:7 (כְּפֶלַח הָרִמּוֹן רַקָּתֵךְ מִבַּעַד לְצַמָּתֵךְ 'like a piece of a pomegranate are your temples behind your locks'), which makes it an appropriate choice for inclusion in Ram's speech.

21 This comparison lacks a direct basis in the original, which does not refer to Romeo at this point, but only to Rosaline: 'And wish his mistress were that kind of fruit/As maids call medlars when they laugh alone' (2.1.35–6). Salkinson may have chosen to insert this reference to palm branch here because its shape evokes the bawdy connotations of the original lines more clearly than 'pomegranate' (see preceding note).

	Or she a flower,[22] and he the bud in the middle.[23]	אוֹ הִיא לְפֶרַח[22] וְהוּא לְכַפְתֹּר בַּתָּוֶךְ.[23]	
	May it be for you Ram as you desire, and may the night be pleasant for you	יְהִי לְךָ רָם כַּאֲשֶׁר חָפַצְתָּ וְיֶעֱרַב לְךָ הַלַּיְלָה	
	As for me, I am going to my bed; I shall not lodge on the cold street.	וַאֲנִי הוֹלֵךְ לְמִשְׁכָּבִי וְלֹא אָלִין בָּרְחוֹב בַּקָּרָה.	
	Arise, Benaiah, let us go.	קוּמָה בְנָיָה וְנֵלֵכָה.	
BENAIAH	I am going with you;	הִנְנִי הוֹלֵךְ אִתְּךָ;	בניה
	For it is pointless to seek a man who seeks to sit in secrecy.	כִּי חִנָּם יְבַקֵּשׁ אִישׁ, הַמְבַקֵּשׁ בְּמִסְתָּר שָׁבֶת.	
	(Exeunt)	(הולכים)	
SCENE 2	*Abiel's vineyard*	כרם אביעל	מחזה ב'
RAM	A man who has not known affliction laughs at a sore or a scar	אִישׁ לֹא יָדַע נֶגַע, יִשְׂחַק לְבַהֶרֶת וְצָרֶבֶת.	רם
	(Jael looks down from the window)	(יעל נשקפה בעד החלון)	
	But what is that light there that spills out of the window there?	אַךְ מֶה הָאוֹר הַהוּא שָׁם בְּעַד הַחַלּוֹן יִבָּקֵעַ?	
	The window is the face of the east, and Jael is the sun shining there	הַחַלּוֹן הוּא פְּנֵי הַמִּזְרָח וְיָעֵל שָׁם שֶׁמֶשׁ זֹרַחַת	
	Arise, my light, my sun! And the moon will not shine its light	קוּמִי אוֹרִי שִׁמְשִׁי! וְהַלְּבָנָה לֹא תַגִּיהַּ אוֹרָהּ	
	It is brokenhearted from its jealousy of your beauty, **and its face grows pale**[24]	מִקִּנְאָתָהּ בְּיָפְיֵךְ נְכֵאָה הִיא וּפָנֶיהָ יֶחֱוָרוּ[24]	
	For in its heart it says that you are its maidservant yet more beautiful than it is.	כִּי בְלִבָּהּ תֹּאמַר שִׁפְחָתָהּ אַתְּ וְיָפָה מִמֶּנָּה.	
	Do not be a maidservant to such a jealous mistress as it.	אַל לָךְ הֱיוֹת שִׁפְחָה לְבַעֲלַת קִנְאָה כָּמוֹהָ.	
	For out of jealousy it is full of greenish sores	כִּי אַךְ מִקִּנְאָה הִיא מְלֵאָה בֶּהָרוֹת יְרַקְרַקּוֹת	

22 This is Salkinson's equivalent of Shakespeare's 'open-arse' (2.1.38), a slang equivalent of 'medlar' (Crystal and Crystal 2002: 305). The word 'flower' in Hebrew does not have the explicit connotations of 'open-arse', but taken together with 'bud' (see next note) this translation may be an attempt to suggest the lewd associations of the original.

23 This is Salkinson's equivalent of Shakespeare's 'poperin pear' (2.1.38). As in the case of 'flower' discussed in the preceding note, 'bud' does not constitute the same type of obvious ribald pun as 'poperin pear', but taken together 'flower' and 'bud' are likely to have been intended to evoke similar connotations to the original.

24 Isa. 29:22 וְלֹא עַתָּה פָּנָיו יֶחֱוָרוּ 'nor will his face now grow pale'.

But not so you, for you are entirely beautiful and pure –	לֹא כֵן אַתְּ, כִּי כֻלָּךְ יָפָה וּבָרָה –
This is **my love**![25] This is the one **whom my soul loves**![26]	זוּ הִיא רַעְיָתִי[25]! זוּ הִיא שֶׁאָהֲבָה נַפְשִׁי![26]
If only she would say, '**My beloved is mine and I am his**'.[27]	מִי יִתֵּן וְגַם הִיא תֹאמַר, דּוֹדִי לִי וַאֲנִי לוֹ.[27]
Her lips move as she speaks, but her voice cannot be heard[28]	שְׂפָתֶיהָ נָעוֹת כִּמְדַבֶּרֶת אַךְ קוֹלָהּ לֹא יִשָּׁמֵעַ[28]
She bats her eyelids;[29] I shall respond to her;	עַפְעַפֶּיהָ הִיא מְשַׂקֶּרֶת,[29] הִנְנִי לַהֲשִׁיבָהּ דָּבָר;
Indeed her words are not for me, so how can I approach like one **fierce of countenance**?[30, 31]	אָכֵן מִלֶּיהָ לֹא אֵלַי, וְאֵיךְ אָבוֹא כְּעַז פָּנִים?[30, 31]
This is nothing other than two twinkling stars	אֵין זֹאת כִּי אִם שְׁנֵי כוֹכָבִים נֹצְצִים
That, having some business,[32] have asked her to stand in their place[33]	אֲשֶׁר שִׂיחַ וָשִׂיג לָמוֹ,[32] בִּקְשׁוּהָ לַעֲמֹד בִּמְקוֹמָם[33]
And to shine with her two eyes, until they return to their course.	וּלְהָאִיר בִּשְׁתֵּי עֵינֶיהָ, עַד אֲשֶׁר יָשׁוּבוּ לִמְסִלּוֹתָם.
How comely is this substitution! Her eyes shine light in the firmament	מַה־נָּאוָה הַתְּמוּרָה הַזֹּאת! עֵינֶיהָ מְאִירוֹת בָּרָקִיעַ
And the stars are fixed in her head; they are ashamed of the light of her face	וְהַכּוֹכָבִים תְּקוּעִים בְּרֹאשָׁהּ; הֵם יֵבוֹשׁוּ מֵאוֹר פָּנֶיהָ

---

25 Song of Songs 1:9, 15, 2:2, 10, 13, 4:1, 7, 5:2, 6:4.

26 Song of Songs 1:7, 3:1, 2, 3.

27 Song of Songs 6:3 אֲנִי לְדוֹדִי וְדוֹדִי לִי 'I am my beloved's and he is mine'.

28 1 Sam. 1:13 וְחַנָּה הִיא מְדַבֶּרֶת עַל־לִבָּהּ רַק שְׂפָתֶיהָ נָּעוֹת וְקוֹלָהּ לֹא יִשָּׁמֵעַ 'now Hannah was speaking in her heart; her lips moved, but her voice could not be heard'. Cf. Shakespeare's 'She speaks, yet she says nothing' (2.2.12). Salkinson's rendition serves to draw a parallel between Jael and the biblical heroine Hannah whose silent entreaty is renowned in the rabbinic tradition as the model of Jewish prayer (see Kadari 2009).

29 Isa. 3:16 וַתֵּלַכְנָה נטוות נְטוּיוֹת גָּרוֹן וּמְשַׂקְּרוֹת עֵינָיִם 'and they walk with necks stretched forth and bat their eyes'.

30 Deut. 28:50; Dan. 8:23.

31 This and the next line form a rhyming couplet, mirroring Shakespeare's 'bright/night' (2.2.21–2). Note that the Hebrew and English rhyming couplets do not correspond in terms of meaning; the actual Hebrew translation of the English rhyming couplet is several lines further on and does not rhyme.

32 1 Kings 18:27 כִּי שִׂיחַ וְכִי־שִׂיג לוֹ 'indeed he has some business'.

33 This and the next line form a rhyming couplet, mirroring Shakespeare's 'hand/hand' (2.2.23–4). As in the case of the rhyme discussed in note 31, the Hebrew and English rhyming couplets do not correspond in terms of meaning; the actual Hebrew translation of the English rhyming couplet is several lines further on and does not rhyme. (Salkinson does not typically recognize words rhyming with themselves, such as 'hand/hand', as rhymes in his own text.)

	As a torch is ashamed of the daylight, and from her eyes in the heights of the heavens	כְּלַפִּיד יֵבוֹשׁ מֵאוֹר יוֹם, וּמֵעֵינֶיהָ בִּרוּם שְׁחָקִים	
	Radiance and light flow until **the birds of the heavens**	יִזַּל נֹגַהּ וּנְהָרָה עַד אֲשֶׁר **עוֹף הַשָּׁמַיִם**	
	Sing among the branches,[34] for the **night shines like the day.**[35]	**מִבֵּן עֳפָאִים יִתְּנוּ קוֹל,**[34] **כִּי הַלַּיְלָה כַּיּוֹם יָאִיר.**[35]	
	And now she has leaned her cheek on the palm of her hand	וְעַתָּה סָמְכָה אֶת לֶחֱיָהּ עַל כַּף יָדָהּ	
	If only I could become **the skins of kid goats**[36]	לוּ הָיִיתִי אֲנִי **לְעֹרֹת גְּדָיֵי הָעִזִּים**[36]	
	And gloves upon her hand, and her cheek would lean upon me.	וּלְבָתֵּי כַף עַל יָדֶיהָ. וְעָלַי תִּסְמֹךְ לֶחֱיָהּ.	
JAEL	**Woe is me!**[37]	**אַלְלַי לִי!**[37]	יעל
RAM	She has begun to speak.	הִיא פָּתְחָה לְדַבֵּר.	רם
	Continue, angel of God! Continue, speak, speak	הוֹסִיפִי, מַלְאַךְ אֱלֹהִים! הוֹסִיפִי דַּבְּרִי דַּבֵּרִי	
	For you have been revealed to me tonight in all majesty and glory.	כִּי נִגְלֵית אֵלַי הַלַּיְלָה בְּכָל הוֹד וְתִפְאָרֶת.	
	Like a winged messenger on high **riding on a swift cloud**[38]	כְּצִיר בַּעַל כְּנָפַיִם מִמָּרוֹם **רֹכֵב עַל עָב קַל**[38]	
	He flies and breaks through the heavens before the eyes of **mortals**[39]	יָעוּף יַבְקִיעַ שְׁחָקִים לְעֵינֵי **בְּנֵי תְמוּתָה**[39]	
	Who watch and look at him and are amazed at the sight of him	אֲשֶׁר יֶחֱזוּ יַבִּיטוּ בוֹ וְעַל מַרְאֵהוּ יִשְׁתָּאוּ	
	So you stand above me and I raise my eyes to you.	כֵּן תַּעַמְדִי מִמַּעַל לִי וְאֵלַיִךְ עֵינַי נָשָׂאתִי.	
JAEL	Oh, son of Abiram! Why are you called Ram?	הוֹי בֶּן אֲבִירָם! לָמָּה קָרְאוּ לְךָ רָם?	יעל
	Say to your father, **'I have never seen you'**[40] and you will no longer be called Ram	אֱמֹר לְאָבִיךָ **לֹא רְאִיתִיךָ**[40] וְלֹא רָם יֵאָמֵר עוֹד שְׁמֶךָ	
	And if not, swear to me with an oath of love	וְאִם אַיִן, הִשָּׁבְעָה לִי בִּשְׁבוּעַת הָאַהֲבָה	

---

34 Ps. 104:12 עֲלֵיהֶם עוֹף־הַשָּׁמַיִם יִשְׁכּוֹן מִבֵּין עֳפָאיִם יִתְּנוּ־קוֹל 'upon them the birds of the heavens dwell; they sing among the branches'.

35 Ps. 139:12.

36 Gen. 27:16.

37 Mic. 7:1; Job 10:15.

38 Isa. 19:1.

39 Ps. 79:11, 102:21 (102:20 in English Bibles).

40 Job 8:18 (in the context of disowning).

	And I shall not be the daughter of Abiel; there will be no mention of him in my name.[41]	וַאֲנִי בַּת אֲבִיעֵל לֹא אֶהְיֶה, אֵין זֵכֶר לוֹ בִּשְׁמִי.[41]	
RAM *(To himself)*	Shall I continue to listen, or respond to her now?	הַאוֹסִיף לִשְׁמֹעַ, אוֹ אָשֵׁב לָהּ עָתָּה?	רם (אל עצמו)
JAEL	Only your name **stands as an adversary against me on the way**[42]	רַק שִׁמְךָ הוּא הַנִּצָּב לְשָׂטָן לִי בַּדָּרֶךְ[42]	יעל
	If you were not called an Abiramite, I would honour you as you are honoured.	לוּ אֲבִירָמִי לֹא נִקְרֵאתָ, אוֹקִירְךָ כַּאֲשֶׁר יָקַרְתָּ.	
	What is the name Abiram? It is nor hand nor foot	מַה שֵּׁם אֲבִירָם? לֹא יָד וְלֹא רֶגֶל הוּא	
	Nor arm nor face, nor any other part	לֹא זְרוֹעַ וְלֹא פָּנִים וְלֹא חֵלֶק אַחֵר	
	From among the parts of man; choose a new name for yourself	מֵחֶלְקֵי נֶפֶשׁ הָאָדָם; בְּחַר לְךָ שֵׁם חָדָשׁ	
	For what is a name? If you change the name of the rose	כִּי מָה הוּא הַשֵּׁם? אִם תְּשַׁנֶּה שֵׁם הַשּׁוֹשַׁנָּה	
	It will not change its appearance and its scent will be as pleasant as formerly	הִיא לֹא תְשַׁנֶּה אֶת פָּנֶיהָ וְרֵיחָהּ יֶעֱרַב כְּבַתְּחִלָּה	
	And so Ram's sense will remain in him, if he is no longer called Ram	וְכֵן טַעַם רָם יַעֲמָד בּוֹ, אִם רָם לֹא עוֹד יִקָּרֵא	
	And he will not exchange his worth when he exchanges his name	וְחִין עֶרְכּוֹ לֹא יָמֵר בְּהָמִיר אֶת שְׁמוֹ	
	Erase your name, Ram, and instead of this name	מְחֵה רָם אֶת שִׁמְךָ וְתַחַת הַשֵּׁם הַזֶּה	
	Which is not **your flesh and blood**,[43] I shall be **your flesh and blood**.[44]	אֲשֶׁר אֵינֶנּוּ עַצְמְךָ וּבְשָׂרְךָ,[43] עַצְמְךָ וּבְשָׂרְךָ[44] אֶהְיֶה אָנִי.	
RAM	I take you today at your word	לְקַחְתִּיךְ הַיּוֹם בִּדְבָרֵךְ	רם
	You are mine and I am yours, and I make your covenant[45] with a new name	אַתְּ לִי וַאֲנִי לָךְ וּבְשֵׁם חָדָשׁ כָּרַתִּי בְּרִיתֵךְ[45]	

41 Cf. Shakespeare's 'And I'll no longer be a Capulet' (2.2.36). Salkinson's replacement is appropriate for his translation given that the Hebrew version of Capulet, Abiel, means 'Jael's father'.

42 Num 22:22 וַיִּתְיַצֵּב מַלְאַךְ יְהוָה בַּדֶּרֶךְ לְשָׂטָן לוֹ 'and the angel of the Lord stood on the way as an adversary against him'.

43 2 Sam. 5:11; 1 Chron. 11:1.

44 2 Sam. 5:11; 1 Chron. 11:1.

45 Cf. Shakespeare's 'Call me but love and I'll be new baptized' (2.2.50). The covenant can be regarded as a fitting Jewish dynamic equivalent of Christian baptism because it is the model used to describe the relationship between God and Israel. This covenantal model is mentioned on numerous occasions throughout biblical, rabbinic, and later Hebrew literature (Weinfeld 2007).

	And the name Ram will not be mentioned, will not be heard from my mouth.	וְשֵׁם רָם לֹא יִזָּכֵר, לֹא יִשָּׁמַע עַל פִּי.	
JAEL	But who and what are you, that you have come **in the middle of the night**[46]	אַךְ מִי וּמָה אַתָּה, כִּי בָאתָ בְּאִישׁוֹן לַיְלָה[46]	יעל
	To set a snare for me and enter into my confidence?	לְהִתְנַקֵּשׁ בִּי וְלָבוֹא בְּסוֹדִי?	
RAM	I am a nameless son	בֵּן בְּלִי שֵׁם אָנִי	רם
	For my name is scorned in my eyes just as it is despised in your eyes[47]	כִּי שְׁמִי נִבְזֶה בְּעֵינַי כַּאֲשֶׁר נִמְאָס הוּא בְּעֵינַיִךְ[47]	
	If it were written in ink, I would erase it from the book.	לוּ הָיָה כָתוּב בִּדְיוֹ מָחִיתִי אוֹתוֹ מִן הַסֵּפֶר.	
JAEL	My ear has not yet heard a hundred words from your mouth	מֵאָה מִלִּין עוֹד לֹא שָׁמְעָה אָזְנִי מִפִּיךָ	יעל
	But I know the voice; why, you are Ram son of Abiram!	אַךְ יָדַעְתִּי אֶת הַקּוֹל הֲלֹא רָם בֶּן אֲבִירָם אָתָּה!	
RAM	Who is Ram and who is Abiram? Why, you hate them both.	מִי רָם וּמִי אֲבִירָם? הֲלֹא שָׂנֵאת אֶת שְׁנֵיהֶם.	רם
JAEL	But tell me how you have come and why you have come here?	אַךְ הַגֵּד אֵיךְ בָּאתָ וְלָמָּה בָאתָ פֹּה?	יעל
	Indeed, the wall is high; who can ascend it	הֵן הַחוֹמָה רָמָה מִי יוּכַל לַעֲלוֹת עָלֶיהָ	
	And death lies in wait for you in the vineyard; if the members of my household find you they will kill you.	וְהַמָּוֶת אֹרֵב לְךָ בַּכֶּרֶם; אִם יִמְצָאוּךָ בְּנֵי בֵיתִי וַהֲרָגוּךָ.	
RAM	Wings of love have carried me, and have brought me up over the wall	כַּנְפֵי אַהֲבָה נְשָׂאוּנִי וְהֶעֱלוּנִי עַל הַחוֹמָה	רם
	For wall and fence cannot stop love.	כִּי חוֹמָה וָגֶדֶר, לֹא יַעַצְרוּן אֶת הָאַהֲבָה.	
	Love has great power and can do anything	הָאַהֲבָה כֹּחָהּ רַב לָהּ וְיָדָהּ כֹּל תּוּכָל	
	And therefore all of my enemies are not a terror to me.[48]	וְלָכֵן כָּל שֹׂנְאֵי נַפְשִׁי אֵינָם לִי לִמְחִתָּה.[48]	
JAEL	If they see you, you will be killed at once.	אִם הֵם יִרְאוּךָ כְּרֶגַע אַתָּה מוּמָת.	יעל
RAM	I fear one of your eyes, but not twenty swords of my enemies	מֵאַחַת מֵעֵינַיִךְ אֵחַתָּה וְלֹא מֵעֶשְׂרִים חַרְבוֹת שֹׂנְאָי	רם

46 Prov. 7:9.
47 Salkinson has omitted Shakespeare's 'dear saint' (2.2.55) from this line.
48 Salkinson has not reproduced the rhyme 'me/thee' between this and the next line in the source text (2.2.69–70).

	Set your eye favourably upon me, and their hatred will be in my eyes like straw to a stone.	שִׂימִי עֵינֵךְ עָלַי* לְטוֹבָה וְשִׂנְאָתָם לְעֵינַי כְּקַשׁ לְאָבֶן.	
JAEL	Nevertheless I fear for your life, lest they see you here.	בְּכָל זֹאת יָרֵאתִי לְנַפְשְׁךָ, פֶּן יִרְאוּךָ הֲלֹם.	יעל
RAM	The night is a hiding place for me; in its wings it hides me from their eyes	הַלַּיְלָה לְסֵתֶר לִי בִּכְנָפָיו יַסְתִּירֵנִי מֵעֵינֵיהֶם	רם
	If only you love me, I shall not fear them finding me	אִם אַךְ אַתְּ אֲהַבְתִּנִי, לֹא אִירָא כִּי יִמְצָאֻנְנִי	
	It would be better for me to fall victim to the edge of the sword of their hatred	טוֹב לִי לִנְפֹּל חָלָל לְפִי חֶרֶב שִׂנְאָתָם	
	Than to live many long days without **the beloved of my soul.**[49]	מֵהַאֲרִיךְ יָמִים רַבִּים וִידִידוּת נַפְשִׁי[49] אֶחְסָר.	
JAEL	Who showed you this place that you have found?	מִי הֶרְאָה לְךָ הַמָּקוֹם הַזֶּה אֲשֶׁר מָצָאתָ?	יעל
RAM	The love of my heart guided me to spy out and search for your dwelling place	אַהֲבַת לִבִּי הִטַּתְנִי לָתוּר וְלִדְרֹשׁ לְשִׁכְנֵךְ	רם
	It gave me counsel, and I paid heed and found it.	הִיא נָתְנָה לִי עֵצָה וַאֲנִי נָתַתִּי עֵינַי וָאֶמְצָא.	
	For if you lived in distant lands by the last sea	כִּי אִם שָׁכַנְתְּ בַּמֶּרְחַקִּים לְחוֹף הַיָּם הָאַחֲרוֹן	
	I would go to sea in a ship, even though I am no sailor or captain	אָז יָרַדְתִּי הַיָּם בָּאֳנִיָּה, אַף כִּי מַלָּח וְחֹבֵל אֵינֶנִּי	
	And I would risk my life[50] to find so great a treasure as you.	וָאַשְׁלִיךְ נַפְשִׁי מִנֶּגֶד[50] לִמְצוֹא אוֹצָר רָב כָּמוֹךְ.	
JAEL	Why, I know that the night is like a veil upon my face	הֲלֹא יָדַעְתִּי כִּי הַלַּיְלָה כַּצָּעִיף עַל פָּנַי	יעל
	For were it not so, my cheeks would redden from shame	כִּי לוּלֵי כֵן אָדְמוּ לְחָיַי מִבּוּשָׁה	
	Because of everything that I have declared to you from my mouth here tonight.	עַל כָּל אֲשֶׁר הִשְׁמַעְתִּיךָ מִפִּי בָּזֶה הַלַּיְלָה.	
	If only I had spoken to you **one way with the mouth and one way with the heart;**[51]	לוּ דִבַּרְתִּי אֵלֶיךָ אַחַת בְּפֶה וְאַחַת בְּלֵב;[51]	

49 Jer. 12:7.

50 Judg. 9:17 וַיַּשְׁלֵךְ אֶת־נַפְשׁוֹ מִנֶּגֶד 'and he risked his life'.

51 This appears in various locations in medieval Hebrew literature; for example, Rashi to Gen. 37:4.

* עָלַי

If only I could now deny everything which I have declared to you here –	לוּ יָכֹלְתִּי לְכַחֵשׁ עַתָּה כֹּל אֲשֶׁר הִשְׁמַעְתִּיךָ בָּזֶה –
But what does a maiden like me have to do with **the way of all the earth**![52] –	אַךְ מַה לְנַעֲרָה כָּמֹנִי וּלְדֶרֶךְ כָּל הָאָרֶץ![52] –
Do you really love me? I know that you will say 'yes'	הַאַתָּה בֶּאֱמֶת אֲהַבְתַּנִי? יָדַעְתִּי כִּי תֹאמַר „הֵן"
And I shall believe your words; therefore, do not swear to me	וַאֲנִי אַאֲמִין בִּדְבָרֶיךָ אָכֵן אַל תִּשָּׁבַע לִי
Lest you give me false hope, for I have heard people say	פֶּן תַּשְׁלֶה אֹתִי, כִּי שָׁמַעְתִּי אֹמְרִים
The heavenly host[53] laughs at the breach of love's covenant.	צְבָא הַמָּרוֹם[53] יִשְׂחֲקוּ לִתְנוּאַת בְּרִית אֲהָבִים.
Please, dear Ram, if your love is sincere	נָא רָם הַיָּקָר, אִם אַהֲבָתְךָ תְּמִימָה
Tell me so with faithful, **pure speech**.[54]	הַגֵּד לִי כֵּן בְּשָׂפָה בְרוּרָה[54] נֶאֱמָנָה.
And if you say in your heart that I have been captured too easily,	וְכִי תֹאמַר בִּלְבָבְךָ כִּי עַל נְקַלָּה נִשְׁבֵּיתִי
I shall also do this: I shall put on **an angry countenance**[55]	גַּם אֲנִי אֶעֱשֶׂה זֹאת: אֶלְבַּשׁ פָּנִים נִזְעָמִים[55]
I shall choose the way of stubbornness and **go contrarily against you**[56]	אֶבְחַר בְּדֶרֶךְ עִקְּשׁוּת וְהָלַכְתִּי עִמְּךָ בְּקֶרִי[56]
Then you will fall to my feet and beseech me with your love.	אָז תִּפֹּל לְרַגְלַי וְתִתְחַנֵּן אֵלַי בְּאַהֲבָתֶךָ.
Indeed it is true, son of Abiram, that I love you very much	הֵן אֱמֶת בֶּן אֲבִירָם, כִּי אֶרְחָמְךָ עַד מְאֹד
And therefore you may rebuke, saying that I am light[57]	וְלָכֵן תּוּכַל לְהוֹכִיחַ לֵאמֹר כִּי קַלָּה[57] אָנִי

52 Gen. 19:31; Josh. 23:14; 1 Kings 2:2.

53 This replaces Shakespeare's 'Jove' (2.2.93). Salkinson has preserved the sense of the original in that Jove or Jupiter, the Greco-Roman sky god, can be equated with the 'heavenly host', a term for God's army of angels mentioned in Isa. 24:21 and on numerous occasions in rabbinic, medieval, and early modern Hebrew literature.

54 Zeph. 3:9.

55 Prov. 25:23.

56 Lev. 26:27 וַהֲלַכְתֶּם עִמִּי בְּקֶרִי 'and you go contrarily against Me'.

57 This corresponds to Shakespeare's 'light' (2.2.99), used in the sense of 'wanton' (Weis 2012: 193, note 99). While the Hebrew adjective is not typically used in this particular sense, it can convey a variety of closely related negative meanings including 'trifling', 'insubstantial', etc.

	But know, my friend, that you will find my heart more faithful before you	אַךְ דַּע לְךָ יְדִידִי, כִּי תִמְצָא לְבָבִי נֶאֱמָן לְפָנֶיךָ	
	Than the heart of all the women who know how to act like a stranger in the sight of the eye.	מִלֵּב כָּל הַנָּשִׁים הַיֹּדְעוֹת לְהִתְנַכֵּר לְמַרְאֵה עָיִן.	
	But I admit that you would have found me acting like a stranger as well	וַאֲנִי אוֹדֶה, כִּי מִתְנַכֵּרָה מְצָאתַנִי גַּם אָנִי	
	Had you not first heard my words from the bottom of my heart	לוּלֵא קִדַּמְתָּ לְהַקְשִׁיב דְּבָרַי מִמְּקוֹר לְבָבִי	
	Before it became known to me that you were listening in secret.	בְּטֶרֶם נוֹדַע לִי כִּי מַקְשִׁיב אַתָּה בַּסָּתֶר.	
	But since you came into my confidence **in the middle of the night and the darkness**[58]	וְאַחֲרֵי אֲשֶׁר בָּאתָ בְּסוֹדִי **בְּאִישׁוֹן לַיְלָה וַאֲפֵלָה**[58]	
	Please do not say that my love is hasty and light.[59]	אַל נָא תֹאמַר כִּי אַהֲבָתִי מְבֹהֶלֶת וְקַלָּה.[59]	
RAM	Indeed I swear my lady, on **the moon going in brightness**[60] there	הֵן נִשְׁבַּע אֲנִי גְּבִרְתִּי, **בַּיָּרֵחַ** שָׁם **יָקָר הוֹלֵךְ**[60]	רם
	From the brightness of whose presence[61] the tops of the trees appear white as silver –	**אֲשֶׁר מִנֹּגַהּ נֶגְדּוֹ**[61] יַלְבִּינוּ רָאשֵׁי הָעֵצִים כַּכָּסֶף –	
JAEL	Please do not swear on the moon, on the moon which shifts	אַל נָא תִשָּׁבַע בַּיָּרֵחַ, בַּיָּרֵחַ אֲשֶׁר חֲלִיפוֹת לוֹ	יעל
	And which changes its face from time to time in its cycle	וַאֲשֶׁר יְשַׁנֶּה פָּנָיו מֵעֵת אֶל עֵת בִּתְקוּפָתוֹ	
	Lest your love also change its face as it does.	פֶּן אַהֲבָתְךָ תְּשַׁנֶּה פָּנֶיהָ גַּם הִיא כָּמוֹהוּ.	
RAM	So what shall I swear on?	וּבַמֶּה אִשָּׁבֵעַ?	רם
JAEL	Do not swear on anything	אַל תִּשָּׁבַע בִּמְאוּמָה	יעל
	Indeed if you desire, swear to me on yourself	אָכֵן אִם חָפַצְתָּ, הִשָּׁבְעָה לִי בְּנַפְשֶׁךָ	
	Which I honour like God,[62] and I shall trust in your words.	אֲשֶׁר אֲכַבְּדֶנָּה כֵּאלֹהִים,[62] וַאֲנִי בִּדְבָרֶיךָ אֶבְטָח.	
RAM	On my life, which is bound to your life –	חֵי נַפְשִׁי הַקְּשׁוּרָה בְּנַפְשֶׁךָ –	רם

58 Prov. 7:9.

59 See note 57.

60 Job 31:26 וְיָרֵחַ יָקָר הֹלֵךְ 'and the moon going in brightness'.

61 2 Sam. 22:13; Ps. 18:13 (18:12 in English Bibles).

62 Cf. Shakespeare's 'the god of my idolatry' (2.2.114). Salkinson may have simplified the text in this way because the notion of Jael honouring Ram like God would have sufficed to convey the image of idolatry to his readers without the need for further detail.

JAEL	Desist, do not bring forth an oath from your mouth –	הֶרֶף, אַל תּוֹצִיא שְׁבוּעָה מִפִּיךָ –	יעל
	Although I rejoice over you, I do not rejoice over our covenant	אַף כִּי שַׂשְׂתִּי עָלֶיךָ, לֹא אָשִׂישׂ עַל בְּרִיתֵנוּ	
	Which we have made tonight, for it was made in haste	אֲשֶׁר עָשִׂינוּ הַלַּיְלָה כִּי נֶעֶשְׂתָה בְּחִפָּזוֹן	
	Without steady counsel, and it is as hasty as lightning	בְּלִי עֵצָה נְכוֹנָה וּמְבֹהֶלֶת הִיא כַּבָּרָק	
	Which flashes for a moment and is gone before the one who has seen it can say	אֲשֶׁר רֶגַע יִבְרֹק וְאֵינֶנּוּ טֶרֶם יַגִּיד הָרֹאֶה	
	'My eyes have seen light' – go in peace, my friend,	„עֵינַי רָאוּ אוֹר" – לֵךְ לְךָ לְשָׁלוֹם יְדִידִי	
	And **I shall watch and hope**[63] that **you will return at this time next year**[64]	**וַאֲנִי אֲצַפֶּה אוֹחִילָה**[63] **כִּי תָשׁוּב כָּעֵת חַיָּה**[64]	
	And the blossom of our love **in the clear heat**[65] becomes **a ripening fruit**.[66]	וְנֵץ אַהֲבָתֵנוּ **בְּחֹם צַח**[65] יִהְיֶה **בֹסֶר גֹּמֵל**.[66]	
	Go, restore your soul with sleep after the toil which you have done[67]	לֵךְ הָשֵׁב נַפְשְׁךָ בַּשֵּׁנָה אַחֲרֵי הֶעָמָל עָמַלְתָּ[67]	
	Just as you have restored my soul and reserved some of your spirit for me.	כַּאֲשֶׁר הֵשַׁבְתָּ נַפְשִׁי וּמֵרוּחֲךָ עָלַי אָצַלְתָּ.	
RAM	Would you leave me now, for naught, without recompense?	הַאִם תַּעַזְבִינִי עַתָּה, חִנָּם אֵין גְּמוּל?	רם
JAEL	What power do I have to recompense you tonight?	מַה־יֵּשׁ בְּיָדִי לִגְמֹל עִמְּךָ הַלַּיְלָה?	יעל
RAM	The faithful oath of your covenant in exchange for my oath.	שְׁבוּעַת בְּרִיתֵךְ הַנֶּאֱמָנָה תְּמוּרַת שְׁבוּעָתִי.	רם
JAEL	I raised my hand in an oath before you asked it of me	הֲרִימוֹתִי יָדִי בִּשְׁבוּעָה טֶרֶם שָׁאַלְתָּ מִמֶּנִּי	יעל
	But I wish it had not come out of my mouth until now.	אַךְ מִי יִתֵּן וְלֹא יָצְאָה מִפִּי עַד כֹּה.	
RAM	Do you regret that it came out of your mouth? Please tell me why.	הֲנִחַמְתְּ כִּי יָצְאָה מִפִּיךְ? הַגִּידִי נָא מַדּוּעַ.	רם

63 Mic. 7:7 וַאֲנִי֙ בַּיהוָ֣ה אֲצַפֶּ֔ה אוֹחִ֖ילָה לֵאלֹהֵ֣י יִשְׁעִ֑י 'and I shall watch for the Lord; I shall wait for the God of my salvation'.

64 Gen. 18:10 שׁ֣וֹב אָשׁ֤וּב אֵלֶ֙יךָ֙ כָּעֵ֣ת חַיָּ֔ה 'I shall indeed return to you at this time next year'.

65 Isa. 18:4 כְּחֹ֥ם צַח֙ 'in the clear heat'.

66 Isa. 18:5.

67 This and the next line form a rhyming couplet, mirroring Shakespeare's 'rest/breast' (2.2.123–4).

JAEL	Because I desire to make the oath again with **a willing spirit**[68]	יַעַן חָפַצְתִּי לְהוֹצִיא הַשְּׁבוּעָה עוֹד בְּרוּחַ נְדִיבָה[68]	יעל
	For with everything that I have brought forth there still remains much in me[69]	כִּי בְּכָל אֲשֶׁר הוֹצֵאתִי עוֹד נִשְׁאַר רַב עִמָּדִי[69]	
	My willingness is broader than the sea,[70] and my love is deeper than the watery abyss	רְחָבָה נִדְבָתִי מִנִּי יָם[70] וְאַהֲבָתִי מִתְּהוֹם עֲמֻקָּה	
	And the more I continue to bring it forth, **the more it multiplies and spreads**[71] within me.[72]	וְכַאֲשֶׁר אוֹסִיף לְהוֹצִיאָהּ, כֵּן תִּרְבֶּה וְתִפְרֹץ[71] בְּקִרְבִּי.[72]	
	(The nurse calls from within)	(האומנת קוראת מלפנים)	
	I hear a voice from within; go in peace, my beloved –	קוֹל אֲנִי שֹׁמַעַת מִלִּפְנִים; לֵךְ לְשָׁלוֹם יְדִיד נַפְשִׁי –	
	I am coming, Nurse – be sincere, son of Abiram!	הִנְנִי בָּאָה אֹמֶנֶת – הֱיֵה תָמִים בֶּן אֲבִירָם!	
	But stay a little while yet, for I shall come here again.	אַךְ עֲמֹד עוֹד מְעַט, כִּי עוֹד אָבוֹא הֵנָּה.	
	(She exits from the window)	(היא הולכת מעל החלון)	
RAM	Oh, **twilight that I have longed for**,[73] **night of vigil**![74] I fear greatly	הֶאָח נֶשֶׁף חִשְׁקִי,[73] לֵיל שִׁמֻּרִים![74] יָרֵאתִי מְאֹד	רם
	That it is a dream which I see in this vision of the night	כִּי חֲלוֹם אֲנִי רֹאֶה בְּחֶזְיוֹן הַלַּיְלָה הַזֶּה	
	The vision is too agreeable and pleasant to be so while waking.	נֶחְמָד וְנָעִים הַמַּחֲזֶה מֵהֱיוֹת כֵּן בְּהָקִיץ.	
	(Jael re-enters)	(יעל שבה)	
JAEL	There is yet one word to tell you; afterwards go in peace.	עוֹד דָּבָר אֶחָד לְהַגִּידְךָ, אַחַר תֵּלֵךְ לְשָׁלוֹם.	יעל
	If your love is pure and you desire to wed me,	אִם אַהֲבָתְךָ זַכָּה וְלָקַחַת אֹתִי חָפַצְתָּ.	
	Set the place and the day for our wedding	הַגְבֵּל אֶת הַמָּקוֹם וְאֶת הַיּוֹם לַחֲתֻנָּתֵנוּ	

68 Ps. 51:14 (51:12 in English Bibles).

69 This rhymes with the last word two lines beneath (which itself forms a rhyming couplet with the line following it; see note 72). This may be an attempt to replicate in some measure Shakespeare's rhyming couplet 'sea/thee' (2.2.133–4), which corresponds in meaning to the two Hebrew lines following this one.

70 Job 11:9 וּרְחָבָה מִנִּי־יָם 'and broader than the sea'.

71 Exod. 1:12 כֵּן יִרְבֶּה וְכֵן יִפְרֹץ 'the more it multiplied and spread'.

72 This and the next line form a rhyming couplet, mirroring Shakespeare's 'adieu/true' (2.2.136–7).

73 Isa. 21:42.

74 Exod. 12:42.

	And inform me of all this tomorrow by the hand of one of the youths	וְהוֹדִיעֵנִי כָּל זֶה לְמָחָר בְּיַד אַחַד הַנְּעָרִים	
	Whom I shall send to you; and I shall be yours, and all that is mine	אֲשֶׁר אֶשְׁלָחֶנּוּ אֵלֶיךָ; וּלְךָ אֲנִי וְכָל אֲשֶׁר לִי	
	You will be the chief at my head, and **where you go, I shall go**.[75]	אַתָּה אַלּוּף לְרֹאשִׁי וּבַאֲשֶׁר תֵּלֵךְ אֵלֵכָה.[75]	
THE NURSE *(From within)*	Jael, my lady!	יָעֵל* גְּבִרְתִּי!	האומנת (מלפנים)
JAEL	I'll come at once – but if **there is another spirit with you**[76]	אֲנִי אָבוֹאָה כְּרֶגַע – וְאִם רוּחַ אַחֶרֶת אִתְּךָ[76]	יעל
	Please listen to me –	נָא שְׁמָעֵנִי –	
THE NURSE *(From within)*	My lady!	גְּבִרְתִּי!	האומנת (מלפנים)
JAEL	Wait for me a moment and I'll come –	חַכִּי לִי מְעַט רֶגַע וְאָבוֹאָה –	יעל
	Let me be,[77] and leave me **in the bitterness of my soul**[78]	חֲדַל לְךָ מִמֶּנִּי[77] וְעָזְבֵנִי בְּמַר נַפְשִׁי[78]	
	And tomorrow I shall send the youth to you.	וּלְמָחָר אֶשְׁלַח לְךָ אֶת הַנָּעַר.	
RAM	Indeed I swear[79] –	הֵן בִּי נִשְׁבַּעְתִּי[79] –	רם
JAEL	Go, **and may your sleep be sweet**,[80] a thousand times in accordance with my blessing.	לְכָה וְעָרְבָה שְׁנָתְךָ,[80] אֶלֶף פְּעָמִים כְּבִרְכָתִי.	יעל
	(Exits from the window)	(הולכת מעל החלון)	
RAM	Without the light of your face, how can my sleep be pleasant?	בִּלְעֲדֵי אוֹר פָּנַיִךְ, אֵיךְ תֶּעֱרַב שְׁנָתִי.	רם
	A boy goes to his school in sadness; afterwards he goes out to freedom[81]	יֶלֶד יֵלֵךְ לְבֵית סִפְרוֹ בְּעֹצֶב, אַחַר יֵצֵא לִרְוָחָה[81]	

75 Ruth 1:16 אֶל־אֲשֶׁר תֵּלְכִי אֵלֵךְ 'where you go, I shall go'.
76 Num. 14:24 הָיְתָה רוּחַ אַחֶרֶת עִמּוֹ 'there was another spirit with him' (i.e., another attitude).
77 Job 7:16 חֲדַל מִמֶּנִּי 'let me be'.
78 Job 7:11, 10:1.
79 This rhymes with the following two lines. In this respect it mirrors the original 'night/light' (2.2.154–5), except that in Salkinson's version the rhyme starts a line earlier and extends over three lines rather than two.
80 Prov. 3:24.
81 This and the next line form a rhyming couplet, mirroring Shakespeare's 'books/looks' (2.2.156–7).

* יָעֵל

	And a man meets his beloved in joy but parts in **sorrow and sighing**.[82]	וְאִישׁ יִפְגֹּשׁ אֲהֻבָתוֹ בְּשָׂשׂוֹן וְיִפָּרֵד בְּיָגוֹן **וַאֲנָחָה**.[82]	
	(He goes slowly on his way)	(הוא הולך אט לדרכו)	
	(Jael re-enters)	(יעל שבה)	
JAEL	Listen, Ram; come back! If only I had the voice of a falcon[83]	הַקְשִׁיבָה רָם; שׁוּבָה! מִי יִתֵּן לִי קוֹל אַיָּה[83]	יעל
	To whistle and to bring back this pleasant hawk.	לִשְׁרֹק וּלְהָשִׁיב אֶת הַנֵּץ הַנָּעִים הַזֶּה.	
	But a trapped maiden like myself has no way to make her voice heard	אַךְ נַעֲרָה עֲצוּרָה כָּמוֹנִי אֵין לָהּ לְהַשְׁמִיעַ קוֹלָהּ	
	Except **as a ghost from the earth**![84] For if it were not so	כִּי אִם **כְּאוֹב מֵאֶרֶץ**![84] כִּי לוּלֵי כֵן	
	I would raise my voice with force and call out the name of Ram my chosen one	הֲרִימֹתִי קוֹלִי בַּכֹּחַ וָאֶקְרָא בְּשֵׁם רָם בְּחִירִי	
	Until the valley opposite[85] split apart at my voice.	עַד אֲשֶׁר הַבִּקְעָה מִנֶּגֶד[85] תִּבָּקַע לְקוֹלִי.	
RAM	The voice is the voice of **the beloved of my soul**;[86] she is calling my name	הַקּוֹל קוֹל **יְדִידוּת נַפְשִׁי**,[86] הִיא קֹרַאת* בִּשְׁמִי	רם
	How agreeable and pleasant is the voice of love at night.	מָה עָרֵב וְנָעִים קוֹל דֹּדִים בַּלַּיְלָה.	
	Like the sound of skilful playing to a listening ear.	כְּקוֹל מֵטִיב נַגֵּן עֲלֵי אֹזֶן שֹׁמָעַת.	
JAEL	Ram!	רָם!	יעל
RAM	Here I am, **graceful doe**.[87]	הִנְנִי **יַעֲלַת חֵן**.[87]	רם
JAEL	At what time tomorrow shall I send the youth to you?	בְּאֵיזֶה זְמַן לְמָחָר, אֶשְׁלַח לְךָ אֶת הַנָּעַר?**	יעל
RAM	In the morning.	בַּבֹּקֶר.	רם
JAEL	And the time until the morning will be as prolonged for me as twenty years	וְהָעֵת עַד הַבֹּקֶר תִּמָּשֵׁךְ לִי כְּעֶשְׂרִים שָׁנָה	יעל
	Admittedly I have forgotten why I called you to come back.	אוּלָם שָׁכַחְתִּי לָמָּה זֶה קְרָאתִיךָ לָשׁוּב.	

82 Isa. 35:10, 51:11.

83 This bird is mentioned three times in the Hebrew Bible (Lev. 11:14; Deut. 14:13; Job 28:7). It is translated as 'kite' in some English Bible versions (e.g., the King James Bible). Salkinson's 'falcon' replaces Shakespeare's 'falconer' (2.2.158), and as such lends a very different sense to the line, evoking the image of one bird summoning another.

84 Isa. 29:4.

85 Cf. Shakespeare's 'the cave where Echo lies' (2.2.161). This is in keeping with Salkinson's strategy of removing references to Classical mythological figures.

86 Jer. 12:7.

87 Prov. 5:19. Cf. Shakespeare's 'my nyas' (2.2.167), i.e., fledgling hawk. As in many other cases, Salkinson has not retained Shakespeare's hawking imagery, which would lack relevance for his audience. See also First Part, note 171.

* קֹרֵאת

** הַנָּעַר

RAM	I shall stand here until the matter comes to your mind.	הִנְנִי אֶעֱמֹד פֹּה, עַד עֲלוֹת הַדָּבָר עַל לִבֵּךְ.	רם
JAEL	And I shall continue to forget, so that you might continue to stand	וַאֲנִי אוֹסִיף לִשְׁכֹּחַ לְמַעַן תּוֹסֵף לַעֲמֹד	יעל
	And only this I remember, that I long for your closeness.	וְרַק זֹאת אֶזְכְּרָה, כִּי קִרְבָתְךָ תָּאַבְתִּי.	
RAM	And I shall continue to stand so that you might continue to forget	וַאֲנִי אוֹסִיף לַעֲמֹד לְמַעַן תּוֹסִיפִי לִשְׁכֹּחַ	רם
	And I shall also forget everything, except for this place.	וְגַם אֲנִי אֶשְׁכַּח הַכֹּל, בִּלְתִּי מְקוֹמִי זֶה.	
JAEL	I am willing for you to go, because the morning is near	הוֹאַלְתִּי כִּי תֵלֵךְ, יַעַן הַבֹּקֶר קָרוֹב	יעל
	But do not distance yourself further than a bird	אֶפֶס לֹא תִרְחַק לָלֶכֶת, כִּי אִם כְּרְחֹק הַצִּפּוֹר	
	Which is grasped by **a scarlet cord**[88] in the hand of its mistress	הָאֲחוּזָה בְּתִקְוַת שָׁנִי[88] אֲשֶׁר בְּיַד גְּבִרְתָּהּ	
	The bird walks a little bit, like a prisoner with his leg in a chain[89]	הַצִּפּוֹר תְּדַדֶּה מְעַט מְעַט, כְּאַסִּיר רַגְלוֹ בַּכֶּבֶל[89]	
	And it returns from time to time because it is pulled by the rope	וְתָשׁוּב כְּפַעַם בְּפַעַם כִּי תִמָּשֵׁךְ בַּחֶבֶל	
	Since its lady, out of the jealousy of her love, will not set it free.	יַעַן גְּבִרְתָּהּ מִקִּנְאַת אַהֲבָה לֹא תְשַׁלְּחֶנָּה לַחָפְשִׁי.	
RAM	If only I were the bird.	מִי יִתֵּן וְהָיִיתִי אֲנִי הַצִּפּוֹר.	רם
JAEL	My desire is like your desire, chosen one of my soul;	חֶפְצִי כְּחֶפְצְךָ בְּחִיר נַפְשִׁי;	יעל
	Though I worry that I might kill you with my excessive fondness.	אֶפֶס דָּאַגְתִּי פֶּן אֲמִיתְךָ בְּרֹב שַׁעֲשֻׁעַי.	
	Now descend, Ram, turn around, go in peace.	עַתָּה רְדָה רָם, סֹב לֶךְ־לְךָ לְשָׁלוֹם.	
	To bless you and send you away in peace is a joy, but it ends with a sigh[90]	לְבָרֶכְךָ וּלְשַׁלֵּחֲךָ בְּשָׁלוֹם, מָשׂוֹשׂ הוּא וְאַחֲרִיתוֹ אֲנָחָה[90]	
	Therefore I shall detain you and bless you until **the sun shines**.[91]	לָכֵן אֶעֱצָרְךָ וַאֲבָרֶכְךָ עַד אֲשֶׁר הַשֶּׁמֶשׁ זָרְחָה.[91]	
	(Exits from the window)	(הולכת מעל החלון)	
RAM	May peace reside in your heart **and slumber on your eyelids**,[92] beloved![93]	יִשְׁכּוֹן שָׁלוֹם בְּלִבֵּךְ וּתְנוּמָה עַל עַפְעַפַּיִךְ[92] רַחֲמָה![93]	רם

88 Josh. 2:21 וַתִּקְשֹׁר אֶת־תִּקְוַת הַשָּׁנִי בַּחַלּוֹן 'and she tied the scarlet cord in the window'.
89 This and the next line form a rhyming couplet. There is no precedent for this in the source text 'gyves/again' (2.2.179–80).
90 This and the next line form a rhyming couplet, mirroring Shakespeare's 'sorrow/morrow' (2.2.184–5).
91 2 Kings 3:22.
92 Prov. 6:4 וּתְנוּמָה לְעַפְעַפֶּיךָ 'nor slumber to your eyelids'.
93 This and the next line form a rhyming couplet, mirroring Shakespeare's original 'breast/rest' (2.2.186–7).

	If only I were peace and slumber and dwelled in pleasantness there[94] –	לוּ הָיִיתִי אֲנִי שָׁלוֹם וּתְנוּמָה וְשָׁכַנְתִּי בַּנְּעִימִים שָׁמָּה[94] –	
	Now I shall go to the chamber of the priest,[95] who teaches about the secret of redemption,[96]	עַתָּה אֵלֵךְ לְלִשְׁכַּת הַכֹּהֵן,[95] הַמּוֹרֶה סוֹד הַגְּאֻלָּה.[96]	
	To tell him the matters of the covenant and to ask his advice and counsel.	לְסַפֵּר לוֹ דִּבְרֵי הַבְּרִית וְלִשְׁאוֹל מִפִּיו עֵצָה וְתַחְבֻּלָה.	
	(Exits)	(הולך)	
SCENE 3	*Chamber of Rezin[97] the priest (Rezin with a basket on his arm)*	לשכת רצין[97] הכהן (רצין וסל על ידו)	מחזה ג'
REZIN	The dawn has opened its eyelids; **it is peering through the lattice**[98, 99, 100]	הַשַּׁחַר פָּקַח עַפְעַפָּיו, יָצִיץ מִבֵּין הַחֲרַכִּים[98,99,100]	רצין
	It scatters the eastern clouds, turns its eye to the dark places	יָפִיץ עַנְנֵי קָדִים, יִתֵּן עֵינוֹ בַּמַּחֲשַׁכִּים	
	The night moves like a drunkard and does not stand still in the dark	הַלַּיְלָה יָנוּעַ כַּשִּׁכּוֹר וְלֹא יַעֲמֹד אָמֶשׁ	
	For it retreats from the wheels of the sun's chariot[101]	כִּי יִסּוֹג לְאָחוֹר מִגַּלְגַּלֵּי מֶרְכֶּבֶת הַשָּׁמֶשׁ.[101]	
	Indeed before light dawns, ere it sends out its heat[102]	אַךְ טֶרֶם יִבָּקַע אוֹר, עַד לֹא יִשְׁלַח חֻמּוֹ[102]	
	To make the day rejoice, to dry out all moisture until it is gone.	לְשַׂמַּח אֶת הַיּוֹם, לְיַבֵּשׁ כָּל לֵחַ עַד תֻּמּוֹ.	

94 In the Arden edition, based on the Second Quarto (and also corresponding to the First Folio), Romeo speaks four lines here (2.2.188–91) that Salkinson instead assigns to the opening of Rezin's speech at the beginning of the following scene; see note 99.

95 This corresponds to Shakespeare's 'my ghostly sire' (2.2.192). See First Part, note 268 for further discussion of the Hebrew term כֹּהֵן 'priest'.

96 This and the next line form a rhyming couplet, mirroring Shakespeare's 'cell/tell' (2.2.192–3). Salkinson most likely inserted the phrase 'who teaches the secret of redemption', which is not based on the original, for purposes of the rhyme.

97 The name of an eighth-century BCE king of the biblical kingdom of Aram who attacked Judah (2 Kings 15:37). There is no obvious correspondence in sound or meaning between this name and Shakespeare's Laurence. It is possible that Salkinson chose the name Rezin as a veiled reference to the character's status as a Catholic friar, because in Jewish sources Aram was sometimes associated with Rome and Christianity (Jastrow 1903: 123), but this is uncertain. This would fit in with Salkinson's description of Rezin as a 'Christian priest' in the list of characters at the beginning of the play.

98 Song of Songs 2:9 מֵצִיץ מִן־הַחֲרַכִּים 'he is peering through the lattice'.

99 In the Arden edition, which is based on the Second Quarto and also corresponds to the First Folio, this and the following three lines are spoken by Romeo at the end of the previous scene (2.2.188–91). The fact that Salkinson places them here suggests that he was working from an English edition based on the Second, Third, or Fourth Folio, in which these lines are spoken by Friar Laurence.

100 This and the next three lines form a pair of rhyming couplets, mirroring Shakespeare's 'night/light', 'reels/wheels' (2.2.188–91).

101 This is Salkinson's culturally neutral equivalent of Shakespeare's 'Titan's wheels' (2.2.191).

102 This and the next line form a rhyming couplet, mirroring Shakespeare's 'eye/dry' (2.3.1–2).

I shall gather lights in my basket, evil and bitter herbs[103]	אֲלַקֵּט אוֹרוֹת בְּסַלִּי, סַמִּים רָעִים וּמָרִים[103]
And blossoms that give off a scent of precious perfumes.	וְנִצָּנִים נֹתְנֵי רֵיחַ עִם בְּשָׂמִים יְקָרִים.
The earth is the mother of nature, and nature is buried in the earth.[104]	הָאֲדָמָה אֵם לְטֶבַע וְהַטֶּבַע בָּאֲדָמָה תִּקָּבֵר[104]
She is the womb of everything that is born, and also a burial site	הִיא רֶחֶם לְכָל נוֹלָד וְגַם אֲחֻזַּת קָבֶר
Her womb is always great,[105] and her children are most diverse[106]	רַחְמָהּ הֲרַת עוֹלָם[105] וְשׁוֹנִים שׁוֹנִים יְלָדֶיהָ[106]
They all satiate themselves with her bread, and drink their fill from the milk of her breasts	כֻּלָּם מִלַּחְמָהּ יִשְׂבָּעוּ יִרְווּ מֵחֲלֵב שָׁדֶיהָ
Many of them are honourable, each with its own worth[107]	רַבִּים מֵהֶם נִכְבָּדִים וְאִישׁ אִישׁ הַיִּתְרוֹן בּוֹ הוּא[107]
They differ from each other, each according to its kind, none created in vain	וְהֵם שׁוֹנִים לְמִינֵיהֶם, אֵין אֶחָד נִבְרָא לַתֹּהוּ
Who can match the worth of herbs; how exalted is their work![108]	מִי יַעֲרֹךְ יִתְרוֹן הַסַּמִּים, פְּעֻלָּתָם מַה־נִּשְׂגָּבָה![108]
Or **the strength of stones**[109] by the thousands, and **the plants of the field by the myriads**![110]	אוֹ כֹּחַ אֲבָנִים[109] לַאֲלָפִים, וְצֶמַח הַשָּׂדֶה לִרְבָבָה![110]
Even the lowest of the low which the earth abhors[111]	גַּם שָׁפָל בַּשְּׁפָלִים אֲשֶׁר אֶרֶץ זִהֲמַתּוּ[111]
The root of the matter is found in it[112] to benefit the mother who bore him	שֹׁרֶשׁ דָּבָר נִמְצָא בוֹ[112] לְהוֹעִיל לְאֵם יְלָדַתּוּ
And everything created on the earth which is considered a precious gift[113]	וְכָל הַנּוֹצָר בָּאָרֶץ הַנֶּחְשָׁב לְמַתָּנָה יְקָרָה[113]

103 This and the next line form a rhyming couplet, mirroring Shakespeare's 'ours/flowers' (2.3.3–4).
104 This and the next line form a rhyming couplet, mirroring Shakespeare's 'tomb/womb' (2.3.5–6).
105 Jer. 20:17.
106 This and the next line form a rhyming couplet, mirroring Shakespeare's 'kind/find' (2.3.7–8).
107 This and the next line form a rhyming couplet, mirroring Shakespeare's 'excellent/different' (2.3.9–10).
108 This and the next line form a rhyming couplet, mirroring Shakespeare's 'lies/qualities' (2.3.11–12).
109 Job 6:12.
110 Ezek. 16:7 רְבָבָה כְּצֶמַח הַשָּׂדֶה נְתַתִּיךְ 'I have caused you to multiply [lit. grow by the myriads] like the plants of the field'.
111 This and the next line form a rhyming couplet, mirroring Shakespeare's 'live/give' (2.3.13–14).
112 Job 19:28 וְשֹׁרֶשׁ דָּבָר נִמְצָא־בִי 'as the root of the matter is found in me'.
113 This and the next line form a rhyming couplet, mirroring Shakespeare's 'use/abuse' (2.3.15–16).

	Turns into **a stone of stumbling**[114] when it corrupts its straight path.	יִתְהַפֵּךְ לְאֶבֶן נֶגֶף[114] בְּהַשְׁחִיתוֹ אֶת דַּרְכּוֹ הַיְשָׁרָה.	
	Even justice not in its time is regarded as wickedness[115]	גַּם צֶדֶק לֹא בְעִתּוֹ יֵחָשֵׁב כְּמוֹ רֶשַׁע[115]	
	And an evildoer who does noble things is elevated as **one whose transgression is forgiven.**[116]	וְעַוָּל עֹשֶׂה נְדִיבוֹת יְרוֹמָם כִּנְשׂוּי פֶּשַׁע.[116]	
	Consider this tender blossom still in its greenness[117]	הִתְבּוֹנֵן בַּצִּיץ הָרַךְ הַזֶּה עוֹדוֹ בְאִבּוֹ[117]	
	In it is concealed **the elixir of death**[118] and **the elixir of life**[119] is also in its heart	בּוֹ סָפוּן סַם מָוֶת[118] וְגַם סַם חַיִּים[119] בְּלִבּוֹ	
	If a man smells it, its good scent gladdens him[120]	אִם יָרִיחַ בּוֹ אִישׁ, רֵיחוֹ הַטּוֹב יְשַׂמְּחֶנּוּ[120]	
	But if he tastes its drink, it is poison and kills him.	וְאִם יִטְעַם שִׁקּוּיוֹ, רוֹשׁ הוּא וִימִיתֶנּוּ	
	So is the good and evil inclination;[121] two warriors, hawks[122]	כֵּן יֵצֶר טוֹב וָרָע,[121] שְׁנֵי גִבּוֹרִים נִצִּים[122]	
	Fight in man's heart as in the heart of herbs and blossoms	נִלְחָמִים בְּלֵב הָאָדָם כְּמוֹ בְּלֵב סַמִּים וָצִיצִים	
	And if the evil lifts up its head and the good sinks down below[123]	וְאִם הָרַע יָרִים רֹאשׁ וְהַטּוֹב יִשְׁקַע מִתָּחַת[123]	
	Then the man's end is near and the plant dies, into the grave.	אָז קָרוֹב קֵץ הָאָדָם וְהַמַּטָּע יָמוּת לַשָּׁחַת.	
RAM	Greetings to you, father![124]	הֲשָׁלוֹם לְךָ אַבָּא![124]	רם

114 Isa. 8:14.
115 This and the next line form a rhyming couplet, mirroring Shakespeare's 'misapplied/dignified' (2.3.17–18).
116 Ps. 32:1.
117 This and the next line form a rhyming couplet, mirroring Shakespeare's 'flower/power' (2.3.19–20).
118 Mishnah *Ḥullin* 3:5.
119 Babylonian Talmud *Yoma* 72b.
120 This and the next line form a rhyming couplet, mirroring Shakespeare's 'part/heart' (2.3.21–2).
121 This refers to a principle in Jewish thought that all humans are born with two opposing inclinations, one to do good and the other to do evil, and must strive throughout their lives to keep the evil inclination under control. This concept is mentioned in the Mishnah (*Berakhot* 9:5) and in numerous other locations in rabbinic and later Jewish literature.
122 This and the next line form a rhyming couplet, mirroring Shakespeare's 'still/will' (2.3.23–4). Salkinson's seemingly unmotivated use of the word 'hawks' here is most likely rooted in the need to find a suitable rhyme.
123 This and the next line form a rhyming couplet, mirroring Shakespeare's 'predominant/plant' (2.3.25–6).
124 This forms a rhyming couplet with the following line. There is no precedent for this in Shakespeare's 'father/me' (2.3.27–8).

REZIN	Welcome![125]	בָּרוּךְ הַבָּא![125]	רצין
	Who enquires after my wellbeing at dawn, with sweetness and great pleasantness?	מִי דֹרֵשׁ שְׁלוֹמִי בַּשַּׁחַר, בְּמֶתֶק וּנְעִימָה רַבָּה?	
	Have you, my son, left your bed while it is still night?[126]	הַאַתָּה בְּנִי בְּעוֹד לַיְלָה עָזַבְתָּ מִשְׁכָּבֶךָ?[126]	
	It is nothing other than **agitated sorrow**[127] in your heart.	אֵין זֶה כִּי אִם כְּאֵב נֶעְכָּר[127] בִּלְבָבֶךָ.	
	An old heart full of worry seeks a resting place but there is none[128]	לֵב זָקֵן מָלֵא דְאָגָה יְבַקֵּשׁ מָנוֹחַ וָאָיִן[128]	
	Where worry dwells, there sleep flees from the eye.	בַּאֲשֶׁר הַדְּאָגָה תִּשְׁכֹּן, שָׁם תִּדַּד שֵׁנָה מֵעָיִן.	
	But one possessed of the power and soul of youth does not know distress[129]	אַךְ בַּעַל כֹּחַ נְעוּרִים וְנֶפֶשׁ לֹא תֵדַע מְצוּקָה[129]	
	He lies down in safety and his sleep is sweet for him.	הוּא יִשְׁכַּב לָבֶטַח וּשְׁנָתוֹ עָלָיו מְתוּקָה.	
	But you, because you have risen early, and have come to me in the darkness[130]	וְאַתָּה כִּי הִשְׁכַּמְתָּ וַתָּבוֹא אֵלַי בַּאֲפֵלָה[130]	
	By this I know that you have been afflicted and woe **is hurling you violently**[131]	בְּזֹאת יָדַעְתִּי כִּי עֻנֵּיתָ וְעָמָל מְטַלְטֶלְךָ טַלְטֵלָה[131]	
	And if it is not so, Ram, I shall tell you where you were[132]	וְאִם לֹא כֵן רָם, אַגִּדְךָ אֵיפֹה הָיִיתָ[132]	
	For you have wandered the whole night and have not been to your bed.	כִּי נָדַדְתָּ כָּל הַלַּיְלָה וְעַל יָצוּעַ לֹא עָלִיתָ.	
RAM	My rest was pleasant for me, although I have not seen sleep.[133]	מְנוּחָתִי עָרְבָה לִי, אַף כִּי לֹא רָאִיתִי שֵׁנָה.[133]	רם
REZIN	May God forgive iniquity – were you with Shoshannah?	הָאֱלֹהִים יְכַפֵּר עָוֹן – הַאִם הָיִיתָ עִם שׁוֹשַׁנָּה?	רצין

125 This replaces Shakespeare's '*Benedicite*'. Salkinson's substitution of the Hebrew greeting for the original Latin is in keeping with his strategy of replacing Latin and French elements with Hebrew ones, thereby homogenizing the linguistic variation present in the source text.
126 This and the next line form a rhyming couplet, mirroring Shakespeare's 'head/bed' (2.3.29–30).
127 Ps. 39:3 וּכְאֵבִי נֶעְכָּר 'and my sorrow was agitated'.
128 This and the next line form a rhyming couplet, mirroring Shakespeare's 'eye/lie' (2.3.31–2).
129 This and the next line form a rhyming couplet, mirroring Shakespeare's 'brain/reign' (2.3.33–4).
130 This and the next line form a rhyming couplet, mirroring Shakespeare's 'assure/distemperature' (2.3.35–6).
131 Isa. 22:17.
132 This and the next line form a rhyming couplet, mirroring Shakespeare's 'right/tonight' (2.3.37–8).
133 This and the next line form a rhyming couplet, mirroring Shakespeare's 'mine/Rosaline' (2.3.39–40).

RAM	I was not with Shoshannah, not so, my father,[134]	עִם שׁוֹשַׁנָּה לֹא הָיִיתִי, לֹא כֵן אָבִי,[134]	רם
	I have forgotten like a dead man from my mind[135] that name which recalls woe.	הַשֵּׁם הַהוּא הַמַּזְכִּיר עָמָל **שָׁכַחְתִּי כַּמֵּת מִלְּבָבִי**.[135]	
REZIN	The matter is good, my son, but where were you, tell me.[136]	טוֹב הַדָּבָר בְּנִי, וְאֵיפֹה הָיִיתָ הוֹדִיעֵנִי.[136]	רצין
RAM	I shall tell you, before you ask me again;	זֹאת אַגִּיד לְךָ, טֶרֶם שֵׁנִית תִּשְׁאָלֵנִי;	רם
	At a time of **feasting and gladness**[137] I met my enemy[138]	אֲנִי לְעֵת **מִשְׁתֶּה וְשִׂמְחָה**[137] אֶת אוֹיְבִי פָּגַעְתִּי[138]	
	He drew his bow and broke through **the covering of my heart**[139]	הוּא דָרַךְ קַשְׁתּוֹ **וּסְגוֹר לְבָבִי**[139] הִבְקִיעַ	
	And I shot my arrow and wounded him	וַאֲנִי יָרִיתִי חִצִּי וּפֶצַע בּוֹ פָּצַעְתִּי	
	But you, faithful physician, will save us both	אַךְ אַתָּה רוֹפֵא נֶאֱמָן לִשְׁנֵינוּ יָדְךָ תּוֹשִׁיעַ	
	The path of revenge is distant from me; look, please look, my father,[140]	דֶּרֶךְ נְקָמָה רְחֹקָה מֶנִּי, רְאֵה נָא רְאֵה אָבִי[140]	
	I seek medicine for the affliction of an enemy as for the affliction of my own heart.	תְּרוּפָה לְנֶגַע אוֹיֵב אֲבַקֵּשׁ כְּמוֹ לְנֶגַע לְבָבִי.	
REZIN	Speak, my son, with **pure speech**;[141] let the parables and riddles be[142]	דַּבֵּר בְּנִי **בְּשָׂפָה בְרוּרָה**[141] לִמְלִיצָה חִידָה הַנִּיחָה[142]	רצין
	If one confesses and repents[143] in riddles, the pardon will also be like a riddle.	**מוֹדֶה וְעֹזֵב**[143] בְּחִידוֹת, כַּחִידָה תְּהִי גַּם הַסְּלִיחָה.	
RAM	Therefore know with certainty that my soul desires[144]	לָכֵן דַּע נֶאֱמָנָה, כִּי בַת אֲבִיעֵל הַיְחִידָה[144]	רם
	The only daughter of Abiel with a great and pure love	חָשְׁקָה נַפְשִׁי בָּהּ בְּאַהֲבָה רַבָּה וּטְהוֹרָה	

134 This and the next line form a rhyming couplet, mirroring Shakespeare's 'no/woe' (2.3.41–2).

135 Ps. 31:13 (31:12 in English Bibles) נִשְׁכַּחְתִּי כְּמֵת מִלֵּב 'I have been forgotten from the mind like a dead man'.

136 This and the next line form a rhyming couplet, mirroring Shakespeare's 'then/again' (2.3.43–4).

137 Esther 9:17, 18, 22.

138 This and the following three lines form an ABAB rhyming pattern, echoing the English except that the latter consists of two rhyming couplets: 'enemy/me', 'remedies/lies' (2.3.45–8).

139 Hosea 13:8 וְאֶקְרַע סְגוֹר לִבָּם 'and I shall tear open the covering of their heart'.

140 This and the next line form a rhyming couplet, mirroring Shakespeare's 'lo/foe' (2.3.49–50).

141 Zeph. 3:9.

142 This and the next line form a rhyming couplet, mirroring Shakespeare's 'drift/shrift' (2.3.51–2).

143 Prov. 28:13.

144 This and the following three lines form an ABAB rhyming pattern, echoing the English except that the latter consists of two rhyming couplets: 'set/Capulet', 'mine/combine' (2.3.53–6).

	And she is also bound to me; she is my beloved	וְגַם הִיא קְשׁוּרָה בִי, לִי הִיא הַיְדִידָה	
	Nothing is lacking, except the bond according to the Law[145]	אֵין מַחְסֹר כָּל דָּבָר, בִּלְתִּי הַקֶּשֶׁר לְפִי הַתּוֹרָה[145]	
	But when, where, and how I saw her, fell in love with her, and betrothed her[146]	אַךְ מָתַי, אָנָה וְאֵיךְ רְאִיתִיהָ, אֲהַבְתִּיהָ וְאֵרַשְׂתִּיהָ[146]	
	I shall inform you at a different time, or you will hear it from her mouth.	אַשְׁמִיעֲךָ לְעֵת אַחֶרֶת, אוֹ תִּשְׁמַע מִפִּיהָ.	
	Just please consent, instructor of justice and faith![147]	רַק אָנָּא הוֹאֶל נָא, מוֹרֶה צֶדֶק וֶאֱמוּנָה![147]	
	To bring us on this day into the tradition of the wedding covenant.	לַהֲבִיאֵנוּ בַּיּוֹם* הַזֶּה, בְּמָסֹרֶת בְּרִית הַחֲתֻנָּה.	
REZIN	Oh! My heart pricks me[148] at this hasty change[149]	אֲהָהּ! לִבִּי יִשְׁתּוֹנֵן[148] לִתְמוּרָה זוֹ מְבֹהֶלֶת[149]	רצין
	How you have abandoned your beloved Shoshannah like a withering rose.	אֵיךְ שׁוֹשַׁנָּה אֲהֻבָתְךָ, עָזַבְתָּ כְּשׁוֹשַׁנָּה נֹבֶלֶת.	
	Young people go mad in their love as if **overcome with wine**[150, 151]	בְּנֵי הַנְּעוּרִים בְּאַהֲבָתָם יִשְׁתַּגְּעוּ כַּהֲלוּמֵי יָיִן[150, 151]	
	But love does not lodge in their hearts, only rests upon the eye.	וְאַהֲבָה לֹא תָלִין בְּלִבָּם, רַק רֹבֶצֶת עֲלֵי עָיִן.	
	How many tears[152] have you poured like rain on a garden[153]	כַּמָּה מֵי דִמְעָה[152] שָׁפַכְתָּ כַּמָּטָר עַל גַּנָּה[153]	
	Arousing **mercy and compassion**[154] to turn Shoshannah's heart.	לְעוֹרֵר חֶסֶד וְרַחֲמִים[154] לְהַטּוֹת אֶת לֵב שׁוֹשַׁנָּה.	

145 Alternatively, 'according to the Torah'. Cf. Shakespeare's 'holy marriage' (2.3.57). The word תּוֹרָה typically means 'law' or 'instruction' when appearing in the Hebrew Bible, but in postbiblical Hebrew it generally denotes the Torah (which in its narrow sense refers to the Pentateuch and in its broader sense the whole of Jewish law and tradition). Salkinson's readers would have been aware of both the biblical and postbiblical meanings of the word, but the postbiblical sense would have been salient, as the phrase 'according to the Torah' is commonly used in Jewish texts and speech.

146 This and the next line form a rhyming couplet, mirroring Shakespeare's 'how/vow' (2.3.57–8).

147 This and the next line form a rhyming couplet, mirroring Shakespeare's 'pray/today' (2.3.59–60).

148 This neutral expression replaces Shakespeare's 'Holy Saint Francis' (2.3.61).

149 This and the next line form a rhyming couplet, mirroring Shakespeare's 'here/dear' (2.3.61–2).

150 Isa. 28:1.

151 This and the next line form a rhyming couplet, mirroring Shakespeare's 'lies/eyes' (2.3.63–4).

152 Salkinson has omitted the Catholic exclamation 'Jesu Maria' that appears directly before this mention of tears in the original.

153 This and the next line form a rhyming couplet, mirroring Shakespeare's 'brine/Rosaline' (2.3.65–6).

154 Zech. 7:9; Ps. 103:4.

* בַּיּוֹם

	What is the profit in the **drops of water**[155] that you have spilled from the spring of your eyes[156]	מַה־בֶּצַע בְּנִטְפֵי מַיִם[155], מִמְּקוֹר עֵינֶיךָ זָרַמְתָּ[156]	
	To grow a plant of love from which you have not tasted	לְהַצְמִיחַ צֶמַח אַהֲבָה, מִמֶּנָּה לֹא טָעַמְתָּ	
	Your sighs have not yet dried up; they have risen like steam into the eye of the sun[157]	עוֹד לֹא יָבְשׁוּ אַנְחוֹתֶיךָ עָלוּ כְּאֵד לְעֵין הַשֶּׁמֶשׁ[157]	
	My ears still tingle at the sound of your wailing; you wailed last night	עוֹד תִּצַּלְנָה אָזְנַי לְקוֹל יִלְלָתְךָ הֵילַלְתָּ אֶמֶשׁ	
	Where, then, has the sorrow fled? How has the weeping been forgotten?[158]	אַיֵּה אֵיפוֹ נָס הַיָּגוֹן? אֵיךְ נִשְׁכַּח הַבֶּכִי?[158]	
	You are still stained with tears; they have not yet been wiped from your cheek.	עוֹד נִכְתָּם הַדֶּמַע, לֹא נִמְחָה מֵעַל הַלֶּחִי.	
	If you are Ram, and from your mouth has come forth **mourning and woe**[159, 160]	אִם אַתָּה הוּא רָם, וּמִפִּיךָ יָצָא הֶגֶה וָהִי[159, 160]	
	You have no woman on earth except for Soshannah alone	אֵין לְךָ אִשָּׁה בָּאָרֶץ, בִּלְתִּי שׁוֹשַׁנָּה לְבַדָּהּ הִיא	
	But now, are you changed? – Tell me, lad, truthfully![161]	ועַתָּה* הַאִם שָׁנִיתָ? – הַגֵּד לִי בָּחוּר בְּמֵישָׁרִים![161]	
	Who can mock fallen women if there is no strength in men.	מִי יָבוּז לַנָּשִׁים נֹפְלוֹת, אִם אֵין כֹּחַ בַּגְּבָרִים.	
RAM	When I loved Shoshannah, you chastised me relentlessly.[162]	כַּאֲשֶׁר אָהַבְתִּי אֶת שׁוֹשַׁנָּה יִסַּרְתַּנִי מֵאֵין הֲפֻגָה.[162]	רם
REZIN	Not because you loved, but rather because you were like a madman.	לֹא בַאֲשֶׁר אָהַבְתָּ, בִּלְתִּי בַּאֲשֶׁר הָיִיתָ כִּמְשֻׁגָּע.	רצין
RAM	Why, you commanded me to bury my love **in the river of forgetfulness.**[163, 164]	הֲלֹא צִוִּיתָ לְקַבֵּר אַהֲבָתִי בְּנַחַל הַנְּשִׁיָּה.[163, 164]	רם

155 Job 36:27.
156 This and the next line form a rhyming couplet, mirroring Shakespeare's 'waste/taste' (2.3.67–8).
157 This and the next line form a rhyming couplet, mirroring Shakespeare's 'clears/ears' (2.3.69–70).
158 This and the next line form a rhyming couplet, mirroring Shakespeare's 'sit/yet' (2.3.71–2).
159 Ezek. 2:10.
160 This and the next line form a rhyming couplet, mirroring Shakespeare's 'thine/Rosaline' (2.3.73–4).
161 This and the next line form a rhyming couplet, mirroring Shakespeare's 'then/men' (2.3.75–6).
162 This and the next line form a rhyming couplet, mirroring Shakespeare's 'Rosaline/mine' (2.3.77–8).
163 Ps. 88:13 (88:12 in English Bibles) בְּאֶרֶץ נְשִׁיָּה 'in the land of forgetfulness' (a euphemism for the world of the dead; cf. Eccles. 9:5).
164 This and the next line form a rhyming couplet, mirroring Shakespeare's 'love/have' (2.3.79–80).

* וְעַתָּה

REZIN	Not to bury one and raise another up from the grave.	לֹא לְקַבֵּר אַחַת וּלְהַעֲלוֹת מִקֶּבֶר אֶת הַשְּׁנִיָּה.	רצין
RAM	Leave off chastisement this time and **spare the rod**[165] of punishment[166]	עֲזֹב תּוֹכֵחָה הַפַּעַם וַחֲשׂךְ שֵׁבֶט[165] בִּקֹּרֶת[166]	רם
	This damsel that I desire, she is not like the damsel I left	עַלְמָה זוּ אִוִּיתִיהָ, אֵינֶנָּה כָּעַלְמָה הָעֲזוּבָה	
	She shows compassion and is shown compassion, and loves as she is loved	הִיא מְרַחֶמֶת וְרֻחָמָה וְאֹהֶבֶת כַּאֲשֶׁר הִיא אֲהוּבָה	
	Not so was the other one.	לֹא כֵן הָיְתָה הָאַחֶרֶת.	
REZIN	She knew that your love was like the voice of joy and prayer[167]	הִיא יָדְעָה כִּי אַהֲבָתְךָ כְּקוֹל רִנָּה וּתְפִלָּה[167]	רצין
	Like **a learned tongue**[168] in the mouth of a child without understanding the interpretation of the word	כִּלְשׁוֹן לִמּוּדִים[168] בְּפִי יֶלֶד, מִבְּלִי הָבִין פִּתְרוֹן הַמִּלָּה	
	But come with me, son trifling as chaff in a storm[169]	אַךְ לְכָה אִתִּי בֵּן קַל כַּמֹּץ בִּסְעָרָה[169]	
	On account of one matter I shall be a help to you in distress	בַּעֲבוּר דָּבָר אֶחָד אֶהְיֶה לְךָ לְעֵזֶר בַּצָּרָה	
	Perhaps as a result of your wedding quarrel and strife will cease[170]	אוּלַי עֵקֶב חֲתֻנָּתְךָ, יֶחְדַּל רִיב וּמְדָנִים[170]	
	And your fathers' enmity will retreat because of the children's love.	וְאֵיבַת אֲבוֹתֵיכֶם תָּסוּר מִפְּנֵי אַהֲבַת הַבָּנִים.	
RAM	I am in a great rush, and in my haste I am babbling.[171]	אָץ אֲנִי מְאֹד וּבְחָפְזִי אֲנִי בוֹטֶה.[171]	רם
REZIN	One who is cunning makes his way, but one who rushes sins with his legs.	עָרוּם יְפַלֵּס דַּרְכּוֹ וְאָץ בְּרַגְלַיִם חוֹטֵא.	רצין
	(Exeunt)	(הולכים)	

165 Prov. 13:24 חוֹשֵׂךְ שִׁבְטוֹ שׂוֹנֵא בְנוֹ 'he who spares the rod hates his child'.
166 This and the following three lines form an ABAB rhyming pattern, mirroring the English except that the latter is composed of a rhyming couplet: 'now/allow' (2.3.81–2). Salkinson's speech has four lines, whereas Shakespeare's has three.
167 This and the next line form a rhyming couplet, mirroring Shakespeare's 'well/spell' (2.3.83–4).
168 Isa. 50:4.
169 This and the next line form a rhyming couplet, mirroring Shakespeare's 'me/be' (2.3.85–6).
170 This and the next line form a rhyming couplet, mirroring Shakespeare's 'prove/love' (2.3.87–8).
171 This and the next line form a rhyming couplet, mirroring Shakespeare's 'haste/fast' (2.3.89–90).

SCENE 4	*Street (Benaiah and Meraioth)*	רחוב (בניה ומריות)	מחזה ד'
MERAIOTH[172]	Where[173] is Ram hiding? Did he stay in his house tonight?	אָן[173] רָם מִסְתַּתֵּר? הֲלָן הַלַּיְלָה הַזֶּה בְּבֵיתוֹ?	מריות[172]
BENAIAH	He did not stay in his father's house, so I heard from the mouth of his men.	לֹא לָן בְּבֵית אָבִיו, כֵּן שָׁמַעְתִּי מִפִּי אֲנָשָׁיו.	בניה
MERAIOTH	That maiden Shoshannah, **stiff-necked**[174] and white of face	הַנַּעֲרָה הַהִיא שׁוֹשַׁנָּה, קְשַׁת עֹרֶף[174] וּלְבֶנֶת פָּנִים	מריות
	Indeed tortures his soul to the point of driving him mad.	עַנֵּה תְעַנֶּה אֶת נַפְשׁוֹ, עַד לְשַׁנּוֹת אֶת טַעְמוֹ.	
BENAIAH	Tubal, who is kin to old Abiel, sent a letter to his father's house.	תּוּבַל הַקָּרוֹב לַאֲבִיעֵל הַזָּקֵן, שָׁלַח מִכְתָּב לְבֵית אָבִיו.	בניה
MERAIOTH	It is a letter of summons, to face him in battle.	מִכְתַּב קְרִיאָה הוּא, לְהִתְרָאוֹת פָּנִים אִתּוֹ בַּקְּרָב.	מריות
BENAIAH	And Ram will answer the summons.	וְרָם יַעֲנֶה אֶת הַקְּרִיאָה.	בניה
MERAIOTH	Any man who knows how to write can write a response.	כָּל אִישׁ הַיֹּדֵעַ לִכְתֹּב יוּכַל לִכְתֹּב מַעֲנֶה.	מריות
BENAIAH[175]	He will answer the summons and will come to face him.	הוּא יַעֲנֶה אֶת הַקְּרִיאָה וְיָבוֹא לְהִתְרָאוֹת פָּנִים.	בניה[175]
MERAIOTH[176]	I am distressed for the wretch, for **he has surely been torn to pieces**.[177]	צַר לִי עַל הָאֻמְלָל, כִּי טָרֹף טֹרַף[177] הוּא.	מריות[176]
	A pure maiden has pierced him through with the flaming arrows of her black eyes	נַעֲרָה זַכָּה דְּקָרַתְהוּ בְּזִיקֵי עֵינֶיהָ הַשְּׁחֹרוֹת	
	An arrow of **love songs**[178] has entered his flesh through his ear	חֵץ שִׁיר עֲגָבִים[178] בָּא בִּבְשָׂרוֹ דֶּרֶךְ אָזְנוֹ	
	And his heart has been split by arrows from the hand of the blind archer	וּלְבָבוֹ נִבְקַע בִּבְנֵי אַשְׁפָּה מִיַּד הָעִוֵּר הָרֹבֶה קַשָּׁת	
	So how can he involve himself in fighting against Tubal?	וְאֵיךְ יִתְעָרֵב הוּא לְהִלָּחֵם עִם תּוּבַל?	

172 This speech is prose in the original (2.4.1–2).
173 Cf. Shakespeare's 'Where the devil'; Salkinson has transformed this into a neutral interrogative.
174 Exod. 33:3 עַם־קְשֵׁה־עֹרֶף 'a stiff-necked people'; also Exod. 33:5, 34:9; Deut. 9:13.
175 This speech is prose in the original (2.4.11–12).
176 This speech is prose in the original (2.4.13–17).
177 Gen. 37:33, 44:28.
178 Ezek. 33:32.

BENAIAH	But who is Tubal, and what is his power?	אַךְ מִי תּוּבַל וּמַה־כֹּחוֹ?	בניה
MERAIOTH[179]	He is more powerful than the commander of the grasshopper army[180]	רַב כֹּחַ הוּא מִשַּׂר צְבָא הַחֲגָבִים[180]	מריות[179]
	And he is greatly praised among **damsels playing timbrels**[181]	וּמְהֻלָּל הוּא בַּתִּשְׁבָּחוֹת בְּתוֹךְ **עֲלָמוֹת תּוֹפֵפוֹת**[181]	
	For he wages war like **one who strums upon the harp**[182]	כִּי יַעֲשֶׂה מִלְחָמָה **כְּפֹרֵט עַל פִּי הַנָּבֶל**[182]	
	Who keeps the time of playing note by note by the book	אֲשֶׁר יִשְׁמֹר מוֹעֵד הַנְּגִינָה אוֹת בְּאוֹת מִפִּי הַסֵּפֶר	
	He raises and lowers his voice and rests once or twice according to the rules.	יָרִים יוֹרִיד קוֹלוֹ וְיָנוּחַ אַחַת וּשְׁתַּיִם כַּמִּשְׁפָּט.	
	And the third time he plunges his sword into the heart of his enemy	וּבַשְּׁלִישִׁית יִתְקַע חַרְבּוֹ בְּלֵב אִישׁ מִלְחַמְתּוֹ	
	Who has approached him and remained unharmed? Even **a bud and blossom**[183]	מִי הִקְרִיב אֵלָיו וַיִּשְׁלָם? גַּם **כַּפְתּוֹר וָפֶרַח**[183]	
	Cannot withstand him, **and wherever he turns, he inflicts punishment**[184]	לֹא יִתְיַצְּבוּ בְּפָנָיו **וּבְכֹל אֲשֶׁר יִפְנֶה יַרְשִׁיעַ**[184]	
	He is a goring[185] man, a goring man from his youth	אִישׁ נַגָּח[185] הוּא, אִישׁ נַגָּח הוּא מִנְּעֻרָיו	
	Noble and a son of great men, one who knows **the speech of date palms and demons**[186]	שׁוֹעַ וּבֶן גְּדוֹלִים, יֹדֵעַ **שִׂיחַת דְּקָלִים וְשֵׁדִים**[186]	

179 This speech is prose in the original (2.4.19–26).

180 Cf. Shakespeare's 'Prince of Cats' (2.4.19). Grasshoppers are mentioned twice in the Hebrew Bible, in Num. 13:33 and Isa. 40:22. In both cases they are depicted as small and insignificant, which may have inspired Salkinson to select them in the present context.

181 Ps. 68:26 (68:25 in English Bibles).

182 Amos 6:5 הַפֹּרְטִים עַל־פִּי הַנָּבֶל 'those who strum upon the harp'.

183 Exod. 25:33, 37:19.

184 1 Sam. 14:47.

185 This term appears in Exod. 21:29 and 21:36, and refers to an ox that habitually gores.

186 Babylonian Talmud *Bava Batra* 134a, *Sukkah* 28a שיחת שדים ושיחת דקלים 'the speech of demons and the speech of date palms'.

	And all the words of the Frenchmen[187] that they call out **on the day of battle**[188]	וְכָל מִלּוֹת הַצָּרְפָתִים[187] אֲשֶׁר יִקְרְאוּ בְּיוֹם נָשֶׁק[188]	
	Are not concealed from him.[189]	לֹא נֶעֶלְמוּ מֵאִתּוֹ.[189]	
BENAIAH	Behold, Ram is coming, Ram is coming, behold.	הִנֵּה רָם בָּא, רָם הִנֵּה בָא.	בניה
MERAIOTH[190]	Ram's face is sad, he is low and not elevated[191]	רָם פָּנָיו רָעִים, שָׁפֵל הוּא וְלֹא רָם[191]	מריות[190]
	Why is he so meagre? Meagre of flesh like a thin fish.	מַדּוּעַ הוּא כָּכָה דַל? דַּל בָּשָׂר כְּדָג רָזֶה.	
	And **the expression of his face testifies against him**[192] that he is now composing poems	וְהַכָּרַת פָּנָיו תַּעֲנֶה בּוֹ[192] כָּעֵת יְחַבֵּר שִׁירִים	
	Like the poems of the poet Petrarch to his beloved Laura[193]	כְּשִׁירוֹת פֶּטְרַארְךְ הַמְשׁוֹרֵר אֶל לוֹרָה אֲהוּבָתוֹ[193]	
	But what is Laura worth compared to Ram's gorgeous beloved?	אַךְ מָה עֶרֶךְ לוֹרָה לַאֲהוּבַת רָם הַיְפֵה־פִיָּה	
	Why, she stands before her like one of the royal perfumers.[194]	הֲלֹא כְּאַחַת הָרַקָּחוֹת[194] תַּעֲמֹד הִיא לְפָנֶיהָ.	
	Dida[195] the wanderer beautifies herself in vain, and Cleopatra's[196] charm is a lie	דִּידָה[195] נוֹדֵדָה תִּתְיַפֶּה לַשָּׁוְא וְחֵן קְלֵיאָפַּטְרָה[196] שָׁקֶר	

187 Cf. Shakespeare's '*passado*' and '*punto reverso*' (2.4.26); note that the terms in the original derive from Italian, not French.

188 Ps. 140:8 (140:7 in English Bibles).

189 Salkinson has omitted the next nine lines (2.4.28–35) consisting primarily of a prose speech by Mercutio which is replete with wordplays. This omission is an example of the translational difficulties posed by Mercutio's speeches which Salkinson lamented in his introduction to *Ram and Jael*.

190 All lines from here until the nurse and Peter's arrival are prose in the original (2.4.36–109).

191 Cf. Shakespeare's 'Without his roe, like a dried herring' (2.4.37). Salkinson has found a Hebrew equivalent for Shakespeare's use of 'roe' as a pun on 'Romeo' (mentioned in the preceding line): in Hebrew רָם, as well as a personal name, is a participial form meaning 'elevated'.

192 Isa. 3:9 הַכָּרַת פְּנֵיהֶם עָנְתָה בָּם 'the expression of their faces testifies against them'.

193 This is one of the only cases where Salkinson has retained the non-Jewish cultural reference present in the original text, perhaps because the allusion is to a prominent member of the European literary canon venerated by Maskilic authors.

194 1 Sam. 8:13; this word denotes girls employed to mix perfume in the royal household (Koehler and Baumgartner 2001, 2: 1290); Salkinson uses it as a replacement for Shakespeare's 'kitchen wench' (2.4.40).

195 This corresponds to Shakespeare's 'Dido' (2.4.41), the Queen of Carthage. This name is not a feature of Jewish literature; Salkinson has changed the final vowel from -o to -a, which is the standard Hebrew feminine marker, but has not otherwise domesticated it. The reason for this is unclear, but it is possible that he chose to retain it because it refers to a historical figure rather than a mythological one.

196 Cleopatra is mentioned in the Babylonian Talmud (*Sanhedrin* 90b), in which she has a short conversation with the sage Rabbi Meir.

	And who are Helena[197] and Hera,[198] daughters of whoredom and **lewd women!**[199]	וּמִי הֵילֶנִי[197] וְהֵירָה,[198] בְּנוֹת זְנוּנִים **וְאִשֹּׁת הַזִּמָּה!**[199]	
	And Thisbe,[200] **one eye painted,**[201] **of what account is she?**[202]	וטִסְבֵּי,[200] **עַיִן אַחַת בַּפּוּךְ,**[201] **בַּמֶּה נֶחְשָׁבָה הִיא?**[202]	
	(To Ram upon his entrance)	(אל רם בבואו)	
	Greetings to you,[203] Frenchman! Greetings to your red trousers![204, 205]	הֲשָׁלוֹם לְךָ[203] צָרְפָתִי! הֲשָׁלוֹם לְמִכְנָסֶיךָ הָאֲדֻמּוֹת![204, 205]	
RAM[206]	I am happy to see your faces, my brothers and companions both.	שָׂמַחְתִּי לִרְאוֹת פְּנֵיכֶם אַחַי וְרֵעַי גַּם שְׁנֵיכֶם.	רם[206]
	I have donned the red trousers not in order for you to look at me	מִכְנְסֵי הָאֲדֻמּוֹת לָבַשְׁתִּי, לֹא בַּעֲבוּר תַּבִּיטוּ בִי אַתֶּם	
	But in order to attract the eyes of this woman who is coming towards us	כִּי אִם לִמְשׁוֹךְ עֵינֵי הַזֹּאת הַבָּאָה לִקְרָאתֵנוּ	
	Who **has ornaments on**[207] and is dressed in crimson and purple	אֲשֶׁר **עֶדְיָהּ עָלֶיהָ**[207] וּלְבוּשָׁהּ שָׁנִי וְאַרְגָּמָן	

197 Cf. Shakespeare's 'Helen' (2.4.42). While the reference in the English source text is to Helen of Troy, Salkinson's Helena is the Queen of Adiabene, who converted to Judaism in c. 30 CE. Queen Helena is mentioned in the Mishnah (*Yoma* 3:10 and *Nazir* 3:6). See Schalit and Gibson (2007) for further details.

198 Cf. Shakespeare's 'Hero' (2.4.42), from the Greek myth of Hero and Leander. As in the case of Dida, this name does not appear in Jewish literature; again, Salkinson has changed the final vowel from -o to -a, which is the standard Hebrew feminine marker, but has not otherwise domesticated it. While Hero is not a historical figure, Salkinson may have decided not to Judaize it because it appears as part of a list of names of historical and literary personages. The fact that Hero was a mortal rather than a god may have made him feel more comfortable forgoing domestication.

199 Ezek. 23:44.

200 Cf. Shakespeare's 'Thisbe' (2.4.42), the tragic heroine of the story of Pyramus and Thisbe from Ovid's *Metamorphoses*. As in the case of Dida and Hera, this name does not appear in Jewish literature; again, Salkinson may have chosen to retain it because he thought that it was more appropriate than a domesticated equivalent within the context of this list of historical and literary personages. As in the case of Hera, the fact that Thisbe was a mortal rather than a god may have made domestication a less pressing concern.

201 Jer. 4:30 כִּי־תִקְרְעִי בַפּוּךְ עֵינַיִךְ לַשָּׁוְא 'that you enlarge your eyes with paint in vain'.

202 Isa. 2:22 כִּי־בַמֶּה נֶחְשָׁב הוּא 'for of what account is he?'

203 Cf. Shakespeare's 'Signor Romeo, *bonjour*' (2.4.43–4). Salkinson has replaced the French greeting with a Hebrew one, in keeping with his general strategy of homogenizing linguistic variation within the source text.

204 Cf. Shakespeare's 'French slop' (2.4.44–5), i.e., French trousers. Salkinson's motivation for replacing 'French' with 'red' may be rooted in a desire to insert a comedic component into his translation in order to compensate for his subsequent omission of a large section of source text (see next note).

205 Salkinson has omitted the next 52 lines of the source text, beginning with the last sentence of 2.4.45 and ending with 2.4.96, which consist primarily of a bantering exchange between Romeo and Mercutio. The omission is most likely due to the fact that, as in the case discussed in note 189, the English lines include numerous puns that Salkinson found difficult to translate.

206 This speech has little basis in the original, which consists solely of 'Here's goodly gear!/A sail, a sail' (2.4.97–8). The motivation for Salkinson's expansion, including a reference to the red trousers and a comically exaggerated description of the nurse's larger-than-life appearance, may be rooted in a desire to make up for omitting the source text's witty repartee between Romeo and Mercutio (see notes 204 and 205) by injecting an element of comedy into the translation.

207 Exod. 33:4 וְלֹא־שָׁתוּ אִישׁ עֶדְיוֹ עָלָיו 'and no one put on his ornaments'.

	Who looks down **like a merchant's ship**[208] and is **as awesome as an army with banners.**[209]	הַנִּשְׁקָפָה כָּאֳנִיַּת* סוֹחֵר[208] וַאֲיֻמָּה כַּנִּדְגָּלוֹת.[209]	
MERAIOTH	Make way for the ship! A ship with an oar behind it.	פַּנּוּ מָקוֹם לָאֳנִיָּה! אֳנִיָּה וּמָשׁוֹט אַחֲרֶיהָ.	מריות
	(The nurse with her attendant Peter[210]*)*	(האומנת עם פֶּטֶר[210] משרתה)	
THE NURSE[211]	Peter!	פֶּטֶר!	האומנת[211]
PETER	Here I am.	הִנֵּנִי.	פטר
THE NURSE	Give me the fan.	תֶּן לִי אֶת הַמְנַשֵּׁב רוּחַ.	האומנת
MERAIOTH	Give her the fan, dear Peter	תֶּן לָהּ פֶּטֶר הַיָּקָר, אֶת הַמְנַשֵּׁב רוּחַ	מריות
	So that it may be **an eye-covering**[212] for her, because its face is better than her face.[213]	וְהָיָה לָהּ לִכְסוּת עֵינַיִם,[212] כִּי פָּנָיו טוֹבִים מִפָּנֶיהָ.[213]	
THE NURSE	Who is this man who dares to provoke me?	מִי הוּא הָאִישׁ הַזֶּה אֲשֶׁר יָעֹז לְהִתְגָּרוֹת בִּי?	האומנת
RAM	He is **a formed weapon,**[214] which God created	הוּא כְּלִי יוּצַר,[214] אֲשֶׁר יָצַר אֱלֹהִים	רם
	In order to destroy the work of His hands.	לְהַשְׁחִית מַעֲשֵׂה יָדָיו.	
MERAIOTH[215]	Do well with your tongue, Frenchman, and speak honour[216] before the old lady	הֵטִיבָה לְשׁוֹנְךָ צָרְפָתִי וְדַבֵּר נֶגֶד הַזְּקֵנָה כָּבוֹד[216]	מריות[215]

208 Prov. 31:14 הָיְתָה כָּאֳנִיּוֹת סוֹחֵר 'she is like the merchants' ships'.

209 Song of Songs 6:4, 10.

210 This is not a Hebrew name. As such, it could be interpreted as a straightfoward transliteration of the source text's 'Peter', which would be a departure from Salkinson's usual strategy of Hebraizing characters' names (the only other such cases are Balthasar in this play (First Part, note 18) and Marcos in *Ithiel* (First Part, note 155). However, it is a Hebrew word meaning 'firstborn' (commonly used with reference to livestock), and Salkinson may have chosen to retain it in his translation because of this somewhat comedic association.

211 All lines from here until Ram's mention of Rezin are prose in the original (2.4.98–172) (although some of these lines are missing from Salkinson's version; see notes 213 and 215).

212 Gen. 20:16.

213 Salkinson has omitted the next five lines of source text, consisting of a punning dialogue between Mercutio and Nurse (2.4.105–9). This is most likely because, as in the case of other such omissions, he found the language difficult to translate.

214 Isa. 54:17.

215 Salkinson has created this speech based on a fusion of two separate utterances by Mercutio appearing later in the original, namely 'No hare, sir, unless a hare, sir, in a lenten pie, that is something stale and hoar ere it be spent' (2.4.128–9) and 'Farewell, ancient lady, farewell lady, "lady, lady"' (2.4.137–8). Salkinson's version of the first line is very different from the English, including another mention of Ram as a 'Frenchman' and omitting the original reference to Lent; the only resemblance it bears to the source text is the allusion to the nurse's age. Salkinson seems to have placed this speech here in order to hasten Meraioth's exit, as he found the character's lines particularly challenging to translate.

216 This is a pun based on the fact that the Hebrew word for 'honour' can also mean 'heavy weight' or 'burden' (see next note).

* כָּאֳנִיַּת

	The lady is weighty[217] *(in a singing voice)*, lady, lady, lady!	כְּבוּדָה[217] הִיא הַגְּבִירָה (בקול שיר) גְּבִירָה, גְּבִירָה, גְּבִירָה!	
	(Meraioth and Benaiah exit)	(מריות ובניה הולכים)	
THE NURSE	Can you tell me where I might find the youth Ram?	הֲתַגִּיד לִי אָנָה אֶמְצָא אֶת רָם הַנַּעַר?	האומנת
RAM	I hereby tell you, that I am he;	הִנְנִי מַגִּיד לָךְ, כִּי אֲנִי אֲנִי הוּא;	רם
	I am very sorry that I have no other name.	צַר לִי מְאֹד כִּי אֵין לִי שֵׁם אַחֵר.	
THE NURSE	You have spoken well.[218]	הֱטִיבֹתָ לְדַבֵּר.[218]	האומנת
	But what do I have to do with this villain	אַךְ מַה־לִּי וּלְבֶן בְּלִיַּעַל הַזֶּה	
	Who has spread mockery and poured scorn like **a fool**?[219]	אֲשֶׁר הֵפִיחַ לָצוֹן וְשָׁפַךְ בּוּז **כְּאַחַד הָרֵקִים**?[219]	
	Am I like one of the damsels, like one of the girls of his age	הַאֲנִי כְּאַחַת הָעֲלָמוֹת, כְּאַחַת מִבְּנוֹת גִּילוֹ	
	With whom he amuses himself for a moment and scoffs at for a moment?	אֲשֶׁר רֶגַע יִשְׁתַּעֲשַׁע וָרֶגַע יְצַחֵק בָּהֶן?	
	My wrath is at you, Peter, for you saw a strange man	חֲמָתִי עָלֶיךָ פֶּטֶר, כִּי רָאִיתָ אִישׁ זָר	
	Coming to satiate his eye with me, and you stood opposite	הַבָּא לְהַשְׂבִּיעַ עֵינוֹ בִי וְאַתָּה עָמַדְתָּ מִנֶּגֶד	
	Like a man who cannot save.[220]	**כְּגֶבֶר לֹא יוּכַל לְהוֹשִׁיעַ.**[220]	
PETER	I have never seen a man come to satiate his eye with you;	מֵעוֹדִי לֹא רָאִיתִי אִישׁ בָּא לְהַשְׂבִּיעַ עֵינוֹ בָךְ;	פטר
	If I saw him, I would not be too weak to draw my sword	לוּ רָאִיתִי אוֹתוֹ, לֹא קָצְרָה יָדִי מֵהָרִיק חַרְבִּי	
	And show him who I am. For to save an oppressed man from the hand of his oppressor	וּלְהַרְאוֹתוֹ מִי אָנִי. כִּי לְהַצִּיל עָשׁוּק מִיַּד עֹשְׁקוֹ	
	As long as it is **according to the law and the commandment**,[221] there is none better than me.	אִם רַק **כַּתּוֹרָה וְכַמִּצְוָה**[221] הוּא, אֵין טוֹב מִמֶּנִּי.	

217 This is a pun linked to the noun כָּבוֹד 'honour' in the previous line (see preceding note).

218 This is a complete single-line speech in the original, 'You say well' (2.4.120). Salkinson has merged it with a later speech by the nurse (2.4.144) and omitted the intervening lines (2.4.121–43), except for Meraioth/Mercutio's lines (2.4.128–9 and 2.4.137–8) mentioned in note 215.

219 2 Sam. 6:20.

220 Jer. 14:9 כְּגִבּוֹר לֹא־יוּכַל לְהוֹשִׁיעַ 'like a warrior who cannot save'.

221 2 Chron. 14:3 (14:4 in English Bibles) הַתּוֹרָה וְהַמִּצְוָה 'the law and the commandment'.

THE NURSE	That worthless mocker **has provoked my bitter anger**[222]	הַלֵּץ הַנָּבָל הַהוּא, הִכְעִיס אֹתִי תַּמְרוּרִים[222]	האומנת
	A fire is kindled in my anger,[223] **and my knees are knocking against each other**[224]	אֵשׁ קָדְחָה בְאַפִּי[223] וְאַרְכֻּבוֹתַי דָּא לְדָא נָקְשָׁן[224]	
	But his day will yet come, **and I shall look upon his wretchedness.**[225]	אַךְ עוֹד יָבֹא יוֹמוֹ וַאֲנִי אֶרְאֶה בְּרָעָתוֹ.[225]	
	Now please, my lord, let me speak a word in your ears	עַתָּה בִּי אֲדֹנִי, תֶּן לִי לְדַבֵּר דָּבָר בְּאָזְנֶיךָ	
	As I have already said, my lady sent me to see you	כַּאֲשֶׁר כְּבָר אָמַרְתִּי, גְּבִרְתִּי שְׁלָחַתְנִי לִרְאוֹת פָּנֶיךָ	
	But the matter which she commanded me to tell you, I shall keep in my heart;	וְהַדָּבָר אֲשֶׁר צִוְּתָה לְהַגִּדְךָ, אֹתוֹ אֶשְׁמֹר בִּלְבָבִי;	
	Only this shall I say at the beginning, if you lead my lady astray	אֶפֶס זֹאת אַגִּיד בַּתְּחִלָּה, אִם תַּנְחֶה אֶת גְּבִרְתִּי	
	To a false paradise, because you delude her in the end,	אֶל גַּן עֵדֶן אַכְזָב, כִּי תַשְׁלֶה אֹתָהּ בָּאַחֲרוֹנָה	
	Your glory will not be on this path[226]	לֹא תִהְיֶה תִּפְאַרְתְּךָ עַל הַדֶּרֶךְ הַזֹּאת[226]	
	For the damsel is **tender and delicate,**[227] and **anyone who touches her for ill**	כִּי הָעַלְמָה רַכָּה וַעֲנֻגָּה[227] וְכָל הַנֹּגֵעַ בָּהּ לְרָעָה	
	Is like one who touches the apple of my eye.[228]	כְּנֹגֵעַ בְּבָבַת עֵינִי.[228]	
RAM	Please greet your lady in my name	פִּקְדִי נָא אֶת גְּבִרְתֵּךְ בִּשְׁמִי לְשָׁלוֹם	רם
	And I say to you: A man **intoxicates with love.**[229]	וַאֲנִי אֹמֵר לָךְ: אִישׁ מַשְׁגֶּה בְּאַהֲבָה.[229]	
THE NURSE	How beautiful are your words that come forth from a faithful heart	מַה יָּפוּ דְבָרֶיךָ הַיּוֹצְאִים מִלֵּב נֶאֱמָן	האומנת

222 Hosea 12:15 (12:14 in English Bibles) הִכְעִיס אֶפְרַיִם תַּמְרוּרִים 'Ephraim has provoked bitter anger'.

223 Deut. 32:22; Jer. 15:14.

224 Dan. 5:6 וְאַרְכֻבָּתֵהּ דָּא לְדָא נָקְשָׁן 'and his knees knocked against each other'. This is the only example in Salkinson's translations of *shibbuṣ* from an Aramaic portion of the Hebrew Bible.

225 Num. 11:15 וְאַל־אֶרְאֶה בְּרָעָתִי 'and let me not look upon my wretchedness'.

226 Judg. 4:9 לֹא תִהְיֶה תִּפְאַרְתְּךָ עַל־הַדֶּרֶךְ אֲשֶׁר אַתָּה הוֹלֵךְ 'your glory will not be on the path that you are going on'.

227 Isa. 47:1.

228 Zech. 2:12 (2:8 in English Bibles) כִּי הַנֹּגֵעַ בָּכֶם נֹגֵעַ בְּבָבַת עֵינוֹ 'for whoever touches you touches the apple of his own eye'.

229 Prov. 5:19 בְּאַהֲבָתָהּ תִּשְׁגֶּה תָמִיד 'may you always be intoxicated in her love'.

	How much she will rejoice and take delight to lie in your bosom.	כַּמָּה תִּשְׂמַח וְתִתְעַלֵּס, לִהְיוֹת שֹׁכֶבֶת חֵיקֶךָ.	
RAM	What will you tell her; indeed, you have not understood my word.	מַה־תֹּאמְרִי לָהּ, הֵן לֹא הֵבַנְתְּ דְּבָרִי.	רם
THE NURSE	I have understood your word well, and I shall tell it to her	הֲבִנֹתִי דְבָרְךָ הֵיטֵב וְאֹתוֹ אַגִּיד לָהּ	האומנת
	Just as you told me here that **you are intoxicated in her love.**[230]	כַּאֲשֶׁר הִגַּדְתָּ בָּזֶה, כִּי תִשְׁגֶּה בְּאַהֲבָתָהּ.[230]	
	So speaks an honourable man who desires to take a wife.	כָּזֹאת יְדַבֵּר אִישׁ נִכְבָּד הֶחָפֵץ לָקַחַת אִשָּׁה.	
RAM	Tell her to ask permission to come today to the prayerhouse	אִמְרִי לָהּ לְבַקֵּשׁ רִשְׁיוֹן לָבֹא הַיּוֹם לְבֵית הַתְּפִלָּה	רם
	To confess at noon and there in the chamber of Rezin the priest[231]	לְהִתְוַדּוֹת בַּצָּהֳרַיִם וְשָׁם בְּלִשְׁכַּת רְצִין הַכֹּהֵן[231]	
	She shall confess and enter into a covenant with me –	תִּתְוַדֶּה וְתָבוֹא בִּבְרִית אִתִּי–	
	And take this for yourself as your payment.	וְהֵא לָךְ זֹאת בִּשְׂכָרֵךְ.	
THE NURSE	I shall not take anything from your hand, not even a single coin.[232]	לֹא אֶקַּח מִיָּדְךָ מְאוּמָה, אַף לֹא אֲגוֹרָה[232] אֶחָת.	האומנת
RAM	But I say that you must take it from my hand.	וַאֲנִי הִנְנִי מַגִּיד כִּי תִקְחִי מִיָּדִי.	רם
THE NURSE	Is it today at noon? Why, she will come as you have said.	הַאִם הַיּוֹם בַּצָּהֳרַיִם? הֲלֹא תָבֹא כַּאֲשֶׁר אָמַרְתָּ.	האומנת
RAM	And you, dear Nurse, stand behind the wall[233]	וְאַתְּ אֹמֶנֶת הַיְקָרָה תַּעַמְדִי מֵאַחֲרֵי הַכֹּתֶל[233]	רם
	Near the priest's chamber and there you will find my servant	אֵצֶל לִשְׁכַּת הַכֹּהֵן וְשָׁם תִּמְצְאִי אֶת עַבְדִּי	
	Who will bring you ropes bound together in the manner of a ladder	אֲשֶׁר יָבִיא לָךְ עֲבֹתִים קְשׁוּרִים כְּמַעֲשֵׂה הַסֻּלָּם	

230 Prov. 5:19 בְּאַהֲבָתָהּ תִּשְׁגֶּה תָמִיד 'may you always be intoxicated in her love'.
231 Cf. Shakespeare's 'Friar' (2.4.174).
232 This word appears only once in the Hebrew Bible, in 1 Sam. 2:36. It is typically translated either as 'small amount of money', 'piece of silver', or 'payment'.
233 Cf. Shakespeare's 'abbey wall' (2.4.179); Salkinson has omitted the reference to the Christian institution.

	That is the ladder on which I shall ascend to **my greatest joy**[234] tonight.	הוּא הַסֻּלָּם אֶעֱלֶה בּוֹ אֶל רֹאשׁ **שִׂמְחָתִי**[234] הַלָּיְלָה.	
	Just keep the secret, and know that there is payment for your toil.	רַק שִׁמְרִי אֶת הַסּוֹד וּדְעִי כִּי יֵשׁ שָׂכָר לַעֲמָלֵךְ.	
	Now go in peace, and greet your mistress.	עַתָּה לְכִי לְשָׁלוֹם וּפִקְדִי אֶת גְּבִרְתֵּךְ.	
THE NURSE	May the LORD give you His blessing; but please listen to me.	יְצַו הַשֵּׁם בִּרְכָתוֹ עָלֶיךָ; אַךְ אָנָּא שְׁמָעֵנִי.	האומנת
RAM	Speak, **woman of valour**.[235]	דַּבְּרִי **אֵשֶׁת חַיִל**.[235]	רם
THE NURSE	Is your servant faithful, and will not reveal a secret?	הַאִם עַבְדְּךָ נֶאֱמָן הוּא וְלֹא יְגַלֶּה סוֹד?	האומנת
	Haven't you heard any of the proverbs of the masses?	הַאִם לֹא שָׁמַעְתָּ מִמִּשְׁלֵי הֶהָמוֹן מְאוּמָה?	
	'Two can keep a secret if one of them goes to the grave.'	„שְׁנַיִם יִצְפְּנוּ סוֹד, אִם אֶחָד מֵהֶם יֵרֵד דּוּמָה".	
RAM	I vouch for my servant with my life; **like a mute, he will not open his mouth**.[236]	אֶת עַבְדִּי בְּנַפְשִׁי אֶעֶרְבֶנּוּ, **כְּאִלֵּם לֹא יִפְתַּח פִּיו**.[236]	רם
THE NURSE[237]	My lady is unique among women, unique among all charming girls	גְּבִרְתִּי אַחַת הִיא בַּנָּשִׁים, אַחַת בְּכָל בְּנוֹת חֵן	האומנת[237]
	If you had seen her in her childhood, at that time when she had just started to babble!	לוּ רָאִיתָ אֹתָהּ בְּיַלְדוּתָהּ, כַּאֲשֶׁר הֵחֵלָּה אָז לְבַטֵּא!	
	If you had heard the prattling of her lips, which was sweeter than any **pleasant words**,[238]	לוּ שָׁמַעְתָּ לַהַג שְׂפָתֶיהָ, אֲשֶׁר עָרֵב מִכָּל **אִמְרֵי נֹעַם**,[238]	
	And even Paris, one of the noblemen, of the aristocrats who are in our city	וְגַם פָּרִיז מִבְּנֵי הָאֲצִילִים, מֵהַפַּרְתְּמִים אֲשֶׁר בְּעִירֵנוּ	
	Yearns and lies in wait to catch this fish on his hook	יִתְאָו יֶאֱרֹב לִמְשׁוֹךְ הַדָּגָה הַזֹּאת בְּחַכָּתוֹ	
	But she spurns him, and will not consider him	אַךְ הִיא תִּמְאַס בּוֹ וְלֹא תַבִּיט אֵלָיו	

234 Ps. 137:6.
235 Prov. 12:4, 31:10; Ruth 3:11.
236 Ps. 38:14 (38:13 in English Bibles).
237 This speech is prose in the original (2.4.191–9).
238 Prov. 15:26, 16:24.

	For **she utterly abhors him; she utterly detests him**[239] as an abomination.	כִּי תַעֵב תְּתַעֲבֶנּוּ, כְּשֶׁקֶץ שַׁקֵּץ תְּשַׁקְּצֶנּוּ.[239]	
	How many times have I mocked her, until I angered her	כַּמֶּה פְּעָמִים הֵתַלְתִּי בָהּ, עַד אֲשֶׁר הִכְעַסְתִּיהָ	
	Saying, Paris is the man **under whose wings she should find shelter**[240]	לֵאמֹר פָּרִיז הוּא הָאִישׁ אֲשֶׁר בִּכְנָפָיו תֶּחְסֶה[240]	
	And as for her, her face grew pale from anger like a white handkerchief[241]	וְהִיא חָוְרוּ פָנֶיהָ מִכַּעַס כְּמִטְפַּחַת לְבָנָה[241]	
	Like **fine Egyptian linen**[242] on a cow's table.	כְּמוֹ אֵטוּן מִצְרַיִם[242] עַל שֻׁלְחַן פָּרָה.	
RAM	A cow does not have a table; maybe King Pharaoh.[243]	פָּרָה אֵין לָהּ שֻׁלְחָן, אוּלַי פַּרְעֹה[243] הַמֶּלֶךְ.	רם
THE NURSE	But tell me, what is the first letter of your name?	אַךְ הַגִּידָה לִי, מֶה הָאוֹת הָרִאשׁוֹן מִשְּׁמֶךָ?	האומנת
	Is it like the first letter of the names 'friend' and 'shepherd'?[244]	הַאִם כְּאוֹת הָרִאשׁוֹן הוּא מִשְּׁמוֹת רֵעַ וָרֹעֶה?[244]	
RAM	Why do you ask such a thing? *Resh* is the first of the three names.	לָמָּה תִדְרְשִׁי כָזֹאת? ר הוּא הָרִאשׁוֹן לִשְׁלֹשֶׁת הַשֵּׁמוֹת.	רם
THE NURSE	**Get out**,[245] mocker, I know that the letter *resh*	גֶּשׁ־הָלְאָה[245] מִתְלוֹצֵץ, יָדַעְתִּי כִּי אוֹת ר	האומנת
	Is the first of the name of a small dog that belongs to my lady[246]	הוּא הָרִאשׁוֹן לְשֵׁם כֶּלֶב קָטֹן אֲשֶׁר לִגְבִרְתִּי[246]	

239 Deut. 7:26 שַׁקֵּץ | תְּשַׁקְּצֶנּוּ וְתַעֵב | תְּתַעֲבֶנּוּ 'you shall utterly detest it and utterly abhor it'.

240 Ps. 91:4 וְתַחַת־כְּנָפָיו תֶּחְסֶה 'and under his wings you will find refuge'; Ruth 2:12 אֲשֶׁר־בָּאת לַחֲסוֹת תַּחַת־כְּנָפָיו 'under whose wings you have come to find refuge'.

241 This word appears twice in the Hebrew Bible (Isa. 3:22 and Ruth 3:15), where it means 'shawl' or 'cloak'. From the rabbinic period onwards it more commonly means 'handkerchief'; Salkinson is using it in the latter sense.

242 Prov. 7:16.

243 This is a pun based on the similarity in sound between פָּרָה *para* 'cow' and פַּרְעֹה *par'o* 'Pharaoh'. This line lacks a basis in the original, and it is unclear why Salkinson has inserted it, unless he felt that the Hebrew translation of the upcoming wordplay centred on the English letter *r* (see next note) did not sufficiently echo the punning nature of the original and needed reinforcement.

244 Both of these Hebrew words start with the letter *resh*, corresponding to the English *r*. This is Salkinson's equivalent to Shakespeare's 'Doth not rosemary and Romeo begin both with a letter?' (2.4.198–9).

245 Gen. 19:9.

246 This corresponds to Shakespeare's 'Ah, mocker, that's the dog's name' (2.4.201). The English line is based on a pun between the letter *r* and the 'arr' sound made by snarling dogs (Weis 2012: 224, notes 201–4). This meaning is lost in Hebrew, so Salkinson has changed generic 'dog' to 'small dog belonging to my lady', suggesting that Jael has a dog whose name starts with the letter *resh*.

	But there is no *resh* in your name. Indeed, in any case	אַךְ אֵין ר בִשְׁמֶךָ. אוּלָם בֵּין כֹּה וָכֹה	
	If only you could hear with your own ears as my lady sings	לוּ שָׁמַעְתָּ בְּאָזְנֶיךָ עֵת תָּשִׁיר גְּבִרְתִּי*	
	'Ram, my friend, my shepherd – Ram, my friend, my shepherd'	„רָם רֵעִי רֹעִי – רָם רֵעִי רֹעִי"	
	I know that you would take pleasure in it. And she told me	יָדַעְתִּי כִּי הִתְעַנַּגְתָּ. וְהִיא הִגִּידָה לִּי	
	That the first letter of these three names is the same.	כִּי הָאוֹת הָרִאשׁוֹן לִשְׁלֹשֶׁת הַשֵּׁמוֹת הָאֵלֶּה אֶחָד.	
RAM	Please mention me to your lady.	הַזְכִּירֵנִי נָא אֶל גְּבִרְתֵּךְ.	רם
THE NURSE	I shall mention your name **evening, morning, and noon**.[247] – *(Ram exits)*	אֶת שִׁמְךָ אַזְכִּיר עֶרֶב בֹּקֶר וְצָהֳרָיִם[247] – (רם הולך)	האומנת
	Peter!	פֶּטֶר!	
PETER	Here I am.	הִנֵּנִי.	פטר
THE NURSE	Take the fan and go before me. *(Exeunt)*	קַח לְךָ אֶת הַמְנַשֵּׁב רוּחַ וְלֵךְ לְפָנָי. (הולכים)	האומנת
SCENE 5	*Abiel's vineyard*	כרם אביעל	מחזה ה'
JAEL	Indeed at the ninth hour I sent the nurse	הֵן בְּשָׁעָה הַתְּשִׁיעִית שָׁלַחְתִּי אֶת הָאֹמֶנֶת	יעל
	And within half an hour she promised me to return	וּבְמֶשֶׁךְ חֲצִי שָׁעָה הִבְטִיחָה לִי לָשׁוּב	
	Perhaps she has not found him – but the matter is not so	אוּלַי לֹא מָצְאָה אֹתוֹ – אַךְ לֹא כֵן הַדָּבָר	
	It is only that she limps, and love demands **messengers as swift**[248]	רַק צֹלֵעָה הִיא וְהָאַהֲבָה דֹּרֶשֶׁת צִירִים קַלִּים[248]	
	As thoughts that run ten times faster than the sun's rays	כְּמַחְשָׁבוֹת הַמְמַהֲרוֹת לָרוּץ עֶשֶׂר פְּעָמִים מִקַּוֵּי הַשֶּׁמֶשׁ	
	Which run to drive out the shadows from **dark mountains**.[249]	הָרָצִים לְהַבְרִיחַ הַצְּלָלִים מֵעַל הָרֵי נָשֶׁף.[249]	
	Because of this **doves and young pigeons**[250] are chosen	בַּעֲבוּר זֹאת נִבְחֲרוּ תּוֹרִים וּבְנֵי יוֹנָה[250]	

247 Ps. 55:18 (55:17 in English Bibles) עֶרֶב וָבֹקֶר וְצָהֳרַיִם 'evening and morning and noon'.
248 Isa. 18:2 מַלְאָכִים קַלִּים 'swift messengers' (the synonym צִירִים appears earlier in the verse).
249 Jer. 13:16.
250 Lev. 5:7 שְׁתֵּי תֹרִים אוֹ־שְׁנֵי בְנֵי־יוֹנָה 'two doves or two young pigeons'

* גְּבִרְתִּי

Those possessed of wing and feather, to pull the wagon of love	בַּעֲלֵי אֵבֶר וָנֹצָה, לִמְשׁוֹךְ הָעֲגָלָה לְאַהֲבַת דּוֹדִים
And all messengers of love are possessed of arrows and have wings[251]	וְכָל מַלְאֲכֵי הָאַהֲבָה בַּעֲלֵי חִצִּים וּכְנָפַיִם לָמוֹ[251]
And behold, the sun in its cycle has risen up to the height of the chariot-wheel	וְהִנֵּה הַשֶּׁמֶשׁ בִּתְקוּפָתוֹ עָלָה עַד מְרוֹם הַגַּלְגָּל
And from the ninth hour until now it has been three long hours	וּמִשָּׁעָה הַתְּשִׁיעִית עַד הֵנָּה שָׁלֹשׁ שָׁעוֹת אֲרֻכּוֹת
And she still has not returned. If she had a warm heart	וְעוֹדֶנָּה לֹא שָׁבָה. לוּ הָיָה לָהּ לֵב חַם
And youthful blood in her veins, her feet would not have delayed until now	וּדְמֵי נְעוּרִים בְּעוֹרְקֶיהָ לֹא אֶחֱרוּ פְּעָמֶיהָ עַד הֵנָּה
For she would have hastened on her way like a catapult from the slinger's hand	כִּי הָיְתָה מְבֹהֶלֶת בְּדַרְכָּהּ כְּכַדּוּר מִיַּד הַקַּלָּע
To bring the words to the one **whom my soul loves**[252]	לְהָבִיא אֶת הַדְּבָרִים אֶל **שֶׁאָהֲבָה נַפְשִׁי**[252]
And to return to inform me at once of **what he answered and what he spoke**[253]	וְלָשׁוּב* לְהַשְׁמִיעֵנִי כְּרֶגַע, **מֶה עָנָה וּמַה־דִּבֵּר.**[253]
But the old are not living; they have **a different spirit**[254, 255]	אַךְ הַזְּקֵנִים אֵינָם חַיִּים, **אִתָּם רוּחַ אַחֶרֶת**[254, 255]
They move heavily from their place; their soul is a burden and their foot is lead.	בִּכְבֵדוּת יָמוּשׁוּ מִמְּקוֹמָם נַפְשָׁם מַעֲמָסָה וְרַגְלָם עֹפָרֶת.
But here she comes –	אַךְ הִנֵּה בָּאָה –
(The nurse and Peter)	(האומנת ופטר)
My nurse! My nurse! Are you well? What are the tidings in your mouth?	אֹמַנְתִּי! אֹמַנְתִּי! הֲשָׁלוֹם? מַה־בְּשׂוֹרָה בְּפִיךְ
Have you seen him? Tell the servant to go.	הֲרָאִית אֶת פָּנָיו? אִמְרִי לַנַּעַר וְיַעֲבֹר.

---

251 This corresponds to Shakespeare's 'And therefore hath the wind-swift Cupid wings' (2.5.8); as usual, Salkinson has omitted the mythological reference.

252 Song of Songs 1:7, 3:1, 2, 3.

253 Jer. 23:35 מֶה־עָנָה יְהוָה וּמַה־דִּבֶּר יְהוָה 'what has the LORD answered, and what has the LORD spoken?'

254 Num. 14:24.

255 This and the next line form a rhyming couplet, mirroring Shakespeare's 'dead/lead' (2.5.16–17).

* לְשׁוּב

THE NURSE	Peter, go and stand by the gate. *(Peter exits)*	פֶּטֶר לֵךְ וַעֲמֹד עַל יַד הַשָּׁעַר. (פטר הולך)	האומנת
JAEL	Now my nurse, my comfort – but **why is your face sad**?[256]	עַתָּה אֹמַנְתִּי נֶחָמָתִי – אַךְ מַדּוּעַ **פָּנַיִךְ רָעִים**?[256]	יעל
	If there are bad tidings in your mouth, inform me of them with favourable lips	אִם בְּשׂוֹרָה רָעָה בְּפִיךְ, הַשְׁמִיעִנִי בְּשִׂפְתֵי רָצוֹן	
	And if they are good, why do you vex me with **a broken spirit**?[257]	וְאִם טוֹבָה הִיא, לָמָּה תְּעַצְּבִנִי **בְּרוּחַ נְכֵאָה**.[257]	
THE NURSE	Indeed my soul is weary; wait for me a little while	הֵן נַפְשִׁי עָיְפָה, חַכִּי לִי מְעַט רֶגַע	האומנת
	The exertion of the way has been too much for me; all of **my bones have wasted away**.[258]	עֲמַל הַדֶּרֶךְ רַב מִמֶּנִּי, כָּל **עֲצָמַי עָשֵׁשׁוּ**.[258]	
JAEL	Give me the word of your tidings and I shall give you my bones	תְּנִי לִי דְּבַר בְּשׂרָתֵךְ וַאֲנִי אֶתֵּן לָךְ עֲצָמָי	יעל
	But please, my nurse, my dear nurse, please speak.	אַךְ אָנָּא אֹמַנְתִּי, אֹמַנְתִּי הַיְקָרָה, נָא דַּבֵּרִי.	
THE NURSE	Why are you pressing me?[259] Wait for me a little while longer.	לָמָּה זֶה תָּאִיצִי בִי?[259] חַכִּי לִי עוֹד מְעָט.	האומנת
	Do you not see that **there is no breath left in me**?[260]	הַאִם לֹא תִרְאִי, כִּי **לֹא נוֹתְרָה בִּי נְשָׁמָה**?[260]	
JAEL	How can you tell me that there is no breath left in you	אֵיךְ תּוּכְלִי לְהַגִּיד, כִּי לֹא נוֹתְרָה בָךְ נְשָׁמָה	יעל
	When there is breath in you to tell me that there is no breath left in you?	וּנְשָׁמָה בָךְ לְהַגִּיד, כִּי לֹא נוֹתְרָה בָךְ נְשָׁמָה?	
	Out of impatience you refuse to give an answer to my question	מִקֹּצֶר רוּחַ תִּמָּנְעִי מִתֵּת מַעֲנֶה לְשַׁאֲלָתִי	
	While **you are multiplying words**[261] for nothing on the matter of impatience	**וּמִלִּין תַּכְבִּירִי**[261] חִנָּם עַל דְּבַר קֹצֶר רוּחַ	
	Just tell me this, are your tidings good or bad?	רַק זֹאת הַגִּידִי לִי, הֲטוֹבָה בְּשׂרָתֵךְ אוֹ רָעָה?	
	Say good or bad and I shall be silent and wait for you,	אִמְרִי טוֹבָה אוֹ רָעָה וַאֲנִי אֶשְׁקֹט וְאֶתְחוֹלֵל לָךְ,	

---

256 Neh. 2:2 מַדּ֤וּעַ ׀ פָּנֶ֣יךָ רָעִ֗ים 'why is your face sad'.
257 Prov. 15:13, 17:22, 18:14.
258 Ps. 31:11 (31:10 in English Bibles).
259 Cf. Shakespeare's 'Jesu, what haste!' (2.5.29). Salkinson has omitted the Catholic oath.
260 1 Kings 17:17 לֹא־נֽוֹתְרָה־בּ֖וֹ נְשָׁמָֽה 'there was no breath left in him'.
261 Job 35:16 מִלִּ֣ין יַכְבִּֽר 'he multiplies words'.

	Please say and calm me down. Are they good or bad?	אָנָּא אִמְרִי וְהַרְגִּיעִנִי. הֲטוֹבָה הִיא אִם רָעָה?	
THE NURSE[262]	It is just as easy for me to choose one of these two paths	נָקֵל לִי לִבְחֹר אַחַת מִשְּׁתֵּי הַדְּרָכִים הָאֵלֶּה	האומנת[262]
	As it is for you to choose one of the men to marry.	כַּאֲשֶׁר נָקֵל לָךְ לִבְחֹר אִישׁ מֵהָאֲנָשִׁים לְהִבָּעֵל לוֹ.	
	Behold, your chosen one Ram has more **beautiful eyes**[263] than many	הִנֵּה רָם בְּחִירֵךְ יְפֵה עֵינַיִם[263] הוּא מֵרַבִּים	
	Indeed his legs, his hands, and his feet, **nothing on earth is their equal**[264]	אַךְ שׁוֹקָיו יָדָיו וְרַגְלָיו, אֵין עַל עָפָר מָשְׁלָם[264]	
	He does not know flattery, and is not much for **pleasant words**[265]	הוּא חֲלָקוֹת לֹא יֵדַע וְאִמְרֵי נֹעַם[265] לֹא יַרְבֶּה	
	Yet all those who see him perceive that he is **an unblemished lamb**[266]	וְכָל רֹאָיו יֶחֱזוּ בוֹ כִּי הוּא שֶׂה תָּמִים.[266]	
	Go, my delightful girl, serve the LORD and be well	לְכִי לָךְ בַּת שַׁעֲשׁוּעַי, עִבְדִי אֵת אֲדֹנָי וְטוֹב לָךְ	
	Where did you eat at noon?	אָנָה אָכַלְתְּ בַּצָּהֳרָיִם?	
JAEL	Desist, all these things I knew long ago	הַרְפִּי, כָּל אֵלֶּה יָדַעְתִּי מֵאָז	יעל
	But what did he answer regarding the matter of the wedding?	אַךְ מַה עָנָה הוּא עַל דְּבַר הַחֲתֻנָּה?	
	What did he say about this?	מַה־דִּבֶּר עַל זֹאת?	
THE NURSE	Oh, **my head, my head**![267] My head is splitting into pieces	הָהּ רֹאשִׁי רֹאשִׁי![267] רֹאשִׁי יִבָּקַע לִבְקִיעִים	האומנת
	And my shoulder **is like to break apart**;[268] my shoulder is going to fall off my back.	וּכְתֵפִי מְחַשֶּׁבֶת לְהִשָּׁבֵר,[268] כְּתֵפִי מִשִּׁכְמָהּ תִּפּוֹל.	

262 This speech is prose in the original (2.5.38–45).
263 1 Sam. 16:12.
264 Job 41:25 (41:33 in English Bibles) אֵֽין־עַל־עָפָר מָשְׁלוֹ ‘nothing on earth is his equal’.
265 Prov. 15:26, 16:24.
266 Exod. 12:5.
267 2 Kings 4:19.
268 Jonah 1:4 וְהָאֳנִיָּה חִשְּׁבָה לְהִשָּׁבֵר ‘and the ship was like to break apart’.

May the One Who Deals Bountifully not deal bountifully with you as He has with me

אַל יִגְמָלֵךְ הַגֹּמֵל גְּמוּל כַּאֲשֶׁר גָּמַלְתְּ עָלָי

For you have sent me here and there in order to bring me **to the gates of death**.[269]

כִּי שְׁלַחְתִּנִי הֵנָּה וָהֵנָּה לַהֲבִיאֵנִי עַד שַׁעֲרֵי מָוֶת.[269]

JAEL I am distressed, I am greatly distressed, that there is no peace in your bones

יעל צַר לִי, צַר לִי מְאֹד, כִּי אֵין שָׁלוֹם בַּעֲצָמָיִךְ

But tell me, my nurse, what did the man of my covenant say?

אַךְ אִמְרִי לִי אֹמַנְתִּי מַה־דִּבֵּר אִישׁ בְּרִיתִי?

THE NURSE The man of your covenant speaks like **a blameless and upright man**[270]

האומנת אִישׁ בְּרִיתֵךְ מְדַבֵּר, כְּאִישׁ תָּם וְיָשָׁר[270]

Like one with **a faithful spirit**,[271] like one with **a willing heart**,[272] like one with **beautiful eyes**[273]

כְּנֶאֱמַן רוּחַ,[271] כִּנְדִיב לֵב,[272] כִּיפֵה עֵינַיִם[273]

And also, on my life! Indeed he speaks as a valiant man.[274]

וְגַם חֵי נַפְשִׁי! כִּי כְּבֶן חַיִל יְדַבֵּר?[274]

Where is your mother?

אֵיפֹה הִיא אִמֵּךְ?

JAEL Where is my mother? Where indeed might she be?

יעל אֵיפֹה הִיא אִמִּי? אֵיפֹה הָיֹה תִהְיֶה?

She is sitting inside the house.

הִיא יֹשֶׁבֶת בְּתוֹךְ הַבָּיִת.

What has become of you, that you respond so strangely?

מֶה הָיָה לָךְ, כִּי תְשִׁיבִי זָרוֹת כָּאֵלֶּה*?

'The man of your covenant speaks like a man of valour – where is your mother?'

„אִישׁ בְּרִיתֵךְ כְּבֶן חַיִל יְדַבֵּר – אֵיפֹה הִיא אִמֵּךְ?"

THE NURSE But why are you speaking in haste?[275] Are you intent on fighting with me?

האומנת וּמדוּעַ** בְּחִפָּזוֹן תְּדַבֵּרִי[275]? הַהוֹאַלְתְּ לְהִתְקוֹטֵט בִּי?

Is this the balm for my pain, and the medicine for my bones?

הֲזֶה הוּא הַצֳּרִי לְמַכְאֹבִי וְרִפְאוּת לְעַצְמוֹתָי?

Next time you go on this errand instead of me.

בִּמְלַאֲכוּת זֹאת שֵׁנִית, תֵּלְכִי אַתְּ וְלֹא אָנִי.

269 Ps. 107:18.
270 Job 1:8, 2:3.
271 Prov. 11:13.
272 Exod. 35:22; 2 Chron. 29:31.
273 1 Sam. 16:12.
274 The Hebrew has a question mark here, but the utterance seems to be a statement.
275 Cf. Shakespeare's 'O God's Lady' (2.5.61); Salkinson has removed the reference to the Virgin Mary.

* כָּאֵלֶּה
** וּמַדּוּעַ

JAEL	That's enough for us of this confusion; tell me, what did Ram say?	רַב לָנוּ מְבוּכָה זוּ; הַגִּידִי מַה־דִּבֶּר רָם?	יעל
THE NURSE	Do you have permission to go to the prayerhouse today?	הֲיֵשׁ רִשְׁיוֹן בְּיָדֵךְ לָלֶכֶת הַיּוֹם לְבֵית הַתְּפִלָּה?	האומנת
JAEL	Yes.	הֵן.	יעל
THE NURSE	If so, hurry, go to the chamber of Rezin the priest	אִם כֵּן מַהֲרִי לְכִי אֶל לִשְׁכַּת רְצִין הַכֹּהֵן	האומנת
	There you will find the man, and there too you will become his wife.	שָׁם תִּמְצְאִי אֶת הָאִישׁ וְגַם שָׁם תִּהְיִי לוֹ לְאִשָּׁה.	
	See how your cheeks have reddened from the heat of your young blood	רְאִי אֵיךְ אָדְמוּ לְחָיַיִךְ מֵחֹם דְּמֵי נְעוּרָיִךְ	
	I know that your face reddens like crimson at a piece of news.	יָדַעְתִּי כִּי לְדָבָר חָדָשׁ פָּנַיִךְ כַּשָּׁנִים יַאֲדִימוּ.	
	Hurry to the prayerhouse,[276] whereas I shall go a different way	מַהֲרִי לְבֵית הַתְּפִלָּה[276] וַאֲנִי אֵלֵךְ דֶּרֶךְ אַחֶרֶת	
	I must bring the ladder on which your beloved will ascend	עָלַי לְהָבִיא אֶת הַסֻּלָּם, בּוֹ יַעֲלֶה יְדִידֵךְ	
	In the middle of the night and the darkness,[277] like one ascending to a bird's nest.	**בְּאִישׁוֹן לַיְלָה וַאֲפֵלָה**,[277] כְּעֹלֶה אֶל קַן צִפּוֹר.	
	I am an ass of burden and through my toil your lover will find you[278]	אֲנִי חֲמוֹר לְמַשָּׂא וּבַעֲמָלִי מְאַהֲבֵךְ יִמְצָאֵךְ[278]	
	But when night comes, *you* will lie under your burden.	אַךְ בְּבוֹא הַלַּיְלָה תִּרְבְּצִי אַתְּ תַּחַת מַשָּׂאֵךְ.	
	Go, my daughter, to the prayerhouse; as for me, my mealtime is approaching.[279]	לְכִי בִתִּי לְבֵית הַתְּפִלָּה וַאֲנִי עֵת אֲרֻחָתִי קְרוֹבָה.[279]	
JAEL	I shall hurry to **my greatest joy**,[280] and farewell, my good nurse! *(Exits)*	אָחִישָׁה **לְרֹאשׁ שִׂמְחָתִי**[280] וְשָׁלוֹם לְאֹמַנְתִּי הַטּוֹבָה! (הולכות)	יעל

276 Cf. Shakespeare's 'church' (2.5.72); Salkinson's version is religiously neutral.
277 Prov. 7:9.
278 This and the next line form a rhyming couplet, mirroring Shakespeare's 'delight/night' (2.5.75–6).
279 This and the next line form a rhyming couplet, mirroring Shakespeare's 'cell/farewell' (2.5.77–8).
280 Ps. 137:6.

SCENE 6	*Prayerhouse chamber (Rezin and Ram)*	לשכת בית התפלה (רצין ורם)	מחזה ו'
REZIN	May the heavens pour out a blessing, and may the pleasantness of the LORD be upon us	הַשָּׁמַיִם יָרִיקוּ בְּרָכָה וִיהִי נֹעַם אֲדֹנָי עָלֵינוּ	רצין
	Without visiting with afflictions our deeds that we do today.	לִבְלִי יִפְקֹד בִּנְגָעִים מַעֲשֵׂנוּ שֶׁאָנוּ עֹשִׂים הַיּוֹם.	
RAM	**Amen and amen**![281] But of what account	אָמֵן וְאָמֵן![281] אַךְ כָּל נְגָעִים וּמַכְאוֹבוֹת	רם
	Are all afflictions and pains compared to the greatest of delights	בַּמֶּה נֶחְשְׁבוּ הֵם לְנֶגֶד רֹאשׁ הַתַּעֲנוּגִים	
	Which seeing her face will give me in one moment?	אֲשֶׁר רְאוֹת פָּנֶיהָ תִּתֶּן לִי בְּרֶגַע אֶחָד?	
	Please unite our two hearts in the bond of holy covenant	יַחֵד נָא לִבּוֹת שְׁנֵינוּ בְּקֶשֶׁר בְּרִית הַקֹּדֶשׁ	
	And I shall not fear the sword of the angel of death that might come	וּמִפְּנֵי חֶרֶב מַלְאַךְ הַמָּוֶת לֹא אִירָא כִּי יָבוֹא	
	It is enough for me, enough to say: Jael is mine.	רַב לִי, רַב, לֵאמֹר: יָעֵל לִי הִיא.	
REZIN	The end of such bursting desire will be **burst upon burst**[282]	תַּאֲוָה פְּרוּצָה כָּזֹאת, אַחֲרִיתָהּ פֶּרֶץ עַל פָּרֶץ[282]	רצין
	For like fire and gunpowder the ones who desire will burst	כִּי כָּאֵשׁ וַאֲבַק הַשְּׂרֵפָה יִתְפָּרְצוּ בְּנֵי הַחֵשֶׁק	
	They will unite, will kiss each other, and like smoke will be consumed together.	יִתְאַחֲדוּ יִשְׁקוּ זֶה לָזֶה וְכֶעָשָׁן יַחְדָּו יָסוּפוּ.	
	Even honey can become loathsome because of its great sweetness	גַּם הַדְּבַשׁ יִהְיֶה לְזָרָא מִפְּנֵי מָתְקוֹ כִּי רָב	
	And when we eat too much of it, we become satiated with it and vomit it.	וְכִי נֹאכַל מִמֶּנּוּ יֶתֶר מִדַּי, נִשְׂבָּעֶנּוּ וּנְקִיאֶנּוּ.	
	Therefore love calmly and your love will not become loathsome[283]	לָכֵן אֱהַב בְּנַחַת וְאַהֲבָתְךָ לֹא תִהְיֶה לְזָרָא[283]	
	While the hasty man is as late as the lazy man to arrive at the target.	וְהַנִּמְהָר יְאַחֵר כְּעָצֵל מִבּוֹא אֶל הַמַּטָּרָה.	
	(Jael enters)	(יעל באה)	

281 Ps. 41:14 (41:13 in English Bibles), 72:19, 89:53 (89:52 in English Bibles).
282 Job 16:14 פֶּרֶץ עַל־פְּנֵי־פָרֶץ 'burst upon burst'.
283 This and the next line form a rhyming couplet, mirroring Shakespeare's 'so/slow' (2.6.14–15).

	Behold, the bride comes, **as swift-footed as a deer**[284]	הִנֵּה הַכַּלָּה בָּאָה, קַלָּה בְּרַגְלֶיהָ כְּאַחַד הָאַיָּלִים[284]	
	But what is swifter than breath?[285] And many people become worthless through **vanity of vanities.**[286]	אַךְ מַה־קַּל מֵהֶבֶל?[285] וְרַבִּים יֶהְבָּלוּ בַּהֲבֵל הֲבָלִים.[286]	
	(Jael gives her hand to Ram and afterwards to Rezin)	(יעל נותנת ידה אל רם ואחרי כן אל רצין)	
JAEL	Greetings, my honourable teacher.	שָׁלוֹם לְמוֹרִי הַנִּכְבָּד.	יעל
REZIN	Ram answers your greeting, my daughter, for himself and also for me.	רָם יַעֲנֶה שָׁלוֹם לָךְ בִּתִּי, בַּעֲדוֹ וְגַם בַּעֲדִי.	רצין
JAEL	My greetings to you both, or else his greeting would turn back to him.	בִּרְכַּת שְׁלוֹמִי לִשְׁנֵיכֶם, לוּלֵא כֵן בִּרְכָתוֹ אֵלָיו תָּשׁוּב.	יעל
RAM	If your cup of joy, my bride, runs over like my cup of joy	אִם כּוֹס שִׂמְחָתֵךְ, כַּלָּתִי, רְוָיָה כְּכוֹס שִׂמְחָתִי	רם
	And there is **a learned tongue**[287] in your mouth to magnify and glorify the joy	וּלְשׁוֹן לִמּוּדִים[287] בְּפִיךְ לְהַגְדִּיל וּלְהַאֲדִיר הַשִּׂמְחָה.	
	Please **let me hear your voice, for it is sweet,**[288] making our hearts rejoice	הַשְׁמִיעִינוּ נָא קוֹלֵךְ כִּי עָרֵב[288] לְהַרְנִין אֶת לִבֵּנוּ	
	At this **favourable time**[289] and **this good union.**[290]	בְּעֵת רָצוֹן[289] זֹאת וְהַדֶּבֶק הַטּוֹב הַזֶּה.[290]	
JAEL	The rich man boasts of his possessions, not of the blossoms in his field	הֶעָשִׁיר יִתְהַלֵּל בִּנְכָסָיו וְלֹא בְּפִרְחֵי שָׂדֵהוּ	יעל
	He who can count the number of his possessions is poor and needy	וְהַיּוֹדֵעַ לִמְנוֹת מִסְפָּר* קִנְיָנָיו הוּא עָנִי וְאֶבְיוֹן	
	Whereas I in my love have found wealth beyond measure and weight.	וַאֲנִי בְּאַהֲבָתִי מָצָאתִי הוֹן לְאֵין מִדָּה וּמִשְׁקָל.	
	And if I were to go to count it, not even half could be tallied.	וְאִם אָבוֹא לִמְנוֹתוֹ לֹא יְסֻפַּר אַף הַחֲצִי.	
REZIN	Stand and I shall bring you into the covenant, for the appointed time must not be delayed.	עִמְדוּ וַאֲבִיאֲכֶם בַּבְּרִית, כִּי אֵין לְאַחֵר הַמּוֹעֵד.	רצין

---

284 Abarbanel to Amos 2 קל ברגליו כאחד האילים 'as swift-footed as a deer'. Cf. 2 Sam. 2:18 קַל בְּרַגְלָיו כְּאַחַד הַצְּבָיִם 'as swift-footed as a gazelle'.
285 Can also be translated as 'vanity' (in the sense of 'pointlessness') depending on the context.
286 Eccles. 1:2, 12:8.
287 Isa. 50:4.
288 Song of Songs 2:14 הַשְׁמִיעִינִי אֶת־קוֹלֵךְ כִּי־קוֹלֵךְ עָרֵב 'let me hear your voice, for your voice is sweet'.
289 Isa. 49:8.
290 Isa. 41:7 אֹמֵר לַדֶּבֶק טוֹב הוּא 'he says of the welding, "it is good"'; this citation is used idiomatically to indicate acceptance of a marriage match (Even-Shoshan 2003, 1: 292).

* מִסְפָּר

Behold, as you hear two or three words come out of my mouth[291]

הִנֵּה כְּשָׁמְעֲכֶם יֹצְאִים מִפִּי דְבָרִים שְׁנַיִם שְׁלֹשָׁה[291]

You will become one flesh[292] according to our holy Law.[293]

וִהְיִיתֶם לְבָשָׂר אֶחָד[292] לְפִי תוֹרָתֵנוּ[293] הַקְּדוֹשָׁה.

(Exeunt)

(הולכים)

End of Second Part.

תם חלק שני.

---

291 This and the next line form a rhyming couplet, mirroring Shakespeare's 'alone/one' (2.6.36–7).
292 Gen. 2:24 וְהָיוּ לְבָשָׂר אֶחָד 'and they will become one flesh'.
293 Alternatively, 'our holy Torah' (see note 145). Cf. Shakespeare's 'holy church' (2.6.37).

Third Part

חלק שלישי

SCENE I	*A street in Verona (Meraioth, Benaiah, and attendants)*	רחוב בוירונה (מריות בניה ומשרתים)	מחזה א'
BENAIAH	Please, Meraioth, my friend, come, let us return home	נָא מְרָיוֹת יְדִידִי, לְכָה וְנָשׁוּבָה הַבַּיְתָה	בניה
	Behold, the heat of the day is great, and the Abiels are all around outside	הִנֵּה חֹם הַיּוֹם גָּדוֹל וְהָאֲבִיעֵלִים סְבִבִים בַּחוּץ	
	And if we meet them, they will stir up **quarrel and strife**[1,2]	וְאִם נִפְגֹּשׁ אֹתָם יְחַרְחֲרוּ רִיב וּמָדוֹן[1,2]	
	For the heat will boil their blood and strike them with madness.	כִּי הַחֹם יַרְתִּיחַ דָּמָם וְיַכֶּה אֹתָם בְּשִׁגָּעוֹן.	
MERAIOTH[3]	You are like one of the men who come to the winehouse	אַתָּה כְּאַחַד הָאֲנָשִׁים הַבָּא אֶל בֵּית הַיַּיִן	מריות[3]
	There he hangs his sword on the peg, telling it, relax and be silent	שָׁם יִתְלֶה חַרְבּוֹ עַל הַיָּתֵד לֵאמֹר הֵרָגְעִי וָדֹמִּי	
	Yet before he has emptied the cup into his mouth twice	וּבְטֶרֶם יָרִיק הַכּוֹס לְתוֹךְ פִּיו פַּעֲמַיִם	
	He arises like a soldier and draws[4] his sword against the pourer of his drink.	יָקוּם כְּאִישׁ חַיִל וְיָרִיק[4] חַרְבּוֹ לִקְרַאת מַשְׁקֵהוּ.	
BENAIAH	Am I like this soldier?	הַאֲנִי הוּא כְּאִישׁ חַיִל הַזֶּה.	בניה
MERAIOTH[5]	You are quick to anger, like one of the Italians[6]	אַתָּה הוּא מְהִיר־חֵמָה, כְּאַחַד מִבְּנֵי אִטַלְיָאָה[6]	מריות[5]
	Your heart grows hot[7] in your anger, and you become angry when your heart grows hot.	לִבְּךָ* יֵחַם[7] בְּעֶבְרָתְךָ וּמִתְעַבֵּר כַּאֲשֶׁר יֵחַם לִבְּךָ.	
BENAIAH	And what else is under your tongue?	וּמָה עוֹד תַּחַת לְשׁוֹנֶךָ?	בניה

1 Hab. 1:3.

2 This and the next line form a rhyming couplet. There is no precedent for this in Shakespeare's 'brawl/stirring' (3.1.3–4).

3 This speech is prose in the original (3.1.5–9).

4 In Hebrew this is a pun on 'empties' in the previous line, as the same verb means 'empty' and 'draw a sword'.

5 This speech is prose in the original (3.1.11–13).

6 Cf. Shakespeare's 'as any in Italy' (3.1.12); Salkinson's phrasing suggests that he intends the characters in his translation to be understood as Italian Jews (with their biblical names, Hebrew speech, and Jewish customs), as opposed to the non-Jewish Italians referred to here.

7 Deut. 19:6 כִּי־יֵחַם לְבָבוֹ 'while his heart is hot' (i.e., while angry).

* לְבָבְךָ

MERAIOTH[8] If there were two like you, not even one would remain	מריות[8] לוּ הָיוּ שְׁנַיִם כָּמוֹךָ, לֹא נִשְׁאַר אַף אֶחָד
For one man would seize his fellow's side and they would both die at once.	כִּי יַחֲזִיקוּ אִישׁ בְּצַד רֵעֵהוּ וְיָמוּתוּ שְׁנֵיהֶם כְּרָגַע.
Why, you would quarrel with one man because he has	הֲלֹא אַתָּה תָּרִיב בְּאִישׁ עַל אֲשֶׁר יֶשׁ לוֹ
One more hair in his beard, or one less than you;	שֵׂעָר אֶחָד יֶתֶר בִּזְקָנוֹ, אוֹ אֶחָד חָסֵר מֵאֲשֶׁר לָךְ;
With another you would quarrel because he cracked a nut	עִם הַשֵּׁנִי תָּרִיב עַל אֲשֶׁר נִפֵּץ אֱגוֹז אֱחָד*
On the grounds that your eye looks like that nut;	בְּאָמְרְךָ כִּי מַרְאֵה עֵינֶיךָ כְּעֵין הָאֱגוֹז הַהוּא;
Like an egg full of yolk, so your head is full of quarrels	כְּבֵיצָה מְלֵאָה חֶלְמוֹן, כֵּן רֹאשְׁךָ מָלֵא מְדָנִים
Even though your head has been struck and beaten like an egg yolk in your quarrels;	אַף כִּי הָלְמוּ רֹאשְׁךָ וְנִפְעַמְתָּ כְּחֶלְמוֹן בֵּיצָה בִּמְדָנֶיךָ;
Once you grumbled at an elderly wayfarer	פַּעַם אַחַת הֲלִינֹתָ עַל זָקֵן עֹבֵר אֹרַח
Because with his sneezes he woke your dog who was sleeping on the street;	יַעַן כִּי בַּעֲטִישֹׁתָיו הֵקִיץ כַּלְבְּךָ הַיָּשֵׁן בָּרְחוֹב;
You caused anguish to a certain tailor with words that **go down into the innermost parts of the belly**[9]	אֶת לֵב חַיָּט פְּלֹנִי הִכְאַבְתָּ בִּדְבָרִים יֹרְדִים חַדְרֵי בָטֶן[9]
And what was his crime? That he wore a new cloth tunic	וּמֶה הָיָה פִּשְׁעוֹ? כִּי לָבַשׁ כְּתֹנֶת בַּד חֲדָשָׁה
And did not save it for Passover.[10] And moreover you did not pardon a shoemaker	וְלֹא שָׁמַר עַד חַג הַמַּצּוֹת.[10] גַּם רַצְעָן אֶחָד לֹא נִקֵּיתָ
Because he tied his old shoes with a new lace	בַּעֲבוּר כִּי קָשַׁר בִּשְׂרוֹךְ חָדָשׁ אֶת מִנְעָלָיו הַיְשָׁנִים
And you are the man who comes to instruct me	וְאַתָּה הוּא הָאִישׁ הַבָּא לְהוֹרוֹת לִי מוּסָר

8 This speech is prose in the original (3.1.15–32).
9 Prov. 18:8 וְהֵם יָרְדוּ חַדְרֵי־בָטֶן 'and they go down into the innermost parts of the belly'; also Prov. 26:22.
10 Cf. Shakespeare's 'Easter' (3.1.28). Passover falls at the same time of year as and is the historical setting for Easter; as such it is an appropriate domesticating translation choice.

* אֶחָד

	To desist from **quarrel and contention?**[11]	לַחְדֹּל מֵרִיב וָמַצָּה.[11]	
BENAIAH[12]	If I too were a man of strife like yourself	אִם אִישׁ מָדוֹן כָּמוֹךָ הָיִיתִי גַּם אָנִי	בניה[12]
	No man would give **a homer of barley**[13] for the length of my life	חֹמֶר שְׂעֹרִים[13] לֹא יִתֵּן אִישׁ בְּעַד אֹרֶךְ חַיָּתִי	
	For my time would not last longer than a handbreadth[14] and a quarter.	כִּי עִתִּי לֹא תִמָּשֵׁךְ יוֹתֵר מִטֶּפַח[14] וָרֹבַע.	
MERAIOTH	**A homer of barley**[15] for an ass.[16]	חֹמֶר שְׂעֹרִים[15] לַחֲמוֹר.[16]	מריות
BENAIAH	By the life of my head! Indeed the Abiels are coming.	בְּחַיֵּי רֹאשִׁי! כִּי הָאֲבִיעֵלִים בָּאִים.	בניה
MERAIOTH	By the life of my foot! Indeed I do not fear them.	בְּחַיֵּי רַגְלִי! כִּי אֵינֶנִּי יָרֵא מִפְּנֵיהֶם.	מריות
	(Tubal and his men)	(תובל ואנשיו)	
TUBAL	Follow me and I shall speak with these men –	לְכוּ אַחֲרַי וַאֲדַבֵּר אֶת הָאֲנָשִׁים הָאֵלֶּה –	תובל
	May you be well, honourable men! I have a word for one of you.	שְׁלוֹמְכֶם יִשְׂגֶּה מְכֻבָּדִים! דָּבָר לִי אֶל אֶחָד מִכֶּם.	
MERAIOTH[17]	Only one word? And only for one of us?	רַק דָּבָר אֶחָד? וְרַק אֶל אֶחָד מֵאִתָּנוּ?	מריות[17]
	Add something to the one word	הוֹסֵף דָּבָר מָה אֶל הַדָּבָר הָאֶחָד	
	Say a short word and strike a great blow.	אֱמֹר מִלָּה קְצָרָה וְהַךְ מַכָּה רַבָּה.	
TUBAL[18]	I am prepared to act in accordance with your word, if you give me a pretext.	נָכוֹן אֲנִי לַעֲשׂוֹת כִּדְבָרְךָ, אִם תִּתֶּן לִי תֹּאֲנָה.	תובל[18]
MERAIOTH[19]	Why can't you find a pretext for yourself, without me delivering it to your hand?	לָמָּה לֹא תִמְצָא לְךָ תֹּאֲנָה, מִבְּלִי תִתָּה אֲנִי לְיָדֶךָ?	מריות[19]

11 Isa. 58:4.

12 This speech is prose in the original (3.1.30–2).

13 Lev. 27:16; Hosea 3:2. A homer is a biblical measurement equivalent to approximately 394 litres.

14 A biblical measurement equivalent to approximately 9cm.

15 Lev. 27:16; Hosea 3:2. A homer is a biblical measurement equivalent to approximately 394 litres.

16 This is a pun based on the sound correspondence between חֹמֶר *ḥomer* 'barley' and חֲמוֹר *ḥamor* 'ass'. Salkinson is echoing Shakespeare's wordplay 'The fee-simple? O simple!' (3.1.33).

17 This speech is prose in the original (3.1.38–9).

18 This speech is prose in the original (3.1.40–1).

19 This speech is prose in the original (3.1.42–3).

TUBAL	I hear Ram's tunes from your mouth; do you assist him?	נְגִינוֹת רָם אֲנִי שֹׁמֵעַ מִפִּיךָ, הַאַתָּה עֹזֵר לוֹ?	תובל
MERAIOTH[20]	I help him with his tunes, so that you might dance for us	אֲנִי עֹזֵר לוֹ לְנַגֵּן, לְמַעַן תִּרְקֹד לָנוּ אָתָּה	מריות[20]
	And if you do not dance, I **shall turn your dancing to mourning**.[21, 22]	וְאִם לֹא תִרְקֹד, אֶהְפֹּךְ מְחוֹלְךָ לְאֵבֶל.[21, 22]	
BENAIAH	Here we are on the street and many are listening to our voice	פֹּה אֲנַחְנוּ בָּרְחוֹב וְרַבִּים מַקְשִׁיבִים לְקוֹלֵנוּ	בניה
	Come, let us depart from here to a quiet place	לְכוּ וְנֵלְכָה מִזֶּה לְאַחַד הַמְּקוֹמוֹת הַשְּׁקֵטִים	
	And quietly present your arguments and grievances there without restraint	וּבְהַשְׁקֵט הַגִּישׁוּ שָׁם עֲצֻמוֹתֵיכֶם וְדִין וּדְבָרִים בְּאֵין מוֹנֵעַ	
	Or depart, each man to his house, for the eyes of all the people are upon us.	אוֹ סוּרוּ אִישׁ אִישׁ לְבֵיתוֹ כִּי עֵינֵי כָל הָעָם עָלֵינוּ.	
MERAIOTH	Eyes were given to the people to look, so why should they not look in accordance with their desire?	עֵינַיִם נִתְּנוּ לָעָם לִרְאוֹת וְלָמָּה לֹא יִרְאוּ כִּרְצוֹנָם?	מריות
	On account of the people's eyes and ears, I shall not depart.	לְמַעַן עֵינֵי הָעָם וְאָזְנֵיהֶם, לֹא אָסוּרָה אָנִי.	
	(Ram enters)	(רם בא)	
TUBAL	Go in peace, my lord; behold, I have found my lad there.	לֶךְ־לְךָ לְשָׁלוֹם אֲדֹנִי, הֵן מָצָאתִי שָׁם אֶת נַעֲרִי.	תובל
MERAIOTH	May **the king of terrors**[23] take me if this lad is your attendant	יִקָּחֵנִי מֶלֶךְ בַּלָּהוֹת![23] אִם הַנַּעַר הַזֶּה מְשָׁרְתֶךָ	מריות
	Except when you go forth to battle; then he goes forth after you	בִּלְתִּי בְּצֵאתְךָ אֶל הַמַּעֲרָכָה אָז יֵצֵא אַחֲרֶיךָ	
	As a lad after his master.	כְּנַעַר אַחֲרֵי אֲדֹנָיו.	
TUBAL	Why, you know, Ram, that I hate you with a deathly hatred	הֲלֹא יָדַעְתָּ רָם, כִּי שִׂנְאַת מָוֶת שְׂנֵאתִיךָ	תובל

20 This speech is prose in the original (3.1.45–8).
21 Lam. 5:15 נֶהְפַּךְ לְאֵבֶל מְחֹלֵנוּ 'our dancing has turned to mourning'.
22 Cf. Shakespeare's 'Zounds, "consort"!' (3.1.48); Salkinson has removed the Christian oath.
23 Job 18:14 (an epithet for Death; see Gruber 2004: 1528).

	And you shall no longer be called Ram; rather, your name shall be villain.[24]	וְלֹא יִקָּרֵא עוֹד שִׁמְךָ רָם וְהָיָה שִׁמְךָ נָבָל.[24]	
RAM	I am willing to love you with a love greater than your hatred	יֵשׁ אֶת נַפְשִׁי לֶאֱהֹב אֹתְךָ אַהֲבָה גְדוֹלָה מִשִּׂנְאָתְךָ	רם
	Therefore I shall calm my wrath and not consider it as an iniquity of yours	לָכֵן אַשְׁבִּיחַ חֲמָתִי וְלֹא אֶחְשָׁב לְךָ לְעָוֹן	
	That you have scorned my name, although I am not a villain	כַּאֲשֶׁר בָּזִיתָ אֶת שְׁמִי וַאֲנִי נָבָל אֵינֶנִּי	
	Therefore depart in peace, for you do not know who I am.	לָכֵן סֹב לְךָ בְּשָׁלוֹם, כִּי לֹא יָדַעְתָּ מִי אָנִי.	
TUBAL	None of these will benefit you, and I shall not forgive you	כָּל אֵלֶּה לֹא יוֹעִילוּךָ וְלֹא אֶשָּׂא פָּנֶיךָ	תובל
	For the evil that you have done to me – **draw your sword**[25] and come forth.	בַּעֲבוּר הָרָעָה שֶׁעָשִׂיתָ לִי – שְׁלֹף חַרְבְּךָ[25] וָצֵאָה.	
RAM	The matter is not so; I have never done you evil	לֹא כֵן הַדָּבָר; מֵעוֹדִי לֹא עָשִׂיתִי לְךָ רָעָה	רם
	And moreover my love for you is greater than you reckon	וְגַם אַהֲבָתִי גְדוֹלָה אֵלֶיךָ מֵאֲשֶׁר תַּחְשֹׁב אַתָּה	
	Because you do not know from whom the reason for this love derives.	כִּי אֵינְךָ יֹדֵעַ מִמִּי הָיְתָה סִבָּה לְאַהֲבָה זוּ.	
	Know, Abielite, that your name is more precious to me than my name	דַּע לְךָ אֲבִיעֵלִי, כִּי שִׁמְךָ יָקָר לִי מִשְּׁמִי	
	And therefore I shall wait for you to reconcile yourself with me.	וְלָכֵן אוֹחִילָה כִּי תִרְצֵנִי.	
MERAIOTH[26]	Who surrenders with such scorned and despised humility	מִי יִכָּנַע בַּעֲנָוָה בְזוּיָה וְנִמְאָסָה כָּזֹאת	מריות[26]
	The edge of the sword will inform us who is righteous in his quarrel	פִּי הַחֶרֶב יְחַוֶּה לָנוּ מִי צַדִּיק בְּרִיבוֹ	

24 This word corresponds directly to Shakespeare's 'villain' (3.1.60). It is also the name of a biblical character, the first husband of King David's wife Abigail (initially mentioned in 1 Samuel 25:3 and appearing throughout 1 Samuel 25); Nabal's character is in keeping with the name's meaning.

25 Judg. 9:54; 1 Sam. 31:4; 1 Chron. 10:4.

26 This speech is a modified conflation of two separate English speeches by Mercutio (3.1.72–4 and 76–81, the latter in prose); Salkinson has omitted Tybalt's intervening line (3.1.75).

	Come, valiant warrior, who has **struggled with grasshoppers and prevailed**[27]	הָבָה גִּבּוֹר חַיִל, אֲשֶׁר שָׂרִיתָ עִם חֲגָבִים וַתּוּכָל[27]	
	Draw – and let us face each other!	שְׁלֹף – וְנִתְרָאֶה פָנִים!	
TUBAL	I am coming for you. *(They both draw their swords)*	הִנְנִי לִקְרָאתֶךָ. (שניהם שולפים חרבותם)	תובל
RAM	Meraioth, my friend, desist, **put your sword back in its sheath.**[28]	מְרָיוֹת יְדִיד נַפְשִׁי, הֶרֶף, הָשֵׁב חַרְבְּךָ אֶל נְדָנָהּ.[28]	רם
MERAIOTH	Hurry, hasten, Tubal, lest you be stabbed at once.	מַהֲרָה חוּשָׁה תּוּבַל, פֶּן תִּדָּקֵר כְּרָגַע.	מריות
	(They fight each other)	(נלחמים יחדו)	
RAM	Come, Benaiah, between them; knock the weapons from their hand –	בֹּא בְנָיָה בֵּינֵיהֶם, הַפֵּל כְּלֵי הַנֶּשֶׁק מִיָּדָם –	רם
	Be ashamed and disgraced[29] by your deeds, do not commit such ignominy	בּוֹשׁוּ הִכָּלְמוּ[29] מִמַּעֲשֵׂיכֶם, עַל תַּעֲשׂוּ נְאָצָה כָּזֹאת	
	Tubal! Meraioth! Why are you violating the prince's command	תּוּבַל! מְרָיוֹת! לָמָּה אַתֶּם עֹבְרִים אֶת פִּי הַנָּסִיךְ	
	Gathering together and waging battle on the streets of Verona?	לְהִתְגּוֹדֵד וְלַעֲרֹךְ קְרָב בְּחוּצוֹת וֵירוֹנָה?	
	Desist, Tubal, let it be, Meraioth my friend.	הֶרֶף תּוּבַל, הַנִּיחָה מְרָיוֹת יְדִידִי.	
	(Tubal and his men exit)[30]	(תובל ואנשיו הולכים)[30]	
MERAIOTH	I have been struck down. –	נִגָּפְתִּי. –	מריות
	Cursed be both ancestral houses together! I am dying.	אֲרוּרִים שְׁנֵי בָּתֵּי הָאָבוֹת יַחְדָּו! הִנְנִי מֵת.	
	Has he left here **and not one of his hairs has fallen to the ground?**[31]	הַהוּא יָצָא מִזֶּה וְלֹא נָפַל מִשַּׂעֲרָתוֹ אָרְצָה?[31]	

27 Gen. 32:29 כִּי־שָׂרִיתָ עִם־אֱלֹהִים וְעִם־אֲנָשִׁים וַתּוּכָל 'for you have struggled with God and with men and have prevailed'.
28 1 Chron. 21:27 וַיָּשֶׁב חַרְבּוֹ אֶל־נְדָנָהּ 'and he put his sword back in its sheath'.
29 Ezek. 36:32 בּוֹשׁוּ וְהִכָּלְמוּ 'be ashamed and disgraced'.
30 This translation follows the Folio version; the Second Quarto has a different stage direction followed by Petruchio's 'Away, Tybalt!' (3.1.90), which does not appear here.
31 1 Kings 1:52 לֹא־יִפֹּל מִשַּׂעֲרָתוֹ אָרְצָה 'not one of his hairs will fall to the ground'.

BENAIAH	What is this matter, have you been struck down?	מָה הַדָּבָר הַזֶּה, הַאִם נִגַּפְתָּ?	בניה
MERAIOTH	One scratch in my flesh, a scratch that **will cost me my life**[32]	שֶׂרֶט אֶחָד בִּבְשָׂרִי, שֶׂרֶט אֲשֶׁר **בְּנַפְשִׁי הוּא**[32]	מריות
	(To his attendant) Go and call the doctor for me. *(The servant exits)*	(אל משרתו) לֵךְ וּקְרָא לִי אֶת הָרֹפֵא. (המשרת הולך)	
RAM	Please be courageous, Meraioth; the wound is not great.	הִתְחַזֵּק נָא מְרָיוֹת הַפֶּצַע אֵינֶנּוּ גָּדוֹל.	רם
MERAIOTH[33]	It is not as deep as a well and it is not as wide as **the entrance to the Hall**[34]	אֵינֶנּוּ עָמֹק כִּבְאֵר וְאֵינֶנּוּ רָחָב כְּפֶתַח **הָאוּלָם**[34]	מריות[33]
	But it is enough to end my life. Come here and ask tomorrow	אַךְ דַּי הוּא לְבַצְּעֵנִי. בּוֹאוּ הֵנָּה וְשַׁאֲלוּ לְמָחָר	
	And you will find me like **a silent man who is considered wise.**[35]	וְתִמְצָאוּנִי כְּאִישׁ **מַחֲרִישׁ אֲשֶׁר לְחָכָם יֵחָשֵׁב.**[35]	
	The mocker is no more, the mockery is finished – cursed be both ancestral houses!	אָפֵס הַלֵּץ, כָּלָה לָצוֹן – אֲרוּרִים שְׁנֵי בָּתֵּי הָאָבוֹת!	
	How can a despicable dog,[36] how can a cat, a rat, or a mouse	אֵיךְ כֶּלֶב נִמְאָס,[36] אֵיךְ חָתוּל חֹלֶד וְעַכְבָּר	
	Make a fatal scratch on a man from which he would die	יִשְׂרֹט שֶׂרֶטֶת בְּנֶפֶשׁ אָדָם אֲשֶׁר יָמוּת בָּהּ	
	Behold, that dog learned to bark and not to bite	הֵן הַכֶּלֶב הַהוּא לָמַד לִנְבּוֹחַ וְלֹא לִנְשֹׁךְ	
	But you, the middlemen, when you came between us	אַךְ אַתֶּם אַנְשֵׁי הַבֵּינַיִם, כַּאֲשֶׁר בָּאתֶם בֵּינֵינוּ	
	You helped with your arms to stab me.	עֲזַרְתֶּם בִּזְרוֹעוֹתֵיכֶם לְדָקְרֵנִי.	
RAM	My intention was for good.	מַחֲשַׁבְתִּי הָיְתָה לְטוֹבָה.	רם
MERAIOTH	Please bring me, Benaiah, to some house	הֲבִיאֵנִי נָא בְּנָיָה, אֶל אֵיזֶה בַּיִת	מריות
	For I am dying – cursed be both your ancestral houses!	כִּי גֹוֵעַ אָנִי – אֲרוּרִים שְׁנֵי בָּתֵּי אֲבוֹתֵיכֶם!	

32 Prov. 7:23 וְלֹא־יָדַע כִּי־בְנַפְשׁוֹ הוּא 'and he does not know that it will cost him his life'.
33 This speech is prose in the original (3.1.98–105).
34 Mishnah *Middot* 3:7 פתחו של אולם 'the entrance to the Hall' (of the Temple in Jerusalem). Cf. Shakespeare's 'church door' (3.1.99).
35 Prov. 17:28 גַּם אֱוִיל מַחֲרִישׁ חָכָם יֵחָשֵׁב 'even a silent fool is considered wise'.
36 Cf. Shakespeare's 'Zounds, a dog' (3.1.102).

	They have made my flesh into food for maggots and worms	הֵם נָתְנוּ בְשָׂרִי לְמַאֲכַל רִמָּה וְתוֹלֵעָה	
	And may a sword devour both the houses. – *(Benaiah and his servants lead Meraioth off)*	וְחֶרֶב תֹּאכַל אֵת שְׁנֵי הַבָּתִּים. – (בניה ומשרתיו מוליכים את מריות)	
RAM	Meraioth, who is kinsman of the Prince's house and **a friend like a brother**[37] to me	מְרָיוֹת הַקָּרוֹב לְבֵית הַנָּסִיךְ **וְרֵעַ כְּאָח לִי**[37]	רם
	Was dealt a mortal blow while **defending my cause**[38]	הֻכָּה מַכַּת מָוֶת כַּאֲשֶׁר **רָב אֶת רִיבִי**[38]	
	And Tubal, whom I almost considered my **flesh and blood**[39]	וְתוּבַל אֲשֶׁר כִּמְעַט חֲשַׁבְתִּיו **לִשְׁאֵרִי וּבְשָׂרִי**[39]	
	Maligned my name and **besmirched me.**[40]	נָתַן אֶת שְׁמִי לִשְׁמְצָה **וַיַּשְׁלֵךְ עָלַי שִׁקּוּצִים.**[40]	
	Oh, my beautiful Jael! Your beauty has softened my heart	הוֹי יָעֵל יָפָתִי! יָפְיֵךְ הֵרַךְ לִבִּי	
	You have turned the arrow of my might into straw, and the stones of my sling into chaff.	חֵץ גְּבוּרָתִי הָפַכְתְּ לְקַשׁ וְאַבְנֵי קַלְעִי לַמֹּץ.	
	(Benaiah re-enters)	(בניה שב)	
BENAIAH	Ram, Ram my brother! Meraioth has been snatched away **before his time**[41]	רָם, רָם אָחִי! מְרָיוֹת נִסְפָּה **בְּלֹא יוֹמוֹ**[41]	בניה
	With the strength of his lofty spirit he has split the clouds and ascended	בְּעֹז רוּחוֹ הַנַּעֲלָה בָּקַע עָבִים וַיַּעַל	
	He has scorned dwelling on earth and has made his seat in the heavens.	בָּז לָשֶׁבֶת בָּאָרֶץ וַיִּתֵּן כִּסְאוֹ בַּשְּׁחָקִים.	
RAM	The destroyer started with one, but will yet strike down several[42]	הַמַּשְׁחִית הֵחֵל בְּאֶחָד וְעוֹד יִגֹּף אֲחָדִים[42]	רם

37 Ps. 35:14.
38 Jer. 51:36 הִנְנִי־רָב אֶת־רִיבֵךְ 'I shall defend your cause'.
39 Prov. 5:11 בְּשָׂרְךָ וּשְׁאֵרֶךָ 'your flesh and body' (used literally in this verse, but idiomatically in Salkinson's text).
40 Nah. 3:6 וְהִשְׁלַכְתִּי עָלַיִךְ שִׁקֻּצִים 'and I shall besmirch you'.
41 Job 15:32.
42 This and the next three lines form two rhyming couplets; cf. Shakespeare's 'depend/end' (3.1.121–2). Salkinson has added an extra two lines to this speech. The reason for this is unclear as the added lines do not appear in the Folio or Quarto versions.

	The quiver of time is open, like a belly full of children;	אַשְׁפַּת הַזְּמָן פְּתוּחָה, כַּבֶּטֶן מְלֵאָה יְלָדִים;	
	This one has burst forth first, his father's firstborn son	זֶה פָּרַץ רִאשׁוֹנָה, בֵּן בְּכוֹר לְאָבִיהוּ	
	And the hand of each child is grasping the heel of his brother.[43]	וְיַד יֶלֶד יֶלֶד, אֹחֶזֶת בַּעֲקֵב אָחִיהוּ.[43]	
	(Tubal re-enters)	(תובל שב)	
BENAIAH	Behold, Tubal in his fury comes again.[44]	הִנֵּה תוּבַל בְּזַעְמוֹ בָּא עוֹד הַפָּעַם.[44]	בניה
RAM	He lives in his haughtiness, while Meraioth has fallen by the sword –	הוּא חַי בְּגַאֲוָתוֹ וּמְרָיוֹת נָפַל לְפִי חָרֶב –	רם
	Depart, compassion, from my eyes; mercy, leave me	סוּרִי חֶמְלָה מֵעֵינַי, חֲנִינָה צְאִי מֵעַל פָּנָי	
	I shall don zeal as my garment and in a consuming fire I shall exhaust my wrath –	קִנְאָה אֶלְבַּשׁ כְּמַדַּי וּבְאֵשׁ אֹכְלָה אֲכַלֶּה חֲמָתִי –	
	Tubal! You have reviled me for nothing; say that you regret it	תּוּבַל! אַתָּה חֵרַפְתַּנִי חִנָּם, אֱמֹר כִּי נִחַמְתָּ	
	For Meraioth's soul is still floating over our heads	כִּי נֶפֶשׁ מְרָיוֹת עוֹד מְרַחֶפֶת מֵעַל לְרֹאשֵׁנוּ	
	And waiting until your soul leaves, to keep it company there	וּמְיַחֶלֶת עַד צֵאת נַפְשְׁךָ, לְהִתְרֹעֵעַ שָׁם עִמָּהּ	
	For you or I, or both of us together	כִּי אַתָּה אוֹ אֲנִי, אוֹ שְׁנֵינוּ יַחְדָּו	
	Shall keep it company momentarily.	נִתְרֹעֵעַ עִמָּהּ כְּרָגַע.	
TUBAL	Despoiled lad! Behold, you were his friend in life	נַעַר שָׁדוּד! הֵן רֵעוֹ הָיִיתָ בַּחַיִּים	תובל
	Therefore in his death, you shall not be separated from him.	עַל כֵּן בְּמוֹתוֹ, לֹא תִפָּרֵד מִמֶּנּוּ אָתָּה.	
RAM	The sword will decide our case. *(They fight each other and Tubal falls)*	הַחֶרֶב תַּחֲרֹץ דִּינֵנוּ. (נלחמים יחדו ותובל נופל)	רם
BENAIAH	Go from here, Ram, flee at once	לֵךְ מִזֶּה רָם, בְּרַח לְךָ כְּרָגַע	בניה
	Behold, the residents of the city are coming and Tubal lies dead.	הִנֵּה בְּנֵי הָעִיר בָּאִים וְתוּבַל שׁוֹכֵב מֵת.	

---

43 This is a reference to Gen. 25:26 וְיָדוֹ אֹחֶזֶת בַּעֲקֵב עֵשָׂו 'and his hand was grasping Esau's heel', referring to the patriarch Jacob when he was born.

44 Salkinson's text has no rhyming couplet here, in contrast to Shakespeare's 'again/slain' (3.1.123–4).

	Do not stand as if stunned – if you are found here	אַל תַּעֲמֹד כְּמִשְׁתּוֹנֵן – אִם תִּמָּצֵא פֹּה	
	You will surely die today according to the prince's commandment	מוֹת תָּמוּת כַּיּוֹם* לְפִי מִצְוַת הַנָּסִיךְ	
	Arise, **flee for your life.**[45, 46]	קוּם הִמָּלֵט עַל נַפְשֶׁךָ.[45, 46]	
RAM	Woe to **a foolish son**[47] who prospers like me!	אוֹי לְבֵן כְּסִיל[47] מַצְלִיחַ כָּמֹנִי!	רם
BENAIAH	Why do you still tarry? *(Ram exits)*	לָמָּה זֶה עוֹד תִּתְמַהְמֵהַּ? (רם הולך)	בניה
	(A crowd of people and city officials)	(המון העם ושוטרי העיר)	
THE CHIEF OFFICIAL	Which way did he flee, the one who struck Meraioth	אֵיזֶה דֶרֶךְ נָס הוּא אֲשֶׁר הִכָּה אֶת מְרָיוֹת	ראש השוטרים
	He is the murderer Tubal, which way did he flee?[48]	הוּא תוּבַל הָרֹצֵחַ, אֵיזֶה דֶרֶךְ נָס?[48]	
BENAIAH	There lies Tubal, the man whom you seek.	שָׁם שׁוֹכֵב תּוּבַל, הָאִישׁ אֲשֶׁר אַתָּה מְבַקֵּשׁ.	בניה
THE OFFICIAL	Arise, come with me, quick, stand on your feet	קוּם בֹּא אִתִּי, מַהֵר עֲמֹד עַל רַגְלֶיךָ	השוטר
	Why, I command you in the prince's name.[49]	הֲלֹא בְּשֵׁם הַנָּסִיךְ צִוִּיתִיךָ.[49]	
	(The prince with his men, Abiram, Abiel, and their wives with the members of their household)	(הנסיך עם אנשיו ואבירם ואביעל ונשותיהם עם בני ביתם)	
THE PRINCE	Who are they that have burst out to wreak destruction on our streets?	מִי הֵמָּה אֲשֶׁר פָּרְצוּ לִפְרֹעַ פְּרָעוֹת בִּרְחוֹבוֹתֵינוּ?	הנסיך
BENAIAH[50]	Please, my lord prince! I am prepared to tell **in the bitterness of my soul**[51]	בִּי אֲדֹנִי הַנָּסִיךְ! הִנְנִי נָכוֹן לְהַגִּיד בְּמַר נַפְשִׁי[51]	בניה[50]

45 Gen. 19:17.
46 Salkinson's text has no rhyming couplet here, in contrast to Shakespeare's 'away/stay' (3.1.137–8).
47 Prov. 10:1, 17:25, 19:13.
48 The Hebrew text has no rhyming couplet here, in contrast to Shakespeare's 'he/me' (3.1.140–1).
49 The Hebrew text has no rhyming couplet here, in contrast to Shakespeare's 'obey/fray' (3.1.142–3).
50 Salkinson has not included any rhyming couplets in this speech, in contrast to Shakespeare's 'all/brawl' and 'Romeo/Mercutio' (3.1.144–5 and 146–7).
51 Job 7:11, 10:1.

* כַּיּוֹם

	Of the horrors that have been committed from the beginning to the end.	הַמּוֹרָאִים אֲשֶׁר נַעֲשׂוּ מֵהָחֵל וְעַד כָּלָה.	
	There lies the man whom the lad Ram killed	שָׁם שׁוֹכֵב הָאִישׁ אֲשֶׁר רָם הַנַּעַר הֲרָגוֹ	
	Because he had killed Meraioth, **a mighty man of valour**[52]	עַל אֲשֶׁר הָרַג אֶת מְרָיוֹת אִישׁ גִּבּוֹר חַיִל[52]	
	Who is kin to my lord the prince.	הַקָּרוֹב לַאֲדֹנִי הַנָּסִיךְ.	
ABIEL'S WIFE	Tubal – Tubal is dead – Tubal, my brother's son[53] –	תּוּבַל – תּוּבַל מֵת – תּוּבַל בֶּן אָחִי[53] –	אשת אביעל
	See, my lord the prince! See, look, my husband!	רְאֵה אֲדֹנִי הַנָּסִיךְ! רְאֵה הַבִּיטָה בַּעֲלִי!	
	Oh, there is spilled the blood of my brother's son, whom I love	הָהּ שָׁם שָׁפוּךְ דַּם בֶּן אָחִי אֲשֶׁר אָהַבְתִּי	
	Please, my lord! Command **according to the greatness of your mercy**[54]	הוֹאֶל־נָא אֲדֹנִי! צַוֵּה כְּגֹדֶל חַסְדֶּךָ[54]	
	And let the blood of the house of Abiram be spilled to atone for this blood.	וְדַם בֵּית אֲבִירָם יִשָּׁפֵךְ לְכַפֵּר עַל הַדָּם הַזֶּה.	
	My brother's son! – My brother's son, **my flesh and blood!**[55]	בֶּן אָחִי! – בֶּן אָחִי עַצְמִי וּבְשָׂרִי![55]	
THE PRINCE	Tell me, Benaiah, what happened from beginning to end?	הַגֵּד בְּנָיָה, מֶה הָיָה הַדָּבָר מֵהָחֵל וְעַד כַּלֵּה?	הנסיך
BENAIAH	Tubal, who has fallen here, fell by Ram's hand	תּוּבַל הַנֹּפֵל פֹּה נָפַל בְּיַד רָם	בניה
	That is the same Ram who, when he encountered him, spoke to him tenderly	הוּא רָם אֲשֶׁר בְּפִגְעוֹ בוֹ, דִּבֶּר אֵלָיו רַכּוֹת	

52 Ruth 2:1.

53 The last word in this line rhymes with the last word in the following two lines, mirroring Shakespeare's 'child/spilled' (3.1.148–9) except that the latter is a rhyming couplet. Salkinson may have added the third rhyming line to compensate for the fact that there are no further rhymes in this speech, in contrast to Shakespeare's 'true/Montague' (3.1.150–1) and 'fray/slay' (3.1.153–4), the latter split between Capulet's wife and Benvolio. This discrepancy most likely reflects a difficulty in finding suitable rhymes while maintaining the desired meaning.

54 Num. 14:19.

55 Gen. 29:14; 2 Sam. 19:13, 14 (19:12, 13 in English Bibles).

Saying to relent from a quarrel which has no basis	לֵאמֹר לַחְשׂךְ מֵרִיב אֲשֶׁר אֵין לוֹ כָּל יְסוֹד
And that it would be fitting for him to guard himself, so as not to violate the prince's command	וְכִי נָכוֹן לוֹ לְהִשָּׁמֵר, לִבְלִי עֲבֹר מִצְוַת הַנָּסִיךְ
And even though he implored him with **a willing spirit**[56] and a beseeching tongue	וְאַף כִּי הִפְצִיר בּוֹ **בְּרוּחַ נְדִיבָה**[56] וּבִלְשׁוֹן תַּחֲנוּנִים
His words fell to the ground, for Tubal in his haste **stiffened his neck**[57]	נָפְלוּ דְבָרָיו אַרְצָה, כִּי תּוּבַל בְּחָפְזוֹ **הִקְשָׁה עָרְפּוֹ**[57]
And was like a deaf man; he would not listen to **words of peace and truth**[58]	וַיְהִי כְּחֵרֵשׁ לֹא יִשְׁמַע **לְדִבְרֵי שָׁלוֹם וֶאֱמֶת**[58]
And he made **the point of his sword**[59] fly, **tearing the covering of Meraioth's heart**[60]	וַיְעוֹפֵף **בְּאִבְחַת חַרְבּוֹ**,[59] **לִקְרֹעַ סְגוֹר לֵב מְרָיוֹת**[60]
And Meraioth too brandished his weapon, weapon against weapon	וּמְרָיוֹת הֵנִיף נִשְׁקוֹ גַּם הוּא, נֶשֶׁק לִקְרַאת נָשֶׁק
And stood opposite him **like a mighty expert man**[61] **made without fear**[62]	וַיַּעֲמֹד נֶגְדּוֹ **כְּגִבּוֹר מַשְׂכִּיל**[61] **הֶעָשׂוּי לִבְלִי חָת**[62]
With one of his hands he drove back **the one who sought to take his life**[63]	בְּיָדוֹ הָאַחַת מֵשִׁיב אֶת **הַמְבַקֵּשׁ נַפְשׁוֹ, לִסְפּוֹתָהּ**[63]
While with his other hand he sought the life of his enemy	וּבְיָדוֹ הַשֵּׁנִית מְבַקֵּשׁ אֶת נֶפֶשׁ אִישׁ מִלְחַמְתּוֹ
But Tubal also drove him back, because he knew how to heed a warning	אַךְ גַּם תּוּבַל הֱשִׁיבוֹ אָחוֹר כִּי יָדַע לְהִזָּהֵר
And meanwhile Ram raised his voice mightily	וּבֵין כֹּה וָכֹה וְרָם נָתַן קוֹלוֹ בַּכֹּחַ

56 Ps. 51:14 (51:12 in English Bibles).

57 Jer. 19:15 הִקְשׁוּ אֶת־עָרְפָּם 'they have stiffened their necks'.

58 Esther 9:30.

59 Ezek. 21:20 (21:15 in English Bibles) אִבְחַת־חָרֶב 'the point of the sword'. The meaning of this phrase is uncertain; this translation follows the King James Bible, but other possibilities include 'the fear of the sword' (Geneva Bible), 'the threat of the sword' (New English Bible), and 'the glittering sword' (English Standard Version).

60 Hosea 13:8 וְאֶקְרַע סְגוֹר לִבָּם 'and I shall tear open the covering of their heart'.

61 Jer. 50:9.

62 Job 41:25 (41:33 in English Bibles).

63 Ps. 40:15 (40:14 in English Bibles) מְבַקְשֵׁי נַפְשִׁי לִסְפּוֹתָהּ 'those who seek to take my life'.

	'Cease, brothers! Cease doing evil!' And swift as an eagle he turned aside	„חִדְלוּ אַחִים! חִדְלוּ הָרֵעַ!" וְקַל כַּנֶּשֶׁר שָׁט	
	And stood between the fighters to knock the instruments of death from their hand	וַיַּעֲמֹד בֵּין הַלֹּחֲמִים לְהַפִּיל כְּלֵי הַמָּוֶת מִיָּדָם	
	But then Tubal's sword struck Meraioth's living soul	וַתִּפְגַּע אָז חֶרֶב תּוּבַל בְּנֶפֶשׁ חַיַּת מְרָיוֹת	
	And Tubal saw and fled, but afterwards he returned to Ram	וְתוּבַל רָאָה וַיָּנָס וְאַחַר שָׁב אֶל רָם	
	Upon whom the spirit of jealousy had come[64] and who bore a grudge in his heart	אֲשֶׁר רוּחַ קִנְאָה עֲבָרוֹ[64] וְנָקָם שָׁמַר בְּלִבּוֹ	
	Then they both burst forth like lightning, one man against his fellow	אָז פָּרְצוּ שְׁנֵיהֶם כַּבְּרָקִים אִישׁ לִקְרַאת רֵעֵהוּ	
	And before I could separate them Tubal bowed over and fell down dead.	וּבְטֶרֶם יָכֹלְתִּי לְהַפְרִידָם כָּרַע תּוּבַל נָפַל מֵת.	
	As for Ram, he fled; my eye has not seen him again[65]	וְרָם בָּרַח לוֹ, לֹא רָאַתְהוּ עוֹד עֵינִי[65]	
	These are words of truth, and if they are a lie you may surely kill me.	אֵלֶּה דִּבְרֵי אֱמֶת, וְאִם שֶׁקֶר הָרֹג הָרְגֵנִי.	
ABIEL'S WIFE	He is from Abiram's family and in his love he is twisting his words[66]	הוּא מִמִּשְׁפַּחַת אֲבִירָם וּבְאַהֲבָתוֹ יְסַלֵּף דְּבָרָיו[66]	אשת אביעל
	His tongue speaks falsehoods and his face testifies to his lies	לְשׁוֹנוֹ תְּדַבֵּר כְּזָבִים וּבְפָנָיו יַעֲנוּ שְׁקָרָיו	
	Not with the hand of one man was Tubal struck a winning blow	לֹא בְּיַד אֶחָד הֻכָּה תּוּבַל מַכָּה נִצַּחַת	
	Roughly twenty men fought and killed a single soul	כְּעֶשְׂרִים אֲנָשִׁים נִלְחֲמוּ וְרָצְחוּ נֶפֶשׁ אַחַת	
	And **the voice of his blood cries out**[67] to the prince, **it will not give you rest**[68]	וְקוֹל דָּמָיו צֹעֲקִים[67] לַנָּסִיךְ, לֹא יִתְּנוּ לְךָ דֳּמִי[68]	

64 Num. 5:14 וְעָבַר עָלָיו רוּחַ־קִנְאָה 'and the spirit of jealousy comes upon him'; see also Num. 5:30.

65 This forms a rhyming couplet with the next line, mirroring Shakespeare's 'fly/die' (3.1.176–7).

66 This speech is composed of three rhyming couplets, mirroring Shakespeare's 'Montague/true', 'strife/life', 'give/live' (3.1.178–83).

67 Gen. 4:10 קוֹל דְּמֵי אָחִיךָ צֹעֲקִים אֵלַי מִן־הָאֲדָמָה 'the voice of your brother's blood cries out to me from the ground' (referring to Abel, who has just been killed by his brother Cain).

68 Isa. 62:7 וְאַל־תִּתְּנוּ דֳמִי לוֹ 'and do not give him rest'.

	'Ram killed me, and Ram's blood must be spilled like my blood'.	„רָם הֵמִית אֹתִי וְדַם רָם יִשָּׁפֵךְ כְּדָמִי".	
THE PRINCE	Tubal struck Meraioth and Ram struck Tubal[69]	תּוּבַל הִכָּה אֶת מְרָיוֹת וְרָם הִכָּה אֶת תּוּבָל[69]	הנסיך
	And on whose head is the bloodguilt? Who should be brought to slaughter?	וּבְרֹאשׁ מִי הַדָּם? מִי לַטֶּבַח יוּבָל?	
ABIRAM	And **the voice of Meraioth's blood cries out bitterly from the ground**[70, 71]	וְקוֹל דְּמֵי מְרָיוֹת מִן הָאֲדָמָה מַר צֹרֵחַ[70, 71]	אבירם
	'Not my friend Ram, who destroyed the murderer	„לֹא רָם אֹהֲבִי, אֲשֶׁר הִשְׁמִיד אֶת הָרֹצֵחַ	
	For he acted as a judge in his zeal and this is his only sin.'	כִּי עָשָׂה כַּשּׁוֹפֵט בְּקִנְאָתוֹ וְזֶה כָּל חַטָּאתוֹ"	
THE PRINCE	Because of this sin of his which is not large[72]	עֵקֶב חַטָּאתוֹ זֹאת אֲשֶׁר לֹא גְדוֹלָה[72]	הנסיך
	We pronounce this judgement, that he shall go into exile	חָרַצְנוּ מִשְׁפָּט זֶה כִּי יֵלֵךְ בַּגּוֹלָה	
	The blows of your hand,[73] men of violence, **have brought down many victims**[74]	תִּגְרַת יֶדְכֶם[73] אַנְשֵׁי חָמָס, רַבִּים חֲלָלִים הִפִּילָה[74]	
	Including **my flesh and blood**,[75] **wallowing in blood in the road**[76]	וְגַם עַצְמִי וּבְשָׂרִי,[75] מִתְגּוֹלֵל בַּדָּם בַּמְסִלָּה[76]	
	Indeed I impose a ransom upon you and set a large fine	אַךְ כֹּפֶר שַׁתִּי עֲלֵיכֶם וְכֶסֶף עֲנוּשִׁים הִרְבֵּתִי	
	So that **you might smite your thigh**[77] and wail over my dead one	לְמַעַן תִּסְפְּקוּ עַל יָרֵךְ[77] וְתֵילִילוּ עַל מֵתִי	

69 This forms a rhyming couplet with the next line, mirroring Shakespeare's 'Mercutio/owe' (3.1.184–5).

70 Gen. 4:10 קוֹל דְּמֵי אָחִיךָ צֹעֲקִים אֵלַי מִן־הָאֲדָמָה 'the voice of your brother's blood cries out to me from the ground' (referring to Abel, who has just been killed by his brother Cain); Zeph. 1:14 קוֹל יוֹם יְהוָה מַר צֹרֵחַ שָׁם גִּבּוֹר 'the voice of the day of the Lord, wherein the mighty man cries bitterly'.

71 This forms a rhyming couplet with the next line, mirroring Shakespeare's 'friend/end' (3.1.186–7).

72 This speech is composed of six rhyming couplets, mirroring Shakespeare's 'offence/hence', 'proceeding/a-bleeding', 'fine/mine', 'excuses/abuses', 'haste/last', 'will/kill' (3.1.188–99).

73 Ps. 39:11 (39:10 in English Bibles) מִתִּגְרַת יָדְךָ 'from the blows of Your hand'.

74 Prov. 7:26.

75 Gen. 29:14; 2 Sam. 19:13, 14 (19:12, 13 in English Bibles).

76 2 Sam. 20:12 מִתְגֹּלֵל בַּדָּם בְּתוֹךְ הַמְסִלָּה 'wallowing in blood in the middle of the road'.

77 Jer. 31:19 סָפַקְתִּי עַל־יָרֵךְ 'I smote my thigh' (in grief).

	Prayers I shall not hear, like a deaf man; I shall not have mercy on wickedness	תְּפִלָּה לֹא אֶשְׁמַע כְּחֵרֵשׁ, לֹא אָחֹן רֶשַׁע	
	And rivers of tears and beseeching cannot erase a crime	וְנַחֲלֵי דִמְעָה וְתַחֲנוּנִים לֹא יִמְחוּ פֶּשַׁע	
	And as for you, do not entreat me, do not raise **a voice of wailing**[78]	וְאַתֶּם אַל תִּפְגְּעוּ בִי, אַל תִּשְׂאוּ קוֹל נְהִי[78]	
	Ram shall surely be exiled, or **let his blood be upon his own head**.[79]	רָם גָּלֹה יִגְלֶה, אוֹ דָּמוֹ בְרֹאשׁוֹ יְהִי.[79]	
	Remove the slain man's bones from here and take instruction from the matter of the strife	שְׂאוּ עַצְמוֹת הַמֻּכֶּה מִזֶּה וּקְחוּ מוּסָר מִדְּבַר הַמָּדוֹן	
	And know that he who has mercy on a murderer is like **one who ends a life maliciously**.[80]	וּדְעוּ כִּי הַחֹנֵן רֹצֵחַ, הוּא כְּמַכֵּה נֶפֶשׁ בְּזָדוֹן.[80]	
	(Exeunt)	(הולכים)	
SCENE 2	*A chamber in Abiel's house*	חדר בבית אביעל	מחזה ב׳
JAEL	Hurry, chariot of the sun, complete the day's cycle	חוּשִׁי מֶרְכֶּבֶת הַשֶּׁמֶשׁ, כַּלִּי אֵת תְּקוּפַת הַיּוֹם	יעל
	Who[81] would brandish a whip at horses of fire while the wheels rise like a storm	מִי[81] יָנִיף שׁוֹט לְסוּסֵי אֵשׁ וְהָאוֹפַנִּים יַעֲלוּ כַּסּוּפָה	
	Because the sun[82] strives for its shelter, for its tent at the end of the day	כִּי הַשֶּׁמֶשׁ[82] שׁוֹאֵף לִמְלוּנָתוֹ, לְאָהֳלוֹ בְּאַחֲרִית יָם	
	And we yearn for the night, for the night that attends to lovers	וַנַּחְנוּ לַלַּיְלָה נִתְאַוֶּה, לַלַּיְלָה הָאֹמֵן אֶת הַנֶּאֱהָבִים	
	For it unfurls **the veil that is spread over all faces**[83]	כִּי הוּא יִפְרֹשׂ הַמַּסֵּכָה הַנְּסוּכָה עַל כָּל פָּנִים[83]	
	So that Ram might come to embrace me when no eye sees.	לְמַעַן יָבוֹא רָם לְחַבְּקֵנִי וְאֵין עַיִן רֹאָה.	

78 Jer. 9:18 (9:19 in English Bibles).
79 Ezek. 33:4 דָּמוֹ בְרֹאשׁוֹ יִהְיֶה 'his blood shall be upon his own head'.
80 Gersonides to 1 Kings 1:50.
81 Cf. Shakspeare's 'Phaeton' (3.2.3); as usual, Salkinson has removed the Classical mythological reference.
82 Cf. Shakespeare's 'Phoebus' (3.2.2), i.e., Apollo, the Greco-Roman sun god.
83 Isa. 25:7 וְהַמַּסֵּכָה הַנְּסוּכָה עַל־כָּל־הַגּוֹיִם 'and the veil which is spread over all the nations'.

Lovers wait for the season of night, saying, **no eye will see us**[84]

הַנֶּאֱהָבִים לְעוֹנַת לַיְלָה יְחַכּוּ, לֵאמֹר לֹא תְשׁוּרֵנוּ עָיִן[84]

In their beauty they see light, so what use have they for the light of the sun?

הֵם בְּיָפְיָם יִרְאוּ אוֹר, וּמַה לָּהֶם וּלְאוֹר שֶׁמֶשׁ?

Love is struck by blindness, and the night suits it

הָאַהֲבָה מֻכָּה בְסַנְוֵרִים וְהַלַּיְלָה לָהּ יָאֲתָה

Therefore I call to you, O night, to teach me the way of women

לָכֵן אֵלֶיךָ הַלַּיְלָה אֶקְרָא, לְהוֹרוֹת לִי דֶּרֶךְ נָשִׁים

For as a **dark yet comely**[85] woman you are full of knowledge.

כִּי כְאִשָּׁה **שְׁחוֹרָה וְנָאוָה**[85] הִנְּךָ מָלֵא דָעַת.

To teach me to acquire a master over me for the price of my pure virginity

לְלַמְּדֵנִי לִקְנוֹת אַלּוּף לְרֹאשִׁי בִּדְמֵי בְתוּלַי הַטְּהוֹרִים

But cover my face with a veil, for it reddens from shame

אַךְ כַּסֵּה בַצָּעִיף פָּנַי, כִּי יַאֲדִימוּ מִבּוּשָׁה

Until little by little I learn to know a man.

עַד אֲשֶׁר עַל יָד עַל יָד, אֶלְמַד לָדַעַת אִישׁ.

If one does something and repeats it, he is given his due in the end:

הָעֹשֶׂה דָבָר וְשׁוֹנֶה נַעֲשֶׂה לוֹ כְּחֹק בְּאַחֲרִיתוֹ:

Come to me tonight, come to me, Ram, my chosen one

בֹּא אֵלַי הַלַּיְלָה, בֹּא אֵלַי רָם בְּחִירִי

You are a shining light, you are my sun in my darkness

אַתָּה אוֹר זוֹרֵחַ, אַתָּה שִׁמְשִׁי בְּחָשְׁכִּי

Like snow on a raven's back, so you rest on the wings of night

כַּשֶּׁלֶג עַל גַּב עוֹרֵב, כֵּן תָּנוּחַ עַל כַּנְפֵי לַיְלָה

Please come, night of my desire and bring me Ram

בּוֹא נָא לֵיל חִשְׁקִי וְהָבֵא לִי אֶת רָם

And when his time comes and he is taken away,[86] cut him into pieces

וְכַאֲשֶׁר יָבוֹא יוֹמוֹ וְנִסְפָּה[86] נַתַּח אֹתוֹ לִנְתָחָיו

And set the pieces in the wheel so that they might shine like the stars in the firmament

וְהַנְּתָחִים תִּתְקַע בַּגַּלְגַּל וְיַזְהִרוּ כַּכּוֹכָבִים בָּרָקִיעַ

And from that day onwards all men

וּמִיּוֹם הַהוּא וָמַעְלָה כָּל בְּנֵי הָאָדָם

---

84 Job 24:15 לֹא־תְשׁוּרֵנִי עָיִן 'no eye will see me'.

85 Song of Songs 1:5 שְׁחוֹרָה אֲנִי וְנָאוָה 'I am dark yet comely'.

86 Cf. Shakespeare's 'when I shall die' (3.2.21); Salkinson's version lacks the double-entendre present in the source text (see Weis 2012: 249, note 21).

	Will love night more than day, for they will rejoice in the stars of light	לַיְלָה מִיּוֹם יֶאֱהָבוּ, כִּי יָשִׂישׂוּ בְּכוֹכְבֵי אוֹר
	And will no longer bow down to the sun; they will surely scorn it. –	וְלֹא יִשְׁתַּחֲווּ עוֹד לַשֶּׁמֶשׁ, בּוֹז יָבוּזוּ לוֹ. –
	Now I have bought an abode of love but have not dwelled in it	וַאֲנִי קָנִיתִי מִשְׁכַּן יְדִידוֹת וְלֹא שָׁכַנְתִּי בוֹ
	I have been placed **like clay in the potter's hand but he has not made me into a vessel**[87]	הִתְמַכַּרְתִּי כַּחֹמֶר לְיַד הַיּוֹצֵר וְלֹא עָשַׂנִי כֶּלִי[87]
	Like the length of the night to a child before **a day of feasting and gladness**[88]	כְּאֹרֶךְ הַלַּיְלָה לַיֶּלֶד לִפְנֵי יוֹם מִשְׁתֶּה וְשִׂמְחָה[88]
	Whose parents have made a new **coat of many colours**[89] for him	אֲשֶׁר אֲבוֹתָיו עָשׂוּ לוֹ כְּתֹנֶת פַּסִּים[89] חֲדָשָׁה
	But he cannot wear it before the appointed time arrives	וְאֵין לוֹ לִלְבֹּשׁ אֹתָהּ טֶרֶם בָּא הַמּוֹעֵד
	That is how long this day is to me – but my nurse approaches me	כֵּן יֶאֱרַךְ לִי הַיּוֹם הַזֶּה – אַךְ אֹמַנְתִּי לִקְרָאתִי
	And her mouth is full of news and every mouth which mentions Ram's name	וּפִיהָ מָלֵא חֲדָשׁוֹת וְכָל פֶּה הַמַּזְכִּיר שֵׁם רָם
	Speaks as clearly in my ears as **an interceding angel**[90] on high.	הוּא דֹבֵר צַחוֹת בְּאָזְנַי כְּמַלְאָךְ מֵלִיץ[90] בַּמָּרוֹם.
	(The nurse enters with ropes in her hand)	(האומנת באה ועבותים בידיה)
	What do you have to say, my nurse? What are those in your hand?	מַה־בְּפִיךְ אֹמַנְתִּי?מָה אֵלֶּה בְּיָדֵיךְ?
	Are they the ropes which Ram commanded you to bring?	הַאִם הָעֲבֹתִים הֵם, אֲשֶׁר צִוָּה רָם לַהֲבִיאָם?
THE NURSE	They are the ropes to be hanged on – *(Throws them to the ground)*	האומנת הֵם הָעֲבֹתִים לְהֵחָנֵק בָּם – (משלכת אותם ארצה)

87 Liturgical poem sung at the Yom Kippur evening service כחומר ביד היוצר 'like clay in the potter's hand'. Cf. Jer. 18:4 וְנִשְׁחַת הַכְּלִי אֲשֶׁר הוּא עֹשֶׂה בַּחֹמֶר בְּיַד הַיּוֹצֵר 'and the vessel which he was making from the clay was ruined in the potter's hand'.

88 Esther 9:17, 18.

89 Gen. 37:7; 2 Sam. 13:18.

90 Job 33:23.

JAEL	Woe is me! What has happened to us? Why do you wring your hands?	אוֹי לִי! מַה־קָּרָה לָנוּ? לָמָּה תִּסְפְּקִי כַּפָּיִךְ?	יעל
THE NURSE	Woe unto us this day! He is dead, he is dead, he is dead!	אוֹי לָנוּ הַיּוֹם! הוּא מֵת, הוּא מֵת, הוּא מֵת!	האומנת
	Woe is us, for we are done for! We are done for, done for, my lady!	אוֹי לָנוּ כִּי אָבָדְנוּ! אָבַדְנוּ אָבַדְנוּ גְּבִרְתִּי!	
	Cursed be this day! He has fallen slain, dead!	אָרוּר הַיּוֹם הַזֶּה! הוּא נָפַל חָלָל מֵת!	
JAEL	Could such wrath, such cruelty come forth from the heavens?	הַאִם מִן הַשָּׁמַיִם תֵּצֵא חֵמָה, אַכְזְרִיּוּת כָּזֹאת?	יעל
THE NURSE	Not from the heavens, but rather from Ram's hand it has come forth	לֹא מִן הַשָּׁמַיִם, כִּי אִם מִיַּד רָם יָצָאָה	האומנת
	Who would have said to us that Ram would do such a thing –	מִי מִלֵּל לָנוּ כִּי רָם יַעֲשֶׂה כָּזֹאת –	
	Oh, son of Abiram!	אֲהָהּ בֶּן אֲבִירָם!	
JAEL	What do you have against me, cursed woman, that you have come to afflict me today?	מַה־לִּי וָלָךְ אֲרוּרָה! כִּי בָאת לְעַנּוֹתֵנִי כַּיּוֹם הַזֶּה?	יעל
	You are speaking like one of the daughters of Sheol, **killing me with the breath of your lips.**[91]	כְּאַחַת מִבְּנוֹת הַשְּׁאוֹל תְּדַבְּרִי לַהֲמִתֵנִי **בְּרוּחַ שְׂפָתָיִךְ.**[91]	
	Has Ram laid a hand on himself? Tell me if it is so	הֲשָׁלַח רָם יָד בְּנַפְשׁוֹ? הַגִּידִי אִם כֵּן הוּא	
	And that word will be like a sharp sword adding to the slain ones	וְהַמִּלָּה הַזֹּאת תִּהְיֶה כְּחֶרֶב חַדָּה לְהוֹסִיף חֲלָלִים	
	Life and death are in the power of the tongue,[92] in the power of a single word[93]	**חַיִּים וָמָוֶת בְּיַד הַלָּשׁוֹן**[92] בְּיַד מִלָּה אַחַת[93]	
	Say the word and **it will bring me down into the pit of destruction.**[94]	הוֹצִיאִי אֶת הַמִּלָּה **וְהִיא תוֹרִידֵנִי לִבְאֵר שָׁחַת.**[94]	
THE NURSE	I saw his wound, my eyes saw the wound	אֲנִי רָאִיתִי אֶת מַכָּתוֹ, עֵינַי רָאוּ אֶת הַמַּכָּה	האומנת

91 Isa. 11:4 וּבְרוּחַ שְׂפָתָיו יָמִית רָשָׁע 'and with the breath of his lips he will kill the wicked'.
92 Prov. 18:21 מָוֶת וְחַיִּים בְּיַד־לָשׁוֹן 'death and life are in the power of the tongue'.
93 This and the next line form a rhyming couplet, mirroring Shakespeare's 'no/woe' (3.2.50–1).
94 Ps. 55:24 (55:23 in English Bibles) וְאַתָּה אֱלֹהִים ׀ תּוֹרִדֵם ׀ לִבְאֵר שַׁחַת 'and You, God, will bring them down into the pit of destruction'.

	A bleeding wound[95] in his flesh, at his mighty heart	מַכָּה טְרִיָּה[95] בִּבְשָׂרוֹ, לְנֹכַח לִבּוֹ הַכַּבִּיר	
	The whiteness of his face was like ash, and his tunic was **rolled in blood**[96]	לֹבֶן פָּנָיו כָּאֵפֶר וְכֻתָּנְתּוֹ מְגוֹלָלָה בְּדָמִים[96]	
	Slain by the sword,[97] slain, dead, a corpse, **a corpse trampled underfoot**.[98]	חֲלַל חֶרֶב,[97] חָלָל מֵת, פֶּגֶר, פֶּגֶר מוּבָס[98]	
	All this my eyes saw, until **agony seized me**.[99]	כָּל זֹאת רָאוּ עֵינַי, עַד אֲשֶׁר אֲחָזַנִי הַשָּׁבָץ.[99]	
JAEL	Split, my heart, into pieces; crumble, all my bones	הִתְבַּקַּע לְבָבִי לִבְקִיעִים, הִתְפּוֹרֵרְנָה כָּל עַצְמוֹתַי	יעל
	It is too much for you to see, my eyes; let me alone, breath of my nose	רַב לָכֶן עֵינַי מֵרְאוֹת, חִדְלִי מִמֶּנִּי נִשְׁמַת אַפִּי	
	For **a clod of dust**[100] like me establish a gravestone as a memorial[101]	לְגוּשׁ עָפָר[100] כָּמוֹנִי, הַצִּיבוּ מַצֶּבֶת קְבֻרָה לְזִכָּרוֹן[101]	
	For what else is my desire, except to lie with him in the coffin.	וּמַה חֶפְצִי עוֹד, בִּלְתִּי לִשְׁכַּב עִמּוֹ בָּאָרוֹן.	
THE NURSE	Tubal, Tubal, my friend, Tubal, chief among those who ever loved me!	תּוּבַל, תּוּבַל אֹהֲבִי, תּוּבַל רֹאשׁ מְאַהֲבַי בְּעוֹלָמִי	האומנת
	How pleasant you were to me, how honourable you were, honourable man,	מַה־נָּעַמְתָּ לִי, מַה־נִּכְבַּדְתָּ אִישׁ נִכְבָּד,	
	Is it for this that I have lived so many days, to see your death?	הֲבַעֲבוּר זֹאת הֶאֱרַכְתִּי יָמִים לִרְאוֹת מוֹתְךָ אָתָּה?	
JAEL	What is this storm that is coming from the other side?	מָה הַסַּעַר הַזֶּה הַנֵּעוֹר מֵעֵבֶר הַשֵּׁנִי?	יעל
	Has Ram been killed and Tubal is also dead?	הַאִם רָם נֶהֱרַג וְגַם תּוּבַל מֵת?	

95 Isa. 1:6.
96 Isa. 9:4 (9:5 in English Bibles).
97 Num. 19:16.
98 Isa. 14:19.
99 2 Sam. 1:9. See *Ithiel*, Fourth Part, note 10 for a different use of this citation.
100 Job 7:5.
101 This and the next line form a rhyming couplet, mirroring Shakespeare's 'here/bier' (3.2.59–60).

	Tubal is my age and my brother,[102] and Ram is **the beau of my youth**[103]	תּוּבַל בֶּן גִּילִי וְאָחִי[102] וְרָם **אַלּוּף נְעוּרָי**[103]	
	So why does the trumpet not sound that the day of dread has come?	וְלָמָּה לֹא יִתָּקַע בַּשּׁוֹפָר כִּי יוֹם הַנּוֹרָא בָּא?	
	Who is still living, if they have both gone and are no more?	מִי יִחְיֶה עוֹד, אִם שְׁנֵיהֶם הָלְכוּ וְאֵינָם?	
THE NURSE	Tubal was struck down and is dead, whereas Ram, who struck him down, will surely go into exile.	תּוּבַל הֻכָּה וָמֵת וְרָם מַכֵּהוּ גָּלֹה יִגְלֶה.	האומנת
JAEL	Did Ram's hand spill Tubal's blood?	הַאִם דְּמֵי תוּבַל, יַד רָם שָׁפָכָה?	יעל
THE NURSE	His hand did this, his hand spilled the blood.	יָדוֹ עָשְׂתָה זֹאת יָדוֹ שָׁפְכָה אֶת הַדָּם.	האומנת
JAEL	Oh, serpent's heart, while the face is the face of **a beloved man**[104]	הוֹי לֵב תַּנִּין וְהַפָּנִים פְּנֵי **אִישׁ חֲמֻדוֹת**[104]	יעל
	Who has seen such **a viper's den**[105] in the form of a palace like your body?	מִי רָאָה מְאוּרַת **צִפְעוֹנִי**[105] בְּתַבְנִית הֵיכָל כִּגְוִיָּתְךָ?	
	A **beautiful-eyed**[106] cruel man, **an adversary and enemy**[107] in the likeness of an angel's face	אַכְזָר **יְפֵה עֵינַיִם**,[106] **צַר וְאוֹיֵב**[107] בִּדְמוּת פְּנֵי מַלְאָךְ	
	A raven in a dove's feathers, a mauling wolf in a ewe's skin	עוֹרֵב בְּנוֹצַת יוֹנָה, זְאֵב טֹרֵף בְּעוֹר כִּבְשָׂה	
	An evil beast from the woods in the image of the face of God.	חַיָּה רָעָה מִיַּעַר בְּצֶלֶם פְּנֵי אֱלֹהִים.	
	You are the opposite **in the heart from your outward appearance**[108]	**הֶפֶךְ אַתָּה לַלֵּבָב מֵאֲשֶׁר תֵּרָאֶה לָעֵינָיִם**[108]	

102 Cf. Shakespeare's 'cousin' (3.2.66); see First Part, note 65.
103 Jer. 3:4.
104 Dan. 10:11, 19.
105 Isa 11:8.
106 1 Sam. 16:12.
107 Esther 7:6.
108 1 Sam. 16:7 הָאָדָם יִרְאֶה לַעֵינַיִם וַיהוָה יִרְאֶה לַלֵּבָב 'man sees the outward appearance, but the LORD sees the heart'.

	An honourable holy man[109] of the Lord on the outside, while your insides are **an abomination of desolation.**[110]	קְדוֹשׁ[109] אֲדֹנָי מְכֻבָּד מִחוּץ וְתוֹכְךָ **שִׁקּוּץ מְשׁוֹמֵם.**[110]	
	How has the Rock[111] taken dust from the earth of paradise	אֵיךְ לָקַח הַצּוּר[111] עָפָר מֵאַדְמַת גַּן הָעֵדֶן	
	And wondrously made your body glorious like **the seal of perfection**[112]	וַיַּפְלִיא לַעֲשׂוֹת גְּוִיָּתְךָ **כְּחוֹתַם תָּכְנִית**[112] לְהִתְפָּאֵר	
	And afterwards blown breath into your nostrils from the valley of the dead –	וְאַחֲרֵי כֵן נָפַח בְּאַפֶּיךָ רוּחַ מֵעֵמֶק רְפָאִים –	
	Who has seen a book full of **devouring words**[113]	מִי רָאָה סֵפֶר מָלֵא **דִבְרֵי בָלַע**[113]	
	In a gold embroidered handkerchief? How in **a tower of strength,**[114]	בְּמִטְפַּחַת זָהָב וְרִקְמָה? אֵיךְ **בְּמִגְדַּל עֹז,**[114]	
	In a temple where everyone speaks of glory[115] can there dwell such deceit as this?	**בְּהֵיכָל כֻּלּוֹ אֹמֵר כָּבוֹד**[115] תֵּשֵׁב מִרְמָה כָּמֹהָ?	
THE NURSE	There is no more confidence, for **all men are liars**[116]	אֵין בִּטָּחוֹן עוֹד, כִּי **כָל הָאָדָם כֹּזֵב**[116]	האומנת
	There is no truth, there is no faith, **the faithful have vanished from among the sons of men**[117]	אֵין אֱמֶת, אֵין אֱמוּנָה, **פַּסּוּ אֱמֻנִים מִבְּנֵי אָדָם**[117]	
	All speak lies, all swear falsely	כֻּלָּם שָׁוְא יְדַבֵּרוּ, כֻּלָּם נִשְׁבָּעִים לַשָּׁקֶר	
	All are hypocrites – but hurry, my servant, where are you?	כֻּלָּם חַנְפֵי לֵב – אַךְ חוּשָׁה מְשָׁרְתִי, אַיֶּכָּה?	
	Hurry, **sustain me with a raisin cake**[118] – all the woes and distresses and groaning	חוּשָׁה **סַמְּכֵנִי בָּאֲשִׁישָׁה**[118] – כָּל הַצָּרוֹת וְהַמְּצוּקוֹת וְהָאֲנָחוֹת	

109 Cf. Shakespeare's 'saint' (3.2.79).
110 Dan. 11:31.
111 A name for God; see Deut. 32:4.
112 Ezek. 28:12.
113 Ps. 52:6 (52:4 in English Bibles).
114 Judg. 9:51; Ps. 61:4 (61:3 in English Bibles); Prov. 18:10.
115 Ps. 29:9 וּבְהֵיכָלוֹ כֻּלּוֹ אֹמֵר כָּבוֹד 'and in His temple everyone speaks of glory'.
116 Ps. 116:11.
117 Ps. 12:2 (12:1 in English Bibles).
118 Song of Songs 2:5 סַמְּכוּנִי בָּאֲשִׁישׁוֹת 'sustain me with raisin cakes'. Cf. Shakespeare's 'give me some aqua vitae' (3.2.88).

	They have all come upon me, and I have grown old before my old age	עָלַי הָיוּ כֻלָּנָה וָאֶזְקַן בְּלֹא עֵת זִקְנָתִי	
	May disgrace descend upon Ram!	חֶרְפָּה תִּפֹּל עַל פְּנֵי רָם!	
JAEL	May your tongue rot in your mouth for this curse of yours	תִּמַּק לְשׁוֹנֵךְ בְּפִיךְ תַּחַת קִלְלָתֵךְ זֹאת	יעל
	Disgrace will not descend upon Ram, for it fears to approach him	חֶרְפָּה לֹא תִפֹּל עַל פָּנָיו, כִּי יָרֵאָה לָגֶשֶׁת אֵלָיו	
	Nothing but honour and splendour will crown him and a throne is prepared for him	אַךְ כָּבוֹד וְהָדָר יְעַטְּרֵהוּ וְכִסֵּא נָכוֹן לוֹ	
	Like a king who rules over all. – How foolish I was to revile his name!	כְּמֶלֶךְ מֹשֵׁל בַּכֹּל. – אֵיךְ נִבְעַרְתִּי לְנַבֵּל שְׁמוֹ!	
THE NURSE	Do you honour the name of the one who murdered your brother?[119]	הֲתִתְּנִי כָבוֹד לִשְׁמוֹ אֲשֶׁר רָצַח נֶפֶשׁ אָחִיךְ?[119]	האומנת
JAEL	Would I defame the name of my husband? Oh, my husband!	הַאֶתֵּן שֵׁם בַּעֲלִי לִנְאָצָה? – הוֹי בַּעֲלִי!	יעל
	Who would bring your name upon his lips in honour and glory	מִי יִשָּׂא שִׁמְךָ* עַל שְׂפָתָיו לְכָבוֹד וְלִתְהִלָּה	
	When your wife on her wedding day mentions it with gnashing of teeth?	וְאִשְׁתְּךָ בְּיוֹם חֲתֻנָּתָהּ תַּזְכִּירֶנּוּ בַּחֲרֹק שִׁנַּיִם?	
	But why, villain, did you strike down my brother?[120]	אַךְ עַל מַה בְּלִיַּעַל הִכִּיתָ נֶפֶשׁ אָחִי?[120]	
	Admittedly, if you had not struck him down, my brother[121] the villain would have taken your life.	אוּלָם לוּלֵא הִכִּיתוֹ, הָיָה אָחִי[121] הַבְּלִיַּעַל לָקַחַת נַפְשְׁךָ.	
	So therefore it is not in mourning that my eyes shed a tear	לָכֵן אֵיפֹה לֹא לְסִפֵּד תֵּרַדְנָה עֵינַי דִּמְעָה	
	But rather, they are tears of joy and a time of dancing	כִּי דִמְעוֹת שִׂמְחָה הֵנָּה וְעֵת רְקוֹד	

119 Cf. Shakespeare's 'cousin' (3.2.96); see First Part, note 65.
120 Cf. Shakespeare's 'cousin' (3.2.100); see First Part, note 65.
121 Cf. Shakespeare's 'cousin' (3.2.101); see First Part, note 65.

* שִׁמְךָ

Because my husband lives, he whom Tubal sought to kill	כִּי בַּעֲלִי חַי אֲשֶׁר תּוּבַל בִּקֵּשׁ לְהָרְגוֹ
And because Tubal is dead, he who sought to kill my husband	וְכִי תּוּבַל מֵת אֲשֶׁר בִּקֵּשׁ לַהֲרֹג אֶת בַּעֲלִי
So why am I still weeping, why **is my heart faint**[122]	וְלָמָּה אֲנִי בְּכִיָּה עוֹד, לָמָּה זֶה לִבִּי דַוָּי[122]
And I do not rejoice in my suffering which has befallen me so pleasantly?	וְלֹא אֶשְׂמַח בְּחֶבְלִי אֲשֶׁר נָפַל לִי בַּנְּעִימִים?
But I heard another word, a word more bitter than Tubal's death	אַךְ עוֹד דָּבָר שָׁמַעְתִּי, דָּבָר מַר מִמּוֹת תּוּבָל
And it is like **a sword in my bones**;[123] I cannot remove it from my heart	וְהוּא כְּרֶצַח בְּעַצְמוֹתַי,[123] לַהֲסִירוֹ מִלִּבִּי לֹא אוּכָל
For it oppresses me like **a lower millstone**,[124] like **a sin worthy of death**[125]	כִּי יְצִיקֵנִי כְּפֶלַח תַּחְתִּית,[124] כְּחֵטְא מִשְׁפַּט מָוֶת[125]
Which oppresses the heart of sinners: it is this evil word	אֲשֶׁר יָצִיק לֵב הַחַטָּאִים: הוּא הַדָּבָר הָרָע הַזֶּה
That after Tubal's death Ram is to go into exile.	כִּי אַחֲרֵי מוֹת תּוּבַל יֵלֵךְ רָם בַּגּוֹלָה.
This word **pierces my kidneys**[126] tens of thousands of times more than Tubal's death	אֹמֶר הַזֶּה יְפַלַּח כִּלְיוֹתַי[126] רִבְבוֹת פְּעָמִים מִמּוֹת תּוּבָל
At the death of my brother Tubal, **I find woe and sorrow**[127] enough.	בְּמוֹת תּוּבַל אָחִי, צָרָה וְיָגוֹן אֶמְצָא[127] לְמַדַּי.
But if it is the way of woes **for each one to love its fellow**[128]	וְאִם דֶּרֶךְ הַצָּרוֹת לֶאֱהֹב אִשָּׁה אֶת רְעוּתָהּ[128]
And woe comes on top of woe, disaster on top of disaster	וְצָרָה עַל צָרָה תָּבוֹא, הֹוָה עַל הֹוָה
Why did the messenger stop when she gave me the tidings	מַדּוּעַ חָדְלָה הַמְבַשֶּׂרֶת, לְעֵת בִּשְּׂרָה לִי הַבְּשֹׂרָה
That Tubal was dead, and not go on to say	כִּי תּוּבַל מֵת, וְלֹא הוֹסִיפָה לֵאמֹר

122 Jer. 8:18; Lam. 1:22.
123 Ps. 42:11 (42:10 in English Bibles).
124 Job 41:16 (41:24 in English Bibles).
125 Deut. 21:22.
126 Job 16:13.
127 Ps. 116:3.
128 Exod. 11:2.

	That my father too was dead, or my mother, or even both of them?	גַּם אָבִי מֵת אוֹ אִמִּי, אוֹ גַם שְׁנֵיהֶם?	
	But she said that Ram will surely go into exile	אַךְ הִיא אָמְרָה כִּי רָם גָּלֹה יִגְלֶה	
	The word of this report, it is as if I had heard	דְּבַר הַשְּׁמוּעָה הַזֹּאת, הוּא כְּאִלּוּ שָׁמַעְתִּי לֵאמֹר	
	That my father and mother and Tubal and Ram and Jael are all slain, dead.	אָבִי וְאִמִּי וְתוּבַל וְרָם וְיָעֵל כֻּלָּם חֲלָלִים מֵתִים.	
	'Ram will surely go into exile' and Jael will be left **as a widow whose husband is alive**[129, 130]	„רָם גָּלֹה יִגְלֶה" וְיָעֵל **בְּאַלְמְנוּת חַיּוּת**[129] תִּשָּׁאֵר[130]	
	This is like a spear in my belly, my heart is pierced by an arrow	זֶה כַּחֲנִית בְּבִטְנִי, מֵחֵץ לִבִּי יִדָּקֵר	
	My destruction is as vast as the ocean; it cannot be measured, cannot be fathomed	גָּדוֹל שִׁבְרִי כַּיָּם, לֹא יִמַּד לֹא יֵחָקֵר	
	There is not a word on my tongue[131] to tell of my woe enough to explain it. –	**אֵין מִלָּה בִּלְשׁוֹנִי,**[131] לְהַגִּיד צָרָתִי דֵּי בָאֵר. –	
	Tell me, my nurse, where are my father and my mother?	הַגִּידִי לִי אֹמַנְתִּי, אַיֵּה אָבִי וְאִמִּי?	
THE NURSE	They went to mourn for Tubal, to spill a tear over his blood	הֵם הָלְכוּ לִסְפֹּד לְתוּבַל, לִשְׁפֹּךְ דִּמְעָה עַל דָּמוֹ	האומנת
	And I shall take you to them, if you would go with me.	וַאֲנִי אוֹלִיכֵךְ אֲלֵיהֶם, אִם תֵּלְכִי עִמִּי.	
JAEL	They spill their tears over the one who is going to his eternal home[132]	יִשְׁפְּכוּ הֵם דִּמְעָתָם עַל הַהוֹלֵךְ לְבֵית עוֹלָמוֹ[132]	יעל
	Whereas I shall keep my tears for the one who is going down living to Sheol	וַאֲנִי דִּמְעָתִי אֶשְׁמֹר לַיּוֹרֵד חַיִּים שְׁאוֹלָה	

129 2 Sam. 20:3.

130 This and the next three lines form two rhyming couplets, mirroring Shakespeare's 'bound/sound' (3.2.125–6), except that Salkinson's rhyme extends over four lines whereas Shakespeare's is composed only of two.

131 Ps. 139:4.

132 While this does not rhyme with the last word on the next line visually or in Modern Hebrew pronunciation, it does form a near rhyme in Ashkenazic pronunciation, mirroring Shakespeare's 'spent/banishment' (3.2.130–1).

	Take the ropes away from here, the ropes which are as humiliated as me[133]	שְׂאִי אֶת הָעֲבֹתִים מִזֶּה, הָעֲבֹתִים הַנִּכְלָמִים כָּמוֹנִי[133]	
	For they were brought in order to become a ladder, to raise up Ram to my palanquin	כִּי הוּבְאוּ לִהְיוֹת לְסֻלָּם, לְהַעֲלוֹת אֶת רָם לְאַפִּרְיוֹנִי	
	And they groan with me, for Ram is going into exile.[134]	וְהֵם נֶאֱנָחִים עִמָּדִי, כִּי רָם הוֹלֵךְ בַּגּוֹלָה.[134]	
	Please bring me to my bed, where I hoped to become a man's wife	הֲבִיאִנִי נָא אֶל יְצוּעִי, שָׁם קִוִּיתִי לִהְיוֹת בְּעוּלָה	
	But there I shall perish, I shall die a virgin widow.	וְשָׁם אֶגְוָעָה אָמוּתָה אִשָּׁה אַלְמָנָה בְּתוּלָה.	
	She shall not be wife to Ram, but rather to death.[135]	לֹא לְרָם הִיא, כִּי אִם לַמָּוֶת תִּבָּעֵל.[135]	
THE NURSE	Come on, come into your room and I shall bring comfort to you	לְכִי בֹּאִי בְּחַדְרֵךְ וַאֲנִי אָבִיא לָךְ נֹחַם	האומנת
	You will see Ram tonight, because I know where he is[136]	אֶת רָם תִּרְאִי הַלַּיְלָה כִּי אֶת מְקוֹמוֹ יָדַעְתִּי[136]	
	He is hiding in the priest's chamber; I shall go and bring him to you.	הוּא נֶחְבָּא בְּלִשְׁכַּת הַכֹּהֵן, אֵלֵךְ וְאֵלַיִךְ אֲבִיאֶנּוּ.	
JAEL	Go, seek him and give him my ring	לְכִי בַּקְּשִׁי פָנָיו וּתְנִי לוֹ אֶת טַבַּעְתִּי	יעל
	Tell him that he must visit me before he goes and is no more.	אִמְרִי לוֹ כִּי יְשַׁחֲרֵנִי טֶרֶם יֵלֵךְ וְאֵינֶנּוּ.	
	(Both exit)	(הולכות שתיהן)	
THIRD SCENE	*The priest's chamber (Rezin and Ram)*	לשכת הכהן (רצין ורם)	מחזה שלישי

133 This and the next line form a rhyming couplet, mirroring Shakespeare's 'beguiled/exiled' (3.2.132–3).

134 This forms a near rhyme with the following two lines, which themselves comprise a rhyming couplet; cf. Shakespeare's 'bed/widowed' (3.2.134–5).

135 Due to the fact that the rhyme scheme in this speech is different in Salkinson's version than in Shakespeare's, this final line does not rhyme with anything, whereas in the source text the last two lines form a rhyming couplet 'bed/maidenhead' (3.2.136–7).

136 This and the following three lines form an ABAB rhyme, mirroring Shakespeare's 'night/cell/knight/farewell' (3.2.140–3).

REZIN	Approach me, Ram, approach me, **misfortunate man**.[137]	רצין גְּשָׁה לִי רָם, גְּשָׁה לִי **גֶּבֶר לֹא יִצְלָח**[137]
	Misfortune and destruction pursue you, and the hand of love is upon you for ill	אֵיד וָשֶׁבֶר יִרְדְּפוּךָ וְיַד הָאַהֲבָה בְּךָ לְרָעָה
	You call grief 'my sister', and woe 'the wife of my covenant'.	אֲחוֹתִי תִּקְרָא לְתוּגָה וּלְצָרָה אֵשֶׁת בְּרִיתִי.
RAM	Of what would you inform me, my father? What is the prince's judgement?	רם מַה־תַּשְׁמִיעֵנִי אָבִי? מַה מִשְׁפַּט הַנָּסִיךְ?
	Is there another new woe that desires me	הֲיֵשׁ עוֹד צָרָה חֲדָשָׁה, אֲשֶׁר תִּמְצָא בִי חֵפֶץ
	Of which I do not know thus far?	אֲשֶׁר לֹא יָדַעְתִּי עַד כֹּה?
REZIN	Are you lacking in woes? – Listen to me, my dear son	רצין הַחֲסַר צָרוֹת אַתָּה? – שְׁמָעֵנִי בְּנִי הַיָּקָר
	For I shall inform you of what has been decreed upon you from the mouth of the prince.	כִּי אַשְׁמִיעֲךָ מַה־נִּגְזַר עָלֶיךָ מִפִּי הַנָּסִיךְ.
RAM	What is the decree, if not a decree equal to a death sentence?	רם מָה הִיא הַגְּזֵרָה, אִם לֹא גְּזֵרָה שָׁוָה לְמִשְׁפַּט* מָוֶת?
REZIN	The prince has lightened your sentence for he has had mercy upon you	רצין הַנָּסִיךְ הֵקַל מִשְׁפָּטְךָ כִּי הִטָּה אֵלֶיךָ חָסֶד
	You shall not go into **the valley of the shadow of death**,[138] but rather into exile.	לֹא **בְּגֵיא צַלְמָוֶת**[138] כִּי אִם בַּגּוֹלָה תֵּלֵךְ.
RAM	Be merciful to me and say death, and do not mention to me the word exile	רם חָנֵּנִי וֶאֱמֹר מָוֶת וְאַל תַּזְכֶּר־לִי שֵׁם גּוֹלָה
	The valley of the shadow of death[139] would be better for me than wandering in exile	טוֹב לִי **גֵּיא צַלְמָוֶת**[139] מִנּוֹעַ וָנוּד בַּגּוֹלָה
	The name of exile is dreadful and terrible, and more bitter to me than **the bitterness of death**.[140]	שֵׁם גּוֹלָה נוֹרָא וְאָיֹם וּמַר לִי **מִמַּר הַמָּוֶת**.[140]

137 Jer. 22:30.
138 Ps. 23:4.
139 Ps. 23:4.
140 1 Sam. 15:32.

* מִשְׁפַּט

REZIN	You have only been banished from the city of Verona, therefore do not fear	רַק מֵעִיר וֵירוֹנָה נִגְרַשְׁתָּ, לָכֵן אַל תִּירָא	רצין
	For the land is spacious, and you still have hope.	כִּי הָאָרֶץ רַחֲבַת יָדַיִם וְעוֹד יֵשׁ לְךָ תִּקְוָה.	
RAM	All the earth outside of the city of Verona is **formless and void**[141]	כָּל הָאָרֶץ מִחוּץ לָעִיר וֵירוֹנָה **תֹּהוּ וָבֹהוּ**[141]	רם
	It can be considered as **Sheol and destruction**,[142] as burning fire in hell	**כִּשְׁאוֹל וַאֲבַדּוֹן**[142] תֵּחָשֵׁב, כְּזַלְעֲפוֹת אֵשׁ בְּגֵיהִנֹּם	
	And if I am banished from the city of Verona to settle in some place	וְכִי אֲגֹרַשׁ מֵעִיר וֵירוֹנָה לִשְׁכֹּן בְּאַחַד הַמְּקוֹמוֹת	
	Why, I have been banished from the land of the living to settle like a dead man in the grave	הִנְנִי נִגְרַשְׁתִּי מֵאֶרֶץ חַיִּים לִשְׁכֹּן כַּמֵּת בַּקֶּבֶר	
	For Verona is my life's home, and my exile is death	כִּי וֵירוֹנָה בֵּית חַיַּי וְגָלוּתִי הוּא הַמָּוֶת	
	And you cut off my head today with a golden axe	וְאַתָּה תִּכְרֹת רֹאשִׁי כַּיּוֹם בְּגַרְזֶן זָהָב	
	And raise your voice in laughter saying that you are merciful.	וְתִתֵּן קוֹלְךָ בִּשְׂחוֹק לֵאמֹר כִּי לְךָ הַחֶסֶד.	
REZIN	Does one who has been treated mercifully scorn mercy? Does the one who has been treated compassionately mock compassion?	הֲיָחֹן בּוֹזֶה חֲנִינָה? לֹעֵג לְרַחֲמִים הַיְרֻחָם?	רצין
	Why, you have committed **a sin worthy of death**[143] because you spilled blood	**הֵן חֵטְא מִשְׁפַּט מָוֶת**[143] בְּךָ כִּי דָם שָׁפָכְתָּ	
	But the prince **delights in kindness**;[144] he has given you the chance to flee	וְהַנָּסִיךְ **חָפֵץ חֶסֶד הוּא**[144] נָתַן לְךָ יָדַיִם לָנוּס	
	So that you might save yourself as in one of the cities of refuge[145]	לְמַעַן תִּנָּצֵל נַפְשְׁךָ כְּמוֹ בְּאַחַת עָרֵי מִקְלָט[145]	

141 Gen. 1:2; Jer. 4:23.

142 Prov. 15:11. Cf. Shakespeare's 'purgatory' (3.3.18), which does not have a direct biblical parallel.

143 Deut. 21:22.

144 Mic. 7:18.

145 This refers to the six cities set aside under biblical law as places of asylum to which perpetrators of manslaughter could flee (Num. 35:11, 13, 14).

	Yet you do not recognize his kindness.	וְאַתָּה אֶת חַסְדּוֹ לֹא תַכִּיר.	
RAM	It is **a furnace of affliction**[146] rather than mercy and kindness	**כּוּר עֹנִי**[146] הוּא וְלֹא חֶסֶד וַחֲנִינָה	רם
	Why, Jael lives here, and this city is like the garden of the LORD	הֵן יָעֵל יֹשֶׁבֶת פֹּה וְהָעִיר הַזֹּאת כְּגַן אֲדֹנָי	
	And every creeping creature, abomination, and mouse, **every unclean thing**[147]	וְכָל רֶמֶשׂ שֶׁקֶץ וְעַכְבָּר, **כָּל דָּבָר טָמֵא**[147]	
	Can **walk to and fro in the garden**[148] and behold the pleasantness of her face	יוּכַל **לְהִתְהַלֵּךְ בַּגָּן**[148] וְלַחֲזוֹת בְּנֹעַם פָּנֶיהָ	
	But Ram cannot **set the sole of his foot**[149] here.	אַךְ רָם אֵין לוֹ פֹּה **מִדְרַךְ כַּף רָגֶל**.[149]	
	The flies are like honourable free men; they are free	הַזְּבוּבִים כִּבְנֵי חוֹרִים נִכְבָּדִים חָפְשִׁים הֵם	
	To approach Jael, to take delight in the whiteness of her hands	לָגֶשֶׁת אֶל יָעֵל, לְהִתְעַנֵּג עַל לִבְנַת יָדֶיהָ	
	And moreover at a suitable time during sleep, or even while awake,	וְגַם לְעֵת מְצֹא בַּשֵּׁנָה, אוֹ גַּם בְּהָקִיץ	
	They can steal in to kiss her mouth and to suck the pure honey of her lips	יִתְגַּנְּבוּ לְנַשֵּׁק אֶת פִּיהָ וְלָמֹץ נֹפֶת שְׂפָתֶיהָ	
	But Ram himself is trapped like a sinning soul in Sheol	אַךְ רָם לְבַדּוֹ עָצוּר כַּנֶּפֶשׁ הַחֹטֵאת בִּשְׁאוֹל	
	He cannot enter the city, cannot approach her	לֹא יוּכַל לָבוֹא בָּעִיר, בַּל קְרֹב אֵלֶיהָ	
	The flies can approach and touch her, but Ram cannot approach	הַזְּבוּבִים יִקְרְבוּ יִגְּעוּ בָהּ אַךְ רָם בַּל יִקְרַב	
	For he is driven out and chased off, and banishment and excommunication are upon him.	כִּי מֻדָּח וּמְנֻדֶּח הוּא וְנִדּוּי וְשַׁמְתָּא עָלָיו.	
	So how can you say that my exile is not my death?	וְאֵיךְ תֹּאמַר אַתָּה כִּי גָלוּתִי לֹא מוֹתִי הוּא?	
	Do you not have **a cup of poison**,[150] or a sharp knife	הַאֵין לְךָ **סַף רַעַל**,[150] אוֹ מַאֲכֶלֶת חַדָּה	

146 Isa. 48:10.
147 Lev. 5:2.
148 Gen. 3:8 מִתְהַלֵּךְ בַּגָּן 'walking to and fro in the garden'.
149 Deut. 2:5.
150 Zech. 12:2.

	Or some instrument of death to kill me with one blow	אוֹ אֵיזֶה כְּלִי־מָוֶת לַהֲמִיתֵנִי בְּמַכָּה אַחַת	
	And not to afflict my soul with exile, banishment, and excommunication	וְלֹא לְעַנּוֹת נַפְשִׁי בְּגָלוּת נִדּוּי וְשַׁמְתָּא	
	These dreadful judgements at whose mere mention	מִשְׁפָּטִים נוֹרָאִים אֵלֶּה אֲשֶׁר רַק לְזִכְרָם	
	The ghosts tremble underneath[151] and Sheol quakes at them?	הָרְפָאִים יְחֹלָלוּ מִתַּחַת[151] וּשְׁאוֹל תִּרְגַּז לִקְרָאתָם?	
	Why, you are a holy man of God, a doctor for the illnesses of the soul	הֲלֹא אִישׁ אֱלֹהִים קָדוֹשׁ אַתָּה, רֹפֵא תַחֲלוּאֵי הַנֶּפֶשׁ	
	Who pardons iniquities **for those who repent from sin**[152] and is also a faithful friend to me	הַסֹּלֵחַ עֲוֹנוֹת לְשָׁבֵי פֶשַׁע[152] וְגַם אֹהֵב נֶאֱמָן לְנַפְשִׁי	
	How do you presume to crush me with such words?	אֵיךְ מְלָאֲךָ לִבְּךָ לְדַכְּאֵנִי בְּמִלִּים כָּאֵלֶּה?	
REZIN	Senseless lad, listen to what I have to say too.	נַעַר סָר טַעַם, שְׁמָעֵנִי מַה בְּפִי גַּם אָנִי.	רצין
RAM	When you open your lips you will inform me further about exile.	כִּי תִפְתַּח שְׂפָתֶיךָ עַל גָּלוּת תַּשְׁמִיעֵנִי עוֹד.	רם
REZIN	I shall give you **oil and balm**[153] for the wound of exile	אֲנִי אֶתֵּן לְךָ שֶׁמֶן וָצֳרִי[153] לְמַכַּת הַגָּלוּת	רצין
	To be a remedy for you even as you go into exile	לִהְיוֹת לְמַרְפֵּא לְךָ אַף כִּי תֵלֵךְ בַּגּוֹלָה	
	It is the balm of understanding and **the precious oil**[154] **from the spring of wisdom.**[155]	הוּא צֳרִי הַשֵּׂכֶל וְהַשֶּׁמֶן הַטּוֹב[154] מִמְּקוֹר הַחָכְמָה.[155]	
RAM	Again you have come to mention the matter of exile to me	עוֹד הַפַּעַם בָּאתָ לְהַזְכִּירֵנִי עַל דְּבַר הַגָּלוּת	רם
	What use have I for wisdom? **Hang it up before the sun**[156]	מַה־לִּי וְלַחָכְמָה? הוֹקַע אֹתָהּ נֶגֶד הַשָּׁמֶשׁ[156]	
	Does it have the power to build me a new Verona	הֲיֵשׁ לְאֵל יָדָהּ לִבְנוֹת לִי וֵירוֹנָה חֲדָשָׁה	
	And to create another Jael, or to move the prince's heart	וְלִבְרוֹא יָעֵל אַחֶרֶת, אוֹ לְהַטּוֹת לֵב הַנָּסִיךְ	

151 Job 26:5.
152 Isa. 59:20.
153 Ezek. 27:17.
154 Isa 39:2.
155 Alshekh to Isa. 44.
156 Num. 25:4 וְהוֹקַע אוֹתָם לַיהוָה נֶגֶד הַשָּׁמֶשׁ 'and hang them up for the Lord before the sun'.

To remove the evil of the decree?[157] None of these is in its power

לְהַעֲבִיר רֹעַ הַגְּזֵרָה?[157] אֵין כָּל אֵלֶּה בְּיָדָהּ

For **wisdom has no advantage over folly**[158]

כִּי מוֹתָר הַחָכְמָה מִן הַסִּכְלוּת אָיִן[158]

Therefore listen to me and be silent, and you will be considered a wise man.

לָכֵן שְׁמָעֵנִי וְהַחֲרֵשׁ וּלְאִישׁ חָכָם תֵּחָשֵׁב.

REZIN I know that madmen **have ears but do not hear.**[159]

רצין יָדַעְתִּי כִּי הַמְשֻׁגָּעִים אָזְנַיִם לָהֶם וְלֹא יִשְׁמָעוּ.[159]

RAM Because the clear-sighted **have eyes but do not see.**[160]

רם יַעַן כִּי הַפִּקְחִים עֵינַיִם לָהֶם וְלֹא יִרְאוּ.[160]

REZIN Come, let us consult together, Ram, regarding your position.

רצין לְכָה נָּא וְנִוָּעֲצָה רָם, עַל אֹדֹת מַעֲמָדֶךָ.

RAM Do not speak a word which you do not know yourself

רם אַל תְּדַבֵּר דָּבָר אֲשֶׁר בְּנַפְשְׁךָ לֹא תֵדָעֶנּוּ

And do not judge a man's position until you arrive in his place.[161]

וְאַל תָּדִין מַעֲמַד אִישׁ עַד שֶׁתַּגִּיעַ לִמְקוֹמוֹ.[161]

If you were a young man like me and Jael's soul was bound to your soul

לוּ בָחוּר הָיִיתָ כָּמוֹנִי וְנֶפֶשׁ יָעֵל קְשׁוּרָה בְנַפְשֶׁךָ

And on this day, your wedding day, Tubal was struck down by your hand;

וּבְיוֹם זֶה יוֹם חֲתֻנָּתְךָ הֻכָּה תוּבַל בְּיָדֶיךָ;

Your love was as strong as death[162] and it was decreed upon you to go into exile,

אַהֲבָתְךָ עַזָּה כַמָּוֶת[162] וְנִגְזַר עָלֶיךָ לָלֶכֶת גּוֹלָה,

Then you would have the right to speak, to pull out the hair of your head

אָז הָיְתָה לְךָ הַצְּדָקָה לְדַבֵּר, לִמְרֹט שְׂעַר רֹאשֶׁךָ

To wallow in the dust and to lie out flat, as I do here

לְהִתְפַּלֵּשׁ בֶּעָפָר וּלְהִשְׁתַּטֵּחַ, כַּאֲשֶׁר אֲנִי עֹשֶׂה בָזֶה

To take my measure on the ground to be the measure of my grave.

לִנְטוֹת קַו מִדָּתִי עַל הָאָרֶץ לִהְיוֹת לִי לְמִדַּת קָבֶר.

157 This is based on ותשובה וצדקה ותפילה מעבירין את רוע הגזירה 'but repentence, prayer, and charity remove the evil of the decree', from *Unetane Toqef*, a medieval composition forming part of the Rosh HaShanah (Jewish New Year) liturgy.

158 Eccles. 2:13 וְרָאִיתִי אָנִי שֶׁיֵּשׁ יִתְרוֹן לַחָכְמָה מִן־הַסִּכְלוּת 'and I saw that wisdom has an advantage over folly'.

159 Jer. 5:21; Ps. 115:6.

160 Jer. 5:21; Ps. 115:5.

161 Mishnah *Avot* 2:5 ואל תדין את חברך עד שתגיע למקומו 'and do not judge your fellow until you arrive in his place'.

162 Song of Songs 8:6 עַזָּה כַמָּוֶת אַהֲבָה 'love is as strong as death'.

	(Falls and lies out flat on the ground) (Sound of someone knocking outside)	(נופל ומשתטח על הארץ) (קול דופק מחוץ)	
REZIN	Behold, someone is knocking; arise and hide.	הִנֵּה אִישׁ דֹּפֵק, קוּם לְךָ וְהִסָּתֵר.	רצין
RAM	I shall not hide, unless my lament and sighing	אֲנִי לֹא אֶסָּתֵר, בִּלְתִּי אִם שִׂיחִי וְאֶנְקָתִי	רם
	Rise up like steam from the depths of my heart and become a shelter for me	כָּאֵד יַעֲלוּ מֵעֹמֶק לִבִּי וְהֵם יִהְיוּ לִי לְסִתְרָה	
	(Sound of someone knocking outside)	(קול דופק מחוץ)	
REZIN	Men are pounding on the door; hide lest you be caught –	אֲנָשִׁים מִתְדַּפְּקִים עַל הַדֶּלֶת, הִסָּתֵר פֶּן תִּלָּכֵד –	רצין
	Who knocks there? I'm coming at once –	מִי דֹפֵק שָׁמָּה? הִנֵּה אֲנִי בָּא כְּרֶגַע –	
	Go quickly and hide in the library –	לֵךְ מַהֵר וְהֵחָבֵא בְּבֵית עֵקֶד הַסְּפָרִים –	
	Who knocks there forcefully? Who are you there?	מִי דֹפֵק שָׁם בְּחָזְקָה? מִי אַתָּה שָׁמָּה?	
	From where do you come, and what do you seek here?	אֵי מִזֶּה תָבוֹא וּמַה־תְּבַקֵּשׁ הֲלֹם?	
THE NURSE *(Outside)*	Open up for me, and you will know who I am and what I have to say	פְּתַח לִי וְתֵדַע מִי אֲנִי וּמַה־בְּפִי	האומנת (מחוץ)
	Why, I come from the lady Jael.	הֲלֹא מִיָּעֵל הַגְּבִירָה אֲנִי בָּאָה.	
REZIN	Come into the house in peace.	בּוֹאִי הַבַּיְתָה בְּשָׁלוֹם.	רצין
THE NURSE	Tell me, man of God! Please tell me, holy man of the LORD![163]	הַגִּידָה לִּי אִישׁ הָאֱלֹהִים! הַגֶּד־נָא קְדוֹשׁ אֲדֹנָי![163]	האומנת
	Where is the lady's husband? Where is the son of Abiram?	אֵיכֹה בַּעַל הַגְּבִירָה? אֵיכֹה בֶּן אֲבִירָם?	
REZIN	He is lying in his tears there **drunk, but not with wine**.[164]	הוּא שֹׁכֵב בְּדִמְעָתוֹ שָׁם שִׁכּוֹר וְלֹא מִיָּיִן.[164]	רצין
THE NURSE	He is like the lady, and the lady is also like him.	הוּא כְּמוֹ הַגְּבִירָה וְהַגְּבִירָה גַּם הִיא כָּמוֹהוּ.	האומנת

163 Cf. Shakespeare's 'holy Friar' (3.3.81).

164 Isa. 51:21 שְׁכֻרַת וְלֹא מִיָּיִן 'drunk, but not with wine'.

REZIN	They have one soul and one spirit and one heart.	נֶפֶשׁ אַחַת לִשְׁנֵיהֶם וְרוּחַ אֶחָד וְלֵב אֶחָד.	רצין
THE NURSE	She is also lying like him;	גַּם הִיא שׁוֹכֶבֶת כָּמוֹהוּ;	האומנת
	Crying, wailing, and weeping; weeping, wailing, and crying –	זָעֹק הֵילֵל וּבָכֹה, בָּכֹה הֵילֵל וְזָעֹק –	
	Arise, my lord, stand up on your feet, be a man	קוּמָה אֲדֹנִי, עֲמֹד עַל רַגְלֶיךָ הֱיֵה לְאִישׁ	
	Arise, Ram, for Jael, for her be a man	קוּם רָם לְמַעַן יָעֵל, לְמַעֲנָהּ הֱיֵה לְאִישׁ	
	How **have you fallen astoundingly**[165] and lie **like a man without strength**.[166]	אֵיךְ נָפַלְתָּ פְּלָאִים[165] וַתִּשְׁכַּב כְּגֶבֶר אֵין אֱיָל.[166]	
RAM *(Arising)*	The nurse?!	הָאֹמֶנֶת?!	רם (בקומו)
THE NURSE	My lord, my lord, this is my only comfort in my misery	אֲדֹנִי אֲדֹנִי, זֹאת כָּל נֶחָמָתִי בְעָנְיִי	האומנת
	That everything has an end; why, it is death.	כִּי לְכָל דָּבָר יֵשׁ קֵץ, הֲלֹא הוּא הַמָּוֶת.	
RAM	Are you speaking about Jael? How is she now?	עַל אֹדֹת יָעֵל תְּדַבֵּרִי? אֵיךְ הִיא עַתָּה?	רם
	Does she regard me as a murderer, since I have spilled blood	הֲתַחְשֹׁב אֹתִי לְרֹצֵחַ, אַחֲרֵי אֲשֶׁר דָּם שָׁפַכְתִּי	
	The blood of **her flesh and blood,**[167] **and have turned our youthful joy into mourning?**[168]	דַּם שְׁאֵרָהּ וּבְשָׂרָהּ,[167] וּשְׂשׂוֹן נְעוּרֵנוּ לְאֵבֶל הָפַכְתִּי[168]	
	Where, then, is she, the sorrowful one? What is she doing?	אָנָה אֵיפוֹ הִיא הָעֲצוּבָה? מָה הִיא עֹשָׂה?	
	What does my secret wife say regarding our concealed[169] love?	מָה אֵשֶׁת סִתְרִי אֹמֶרֶת לְאַהֲבָתֵנוּ הַמְּסֻתָּרֶת?[169]	
THE NURSE	She says nothing, but has indeed been weeping all night	הִיא אֵינֶנָּה אֹמֶרֶת מְאוּמָה וּבָכֹה תִבְכֶּה כָּל הַלַּיְלָה	האומנת

165 Lam. 1:9 וַתֵּרֶד פְּלָאִים 'and she fell astoundingly'.
166 Ps. 88:5 (88:4 in English Bibles).
167 Prov. 5:11 בְּשָׂרְךָ וּשְׁאֵרֶךָ 'your flesh and body' (used literally in this verse, but idiomatically in Salkinson's text).
168 Jer. 31:13 וְהָפַכְתִּי אֶבְלָם לְשָׂשׂוֹן 'and I shall turn their mourning into joy'.
169 Cf. Shakespeare's 'cancelled' (3.3.97), i.e., invalidated or annulled (Weis 2012: 264, note 97, and Crystal and Crystal 2002: 62); in Salkinson's version, the love is concealed rather than invalidated.

	She arises from the bed and falls and arises again.	תָּקוּם מֵעַל הַמִּטָּה וְתִפֹּל וְתָקוּם עוֹד הַפַּעַם.	
	Tubal, she says, and her eyes indeed shed tears	תּוּבַל תַּעֲלֶה עַל שְׂפָתֶיהָ וְדָמֹעַ תִּדְמַע עֵינָהּ	
	And then she cries out, Ram, and falls again.	וְאַחֲרֵי כֵן תִּזְעַק רָם וְתִפֹּל עוֹד הַפָּעַם.	
RAM	My name is a lead bullet from a gun	שְׁמִי הוּא כַּדּוּר עֹפֶרֶת מִקְנֵה רֹבֶה	רם
	Which has torn **the covering of her heart**,[170] like my cursed hand	אֲשֶׁר קָרַע סְגוֹר לִבָּהּ,[170] כְּמוֹ יָדִי הָאֲרוּרָה	
	Which tore her brother's heart. Tell me, righteous priest	אֲשֶׁר קָרְעָה לֵב אָחִיהָ. הַגֶּד לִי כֹּהֵן צֶדֶק	
	In which part of my body my name resides?	בְּאֵיזֶה חֵלֶק מִגְּוִיָּתִי יִשְׁכֹּן שְׁמִי שָׁם?	
	So that I might destroy that abode which I had	וְאַחֲרִיב אֶת הַמִּשְׁכָּן הַהוּא אֲשֶׁר הָיָה לִי	
	In my anger and my wrath.[171] *(Draws his sword)*	עַל אַפִּי וְעַל חֲמָתִי.[171] (שולף את חרבו)	
REZIN	Stay your hand, despairing man, **empty-headed man**[172] with no sense	הָשֵׁב יָדְךָ אִישׁ נוֹאָשׁ, אִישׁ נָבוּב[172] וְאֵין לֵב	רצין
	Are you a man? The form of your face is like that of a man	הַאִם אִישׁ אַתָּה? תֹּאַר פָּנֶיךָ כִּפְנֵי אִישׁ	
	Yet the tears of your eyes say that you have become a woman	וְנִטְפֵי עֵינֶיךָ יֹאמְרוּן כִּי הָיִיתָ לְאִשָּׁה	
	Your wrath is like a wild ass of a man, like the wrath of **a beast of Lebanon**[173]	חֲמַת אַפְּךָ כְּפֶרֶא אָדָם, כַּחֲמַת חַיַּת לְבָנוֹן[173]	
	The soul of **a beast of the forest**[174] in the likeness of a man's face.	נֶפֶשׁ חַיָּה מֵחַיְתוֹ יַעַר[174] בִּדְמוּת פְּנֵי גֶבֶר.	
	I am dismayed to see that it is thus for you, **it would not be believed if it were told.**[175]	נִבְהַלְתִּי מֵרְאוֹת שֶׁכָּכָה לְּךָ, לֹא יְאֻמַּן כִּי יְסֻפָּר.[175]	
	By the Temple service![176] Indeed you are inferior to what I had considered you to be until now	הָעֲבוֹדָה![176] כִּי נֹפֵל אַתָּה מֵאֲשֶׁר חֲשַׁבְתִּיךָ עַד כֹּה	

170 Hosea 13:8 וְאֶקְרַע סְגוֹר לִבָּם 'and I shall tear open the covering of their heart'.
171 Jer. 32:31.
172 Job 11:12.
173 2 Chron. 25:18 חַיַּת הַשָּׂדֶה אֲשֶׁר בַּלְּבָנוֹן 'a wild beast in Lebanon'.
174 Ps. 50:10, 104:20.
175 Hab. 1:5 לֹא תַאֲמִינוּ כִּי יְסֻפָּר 'you would not believe it if it were told'.
176 This is a Talmudic oath (Even-Shoshan 2003, 4: 1334); Salkinson has Judaized Shakespeare's overtly Catholic oath 'by my holy order' (3.3.113). Cf. Fifth Part, note 30.

You have already taken Tubal's life; do you mean to take your own as well	הֵן נֶפֶשׁ תּוּבַל לָקַחְתָּ, הֲתֹאמַר לָקַחַת גַּם נַפְשֶׁךָ
And also take Jael's life, which is bound to yours	וְלָקַחַת גַּם נֶפֶשׁ יָעֵל אֲשֶׁר* קְשׁוּרָה הִיא בְּנַפְשֶׁךָ
For your life is her life, and with you she too will die.	כִּי חַיָּתְךָ חַיֶּיהָ וְעִמְּךָ תָּמוּת גַּם הִיא.
Why do you curse your birth and profane **earth and heavens**[177]	לָמָּה זֶה תְּקַלֵּל לֵדָתְךָ וְתָאֹר **אֶרֶץ וְשָׁמַיִם**[177]
As if you desired to shake yourself free from the three of them, even though they have all as one	כְּמוֹ לְהִתְנַעֵר מִשְּׁלָשְׁתָּם חָפַצְתָּ וְהֵם כֻּלָּם כְּאֶחָד
Been given to you as a blessing? Be ashamed and humiliated by your deeds	נְתוּנִים לְךָ לִבְרָכָה? בּוֹשׁ וְהִכָּלֵם מִמַּעֲשֶׂיךָ
Because you have covered the beauty of your face, your prodigious love, and your intellect	כִּי עַל הַדְרַת פָּנֶיךָ וְעַל רֹב אַהֲבָתְךָ וְשִׂכְלֶךָ
With a great shame and disgrace which cannot be erased.	הֶעֱטִיתָ בּוּשָׁה גְדוֹלָה וְחֶרְפָּה אֲשֶׁר לֹא תִמָּחֶה.
Indeed in intellect, good looks, and love you have **ten shares**,[178]	הֵן בְּשֵׂכֶל בְּיֹפִי וּבְאַהֲבָה לְךָ **עֶשֶׂר יָדוֹת**[178]
Yet you do not know how to find advantage in one of them.	וְאֵין אַתָּה יֹדֵעַ לִמְצוֹא יִתְרוֹן בְּאֶחָד מֵהֶם.
You are a miserly rich man and your money is of no benefit to you	עָשִׁיר כִּילַי אַתָּה וְכַסְפְּךָ לֹא לְהוֹעִיל לְךָ
The beauty of your glorious face is like a wax mask	יִפְעַת הֲדַר פָּנֶיךָ כִּפְנֵי מַסֵּכַת דּוֹנָג
It is beautiful to the eyes, but it has no spirit	יָפָה הִיא לָעֵינַיִם וְכָל רוּחַ אֵין בָּהּ
And as for your exceeding love for Jael which you swore to her on your life	וְרֹב אַהֲבָתְךָ לְיָעֵל אֲשֶׁר נִשְׁבַּעְתָּ לָהּ בְּנַפְשֶׁךָ
You swore it in vain and falsely, for with your hand you have killed her	נִשְׁבַּעְתָּ לַשָּׁוְא וָשֶׁקֶר, כִּי בְיָדְךָ הֵמַתָּה אֹתָהּ

177 Gen. 2:4; Ps. 148:13.
178 2 Sam. 19:44 (19:43 in English Bibles).

* אֲשֶׁר

And your intellect, which gloriously crowns your beauty and love	וְשִׂכְלְךָ כְּלִיל תִּפְאֶרֶת לְרֹאשׁ יֹפִי וְאַהֲבָה
You have destroyed completely, like **a vessel in which there is no pleasure**[179]	שִׁחַתָּ אֹתוֹ כָּלִיל, **כִּכְלִי אֵין חֵפֶץ בּוֹ**[179]
And it has become like gunpowder in a foolish soldier's pouch	וְנֶהְפַּךְ כַּאֲבַק הַשְּׂרֵפָה בְּיַלְקוּט אִישׁ חַיִל אֱוִילִי
Which **has gone forth like lightning**[180] and devoured its owner	**אֲשֶׁר יָצָא כַבָּרָק**[180] וַיֹּאכַל אֶת נֶפֶשׁ בְּעָלָיו
So the light of your intellect has become **a flame of consuming fire**[181]	כֵּן אוֹר שִׂכְלְךָ הָיָה **לְלַהַב אֵשׁ אֹכֵלָה**[181]
Consuming not your enemies, but rather yourself.	לֹא לֶאֱכֹל אֶת צָרֶיךָ, כִּי אִם אֶת נַפְשֶׁךָ.
Therefore awaken, son of Abiram! **Gird your loins like a man**[182]	לָכֵן עוּרָה בֶּן אֲבִירָם! **אֱזָר כַּגֶּבֶר חֲלָצֶיךָ**[182]
The **graceful doe**[183] whom you love and for whom you are lying like a dead man	**יַעֲלַת חֵן**[183] אֲשֶׁר אָהַבְתָּ וַאֲשֶׁר לְמַעֲנָהּ תִּשְׁכַּב כַּמֵּת
Is still alive! Remember this and rejoice, young man!	עוֹדֶנָּה בַּחַיִּים חַיָּתָהּ! זְכָר־זֹאת וּשְׂמַח בָּחוּר!
Tubal came to kill you, so you rose early and killed him[184]	**תּוּבַל בָּא לְהָרְגְךָ וְאַתָּה הִשְׁכַּמְתָּ וַתַּהַרְגֵהוּ**[184]
Remember this and rejoice, young man! According to the law of the land	זְכָר־זֹאת וּשְׂמַח בָּחוּר! לְפִי מִשְׁפַּט הָאָרֶץ
You were **condemned to death**,[185] but by **the law of kindness**[186] you have been banished from the city	**בֶּן מָוֶת**[185] הָיִיתָ **וּבְתוֹרַת חֶסֶד**[186] נִגְרַשְׁתָּ מֵעִיר
And you have had your life as a prize of war;[187] remember this and rejoice, young man!	**וַתְּהִי לְךָ נַפְשְׁךָ לְשָׁלָל**;[187] זְכָר־זֹאת וּשְׂמַח בָּחוּר!

179 Jer. 22:28, 48:38; Hosea 8:8.

180 Zech. 9:14.

181 Joel 2:5.

182 Job 38:3, 40:7.

183 Prov. 5:19; see First Part, note 171.

184 Babylonian Talmud *Berakhot* 58a הבא להרגך השכם והרגו 'if a man comes to kill you, rise early and kill him first'. This is a well-known principle in Jewish law.

185 1 Sam. 20:31; 2 Sam. 12:5.

186 Prov. 31:26.

187 Jer. 39:18 וְהָיְתָה לְךָ נַפְשְׁךָ לְשָׁלָל 'and you shall have your life as a prize of war'.

Behold, you bear a bag of many blessings on your shoulders,	הֵן צְרוֹר בְּרָכוֹת רַבּוֹת תִּשָּׂא עַל שִׁכְמֶךָ
And everywhere you go kindness and love pursue you	וּבְכָל אֲשֶׁר אַתָּה הוֹלֵךְ חֶסֶד וִידִידוֹת יִרְדְּפוּךָ
But like a froward girl who gnashes and hisses with the abundance of everything	רַק כְּיַלְדָּה שׁוֹבֵבָה חֹרֶקֶת שֹׁרֶקֶת מֵרֹב כֹּל
So you complain about your love and your happiness which is so great	כֵּן תִּתְאוֹנֵן עַל אַהֲבָתְךָ וְעַל אָשְׁרְךָ כִּי רָב
Therefore I say, guard yourself, my friend	עַל כֵּן אֲנִי אֹמֵר, הִשָּׁמֶר לְךָ יְדִידִי
Because men who complain for nothing do not have a good end	כִּי אֲנָשִׁים מִתְאוֹנְנִים חִנָּם אַחֲרִיתָם לֹא טוֹבָה
Arise, go to **the one whom your soul loves**[188] as discussed	קוּם לֵךְ אֶל **שֶׁאָהֲבָה נַפְשֶׁךָ**[188] כְּפִי הַמְדֻבָּר
Ascend to her, to the upper chamber, and speak words of comfort to her heart	עֲלֵה אֵלֶיהָ אֶל הָעֲלִיָּה וְדַבֵּר תַּנְחוּמִים עַל לִבָּהּ
But do not dawdle there lest the watchmen come	אָכֵן אַל תִּתְמַהְמַהּ שָׁם פֶּן יָבוֹאוּ הַשֹּׁמְרִים
For they will not let you pass to the city of Mantua	כִּי הֵם לֹא יִתְּנוּךָ לַעֲבֹר לְעִיר מַנְטוּבָה
And you will dwell in that city, until we find **a favourable time**[189]	וְאַתָּה בָּעִיר הַהִיא תֵּשֵׁב, עַד נִמְצָא לָנוּ **עֵת רָצוֹן**[189]
To announce at **the gate of Bath-rabbim**[190] that your wedding was **according to the law**[191]	לְהַגִּיד **בְּשַׁעַר בַּת רַבִּים**[190], כִּי חֲתֻנָּתְךָ הָיְתָה **כַּדָּת**[191]
And also to make peace between all **those who quarrel with you**[192]	וְגַם לַעֲשׂוֹת שָׁלוֹם בֵּין כָּל **אַנְשֵׁי מַצֻּתֶךָ**[192]
And to reconcile you to the prince so that he restores you to your position	וּלְהִתְרַצּוֹת אֶל הַנָּסִיךְ עַד אֲשֶׁר יְשִׁיבְךָ עַל כַּנֶּךָ
Then your heart will swell from joy when you return to your native city	אָז יִרְחַב לִבְּךָ מִשָּׂשׂוֹן בְּשׁוּבְךָ לְעִיר מוֹלַדְתֶּךָ
For the gladness will be twenty thousand times greater	כִּי גְדוֹלָה תִּהְיֶה הַשִּׂמְחָה עֶשְׂרִים אֶלֶף פְּעָמִים

188 Song of Songs 1:7, 3:1, 2, 3.
189 Isa. 49:8.
190 Song of Songs 7:5 (7:4 in English Bibles). Bath-rabbim, which literally means 'daughter of many', is the name of one of the gates in the biblical city of Heshbon, mentioned in the same verse.
191 Esther 1:8, 4:16.
192 Isa. 41:12.

	Than your sorrow on this day, the day when you depart for the city of refuge[193] –	מִיגוֹנֵךְ בַּיּוֹם הַזֶּה, יוֹם צֵאתֵךְ לְעִיר הַמִּקְלָט[193] –	
	As for you, Nurse, depart before him and mention me to your lady	וְאַתְּ אֹמֶנֶת צְאִי לְפָנָיו וְהִזְכַּרְתִּנִי אֶל גְּבִרְתֵּךְ	
	Tell her to act wisely and to hasten to send the members of the household to their beds	אִמְרִי לָהּ לְהִתְחַכֵּם וּלְהָחִישׁ לִשְׁלֹחַ בְּנֵי הַבַּיִת לְמִשְׁכָּבָם	
	And they, out of sadness and sorrow, will be willing to obey her	וְהֵם מֵעֶצֶב וְיָגוֹן יֵאֹתוּ לִשְׁמֹעַ בְּקוֹלָהּ	
	For behold, Ram is coming.	כִּי רָם הִנֵּה בָּא.	
THE NURSE	**Great in counsel**?[194] You have wisdom, **counsel, and sound judgement**[195]	גְּדוֹל הָעֵצָה?[194] לָךְ חָכְמָה עֵצָה וְתוּשִׁיָּה[195]	האומנת
	Here I would be willing to sit all night, for your words are pleasant	פֹּה אוֹיתִי שֶׁבֶת כָּל הַלַּיְלָה, כִּי עֲרֵבִים דְּבָרֶיךָ	
	The sweetness of hearty counsel.[196] – Why, you will come, won't you, my lord Ram	מֶתֶק עֲצַת נָפֶשׁ.[196] – הֲלֹא תָבוֹא רָם אֲדֹנִי	
	I shall go to my mistress to tell her that you are coming.	הִנְנִי הוֹלֶכֶת לִגְבִרְתִּי לֵאמֹר לָהּ כִּי בָא אָתָּה.	
RAM	Please act in accordance with your word, and tell her that I am prepared	עֲשִׂי נָא כִּדְבָרֵךְ וְאִמְרִי לָהּ כִּי נָכוֹן אֲנִי	רם
	To hear scolding from her mouth.	לִשְׁמֹעַ גְּעָרָה מִפִּיהָ.	
THE NURSE	Take my lady's ring, which she sent you as a token	הֵא לְךָ טַבַּעַת גְּבִרְתִּי, אֲשֶׁר שָׁלְחָה לְךָ לְאוֹת	האומנת
	But hurry and come, for the night is passing by.	אַךְ חוּשָׁה וָבוֹאָה, כִּי הַלַּיְלָה הוֹלֵךְ וְעֹבֵר.	
RAM	By this my spirit lives, and my soul has returned to its strength.	בָּזֹאת חָיְתָה רוּחִי וַתָּשָׁב נַפְשִׁי לְאֵיתָנָהּ.	רם

193 See note 145.
194 Jer. 32:19.
195 Prov. 8:14.
196 Prov. 27:9 וּמֶתֶק רֵעֵהוּ מֵעֲצַת־נָפֶשׁ 'and the sweetness of a man's friend by hearty counsel'.

REZIN	Now go in peace, **be strong and courageous**[197] so that it may go well with you.	עַתָּה לֵךְ לְשָׁלוֹם, חֲזַק וֶאֱמָץ[197] וְטוֹב לָךְ.	רצין
	Before the morning dawns rise early and set out for Mantua	בְּטֶרֶם אוֹר הַבֹּקֶר תַּשְׁכִּים וְתָשִׂים לְמַנְטוּבָה פְּעָמֶיךָ	
	And if you do not rise early, disguise yourself in a woman's garment[198]	וְאִם לֹא תַשְׁכִּים, הִתְחַפֵּשׂ בְּשִׂמְלַת אִשָּׁה[198]	
	So that the watchmen do not recognize you. Meanwhile, I shall find one loyal to your house	לְבִלְתִּי יַכִּירוּךָ הַשֹּׁמְרִים. וַאֲנִי אֶמְצָא נֶאֱמָן בֵּיתֶךָ	
	By whose hand I may inform you from time to time	אֲשֶׁר עַל יָדוֹ אוֹדִיעֲךָ כְּפַעַם בְּפַעַם	
	Everything that happens here until your desire comes to light.	כָּל אֲשֶׁר יִקְרֶה פֹּה עַד חֶפְצְךָ לָאוֹר יֵצֵא.	
	Give me your hand and go in peace, for the appointed time has come.	הַב לִי יָדְךָ וְלֵךְ בְּשָׁלוֹם כִּי בָא מוֹעֵד.	
RAM	And peace to you too. – If only the morning were not waiting there for my arrival	וְגַם אַתָּה שָׁלוֹם. – לוּלֵא לְבוֹאִי מְיַחֶלֶת שָׁם	רם
	Through the lattice,[199] like a messenger of God in a vision[200]	הַצְּפִירָה בְּעַד הָאֶשְׁנָב,[199] כְּמַלְאַךְ אֵל בֶּחָזוֹן[200]	
	My heart would not allow me to part from you in haste. *(Exeunt)*	לֹא נְתָנַנִי לִבִּי לְהִתְפָּרֵד מִמְּךָ בְּחִפָּזוֹן. (הולכים)	
FOURTH SCENE	*Abiel's house (Abiel and his wife with Paris)*	בית אביעל (אביעל ואשתו עם פריז)	מחזה רביעי
ABIEL	Many woes have engulfed us and we have not seen relief thus far	צָרוֹת רַבּוֹת אֲפָפוּנוּ וּרְוָחָה לֹא רָאִינוּ עַד כֹּה	אביעל
	And we have not found **a favourable time**[201] for our daughter **to be spoken for**[202]	וְלֹא מָצָאנוּ עֵת רָצוֹן[201] לְבִתֵּנוּ שֶׁיְּדֻבַּר בָּהּ[202]	

197 Deut. 31:7, 23; Josh. 1:6, 7, 9, 18; 1 Chron. 22:13.

198 There is no basis for this in the source text, nor in the Schlegel-Tieck German translation.

199 Judg. 5:28.

200 This and the next line form a rhyming couplet, mirroring Shakespeare's 'me/thee' (3.3.172–3). Note that Salkinson's rhyme is in the last two lines of the speech, whereas Shakspeare's is in the first two.

201 Isa. 49:8.

202 Song of Songs 8:8.

	Her spirit is bitter over Tubal, who was of her age and family	נַפְשָׁהּ מָרָה לָהּ לְתוּבַל בֶּן גִּילָהּ וּמִשְׁפַּחְתָּהּ	
	And I also loved him, but man's end is to die.	וְגַם אָנֹכִי אֲהַבְתִּיהוּ, אַךְ סוֹף הָאָדָם לָמוּת.	
	You will not see my daughter tonight, for she will not come out of her room	אֶת בִּתִּי לֹא תִרְאֶה הַלַּיְלָה, כִּי לֹא תֵצֵא מֵחָדֶר	
	And if you were not here, I would also already be in bed	וְלוּלֵא הָיִיתָ פֹּה כְּבַר הָיִיתִי בַּמִּטָּה גַּם אָנִי	
	For it is close to midnight.	כִּי חֲצִי הַלַּיְלָה קָרוֹב.	
PARIS	**Pleasant words**[203] in a time of distress are words not in their time	דִּבְרֵי חֵשֶׁק[203] בְּעֵת צָרָה הֵם דְּבָרִים לֹא בְעִתָּם	פריז
	Take my blessing, my lady, **and lie down, and may your sleep be sweet**[204]	קְחִי אֶת בִּרְכָתִי גְּבִרְתִּי, וְשָׁכַבְתְּ וְעָרְבָה שְׁנָתֵךְ[204]	
	And tomorrow mention me to your daughter.	וּלְמָחָר הַזְכִּירְנִי אֶל בִּתֵּךְ.	
ABIEL'S WIFE	So I shall do in accordance with your word, and tomorrow in the morning **I shall ask her consent**[205]	כֵּן אֶעֱשֶׂה כִּדְבָרְךָ וּלְמָחָר בַּבֹּקֶר אֶשְׁאַל אֶת פִּיהָ[205]	אשת אביעל
	For at this time we are all desolate and it is bitter for her.	כִּי בָעֵת כֻּלָּנוּ שׁוֹמֵמִים וְהִיא מַר לָהּ.	
ABIEL	Listen to me, Lord Paris, indeed my daughter's desire is as mine	שְׁמָעֵנִי פָּרִיז הַשָּׂר, הֵן רְצוֹן בִּתִּי כִּרְצוֹנִי	אביעל
	For she obeys my command, therefore I am prepared to give her to you	כִּי תָסוּר לְמִשְׁמַעְתִּי, לָכֵן נָכוֹן אֲנִי לְתִתָּהּ לְךָ	
	For the one to whom I give her, I know that she will be his.	כִּי אֶל אֲשֶׁר אֶתְּנֶנָּה, יָדַעְתִּי כִּי לוֹ תֶהִי.	
	Go, my wife, to her chamber before you go to your bed	בּוֹאִי אִשְׁתִּי אֵלֶיהָ הַחַדְרָה טֶרֶם תֵּלְכִי לְמִשְׁכָּבֵךְ	
	And tell her the desire of my son Paris' heart	וְהַגִּידִי לָהּ אֶת חֵפֶץ לֵב פָּרִיז בְּנִי	

203 Eccles. 12:10.
204 Prov. 3:24 וְשָׁכַבְתָּ וְעָרְבָה שְׁנָתֶךָ 'you shall lie down and your sleep shall be sweet'.
205 Gen. 24:57 וְנִשְׁאֲלָה אֶת־פִּיהָ 'and we shall ask her consent'.

	For Wednesday – have you been listening to me?	כִּי יוֹם הָרְבִיעִי בְּשְׁבוּעַ – הַאִם הֶאֱזַנְתְּ אֵלָי?	
	Wednesday is – but wait	יוֹם הָרְבִיעִי בְּשְׁבוּעַ הוּא – אַךְ הֶרֶף	
	What is today?	מָה הַיּוֹם הַזֶּה?	
PARIS	Today is Monday.	הַיּוֹם* יוֹם שֵׁנִי.	פריז
ABIEL	Wednesday is not suitable, for it is close	לֹא נָכוֹן יוֹם הָרְבִיעִי, כִּי קָרוֹב הוּא	אביעל
	But Thursday will be the day of her wedding	אֲבָל יוֹם הַחֲמִישִׁי, הוּא יוֹם חֲתֻנָּתָהּ	
	On that very day she will be wed to this lord	בְּעֶצֶם הַיּוֹם הַהוּא תִּבָּעֵל אֶל הַשָּׂר הַזֶּה	
	But what do you say, are you prepared for Thursday	אַךְ מַה־תֹּאמַר אַתָּה, הֲתִהְיֶה נָכוֹן לַיּוֹם הַחֲמִישִׁי	
	Or do you desire to delay the appointed time? The number of wedding guests	אוֹ חָפַצְתָּ לְאַחֵר הַמּוֹעֵד? מִסְפַּר קְרוּאֵי הַחֲתֻנָּה	
	Will be very small for us, two or three friends, not more	יִהְיֶה לָנוּ מְעַט מְאֹד, שְׁנַיִם שְׁלֹשָׁה רֵעִים לֹא יוֹתֵר	
	Lest those who talk say: we are holding a banquet and festival	פֶּן יֹאמְרוּ הָאֹמְרִים: אָנוּ עֹשִׂים מִשְׁתֶּה וְהִלּוּלִים	
	And not paying heed to Tubal, **our flesh and blood**,[206] who is dead	וְלֹא נָשִׂים לֵב לְתוּבַל עַצְמֵנוּ וּבְשָׂרֵנוּ[206] כִּי מֵת	
	Therefore let six or seven guests gather and that will be enough for us.	לָכֵן יִתְאַסְּפוּ שִׁשָּׁה אוֹ שִׁבְעָה קְרוּאִים וְדַיֵּנוּ.	
	Speak, dear Paris, is Thursday good in your eyes?	דַּבֵּר פָּרִיז הַיָּקָר, הֲיִיטַב בְּעֵינֶיךָ יוֹם הַחֲמִישִׁי?	
PARIS	What can I say: if only Thursday were tomorrow.	מָה אֲדַבֵּר: מִי יִתֵּן וְהָיָה יוֹם הַחֲמִישִׁי לְמָחָר.	פריז
ABIEL	Now go in peace and Thursday will be the day.	עַתָּה לֵךְ בְּשָׁלוֹם וְיוֹם הַחֲמִישִׁי הוּא הַיּוֹם.	אביעל
	Speak, my wife, with Jael, before you go to your bed	דַּבְּרִי אִשְׁתִּי עִם יָעֵל, טֶרֶם תֵּלְכִי לְמִטָּתֵךְ	
	So that she may know that Thursday is to be her bridal day.	לְמַעַן תֵּדַע כִּי יוֹם הַחֲמִישִׁי הוּא יוֹם כְּלוּלוֹתֶיהָ.	

206 Gen. 29:14 עַצְמִי וּבְשָׂרִי 'my flesh and blood'; also 2 Sam. 19:13, 14 (19:12, 13 in English Bibles).

* היום

	Go in peace, my lord – bring a light to the bedroom	לֶךְ־לְךָ לְשָׁלוֹם אֲדֹנִי – הָבִיאוּ נֵר לַחֲדַר הַמִּטּוֹת	
	The night has almost passed; soon we will see the dawn;	הַלַּיְלָה כִּמְעַט עָבַר, עוֹד מְעַט וְנִרְאֶה שָׁחַר,	
	Go, lie down in peace.	לְכוּ שִׁכְבוּ בְשָׁלוֹם.	
	(All exit)	(הולכים כולם)	
SCENE 2[207]	*The lattice of Jael's upper chamber, which overlooks the vineyard (Ram and Jael)*	שבכה בעלית יעל הנשקפה אל הכרם (רם ויעל)	מחזה ב'[207]
JAEL	Dawn has not yet broken; would you go now?	הַשַּׁחַר עוֹד לֹא עָלָה, הַאִם תֵּלֵךְ עַתָּה?	יעל
	The voice which rings in your ears is the voice of the nightingale	הַקּוֹל אֲשֶׁר יְצַלְצֵל בְּאָזְנֶיךָ הוּא קוֹל הַזָּמִיר	
	Which gives its songs in the night[208] from the pomegranate tree there	הַנֹּתֵן זְמִירוֹתָיו בַּלַּיְלָה[208] מֵעֵץ הָרִמּוֹן שָׁמָּה	
	And not the voice of the bird which twitters in the early morning[209]	וְלֹא קוֹל הַצִּפּוֹר אֲשֶׁר יְצַפְצֵף לִפְנוֹת בֹּקֶר[209]	
	As you thought in your fear. Believe me, my beloved	כַּאֲשֶׁר חָשַׁבְתָּ בְּחֶרְדָתֶךָ. הַאֲמֶן לִי יְדִיד נַפְשִׁי	
	It is the voice of the nightingale, and the night is yet long.	הוּא קוֹל הַזָּמִיר וְעוֹד הַלַּיְלָה גָּדוֹל.	
RAM	It is the voice of the bird that awakens the dawn	הוּא קוֹל הַצִּפּוֹר הַמֵּעִיר אֶת הַשַּׁחַר	רם
	And not the voice of the nightingale; look, beloved of my soul	וְלֹא קוֹל הַזָּמִיר; רְאִי אֲהֻבַת נַפְשִׁי	
	Over there white spots, because they are jealous of us,	שָׁם בֶּהָרוֹת לְבָנוֹת, כִּי מְקַנְּאוֹת בָּנוּ,	
	Assemble like a wreath on the edges of the clouds in the east	תִּסְתַּפַּחְנָה כַּזֵּר עַל שׁוּלֵי הָעֲנָנִים מִקֶּדֶם	

207 Sic; should read 'SCENE 5'.
208 Job 35:10 נֹתֵן זְמִרוֹת בַּלָּיְלָה 'the one who gives songs in the night'.
209 Cf. Shakespeare's 'lark' (3.5.2). The Hebrew term עפרוני 'lark' is a modern innovation (Even-Shoshan 2003, 4: 1407) which was not yet standard in Salkinson's time; given the lack of a precise equivalent for the English, Salkinson has chosen to provide a description of the lark's characteristics.

	The nighttime candles have gone out and the dawn **is leaping over the mountains**[210]	נֵרוֹת הַלַּיְלָה תַּמּוּ וְעַמּוּד הַשַּׁחַר **מְדַלֵּג עַל הֶהָרִים**[210]	
	If I move on from here, I shall not die, but if I stay, I shall not live.[211]	אִם אֶעֱבֹר מִזֶּה לֹא אָמוּת וְאִם אֶעֱמֹד לֹא אֶחְיֶה.[211]	
JAEL	I know that that light is not the light of morning	הָאוֹר הַהוּא יָדַעְתִּי כִּי אֵינֶנּוּ אוֹר בֹּקֶר	יעל
	It is a burning torch which the sun has spewed out	הוּא לַפִּיד אֵשׁ אֲשֶׁר הֵקִיא הַשֶּׁמֶשׁ מִקִּרְבּוֹ	
	To be **a lamp unto your feet**[212] tonight to guide you on the way to Mantua	לִהְיוֹת **נֵר לְרַגְלְךָ**[212] הַלַּיְלָה לְהוֹרוֹתְךָ הַדֶּרֶךְ לְמַנְטוּבָה	
	Therefore stay yet with me, for it is not time to leave.	לָכֵן עֲמֹד עוֹד אֶצְלִי, כִּי אֵין עֵת לַעֲבֹר.	
RAM	Here I stand, and when they find me and kill me	פֹּה הִנְנִי עֹמֵד; וְכִי יִמְצָאוּנִי וְיִקְטְלוּנִי	רם
	I shall die with a glad heart, because I have stayed here at your desire	אָמוּת בְּלֵב שָׂמֵחַ, יַעַן לִרְצוֹנֵךְ עָמַדְתִּי פֹּה	
	And now I say, the white spots over there	וְעַתָּה אֲנִי אֹמֵר, הַבֶּהָרוֹת הַלְּבָנוֹת שָׁם	
	Are not **the eyelids of dawn**,[213] moreover the voice which I heard	אֵינָן **עַפְעַפֵּי שַׁחַר**,[213] גַּם הַקּוֹל אֲשֶׁר שָׁמַעְתִּי	
	Twittering in the firmament above our heads is the voice of the nightingale	מְצַפְצֵף בָּרָקִיעַ מֵעַל לְרָאשֵׁנוּ, הוּא קוֹל הַזָּמִיר	
	And not the voice of the bird which sings the morning song[214]	וְלֹא קוֹל הַצִּפּוֹר אֲשֶׁר יָשִׁיר שִׁיר הַבֹּקֶר[214]	
	And indeed I also long to stay with you rather than to go from here.	וְגַם נִכְסֹף נִכְסַפְתִּי לַעֲמֹד עִמֵּךְ מִלֶּכֶת מִזֶּה.	
	The morning has not come, **let us take our fill of love**,[215] **my love**,[216] in the darkness.[217]	הַבֹּקֶר לֹא אָתָא, **נִרְוֶה דֹדִים**[215] **רַעְיָתִי**[216] בְּמַחֲשַׁכִּים.[217]	

210 Song of Songs 2:8.
211 Salkinson has not replicated Shakespeare's rhyming couplet 'die/I' (3.5.11–12) shared between the last line of this speech and the first line of the next.
212 Ps. 119:105 נֵר־לְרַגְלִי דְבָרֶךָ 'Your word is a lamp unto my feet'.
213 Job 3:9, 41:10 (41:18 in English Bibles). Salkinson has omitted Shakespeare's ''tis but the pale reflex of Cynthia's brow' (3.5.20) here, in keeping with his usual domesticating treatment of Classical references.
214 Cf. Shakespeare's 'that is not the lark' (3.5.21); see note 209.
215 Prov. 7:18.
216 Song of Songs 1:9, 15, 2:2, 10, 13, 4:1, 7, 5:2, 6:4.
217 This and the next line form a rhyming couplet, mirroring Shakespeare's 'day/away' (3.5.25–6).

JAEL	Flee, my love, the sun **is peering through the lattice**[218]	בְּרַח לְךָ דוֹדִי, הַשֶּׁמֶשׁ מֵצִיץ מִן הַחֲרַכִּים[218]	יעל
	And moreover the voice of the bird is a voice that tears the ear and heart	גַּם קוֹל הַצִּפּוֹר הוּא, קוֹל קֹרֵעַ אֹזֶן וָלֵב	
	It always used to have **a beautiful voice and play well**[219]	הוּא הָיָה מֵעוֹדוֹ יְפֵה קוֹל מֵטִיב נַגֵּן[219]	
	But now I take no pleasure in it, because it has become the sound of the trumpet	וְעַתָּה אֵין לִי חֵפֶץ בּוֹ, כִּי נֶהְפַּךְ לְקוֹל שׁוֹפָר	
	The sound of destruction and trembling, which comes to separate those who cleave together	לְקוֹל שֶׁבֶר וּרְעָדָה, הַבָּא לְהַפְרִיד בֵּין הַדְּבֵקִים	
	But the dawn is growing lighter on the mountain and the lowlands[220]	אַךְ עַמּוּד הַשַּׁחַר הוֹלֵךְ וָאוֹר בָּהָר וּבַשָּׁפֶל[220]	
	Hurry, hasten to Mantua and do not let yourself die.	מַהֲרָה חוּשָׁה לְמַנְטוּבָה וְאַל תִּתֵּן נַפְשְׁךָ לַמָּוֶת.	
RAM	It is **a pillar of cloud**[221] to me, a cloud of darkness and gloom	עַמּוּד עָנָן[221] הוּא לִי, עָנָן חשֶׁךְ וַעֲרָפֶל	רם
	The day has darkened over me and morning has turned into the shadow of death for me.	חָשַׁךְ עָלַי הַיּוֹם וּבֹקֶר נֶהְפַּךְ לִי לְצַלְמָוֶת.	
THE NURSE	Jael!	יָעֵל!	האומנת
JAEL	My nurse?	אֹמַנְתִּי?	יעל
THE NURSE	Guard yourself Jael, your lady mother is about to come into the chamber	הִשָּׁמְרִי לָךְ יָעֵל, אִמֵּךְ הַגְּבִירָה בָּאָה הַחֶדְרָה	האומנת
	The sun goes forth over the land and my lord Ram has not yet left.[222]	הַשֶּׁמֶשׁ יָצָא עַל הָאָרֶץ וְעוֹד לֹא יָצָא רָם אֲדֹנִי.[222]	
JAEL *(Opens the window)*	Please come, light of day, and leave, light of my soul, from my window.	בּוֹא נָא אוֹר הַיּוֹם וְאוֹר נַפְשִׁי צֵא מֵחַלּוֹנִי.	יעל (פותחת את החלון)

218 Song of Songs 2:9.

219 Ezek. 33:32 יְפֵה קוֹל וּמֵטִב נַגֵּן 'a beautiful voice and plays well'.

220 This and the next three lines form an ABAB rhyming pattern, mirroring Shakespeare's 'affray/day', 'grows/woes' (3.5.33–6) except that the latter is composed of two rhyming couplets.

221 This refers to the pillar of cloud in which God travelled alongside the Israelites after their exodus from Egypt (Exod. 13:21; mentioned also in Num. 12:5; Deut. 31:15; Ps. 99:7; Neh. 9:12).

222 This and the next line form a rhyming couplet, mirroring Shakespeare's 'about/out' (3.5.40–1).

RAM	On my only life! Jael, **my flesh and blood**[223, 224]	חַיֵּי נַפְשִׁי יְחִידָתִי! יָעֵל **עַצְמִי וּבְשָׂרִי**[223, 224]	רם
	I shall but kiss you this once and leave, for this is my only recompense. *(Exits from the window)*	אֶשָּׁקֵךְ אַךְ הַפַּעַם וְאֵצֵא כִּי זֶה כָּל שְׂכָרִי. (יוצא מן החלון)	
JAEL	Will you leave, will you forsake me now, my beau, **the husband of my youth**[225]	הֲתֵצֵא הֲתַעַזְבֵנִי עַתָּה אַלּוּפִי **בַּעַל נְעוּרָי**[225]	יעל
	Will you not make known to me how you are faring every day at every hour	הֲלֹא תוֹדִיעֵנִי מִשְּׁלוֹמְךָ יוֹם יוֹם בְּכָל שָׁעָה	
	For every hour in my love will be in my eyes like many days	כִּי כָל שָׁעָה בְּאַהֲבָתִי תִּהְיֶה בְעֵינַי כְּיָמִים רַבִּים	
	And therefore you will find upon your return that **I have grown old, advanced in years**.[226]	וְלָכֵן תִּמְצָאֵנִי בְשׁוּבְךָ כִּי **זָקַנְתִּי בָּאתִי בַּיָּמִים**.[226]	
RAM	Trust in me, **the one whom my soul loves**,[227] when I find the opportunity	בִּטְחִי בִי **שֶׁאָהֲבָה נַפְשִׁי**,[227] כַּאֲשֶׁר אֶמְצָא לִי יָדַיִם	רם
	I shall not desist from asking how you are faring and from making known to you how it goes with me.	לֹא אֶרֶף מִדְּרשׁ שְׁלוֹמֵךְ וּמֵהוֹדִיעֵךְ מָה עִמָּדִי.	
JAEL	Do you think that you will return to me and I shall see your face again?	הֲתַחְשֹׁב כִּי תָשׁוּב אֵלַי וְעוֹד אוֹסִיף רְאוֹת פָּנֶיךָ?	יעל
RAM	I trust that we shall see relief, and that this woe and distress[228]	בָּטַחְתִּי כִּי נִרְאֶה הָרְוָחָה וְזֹאת הַצָּרָה וְהַמְּצוּקָה[228]	רם
	Will become for us in the coming days good and sweet discourse.	תִּהְיֶה לָנוּ בַּיָּמִים הַבָּאִים לְשִׂיחָה טוֹבָה וּמְתוּקָה.	
JAEL	Yet my heart tells me terrible things; **God's terrors array themselves against me**[229, 230]	וּלְבָבִי יַגִּיד לִי נוֹרָאוֹת, **בִּעוּתֵי אֱלוֹהַּ יַעַרְכוּנִי**[229, 230]	יעל

223 Gen. 29:14; 2 Sam. 19:13, 14 (19:12, 13 in English Bibles).

224 This and the next line form a rhyming couplet, mirroring Shakespeare's 'descend/friend' (3.5.42–3). Note, however, that in Salkinson's version the couplet is contained within Ram's two-line speech, whereas in Shakespeare's it is split between Romeo (whose speech consists of a single line) and Juliet.

225 Joel 1:8 בַּעַל נְעוּרֶיהָ 'the husband of her youth'.

226 Josh. 23:2.

227 Song of Songs 1:7, 3:1, 2, 3.

228 This and the next line form a rhyming couplet. There is no precedent for this in the source text 'serve/come' (3.5.52–3).

229 Job 6:4.

230 This and the next three lines form an ABBA rhyming sequence, which partially mirrors the source text's 'soul/low' (3.5.54–5), except that the latter consists of a single rhying couplet. ('Soul/low' was considered a workable rhyme in Shakespeare's day; see Weis 2012: 420.)

	For as you have descended and stand at the bottom of the steps	כִּי כַאֲשֶׁר יָרַדְתָּ וַתַּעֲמֹד בִּשְׁפַל הַמַּדְרֵגָה	
	Your face looks to me like a dead man, like a slain man lying in **the valley of slaughter**[231]	נִרְאוּ לִי פָּנֶיךָ כַּמֵּת, כְּחָלָל שֹׁכֵב בְּגֵיא הַהֲרֵגָה[231]	
	And I do not know whether your face has grown pale, or my eyes have deceived me.	וְלֹא יָדַעְתִּי אִם חָוְרוּ פָּנֶיךָ, אוֹ עֵינַי רִמּוּנִי.	
RAM	Such a thing I too have seen in your face from where I stand[232]	כָּזֹאת חָזִיתִי בְּפָנַיִךְ גַּם אֲנִי מִמַּעֲמָדִי[232]	רם
	Trembling has gripped me[233] and I do not know what is wrong with me	פַּלָּצוּת בִּעֲתָתְנִי[233] וְלֹא יָדַעְתִּי מָה עִמָּדִי	
	This is nothing but sorrow, sucking our lifeblood	אֵין זֶה כִּי אִם הַיָּגוֹן, יוֹנֵק דַּם חַיֵּינוּ	
	Live, my soul's beloved! And may the merciful father have mercy upon us.	חֲיִי רַעְיַת נַפְשִׁי! וַאֲבִי הָרַחֲמִים יְרַחֲמֵנוּ.	
	(Exits through the vineyard)	(הולך דרך הכרם)	
JAEL	Men say that the prince of fortune is lucky	בְּנֵי אָדָם אֹמְרִים בַּעַל גַּד שַׂר הַמַּזָּלוֹת	יעל
	He is fickle and strange and trifling, frivolous in doing good and evil	הוּא הֲפַכְפַּךְ וָזָר וְקַל בְּדַעְתּוֹ לְהֵיטִיב וּלְהָרַע	
	If so, what could he have to do with my husband, a man who stands by his opinion	אִם כֵּן מַה־לּוֹ וּלְבַעֲלִי אִישׁ עֹמֵד עַל דַּעְתּוֹ?	
	Indeed luck is quick to do good and quick to pour out its anger	אַךְ גַּד מָהִיר לְהֵיטִיב וּמָהִיר לִשְׁפֹּךְ חֲרוֹנוֹ	
	It has pushed him away in its rage and will restore him in accordance with its desire.	הוּא הֲדָפוֹ בְּזַעְמוֹ וְהוּא יְשִׁיבֶנּוּ בִּרְצוֹנוֹ.	
ABIEL'S WIFE *(Outside)*	My daughter, are you not sleeping?	בִּתִּי הַאִם לֹא יְשֵׁנָה אָתְּ?	אשת אביעל (מחוץ)

231 Jer. 7:32, 19:6.

232 This and the next three lines form two rhyming couplets, mirroring Shakespeare's 'you/adieu' (3.5.58–9) except that the latter consists of a single rhyming couplet (which makes up the whole of the speech). Salkinson has expanded the speech by two lines, but has not altered the meaning in any significant sense.

233 Isa. 21:4.

JAEL	Is it my mother's voice?	הֲקוֹל אִמִּי הוּא?	יעל
	Has she risen from her bed, or has she not lain down tonight	הַאִם קָמָה מִמִּשְׁכָּבָהּ, אוֹ לֹא שָׁכְבָה הַלָּיְלָה	
	I cannot know what her desire is at such a time.	דַּעַת לֹא אוּכַל, מַה חֶפְצָהּ לְעֵת כָּזֹאת.	
	(Abiel's wife enters)	(אשת אביעל באה)	
ABIEL'S WIFE	What is wrong with you, Jael?	מַה לָּךְ יָעֵל?	אשת אביעל
JAEL	I am not well, my mother.	אֵין שָׁלוֹם לִי אִמִּי.	יעל
ABIEL'S WIFE	How long will you mourn over Tubal's death?	עַד מָתַי תִּתְאַבְּלִי עַל מוֹת תּוּבַל	אשת אביעל
	If you wash his flesh in your tears indeed he will not arise	אִם תִּרְחֲצִי בְּשָׂרוֹ בְּדִמְעָתֵךְ קוּם לֹא יָקוּם	
	Therefore **give yourself respite**,[234] do not shed tears in vain.	לָכֵן **תְּנִי פוּגַת לָךְ**,[234] אַל תּוֹרִידִי דִמְעָה לַשָּׁוְא.	
	Mourning according to the measure is a sign of great love	אֵבֶל לְפִי הַמִּדָּה, הוּא אוֹת לְאַהֲבָה רַבָּה	
	But mourning in excess of the measure is a sign of little intellect.	וְאֵבֶל יֶתֶר עַל הַמִּדָּה, אוֹת לְשֵׂכֶל מְעָט.	
JAEL	The destruction is too great to bear, so how can I not mourn?	הַשֶּׁבֶר גָּדוֹל מִנְּשֹׂא וְאֵיךְ לֹא אֶתְאַבֵּל.	יעל
ABIEL'S WIFE	Your mourning will not benefit the one for whom you mourn	אֶבְלֵךְ לֹא לְהוֹעִיל לַאֲשֶׁר עָלָיו תִּתְאַבֵּלִי	אשת אביעל
	For one who goes down into the silence of the grave knows nothing.	כִּי יוֹרֵד דּוּמָה אֵינֶנּוּ יוֹדֵעַ מְאוּמָה.	
JAEL	My heart knows my bitterness of spirit; I cannot restrain myself	לִבִּי יוֹדֵעַ מָרַת נַפְשִׁי, הִתְאַפֵּק לֹא אוּכַל	יעל
	Therefore I indeed weep over my friend's destruction.	עַל כֵּן בָּכֹה אֶבְכֶּה עַל שֶׁבֶר אֹהֲבִי.	
ABIEL'S WIFE	Not over his death, my daughter, **does your eye stream relentlessly**[235]	לֹא עַל מוֹתוֹ בִּתִּי, **עֵינֵךְ נִגָּרָה מֵאֵין הֲפֻגוֹת**[235]	אשת אביעל

234 Lam. 2:18 אַל־תִּתְּנִי פוּגַת לָךְ 'give yourself no respite'.
235 Lam. 3:49 עֵינִי נִגְּרָה וְלֹא תִדְמֶה מֵאֵין הֲפֻגוֹת 'my eye flows and does not cease, relentlessly'.

	But rather over the villain who killed him and still lives.	בִּלְתִּי עַל הַבְּלִיַּעַל שֶׁהֱמִיתוֹ וְהוּא עוֹדֶנּוּ חָי.	
JAEL	Who is the villain, my mother?	מִי הוּא הַבְּלִיַּעַל אִמִּי?	יעל
ABIEL'S WIFE	He is the villain Ram.	הוּא רָם הַבְּלִיַּעַל.	אשת אביעל
JAEL	*(To herself)* He is as far from a villain as the east is far from the west –	(אל עצמה) רָחוֹק הוּא מִבְּלִיַּעַל* כִּרְחֹק מִזְרָח מִמַּעֲרָב –	יעל
	(To her mother) God will pardon him, and I have already forgiven him	(אל אמה) הָאֱלֹהִים יְכַפֵּר בַּעֲדוֹ וַאֲנִי כְּבָר נָשָׂאתִי פָנָיו	
	Although there is no man who pains my heart as he does.	אַף כִּי אֵין אִישׁ אֲשֶׁר יַכְאִיב לִבִּי כָּמוֹהוּ.	
ABIEL'S WIFE	Because he is a killer.	יַעַן הֹרֵג נְפָשׁוֹת הוּא.	אשת אביעל
JAEL	How great is my desire that others' hands not touch him	מַה־גָּדְלָה תְשׁוּקָתִי לִבְלִי תִגַּע בּוֹ יַד אֲחֵרִים	יעל
	But rather that he fall into my hand to do with him in accordance with my desire	כִּי אִם יִפֹּל בְּיָדִי לַעֲשׂוֹת בּוֹ כִּרְצוֹנִי	
	To exact vengeance from him and to redeem my brother's[236] spilled blood.	לִנְקֹם נָקָם מִמֶּנּוּ וְלִגְאֹל דַּם אָחִי[236] הַשָּׁפוּךְ.	
ABIEL'S WIFE	Do not fear, my daughter, behold, we shall find an opportunity	אַל תִּירְאִי בִתִּי, הִנֵּה נִמְצָא לָנוּ יָדַיִם	אשת אביעל
	To take revenge against him, but cease crying	לַעֲשׂוֹת נְקָמָה בּוֹ אַךְ מִנְעִי קוֹלֵךְ מִבֶּכִי	
	Behold, I shall send to Mantua, where the murderer has gone into exile	הִנֵּה אֶשְׁלַח לְמַנְטוֹבָה, לַאֲשֶׁר גָּלָה שָׁם הָרֹצֵחַ	
	And there is a man known to us there who will give him **the cup of our wrath**[237] to drink	וְשָׁם אִישׁ יָדוּעַ לָנוּ אֲשֶׁר יַשְׁקֶנּוּ כּוֹס חֲמָתֵנוּ[237]	
	And he too will go to the place where Tubal went, to be with him	וְאֶל אֲשֶׁר הָלַךְ תּוּבַל יֵלֵךְ גַּם הוּא לִהְיוֹת עִמּוֹ	

236 Cf. Shakespeare's 'cousin' (3.5.86); see First Part, note 65.
237 Isa. 51:22 כּוֹס חֲמָתִי 'the cup of my wrath'; see also Isa. 51:17.

* מִבְּלִיַּעַל

	Then you will see and shine,[238] and your eye will be sated with our enemy.[239]	אָז תִּרְאִי וְנָהַרְתְּ[238] וְעֵינֵךְ תִּשְׂבַּע בְּאוֹיְבֵנוּ.[239]	
JAEL	My eye will not be sated with Ram until I see him dead	עֵינִי לֹא תִשְׂבַּע בְּרָם עַד אֲשֶׁר אֶרְאֶנּוּ מֵת	יעל
	For the death of **my flesh and blood**[240] does not give me rest	כִּי מוֹת שְׁאֵרִי וּבְשָׂרִי[240] לֹא יִתֶּן לִי מְנוּחָה	
	And now if you have a man, a loyal messenger to send	וְעַתָּה אִם יֶשׁ לָךְ אִישׁ, צִיר נֶאֱמָן לְשָׁלְחָיו	
	I shall prepare cup of poison to give to Ram to drink	אָכִין אֲנִי כּוֹס רַעַל לְהַשְׁקוֹת אֶת רָם	
	And when he tastes of it he will sleep and awaken no more.	וְכִי יִטְעַם מִמֶּנּוּ מְאוּמָה יִישַׁן וְלֹא יִיקַץ עוֹד.	
	How bitter is my heart when I hear the name of Ram from a mouth other than my own[241]	מַה־יִּתְמַרְמַר לִבִּי בְּשָׁמְעִי שֵׁם רָם מִפִּי זוּלָתִי[241]	
	And I cannot find a way to calm **the fire of my zeal**[242] against him	וַאֲנִי לֹא אוּכַל לָבוֹא לְשַׁכֵּךְ אֵשׁ קִנְאָתִי[242] בוֹ	
	And to atone for the blood, the blood of my brother[243] whom I love.	וּלְכַפֵּר עַל הַדָּם, דַּם אָחִי[243] אֲשֶׁר אָהַבְתִּי.	
ABIEL'S WIFE	Prepare **the poison of death,**[244] and I shall send **the messenger of death**[245]	הָכִינִי אֶת סַם הַמָּוֶת[244] וְאֶת מַלְאַךְ הַמָּוֶת[245] אֶשְׁלַח אָנִי	אשת אביעל
	And now listen to me, my daughter, for there are good tidings in my mouth.	וְעַתָּה שִׁמְעִי לִי בִתִּי, כִּי בְּשׂוֹרָה טוֹבָה בְּפִי.	
JAEL	Good tidings are welcome at such a time of distress.	בְּשׂוֹרָה טוֹבָה נָאוָה לְעֵת צָרָה כָּזֹאת	יעל

238 Isa. 60:5.
239 Salkinson has not reproduced Shakespeare's same-word rhyming couplet 'satisfied/satisfied' (3.5.92–3).
240 Prov. 5:11 בְּשָׂרְךָ וּשְׁאֵרֶךָ 'your flesh and body' (used literally in this verse, but idiomatically in Salkinson's text).
241 This and the following two lines form an ABA rhyme, mirroring Shakespeare's 'him/cousin/him' (3.5.100–2); this is unusual as Salkinson does not typically reproduce same-word rhymes.
242 Ezek. 36:5; Zeph. 3:8.
243 Cf. Shakespeare's 'cousin' (3.5.101); see First Part, note 65.
244 Mishnah *Ḥullin* 3:5.
245 Prov. 16:14 מַלְאֲכֵי־מָוֶת 'messengers of death'. This phrase is also very commonly used in postbiblical texts in the sense of 'angel of death', and both the senses 'messenger' and 'angel' would have been apparent to Salkinson's readers.

	But what is the message? Tell me, my lady mother.	אַךְ מָה הִיא הַבְּשׂוֹרָה? סַפְּרִי לִי אִמִּי הַגְּבִירָה.	
ABIEL'S WIFE	You know that your father seeks your wellbeing and your good all the days	יָדַעַתְּ כִּי אָבִיךְ דֹּרֵשׁ שְׁלוֹמֵךְ וְטוּבֵךְ כָּל הַיָּמִים	אשת אביעל
	And he has sought and found a fitting day **to turn your mourning into joy**[246]	וְהוּא בִּקֵּשׁ וַיִּמְצָא יוֹם נָכוֹן לַהֲפֹךְ אֶבְלֵךְ לְשָׂשׂוֹן[246]	
	It is the day which you have not expected, and which had not entered my mind either.	הוּא הַיּוֹם שֶׁלֹּא קִוִּית וְלֹא עָלָה עַל לִבִּי גַּם אָנִי.	
JAEL	If only it were a good day, but which is it?	מִי יִתֵּן וְהָיָה לְיוֹם טוֹב; אַךְ אֵיזֶה הוּא?	יעל
ABIEL'S WIFE	This coming Thursday in the morning	בְּיוֹם הַחֲמִישִׁי בַּשָּׁבוּעַ בַּבֹּקֶר הַבָּא עָלֵינוּ לְטוֹבָה	אשת אביעל
	A young man, praiseworthy in grace, beauty, and wealth will come to our house	יָבוֹא לְבֵיתֵנוּ בָּחוּר מְהֻלָּל בְּחֵן בְּיֹפִי וּבְעֹשֶׁר	
	He is Lord Paris, **a rod from the stem of the prince**[247]	הוּא פָּרִיז הַשָּׂר, **חֹטֶר מִגֶּזַע הַנָּסִיךְ**[247]	
	And he will take you to the Temple[248] of **Michael the Prince of the Presence**[249]	וְהוּא יוֹלִיכֵךְ לְמִקְדָּשׁ[248] אֲשֶׁר **לְמִיכָאֵל שַׂר הַפָּנִים**[249]	
	As a resplendent and joyful bride, to enter into a covenant with you there.	כְּכַלָּה הֲדוּרָה וּשְׂמֵחָה לָבוֹא שָׁם אִתֵּךְ בִּבְרִית.	

246 Jer. 31:13 וְהָפַכְתִּי אֶבְלָם לְשָׂשׂוֹן 'and I shall turn their mourning into joy'.

247 Isa. 11:1 חֹטֶר מִגֵּזַע יִשָׁי 'a rod from the stem of Jesse' (a messianic prophecy referring to a king of the Davidic line).

248 Cf. Shakespeare's 'church' (3.5.114). Salkinson's version refers to the Temple in Jerusalem, which was destroyed by the Romans in 70 CE but has remained the symbolic heart of the Jewish people and religion until the present day and is recalled on multiple occasions in the daily liturgy. See also note 250.

249 Cf. Shakespeare's 'Saint Peter' (3.5.114). The angel Michael is mentioned in various places in the Hebrew Bible (most famously in the Book of Daniel) as well as in rabbinic literature (*Midrash Rabba* 2:20) as God's right-hand ministering angel. However, this specific phrase 'Michael, the Prince of the Presence' is a reference to the extremely prominent exegetical work of the eleventh-century scholar Rashi, as his commentary on the book of Isaiah (63:9) is the most well-known Jewish source in which this particular wording appears. Jews traditionally study the Hebrew Bible together with Rashi's commentary, and therefore this reference would have been immediately recognizable to Salkinson's audience. While the Archangel Michael also has a place in various Christian traditions, appearing in the Book of Revelation (12:7–9) as one of the leaders of God's army against Satan and revered in later Christian theology, the conscious decision to employ the precise phrasing from Rashi's commentary underscores the fact that Salkinson intended his translation for a Jewish readership.

JAEL	By the name of the Temple![250] And by the name of Michael the Prince of the Presence![251]	בְּשֵׁם בֵּית הַמִּקְדָּשׁ![250] וּבְשֵׁם מִיכָאֵל שַׂר הַפָּנִים![251]	יעל
	Indeed he shall not take me as a joyous bride to enter into a covenant with him	כִּי לֹא יוֹלִיכֵנִי כְּכַלָּה שְׂמֵחָה לָבוֹא אִתּוֹ בַּבְּרִית	
	Such knowledge is too wondrous for me;[252] why should I hurry to marry the man	פְּלִיאָה דַעַת מִמֶּנִּי[252] לָמָּה אָחִישׁ לְהִנָּשֵׂא לָאִישׁ	
	Before he has told me that he desires me	טֶרֶם הִגִּיד לִי כִּי נַפְשׁוֹ חָשְׁקָה בִי	
	And before he has asked me whether I desire him.	וְטֶרֶם שָׁאַל אֶת פִּי, אִם חָפַצְתִּי בוֹ.	
	Please, my lady mother, tell my father these words	בִּי אִמִּי הַגְּבִירָה, הַגִּידִי לְאָבִי כַּדְּבָרִים הָאֵלֶּה	
	I am tender in years and my time has not yet come	רַכָּה בְשָׁנִים אֲנִי וְעוֹד לֹא בָאָה עִתִּי	
	And if my day comes I shall marry Ram, whom I hate,	וְאִם יָבוֹא יוֹמִי אֶנָּשֵׂא לְרָם אֲשֶׁר שָׂנֵאתִי	
	Rather than marry Paris his chosen one – these are my tidings.	מֵהִנָּשֵׂא לְפָרִיז בְּחִירוֹ – זֹאת הִיא בְּשֹׂרָתִי	
	Tidings for tidings.	בְּשֹׂרָה תַּחַת בְּשֹׂרָה.	
ABIEL'S WIFE	Behold, your father is coming; tell him what you have to say	הִנֵּה אָבִיךְ בָּא, הַגִּידִי לוֹ מַה־בְּפִיךְ	אשת אביעל
	And afterwards see what tidings there are for you.	וְאַחֲרֵי כֵן תִּרְאִי מַה־בְּשֹׂרָה לָךְ מֹצֵאת.	
	(Abiel and the nurse)	(אביעל והאומנת)	
ABIEL	After the sun goes down, the heavens let drops of dew fall	אַחֲרֵי בוֹא הַשֶּׁמֶשׁ, שְׁחָקִים יַרְעִיפוּ רְסִיסֵי טָל	אביעל
	But since my brother's son went down, the rain has been flooding relentlessly	וְכַאֲשֶׁר שָׁקַע בֶּן אָחִי, הַגֶּשֶׁם שֹׁטֵף מֵאֵין הֲפֻגוֹת	

250 Cf. Shakespeare's 'church' (3.5.116); this expression refers even more unambiguously than the previous one (see note 248) to the Temple in Jerusalem; the collocation is a postbiblical one that is used invariably in this capacity, in contrast to the single word מִקְדָּשׁ appearing above, which could theoretically simply mean 'sanctuary'.

251 Cf. Shakespeare's 'Saint Peter' (3.5.116); see note 249.

252 Ps. 139:6.

	The water still floods through your waterspouts, my daughter	עוֹד הַמַּיִם שֹׁטְפִים דֶּרֶךְ צִנּוֹרַיִךְ בִּתִּי	
	Like **a flowing brook**[253] **and does not deceive**.[254] Behold, your body is small	**כְּנַחַל נוֹבֵעַ**[253] **וְלֹא יְכַזֵּב**.[254] הֵן גְּוִיָּתֵךְ קְטַנָּה	
	Yet it contains within it water and a storm wind and a ship	וְהִיא תָּכִיל בְּקִרְבָּהּ יָם וְרוּחַ סְעָרָה וּסְפִינָה	
	The waters of your eyes that go to and fro resemble the sea	מֵימֵי עֵינַיִךְ הַהוֹלְכִים הָלוֹךְ וָשׁוֹב דֹּמִים לַיָּם	
	Your groaning a storm wind, and your soul a storm-tossed ship	אֶנְקָתֵךְ לְרוּחַ סְעָרָה וְנַפְשֵׁךְ לָאֳנִיָּה סֹעֲרָה	
	On these salty waters, and in the absence of **one to turn the storm to calm**[255]	בַּמַּיִם הַמְּלוּחִים הָאֵלֶּה, וּבְאֵין **מֵקִים הַסְּעָרָה לִדְמָמָה**[255]	
	Your ship circles and sways and is broken in the heart of the sea. –	אֳנִיָּתֵךְ תָּחוֹג וְתָנוּעַ וְתִשָּׁבֵר בְּלֶב־הַיָּם. –	
	Have you told her, my wife, the matter that we have decided?	הֲהִגַּדְתְּ לָהּ אִשְׁתִּי, אֵת הַדָּבָר אֲשֶׁר חָרַצְנוּ?	
ABIEL'S WIFE	She answered to thank you but that she will not be able to fulfil your desire	הִיא עָנְתָה לְהוֹדוֹת לָךְ וּלְמַלֵּא רְצוֹנְךָ לֹא תוּכָל	אשת אביעל
	Leave this foolish girl, let the grave and not a man[256] take her.	הַנַּח לָאִוֶּלֶת הַזֹּאת, קֶבֶר וְלֹא גֶּבֶר[256] יִקָּחֶנָּה.	
	(She makes to exit)	(היא רוצה ללכת)	
ABIEL	You have spoken well, my wife; I am going with you –	הֵיטַבְתְּ לְדַבֵּר אִשְׁתִּי, הִנְנִי הוֹלֵךְ עִמָּךְ –	אביעל
	Does she not intend to marry and to thank us for our gracious act?	הַאֵין נַפְשָׁהּ לְהִנָּשֵׂא וּלְהוֹדוֹת לָנוּ עַל תַּגְמוּלֵנוּ?	
	Does she not consider it a blessing, pride, and glory	הַאִם לֹא תַחְשֹׁב לִבְרָכָה לְגָאוֹן וּלְתִפְאֶרֶת	

253 Prov. 18:4.

254 Hab. 2:3.

255 Ps. 107:29 יָקֵם סְעָרָה לִדְמָמָה 'He turns the storm to calm'.

256 The Hebrew words for 'grave' and 'man' rhyme, creating an internal play on words lacking direct precedent in the source text.

	That we have found for her a husband perfect in **his graceful proportion**[257]	כִּי מָצָאנוּ לָהּ בַּעַל כָּלִיל בְּחִין עֶרְכּוֹ[257]	
	When she is not even fit to be a maidservant?	וְלָהּ אֵין צְדָקָה לִהְיוֹת אַף כְּאַחַת הַשְּׁפָחוֹת?	
JAEL	I cannot be proud because you have acted graciously towards me	לְהִתְגָּאוֹת לֹא אוּכַל עַל אֲשֶׁר גְּמַלְתֶּם עָלָי	יעל
	I only desire to thank you for taking the trouble	רַק לְהוֹדוֹת לָכֶם חָפַצְתִּי עֵקֶב אֲשֶׁר עֲמַלְתֶּם	
	How can I be proud of a matter which I hate	אֵיךְ אֶתְגָּאֶה עַל דָּבָר אֲשֶׁר שָׂנְאָה נַפְשִׁי	
	Even though I thank you for that which I hate	אַף כִּי אוֹדֶה לָכֶם עַל זֶה אֲשֶׁר שָׂנֵאתִי	
	Since I know that you consider it to be good.	אַחֲרֵי אֲשֶׁר יָדַעְתִּי כִּי חֲשַׁבְתֶּם לְטוֹבָה.	
ABIEL	Who is this that I am hearing? Thinking too deep, too deep to fathom	מִזֶּה אֲנִי שֹׁמֵעַ? הִגָּיוֹן עָמֹק עָמֹק מֵחֵקֶר	אביעל
	Who could understand these 'I am proud and I desire to thank you	מִי יָבִין אֵלֶּה „אֶתְגָּאֶה, וּלְהוֹדוֹת חָפַצְתִּי,	
	But nevertheless I am not proud, nor do I thank,	וּבְכָל זֹאת לֹא אֶתְגָּאֶה, אַף לֹא אוֹדֶה,	
	Even though I thank; listen to me, **noble daughter**[258]	אַף כִּי אוֹדֶה" שְׁמָעִנִי בַּת נָדִיב[258]	
	Do not continue to thank me, do not continue to be proud	אַל תּוֹסִיפִי לִי לְהוֹדוֹת, אַל תּוֹסִיפִי לְהִתְגָּאוֹת	
	Just prepare your heap of bones	רַק הָכִינִי אֶת גַּל הָעֲצָמוֹת אֲשֶׁר לְנַפְשֵׁךְ	
	Bone to bone, for Thursday morning	עֶצֶם אֶל עַצְמוֹ לְיוֹם הַחֲמִישִׁי בַּבֹּקֶר	
	To go with Paris to the Temple of the Prince of the Presence[259]	לָלֶכֶת עִם פָּרִיז לְמִקְדַּשׁ שַׂר הַפָּנִים[259]	
	And if you refuse to go, I'll drag you **like an abominable branch**[260]	וְאִם תְּמָאֲנִי לָלֶכֶת, אֶסְחָבֵךְ כְּנֵצֶר נִתְעָב[260]	
	Like a corpse trampled underfoot,[261] a sprawling carcass, shame of your father's house!	כְּפֶגֶר מוּבָס,[261] נְבֵלָה סְרוּחָה, קְלוֹן בֵּית אָבִיךְ!	

257 Job 41:4 (41:12 in English Bibles).
258 Song of Songs 7:2 (7:1 in English Bibles).
259 Cf. Shakespeare's 'Saint Peter's church' (3.5.154); see notes 248 and 249.
260 Isa. 14:19.
261 Isa. 4:19.

ABIEL'S WIFE	Be ashamed and humiliated by your words; have you lost your senses?	בּוֹשׁ וְהִכָּלֵם מִדְּבָרֶיךָ, הַאִם שִׁנִּיתָ טַעֲמֶךָ?	אשת אביעל
JAEL	But please, my father, on my knees I hereby bend	אַךְ אָנָּא אָבִי, עַל בִּרְכַּי הִנְנִי כֹּרַעַת	יעל
	Please be kind enough to let me speak a word.	הוֹאֶל־נָא בְּחַסְדְּךָ וְתֶן לִי לְדַבֵּר דָּבָר.	
ABIEL	Hang yourself and be silent, **false seed**![262] Daughter **of a perverse and rebellious woman**![263]	הֵחָנְקִי וָדֹמִּי זֶרַע שָׁקֶר![262] **בַּת נַעֲוַת הַמַּרְדּוּת**![263]	אביעל
	What use have I for **worn out rags**,[264] **a filthy cloth**[265] like you?	מַה־לִּי וְלִבְלוֹאֵי סְחָבוֹת,[264] לְבֶגֶד עִדִּים[265] כָּמוֹךְ?	
	Now choose: **go out as a bride towards the groom**[266]	עַתָּה בַּחֲרִי לָךְ: צְאִי כְּכַלָּה לִקְרַאת הֶחָתָן[266]	
	Or go out from my presence and I shall see you no more	אוֹ צְאִי מֵעַל פָּנַי וְלֹא אוֹסִיף לִרְאוֹתֵךְ	
	Do not speak a word, do not give me a response	אַל תְּדַבְּרִי דָּבָר, אַל תָּשִׁיבִי לִי מַעֲנֶה	
	And do not open your mouth, lest I stretch out my upraised hand. –	וְאַל תִּפְצִי פֶּה, פֶּן אֶשְׁלַח יָדִי הַנְּטוּיָה. –	
	How we have erred in complaining that **the Lord has withheld from us**	אֵיךְ שָׁגִינוּ לְהִתְאוֹנֵן, כִּי אֲדֹנָי מָנַע מִמֶּנּוּ	
	Fruit of the womb[267] apart from this one; now we have seen with our own eyes	פְּרִי בֶטֶן[267] בִּלְעֲדֵי זֹאת. עַתָּה רָאִינוּ בְּעֵינֵינוּ	
	That even this one is excessive for us, for she has become a curse	כִּי גַּם זֹאת לְיִתְרָה לָנוּ, כִּי לִקְלָלָה הָיְתָה	

262 Isa. 57:4.

263 1 Sam. 20:30.

264 Jer. 38:12.

265 Isa. 64:5 (64:6 in English Bibles).

266 Cf. Shakespeare's 'get thee to church a' Thursday' (3.5.161). Salkinson's Judaized equivalent is traceable to Babylonian Talmud *Berakhot* 59b חתן לקראת כלה 'a groom towards a bride' and Alshekh to Ps. 14 יצא כחתן לקראת כלה 'he will go out as a groom towards a bride'.

267 Gen. 30:2 הֲתַחַת אֱלֹהִים אָנֹכִי אֲשֶׁר־מָנַע מִמֵּךְ פְּרִי־בָטֶן 'am I in place of God, who has withheld from you the fruit of the womb?'

	And not a blessing in our house – cursed be the villainous daughter!	וְלֹא לִבְרָכָה בְּבֵיתֵנוּ – אֲרוּרָה בַּת הַבְּלִיַּעַל! –	
THE NURSE	May the God of the heavens pour His blessing upon her –	אֵל אֱלֹהֵי הַשָּׁמַיִם יָרִיק עָלֶיהָ בִּרְכָתוֹ –	האומנת
	The matter is not good, my lord, to bring disaster upon her with both hands.	לֹא טוֹב הַדָּבָר אֲדֹנִי, לַהֲדִיחָהּ בִּשְׁתֵּי יָדַיִם.	
ABIEL	What is wrong with you, wisest of women? Put a lock on your mouth	מַה־לָּךְ חַכְמַת הַנָּשִׁים? שִׂימִי מַסְגֵּר לְפִיךְ	אביעל
	Or preach your wise words in the women's banquet house.	אוֹ הַטִּיפִי שֵׂכֶל מִלַּיִךְ בְּבֵית מִשְׁתֵּה הַנָּשִׁים.	
THE NURSE	My lips speak no wrong.	שְׂפָתַי לֹא תְדַבֵּרְנָה עַוְלָה.	האומנת
ABIEL	Go in the name of the LORD.	לְכִי לָךְ בְּשֵׁם אֲדֹנָי.	אביעל
THE NURSE	May I not speak a word?	הַאֵין לִי לְדַבֵּר דָּבָר?	האומנת
ABIEL	Be silent, fool, clamorous woman!	הַחֲרִישִׁי פְּתַיָּה, אִשָּׁה הֹמִיָּה!	אביעל
	Make a speech over a cup of wine in the neighbour women's houses	עַל סֵפֶל יַיִן בְּבָתֵּי הַשְּׁכֵנוֹת תִּנְאֲמִי נְאֻם	
	We have no need now.	וְלָנוּ אֵין מַחְסוֹר עָתָּה.	
ABIEL'S WIFE	**Your heart is hot within you**;[268] that's enough from you, my husband.	לִבְּךָ חַם בְּקִרְבְּךָ[268] רַב לְךָ בַּעֲלִי.	אשת אביעל
ABIEL	My heart burns within me, and I am mad from the sight of my eye	לִבִּי בֹעֵר בְּקִרְבִּי וּמְשֻׁגָּע אֲנִי מִמַּרְאֵה עֵינִי	אביעל
	Indeed by day or night, at twilight or in the morning	הֵן בַּיּוֹם אוֹ בַלַּיְלָה בַּנֶּשֶׁף אוֹ בַבֹּקֶר	
	In the house or outside, while I am sitting alone or in company	בַּבַּיִת אוֹ בַחוּץ, בְּשִׁבְתִּי בָדָד וּבְקָהָל	
	Whether waking or sleeping, I have thought only one thing	בֵּין עֵר בֵּין יָשֵׁן חָשַׁבְתִּי רַק מַחֲשָׁבָה אַחַת	
	When will I succeed in my desire to marry her off	לְמָתַי יִצְלַח חֶפְצִי בְיָדִי לָתֵת אֹתָהּ לְבַעַל	

268 Ps. 39:4 (39:3 in English Bibles) חַם־לִבִּי | בְּקִרְבִּי 'my heart was hot within me'.

And after I found **a man after my own heart**,[269] from a family of princes	וְאַחֲרֵי אֲשֶׁר מָצָאתִי אִישׁ כִּלְבָבִי[269] מִמִּשְׁפַּחַת שָׂרִים
A man of wealth and riches, **tender in years yet great in wisdom**,[270]	בַּעַל עֹשֶׁר וּנְכָסִים רַךְ בְּשָׁנִים וְאַב בְּחָכְמָה[270]
He is also a mighty man of valour, **with beautiful eyes and a comely appearance**[271]	גַּם גִּבּוֹר חַיִל הוּא, יְפֵה עֵינַיִם וְטוֹב רֹאִי[271]
For he is perfect in his splendour[272] – after all these things	כִּי כָלִיל הוּא בַּהֲדָרוֹ[272] – וְאַחֲרֵי כָל אֵלֶּה
This daughter of my sorrow[273] dares, between her groans, to say	תָּעִיז בַּת אוֹנִי[273] הַזֹּאת, כַּאֲנָקָה בְּנַאֲקוֹתֶיהָ לֵאמֹר
'I shall not take this blessing, I am tender in years	„לֹא אֶקַּח הַבְּרָכָה הַזֹּאת, רַכָּה אֲנִי בְּשָׁנִים
The **time of love**[274] has not arrived, and I cannot marry	עֵת דֹּדִים[274] לֹא בָאָה וּלְהִנָּשֵׂא לֹא אוּכָל
Forgive me my father, for I do not desire him'	סְלַח לִי אָבִי, כִּי לֹא חָפַצְתִּי בוֹ"
And I say to you, if you refuse to marry	וַאֲנִי אֹמֵר לָךְ, אִם תְּמָאֲנִי לְהִנָּשֵׂא
I forgive you in accordance with your word,[275] but go graze in such place as you can find;	סָלַחְתִּי לָךְ כִּדְבָרֵךְ,[275] רַק לְכִי לִרְעוֹת בַּאֲשֶׁר תִּמְצָאִי
You shall not live with me in the house. Look what is before you	וְאִתִּי לֹא תֵשְׁבִי בַּבָּיִת. רְאִי אֶת אֲשֶׁר לְפָנַיִךְ
Consider again, for I am not accustomed to jesting	הִתְבּוֹנְנִי עוֹד הַפַּעַם, כִּי לֹא הִסְכַּנְתִּי לְצַחֵק
Behold, Thursday is close; pay heed and take counsel	הֵן יוֹם הַחֲמִישִׁי קָרוֹב, שִׁיתִי לִבֵּךְ וַעֲצִי עֵצָה
If you are to be my daughter then I shall give you to the man of my choice	אִם תִּהְיִי לִי לְבַת אָז אֶתְּנֵךְ לְאִישׁ בְּחִירִי

269 1 Sam. 13:14 אִישׁ כִּלְבָבוֹ 'a man after his own heart'.
270 *Sifre* to Deut. 1; Genesis Rabbah 50; Rashi to Gen. 41.
271 1 Sam. 16:12.
272 Ezek. 16:14 כִּי | כָּלִיל הוּא בַּהֲדָרִי 'for it was perfect through my splendour'.
273 This is a reference to Gen. 35:18, in which the matriarch Rachel names her second son 'Ben-oni' (lit. 'son of my sorrow') as she is dying in childbirth.
274 Ezek. 16:8.
275 Num. 14:20 סָלַחְתִּי כִּדְבָרֶךָ 'I have forgiven in accordance with your word'.

	And if not, go hang yourself, or **go from house to house**[276]	וְאִם אַיִן, לְכִי הֵחָנְקִי, אוֹ סֹבִּי עַל הַפְּתָחִים[276]	
	And die of hunger on the city streets, for on my life!	וּמוּתִי בְרָעָב בִּרְחוֹבוֹת קִרְיָה, כִּי חֵי נַפְשִׁי!	
	I shall not be your father and I shall not give you **a portion or inheritance**[277]	אִם אֶהְיֶה לָךְ לְאָב וְאִם אֶתֵּן לָךְ חֵלֶק וְנַחֲלָה[277]	
	Of that with which God has graced me. Now know and believe	מֵאֲשֶׁר חֲנַנִי אֱלֹהִים. עַתָּה דְעִי לָךְ וְהַאֲמִינִי	
	That I have not sworn falsely.	כִּי לֹא נִשְׁבַּעְתִּי לַשָּׁקֶר.	
	(Exits)	(הולך)	
JAEL	Are there no merciful eyes in the heavens to see my pain	הַאֵין עֵינֵי רַחֲמִים בַּשְּׁחָקִים לִרְאוֹת אֶת מַכְאֹבִי	יעל
	And **the plague of my heart**?[278] Oh, my mother, mother who gave me birth!	וְאֶת נֶגַע לְבָבִי?[278] הוֹי אִמִּי, אֵם הוֹרָתִי!	
	Do not cast me away! Postpone the wedding date	אַל תַּשְׁלִיכִינִי אַתְּ! הַעֲבִירִי מוֹעֵד הַחֲתֻנָּה	
	By a month, **at least ten days**,[279] and if you will not do so for me	חֹדֶשׁ יָמִים אוֹ עָשׂוֹר[279] וְאִם לֹא תַעֲשִׂי לִי כָּכָה	
	Put my bed in the grave of my brother Tubal	שִׂימִי אֶת יְצוּעִי בְּקֶבֶר תּוּבַל אָחִי	
	And there I shall lie with him on the day appointed for my wedding.	וְשָׁם אֶשְׁכְּבָה עִמּוֹ לְיוֹם מוֹעֵד חֲתֻנָּתִי.	
ABIEL'S WIFE	Do not entreat me for I shall not say a word	אַל תִּפְגְּעִי בִי כִּי לֹא אֲדַבֵּר דָּבָר	אשת אביעל
	Do what is good in your eyes, for you are not my daughter.	עֲשִׂי אֶת הַטּוֹב בְּעֵינַיִךְ, כִּי לֹא בִתִּי אָתְּ.	
	(Exits)	(הולכת)	
JAEL	Oh, God! What shall I do, my nurse?	אֲהָהּ אֵל אֱלֹהִים! מָה אֶעֱשֶׂה אֹמַנְתִּי?	יעל

276 Tosefta *Pe'a* 4:8 מסבב על הפתחים 'going from house to house'.
277 Gen. 31:14; Deut. 10:9, 12:12, 14:27, 29.
278 1 Kings 8: 38 נֶגַע לְבָבוֹ 'the plague of his own heart'.
279 Gen. 24:55.

	How can I escape from a snare in which I have been trapped like a bird?	אֵיךְ אֲמַלֵּט מִפַּח, בּוֹ כְּצִפּוֹר נִלְכַּדְתִּי?	
	Indeed, my husband is alive on the earth and my oath is a testimony on high	הֵן בַּעֲלִי חַי בָּאָרֶץ וּשְׁבוּעָתִי עֵדוּת בַּמָּרוֹם	
	And as long as he still lives and has not ascended on high	וְכָל עוֹד הוּא חַי וְלַמָּרוֹם לֹא עָלָה	
	Who can disallow my oath, who can undo the bond of my covenant?	מִי יָנִיא שְׁבוּעָתִי, מִי יַתִּיר קֶשֶׁר בְּרִיתִי?	
	Give me counsel, give me help in distress;	תְּנִי לִי עֵצָה, תְּנִי לִי עֶזְרָה בַּצָּרָה;	
	Will it issue from the Mouth Most High to plant snares at my feet,	הֲמִפִּי עֶלְיוֹן יֵצֵא לִטְמוֹן מוֹקְשִׁים לְרַגְלַי,	
	To pursue dry straw, to harass a windblown leaf[280] like me?	לִרְדֹּף קַשׁ יָבֵשׁ, לַעֲרֹץ עָלֶה נִדָּף[280] כָּמוֹנִי?	
	To whom can I turn now, **from where will my help come?**[281]	אֶל מִי אֶפְנֶה עַתָּה, מֵאַיִן יָבוֹא עֶזְרִי?[281]	
	Is there nothing, my nurse, is there nothing you can say to comfort me?	הַאֵין דָּבָר אֹמַנְתִּי, הַאֵין דָּבָר בְּפִיךְ לְנַחֲמֵנִי?	
THE NURSE	Certainly there is, there is, but please listen to me:	אָמְנָם יֵשׁ וָיֵשׁ, אַךְ לוּ שְׁמָעֵנִי:	האומנת
	Indeed Ram is shut up in exile and **it is known in all the earth**[282]	הֵן רָם עָצוּר בַּגּוֹלָה **וּמוּדַעַת זֹאת בְּכָל הָאָרֶץ**[282]	
	That he does not dare to return to see you	כִּי לֹא יָעִיז לָשׁוּב לִרְאוֹת אֶת פָּנַיִךְ	
	And if he does indeed come, he will come only like a thief in secret.	וְאִם בּוֹא יָבוֹא, יָבוֹא אַךְ כְּגַנָּב בַּסָּתֶר.	
	In respect of which my counsel is to become wife to Lord Paris	אֲשֶׁר לְזֹאת עֲצָתִי, לִהְיוֹת לְאִשָּׁה לְפָרִיז הַשָּׂר	
	For he is an honourable man and wondrously desirable	כִּי הוּא אִישׁ נִכְבָּד וְנֶחְמָד עַד לְהַפְלִיא	
	And indeed Ram next to him is only a potsherd next to gold	וְאַף רָם לִקְרָאתוֹ רַק חֶרֶס לִקְרַאת זָהָב	

280 Job 13:25 הֶעָלֶה נִדָּף תַּעֲרוֹץ וְאֶת־קַשׁ יָבֵשׁ תִּרְדֹּף 'will you harass a windblown leaf, and will you pursue dry straw?'
281 Ps. 121:1.
282 Isa. 12:5.

	His eyes are burning torches and sparkle more than the eagle's eyes	עֵינָיו לַפִּידִים בֹּעֲרִים וְנֹצְצִים מֵעֵינֵי הַנָּשֶׁר	
	I have never seen anyone with such **beautiful eyes**[283] as he	מֵעוֹדִי לֹא רָאִיתִי יְפֵה עֵינַיִם[283] כָּמוֹהוּ	
	May God do thus to me[284] if the second husband	כֹּה יַעֲשׂוּן לִי אֱלֹהִים![284] אִם לֹא הַבַּעַל הַשֵּׁנִי	
	Is not better than the first, and if it is not so in your eyes	הוּא טוֹב מִן הָרִאשׁוֹן וְאִם לֹא כֵן הוּא בְּעֵינַיִךְ	
	Why the first one is dead, for even if he lives	הֲלֹא הָרִאשׁוֹן מֵת: כִּי אַף אִם חַי הוּא	
	He is like a dead man to you, for he is of no benefit to you.	נֶחְשָׁב לָךְ כַּמֵּת, כִּי לָךְ הוּא לֹא לְהוֹעִיל.	
JAEL	Are you saying such things with all your heart?	הַאִם בְּכָל לְבָבֵךְ אַתְּ דֹּבֶרֶת כָּאֵלֶּה?	יעל
THE NURSE	May God do thus to me and more also[285]	כֹּה יַעֲשׂוּן לִי אֱלֹהִים וְכֵן יוֹסִיפוּן לִי[285]	האומנת
	If I have not said such things with all my heart and all my soul.	אִם לֹא בְּכָל לְבָבִי וּבְכָל נַפְשִׁי דִּבַּרְתִּי כָּאֵלֶּה.	
JAEL	Amen!	אָמֵן!	יעל
THE NURSE	What did you answer?	מָה עָנִית?	האומנת
JAEL	Why, your counsel is marvellously good, and most marvellous	הֲלֹא עֲצָתֵךְ טוֹבָה הַפְלֵא וָפֶלֶא עַד מְאֹד	יעל
	Go and say to my mother: because I have vexed my father	לְכִי וְאִמְרִי לְאִמִּי: יַעַן כִּי הִכְעַסְתִּי אֶת אָבִי	
	I shall go to the house of God to confess my iniquity	אֵלְכָה בֵּית הָאֱלֹהִים לְהִתְוַדּוֹת אֶת עֲוֹנִי	
	So that I may be forgiven.	וְנִסְלַח לִי.	
THE NURSE	Thus you must do, as you have spoken; as for me, I am going.	כֵּן תַּעֲשִׂי כַּאֲשֶׁר דִּבַּרְתְּ וַאֲנִי הִנְנִי הוֹלֶכֶת.	האומנת
	(Exits)	(הולכת)	
JAEL	The primeval serpent speaks through her mouth, the enemy, oppressor of men's souls	הַנָּחָשׁ הַקַּדְמֹנִי דִּבֵּר בְּפִיהָ, הַצָּר הַצֹּרֵר נֶפֶשׁ הָאָדָם	יעל

283 1 Sam. 16:12.

284 This is part of a biblical oath formula appearing in 2 Sam. 3:35, 19:14 (19:13 in English Bibles); 1 Kings 2:23; 2 Kings 6:31.

285 This is the full oath formula mentioned in the preceding note.

Cursed by the Lord – and it has become a trifling matter in her eyes to deceive me	אֲשֶׁר אֵרֲרוֹ אֲדֹנָי – וַתְּהִי הַנְּקַלָּה בְּעֵינֶיהָ לְהַשִּׁיאֵנִי
To violate the oath of covenant, for she also lashed out with her tongue	לְהָפֵר שְׁבוּעַת הַבְּרִית, כִּי גַּם שָׁלְחָה לְשׁוֹנָהּ
To scorn my husband's name; a thousand times she said yesterday	לָתֵת שֵׁם בַּעֲלִי לָבוּז; אֶלֶף פְּעָמִים אָמְרָה אֶתְמוֹל
That **he cannot be valued with the gold of Ophir**,[286] yet today he is **a potsherd with the potsherds of the earth**[287]	כִּי לֹא יְסֻלֶּה בְּכֶתֶם אוֹפִיר[286] וְהַיּוֹם חֶרֶס הוּא אֶת חַרְסֵי אֲדָמָה[287]
I have had enough compassion, **counsel, and sound wisdom**[288] from your mouth, my nurse	רַב לִי נֹחַם עֵצָה וְתוּשִׁיָּה[288] מִפִּיךְ אֹמַנְתִּי
Here is **the Rock of Divisions**,[289] for **the partnership has been dissolved.**[290]	פֹּה הוּא סֶלַע הַמַּחְלְקוֹת,[289] כִּי נִתְפָּרְדָה הַחֲבִילָה.[290]
Now I shall go to the **priest of God Most High**[291]	עַתָּה אֵלְכָה לִי אֶל הַכֹּהֵן לְאֵל עֶלְיוֹן[291]
Perhaps he will help me to free me from my distress[292]	אוּלַי יַעֲזָר־לִי לְחַלֵּץ נַפְשִׁי מִמְּצוּקָתִי[292]
And if not, my own hand will save me, to die in my blamelessness.	וְאִם אַיִן, יָדִי תוֹשִׁיעַ לִי לָמוּת בְּתֻמָּתִי.
(Exits)	(הולכת)

286 Job 28:16 לֹא־תְסֻלֶּה בְּכֶתֶם אוֹפִיר 'it cannot be valued with the gold of Ophir'. Ophir is a region renowned in the Hebrew Bible for its wealth.

287 Isa. 45:9 חֶרֶשׂ אֶת־חַרְשֵׂי אֲדָמָה 'a potsherd with the potsherds of the earth'.

288 Prov. 8:14.

289 1 Sam. 23:28; this refers to the place where Saul was obliged to stop his ongoing pursuit of David and go to fight the Philistines. In some English Bible versions (e.g., Geneva Bible, King James Bible, New International Version) the name is not translated but appears in transliteration as Sela-hammahlekoth or similar.

290 Babylonian Talmud *Giṭṭin* 59b.

291 Gen. 14:18.

292 This and the next line form a rhyming couplet, mirroring Shakespeare's 'remedy/die' (3.5.242-3). This was a workable rhyme in Shakespeare's day (Weis 2012: 420).

Fourth Part

חלק רביעי

SCENE I	*(Rezin and Paris)*	(רצין ופריז)	מחזה א'
REZIN	On Thursday? Why, it is very close.	הַאִם בַּיּוֹם הַחֲמִישִׁי? הֲלֹא קָרוֹב הוּא מְאֹד.	רצין
PARIS	So my father Abiel desires, and as for me, I have no desire	כֵּן חָפֵץ אֲבִיעֵל אָבִי וַאֲנִי אֵין לִי חֵפֶץ	פריז
	To hinder or persuade him to postpone the appointed time.	לַעֲצֹר וּלְפַתּוֹתוֹ כִּי יַרְחִיק אֶת הַמּוֹעֵד.	
REZIN	You, my lord, said to me that you have not asked the maiden's consent	אַתָּה אֲדֹנִי אָמַרְתָּ לִי, כִּי פִּי הַנַּעֲרָה לֹא שָׁאַלְתָּ	רצין
	And you do not know what is in her heart: the matter is not fitting in my eyes	וְלֹא יָדַעְתָּ אֶת לִבָּהּ: לֹא נָכוֹן הַדָּבָר בְּעֵינַי	
	For **this is not the way.**[1]	כִּי לֹא זֹה הַדֶּרֶךְ.[1]	
PARIS	**She is weeping for Tubal; she refuses to be comforted**[2] thus far	הִיא מְבַכָּה עַל תּוּבַל, מֵאֲנָה לְהִנָּחֵם[2] עַד כֹּה	פריז
	And I have spoken with her but very little	וַאֲנִי לֹא דִבַּרְתִּי עִמָּהּ כִּי אִם מְעַט מִזְעָר	
	For words of love[3] are not pleasant to one bitter of soul	כִּי דִבְרֵי אַהֲבָה[3] אֵינָם נְעִימִים לְמָרַת נָפֶשׁ	
	But her father was concerned for her, lest the sorrow overwhelm her	אֶפֶס אָבִיהָ דָּאַג לָהּ פֶּן תִּגְבַּר עָלֶיהָ הַתּוּגָה	
	Therefore in his wisdom he appointed a close day for her wedding	לָכֵן יָעַד הוּא בְּחָכְמָתוֹ יוֹם חֲתֻנָּתָהּ מִקָּרוֹב	
	For only when she is sitting alone **does it grieve her in her heart**[4]	כִּי רַק בְּשִׁבְתָּהּ בָּדָד תִּתְעַצֵּב אֶל לִבָּהּ[4]	
	But in her husband's house quick as lightning she will forget **sorrow and sighing.**[5]	אַךְ בְּבֵית בַּעֲלָהּ חִישׁ קַל תִּשְׁכַּח יָגוֹן וַאֲנָחָה.[5]	
	This is the secret of the matter, why the wedding is close.	זֶה הוּא סוֹד הַדָּבָר, לָמָּה הַחֲתֻנָּה קְרוֹבָה.	

1 2 Kings 6:19.
2 Jer. 31:15 רָחֵל מְבַכָּה עַל־בָּנֶיהָ מֵאֲנָה לְהִנָּחֵם 'Rachel is weeping for her children; she refuses to be comforted'.
3 Cf. Shakespeare's 'Venus'; Salkinson has omitted the Classical mythological reference.
4 Gen. 6:6 וַיִּתְעַצֵּב אֶל־לִבּוֹ 'and it grieved Him in His heart'.
5 Isa. 35:10, 51:11.

REZIN *(To himself)*	If only I did not know the secret, why the wedding is distant –	מִי יִתֵּן וְלֹא יָדַעְתִּי הַסּוֹד, לָמָּה הַחֲתֻנָּה רְחוֹקָה –	רצין (אל עצמו)
	Look, my lord, behold, the damsel is coming into the chamber.	רְאֵה נָא אֲדֹנִי, הִנֵּה הָעַלְמָה בָּאָה אֶל הַלִּשְׁכָּה.	
	(Jael enters)	(יעל באה)	
PARIS	I rejoice to see your face here, my beautiful bride.[6]	שָׂמַחְתִּי לִרְאוֹת פָּנַיִךְ פֹּה כַּלָּתִי יָפָתִי.[6]	פריז
JAEL	That will be my title when the day of my wedding comes.	כֵּן יִהְיֶה שְׁמִי כַּאֲשֶׁר יָבוֹא יוֹם חֲתֻנָּתִי.	יעל
PARIS	Thursday is close, and then the matter will come and take place.	יוֹם הַחֲמִישִׁי קָרוֹב וְאָז יָבוֹא וְיָקוּם הַדָּבָר.	פריז
JAEL	When it is fitting for it to come, so it shall come and so it shall take place.	כַּאֲשֶׁר נָכוֹן לָבוֹא, כֵּן יָבוֹא וְכֵן יָקוּם.	יעל
REZIN	**The entrance into your word**[7] is enough for one who understands.	פֵּתַח דִּבַרְכֶם[7] רַב לְמֵבִין.	רצין
PARIS	Have you come to confess here before the priest?	הֲבָאתְ* לְהִתְוַדּוֹת פֹּה לִפְנֵי הַכֹּהֵן?	פריז
JAEL	To answer you this is like confessing before you.	לְהָשִׁיב לְךָ זֹאת, הוּא כְּהִתְוַדּוֹת לְפָנֶיךָ.	יעל
PARIS	Go and confess before him, and tell him that you love me.	לְכִי וְהִתְוַדִּי לְפָנָיו וְהַגִּידִי לוֹ כִּי אֲהַבְתִּנִי.	פריז
JAEL	I shall confess before you that I love him.	הִנְנִי לְהִתְוַדּוֹת לְפָנֶיךָ, כִּי אָהַבְתִּי אֹתוֹ.	יעל
PARIS	And likewise you will confess before him that you love me.	וְכֵן תִּתְוַדִּי לְפָנָיו, כִּי אֹתִי אָהַבְתְּ.	פריז
JAEL	The matter would be better if I were to tell such things **by the walls**[8]	טוֹב יִהְיֶה הַדָּבָר, אִם אַגִּיד כֵּן אֵצֶל הַקִּירוֹת[8]	יעל

6 This and the next line form a rhyming couplet, mirroring either 'wife/wife' (4.1.18–19) or 'next/text' (4.1.20–1) in the source text. In terms of meaning, Salkinson's rhyme corresponds to Shakespeare's 'wife/wife', but the fact that Salkinson did not typically recognize the original's same-word pairs as rhymes, combined with the fact that he did not attempt to find a separate rhyme for his next two lines, suggest that he may have instead had 'next/text' in mind as his model.

7 Ps. 119:130 פֵּתַח דְּבָרֶיךָ 'the entrance into your words'.

8 Ezekiel 33:30 בְּנֵי עַמְּךָ הַנִּדְבָּרִים בְּךָ אֵצֶל הַקִּירוֹת וּבְפִתְחֵי הַבָּתִּים 'the members of your people are speaking about you by the walls and at the entrances to the houses'. This biblical reference to speaking about someone behind their back retains the sense of Shakespeare's 'being spoke behind your back' (4.1.28).

* הֲבָאת

	Rather than telling it to your face.	מֵאֲשֶׁר אַגִּיד בְּפָנֶיךָ.	
PARIS	**The expression of your face testifies against it**[9] that it has suffered from a surfeit of tears.	הַכָּרַת פָּנַיִךְ תַּעֲנֶה בָּם[9] כִּי סָבְלוּ מֵרֹב דִּמְעָה.	פריז
JAEL	My tears must not boast that they have prevailed over my face	אֵין לְדִמְעוֹתַי לְהִתְפָּאֵר כִּי גָבְרוּ עַל פָּנַי	יעל
	Since even in the beginning, **of what account was my face?**[10]	**אַחֲרֵי אֲשֶׁר גַּם בַּתְּחִלָּה פָּנַי בַּמֶּה נֶחְשָׁבוּ.**[10]	
PARIS	With this you have spoken wicked slander against your face.	בְּזֹאת הוֹצֵאת דִּבָּה רָעָה עַל פָּנָיִךְ.	פריז
JAEL	I spoke against my face, but it was not false slander.	נֶגֶד פָּנַי דִּבַּרְתִּי וְלֹא דִבַּת שֶׁקֶר הִיא.	יעל
PARIS	Your face is mine, for you have become my treasure	פָּנַיִךְ לִי הֵם, כִּי הָיִיתְ* לִי סְגֻלָּה	פריז
	And you have spoken wicked slander against my allotted possession.	וְדִבָּה רָעָה הוֹצֵאתְ** עַל חֶבֶל נַחֲלָתִי.	
JAEL	Perhaps the matter is so, for my face does not belong to me –	אוּלַי כֵּן הַדָּבָר, כִּי פָּנַי לֹא לִי הֵמָּה –	יעל
	And now, my father and teacher, is this time suitable for you	וְעַתָּה אָבִי וּמוֹרִי, הַנְכוֹנָה לְךָ הָעֵת הַזֹּאת	
	Or should I return to you at twilight?[11]	אוֹ אָשׁוּב אָבוֹא אֵלֶיךָ בֵּין הָעַרְבָּיִם?[11]	
REZIN	I am ready to serve you, my sad-spirited daughter –	הִנְנִי נָכוֹן לְשָׁרְתֵךְ בִּתִּי עֲצוּבַת רוּחַ –	רצין
	Please, sir, please let me fulfil the duty of my office.	בִּי הַשָּׂר הַנִּיחֵנִי נָא לְמַלֵּא מִשְׁמֶרֶת פְּקוּדָתִי.	
PARIS	God forbid that I should be an obstacle interfering with the holy work –	חָלִילָה לִּי לִהְיוֹת לְשָׂטָן לְהַפְרִיעַ עֲבֹדַת הַקֹּדֶשׁ –	פריז
	On Thursday morning I shall come to awaken you, Jael, from your sleep.	בַּיּוֹם הַחֲמִישִׁי בַּבֹּקֶר אָבוֹא לְהָעִירֵךְ יָעֵל מִשְּׁנָתֵךְ	
	I'll depart from you. *(Kisses her and exits)*	הִנְנִי יוֹצֵא מֵאֵת פָּנָיִךְ. (נושק לה והולך)	
JAEL	Close the door and sit to weep with me	סְגוֹר אֶת הַדֶּלֶת וְשֵׁב לִבְכּוֹת עִמִּי	יעל
	There is no more hope, there is no medicine and no help.	אֵין תִּקְוָה עוֹד, אֵין תְּרוּפָה וְאֵין עֵזֶר.	

---

9 Isa. 3:9 הַכָּרַת פְּנֵיהֶם עָנְתָה בָּם 'the expression of their faces testifies against them'.
10 Isa. 2:22 כִּי־בַמֶּה נֶחְשָׁב הוּא 'for of what account is he?'
11 Cf. Shakespeare's 'at evening mass' (4.1.38); Salkinson has replaced the explicitly Catholic reference with a religiously neutral one that preserves the temporal sense of the original.

* הָיִית
** הוֹצֵאת

REZIN	Oh, Jael, my daughter! I know your pain	הוֹי יָעֵל בִּתִּי! נַפְשִׁי יֹדַעַת מַכְאוֹבֵךְ	רצין
	I am distressed at your distress, for it has touched my very heart	צַר לִי בְּצָרָתֵךְ, כִּי נָגְעָה עַד לִבִּי	
	You have been brought **between the straits**[12] and you have no refuge or sanctuary	בֵּין הַמְּצָרִים[12] הוּבֵאת וְאֵין לָךְ מָנוֹס וּמִפְלָט	
	For Thursday is the day that I heard	כִּי הַיּוֹם הַחֲמִישִׁי הוּא הַיּוֹם אֲשֶׁר שָׁמַעְתִּי	
	Which they have set as your appointed time for this lord to take you to wife.	אֲשֶׁר קָרְאוּ עָלַיִךְ מוֹעֵד, כִּי יִבְעָלֵךְ הַשָּׂר הַזֶּה.	
JAEL	Please do not tell me,[13] for I have heard this thing	אָנָּא אַל תַּגֶּד־לִי,[13] כִּי שָׁמַעְתִּי הַדָּבָר הַזֶּה	יעל
	Unless you know a remedy and can heal my wound.	בִּלְתִּי אִם מָזוֹר יָדַעְתָּ וְתַעֲלֶה אֲרֻכָה לְשִׁבְרִי.	
	If your wisdom is not sufficient to bring me salvation	אִם חָכְמָתְךָ אֵין דֵּי לְהָבִיא לִי תְּשׁוּעָה	
	Say that I am wise enough to find guidance for myself	אֱמֹר כִּי חָכַמְתִּי אֲנִי לִמְצוֹא לִי תַחְבּוּלָה	
	And this knife will bind my wound with a single blow.	וְזֹאת הַמַּאֲכֶלֶת תַּחֲבֹשׁ בְּמַכָּה אַחַת אֶת מַכָּתִי.	
	Behold, God has linked my heart and Ram's heart with bonds of love	הֵן לִבִּי וְלֵב רָם חִבֵּר אֱלֹהִים בְּחַבְרוֹת אַהֲבָה	
	And with the tie and **the bond of the covenant**[14] you yourself linked our hands	וּבְמָסֹרֶת הַבְּרִית[14] וְהַקֶּשֶׁר חִבַּרְתָּ אֶת יָדֵינוּ אַתָּה	
	So before my hand severs the tie, to make another tie,	וּבְטֶרֶם תְּנַתֵּק יָדִי הַקֶּשֶׁר לַעֲשׂוֹת קֶשֶׁר אַחֵר	
	Before my heart grows unfaithful, whoring after a strange man	בְּטֶרֶם לִבִּי יִמְעַל מַעַל לִזְנוֹת אַחֲרֵי אִישׁ זָר	
	This knife is raised to devour them both.	הַמַּאֲכֶלֶת הַזֹּאת נְטוּיָה לֶאֱכֹל אֶת שְׁנֵיהֶם.	
	And now, give me counsel, for **there is wisdom with the aged**[15]	וְעַתָּה עֵצָה לִי עֵצָה, כִּי בִישִׁישִׁים חָכְמָה[15]	

12 Lam. 1:3; translated as 'in the midst of her distress' in some English Bible versions (e.g., New Revised Standard Version, New International Version, English Standard Version).

13 Cf. Shakespeare's 'Tell me not, Friar' (4.1.50).

14 Ezek. 20:37.

15 Job 12:12.

	But if not, look, this knife **will bring me forth into a broad space**[16]	וְאִם אַיִן, רְאֵה הַשַּׂכִּין הַזֶּה **יוֹצִיאֵנִי לַמֶּרְחָב**[16]	
	And that which you have not been able to do by means of **counsel and sound wisdom**[17]	וְאֵת אֲשֶׁר לֹא יָכֹלְתָּ עֲשׂוֹת בְּדֶרֶךְ **עֵצָה וְתוּשִׁיָּה**[17]	
	With all your days and your wisdom, my hand will surely be able to do.	עִם כָּל יָמֶיךָ וְחָכְמָתֶךָ, יָדִי יָכֹל תּוּכָל.	
	Now hurry, speak, for I have already decreed my judgement[18]	עַתָּה דַּבֵּר חוּשָׁה, כִּי מִשְׁפָּטִי כְּבָר חָרַצְתִּי[18]	
	And if you have no counsel, I desire to die.	וְאִם אֵין עֵצָה בְּפִיךָ, אֲנִי לָמוּת חָפַצְתִּי.	
REZIN	Wait, my daughter, something like a **door of hope**[19] appears to me from afar	הוֹחִילִי בִתִּי, כְּפֶתַח **תִּקְוָה**[19] נִרְאֶה לִּי מֵרָחוֹק	רצין
	But in order to arrive at the desired haven you must do a terrible thing	אַךְ לָבוֹא לִמְחוֹז הַחֵפֶץ עָלַיִךְ לַעֲשׂוֹת דָּבָר נוֹרָא	
	Almost like that thing from which we strive to escape	כִּמְעַט כַּדָּבָר הַזֶּה שֶׁאָנוּ חֹתְרִים לְהִמָּלֵט מִיָּדוֹ.	
	Behold, you have the courage of spirit to kill yourself	הֵן יֶשׁ־לָךְ אֹמֶץ רוּחַ לְאַבֵּד אֶת נַפְשֵׁךְ	
	In order not to marry Paris, because it is a disgrace in your eyes	לְמַעַן בַּל תִּנָּשְׂאִי לְפָרִיז, יַעַן חֶרְפָּה הִיא בְּעֵינַיִךְ	
	So you can indeed find the courage **to risk your life**[20]	אַף כִּי תִמְצְאִי אֹמֶץ **לְהַשְׁלִיךְ נַפְשֵׁךְ מִנֶּגֶד**[20]	
	In order to escape the disgrace which is more bitter to you than death.	לְמַעַן תִּמָּלְטִי מִן הַחֶרְפָּה אֲשֶׁר מָרָה הִיא לָךְ מִמָּוֶת.	
	So now, if you are prepared, command and I shall help you.	וְעַתָּה אִם לִבֵּךְ נָכוֹן, צַוִּי וְהִנְנִי לָךְ לַעֲזֹר.	
JAEL	Command me to cast myself down from the top of the tower there	צַוֵּה לִי לְהִתְנַפֵּל מֵעַל רֹאשׁ הַמִּגְדָּל שָׁמָּה	יעל
	Rather than to become Paris' wife; command me to sojourn in robbers' lairs	מִהְיוֹת לְפָרִיז לְאִשָּׁה; צַוֵּה לִי לָגוּר בִּמְעוֹנוֹת שׁוֹדְדִים	

16 Ps. 18:20 (18:19 in English Bibles) וַיּוֹצִיאֵנִי לַמֶּרְחָב 'He brought me forth into a broad place'.
17 Prov. 8:14.
18 This forms a rhyming couplet with the next line, mirroring Shakespeare's 'die/remedy' (4.1.66–7).
19 Hosea 2:17 (2:15 in English Bibles).
20 Judg. 9:17 וַיַּשְׁלֵךְ אֶת־נַפְשׁוֹ מִנֶּגֶד 'and he risked his life'.

	In a desert of serpents and scorpions, **in an asp's hole and a viper's nest**;[21]	בְּמִדְבַּר נְחָשִׁים וְעַקְרַבִּים, בְּחֹר פֶּתֶן וּמְאוּרַת צִפְעוֹנִי;[21]	
	Or imprison me in fetters and throw me among **raging bears**;[22]	אוֹ אֲסָרֵנִי בְזִקִּים וְהַשְׁלִיכֵנִי בֵּין דֻּבִּים שׁוֹקְקִים;[22]	
	Or to be shut up to spend the whole night in a house of corpses	אוֹ לִהְיוֹת עֲצוּרָה לָלוּן כָּל הַלַּיְלָה בְּבָתֵּי מֵתִים	
	Full of bones rich in marrow, skulls, and rotting shankbones;	מְלֵאִים עֲצָמוֹת מְמֻחָיִם, גֻּלְגָּלוֹת, וְשׁוֹקַיִם נִסְרָחוֹת;	
	Or give me the word to descend into a new grave	אוֹ תְּנָה לִי אֹמֶר לָרֶדֶת בְּקֶבֶר חָדָשׁ	
	To wrap myself in a single shroud with the corpse lying there –	לְהִתְעַטֵּף בְּתַכְרִיךְ אֶחָד עִם הַמֵּת הַשּׁוֹכֵב שָׁם –	
	Words which, upon hearing them, trembling seizes me and I convulse –	דְּבָרִים אֲשֶׁר לִשְׁמַע אֹזֶן רְעָדָה אֲחָזַתְנִי וָאֶתְחַלְחָל –	
	All these I would do today and would not cry out and would not complain	כָּל אֵלֶּה אֶעֱשֶׂה הַיּוֹם וְלֹא אֶזְעַק וְלֹא אֶתְאוֹנָן	
	If only I might have hope to live like an upright and blameless wife	רַק אִם יֵשׁ לִי תִקְוָה לָשֶׁבֶת כְּאִשָּׁה יְשָׁרָה וּנְקִיָּה	
	With my husband **whom my soul loves**.[23]	עִם בַּעֲלִי שֶׁאָהֲבָה נַפְשִׁי.[23]	
REZIN	Return to your house with a laughing face and reconcile yourself with your father, saying	שׁוּבִי לְבֵיתֵךְ בְּפָנִים שׂחֲקִים וְהִתְרַצִּי אֶל אָבִיךְ לֵאמֹר	רצין
	That you will marry Paris; and tomorrow, which is Wednesday,	כִּי תִנָּשְׂאִי לְפָרִיז; וּלְמָחָר הוּא יוֹם הָרְבִיעִי	
	Do not let your nurse lie down with you in the bedchamber	אַל תִּתְּנִי לְאֹמַנְתֵּךְ בַּלַּיְלָה לִשְׁכַּב עִמֵּךְ בַּחֲדַר הַמִּטּוֹת	
	But rather, lie down alone, and take this jar to your bed	כִּי אִם שִׁכְבִי לְבָדָד וְצִנְצֶנֶת הַזֹּאת קְחִי לְמִטָּתֵךְ	
	And when you lie down, drink the mixture from the jar	וְהָיָה כַּאֲשֶׁר תִּשְׁכְּבִי תִּשְׁתִּי אֶת הַמֶּסֶךְ מֵהַצִּנְצֶנֶת	
	Quick as lightning your tendons will be filled with a cold spirit, **a spirit of deep sleep**[24]	חִישׁ קַל יִמָּלְאוּ גִידַיִךְ רוּחַ קָרָה רוּחַ תַּרְדֵּמָה[24]	
	The blood will freeze, it will not run and will not beat in your veins	הַדָּם יִקְפָּא לֹא יָרוּץ וְלֹא יִדְפֹּק בְּעוֹרְקַיִךְ	

21 Isa. 11:8 וְשִׁעֲשַׁע יוֹנֵק עַל־חֻר פָּתֶן וְעַל מְאוּרַת צִפְעוֹנִי גָּמוּל יָדוֹ הָדָה 'and the nursing child shall play on the asp's hole, and the weaned child shall put his hand on the viper's nest'.

22 Prov. 28:15 דֹב שׁוֹקֵק 'a raging bear'.

23 Song of Songs 1:7, 3:1, 2, 3.

24 Isa. 29:10.

The heat of the flesh will pass and the blush of the lips and the cheeks will depart	חֹם הַבָּשָׂר יַעֲבֹר וְאֹדֶם הַשְּׂפָתַיִם וְהַלְּחָיַיִם יָסוּר
No breath will remain in you, and the shadow of death will rest upon your eyelids	לֹא תִשָּׁאֶר בָּךְ נְשָׁמָה וְעַל עַפְעַפֵּי עֵינַיִךְ צַלְמָוֶת
The only small dominion in this small body of yours	כָּל הַמַּמְלָכָה הַקְּטַנָּה בִּגְוִיָּתֵךְ הַקְּטַנָּה הַזֹּאת
Will be the command of its life spirit, there will be no other prince or servant	תַּפְקִיד רוּחַ חַיֶּיהָ, אֵין שַׂר וְאֵין עֶבֶד עוֹד
There will be no authority and no service, **and there shall be none shut up or left at large**[25]	אֵין מִשְׂרָה וְאֵין עֲבֹדָה וְאֶפֶס עָצוּר וְעָזוּב[25]
Every joint, every member will be cold and heavy, it will not move, like a corpse	כָּל פֶּרֶק כָּל אֵבֶר קַר וְכָבֵד לֹא יָנוּעַ כַּמֵּת
And in the image of a lifeless form you will lie for forty-two hours	וּבִדְמוּת תַּבְנִית הַמָּוְתָה תִּשְׁכְּבִי אַרְבָּעִים וּשְׁתֵּי שָׁעוֹת
But afterwards you will awaken and arise as if from a sweet sleep.	וְאַחֲרֵי כֵן תָּקִיצִי וְתָקוּמִי כְּמוֹ מִשֵּׁנָה מְתוּקָה.
And when Paris comes on Thursday morning	וְהָיָה כַּאֲשֶׁר יָבוֹא פָּרִיז בְּיוֹם הַחֲמִישִׁי בַּבֹּקֶר
To wake you from sleep, he will find you dead in the bed	לְהָעִיר אֹתָךְ מִשֵּׁנָה יִמְצָאֵךְ מֵתָה בַּמִּטָּה
Then they will dress you in linen garments and bear you in an open coffin	אָז יַלְבִּשׁוּךְ בִּגְדֵי בַד וְיִשָּׂאוּךְ בְּאָרוֹן פָּתוּחַ
In the manner of the people of our place[26] – to the cavern[27] of your forefathers' graves	כְּדֶרֶךְ אַנְשֵׁי מְקוֹמֵנוּ[26] – אֶל מְעָרַת[27] קִבְרֵי אֲבוֹתַיִךְ

25 Deuteronomy 32:36.

26 This custom clashes with that of Jewish tradition, according to which coffins are always closed and the deceased may not be viewed. Salkinson has chosen to retain this detail of the source text, but has rephrased it from Shakespeare's 'Then, as the manner of our country is,/In thy best robes, uncovered on the bier' (4.1.109–10), moving the reference to the manner of the country from the beginning of the unit until the end. This change has the effect of drawing attention to the uncovered coffin as a custom of the land (rather than both the robes and the bier). Salkinson may have done this in order subtly to highlight the fact that this is a custom of the local Italian non-Jews, rather than a Jewish custom. In addition, he has changed Shakespeare's 'best robes' to 'linen garments', a reference to the Jewish practice of clothing the dead in a plain linen shroud (Hillers and Kashani 2007: 293). These decisions result in a text reflecting a singular fusion of Jewish and non-Jewish funeral customs.

27 Cf. Shakespeare's 'vault' (4.1.111); Salkinson's translation is a reference to the biblical practice of burying the dead in family caves, most famously the Cave of Machpelah which the patriarch Abraham purchased as a family tomb (see Gen. 23).

	The Abiels **from generation to generation.**[28] And meanwhile	הֵם הָאֲבִיעֶלִים מִדֹּר דֹּר.[28] וַאֲנִי בֵּין כֹּה וָכֹה	
	Before you awaken from your sleep, I shall send a letter to Ram	עַד לֹא תָקִיצִי מִשְּׁנָתֵךְ אֶשְׁלַח מִכְתָּב אֶל רָם	
	And make known to him everything that has been done, and he will hurry to come here	וְאוֹדִיעֶנּוּ כָּל אֲשֶׁר נַעֲשָׂה וְהוּא יָחִישׁ לָבוֹא הֲלֹם	
	And he and I together will keep watch when you awaken from your deep sleep	וַאֲנִי וְהוּא יַחְדָּו נִשְׁמֹר עֵת תִּתְעוֹרְרִי מִתַּרְדֵּמָתֵךְ	
	And on that very night you will travel with Ram to Mantua.	וּבְעֶצֶם הַלַּיְלָה הַהוּא תַּעַבְרִי עִם רָם לְמַנְטוּבָה.	
	This is the way in which the disgrace will be removed from you	זֹאת הִיא הַדֶּרֶךְ אֲשֶׁר נָגֹל מֵעָלַיִךְ הַחֶרְפָּה	
	If only your heart stays steady, and you do not know fright	אִם רַק לִבֵּךְ בְּאֵיתָן יֵשֵׁב, וְלֹא תֵדְעִי מְחִתָּה	
	Nor the fear of a woman's heart to carry out this scheme.	וְלֹא פַּחַד לֵב נָשִׁים לְבַצַּע אֶת הַמְּזִמָּה הַזֹּאת.	
JAEL	Give it to me, give it to me, and do not mention the name of fear.	תֶּן לִי תֶּן לִי, וְאַל תִּזְכֹּר שֵׁם פַּחַד.	יעל
REZIN	Here it is, and go in peace, go with this strength of yours and be saved	הֵא לָךְ וּלְכִי לְשָׁלוֹם, לְכִי בְּכֹחֵךְ זֶה וְתִוָּשֵׁעִי	רצין
	Meanwhile, I shall quickly send one of the sons of the prophets[29] to Mantua.[30]	וַאֲנִי אֶשְׁלַח מְהֵרָה אֶחָד מִבְּנֵי הַנְּבִיאִים[29] לְמַנְטוּבָה.[30]	
JAEL	May love give strength, and may the Gods of love give salvation.	הָאַהֲבָה תִּתֵּן אֱיָל וְלֵאלֹהֵי הָאַהֲבָה הַתְּשׁוּעָה.	יעל
	And you, my dear father, farewell! *(Both exit)*	וְאַתָּה אָבִי הַיָּקָר שָׁלוֹם! (הולכים שניהם)	
SCENE 2	*Abiel's house (Abiel and his wife and the nurse with servants)*	בית אביעל (אביעל ואשתו והאומנת עם עבדים)	מחזה ב'

28 Exod. 17:16.

29 Cf. Shakespeare's 'friar' (4.1.123); Salkinson has replaced this explicitly Catholic term with a biblical expression used to denote the desciples of a prophet (see, e.g., 1 Kings 20:35; 2 Kings 2:15).

30 This and the next line form a rhyming couplet, mirroring Shakespeare's 'lord/afford' (4.1.124–5).

ABIEL *(To one servant)*	Go and call all the men listed here by their names.	לֵךְ וּקְרָא אֵת כָּל הָאֲנָשִׁים הַנְּקוּבִים פֹּה בִּשְׁמוֹתָם.	אביעל (לעבד אחד)
	(To a second servant) Go and hire for me twenty expert bakers and cooks.	(לעבד שני) לֵךְ וּשְׂכָר לִי עֶשְׂרִים אֹפִים וּמְבַשְּׁלִים מְבִינִים.	
THE SECOND SERVANT[31]	They will all be experts, for I shall test them first	כֻּלָּם יִהְיוּ מְבִינִים כִּי אֶבְחָנֵם בַּתְּחִלָּה[31]	העבד השני
	To see if they are experts at licking their fingers.	אִם מְבִינִים הֵם לְלַקֵּק אֵת אֶצְבְּעוֹתֵיהֶם.	
ABIEL	How will they be tested by that?	אֵיךְ יִבָּחֲנוּ בָּזֹאת?	אביעל
THE SECOND SERVANT[32]	A cook who is not expert in licking his fingers is senseless	מְבַשֵּׁל בִּלְתִּי מֵבִין לְלַקֵּק אֶצְבְּעוֹתָיו הוּא חֲסַר טָעַם	העבד השני[32]
	And such a senseless cook as this I shall not take with me.	וּמְבַשֵּׁל חֲסַר טַעַם כָּזֶה לֹא אֶקָּחֶנּוּ* עִמָּדִי.	
ABIEL	Go forth, go forth on your way – *(The second servant exits)*	צֵא צֵא לְדַרְכֶּךָ – (העבד השני הולך)	אביעל
	We shall not be able to prepare everything that we need in such a short time	לֹא נוּכַל לְהָכִין כָּל דֵּי מַחְסֹרֵנוּ בְּעֵת קְצָרָה כָּזֹאת	
	Has my daughter gone to Rezin the priest?	הַאִם הָלְכָה בִתִּי אֶל רְצִין הַכֹּהֵן?	
THE NURSE	Yes, she has gone.	הֵן, הִיא הָלָכָה.	האומנת
ABIEL	Perhaps this priest will benefit the perverse-hearted and stiff-necked girl	אוּלַי הַכֹּהֵן הַזֶּה יוֹעִיל לְנַעֲוַת לֵב וּקְשַׁת עֹרֶף	אביעל
	This **rebellious daughter**.[33]	**הַבַּת הַשּׁוֹבֵבָה**[33] הַזֹּאת.	
THE NURSE	Behold, she returns, and her face is favourable	הִנֵּה הִיא שָׁבָה וּפָנֶיהָ מְפִיקִים רָצוֹן	האומנת
	The peace-loving priest has restored her heart to her parents.	הַכֹּהֵן הָרֹדֵף שָׁלוֹם הֵשִׁיב לִבָּהּ אֶל אֲבוֹתֶיהָ.	
	(Jael enters)	(יעל באה)	

31 This speech is prose in the original (4.2.3–4).
32 This speech is prose in the original (4.2.6–8).
33 Jer. 31:22, 49:4.

* אֶקָּחֶנּוּ

ABIEL	From whence comes the wayward heifer? From which **valley of vision**[34] do you come?	מֵאַיִן עֶגְלָה סֹרֵרָה? מֵאֵיזֶה גֵיא חִזָּיוֹן[34] בָּאת?	אביעל
JAEL	I come from the house of God, where I learned to repent of my iniquity	מִבֵּית הָאֱלֹהִים בָּאתִי, שָׁם לָמַדְתִּי לָשׁוּב מֵעֲוֹנִי	יעל
	For I have rebelled against your word and have not obeyed my parents	כִּי מָרִיתִי אֶת פִּיךָ וְלֹא שָׁמַעְתִּי בְּקוֹל הוֹרָי	
	But here I fall on my face as the man of God commanded me	וְהִנְנִי נֹפֶלֶת עַל אַפִּי כַּאֲשֶׁר צִוַּנִי אִישׁ הָאֱלֹהִים	
	Saying: **I pray you, pardon my sin**[35] just this once	לֵאמֹר: **אָנָּא שָׂא נָא אֵת חַטָּאתִי**[35] אַךְ הַפָּעַם	
	And from this day forth I shall keep the commandment of your mouth.	וּמִיּוֹם הַזֶּה וָמַעְלָה אֵת מִצְוַת פִּיךָ אֶשְׁמֹרָה.	
ABIEL	Summon Paris for me, go and tell him this	קִרְאוּ לִי לְפָרִיז, לְכוּ הַגִּידוּ לוֹ זֹאת	אביעל
	As for me, I shall not rest until tomorrow's morning light	וַאֲנִי לֹא אֶשְׁקֹט עַד אוֹר הַבֹּקֶר לְמָחָר	
	Which will illuminate my eyes to see them emerging from their wedding canopy.[36]	אֲשֶׁר יָאִיר עֵינַי לִרְאוֹתָם יוֹצְאִים מֵחֻפָּתָם.[36]	
JAEL	I saw the lord's face in the chamber of Rezin the priest	אֶת פְּנֵי הַשָּׂר רָאִיתִי בְּלִשְׁכַּת רְצִין הַכֹּהֵן	יעל
	And I spoke many words of love and affection to him there	וְשָׁם הִרְבֵּיתִי לְדַבֵּר עִמּוֹ דִּבְרֵי יְדִידוֹת וַאֲהָבִים	
	Without transgressing the limit of the laws of modesty.	מִבְּלִי עֲבֹר אֶת הַגְּבוּל אֲשֶׁר לְחֹק הָעֲנָוָה.	
ABIEL	**How good and how pleasant**[37] is the matter; arise, my daughter	מַה־טּוֹב וּמַה־נָּעִים[37] הַדָּבָר, קוּמִי לָךְ בִּתִּי	אביעל
	This is what I have desired – summon Paris for me	זֶה הוּא אֲשֶׁר חָפַצְתִּי – קִרְאוּ לִי לְפָרִיז	
	Hurry, go, why, I've commanded you; bring him to me	מַהֲרוּ לְכוּ הֲלֹא צִוִּיתִיכֶם, הָבִיאוּ אֹתוֹ אֵלָי	

34 Isa. 22:1, 5.

35 1 Sam. 15:25.

36 Cf. Shakespeare's 'I'll have this knot knit up tomorrow' (4.2.24). Salkinson's mention of the traditional canopy under which the couple and close family stand during a Jewish wedding ceremony serves to transform the reference into a specifically Jewish one.

37 Ps. 133:1.

	On my life! The holy priest of my LORD[38] is honourable	חֵי נַפְשִׁי! כִּי הַכֹּהֵן קְדוֹשׁ אֲדֹנָי[38] מְכֻבָּד הוּא	
	And may all the city's inhabitants honour his name.	וְכָל יוֹשְׁבֵי הָעִיר יִתְּנוּ כָבוֹד לִשְׁמוֹ.	
JAEL	Will you go with me, my nurse, to the upper chamber	הֲתֵלְכִי אִתִּי אֹמַנְתִּי, אֶל חֲדַר הָעֲלִיָּה	יעל
	To see which of the garments, jewels, and sashes	לִרְאוֹת אֶת הַבְּגָדִים, אֶת הָעֲדָיִים וְאֵת הַקִּשּׁוּרִים	
	Are best for me to wear tomorrow?	אֵיזֶה מֵהֶם טוֹבִים, כִּי אֶשָּׂאֵם בְּיוֹם מָחָר.	
ABIEL'S WIFE	Not today, we still have much time	לֹא בַּיּוֹם הַזֶּה, עוֹד עֵת רַב לָנוּ	אשת אביעל
	To see them tomorrow.	לִרְאוֹתָם בְּיוֹם מָחָר.	
ABIEL	Go with her, Nurse; tomorrow morning we shall go to the prayerhouse.[39]	לְכִי אִתָּהּ אֹמֶנֶת, לְמָחָר בַּבֹּקֶר בֵּיתָה הַתְּפִלָּה[39] נֵלֵךְ.	אביעל
	(Jael and the nurse exit)	(יעל והאומנת הולכות)	
ABIEL'S WIFE	Why, the time is too short for us to prepare everything	הֲלֹא הָעֵת תִּקְצַר לָנוּ מֵהָכִין אֶת הַכֹּל	אשת אביעל
	For night is near.	כִּי הַלַּיְלָה קָרוֹב.	
ABIEL	Desist, I am hereby ready to perform every task	הַרְפִּי, אֲנִי הִנְנִי נָכוֹן לַעֲשׂוֹת בְּכָל מְלָאכָה	אביעל
	Trust me, wife, that nothing will be lacking.	בִּטְחִי בִי אִשָּׁה, כִּי דָבָר לֹא יֶחְסָר.	
	Go help Jael choose her bridal garments	לְכִי לַעֲזֹר לְיָעֵל לִבְחֹר בִּגְדֵי כְלוּלוֹתֶיהָ	
	And I shall toil here all night – do not mock me	וַאֲנִי אֶשְׁקֹד פֹּה כָּל הַלַּיְלָה – אַל תִּלְעֲגִי לִי	
	Behold, this time I want to be the mistress of the house in your stead.	הִנֵּה חָפַצְתִּי הַפַּעַם לִהְיוֹת בַּעֲלַת הַבַּיִת תַּחְתָּיִךְ.	
	But what has become of them? They have all gone and are not here	אַךְ מֶה הָיָה לָהֶם? כֻּלָּם הָלְכוּ וְאֵינָם	
	I shall go on my own feet to see and speak with Lord Paris	אֲנִי אֵלֵךְ בְּרַגְלַי לִרְאוֹת וּלְדַבֵּר עִם פָּרִיז הַשָּׂר	

38 Cf. Shakespeare's 'this reverend holy friar' (4.2.31).

39 Cf. Shakespeare's 'we'll to church tomorrow' (4.2.37).

	In order that he might be prepared for the morning – indeed, the vigour of youth has returned to me[40]	לְמַעַן יִהְיֶה נָכוֹן לַבֹּקֶר – הֵן שָׁב אֵלַי כֹּחַ נְעוּרִים[40]	
	Since the maiden repented **to follow the best of young men.**[41]	מֵעֵת שָׁבָה הַנַּעֲרָה **לָלֶכֶת אַחֲרֵי הַטּוֹב בַּבַּחוּרִים.**[41]	
	(Abiel and his wife exit)	(אביעל ואשתו הולכים)	
SCENE 3	*Jael's chamber (Jael and the nurse)*	חדר יעל (יעל והאומנת)	מחזה ג'
JAEL	These linen garments are the best of them all	מַלְבּוּשֵׁי שֵׁשׁ אֵלֶּה הֵם הַטּוֹבִים מִכֻּלָּם	יעל
	But my dear nurse, leave me alone tonight	אַךְ אֹמַנְתִּי הַיְקָרָה, הַנִּיחִנִי לְבָדָד בַּלַּיְלָה הַזֶּה	
	For after all, you know my position and all **the sins of my youth**[42]	כִּי אַתְּ הֲלֹא יָדַעַתְּ מַעֲמָדִי וְכָל **חַטֹּאת נְעוּרַי**[42]	
	And I have many things to petition the God of mercy	וְרַבּוֹת לִי לְהַעְתִּיר אֶל אֱלֹהֵי הָרַחֲמִים	
	To guide me on the path on which I must go, for my path is not paved.	לְהַדְרִיכֵנִי בְּדֶרֶךְ אֵלֵךְ, כִּי דַרְכִּי לֹא סְלוּלָה.	
	(Abiel's wife enters)	(אשת אביעל באה)	
ABIEL'S WIFE	Have you not yet finished your business? Can I help you?	הַעוֹד לֹא כִלִּיתֶן מַעֲשֵׂיכֶן? הַאוּכַל לַעֲזֹר לָכֶן?	אשת אביעל
JAEL	Please don't, my lady mother; we have already chosen	אַל נָא אִמִּי הַגְּבִירָה, כְּבָר בָּחַרְנוּ לָנוּ	יעל
	Each thing with certainty as befits us for tomorrow.	דָּבָר דָּבָר אֶל נָכוֹן כְּנָאוָה לָנוּ לְיוֹם מָחָר.	
	Now, please leave me to be on my own	עַתָּה אָנָּא הַנִּיחִנִי נָא לִהְיוֹת לְבַדִּי	
	And take the nurse to stay up with you tonight	וְאֶת הָאֹמֶנֶת קְחִי לִשְׁקֹד עִמָּךְ בַּלַּיְלָה הַזֶּה	

40 This and the next line form a rhyming couplet. There is no precedent for this in Shakespeare's 'light/reclaimed' (4.2.46–7).

41 Ruth 3:10 לְבִלְתִּי־לֶכֶת אַחֲרֵי הַבַּחוּרִים 'not following the young men'.

42 Ps. 25:7.

	Because there is too much work for you to prepare everything	כִּי הַמְּלָאכָה רַבָּה מִכֶּן לְהָכִין כָּל דָּבָר	
	For the occasion that has suddenly descended upon us.	לַמּוֹעֵד הַבָּא עָלֵינוּ פִּתְאֹם.	
ABIEL'S WIFE	Go to your bed in peace and may your rest be pleasant	לְכִי אֶל מִשְׁכָּבֵךְ בְּשָׁלוֹם וְהַמְּנוּחָה תֶּעֱרַב לָךְ	אשת אביעל
	For you need it. *(Abiel's wife and the nurse exit)*	כִּי אֹתָהּ אַתְּ מְבַקֶּשֶׁת. (אשת אביעל והאומנת הולכות)	
JAEL	Go in peace! – God knows when I shall see you again –	לֵכְנָה בְשָׁלוֹם! – הָאֱלֹהִים יֹדֵעַ מָתַי אוֹסִיף לִרְאוֹתְכֶן –	יעל
	Something like a cold wind spreads through my tendons, **and my sinews take no rest**[43]	כְּרוּחַ קַר יָפוּחַ בְּגִידַי וְעוֹרְקַי לֹא יִשְׁכָּבוּן[43]	
	My heat disappears from its place[44] and my blood is like frost and ice	חֲמִּי נִדְעַךְ מִמְּקוֹמוֹ[44] וְדָמִי כְּקִפָּאוֹן וָקָרַח	
	I shall call to my mother to return to me to comfort me in a time of distress.	אֶקְרָא לְאִמִּי לָשׁוּב אֵלַי לְנַחֲמֵנִי בְּעֵת צָרָה.	
	My nurse! – But what use have I for the nurse now?	אֹמַנְתִּי! – אַךְ מַה־לִּי וְלָאֹמֶנֶת עַתָּה?	
	I shall drink the cup of poison myself, and let no stranger interfere with me	כּוֹס הַחֵמָה לְבַדִּי אֶשְׁתֶּה וְזָר לֹא יִתְעָרֵב עִמִּי	
	Here is the jar, here is the **potion for my bones.**[45]	פֹּה הִיא הַצִּנְצֶנֶת, פֹּה הַשִּׁקּוּי לְעַצְמוֹתַי.[45]	
	But if the potion is insipid and of no effect	אַךְ אִם הַשִּׁקּוּי תָּפֵל וּפְעוּלָּתוֹ תָּשׁוּב רֵיקָם	
	Then they will force me to marry Paris **with a strong hand**[46]	אָז הֵם יְאַלְּצוּנִי לְהִבָּעֵל לְפָּרִיז בְּיָד חֲזָקָה[46]	
	Indeed this shall not be; this dagger is ready to help me.	זֹאת הָיֹה לֹא תִהְיֶה, הַכִּידוֹן הַזֶּה נָכוֹן לְעָזְרֵנִי.	
	(Places the dagger next to her)	(תניח את הכידון אצלה)	

43 Job 30:17.
44 Job 6:17 בְּחֻמּוֹ נִדְעֲכוּ מִמְּקוֹמָם 'when it is hot they disappear from their place'.
45 Prov. 3:8 וְשִׁקּוּי לְעַצְמוֹתֶיךָ 'and a potion for your bones'.
46 Exod. 3:19, 6:1, 13:9; Deut. 5:15, 6:21, 7:8, 9:26, 26:8; Ezek. 20:33–4; Ps. 136:12; Dan. 9:15.

But perhaps **there is death in the jar**,[47] for the priest[48] is indeed cunning

אַךְ אוּלַי מָוֶת בַּצִּנְצֶנֶת,[47] כִּי הַכֹּהֵן[48] עָרֹם יַעְרִים

And he desires to kill me, because he fears for his life

וְחָפֵץ הוּא לַהֲמִיתֵנִי, כִּי יָרֵא הוּא לְנַפְשׁוֹ

Lest I marry Paris and his disgrace be revealed in public

פֶּן אֶנָּשֵׂא לְפָרִיז וְחֶרְפָּתוֹ תִּגָּלֶה בַּקָּהָל

When my first marriage, which was performed by his hand in secret, becomes known.

בְּהִוָּדַע חֲתֻנָּתִי הָרִאשׁוֹנָה שֶׁהָיְתָה עַל יָדוֹ בַּסָּתֶר.

I fear this; nevertheless, I fear in vain

מִדָּבָר הַזֶּה פַּחַד לִבִּי; בְּכָל זֹאת פַּחְדְּתִּי לַשָּׁוְא

Until now I have found his heart faithful in all his ways

עַד הֵנָּה מָצָאתִי אֶת לְבָבוֹ נֶאֱמָן בְּכָל דְּרָכָיו

But now the righteous priest is to have become **a bloody and deceitful man**?[49]

וְעַתָּה נֶהְפַּךְ כֹּהֵן צֶדֶק **לְאִישׁ דָּמִים וּמִרְמָה**?[49]

This cannot be so,[50] I shall not ascribe to him things

זֹאת לֹא זֹאת,[50] לֹא אֲחַפֵּא עָלָיו דְּבָרִים

Which are not so. –

אֲשֶׁר לֹא כֵן. –

But what will happen if they lower me into the grave in the cavern[51]

אַךְ מַה־יִּהְיֶה כַּאֲשֶׁר יוֹרִידוּנִי בְּקֶבֶר הַמְּעָרָה[51]

And I awaken before Ram comes to redeem me?

וַאֲנִי אָקִיץ טֶרֶם יָבוֹא רָם לִגְאֹל אֶת גְּאֻלָּתוֹ?

Why, then I shall suffocate in this courtyard of death

הֲלֹא אָז תֵּחָנֵק נַפְשִׁי בַּחֲצַר מָוֶת הַזֶּה

For the cavern is full of thick vapours **from one end to the other**[52]

כִּי הַמְּעָרָה מְלֵאָה אֵד עָב **מִפֶּה אֶל פֶּה**[52]

No **fresh wind**[53] enters there, and when Ram arrives there

רוּחַ צַח[53] לֹא יָבוֹא שָׁם וְכַאֲשֶׁר רָם יָבוֹא שָׁמָּה

He will find me dead. And even if I am still alive

יִמְצָא אֹתִי מֵתָה. וְאַף אִם עוֹדֶנִּי בַּחַיִּים

47 2 Kings 4:40 מָוֶת בַּסִּיר 'there is death in the pot' (referring to poison in a pot of stew).
48 Cf. Shakespeare's 'Friar' (4.3.24).
49 Ps. 5:7 (5:6 in English Bibles).
50 Ezek. 21:31 (21:26 in English Bibles).
51 See note 27.
52 Ezra 9:11.
53 Jer. 4:11. In this verse, the word צַח is typically translated as 'dry', 'burning', or 'searing', but it additionally means 'fresh' or 'clean'.

Why, the dread of death will terrify me more than fear of the night	הֲלֹא אֵימַת מָוֶת תְּבַעֲתֵנִי מִפַּחַד בַּלַּיְלָה
In this terrible place in which are buried	בַּמָּקוֹם הַנּוֹרָא הַזֶּה אֲשֶׁר שָׁם קְבוּרִים
The bones of my fathers' fathers and the members of my family from yesteryear;	עַצְמוֹת אֲבוֹת אֲבוֹתַי וּבְנֵי מִשְׁפַּחְתִּי מִשָּׁנִים קַדְמֹנִיּוֹת;
Tubal has been interred there in his blood and **his flesh rots away**[54] in his shrouds;	שָׁם הוּרַד תּוּבַל בְּדָמוֹ וְהָמֵק בְּשָׂרוֹ[54] בְּתַכְרִיכָיו;
I have heard that the ghosts gather together there at night.	שָׁם הָרְפָאִים שָׁמַעְתִּי יִתְאַסְּפוּ יַחְדָּו בַּלֵּילוֹת.
Woe, who can live in fear and **the terrors of the shadow of death**[55]	אוֹי מִי יִחְיֶה בְּחַתְחַתִּים וּבַלְהוֹת צַלְמָוֶת[55]
Driven into the dimness of darkness and anguish,[56] smoke, stink of decay, and stench;	בִּמְעוּף צוּקָה וַאֲפֵלָה מְנֻדָּח[56] קִיטוֹר צַחֲנָה וּבָאְשָׁה;
Who can stand and listen to the whistles of the ghosts	מִי יוּכַל לַעֲמֹד וְלִשְׁמֹעַ שְׁרִיקוֹת הָרְפָאִים
Why, they are like the groans of mandrakes*) when they are torn from their roots	הֲלֹא הֵנָּה כְּנַאֲקוֹת הַדּוּדָאִים*) לְעֵת יֵעָקְרוּ מִשָּׁרְשָׁם
At which anyone who hears them goes mad. And even if it is not this	אֲשֶׁר כָּל הַשּׁוֹמֵעַ יִשְׁתַּגֵּעַ. וְאַף אִם אֵין זֹאת
Why, an evil spirit dwelling between the graves will terrify me,	הֲלֹא רוּחַ רָעָה הַשֹּׁכֶנֶת בֵּין הַקְּבָרִים תְּבַעֲתֵנִי,
I shall let my spittle run over my lips, and go mad among the bones of the dead,	אוֹרִיד רִירִי עַל שְׂפָתַי וּבְעַצְמוֹת הַמֵּתִים אֶתְהוֹלָל,
I shall throw Tubal out of his coffin, to provoke him	אֶת תּוּבַל אַשְׁלִיךְ מֵאֲרוֹנוֹ לְהִתְגָּרוֹת בּוֹ
And in my burning wrath I shall seize a thigh or cheek of one of my forefathers	וּבַחֲרוֹת אַפִּי אַחֲזִיק בְּשׁוֹק אוֹ בִלְחִי מֵאַחַד אֲבוֹתַי

54 Zech. 14:12.

55 Job 24:17.

56 Isa. 8:22.

*) Mandrakes, according to the popular belief in Shakespeare's day, made a groaning sound like animals when they were torn from their roots, and all who heard their groaning went mad at the sound. [Salkinson's note]

*) הדודאים Mandrakes לפי אמונת ההמון בימי שעקספער, השמיעו קול נאקה כבעלי חיים לעת נעקרו משרשם וכל השומעים את נאקתם השתגעו למשמע אזנם.

	And smash my skull – but what is this I see?	וַאֲרַצֵּץ אֶת גֻּלְגָּלְתִּי – אַךְ מַה־זֶּה אֲנִי רֹאָה	
	Tubal's spirit is awakening in his rage, roaming towards Ram	רוּחַ תּוּבַל יֵעוֹר בְּזַעְמוֹ, יָשׁוּט לִקְרַאת רָם	
	Because he stabbed him with the edge of his sword – **stand back**,[57] Tubal!	עַל אֲשֶׁר דְּקָרוֹ בְּפִי חַרְבּוֹ – **גֶּשׁ־הָלְאָה**[57] תּוּבַל!	
	I have come to help you, my husband; for you I drink the jar.	לְעֶזְרֵךְ בַּעְלִי בָּאתִי, לְמַעַנְךָ אֲנִי שׁוֹתָה הַצִּנְצֶנֶת.	
	(Empties the jar into her mouth and falls upon the bed)	(מריקה את הצנצנת לתוך פיה ונופלת על המטה)	
SCENE 4	*Abiel's house (Abiel's wife and the nurse)*	בית אביעל (אשת אביעל והאומנת)	מחזה ד'
ABIEL'S WIFE	Take the keys and bring us **various spices and perfumes**.[58]	קְחִי אֶת הַמַּפְתְּחוֹת וְהָבִיאִי לָנוּ **זְנִים וּבְשָׂמִים**.[58]	אשת אביעל
THE NURSE	The bakers are asking there for **oil and honey**[59] for the cakes	הָאֹפִים מְבַקְּשִׁים שָׁם **שֶׁמֶן וּדְבַשׁ**[59] לְתֻפִּינִים	האומנת
	And **almonds and pomegranates**[60] for the delicacies.	**וּשְׁקֵדִים וְרִמּוֹנִים**[60] לְמִגְדִּים.	
ABIEL	Hurry, hasten, bakers – hurry, graceful daughters	עוּשׁוּ חוּשׁוּ אֹפִים – מַהֵרְנָה בְּנוֹת חֵן	אביעל
	The cock has called twice now, and the bell has tolled	הַתַּרְנְגוֹל קָרָא זֶה פַּעֲמַיִם וְהַפַּעֲמוֹן נָתַן קוֹלוֹ	
	For the third watch is starting – go, see, beautiful one[61]	כִּי אַשְׁמֹרֶת הַשְּׁלִישִׁית בָּאָה – לְכִי רְאִי יְפֵה־פִיָּה[61]	
	Whether that which is being **baked in the oven**[62] is as it should be.	**אִם מַאֲפֵה הַתַּנּוּר**[62] כַּמִּשְׁפָּט.	

57 Gen. 19:9.
58 2 Chron. 16:14 בְּשָׂמִים וּזְנִים 'perfumes and various spices'.
59 Jer. 41:8; Ezek. 16:19.
60 Tosefta *Terumot* 2:4; Babylonian Talmud *Shabbat* 22a.
61 Cf. Shakespeare's 'Angelica' (4.4.5).
62 Lev. 2:4 מַאֲפֵה תַנּוּר 'baked in an oven'.

THE NURSE	Why are you looking at the cooking pot, my lord? Why are you looking at the stove?	מַה־תַּבִּיט בַּפָּרוּר אֲדֹנִי? מַה־תַּבִּיט בְּכִירַיִם?	האומנת
	Is the way of women upon you?[63] Please go to your bed	הֲדֶרֶךְ נָשִׁים לָךְ?[63] לֶךְ־נָא אֶל מִשְׁכָּבְךָ	
	And may your eyes see sleep, lest you fall ill on the morrow.	וּרְאֵה שֵׁנָה בְעֵינֶיךָ פֶּן תֶּחֱלֶה בְּיוֹם מָחָר.	
ABIEL	How many nights have I kept guard and not seen sleep in my eyes	כַּמֶּה לֵילוֹת שָׁמַרְתִּי וְלֹא רָאִיתִי שֵׁנָה בְעֵינָי	אביעל
	For I was pursuing small delights, and I have never fallen ill	כִּי רָדַפְתִּי תַעֲנוּגוֹת קְטַנּוֹת וְלֹא חָלִיתִי מֵעוֹדִי	
	Yet now I should fall ill on the morrow because I have not slept tonight?	וְעַתָּה אֶחֱלֶה לְמָחָר כִּי לֹא יָשַׁנְתִּי הַלַּיְלָה?	
ABIEL'S WIFE	I know that you have lain in wait at night from the days of your youth	יָדַעְתִּי כִּי אוֹרֵב בַּלֵּילוֹת הָיִיתָ מִימֵי נְעוּרֶיךָ	אשת אביעל
	And you have kept guard in order to hunt **a silly dove**[64]	וְלָצוּד יוֹנָה פוֹתָה[64] שָׁמַרְתָּ אַשְׁמֻרוֹת עַל הַמִּשְׁמָר	
	But such times are no more, and I shall guard you from keeping guard.	אַךְ עִתּוֹת כָּאֵלֶּה אֵין עוֹד וּמֵאַשְׁמֻרוֹת אֲנִי אֶשְׁמְרֶךָּ.	
	(Abiel's wife and the nurse exit)	(אשת אביעל והאומנת הולכות)	
ABIEL	This is the way of women, it is jealousy, and it will become a lament –	זֹאת דֶּרֶךְ נָשִׁים, קִנְאָה הִיא וַתְּהִי לְקִינָה –	אביעל
	(Servants bearing meat-forks, wood, and baskets)	(עבדים נושאים מזלגות עצים וסלים)	
	What are you bearing?	מָה אַתֶּם נֹשְׂאִים?	
FIRST SERVANT	A basket for the cooking women's house, but I do not know what is inside it.	סַל לְבֵית הַמְבַשְּׁלוֹת וְאֵינֶנִּי יוֹדֵעַ מַה־בְּתוֹכוֹ.	עבד אחד

63 Gen. 31:35 כִּי־דֶרֶךְ נָשִׁים לִי 'for the way of women is upon me' (spoken by the matriarch Rachel).
64 Hosea 7:11.

ABIEL	Pave a road for one bearing a basket,[65] so that he might go quickly	סֹלּוּ מְסִלָּה לְנֹשֵׂא סַל,[65] לְמַעַן יְמַהֵר לָכֶת	אביעל
	(To a second servant) Your wood is wet; go call Peter	(לעבד שני) עֵצֶיךָ לַחִים הֵם לְכָה קְרָא אֶל פֶּטֶר	
	And he will show you dry wood.	וְהוּא יוֹרְךָ עֵצִים יְבֵשִׁים.	
THE SECOND SERVANT	What might you have to do with Peter, my lord? Behold, I am here	מַה־לְּךָ אֲדֹנִי וּלְפֶטֶר? אֲנִי הִנְנִי פֹה	העבד השני
	And no dry block of wood is missing.	וּבוּל עֵץ יָבֵשׁ לֹא יֶחְסָר.	
ABIEL	Your mouth has testified against you that you are a block of wood[66] –	פִּיךָ עָנָה בְךָ כִּי בוּל עֵץ אָתָּה[66] –	אביעל
	But **the morning has dawned**,[67] and Paris is to come with the musicians	אַךְ הַבֹּקֶר אוֹר[67] וּפָרִיז יָבוֹא עִם הַמְנַגְּנִים	
	For so he told me, and I also hear the sound of his footsteps.	כִּי כֵן הִגִּיד לִי וְגַם קוֹל פְּעָמָיו אֲנִי שׁוֹמֵעַ.	
	(The sound of singing outside)	(קול זמרה מחוץ)	
	Nurse! – Wife! – Where are you, Nurse?	אֹמֶנֶת! – אִשָּׁה! – אַיֵּה אֵיפֹה אַתְּ אֹמֶנֶת?	
	(The nurse re-enters)	(האומנת שבה)	
	Go wake up Jael, put her bridal garments on her	לְכִי הָעִירִי אֶת יָעֵל, שִׁיתִי בִגְדֵי כְלוּלֹתֶיהָ עָלֶיהָ	
	And I shall go to Paris and converse with him a little	וַאֲנִי אֵלֵךְ לִקְרַאת פָּרִיז וְאָשִׂיחָה עִמּוֹ מְעָט	
	Hurry, hasten, why do you stand, behold, the groom is coming	מַהֲרִי חוּשִׁי לָמָּה תַעֲמֹדִי, הֶחָתָן הִנֵּה בָא	
	Hurry, I command you. *(Exeunt)*	מַהֲרִי הֲלֹא צִוִּיתִיךְ. (הולכים)	
SCENE 5	*Jael lies in her bedchamber (The nurse enters)*	יעל שוכבת בחדר מטתה (האומנת באה)	מחזה ה'

65 This line contains a play on words based on a sound correspondence and shared etymology between the verbal root ס.ל.ל. 'to pave' and the nouns מְסִלָּה 'road' and סַל 'basket'. This wordplay most likely represents an attempt to find an equivalent for Shakespeare's pun between 'logs' (4.4.15, 17) and 'loggerhead' (4.4.19), which begins in the corresponding line (given that the Hebrew translation of the latter exchange is not itself a pun).

66 Salkinson has omitted Shakespeare's 'Mass, and well said' (4.4.19).

67 Gen. 44:3.

THE NURSE	Lady! Delicate bride! – **Blessed above women be Jael!**[68] –	גְּבִירָה! כַּלָּה עֲדִינָה! – תְּבֹרַךְ מִנָּשִׁים יָעֵל![68] –	האומנת
	Innocent sleeping ewe-lamb – is it time for you to sleep? It is a disgrace	כִּבְשָׂה תְּמִימָה יְשֵׁנָה – הַעֵת לָךְ לִישׁוֹן? חֶרְפָּה הִיא	
	It is a disgrace for you, my only one; when will you arise, bride?	חֶרְפָּה הִיא לָךְ יְחִידָתִי, מָתַי תָּקוּמִי כַּלָּה?	
	There is no word on your tongue, for the sleep is sweet for you	אֵין מִלָּה בִלְשׁוֹנֵךְ, כִּי הַשֵּׁנָה לָךְ מְתוּקָה	
	Continue to sleep a long sleep, as long as seven days	הוֹסִיפִי לִישׁוֹן שֵׁנָה אֲרֻכָּה עַד שִׁבְעַת יָמִים	
	For I know well that on the next night	כִּי נַפְשִׁי יֹדַעַת מְאֹד, כִּי בַלַּיְלָה הַבָּא	
	Paris will rob your sleep from your eyes and will not give you rest	יִגְזַל פָּרִיז שְׁנָתֵךְ מֵעֵינַיִךְ וְלֹא יִתֵּן לָךְ מְנוּחָה	
	Perhaps I have sinned with my lips, but there is forgiveness with the Lord –	אוּלַי חָטָאתִי בִשְׂפָתַי, אַךְ עִם אֲדֹנָי הַסְּלִיחָה –	
	How sleep has overcome her – I shall wake her, for the appointed time has come	אֵיךְ גָּבְרָה עָלֶיהָ הַשֵּׁנָה – אָעִירָהּ כִּי בָא מוֹעֵד	
	Arise, my lady, arise lest you be put to shame by the lord	קוּמִי לָךְ גְּבִרְתִּי קוּמִי פֶּן תֵּבוֹשִׁי מִפְּנֵי הַשָּׂר	
	When he finds you in bed? Is it not so, Jael?	כִּי יִמְצָאֵךְ בַּמִּטָּה? הַאֵין זֹאת יָעֵל?	
	But what is this? Has she donned linen garments	אַךְ מַה־זֹּאת? הַאִם לָבְשָׁה בִּגְדֵי שֵׁשׁ	
	And adorned herself with her jewels and sashes, and then gone to sleep again?	וַתַּעַד עֶדְיָהּ וְקִשּׁוּרֶיהָ וַתִּישַׁן פַּעַם שֵׁנִית?	
	Such knowledge is too wondrous for me;[69] I shall quickly wake her so that I may know	פְּלִיאָה דַעַת מִמֶּנִּי,[69] אָעִירָהּ מַהֵר וְאֵדָעָה	
	My lady, my lady, my lady, arise! –	גְּבִרְתִּי, גְּבִרְתִּי, גְּבִרְתִּי קוּמִי! –	
	What do my eyes see? Oh, oh! Come, help!	מָה עֵינַי תִּרְאֶינָה? הוֹ הוֹ! בּוֹאוּ הוֹשִׁיעוּ!	

68 Judg. 5:24.
69 Ps. 139:6.

	The bride is dead, she is dead in the bed!	הַכַּלָּה מֵתָה הִיא, מֵתָה הִיא בַּמִּטָּה	
	Woe to me that I was born – support me, lest I die	אוֹי לִי כִּי נוֹלַדְתִּי – סַמְכוּנִי פֶּן אֶגְוָע	
	Oh, lord! Oh, lady!	הוֹי אָדוֹן! הוֹי גְּבִירָה!	
	(Abiel's wife enters)	(אשת אביעל באה)	
ABIEL'S WIFE	What is this noise?	מָה הַקּוֹל הַזֶּה?	אשת אביעל
THE NURSE	This is a day of distress.	יוֹם צָרָה הַיּוֹם הַזֶּה.	האומנת
ABIEL'S WIFE	What has happened?	מַה־נִּהְיָתָה?	אשת אביעל
THE NURSE	Look what has happened – a day of **distress and anguish**![70]	רְאִי מַה־נִּהְיָתָה – יוֹם צָרָה וְצוּקָה![70]	האומנת
ABIEL'S WIFE	Woe, woe, woe! – My daughter, my only daughter	אוֹיָה אוֹיָה אוֹיָה! – בִּתִּי בִּתִּי יְחִידָתִי	אשת אביעל
	Come back, live, my daughter, open your eyes, oh, I shall die with you –	שׁוּבִי, חֲיִי בִּתִּי, פִּקְחִי עֵינַיִךְ, אוֹ עִמֵּךְ אָמוּתָה –	
	Help! – Help! –	הוֹשִׁיעָה! – הוֹשִׁיעָה! –	
	(Abiel enters)	(אביעל בא)	
ABIEL	Why do you delay? Bring Jael	לָמָּה זֶה תְּאַחֵרְנָה? הֲבִיאֶינָה אֶת יָעֵל	אביעל
	Behold, the groom has arrived.	הֶחָתָן הִנֵּה בָא.	
THE NURSE	She has perished and died – woe to this day!	הִיא גָוְעָה וַתָּמָת – אוֹי לַיּוֹם הַזֶּה.	האומנת
ABIEL'S WIFE	Woe to this day! She is dead, dead!	אוֹי לַיּוֹם הַזֶּה! מֵתָה הִיא מֵתָה!	אשת אביעל
ABIEL	Leave her to me so that I may see – her flesh is cold as ice	הֲנִיחֶינָה לִי וְאֶרְאֶה – בְּשָׂרָהּ קַר כַּקָּרַח	אביעל
	Her blood has frozen in her veins, every limb and joint is stiff	דָּמֶיהָ קָפְאוּ בְּעוֹרְקֶיהָ, כָּל אֵבֶר וָפֶרֶק קָשֶׁה	
	Her breath has left her, has long ago left her lips	רוּחָהּ עָזְבָה אֹתָהּ, עָזְבָה אֶת שְׂפָתֶיהָ זֶה־כַּמָּה	
	Like **the frost of heaven**[71] falling on **the flowers of the field**[72]	כִּכְפוֹר שָׁמַיִם[71] נֹפֵל עֲלֵי צִיץ הַשָּׂדֶה[72]	

70 Isa. 30:6; Prov. 1:27.
71 Job 38:29.
72 Isa. 40:6; Ps. 103:15.

	So does death lie upon her.	כֵּן רָבַץ הַמָּוֶת עָלֶיהָ.	
THE NURSE	Oh, day of **distress and anguish**.[73]	הוֹי יוֹם צָרָה וְצוּקָה.[73]	האומנת
ABIEL'S WIFE	Time of **darkness and the shadow of death**.[74]	עֵת חֹשֶׁךְ וְצַלְמָוֶת.[74]	אשת אביעל
ABIEL	Death has devoured my only daughter and summoned me for weeping and mourning	הַמָּוֶת טָרַף יְחִידָתִי וַיִּקְרָאֵנִי לִבְכִי וּלְאֵבֶל	אביעל
	But **it has made my tongue cleave to the roof of my mouth**;[75] like a mute I am unable to speak.	וְהוּא הִדְבִּיק לְשׁוֹנִי לְחִכִּי,[75] כְּאִלֵּם לֹא אוּכַל דַּבֵּר.	
	(Rezin the priest and Paris with musicians enter)	(רצין הכהן ופריז עם מנגנים באים)	
REZIN	Let us go! Is the bride ready to go to the house of God?[76]	הָבָה! הַנְכוֹנָה הַכַּלָּה לָבוֹא לְבֵית הָאֱלֹהִים?[76]	רצין
ABIEL	She is ready to go, but she will never return from there –	הִיא נְכוֹנָה לָבוֹא וְלֹא תָשׁוּב מִשָּׁם עַד עוֹלָם –	אביעל
	Oh, my son, my son, the night before the day of the wedding	הוֹי בְּנִי בְּנִי, הַלַּיְלָה לִפְנֵי יוֹם הַחֲתֻנָּה	
	Death came to your bride, look, there she lies	בָּא הַמָּוֶת אֶל כַּלָּתְךָ, רְאֵה שָׁם הִיא שֹׁכֶבֶת	
	Like the rose of Sharon[77] she was budding, **but it, being stronger than her, has forced itself upon her**[78]	כַּחֲבַצֶּלֶת הַשָּׁרוֹן[77] פָּרְחָה וְהוּא הֶחֱזִיק בָּהּ וַיְעַנֶּהָ[78]	
	Death is my son-in-law, death will be my heir	הַמָּוֶת הוּא חֲתָנִי, הַמָּוֶת הוּא יוֹרֵשׁ אֹתִי	
	It has taken my daughter for itself, it will take my life	הוּא לָקַח לוֹ אֶת בִּתִּי, הוּא יִקַּח אֶת נַפְשִׁי	
	I shall die now and leave everything in its hand.	אָמוּתָה הַפַּעַם וְאֶעֱזֹב אֶת כֹּל בְּיָדוֹ.	

73 Isa. 30:6; Prov. 1:27.
74 Ps. 107:10, 14; Job 3:5, 10:21.
75 Ps. 137:6 תִּדְבַּק־לְשׁוֹנִי ׀ לְחִכִּי 'may my tongue cleave to the roof of my mouth'.
76 Cf. Shakespeare's 'to church' (4.5.33).
77 Song of Songs 2:1.
78 2 Sam. 13:14 וַיֶּחֱזַק מִמֶּנָּה וַיְעַנֶּהָ 'but he, being stronger than her, forced himself upon her'.

PARIS	How I have waited, how I have anticipated[79]	עַד כַּמָּה הוֹחַלְתִּי, עַד כַּמָּה צִפִּיתִי[79]	פריז
	For this day to come, yet now *this* is the day for which I had hoped.	מָתַי יָבוֹא הַיּוֹם הַזֶּה וְהוּא הַיּוֹם שֶׁקִּוִּיתִי.	
ABIEL'S WIFE	Cursed be this day! Let it be a damnation and a curse in the land	אָרוּר הַיּוֹם הַזֶּה! יְהִי לִמְאֵרָה וְלִקְלָלָה בָּאָרֶץ	אשת אביעל
	Let evil angels terrify it and let no blessing come upon it	יְבַעֲתֻהוּ מַלְאֲכֵי* רָעִים וּבְרָכָה אַל תָּבוֹא בּוֹ	
	It is a more evil and bitter day than all the days of trouble in the world.	הוּא יוֹם רַע וָמַר מִכָּל יְמוֹת עָמָל בֶּחָלֶד.	
	Just one daughter, just one single, tender girl	רַק בַּת אַחַת, רַק יַלְדָּה רַכָּה יְחִידָה	
	Did I have in my time, to restore my spirit	הָיְתָה לִּי בְּעוֹלָמִי לִהְיוֹת לִי לִמְשִׁיבַת נָפֶשׁ	
	But death, bitter and cruel, has torn her from my hand.	וְהַמָּוֶת מַר וְאַכְזָרִי טָרַף אֹתָהּ מִיָּדִי.	
THE NURSE	**Woe is me,**[80] woe and sorrow! Woe to this day!	**אַלְלַי לִי,**[80] אוֹי וַאֲבוֹי! אוֹי לַיּוֹם הַזֶּה!	האומנת
	Woe to my eyes, which see this; I have never seen such a thing	אוֹי לְעֵינַי הָרֹאוֹת זֹאת, לֹא רָאִיתִי כֵן מֵעוֹדִי	
	Oh, day of rage and anger, day of fury and disgrace	אֲהָהּ יוֹם זַעַף וְחָרוֹן, יוֹם רֹגֶז וּנְאָצָה	
	Who has seen such a day, **it is terrible and dreadful**[81]	מִי רָאָה יוֹם כָּזֶה, **אָיֹם וְנוֹרָא הוּא**[81]	
	As destruction from the Almighty it has come;[82] as for that day, **let it not be blessed.**[83]	**כְּשׁוֹד מִשַּׁדַּי בָּא,**[82] הַיּוֹם הַהוּא **אַל יְהִי בָּרוּךְ.**[83]	
PARIS	**Death, the king of terrors,**[84] **has swallowed me, it has devoured me, it has crushed me**	**בְּלָעַנִי אֲכָלַנִי הֲמָמַנִי הַמָּוֶת מֶלֶךְ בַּלָּהוֹת**[84]	פריז

79 This and the next line form a rhyming couplet. There is no precedent for this in Shakespeare's 'face/this' (4.5.41–2).
80 Mic. 7:1; Job 10:15.
81 Hab. 1:7.
82 Isa. 13:16; Joel 1:15.
83 Jer. 20:14.
84 Job 18:14.

* מַלְאֲכֵי

	It has made me an empty vessel,[85] a vessel full of shame and humiliation	כְּלִי רִיק הִצִּיגַנִי,[85] כְּלִי מָלֵא בוּשָׁה וּכְלִמָּה	
	What is my life that I should hope,[86] what is my hope, that I should live?	מֶה חַיַּי כִּי אֲיַחֵל,[86] מַה־תּוֹחַלְתִּי כִּי אֶחְיֶה	
	Where is my love! Where is my life! My life is not alive	אֵי אַהֲבָתִי! אֵי חַיָּתִי! חַיָּתִי אֵינֶנָּה בַּחַיִּים	
	And my love descends into the grave.	וְאַהֲבָתִי יֹרֶדֶת קָבֶר.	
ABIEL	I am spurned, **I am broken and feeble;**[87] I have fallen, I cannot get up	נִמְאַסְתִּי נִדְכֵּיתִי נְפוּגֹתִי,[87] נָפַלְתִּי לֹא אוּכַל קוּם	אביעל
	Oh, day of rage! Why **have you called an appointed time against me**[88]	הוֹי יוֹם זַעַם! מַדּוּעַ קָרָאתָ עָלַי מוֹעֵד[88]	
	To destroy me, to destroy my house and **turn my feast into mourning?**[89]	לְהַשְׁמִידֵנִי, לְהַשְׁמִיד בֵּיתִי וְלַהֲפֹךְ חַגִּי לְאֵבֶל?[89]	
	My daughter, my daughter Jael! You are not Jael, but rather my life	בִּתִּי בִּתִּי יָעֵל! – לֹא יָעֵל, בִּלְתִּי נַפְשִׁי אָתְּ	
	For your death is my death, and having been bereaved I perish[90] –	כִּי מוֹתֵךְ מוֹתִי וְכַאֲשֶׁר שָׁכֹלְתִּי אָבָדְתִּי[90] –	
	My daughter, my daughter has perished, and with my daughter my delight has also been buried.	בִּתִּי בִּתִּי אָבְדָה וְעִם בִּתִּי נִקְבְּרָה תַּאֲוָתִי.	
REZIN	That's enough from you, **those who curse the day**![91] Do not make the sound of your wailing heard	רַב לָכֶם אֹרְרֵי יוֹם![91] אַל תַּשְׁמִיעוּ קוֹל יִלְלַתְכֶם	רצין
	With the sound of mournful wailing the break will not heal.	בְּקוֹל יִלְלַת שֶׁבֶר לֹא תַעֲלֶה אֲרֻכָה לַשָּׁבֶר.	
	Jael had three masters: her mother, her father, and her God	שְׁלֹשָׁה אֲדֹנִים הָיוּ לְיָעֵל: אִמָּהּ אָבִיהָ וֵאלֹהֶיהָ	
	But now she has one master, **for God has taken her**[92]	וְעַתָּה אָדוֹן אֶחָד לָהּ, כִּי לָקַח אֹתָהּ אֱלֹהִים[92]	

85 Jer. 51:34 אֲכָלַנִי הֲמָמַנִי נְבוּכַדְרֶאצַּר מֶלֶךְ בָּבֶל הִצִּיגַנִי כְּלִי רִיק בְּלָעַנִי 'Nebuchadrezzar the king of Babylon has devoured me, he has crushed me, he has made me an empty vessel, he has swallowed me'.
86 Job 6:11 מַה־כֹּחִי כִּי־אֲיַחֵל 'what is my strength, that I should hope'.
87 Ps. 38:9 (38:8 in English Bibles) נְפוּגוֹתִי וְנִדְכֵּיתִי 'I am feeble and broken'.
88 Lam. 1:15 קָרָא עָלַי מוֹעֵד 'He has called an appointed time against me'.
89 Amos 8:10 וְהָפַכְתִּי חַגֵּיכֶם לְאֵבֶל 'and I shall turn your feasts into mourning'.
90 This and the next line form a rhyming couplet, mirroring Shakespeare's 'dead/buried' (4.5.63–4).
91 Job 3:8.
92 Gen. 5:24 כִּי־לָקַח אֹתוֹ אֱלֹהִים 'for God took him'.

And it is better for her now than previously; one master is better than three.	וְטוֹב לָהּ עַתָּה מֵאָז, טוֹב אָדוֹן אֶחָד מִשְּׁלֹשָׁה.
Your portion in her you could not save from death	חֶלְקְכֶם בָּהּ אַתֶּם, לֹא יְכָלְתֶּם לְהַצִּיל מִמָּוֶת
But the portion which belongs to the LORD is preserved for eternal life	וְהַחֵלֶק אֲשֶׁר לַאֲדֹנָי הוּא שָׁמוּר לְחַיֵּי נֶצַח
Indeed, to magnify and elevate her was your whole desire	הֵן לְגַדֵּל וּלְרוֹמֵם אֹתָהּ, הָיָה כָּל חֶפְצֶכֶם*
Yet now that she is elevated, for she has ascended on high	וְאַחֲרֵי אֲשֶׁר רָמָה הִיא, כִּי עָלְתָה לַמָּרוֹם
You weep and rage as if you view her happiness with hostility.	תִּבְכּוּ אַתֶּם וְתִתְמַרְמְרוּ כְּמוֹ רָעָה עֵינְכֶם בְּאָשְׁרָהּ.
You have been intoxicated in your daughter's love;[93] this love is not good	**שְׁגִיתֶם בְּאַהֲבַת בִּתְּכֶם**,[93] לֹא טוֹבָה הָאַהֲבָה הַזֹּאת
She is **bound in the bundle of life**,[94] so what else do you desire?	הִיא **צְרוּרָה בִּצְרוֹר הַחַיִּים**[94] וּמַה־תַּחְפְּצוּ עוֹד?
A woman married to a husband cannot delight in his love forever	אִשָּׁה בְּעוּלַת בַּעַל לֹא תִתְעַנַּג בְּאַהֲבָתוֹ לָנֶצַח
But **happy is the woman whose husband is her maker**,[95] the LORD.	אַךְ **אַשְׁרֵי הָאִשָּׁה אֲשֶׁר בְּעָלֶיהָ עֹשֶׂיהָ**[95] אֲדֹנָי.
Therefore wipe your tears; put blossoms and flowers[96]	עַל כֵּן מְחוּ דִמְעַתְכֶם; שִׂימוּ צִיצִים וּפְרָחִים[96]
Upon your beloved daughter, and bear her in her bridal garments	עַל בִּתְּכֶם הָאֲהוּבָה וּשְׂאוּ אֹתָהּ בְּבִגְדֵי כְלוּלֹתֶיהָ

93 Prov. 5:19 בְּאַהֲבָתָהּ תִּשְׁגֶּה תָמִיד 'may you always be intoxicated in her love'.

94 1 Sam. 25:29. In the biblical verse this expression is a metaphor for long life, but in postbiblical Jewish tradition it denotes the afterlife (Bar-Efrat 2004: 609–10); Salkinson is using it in the latter sense.

95 Ps. 1:1 אַשְׁרֵי־הָאִישׁ אֲשֶׁר ׀ לֹא הָלַךְ בַּעֲצַת רְשָׁעִים 'happy is the man who has not walked in the counsel of the wicked'.

96 Cf. Shakespeare's 'rosemary' (4.5.79), a symbol of remembrance (Weis 2012: 309, note 79). Flowers are not traditionally a feature of Jewish funerals. As in the case of the open coffin mentioned in note 26, Salkinson has not substituted Shakespeare's reference with a Jewish equivalent. However, he has replaced the mention of a specific herb, which would likely have meant little to readers, with one of generic 'blossoms and flowers', which would have been identifiable as a Christian funeral custom.

* חֶפְצְכֶם

Perfumed with myrrh and frankincense[97] to **the house appointed for all the living.**[98]

מְקֻטֶּרֶת מוֹר וּלְבוֹנָה[97] לְבֵית מוֹעֵד לְכָל חָי.[98]

Eyes of flesh[99] **weep abundantly**[100] for the one **going to his eternal home**[101, 102]

עֵינֵי בָשָׂר[99] יוֹרְדוֹת בַּבֶּכִי,[100] לַהוֹלֵךְ אֶל בֵּית עוֹלָמוֹ[101, 102]

But for **those who have knowledge of the Most High,**[103] tears are laughter.

אַךְ יֹדְעֵי דַעַת עֶלְיוֹן,[103] דְּמָעוֹת מִשְׂחָק לָמוֹ.

ABIEL My house, a house of feasting, has turned into a house of mourning

אביעל בֵּיתִי בֵּית מִשְׁתֶּה נֶהְפַּךְ לְבֵית אֵבֶל

Merrymaking and dancing into laments, and **damsels playing timbrels**[104] into professional mourning women

הִלּוּלִים וּמְחוֹלוֹת לְקִינוֹת וַעֲלָמוֹת תּוֹפֵפוֹת[104] לִמְקֹנְנוֹת

Robes and precious gifts into **sackcloth and ashes,**[105] and the wedding canopy[106] into a coffin and shroud

שְׂמָלוֹת וּמִגְדָּנוֹת לְשַׂק וָאֵפֶר[105] וְחֻפָּה[106] לְאָרוֹן וְתַכְרִיכִים

Joyous cries of young men into an elegy and songs of joy into **sorrow and sighing**[107]

מִצְהֲלוֹת בַּחוּרִים לְמִסְפֵּד וְשִׁירֵי שָׂשׂוֹן לְיָגוֹן וַאֲנָחָה[107]

Perfumes and various prepared spices[108] to fill the bed of my dead one in the grave

בְּשָׂמִים וּזְנִים מְרֻקָּחִים[108] לְמַלֵּא מִשְׁכַּב מֵתִי בַּקֶּבֶר

And blossoms and flowers and sashes into **an ornament of grace**[109] for burial

וְצִיצִים וּפְרָחִים וְקִשּׁוּרִים לְלִוְיַת חֵן[109] לִקְבוּרָה

All the valuables which I prepared have changed and become the opposite.

כָּל הַכְּבֻדָּה אֲשֶׁר הֲכִינוֹתִי שִׁנְּתָה פָּנֶיהָ וַתְּהִי לְהֶפֶךְ.

---

97 Song of Songs 3:6.
98 Job 30:23 (a reference to death). Cf. Shakespeare's 'to church' (4.5.81).
99 Job 10:4.
100 Isa. 15:3 יֹרֵד בַּבֶּכִי 'weeping abundantly'.
101 Alshekh to Isa. 51, Prov. 6, Eccles. 12.
102 This and the next line form a rhyming couplet, mirroring Shakespeare's 'lament/merriment' (4.5.82–3).
103 Num. 24:16.
104 Ps. 68:26 (68:25 in English Bibles).
105 Isa. 58:5; Esther 4:1, 3; Dan. 9:3 (a biblical sign of mourning).
106 See note 36.
107 Isa. 35:10, 51:11.
108 2 Chron. 16:14.
109 Prov. 1:9, 4:9.

REZIN	Go, my lord Abiel, prepare yourself, you and your wife	לֵךְ אֲבִיעֵל אֲדֹנִי, הִכּוֹן לְךָ אַתָּה וְאִשְׁתֶּךָ	רצין
	And Lord Paris with you; be prepared, the three of you	וְהַשָּׂר* פָּרִיז עִמָּכֶם; הֱיוּ נְכוֹנִים שְׁלָשְׁתְּכֶם	
	To follow the coffin to the grave there in the cavern.	לָצֵאת אַחֲרֵי הָאָרוֹן אֶל הַקֶּבֶר שָׁם בַּמְּעָרָה.	
	Behold, anger looks down from above and the heavens thunder[110]	הִנֵּה קֶצֶף נִשְׁקָף מֵעָל וְשָׁמַיִם רָעֲמוּ רָעַם[110]	
	Declare the heavens innocent and do not hate the LORD's discipline	הַצְדִּיקוּ דִּין שָׁמַיִם וּמוּסַר אֲדֹנָי אַל תִּשְׂנָאוּ	
	For if you provoke further anger, the fury will not pass	כִּי אִם עוֹד תַּקְצִיפוּ, לֹא יַעֲבֹר זָעַם	
	Therefore let yourselves take instruction, give in, **tremble, and do not sin.**[111]	לָכֵן הִוָּסְרוּ הִכָּנְעוּ רִגְזוּ אַל תֶּחֱטָאוּ.[111]	
	(All exit)	(כלם הולכים)	

End of Second[112] Part.[113] — תם חלק שני.[112,113]

110 This and the next three lines form an ABAB rhyming sequence, which resembles Shakespeare's 'ill/will' (4.5.94–5) except that the latter is a single rhyming couplet.

111 Ps. 4:5 (4:4 in English Bibles) רִגְזוּ וְאַל־תֶּחֱטָאוּ 'tremble and do not sin'.

112 Sic; should be Fourth Part.

113 Salkinson has omitted the rest of this scene (4.5.100–41), which consists of an exchange between Peter and the musicians. The omitted lines appear in the Quarto and Folio versions, and as such would most likely have been printed in the English version which Salkinson utilized. His decision not to translate these lines (which are not explicitly essential to the plot of the play) may be rooted in the fact that they contain a number of puns and would therefore have been difficult to render into Hebrew.

* וְהַשָּׂר

Fifth Part / חלק חמישי

SCENE I	*A street in Mantua*	(רחוב במנטובה)	מחזה א'
RAM	If **visions of the night**[1] are honest and faithful	אִם חֶזְיוֹנוֹת לַיְלָה[1] כֵּנִים הֵם וְנֶאֱמָנִים	רם
	And dreams **when deep sleep falls**[2] do not speak falsely	וַחֲלוֹמוֹת בִּנְפֹל תַּרְדֵּמָה[2] לֹא שָׁוְא יְדַבֵּרוּ	
	Then my waiting will not be prolonged, and my salvation is close.	אָז לֹא תִמָּשֵׁךְ תּוֹחַלְתִּי וּתְשׁוּעָתִי קְרוֹבָה לָבוֹא.	
	Because of this, this morning a new spirit has come upon me	לָזֹאת בַּבֹּקֶר הַזֶּה, רוּחַ חֲדָשָׁה לָבְשָׁה אֹתִי	
	And in my mind I imagine that my love sits before me	וּבְקֶרֶב לְבָבִי דִּמִּיתִי כִּי אֲהֻבָתִי לְפָנַי יֹשֶׁבֶת	
	Like a queen in the inner chamber of a palace, and I have become like a king	כְּמַלְכָּה בְּהֵיכָל פְּנִימָה וָאֱהִי בְעֵינַי כְּמֶלֶךְ	
	For in my dream I saw that I was dead	כִּי בַּחֲלוֹמִי רָאִיתִי וְהִנֵּה אָנֹכִי מֵת	
	(How strange is the dream which a dead man can see)	(מַה־זָּר הַחֲלוֹם אֲשֶׁר הַמֵּת יוּכַל לִרְאוֹת)	
	When behold, Jael came **and kissed me with the kisses of her mouth**[3]	וְהִנֵּה יָעֵל בָּאָה וַתְּנַשְּׁקֵנִי מִנְּשִׁיקוֹת פִּיהָ[3]	
	And when her lips touched my lips, she restored my life to me	וּבִנְגֹעַ שְׂפָתֶיהָ בִּשְׂפָתַי הֵשִׁיבָה לִי אֶת נִשְׁמָתִי	
	And I tasted the sweetness of her lips and the honey of her mouth like **the precious things of heaven**[4]	וָאֶטְעַם מֶתֶק שְׂפָתֶיהָ וְנֹפֶת פִּיהָ כְּמֶגֶד שָׁמַיִם[4]	
	Which cannot be told. And now, what can I say	אֲשֶׁר לֹא יְסֻפַּר. וְעַתָּה מָה אֹמַר וַאֲדַבֵּר	
	If the shadow of love is sweeter than any pure honey	אִם צֵל הָאַהֲבָה מָתוֹק מִכָּל נֹפֶת	
	How sweet is love!	מַה מְּתוּקָה הִיא הָאַהֲבָה!	

1 Job 4:13.
2 Job 4:13.
3 Song of Songs 1:2 יִשָּׁקֵנִי מִנְּשִׁיקוֹת פִּיהוּ 'let him kiss me with the kisses of his mouth'.
4 Deut. 33:13.

	(Balthasar enters)	(בלטאזר בא)	
	Greetings, Balthasar! What have you brought me from Verona?	הֲשָׁלוֹם בֶּלְטַאזָר? מָה הֵבֵאתָ לִי מִוֵּירוֹנָה?	
	Are there no letters in your hand from the priest for me?	הַאֵין בְּיָדְךָ אִגְּרוֹת מֵאֵת הַכֹּהֵן אֵלָי?	
	How fares my bride? Does my father still live?	מַה־שְּׁלוֹם כַּלָּתִי? הַעוֹד אָבִי חָי?	
	And I ask again: how fares my bride Jael?	וְהִנְנִי מוֹסִיף לִשְׁאוֹל: הֲשָׁלוֹם לְיָעֵל כַּלָּתִי?	
	For she is my only desire and if she is well	כִּי הִיא כָּל חֶפְצִי וְאִם שָׁלוֹם לָהּ	
	I shall be well, and shall know no evil.	שָׁלוֹם יִהְיֶה לִּי וְלֹא אֵדַע כָּל רָע.	
BALTHASAR	She and you both fare well, and shall know no evil	שָׁלוֹם גַּם לָהּ וָלָךְ וְלֹא תֵּדַע כָּל רָע	בלטאזר
	For she has been gathered in peace to the graves of her forefathers	כִּי הִיא נֶאֶסְפָה בְשָׁלוֹם אֶל קִבְרוֹת אֲבוֹתֶיהָ	
	And her spirit has ascended on high to the God who had given it to her	וְרוּחָהּ עָלְתָה לַמָּרוֹם אֶל הָאֱלֹהִים אֲשֶׁר נְתָנָהּ	
	When I saw this, I hastened to come and tell you	אֲנִי בִּרְאוֹתִי זֹאת מִהַרְתִּי לָבוֹא וּלְהַגֶּד לָךְ	
	Even though it distresses me to report such tidings	אַף כִּי צַר לִי לְבַשֶּׂרְךָ בְּשֹׂרָה כָּזֹאת	
	But you commanded me to tell you everything which has happened.	אַךְ אַתָּה צִוִּיתַנִי לְהַגִּדְךָ כָּל אֲשֶׁר נַעֲשָׂה.	
RAM	If the matter is so, whom else have I to fear?	אִם כֵּן הַדָּבָר, מִמִּי אִירָא עוֹד?	רם
	Those who dwell on earth are as nothing to me, and I charge the heavenly host with folly –	יֹשְׁבֵי הָאָרֶץ כְּאַיִן לִי וּבִצְבָא הַמָּרוֹם אָשִׂים תָּהֳלָה –	
	As for you, bring a scroll of paper, a pen, and ink to my lodgings	וְאַתָּה הָבֵא לְבֵית מְלוֹנִי גִּלָּיוֹן עֵט וּדְיוֹ	
	And hire horses for me, because I must go to Verona tonight.	וּשְׂכָר לִי סוּסִים כִּי עָלַי לָבוֹא לְוֵירוֹנָה הַלָּיְלָה.	
BALTHASAR	Please, my lord, listen to me; before you do anything	אָנָּא אֲדֹנִי שְׁמָעֵנִי, טֶרֶם תַּעֲשֶׂה דָּבָר	בלטאזר

	Ponder the path of your ways,[5] for your face testifies against you	פַּלֵּס מַעְגַּל דְּרָכֶיךָ,[5] כִּי פָנֶיךָ יְעִידוּן בְּךָ	
	That you are considering doing an evil thing.	כִּי חשֵׁב אַתָּה לַעֲשׂוֹת דָּבָר רָע.	
RAM	Desist, put your hand over your mouth and do as you have been commanded	הֶרֶף, שִׂים יָדְךָ עַל פִּיךָ וַעֲשֵׂה כַּאֲשֶׁר צֻוֵּיתָ	רם
	For you have mistaken what you saw. But tell me	כִּי שָׁגִיתָ לְמַרְאֵה עֵינֶיךָ. אַךְ הַגִּידָה לִּי	
	Are the priest's letters not in your hand?	הַאֵין אִגְּרוֹת הַכֹּהֵן בְּיָדֶךָ?	
BALTHASAR	There are no letters in my hand, my lord.	אֵין אִגְּרוֹת בְּיָדִי אֲדֹנִי.	בלטאזר
RAM	If so, then, go forth and bring me the horses	אִם כֵּן אֵיפֹא צֵא וְהָבֵא לִי אֶת הַסּוּסִים	רם
	And I shall come quickly after you. *(Balthasar exits)*	וַאֲנִי אָבוֹא אַחֲרֶיךָ מְהֵרָה. (בלטאזר הולך)	
	I am coming to you, Jael, and I shall lie with you tonight.	הִנְנִי בָא אֵלַיִךְ יָעֵל, וְשָׁכַבְתִּי עִמֵּךְ הַלַּיְלָה.	
	And now I shall turn my attention to how I may succeed in my desire.	וְעַתָּה אָשִׂים לֵב בַּמֶּה יִצְלַח חֶפְצִי בְּיָדִי.	
	Why, a man despairing of life as I am today	הֲלֹא גֶבֶר נוֹאָשׁ מֵחַיִּים כָּמוֹנִי הַיּוֹם הַזֶּה	
	Is quick in thinking of how to take his own life.	מְהִיר תַּחְבּוּלָה הוּא בַּמֶּה לְאַבֵּד אֶת נַפְשׁוֹ.	
	Behold, I remember the apothecary whom I saw	הִנֵּה זֹכֵר אֲנִי אֶת הָרֹקֵחַ אֲשֶׁר רָאִיתִי	
	He is **poor and needy**[6] and gathers **mountain herbs**[7]	דַּל וְאֶבְיוֹן[6] הוּא וּמְלַקֵּט עִשְּׂבוֹת הָרִים[7]	
	His eyebrows are long and his garments are worn and patched	גַּבּוֹת עֵינָיו אֲרֻכּוֹת וּבְגָדָיו בָּלִים וּמְטֻלָּאִים	
	Meagreness and misfortune greet him and want follows at his feet	רָזוֹן וּמִגְעֶרֶת יְקַדְּמוּ פָנָיו וְיֵצֵא מַחְסֹר לְרַגְלָיו	

5 Prov. 4:26 פַּלֵּס מַעְגַּל רַגְלֶךָ וְכָל־דְּרָכֶיךָ יִכֹּנוּ 'ponder the path of your feet, and let all your ways be established'.
6 Ps. 72:13, 82:4.
7 Prov. 27:25.

And in his shop I have seen a tortoise and **a serpent upon a pole**[8]	וּבַחֲנוּתוֹ רָאִיתִי צָב **וְשָׂרָף עַל נֵס**[8]
A few embalmed fish and old **empty pitchers**[9]	דָּגִים חֲנֻטִים אֲחָדִים **וְכַדִּים רֵיקִים**[9] יְשָׁנִים
As well as broken vessels **and torn and mended drinking skins**[10]	גַּם שִׁבְרֵי כֵלִים **וְנֹאדוֹת מְבֻקָּעִים וּמְצֹרָרִים**[10]
And on the windowsill a bit of seed **scattered and separated**[11]	וְעַל סְעִיף הַחַלּוֹן מְעַט זֶרַע **מְפֻזָּר וּמְפֹרָד**[11]
Four or five olive berries[12] and the ends of tendons and threads	**גַּרְגְּרִים אַרְבָּעָה חֲמִשָּׁה**[12] וּקְצוֹת יְתָרִים וּפְתִילִים
And old pots of rose ointments to attract the customers' eyes	וּמֶרְקָחוֹת שׁוֹשַׁנִּים יְשָׁנוֹת לִמְשׁוֹךְ עֵינֵי הַקּוֹנִים.
And when I examined this shop, I said to myself	וְכַאֲשֶׁר הִתְבּוֹנַנְתִּי בַּחֲנוּת זוֹ, דִּבַּרְתִּי עִם לִבִּי
If a man were seeking to take a **poison of death**[13] today	לוּ יִדְרֹשׁ אִישׁ לָקַחַת **סַם הַמָּוֶת**[13] הַיּוֹם
This shop owner in his poverty would be prepared to sell it	בַּעַל הַחֲנוּת בְּרֵישׁוֹ זֶה יִהְיֶה נָכוֹן לְמָכְרוֹ
Even though in Mantua it is **a sin worthy of death**[14] for those who sell it.	אַף כִּי בְּמַנְטוּבָה **חֵטְא מִשְׁפַּט מָוֶת**[14] הוּא לְמוֹכְרָיו.
This thought entered my mind before I knew	מַחְשָׁבָה זוֹ עָלְתָה עַל לִבִּי טֶרֶם יָדְעָה נַפְשִׁי
That I would be the one buying from this seller.	כִּי אֲנִי אֶהְיֶה הַקּוֹנֶה מִיַּד הַמּוֹכֵר הַזֶּה.
Here is his house, but the poor man has locked his shop	פֹּה הוּא בֵיתוֹ אַךְ הַמִּסְכֵּן נָעַל חֲנוּתוֹ
For it is a holiday today. *(Knocks on the door)*	כִּי חַג הַיּוֹם הַזֶּה. (דופק אל הדלת)
Where are you, apothecary? Open the door for me!	אֵי אַתָּה רֹקֵחַ? פְּתַח לִי הַדֶּלֶת!

8 Num. 21:8 עֲשֵׂה לְךָ שָׂרָף וְשִׂים אֹתוֹ עַל־נֵס 'make for yourself a serpent and set it upon a pole' (as a cure for a plague of serpents sent by God).

9 Judg. 7:16.

10 Josh. 9:4 וְנֹאדוֹת יַיִן בָּלִים וּמְבֻקָּעִים וּמְצֹרָרִים 'and worn wineskins, torn and mended'.

11 Esther 3:8.

12 Isa. 17:6 שְׁנַיִם שְׁלֹשָׁה גַּרְגְּרִים בְּרֹאשׁ אָמִיר אַרְבָּעָה חֲמִשָּׁה בִּסְעִפֶיהָ פֹּרִיָּה 'two or three olive berries on the top of the uppermost bough, four or five on its fruitful branches'.

13 Mishnah *Ḥullin* 3:5.

14 Deut. 21:22.

<table>
<tr><td>THE APOTHECARY</td><td>Who is calling there with all his voice?</td><td>מִי הוּא הַקֹּרֵא שָׁם בִּמְלֹא קוֹלוֹ?</td><td>הרוקח</td></tr>
<tr><td>RAM</td><td>Come to me, man – I know that you are poor</td><td>בּוֹא אֵלַי בֶּן אָדָם – יָדַעְתִּי כִּי רָשׁ אָתָּה</td><td>רם</td></tr>
<tr><td></td><td>Take forty shekels[15] of gold for yourself, and in exchange for them give me</td><td>הֵא לְךָ אַרְבָּעִים שִׁקְלֵי[15] זָהָב וְאַתָּה תִּתֵּן לִי תַּחְתָּם</td><td></td></tr>
<tr><td></td><td>A few drops of poison that will kill the one who drinks it</td><td>מְעַט נִטְפֵי רַעַל אֲשֶׁר יָמִית אֶת שֹׁתֵהוּ</td><td></td></tr>
<tr><td></td><td>Who despises his life and whose soul has become a burden to him</td><td>אֲשֶׁר קָץ בְּחַיָּיו וְנַפְשׁוֹ לוֹ לְמַעֲמָסָה</td><td></td></tr>
<tr><td></td><td>So that it might mix with his blood and touch all of his veins</td><td>כִּי יִתְעָרֵב בְּדָמוֹ וְיִגַּע בְּכָל עוֹרְקָיו</td><td></td></tr>
<tr><td></td><td>Until he quickly dies and his spirit leaves his body</td><td>עַד אֲשֶׁר יָחִישׁ לִגְוֹעַ וְרוּחוֹ תֵּצֵא מִגְּוִיָּתוֹ</td><td></td></tr>
<tr><td></td><td>Like gunpowder from a gun as it fires.</td><td>כַּאֲבַק הַשְּׂרֵפָה מִתּוֹךְ קְנֵה הָרֹבֶה בְּהֲרִיחוֹ אֵשׁ.</td><td></td></tr>
<tr><td>THE APOTHECARY</td><td>I have such poisons, but I cannot sell them</td><td>יֶשׁ לִי סַמִּים כָּאֵלֶּה אַךְ לֹא אוּכַל לְמָכְרָם</td><td>הרוקח</td></tr>
<tr><td></td><td>For according to the law of the land the seller must surely be put to death.</td><td>כִּי לְפִי מִשְׁפַּט הָאָרֶץ מוֹת יוּמַת הַמּוֹכֵר.</td><td></td></tr>
<tr><td>RAM</td><td>You are impoverished, you have nothing, yet you fear death?</td><td>רָשׁ אֵין כֹּל לְךָ וּמִפְּנֵי הַמָּוֶת אַתָּה יָרֵא?</td><td>רם</td></tr>
<tr><td></td><td>Behold, you lack bread and you have no robe.</td><td>הֵן לֶחֶם תֶּחְסַר וְשִׂמְלָה לְךָ אָיִן.</td><td></td></tr>
<tr><td></td><td>Your bones are as dry as potsherds, and your flesh is like a drinking skin in the smoke[16]</td><td>יָבְשׁוּ כַּחֶרֶשׂ עַצְמוֹתֶיךָ וּבְשָׂרְךָ כְּנֹאד בְּקִיטוֹר[16]</td><td></td></tr>
<tr><td></td><td>You are hated by men and relatives do not love you</td><td>שָׂנוּא אַתָּה לִבְנֵי אָדָם וּקְרוֹבִים לֹא יֶאֱהָבוּךָ</td><td></td></tr>
<tr><td></td><td>Dogs bark at you and youths cast stones at you.</td><td>כְּלָבִים נֹבְחִים אַחֲרֶיךָ וּנְעָרִים יַדּוּ אֶבֶן בָּךְ.</td><td></td></tr>
</table>

15 Cf. Shakespeare's 'ducats' (5.1.59). A shekel is a biblical weight (commonly used with reference to silver and gold) corresponding to approximately ten grams.

16 Ps. 119:83.

	The laws of the earth were not made for you to become wealthy	חֻקֵּי הָאָרֶץ לֹא נַעֲשׂוּ לְמַעַן תַּעְשֵׁר אַתָּה	
	And the earth does not rush to find out if you are sated or hungry	וְהָאָרֶץ לֹא תָחוּשׁ לָדַעַת אִם תִּשְׂבַּע וְאִם תִּרְעַב	
	So why should you rush to keep the law of the land?	וְלָמָּה תָחוּשׁ אַתָּה לִשְׁמֹר מִשְׁפַּט הָאָרֶץ?	
	Take the gold from my hand, and be poor no longer.	קַח אֶת הַזָּהָב מִיָּדִי וְעָנִי אַל תִּהְיֶה עוֹד.	
THE APOTHECARY	I take the gold because I am a pauper	הִנְנִי לֹקֵחַ אֶת הַזָּהָב מֵאֲשֶׁר אֲנִי עָנִי	הרוקח
	Rather than out of my heart's desire.	וְלֹא בְּחֵפֶץ לִבִּי.	
RAM	I pay the pauper, rather than your heart's desire.	אֶל הֶעָנִי אֲנִי מְשַׁלֵּם וְלֹא אֶל חֵפֶץ לִבֶּךָ.	רם
THE APOTHECARY	Put these drugs in a cup of water or mixed wine	שִׂים הַסַּמִּים הָאֵלֶּה בְּכוֹס מַיִם אוֹ מִמְסָךְ	הרוקח
	Until they melt; then drink from the mixture	עַד אֲשֶׁר יִמַּסּוּ, אַחַר תִּשְׁתֶּה מִן הַמֶּזֶג	
	And **even if your strength is like the strength of stones,**[17] **you will be cut off from the earth**[18] at once.	וְאִם גַּם כֹּחַ אֲבָנִים כֹּחֲךָ[17] תִּכָּחֵד מִן הָאָרֶץ[18] כְּרָגַע.	
RAM	The gold which you took is **a cup of poison**[19] for men	הַזָּהָב אֲשֶׁר לָקַחְתָּ הוּא סַף רַעַל[19] לְאָדָם	רם
	It has cast down many more victims, and more numerous are all its slain[20] in the world	רַבִּים חֲלָלִים הִפִּיל וַעֲצוּמִים הֲרָגָיו[20] בְּתֵבֵל	
	Than the victims of poisons such as those that you have no leave to sell	מֵחַלְלֵי הַסַּמִּים כָּאֵלֶּה שֶׁאֵין מִשְׁפָּט לְךָ לְמָכְרָם	
	I sold you the **poison of death,**[21] I and not you	סַם הַמָּוֶת[21] מָכַרְתִּי לְךָ אָנֹכִי וְלֹא אַתָּה	

17 Job 6:12 אִם־כֹּחַ אֲבָנִים כֹּחִי 'is my strength the strength of stones'.
18 Exod. 9:15.
19 Zech. 12:2.
20 Prov. 7:26 כִּי־רַבִּים חֲלָלִים הִפִּילָה וַעֲצֻמִים כָּל־הֲרֻגֶיהָ 'for she has cast down many victims; numerous are all her slain'.
21 Mishnah *Ḥullin* 3:5.

	Go in peace! Buy food and clothing for yourself	לֶךְ־לְךָ לְשָׁלוֹם! קְנֵה לְךָ מָזוֹן וּבֶגֶד	
	And be healthy –	וֶהֱיֵה בָּרִיא אוּלָם –	
	As for you, jar of poison, your name is not **poison of death**[22]	וְאַתְּ צִנְצֶנֶת הַסַּמִּים לֹא סַם מָוֶת[22] שְׁמֵךְ	
	But rather elixir of life, because you are a remedy for my soul	כִּי אִם סַם חַיִּים כִּי מַרְפֵּא לְנַפְשִׁי אָתְּ	
	And I shall bring you to Jael's grave, to finish feast and dinner[23]	וְעַד קֶבֶר יָעֵל אֲבִיאֵךְ, לְכַלּוֹת מִשְׁתֶּה וַאֲרוּחָה[23]	
	There you will become pure honey in my mouth and there I shall find rest for myself. *(Exeunt)*	שָׁם תִּהְיִי לְנֹפֶת בְּפִי וְשָׁם אֶמְצָא לִי מְנוּחָה. (הולכים)	
SCENE 2	*Verona. Chamber of Rezin the priest (Hanan[24] the priest enters)*	וירונה לשכת רצין הכהן (חנן[24] הכהן בא)	מחזה ב'
HANAN	Where is my brother Rezin? Where is the righteous priest?[25]	אֵי רְצִין אָחִי? אֵי כֹּהֵן צֶדֶק?[25]	חנן
	(Rezin enters)	(רצין בא)	
REZIN	**The voice is the voice of Hanan**[26] – have you come from Mantua?	הַקּוֹל קוֹל חָנָן[26] הוּא – הַאִם מִמַּנְטוּבָה בָּאתָ?	רצין
	What did Ram say to you? Or is his letter in your hand?	מַה־דִּבֶּר אֵלֶיךָ רָם? אוֹ הֲיֵשׁ מִכְתָּבוֹ בְּיָדֶךָ?	
HANAN	Indeed I went to seek a brother walking barefoot like myself[27]	הָלוֹךְ הָלַכְתִּי לְבַקֵּשׁ אָח הוֹלֵךְ יָחֵף כָּמוֹנִי[27]	חנן
	To go with me to Mantua, and I found him in a certain house	לָלֶכֶת אִתִּי לְמַנְטוּבָה וָאֶמְצָאֵהוּ בְּבַיִת אֶחָד	
	To which he had gone to visit someone lying on his deathbed	אֲשֶׁר בָּא שָׁם לְבַקֵּר שֹׁכֵב עַל עֶרֶשׂ דְּוָי	
	And the city guards saw and said that we had come to a house	וְנֹטְרֵי הָעִיר רָאוּ וַיֹּאמְרוּ כִּי בָאנוּ לְבַיִת	

22 Mishnah *Ḥullin* 3:5.

23 This and the next line form a rhyming couplet, mirroring Shakespeare's 'me/thee' (5.1.85–6).

24 This is the name of a number of minor biblical characters; for example, one of the Levites who helped Ezra explain the Law to the people (Neh. 8:7). Salkinson most likely selected it as a translation of Shakespeare's 'John' because it (or, more typically, its variant יוֹחָנָן 'Johanan') is the usual Hebrew equivalent of this name.

25 Cf. Shakespeare's 'Holy Franciscan friar' (5.2.1).

26 Gen. 27:22 הַקֹּל קוֹל יַעֲקֹב 'the voice is the voice of Jacob'.

27 Cf. Shakespeare's 'one of our order' (5.2.6); Salkinson has neutralized the explicitly Catholic associations of this phrase.

	In which there was cholera,[28] and therefore they closed the door upon us	אֲשֶׁר הַחֳלִי־רַע[28] בְּתוֹכוֹ וְלָכֵן סָגְרוּ עָלֵינוּ הַדֶּלֶת	
	And did not let us go out lest the plague[29] break out because of us	וְלֹא נְתָנוּנוּ לָצֵאת פֶּן תִּפְרֹץ הַמַּגֵּפָה[29] לְרַגְלֵנוּ	
	So we were shut up there and I could not go to Mantua.	וַנִּהְיֶה עֲצוּרִים שָׁם וְלֹא יָכֹלְתִּי לָלֶכֶת לְמַנְטוֹבָה.	
REZIN	So with whom did you send my letter to Ram?	וְעַל יַד מִי שָׁלַחְתָּ אֶת מִכְתָּבִי אֶל רָם?	רצין
HANAN	They did not let me send it; here it is before you	לֹא נְתָנוּנִי לְשָׁלְחֵהוּ, הִנֵּה הוּא פֹּה לְפָנֶיךָ	חנן
	I could not even find a messenger to return it to you	וְגַם שָׁלִיחַ לַהֲשִׁיבוֹ אֶל יָדְךָ לֹא מָצָאתִי	
	For the fear of the plague was great in the city.	כִּי יִרְאַת הַמַּגֵּפָה הָיְתָה גְדוֹלָה בָּעִיר.	
REZIN	It is bad fortune; by the Temple service![30] For this letter	מִקְרֶה לֹא טוֹב הוּא; הָעֲבוֹדָה![30] כִּי הַמִּכְתָּב הַזֶּה	רצין
	Is most precious and important, and needed to be sent.	הוּא יָקָר וְנִכְבָּד מְאֹד וְנָחוּץ הָיָה לְהִשְׁתַּלֵּחַ.	
	Now I fear greatly that a disaster may befall us.	עַתָּה יָרֵאתִי מְאֹד פֶּן יִמְצָאֵנוּ אָסוֹן.	
	Please hurry, my brother Hanan, and seek an axe and hammers	חוּשָׁה נָּא חָנָן אָחִי, וּבַקֵּשׁ מַעֲצָר וּמַקָּבוֹת	
	And bring them to me in the chamber.	וַהֲבִיאֵם אֵלַי אֶל הַלִּשְׁכָּה.	
HANAN	I am going, my brother, and I shall bring them to you in accordance with your word.	הִנְנִי הוֹלֵךְ אָחִי, וַאֲבִיאֵם אֵלֶיךָ כִּדְבָרֶךָ.	חנן
	(Exits)	(הולך)	
REZIN	Meanwhile, I shall go on my own to the grave in the cavern	וַאֲנִי אֵלֵךְ לְבַדִּי אֶל הַקֶּבֶר בַּמְּעָרָה	רצין
	For in another three hours Jael's soul will return to her body	כִּי בְעוֹד שָׁלֹשׁ שָׁעוֹת תָּשׁוּב נֶפֶשׁ יָעֵל אֶל קִרְבָּהּ	

28 Cf. Shakespeare's 'the infectious pestilence' (5.2.10). Cholera was the most common infectious disease affecting Eastern European Jews in the second half of the nineteenth century (see Markel 1997: esp. 87–8). Cf. *Ithiel*, First Part, note 267.

29 The Hebrew term can denote any serious contagious disease.

30 This is a Talmudic oath (Even-Shoshan 2003, 4: 1334); Salkinson has Judaized Shakespeare's overtly Catholic oath 'by my brotherhood' (5.2.17). Cf. Third Part, note 176.

	And she will grumble to me that Ram did not come at the appointed time	וְהִיא תָלִין עָלַי כִּי לֹא בָא רָם לַמּוֹעֵד	
	For I have not informed him of anything that has happened	כִּי לֹא הוֹדַעְתִּי אֹתוֹ דָבָר מִכֹּל אֲשֶׁר נָפָל	
	But I shall write again and send a messenger to Mantua.	אַךְ אֲנִי אֶכְתֹּב עוֹד וְצִיר אֶשְׁלַח לְמַנְטוּבָה.	
	A precious soul[31] is lying in a coffin, like a soul **cut off out of the land of the living**[32, 33]	נֶפֶשׁ יְקָרָה[31] שֹׁכֶבֶת בְּאָרוֹן, כְּנֶפֶשׁ מֵאֶרֶץ חַיִּים נִגְזֶרֶת[32, 33]	
	And until Ram arrives, she will be kept watch over in the chamber with me. *(Exits)*	וְעַד בּוֹא רָם בַּלִּשְׁכָּה אִתִּי תִּהְיֶה לְמִשְׁמֶרֶת. (הולך)	
SCENE 3	*Graveyard in which there is a tower and cavern, the burial site of the Abiels (Paris with a youth in whose hand is a torch and bunch of flowers)*	שדה קברות ובתוכו מגדל ומערה אחוזת קברי האביעלים (פריז עם נער אשר בידו לפיד וצרור פרחים)	מחזה ג'
PARIS	Give me the torch, and leave my presence	תֶּן לִי אֶת הַלַּפִּיד וְאַתָּה לֶךְ־לְךָ מִנֶּגֶד	פריז
	But I misspoke; put out the torch	אַךְ לֹא כֵן דִּבַּרְתִּי, כַּבֵּה אֶת הַלַּפִּיד	
	So that no one's eye sees, and lie there on the ground	לִבְלִי תִרְאֵנִי עֵין אָדָם וְשְׁכַב שָׁם עַל הָאָרֶץ	
	And listen carefully behind the thicket and if a man comes	וְהַטֵּה אָזְנֶיךָ מֵאַחֲרֵי הַסְּבָךְ וְהָיָה כִּי יָבוֹא אִישׁ	
	And treads over the ground[34] whose clods have crumbled	וְיִצְעַד עַל פְּנֵי הַקַּרְקַע[34] אֲשֶׁר רְגָבָיו הִתְפּוֹרָרוּ	
	And which is as hollow as a sieve and riddled with holes and graves	וְנָקוּב הוּא כַּכְּבָרָה וּנְבוּב מְחִלּוֹת וּקְבָרִים	
	Only then, when you hear the sound of footsteps, whistle with your mouth	הֲלֹא תִשְׁמַע קוֹל הַצְּעָדָה וְשָׁרַקְתָּ בְּמוֹ פִיךָ	
	As a sign for me that a man's feet are in the courtyard of death	לִהְיוֹת לִי לְאוֹת כִּי רַגְלֵי אָדָם בַּחֲצַר מָוֶת	

31 Prov. 6:26.
32 Isa. 53:8 כִּי נִגְזַר מֵאֶרֶץ חַיִּים 'for he was cut off out of the land of the living'.
33 This and the next line form a rhyming couplet, mirroring Shakespeare's 'come/tomb' (5.2.28–9).
34 Cf. Shakespeare's 'churchyard' (5.3.5).

	And now, give me the flowers, and go, do as I have commanded you.	וְעַתָּה תֶּן לִי הַפְּרָחִים וְלֵךְ עֲשֵׂה כַּאֲשֶׁר צִוִּיתִיךָ.	
	The youth (to himself)	הנער (אל עצמו)	
	I almost fear to stand in the courtyard of death[35] by myself	כִּמְעַט יָרֵאתִי לַעֲמֹד בַּחֲצַר מָוֶת[35] לְבַדִּי	
	But I shall go and do as my master has commanded me. *(Exits)*	אַךְ אֵלֵךְ וְאֶעֱשֶׂה כַּאֲשֶׁר צִוַּנִי אֲדֹנִי. (הולך)	
PARIS	Every flower, **O beauty**![36] I shall glorify your wedding canopy[37] with blossoms[38]	הַצְּבִי[36] כָּל פֶּרַח! חֻפָּתֵךְ[37] אֲפָאֵר בַּנִּצָּנִים[38]	פריז
	Woe is me, woe is me! Your wedding canopy is dust and stones	אוֹי לִי אוֹי לִי! חֻפָּתֵךְ עָפָר וַאֲבָנִים	
	Here each night I shall pour out my heart in my sighing	פֹּה בְּכָל לַיְלָה אֶשְׁפֹּךְ לִבִּי בְּאַנְחָתִי	
	My lament will drop as the rain,[39] like the dew **I shall water you with my tears**[40]	מִסְפְּדִי יַעֲרֹף כַּמָּטָר[39] כַּטַּל אֲרַיָּוֵךְ דִּמְעָתִי[40]	
	At midnight my abandoned desolate soul will arise[41]	חֲצוֹת לַיְלָה תָּקוּם נַפְשִׁי הָעֲזוּבָה הַשֹּׁמֵמָה[41]	
	And **with weeping and moaning**[42] I shall sacrifice for you **plaited chains**[43] of flowers	וּבִבְכִי וַאֲנָקָה[42] אַקְרִיב לָךְ שַׁרְשֹׁת גַּבְלֻת[43] פֶּרַח	
	And I shall raise up a dirge and lament for twelve months	וְאֶשָּׂא נְהִי וְקִינָה מֶשֶׁךְ שְׁנֵים עָשָׂר יֶרַח	
	This I vow, Jael, and as I have vowed so I shall fulfil.	זֶה נָדַרְתִּי יָעֵל, וַאֲשֶׁר נָדַרְתִּי אֲשַׁלֵּמָה.	
	(The youth whistles with his mouth)	(הנער שורק בפיו)	

35 Cf. Shakespeare's 'in the churchyard' (5.3.11).

36 2 Sam. 1:19 (David's lament for Saul and Jonathan).

37 Cf. Shakespeare's 'thy bridal bed' (5.3.12). See Fourth Part, note 36 for discussion of 'wedding canopy'.

38 This and the next three lines form two rhyming couplets, mirroring Shakespeare's 'strew/stones/dew/moans' (5.3.12–15) except that the latter is composed of an ABAB pattern.

39 Deut. 32:2 יַעֲרֹף כַּמָּטָר לִקְחִי 'My teaching shall drop as the rain'.

40 Isa. 16:9.

41 This and the next three lines form an ABBA rhyming pattern, mirroring Shakespeare's 'keep/weep' (5.3.16–17) except that the latter consists of a single rhyming couplet. Salkinson has turned Shakespeare's two lines into four; the discrepancy most likely reflects a difficulty in conveying the necessary information and finding suitable rhymes within the space of the original two lines.

42 Mal. 2:13.

43 Exod. 28:22.

	The youth has given me a sign that he has heard the sound of footsteps[44]	הַנַּעַר נָתַן לִי אוֹת כִּי שָׁמַע קוֹל צְעָדָה[44]	
	Who would dare to come here, to be an adversary against me tonight	מִי יָעִיז לָגֶשֶׁת הֲלֹם לִהְיוֹת לְשָׂטָן לִי הַלַּיְלָה	
	When I have come to the grave to fulfil the vow of my love	וַאֲנִי בָאתִי אֶל הַקֶּבֶר, לְשַׁלֵּם נֶדֶר אַהֲבָתִי	
	But behold, a man is coming, and moreover there is a torch in his hand	אַךְ אִישׁ הִנֵּה בָא וְגַם לַפִּיד בְּיָדוֹ	
	I shall retreat for a moment and hide in the wings of night.	אָשׁוּב לְאָחוֹר רֶגַע וְאֶסָּתֵר בְּכַנְפֵי לָיְלָה.	
	(Retreats)	(שב לאחור)	
	(Ram and Balthasar enter with a torch and axes and various iron tools)	(רם ובלטאזר באים עם לפיד וקרדומות וכלי ברזל שונים)	
RAM	Give me the iron tools and take this letter	תֶּן לִי כְּלֵי הַבַּרְזֶל וְקַח אֶת הַמִּכְתָּב הַזֶּה	רם
	And tomorrow morning see to transmit it to the hand of my lord father	וּלְמָחָר בַּבֹּקֶר רְאֵה לְמָסְרוֹ לְיַד אָבִי אֲדֹנִי	
	Give me the torch, and I adjure you to stand afar	תְּנָה לִי אֶת הַלַּפִּיד וְהִנְנִי מַשְׁבִּיעֲךָ לַעֲמֹד מֵרָחוֹק	
	Guard yourself from descending after me, for **your blood will be on your head**.[45]	הִשָּׁמֶר־לְךָ מֵרֶדֶת אַחֲרַי כִּי דָמְךָ יִהְיֶה **בְרֹאשֶׁךָ**.[45]	
	If you see or hear something, do not move from your place	אִם תִּרְאֶה וְתִשְׁמַע דָּבָר אַל תָּנוּעַ מִמְּקוֹמְךָ	
	And do not approach in order to stop my labour, for **it will cost you your life**[46]	וְאַל תִּגַּשׁ לְהַשְׁבִּית מְלַאכְתִּי כִּי **בְנַפְשְׁךָ הוּא**[46]	
	As for me, **I shall go down to the chambers of death**[47] to see my bride	וַאֲנִי יֹרֵד **בְּחַדְרֵי* מָוֶת**[47] לִרְאוֹת אֶת פְּנֵי כַלָּתִי	
	And also to remove from her finger a ring with a precious stone	וְגַם לְהָסִיר מֵאֶצְבָּעָהּ טַבַּעַת אֶבֶן יְקָרָה	
	Which will benefit me for I shall indeed divine with it	אֲשֶׁר תִּהְיֶה לְהוֹעִיל לִי כִּי נַחֵשׁ אֲנַחֵשׁ בָּהּ	

---

44 In the Ashkenazic Hebrew pronunciation this and the next line form a rhyming couplet, mirroring Shakespeare's 'tonight/rite' (5.3.19–20).

45 1 Kings 2:37.

46 Prov. 7:23 וְלֹא־יָדַע כִּי־בְנַפְשׁוֹ הוּא 'and he does not know that it will cost him his life'.

47 Prov. 7:27 דַּרְכֵי שְׁאוֹל בֵּיתָהּ יֹרְדוֹת אֶל־חַדְרֵי־מָוֶת 'her house is the way to Sheol, going down to the chambers of death'.

* בְּחַדְרֵי

	Now go and stand afar, and do not forget that I have warned you	עַתָּה לֵךְ וַעֲמֹד מִנֶּגֶד וְאַל תִּשְׁכַּח כִּי הִזְהַרְתִּיךָ	
	That if you presume to approach and to see what I shall do further	כִּי אִם תָּזִיד לָגֶשֶׁת וְלִרְאוֹת מָה אוֹסִיף לַעֲשׂוֹת	
	I testify to you today that I shall cut your flesh to pieces	הַעִידֹתִי בְךָ הַיּוֹם כִּי אֶגְזֹר בְּשָׂרְךָ לִגְזָרִים	
	And scatter them over the graves[48] so that **their dust might be made fat.**[49]	וְזֵרִיתִים עַל פְּנֵי הַקְּבָרִים[48] לְמַעַן יְדֻשַּׁן עֲפָרָם.[49]	
	This place is dreadful;[50] my heart is as stormy as the sea	נוֹרָא הַמָּקוֹם הַזֶּה,[50] לְבָבִי סֹעֵר כַּיָּם	
	And **I have no rule over my spirit,**[51] like a hungry leopard in the forest.	וּלְרוּחִי אֵין מַעְצוֹר[51] כְּנָמֵר רָעֵב בַּיָּעַר.	
BALTHASAR	I shall keep your command and shall not be a burden to you.	אֶת פְּקוּדָתְךָ אֶשְׁמֹר וְלֹא אֶהְיֶה עָלֶיךָ לְמַשָּׂא.	בלטאזר
RAM	I shall consider this as righteousness on your part; take this for yourself as a gift	זֹאת אֶחְשָׁב לְךָ לִצְדָקָה וְהֵא לְךָ זֹאת לְמַתָּת	רם
	And now go in peace, and be a successful, **good, and faithful man.**[52]	וְעַתָּה לֵךְ לְשָׁלוֹם וּצְלַח אִישׁ טוֹב וְנֶאֱמָן.[52]	
BALTHASAR *(To himself)*	As for me, I shall hide so that I may see him, **for I fear the wrath**[53, 54]	וַאֲנִי אֶסְתַּתֵּר וְאֶרְאֶנּוּ כִּי יָגוֹרְתִּי מִפְּנֵי הַחֵמָה[53, 54]	בלטאזר (אל עצמו)
	I do not believe his words, for he speaks with cunning	לֹא אַאֲמִין בִּדְבָרוֹ, כִּי יְדַבֵּר בְּעָרְמָה	
	His face testifies evil, and around his eyes is dread	פָּנָיו יַעֲנוּ רָעָה וּסְבִיבוֹת עֵינָיו אֵימָה	

48 Cf. Shakespeare's 'this hungry churchyard' (5.3.36).
49 Isa. 34:7 וְעַפְרָם מֵחֵלֶב יְדֻשָּׁן 'and their dust will be made fat with fatness'.
50 Gen. 28:17.
51 Prov. 25:28 אִישׁ אֲשֶׁר אֵין מַעְצָר לְרוּחוֹ 'a man who has no rule over his spirit'.
52 Babylonian Talmud *Berakhot* 16b.
53 Deut. 9:19 כִּי יָגֹרְתִּי מִפְּנֵי הָאַף וְהַחֵמָה 'for I fear the anger and the wrath'.
54 This and the next three lines form an ABAB rhyming pattern, echoing Shakespeare's 'hereabout/doubt' (5.3.43–4), except that the latter consists of a single rhyming couplet. Salkinson has expanded the speech by two lines, adding details about the specific nature of Balthasar's suspicions regarding Ram's intentions.

	Like one considering destroying himself.	כְּחֹשֵׁב בְּלִבּוֹ לְהַכּוֹת נַפְשׁוֹ עַד חָרְמָה.	
	(Goes and hides)	(הולך ומסתתר)	
RAM	Oh, grave hungry for prey! Gluttonous belly of Sheol!	הוֹי קֶבֶר רָעֵב לְטָרֶף! בֶּטֶן שְׁאוֹל זוֹלֵלָה!	רם
	You have swallowed the best of the earth's delicacies, yet you do not say 'enough'	הַטּוֹב בְּמַעֲדַנֵּי אֶרֶץ בִּלַּעַתְּ* וְלֹא אָמַרְתְּ הוֹן	
	Behold, I shall open your mouth with force and not by your will	הִנֵּה אֶפְתַּח פִּיךְ בְּחָזְקָה וְלֹא לִרְצוֹנֵךְ	
	And place more in your gullet. *(Breaks and opens the door in the tower)*	וְאָשִׁית נוֹסָפוֹת בְּלֹעֵךְ. (שובר ופותח הדלת במגדל)	
PARIS	This is the son of Abiram, who was exiled for his guilt	זֶה הוּא בֶּן אֲבִירָם אֲשֶׁר הָגְלָה בְּאַשְׁמָתוֹ	פריז
	Who killed my bride's brother[55] and she died from sadness and sorrow	אֲשֶׁר הֵמִית אֲחִי[55] כַלָּתִי וְהִיא מֵתָה מֵעֹצֶב וָיָגוֹן	
	And here he comes to the house of bones of the dead	וְהִנֵּה הוּא בָא הֲלֹם לְבָתֵּי עַצְמוֹת הַמֵּתִים	
	To commit a villainous deed – why, I shall catch this villain –	לַעֲשׂוֹת דְּבַר בְּלִיַּעַל – הֲלֹא אֶתְפֹּשׂ בַּבְּלִיַּעַל הַזֶּה –	
	What are you doing here,[56] son of Abiram? What are you doing here, scoundrel?	**מַה־לְּךָ פֹּה**[56] בֶּן אֲבִירָם? מַה־לְּךָ פֹּה נָבָל?	
	Would you chase the bones of the dead? And would you take revenge from **those who sleep in the dust**?[57, 58]	הַעַצְמוֹת הַמֵּתִים תִּרְדֹּף? **וּמִישֵׁנֵי עָפָר**[57] תִּקַּח נָקָם?[58]	
	Come with me, **man condemned to death**,[59] for you shall surely die.	לְכָה אִתִּי **בֶּן מָוֶת**,[59] כִּי מוֹת תָּמוּת.	
RAM	You have spoken truly; I am about to die, for that is why I have come here	כֵּן דִּבַּרְתָּ הִנְנִי אָמוּת כִּי לָכֵן בָּאתִי הֵנָּה	רם
	But I counsel you, noble son, not to fight with me	אַךְ אִיעָצְךָ בֶּן נָדִיב, לִבְלִי תִתְגָּר בִּי	

55 Cf. Shakespeare's 'cousin' (5.3.50); see First Part, note 65.

56 Judg. 18:3; 1 Kings 19:9, 13; Isa. 22:16.

57 This appears in the *Amida*, the central prayer of the daily Jewish liturgy.

58 Salkinson has not reproduced Shakespeare's rhyming couplet in the last two lines of this speech 'thee/die' (5.3.56–7).

59 1 Sam. 20:31; 2 Sam. 12:5.

* בִּלַּעַתְּ

	Better for a man to meet a bear robbed of her whelps than a man despairing of his life[60]	פָּגוֹשׁ דֹּב שַׁכּוּל וְאַל גֶּבֶר נוֹאָשׁ מֵחַיָּיו[60]	
	Turn away from me and pass by; do not anger me further	שְׂטֵה מֵעָלַי וַעֲבֹר, אַל תּוֹסֵף לְהַכְעִיסֵנִי	
	Remember those lying here in their graves	זְכֹר אֶת אֵלֶּה הַשֹּׁכְבִים פֹּה בְּקִבְרֵיהֶם	
	Guard yourself greatly, lest your end be like theirs.	הִשָּׁמֶר־לְךָ מְאֹד פֶּן* תִּהְיֶה אַחֲרִיתְךָ כְּמוֹהֶם.	
	Again I urge you, pleasant and agreeable young man	עוֹד הַפַּעַם אֶפְצַר בְּךָ בָּחוּר נֶחְמָד וְנָעִים	
	Do not ignite my wrath and do not force me to sin further	אַל תַּצִּית חֲמָתִי וְאַל תְּאַלְצֵנִי לַחֲטֹא עוֹד	
	To add iniquity to my iniquity. Please obey me and live	לְהוֹסִיף עָוֹן עַל עֲוֹנִי. שְׁמַע נָא בְּקוֹלִי וֶחְיֵה	
	Flee for your life, which I value more than my own life	הִמָּלֵט עַל נַפְשְׁךָ אֲשֶׁר הוֹקַרְתִּיהָ מִנַּפְשִׁי	
	Because it is for my life and not for yours that I have brought **instruments of violence.**[61]	כִּי לְנַפְשִׁי וְלֹא לְנַפְשְׁךָ כְּלֵי חָמָס[61] הֵבֵאתִי.	
	Please listen to my counsel; pass by from here and live	אָנָּא שְׁמַע לַעֲצָתִי עֲבֹר מִזֶּה וֶחְיֵה	
	And regarding the son of Abiram, open your mouth and call out[62]	וְעַל בֶּן אֲבִירָם, פְּתַח פִּיךָ וּקְרָא־נָא[62]	
	That the madman in his mercy gave you faithful counsel.	כִּי הַמְּשֻׁגָּע בְּחֶמְלָתוֹ יָעַץ לְךָ עֵצָה נֶאֱמָנָה.	
PARIS	I shall not take notice of your words, and all your oaths are in vain	לֹא אָחוּשׁ לִדְבָרֶיךָ וְכָל שְׁבוּעוֹתֶיךָ לָרִיק	פריז
	For I shall take you, criminal, **and present you at the gate of judgement.**[63]	כִּי אוֹבִילְךָ פּשֵׁעַ וְאַצִּיגְךָ בְּשַׁעַר מִשְׁפָּט.[63]	
RAM	Now I am blameless regarding your blood; draw your sword, youth!	נִקֵּיתִי הַפַּעַם מִדָּמְךָ, שְׁלֹף חַרְבְּךָ נַעַר!	רם
	(They fight each other)	(נלחמים יחדיו)	

60 Prov. 17:12 פָּגוֹשׁ דֹּב שַׁכּוּל בְּאִישׁ וְאַל־כְּסִיל בְּאִוַּלְתּוֹ 'better for a man to meet a bear robbed of her whelps than a fool in his folly'.

61 Gen. 49:5.

62 This and the next line form a rhyming couplet, mirroring Shakespeare's 'say/away' (5.3.66–7).

63 Amos 5:15 וְהַצִּיגוּ בַשַּׁעַר מִשְׁפָּט 'and establish judgement at the gate'.

* פֶּן

PARIS' YOUTH	Oh! They are fighting; I shall go and call for the city watchmen.	אֲהָהּ! הֵם נִלְחָמִים אֵלְכָה וְאֶקְרָא לְשֹׁמְרֵי הָעִיר.	נער פריז
	(He exits and Paris falls)	(הוא הולך ופריז נופל)	
PARIS	I have been struck a mortal blow – deal mercifully with me	מַכַּת מָוֶת הֻכֵּיתִי – עֲשֵׂה עִמָּדִי חֶסֶד	פריז
	Open the grave and lay me next to Jael. *(Dies)*	פְּתַח אֶת הַקֶּבֶר וְהַשְׁכִּיבֵנִי אֵצֶל יָעֵל. (מת)	
RAM	Indeed I shall do so – yea, I shall examine his face	אָמְנָם כֵּן אֶעֱשֶׂה – אַךְ אֶתְבּוֹנֵן בְּפָנָיו	רם
	He is Meraioth's kin; Paris is **of the seed of princes**[64]	שְׁאֵר בְּשַׂר מְרָיוֹת הוּא, פָּרִיז מִזֶּרַע הַפַּרְתְּמִים[64]	
	What did my youth say to me, when I was riding on the way	מַה־דִּבֶּר אֵלַי נַעֲרִי, כַּאֲשֶׁר רָכַבְתִּי בַּדֶּרֶךְ	
	And due to the great agitation of my soul I did not listen to his words?	וּמֵרֹב רִגְשַׁת נַפְשִׁי לֹא הִקְשַׁבְתִּי לִדְבָרוֹ?	
	If I am not mistaken, why, he told me	אִם שֹׁגֶה אֵינֶנִּי, הֲלֹא הוּא הִגִּיד לִי	
	That Paris was due to wed Jael.	כִּי נוֹעַד פָּרִיז לָקַחַת לוֹ אֶת יָעֵל.	
	Did he tell me such a thing? Or was I like one dreaming? –	הַאִם הִגִּיד לִי כָּזֹאת? אוֹ כְּחֹלֵם הָיִיתִי? –	
	Or perhaps when I heard that Jael was to be spoken for	אוֹ אוּלַי מֵאֲשֶׁר שָׁמַעְתִּי, כִּי יְדֻבַּר בְּיָעֵל	
	My sense departed from me and I imagined that he had told me this? –	סָר טַעְמִי מִמֶּנִּי וַאֲדַמֶּה שֶׁכֵּן הִגִּיד לִי? –	
	Give me your hand, you are a brother in distress	הָבָה לִי אֶת יָדְךָ, אָח אַתָּה לַצָּרָה	
	Your judgement has been decreed in the same book as mine has been decreed	בְּסֵפֶר אֶחָד נִגְזַר דִּינְךָ כַּאֲשֶׁר נִגְזַר עָלָי	
	And I shall bury you in a grave of strength; but it is not a grave	וַאֲנִי בְּקֶבֶר עֹז אֶקְבָּרֶךָ: אַךְ לֹא קֶבֶר הוּא	
	It is a palace full of light, for there lies Jael	הוּא אַרְמוֹן מָלֵא אוֹר כִּי שָׁם יָעֵל שֹׁכֶבֶת	
	And where she is, her beauty **is like the dawn light, shining ever brighter.**[65]	וּבַאֲשֶׁר הִיא שָׁם יָפְיָהּ **כְּאוֹר נֹגַהּ הוֹלֵךְ וָאוֹר.**[65]	

64 Dan. 1:3 וּמִזֶּרַע הַמְּלוּכָה וּמִן־הַפַּרְתְּמִים 'and of the king's seed, and of the princes'.
65 Prov. 4:18.

Lie here, young man, I have killed you	שְׁכַב פֹּה בָּחוּר, אֲנִי אֹתְךָ הָרַגְתִּי
Behold, I shall bury you, though I too am dead like you.	אֲנִי הִנְנִי מְקַבֶּרְךָ וְגַם אֲנִי מֵת כָּמוֹךָ.
(Lays Paris out next to Jael)	(משכיב את פריז אצל יעל)
Indeed, I have heard people say that a man before his death	הֵן שָׁמַעְתִּי אֹמְרִים אָדָם לִפְנֵי מוֹתוֹ
Finds some small relief, but where is my relief?	יִרְוַח לוֹ מְעָט, וְאַיֵּה אֵיפֹה רַוְחָתִי?
Oh, Jael, my wife! Jael, **whom my soul loves**![66]	הוֹי יָעֵל אִשְׁתִּי! יָעֵל **שֶׁאָהֲבָה נַפְשִׁי**![66]
Even death, which has sucked the sweetness of your lips' breath,	גַּם הַמָּוֶת אֲשֶׁר מָצַץ מֶתֶק רוּחַ שְׂפָתַיִךְ
Has not taken dominion over your beauty, and your splendour has not yet departed	לֹא שָׁלַט עַל יָפְיֵךְ וַהֲדָרֵךְ עוֹד לֹא סָר
Your lips are still as scarlet, and grace rests upon your face	עוֹד שִׂפְתוֹתַיִךְ כַּשָּׁנִים וְחֵן יָלִין עַל פָּנָיִךְ
The sword of death has touched you, but you have not yet been destroyed –	חֶרֶב הַמָּוֶת נָגְעָה בָךְ וְעוֹד לֹא נִכְחַדְתְּ –
Is that you there, Tubal, in **a cloak rolled in blood**?![67]	הַאַתָּה שָׁם תּוּבַל **בְּשִׂמְלָה מְגֹלָלָה בְדָמִים**![67]
I laid my hand on you and snuffed out your life	יָדִי שָׁלַחְתִּי בְךָ וְאֵת נַפְשְׁךָ הִפָּחְתִּי
I struck you down with my sword, and **shortened the days of your youth**[68]	הִפַּלְתִּיךָ לְפִי חַרְבִּי **וִימֵי עֲלוּמֶיךָ הִקְצַרְתִּי**[68]
I hereby lay a hand on myself, **a life for a life**[69]	הִנְנִי שׁוֹלֵחַ יָד בְּנַפְשִׁי **נֶפֶשׁ תַּחַת נָפֶשׁ**[69]
Look, your enemy's soul will be with you in a moment	רְאֵה נֶפֶשׁ אוֹיִבְךָ עִמְּךָ תִּהְיֶה כְּרֶגַע
So what more can I do; how can I find favour with you	וּמָה אוּכַל עֲשׂוֹת עוֹד בַּמֶּה אֶתְרַצֶּה אֵלֶיךָ

66 Song of Songs 1:7, 3:1, 2, 3.
67 Isa. 9:4 (9:5 in English Bibles).
68 Ps. 89:46 (89:45 in English Bibles) הִקְצַרְתָּ יְמֵי עֲלוּמָיו 'you have shortened the days of his youth'.
69 Exod. 21:23; Lev. 24:18.

Forgive me now, my brother,[70] and say that I have calmed your wrath –

סְלַח לִי אָחִי[70] הַפַּעַם וֶאֱמֹר כִּי חֲמָתְךָ הֲנִיחוֹתִי –

At the sight of you, precious Jael, at the lovely sight of you **I am pricked in the heart**[71]

לְמַרְאֵךְ יָעֵל הַיְקָרָה, לְמַרְאֵךְ כִּי נָאוֶה **אֶשְׁתּוֹנָן**[71]

The angel of death has brought you down, yet the radiance of your face has not dimmed

שַׂר הַמָּוֶת הִכְרִיעֵךְ וְזִיו פָּנַיִךְ לֹא הֶחְשִׁיךְ

Before him you have knelt, you have fallen, yet he has not laid his hand upon your beauty;

לְפָנָיו כָּרַעַתְּ נָפַלְתְּ וּבְיָפְיֵךְ לֹא שָׁלַח יָדוֹ;

Admittedly he who has no flesh on his bones

הֲגַם הוּא אֲשֶׁר גְּרָמָיו אֵין בָּשָׂר עָלֵימוֹ

Loves **the daughters of men, for they are fair**[72]

יֶאֱהַב בְּנוֹת הָאָדָם, כִּי טֹבֹת הֵנָּה[72]

So has he brought you to the dungeon in order to take you to his bed?

וַיְבִיאֵךְ לְבֵית הַבּוֹר לְמַעַן יָבוֹא אֵלָיִךְ?

This I feared, so I have come; I shall not part from you again.

זֶה פָּחַדְתִּי וָאָבוֹא; לֹא אֶפָּרֵד מִמֵּךְ עוֹד.

Among maggots and worms, which serve you here

בֵּין רִמָּה וְתוֹלֵעָה הַמְשָׁרְתוֹת פֹּה לְפָנַיִךְ

I shall be a watchman at your head; I shall never depart from here

אֶהְיֶה שׁוֹמֵר לְרֹאשֵׁךְ, לֹא אָמוּשׁ מִזֶּה לָנֶצַח

Here I desire to dwell; this is my rest forever[73]

פֹּה אִוִּיתִי שֶׁבֶת, זֹאת מְנוּחָתִי עֲדֵי עַד[73]

Here I shall cast off the yoke of my life, and all my woes will cease.

פֹּה אֶפְרֹק עֹל חַיַּי וְכָל צָרוֹתַי תִּכְלֶינָה.

My eyes! Look just once more before your light wanes

עֵינַי! רְאֶינָה אַךְ הַפַּעַם טֶרֶם אוֹרְכֶן יֵאָסֵף

And you, my arms, embrace, embrace a last embrace

וְאַתֶּן זְרוֹעוֹתַי חַבֵּקְנָה, חַבֵּקְנָה חִבּוּק אַחֲרוֹן

And you, lips of my mouth, you doors of my breath

וְאַף אַתֵּן שִׂפְתֵי פִּי, אַתֶּן דַּלְתֵי נִשְׁמָתִי

---

70 Cf. Shakespeare's 'cousin' (5.3.101); see First Part, note 65.

71 Ps. 73:21 וְכִלְיוֹתַי אֶשְׁתּוֹנָן 'and I was pricked in the heart'.

72 Gen. 6:2 וַיִּרְאוּ בְנֵי־הָאֱלֹהִים אֶת־בְּנוֹת הָאָדָם כִּי טֹבֹת הֵנָּה 'and the sons of God saw the daughters of men, that they were fair'.

73 Ps. 132:14 זֹאת־מְנוּחָתִי עֲדֵי־עַד פֹּה־אֵשֵׁב כִּי אִוִּתִיהָ 'this is my rest forever; here I shall dwell, for I desired it'.

	Kiss a last kiss before I die and am no more;	נַשֵּׁקְנָה נְשִׁיקָה אַחֲרֹנָה טֶרֶם אֶגְוַע וְאֵינֶנִּי;	
	As a sign that I have paid my debt to the destroying angel	לְאוֹת כִּי שִׁלַּמְתִּי חוֹבִי אֶל שַׂר הַמַּשְׁחִית	
	Who has had a contract with man since the days of old.	אֲשֶׁר עָשָׂה חוֹזֶה עִם הָאָדָם מִימוֹת עוֹלָם.	
	Come, guide! Come, you who lead men **into the valley of the shadow of death**[74]	בּוֹא אַתָּה מְנַהֵל! בּוֹא מְנַהֵג בְּגֵיא **צַלְמָוֶת**[74]	
	And like a sailor on a raging sea lead my storm-tossed ship	וּכְמַלָּח בְּיָם זֹעֵף נְהַג אֳנִיָּתִי הַסֹּעֲרָה	
	Through rocks and cliffs so that it breaks into splinters.	דֶּרֶךְ כֵּפִים וּסְלָעִים לְמַעַן תִּשָּׁבֵר לִרְסִיסִים.	
	(Drinks the poison of death) To your love, Jael, I drink this cup of poison! –	(שותה את סם המות) לְאַהֲבָתֵךְ יָעֵל אֲנִי שֹׁתֶה* כּוֹס הַחֵמָה הַזֹּאת! –	
	The apothecary's words were true; he did not deceive me in his poverty	צָדְקוּ דִבְרֵי הָרֹקֵחַ; בְּעָנְיוֹ לֹא רִמָּנִי	
	His poison has made an end to my life at once, and with a kiss I die. *(Dies)*	סַמָּיו בִּצְעוּנִי כְרֶגַע וּבִנְשִׁיקָה גֹּוֵעַ אֲנִי. (מת)	
	(Rezin enters the graveyard from another side, a torch in his hand, with an axe and hammers)	(רצין בא מעבר אחר אל שדה הקברות ולפיד בידו עם מעצר ומקבות)	
REZIN	The Holy One Most High in heaven![75] Be a shield for me tonight	קָדוֹשׁ עֶלְיוֹן בַּמָּרוֹם![75] הֱיֵה לְמָגֵן לִי הַלַּיְלָה	רצין
	And let the furrows of these graves not be a snare for me	וְתַלְמֵי קְבָרִים אֵלֶּה לֹא יִהְיוּ לִי לְמוֹקֵשׁ	
	Who are you over there?	מִי אַתָּה שָׁמָּה?	
BALTHASAR	A man whose heart is faithful to you, for I know you, my lord.	אִישׁ שֶׁלִּבּוֹ נֶאֱמָן אִתְּךָ, כִּי יְדַעְתִּיךָ אֲדֹנִי.	בלטאזר
REZIN	May the LORD grant you peace; but tell me	יָשֵׂם לְךָ אֲדֹנָי שָׁלוֹם; אַךְ הַגִּידָה לִּי	רצין

74 Ps. 23:4.
75 Cf. Shakespeare's 'Saint Francis be my speed' (5.3.121).

* שֹׁתֶה

	What is that torch burning over there from afar	מָה הַלַּפִּיד הַהוּא הַבֹּעֵר מֵרָחוֹק שָׁמָּה	
	As a lamp that shines **for those who sleep in the dust**,[76] or for maggots and worms?	כַּנֵּר מֵאִיר לִישֵׁנֵי עָפָר,[76] אוֹ לְרִמָּה וְתוֹלֵעָה?	
	If I have not erred in vision, why, it is in the tower of the Abiels.	אִם לֹא שָׁגִיתִי בְרֹאֶה הֲלֹא בְּמִגְדַּל הָאֲבִיעֶלִים הוּא.	
BALTHASAR	You have not erred in vision; my master, whom you love, is there.	לֹא שָׁגִיתָ בְרֹאֶה וְשָׁם אֲדֹנִי אֲשֶׁר אָהַבְתָּ.	בלטאזר
REZIN	And what is your master's name?	וּמַה־שֵּׁם אֲדֹנֶךָ?	רצין
BALTHASAR	Ram.	רָם.	בלטאזר
REZIN	When did he come to the tower?	מָתַי בָּא אֶל הַמִּגְדָּל?	רצין
BALTHASAR	More than half an hour ago.	זֶה יוֹתֵר מֵחֲצִי שָׁעָה.	בלטאזר
REZIN	Come with me to the tower.	לְכָה אִתִּי אֶל הַמִּגְדָּל.	רצין
BALTHASAR	I cannot go, **for it will cost me my life**[77]	לֹא אוּכַל לָלֶכֶת כִּי בְנַפְשִׁי הוּא[77]	בלטאזר
	For I have been commanded by my master to turn away and not to watch him	כִּי מִצְוַת אֲדֹנִי עָלַי לָשׁוּב וְלֹא לְהַבִּיט אַחֲרָיו	
	For if I watch what he is doing there	כִּי אִם אַבִּיט מָה הוּא עֹשֶׂה שָׁם	
	My blood will be on my head.[78]	דָּמִי יִהְיֶה בְרֹאשִׁי.[78]	
REZIN	If so, stay here, and I shall go myself	אִם כֵּן עֲמֹד פֹּה וַאֲנִי אֵלֵךְ לְבַדִּי	רצין
	I fear greatly that evil has been done there.	יָרֵא אֲנִי מְאֹד כִּי רָעָה נֶעֶשְׂתָה שָׁם.	
BALTHASAR	When I lay here by this thicket	כַּאֲשֶׁר שָׁכַבְתִּי פֹּה אֵצֶל הַסְּבַךְ הַזֶּה.	בלטאזר
	I saw as if in a dream that my master struck a man	רָאִיתִי כְּמוֹ בַחֲלוֹם אֲשֶׁר אֲדֹנִי פָּגַע בְּאִישׁ	
	And after they both fought, the other fell by the sword.	וְאַחֲרֵי אֲשֶׁר נִלְחֲמוּ שְׁנֵיהֶם נָפַל הַשֵּׁנִי לְפִי חָרֶב.	
REZIN *(Entering the tower)*	Where are you, Ram?	אַיֶּכָּה רָם?	רצין (בבואו לפני המגדל)

76 This appears in the *Amida*, the central prayer of the daily Jewish liturgy.
77 Prov. 7:23 וְלֹא־יָדַע כִּי־בְנַפְשׁוֹ הוּא 'and he does not know that it will cost him his life'.
78 Ezek. 33:4 דָּמוֹ בְרֹאשׁוֹ יִהְיֶה 'his blood will be on his head'.

	Oh! I see blood on the stones of the path	אֲהָהּ! דָּם אֲנִי רֹאֶה עַל אַבְנֵי הַמְסִלָּה	
	Before the entrance to the tower; what are these swords	לִפְנֵי מְבוֹא הַמִּגְדָּל; מָה הַחֲרָבוֹת הָאֵלֶּה.	
	In the resting house of the dead, with the blood of a slain man upon them?	בְּבָתֵּי מְנוּחוֹת הַמֵּתִים וְדַם חָלָל עֲלֵיהֶן?	
	(As he enters the tower) Ram! Oh, you are dead	(בבואו בתוך המגדל) רָם! אֲהָהּ מֵת אָתָּה	
	And you too, Paris; here you have fallen by the edge of the sword	וְגַם אַתָּה פָּרִיז, פֹּה נָפַלְתָּ לְפִי חָרֶב	
	This day is an evil day, it is an evil time –	יוֹם רַע הַיּוֹם הַהוּא, עֵת רָעָה הִיא –	
	But behold, Jael awakens.	אַךְ יָעֵל הִנֵּה מִתְעוֹרֶרֶת.	
	(Jael arises)	(יעל קמה)	
JAEL	Rezin, restorer of my soul! You have kept your word	רְצִין מֵשִׁיב נַפְשִׁי! מִלֵּאתָ אֶת דְּבָרֶיךָ	יעל
	And I have awoken in the place which you designated for me	וַאֲנִי הֱקִיצֹתִי בַּמָּקוֹם אֲשֶׁר יָעַדְתָּ לִּי	
	Where is Ram? Where is my husband Ram?	אַיֵּה אֵיפֹה רָם? אַיֵּה רָם בַּעֲלִי?	
	(The sound of men's feet is heard outside)	(קול רגלי אנשים נשמע מחוץ)	
REZIN	I hear the sound of men's steps outside	קוֹל צַעֲדֵי אֲנָשִׁים אֲנִי שֹׁמֵעַ מִחוּץ	רצין
	Arise, Jael, and let us leave this **valley of the shadow of death**[79]	קוּמִי יָעֵל וְנֵלְכָה מִגֵּיא צַלְמָוֶת[79] זֶה	
	This is not the place for us, and **this is not the repose.**[80]	לֹא זֶה הַמָּקוֹם לָנוּ וְלֹא זֹאת הַמַּרְגֵּעָה.[80]	
	The ruler over mortal deeds **has thwarted the plans of our hearts**[81]	הַשַּׁלִּיט בְּמַעֲשֵׂי אֱנוֹשׁ, הֵנִיא מַחְשְׁבוֹת לִבֵּנוּ[81]	
	Arise, come with me; your husband lies here dead	קוּמִי לְכִי עִמָּדִי; בַּעֲלֵךְ נֹפֵל פֹּה מֵת	
	And Paris is also dead. I shall take you **to the women's house**[82]	וְגַם פָּרִיז מֵת הוּא וַאֲנִי אוֹלִיכֵךְ לְבֵית הַנָּשִׁים[82]	
	That is to say, the holy women who sit continually before the Lord.[83]	הֲלֹא הֵנָּה נְשֵׁי קֹדֶשׁ הַיֹּשְׁבוֹת לִפְנֵי אֲדֹנָי תָּמִיד.[83]	

79 Ps. 23:4.
80 Isa. 28:12 וְזֹאת הַמַּרְגֵּעָה 'and this is the repose'.
81 Ps. 33:10 יְהוָה הֵפִיר עֲצַת־גּוֹיִם הֵנִיא מַחְשְׁבוֹת עַמִּים 'the Lord nullifies the counsel of the nations; He thwarts the plans of the peoples'.
82 Esther 2:3 אֶל־בֵּית הַנָּשִׁים 'to the women's house'.
83 Cf. Shakespeare's 'a sisterhood of holy nuns' (5.3.157); Salkinson has transformed the explicitly Catholic reference into a vague and religiously neutral one while retaining the general sense of the line.

	Do not ask me anything here; for the watchmen are coming.	אַל תִּשְׁאָלֵנִי פֹּה דָּבָר, כִּי הַשֹּׁמְרִים בָּאִים.	
	(Sound of men's feet outside)	(קול רגלי אנשים מחוץ)	
	Hurry, come with me; I cannot stay here.	מַהֲרִי לְכִי אִתִּי, לֹא אוּכַל לַעֲמֹד פֹּה.	
JAEL	Go on your own; I shall not go with you. *(Rezin exits)*	לֶךְ־לְךָ לְבַדְּךָ, אֲנִי לֹא אֵלֵךְ עִמָּךְ. (רצין הולך)	יעל
	But what is this cup in the hand of **the one whom my soul loves?**[84]	אַךְ מָה הַכּוֹס הַזֹּאת בְּיַד שֶׁאָהֲבָה נַפְשִׁי?[84]	
	A mixture of poisons within it, and with this **he has quickly been cut off and grown weak**[85]	מִמְסַךְ סַמִּים בְּתוֹכָהּ וּבָזֶה גָּז חִישׁ וַיָּעָף[85]	
	How **have you drunk and drained the dregs of the cup of staggering**[86]	אֵיךְ שָׁתִיתָ מָצִיתָ קֻבַּעַת כּוֹס הַתַּרְעֵלָה[86]	
	And have left nothing for me to drink and follow you.	וּמְאוּמָה לֹא הִנַּחְתָּ לִי לִשְׁתּוֹת וְלָבוֹא אַחֲרֶיךָ.	
	Your mouth I shall kiss, Ram, I shall suck the juice of your lips	פִּיךָ אֲנַשֵּׁק רָם, אָמֹץ מִיץ שְׂפָתֶיךָ	
	Perhaps I shall find a sufficient portion for myself in what remains on your lips.	אוּלַי אֶמְצָא דֵּי חֶלְקִי בַּנּוֹתָר עַל הַשְּׂפָתָיִם.	
	(Kisses him) Your lips are moist and hot.	(נושקת אותו) שְׂפָתֶיךָ לַחוֹת וְחַמּוֹת.	
CAPTAIN OF THE WATCHMEN *(Outside)*	Come, guide me, youth, **which way shall we go up?**[87]	לֵךְ נְחֵנִי נַעַר, אֵי־זֶה דֶרֶךְ נַעֲלֶה?[87]	פקיד השומרים (מחוץ)
JAEL	Behold, men are coming; I must hurry to complete my task.	הִנֵּה אֲנָשִׁים בָּאִים אֲמַהֵר לְכַלּוֹת מְלַאכְתִּי.	יעל
	It is good that **you have girded your sword upon your thigh.**[88]	טוֹב כִּי חָגַרְתָּ חַרְבְּךָ עַל יָרֵךְ.[88]	

---

84 Song of Songs 1:7, 3:1, 2, 3.

85 Ps. 90:10 כִּי־גָז חִישׁ וַנָּעֻפָה 'for it is quickly cut off and we fly away'.

86 Isa. 51:17 אֶת־קֻבַּעַת כּוֹס הַתַּרְעֵלָה שָׁתִית מָצִית 'you have drunk and drained to the dregs the cup of staggering'. In English Bible versions the word תַּרְעֵלָה is typically translated as 'staggering', 'reeling', 'trembling', or 'wrath'. However, it literally means 'poison', and this is the sense in which Salkinson is using it.

87 2 Kings 3:8 אֵי־זֶה הַדֶּרֶךְ נַעֲלֶה 'which way shall we go up'.

88 Ps. 45:4 (45:3 in English Bibles) חֲגוֹר־חַרְבְּךָ עַל־יָרֵךְ גִּבּוֹר 'gird your sword upon your thigh, mighty one'.

	(Draws the sword from upon his thigh)	(שולפת החרב מעל ירכו)	
	Return, sword, to your scabbard![89] This is the scabbard that has been prepared for you!	הֵאָסְפִי חֶרֶב אֶל תַּעְרֵךְ![89] זֶה הַתַּעַר הַנָּכוֹן לָךְ!	
	(Plunges the sword into her flesh and falls upon Ram as she dies)	(תוקעת החרב בבשרה ונופלת על רם במותה)	
	(The chief watchman with Paris' youth)	(פקיד השומרים עם הנער אשר לפריז)	
THE YOUTH	There is the place where the torch burns.	שָׁם הוּא הַמָּקוֹם בַּאֲשֶׁר הַלַּפִּיד בֹּעֵר.	הנער
CHIEF WATCHMAN	This is a field of blood; go search in the graveyard[90]	זֶה הוּא שְׂדֵה דָמִים; לְכוּ חַפְּשׂוּ בִּשְׂדֵה הַקְּבָרוֹת[90]	פקיד השומרים
	If you find someone, bring him here.	אִם תִּמְצְאוּ אִישׁ, הָבִיאוּ אֹתוֹ הֵנָּה.	
	(Some of the watchmen exit)	(אחדים מן השומרים הולכים)	
	Whose heart would not feel ill to see **the valley of slaughter**[91]	לֵב מִי לֹא יִדְוֶה לִרְאוֹת גֵּיא הַהֲרֵגָה[91]	
	Here the lord has been struck down and **Ram lies dead**[92]	פֹּה הֻכָּה הַשָּׂר וְרָם נֹפֵל מֵת[92]	
	And upon him Jael lies stabbed through, flowing with hot blood[93]	וְעָלָיו יָעֵל מְדֻקָּרָה זָבַת דָּם חַם[93]	
	As if she has just now died, though she died and was buried	כְּמוֹ מֵתָה עַתָּה וְהִיא מֵתָה וַתִּקָּבֵר	
	Two days ago. – Go tell the prince	זֶה יָמִים שְׁנַיִם. – לְכוּ הַגִּידוּ אֶל הַנָּסִיךְ	
	Call the Abiels so that they might come, tell it in the house of Abiram	קִרְאוּ לָאֲבִיעֵלִים וְיָבוֹאוּ, הַגִּידוּ בְּבֵית אֲבִירָם	
	And the rest of you, go and search wherever you might find.	וְהַנּוֹתָרִים מִכֶּם לְכוּ וְחַפְּשׂוּ* בַּאֲשֶׁר תִּמְצָאוּ.	
	(Some of the watchmen exit)	(מקצת השומרים הולכים)	

89 Jer. 47:6 הֵאָסְפִי אֶל־תַּעְרֵךְ 'return to your scabbard'.
90 Cf. Shakespeare's 'churchyard' (5.3.172).
91 Jer. 7:32, 19:6.
92 Judg. 4:22 וְהִנֵּה סִיסְרָא נֹפֵל מֵת 'and behold, Sisera lay dead'.
93 Salkinson has not reproduced the rhyming couplet 'dead/buried' (5.3.175–6) in the source text.

* וְחַפְּשׂוּ

	In this place a terrible, dreadful deed has been done[94]	בַּמָּקוֹם הַזֶּה נֶעֶשְׂתָה עֲלִילָה נוֹרָאָה אֲיֻמָּה[94]	
	But how it was done I cannot know	אַךְ אֵיךְ נֶעֶשְׂתָה זֹאת דַּעַת לֹא אוּכָלָה	
	Until we enquire and investigate and **bring forth to light that which is hidden**.[95]	עַד נִדְרֹשׁ וְנַחְקֹר וְנוֹצִיא לְאוֹר תַּעֲלֻמָּה.[95]	
	(The watchmen bring Balthasar)	(השומרים מביאים את בלטאזר)	
ONE OF THE WATCHMEN	This is a servant of Ram whom we found in the graveyard.[96]	זֶה עֶבֶד לְרָם אֲשֶׁר מְצָאנֻהוּ בִּשְׂדֵה הַקְּבָרוֹת.[96]	אחד השומרים
CHIEF WATCHMAN	Keep watch over him until the prince arrives.	שִׂימוּ עָלָיו מִשְׁמָר עַד בּוֹא הַנָּסִיךְ.	פקיד השומרים
	(Other watchmen with Rezin)	(שומרים אחרים עם רצין)	
ONE OF THE WATCHMEN	We found this priest[97] coming out of the graveyard[98]	כֹּהֵן[97] זֶה מָצָאנוּ יוֹצֵא מִשְּׂדֵה הַקְּבָרוֹת[98]	אחד השומרים
	And he is **sullen and angry**,[99] sighing and **weeping abundantly**[100]	וְהוּא סָר וְזָעֵף[99] נֶאֱנַח וְיוֹרֵד **בַּבֶּכִי**[100]	
	With an axe and hammers in his hand, these which we have taken from him.	וּבְיָדוֹ מַעֲצָד וּמַקָּבוֹת, אֵלֶּה אֲשֶׁר לָקַחְנוּ מִמֶּנּוּ.	
CHIEF WATCHMAN	In this priest[101] and his tools **there are great searchings of heart**[102]	לַכֹּהֵן[101] הַזֶּה וּלְכֵלָיו גְּדוֹלִים חִקְרֵי לֵב[102]	פקיד השומרים
	Keep watch over him as well.	שִׁמְרוּ גַּם אֹתוֹ.	
	(The prince arrives with his servants)	(הנסיך בא עם משרתיו)	
THE PRINCE	What has happened here, **what thing has been done**[103]	מַה־קָּרָה פֹּה, מֶה הָיָה הַדָּבָר[103]	הנסיך

94 This and the following three lines form an ABA rhyme, mirroring Shakespeare's 'lie/woes/descry' (5.3.179–81).
95 Job 28:11 וְתַעֲלֻמָהּ יֹצִא אוֹר 'and that which is hidden he brings forth to light'.
96 Cf. Shakespeare's 'churchyard' (5.3.182).
97 Cf. Shakespeare's 'friar' (5.3.184).
98 Cf. Shakespeare's 'churchyard' (5.3.186).
99 1 Kings 20:43, 21:4.
100 Isa. 24:7.
101 Cf. Shakespeare's 'friar' (5.3.187).
102 Judg. 5:16.
103 1 Sam. 4:16; 2 Sam. 1:4.

	That they have disturbed my rest, coming at the break of dawn?	כִּי הִפְרִיעוּנִי מִמְּנוּחָתִי לָבוֹא כְּאוֹר הַבֹּקֶר?	
	(Abiel and his wife enter with other people)	(אביעל ואשתו באים עם אנשים אחרים)	
ABIEL	What is this consternation? **Why is the city in such an uproar?**[104]	מָה הַמְּהוּמָה הַזֹּאת? מַדּוּעַ קוֹל הַקִּרְיָה הוֹמָה.[104]	אביעל
ABIEL'S WIFE	People on the street are calling 'Ram', other people 'Jael'	אֲנָשִׁים בָּרְחוֹב קֹרְאִים רָם, אֲנָשִׁים אֲחֵרִים יָעֵל	אשת אביעל
	While some are calling 'Paris', and everyone, **hastened and rushed**[105]	וְאֵלֶּה קֹרְאִים פָּרִיז וְכֻלָּם מְבֹהָלִים **וּדְחוּפִים**[105]	
	Is raging and running towards our tower in the graveyard.	רֹגְשִׁים וְרָצִים אֶל מִגְדָּלֵנוּ בִּשְׂדֵה הַקְּבָרוֹת.	
THE PRINCE	What is the **voice of trembling**[106] that rings in my ears?	מַה־קּוֹל הַחֲרָדָה[106] אֲשֶׁר יְצַלְצֵל בְּאָזְנָי?	הנסיך
CHIEF WATCHMAN	My lord prince! We found Lord Paris	אֲדֹנִי הַנָּסִיךְ! אֶת פָּרִיז הַשָּׂר מְצָאנוּ	פקיד השומרים
	Here **slain by the sword**;[107] next to him the son of Abiram, dead	פֹּה חֲלַל חֶרֶב,[107] אֶצְלוֹ בֶּן אֲבִירָם מֵת	
	And Jael, daughter of Abiel, who died two days ago	וְיָעֵל בַּת אֲבִיעֵל אֲשֶׁר מֵתָה זֶה יוֹמַיִם	
	Flowing with hot blood, as if she had been stabbed through just now.	זָבַת דָּם חַם, כְּמוֹ מְדֻקָּרָה עָתָּה.	
THE PRINCE	Enquire and investigate the matter, from whence this murder has come.	דְּרֹשׁ וַחֲקֹר הַדָּבָר מֵאַיִן בָּא הָרֶצַח הַזֶּה.	הנסיך
CHIEF WATCHMAN	Here is this priest, and this is a servant of the dead Ram	פֹּה הַכֹּהֵן הַזֶּה וְזֶה עֶבֶד לְרָם הַמֵּת	פקיד השומרים
	And in both their hands we found these iron tools	וּבִידֵי שְׁנֵיהֶם מָצָאנוּ כְּלֵי בַרְזֶל אֵלֶּה	
	To open the graves.	לִפְתֹּחַ אֶת הַקְּבָרוֹת.	

104 1 Kings 1:41.
105 Esther 8:14.
106 Jer. 30:5.
107 Num. 19:16.

ABIEL	Look, my wife, oh! Why, our daughter is bleeding	הַבִּיטִי אִשְׁתִּי אֲהָהּ! הֲלֹא בִתֵּנוּ זָבַת דָּם	אביעל
	The sword has been drawn from its scabbard on Ram's thigh	הַחֶרֶב הוּרְקָה מִתַּעְרָהּ אֲשֶׁר עַל יֶרֶךְ רָם	
	And driven into her heart.	וּתְקוּעָה בְּתוֹךְ לִבָּהּ.	
ABIEL'S WIFE	This scene before my eyes is like a bell tolling	הַמַּחֲזֶה הַזֶּה לְעֵינַי, כְּפַעֲמוֹן אֲשֶׁר יִתֵּן קוֹלוֹ	אשת אביעל
	For the professional mourning women and **those skilful in lamentation**[108] to come **bring my grey head down to Sheol.**[109]	לַמְקוֹנְנוֹת וְלַיּוֹדְעֵי נֶהִי[108] לָבוֹא לְהוֹרִיד שֵׂיבָתִי שְׁאוֹלָה.[109]	
	(Abiram and his men enter)	(אבירם ואנשיו באים)	
THE PRINCE	Come here Abiram; you have arisen early at dawn today	בּוֹא הֵנָּה אֲבִירָם, בַּשַּׁחַר הִשְׁכַּמְתָּ הַיּוֹם	הנסיך
	In order to see your son, who arose early in order to close his day at the dawn of his life.	לִרְאוֹת בִּנְךָ אֲשֶׁר הִשְׁכִּים לִסְגֹּר יוֹמוֹ בְּשַׁחֲרוּתוֹ.	
ABIRAM	Oh, my lord prince! My wife died tonight	אוֹיָה אֲדֹנִי הַנָּסִיךְ! אִשְׁתִּי מֵתָה עָלַי הַלַּיְלָה	אבירם
	For she was grieved at the distress of her son, who had been exiled and was no more.	כִּי הִתְעַצְּבָה בְּצָרַת בְּנָהּ אֲשֶׁר גָּלָה וְאֵינֶנּוּ.	
	Is there another pain to be inflicted upon me in my old age?	הֲיֵשׁ עוֹד מַכְאֹב לְהַכְאִיב אֶת נַפְשִׁי לְזִקְנָתִי?	
THE PRINCE	Open your eyes and see.	פְּקַח עֵינֶיךָ וּרְאֵה.	הנסיך
ABIRAM	Rash son! **Why have you done such a thing**[110] to me?	בֵּן נִמְהָר! מַדּוּעַ כָּכָה עָשִׂיתָ[110] לִּי?	אבירם
	Why have you hastened before your father to find a grave for yourself?	מַדוּעַ* מִהַרְתָּ לִפְנֵי אָבִיךָ לִמְצֹא לְךָ קָבֶר?	
THE PRINCE	Put your hand over your mouth; do not cry out	שִׂים יָדְךָ עַל פֶּה, אַל תַּשְׁמִיעַ קוֹל זְעָקָה	הנסיך
	It is time for us to restrain ourselves and not to give vent to all of our feelings	עֵת לָנוּ לְהִתְאַפֵּק וְלֹא לְהוֹצִיא כָּל רוּחֵנוּ	

108 Amos 5:16.
109 Gen. 42:38 וְהוֹרַדְתֶּם אֶת־שֵׂיבָתִי בְּיָגוֹן שְׁאוֹלָה 'you will bring my grey head in sorrow down to Sheol'; Gen. 44:29 וְהוֹרַדְתֶּם אֶת־שֵׂיבָתִי בְּרָעָה שְׁאֹלָה 'and you will bring my grey head in sadness down to Sheol'.
110 1 Kings 1:6.

* מַדּוּעַ

	Until the source is found, from which the evil came forth	עַד אֲשֶׁר נִמְצָא הַמָּקוֹר, מִמֶּנּוּ יָצְאָה הָרָעָה	
	And we remove the shroud cast over the field of graves	**וְנָסִיר אֶת פְּנֵי הַלּוֹט עַל שְׂדֵה הַקְּבָרוֹת**	
	And the veil which is spread over all the nations[111]	**וְאֶת הַמַּסֵּכָה הַנְּסוּכָה עַל הַמַּעֲשִׂים נַעֲשׂוּ פֹּה**[111]	
	Then I shall go before you as a father at the head of mourners	אָז אֵלֵךְ לִפְנֵיכֶם כְּאָב בְּרֹאשׁ אֲבֵלִים	
	Leading you according to the tune of death[112] –	לְנַהֵג אֶתְכֶם עַלְמוּת[112] –	
	Please bring the men whom you suspect	הָבֵא נָא אֵת הָאֲנָשִׁים אֲשֶׁר אַתָּה עוֹיֵן אֹתָם	
	In order that they might be interrogated before me.	לְמַעַן יִבָּחֲנוּ לְפָנָי.	
REZIN	You have set your eyes upon me, and I am the first	עָלַי שַׂמְתֶּם עֵינֵיכֶם וַאֲנִי הוּא הָרִאשׁוֹן.	רצין
	From whom you seek revenge for these people's blood	אֲשֶׁר תִּדְרְשׁוּ מִיָּדִי דַּם הָאֲנָשִׁים הָאֵלֶּה	
	But please know that there is no man on earth	אַךְ דְּעוּ נָא כִּי אֵין אִישׁ בָּאָרֶץ	
	Who guards himself from shedding blood as I do	אֲשֶׁר יִשְׁמֹר אֶת נַפְשׁוֹ מִבּוֹא בְדָמִים כָּמוֹנִי	
	Yet here I stand before you to condemn myself	וַאֲנִי הִנְנִי עֹמֵד לִפְנֵיכֶם לְהַרְשִׁיעַ אֶת נַפְשִׁי	

111 Isa. 25:7 וּבִלַּע בָּהָר הַזֶּה פְּנֵי־הַלּוֹט ׀ הַלּוֹט עַל־כָּל־הָעַמִּים וְהַמַּסֵּכָה הַנְּסוּכָה עַל־כָּל־הַגּוֹיִם 'and on this mountain He will destroy the shroud cast over all the peoples and the veil which is spread over all the nations'.

112 Ps. 9:1 לַמְנַצֵּחַ עַלְמוּת לַבֵּן 'to the chief Musician according to the tune of Muthlabben'. This is the only occurrence of the word עַלְמוּת in the Hebrew Bible (it is a feature of medieval and later Hebrew, but in the meaning of 'youth' or 'youthfulness', which do not seem appropriate here). The Psalm's phrase עַלְמוּת לַבֵּן is enigmatic and has given rise to various explanations. Many English Bible versions, for example, the Geneva Bible, the King James Bible, the New Revised Standard Version, the English Standard Version, and the Jewish Publication Society 1917 Tanakh, interpret it as a personal name Muthlabben. Others, for example, the New International Version, interpret the entire phrase literally as 'upon the death of the son'; this translation also appears in certain ancient Bible translations. Certain translations; for example, the New Revised Standard Version and the New International Version, understand עַל 'upon' in the sense of 'according to' or 'according to the tune of', since the phrase forms part of the Psalm's introductory musical instructions. Some medieval Jewish commentators, such as Ibn Ezra and Dunash ben Labrat, interpret the first word literally as 'upon the death of' and the second word as a personal name, Labben. By contrast, the prominent medieval commentator Rashi interprets the phrase very differently, translating it as 'to brighten the youth' (a reading based on the medieval understanding of the word עַלְמוּת as 'youth' or 'youthfulness' and of לַבֵּן as a form of the root .ל.ב.ן, meaning 'to whiten' or 'to brighten'). Salkinson has selected part of the phrase (leaving off the final word לַבֵּן) in the line corresponding to Shakespeare's 'And lead you even to death' (5.3.220); as such, he seems to have intended the word in the Psalm to serve as a reference to death rather than as a reference to youthfulness or as part of a personal name.

	Though my innocence will also come to light, for I am blameless	וְגַם צִדְקָתִי תֵּצֵא לָאוֹר כִּי נָקִי אָנֹכִי	
	I am both the prosecutor and the defender.	אֲנִי הוּא הַמַּרְשִׁיעַ וַאֲנִי הוּא הַמַּצְדִּיק כְּאֶחָד.	
THE PRINCE	If so, tell us the root of the matter that you know.	אִם כֵּן סַפֵּר לָנוּ שֹׁרֶשׁ הַדָּבָר אֲשֶׁר יָדַעְתָּ.	הנסיך
REZIN	I shall tell everything, but shall not draw out my speech	אֲנִי אַגִּיד אֶת כֹּל וְלֹא אַאֲרִיךְ לָשׁוֹן	רצין
	For out of shortness of breath I cannot speak at length.	כִּי מִקֹּצֶר רוּחַ לְהַרְבּוֹת שִׂיחַ לֹא אוּכָל.	
	Ram, who lies dead here, was husband to Jael	רָם הַמֵּת הַזֶּה הָיָה בַּעַל לְיָעֵל	
	And Jael, who lies dead there, was the wife of his covenant	וְיָעֵל הַמֵּתָה שָׁם הָיְתָה אֵשֶׁת בְּרִיתוֹ	
	For I brought them into the covenant of marriage according to law	כִּי אֲנִי הֵבֵאתִים בִּבְרִית הַחֲתֻנָּה כַּמִּשְׁפָּט	
	And on the day of their concealed marriage Tubal was taken away **before his time**[113]	וּבְיוֹם חֲתֻנָּתָם הַמְּסֻתָּרָה נִסְפָּה תוּבַל **בְּלֹא יוֹמוֹ**[113]	
	And Ram, who killed him, was exiled from his city in **his night of pleasure**[114]	וְרָם אֲשֶׁר הֱמִיתוֹ, גָּלָה מֵעִירוֹ **בְּנֶשֶׁף חִשְׁקוֹ**[114]	
	And it was over him that Jael mourned, not over Tubal's death.	וְעָלָיו הִתְאַבְּלָה יָעֵל וְלֹא עַל מוֹת תּוּבָל.	
	And her parents, who meant to remove the sadness from her heart	וַאֲבוֹתֶיהָ אֲשֶׁר דִּמּוּ לְהָסִיר עֶצֶב מִלִּבָּהּ	
	Promised her to Paris and forced her to marry him	יָעֲדוּ אֹתָהּ לְפָרִיז וַיְאַלְצוּהָ לְהִנָּשֵׂא לוֹ	
	And, being extremely distressed, she came to me in great confusion	וּבְהָצֵר לָהּ מְאֹד בָּאָה אֵלַי בִּמְבוּכָה גְדוֹלָה	
	Asking if I had the power to save her from the second marriage	לֵאמֹר אִם יָדִי מַשֶּׂגֶת לְהַצִּילָהּ מֵחֲתֻנָּה הַשֵּׁנִית	

113 Job 15:32.
114 Isa. 21:4 אֵת נֶשֶׁף חִשְׁקִי שָׂם לִי לַחֲרָדָה 'my night of pleasure he has turned to terror'.

And if not, she would take her own life at once	וְאִם אַיִן, תִּשְׁלַח יָד בְּנַפְשָׁהּ כְּרֶגַע
Therefore I gave her a mixture which I had learned to make	לָכֵן נָתַתִּי מֶסֶךְ בְּיָדָהּ אֲשֶׁר לָמַדְתִּי לַעֲשׂוֹתוֹ
And when she drank from it, a sleep like the sleep of death fell upon her	וְכִשְׁתוֹתָהּ מִמֶּנּוּ נָפְלָה עָלֶיהָ שֵׁנָה כִּשְׁנַת הַמָּוֶת
And she lay in her deep sleep as if dead for two days, as I had planned	וַתִּשְׁכַּב בְּתַרְדֵּמָתָהּ כְּמֵתָה יוֹמַיִם כַּאֲשֶׁר זָמַמְתִּי
And I wrote to Ram to come on this night of distress	וַאֲנִי כָתַבְתִּי אֶל רָם לָבוֹא בְּלֵיל צָרָה הַזֶּה
At the appointed time when she would arise from her grave so that he could take her to his place	לַמּוֹעֵד תָּקוּם מִקִּבְרָהּ לְמַעַן יוֹלִיכֶנָּה לִמְקוֹמוֹ
For after two days she would shake herself free from my mixed wine	כִּי אַחֲרֵי שְׁנֵי יָמִים תִּנָּעֵר מִיֵּין מִסְכִּי
But the messenger with the letter, Hanan the priest,[115]	אֶפֶס שְׁלִיחַ הַמִּכְתָּב, הוּא חָנָן הַכֹּהֵן[115]
Was caught and shut up in the city, and yesterday evening	נִתְפַּשׂ וְנֶעְצַר בָּעִיר וּבְיוֹם אֶתְמוֹל בָּעֶרֶב
He returned my letter to me; therefore I went myself	הֵשִׁיב לִי אֶת מִכְתָּבִי, לָכֵן הָלַכְתִּי לְבַדִּי
Before midnight to be there in the cavern	לִפְנֵי חֲצוֹת הַלַּיְלָה לִהְיוֹת שָׁם בַּמְּעָרָה
At the time when she was to awaken from her sleep, for I intended	לְעֵת תָּעִיר מִשְּׁנָתָהּ, כִּי הָיָה עִם לְבָבִי
To take her and hide her in my house until I found an opportunity	לְהוֹלִיכָהּ וּלְהַסְתִּירָהּ בְּבֵיתִי עַד אֶמְצָא לִי יָדַיִם
To send word and tell Ram; but when I arrived at the place	לִשְׁלֹחַ וּלְהַגִּיד לְרָם; אַךְ בְּבוֹאִי אֶל הַמָּקוֹם
Before she arose from her grave, I found Lord Paris	טֶרֶם קָמָה מִקִּבְרָהּ, מָצָאתִי אֶת פָּרִיז הַשָּׂר
And Ram, the **faithful man**,[116] both of them slain, dead.	וְאֶת רָם אִישׁ אֱמֻנִים[116] שְׁנֵיהֶם חֲלָלִים מֵתִים.

115 Cf. Shakespeare's 'Friar' (5.3.250).
116 Prov. 20:6.

	Then her soul returned to her **and her flesh grew warm**[117] and she came alive.	אָז שָׁבָה נַפְשָׁהּ אֶל קִרְבָּהּ וַיָּחָם בְּשָׂרָהּ[117] וַתֶּחִי.	
	And I urged her to be courageous, to go with me	וְאָנֹכִי הִפְצַרְתִּי בָהּ לְהִתְחַזֵּק לָלֶכֶת עִמִּי	
	And not to despise **the rod of discipline**,[118] for it is the discipline of the LORD.	וְלֹא לָקוּץ בְּשֵׁבֶט מוּסָר,[118] כִּי מוּסַר אֲדֹנָי הוּא.	
	But **a rumbling sound**[119] outside caused me to flee from the cavern	אַךְ קוֹל רַעַשׁ[119] מִחוּץ הִבְרִיחַ אֹתִי מִן הַמְּעָרָה	
	And her soul was bitter, so she refused to go with me	וְהִיא נַפְשָׁהּ מָרָה לָהּ וַתְּמָאֵן לָלֶכֶת עִמִּי	
	And as it looks to me, she took her own life.	וּלְפִי הַנִּרְאֶה בְעֵינַי שָׁלְחָה יָד בְּנַפְשָׁהּ.	
	And regarding the matter of her wedding, which was done **according to the law**,[120]	וְעַל דְּבַר חֲתֻנָּתָהּ אֲשֶׁר נֶעֶשְׂתָה כַּדָּת[120]	
	Her nurse knows, for she was a witness.	אֹמַנְתָּהּ יֹדַעַת זֹאת כִּי הִיא הָיְתָה לְעֵדָה	
	All this I know, and I have told you in faith	כָּל זֹאת יָדַעְתִּי וְסִפַּרְתִּי לָכֶם בֶּאֱמוּנָה	
	And if you have found evil in my deeds and **lay the sin upon me**[121]	וְאִם עָוֶל מְצָאתֶם בְּמַעֲשַׂי וְתָשִׁיתוּ עָלַי חַטָּאת[121]	
	Do with me according to the law; I do not ask for kindness	עֲשׂוּ לִי כַּמִּשְׁפָּט, לֹא אֲבַקֵּשׁ חֶסֶד	
	And I am ready **for my grey head to go down in blood to Sheol.**[122]	וְנָכוֹן אֲנִי בְּשֵׂיבָתִי לָרֶדֶת בְּדָם שְׁאוֹלָה.[122]	
THE PRINCE	Thus far I have known you to be an honourable holy man of the LORD –	עַד הֵנָּה יְדַעְתִּיךָ לִקְדוֹשׁ אֲדֹנָי מְכֻבָּד –	הנסיך
	Bring Ram's servant, and let us hear what he has to say.	הַגִּישׁוּ אֶת עֶבֶד רָם וְנִשְׁמַע מַה־בְּפִיו.	

117 2 Kings 4:34 וַיָּחָם בְּשַׂר הַיָּלֶד 'and the child's flesh grew warm' (when coming back from the dead).
118 Prov. 22:15.
119 Ezek. 3:12.
120 Esther 1:8, 4:16.
121 Num. 12:11 אַל־נָא תָשֵׁת עָלֵינוּ חַטָּאת 'please do not lay the sin upon us'.
122 1 Kings 2:9 וְהוֹרַדְתָּ אֶת־שֵׂיבָתוֹ בְּדָם שְׁאוֹל 'and you must bring his grey head down in blood to Sheol'.

BALTHASAR	When I gave my master the tidings that Jael was dead	כַּאֲשֶׁר בִּשַּׂרְתִּי אֶת אֲדֹנִי כִּי יָעֵל מֵתָה	בלטאזר
	He rushed to return here on horses from Mantua	אָץ לָשׁוּב הֵנָּה עַל סוּסִים מִמַּנְטוֹבָה	
	And came to the graveyard before this tower	וַיָּבוֹא אֶל שְׂדֵה הַקְּבָרוֹת לִפְנֵי הַמִּגְדָּל הַזֶּה	
	And gave me a letter to hurry and deliver to his father	וְלִי נָתַן סֵפֶר לְהָחִישׁ לְמָסְרוֹ בְּיַד אָבִיו	
	And he also commanded me to return to my house, not to watch him	וְגַם צִוַּנִי לָשׁוּב לְבֵיתִי, לִבְלִי הַבֵּט אַחֲרָיו	
	As he entered the cavern, **for it would cost me my life.**[123]	בְּבוֹאוֹ אֶל הַמְּעָרָה כִּי **בְנַפְשִׁי הוּא**.[123]	
THE PRINCE	Give me the letter so that I might see what is written in it –	תֵּן לִי אֶת הַסֵּפֶר וְאֶרְאֶה מַה־כָּתוּב בּוֹ –	הנסיך
	Where is Paris' youth, who called the city watchmen?	אַיֵּה הַנַּעַר לְפָּרִיז אֲשֶׁר קָרָא לְשֹׁמְרֵי הָעִיר?	
	Tell me, you there, what was your master doing here?	הַגֵּד לִי פְּלֹנִי אַלְמֹנִי, מֶה עָשָׂה אֲדֹנְךָ פֹּה?	
THE YOUTH	He had brought flowers to strew over his bride's grave	נִצָּנִים הֵבִיא בְּיָדוֹ לִזְרוֹת עַל קֶבֶר כַּלָּתוֹ	הנער
	And I stood from afar for so I was commanded	וַאֲנִי עָמַדְתִּי מֵרָחוֹק כִּי כֵן צֻוֵּיתִי	
	When lo, a man with a torch in his hand opened the grave	וְהִנֵּה אִישׁ וְלַפִּיד בְּיָדוֹ פָּתַח אֶת הַקֶּבֶר	
	And my master fought with him, **and they brandished their swords before them**[124]	וַיָּרֶב אֲדֹנִי בוֹ **וַיְעוֹפְפוּ חַרְבָּם עַל פְּנֵיהֶם**[124]	
	And I was afraid, and ran and called the watchmen.	וַאֲנִי יָגֹרְתִּי רַצְתִּי וָאֶקְרָא אֶת הַשֹּׁמְרִים.	
THE PRINCE	This letter is testimony that the words of the priest[125] are true	הַסֵּפֶר הַזֶּה לְעֵדוּת כִּי כֵנִים דִּבְרֵי הַכֹּהֵן[125]	הנסיך
	Regarding the secret love and the report of Jael's death	עַל אֹדוֹת הָאַהֲבָה הַמִּסְתָּרָה וּשְׁמוּעַת מוֹת יָעֵל	

123 Prov. 7:23 וְלֹא־יָדַע כִּי־בְנַפְשׁוֹ הוּא 'and he does not know that it will cost him his life'.
124 Ezek. 32:10 בְּעוֹפְפִי חַרְבִּי עַל־פְּנֵיהֶם 'when I brandish my sword before them'.
125 Cf. Shakespeare's 'Friar' (5.3.286).

And it also says that he bought **the poison of death**[126]
וְגַם הוּא מַגִּיד כִּי קָנָה סַם הַמָּוֶת[126]

From a poor apothecary, and that he came to the grave
מֵאֵת רֹקֵחַ עָנִי וְכִי בָא אֶל הַקֶּבֶר

In order to die and lie with Jael – where are you, you who bear a grudge!
לָמוּת וְלִשְׁכַּב עִם יָעֵל – אַיֵּכֶם נֹטְרֵי אֵיבָה!

Where are you, Abiel and Abiram! This is the curse
אַיֶּכֶם אֲבִיעֵל וַאֲבִירָם! זֹאת הִיא הַקְּלָלָה

That lies upon strife, and this is the fruit of the enmity
הָרֹבֶצֶת עַל מְדָנִים וְזֶה פְּרִי הָאֵיבָה

But instead of the wrath of your hatred, which burned like fire,
וְתַחַת חֲמַת שִׂנְאַתְכֶם אֲשֶׁר בָּעֲרָה כָאֵשׁ

The fire of love has gone forth and devoured **those pleasing to your eyes**.[127]
יָצְאָה אֵשׁ הָאַהֲבָה וַתֹּאכַל אֶת מַחְמַדֵּי עֵינֵיכֶם.[127]

And I, because I averred my eyes and did not stop **quarrel and strife**[128]
וַאֲנִי עֵקֶב הֶעֱלַמְתִּי עֵינַי מֵהַשְׁבִּית רִיב וּמָדוֹן[128]

Have lost two young men of my family
אָבְדוּ לִי בַּחוּרִים שְׁנַיִם מִבְּנֵי מִשְׁפַּחְתִּי

We have all been guilty, and the wrath has gone forth over us all.
כֻּלָּנוּ אֲשֵׁמִים הָיִינוּ וְעַל כֻּלָּנוּ יָצָא הַקָּצֶף.

ABIEL Come, my brother Abiram! Give me your hand in peace
אביעל הָבָה אֲבִירָם אָחִי! הָבָה לִּי יָדְךָ לְשָׁלוֹם

This is my daughter's portion; this peace
זֶה חֵלֶק בִּתִּי, זֶה הַשָּׁלוֹם לְבָד

Is all that she has left behind as a memorial – and more I cannot ask for.
הִשְׁאִירָה אַחֲרֶיהָ לְזִכָּרוֹן – וּלְבַקֵּשׁ יֶתֶר לֹא אוּכָל.

ABIRAM Whereas I am prepared to give more than you desire
אבירם וַאֲנִי הִנְנִי נָכוֹן לָתֵת יֶתֶר מֵחֶפְצְךָ

For **out of gold of Ophir**[129] I shall establish a statue in her likeness
כִּי מִזְּהַב אוֹפִיר[129] אָקִים פֶּסֶל תְּמוּנָתָהּ

---

126 Mishnah *Ḥullin* 3:5.
127 Lam. 2:4 כֹּל מַחֲמַדֵּי־עָיִן 'all that were pleasant to the eye'.
128 Hab. 1:3.
129 1 Chron. 29:4. Ophir is a region renowned in the Hebrew Bible for its wealth.

	Made by the greatest craftsman of all the master artisans	עַל יְדֵי הָאָמָן הַגָּדוֹל בְּכָל חַכְמֵי חָרָשִׁים	
	And as long as **the city of Verona stands on its mound**[130]	**וְכָל עוֹד עִיר וֵירוֹנָה תַּעֲמֹד עַל תִּלָּהּ**[130]	
	This statue will be the foremost of all its treasures[131]	יִהְיֶה הַפֶּסֶל הַזֶּה רִאשׁוֹן לְכָל מַחֲמַדֶּיהָ[131]	
	As a memorial for Jael, daughter of truth and faith.	לְאוֹת זִכָּרוֹן לְיָעֵל הַבַּת אֱמֶת וֶאֱמוּנָה.	
ABIEL	And that craftsman shall likewise hew a statue of Ram[132]	וְכֵן גַּם פֶּסֶל רָם, יִפְסֹל הָאָמָן הַהוּא[132]	אביעל
	And both figures will stand **touching each other**[133]	וּשְׁתֵּי הַתְּמוּנוֹת תַּעֲמֹדְנָה **מַשִּׁיקוֹת אִשָּׁה אֶת אֲחוֹתָהּ**[133]	
	In order to commemorate the names of our children, who fell because of our iniquity.	בַּעֲבוּר הַזְכִּיר שֵׁם בָּנֵינוּ אֲשֶׁר נָפְלוּ בַּעֲוֹנֵינוּ.	
THE PRINCE	The morning has brought us peace, but has not wiped away our tears[134]	הַבֹּקֶר הֵבִיא לָנוּ שָׁלוֹם וְדִמְעָתֵנוּ לֹא מָחָה[134]	הנסיך
	And the sun is too ashamed to shine on a day of mourning and sighing.	וְהַשֶּׁמֶשׁ בּוֹשׁ מִזְּרֹחַ בְּיוֹם אֵבֶל וַאֲנָחָה.	
	Go now, each man to his own house, where we shall gather again and converse[135]	לְכוּ עַתָּה אִישׁ לְבֵיתוֹ עוֹד נִתְאַסֵּף וְנָשִׂיחָה[135]	

130 Josh. 11:13 כָּל־הֶעָרִים הָעֹמְדוֹת עַל־תִּלָּם 'all the cities that stood on their mounds'.

131 The corresponding lines in the source text form a rhyming couplet 'set/Juliet' (5.3.301–2). Salkinson has not reproduced this rhyme. Admittedly in the Ashkenazic Hebrew pronunciation the last word of each line would have been pronounced with the same vowel, thus forming a near rhyme, but Salkinson's rhymes typically consist of a matching final consonant as well as vowel, which casts doubt on the possibility that he intended these lines to serve as a rhyming couplet.

132 The equivalent speech in the source text consists of a single rhyming couplet 'lie/enmity' (5.3.303–4). Salkinson has added a line and has not reproduced the rhyming couplet. However, the first and last line of his speech form an ABA near rhyme (the final vowel rhymes, but not the preceding consonant). This may represent an intentional attempt to echo the original; alternatively, it is possible that Salkinson did not recognize Shakespeare's lines as a rhyme, given that 'lie' and 'enmity' would not have rhymed in the late nineteenth century.

133 Ezek. 3:13.

134 This and the next line form a rhyming couplet. Salkinson has expanded this speech from six to ten lines. Shakespeare's speech consists of an ABAB rhyming sequence followed by a final rhyming couplet, so there is no precise equivalent to this initial rhyming couplet in his text (although the couplet's content overlaps with that of the first two lines of Shakespeare's speech).

135 This and the next three lines form an ABAB rhyming pattern, mirroring Shakespeare's 'brings/head/things/punished' (5.3.305–8) – although because Salkinson has added four lines to this speech, the content of these lines does not correspond precisely to that of the equivalent rhyming lines in the source text.

Regarding this evil matter, regarding the deeds of the noblemen	עַל הַדָּבָר הָרָע הַזֶּה, עַל מַעֲשֵׂה הָאֲצִילִים
I shall recompense you according to your deeds,[136] whether punishment or pardon	כְּמַעַלְלֵיכֶם אָשִׁיב לָכֶם,[136] אִם לְעֹנֶשׁ וְאִם לִסְלִיחָה
Kindness is suitable for the blameless one, whereas for the wicked one, the punishment of judges.	חֶסֶד נָכוֹן לַנָּבָר וְלַנָּבָל מוּסַר פְּלִילִים.
Indeed here we shall establish a pillar as a monument in the graveyard[137]	אַךְ פֹּה נָקִים מַצֵּבָה לְצִיּוּן בִּשְׂדֵה הַקְּבָרוֹת[137]
It is a lamentation for all generations, which will be chanted[138] by the male and female singers	קִינָה הִיא לְדֹר דֹּר וְקוֹנְנוּהָ[138] הַשָּׁרִים וְהַשָּׁרוֹת
Oh, Ram and Jael! In their very love they were destroyed[139]	אֲהָהּ רָם וְיָעֵל! בְּעֶצֶם אַהֲבָתָם נִכְחָדוּ[139]
They were lovely and pleasant in their life, and in their death they have not been divided.[140]	הַנֶּאֱהָבִים וְהַנְּעִימִים בְּחַיֵּיהֶם וּבְמוֹתָם לֹא נִפְרָדוּ.[140]
(Exeunt)	(הולכים)

The End of the Book. — תם הספר.

136 Hosea 12:3 (12:2 in English Bibles) כְּמַעֲלָלָיו יָשִׁיב לוֹ 'He will recompense him according to his deeds'.
137 This and the next line form a rhyming couplet. These two lines do not have a parallel in the source text (with respect to both the rhyme and the content).
138 Ezek. 32:16 קִינָה הִיא וְקוֹנְנוּהָ 'this is a lamentation which will be chanted'.
139 This and the next line form a rhyming couplet, mirroring Shakespeare's 'woe/Romeo' (5.3.309–10).
140 2 Sam. 1:23.

References

Ackerman, Susan. 2009. Astarte: Bible. In *Jewish Women: A Comprehensive Historical Encyclopedia*, ed. Paula E. Hyman and Dalia Ofer. http://jwa.org/encyclopedia/article/astarte-bible. Accessed 2 May 2017.

Ahituv, Shmuel. 2007. Azazel. In *Encyclopaedia Judaica*, ed. Michael Berenbaum and Fred Skolnik, 2nd edn, vol. 2, 763–4. Detroit: Macmillan Reference USA.

Almagor, Dan. 1975. שקספיר בספרות העברית בתקופת ההשכלה ובתקופת התחייה: סקירה ביבליוגראפית וביבליוגראפיה [Shakespeare in Hebrew Literature, 1794–1930: Bibliographical Survey and Bibliography]. In ספר היובל לשמעון הלקין: במלאת לו שבעים וחמש שנים [*Festschrift for Shimon Halkin*], eds. Boaz Shahevitch and Menachem Perry, 721–84. Jerusalem: Reuben Mass.

———. 2016. רם-רומיאו ויעל-יוליה חוזרים [Ram-Romeo and Jael-Juliet Return]. *Ha'aretz*, 2 August. www.haaretz.co.il/literature/prose/.premium-1.3024895. Accessed 25 August 2016.

Alterman, Natan. 1950. אותלו [*Othello*]. Merhavia: Sifriat Poalim, HaKibbutz HaArtzi/HaShomer HaTzair. Repr., 1955.

Amit, Yairah. 2004. Judges. In *The Jewish Study Bible*, ed. Adele Berlin and Marc Zvi Brettler, 508–57. Oxford: Oxford University Press.

Arbel, Michal. 2015. הכירו את "איתיאל הכושי מוינעציא", הלוא הוא אותלו [Meet 'Ithiel the Cushite of Venice', i.e., Othello]. *Ha'aretz*, 29 May. www.haaretz.co.il/literature/book-week/.premium-1.2644216. Accessed 25 August 2016.

Armistead, Samuel G. and Joseph H. Silverman. 1965. Christian Elements and De-Christianization in the Sephardic Romancero. In *Collected Studies in Honour of Americo Castro's Eightieth Year*, ed. M. P. Hornik, 21–38. Oxford: Lincombe Lodge Research Library.

Ashkenazi, Yair. 2015. איך נהפך אותלו של שייקספיר לאיתיאל הכושי? [How Did Shakespeare's *Othello* Become *Ithiel the Cushite*?]. *Ha'aretz*, 15 March. www.haaretz.co.il/gallery/literature/.premium-1.2590033. Accessed 25 August 2016.

Ashtor, Eliyahu et al. 2007. Aleppo. In *Encyclopaedia Judaica*, ed. Michael Berenbaum and Fred Skolnik, 2nd edn, vol. 1, 613–17. Detroit: Macmillan Reference USA.

Barb, Isaac. 1883. מקבט [*Macbeth*]. Drohobych: Żupnik and Knoller.

Bar-Efrat, Shimon. 2004. First Samuel. In *The Jewish Study Bible*, ed. Adele Berlin and Marc Zvi Brettler, 558–618. Oxford: Oxford University Press.

Bar-Yosef, Hamutal. 2010. Frishman, David. In *YIVO Encyclopedia of Jews in Eastern Europe*, ed. Jeffrey P. Edelstein et al. www.yivoencyclopedia.org/article.aspx/Frishman_David. Accessed 24 February 2017.

Berlin, Adele and Marc Zvi Brettler. 2004a. Psalms. In *The Jewish Study Bible*, ed. Adele Berlin and Marc Zvi Brettler. Oxford: Oxford University Press.

———, eds. 2004b. *The Jewish Study Bible*. Oxford: Oxford University Press.

Ben-Shushan, Tamar. 2006. חתן דמים: מחקר מיתולוגי בעיצוב רב גרסאי בספרות העברית לדורותיה [*Bridegroom of Blood: A Thematological Multi-Version Investigation Spanning the History of Hebrew Literature*]. PhD dissertation, Bar-Ilan University.

Bornstein, Haim Yehiel. 1900–1. המלט [Hamlet]. In *HaṢefirah* 27 (1): 2; (2): 6; (8): 30; (11): 42; (21): 82; (22): 86; (29): 114; (32): 126; (36): 142; (37): 146; (46): 182; (47): 186; (49): 194; (57): 228; (58): 232; (68): 280); (88): 368; (89): 372; (107): 444; (114): 472; (118): 488; (127): 524; (136): 560; (154): 632; (172): 694; (196): 790; (244): 986 (sic); (250): 920; (261): 962; (270): 998; (277): 1026; (286): 1062; 28 (5): 18; (11): 42; (35): 138; (41): 162; (52); 206; (64): 254; (79): 318; (87): 350; (94): 378; (105): 423; (110): 442; (114): 458; (126): 507; (134): 539; (149): 599; (152): 611; (166): 667; (175): 703; (192): 770; (214): 858; (226): 906; (244): 978; (250): 1002.

Cohen, Israel. 1942. יצחק אדוארד זלקינסון: חייו ומפעלו הספרותי [*Isaac Edward Salkinson: His Life and Literary Work*]. Tel Aviv: Mesillah.

Crystal, David. 2011. Sounding out Shakespeare: Sonnet Rhymes in Original Pronunciation. In *Jezik u upotrebi: primenjena lingvistikja u cast Ranku Bugarskom* [*Language in Use: Applied Linguistics in Honour of Ranko Bugarski*], ed. Vera Vasic, 295–306. Novi Sad and Belgrade: Philosophy Faculties.

Crystal, David and Ben Crystal. 2002. *Shakespeare's Words: A Glossary and Language Companion*. London: Penguin.

Danby, Herbert. 1933. *The Mishnah*. Oxford: Oxford University Press.

Dunlop, John. 1894. *Memories of Gospel Triumphs among the Jews during the Victorian Era*. London: S. W. Partridge and Co.

Eldar, Ilan. 2016. ממנדלסון עד מנדלי: בדרך לעברית החדשה [*From Mendelssohn to Mendele: The Emergence of Modern Literary Hebrew*]. Jerusalem: Carmel.

Eliaz, Raphael, trans. 1957. רומאו ויוליה [*Romeo and Juliet*]. Tel Aviv: HaKibbutz HaMeuchad.

Elkind, Judah Loeb. 1892. מוסר סוררה [*The Disciplining of the Wayward Woman*]. Berditchev: C. Y. Sheftel.

Endelman, Todd M., ed. 1987. *Jewish Apostasy in the Modern World*. New York: Holmes & Meier.

Even-Shoshan, Abraham. 2003. מילון אבן-שושן: מחודש ומעודכן לשנות האלפיים [*The Even-Shoshan Dictionary: Revised and Updated for the Twenty-First Century*], 6 vols., ed. Moshe Azar, Ilana Shamir, and Ya'el Yannai. Israel: HaMilon HeḤadash.

Even-Zohar, Itamar. 1990. The Position of Translated Literature within the Literary Polysystem. *Poetics Today* 11(1): 45–51.

Fassberg, Steven. 2013. Pausal Forms. In *The Encyclopedia of Hebrew Language and Linguistics*, ed. Geoffrey Khan et al., vol. 3, 54–5. Boston: Brill.

Feiner, Shmuel. 2002. *Haskalah and History: The Emergence of a Modern Jewish Historical Consciousness*. Trans. Chaya Naor and Sondra Silverston. Oxford: Littman Library of Jewish Civilization.

Feliks, Jehuda. 2007. Pomegranate. In *Encyclopaedia Judaica*, ed. Michael Berenbaum and Fred Skolnik, 2nd edn, vol. 16, 364–5. Detroit: Macmillan Reference USA.

Frischmann, David. 1924. קוריולנוס [*Coriolanus*]. Warsaw: HaṢefirah.

Frymer, Tikva S. 2007. Ashtoreth. In *Encyclopaedia Judaica*, ed. Michael Berenbaum and Fred Skolnik, 2nd edn, vol. 2, 581–2. Detroit: Macmillan Reference USA.

Gilulah, Devorah. 2013. מאיתיאל הכושי לאותלו של אלתרמן [From *Ithiel the Cushite* to Alterman's *Othello*]. *Bamot uMasakh* 9: 49–58.

Goldberg, Lea. 1936. במות: "אותילו" בתיאטרון עברי בחיפה [Stages: 'Othello' at the Hebrew Theatre in Haifa]. *Davar*, 15 March: 9.

Golomb, Harai. 1998. Shakespearean Re-Generations in Hebrew: A Study in Historical Poetics. In *Strands Afar Remote: Israeli Perspectives on Shakespeare*, ed. Avraham Oz, 255–75. Newark: University of Delaware Press.

Gordon, Samuel Leib. 1899. המלך ליר [*King Lear*]. Warsaw: M. I. Halter and Co.

Grossberg, Daniel. 2004. Lamentations. In *The Jewish Study Bible*, ed. Adele Berlin and Marc Zvi Brettler, 1587–602. Oxford: Oxford University Press.

Gruber, Mayer. 2004. Job. In *The Jewish Study Bible*, ed. Adele Berlin and Marc Zvi Brettler, 1499–562. Oxford: Oxford University Press.

Halkin, Shimon. 1929. הסוחר מונציה [*The Merchant of Venice*]. Berlin: A. J. Stybel.

Haran, Menahem, Menahem Stern, and Gerald Y. Blidstein. 2007. Priests and Priesthood. In *Encyclopaedia Judaica*, ed. Michael Berenbaum and Fred Skolnik, 2nd edn, vol. 16, 513–26. Detroit: Macmillan Reference USA.

Hillers, Delbert Roy and Reuben Kashani. 2007. Burial. In *Encyclopaedia Judaica*, ed. Michael Berenbaum and Fred Skolnik, 2nd edn, vol. 4, 291–4. Detroit: Macmillan Reference USA.

Holtzman, Avner. 2010. Literary Journals: Hebrew Literary Journals. In *YIVO Encyclopedia of Jews in Eastern Europe*, ed. Jeffrey P. Edelstein et al. www.yivoencyclopedia.org/article.aspx/Literary_Journals/Hebrew_Literary_Journals. Accessed 24 February 2017.

Honigmann, E. A. J., ed. 1997. *The Arden Shakespeare: Othello*, 3rd edn. London: Bloomsbury.

Hrushovski-Harshav, Benjamin. 2007. Prosody, Hebrew. In *Encyclopaedia Judaica*, ed. Michael Berenbaum and Fred Skolnik, 2nd edn, vol. 16, 595–623. Detroit: Macmillan Reference USA.

Jastrow, Marcus. 1903. *Dictionary of the Targumim, Talmud Bavli, Talmud Yerushalmi and Midrashic Literature*. Repr., n.p.: Judaica Treasury, 2004.

Kadari, Tamar. 2009. Hannah: Midrash and Aggadah. In *Jewish Women: A Comprehensive Historical Encyclopedia*, ed. Paula E. Hyman and Dalia Ofer. http://jwa.org/encyclopedia/article/asenath-bible. Accessed 25 April 2016.

Kahn, Lily. 2009. *The Verbal System in Late Enlightenment Hebrew*. Leiden: Brill.

———. 2013. Meliṣa. In *The Encyclopedia of Hebrew Language and Linguistics*, ed. Geoffrey Khan et al., vol. 2, 633–4. Boston: Brill.

———. 2015. *A Grammar of the Eastern European Hasidic Hebrew Tale*. Leiden: Brill.

———. 2017. Representations of Italy in the First Hebrew Shakespeare Translations. In *Shakespeare and Italy*, ed. Chris Stamatakis and Enza De Francisci. London: Routledge.

———. Forthcoming a. Biblical Motifs in the First Hebrew Translation of *The Taming of the Shrew*. *Multicultural Shakespeare* 14.

———. Forthcoming b. Domesticating Techniques in the First Hebrew Translation of Hamlet. In *Hamlet Translations*, ed. Márta Minier.

———. Forthcoming c. Kalman Schulman's Hebrew Translation of Josephus's *Jewish War*. In *The Jewish Reception of Josephus*, ed. Andrea Schatz. Leiden: Brill.

Kaufmann, Philipp. 1832. *Othello*. In *Shakspeare's Dramatische Werke*, vol. 2, 1–186. Berlin: Nicolai.

Koehler, Ludwig and Walter Baumgartner. 2001. *The Hebrew and Aramaic Lexicon of the Old Testament*. Rev. Walter Baumgartner and Johann Jakob Stamm with assistance from Benedikt Hartmann et al. Trans. and ed. under the supervision of M. E. J. Richardson. 2 vols. Leiden: Brill.

Lapide, Pinchas. 1984. *Hebrew in the Church: The Foundations of Jewish–Christian Dialogue*. Trans. Erroll F. Rhodes. Grand Rapids, MI: Eerdmans.

Leviant, Curt, ed. and trans. 2003. *King Artus: A Hebrew Arthurian Romance of 1279*. Syracuse: Syracuse University Press.

Levisohn, Shlomo. 1816. מליצת ישורון [*The Meliṣa of Jeshurun*].Vienna: Anton Schmid.

Lieber, Dan. 2007. Strangers and Gentiles. In *Encyclopaedia Judaica*, ed. Michael Berenbaum and Fred Skolnik, 2nd edn, vol. 19, 241–2. Detroit: Macmillan Reference USA.

Malkin, Dov Ber. 1946. מן הצד: שבע דמויות שמצאן שחקן אחד [From the Side: Seven Characters Found by One Actor]. *'Al HaMishmar*, 1 December: 2.

Markel, Howard. 1997. *Quarantine! East European Jewish Immigrants and the New York City Epidemics of 1892*. Baltimore, MD: Johns Hopkins University Press.

Needler, Howard. 1977. Refiguring the Middle Ages: Reflections on Hebrew Romances. *New Literary History* 8(2): 235–55.

Nida, Eugene A. 1964. Principles of Correspondence. Repr. in *The Translation Studies Reader*, ed. Lawrence Venuti, 3rd edn, 141–55. London: Routledge, 2012.

Nida, Eugene A. and Charles R. Taber. 1969. *The Theory and Practice of Translation*. Repr., Leiden: Brill, 2003.

Patterson, David. 1988. *A Phoenix in Fetters: Studies in Nineteenth and Early Twentieth Century Hebrew Fiction*. Savage, MD: Rowman and Littlefield Publishers.

Pelli, Moshe. 1979. *The Age of Haskalah: Studies in Hebrew Literature of the Enlightenment in Germany*. Repr., Lanham, MD: Unversity Press of America, 2006.

———. 1993. On the Role of *Melitzah* in the Literature of Hebrew Enlightenment. In *Hebrew in Ashkenaz: A Language in Exile*, ed. Lewis Glinert, 99–110. New York: Oxford University Press.

Petrovsky-Shtern, Yohanan. 2010. Demons. In *YIVO Encyclopedia of Jews in Eastern Europe*, ed. Jeffrey P. Edelstein et al. www.yivoencyclopedia.org/article.aspx/Demons. Accessed 24 February 2017.

Pym, Anthony. 2010. *Exploring Translation Theories*. London: Routledge.

Rabinowitz, Louis Isaac and David Max Eichhorn. 2007. Proselytes. In *Encyclopaedia Judaica*, ed. Michael Berenbaum and Fred Skolnik, 2nd edn, vol. 16, 587–94. Detroit: Macmillan Reference USA.

Roeh, Y. 1946. אותלו – לאברהם שקלארש [*Othello* – by Avraham Shklarsh]. *Davar*, 21 November: 2.

Rosenzweig, Claudia. 2016. *Bovo d'Antona by Elye Bokher. A Yiddish Romance: A Critical Edition with Commentary*. Leiden: Brill.

Rothkoff, Aaron. 2007. Bat Kol. In *Encyclopaedia Judaica*, ed. Michael Berenbaum and Fred Skolnik, 2nd edn, vol. 3, 213. Detroit: Macmillan Reference USA.

Rovang, Paul R. 2009. Hebraizing Arthurian Romance: The Originality of *Melech Artus*. *Arthuriana* 19(2): 3–9.

Ruderman, David B. 2015. Towards a Preliminary Portrait of an Evangelical Missionary to the Jews: The Many Faces of Alexander McCaul (1799–1863). *Jewish Historical Studies* 47: 48–69.

Sáenz-Badillos, Angel. 1993. *A History of the Hebrew Language.* Trans. John Ewolde. Repr., Cambridge: Cambridge University Press, 2000.

Salkinson, Isaac Edward. 1855. אגרת אל הרומים [*Epistle to the Romans*]. Edinburgh: Robert Young.

———. 1858. סוד הישועה [*The Secret of Salvation*]. Altona, Germany.

———. 1870. ויגרש את האדם [*So He Drove Out the Man*]. Vienna.

———. 1874/2015. איתיאל הכושי מוינציא [*Ithiel the Cushite of Venice*]. Ed. Ilan Bar-Dor, Eran Tzelgov, and Noga Shevach, with an afterword by Aminadav Dikman. Beer Sheva: Raav.

———. 1877. בן קהלת [*The Son of Ecclesiastes*]. Vienna: Georg Brög.

———. 1878/2016. רם ויעל [*Ram and Jael*]. Ed. Ilan Bar-Dor, Eran Tzelgov, and Noga Shevach, with an afterword by Avraham Oz. Beer Sheva: Raav.

Salkinson, Isaac Edward and Christian David Ginsburg. 1885. הברית החדשה: בהעתקה חדשה מלשון יון לישון עבר [*Salkinson-Ginsburg's Hebrew New Testament*]. Vienna: Carl Fromme.

Salsitz, Norman. 2002. *Three Homelands: Memories of a Jewish Life in Poland, Israel, and America*. With Stanley Kaish. Syracuse: Syracuse University Press.

Sarna, Nahum et al. 2007. Enoch. In *Encyclopaedia Judaica*, ed. Michael Berenbaum and Fred Skolnik, 2nd edn, vol. 6, 441–2. Detroit: Macmillan Reference USA.

Schalit, Abraham and Shimon Gibson. 2007. Helena. In *Encyclopaedia Judaica*, ed. Michael Berenbaum and Fred Skolnik, 2nd edn, vol. 6, 781–2. Detroit: Macmillan Reference USA.

Schatz, Andrea. 2009. *Sprache in der Zerstreuung: Di Säkularisierung des Hebräischen im 18. Jahrhundert*. Göttingen: Vandenhoeck & Ruprecht.

Schleiermacher, Friedrich. 1813. On the Different Methods of Translating. Trans. Susan Bernofsky. Repr. in *The Translation Studies Reader*, ed. Lawrence Venuti, 3rd edn, 43–63. London: Routledge, 2012.

Schulman, Alan Richard. 2007. Cush (Kush). In *Encyclopaedia Judaica*, ed. Michael Berenbaum and Fred Skolnik, 2nd edn, vol. 5, 343–4. Detroit: Macmillan Reference USA.

Schwarz, Regina. 2004. Othello and the Horizon of Justice. In *Transcendence: Philosophy, Literature, and Theology Approach the Beyond*, ed. Regina Schwarz, 81–104. New York: Routledge.

Schwarz-Gastine, Isabelle. 2003. Shakespeare on the French Stage: A Historical Survey. In *Four Hundred Years of Shakespeare in Europe*, ed. Juis Pujante and Ton Hoenselaars, 223–40. Newark: University of Delaware Press.

Scolnicov, Hanna. 2001. The Hebrew Who Turned Christian: The First Translator of Shakespeare into the Holy Tongue. *Shakespeare Survey* 54: 182–90.

Shahevitch, Boaz. 1970. On the Nature of the *Melitza*. *Ha-sifrut* 2(3): 664–6.

Shavit, Yaacov. 1993. A Duty Too Heavy to Bear: Hebrew in the Berlin Haskalah, 1783–1819: Between Classic, Modern, and Romantic. In *Hebrew in Ashkenaz: A Language in Exile*, ed. Lewis Glinert, 111–28. New York: Oxford University Press.

Silberbusch, David Isaiah. 1936. מפנקס זכרונותי [*From the Book of My Memoirs*]. Tel Aviv: HaPoel HaTzair; repr. http://benyehuda.org/silberbusch/ishim_umeoraot.html#g. Accessed 24 February 2017.

Singerman, Robert. 1988. Between Western Culture and Jewish Tradition. In *A Sign and a Witness: 2,000 Years of Hebrew Books and Illuminated Manuscripts*, ed. Leonard Singer Gold, 140–54. New York: Oxford University Press.

Standhartinger, Angela. 2009. Asenath: Bible. In *Jewish Women: A Comprehensive Historical Encyclopedia*, ed. Paula E. Hyman and Dalia Ofer. http://jwa.org/encyclopedia/article/asenath-bible. Accessed 31 January 2016.

Ta-Shma, Israel Moses, Shlomo Tal, and Menahem Slae. 2007. Responsa. In *Encyclopaedia Judaica*, ed. Michael Berenbaum and Fred Skolnik, 2nd edn, vol. 17, 228–39. Detroit: Macmillan Reference USA.

Tchernichovsky, Shaul. 1930. הלילה השנים עשר, או: כרצונכם [*Twelfth Night, Or: What You Will*]. Tel Aviv.

Toury, Gideon. 2012. *Descriptive Translation Studies – and Beyond*. Rev. ed. Amsterdam: John Benjamins.

Trachtenberg, Joshua. 2004. *Jewish Magic and Superstition: A Study in Folk Religion*. Philadelphia: University of Pennsylvania Press.

Valles, Margot Behrend. 2013. *Judaized Romance and Romanticized Judaization: Adaptation in Hebrew and Early Yiddish Chivalric Literature*. PhD dissertation, Indiana University.

Venuti, Lawrence. 2008. *The Translator's Invisibility: A History of Translation*. 2nd edn. London: Routledge.

———, ed. 2012. *The Translation Studies Reader*. 3rd edn. London: Routledge.

Walker, James Barr. 1841. *Philosophy of the Plan of Salvation: A Book for the Times*. New York.

Weinfeld, Moshe. 2007. Covenant. In *Encyclopaedia Judaica*, ed. Michael Berenbaum and Fred Skolnik, 2nd edn, vol. 5, 249–53. Detroit: Macmillan Reference USA.

Weis, René, ed. 2012. *The Arden Shakespeare: Romeo and Juliet*. 3rd edn. London: Bloomsbury.

Williams, Simon. 1990. *Shakespeare on the German Stage: Vol. 1: 1586–1914*. Cambridge: Cambridge University Press.

Wolpe, David. 1997. *Hester Panim* in Modern Jewish Thought. *Modern Judaism* 17(1): 25–56.

Zer-Zion, Shelly. 2010. Theater: Hebrew Theater. In *YIVO Encyclopedia of Jews in Eastern Europe*, ed. Jeffrey P. Edelstein et al. www.yivoencyclopedia.org/article.aspx/Theater/Hebrew_Theater. Accessed 24 February 2017.

Zitron, Samuel Leib. 1925. מאחורי-הפרגוד: מומרים, בוגדים, מתכחשים [*Behind the Curtain: Converts, Traitors, Deniers*]. Part 2. Vilnius: Zvi Matz.

Zussman, Ezra. 1946. "אותלו" – שקלארש [Shklarsh – '*Othello*']. *Davar*, 6 December: 4.

www.ingramcontent.com/pod-product-compliance
Lightning Source LLC
LaVergne TN
LVHW090023310826
846742LV00011B/28